RAND McNALLY

WORLD ATLAS

RAND McNALLY & COMPANY
Chicago   New York   San Francisco

CONTENTS

Map Projections. . . . . vi-vii
The Western Hemisphere viii
The Eastern Hemisphere ix

SAGA OF SPACE—*pages x to xxix*

Members of the Universe x
The Milky Way xi
Star Chart for the Northern Skies xii
Star Chart for the Southern Skies xiii
Solar System Chart . . . . xiv-xv
The Solar System—Planet Information Table xvi
Venus, Mars, Jupiter and Saturn xvii
The Saga of Space Exploration xviii
The First Steps Upward xix
Man's Activities in Space xx
America's First Day in Space xxi
Communications Satellites xxii
Project Gemini xxiii
The Moon . . . . xxiv-xv
The Far Side of the Moon. xxvi
Project Apollo xxvii
Interplanetary Probes xxviii
Space Age Glossary xxix

THE POLITICAL WORLD IN MAPS—*pages xxx to 89*

THE WORLD—*pages xxx to 2*

PAGES

Introduction to the Political Maps xxx
Polar Map of the World 1
The World 2

EUROPE—*pages 3 to 14*

Europe 3
British Isles 4
France and the Low Countries 5

Germany, Austria and Switzerland 6
Poland and Czechoslovakia 7
Spain and Portugal 8
Italy 9
Yugoslavia, Hungary, Romania and Bulgaria . . 10
Norway, Sweden and Finland 11
Western Soviet Union 12
Soviet Union 13
Eastern Mediterranean 14

CONTENTS—*continued*

ASIA—*pages 15 to 20*

	PAGES
Israel and Arabia	15
Eurasia	16
China, Mongolia, Korea, Japan and Taiwan	17
Japan and Korea	18
Indonesia and the Philippines	19
India, Pakistan, Burma and Ceylon	20

AFRICA—*pages 21 to 24*

Africa	21
Northwestern Africa	22
Northeastern Africa	23
Central and Southern Africa	24

AUSTRALIA AND NEW ZEALAND—*pages 25 to 26*

Australia	25
Southeastern Australia and New Zealand	26

SOUTH AMERICA—*pages 27 to 32*

South America	27
Central and Southern Argentina and Chile	28
Bolivia, Paraguay, Northern Argentina and Chile	29
Uruguay and Southern Brazil	30
Peru and Ecuador	31
Colombia and Venezuela	32

NORTH AMERICA—*pages 33 to 89*

North America	33
Mexico	34
West Indies	35
Canada	36
British Columbia	37
Alberta	38
Saskatchewan	39
Manitoba	40
Ontario	41
Quebec	42
Maritime Provinces	43
Newfoundland	44
United States	45
Alabama	46
Alaska	47
Arizona	48
Arkansas	49
California	50
Colorado	51
Connecticut	52

NORTH AMERICA—*continued*

	PAGES
Delaware	53
Florida	54
Georgia	55
Hawaii	56
Idaho	57
Illinois	58
Indiana	59
Iowa	60
Kansas	61
Kentucky	62
Louisiana	63
Maine	64
Maryland	53
Massachusetts	65
Michigan	66
Minnesota	67
Mississippi	68
Missouri	69
Montana	70
Nebraska	71
Nevada	72
New Hampshire	73
New Jersey	74
New Mexico	48
New York	75
North Carolina	76
North Dakota	77
Ohio	78
Oklahoma	79
Oregon	80
Pennsylvania	81
Rhode Island	52
South Carolina	82
South Dakota	77
Tennessee	83
Texas	84
Utah	72
Vermont	73
Virginia	85
Washington	86
West Virginia	87
Wisconsin	88
Wyoming	89

CONTENTS—*continued*

PAGES

EXPLANATION OF THE INDEX REFERENCE SYSTEM 90
LIST OF ABBREVIATIONS 91
EXPLANATION OF THE MAP INDEX 92
INDEX 92-185

SELECTED WORLD INFORMATION—*pages 186 to 211*

PAGES

WORLD POLITICAL INFORMATION TABLE 186-190

WORLD FACTS AND COMPARISONS . . 191-193

    MOVEMENTS, MEASUREMENTS, INHABITANTS, SURFACE AND EXTREMES OF TEMPERATURE AND RAINFALL OF THE EARTH; THE CONTINENTS; APPROXIMATE POPULATION OF THE WORLD 1650-1965; LARGEST COUNTRIES OF THE WORLD IN POPULATION; LARGEST COUNTRIES OF THE WORLD IN AREA 191
    PRINCIPAL MOUNTAINS OF THE WORLD 192
    GREAT OCEANS AND SEAS OF THE WORLD 193
    PRINCIPAL LAKES OF THE WORLD 193

PAGES

    PRINCIPAL RIVERS OF THE WORLD 193
    PRINCIPAL ISLANDS OF THE WORLD 193

LARGEST METROPOLITAN AREAS
   AND CITIES OF THE WORLD, 1964 . . 194-195

HISTORICAL GAZETTEER 196-205

PRINCIPAL DISCOVERIES
   AND EXPLORATIONS 206-209

WORLD AIR AND STEAMSHIP
   DISTANCE TABLES 210-211

SELECTED UNITED STATES INFORMATION—*pages 212 to 233*

PAGES

GEOGRAPHICAL FACTS ABOUT
   THE UNITED STATES 212

PLACES OF INTEREST IN
   THE UNITED STATES 213-227

NATIONAL PARKS AND MONUMENTS
   MAP OF THE UNITED STATES 228

UNITED STATES NATIONAL PARK SYSTEM . 229

PAGES

UNITED STATES CLIMATIC AND
   ECONOMIC TABLE 230-231

UNITED STATES POPULATION
   BY STATE OR COLONY 232

UNITED STATES
   STATE GENERAL INFORMATION TABLE . . 233

THE WORLD IN FOCUS—MAPS, TEXT, AND PICTURES—*pages 234 to 294*

PAGES

WORLD POPULATION 234-241
WORLD TRANSPORTATION 242-253
WORLD LANGUAGES 254-259
WORLD RACES 260-267

PAGES

WORLD RELIGIONS 268-275
NATURAL VEGETATION 276-283
WORLD CLIMATES 284-289
WORLD LANDFORMS 290-294

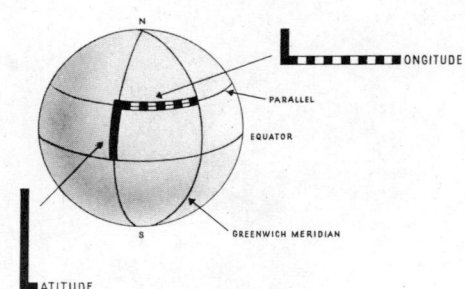

A map projection is merely an orderly system of parallels and meridians on which a flat map can be drawn. There are hundreds of projections, but no one represents the earth's spherical surface without some distortion. The distortion is relatively small for most practical purposes when a small part of the sphere is projected. For larger areas, a sacrifice of some property is necessary.

Most projections are designed to preserve on the flat map some particular property of the sphere. By varying the systematic arrangement or spacing of the latitude and longitude lines, a projection may be made either equal-area or conformal. Although most projections are derived from mathematical formulas, some are easier to visualize if thought of as projected upon a plane, or upon a cone or cylinder which is then unrolled into a plane surface. Thus, many projections are classified as plane (azimuthal), conic, or cylindrical.

SIMPLE CONIC PROJECTIONS

A perspective projection on a tangent cone with the origin point at the center of the globe. At the parallel of tangency, all elements of the map are true angles, distances, shapes, areas. Away from the tangent parallel, distances increase rapidly, giving bad distortion of shapes and areas.

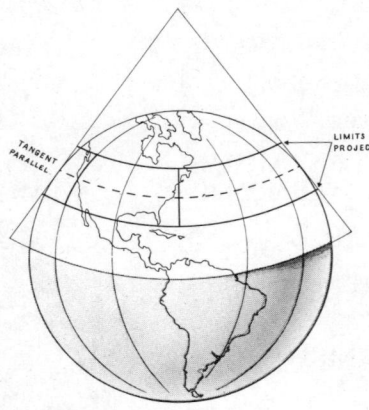

EARTH PROJECTED UPON
A TANGENT CONE

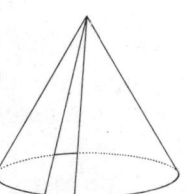

CONE CUT FROM BASE TO APEX

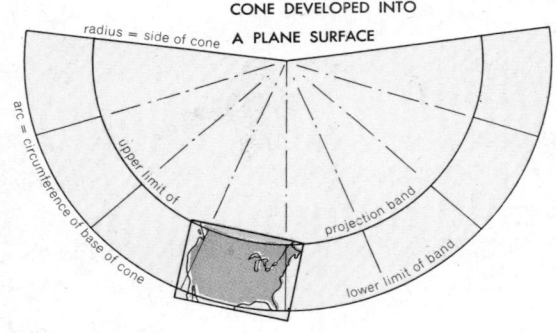

CONE DEVELOPED INTO
A PLANE SURFACE

MODIFIED CONIC PROJECTION

EARTH PROJECTED UPON AN INTERSECTING CONE

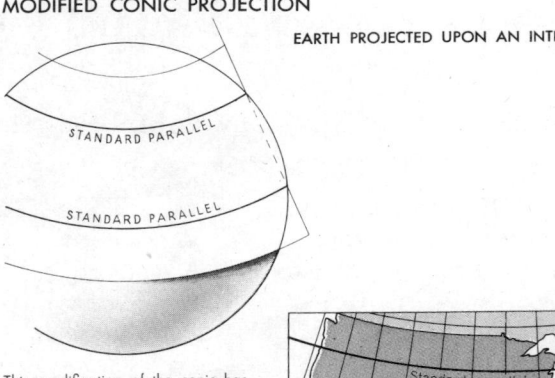

This modification of the conic has two standard parallels, or lines of intersection. It is not an equal-area projection, the space being reduced in size between the standard parallels and progressively enlarged beyond the standard parallels. Careful selection of the standard parallels provides however, good representation for areas of limited latitudinal extent.

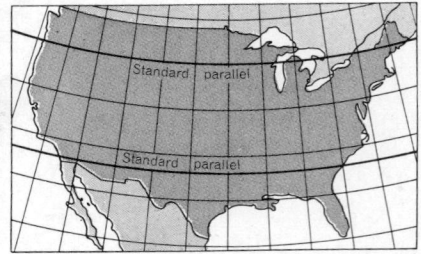

CONIC PROJECTION WITH TWO STANDARD PARALLELS

BONNE PROJECTION

An equal-area modification of the conic principle. Distances are true along all parallels and the central meridian; but away from it, increasing obliqueness of intersections and longitudinal distances, with their attendant distortion of shapes, limits the satisfactory area.

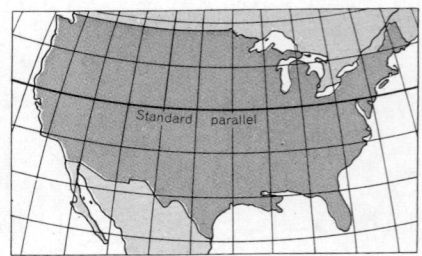

POLYCONIC PROJECTION

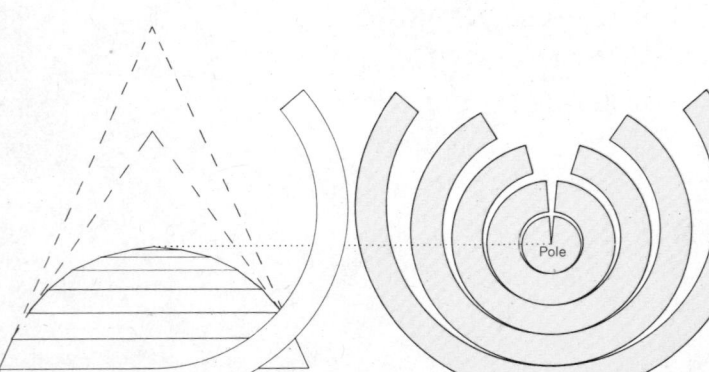

EARTH CONSIDERED AS FORMED
BY BASES OF CONES

DEVELOPMENT OF THE CONICAL BASES

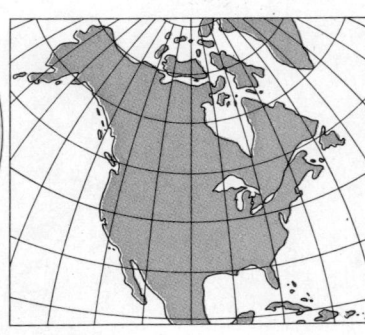

POLYCONIC PROJECTION

This variation is not equal-area. Parallels are nonconcentric circles truly divided. Distances along the straight central meridian are also true, but along the curving meridians are increasingly exaggerated. Representation is good near the central meridian, but away from it there is marked distortion.

TYPICAL PLANE PROJECTIONS

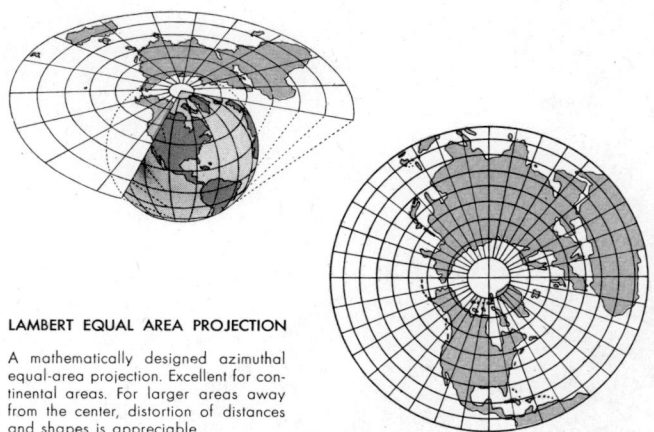

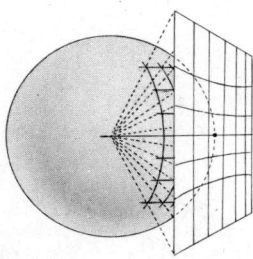

LAMBERT EQUAL AREA PROJECTION

A mathematically designed azimuthal equal-area projection. Excellent for continental areas. For larger areas away from the center, distortion of distances and shapes is appreciable.

GNOMONIC PROJECTION

A geometric or perspective projection on a tangent plane with the origin point at the center of the globe. Shapes and distances rapidly become increasingly distorted away from the center of the projection. Important in navigation, because all straight lines are great circles.

CYLINDRICAL PROJECTIONS

EARTH PROJECTED UPON A CYLINDER

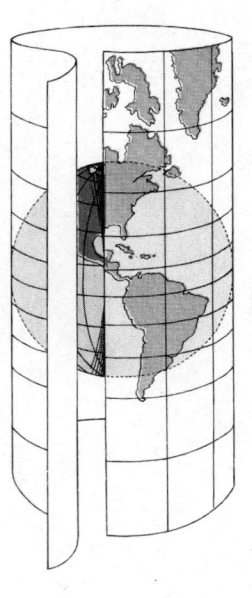

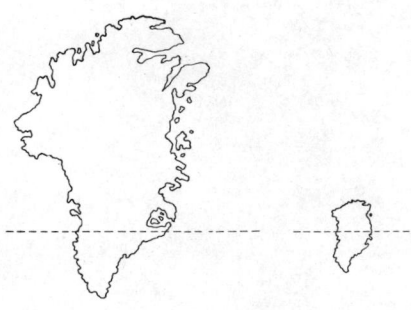

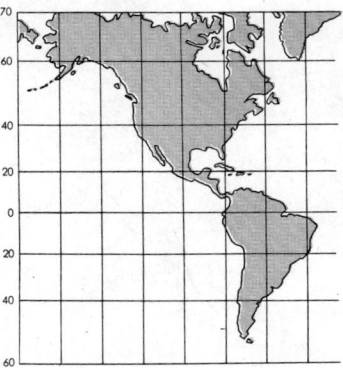

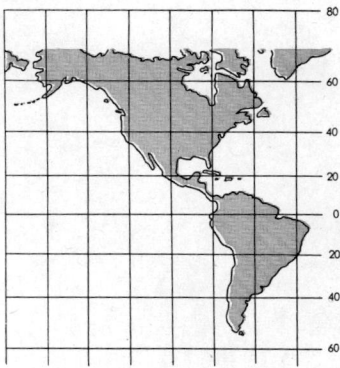

PERSPECTIVE PROJECTION

A perspective projection on a tangent cylinder. Because of rapidly increasing distortion away from the line of tangency and the lack of any special advantage, it is rarely used.

Note the increasing distortion of Greenland (above left) compared to an equal area projection (above right).

MERCATOR CONFORMAL PROJECTION

Mercator's modification increases the longitudinal distances in the same proportion as latitudinal distances are increased. Thus, at any point shapes are true, but areas become increasingly exaggerated. Of value in navigation, because a line connecting any two points gives the true direction between them.

MILLER PROJECTION

This recent modification is neither conformal nor equal-area. Whereas shapes are less accurate than on the Mercator, the exaggeration of areas has been reduced somewhat.

EQUAL AREA PROJECTIONS OF THE WORLD

The earth's surface peeled like the skin from an orange.

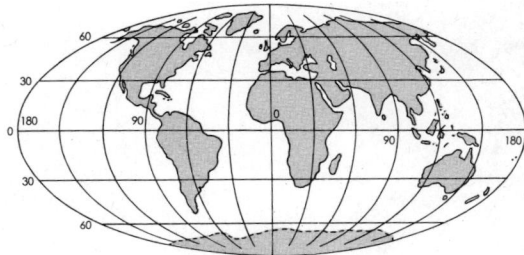

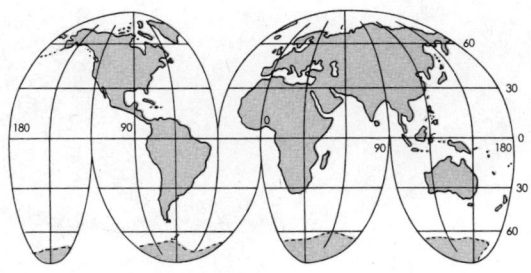

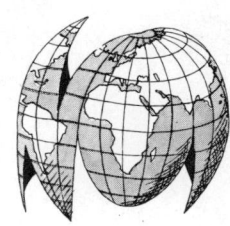

MOLLWEIDE'S HOMOLOGRAPHIC PROJECTION

GOODE'S INTERRUPTED HOMOLOGRAPHIC PROJECTION

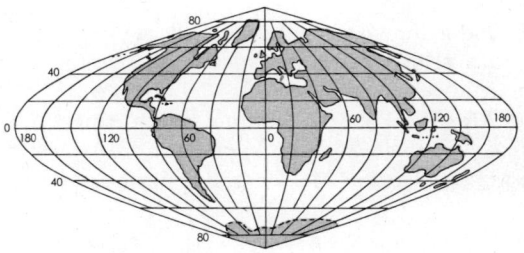

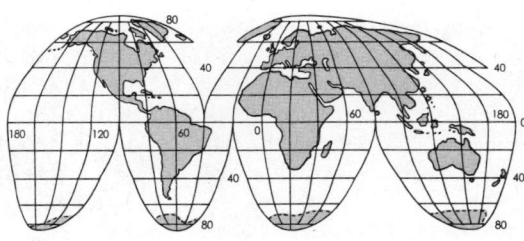

SINUSOIDAL PROJECTION

GOODE'S INTERRUPTED HOMOLOSINE PROJECTION

Although each of these projections is equal-area, differences in the spacing and arrangement of latitude and longitude lines result in differences in the distribution and relative degree of the shape and distance distortion within each grid. On the homolographic, there is no uniformity in scale. It is different on each parallel and each meridian. On the sinusoidal, only distances along all latitudes and the central meridian are true. The homolosine combines the homolographic, for areas poleward of 40°, with the sinusoidal. The principle of interruption permits each continent in turn the advantage of being in the center of the projection, resulting in better shapes.

This distinctive relief interpretation shows the New World as it might be seen from outer space if all hindrances to vision were removed. You can see how the mountain backbone of the Rockies and the Andes stretches nearly from pole to pole, and how the major river systems of the Mississippi-Missouri and the Amazon each drain half a continent.

The face of the land is shown from the ice pack of Greenland and the tundra region of Northern Canada to the great plains of the Midwest and the deserts of southwestern United States and Mexico. The vegetation of South America is depicted from the highlands of Venezuela and the tropical rain forest of the Amazon Valley to the Pampas and Patagonia.

A realistic picture of the Old World is afforded by precise and accurate shaded relief combined with subtly blended colors portraying the face of the land. You can see how the mighty Sahara and the deserts of Arabia confined early civilizations in the Nile and Tigris-Euphrates river valleys.

The topography and vegetation of the earth as shown here reveal something of how such great barriers as the Himalayas, the dense jungles of Africa, and the vast deserts have affected and controlled man's efforts in transportation, communication, and broad cultural interchange.

Members of the Universe

The Universe consists of a vast Space, within which are contained untold numbers of galaxies, billions of stars, planets, asteroids, and other celestial objects of varying sizes, shapes and characteristics.

Among the important members of the Universe are the galaxies, known also as "Universe Islands."

FIGURE 1

COURTESY LICK OBSERVATORY

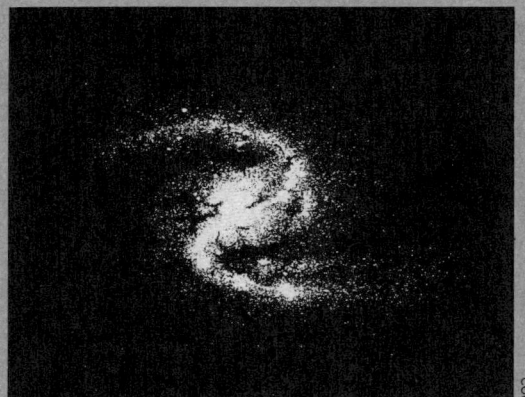

FIGURE 2

FIGURE 3

COURTESY MT. WILSON & MT. PALOMAR OBSERVATORIES

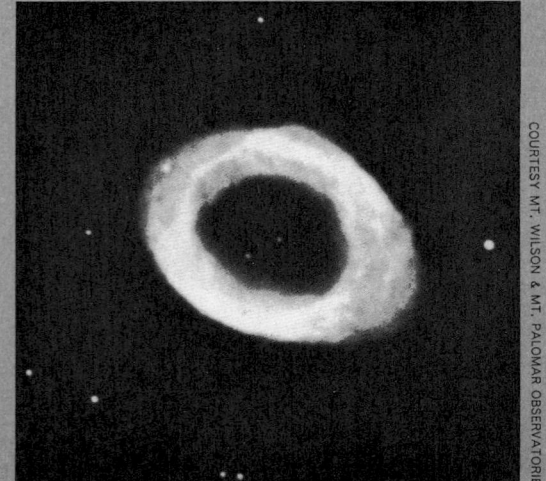

FIGURE 4

COURTESY MT. WILSON & MT. PALOMAR OBSERVATORIES

FIGURE 5

COURTESY MT. WILSON & MT. PALOMAR OBSERVATORIES

A Galaxy is a large community of stars. Several types of Galaxies can be classified by their shape and structure. Thus, our "Milky Way" is a Spiral Galaxy (Figure No. 1). The Sun is a star in the Milky Way and is located over half way out from the center of the Galaxy. In Figure No. 2 the Milky Way is shown as a side view; its diameter approximates 100,000 light years.

There are other types of Galaxies, among them, Barred Spirals (Fig. 3), which have straighter spiral arms than the normal spirals. Also Elliptical galaxies, such as M32, which is located in the region of Andromeda. And, Irregular galaxies, such as the Magellanic Clouds, characterized by having no particular shape. Stars are also grouped close together in Star Clusters (Fig. 4), such as that of Hercules.

In Space, there are also clouds of gases and dust. Any of these clouds are termed Nebula. There are two kinds of them: Diffuse Nebulae and Dark Nebulae. The former are located near a star, which is their source of light (Fig. 5), such as the Ring Nebula in Lyra. Dark Nebulae are those which have no star nearby from which to draw light, (Fig. 6), such as the Horsehead Nebula in Orion.

Our Sun is a smaller than average star. It is completely gaseous and rotates irregularly. The two major portions of the Sun are: its Atmosphere composed of 3 layers, and the Nucleus, or Sun proper. The atmosphere is separated from the Nucleus by the Photosphere, an opaque layer, which does not permit the observer to see under it, (Fig. 7). The effective temperature of the Sun approximates 10,000° F. The amount of energy received from it at the earth's surface is of 1.94 calories per square centimeter per minute.

The upper layer of the Sun's atmosphere registers some very turbulent phenomena known as solar prominences, which resemble flame tongues, streaking upward to tremendous heights dwarfing the size of earth to a mere dot, (Fig. 8).

FIGURE 6

COURTESY MT. WILSON & MT. PALOMAR OBSERVATORIES

FIGURE 7

COURTESY MT. WILSON & MT. PALOMAR OBSERVATORIES

FIGURE 8

COURTESY MT. WILSON OBSERVATORY

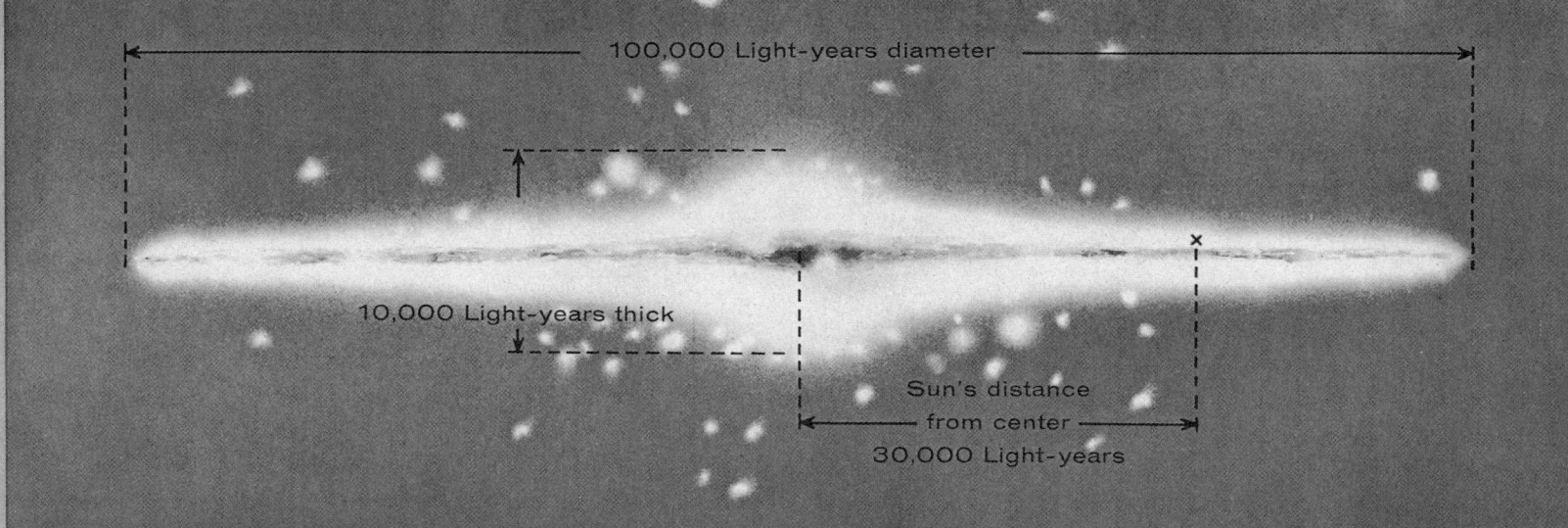

100,000 Light-years diameter

10,000 Light-years thick

Sun's distance
from center
30,000 Light-years

The Milky Way

Above is shown a side view of the Milky Way, as conceived today. In it, the Sun is only one of about 100 billion stars. Below is a "top view" of the Whirlpool galaxy in Canes Venatici, which is very similar to our Milky Way. The Milky Way resembles a huge cartwheel revolving through the intergallactic Space at ponderous velocities. Our Galaxy has enormous quantities of interstellar gas clouds which occur in varying densities and cause the lack of temporary clear vision. (Distances are given in light years. One light year is about six million million miles.)

Photo from Mt. Wilson & Palomar Observatories

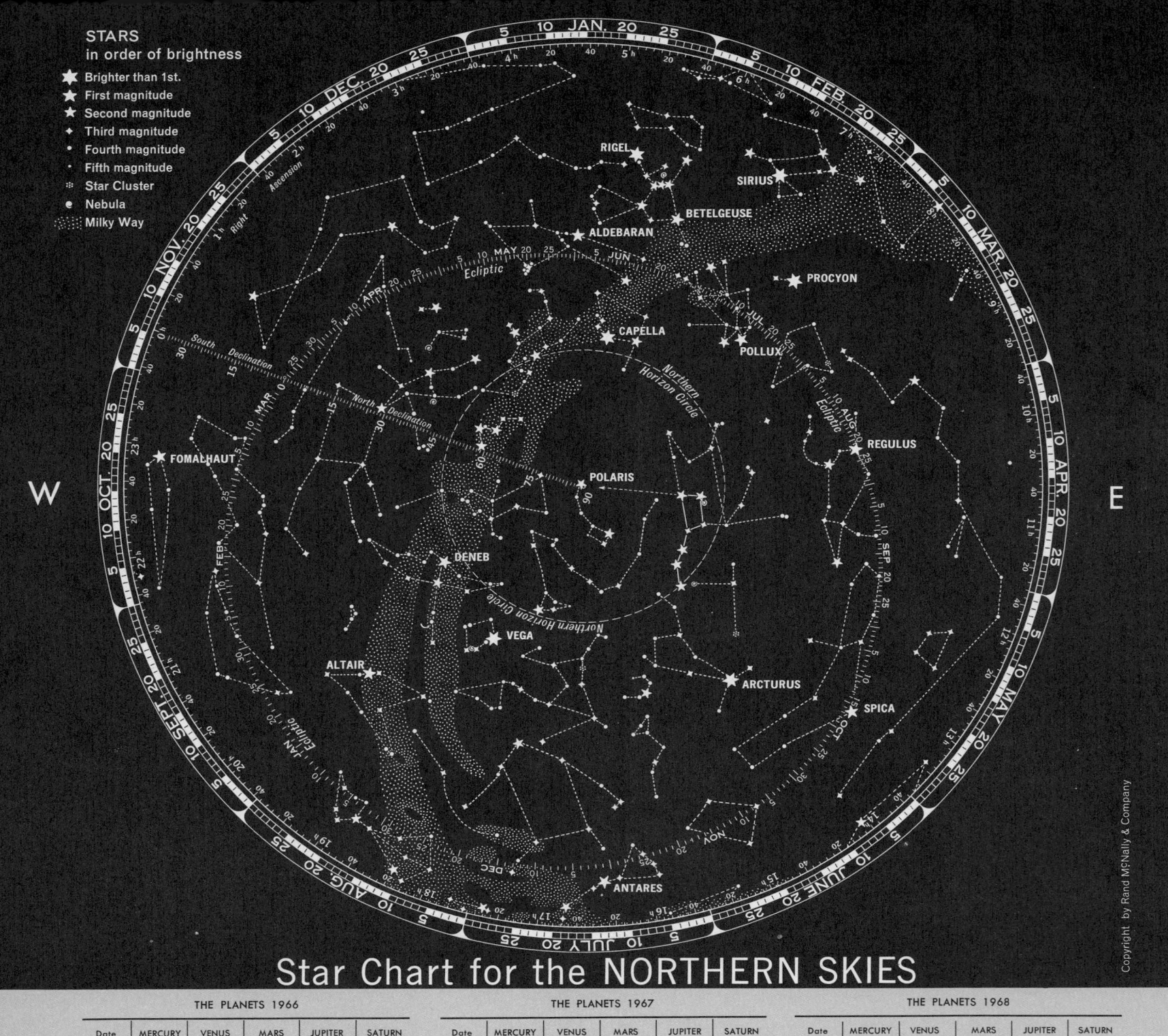

STARS in order of brightness

★ Brighter than 1st.
★ First magnitude
★ Second magnitude
✦ Third magnitude
• Fourth magnitude
· Fifth magnitude
✳ Star Cluster
e Nebula
⋰⋰ Milky Way

W   E

Labeled stars: RIGEL, SIRIUS, BETELGEUSE, ALDEBARAN, PROCYON, CAPELLA, POLLUX, REGULUS, FOMALHAUT, POLARIS, DENEB, VEGA, ALTAIR, ARCTURUS, SPICA, ANTARES

Star Chart for the NORTHERN SKIES

THE PLANETS 1966

Date	MERCURY R.A.	Decl.	VENUS R.A.	Decl.	MARS R.A.	Decl.	JUPITER R.A.	Decl.	SATURN R.A.	Decl.
	h m	°	h m	°	h m	°	h m	°	h m	°
Jan. 1	17 19	22 S	21 02	16 S	20 38	20 S	5 36	23 N	22 58	9 S
15	18 47	24 S	20 53	13 S	21 23	17 S	5 29	23 N	23 03	8 S
Feb. 1	20 44	20 S	20 12	12 S	22 15	12 S	5 23	23 N	23 09	8 S
15	22 22	12 S	19 55	13 S	22 56	8 S	5 22	23 N	23 15	7 S
Mar. 1	23 48	0	20 09	14 S	23 37	3 S	5 23	23 N	23 21	6 S
15	0 13	5 N	20 46	14 S	0 17	1 N	5 27	23 N	23 28	6 S
Apr. 1	23 34	2 S	21 45	12 S	1 04	6 N	5 35	23 N	23 35	5 S
15	23 54	3 S	22 40	8 S	1 44	10 N	5 44	23 N	23 41	4 S
May 1	1 04	4 N	23 45	3 S	2 30	15 N	5 56	23 N	23 48	3 S
15	2 32	13 N	0 43	3 N	3 10	18 N	6 08	23 N	23 52	3 S
June 1	4 58	24 N	1 56	10 N	4 00	21 N	6 23	23 N	23 57	3 S
15	6 58	25 N	2 59	15 N	4 42	23 N	6 37	23 N	0 00	2 S
July 1	8 27	19 N	4 15	20 N	5 30	24 N	6 52	23 N	0 02	2 S
15	8 52	14 N	5 25	22 N	6 11	24 N	7 06	23 N	0 02	2 S
Aug. 1	8 15	15 N	6 54	23 N	7 01	23 N	7 22	22 N	0 01	2 S
15	8 20	18 N	8 06	21 N	7 40	22 N	7 35	22 N	23 59	3 S
Sept. 1	10 07	13 N	9 31	16 N	8 27	20 N	7 50	21 N	23 55	3 S
15	11 47	3 N	10 38	10 N	9 03	18 N	8 00	21 N	23 52	4 S
Oct. 1	13 23	9 S	11 52	2 N	9 42	15 N	8 11	20 N	23 47	4 S
15	14 39	18 S	12 57	5 S	10 16	12 N	8 18	20 N	23 43	4 S
Nov. 1	15 54	23 S	14 16	13 S	10 54	9 N	8 25	20 N	23 40	5 S
15	15 42	20 S	15 26	18 S	11 24	6 N	8 27	19 N	23 38	5 S
Dec. 1	15 07	15 S	16 49	21 S	11 57	2 N	8 27	20 N	23 38	5 S
15	16 12	20 S	18 06	24 S	12 24	1 S	8 24	20 N	23 39	5 S

THE PLANETS 1967

Date	MERCURY R.A.	Decl.	VENUS R.A.	Decl.	MARS R.A.	Decl.	JUPITER R.A.	Decl.	SATURN R.A.	Decl.
	h m	°	h m	°	h m	°	h m	°	h m	°
Jan. 1	18 00	24 S	19 39	23 S	12 55	4 S	8 17	20 N	23 42	4 S
15	19 37	24 S	20 53	19 S	13 18	6 S	8 10	21 N	23 45	4 S
Feb. 1	21 37	16 S	22 16	12 S	13 42	8 S	8 00	21 N	23 51	3 S
15	22 58	6 S	23 21	6 S	13 57	9 S	7 54	21 N	23 56	3 S
Mar. 1	23 04	2 S	0 24	2 N	14 06	10 S	7 49	22 N	0 02	2 S
15	22 24	8 S	1 27	9 N	14 07	10 S	7 46	22 N	0 08	1 S
Apr. 1	22 59	8 S	2 45	17 N	13 54	9 S	7 47	22 N	0 16	1 S
15	0 06	2 S	3 53	22 N	13 36	8 S	7 50	22 N	0 22	0
May 1	1 47	5 N	5 13	25 N	13 25	11 S	7 56	21 N	0 29	1 N
15	3 40	20 N	6 24	26 N	13 00	5 S	8 04	21 N	0 35	1 N
June 1	6 02	26 N	7 45	24 N	12 56	6 S	8 15	20 N	0 41	2 N
15	7 15	23 N	8 46	20 N	13 03	7 S	8 26	20 N	0 45	2 N
July 1	7 29	19 N	9 45	15 N	13 20	9 S	8 39	18 N	0 48	3 N
15	6 57	18 N	10 24	11 N	13 41	12 S	8 51	18 N	0 49	3 N
Aug. 1	7 20	21 N	10 51	4 N	14 13	15 S	9 06	17 N	0 50	3 N
15	8 57	19 N	10 48	1 N	14 44	17 S	9 18	16 N	0 49	2 N
Sept. 1	11 06	7 N	10 13	5 N	15 26	20 S	9 33	15 N	0 46	2 N
15	12 31	3 S	9 51	5 N	16 04	21 S	9 44	14 N	0 42	1 N
Oct. 1	13 53	14 S	10 01	7 N	16 50	24 S	9 57	12 N	0 38	1 N
15	14 47	19 S	10 33	7 N	17 34	25 S	10 07	12 N	0 34	1 N
Nov. 1	14 27	15 S	11 25	2 S	19 15	24 S	10 24	11 N	0 30	0
15	14 07	10 S	12 22	7 S	19 12	25 S	10 24	11 N	0 27	0
Dec. 1	15 24	17 S	13 28	7 S	20 07	22 S	10 29	11 N	0 25	0
15	16 53	23 S	14 29	12 S	20 52	19 S	10 32	10 N	0 25	0

THE PLANETS 1968

Date	MERCURY R.A.	Decl.	VENUS R.A.	Decl.	MARS R.A.	Decl.	JUPITER R.A.	Decl.	SATURN R.A.	Decl.
	h m	°	h m	°	h m	°	h m	°	h m	°
Jan. 1	18 50	25 S	15 49	18 S	21 45	15 S	10 32	10 N	0 26	0
15	20 29	21 S	16 59	21 S	22 26	11 S	10 29	11 N	0 29	1 N
Feb. 1	22 06	11 S	18 28	22 S	23 15	6 S	10 23	11 N	0 33	1 N
15	21 51	9 S	19 42	21 S	23 55	1 S	10 16	12 N	0 38	2 N
Mar. 1	21 17	14 S	20 59	18 S	0 37	4 N	10 09	13 N	0 44	2 N
15	21 59	14 S	22 07	13 S	1 16	8 N	10 02	13 N	0 50	3 N
Apr. 1	23 27	6 S	23 26	5 S	2 03	12 N	9 57	14 N	0 50	3 N
15	0 56	4 N	0 30	2 N	2 43	16 N	9 54	14 N	0 58	4 N
May 1	3 00	18 N	1 43	9 N	3 29	19 N	9 54	14 N	1 05	4 N
15	4 50	25 N	2 49	15 N	4 10	21 N	9 57	14 N	1 12	5 N
June 1	6 04	24 N	4 14	21 N	5 00	23 N	10 03	13 N	1 18	6 N
15	5 58	21 N	5 27	23 N	5 42	24 N	10 10	12 N	1 25	6 N
July 1	5 32	19 N	6 53	24 N	6 29	24 N	10 19	12 N	1 30	7 N
15	6 09	16 N	8 07	21 N	7 03	23 N	10 28	11 N	1 34	7 N
Aug. 1	8 16	19 N	9 33	16 N	7 57	22 N	10 41	9 N	1 38	7 N
15	10 10	13 N	10 35	10 N	8 35	20 N	10 51	8 N	1 38	7 N
Sept. 1	11 56	0	11 56	2 N	9 19	17 N	11 05	7 N	1 37	7 N
15	13 03	9 S	12 59	5 S	9 54	14 N	11 16	6 N	1 34	7 N
Oct. 1	13 50	15 S	14 12	13 S	10 32	11 N	11 29	4 N	1 30	6 N
15	13 23	11 S	15 19	19 S	11 05	7 N	11 40	23 N	1 26	6 N
Nov. 1	14 33	14 S	18 00	25 S	11 52	2 N	11 52	1 N	1 17	5 N
15	14 33	14 S	18 00	25 S	12 15	0	12 01	1 N	1 17	5 N
Dec. 1	16 14	20 S	19 25	25 S	12 50	4 S	12 10	0	1 14	5 N
15	17 49	25 S	20 36	21 S	13 21	7 S	12 17	0	1 13	5 N

STARS
in order of brightness

- ★ Brighter than 1st.
- ★ First magnitude
- ★ Second magnitude
- ◆ Third magnitude
- ● Fourth magnitude
- · Fifth magnitude
- ✳ Star Cluster
- ⊚ Nebula
- ⠿ Milky Way

Star Chart for the SOUTHERN SKIES

A LIST OF THE BRIGHTER STARS

NAME	R.A.*	DECL.**	MAGNITUDE***
Achernar	1 h. 35 m.	S 57° 35'	+1
Acrux	12 h. 22 m.	S 62° 42'	+1
Agena	13 h. 58 m.	S 60° 2'	+1
Aldebaran	4 h. 31 m.	N 16° 22'	+1
Altair	19 h. 47 m.	N 8° 40'	+1
Antares	16 h. 25 m.	S 26° 16'	+1
Arcturus	14 h. 12 m.	N 19° 32'	0
Betelgeuse	5 h. 51 m.	N 7° 23'	+1
Canopus	6 h. 22 m.	S 52° 39'	−1
Capella	5 h. 11 m.	N 45° 55'	0
Deneb	20 h. 39 m.	N 45° 1'	+1
Fomalhaut	22 h. 53 m.	S 29° 59'	+1
Pollux	7 h. 30 m.	N 32° 2'	+1
Procyon	7 h. 37 m.	N 5° 20'	0
Regulus	10 h. 4 m.	N 12° 18'	+1
Rigel	5 h. 11 m.	S 8° 16'	0
Rigil Kentaurus	14 h. 34 m.	S 60° 32'	0
Spica	13 h. 21 m.	S 10° 47'	+1
Sirius	6 h. 42 m.	S 16° 37'	−1.6
Vega	18 h. 34 m.	N 38° 43'	0

*Right Ascension—The distance, in time units, eastward along the Celestial Equator, from the Spring Equinox (Mar. 21 in Ecliptic) to the meridian passing through any given celestial body.

**Declination—The distance, in degrees, northward and southward from the celestial Equator, to any given celestial body. This concept is similar to latitude on earth.

***Magnitude—The relative brightness of celestial bodies, as indicated by a scale of stellar light intensity. The brightest is indicated by a negative number.

DIRECTIONS FOR THE USE OF THE STAR CHARTS

For anyone living in North America, the Star Chart for the NORTHERN SKIES will be most useful. Face north and hold the atlas in a vertical position. Rotate the book until the current date is at the top of the chart. The stars and constellations in the upper two-thirds of the chart are those visible in the sky at about 9 P.M. that night.

The star nearly at the center of the chart is Polaris, the North Star. The stars within the Northern Horizon Circle correspond to the stars that rotate anticlockwise around the North Star, and are always above the horizon for anyone living at 40° North Latitude. The stars to the right of center will be visible in the eastern sky; those to the left of center in the western sky. Stars near the upper edges of the chart will be close to the southern horizon. To visualize the positions of the stars directly overhead and in the southern sky, hold the star chart of the Northern skies overhead with the current date pointing south.

The Star Chart for the SOUTHERN SKIES would be used in similar fashion by anyone living south of the equator.

The positions of the sun and the major planets among the stars for any given date may be added to the charts. Lay a piece of acetate or tracing paper over the chart to be used. Find the sun's position for the day according to the calendar scale along the Ecliptic and mark it with a crayon or wax pencil. Then locate each of the planets along or near the Ecliptic according to its Right Ascension and Declination as given for the nearest date in the table for the current year. Note that Right Ascension is measured eastward from the Declination Scale in hours and minutes from 0 to 24; while Declination is measured in degrees north or south of the celestial equator, 0° on the Declination Scale. Thus Right Ascension on a star chart corresponds to longitude on a map; while Declination corresponds to latitude.

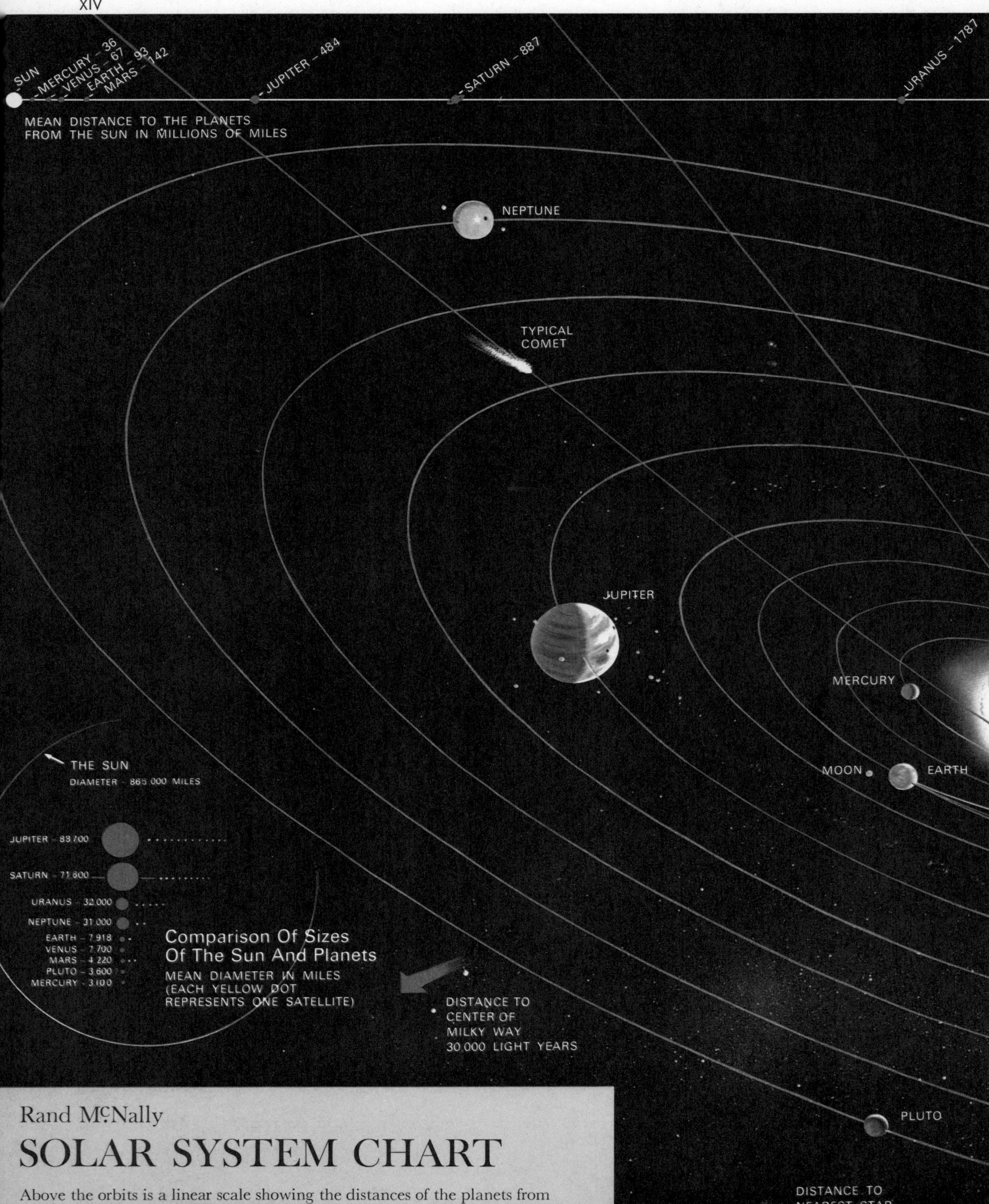

SUN MERCURY – 36 VENUS – 67 EARTH – 93 MARS – 142 JUPITER – 484 SATURN – 887 URANUS – 1787

MEAN DISTANCE TO THE PLANETS
FROM THE SUN IN MILLIONS OF MILES

NEPTUNE

TYPICAL
COMET

JUPITER

MERCURY

MOON EARTH

THE SUN
DIAMETER – 865,000 MILES

JUPITER – 88,700

SATURN – 71,600

URANUS – 32,000

NEPTUNE – 31,000

EARTH – 7,918
VENUS – 7,700
MARS – 4,220
PLUTO – 3,600
MERCURY – 3,100

Comparison Of Sizes
Of The Sun And Planets

MEAN DIAMETER IN MILES
(EACH YELLOW DOT
REPRESENTS ONE SATELLITE)

DISTANCE TO
CENTER OF
MILKY WAY
30,000 LIGHT YEARS

PLUTO

Rand McNally

SOLAR SYSTEM CHART

Above the orbits is a linear scale showing the distances of the planets from
the Sun. At left and below the orbits is a scale of relative planet sizes. In the
main chart neither the orbits nor the sizes of Sun, planets, etc., are in scale.

DISTANCE TO
NEAREST STAR
PROXIMA CENTAURI
4.3 LIGHT YEARS

NEPTUNE – 2797

PLUTO
3675

ANDROMEDA
GALAXY

2,000,000 LIGHT
YEARS DISTANCE

URANUS

MARS

VENUS

ASTEROIDS

SATURN

THE SOLAR SYSTEM

The Solar System, of which the Earth is a part, is depicted graphically on the preceding two pages. This chart simulates the view an observer might expect if situated at a point in space. The system consists of a central star, the Sun, about which moves a family of nine planets, thirty-two moons, thousands of asteroids (or planetoids), and numerous comets and meteor clusters. The planets move around the Sun in nearly circular orbits, lying in approximately the same plane. All revolve in the same direction which is also the direction in which the Sun rotates on its own axis. As the planets' distances from the Sun increase, their respective orbital velocities proportionately decrease. Nearly all of the moons revolve in almost circular orbits along the equatorial planes of their respective planets. One of the exceptions to this rule is the Earth's Moon.

The Planet Information Table below, showing the planets' significant characteristics, will aid in making comparisons between them. The following text sets down further distinguishing characteristics of each. There is one omission, the Earth, which is amply described through the maps of this atlas.

MERCURY: Owing to its small size and consequent low surface gravity, most of its atmosphere escaped into space eons ago. This factor, coupled with a relatively short mean distance from the Sun, has turned Mercury into an arid, Sun-drenched, and most inhospitable world of extremes. On the illuminated side the surface temperature reaches 650° F.

VENUS: It is often called the Earth's "twin sister" because it is so nearly the same size. Venus is shrouded by so dense an atmosphere that its surface has never been seen through telescopes. In 1962, Mariner II spacecraft flew past Venus at a distance of 21,648 miles, and probed the environment of the planet. Thus, it was tentatively determined that the surface temperature might be 800° F., a much higher figure than had been anticipated. It was also ascertained that the dense cloud masses begin at an altitude of 45 miles above the planet's surface, reaching upward to an altitude of 60 miles. Earth-based radar analyses indicate that the surface of Venus might be sandy; alternately some scientists believe that the surface might have oceans and swamps as well as rocky landmasses. Other scientists maintain that the surface might be rocky and wind beaten.

MARS: Mars is the fourth planet in distance from the Sun, and the first located past the Earth. It has several Earth-like features, among them climatic seasons, seasonal water cycles, a surface temperature believed to range from a high of 80° F. to a low of −100° F. Its bright regions suggest the presence of vegetation which changes according to the seasons. Its atmosphere is believed to be thin, yet it is dense enough for clouds to form. Mars has two moons, each less than 10 miles in diameter and located rather near the planet.

JUPITER: Largest of the planets, it is a world of turmoil and change. It rotates so fast that the gases at its surface are forced into bands of turbulent motion. It is believed that it has a small rocky interior surrounded by a huge shell of ice, which in turn is surrounded by layers of solid, then liquid, then gaseous hydrogen topped with clouds of deadly methane and ammonia. The average surface temperature might be about −190° F. Jupiter has twelve moons, three of which are larger than our own.

SATURN: Physically similar to Jupiter, it has a family of nine moons. Due to its greater distance from the Sun, its surface temperature is lower yet, −235° F. Surrounding the planet along its equatorial plane is a ring system with an outside diameter of 175,000 miles. The rings are made up of small solid particles.

URANUS, NEPTUNE, and PLUTO: These are the outer planets of the Solar System. They are also the least-known ones. It is estimated that their surface temperatures drop considerably below −300° F.

PLANET INFORMATION TABLE

PLANET	Mercury	Venus	Earth*	Mars	Jupiter†	Saturn	Uranus	Neptune	Pluto
Number of Natural Satellites per Planet	0	0	1	2	12	9	5	2	0
Mean Diameter (in Miles)	3,100	7,700	7,918	4,220	88,700	71,600	32,000	31,000	3,600
Mean Distance to the Sun (in millions of miles)	36.0	67.25	93.0	141.7	484.0	887.0	1,787.0	2,797.0	3,675.0
Comparative Volume (Earth = 1.00)	0.06	0.92	1.00	0.15	1,318	736	64	60	0.09
Comparative Mass (Earth = 1.00)	0.04	0.81	1.00	0.11	316.94	94.9	14.7	17.2	0.1
Necessary Escape Velocity	2.66	6.38	6.95	3.16	37.0	22.10	13.70	15.40	3.30(?)
Mean Surface Gravity (Earth = 1.00)	0.29	0.86	1.00	0.37	2.64	1.17	0.91	1.12	<0.5
Weight of a Human Being (in pounds)	38	88	100	39	265	117	105	123	55
Rotation on Planet's Own Axis	88.0 days	Unknown	23^{h}56^m	24^{h}37^m	9^{h}50^m	10^{h}14^m	10^{h}45^m	15^{h}48^m	6.39 days
Revolution Around the Sun	88.0 days	224.7 days	365.2 days	687.0 days	11.9 years	29.5 years	84.0 years	164.8 years	248.4 years
Mean Orbital Velocity (in miles per second)	29.76	21.78	18.52	15.00	8.12	6.00	4.23	3.37	2.95
Inclination of Planet's Orbit to the Ecliptic	7°00′	3°24′	0°00′	1°51′	1°18′	2°29′	0°46′	1°47′	17°09′
Inclination of Planet's Equator	0°(?)	32°(?)	23°27′	25°10′	3°07′	26°45′	97°53′	29°	Unknown

*EARTH   †LARGEST PLANET

VENUS

The surface of Venus has never been seen due to the obstructive nature of its upper atmosphere. However, it is believed to have a rugged topography, mostly covered with water. Its upper atmosphere is rich in carbon dioxide, with the occurrence of frequent underlying clouds of formaldehyde droplets. The possibility of organic life is extremely limited. Perhaps there might exist some forms of primitive organic life in association with its extensive water bodies. The Venusian year is composed of 224.7 days. The planet has an orbital velocity of 21.78 miles per second, and any given object would require an escape velocity of 6.4 miles per second to leave the planet as compared with the Earth's 18.5 miles per second and 7.0 miles per second respectively. Venus has no moons.

MARS

The surface of Mars has been the object of extensive studies which seem to indicate the existence of vegetation in both hemispheres. Mars has similar climatic seasons to those of Earth. The Polar caps are easily distinguishable as are their seasonal changes. The surface configurations can be summarized as "debatable in nature." These include a large network of visible lines which at one time were thought to be canals, and regions of four different colors which vary with the seasons. The atmosphere is thinner than that of Earth, nevertheless, it is sufficiently dense to eliminate the need for pressurized suits, although a breathing helmet would still be required. The Martian year consists of 687 days. The planet has an orbital velocity of 15 miles per second and an escape velocity of 3.1 miles per second. This planet has two very small moons.

JUPITER

The surface of this planet has never been seen. Consequently, its visible upper atmosphere has been the object of intensive study. That region of the atmosphere is rich in ammonia, methane and hydrogen. Jupiter rotates more rapidly than Earth and, therefore, its day is only 9.8 hours in length. As a contrast, it takes 11.9 Earth years for Jupiter to travel once around the Sun, with an orbital velocity of about 8 miles per second. The planet requires an escape velocity of 37 miles per second, or over 5 times that required to escape Earth. Jupiter has 12 moons.

SATURN

Saturn's most distinguishing characteristic consists of the three concentric rings that revolve around it. The nearest of these is located a little over 6,000 miles above the planet itself. The rings are extremely thin and are made up of drifting material of varying sizes. Saturn has nine moons. The atmosphere is deep and shows evidence of some turbulence; it does not permit the observation of the actual surface of the planet. It revolves around the Sun once in 29.5 Earth years, with an orbital velocity of 6 miles per second. The escape velocity is 22 miles per second.

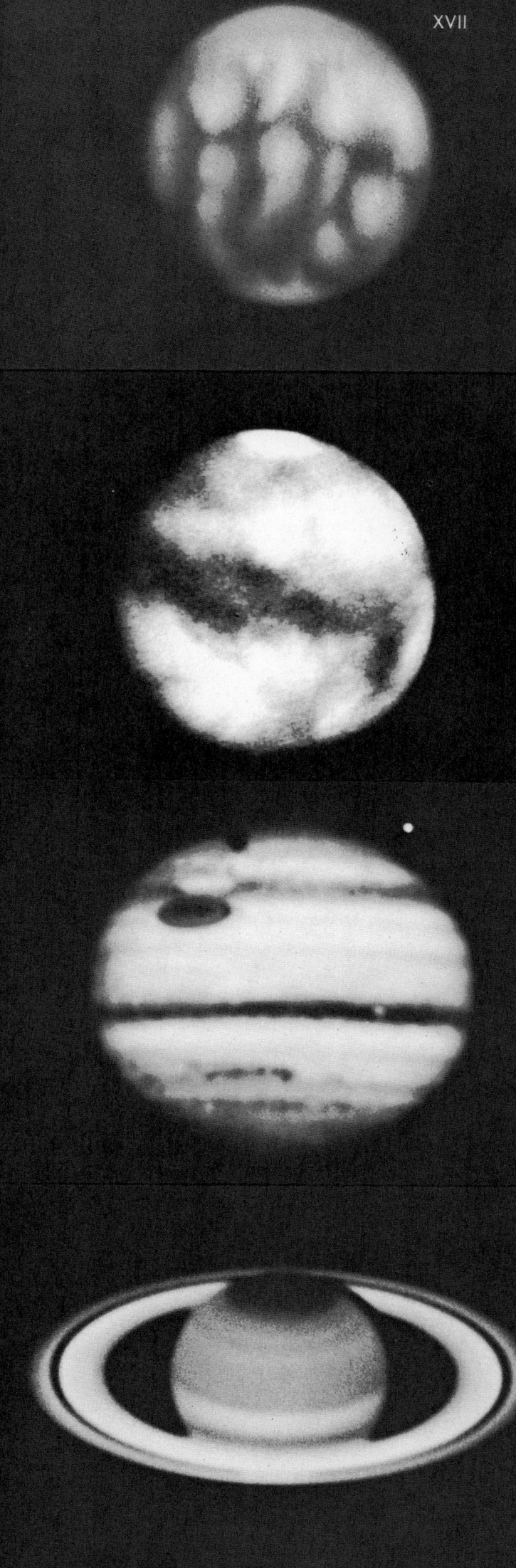

THE SAGA OF SPACE EXPLORATION

Man's exploration of the space above the surface of the Earth, first in, and then beyond the life-giving atmosphere, has been a dramatic experience. In the scientific era in which we live, fundamental knowledge of the Earth's relationship to space will increasingly determine the destiny of man. Already the exploration of space has provided important information concerning the true nature of matter, time, motion, and even life itself. Vast scopes of basic data about many terrestrial as well as extraterrestrial realities are being gathered and processed. Unpredictable benefits for men on Earth will inevitably result from this complex effort.

Man is, now, capable of producing the enormous force required to place a human being in space. Nevertheless, to achieve this goal adequately and safely, it has been necessary first to start with instrumented probes and satellites to gather data helpful in developing the technological ability and equipment. These instrumented probes and satellites have come to number in the hundreds. It is appropriate here to note only the major efforts so far, and their practical returns to man.

Satellites equipped with television cameras and infrared sensors, by observing changing atmospheric conditions which man has no other way of knowing, have made possible vastly improved weather forecasts. These meteorological satellites provide advance warnings of tornadoes, floods, blizzards, and hurricanes, thus enabling people to minimize material loss. Below are examples of the Nimbus and Tiros satellites' photography, which is useful to a great number of Earth scientists in furthering man's understanding of his own planet.

Another example of the practical application of space technology are the communications satellites which have greatly augmented the world's radio and telecommunications facilities. Such satellites as Telstar, Relay, Syncom, and Early Bird have made possible global telecasts which measurably improve the degree of understanding between nations and peoples.

Other applications are navigation satellites which will provide accurate information to any of the hundreds of aircraft that crowd the world's skies, or to the 20,000 surface ships that are estimated to be on the Atlantic Ocean alone at certain times.

There are numerous other benefits which are not of direct application to everyday life, but which are just as important to research in other fields. For example, the astronomical satellites help astronomers overcome the distorting effects of the Earth's atmosphere while studying the heavens. And satellites in general assist in determining exact distances, locations, and precise shapes of land and sea areas on Earth, a boon to the mapmakers.

Beside satellites, there are the space probes through which much information has been gathered. These probes differ from satellites in that they are not intended to achieve moon or planetary orbit. Their purpose is to obtain new data via their instruments. In late 1962 Mariner II was launched and guided toward Venus. As it flew by that planet, Mariner II probed the Venusian environment for new data, and transmitted it back to Earth through 48,000,000 miles of interplanetary space. More recently another Mariner probe has been launched, this time in the direction of Mars. Besides data, it scanned photographically a small portion of the Martian surface. The photographs shown on a later page attest to the success of the Ranger missions to the Moon.

In the not-too-distant future man will launch probes in search of extraterrestrial life. The question of life in space and the question of the origin of life are interwoven. The full understanding of this relationship has innumerable implications in the study of human health and disease.

While these probes are being carried on today, man has taken a few steps toward space on his own. For comparatively brief periods of time astronauts and cosmonauts have reached the fringes of space (Projects Mercury and Vostok) and have even maneuvered outside their spacecraft in orbital flights around the Earth (Projects Gemini and Voskhod). For all purposes, man has been orbited in an artificial moon. In revolving about the Earth, a manned satellite has to obey the same physical laws that a natural satellite must. Consequently, man is being exposed to these new conditions and is, through these orbital missions, in the process of learning how to maneuver and behave effectively while in space.

Project Gemini and two-thirds of Project Apollo are devoted to developing the technical ability to navigate in space prior to a landing on the Moon. Project Apollo with a crew of three is designated to accomplish that. The final objective will be that, upon reaching the Moon's vicinity, the Apollo spacecraft will be swerved into a circular orbit about 100 miles above the lunar surface. Two astronauts will then enter the lunar excursion module portion of Apollo, detach it, and land on a previously chosen location on the Moon, while the third crewman remains in the parent craft which continues to orbit the Moon. After exploring the lunar surface near the landing site, taking pictures, etc., the two astronauts will depart from the Moon and rendezvous with the parent craft. After joining the third astronaut in the parent craft, they will detach from the lunar excursion module and return to Earth.

As man's increasing interest, knowledge, and control of inanimate energy has lead him to exploratory ventures here outlined, so it will carry him to a rendezvous with the secrets of the Universe and to a life still unimaginable.

Nimbus I took this clear picture of the Italian Peninsula and Sicily. Clouds on the right obscure the view of Yugoslavia, Albania, and Greece.

NASA

A photograph of the Red Sea area taken by Tiros I. Major features have been labeled for reference.

A reference map showing the same area photographed by Tiros I.

NASA

© RMcN

TITAN
N.A.S.A.
Type / Intercontinental Ballistic Missile.
Range / 5,500 nautical miles

THOR
U.S. Air Force Photo
Type / Intermediate Ballistic Missile.
Range / 1,500 nautical miles

POLARIS
Offic al U.S. Navy Photo
Type / Intermediate Ballistic Missile.
Range / 1,200 — 1,500 nautical

REDSTONE
N.A.S.A.
Type/Intercontinental Ballistic Missile and Spacecraft.
Range/Restricted information.

THE FIRST STEPS UPWARD

The rocket is, at this time, the only usable means of providing propulsion in the vacuum of space. It needs neither ground, nor water, nor air to push against, as do other vehicles that move by such resistance (such as wheels turning on a roadway or propeller blades churning air or water). The rocket's movement forward is an illustration of the law of reaction; in this case, reaction to the gases which are expelled from the rocket's exhaust. Out in space the rocket is even more efficient than inside a planet's atmosphere.

In space, a rocket engine operates only during part of its journey; the rest of the time the space vehicle keeps moving because it has achieved momentum and there is no air resistance to slow it down. When this stage of flight, the rocket and its contents are in a state of "free fall" and weightlessness.

Traveling through space, man must carry with him absolutely everything he needs—even the air he breathes. He will also need to conserve sufficient fuel for his eventual return to Earth.

JUNO—II
Type/Spacecraft
Range/Restricted information.
N.A.S.A.

VANGUARD
Type / Spacecraft.
Range / Restricted information
Official U.S. Navy Photo

JUPITER-C
Type / Intercontinental Ballistic Missile and Spacecraft.
Range/ 3,300 nautical miles
U.S. Army Photo

ATLAS
Type / Intercontinental Ballistic Missile.
Range / 5,500 nautical miles.
U.S. Air Force Photo

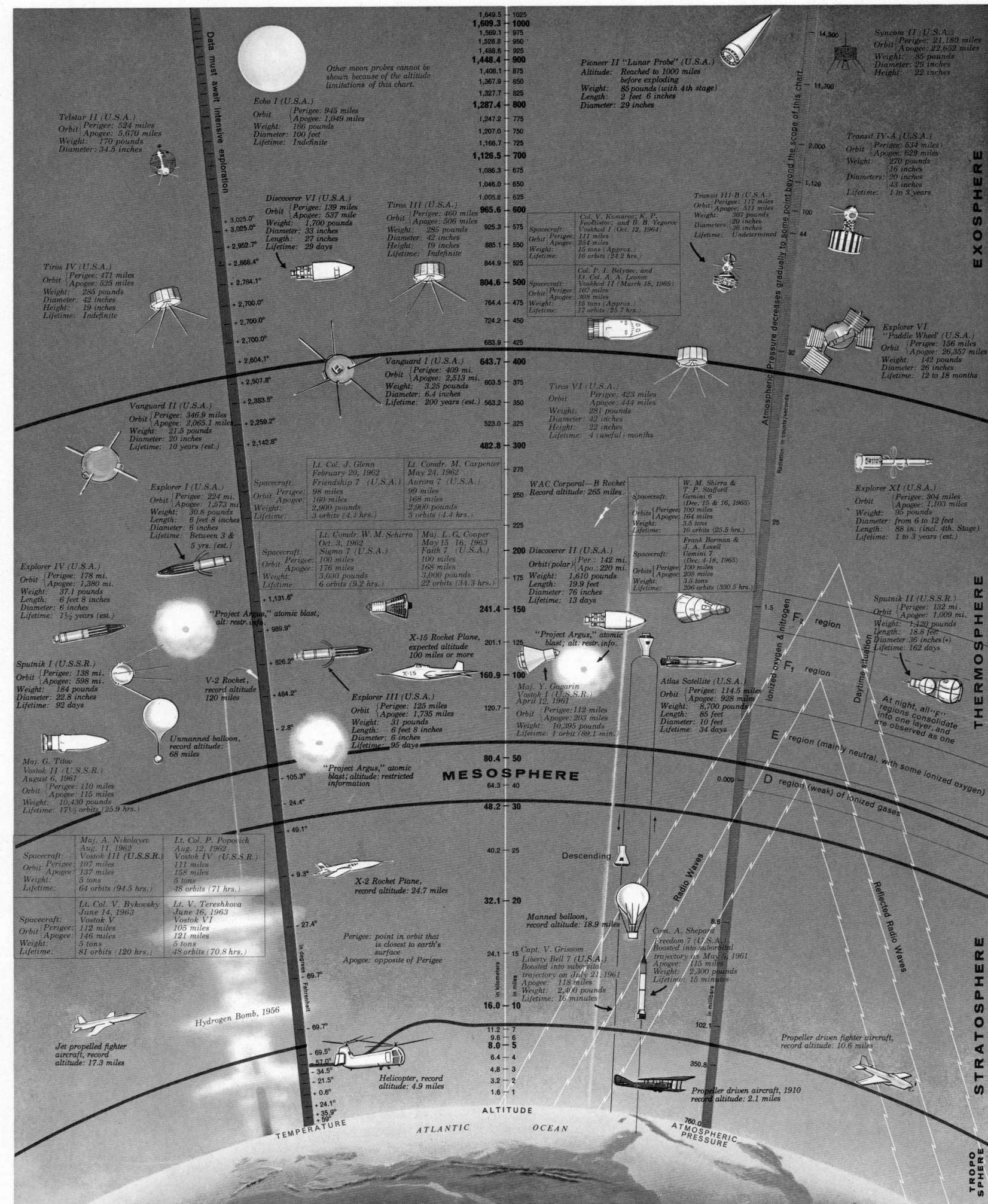

AMERICA'S FIRST DAY IN SPACE

An Atlas-D rocket (360,000 pounds of thrust) launched Lt. Col. J. H. Glenn, aboard spacecraft "Friendship 7", into orbit on February 20, 1962. The principal orbital characteristics of the manned capsule were: perigee, 97.6 miles; apogee, 159.5 miles; average velocity, 17,545 m.p.h.; and inclination, 32.5°.

The capsule afforded a maximum degree of protection for its astronaut against the effects of heat, acceleration changes, and various aerodynamic forces. Within the 9 ft. 6 in. long capsule the temperature averaged about 90°F while traversing over the "night" regions of the Earth and over 100°F while traversing over the "daylight" regions. The separately controlled suit, however, kept astronaut Glenn at a more comfortable 67°F, approximately, while he made valuable observations, performed preassigned experiments on human reaction and adaptation, and took photographs through the porthole. One of the most interesting observations was the phenomenon of numerous small particles of metal-like texture moving at approximately the same velocity as the spacecraft which Glenn encountered in those regions undergoing the process of sunrise.

The re-entry of the capsule began during the end of the third orbit, over the Pacific Ocean, while approaching the West Coast of the United States. This was achieved with the help of the retro-rockets which slowed down the capsule. During re-entry, the temperature rose to about 3,000°F. Subsequently, the spacecraft deployed a parachute for the final descent.

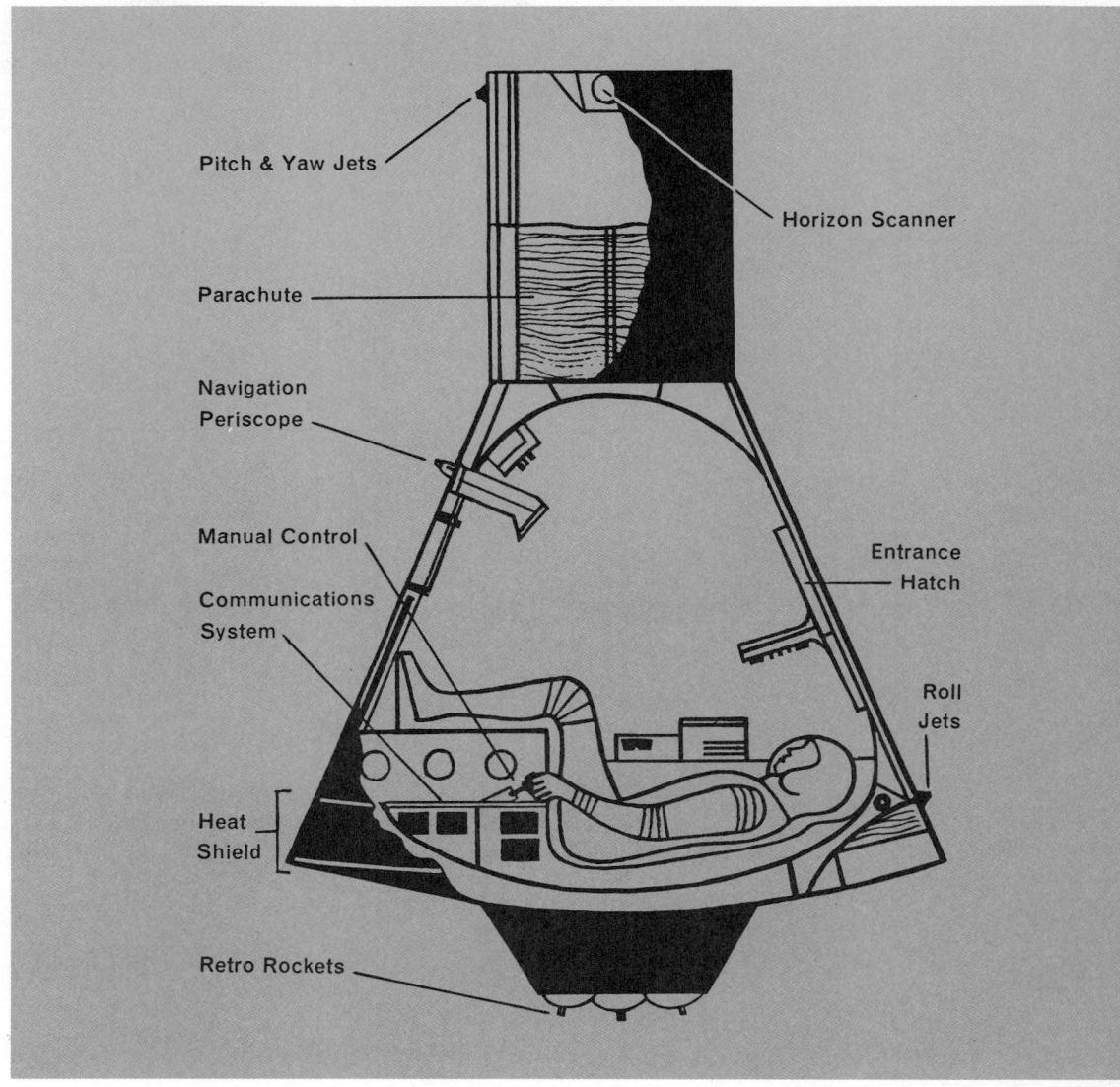

TOP—*Astronaut J. H. Glenn boards "Friendship 7"*

BOTTOM—*Instrument panel of the Mercury capsule*

The beginning of the voyage: lift-off!

TOP—*View of a sunset, taken by J. H. Glenn, from "Friendship 7"*

BOTTOM—*View of the Florida coast taken by J. H. Glenn, at the beginning of his second orbit*

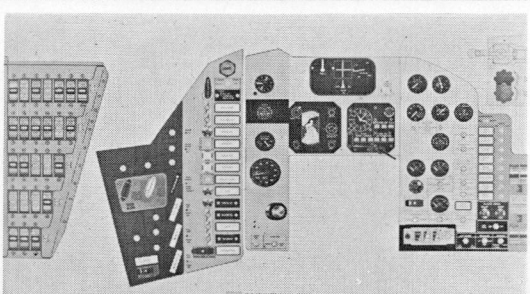

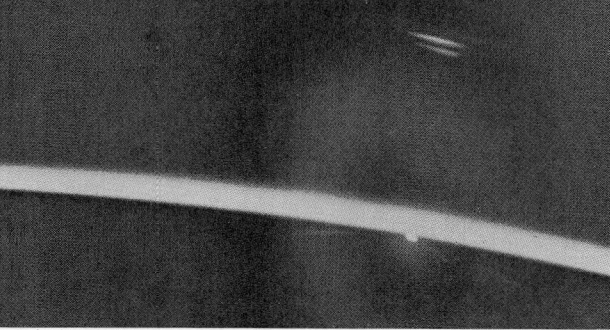

COMMUNICATIONS SATELLITE

Burgeoning telephone and television traffic requirements on overland routes have been met through the use of microwave repeater systems, whose towers are now a familiar site throughout the United States. Microwaves travel in a straight line, and repeaters must be located at intervals of 20 to 30 miles.

Placing a repeater in a satellite, therefore, becomes an economic asset as well as an enormous technical advantage. The horizons, as "seen" from a communications satellite located several thousands of miles above the Earth, spans whole continents and oceans.

The communications satellite era began in 1958, when the Project Score satellite transmitted to the world the now famous Presidential Christmas message. In 1960 Echo I, became the first "passive" communications satellite, and Courier became the first "active" one. Passive satellites merely reflect radio signals, they do not amplify them.

On the other hand, the active communications satellite is equipped with receivers and transmitters for amplifying and retransmitting the received signals. It also has other electronic equipment for control, telemetry and power.

Since the Courier "delayed repeater" satellite, several experimental communications satellites have been orbited, achieving promising degrees of efficiency. Telstar and Relay in 1962, Syncom in 1963 and Early Bird in 1964. Syncom became the first successful attempt at synchronous communications systems.

The development of advanced communications satellites, calls for a system of synchronous satellites such as the one shown on the adjacent diagram. Synchronous or stationary, satellites are those which remain at a designated altitude while completing one revolution around the Earth in 24 hours. In effect, it appears to hover when such a system of satellites is located in an equatorial orbit, at 22,300 miles.

The advantages of the synchronous orbit are that, with only 3 satellites, placed equidistantly, it is theroetically possible to provide almost world coverage. The map below shows the scope of world coverage that an advanced synchronous system is envisaged to provide.

The economics of operational communications satellite system will be dictated by their ability to remain operable for as long as possible. The lifetime of a satellite, in turn, depends on the behavior of its components and on its resistance to hazards such as micrometeorites, etc.

N.A.S.A.

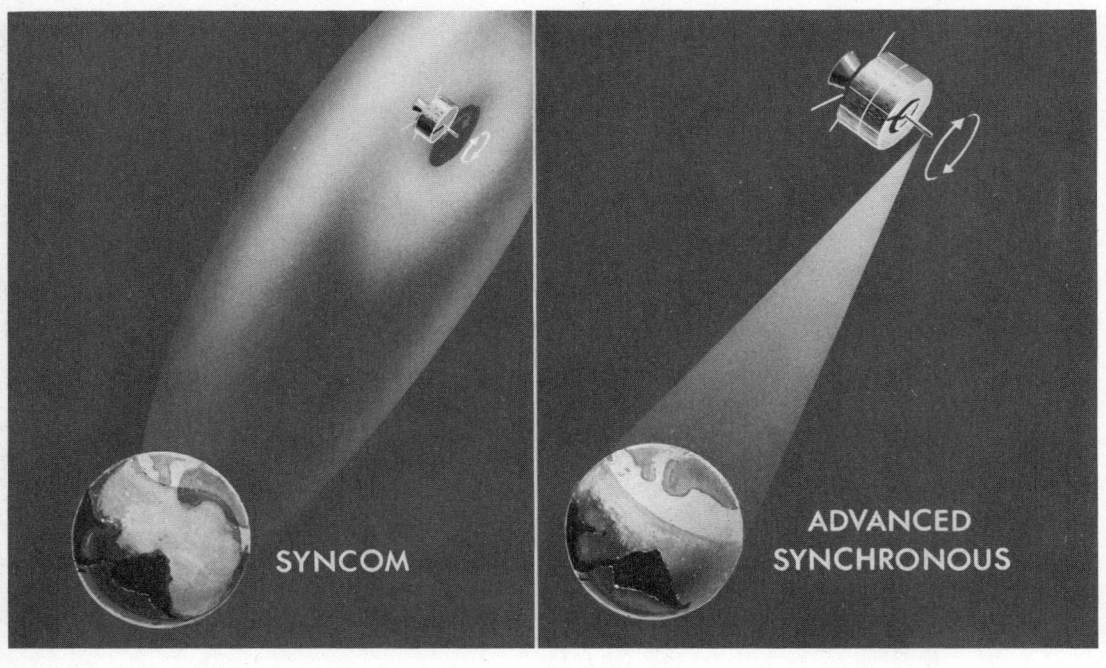

SYNCOM

ADVANCED SYNCHRONOUS

Syncom, on the left, in spin-stabilized. Its antenna radiates uniformly. The Advanced Synchronous satellite, larger and heavier than Syncom, will have a contrarotating antenna that will orient to Earth when transmitting without disturbing the attitude of the satellite.

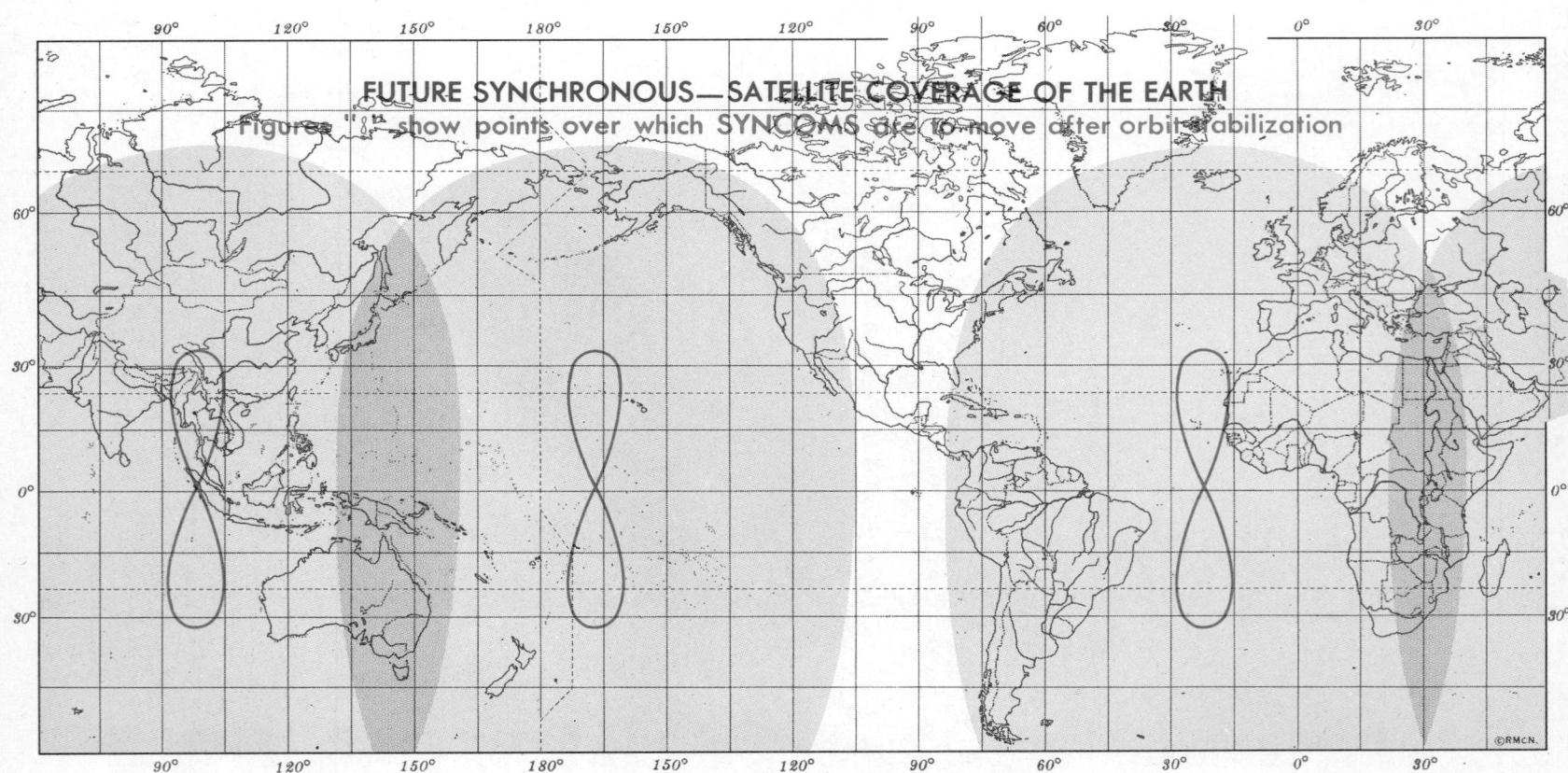

FUTURE SYNCHRONOUS—SATELLITE COVERAGE OF THE EARTH

Figures show points over which SYNCOMS are to move after orbit stabilization

©RMCN.

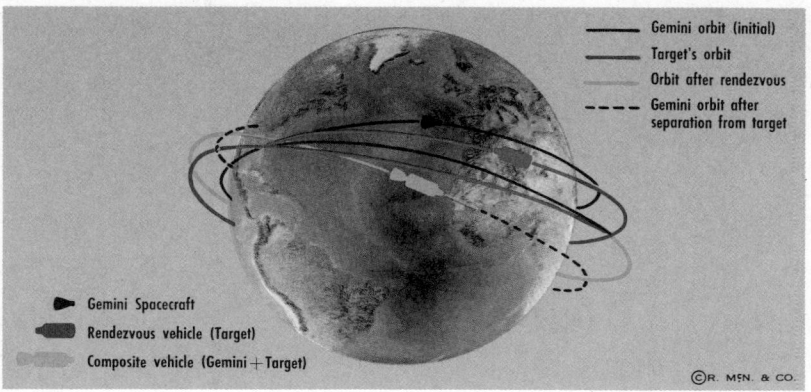

Legend:
- Gemini orbit (initial)
- Target's orbit
- Orbit after rendezvous
- Gemini orbit after separation from target

- Gemini Spacecraft
- Rendezvous vehicle (Target)
- Composite vehicle (Gemini + Target)

©R. M⸱N. & CO.

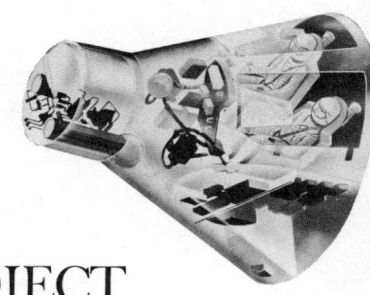

PROJECT GEMINI

N.A.S.A.

The surface details of a small portion of the Earth, photographed by U.S. astronauts

Project Gemini is the nation's current step into manned exploration of space. It employs a two-man space-craft known as Gemini, which is intended for long duration flights. The principal objectives of the project are: to provide manned rendezvous capability and experience, to provide long duration manned flight experience and its technology, to develop space navigation capability, and to collect data on the biological factors involved in prolonged space travel.

The spacecraft is similar to the Mercury capsule, although twice as heavy. It contains 50% more volume, and is about 20% longer. One of the experiments called for an astronaut to step out of the spacecraft, although safely anchored to it.

In 1965, Astronaut Edward White executed his now famous 20 minute "walk in space." Connected to the Gemini spacecraft by a 25-foot "umbilical cord", he floated freely, and performed several manouvering experiments. He also photographed the view shown on this page. Although the view was taken from an altitude of just over 100 miles, it is not possible to readily identify any cultural features. Nevertheless, the view clearly shows the characteristics of the Earth's surface and its principal features, such as mountains, rivers, etc.

In revolving about the Earth, a manned satellite has to obey the same physical laws that a natural satellite must. Consequently, man is being exposed to these new conditions and is, through these orbital missions, in the process of learning how to maneuver and behave effectively while in space.

As the intermediate step between Projects Mercury and Apollo, the objectives of Project Gemini are designed to contribute toward the lunar efforts, with experience and knowledge. This combination of objectives will give the United States the necessary experienced astronauts, who will eventually make the first voyages to the Moon. At the same time, much of the mechanical data collected from the Gemini missions will aid in re-designing and constructing numerous components of the Apollo spacecraft.

N.A.S.A.

Astronaut Edward White, the first American to "walk in space". Behind, the Earth partially covered by clouds.

THE MOON

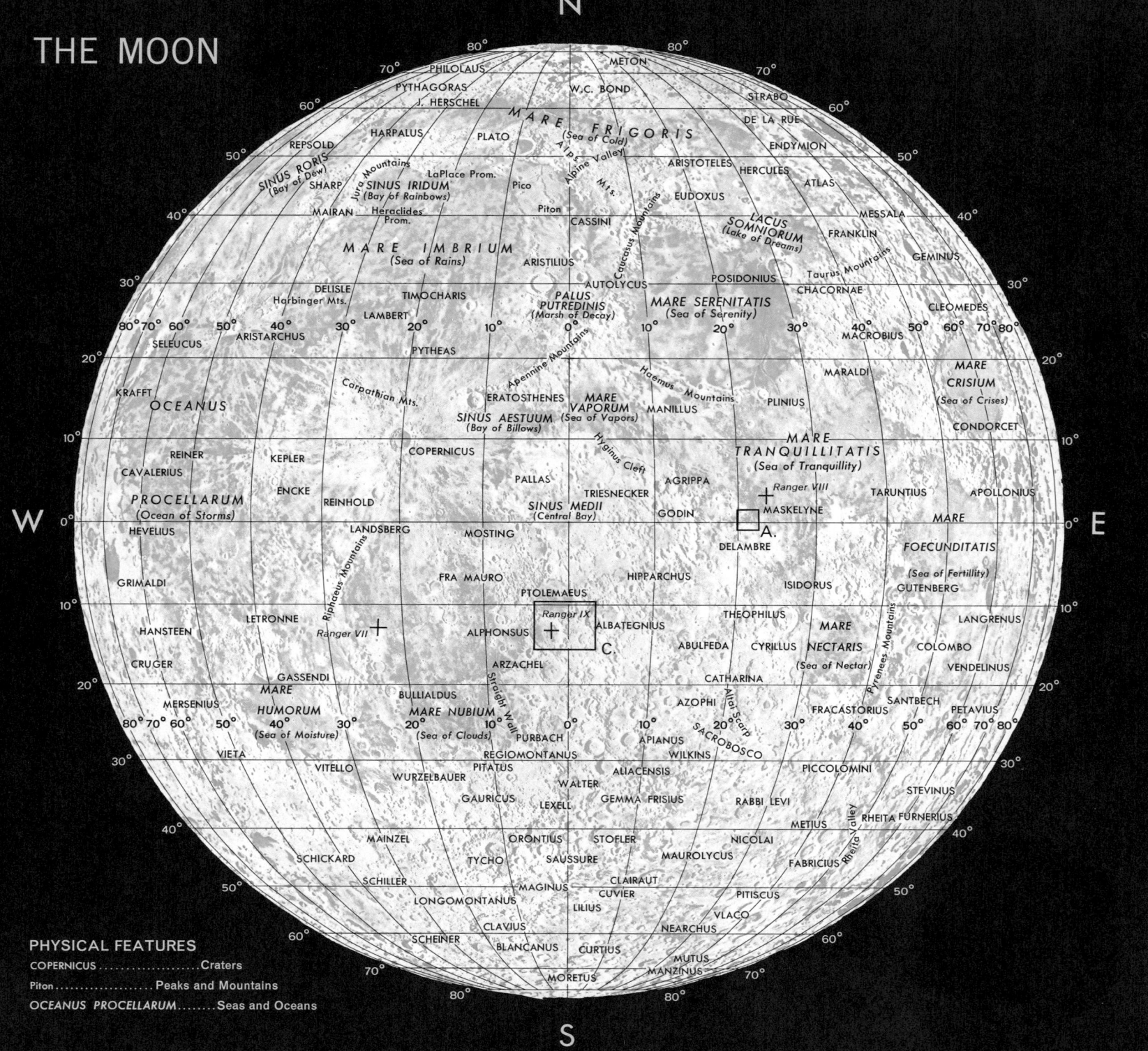

PHYSICAL FEATURES

COPERNICUS . . . . Craters

Piton . . . . Peaks and Mountains

OCEANUS PROCELLARUM . . . . Seas and Oceans

+ = Impact sites of Ranger Spacecraft

The Moon is the only natural satellite of the Earth. In comparison to our planet, the Moon is considerably smaller; its diameter is only 2,160 miles. It travels around the Earth once every 27⅓ days, at an average distance of 238,862 miles. Due to the nature of its orbital behavior, only one half of its surface can be seen from Earth. This half is commonly known as the "face side" or "near side." The relatively short distance to it has made it possible to study its surface details through telescopes. The above map was made from numerous photographs taken through various telescopes.

The Moon is a compact world of steep mountain peaks, mountain ranges, craters of all sizes, barren plains, valleys, clefts, and rills. Among these, the plains are commonly but erroneously called seas and oceans since Galileo thought these plains to be oceans. As part of its environment, the Moon has a very thin atmosphere consisting of rare gases such as argon and krypton. Therefore, there is no weather, no wind. Sound does not propagate. Due to the absence of wind and weather, its surface features have not eroded and consequently have remained unchanged through the ages except for the damage done by meteoroids falling on its surface. Water, which is fundamental to life as we conceive it, is thought to be almost nonexistent. Therefore, astronauts on exploratory ventures, will have to carry their own water, air, and other elements necessary for man's existence.

In recent years some inconclusive evidence shows that the Moon is still undergoing some of its distant-past volcanic activity to which are attributed the large majority of the lunar craters.

The "far side" of the Moon, which is not visible from Earth, remains comparatively unknown save for the photographic evidence gathered by the Russian Lunik III in 1959, which tends to indicate that the "hidden side" isn't very different from the "face side."

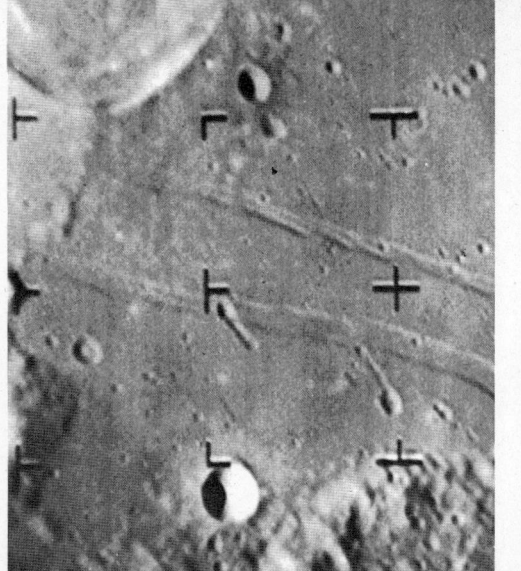

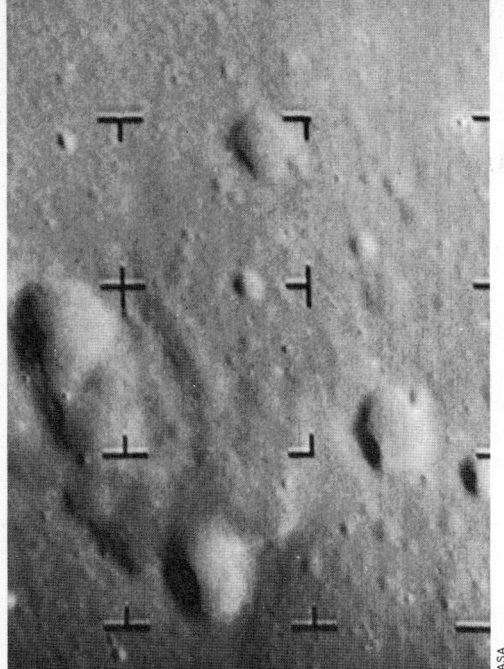

A.   Two photographs by Ranger VIII, February 20, 1965   B.

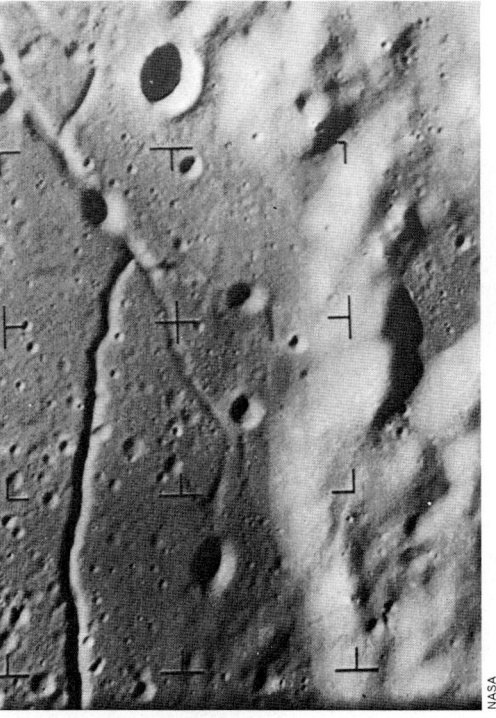

C.   Two photographs by Ranger IX, March 24, 1965   D.

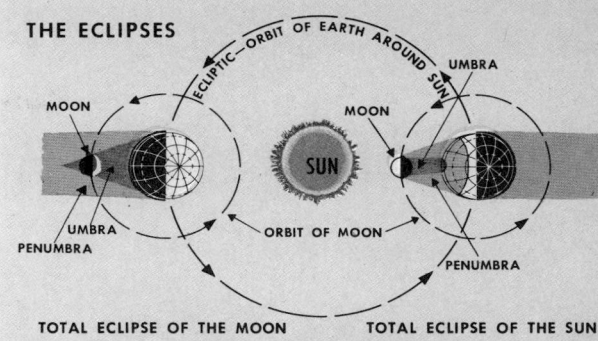

THE ECLIPSES

TOTAL ECLIPSE OF THE MOON
Eclipse of the moon occurs only when moon is full. Moon usually appears dull red during the eclipse due to the refraction of the red rays of the sun by the atmosphere of the earth.

TOTAL ECLIPSE OF THE SUN
Eclipse of the sun occurs only during new moon. Sun is invisible in *umbra* and partly invisible in *penumbra*. Total eclipse is visible only in portion of earth touched by shadow of moon (umbra).

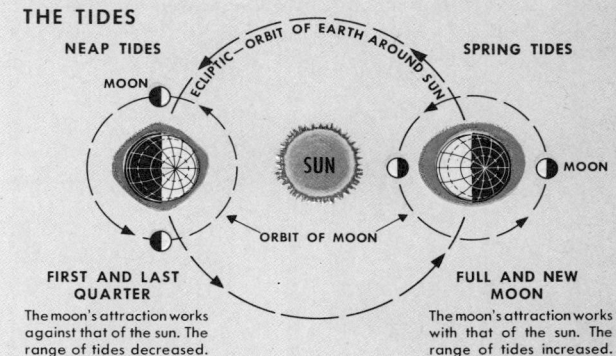

THE TIDES

NEAP TIDES   **SPRING TIDES**

FIRST AND LAST QUARTER
The moon's attraction works against that of the sun. The range of tides decreased.

FULL AND NEW MOON
The moon's attraction works with that of the sun. The range of tides increased.

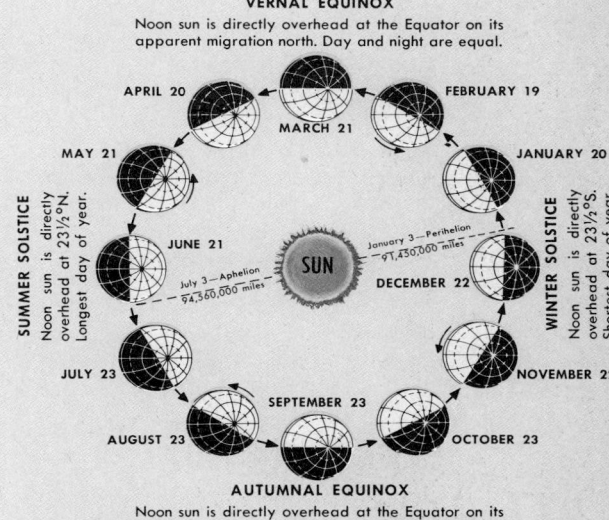

VERNAL EQUINOX
Noon sun is directly overhead at the Equator on its apparent migration north. Day and night are equal.

SUMMER SOLSTICE Noon sun is directly overhead at 23½°N. Longest day of year.

WINTER SOLSTICE Noon sun is directly overhead at 23½°S. Shortest day of year.

AUTUMNAL EQUINOX
Noon sun is directly overhead at the Equator on its apparent migration south. Day and night are equal.

THE SEASONS   Northern Hemisphere

The Ranger program was a National Aeronautics and Space Administration (NASA) project designed to examine the surface of the Moon by means of unmanned spacecraft. Each spacecraft was equipped with a high-resolution, six-camera television system that provided both wide- and narrow-angle coverage. There were three successful Ranger missions. Of these, the last two Rangers, VIII and IX, provided the close-up views shown above. Both missions took place in early 1965.

A. This photograph was taken at an altitude of 151 miles over the lunar surface. The over-all north-south distance is 43 miles. It shows the shoreline of the Sea of Tranquillity, with part of crater Sabine in the northwest corner and the two parallel Hypatia Rills, which extend across the center. Toward the south lies rugged and difficult terrain containing numerous craters.

B. This exposure was taken at an altitude of 27.5 miles. The distance, from north to south, is 4.5 miles. It shows a particularly interesting irregular cluster of depressions which feature gentler slopes than had been anticipated. The surrounding landscape has a frothy appearance of undetermined consistency.

C. This photograph was taken at an altitude of 775 miles. It covers a north-south distance of 123 miles. It shows slightly more than half of two major craters: Ptolomaeus at the top (without significant floor features) and Alphonsus (target of Ranger IX) on the left which shows a rill system and a 3,300-foot central peak.

D. This photograph was taken at an altitude of 115 miles. The over-all north to south distance is 19 miles. It shows the northeastern edge of the floor of the crater Alphonsus and part of the crater's wall. The floor is cut prominently by rills (shown in less detail on figure C.) which are lined with small craterlets that have pocked part of the rills. Surprisingly, the crater walls have gentle slopes and rolling terrain.

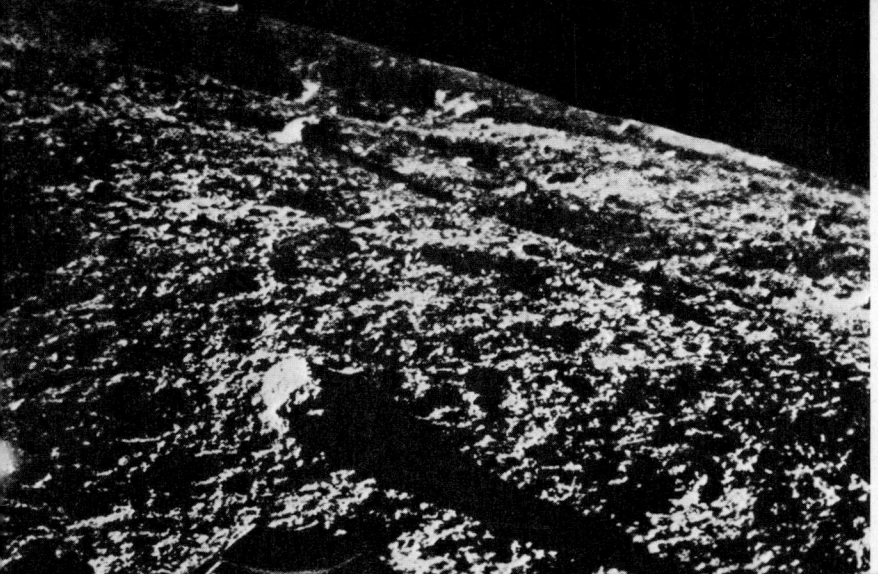

Novosti Press Agency, Moscow

The above view was taken on Feb. 5, 1966 by Russia's Luna-9, which landed on the Ocean of Storms. It shows the surface detail of an area which is known to be relatively even. The rugged appearance is due to the camera being only 2 feet above surface.

N.A.S.A.

This view was photographed on June 2, 1966 by America's Surveyor-I, which landed on another area of the Ocean of Storms. It shows a rock 12 inches long, smaller pebbles, and a small craterlet in the background which has a diameter of about two feet. The camera is 6 feet above surface.

THE FAR SIDE OF THE MOON

The Far Side of the Moon is hidden from our direct view, because of tidal forces that hold the Moon to one rotation on its axis, which takes place in the amount of time that the Moon revolves around the Earth. In the distant past, millions of years ago, the Moon rotated faster than it does now, completing one rotation in a few hours. The force of tidal friction caused by the gravitational pull of the Sun and Earth, have slowed down the Moon and lengthened its period of rotation to its present 27.3 days. Efforts have already been made to discover the nature of the "Far Side of the Moon". On October 1959, Lunik III, a 614 pound Soviet lunar probe, is claimed to have photographed a major portion of the hidden side, using two cameras, as it moved around the Moon. The closest point of approach was at 4,350 miles above the lunar surface. At the time of photography, Lunik III moved along at an altitude which ranged between 37,300 and 43,500 miles above the Moon. The probe took some thirty-two photographs in a 40 minute period. During this time, the cameras were in a line connecting the Sun and the Moon. Thus, the Moon was almost completely illuminated. These photographs were successfully transmitted to Earth a few hours later. The resulting photographs recorded about two-thirds of the Far Side of the Moon, plus a narrow marginal area of the "visible" or "Near Side" part of the lunar surface. Below is one of the best known views taken by Lunik III.

The names it shows are those which soviet scientists asigned to some of the principal surface features of the Far Side. Other photographs permitted soviet scientists to name many more identifyable features.

In general, it was concluded that the Far Side is not very different from the "Near Side". The photographs indicate that similar surface features (craters, seas, mountain ranges, etc.) are to be expected on the Far Side.

Mountain areas appear to predominate, while there are relatively few seas, like those visible on the "Near Side". Large craters stand out sharply. The quality of reflection, on the photographs, tend to indicate that there are numerous smaller craters which do not stand out so sharply.

Several experiments similar to that of Lunik III, with improved instrumentation and camera equipment, will permit selenographers to chart the Far Side of the Moon in the same degree of detail as the visible side or "Near Side."

Far Side of the Moon, taken by Lunik III.

United Press International Photo

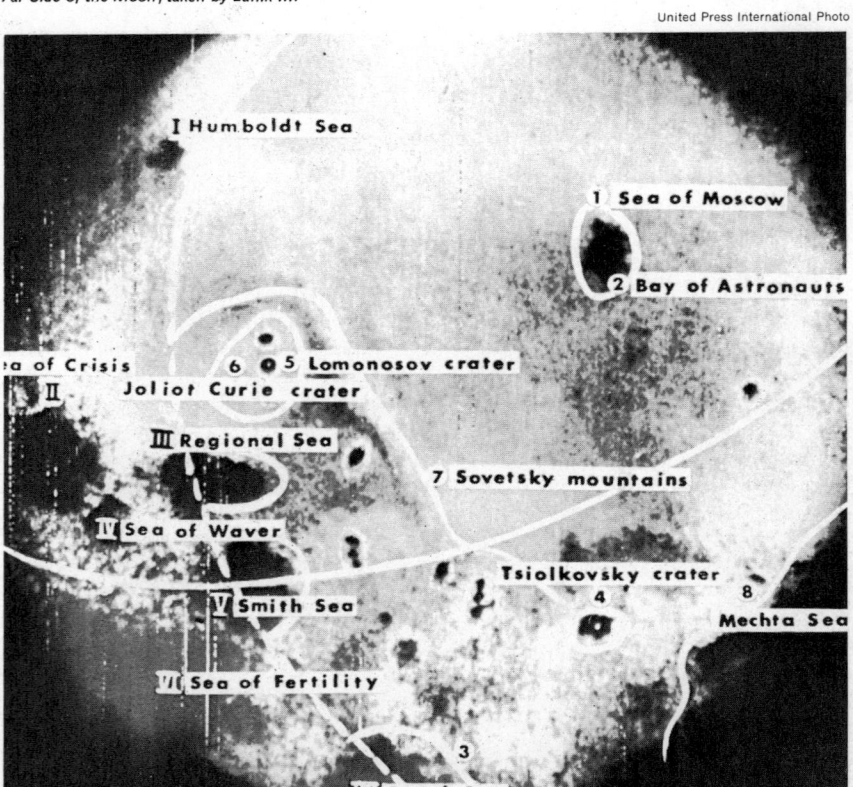

Lunik III photographing the Far Side of the Moon.

Sovfoto

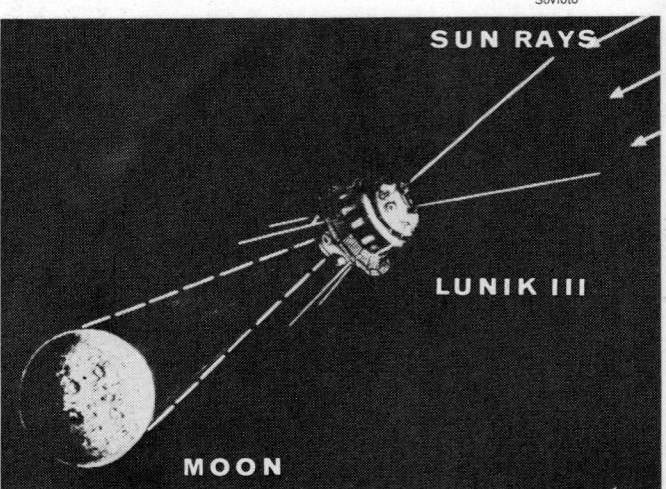

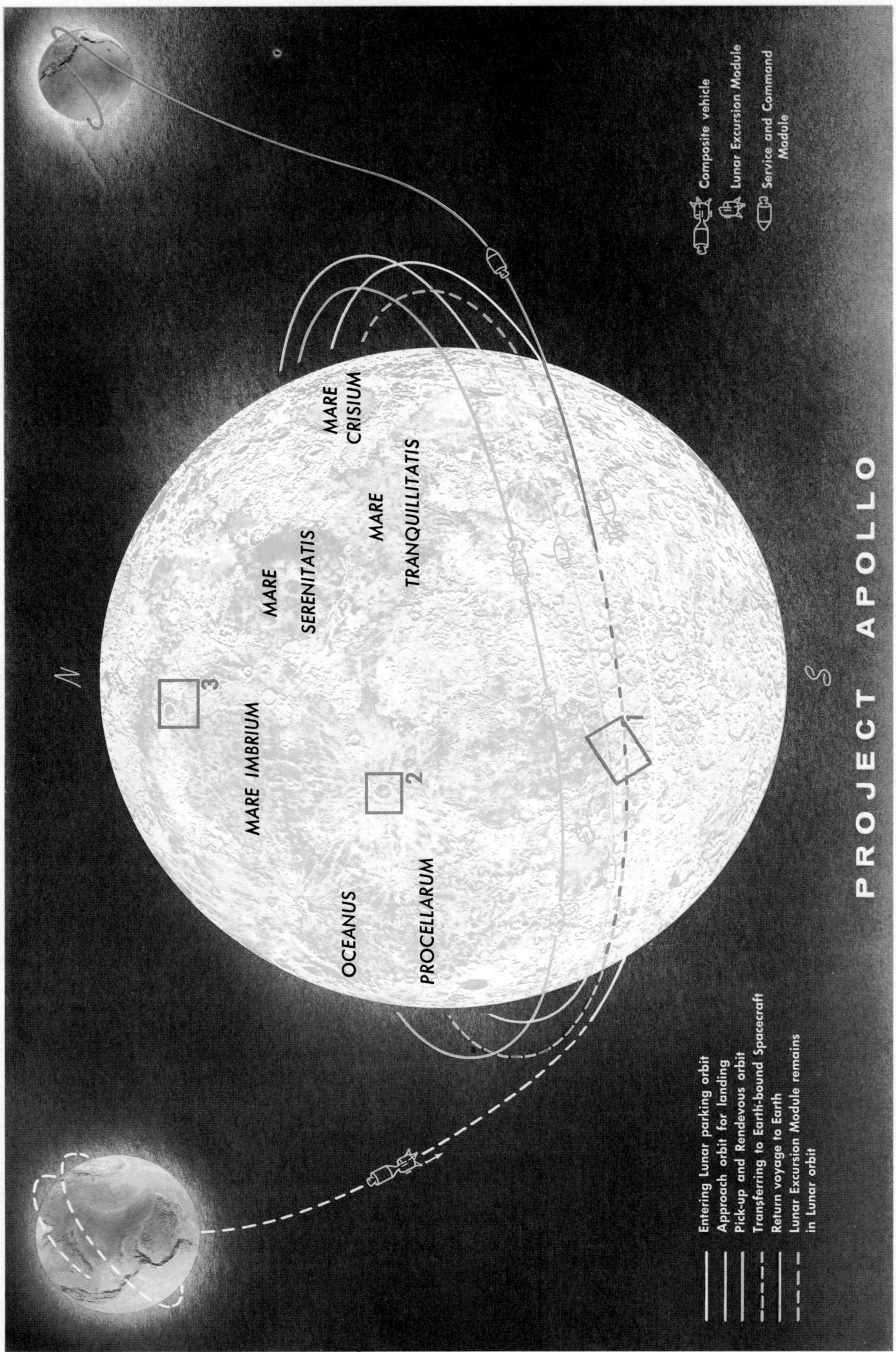

PROJECT APOLLO

MARE CRISIUM

MARE SERENITATIS

MARE TRANQUILLITATIS

MARE IMBRIUM

OCEANUS

PROCELLARUM

N

S

Composite vehicle

Lunar Excursion Module

Service and Command Module

Entering Lunar parking orbit
Approach orbit for landing
Pick-up and Rendevous orbit
Transferring to Earth-bound Spacecraft
Return voyage to Earth
Lunar Excursion Module remains in lunar orbit

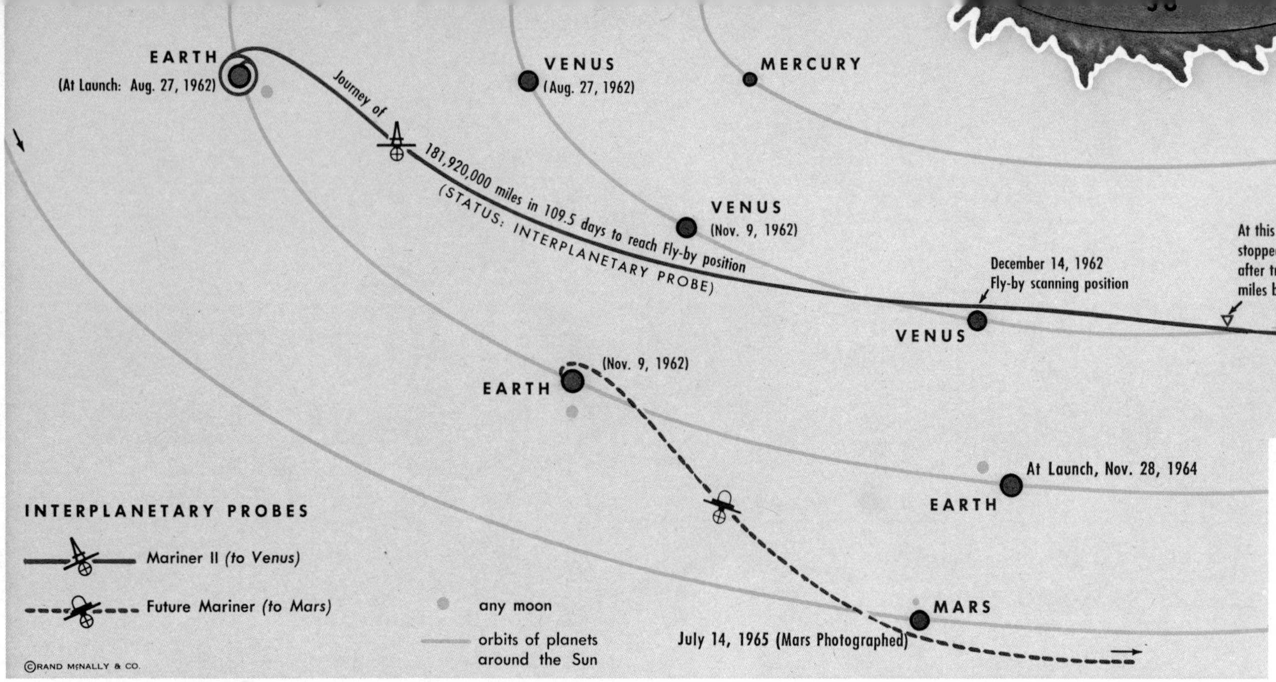

EARTH
(At Launch: Aug. 27, 1962)

MERCURY

VENUS
(Aug. 27, 1962)

VENUS
(Nov. 9, 1962)

VENUS

EARTH
(Nov. 9, 1962)

EARTH

MARS

Journey of
181,920,000 miles in 109.5 days to reach fly-by position
(STATUS: INTERPLANETARY PROBE)

Into orbit around the Sun
(STATUS: ARTIFICIAL PLANETOID)

At this point Mariner II stopped transmitting after traveling 54,225,000 miles beyond Venus

December 14, 1962
Fly-by scanning position

At Launch, Nov. 28, 1964

July 14, 1965 [Mars Photographed]

INTERPLANETARY PROBES

—✧— Mariner II (to Venus)

- -✧- - Future Mariner (to Mars)

● any moon

—— orbits of planets around the Sun

SPACE PROBES

Exploration of space is one of the most difficult technological challenges of our day. The United States is busily engaged in a broad program to explore the Solar System with unmanned instrumented spacecrafts which have come to be known as "space probes". There are various purposes for these probes. Some of these are to provide data concerning surface and environmental characteristics of planets; to provide data about solar plasma; to study the distribution of space hazards such as meteor showers; to provide advance data concerning those regions which one day man might set out to explore. These probes will be our interplanetary eyes, ears and hands until we get there!

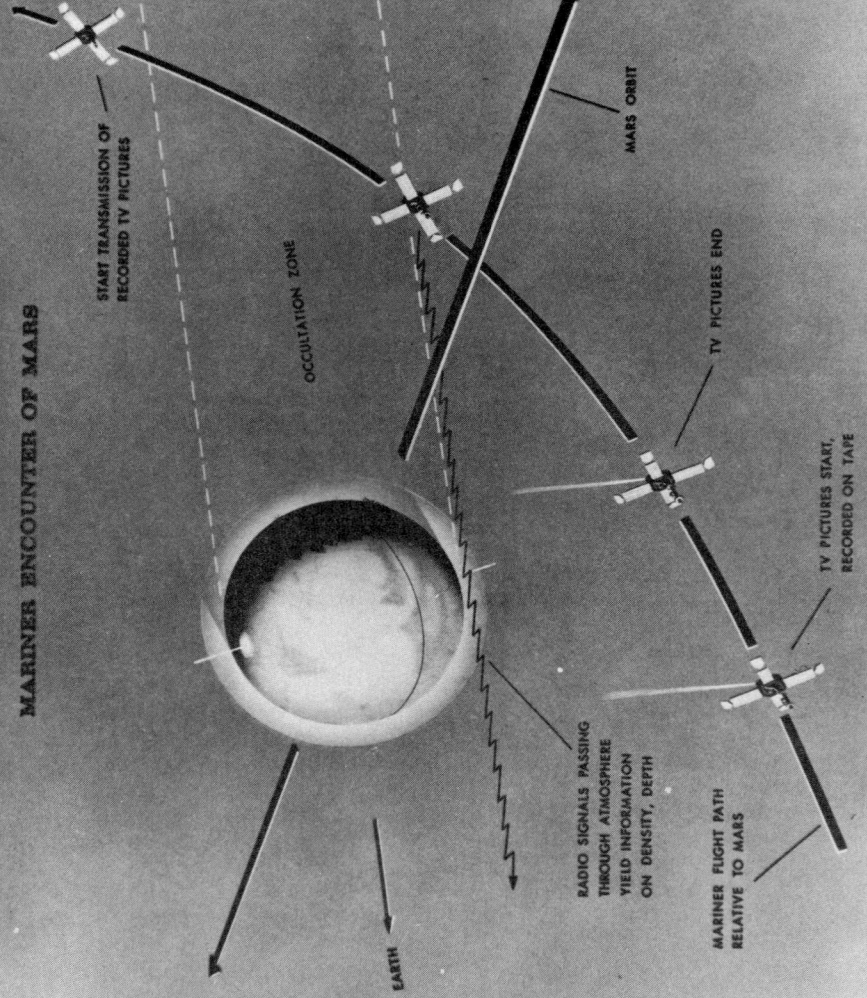

MARINER ENCOUNTER OF MARS

START TRANSMISSION OF RECORDED TV PICTURES

MARS ORBIT

OCCULTATION ZONE

TV PICTURES END

RADIO SIGNALS PASSING THROUGH ATMOSPHERE YIELD INFORMATION ON DENSITY, DEPTH

TV PICTURES START, RECORDED ON TAPE

MARINER FLIGHT PATH RELATIVE TO MARS

EARTH

N.A.S.A.

The approach and encounter between Mariner IV and Planet Mars.

PLANETARY PROBES

On November 28, 1964 Mariner IV, an American planetary probe equipped with television cameras, was launched from Cape Kennedy. Seven and one half months later, on July 14, 1965, it flew-by planet Mars and took 22 photographs. The point of closest approach to the probed planet was about 6,000 miles. Later, the photographs were transmitted to Earth, and are considered among the most significant scientific photographs ever taken.

The spacecraft also gathered data about surface pressure, atmosphere characteristics, corpuscular radiation flow between Earth and Mars, and the extent of trapped radiation in the vicinity of Mars.

With the exception of the photographic reconnaissance and the occultation experiments, the other objectives did not produce sufficient data. The preliminary results of the occultation experiment indicate that the atmosphere (dense portion) extends upward to about 5.5 miles. The Earth's comparable region of the atmosphere measures 13 miles.

The photographic reconnaissance, on the other hand yielded man's first close-up look at Mars. It sampled only 1% of the Martian sur-

face. Many of the 22 photographs revealed the presence of numerous craters, similar in size and appearance to those on our Moon. Most of the craters photographed range, in diameter, from 3 to 75 miles. Their presence, on Mars, raises fundamental questions concerning the planet's evolutionary history. It appears, therefore that Mars is presently an extremely arid planet, though still retaining enough water to support desert-type vegetation. The oceans which were once thought to exist, vanished in ancient times.

N.A.S.A.

The Atlantis region of Mars, between Mare Sirenum and Mare Cimmerium. The North-South distance is 150 miles. Taken from 7,800 miles away, by Mariner IV.

Space Age Glossary

ACCELERATION: Rate of change of velocity. It may be positive, representing a speeding up, or negative, representing a slowing down.

ALBEDO: The ratio between the light reflected from a surface and the light received by it. Thus the Moon, with an albedo of .07, reflects 7 per cent of the sunlight received.

APHELION: That point, in an orbit around the Sun, where a planet, comet, asteroid, etc., is most distant from the Sun. Opposite term: Perihelion.

APOGEE: That point, in an orbit around the Earth, where a satellite is most distant from the Earth. *Opposite term* Perigee.

ARTIFICIAL EARTH SATELLITE: Any one of the man-made objects placed into orbit around the Earth—Sputnik, Explorer, Vanguard, Discoverer, Tiros, etc.

ASTEROID: A small body, larger than a meteoroid, orbiting around the sun. Its name refers to its star-like appearance from Earth.

ASTRONAUTICS: The science of space flight.

ASTRONOMICAL UNIT: The mean distance between Earth and Sun, about 92,900,000 miles.

ASTRONOMY: The study of all celestial bodies; their behavior, composition, relative distances, motion, etc.

ASTROPHYSICS: The science dealing with the principles and applications of physics to problems in astronomy, especially the analysis of light.

ATMOSPHERE: The envelope of gas surrounding a planet, satellite, or a star.

ATMOSPHERE OF THE EARTH: The thin envelope of gases surrounding the Earth.

AURORA (Polaris, Borealis, and Australis): Streams of glowing light in the sky, usually around the polar regions; caused by the symmetrical deflection, toward the poles, of electrically-charged particles received from the Sun.

BALLISTICS: The science dealing with the motions and trajectories of projectiles.

BALLISTIC MISSILE: A missile that progresses in its trajectory with no guidance or propulsion other than that imparted during launching.

BOLIDE: A fireball that explodes in midair. See Fireball.

CELESTIAL EQUATOR: The line constituting the perimeter of the plane of the Earth's equator, as it cuts the Celestial Sphere.

CELESTIAL SPHERE: The apparent sphere of infinite radius on which all celestial objects are assumed to be located for purposes of mapping and identification.

CEPHEID VARIABLE: A giant-type star that undergoes regular periodic changes in brightness due to internal pulsations. It is used in determination of distances.

COMET: A luminous body which moves in an elongated orbit around the sun. Usually it has a long tail which always points away from the Sun.

CONSTELLATION: A configuration of stars associated by patterns in the sky. Constellations can be used to identify areas in the sky like states are used to designate areas in the United States.

COSMIC RAYS: Streams of extremely penetrating and fast electrically-charged particles, which originate in interstellar space.

CRATER: See Lunar Crater.

DECELERATION: Negative acceleration—a slowing down or retardation.

DECLINATION: The distance, in degrees, northward and southward from the celestial equator, to any given celestial body. This concept is similar to latitude on Earth.

DISCOVERER: The name given to the series of U. S. data-gathering Earth satellites having polar orbits.

ECHO: The name given to the series of U. S. Earth satellites designed for use as reflectors in radio communications.

ECLIPTIC: The apparent annual path of the Sun among the stars, defining the center of the zodiac.

ELLIPSE: The geometrical form of the orbit of one celestial body revolving around another. The Earth's orbit around the Sun is an ellipse distorted by the presence of other planets.

ESCAPE VELOCITY: The minimum velocity required by an object (space ship, rocket, etc.) to escape the gravitational attraction of a planet thus leaving its surface.

EXOSPHERE: The outermost region of the Earth's atmosphere. It begins at approximately 625 miles above the Earth's surface.

EXOTIC FUELS: Any of several types of rocket fuels, recently developed, that have components not hitherto used for such purposes.

EXPLORER: The name given to a series of U. S. data-gathering Earth satellites. The Explorer satellites have an equatorial orbit.

FIREBALL: An extremely bright meteor.
See Bolide.

FREE FALL: The condition of unrestricted motion of an object as it travels through space with its propelling force shut off.

GALAXY: An aggregation of millions of stars, gas, and dust. The Milky Way is an example.

GRAVITATION: The force of mutual attraction existing between all objects or matter in the universe. The amount of force depends on the mass of the objects and distance between them.

GRAVITY: The gravitational acceleration of objects toward the Earth, slightly modified by centrifugal force, the shape of the Earth, etc. The term is also applied to a similar force on other bodies (planets, etc.) in space.

GUIDED MISSILE: A self-propelled projectile with a controlled path. The control may be internal or external, and the missile may or may not have a warhead.

INFERIOR PLANETS: Mercury and Venus, between the Earth and the Sun. See Superior Planets.

INTERNATIONAL GEOPHYSICAL YEAR: The eighteen-month interval ending Dec. 31, 1958, during which scientists from many nations cooperated in research activity in geophysics and related fields.

IONOSPHERE: That layer-region of the Earth's atmosphere, consisting mainly of varying layers of ionized gases. It is located between 35 and 235 miles above the Earth's surface.

JET PROPULSION: Propulsion by reaction where the exhaust jet contains matter, such as air, which has not been carried aboard the vehicle. Can be used only in the atmosphere.

LIGHT-YEAR: A measure of distance based on the speed of light. It is about 6 million million miles, the product of 186,000 miles per second (the speed of light) times the number of seconds in a year.

LUNAR CRATER: Generally a circular walled formation, of which there are thousands on the Moon, varying in diameters and depth.

LUNIK: The name given to the Soviet series of lunar probes.

MAGNITUDE: The relative brightness of celestial bodies, as indicated by a scale of stellar light intensity.

MASS: The quantity of matter within an object.

MESOSPHERE: That layer-region of the Earth's atmosphere located between 235 and 630 miles above the Earth's surface.

METEOR: A meteoroid that enters the Earth's atmosphere. It is made luminous by air resistance and may be seen from the Earth's surface momentarily as a streak of light. See Fireball and Bolide.

METEORITE: A meteoroid that has survived a journey through the Earth's atmosphere and has landed on the surface. The largest on display weighs about 34 tons. It is in the American Museum—Hayden Planetarium.

METEOROID: A small solid object in space.

MIDAS: The name given to the U. S. series of Earth satellites designed to detect missile launchings by means of infrared sensors.

MILKY WAY: The luminous belt stretching across the heavens consisting mostly of stars so faint that they cannot be seen individually. This belt defines the central plane of our Galaxy. The Galaxy itself is often loosely referred to as the Milky Way.

NEBULA: A true nebula is a mass of gas in space; it may be bright or dark. Exterior galaxies were thought to be nebulae before modern large telescopes showed them to consist of billions of stars at a great distance. They are still sometimes called "spiral nebulae."

NORTH STAR: Polaris, the star which happens to be nearly over the Earth's north pole at this time in history.

ORBIT: The path described by a celestial body revolving around another; or by an artificial satellite revolving around a celestial body.

PAYLOAD: The weight of all such components, as scientific instruments, radio transmitter, etc., which together will perform a predetermined controllable task. Generally the payload is part of a rocket's last stage, or part of an artificial satellite.

PERIGEE: The point in an orbit around the Earth where a satellite is nearest the Earth. *Opposite term* Apogee.

PERIHELION: The point in an orbit around the Sun where a planet, comet, etc., is nearest the Sun. *Opposite term* Aphelion.

PIONEER: The name given to the U. S. series of lunar probes.

PLANET: One of the dark, mostly solid objects revolving around the Sun, and shining by reflected light. The Earth is a planet.

PROXIMA CENTAURI: Name of the star nearest the Earth, other than the Sun. It is 4.25 light-years away.

RADIATION PRESSURE: The force exerted by light or other electromagnetic radiation in a direction opposite the source.

REVOLUTION: The movement of an object around an external point or object. The Earth revolves around the Sun.

RIGHT ASCENSION: The distance, in time units, counter-clockwise (due east) along the Celestial Equator, from the first point of Aries to the meridian passing through any given celestial body.

ROCKET: A device or vehicle with self-contained material for the production of the jet, which causes the rocket to recoil in the opposite direction of the jet. It does not depend on air or any other exterior medium for its operation.

ROTATION: The motion of an object about an axis through its center of gravity.
Example: The Earth rotates on its axis.

SATELLITE: A body in orbit around a planet. The Moon is the Earth's satellite.

SPACE SHIP: A manned vehicle to be used for interplanetary travel and exploration.

SPACE STATION SATELLITE: A large artificial satellite of the Earth designed for human occupancy.

SPUTNIK: The Russian name for the Soviet series of artificial Earth satellites.

STAR: A self-luminous celestial body, as distinguished from planets which shine by reflected light, and excluding comparatively small objects such as comets and meteors. The Sun is a typical star.

STRATOSPHERE: That layer-region of the Earth's atmosphere located between 13 and 35 miles above the Earth's surface.

SUN, THE: Nearest star to the Earth.

SUPERIOR PLANETS: Those beyond the Earth with respect to distance from the Sun. See Inferior Planets.

THRUST: The recoil of a rocket in one direction caused by expulsion of the jet.

TIROS: The name given to the series of U. S. Meteorological Earth satellites; forerunner of forthcoming geodetical satellites.

TRANSIT: The name given to the series of U. S. Navigational Earth satellites; to be used by ships and aircraft as navigational aids.

TROPOSPHERE: That layer-region of the atmosphere which is in contact with the Earth's surface. It is located between ground level and 6 miles (at the poles) to 13 miles (at the equator) above the Earth's surface.

VANGUARD: The name given to the U. S. Navy's program for launching a series of data-gathering Earth satellites as part of the International Geophysical Year. The name also applies to the rockets used.

ZODIAC: The belt in the sky through which the planets appear to move, as viewed from the Earth. It extends 8° on each side of the Ecliptic.

INTRODUCTION TO THE POLITICAL MAPS

The political maps in this Atlas have been arranged on a regional basis instead of country by country. Each regional map is centered around a major country or an important grouping of countries.

Each of the great land masses of the earth is shown as a whole and then broken down into major regions. All the regional maps for each continent are drawn on the same scale. Thus it is possible to make direct visual comparisons of the sizes of countries and the distances between places, simply by turning from one map to another.

City names on the maps are usually shown with the local or official spelling. Sometimes this official name differs from the form of the name commonly used in English-speaking countries. Whenever the anglicized form of the name of a capital city differs from the official spelling, the official name is included on the maps in parentheses. For other cities, the local official form is given first on the map, with the customary English form in parentheses. Often, where two forms of a name are in common use because of a recent change in sovereignty, an official change in name, or for any other reason, both forms are given on the map.

In general, spellings follow the recommendations of the United States Board on Geographic Names of the Department of the Interior, which determines the official spelling of foreign geographical names for U.S. Government use. For the spelling of place names in the United States, the United States Postal Guide is the authority that is followed.

The political maps carry as many political subdivisions as space will permit. Counties are shown on all state maps in the United States and on most of the maps of Canadian provinces. Other countries may not be mapped on a large enough scale to permit showing present administrative subdivisions. For some of these countries, the names of larger administrative subdivisions appear without the boundaries. In others, regions with historical significance are shown instead of present subdivisions.

The names of physical features on the maps are distinguished by two styles of *italic* type. The type for topographic features, such as mountains, passes, etc., appears in all capital italic letters. Hydrographic features, such as rivers, bays, gulfs, etc., appear in capital and lower case italic letters.

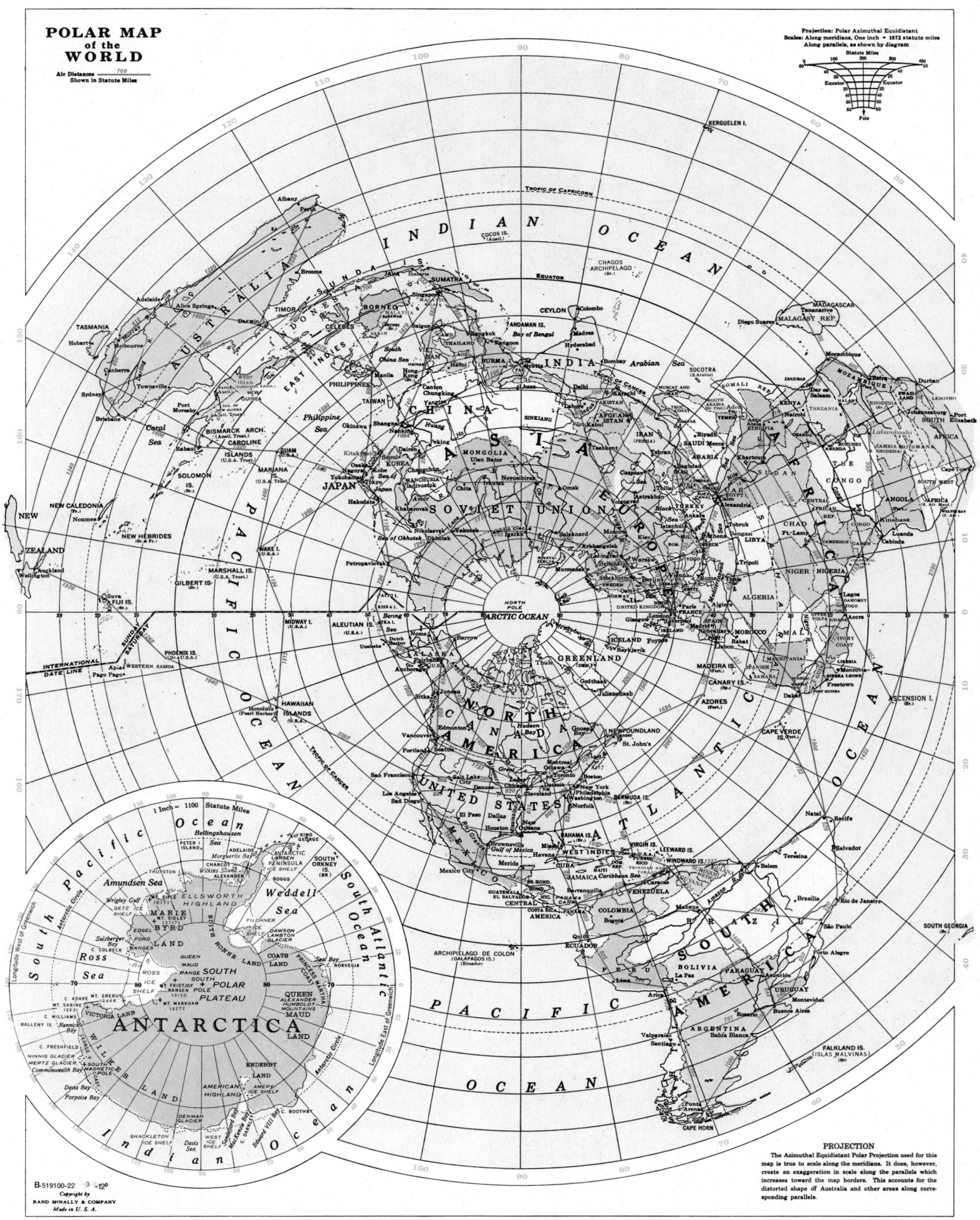

Polar Map of the World

Air Distances — 700 — Shown in Statute Miles

Projection: Polar Azimuthal Equidistant
Scales: Along meridians, One inch = 1872 statute miles
Along parallels, as shown by diagram

PROJECTION

The Azimuthal Equidistant Polar Projection used for this map is true to scale along the meridians. It does, however, create an exaggeration in scale along the parallels which increases toward the map borders. This accounts for the distorted shape of Australia and other areas along corresponding parallels.

1 Inch = 1100 Statute Miles

ANTARCTICA

B-519100-22   -3   -12⁰
Copyright by
RAND McNALLY & COMPANY
Made in U.S.A.

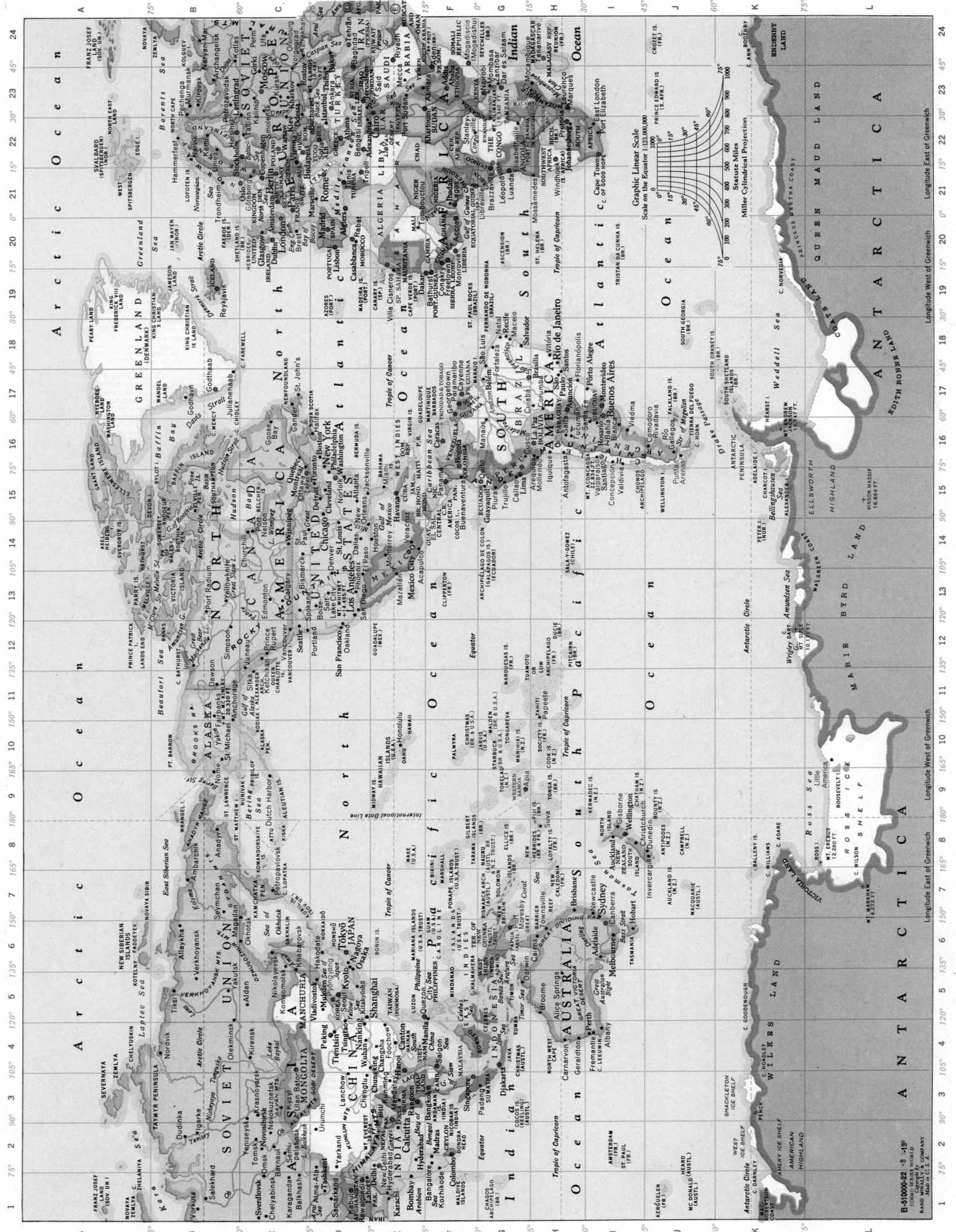

Statute Miles 25 0 25 50 75

Kilometers 25 0 25 50 100

Conic Projection

B-550900-21 -2 2 4°
COSMO SERIES FRANCE
Copyright by
RAND McNALLY & COMPANY
Made in U.S.A.

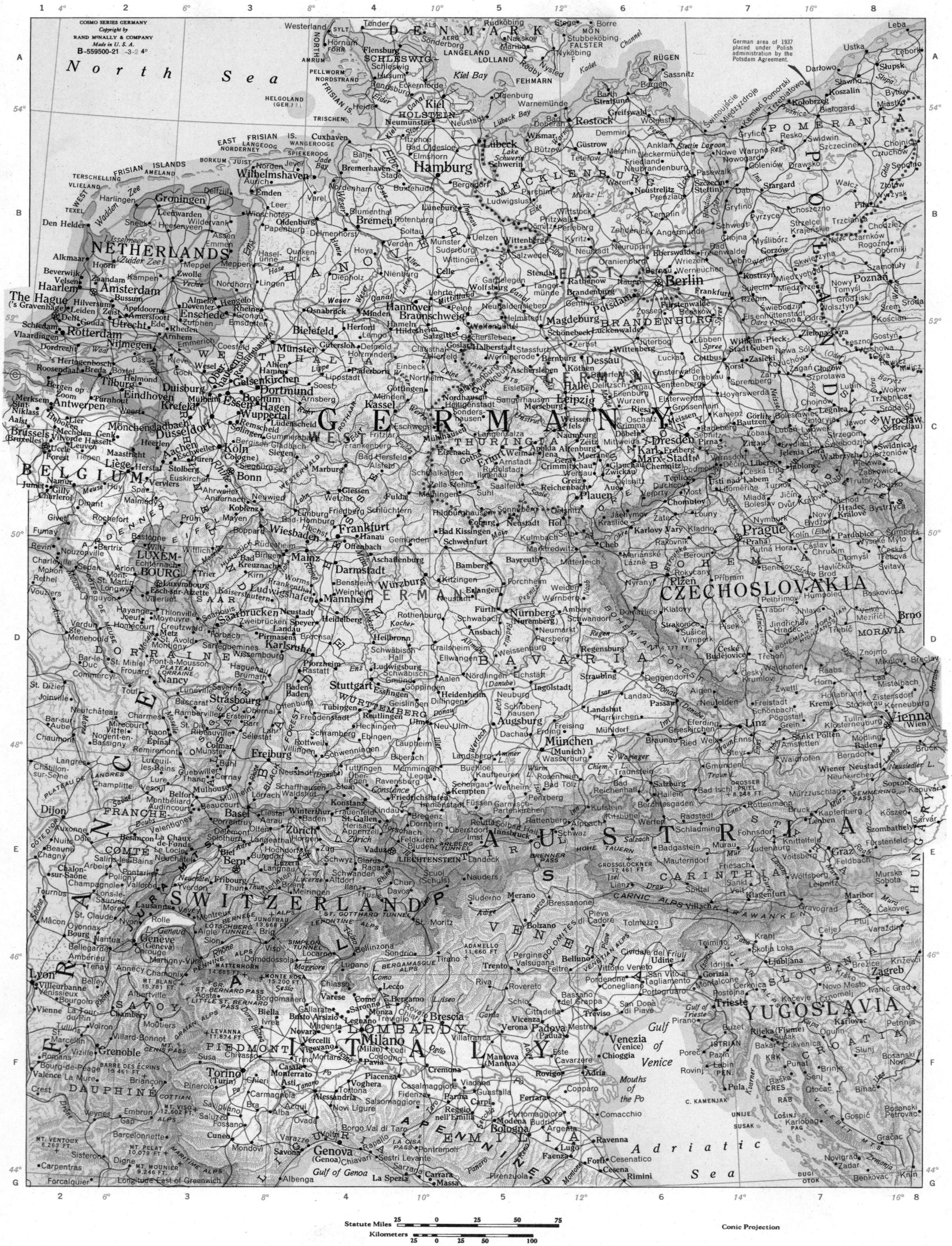

COSMO SERIES GERMANY
Copyright by
RAND McNALLY & COMPANY
Made in U.S.A.
B-559500-21 -3-2 4°

German area of 1937 placed under Polish administration by the Potsdam Agreement.

North Sea

DENMARK

NETHERLANDS

BELGIUM

LUXEMBOURG

FRANCE

GERMANY

WEST GERMANY

EAST GERMANY

POLAND

CZECHOSLOVAKIA

BOHEMIA

MORAVIA

AUSTRIA

SWITZERLAND

LIECHTENSTEIN

ITALY

YUGOSLAVIA

HUNGARY

CROATIA

SLOVENIA

Major cities and labels:

Hamburg, Bremen, Hannover, Berlin, Magdeburg, Leipzig, Dresden, Frankfurt, Köln (Cologne), Bonn, Düsseldorf, Essen, Dortmund, Münster, Bielefeld, Kassel, Mainz, Darmstadt, Mannheim, Stuttgart, Karlsruhe, Nürnberg (Nuremberg), Würzburg, Augsburg, München (Munich), Regensburg, Freiburg, Basel, Zürich, Bern, Genève (Geneva), Vaduz, Innsbruck, Salzburg, Linz, Vienna (Wien), Graz, Klagenfurt, Prague (Praha), Brno, Milano (Milan), Torino (Turin), Genova (Genoa), Bologna, Venezia (Venice), Trieste, Zagreb, Amsterdam, Rotterdam, The Hague ('s Gravenhage), Utrecht, Groningen, Eindhoven, Antwerpen, Brussels (Bruxelles), Liège, Namur, Luxembourg, Nancy, Strasbourg, Metz, Dijon, Lyon, Grenoble, Kiel, Lübeck, Rostock, Schwerin, Stettin (Szczecin), Poznań, Wrocław (Breslau), Brandenburg, Potsdam, Halle, Erfurt, Weimar, Jena, Chemnitz (Karl-Marx-Stadt), Plzen, Wroclaw

MECKLENBURG, POMERANIA, BRANDENBURG, SCHLESWIG, HOLSTEIN, HANOVER, WESTPHALIA, THURINGIA, BAVARIA, WÜRTTEMBERG, SAAR, LORRAINE, SAVOY, PIEDMONT, LOMBARDY, VENETIA, TIROL, CARINTHIA, BOHEMIA, MORAVIA, FRANCHE COMTÉ, DAUPHINÉ

Adriatic Sea

Gulf of Venice

Gulf of Genoa

Mouths of the Po

Statute Miles 25 0 25 50 75
Kilometers 25 0 25 50 100

Conic Projection

Longitude East of Greenwich

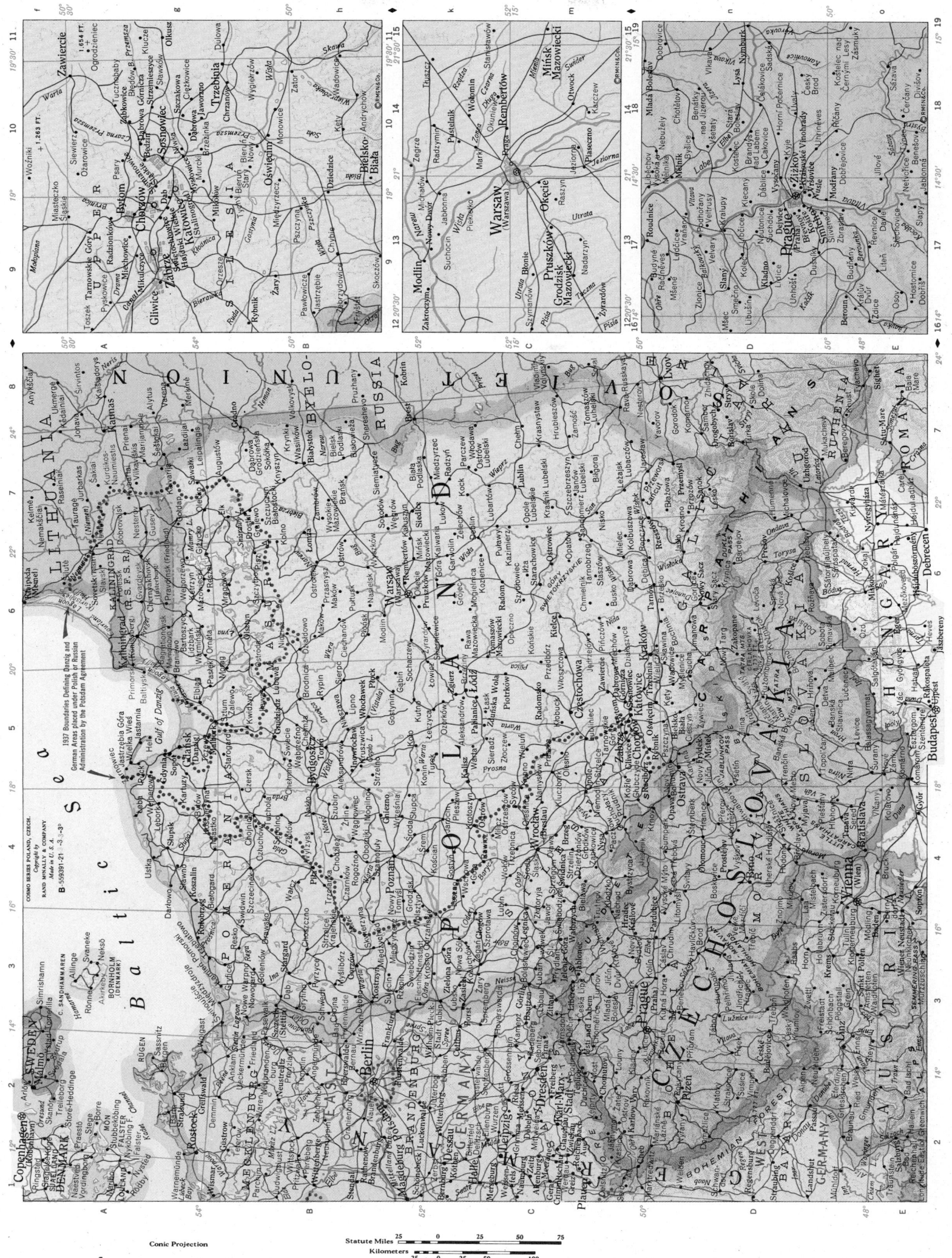

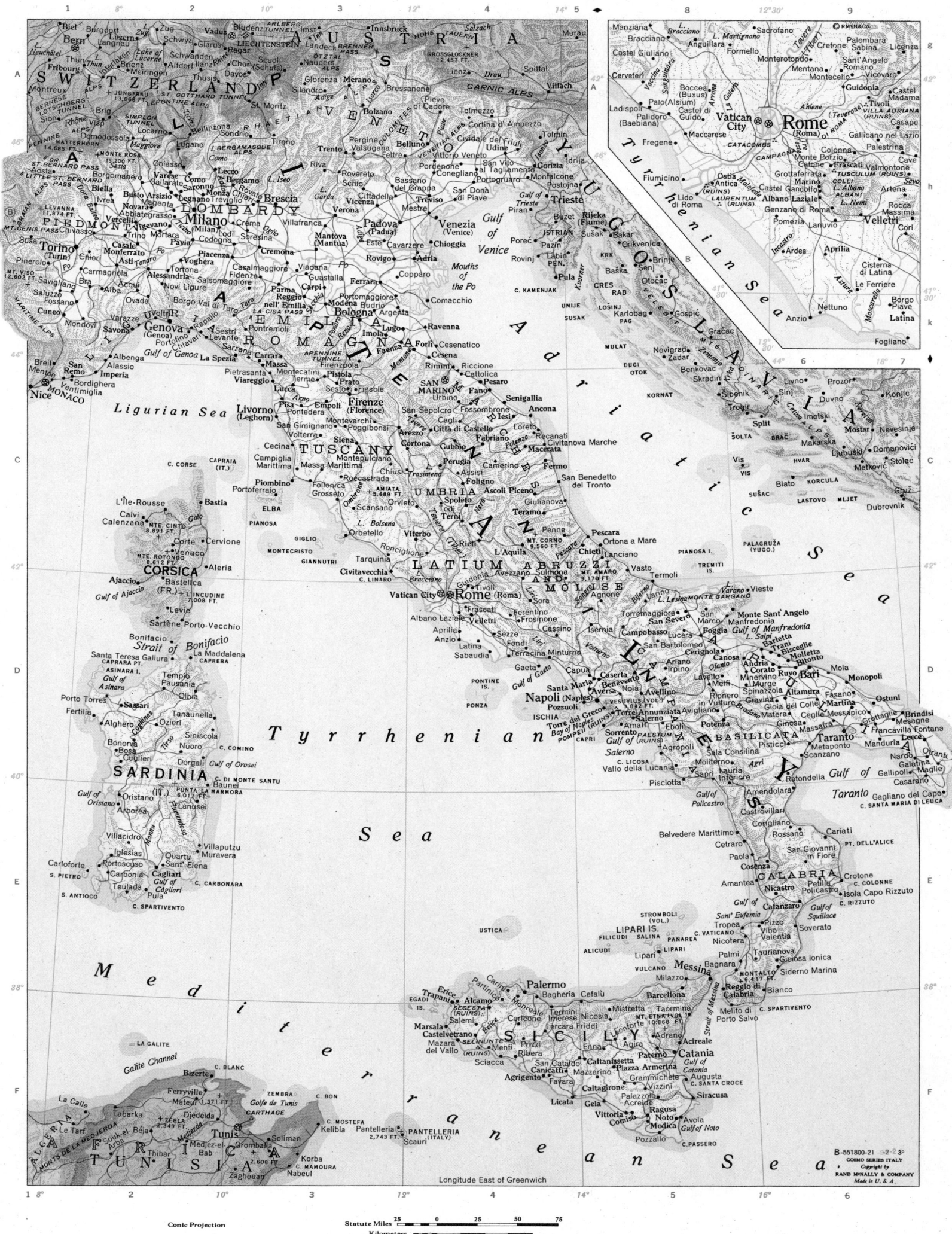

Statute Miles

Kilometers

Conic Projection

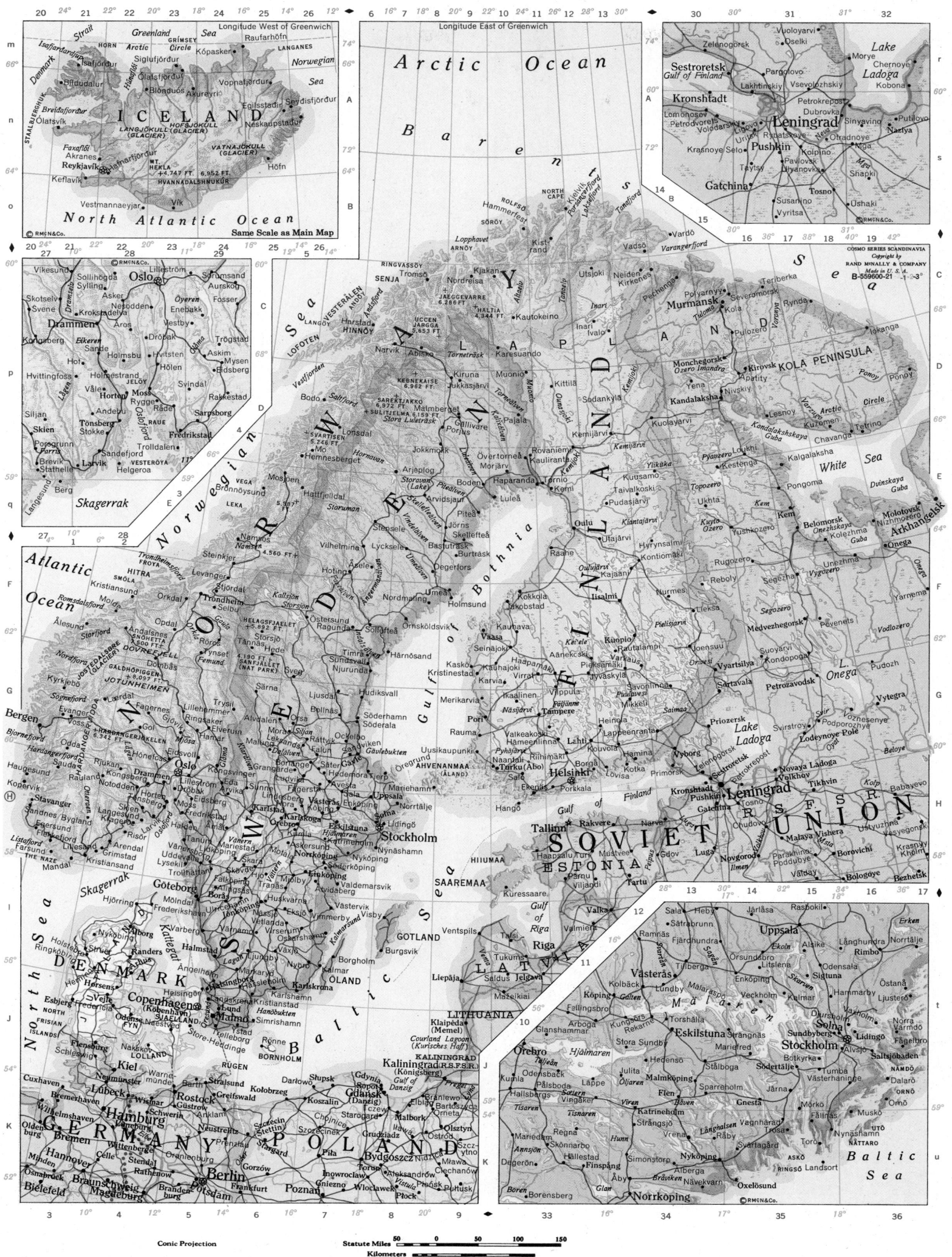

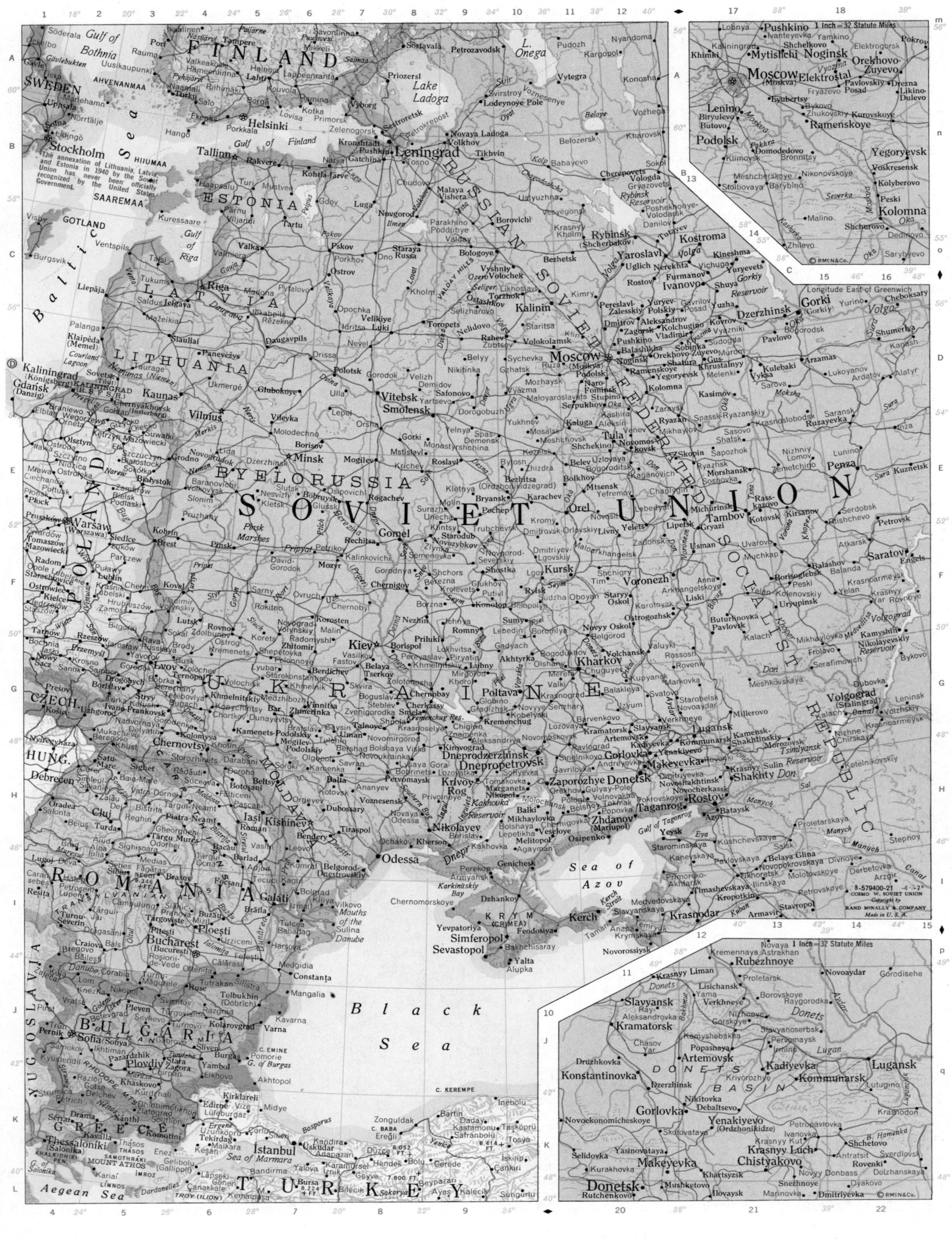

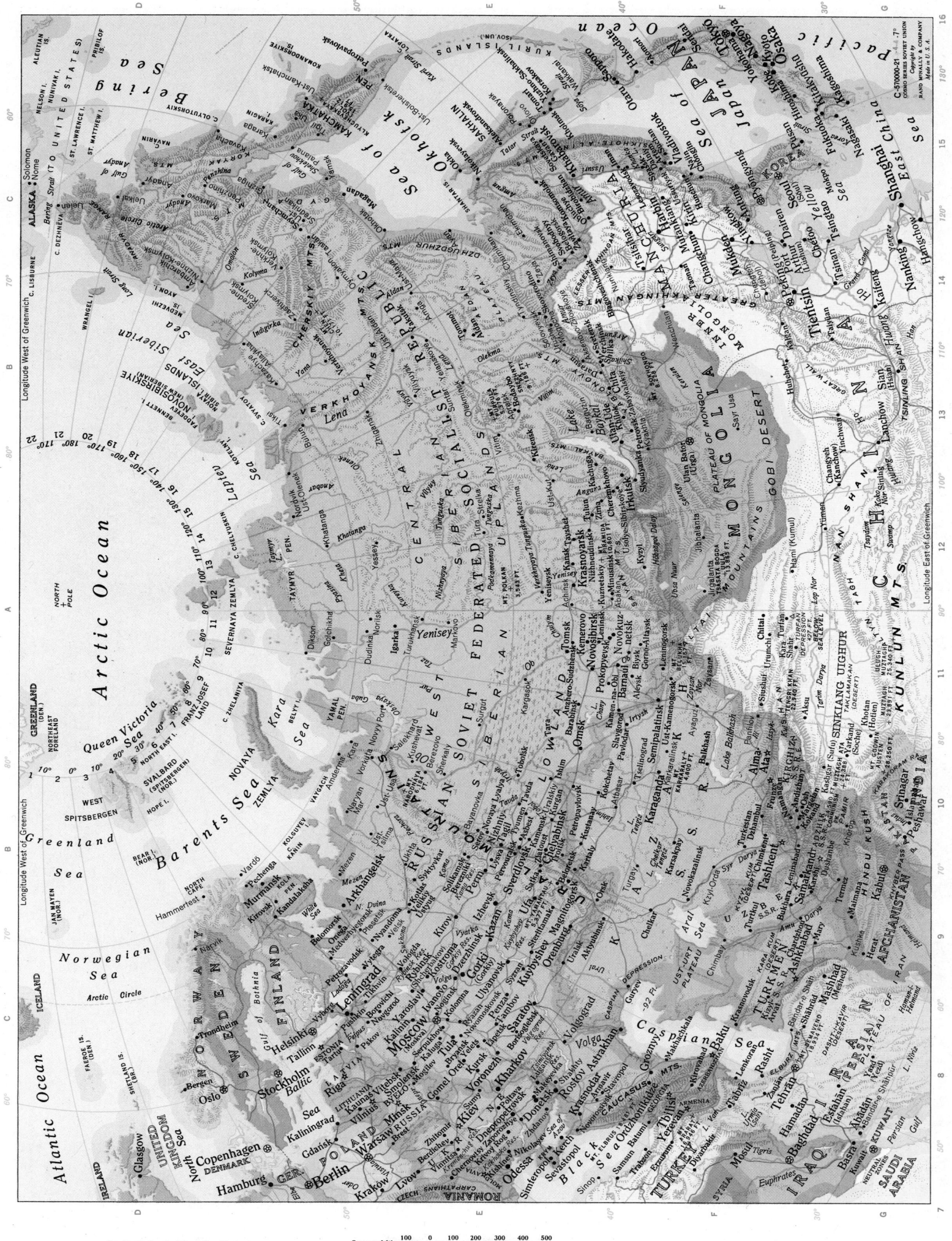

Lambert Azimuthal Equal Area Projection

Statute Miles
100 0 100 200 300 400 500

Kilometers
100 0 100 300 500 700

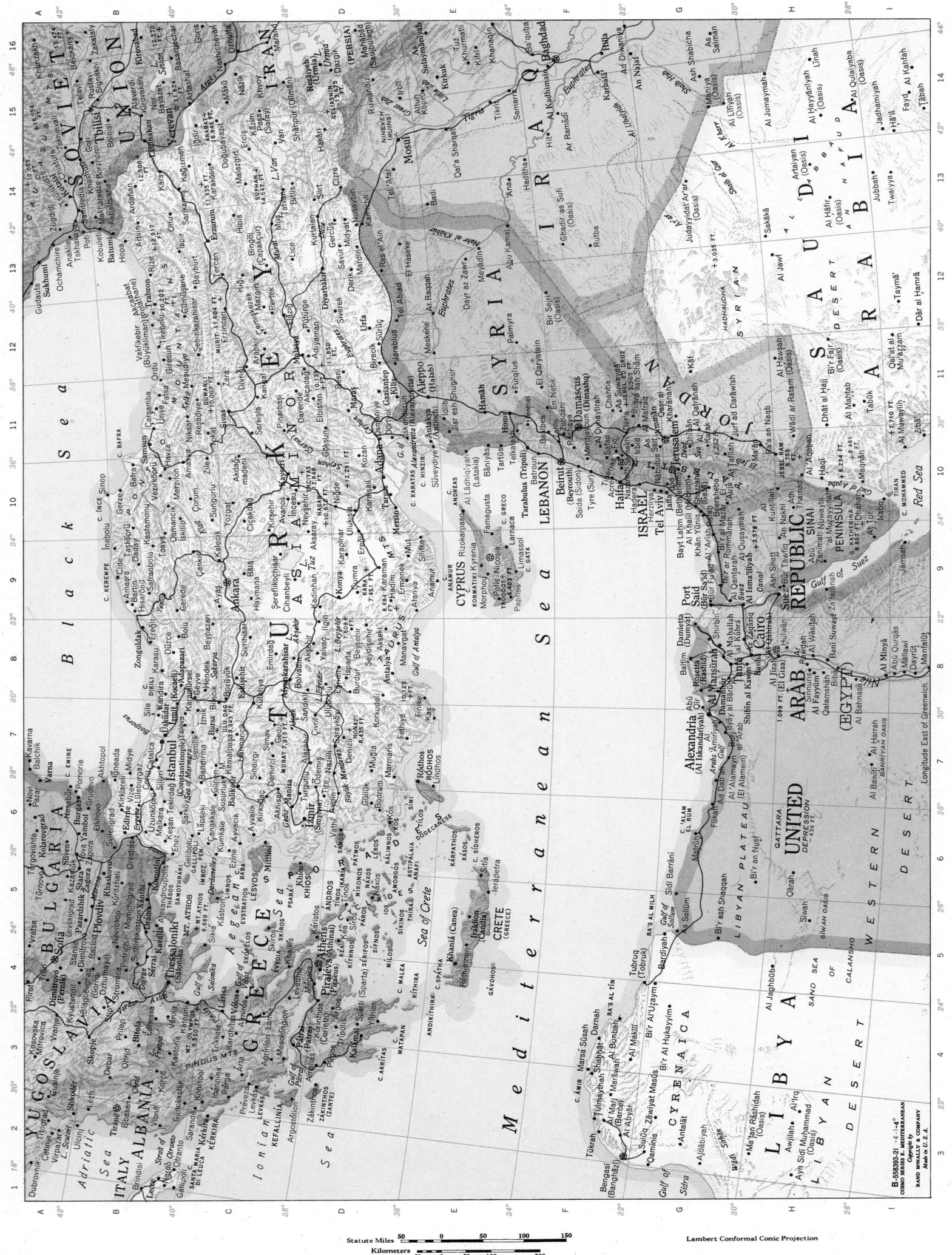

Statute Miles
Kilometers

Lambert Conformal Conic Projection

B-558393-21 -4-¹-4°
COSMO SERIES E. MEDITERRANEAN
Copyright by
RAND McNALLY & COMPANY
Made in U.S.A.

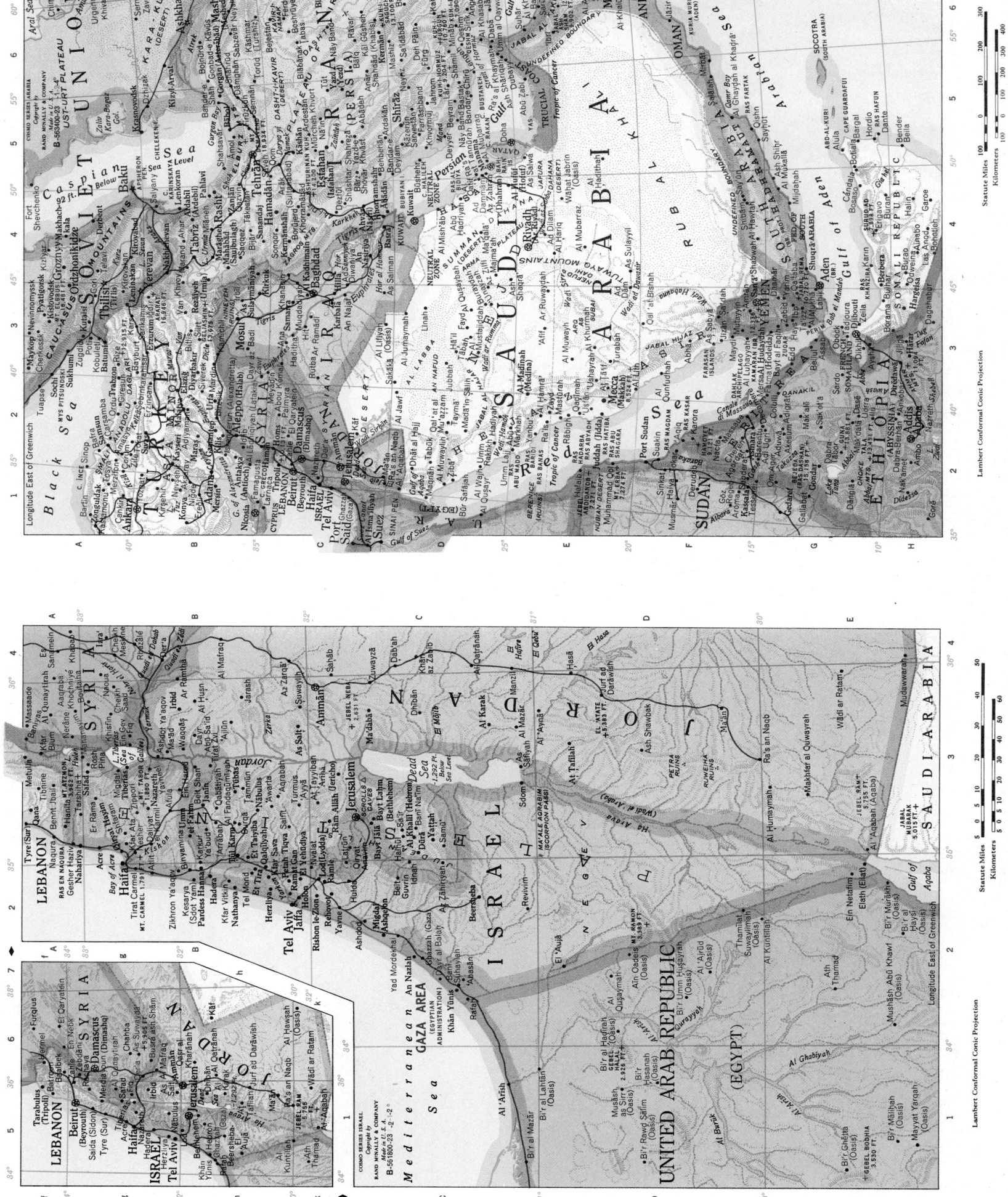

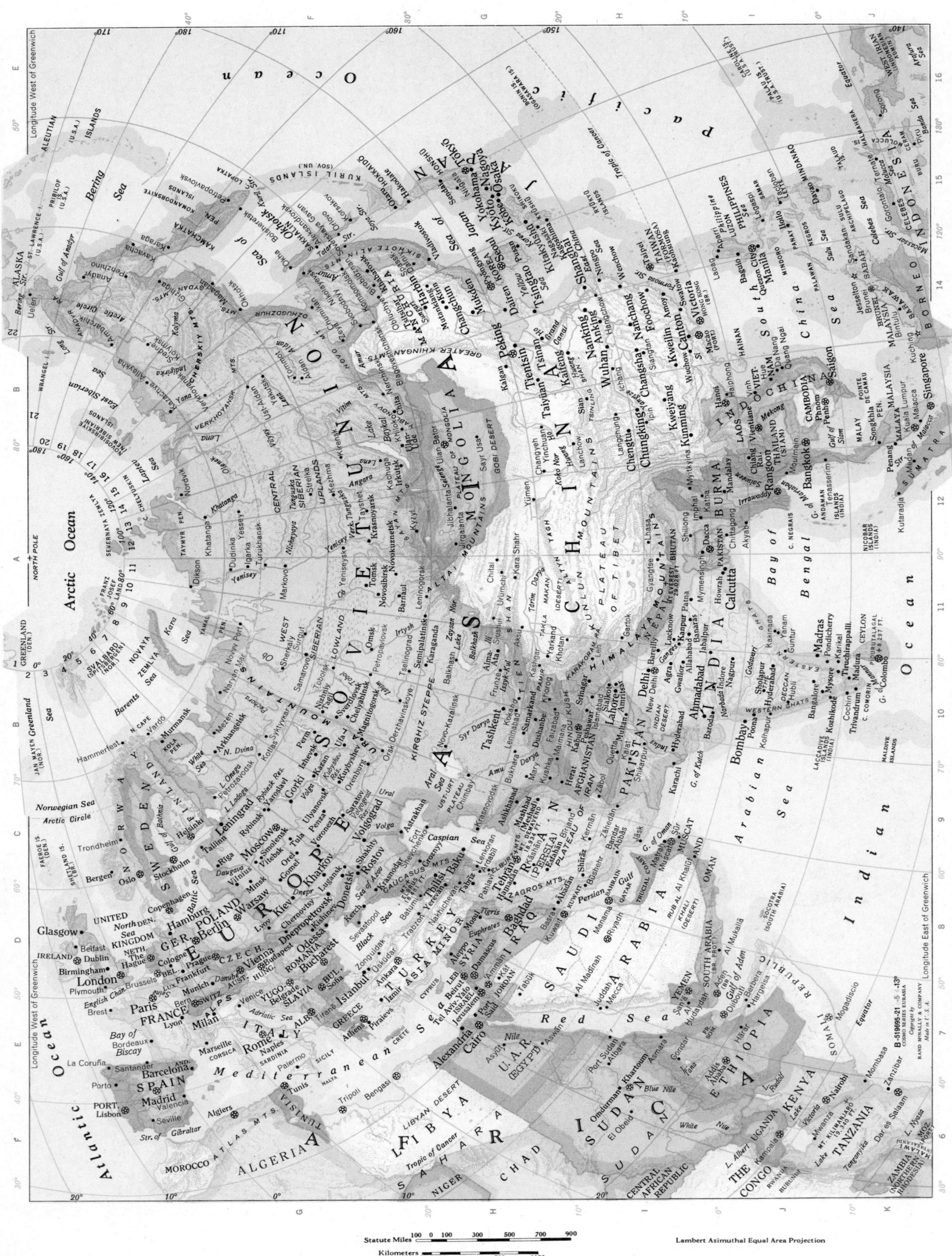

Statute Miles 100 0 100 300 500 700 900

Kilometers 100 0 100 300 700 1100

Lambert Azimuthal Equal Area Projection

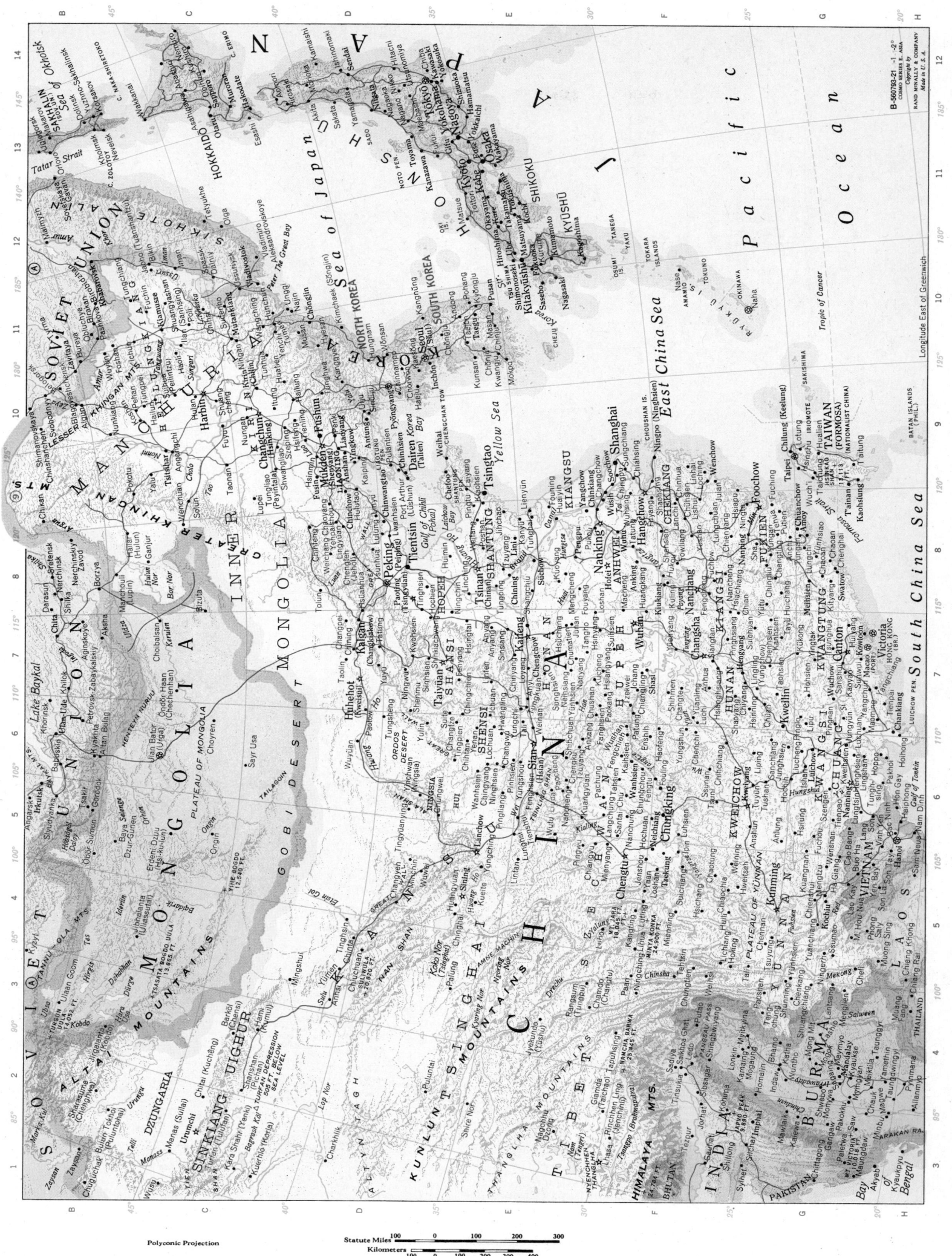

Polyconic Projection

Statute Miles
100   0   100   200   300

Kilometers
100 0 100 200 300 400

Statute Miles   50   0   50   100   150
Kilometers   50   0   50   100   200

Lambert Conformal Conic Projection

B-561900-21   -1 -2 -3°
COSMO SERIES JAPAN, KOREA
Copyright by
RAND McNALLY & COMPANY
Made in U.S.A.

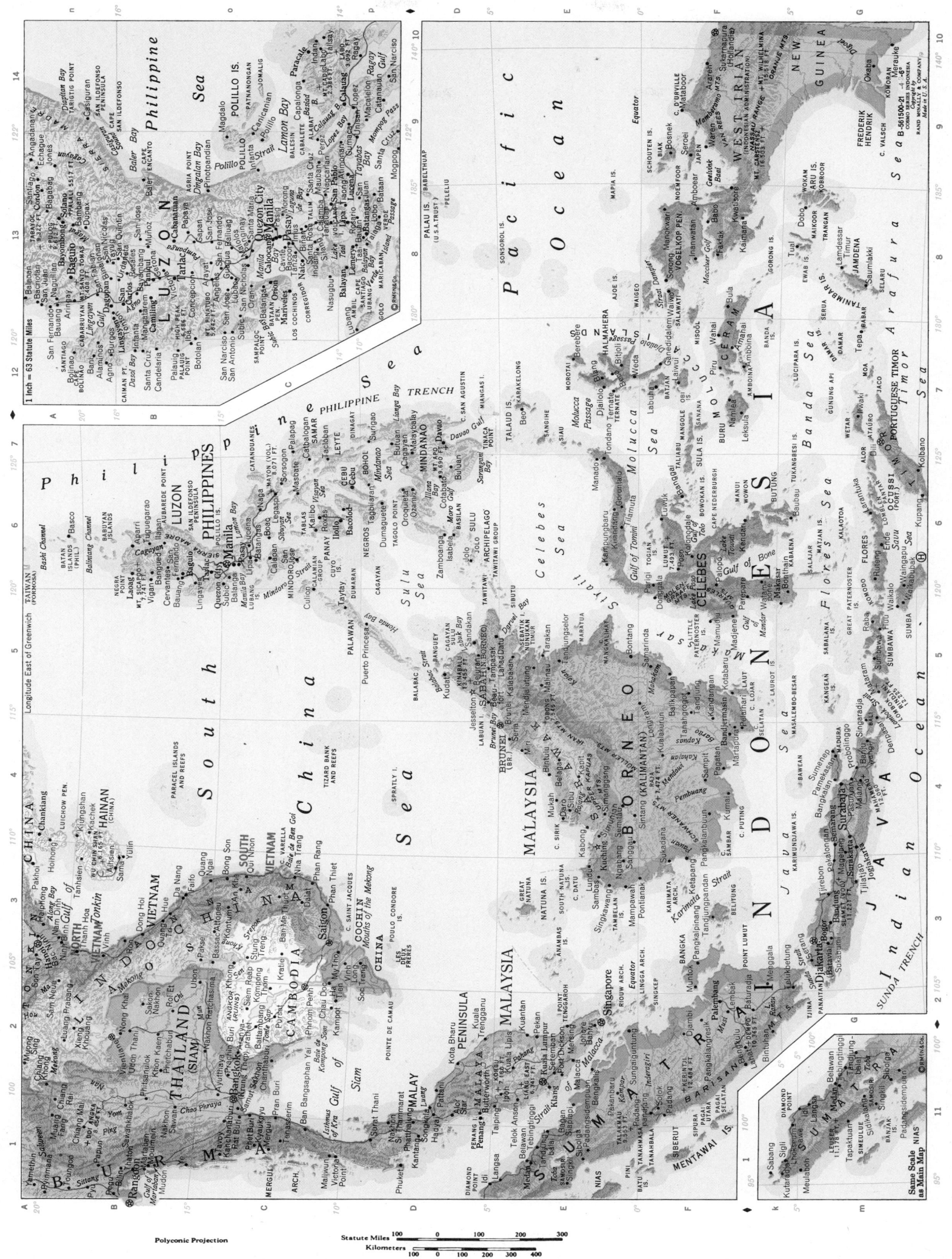

Polyconic Projection

Statute Miles
Kilometers

Same Scale
as Main Map

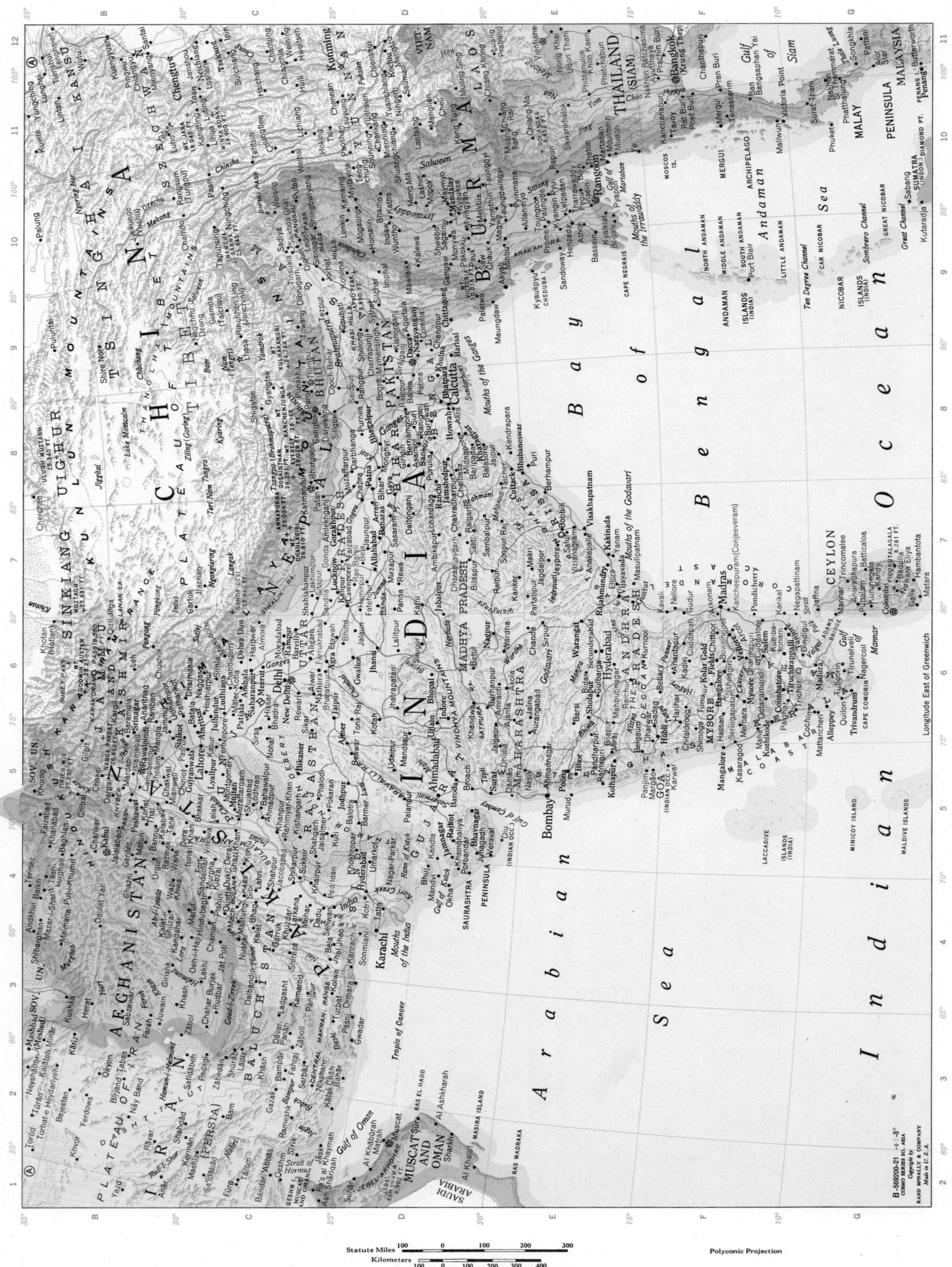

Statute Miles

Kilometers

Polyconic Projection

B-569200-21
COSMO SERIES SO. ASIA
Copyright by
RAND MᶜNALLY & COMPANY
Made in U.S.A.

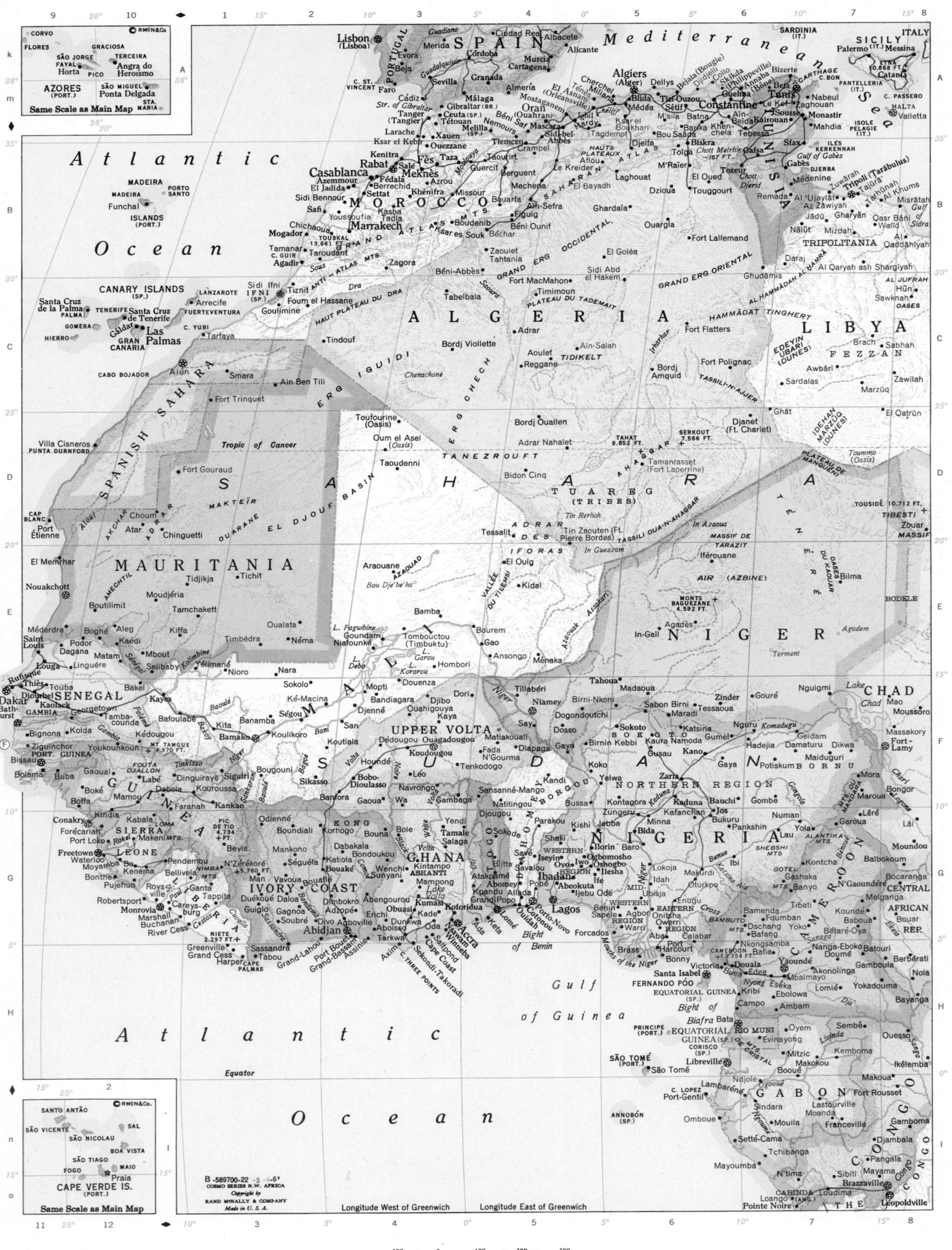

Statute Miles
Kilometers
Sinusoidal Projection

Longitude West of Greenwich   Longitude East of Greenwich

B-589700-22 -3-4-6°
COSMO SERIES N.W. AFRICA
Copyright by
RAND McNALLY & COMPANY
Made in U.S.A.

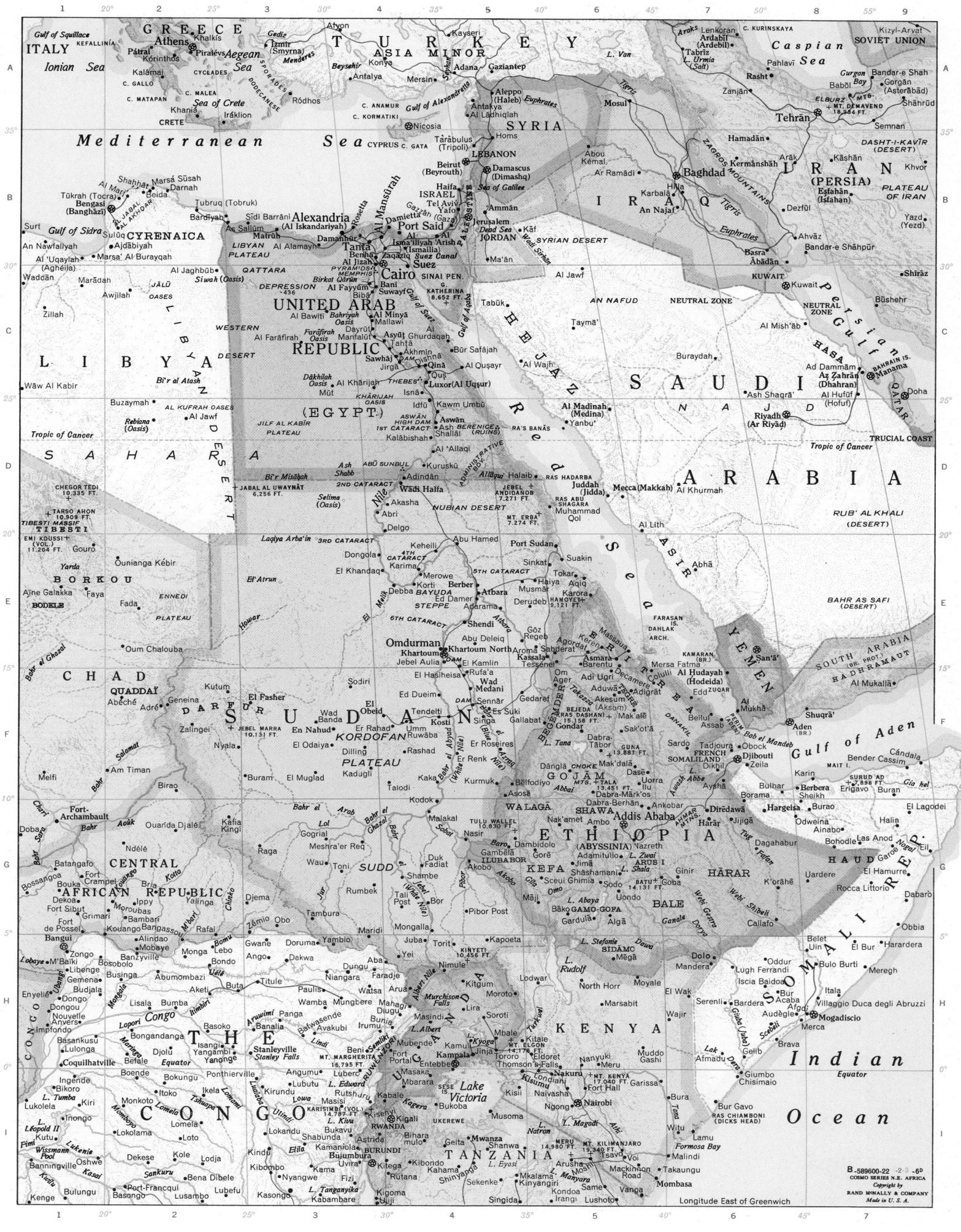

Sinusoidal Projection

Statute Miles 100   0   100   200   300
Kilometers 100 0 100 200 300 400

Longitude East of Greenwich

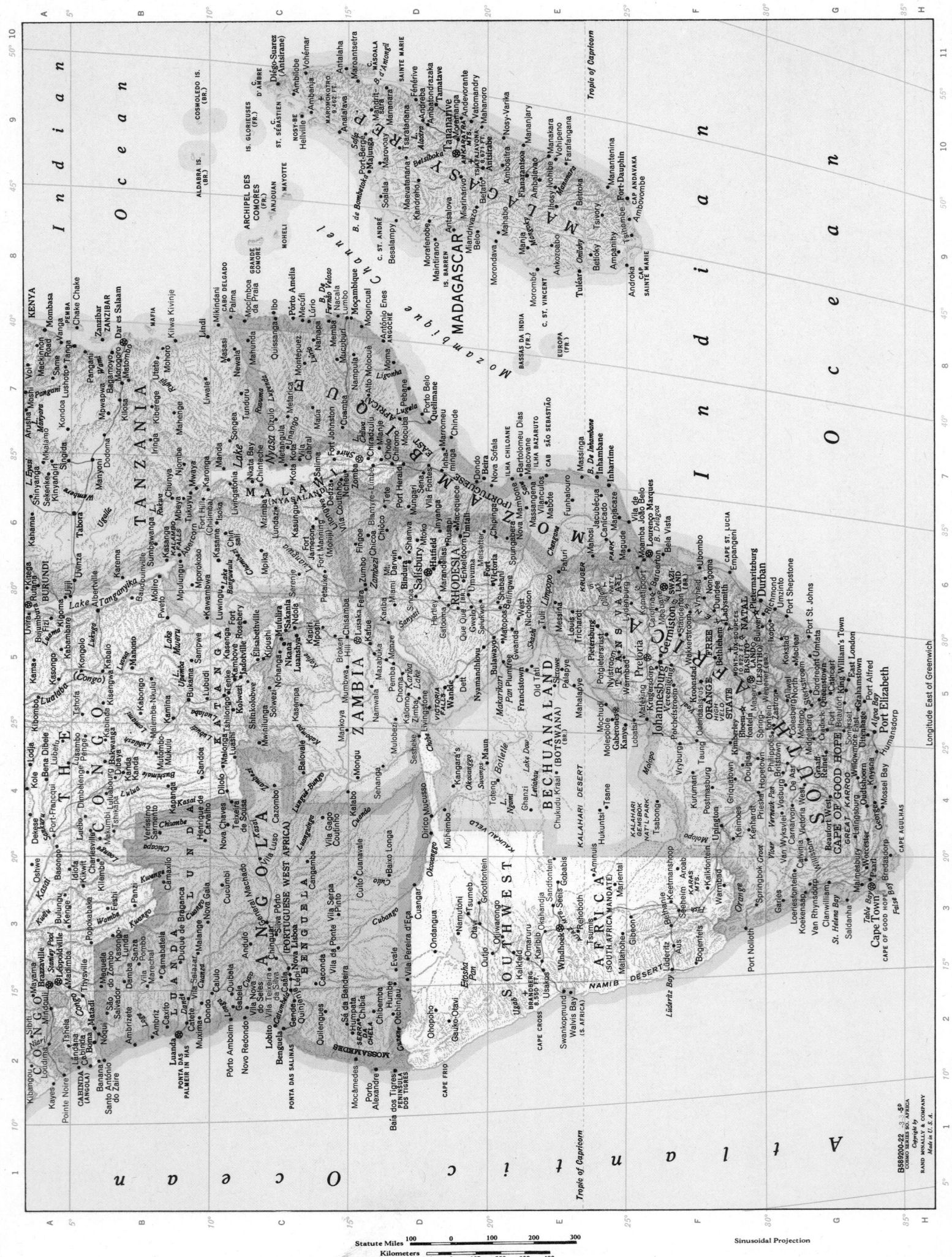

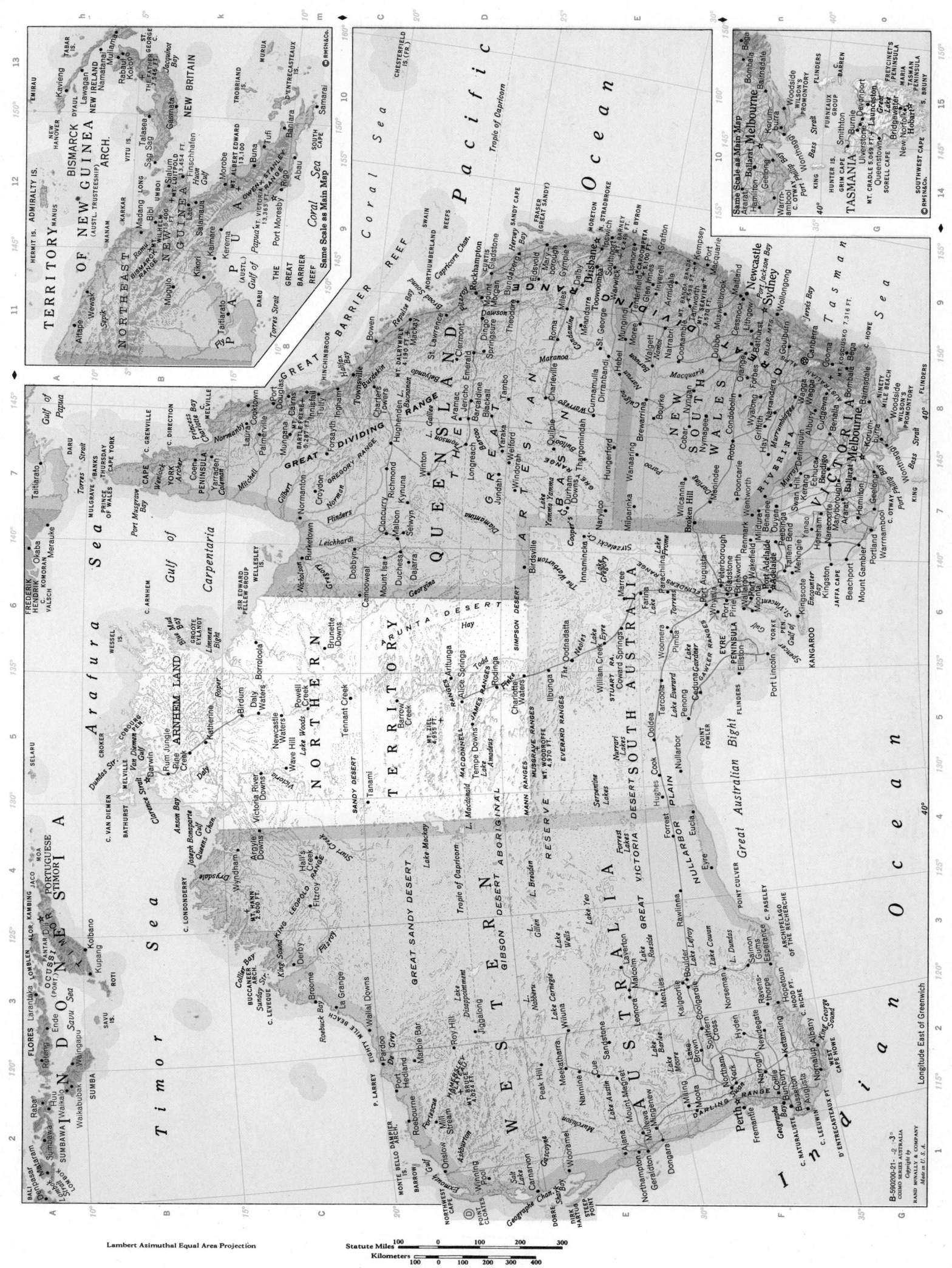

Pacific Ocean

Coral Sea

TERRITORY OF NEW GUINEA
(AUSTL. TRUSTEESHIP)
BISMARCK ARCH.
NEW BRITAIN
NORTHEAST NEW GUINEA
PAPUA (AUSTL.)
Port Moresby
Gulf of Papua
THE GREAT BARRIER REEF

Coral Sea
Same Scale as Main Map

TASMANIA
Melbourne
Ballarat
Geelong
FURNEAUX GROUP
FLINDERS
Launceston
Devonport
Burnie
Queenstown
Hobart
New Norfolk
Bruny
SOUTHWEST CAPE
Same Scale as Main Map

Gulf of Papua
Torres Strait
CAPE YORK PENINSULA

Arafura Sea

Gulf of Carpentaria

INDONESIA
PORTUGUESE TIMOR
Timor Sea

ARNHEM LAND
Darwin
NORTHERN TERRITORY

QUEENSLAND
GREAT DIVIDING RANGE
Brisbane

WESTERN AUSTRALIA
GREAT SANDY DESERT
GIBSON DESERT
GREAT VICTORIA DESERT

SOUTH AUSTRALIA
Lake Eyre
NULLARBOR PLAIN
Great Australian Bight

NEW SOUTH WALES
Sydney
Newcastle
Canberra
VICTORIA
Melbourne

Perth
Fremantle

Indian Ocean

Tasman Sea

Alice Springs
Simpson Desert
Lake Amadeus

Adelaide

Lambert Azimuthal Equal Area Projection

Statute Miles
100   0   100   200   300

Kilometers
100   0   100   200   300   400

Longitude East of Greenwich

B-590200-21- -2- -3-
COSMO SERIES AUSTRALIA
Copyright by
RAND McNALLY COMPANY
Made in U.S.A.

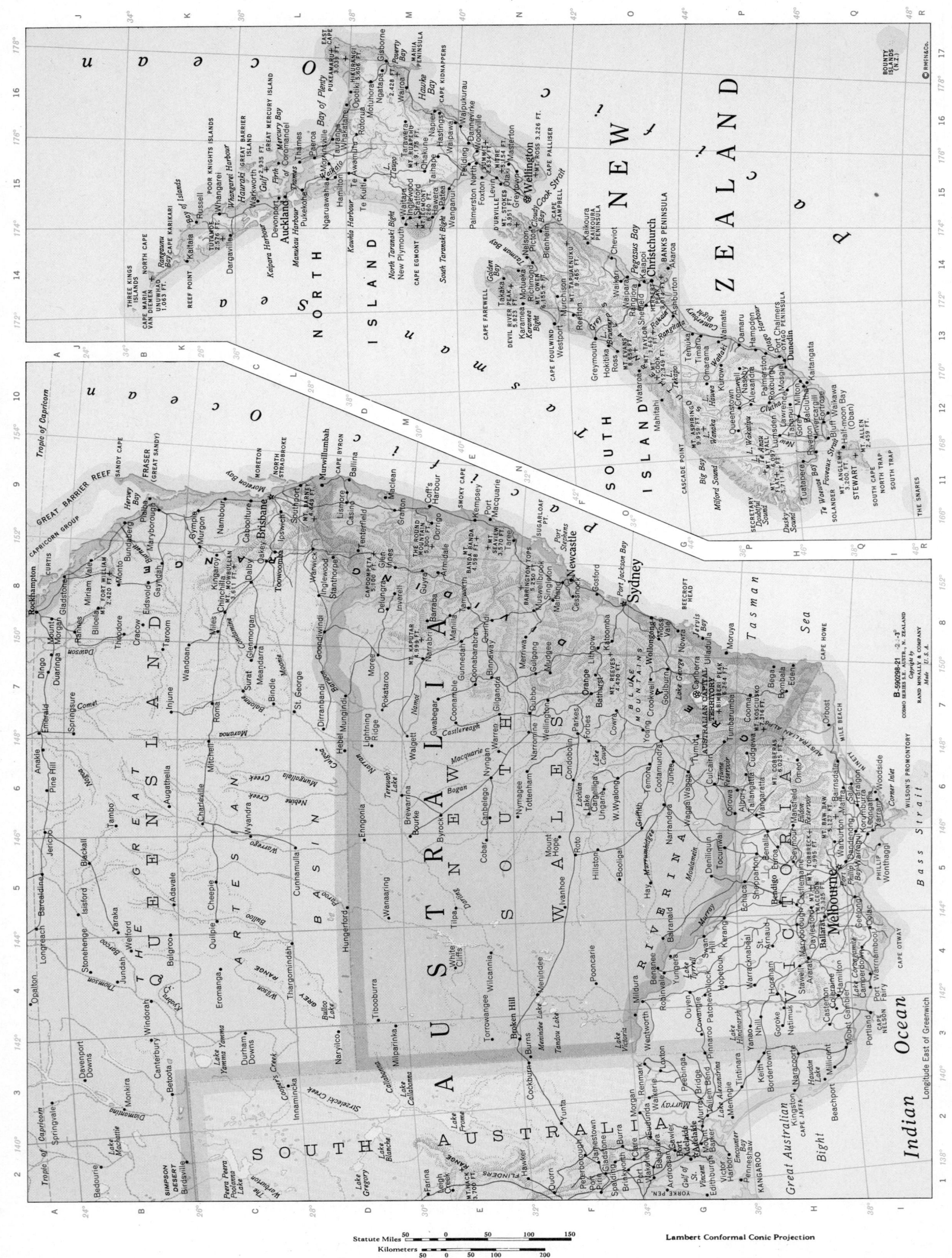

Lambert Conformal Conic Projection

Statute Miles   50   0   50   100   150
Kilometers   50   0   50   100   200

B-590298-21   -2-2³
COSMO SERIES S.E. AUSTR., N. ZEALAND
Copyright by
RAND McNALLY & COMPANY
Made in U.S.A.

BOUNTY
ISLANDS (N.Z.)
©RMN&Co.

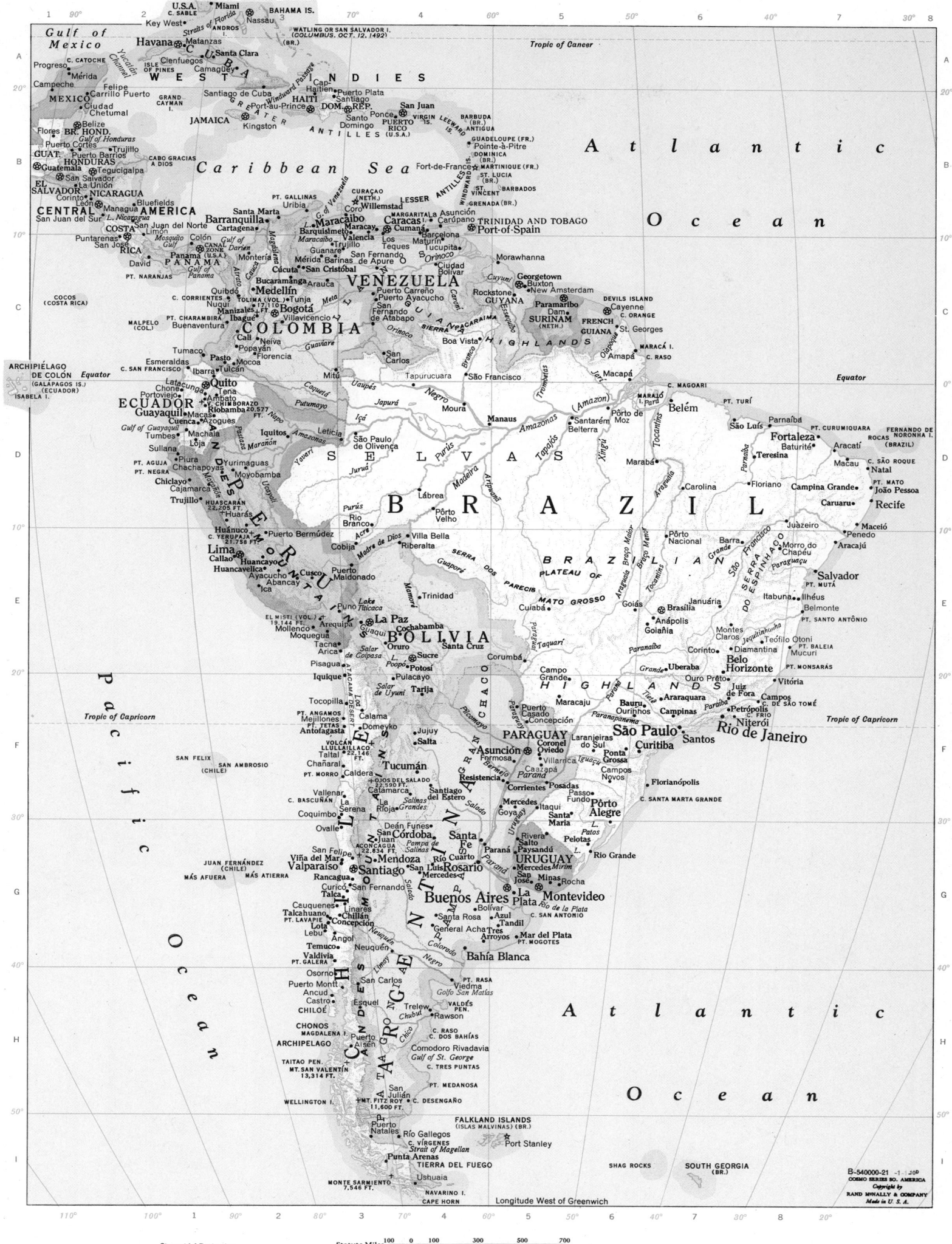

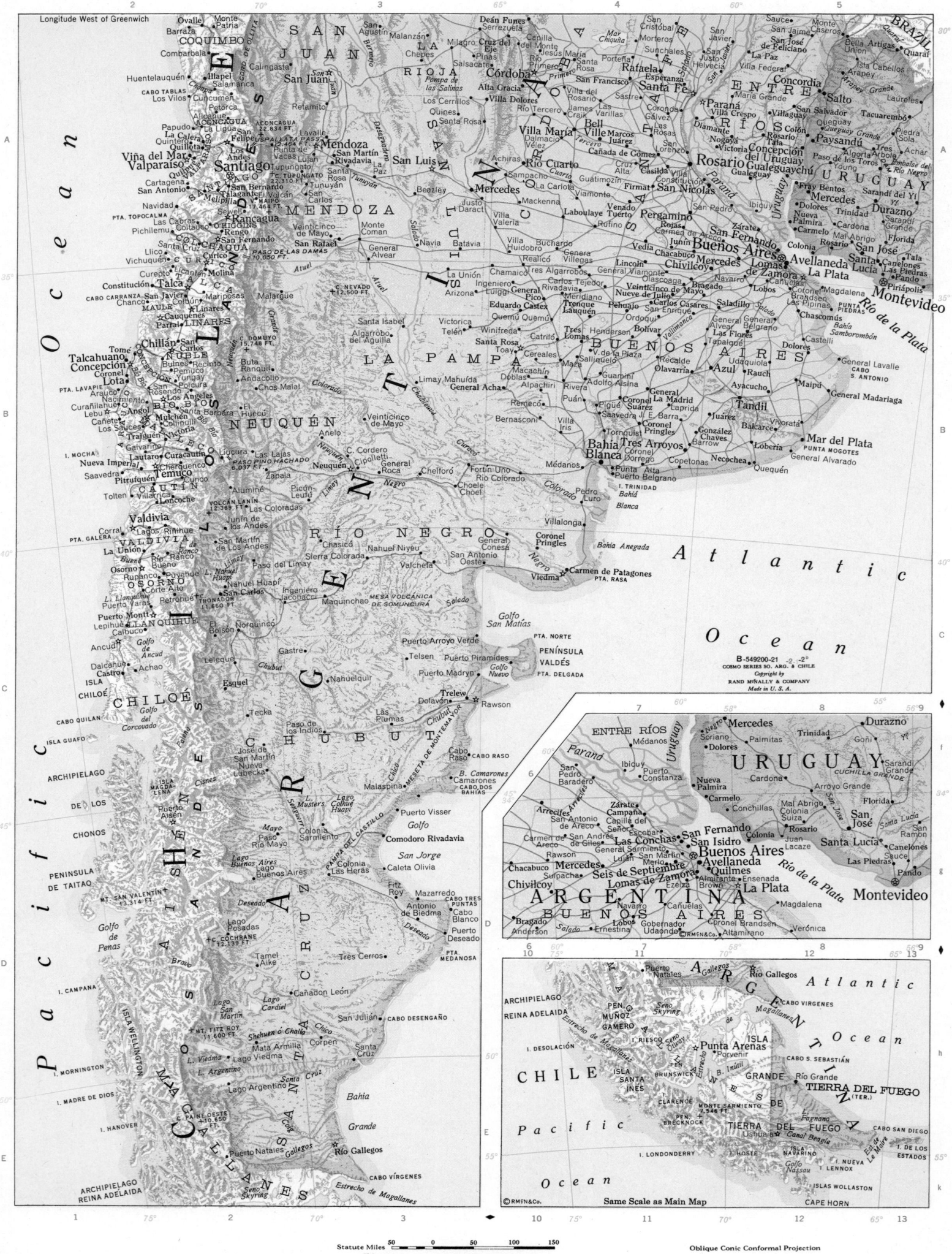

Statute Miles
Kilometers
Oblique Conic Conformal Projection

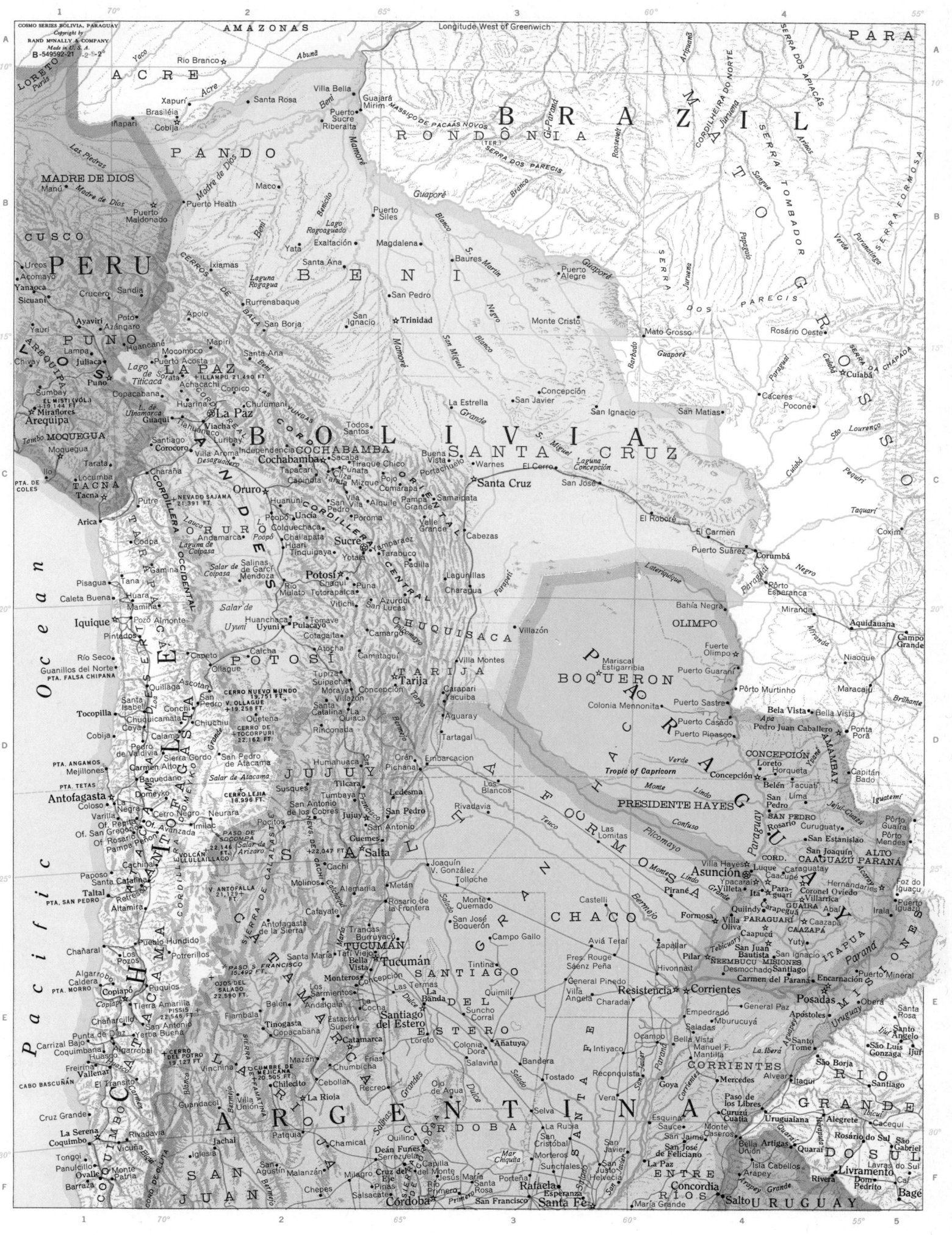

Oblique Conic Conformal Projection

Statute Miles

Kilometers

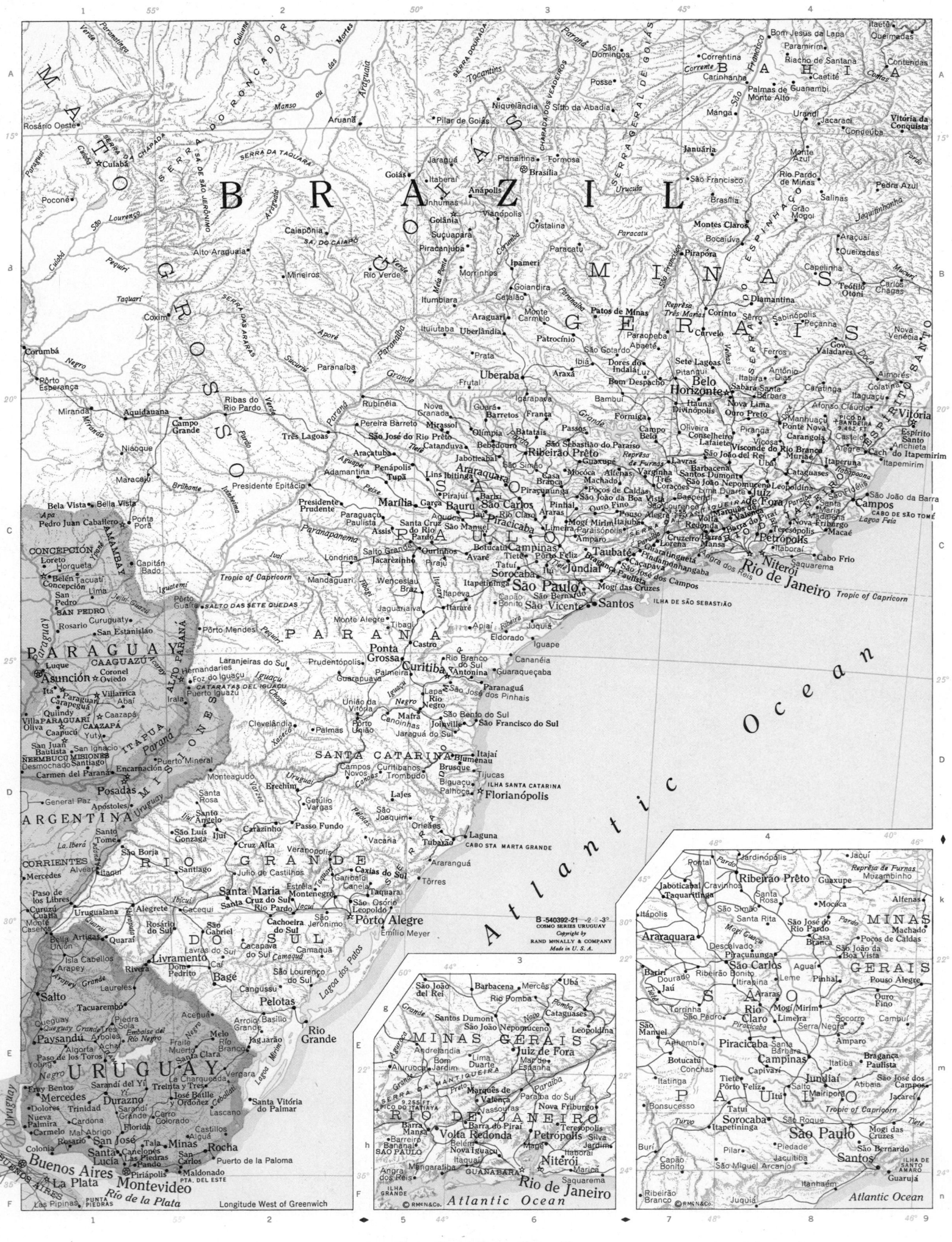

Statute Miles

Kilometers

Oblique Conic Conformal Projection

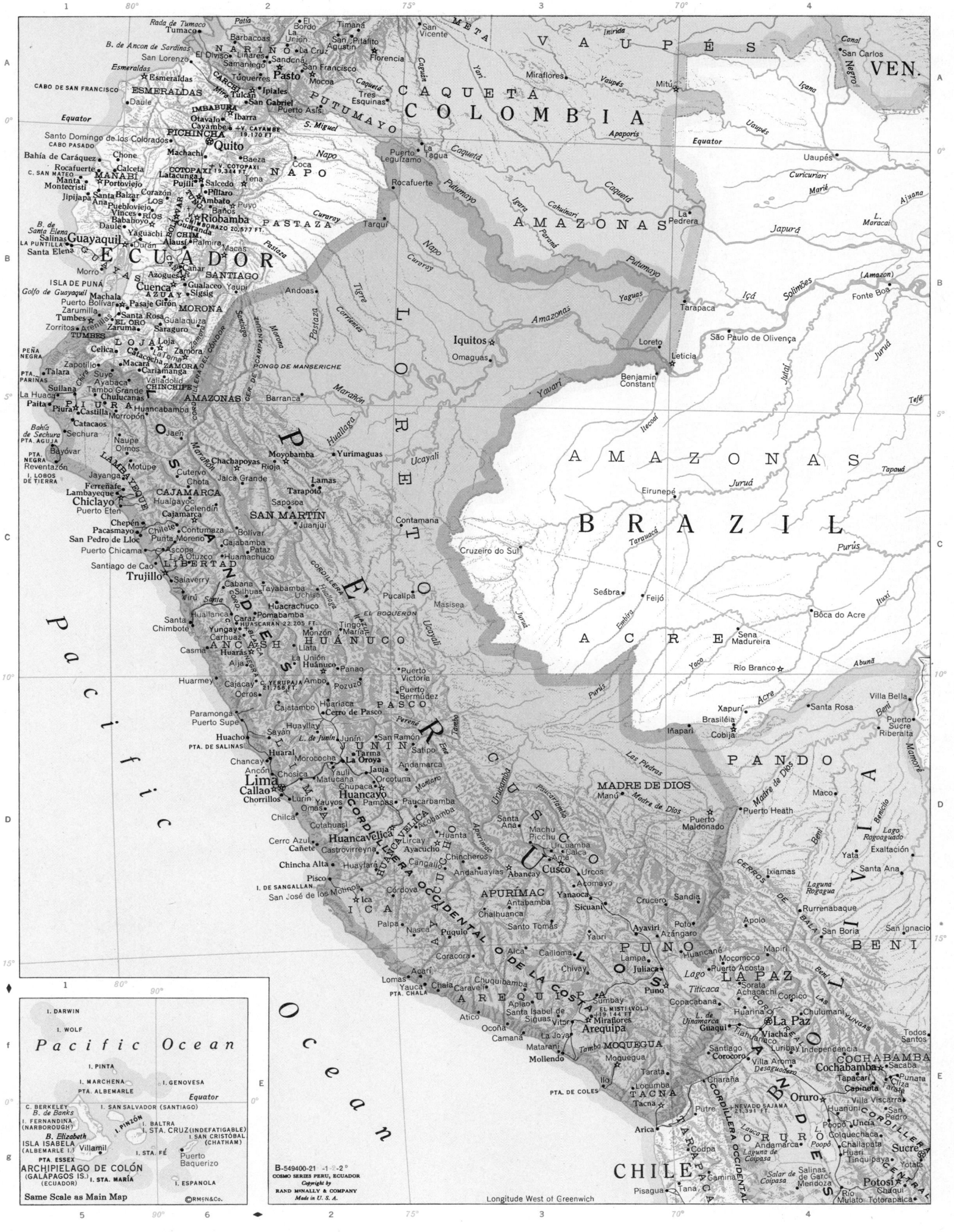

Statute Miles 50 0 50 100 150
Kilometers 50 0 50 100 150 200

Oblique Conic Conformal Projection

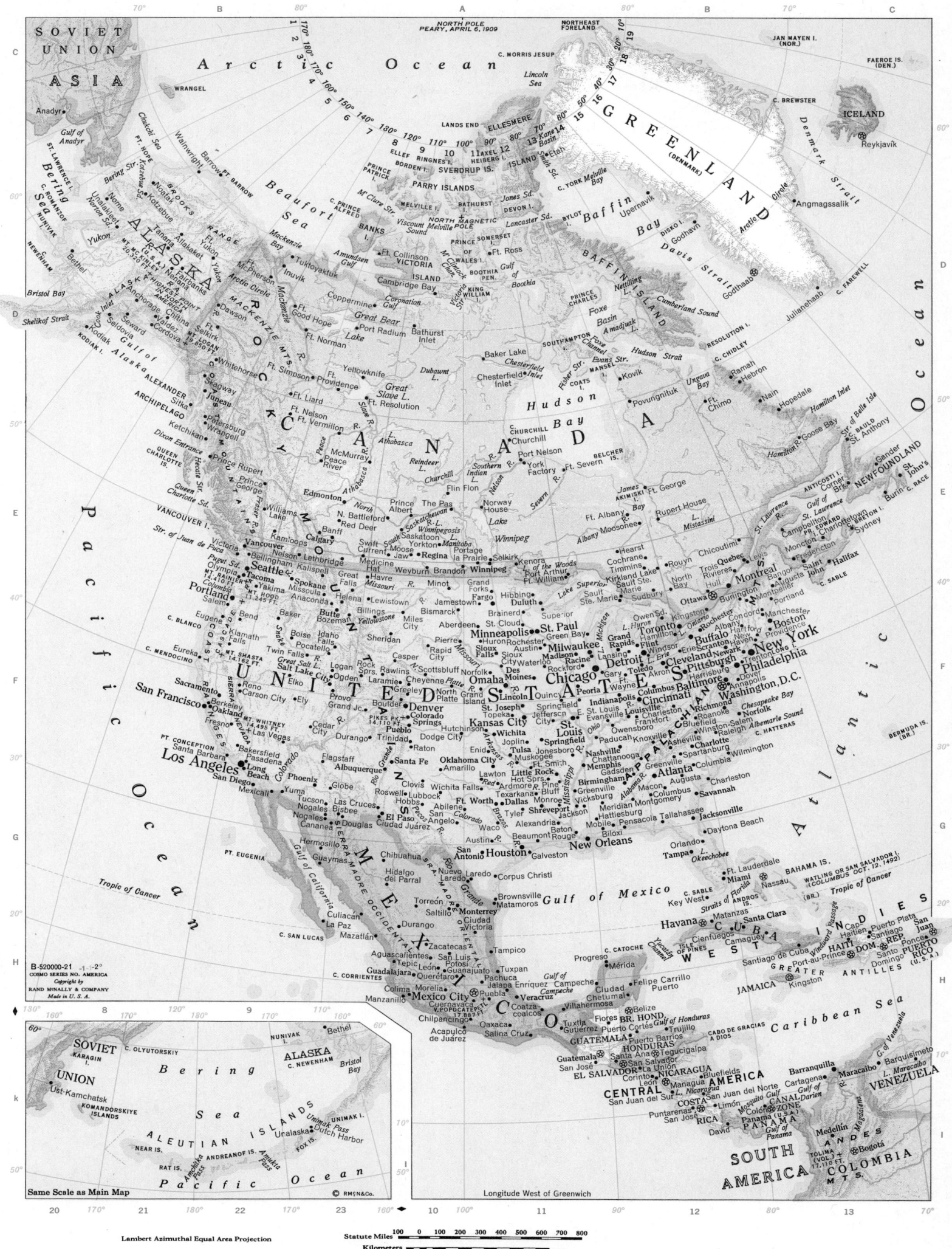

Lambert Azimuthal Equal Area Projection

Statute Miles
100 0 100 200 300 400 500 600 700 800

Kilometers
100 0 100 200 400 600 800 1000

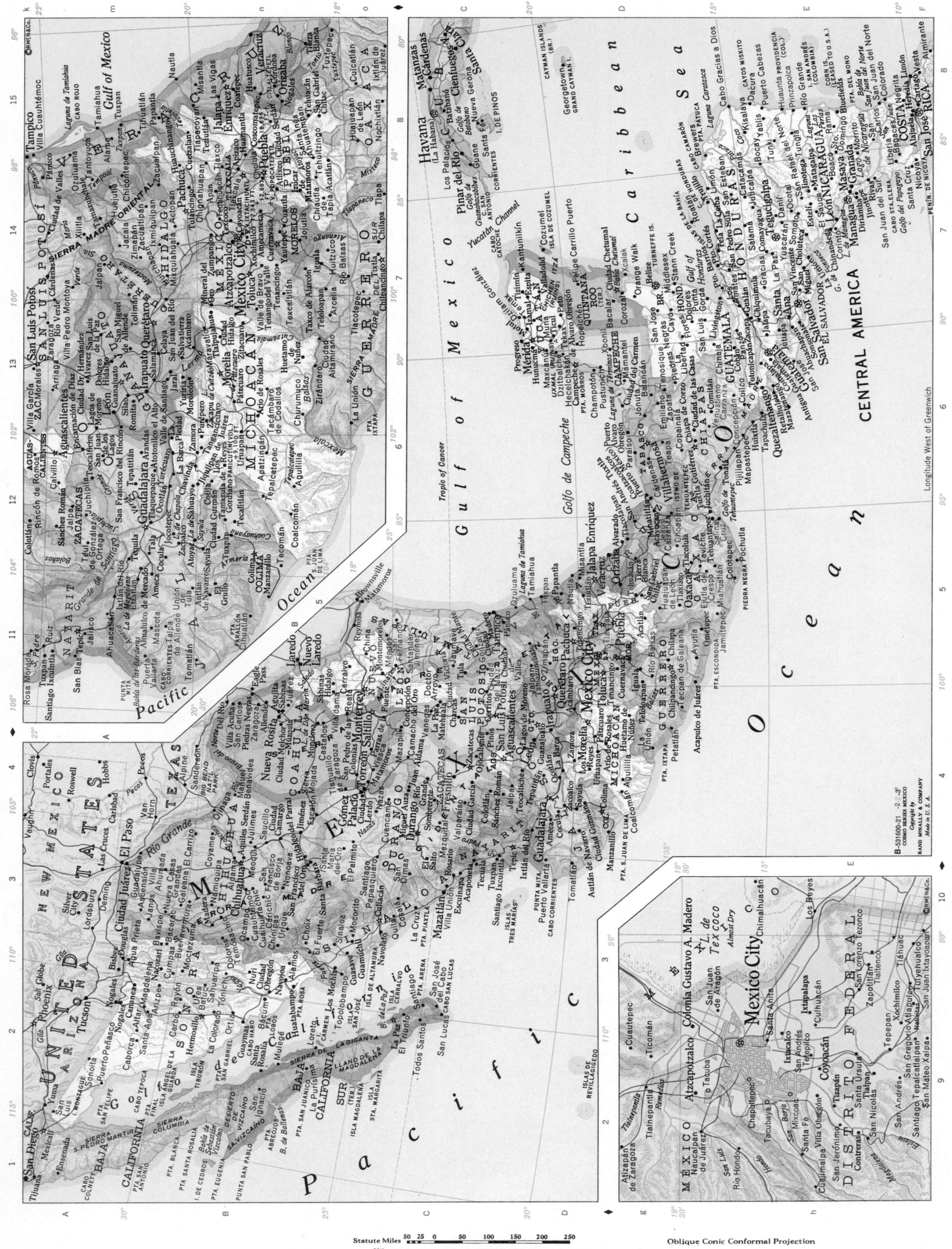

Statute Miles 50 25 0 50 100 150 200 250
Kilometers 50 0 100 200 300

Oblique Conic Conformal Projection

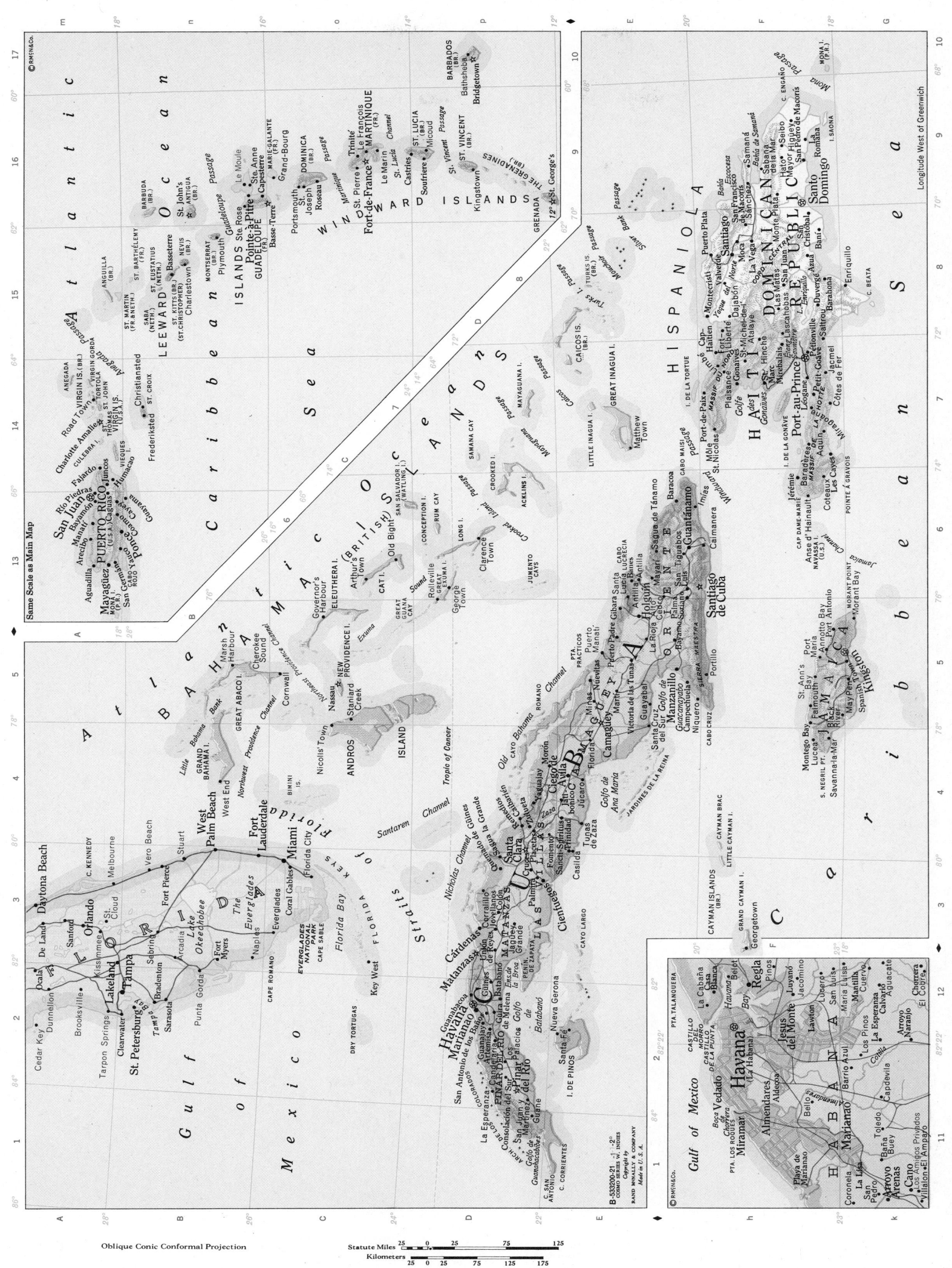

Oblique Conic Conformal Projection

Statute Miles

Kilometers

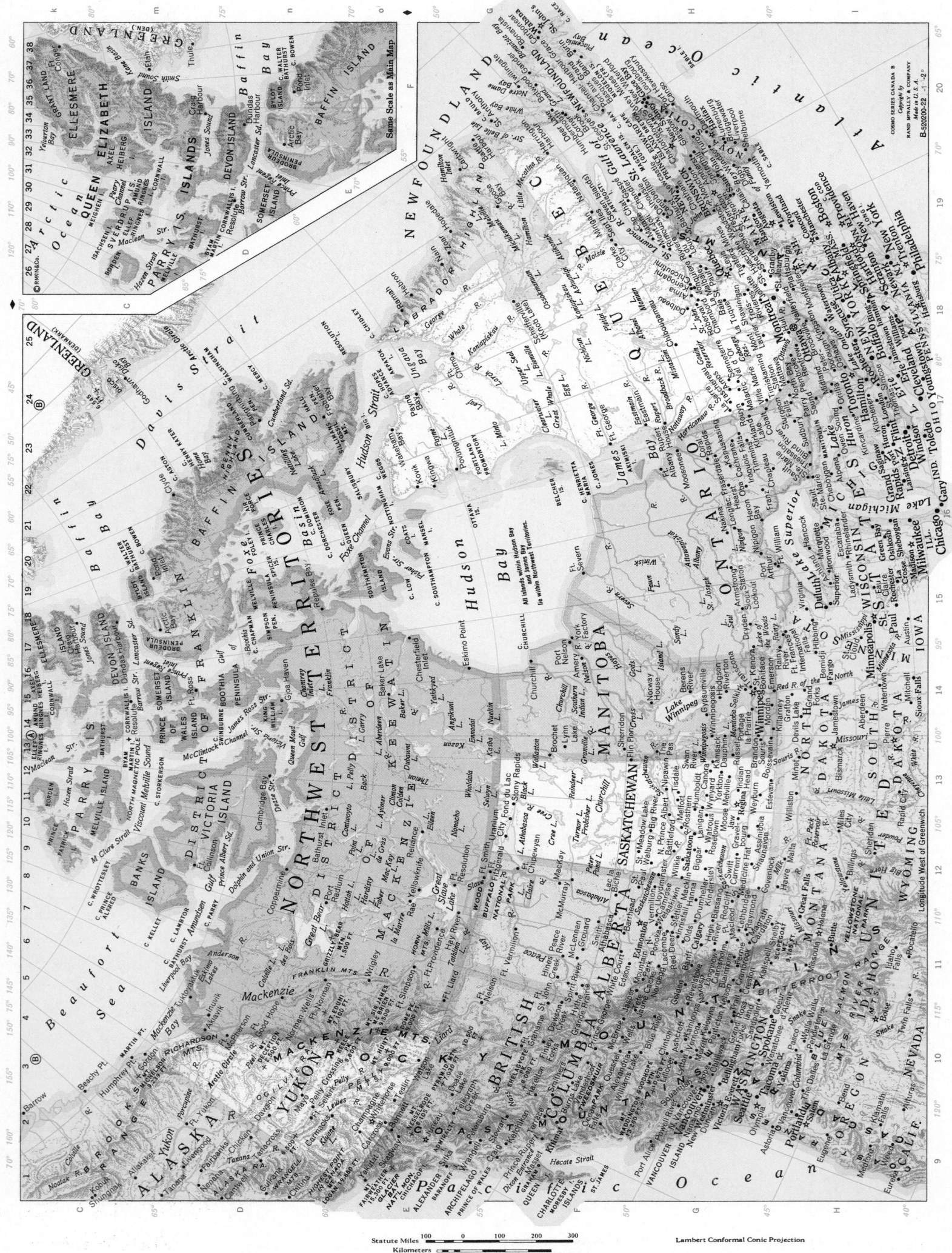

Statute Miles 100 0 100 200 300
Kilometers 100 0 100 200 300 400

Lambert Conformal Conic Projection

Oblique Cylindrical Projection

Statute Miles 10 0 10 20 30 40 50 60 70 80 90 100

Kilometers 10 0 10 20 40 60 80 100 120 140

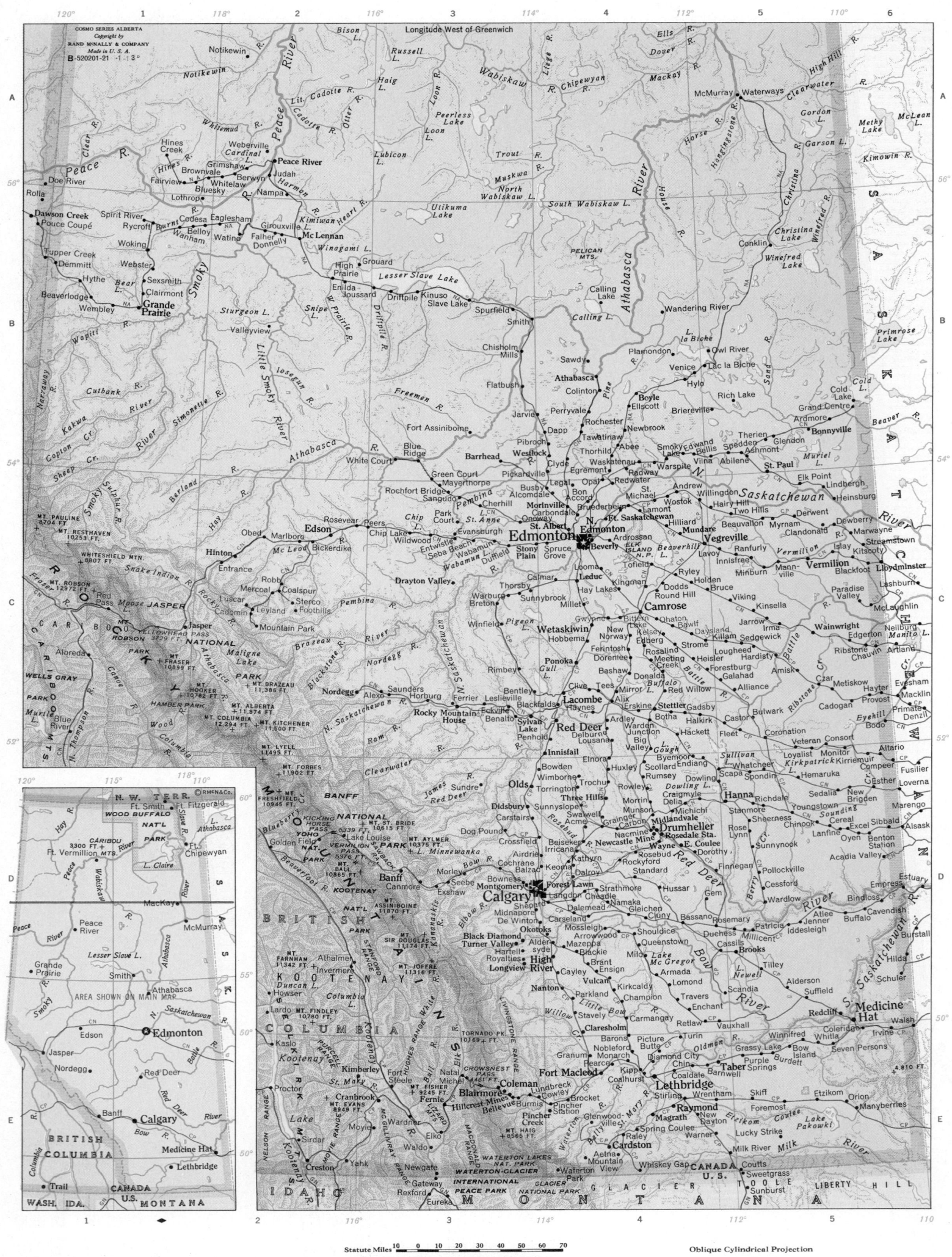

Statute Miles

Kilometers

Oblique Cylindrical Projection

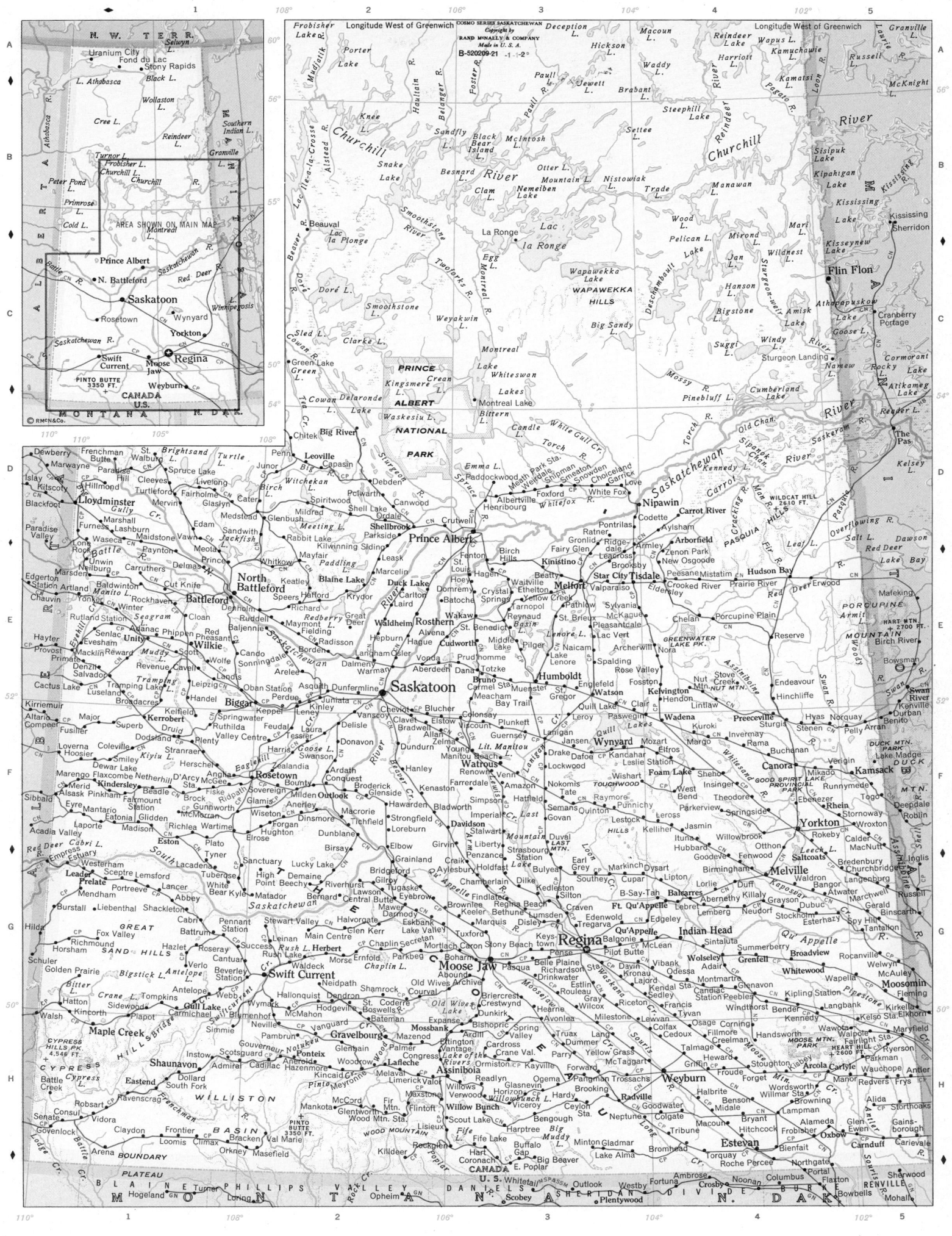

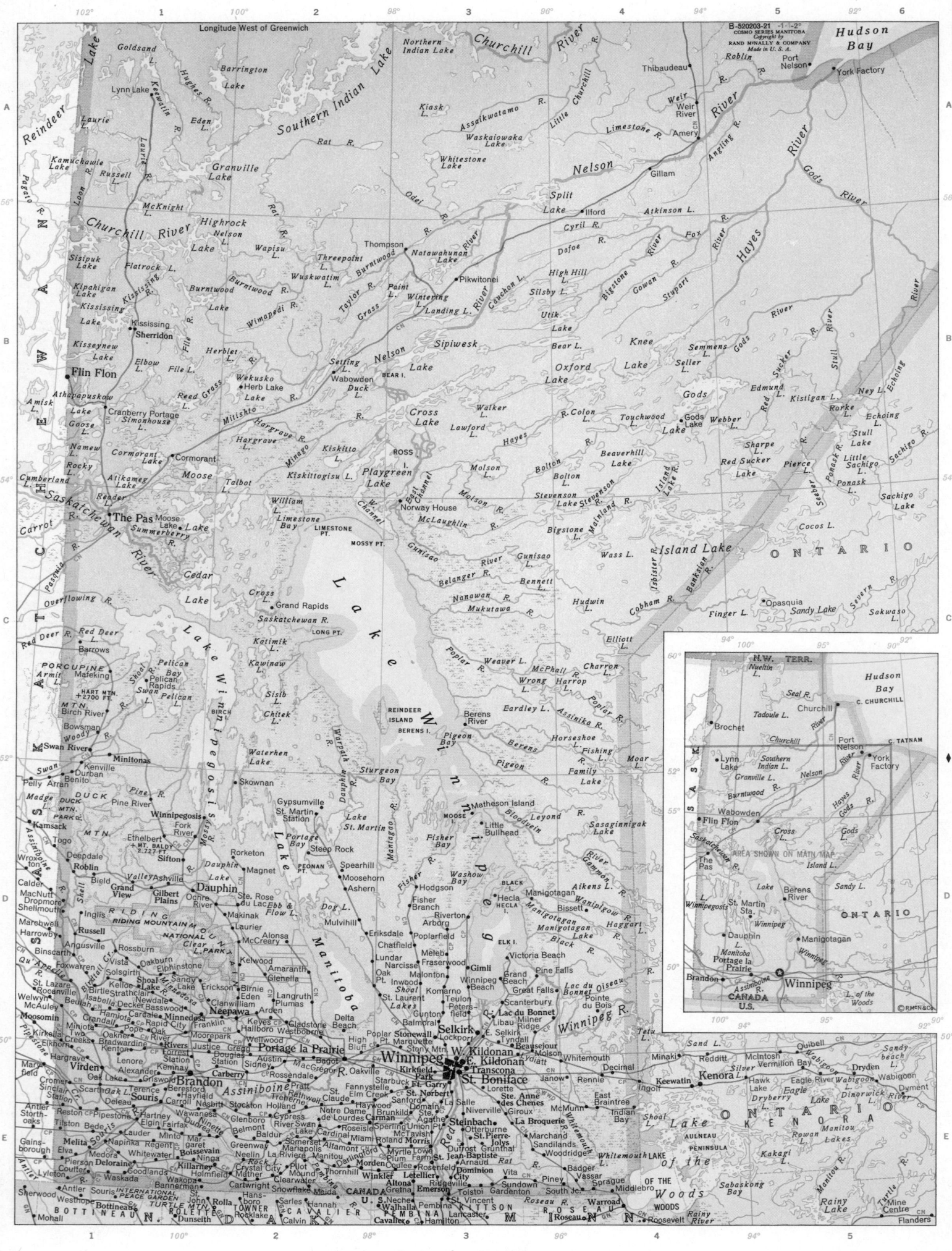

Statute Miles 10 0 10 20 30 40 50 60 70

Kilometers 10 0 10 20 40 60 80 100

Oblique Cylindrical Projection

Oblique Cylindrical Projection

Statute Miles
5 0 5 10 20 30 40 50

Kilometers
5 0 5 15 25 35 45 55 65 75

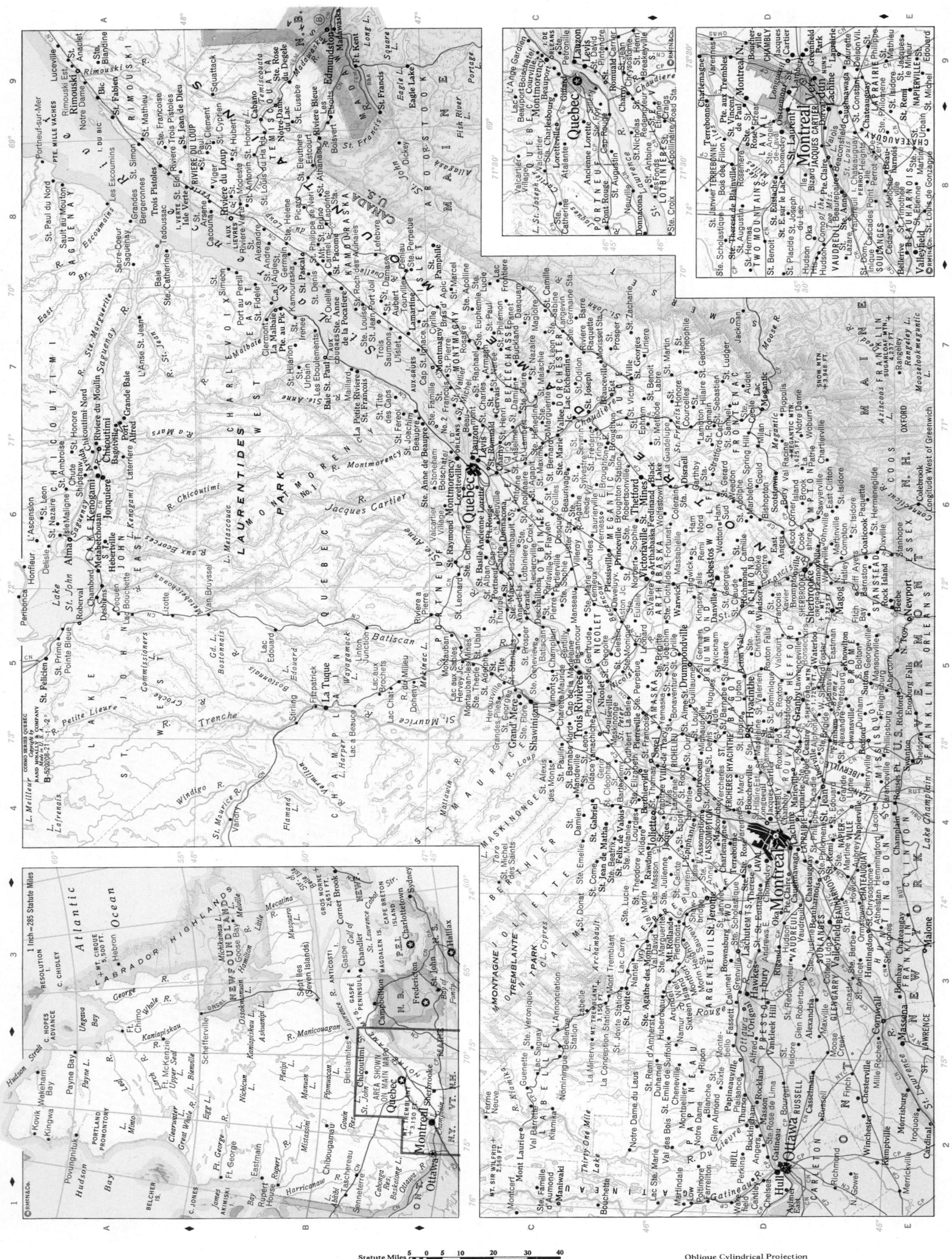

Statute Miles 5 0 5   10   20   30   40

Kilometers 5 0 5   15   25   35   45   55

Oblique Cylindrical Projection

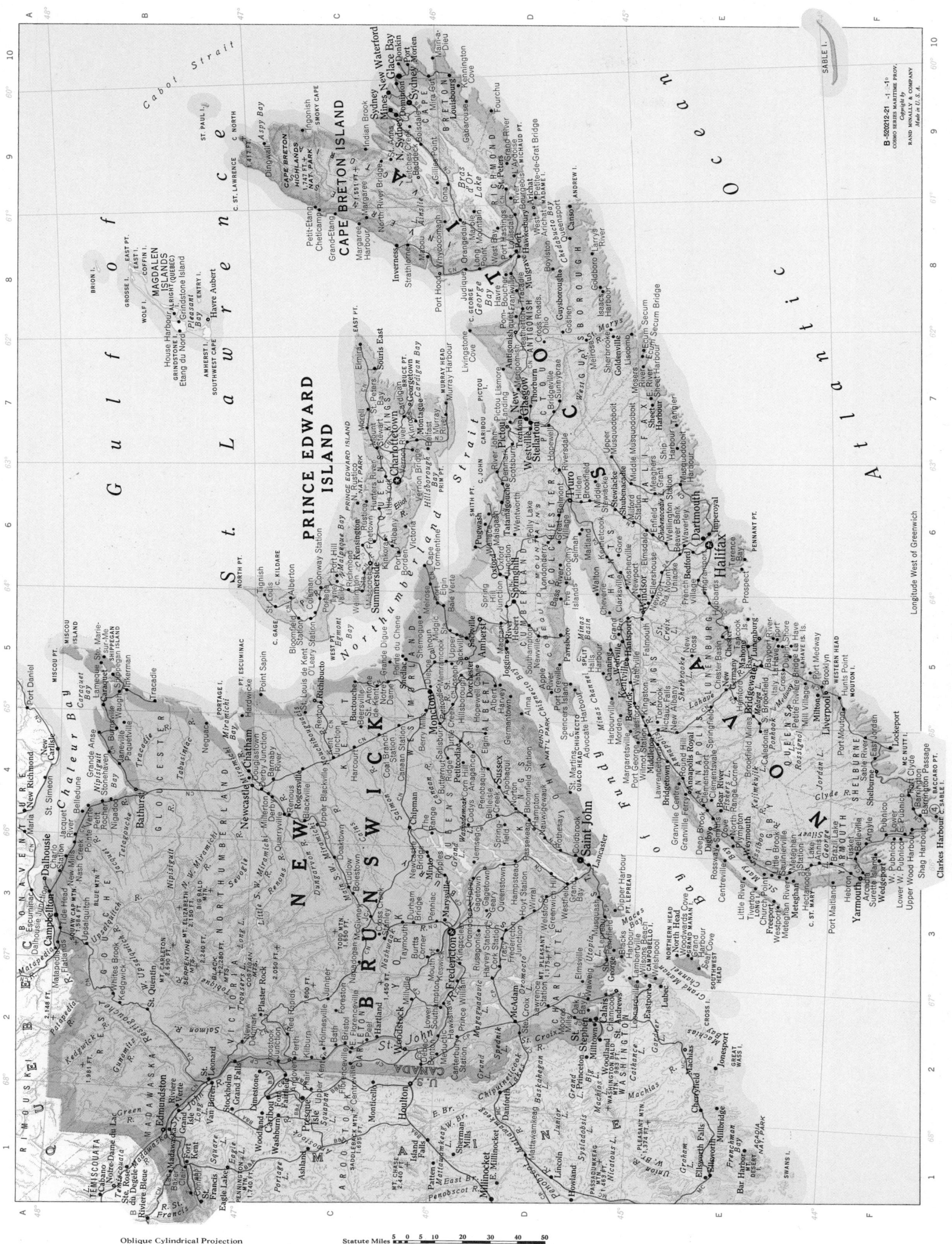

Oblique Cylindrical Projection

Statute Miles 5 0 5 10 20 30 40 50

Kilometers 5 0 5 15 25 35 45 55 65 75

Longitude West of Greenwich

B-520212-21 -1 -1°
COSMO SERIES MARITIME PROV.
Copyright by
RAND M9NALLY & COMPANY
Made in U.S.A.

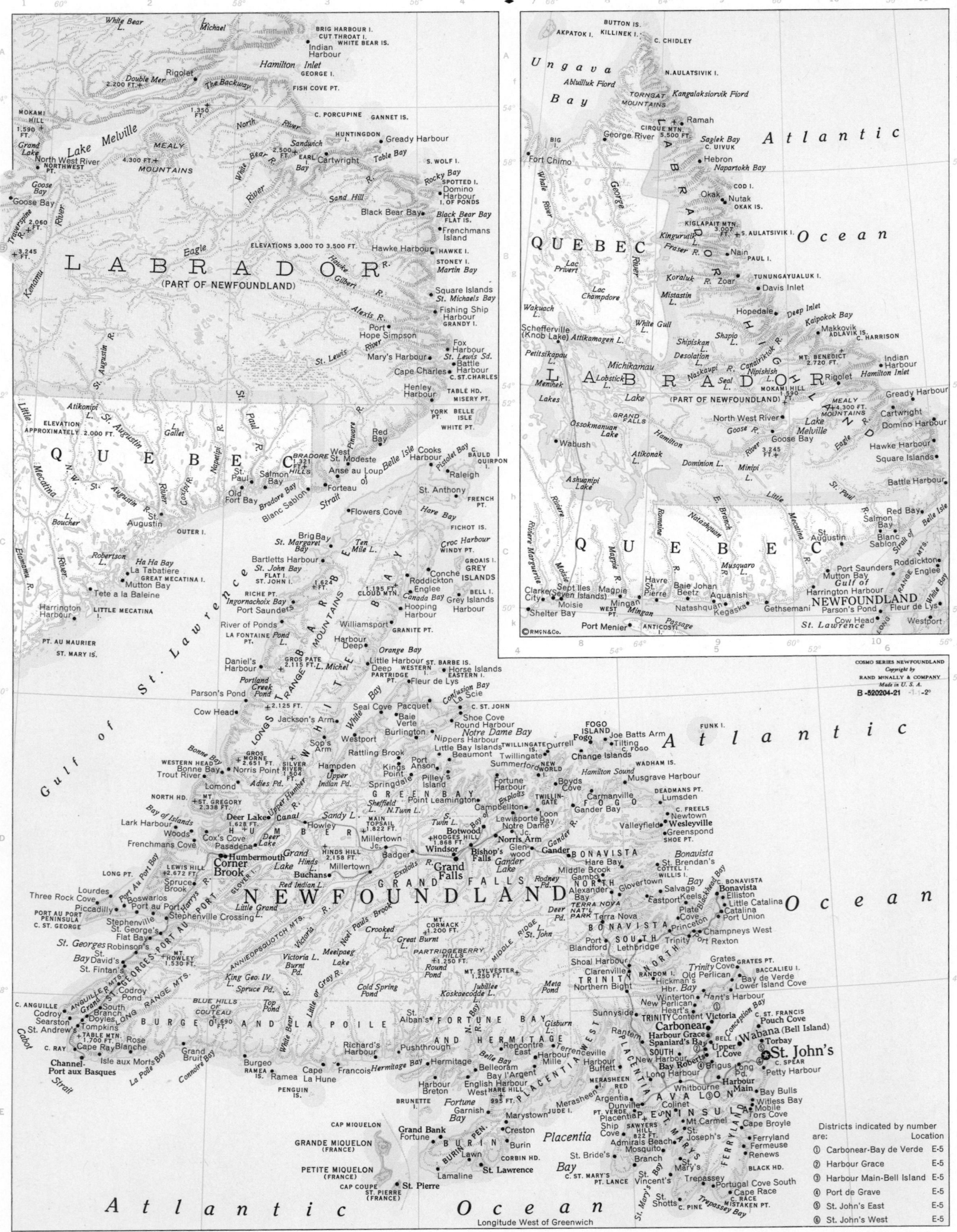

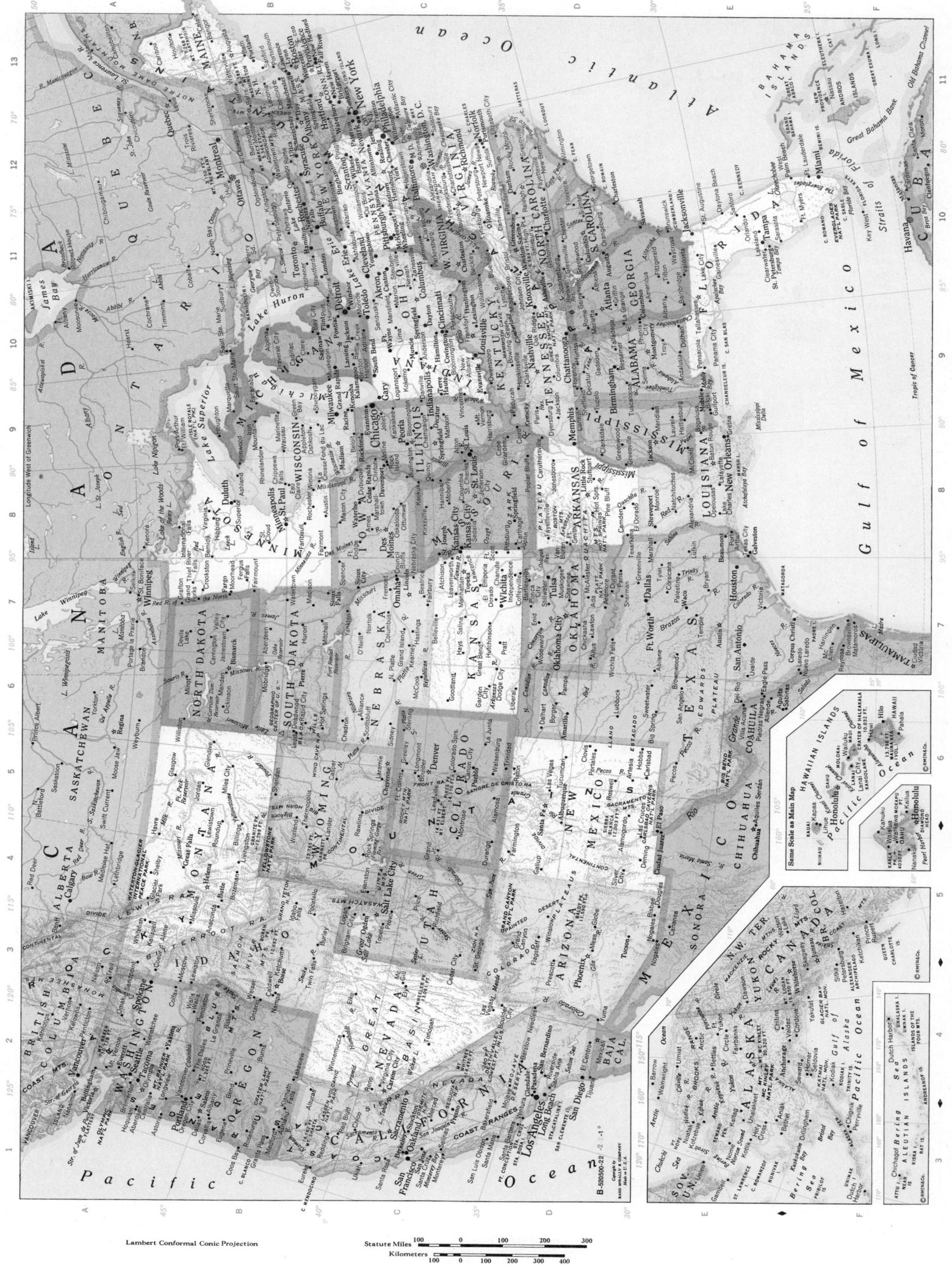

Lambert Conformal Conic Projection

Statute Miles
100   0   100   200   300

Kilometers
100   0   100   200   300   400

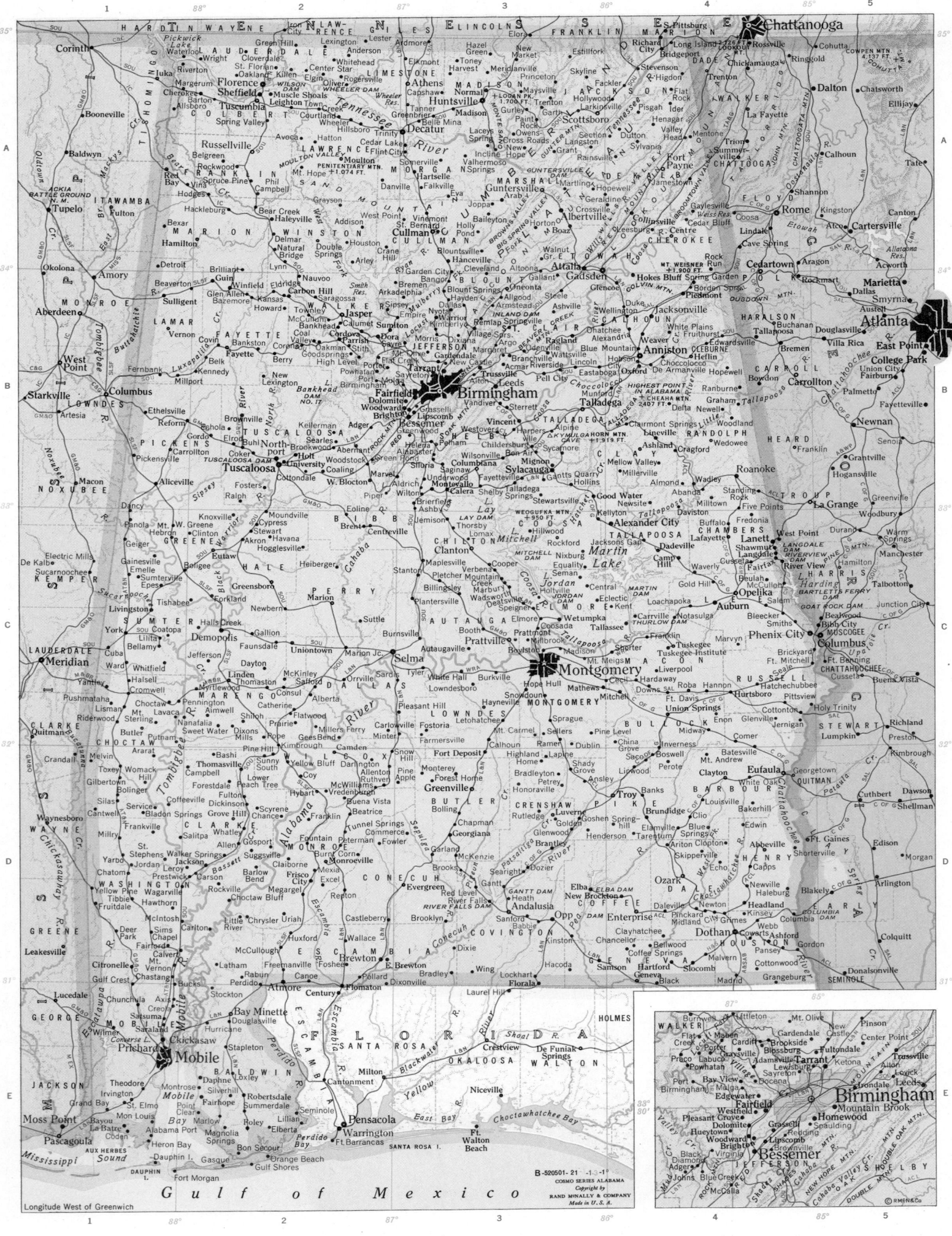

Gulf of Mexico

Statute Miles

Kilometers

Lambert Conformal Conic Projection

B-520501-21 -13-1

COSMO SERIES ALABAMA
Copyright by
RAND McNALLY & COMPANY
Made in U.S.A.

Longitude West of Greenwich

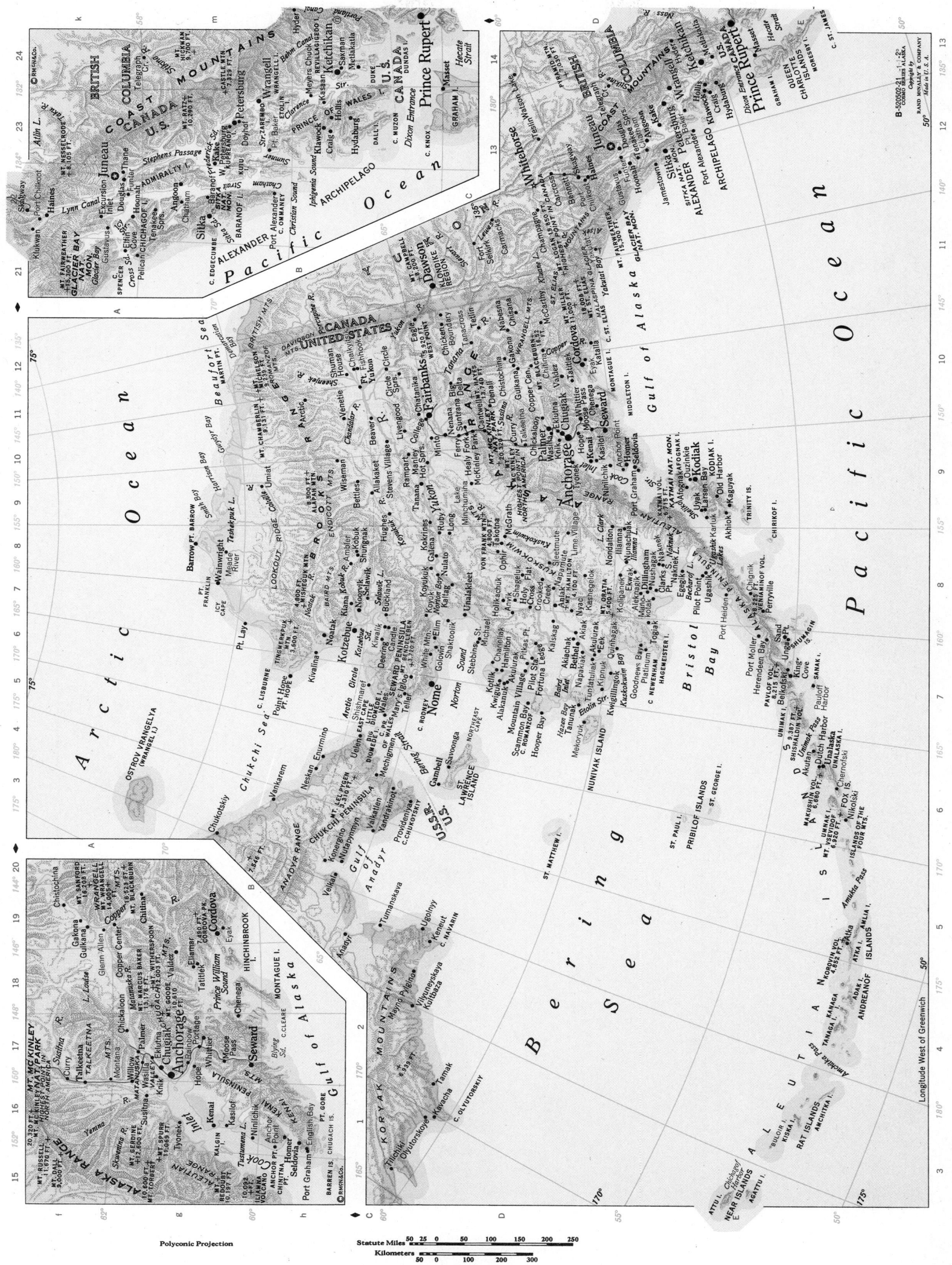

COSMO SERIES ALASKA
B-500502-21 · 1 : 2½
Copyright by
RAND McNALLY & COMPANY
Made in U.S.A.

Polyconic Projection

Statute Miles
50 25 0   50   100   150   200   250

Kilometers
50 0   100   200   300

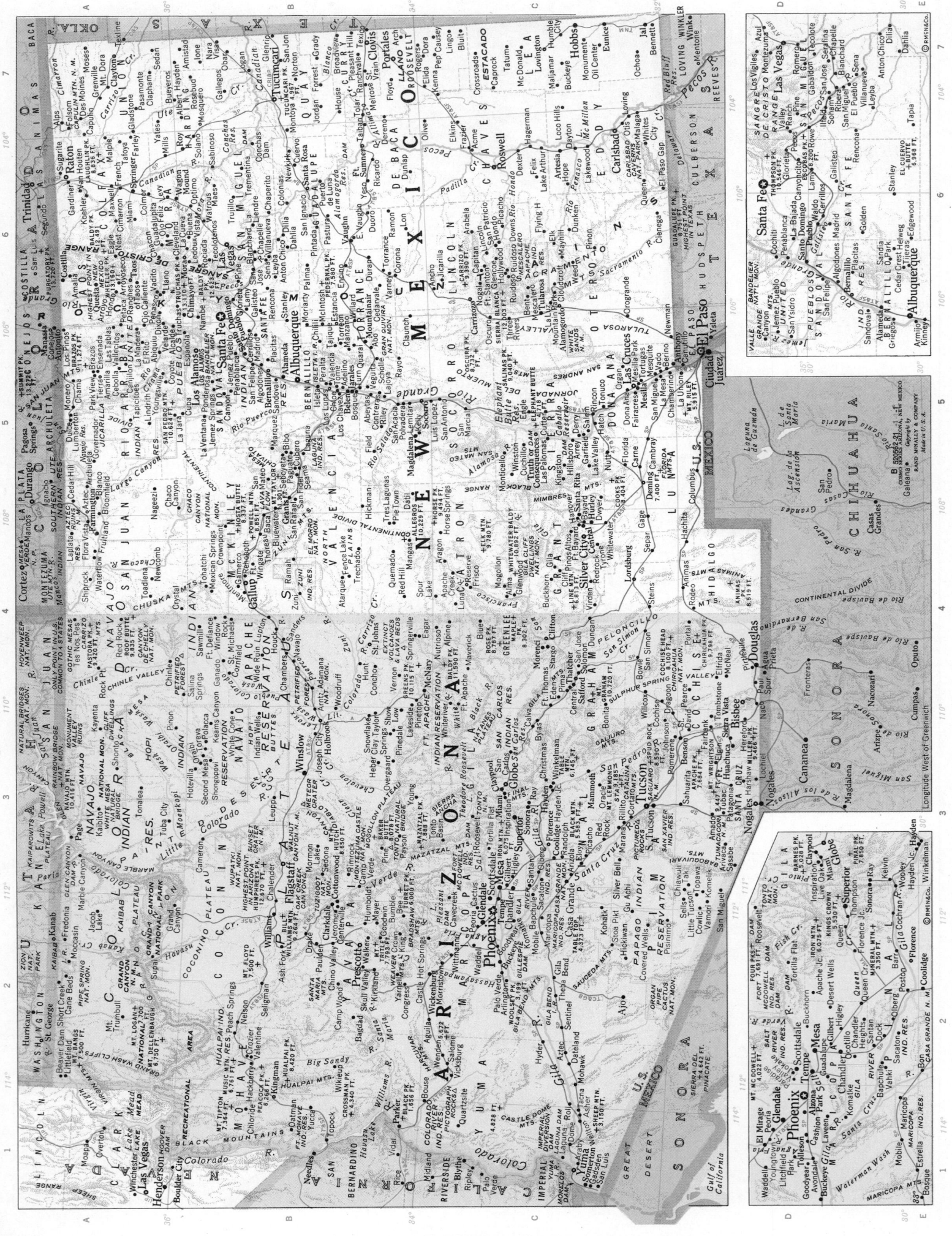

Statute Miles 10 0 10 20 30 40 50 60 70 80 90

Kilometers 10 0 10 20 40 60 80 100 120

Lambert Conformal Conic Projection

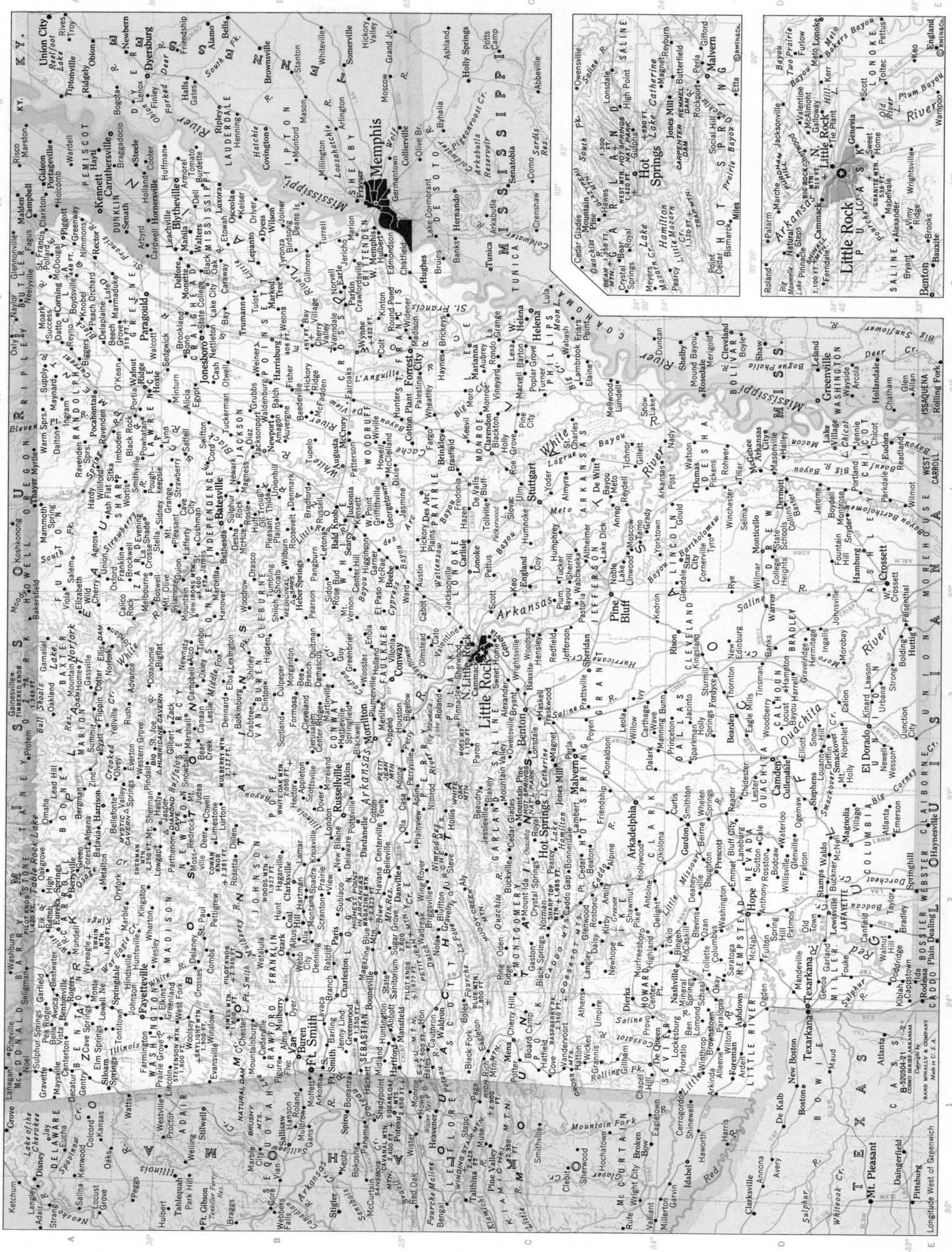

Lambert Conformal Conic Projection

Statute Miles

Kilometers

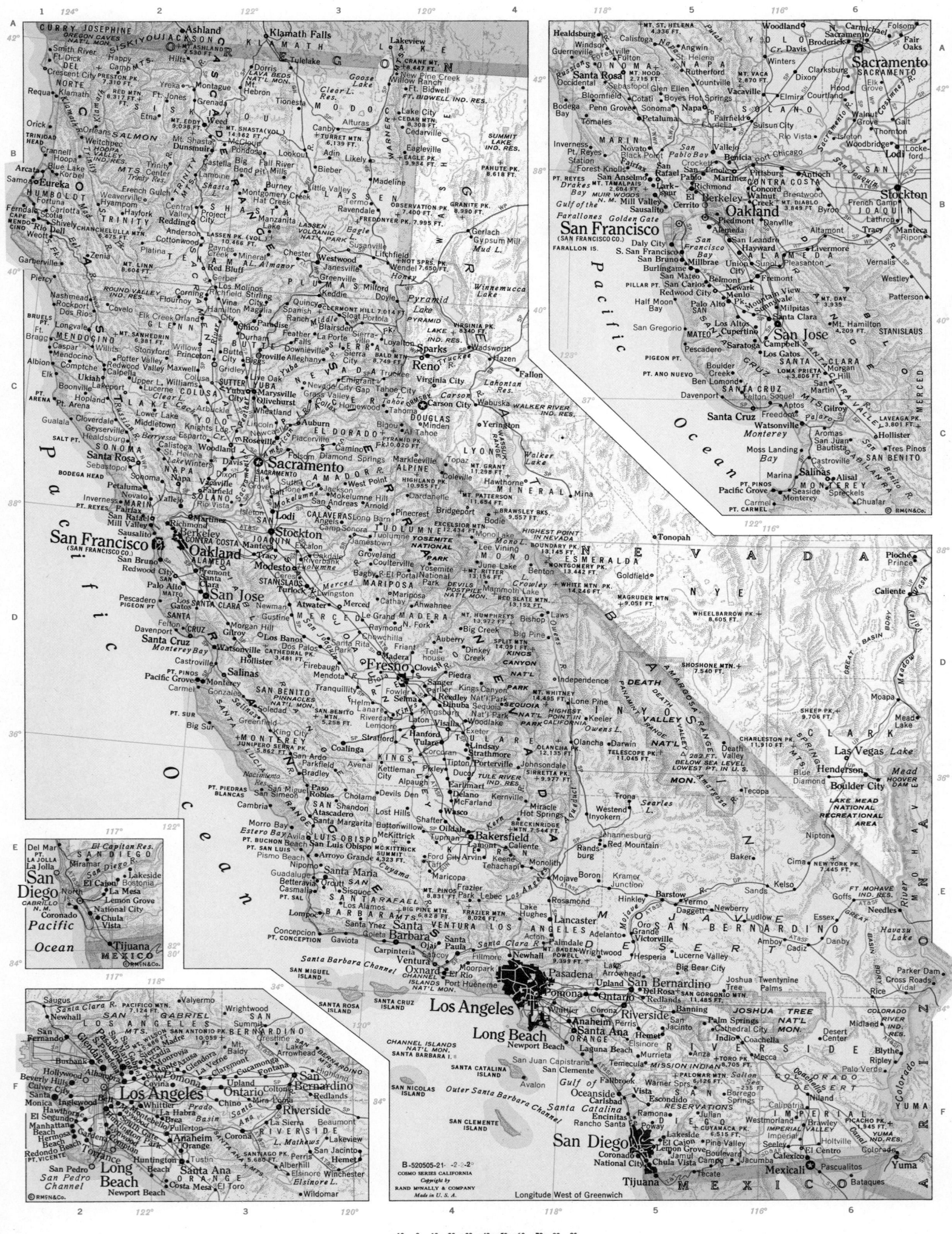

Statute Miles
Kilometers

Lambert Conformal Conic Projection

B-520505-21   -2-2-2°
COSMO SERIES CALIFORNIA
Copyright by
RAND McNALLY & COMPANY
Made in U.S.A.

Longitude West of Greenwich

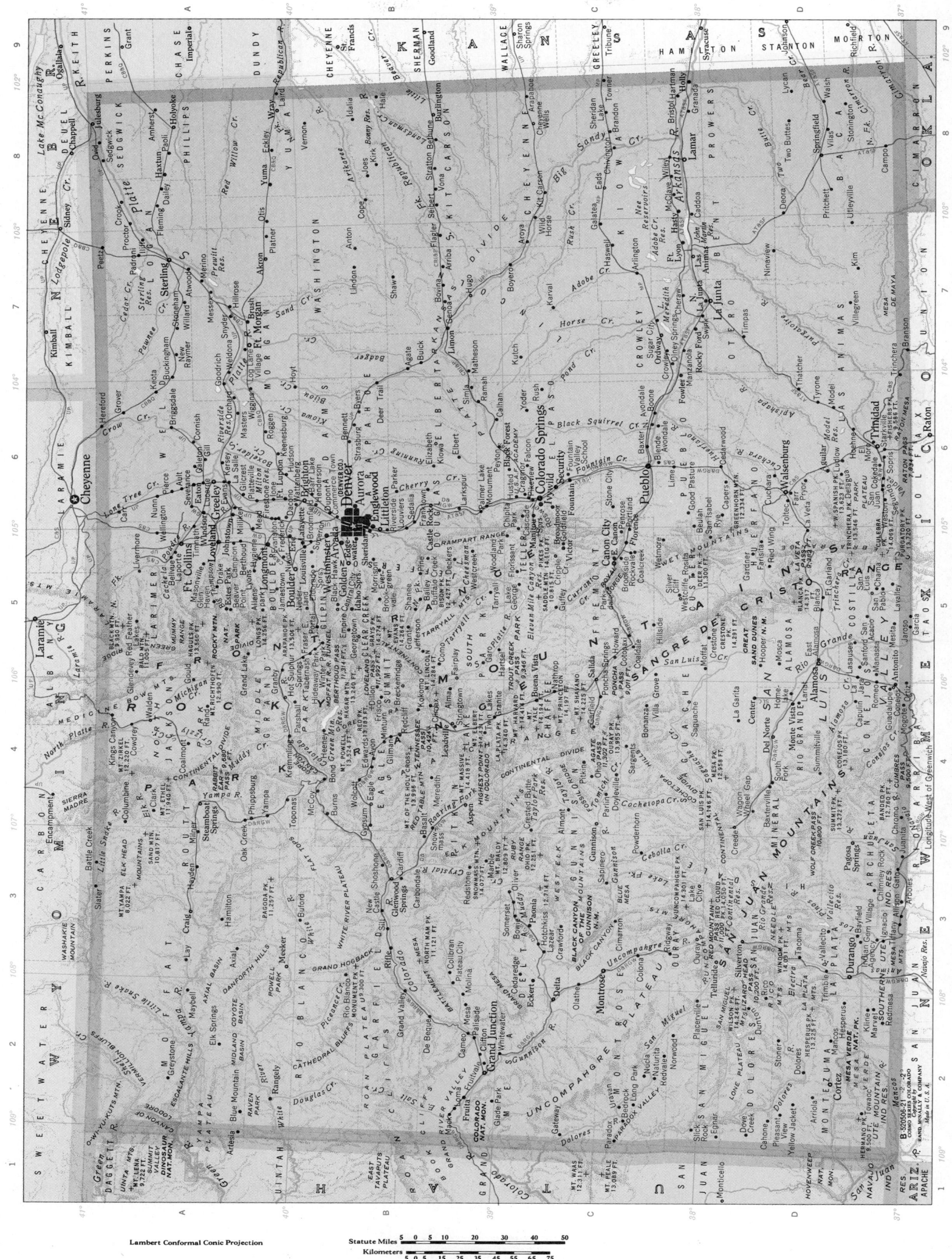

Lambert Conformal Conic Projection

Statute Miles 5 0 5 10 20 30 40 50

Kilometers 5 0 5 15 25 35 45 55 65 75

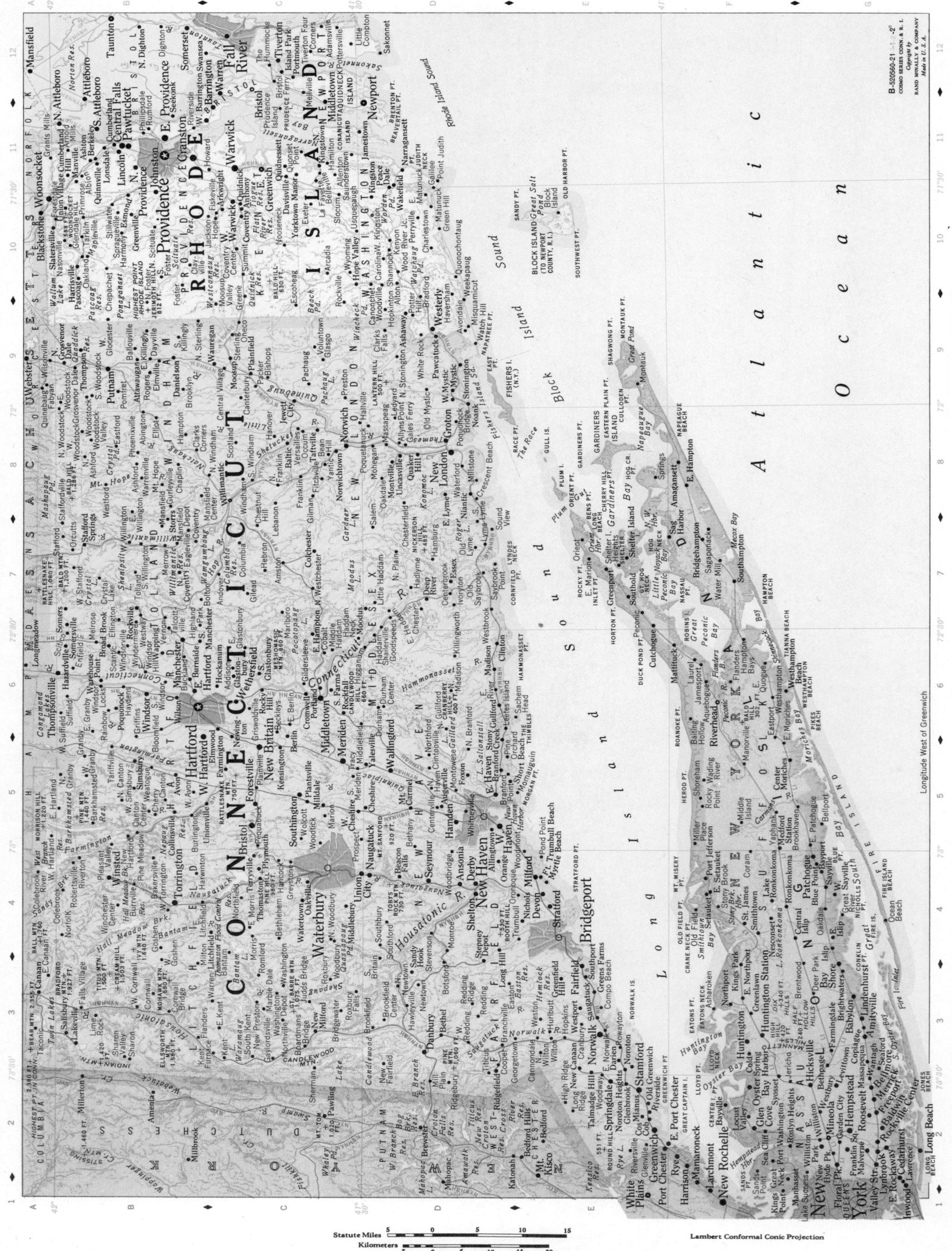

Statute Miles

Kilometers

Lambert Conformal Conic Projection

B-52056O-21-1-2°
COSMO SERIES CONN. & R.I.
Copyright by
RAND McNALLY & COMPANY
Made in U.S.A.

Longitude West of Greenwich

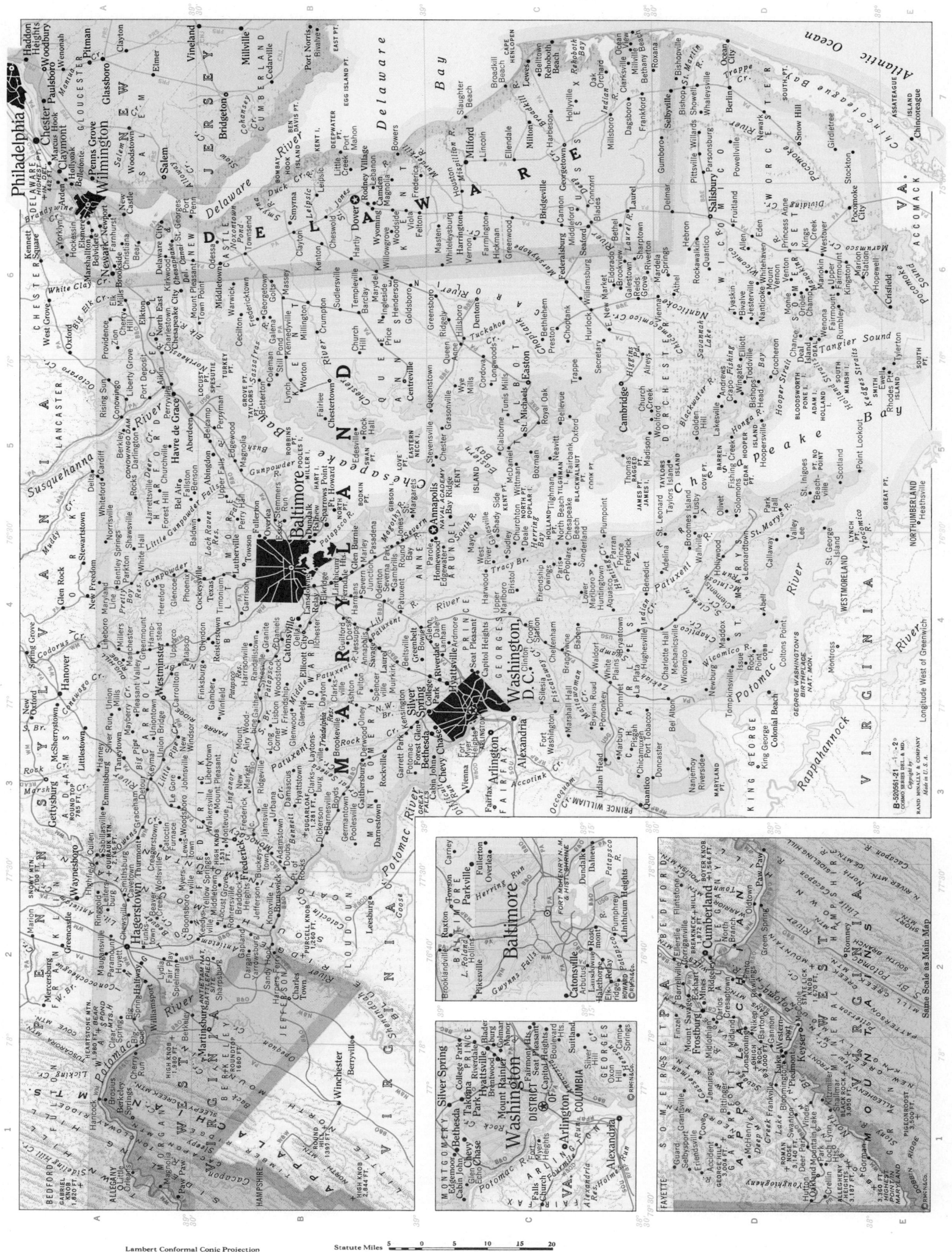

Lambert Conformal Conic Projection

Statute Miles

Kilometers

B-50561-21 -1 -2°
COSMO SERIES 1961. A&D.
RAND MCNALLY & COMPANY
Made in U.S.A.

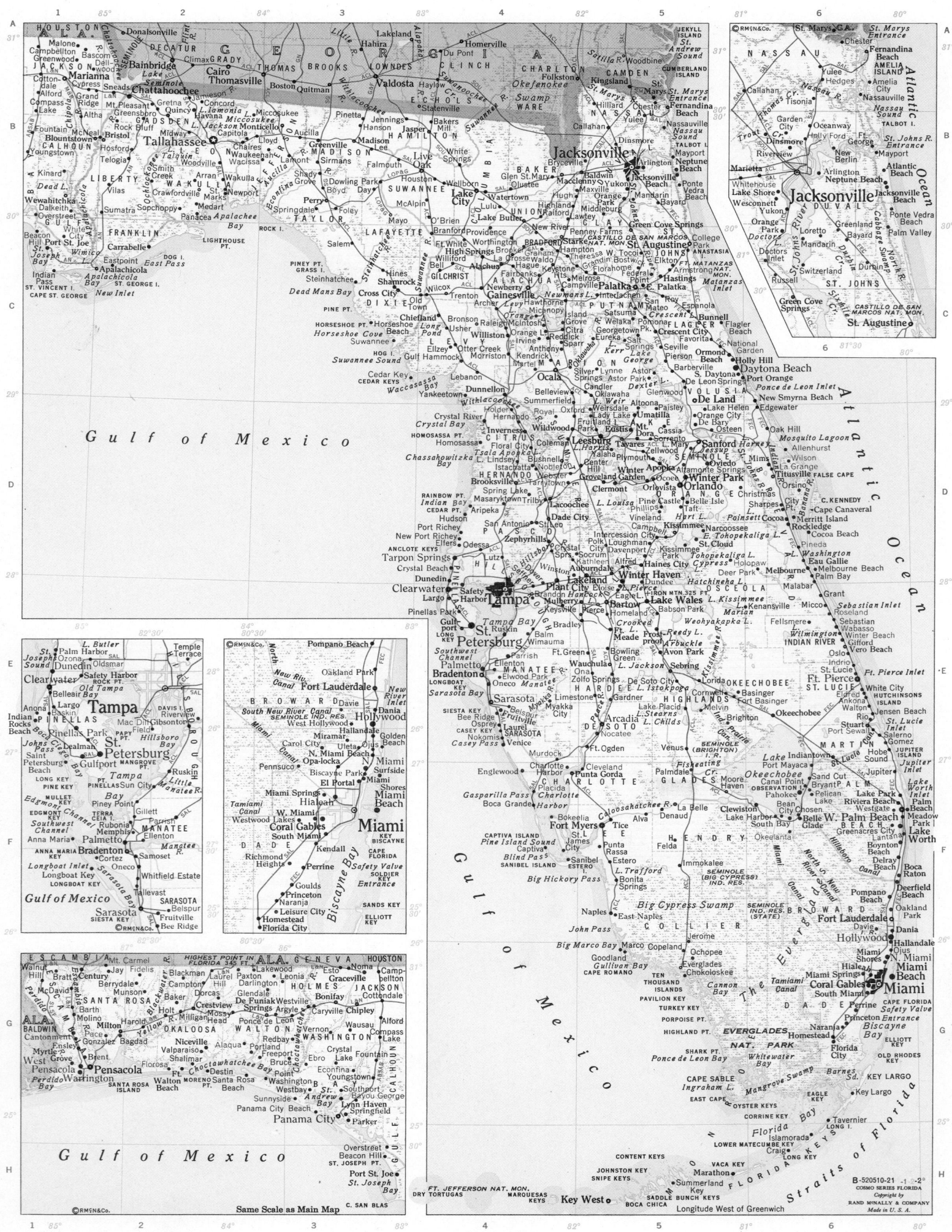

Statute Miles

Kilometers

Lambert Conformal Conic Projection

Same Scale as Main Map

B-520510-21

COSMO SERIES FLORIDA
Copyright by
RAND M^cNALLY & COMPANY
Made in U.S.A.

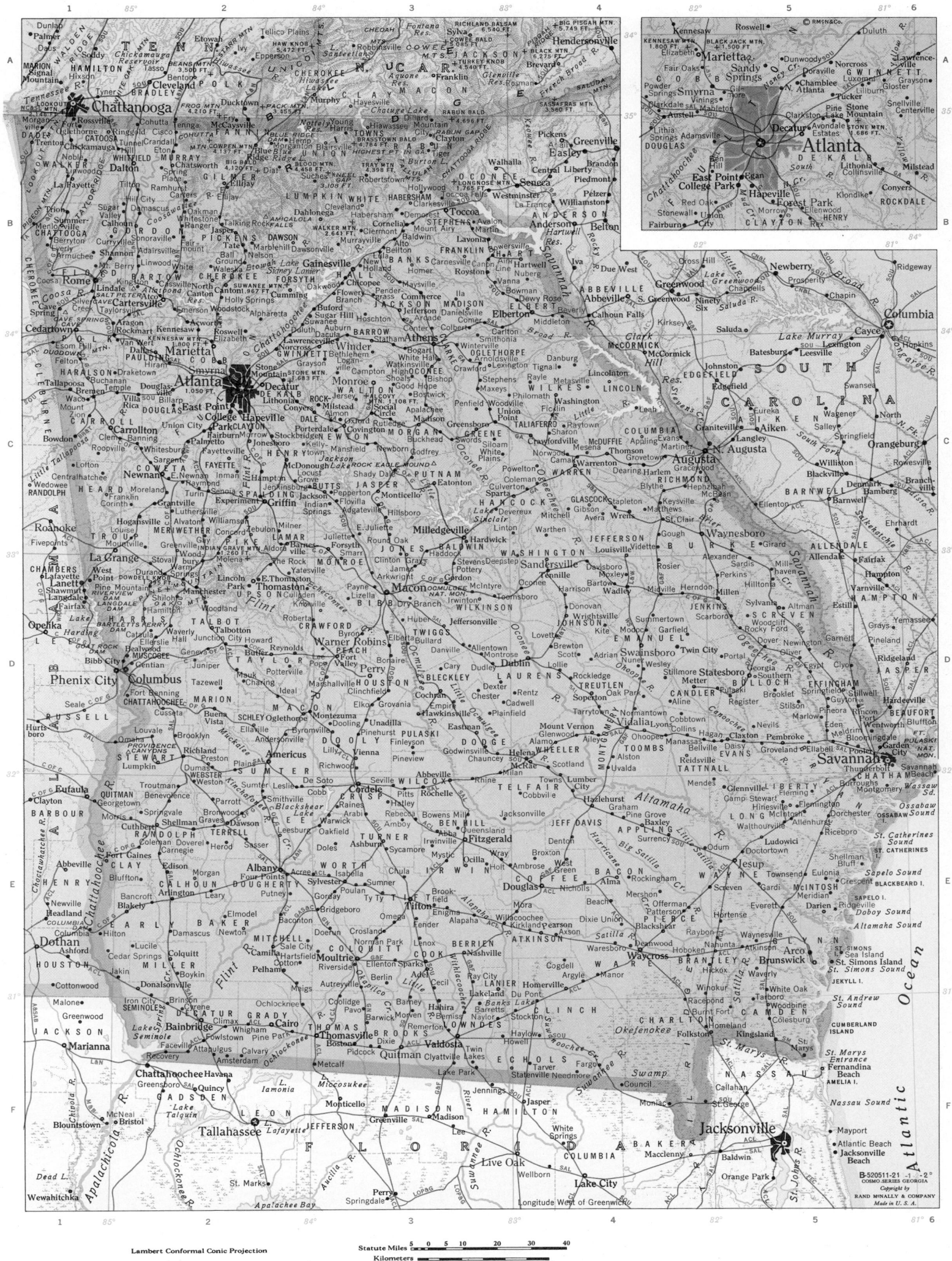

Lambert Conformal Conic Projection

Statute Miles
5 0 5 10 20 30 40

Kilometers
5 0 5 15 25 35 45 55

B-520511-21 -1 -2"
COSMO SERIES GEORGIA
Copyright by
RAND M¢NALLY & COMPANY
Made in U.S.A.

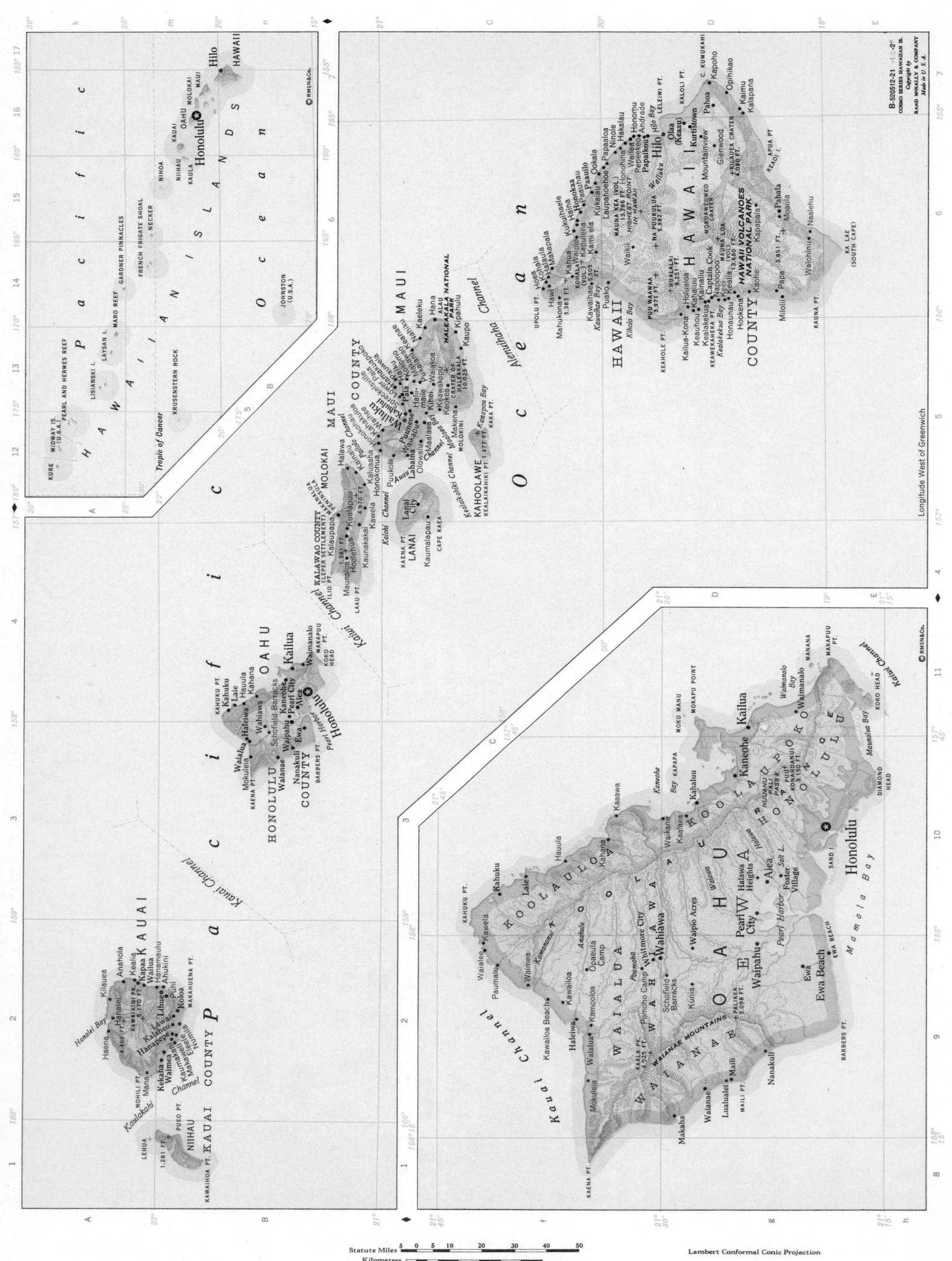

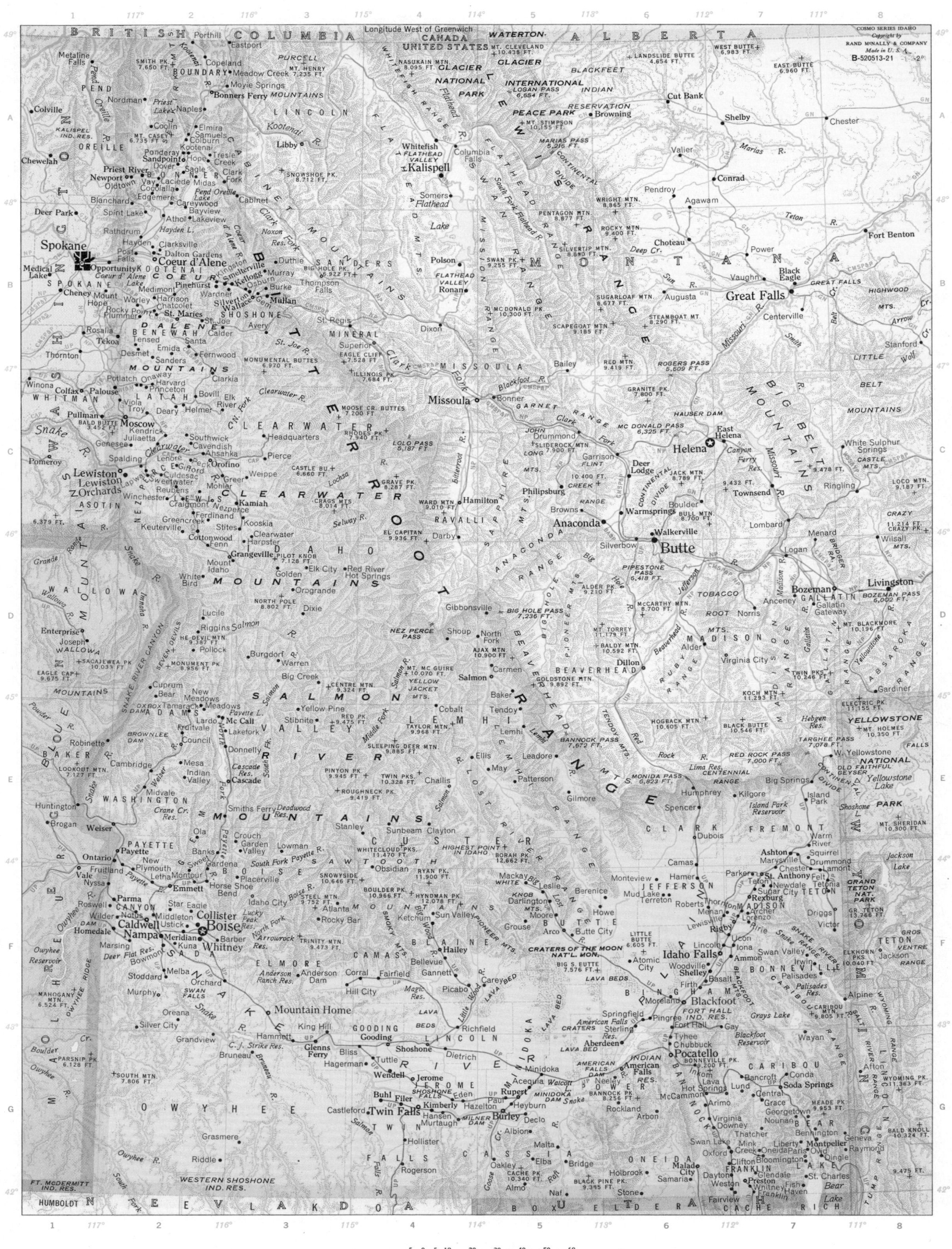

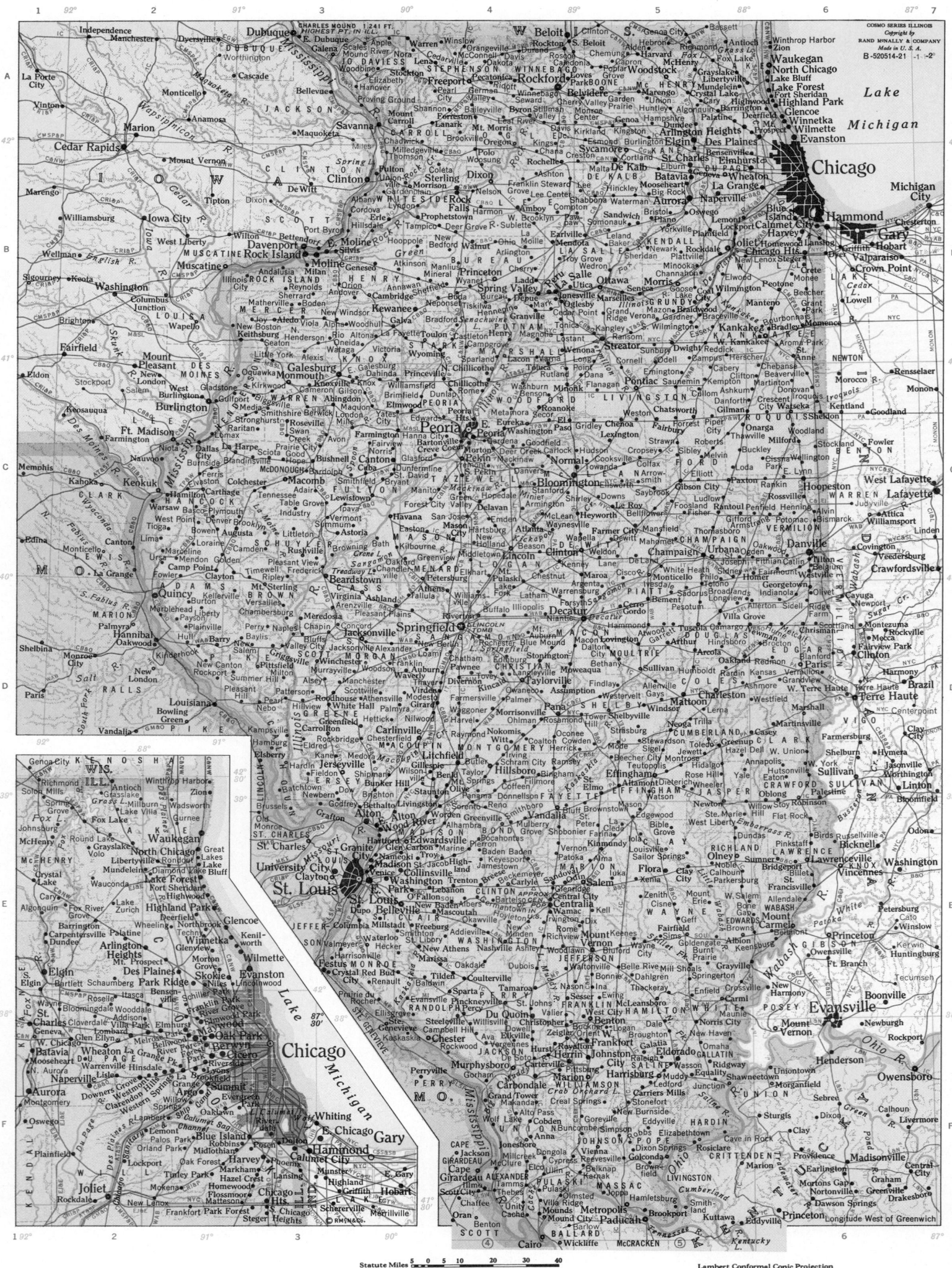

Statute Miles

Kilometers

Lambert Conformal Conic Projection

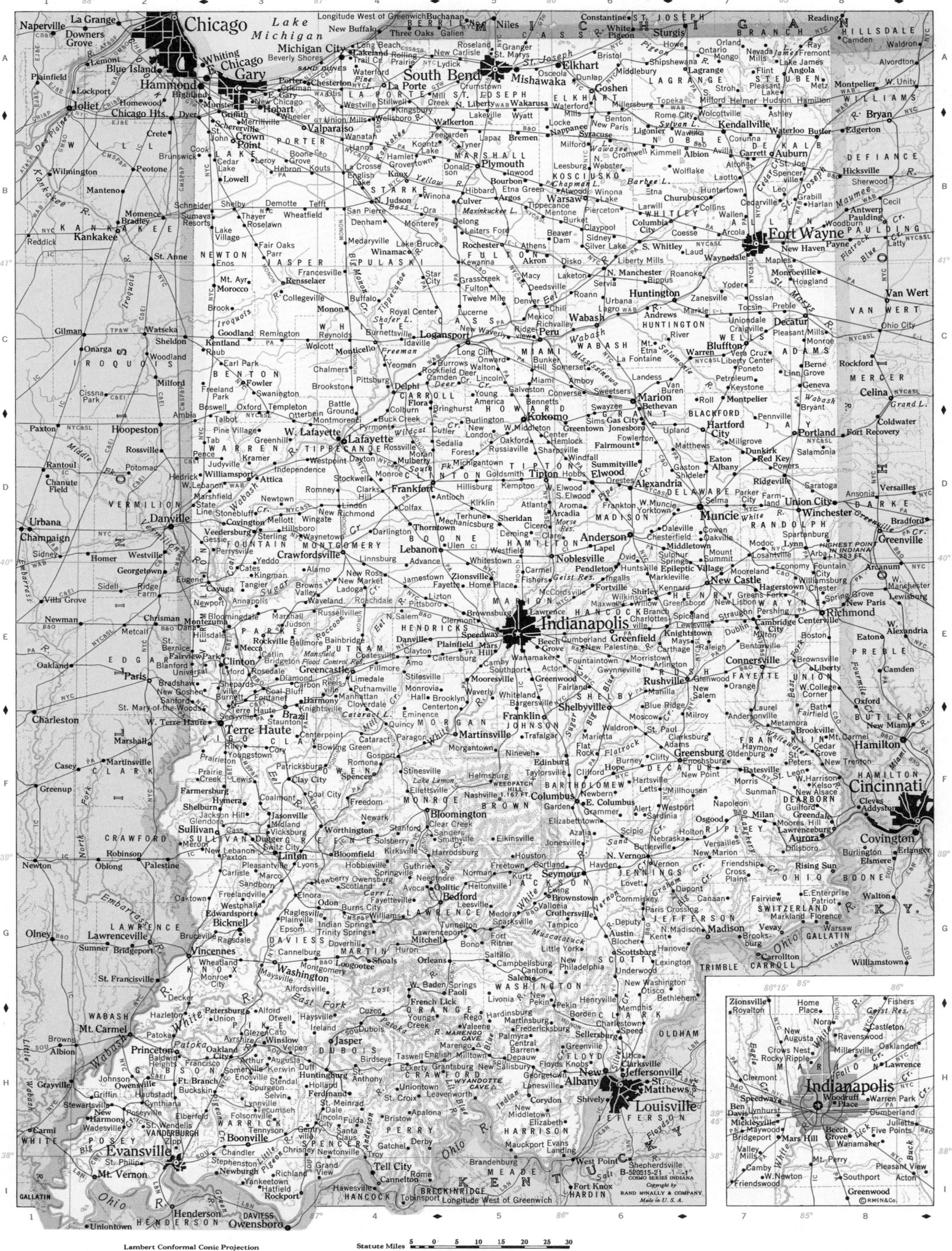

Lambert Conformal Conic Projection

Statute Miles
5 0 5 10 15 20 25 30

Kilometers
5 0 5 15 25 35

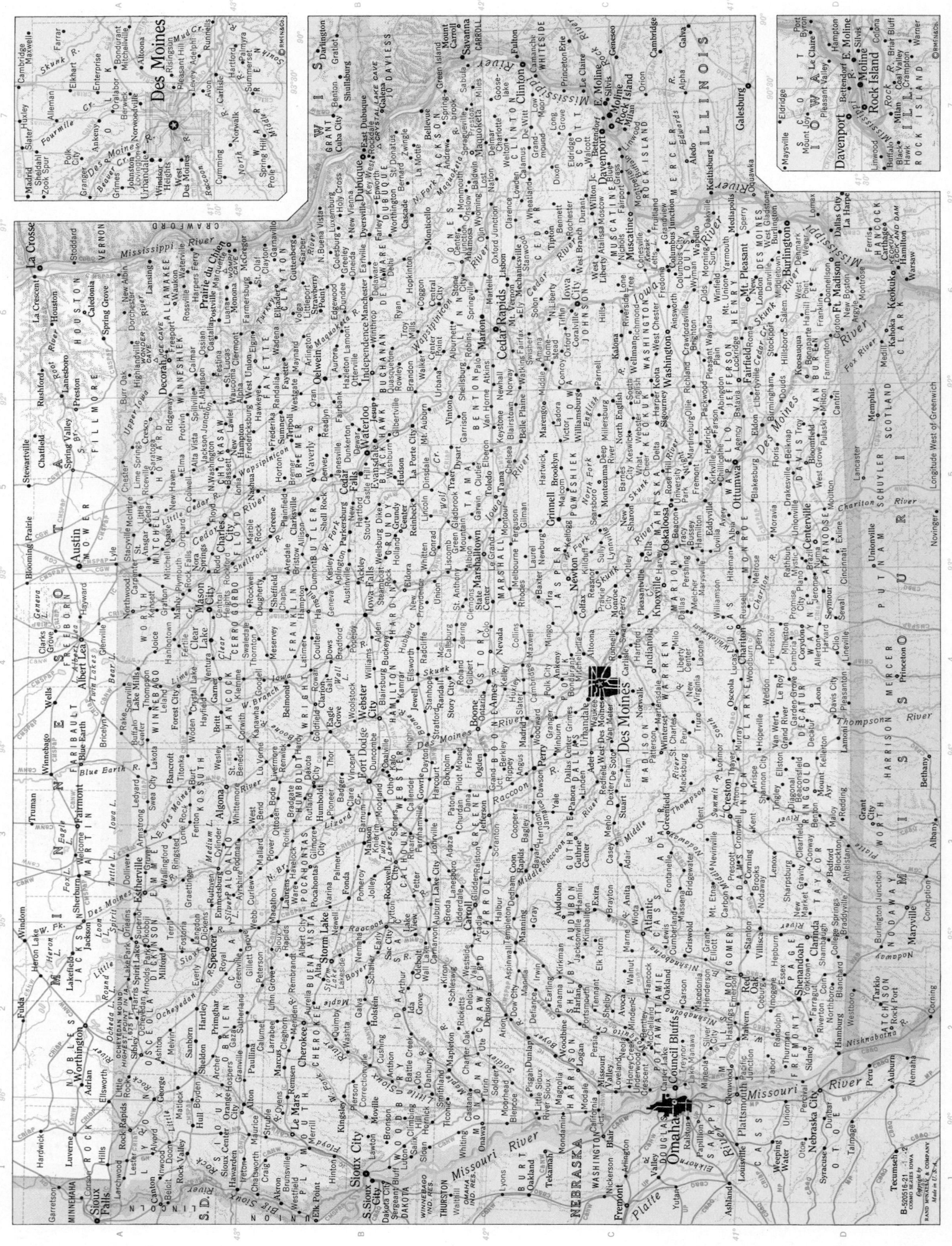

Statute Miles 5 0 5 10 20 30 40
Kilometers 5 0 5 15 25 35 45 55

Lambert Conformal Conic Projection

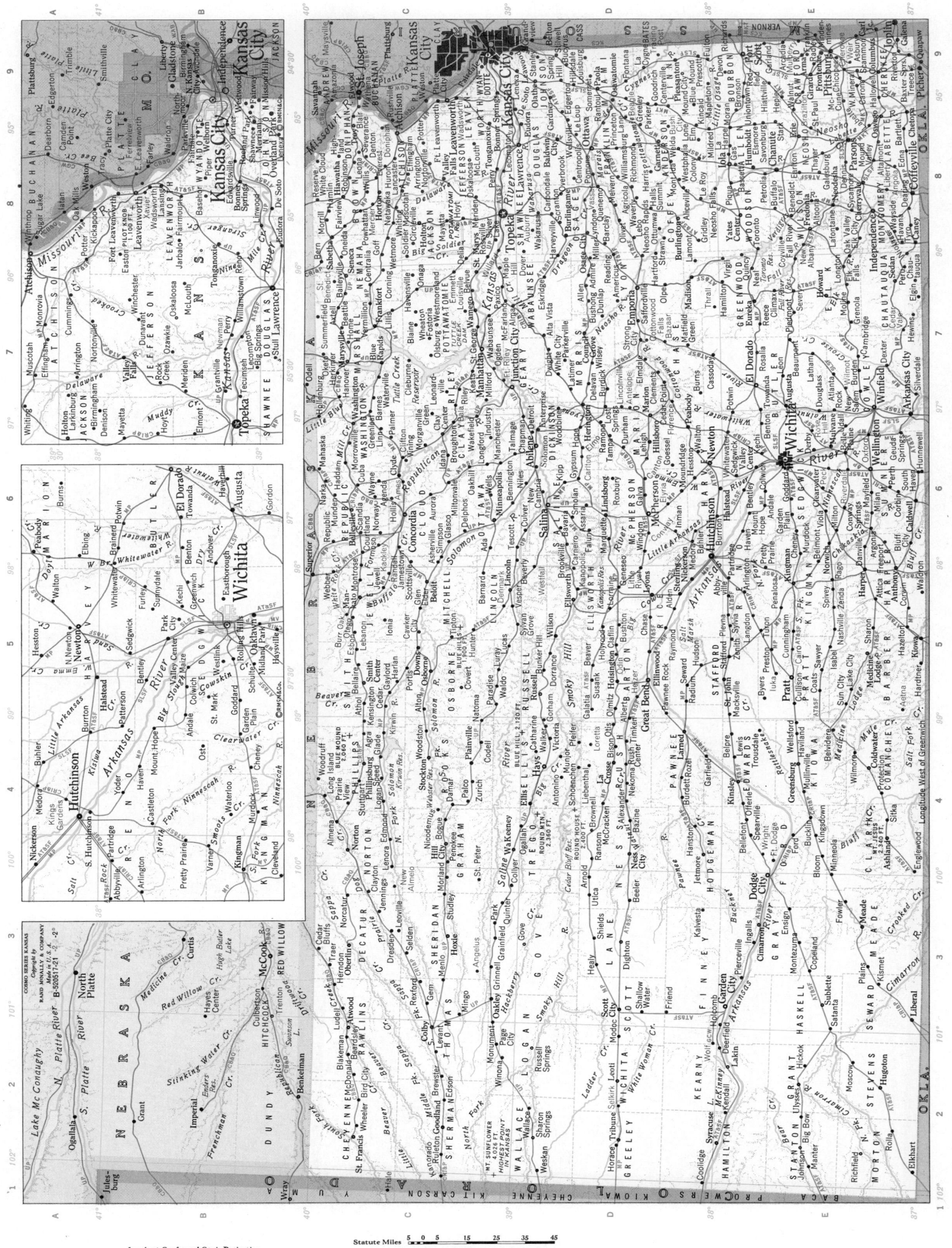

CONCO SERIES KANSAS
Copyright by
RAND McNALLY & COMPANY
Made in U.S.A.
B-500517-21 -2

Lambert Conformal Conic Projection

Statute Miles
5 0 5   15   25   35   45
Kilometers
5 0 5 15 25 35 45 55 65

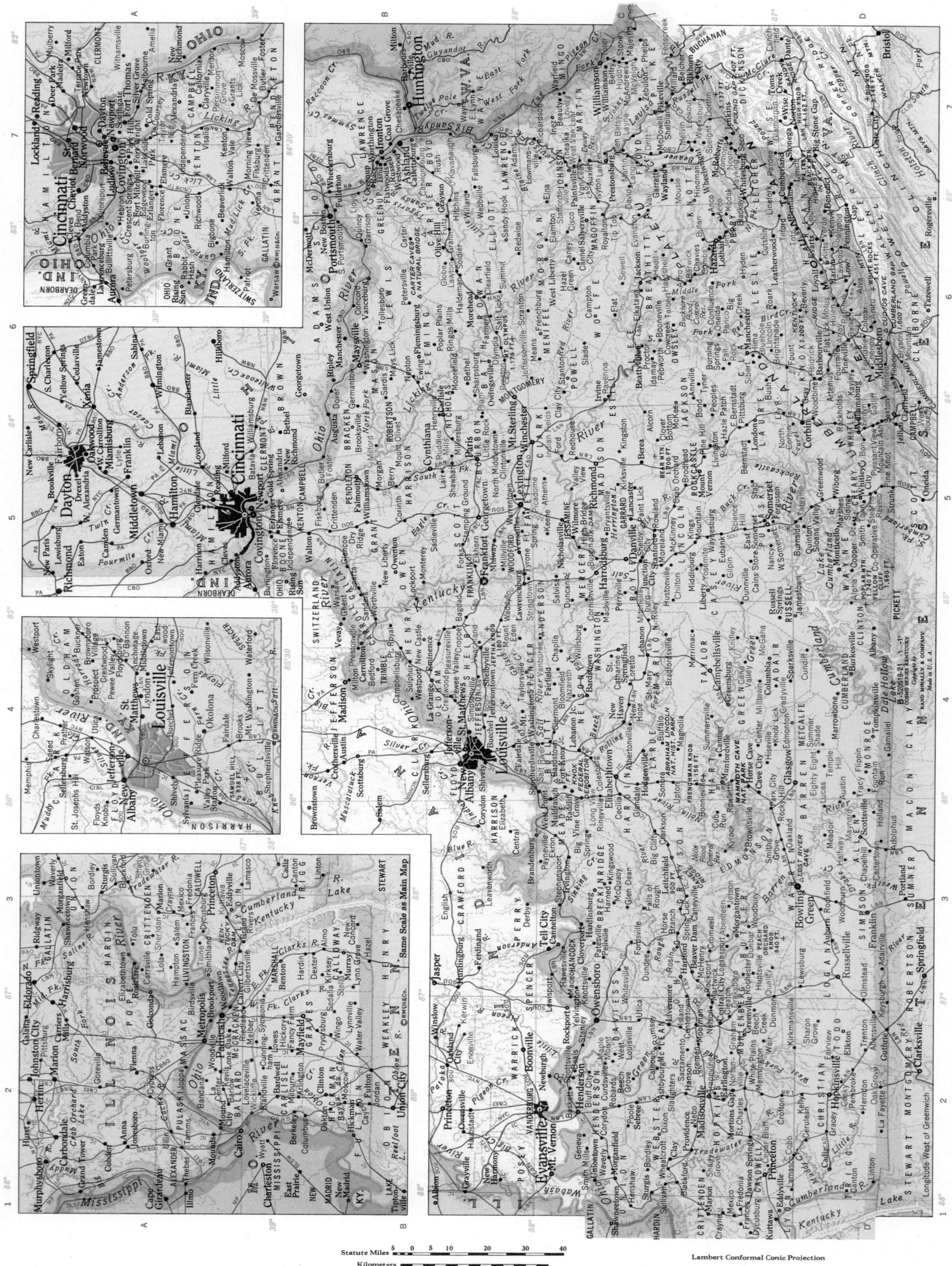

Statute Miles 5 0 5 10 20 30 40

Kilometers 5 0 5 10 20 30 40 50 60

Lambert Conformal Conic Projection

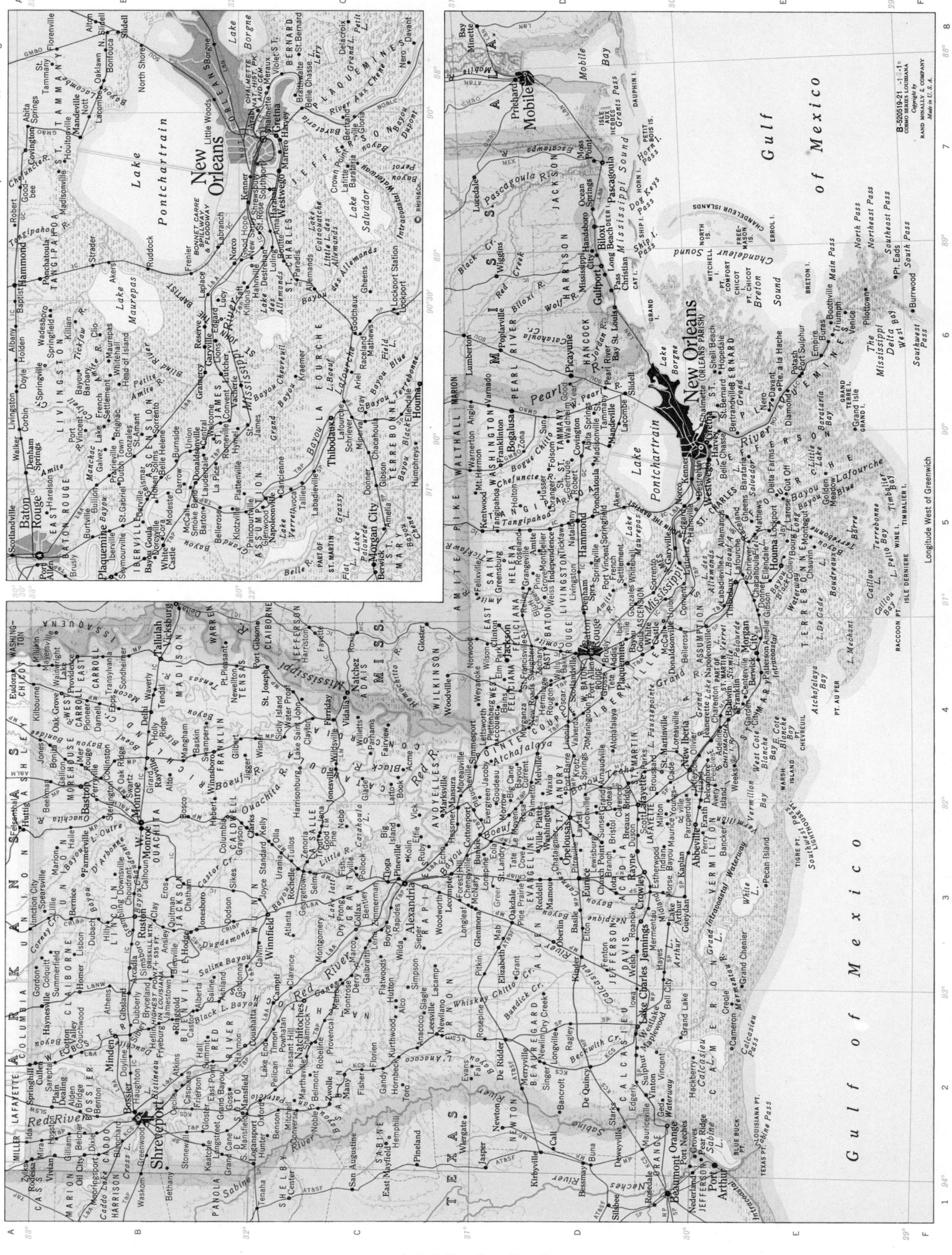

Lambert Conformal Conic Projection

Statute Miles

Kilometers

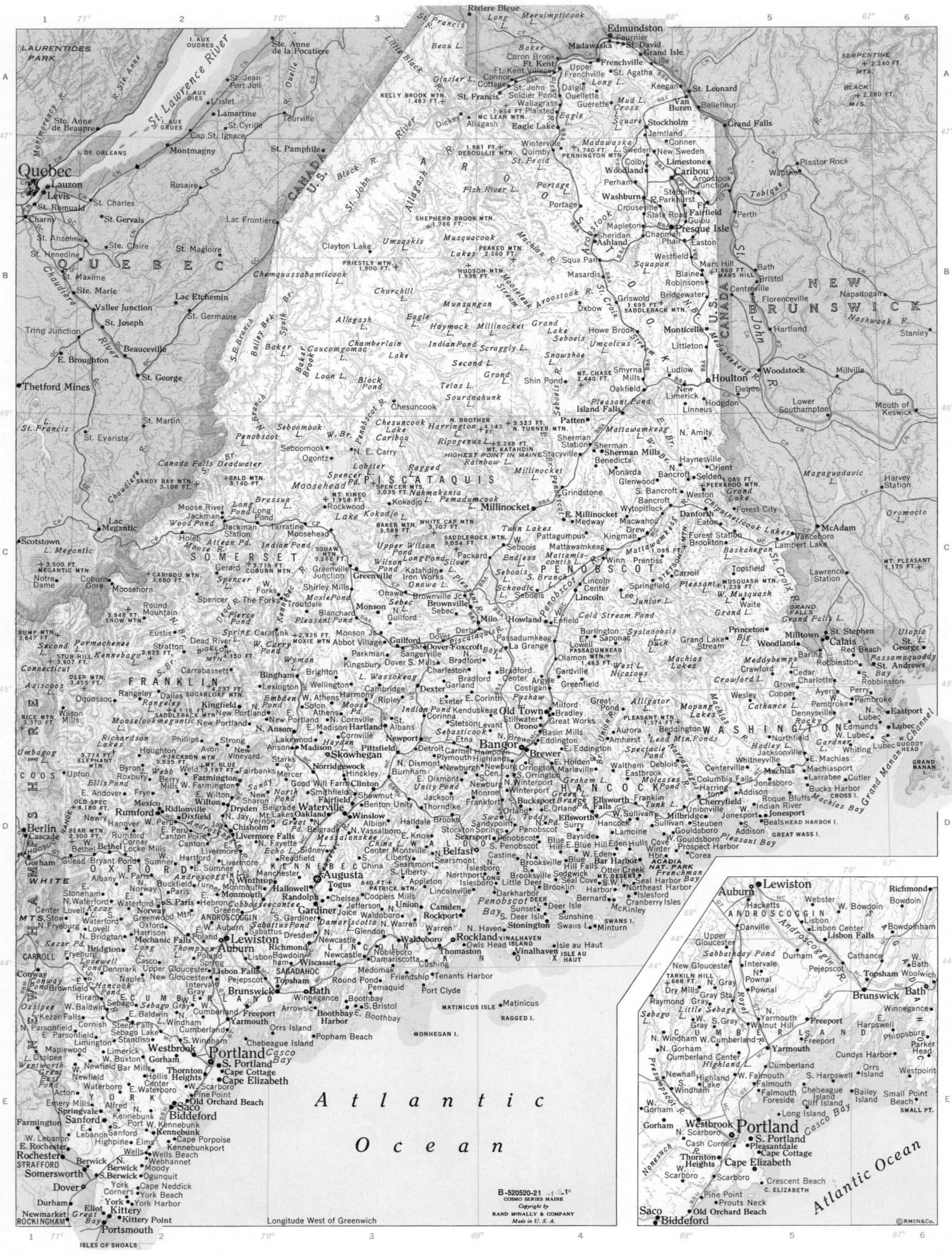

Longitude West of Greenwich

Lambert Conformal Conic Projection

Statute Miles

Kilometers

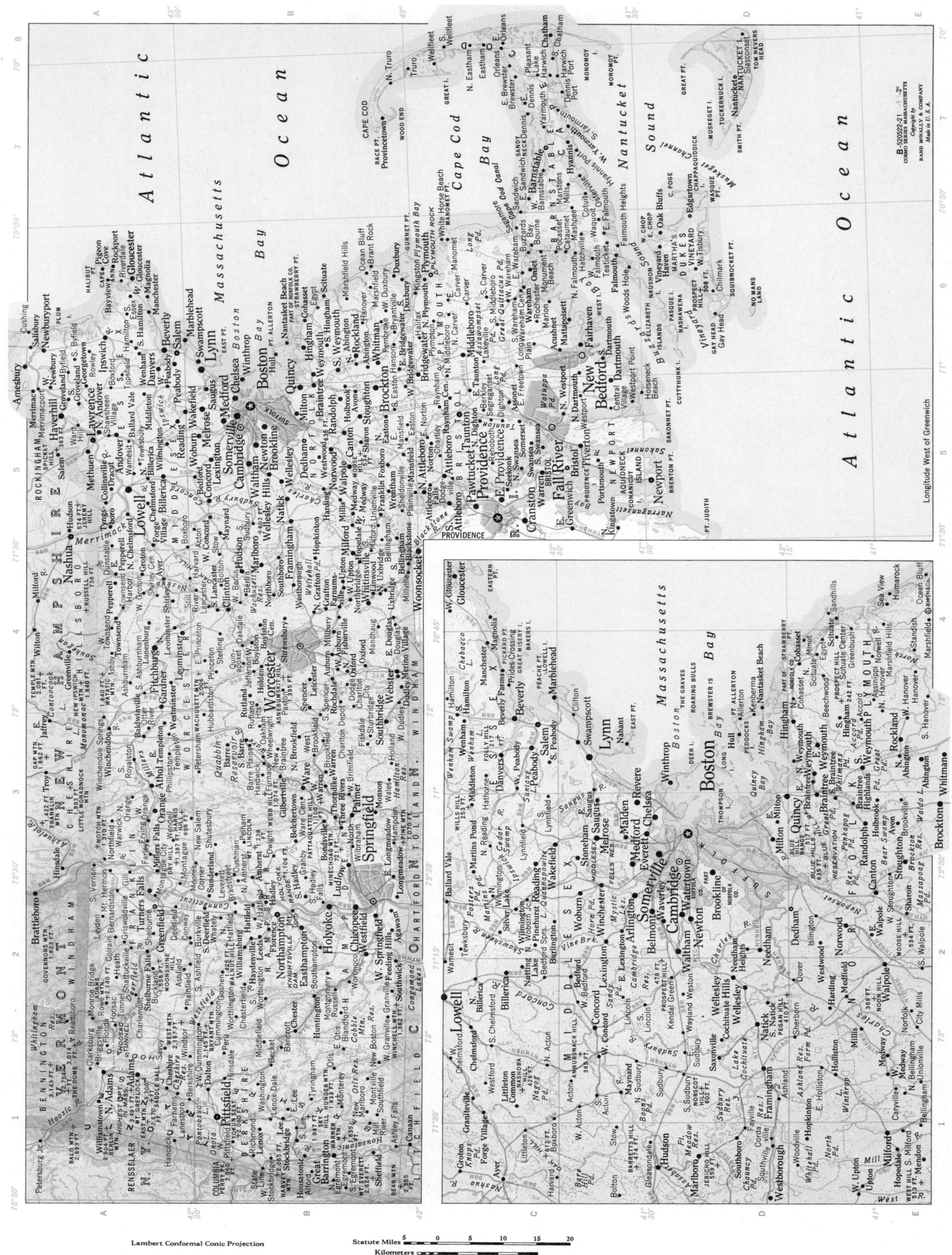

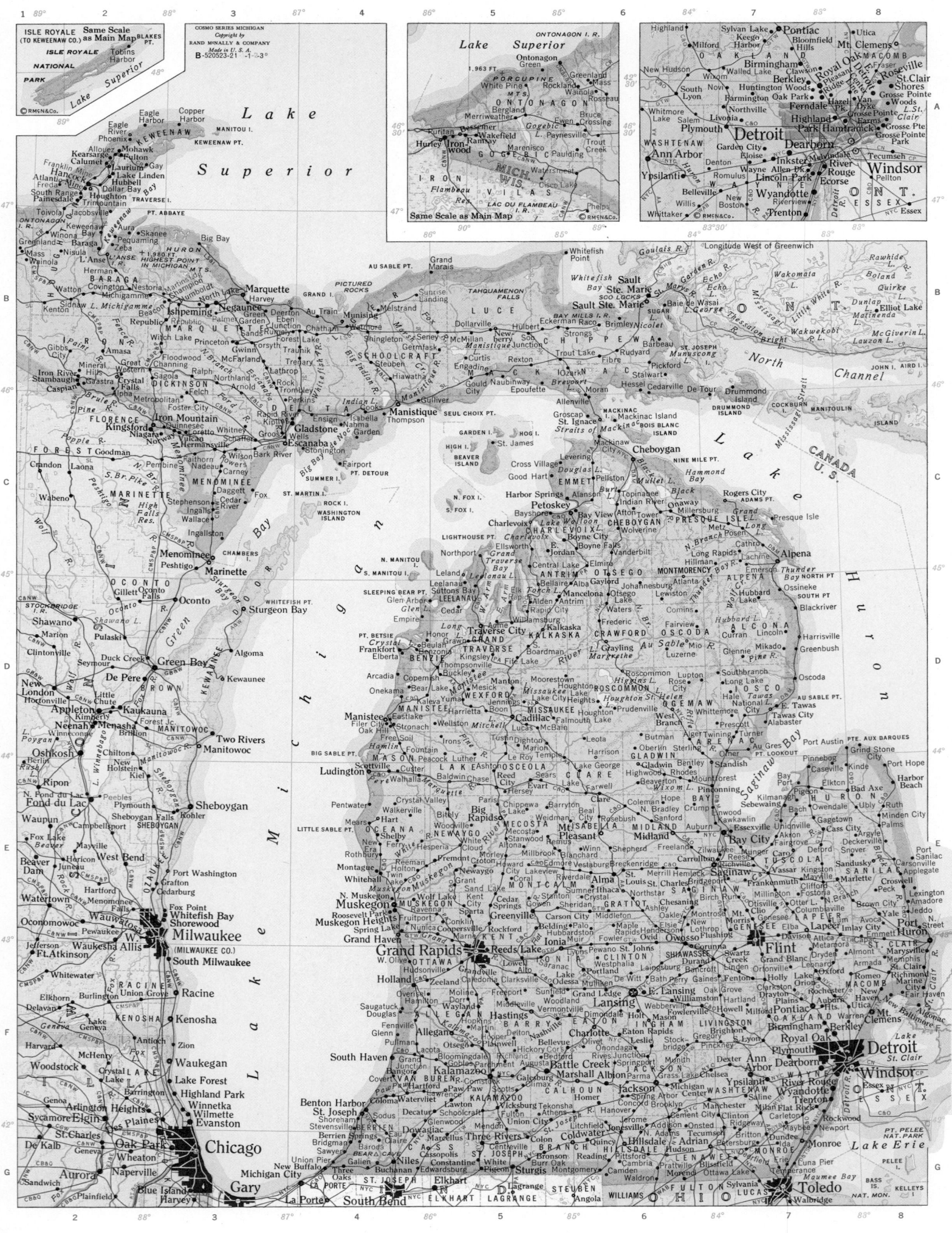

Statute Miles 5 0 5 10   20   30   40   50

Kilometers 5 0 5 15 25 35 45 55 65 75

Lambert Conformal Conic Projection

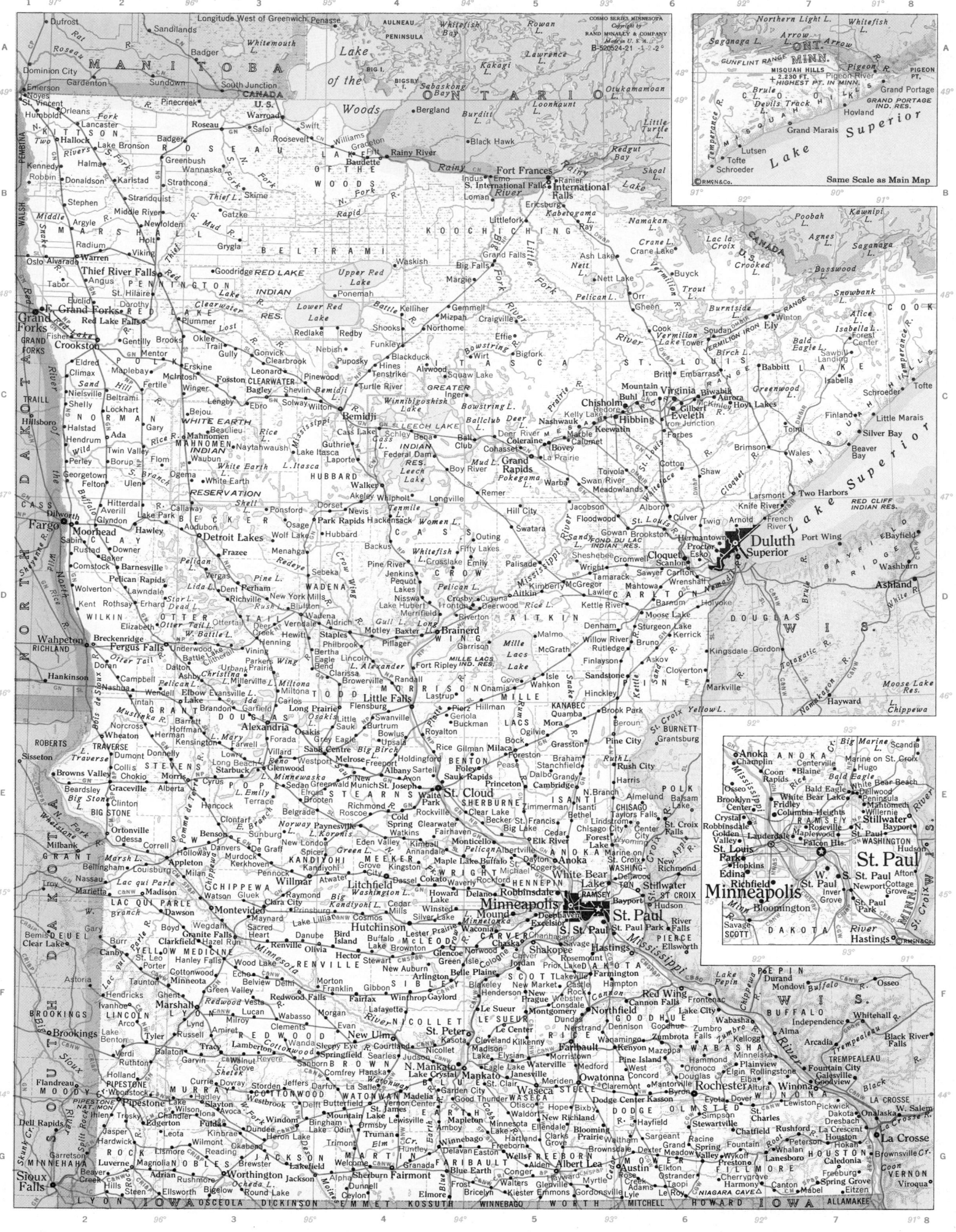

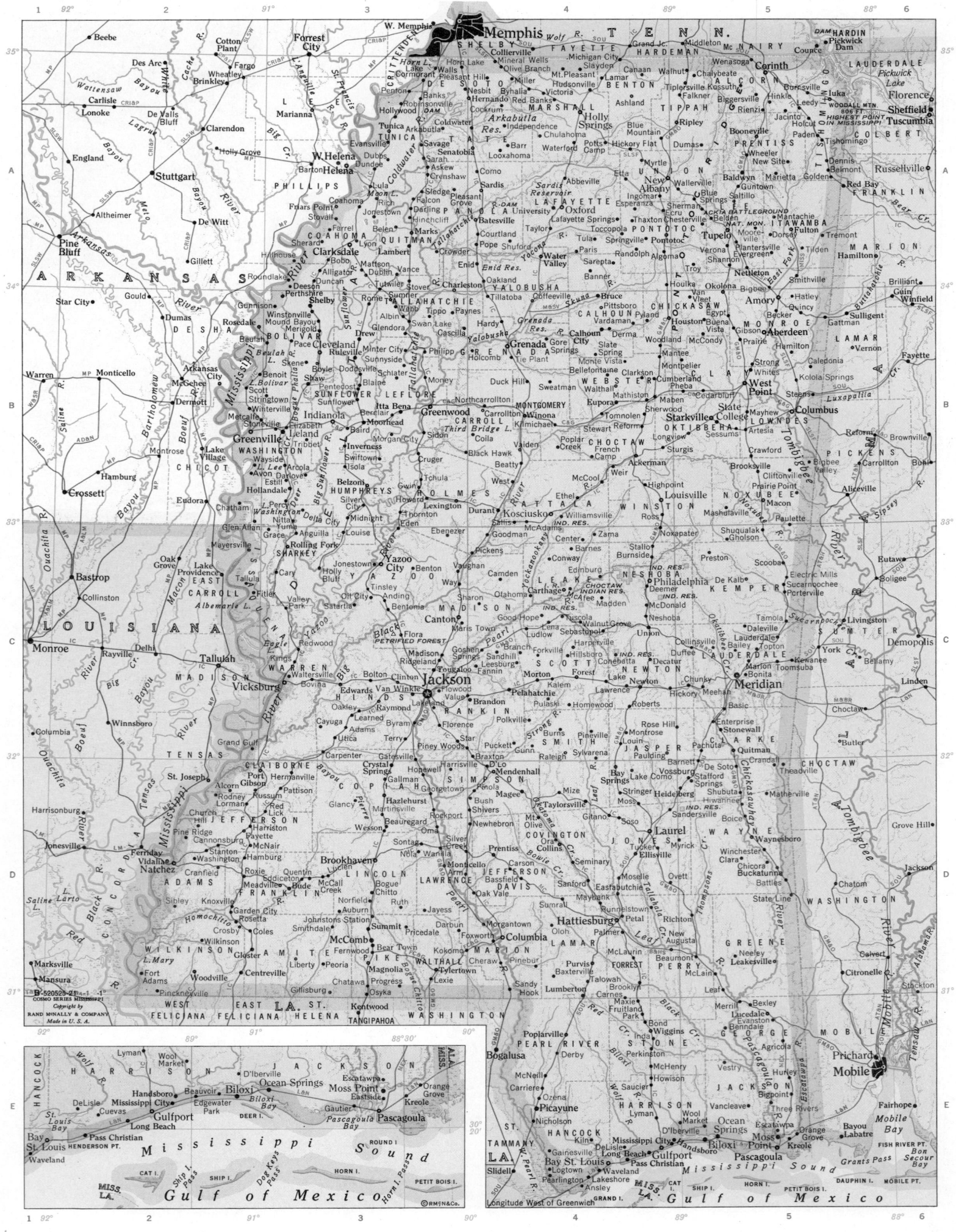

Statute Miles

Kilometers

Lambert Conformal Conic Projection

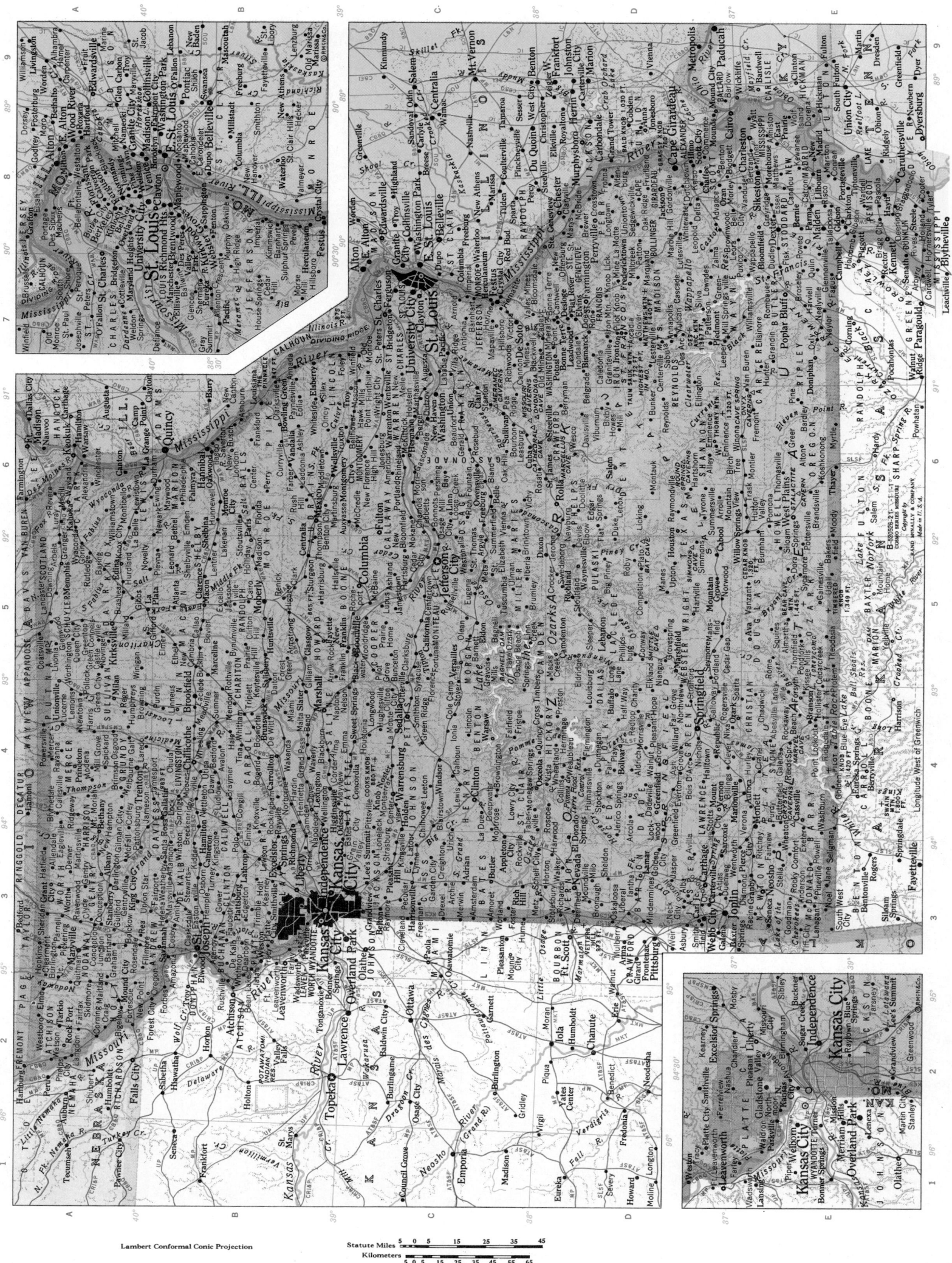

Lambert Conformal Conic Projection

Statute Miles 5 0 5 15 25 35 45

Kilometers 5 0 5 15 25 35 45 55 65

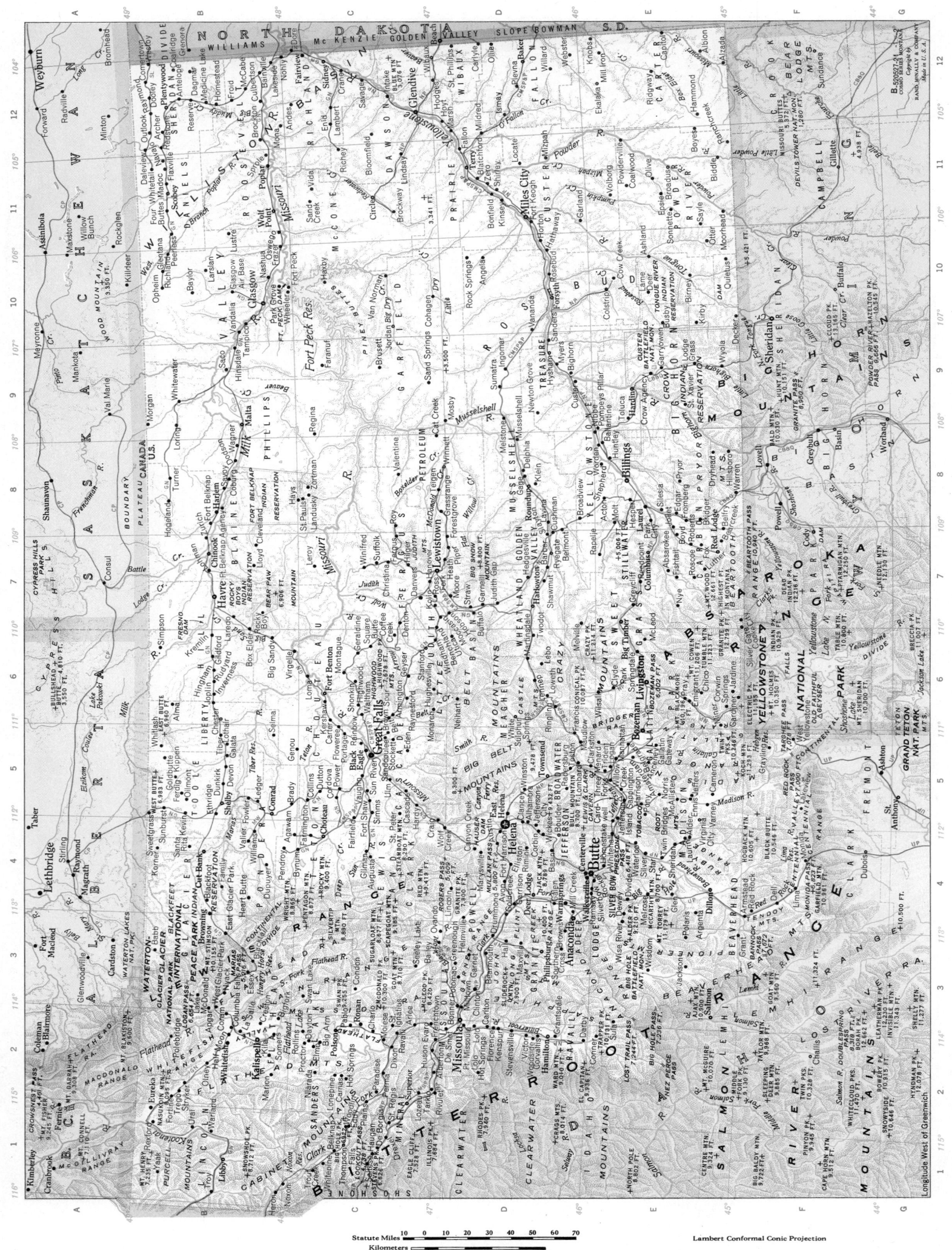

Statute Miles

Kilometers

Lambert Conformal Conic Projection

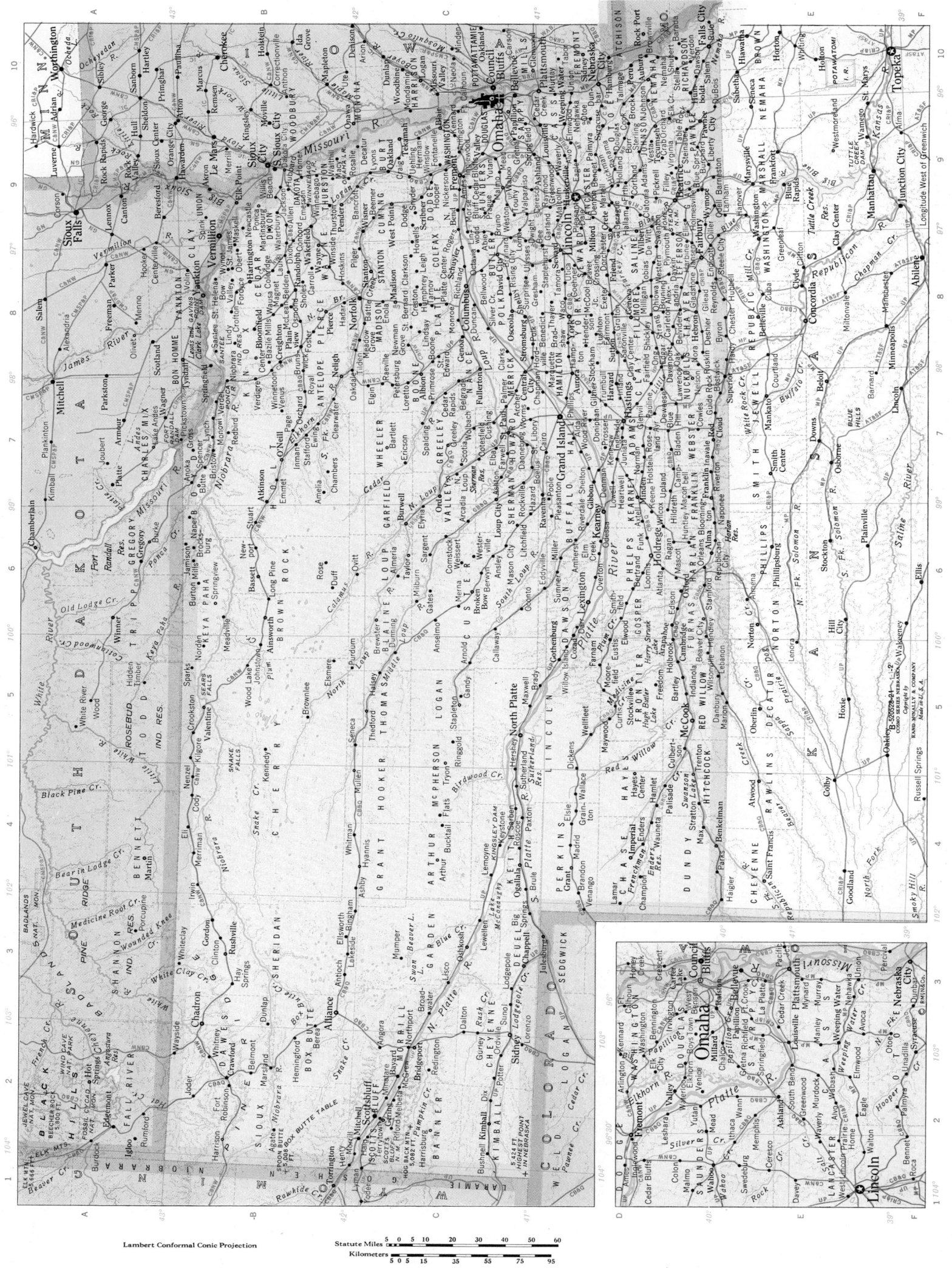

Lambert Conformal Conic Projection

Statute Miles 5 0 5 10   20   30   40   50   60
Kilometers 5 0 5 15   35   55   75   95

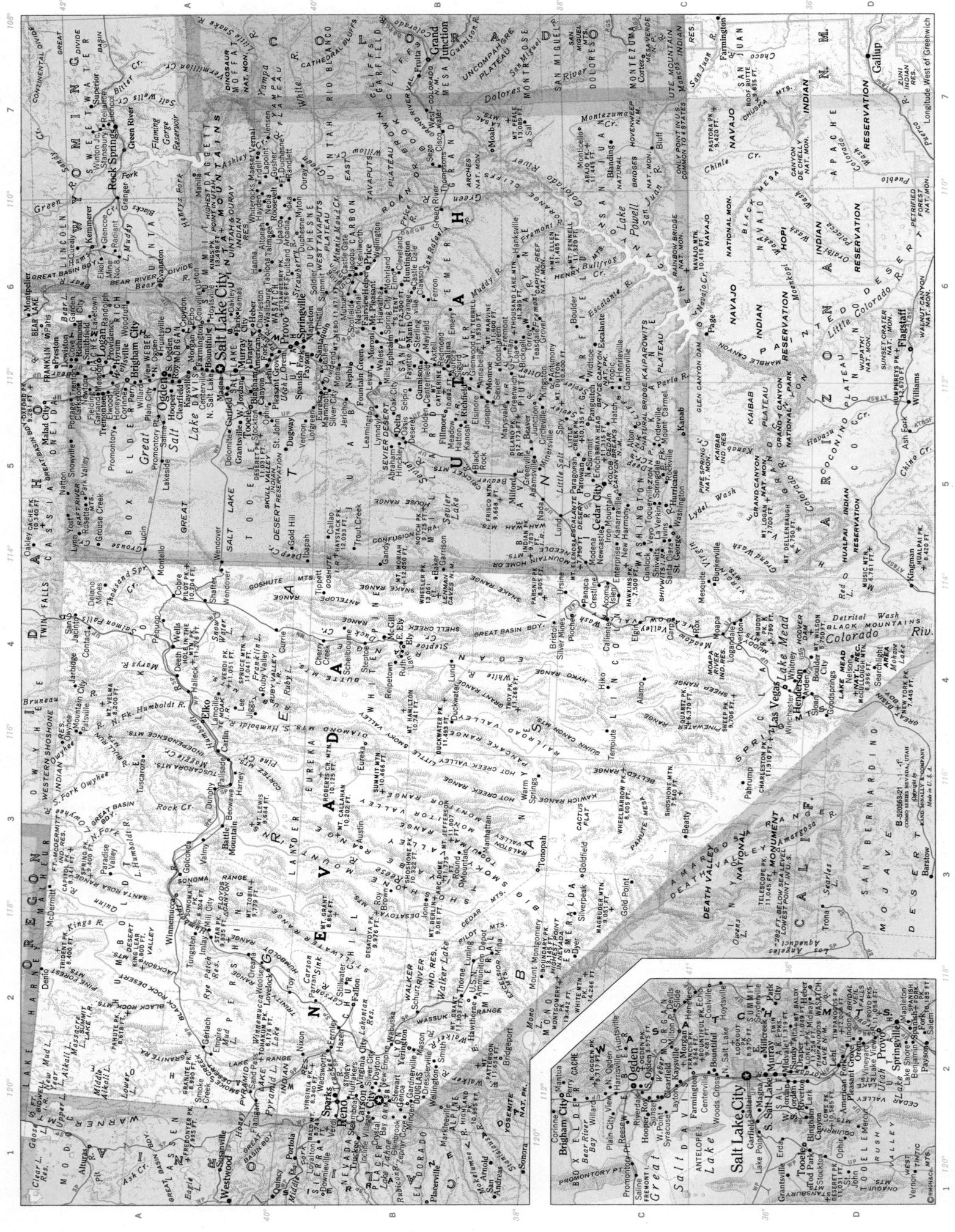

Statute Miles 5 0 5 10 20 30 40 50 60 70 80

Kilometers 50 10 20 40 60 80 100 120

Lambert Conformal Conic Projection

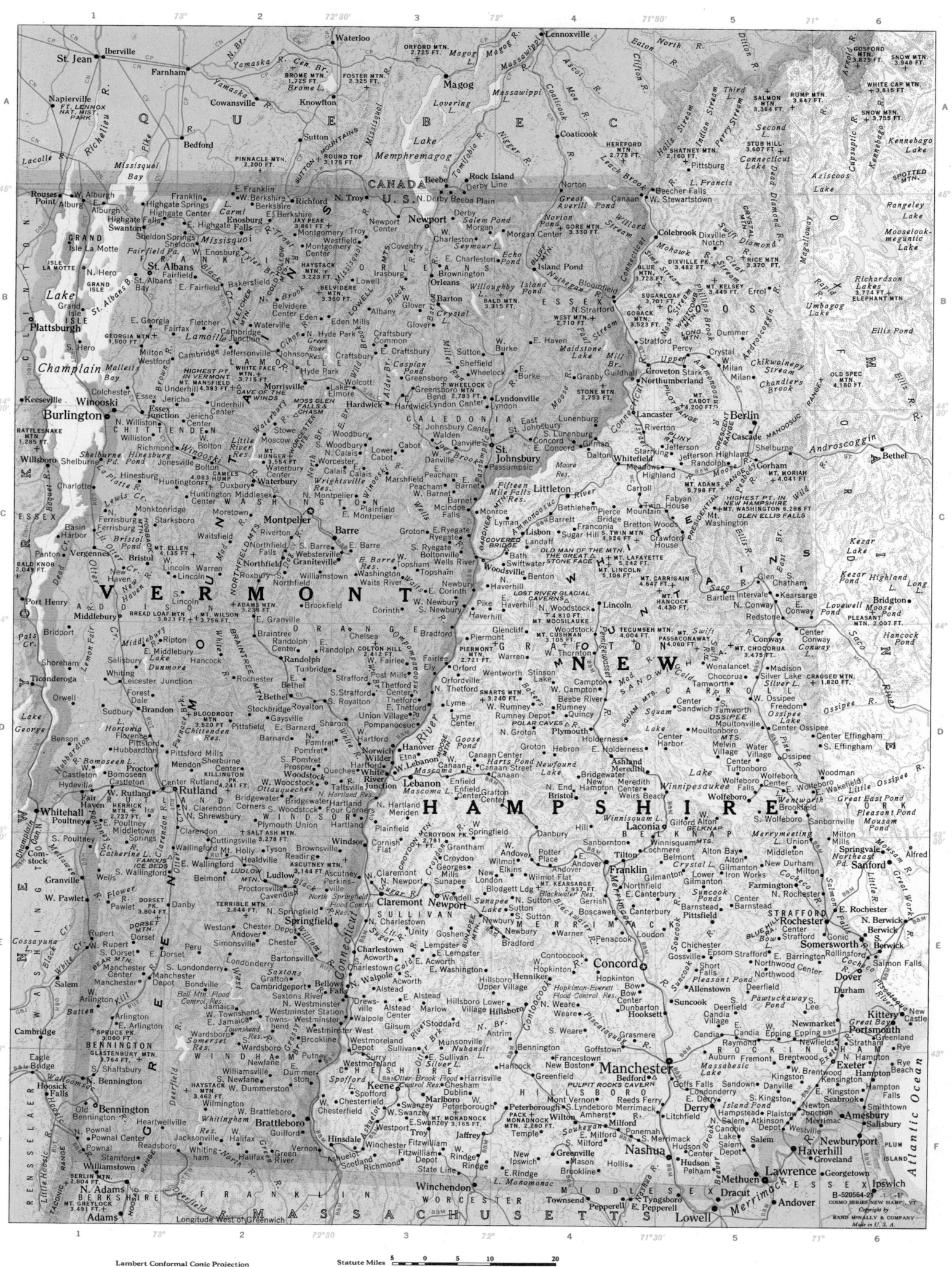

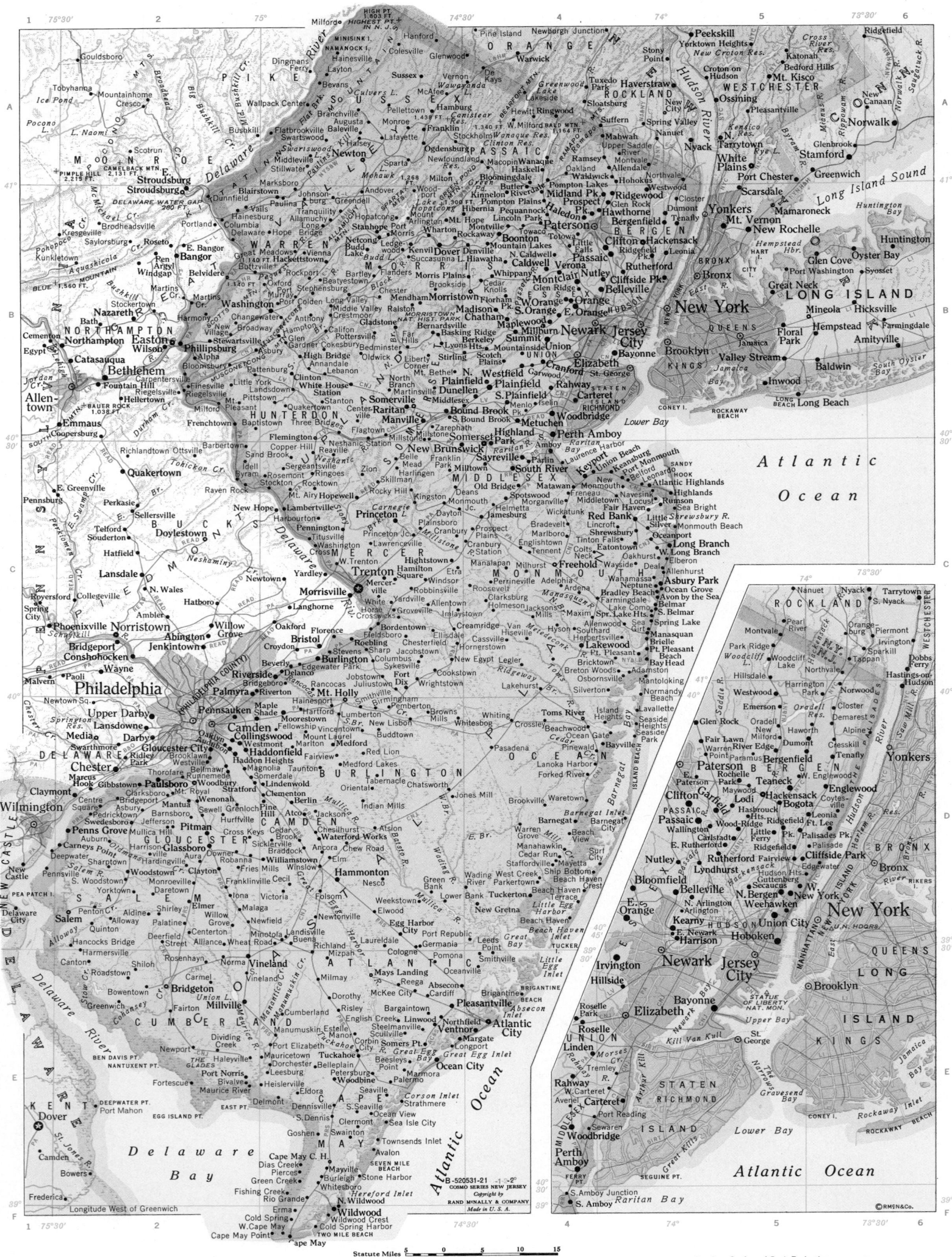

Statute Miles

Kilometers

Lambert Conformal Conic Projection

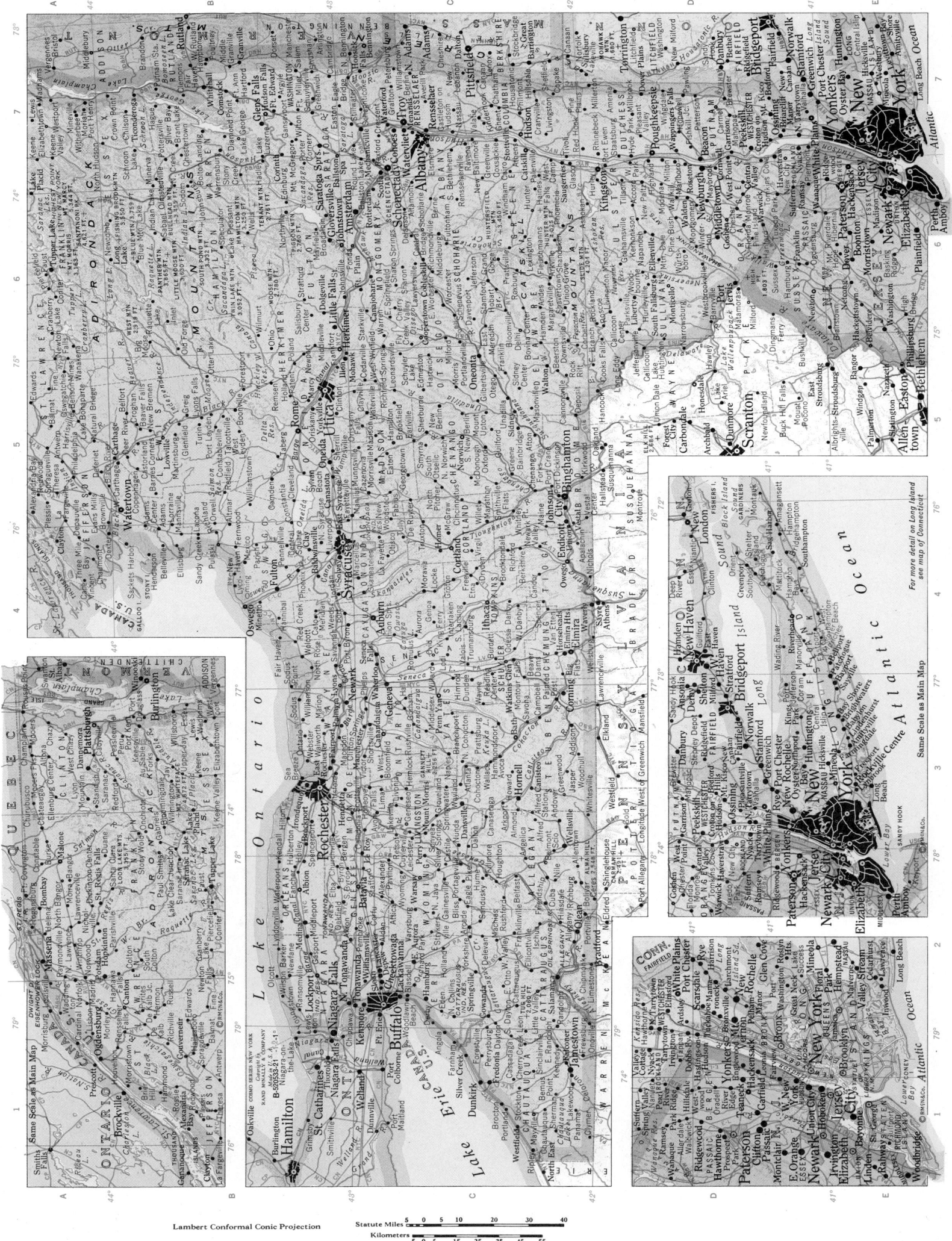

Lambert Conformal Conic Projection

Statute Miles 5 0 5 10 20 30 40

Kilometers 5 0 5 15 25 35 45 55

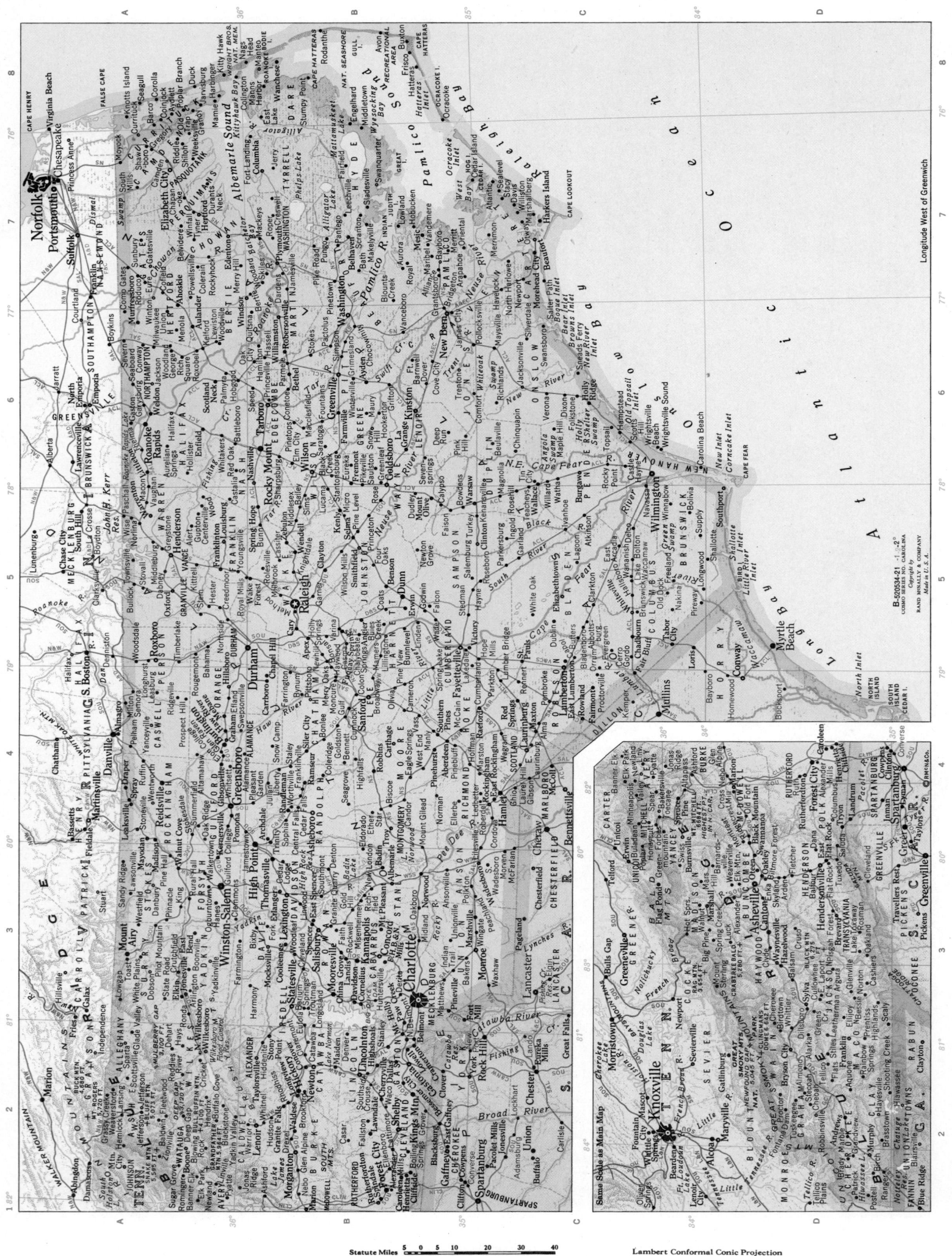

Statute Miles 5 0 5   10   20   30   40
Kilometers 5 0 5   15   25   35   45   55

Lambert Conformal Conic Projection

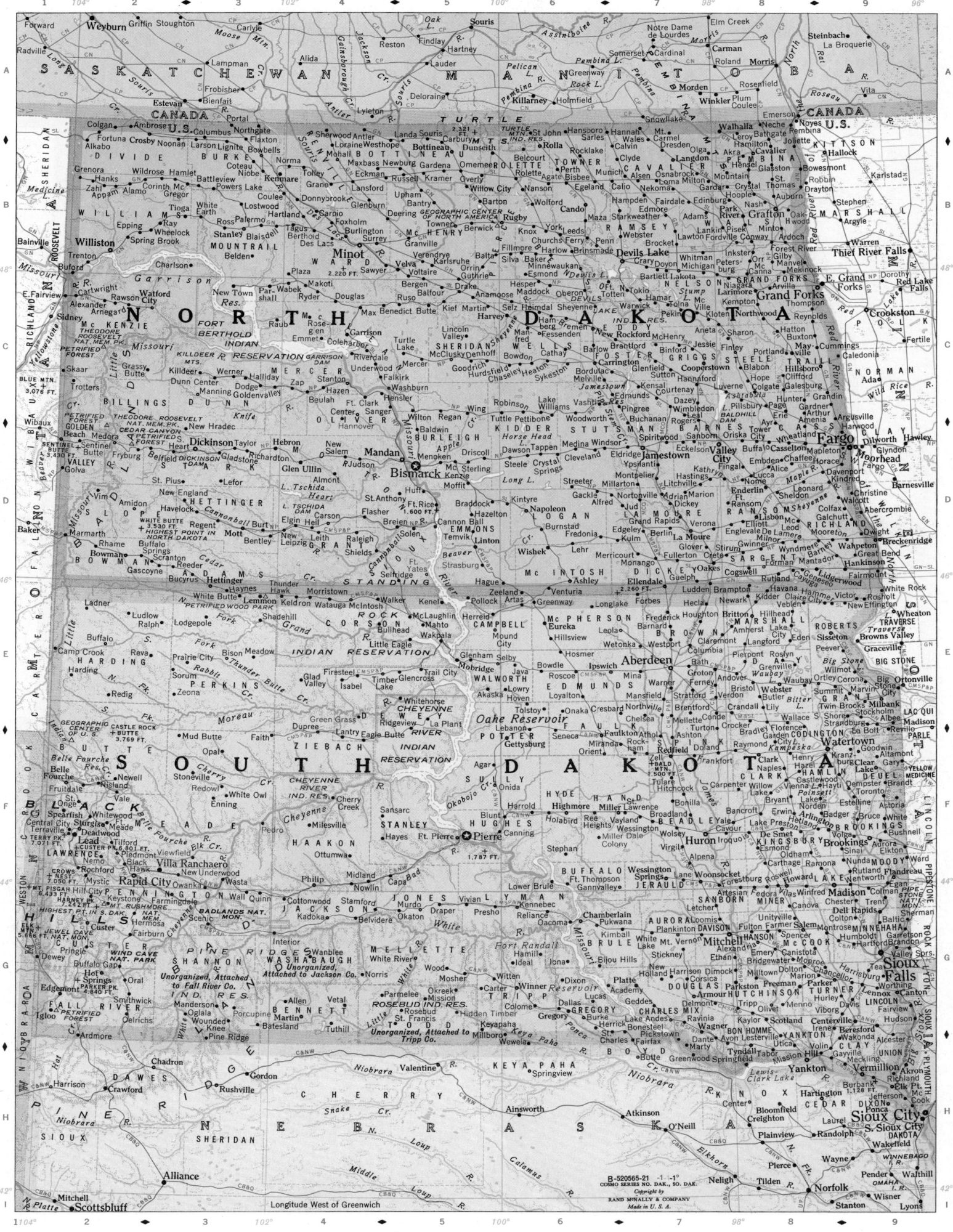

Lambert Conformal Conic Projection

Statute Miles 5 0 5 10 20 30 40 50 60
Kilometers 5 0 5 15 25 35 45 55 75

Longitude West of Greenwich

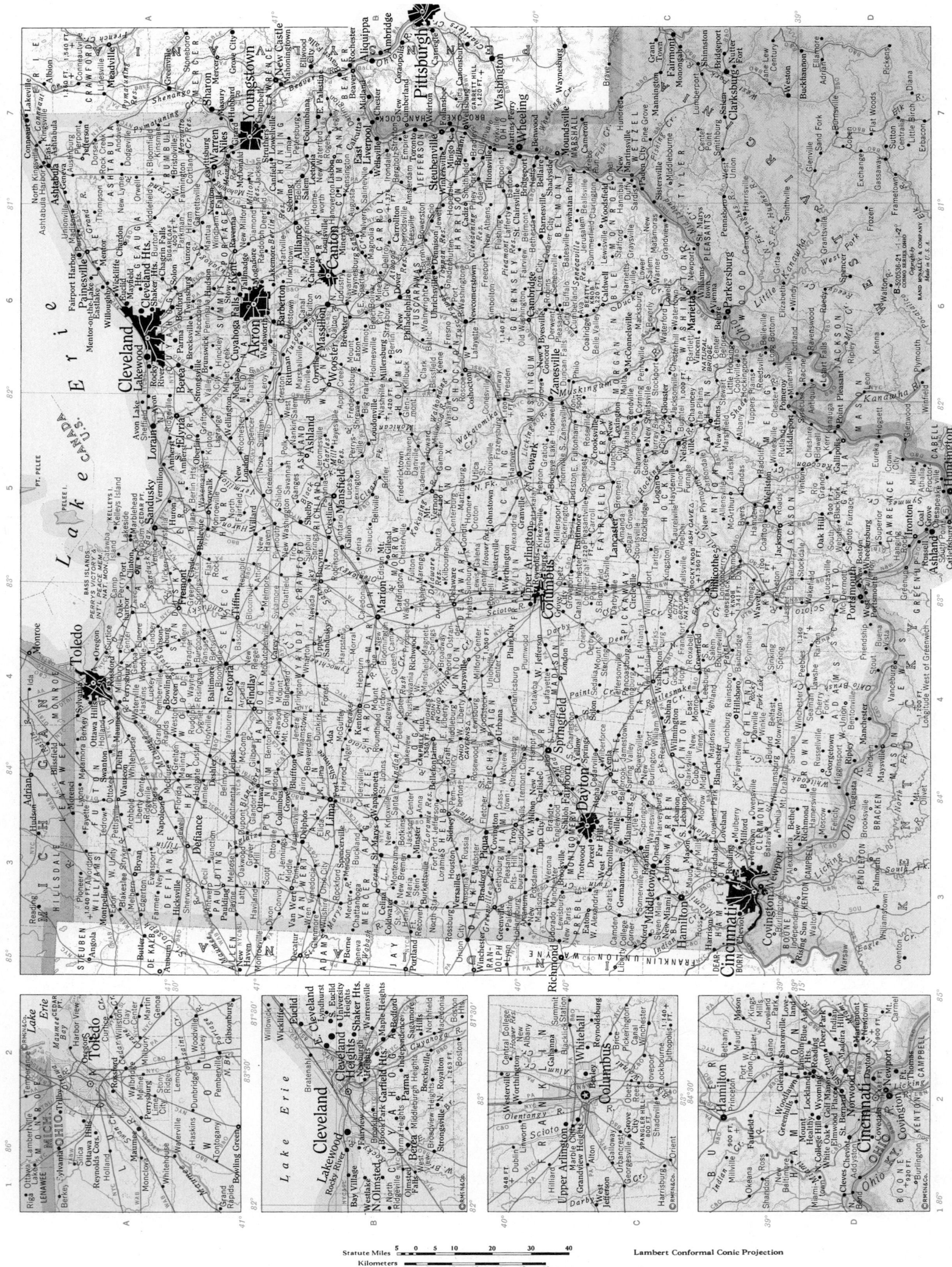

Statute Miles

Kilometers

Lambert Conformal Conic Projection

Lambert Conformal Conic Projection

Statute Miles
5 0 5 10   20   30   40

Kilometers
5 0 5 15   25   35   45   55

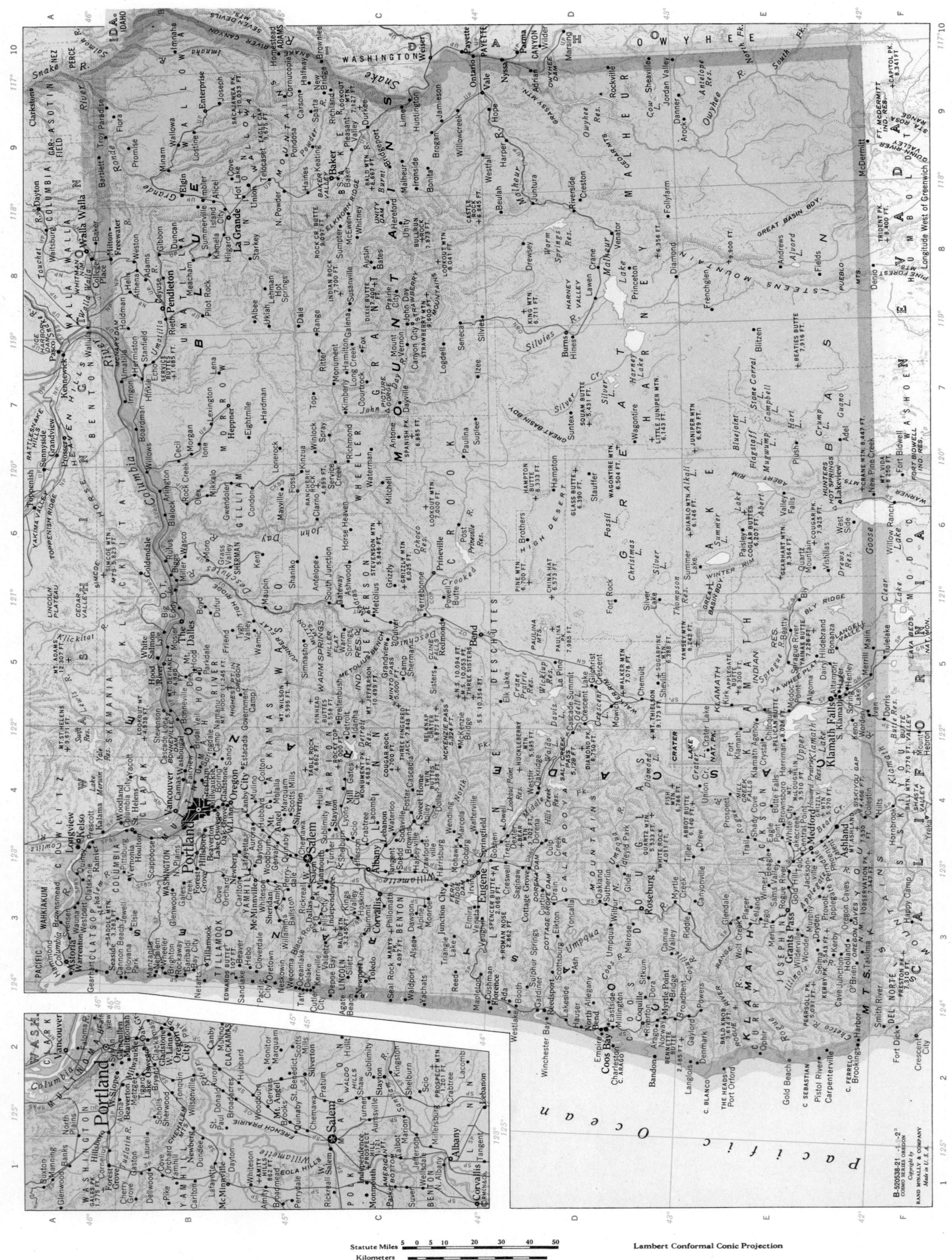

Statute Miles   5 0 5 10   20   30   40   50
Kilometers   5 0 5 15 25 35 45 55 65 75

Lambert Conformal Conic Projection

B-520538-21
COSMO SERIES OREGON
Copyright by
RAND M?NALLY & COMPANY
Made in U.S.A.

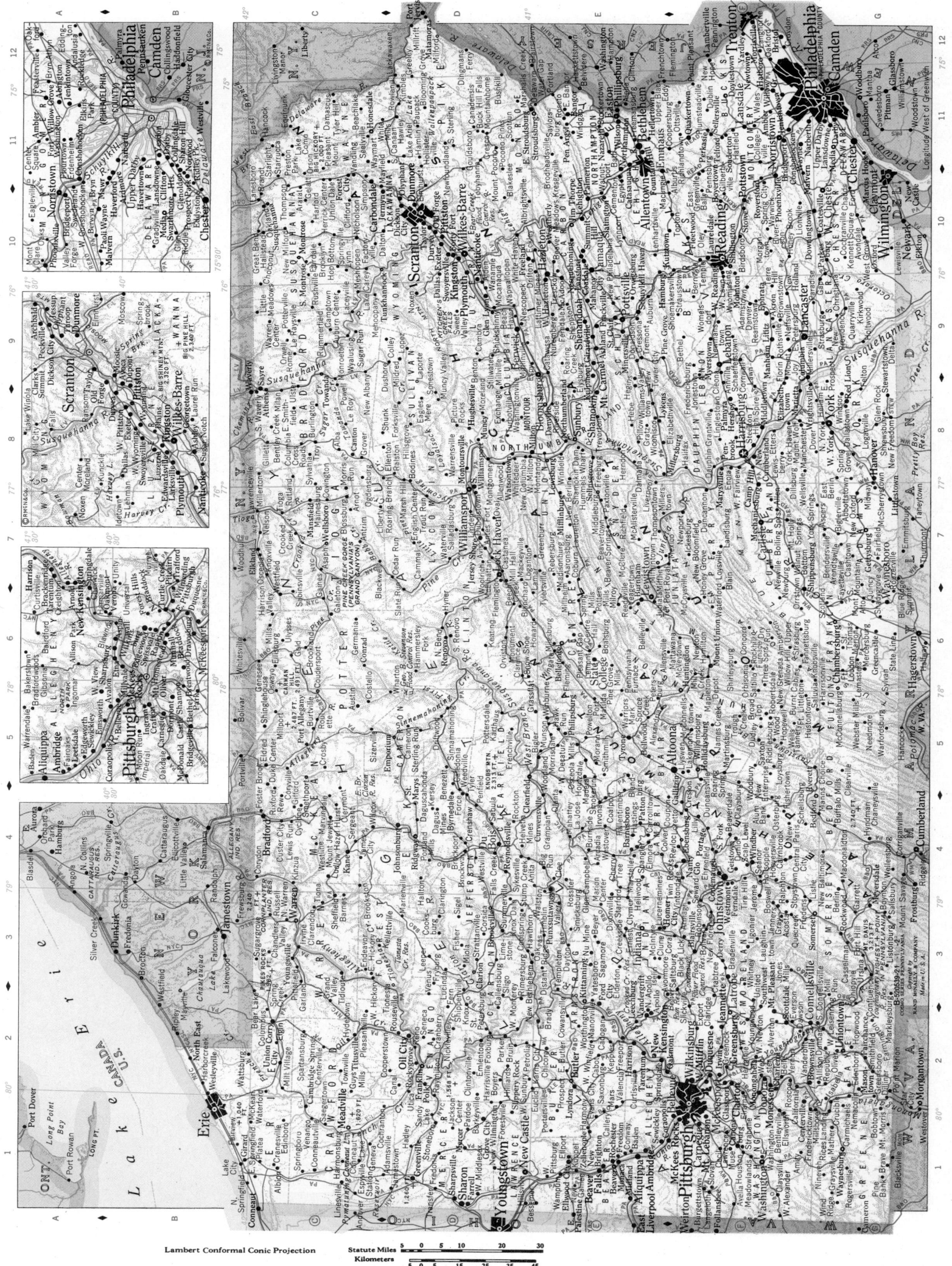

Lambert Conformal Conic Projection

Statute Miles
5 0 5 10 20 30

Kilometers
5 0 5 15 25 35 45

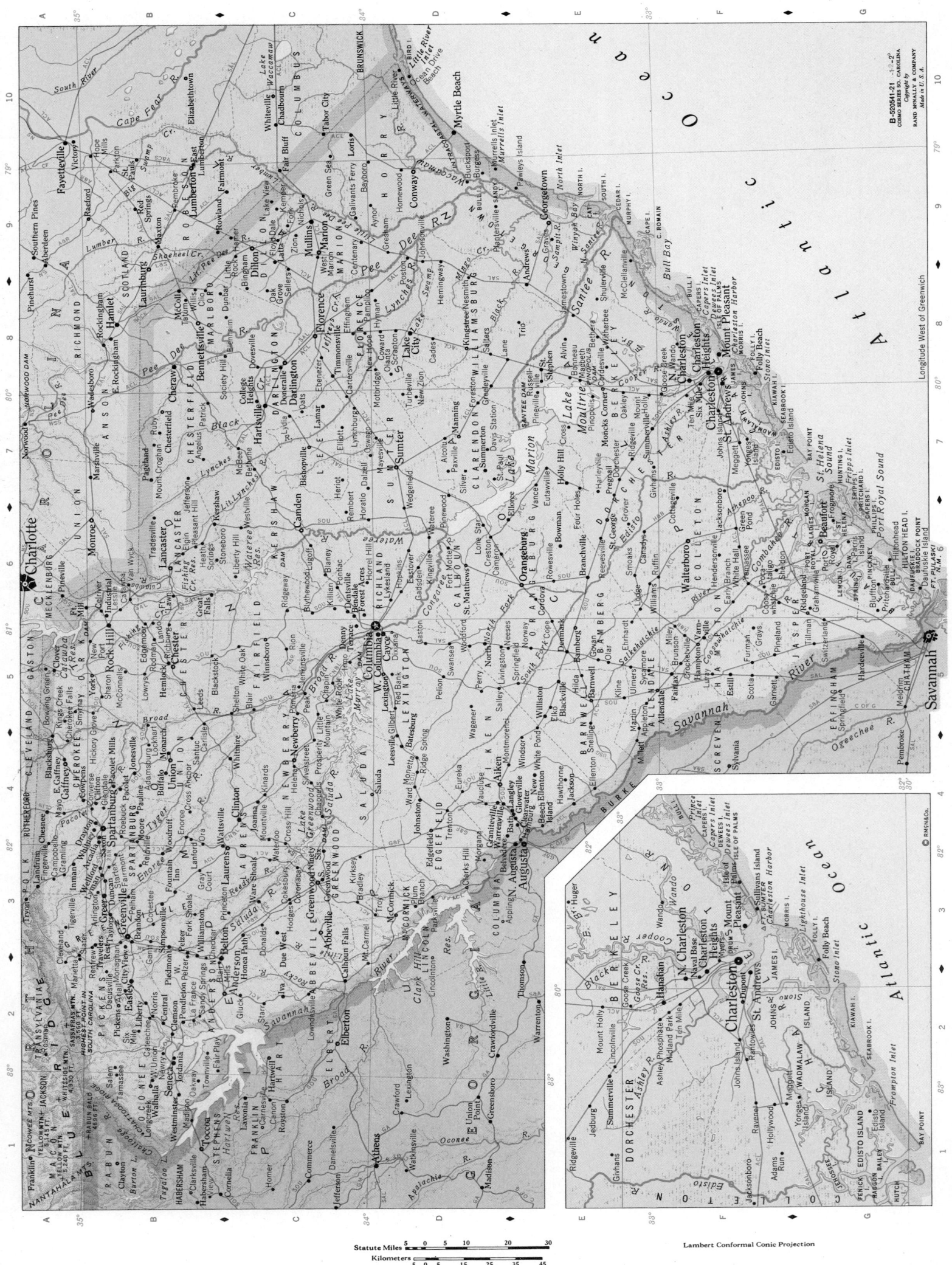

Statute Miles

Kilometers

Lambert Conformal Conic Projection

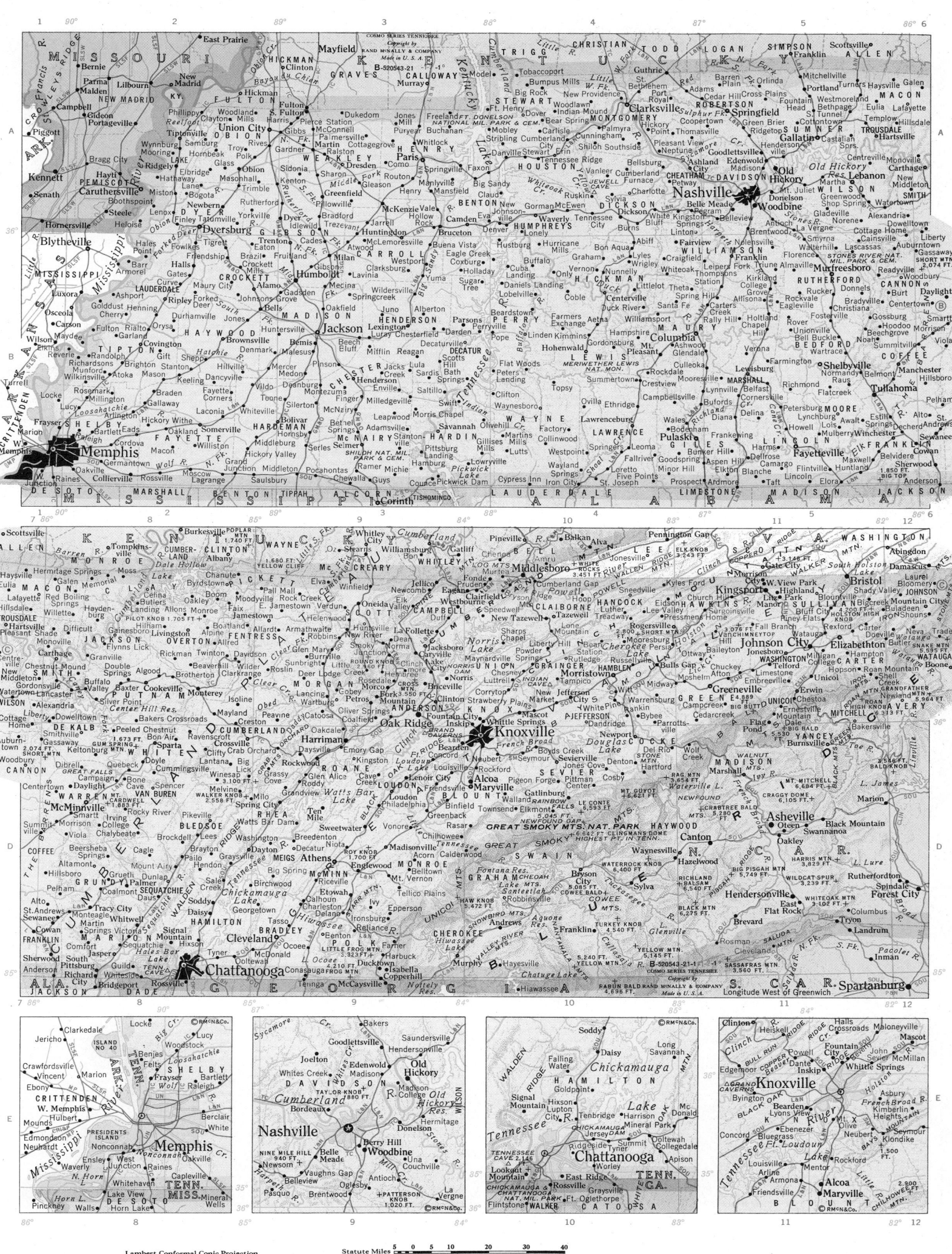

Lambert Conformal Conic Projection

Statute Miles
5 0 5 10 20 30 40

Kilometers
5 0 5 15 25 35 45 55

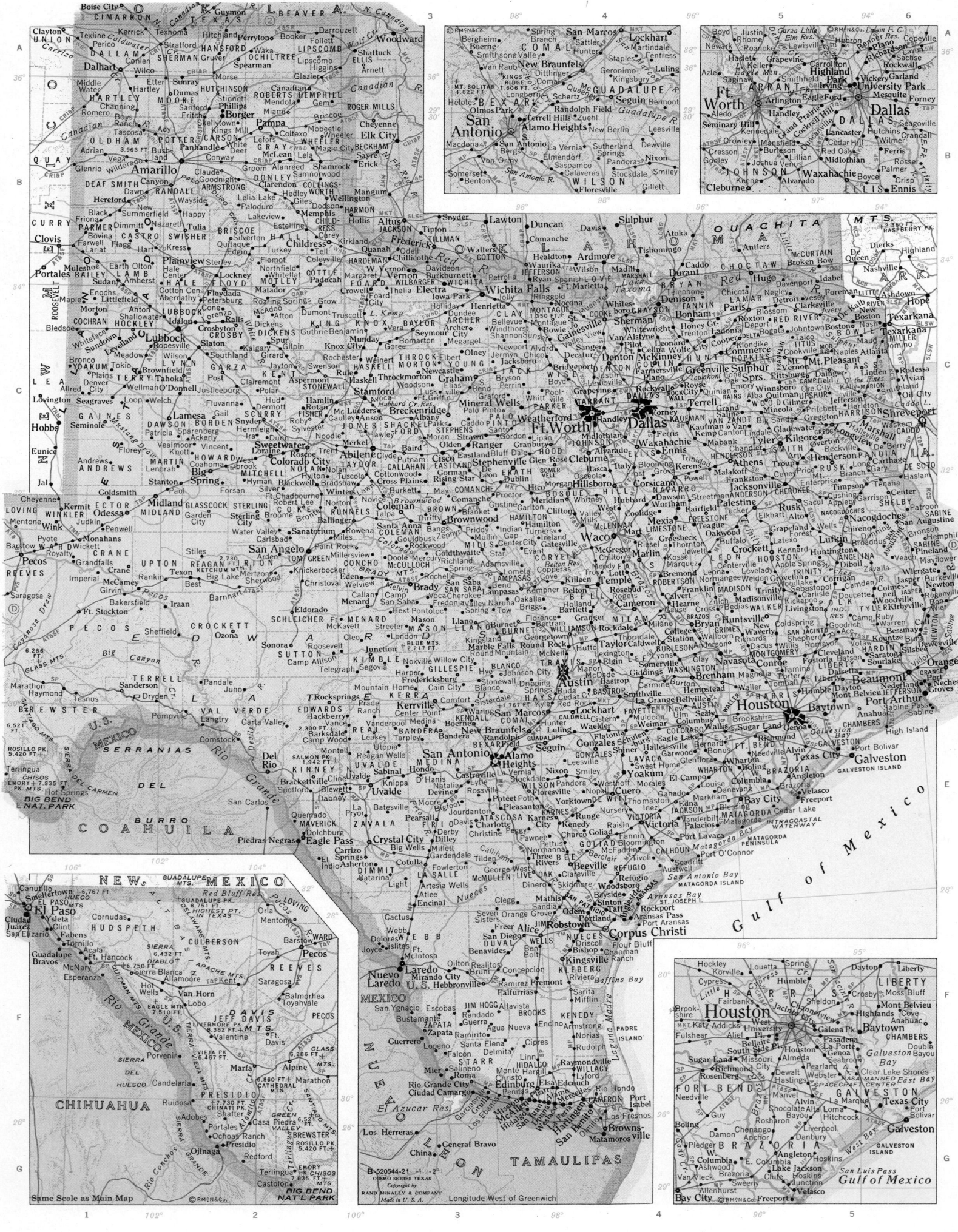

Chesapeake Bay

Norfolk

Newport News

Portsmouth

Hampton

Suffolk

Richmond

Petersburg

Hopewell

Washington, D.C.

Arlington

Alexandria

Annapolis

MD.

W. VA.

TENN.

KY.

N. CAR.

Roanoke

Lynchburg

Danville

Martinsville

Charlottesville

Harrisonburg

Staunton

Fredericksburg

Atlantic Ocean

SHENANDOAH NATIONAL PARK

BLUE RIDGE MOUNTAINS

ALLEGHENY MOUNTAINS

CUMBERLAND PLATEAU

Bristol

Kingsport

Lambert Conformal Conic Projection

Statute Miles
5 0 5 10 20 30 40

Kilometers
5 0 5 15 25 35 45 55

B-500547.21 -1 -2°
Copr. RAND McNALLY VIRGINIA

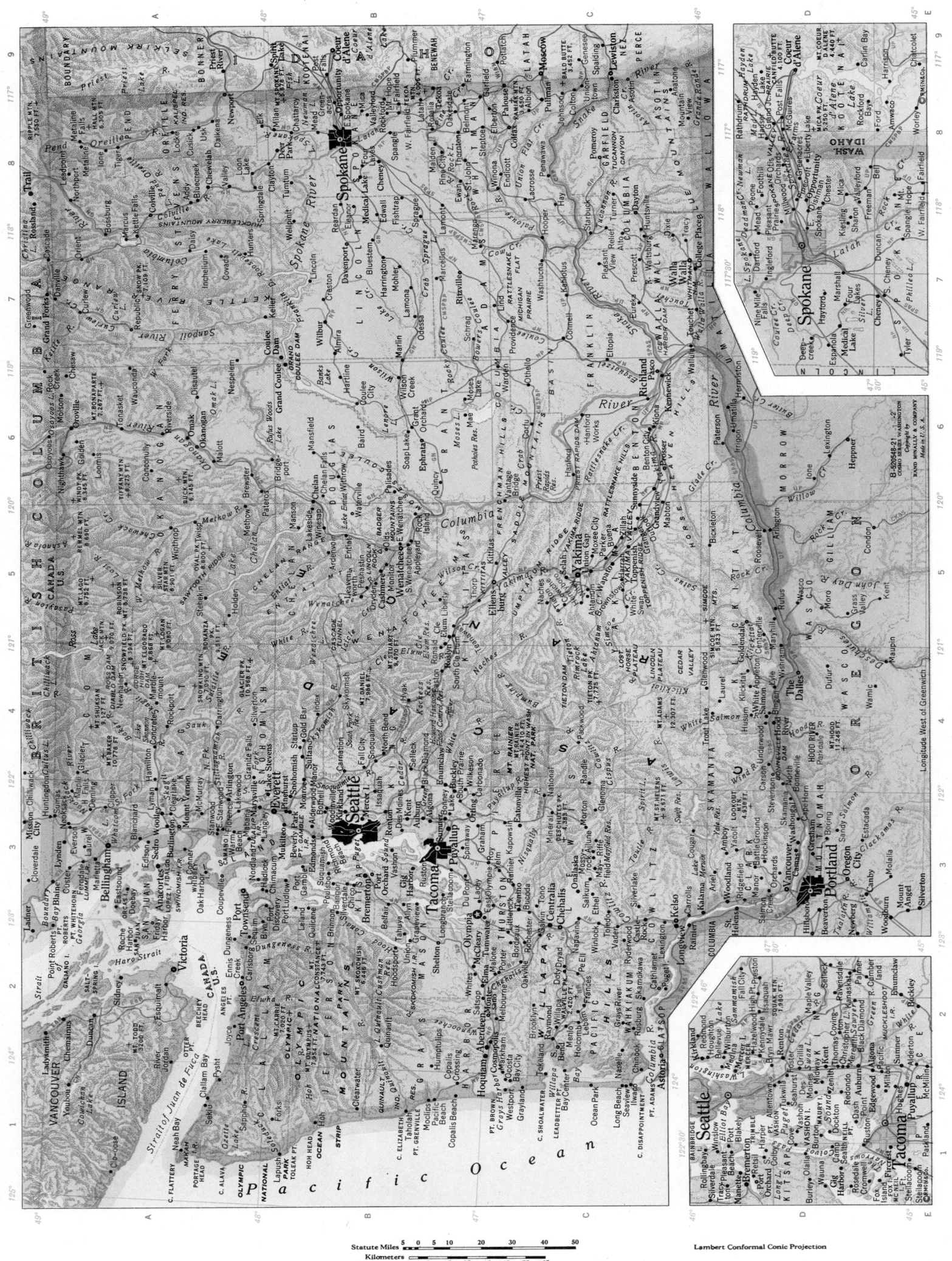

Statute Miles 5 0 5 10   20   30   40   50
Kilometers 5 0 5 15   25   35   45   55   65

Lambert Conformal Conic Projection

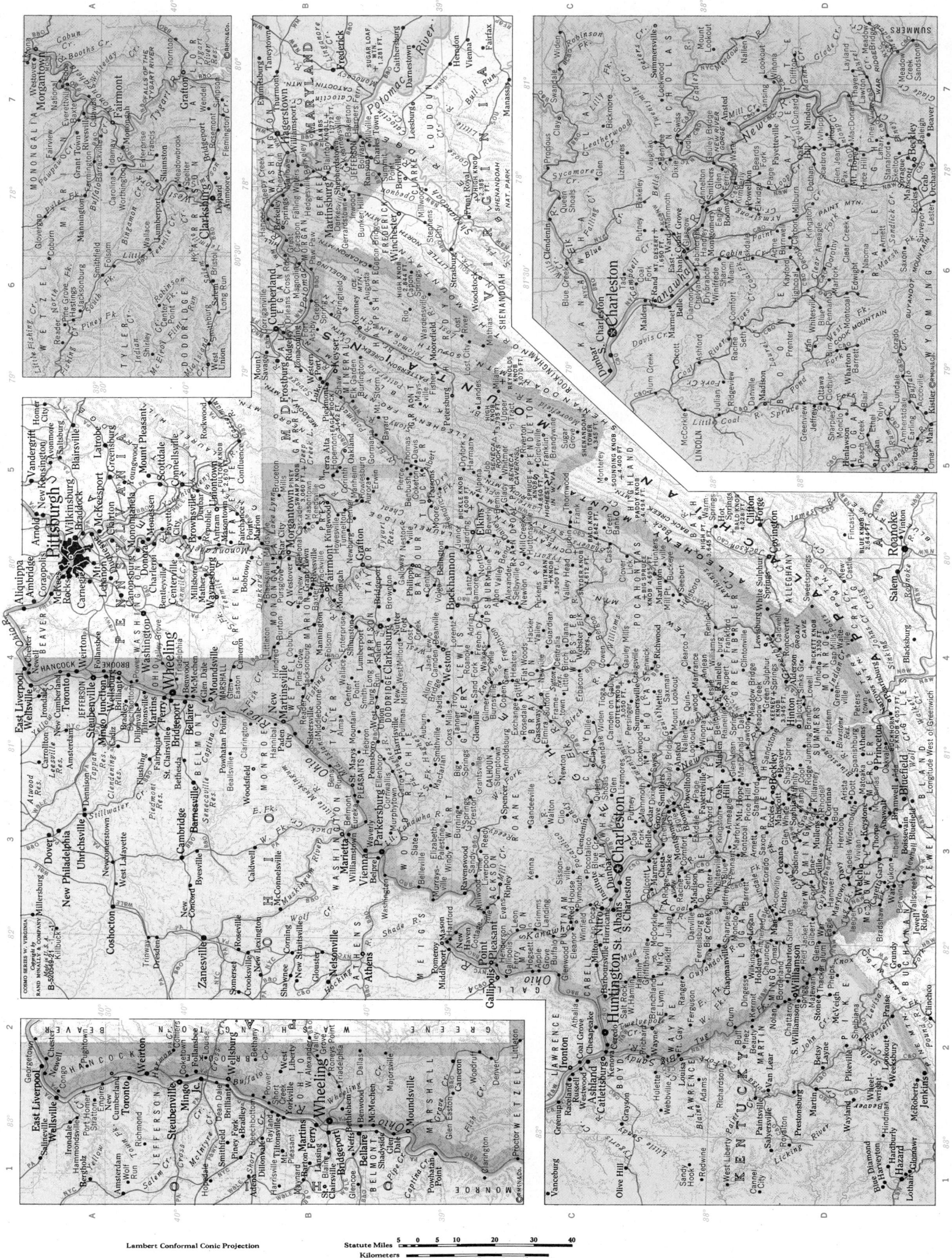

Lambert Conformal Conic Projection

Statute Miles

Kilometers

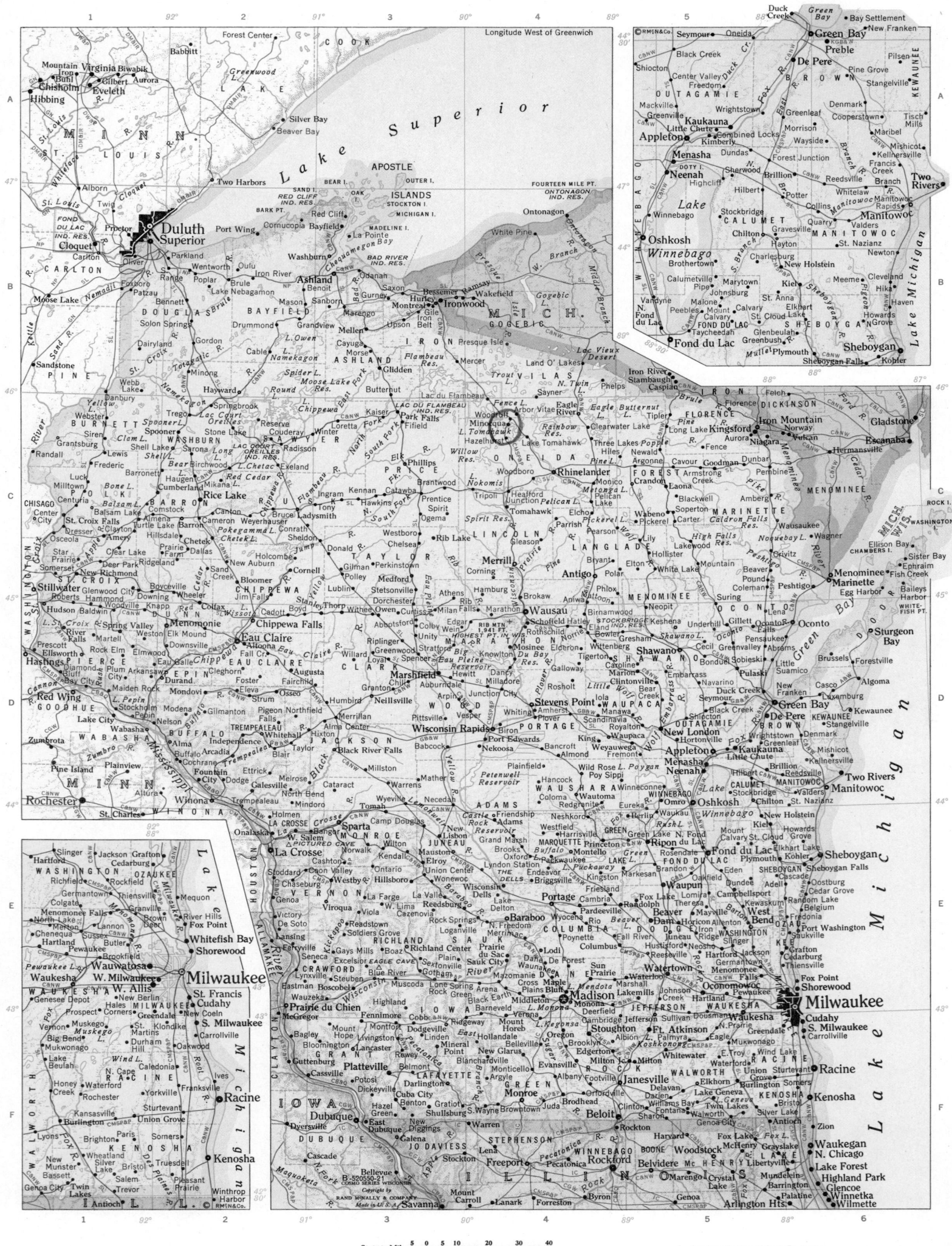

Longitude West of Greenwich

Lake Superior

APOSTLE ISLANDS

Lake Michigan

Statute Miles

Kilometers

Lambert Conformal Conic Projection

Copyright by
RAND McNALLY & COMPANY
Made in U.S.A.
COSMO SERIES WISCONSIN
B-520550-21

B-520551-21-1-2
COSMO SERIES WYOMING
Copyright by
RAND M9NALLY & COMPANY
Made in U.S.A.

Lambert Conformal Conic Projection

Statute Miles

Kilometers

Longitude West of Greenwich

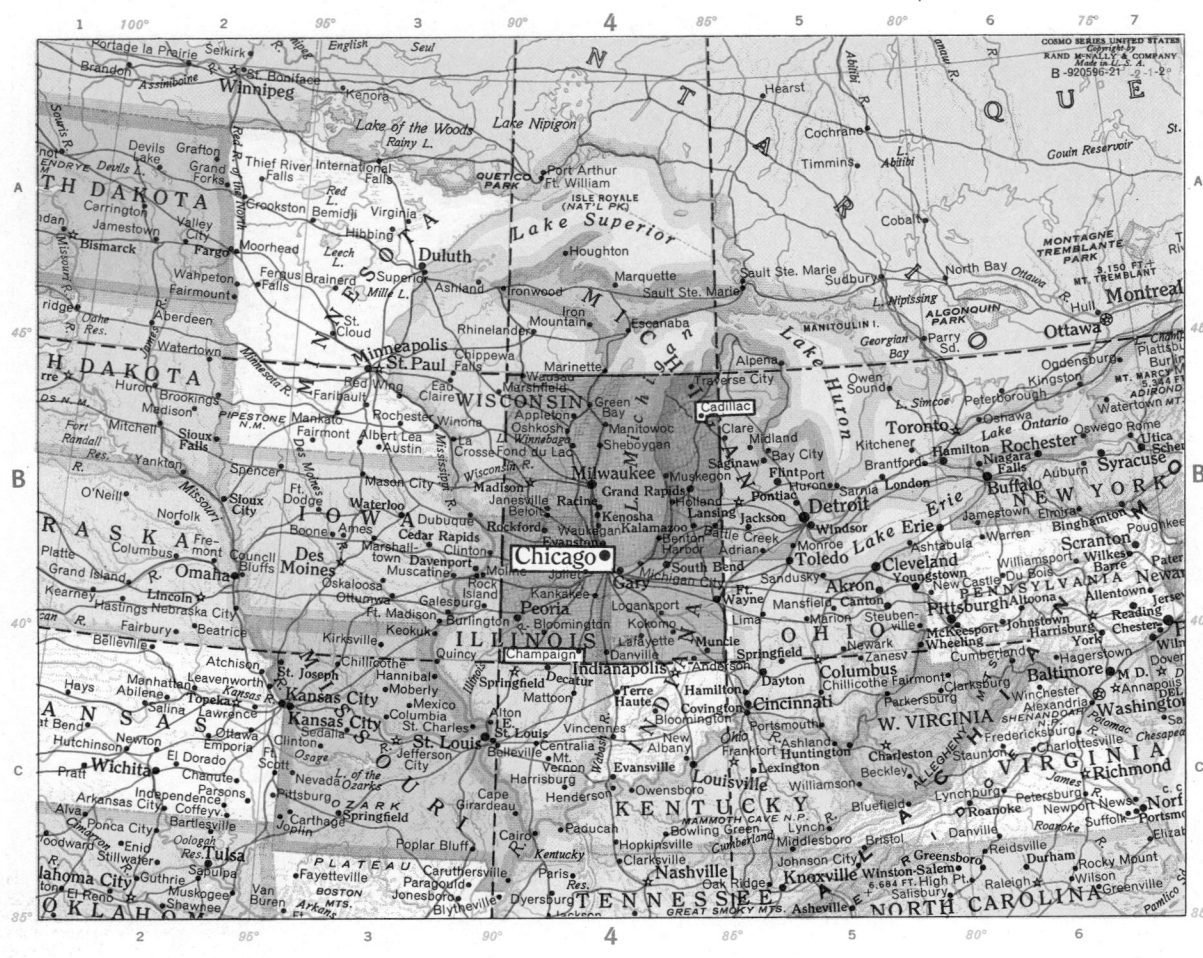

Place	Location	Pop.	Index Key	Page
Cades, Gibson, Tenn., 15			B3	83
➡ Cadillac, Wexford, Mich., 10,112			B4	66
Cádiz, Sp., 117,871			D2	8
Cádiz, prov., Sp., 818,847			*D2	8
Calabogie, lake, Ont., Can.			B8	41
Calais, Washington, Vt., 150 (684▲)			C4	73
Calchaqui, riv., Arg.			E2	29
Calhoun, co., Ala., 95,878			B4	46
Caltanissetta, It., 48,500			F5	9
Cambodia, country, Asia, 3,800,000			C2	19
Campechuela, Cuba, 2,782			E5	35
Campton, Okaloosa, Fla., 100			G2	54
Caney, fork, Tenn.			C8	83
Cannon Falls, Goodhue, Minn., 2,055			F6	67
Capilano, B.C., Can., 800			A9	37
Carbon, Clay, Ind., 409			E3	59
Cardiff, Jefferson, Ala., 202			E4	46
Carlsbad Caverns, nat. park, N. Mex.			C6	48
Caroleen, Rutherford, N.C., 1,168			B2	76
Carouge, Switz., 12,760			E3	6
Casey, co., Ky., 14,327			C5	62
Castleton, Rutland, Vt., 375 (1,902▲)			D2	73
Catacombs, tombs, It.			h9	9
Catharine, Ellis, Kans., 225			D4	61
Caudéran, Fr., 28,715			E3	5
Cavite, Phil., 54,900			o13	19
Cayo Largo, isl., Cuba			E3	35
Cedar Rapids, Linn, Iowa, 92,035			C6	60
Ceduna, Austl., 1,292			F5	25
Centertown, Cole, Mo., 190			C5	69
Ceska Lipa, Czech., 14,000			C3	7
➡ Champaign, Champaign, Ill., 49,583			B4	58
Chandpur, Pak., 32,048			D9	20
Charente-Maritime, dept., Fr., 470,897			*D3	5
Charleston, harbor, S.C.			F8	82
Château-Thierry, Fr., 10,006			C5	5
Chellala, Alg., 2,899			*A5	22
Chernovtsy, Sov. Un., 147,000			G5	12
Cheviot, N.Z., 440			O14	26
Cheyenne, Laramie, Wyo., 43,505			D8	89
Chiapa de Corzo, Mex., 6,972			D6	34
➡ Chicago, Cook, Ill., 3,550,404 (★6,517,600)			B4	58
Chiefland, Levy, Fla., 1,459			C4	54

EXPLANATION OF THE INDEX REFERENCE SYSTEM

The indexing system used in this atlas is based upon the conventional pattern of parallels and meridians used to indicate latitude and longitude. The index sample beside the map indicates that the cities of *Chicago, Cadillac,* and *Champaign* are all located in *B4.* Each index key letter, *in this case "B,"* is placed between corresponding degree numbers of latitude in the vertical borders of the map. Each index key number, *in this case "4,"* is placed between corresponding degree numbers of longitude in the horizontal borders of the map. Crossing of the parallels and meridians above and below the index letter with the meridians on each side of the index number forms a confining "box" in which the given place is certain to be located. It is important to note that location of the place may be anywhere in this confining "box."

Small insets on many foreign maps are indexed independently of the main maps by separate index key letters and figures. All places indexed to these insets are identified by the lower case reference letter in the index key.

Place names are indexed to the location of the city symbol. Political divisions are indexed to the position of the names.

MAP SYMBOLS

CULTURE

Political Boundaries

—·—·—	International
———	State and Provincial
········	County

Cities, Towns, and Villages

Principal Cities

Other cities, towns, and villages are indicated by size of type and symbol according to relative population.

County Seats are indicated by dot-centered symbol.

⊛ Major Capital Cities

☆ Minor Capital Cities

Miscellaneous

National Parks
National Monuments
Indian Reservations
△ Points of Interest
NYC Railroads (Initialed in U.S. and Canada)
Tunnels
Underground or Subway
∴ Ruins
Dikes
Bridges
Dams
■ ⌂ Race Tracks, Buildings, etc.

TOPOGRAPHY

Ranges →
Peaks →
Passes → SOUTH PASS
Point of Elevation above sea level — 8,605 FT. +
Escarpments, Bluffs, Cliffs, and Plateaus — PLATEAU
Glaciers →
Volcanoes →
Lava Flows →
Sand Dunes →
Deserts →

HYDROGRAPHY

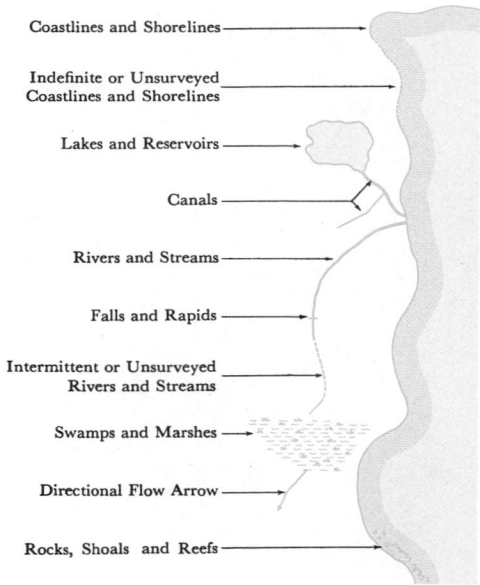

Coastlines and Shorelines →
Indefinite or Unsurveyed Coastlines and Shorelines →
Lakes and Reservoirs →
Canals →
Rivers and Streams →
Falls and Rapids →
Intermittent or Unsurveyed Rivers and Streams →
Swamps and Marshes →
Directional Flow Arrow →
Rocks, Shoals and Reefs →

ABBREVIATIONS

admin	administered
Afg	Afghanistan
Afr	Africa
Ala	Alabama
Alb	Albania
Alg	Algeria
Alsk	Alaska
Alta	Alberta
Am	American
Am. Sam	American Samoa
And	Andorra
Ang	Angola
Ant	Antarctica
Arc	Arctic
arch	archipelago
Arg	Argentina
Ariz	Arizona
Ark	Arkansas
Atl. O	Atlantic Ocean
Aus	Austria
Austl	Australia, Australian
auton	autonomous
Az. Is	Azores Islands
Ba. Is	Bahama Islands
Barb	Barbados
Bas	Basutoland
B. C	British Columbia
Bech	Bechuanaland
Bel	Belgium, Belgian
Bhu	Bhutan
Bis. Arch	Bismarck Archipelago
Bol	Bolivia
Br	British
Braz	Brazil
Br. Hond	British Honduras
Bru	Brunei
Bul	Bulgaria
Bur	Burma
Calif	California
Cam	Cameroon
Camb	Cambodia
Can	Canada
Can. Is	Canary Islands
Cen. Afr. Rep	Central African Republic
Cen. Am	Central America
Cey	Ceylon
co	county
Col	Colombia
Colo	Colorado
Com	Community
Comm	Commonwealth
Con. B	Congo; Capital: Brazzaville
Con. L	Congo, The; Capital: Léopoldville
Conn	Connecticut
cont	continent
C. R	Costa Rica
C. V. Is	Cape Verde Islands
Cyp	Cyprus
C.Z	Canal Zone
Czech	Czechoslovakia
Dah	Dahomey
Dan	Danish
D.C	District of Columbia
Del	Delaware
Den	Denmark
dep	dependency, dependencies
dept	department
dist	district
div	division
Dom. Rep	Dominican Republic
Ec	Ecuador
Eg	Egypt
Eng	England
Equat. Gui	Equatorial Guinea
Eth	Ethiopia
Eur	Europe
excl	excluding
Falk. Is	Falkland Islands
Fed	Federation
Fin	Finland
Fla	Florida
Fr	France, French
Fr. Gu	French Guiana
Fr. Som	French Somaliland
Ga	Georgia
Gam	Gambia
Ger	Germany
Gib	Gibraltar
Grc	Greece
Grnld	Greenland
Guad	Guadeloupe
Guat	Guatemala
Guy	Guyana
Hai	Haiti
Haw	Hawaii
Hond	Honduras
Hung	Hungary
I	Island
I.C	Ivory Coast
Ice	Iceland
Ill	Illinois
incl	includes, including
Ind	Indiana
Indian res	Indian reservation
Indon	Indonesia
I. of Man	Isle of Man
Ire	Ireland
is	islands
isl	island
Isr	Israel
It	Italy
Jam	Jamaica
Jap	Japan
Kans	Kansas
Ken	Kenya
Kor	Korea
Kuw	Kuwait
Ky	Kentucky
La	Louisiana
Leb	Lebanon
Le. Is	Leeward Islands
Lib	Liberia
Liech	Liechtenstein
Lux	Luxembourg
Mad. Is	Madeira Islands
Mala	Malaysia
Malag	Malagasy Republic
Man	Manitoba
Mart	Martinique
Mass	Massachusetts
Maur	Mauritania
Md	Maryland
Medit	Mediterranean
Mex	Mexico
Mich	Michigan
Minn	Minnesota
Miss	Mississippi
Mo	Missouri
Mong	Mongolia
Mont	Montana
Mor	Morocco
Moz	Mozambique
mtn	mount, mountain
mts	mountains
mun	municipality
Mus. & Om	Muscat & Oman
NA	North America
nat. mon	national monument
nat. park	national park
N.B	New Brunswick
N.C	North Carolina
N. Cal	New Caledonia
N. Dak	North Dakota
Nebr	Nebraska
Nep	Nepal
Neth	Netherlands
Nev	Nevada
Newf	Newfoundland
New Hebr	New Hebrides
N. Gui	New Guinea Territory
N.H	New Hampshire
Nic	Nicaragua
Nig	Nigeria
N. Ire	Northern Ireland
N.J	New Jersey
N. Mex	New Mexico
Nor	Norway, Norwegian
N.S	Nova Scotia
N.W. Ter	Northwest Territories
N.Y	New York
N.Z	New Zealand
occ	occupied area
Okla	Oklahoma
Ont	Ontario
Oreg	Oregon
Pa	Pennsylvania
Pac. O	Pacific Ocean
Pak	Pakistan
Pan	Panama
Pap	Papua
Par	Paraguay
par	parish
P.E.I	Prince Edward Island
Phil	Philippines
Pol	Poland
pol. dist	political district
pop	population
Port	Portugal, Portuguese
Port. Gui	Portuguese Guinea
Port. Timor	Portuguese Timor
poss	possession
P.R	Puerto Rico
pref	prefecture
prot	protectorate
prov	province, provincial
pt	point
Que	Quebec
reg	region
rep	republic
res	reservation, reservoir
Rh	Rhodesia
R.I	Rhode Island
Rom	Romania
S. A	South America
S. Afr	South Africa
Sal	El Salvador
Sask	Saskatchewan
Sau. Ar	Saudi Arabia
S.C	South Carolina
Scot	Scotland
S. Dak	South Dakota
Sen	Senegal
S.L	Sierra Leone
Sol. Is	Solomon Islands
Som	Somali Republic
Sov. Un	Soviet Union
Sp	Spain, Spanish
St., Ste	Saint, Sainte
Sud	Sudan
Sur	Surinam
S. W. Afr	South West Africa
Swaz	Swaziland
Swe	Sweden
Switz	Switzerland
Syr	Syria
Tan	Tanzania
Tenn	Tennessee
ter	territories, territory
Tex	Texas
Thai	Thailand
Tr. Coast	Trucial Coast
Trin	Trinidad & Tobago
trust	trusteeship
Tun	Tunisia
Tur	Turkey
U.A.R	United Arab Republic
Ug	Uganda
U.K	United Kingdom
uninc	unincorporated
Ur	Uruguay
U.S	United States
Va	Virginia
Ven	Venezuela
Viet	Vietnam
Vir. Is	Virgin Islands
Vt	Vermont
Wash	Washington
W.I	West Indies
Win. Is	Windward Islands
Wis	Wisconsin
W. Sam	Western Samoa
W. Va	West Virginia
Wyo	Wyoming
Yugo	Yugoslavia

EXPLANATION OF THE MAP INDEX

This universal index includes in a single alphabetical list all important political names that appear on the reference maps. Each place name is followed by its location; the population figure, when available; the map index key; and the page number of the map.

State locations are given for all places in the United States. Province and country locations are given for all places in Canada. All other place name entries show only country locations.

Populations are based upon latest available official census figures and estimates. For some larger cities a second population figure is given accompanied by a star (★). The second figure indicates the population of the city's entire metropolitan area including suburbs, as: Chicago, 3,550,404 (★6,517,600). A triangular symbol (▲) denotes a population figure for an *entire* township, district, or other minor civil division.

The index reference key, always a letter and figure combination, and the map page are the last items in each entry. Because some places are shown on both a main map and an inset map, more than one index key may be given for a single map page. Reference also may be made to more than a single map. In each case,

however, the index key *letter and figure* precede the map *page number* to which reference is made. A lower case key letter indicates reference to an inset map which has been keyed separately.

All major and minor political divisions are followed by both a descriptive term (co., dist., region, prov., dept., state, etc.), indicating political status, and by the country in which they are located. U. S. counties are listed with state locations; all others are given with county references.

Some names are included in the index that were omitted from the maps because of scale size or lack of space. These entries may be identified by an asterisk (*) and reference is given to the approximate location on the map.

A long name may appear on the map in a shortened form, with the full name given in the index. The part of the name not on the map then appears in brackets, thus: St. Gabriel [-de-Brandon].

The system of alphabetizing used in the index is standard. When more than one name with the same spelling is shown, place names are listed *first* and political divisions *second*.

INDEX

A

Aachen, Ger., 169,800..C3 6
Aalen, Ger., 31,800....D5 6
Aalst, Bel., 45,092.....B6 5
Äänekoski, Fin., 7,200.F11 11
Aarau, Switz., 17,045..E4 6
Aargau, canton, Switz.,
  360,940............*E3 6
Ābādān, Iran, 226,103..B7 23
Abaetetuba, Braz.,
  11,196............*D6 27
Abakan, Sov. Un.,
  62,000............D12 13
Abancay, Peru, 6,828..D3 31
Abanilla, Sp., 8,220....C5 8
Abashiri, Jap., 27,800.D12 18
Abbeville, Ala., 2,524..D4 46
Abbeville, Fr., 22,005..B4 5
Abbeville, La., 10,414..E3 63
Abbeville, S.C., 5,436..C3 82
Abbeville, co., S.C.,
  21,417............C3 82
Abbiategrasso, It.,
  21,652............B2 9
Abbotsford, Wis.,1,171.D3 88
Åbenrå, co., Den.,
  48,676............*J3 11
Abeokuta, Nig., 84,451.G5 22
Aberdare, Wales,
  39,044............E5 4
Aberdeen, Idaho, 1,484.G6 57
Aberdeen, Md., 9,679..A5 53
Aberdeen, Miss., 6,450.B5 68
Aberdeen, N.C., 1,531..B4 76
Aberdeen, Scot.,
  185,379............B5 4
Aberdeen, S. Dak.,
  23,073............E7 77
Aberdeen, Wash.,
  18,741............C2 86
Aberdeen, co., Scot.,
  321,757............*B5 4
Abergavenny, Wales,
  9,625.............E5 4
Abernathy, Tex., 2,491.C2 84
Aberystwyth, Wales,
  10,418............D4 4
Abidjan, I.C., 180,000..G4 22
Abilene, Kans., 6,746..D6 61
Abilene, Tex., 90,368..C3 84
Abingdon, Ill., 3,469...C3 58
Abingdon, Va., 4,758...B3 85
Abington, Mass.,
  4,500...........B6, E3 65
Abington, Pa., 8,000..A11 81
Abitibi, co., Que., Can.,
  108,313............*B2 42
Åbo, see Turku, Fin.
Abomey, Dah., 18,900 .G5 22
Abony, Hung., 12,633..B5 10

Abra, prov., Phil.,
  116,700............*B6 19
Abruzzi and Molise,
  reg., It............C4 9
Abruzzi e Molise, pol. dist.,
  It., 1,564,318.......C4 9
Absecon, N.J., 4,320...E3 74
Abu Kamal, Syr.,
  8,200.............E13 14
Åby, Swe., 2,795......u34 12
Acadia, par., La.,
  49,931............D3 63
Acámbaro, Mex.,
  26,011.........C4, m13 34
Acaponeta, Mex., 8,453.C3 34
Acapulco de Juárez,
  Mex., 48,846........D5 34
Acarigua, Ven., 31,737.B4 32
Acatlán [de Osorio],
  Mex., 7,086....D5, n14 34
Acayucan, Mex.,
  12,854............D6 34
Accomack, co., Va.,
  30,635............D7 85
Accoville, W. Va.,
  800...........D3, D5 87
Accra, Ghana, 388,231.G4 22
Achinsk, Sov. Un.,
  57,000............D12 13
Acireale, It., 26,000....F5 9
Ackerman, Miss., 1,382.B4 68
Ackley, Iowa, 1,731....B4 60
Acmetonia, Pa., 1,500.*A6 81
Aconcagua, prov., Chile,
  139,878............A2 28
Acqui, It., 12,200.....B2 9
Acre, Isr., 25,128...g5, B3 15
Acre, state, Braz.,
  160,208............C3 31
Acres Homes, Tex.,
  5,000.............*E5 84
Acton, Ont., Can.,
  3,578.............D4 41
Acton, Eng., 65,274...k11 4
Acton Vale, Que., Can.,
  3,957.............D5 42
Açu, Braz., 8,158.....D7 27
Acushnet, Mass., 3,000.C6 65
Acworth, Ga., 2,359....B2 55
Ada, Ohio, 3,918......B4 78
Ada, Okla., 14,347.....C5 79
Ada, Minn., 2,064.....C2 67
Ada, Yugo., 11,534....C5 10
Adair, co., Iowa, 10,893.C3 60
Adair, co., Ky., 14,699..C4 62
Adair, co., Mo., 20,105.A5 69
Adair, co., Okla.,
  13,112............B7 79

Adairsville, Ga., 1,026..B2 55
Adamantina, Braz.,
  18,164............C2 30
Adams, Mass., 12,391..A1 65
Adams, N.Y., 1,914....B4 75
Adams, Wis., 1,301....E4 88
Adams, co., Colo.,
  120,296............B6 51
Adams, co., Idaho,
  2,978.............E2 57
Adams, co., Ill., 68,467.D2 58
Adams, co., Ind.,
  24,643............C8 59
Adams, co., Iowa,
  7,468.............C3 60
Adams, co., Miss.,
  37,730............D2 68
Adams, co., Nebr.,
  28,944............D7 71
Adams, co., N. Dak.,
  4,449.............D3 77
Adams, co., Ohio,
  19,982............D4 78
Adams, co., Pa., 51,906.G7 81
Adams, co., Wash.,
  9,929.............B7 86
Adams, co., Wis., 7,566.D4 88
Adamstown, Pa., 1,190.F9 81
Adamsville, Ala., 2,095.E4 46
Adamsville, Tenn.,
  1,046.............B3 83
Adana, Tur., 230,000.D10 14
Adapazari, Tur.,
  80,200............B8 14
Addis Ababa, Eth.,
  500,000............G5 23
Addison, Ill., 9,046....F2 58
Addison, N.Y., 2,185...C3 75
Addison, co., Vt.,
  20,076............C1 73
Ad Diwaniya, Iraq,
  27,839............C3 15
Addyston, Ohio, 1,376.D2 78
Adel, Ga., 4,321......E3 55
Adel, Iowa, 2,060......C3 60
Adelaide, Austl., 23,051
  (★630,000).........F6 25
Adelphi, Md., 8,000...*C4 53
Aden, Aden, 99,285....G4 15
Aden, Br. dep., Asia,
  210,000............G4 15
Adena, Ohio, 1,317....B1 78
Adigrät, Eth., 5,000....F5 23
Adi Ugri, Eth., 5,000...F5 23
Adiyaman, Tur.,
  17,000............C12 14
Adjuntas, P.R.,
  5,318.............*m13 35
Admiralty, is., Bis.
  Arch.............h12 25

Adra, Sp., 7,923.......D4 8
Adrano, It., 31,532.....F5 9
Adria, It., 12,100......B4 9
Adrian, Mich., 20,347..G6 66
Adrian, Minn., 1,215...G3 67
Adrian, Mo., 1,082.....C3 69
Adrianople, see Edirne,
  Tur.
Aduwā, Eth., 5,000....F5 23
Affton, Mo., 18,000...*B8 69
Afghanistan, country,
  Asia, 13,000,000....B4 20
Africa, cont., 233,718,700 . 21
Afton, Iowa, 773......C3 60
Afton, N.Y., 956......C5 75
Afton, Okla., 1,111....A7 79
Afton, Wyo., 1,337....C2 89
Afula, Isr., 13,816.....B3 15
Afyonkarahisar, Tur.,
  38,400............C8 14
Agadès, Niger, 4,700...E6 22
Agadir, Mor., 16,695...B3 22
Agana, Guam, 1,642..*F6 2
Agartala, India, 54,878.D9 20
Agawam, Mass., 5,000..B2 65
Agboville, I.C., 13,000..G4 22
Agde, Fr., 7,696.......F5 5
Agematsu, Jap., 4,600.n16 18
Agen, Fr., 32,800......E4 5
Agira, It., 14,079......F5 9
Agnone, It., 9,888.....D5 9
Agra, India, 462,020...C6 20
Agrigento, It., 40,500..F4 9
Agrinion, Grc., 24,763..C3 14
Aguada, P.R., 3,759..*m13 35
Aguadas, Col., 8,064...B2 32
Aguadilla, P.R.,
  15,943............m13 35
Aguascalientes, Mex.,
  126,222.......C4, m12 34
Aguascalientes, state,
  Mex., 236,574...C4, k12 34
Aguilar, Colo., 777.....D6 51
Aguilar, Sp., 13,843....D3 8
Aguilas, Sp., 11,634....D5 8
Agujita, Mex., 5,463...B4 34
Agusan, prov., Phil.,
  272,000............*D7 19
Ahlen, Ger., 40,500....D5 20
Ahmadabad, India,
  1,149,918
  (★1,300,000)........D5 20
Ahmadnagar
  (Ahmednagar),
  India, 119,020.......E5 20
Ahmadpur, Pak.,
  20,423............C5 20
Aho, Jap., 3,210......o15 18
Ahoskie, N.C., 4,583...A7 76
Ahrweiler, Ger., 8,700..C3 6

Ahuachapán, Sal.,
13,298...........*H12 33
Ahualulco de Mercado,
Mex., 8,036........m12 34
Ahvāz, Iran, 120,098...B7 23
Ahvenanmaa, dept., Fin.,
22,787.............*G8 11
Aibonito, P.R., 5,477.*m13 35
Aichi, pref., Jap.,
4,206,313..........*I8 18
Aiea, Haw.,
11,826........B4, G10 56
Aigun, China, 25,000..A10 17
Aikawa, Jap., 7,800....G9 18
Aiken, S.C., 11,243....D4 82
Aiken, co., S.C., 81,038.D4 82
Aiken South, S.C.,
2,980.............*D4 82
Aiken West, S.C.,
2,602.............*D4 82
Aimorés, Braz., 11,448.B4 30
Ain, dept., Fr.,
327,146...........*D6 5
Aïn-Sefra, Alg., 4,637...B4 22
Ainsworth, Nebr.,
1,982.............B6 71
Aire-sur-la-Lys, Fr.,
5,528.............B5 5
Aisén, prov., Chile,
37,085............D2 28
Aisne, dept., Fr.,
512,920...........*C5 5
Aitkin, Minn., 1,829...D5 67
Aitkin, co., Minn.,
12,162............D5 67
Aitolia kai Akarnania,
prov., Grc., 237,738.*C3 14
Aitolikon, Grc., 5,959.*C3 14
Aiud, Rom., 11,886.....B6 10
Aix [-en-Provence], Fr.,
67,943............F6 5
Aix-la-Chapelle, see
Aachen, Ger.
Aix-les-Bains, Fr.,
18,132............E6 5
Aiyina, Grc., 6,217...*D4 14
Aiyion, Grc., 17,762...*C4 14
Ajaccio, Fr., 41,006....D2 9
Ajax, Ont., Can., 7,755.D5 41
Ajigasawa, Jap., 8,100.F10 18
Ajmer, India, 231,240..C5 20
Ajo, Ariz., 7,049......C2 48
Akashi, Jap., 129,780...I7 18
Akçaabat (Polathane),
Tur., 4,414........B12 14
Akershus, co., Nor.,
234,500...........*H4 11
Aketi, Con. L., 12,100..H2 23
Akhaia, prov., Grc.,
239,206...........*C3 14
Akharnai, Grc.,
11,290............*C4 14
Akhisar, Tur., 40,000..C6 14
Akhtyrka, Sov. Un.,
55,200............F10 12
Aki, Jap., 13,100......J6 18
Akita, Jap., 166,000..G10 18
Akita, pref., Jap.,
1,335,580.........*G10 18
Akkeshi, Jap., 16,100.E12 18
Aklavik, N.W. Ter.,
Can., 599..........C5 36
Akola, India, 115,760..D6 20
Akron, Colo., 1,890....A7 51
Akron, Ind., 958......B5 59
Akron, Iowa, 1,351....B1 60
Akron, N.Y., 2,841....B2 75
Akron, Ohio, 290,351
(*573,800).........A6 78
Akron, Pa., 2,167......F9 81
Aksaray, Tur., 20,000.C10 14
Aksehir, Tur., 20,600...C8 14
Aksenovo-Zilovskoye,
Sov. Un., 10,000...D14 13
Aktyubinsk, Sov. Un.,
107,000...........D8 13
Akureyri, Ice., 8,957...n23 11
Akyab, Bur., 42,329...D9 20
Alabama, state, U.S.,
3,266,740............. 46
Alabaster, Ala., 1,623..B3 46
Alachua, Fla., 1,974...C4 54
Alachua, co., Fla.,
74,074............C4 54
Alagoa Grande, Braz.,
12,115...........*D7 27
Alagoas, state, Braz.,
1,271,062.........*D7 27
Alagoinhas, Braz.,
38,246...........*E7 27
Alagón, Sp., 5,270....B5 8
Alajuela, C.R., 19,900..E8 34
Alajuela, prov., C.R.,
232,000...........*E8 34
Al 'Alamayn (El Alamein),
Eg., U.A.R........G7 14
Alamance, co., N.C.,
85,674............B4 76
Alameda, Calif., 63,855.B5 50
Alameda, N. Mex.,
5,000...........B5, D5 48

Alameda, co., Calif.,
908,209...........D3 50
Al 'Āmirīyah, Eg.,
U.A.R., 10,000.....G7 14
Alamo, Calif., 1,791...*B6 50
Alamo, Tenn., 1,665...B2 83
Alamo, Tex., 4,121.....F3 84
Alamogordo, N. Mex.,
21,723............C6 48
Alamo Heights, Tex.,
7,552..........B4, E3 84
Alamosa, Colo., 6,205..D5 51
Alamosa, co., Colo.,
10,000............D5 51
Alanya, Tur., 10,100...D9 14
Al 'Arīsh, Eg., U.A.R.,
10.791............G9 14
Alasehir, Tur., 13,900..C7 14
Alaska, state, U.S.,
226,167............. 47
Alassio, It., 8,544......C2 9
Alatyr, Sov. Un.,
34,700............D16 12
Alava, prov., Sp.,
138,934...........*A4 8
Alba, It., 12,000......B2 9
Albacete, Sp., 59,600...C5 8
Albacete, prov., Sp.,
370,976...........*C5 8
Alba Iulia, Rom.,
14,776............B6 10
Albania, country, Eur.,
1,625,378..........B2 14
Albano, Laziale, It.,
11,700..........D4, h9 9
Albany, Ga., 55,890....E2 55
Albany, Ind., 2,132....D7 59
Albany, Ky., 1,887....D4 62
Albany, Minn., 1,375..E4 67
Albany, Mo., 1,662....A3 69
Albany, N.Y., 129,726
(*592,400).........C7 75
Albany, Oreg.,
12,926.........C1, C3 80
Albany, Tex., 2,174....C3 84
Albany, co., N.Y.,
272,926...........C7 75
Albany, co., Wyo.,
21,290............D7 89
Albany South, Ga.,
1,200............*E2 55
Albay, prov., Phil.,
516,000...........*C6 19
Albemarle, N.C.,
12,261............B3 76
Albemarle, co., Va.,
30,969............D4 85
Albenga, It., 8,700....B2 9
Alberni, B.C., Can.,
4,616.............E5 37
Albert, Fr., 10,247....B5 5
Albert, co., N.B., Can.,
12,485............D5 43
Alberta, prov., Can.,
1,331,944........... 38
Albert Lea, Minn.,
17,108............G5 67
Albertson, N.Y.,
9,700............*G2 52
Albertville, Ala., 8,250.A3 46
Albertville, Con. L.,
29,500............B5 24
Albertville, Fr., 12,159.E7 5
Albi, Fr., 38,709......F5 5
Albia, Iowa, 4,582.....C5 60
Albion, Ill., 2,025.....E5 58
Albion, Ind., 1,325....B7 59
Albion, Mich., 12,749..F6 66
Albion, Nebr., 1,982...C7 71
Albion, N.Y., 5,182....B2 75
Albion, Pa., 1,630.....C1 81
Ålborg, Den., 85,800...I3 11
Ålborg, co., Den.,
232,885............*I3 11
Albox, Sp., 9,908.....D4 8
Albuñol, Sp., 7,989...D4 8
Albuquerque, N. Mex.,
201,189
(*266,300)......B5, D5 48
Alburquerque, Sp.,
9,756.............C2 8
Alburtis, Pa., 1,086...E10 81
Albury, Austl., 22,983..G8 25
Alcalá [de Guadaira], Sp.,
25,000............D3 8
Alcalá de Henares, Sp.,
25,123.........B4, p18 8
Alcalá de los Gazules,
Sp., 9,693.........D3 8
Alcalá la Real, Sp.,
9,979.............D4 8
Alcamo, It., 43,097....F4 9
Alcanar, Sp., 6,944....B6 8
Alcañiz, Sp., 10,035...B5 8
Alcaraz, Sp., 5,864....C4 8
Alcaudete, Sp.,
18,442............D3 8
Alcázar de San Juan,
Sp., 24,963........C4 8

Alcazarquivir, see Ksar
el Kebir, Mor.
Alcira, Sp., 26,669.....C5 8
Alco, La., 40..........C2 63
Alcoa, Tenn.,
6,395.........D10, E11 83
Alcona, co., Mich.,
6,352.............D7 66
Alcorn, co., Miss.,
25,282............A5 68
Alcoy, Sp., 51,096.....C5 8
Aldan, Pa., 4,324.....*G11 81
Aldan, Sov. Un.,
10,000............D15 13
Alden, N.Y., 2,042.....C2 75
Alden, Pa., 1,000......D9 81
Aldershot, Eng., 31,260.E6 4
Alderson, W. Va.,
1,225.............D4 87
Alderwood Manor, Wash.,
4,000.............B3 86
Aledo, Ill., 3,080......B3 58
Alegre, Braz., 7,487....C4 30
Alegrete, Braz., 33,735.D1 30
Aleksandriya, Sov. Un.,
43,300............G9 12
Aleksandrov, Sov. Un.,
30,600............C12 12
Aleksandrovsk
[-Sakhalinskiy],
Sov. Un., 39,400....D17 13
Aleksandrow, Pol.,
7,577.............B5 7
Aleksandrow, Pol.,
6,926.............C5 7
Aleksinac, Yugo., 8,741.D5 10
Alençon, Fr., 25,584...C4 5
Aleppo (Halab), Syr.,
425,500...........D11 14
Alès, Fr., 41,360......E6 5
Alessandria, It., 92,760.B2 9
Ålesund, Nor., 19,200..F2 11
Aleutian, is., Alsk.....E5 47
Alexander, co., Ill.,
16,061............F4 58
Alexander, co., N.C.,
15,625............B2 76
Alexander City, Ala.,
13,140............C4 46
Alexander Mills, N.C.,
947............B2, D4 76
Alexandria, Ont., Can.,
2,487............B10 41
Alexandria (Al
Iskandarīyah), Eg.,
U.A.R., 1,277,819...G7 14
Alexandria, Ind., 5,582.D6 59
Alexandria, Ky.,
1,318..........A7, B5 62
Alexandria, La., 40,279.C3 63
Alexandria, Minn.,
6,713.............E3 67
Alexandria, Rom.,
19,294............D7 10
Alexandria, Va.,
91,023.........B5, C5 85
Alexandria Bay, N.Y.,
1,583...........A5, B1 75
Alexandria Southwest,
La., 2,782........*C3 63
Alexandroupolis, Grc.,
18,712............B5 14
Aleysk, Sov. Un.,
10,000...........D11 13
Alfalfa, co., Okla.,
8,445.............A3 79
Al Farâfirah, Eg.,
U.A.R., 749.......C3 23
Alfaro, Sp., 8,570.....A5 8
Al Fayyūm, Eg., U.A.R.,
84,800............H8 14
Alfenas, Braz.,
16,051.........C3, k9 30
Alfortville, Fr., 32,332.g10 5
Alfred, Ont., Can.,
1,257............B10 41
Alfred, N.Y., 2,807....C3 75
Algarve, prov., Port.,
328,231...........*D2 8
Algarve, reg., Port.,
314,800............D1 8
Algeciras, Sp., 66,317..D3 8
Algemesí, Sp., 19,057...C5 8
Alger, see Algiers, Alg.
Alger, Ohio, 1,068....B4 78
Alger, co., Mich., 9,250.B4 66
Algeria, country, Afr.,
10,003,000.........C3 22
Algiers (Alger), Alg.,
361,285 (*587,570)...A5 22
Algoma, Wis., 3,855...D6 88
Algoma, co., Ont., Can.,
82,059............A2 41
Algona, Iowa, 5,702...A3 60
Algona, Wash.,
1,311..........B3, D2 86
Algonac, Mich., 3,190..F8 66

Algonquin, Ill.,
2,692..........A5, E2 58
Alhama, Sp., 9,849....D4 8
Alhama, Sp., 6,442....D5 8
Alhambra, Calif.,
54,807............F2 50
Alhaurín el Grande,
Sp., 11,525........D3 8
Al Ḩudaydah (Hodeida),
Yemen, 40,000.....F6 23
Al Hufūf (Hofuf), Sau.
Ar., 90,000........D4 15
Alicante, Sp., 121,527..C5 8
Alicante, prov., Sp.,
711,942...........*C5 8
Alice, Tex., 20,861.....F3 84
Alice Southwest, Tex.,
1,813.............*F3 84
Aliceville, Ala., 3,194...B1 46
Aligarh, India, 185,020.C6 20
Alingsås, Swe., 17,500...I5 11
Aliquippa, Pa.,
26,369.........A5, E1 81
Alisal, Calif., 16,473...C1 50
Al Isma'īlīyah, Eg.,
U.A.R., 82,100.....G9 14
Alistrati, Grc., 4,951...B4 14
Aliwal North, S. Afr.,
10,706............G5 24
Al Jawf, Sau. Ar.,
10,000............D2 15
Al Jīzah (El Giza), Eg.,
U.A.R., 98,000.....H8 14
Aljustrel, Port., 5,844..D1 8
Al Kadhimain, Iraq,
126,443...........C3 15
Al Karak, Jordan,
5,539..........C3, h5 15
Al Khalīl (Hebron),
Jordan, 35,983...C3, h5 15
Al Khārijah, Eg.,
U.A.R., 11,155.....C4 23
Alkmaar, Neth., 44,100.A6 5
Al Lādhiqīyah (Latakia),
Syr., 67,600.......E10 14
Allahabad, India,
411,955 (*430,730)...C7 20
Allamakee, co., Iowa,
15,982............A6 60
Allanmyo, Bur.,
15,580............E10 20
Allariz, Sp., 9,403....A2 8
Allaykha, Sov. Un.,
800..............B17 13
Allegan, Mich., 4,827...F5 66
Allegan, co., Mich.,
57,729............F4 66
Allegany, N.Y., 2,064..C2 75
Allegany, co., Md.,
84,169............A1 53
Allegany, co., N.Y.,
43,978............C2 75
Alleghany, co., N.C.,
7,734............A2 76
Alleghany, co., Va.,
12,128............D3 85
Allegheny, co., Pa.,
1,628,587..........E2 81
Allemands, La.,
1,167..........C6, E5 63
Allen, Okla., 1,005....C5 79
Allen, co., Ind.,
232,196...........B7 59
Allen, co., Kans.,
16,369............E8 61
Allen, co., Ky., 12,269..D3 62
Allen, co., Ohio,
103,691...........B3 78
Allen, par., La., 19,867.D3 63
Allendale, N.J., 4,092..A4 74
Allendale, S.C., 3,114...E5 82
Allendale, co., S.C.,
11,362............E5 82
Allende, Mex., 9,938...B4 34
Allen Park, Mich.,
37,494............A7 66
Allenport, Pa., 981...*F2 81
Allenstein, see Olsztyn,
Pol.
Allentown, N.J., 1,393..C3 74
Allentown, Pa., 108,347
(*299,700).........E11 81
Alleppey, India,
138,834...........G6 20
Aller (Cabañaquinta),
Sp., 828...........A3 8
Alliance, Nebr., 7,845..B3 71
Alliance, Ohio, 28,362..B6 78
Allier, dept., Fr.,
380,221...........*D5 5
Allinge, Den., 2,114....A3 7
Allison, Iowa, 952.....B5 60
Allison, Pa., 1,258.....G2 81
Allison Park, Pa., 5,000.A6 81
Alliston, Ont., Can.,
2,426.............C5 41
Al Līth, Sau. Ar.,
10,000............D6 23
Alloa, Scot., 13,895....B5 4
Allouez, Wis., 9,557..*A5 88

Al Luḥayyah, Yemen,
5,000............F3   15
Alma, Ark., 1,370.....B1   49
Alma, Ga., 3,515.....E4   55
Alma, Mich., 8,978....E6   66
Alma, Nebr., 1,342....D6   71
Alma, Wis., 1,008....D2   88
Alma-Ata, Sov. Un.,
508,000...........E10   13
Almada, Port., 11,995..f9   8
Almadén, Sp., 13,443...C3   8
Al Madīnah (Medina),
Sau. Ar., 80,000.....E2   15
Almagro, Sp., 9,681....C4   8
Al Maḥallah al Kubrá,
Eg., U.A.R., 132,300.G8   14
Almansa, Sp., 15,391...C5   8
Al Manṣūrah, Eg.,
U.A.R., 119,000.....G8   14
Al Marj, Libya,
12,000............B2   23
Almeirim, Port., 7,104..C1   8
Almelo, Neth., 51,300..A7   5
Almendralejo, Sp.,
21,884............C2   8
Almería, Sp., 86,808...D4   8
Almería, prov., Sp.,
360,777...........*D4   8
Al Minyā, Eg., U.A.R.,
93,300............C4   23
Almiros, Grc., 7,034....C4   14
Almodóvar, Sp., 14,633.C3   8
Almogía, Sp., 8,341....D3   8
Almon, Ga., 300......C3   55
Almonesson, N.J.,
1,500............*D2   74
Almont, Mich., 1,279...F7   66
Almonte, Ont., Can.,
2,960............B8   41
Almonte, Sp., 11,538...D2   8
Almora, India, 16,004..C6   20
Almoradí, Sp., 3,998...C5   8
Al Mukallā, S. Arabia,
25,000............G4   15
Al Mukhā, Yemen,
5,000............G3   15
Almuñécar, Sp., 6,235..D4   8
Alnwick, Eng., 7,482...C6   4
Aloha, Oreg., 4,000....B2   80
Álora, Sp., 5,960.....D3   8
Alor Star, Mala.,
52,915............D2   19
Alorton (Fireworks),
Ill., 3,282........*E3   7
Alosno, Sp., 5,814.....D2   8
Alpena, Mich., 14,682..C7   66
Alpena, co., Mich.,
28,556............C7   66
Alpes-Maritimes, dept.,
Fr., 618,265.......*F7   5
Alpha, Warren, N.J.,
2,406............B2   74
Alpharetta, Ga., 1,349..B2   55
Alpiarça, Port., 6,680...C1   8
Alpine, Calif., 1,044...*F5   50
Alpine, N.J., 921.....D6   74
Alpine, Tex., 4,740....F2   84
Alpine, co., Calif., 397..C4   50
Alpoca, W. Va., 400...D3   68
Al Qāhirah, see Cairo,
Eg., U.A.R.
Al Qanṭarah, Eg., U.A.R.,
2,000............G9   14
Al Qaṭīf, Sau. Ar.,
5,000............D4   15
Al Qunayṭirah, Syr.,
17,100............F10   14
Alsace, former prov., Fr.,
1,317,000.........C7   5
Alsfeld, Ger., 9,900....C7   5
Alsip, Ill., 3,770.....*F3   58
Alta, Iowa, 1,393.....B2   60
Altadena, Calif.,
40,568............*F2   50
Alta Garcia, Arg.,
11,570............A4   28
Al Tahoe, Calif., 1,500.C4   50
Alta Loma, Tex.,
1,020............G5   84
Altamont, Ill., 1,656...D5   58
Altamont, N.Y., 1,365..C6   75
Altamont, Oreg.,
10,811............E5   80
Altamonte Springs, Fla.,
1,212............D5   54
Altamura, It., 43,735..D6   9
Altavista, Va., 3,299...D3   85
Altdorf, Switz., 7,477..E4   6
Altenburg, Ger.,
46,800............C6   6
Altheimer, Ark., 979...C4   49
Alto, Tex., 869......D5   84
Alto Alentejo, prov.,
Port., 400,374.....*C2   8
Alton, Ill., 43,047.....E3   58
Alton, Iowa, 1,048....B1   59
Altona, Man., Can.,
2,026............E3   40
Altoona, Ala., 744....A3   46
Altoona, Iowa,
1,458............A7, C4   60

Altoona, Pa., 69,407
(*104,500).........E5   81
Altoona, Wis., 2,114...D2   88
Alto Paraná, dept.,
Par., 9,531.......D4   29
Alturas, Calif., 2,819...B3   50
Altus, Okla., 21,225....C2   79
Alula, Som., 1,300....F8   23
Alva, Ky., 700......D6   62
Alva, Okla., 6,258.....A3   79
Alvarado, Mex., 12,424.D5   34
Alvarado, Tex.,
1,907............B5, C4   84
Alvin, Tex., 5,643..E5, F5   84
Alviso, Calif., 1,174...*D3   50
Álvsborg, co., Swe.,
376,500...........*I5   11
Alwar, India, 72,707...C6   20
Al Wāsiṭah, Eg., U.A.R.,
4,000............H8   14
Alytus, Sov. Un., 9,084.A8   7
Amador, co., Calif.,
9,990............C3   50
Amagansett, N.Y.,
1,095............D4   75
Amagasaki, Jap.,
405,955...........o14   18
Amål, Swe., 9,200....H5   11
Amalias, Grc., 15,468..D3   14
Amambay, dept., Par.,
18,160............D4   29
Amantea, It., 5,822....E6   9
Amapá, ter., Braz.,
68,889............C5   27
Amarillo, Tex., 137,969
(*142,500).........B2   84
Amarousion, Grc.,
20,135............C4   14
Amasya, Tur., 28,200.B10   14
Amazonas, comisaría, Col.,
8,120............D3   32
Amazonas, dept., Peru,
100,527...........B2   31
Amazonas, state, Braz.,
721,215...........B3   31
Ambala, India, 76,204..B6   20
Ambarchik, Sov. Un.,
800............C19   13
Ambato, Ec., 33,908...B2   31
Amberg, Ger., 42,500..D5   6
Ambérieu [-en-Bugey],
Fr., 7,748........E6   5
Amberley, Ohio, 2,951.*D2   78
Ambikapur, India,
15,240............D7   20
Ambler, Pa.,
6,765..........A11, F11   81
Amboina, Indon.,
55,263............F7   19
Amboise, Fr., 7,953....D4   5
Amboy, Ill., 2,067.....B4   58
Ambridge, Pa.,
13,865...........A5, E1   81
Ambridge Heights, Pa.,
5,106............*A5   81
Amderma, Sov. Un.,
10,000............C9   13
Ameca, Mex.,
17,396...........C4, m11   34
Amecameca, Mex.,
12,271............n14   34
Amelia, Ohio, 913.....C3   78
Amelia, co., Va., 7,815.D4   85
Amenia, N.Y., 1,769...D7   75
American Falls, Idaho,
2,123............G6   57
American Fork, Utah,
6,373...........A6, D2   72
American Samoa, U.S.
dep., Oceania, 20,051*G9   2
Americus, Ga., 13,472..D2   55
Amersfoort, Neth.,
70,600............A6   5
Amery, Wis., 1,769....C1   88
Ames, Iowa, 27,003....B4   60
Amesbury, Mass.,
10,787............A6   65
Amfissa, Grc., 5,546....C4   14
Amga, Sov. Un., 800...C16   13
Amherst, N.S., Can.,
10,788............D5   43
Amherst, Fla., 1,500..*D6   54
Amherst, Mass., 10,306.B2   65
Amherst, N.Y., 48,000.*C2   78
Amherst, Ohio, 6,750...A5   78
Amherst, Tex., 883....B1   84
Amherst, Va., 1,200...D3   85
Amherst, co., Va.,
22,953............D3   85
Amherstburg, Ont.,
Can., 4,099........E1   41
Amherstdale, W. Va.,
900.........D3, D5   87
Amiens, Fr., 105,433...C5   5
Amite, La., 3,313.....D5   63
Amite, co., Miss.,
15,573............D3   68
Amityville, N.Y.,
8,318.........E3, E7   75
'Ammān, Jordan,
108,304.........C3, h5   15

Ammon, Idaho, 1,882..F7   57
Amory, Miss., 6,474...B5   68
Amos, Que., Can.,
6,080............E9   41
Amoy (Hsiamen), China,
224,300...........G8   17
Amparo, Braz.,
14,382.........C3, m8   30
Amposta, Sp., 8,444...B6   8
Amqui, Que., Can.,
3,247............*B3   42
'Amrān, Yemen, 20,000.F3   15
Amraoti, India,
137,875...........D6   20
Amritsar, India,
376,295...........B5   20
Amsterdam, Neth.,
866,300...........A6   5
Amsterdam, N.Y.,
28,772............C6   75
Amsterdam, Ohio, 931..B7   78
Amstetten, Aus.,
12,086............D7   6
'Ana, Iraq, 5,860.....C3   15
Anaconda, Mont.,
12,054............D4   70
Anacortes, Wash.,
8,414............A3   86
Anadarko, Okla.,
6,299............B3   79
Anadyr, Sov. Un.,
5,000............C20   13
Anaheim, Calif.,
104,184........F3, F5   50
Anahuac, Tex.,
1,985..........E5, F5   84
Anakapalle, India,
46,402............E7   20
Analalava, Malag.,
5,000............C9   24
Anamosa, Iowa, 4,616.B6   60
Anandale, La., 2,827..*C3   63
Anantapur, India,
52,280............F6   20
Anantnag, India,
21,087............B6   20
Ananyev, Sov. Un.,
5,000............H7   12
Anápolis, Braz., 48,847.B3   30
Añatuya, Arg., 9,310...E3   29
Anawalt, W. Va., 1,062 D3   87
Ancash, dept., Peru,
521,661...........C2   31
Anchorage, Alsk., 44,237
(*80,000)......C10, g17   47
Anchorage, Ky., 1,170..A4   62
Anchor Bay Gardens,
Mich., 1,830.......*A8   66
Ancienne Lorette, Que.,
Can., 3,961.......C6, C8   42
Ancon, C.Z., 1,151....B2   32
Ancona, It., 100,485...C4   9
Andalusia, Ala., 10,263.D3   46
Andalusia, reg., Sp.,
5,893,396.........D3   8
Andaman, is., India....F9   20
Anderlecht, Bel.,
94,677............B6   5
Andernach, Ger.,
20,800............C3   6
Anderson, Calif., 4,492.B2   50
Anderson, Ind., 49,061.D6   59
Anderson, Mo., 992....E3   69
Anderson, S.C., 41,316.B2   82
Anderson, co., Kans.,
9,035............D8   61
Anderson, co., Ky.,
8,618............C4   62
Anderson, co., S.C.,
98,478............B2   82
Anderson, co., Tenn.,
60,032............C9   83
Anderson, co., Tex.,
28,162............D5   84
Anderson East Side, Ind.,
3,778............*D6   59
Andes, Col., 6,905.....B2   32
Andhra Pradesh, state,
India, 35,983,447....E6   20
Andizhan, Sov. Un.,
141,000...........E10   13
Andkhui, Afg., 18,438..A4   20
Andong, Kor., 45,700..H4   18
Andorra, And., 600....A6   8
Andorra, country, Eur.,
5,664............A6   8
Andover, Mass., 10,000.A5   65
Andover, N.Y., 1,247...C3   75
Andover, Ohio, 1,116...A7   78
Andraitx, Sp., 5,077....C7   78
Andrew, co., Mo.,
11,062............B3   69
Andrews, Ind., 1,132...C6   59
Andrews, N.C., 1,404..D2   76
Andrews, S.C., 2,995...E8   82
Andrews, Tex., 11,135..C1   84
Andrews, co., Tex.,
13,450............C1   84
Andreyevka, Sov. Un.,
10,000............G11   12
Andria, It., 70,831.....D6   9

Androscoggin, co., Maine,
86,312............D2   64
Andrychow, Pol.,
5,055............h10   7
Andújar, Sp., 26,100...C3   8
Angelholm, Swe.,
12,600............I5   11
Angelica, N.Y., 898....C2   75
Angelina, co., Tex.,
39,814............D5   84
Angels Camp, Calif.,
1,121............C3   50
Angermünde, Ger.,
11,700............B7   6
Angers, Fr., 115,252...D3   5
Angier, N.C., 1,249....B5   76
Anglesey, co., Wales,
51,700............D4   4
Anglet, Fr., 16,150....F3   5
Angleton, Tex.,
7,312.........E5, G5   84
Ango, Con. L........H3   23
Angol, Chile, 14,292...B2   28
Angola, Ind., 4,746....A8   59
Angola, N.Y., 2,499....C1   75
Angola, Port. dep., Afr.,
4,832,677.........C3   24
Angoulême, Fr., 48,190.E4   5
Angra do Heroismo, Port.,
10,296............k10   22
Angra dos Reis, Braz.,
10,634..........C4, h5   30
Angus, co., Scot.,
278,370...........*B5   4
Angwin, Calif., 1,400...A5   50
Anhwei, prov., China,
33,560,000........E8   17
Anina, Rom., 11,837...C5   10
Anita, Iowa, 1,233.....C3   60
Anita, Pa., 550......E4   81
Aniva (Rutaka), Sov.
Un., 10,000........C11   18
Anjo, Jap., 33,000.....o16   18
Anjou, former prov., Fr.,
631,000...........D3   5
Anju, Kor., 21,861.....G2   18
Ankang, China,
105,300...........E8   17
Ankara, Tur., 646,200..C9   14
Ankeny, Iowa,
2,964..........A7, C4   60
Anklam, Ger., 19,400..B6   6
Ankuang, China, 5,000.D1   18
Anmoore, W. Va.,
1,050..........B4, B7   87
Annaba (Bône), Alg.,
114,068...........A6   22
An Najaf, Iraq, 74,089.C3   15
Annalee Heights, Va.,
2,000............*B5   85
Annam, reg., Viet.,
8,000,000.........B3   19
Annandale, Minn., 984.E4   67
Annandale, Va., 5,000..B5   85
Annapolis, Md., 23,385.C5   53
Annapolis, co., N.S., Can.,
22,649............E4   43
Ann Arbor, Mich.,
67,340.........A6, F7   66
An Nasiriya, Iraq,
25,515............C4   15
Anne Arundel, co., Md.,
206,634...........B4   53
Annecy, Fr., 43,255....E7   5
Annemasse, Fr., 13,814.D7   5
Anniston, Ala., 33,657..B4   46
Annonay, Fr., 18,434...E6   5
Annville, Pa., 4,264....F8   81
Anoka, Minn.,
10,562.........E5, E7   67
Anoka, co., Minn.,
85,916............E5   67
Ansbach, Ger., 32,900..D5   6
Anserma, Col., 7,767...B2   32
Anshan, China,
805,000...........C9   17
Anson, Tex., 2,890.....C3   84
Anson, co., N.C.,
24,962............B3   76
Ansong, Kor., 15,800...H3   18
Ansonia, Conn., 19,819.D4   52
Ansonia, Ohio, 1,002...B3   78
Ansted, W. Va.,
1,511..........C3, D7   87
Anta, China, 5,000.....C2   18
Antakya (Antioch), Tur.,
45,800............D11   14
Antalaha, Malag.,
10,300............C10   24
Antalya, Tur.,
51,000............D8   14
Antarctica, cont.......L6   2
Antelope, co., Nebr.,
10,176............B7   71
Antequera, Sp., 29,000.D3   8
Anthon, Iowa, 681....B10   71
Anthony, Kans., 2,744.E5   61
Anthony, N. Mex.,
900............D5   48
Anthony, R.I., 2,800..C10   52

Anthony Wayne Village,
3,000..............*B7   59
Antibes, Fr., 35,439.....F7   5
Antigo, Wis., 9,691....C4   88
Antigonish, N.S., Can.,
4,344..............D7   43
Antigonish, co., N.S.,
Can., 14,360........D8   43
Antigua, Br. dep., N.A.,
54,354.............n16   35
Antigua Guatemala,
Guat., 10,996........E6   34
Antilla, Cuba, 5,786...E6   35
Antilles, see Greater
Antilles and Lesser
Antilles, W.I.
Antioch, Calif., 17,305..B6   50
Antioch, Ill., 2,268.....D2   58
Antioch, see Antakya, Tur.
Antioquia, Col., 3,998..B2   32
Antioquia, dept., Col.,
1,747,580...........B2   32
Antique, prov., Phil.,
239,200............*C6   19
Antlers, Okla., 2,085...C6   79
Antofagasta, Chile,
88,000.............D1   29
Antofagasta, prov., Chile,
214,090............D1   29
Anton, Tex., 1,068.....C1   84
Antonina, Braz., 8,520.D3   30
António Enes, Moz.,
11,628.............D7   24
Antonito, Colo., 1,045..D5   51
Antony, Fr., 46,483....g10   5
Antratsit, Sov. Un.,
5,000.............g22   12
Antrim, co., Mich.,
10,373.............C5   66
Antrim, co., N. Ire.,
273,923............*C3   4
Antsirabe, Malag.,
11,332.............D9   24
Antsirane, see Diégo-
Suarez, Malag.
Antung, China, 360,000.C9   17
Antwerp, see Antwerpen,
Bel.
Antwerp, Ohio, 1,465...A3   78
Antwerpen (Antwerp)
(Anvers), Bel.,
253,295............B6   5
Antwerpen, prov., Bel.,
1,443,355..........*B6   5
Anuradhapura, Cey.,
18,528.............G7   20
Anvers, see Antwerpen,
Bel.
Anyang, China,
124,900............D7   17
Anzhero-Sudzhensk, Sov.
Un., 119,000........D11   13
Anzio, It., 10,000..D4, k9   9
Anzoátegui, state, Ven.,
382,002............B5   32
Aomori, Jap.,
159,000............*F10   18
Aomori, pref., Jap.,
1,426,606..........*F10   18
Aosta, It., 30,127......B1   9
Apache, Okla., 1,455...C3   79
Apache, co., Ariz.,
30,438.............B4   48
Apache Junction, Ariz.,
1,000.............D2   48
Apalachicola, Fla.,
3,099.............C2   54
Apan, Mex., 8,589....n14   34
Aparri, Phil., 14,000...B6   19
Apatin, Yugo., 17,203..C4   10
Apeldoorn, Neth.,
104,900............A6   5
Apex, N.C., 1,368.....B5   76
Apia, W. Sam., 16,000.G9   2
Apizaco, Mex., 15,622.n14   34
Apolda, Ger., 29,300...C5   6
Apollo, Pa., 2,694.....E2   81
Apopka, Fla., 3,578....D5   54
Appalachia, Va., 2,456.B2   85
Appanoose, co., Iowa,
16,015.............D5   60
Appenzell, canton,
Switz., 61,863......*E4   6
Appleton, Minn., 2,172.E2   67
Appleton, Wis., 48,411
(*123,200)......A5, D5   88
Appleton City, Mo.,
1,075.............C3   69
Appleyard, Wash., 950.B5   86
Appling, co., Ga.,
13,246.............E4   55
Appomattox, Va.,
1,184.............D4   85
Appomattox, co., Va.,
9,148.............D4   85
Aprelsk, Sov. Un.,
800..............D14   13
Apt, Fr., 5,521........F6   5
Apulia, reg., It.......D6   9
Apure, state, Ven.,
117,577............B3   32

Apurímac, dept., Peru,
324,338............D3   31
Aquidauana, Braz.,
11,997.............C1   30
Arab, Ala., 2,989......A3   46
Arabi, La., 5,000......C7   63
Arabia, see Saudi Arabia,
Asia.
Aracaju, Braz., 112,516.E7   27
Aracati, Braz., 11,016..D7   27
Araçatuba, Braz.,
53,563.............C2   30
Aracena, Sp., 7,737....D2   8
Arad, Rom., 106,460...B5   10
Aragon, Ga., 1,023.....B1   55
Aragua, state, Ven.,
313,274............A4   32
Araguari, Braz., 35,520.E5   27
Arai, Jap., 9,600......o16   18
Arāk, Iran, 58,998.....B7   23
Aranda de Duero, Sp.,
13,454.............B4   8
Arandas, Mex.,
17,110.............m12   34
Aranjuez, Sp., 27,251..B4   8
Aransas, co., Tex.,
7,006.............E4   84
Aransas Pass, Tex.,
6,956.............F4   84
Aranyaprathet, Thai.,
11,601.............C2   19
Arapahoe, Nebr., 1,084.D6   71
Arapahoe, co., Colo.,
113,426............B6   51
Arapkir, Tur., 6,900...C12   14
Araraquara, Braz.,
58,076.........C3, k7   30
Araras, Braz.,
23,898.........C3, m8   30
Ararat, Austl., 7,934...G7   25
Arauca, Col., 2,028....B3   32
Arauca, intendencia, Col.,
14,080............B3   32
Arauco, prov., Chile,
89,211.............B2   28
Araxá, Braz., 24,041...B3   30
Arbor, N.J., 2,000.....*B4   74
Arboga, Swe., 11,100..t33   11
Arbor, N.J., 2,000.....*B4   74
Arbor Terrace, Mo.,
1,225.............*C7   69
Arbroath, Scot., 19,533.B5   4
Arcachon, Fr., 14,862..E3   5
Arcade, N.Y., 1,930....C2   75
Arcadia, Calif., 41,005..F2   50
Arcadia, Fla., 5,889....E5   54
Arcadia, Ind., 1,271...D5   59
Arcadia, La., 2,547....B3   63
Arcadia, S.C., 2,458...B4   82
Arcadia, Wis., 2,084...D2   88
Arcanum, Ohio, 1,678..C3   78
Arcata, Calif., 5,235...B1   50
Archbald, Pa., 5,471...A9   81
Archbold, Ohio, 2,348..A3   78
Archdale, N.C., 1,520..B4   76
Archer, co., Tex., 6,110.C3   84
Archer City, Tex.,
1,974.............C3   84
Archidona, Sp., 7,962..D3   8
Archuleta, co., Colo.,
2,629.............D3   51
Arcila, Mor., 10,839...E2   8
Arco, Ga., 5,417......E5   55
Arco, Idaho, 1,562.....F5   57
Arcola, Ill., 2,273.....D5   58
Arcos de la Frontera,
Sp., 11,585........D3   8
Arcoverde, Braz.,
18,008............*D6   27
Arcueil, Fr., 20,224....g10   5
Ardabil (Ardebil), Iran,
65,742.............B4   15
Ardatov, Sov. Un.,
5,000.............D16   12
Ardèche, dept., Fr.,
248,516...........*E6   5
Arden, Del., 1,500.....A7   53
Arden Hills, Minn.,
3,930.............*E7   67
Ardennes, dept., Fr.,
300,247............*C6   5
Ardmore, Okla., 20,184.C4   79
Ardmore, Pa., 15,000..B11   81
Ardrossan, Scot., 9,574.C4   4
Ardsley, N.Y., 3,991...D1   75
Arecibo, P.R., 28,826.m13   8
Areia Branca, Braz.,
8,904.............D7   27
Arenac, co., Mich.,
9,860.............D7   66
Arenas de San Pedro,
Sp., 6,001.........B3   8
Arendal, Nor., 11,300..H3   11
Arequipa, Peru, 93,389.E6   31
Arequipa, dept., Peru,
307,943............E3   31
Arezzo, It., 39,000....C3   9
Arganda, Sp., 5,166...p18   8
Argenta, It., 4,600....B3   8
Argentan, Fr., 12,757..C4   5

Argenteuil, Fr.,
82,321.........C5, g10   5
Argenteuil, co., Que.,
Can., 31,830........D3   42
Argentina, country, S.A.,
20,005,691.........C3   28
Argenton [-sur-Creuse],
Fr., 6,344.........D4   5
Argolis, prov., Grc.,
90,145............*D4   14
Argos, Grc., 16,712....D4   14
Argos, Ind., 1,339.....B5   59
Argostolion, Grc.,
8,711.............C3   14
Argyll, co., Scot.,
59,345............*B4   4
Århus, Den., 119,568...I4   11
Århus, co., Den.,
210,409............I4   11
Ariail, S.C., 950......B2   82
Ariano Irpino, It.,
11,300.............D5   9
Arica, Chile, 37,000...C1   29
Ariège, dept., Fr.,
137,192...........*F4   5
Arīḥā (Jericho), Jordan,
41,593.............C3   15
Ario de Rosales, Mex.,
9,196.........D4, n13   34
Arizona, state, U.S.,
1,302,161..........48
Arjay, Ky., 500.......D6   62
Arjona, Col., 12,361...A2   32
Arjona, Sp., 8,154.....D3   8
Arkadelphia, Ark.,
8,069.............C2   49
Arkadhia, prov., Grc.,
135,042...........*D6   14
Arkansas, state, U.S.,
1,786,272..........49
Arkansas, co., Ark.,
23,355............C4   49
Arkansas City, Ark.,
783..............D4   49
Arkansas City, Kans.,
14,262.............E6   61
Arkhangelsk, Sov. Un.,
271,000............C7   13
Arkoma, Okla., 1,862..B7   79
Arkonam, India, 30,658.F6   20
Arkwright, R.I., 1,500.C10   52
Arkwright, S.C., 1,656.*B4   82
Arlanza Village, Calif.,
4,000............*F5   50
Arles, Fr., 29,362.....F6   5
Arlington, Fla.,
19,500.........B5, B6   54
Arlington, Ga., 1,462...E2   55
Arlington, Mass.,
49,953.............C2   65
Arlington, Minn.,
1,601.............F4   67
Arlington, N.Y.,
8,317.............*D7   75
Arlington, Ohio, 955...B4   78
Arlington, S. Dak., 996.F8   77
Arlington, Tex., 44,775.B5   84
Arlington, Vt., 1,111...E1   73
Arlington, Va.,
163,401.........B5, C5   85
Arlington, co., Va.,
163,401............B5   85
Arlington Heights,
Ill., 33,424.....A5, E2   58
Arlington Heights, Ohio,
1,355.............*C3   78
Arlon, Bel., 13,272....C6   5
Arma, Kans., 1,296....E9   61
Armada, Mich., 1,111..F8   66
Armagh, N. Ire., 9,982..C3   4
Armagh, co., N. Ire.,
117,580............*C3   4
Armavir, Sov. Un.,
120,000............I13   12
Armenia, Col., 57,098..C2   32
Armenia (S.S.R.), rep.,
Sov. Un., 1,893,000..A4   15
Armentières, Fr.,
25,248.............B5   5
Armero, Col., 10,258...C3   32
Armidale, Austl.,
12,877.............F9   25
Armijo, N. Mex., 2,500.E5   48
Armona, Calif., 1,302.*D4   50
Armonk, N.Y., 2,000..*D6   75
Armour, S. Dak., 875..G7   77
Armstrong, B.C., Can.,
1,288.............D8   37
Armstrong, Iowa, 958..A3   60
Armstrong, co., Pa.,
79,524.............E3   81
Armstrong, co., Tex.,
1,966.............B2   84
Arnaudville, La., 1,184.D4   63
Arnedo, Sp., 7,958....A4   8
Arnhem, Neth.,
124,800............B6   5
Arnissa, Grc., 2,915...E5   10
Arnold, Mo., 550......C7   69

Arnold, Nebr., 844.....C5   71
Arnold, Pa., 9,437.....A7   81
Arnolds Park, Iowa,
953..............A2   60
Arnouville [-lès-Gonesse],
Fr., 10,227........g10   5
Arnprior, Ont., Can.,
5,474.............B8   41
Arnsberg, Ger., 21,300..C4   6
Arnstadt, Ger., 26,400..C5   6
Aroostook, co., Maine,
106,064............B4   64
Arp, Tex., 812........C5   84
Arrah, India, 76,766...C7   20
Ar Ramādī, Iraq,
67,395.............F14   14
Ar Raqqah, Syr.,
11,411.............E12   14
Arras, Fr., 41,761.....B5   5
Arrecife, Can. Is.,
12,886.............m15   8
Arrecifes, Arg., 7,635..g6   28
Arroyo, P.R., 3,741..*m13   35
Arroyo Grande, Calif.,
3,291.............E3   50
Arsenal, Ark., 1,200...*C3   49
Arta, Grc., 16,899.....C3   14
Arta, prov., Grc.,
82,630............*C3   14
Artem, Sov. Un.,
60,000.............E16   13
Artemisa, Cuba, 17,461.D2   35
Artemovsk, Sov. Un.,
64,000.........G12, q21   12
Artena, It., 7,707.....h9   9
Artesia, Calif., 9,993.*F2   50
Artesia, N. Mex.,
12,000.............C6   48
Arthabaska, Que., Can.,
2,977.............C6   42
Arthabaska, co., Que.,
Can., 45,301.......C5   42
Arthur, Ont., Can.,
1,124.............D4   41
Arthur, Ill., 2,120.....D5   58
Arthur, co., Nebr., 680.C4   71
Artigas, Ur., 18,900...E1   30
Artigas, dept., Ur.,
44,200............*E1   30
Artois, former prov., Fr.,
1,010,000..........B5   5
Arundel Village, Md.,
1,600............*B4   53
Arusha, Tan., 10,038...I5   23
Arvada, Colo., 19,242..B5   51
Arvida, Que., Can.,
14,460.............A6   42
Arvidsjaur, Swe., 2,900.E8   11
Arvika, Swe., 15,800..H5   11
Arvin, Calif., 5,440....E4   50
Arzamas, Sov. Un.,
39,000.............D14   12
Arzúa, Sp., 1,368......A1   8
As, Czech., 9,600......C2   7
Asahigawa, Jap.,
188,309............E11   18
Asan, Guam, 543......*F6   2
Asansol, India, 103,405.D8   20
Asbest, Sov. Un.,
65,000.............D9   13
Asbestos, Que., Can.,
11,083.............D6   42
Asbury Park, N.J.,
17,366.............C4   74
Ascension, par., La.,
27,927.............D5   63
Ascension Isl., Br. dep.,
Atl. O., 210........G20   2
Aschaffenburg, Ger.,
54,100.............D4   57
Aschersleben, Ger.,
34,400.............C5   6
Ascoli Piceno, It.,
29,500.............C4   9
Asenovgrad, Bul.,
20,920.............E7   10
Ashaway, R.I., 1,298..D9   52
Ashburn, Ga., 3,291...E3   55
Ashburnham, Mass., 900
(2,758▲)..........A4   65
Ashburton, N.Z.,
11,602.............O13   26
Ashdown, Ark., 2,725..D1   49
Ashe, co., N.C., 19,768.A2   76
Asheboro, N.C., 9,449..B4   76
Asheboro South, N.C.,
1,515............*B4   76
Asheboro West, N.C.,
1,228............*B4   76
Asherton, Tex., 1,890..E3   84
Asheville, N.C., 60,182
(*105,000)........D3   76
Ashford, Ala., 1,511...D4   46
Ash Grove, Mo., 886..D4   69
Ashikaga, Jap.,
110,972.......H9, m18   18
Ashio, Jap., 16,608...H9   18
Ashkhabad, Sov. Un.,
187,000............F8   13
Ashland, Ala., 1,610...B4   46
Ashland, Ill., 1,064....D3   58

Ashland, Kans., 1,312..E4   61
Ashland, Ky., 31,283...B7   62
Ashland, Maine, 900
  (1,980*)...........B4   64
Ashland, Mass., 7,779..D1   65
Ashland, Nebr.,
  1,989.........C9, E2   71
Ashland, N.H., 1,237..D4   73
Ashland, Ohio, 17,419..B5   78
Ashland, Oreg., 9,119..E4   80
Ashland, Pa., 5,237...E9   81
Ashland, Va., 2,773...D5   85
Ashland, Wis., 10,132..B3   88
Ashland, co., Ohio,
  38,771...........B5   78
Ashland, co., Wis.,
  17,375...........B3   88
Ashland City, Tenn.,
  1,400............A4   83
Ashley, N. Dak., 1,419.D6   77
Ashley, Ohio, 907.....B5   78
Ashley, Pa., 4,258....B8   81
Ashley, co., Ark.,
  24,220...........D4   49
Ashmūn, Eg., U.A.R.,
  26,100..........*G8   14
Ash Shaṭṭ, Eg., U.A.R.,
  2,000............H9   14
Ashtabula, Ohio, 24,559.A7   78
Ashtabula, co., Ohio,
  93,067...........A7   78
Ashton, Idaho, 1,242...E7   57
Ashton, Ill., 1,024....B4   58
Ashton, R.I., 2,000...B11   52
Ashville, Ala., 973....B3   46
Ashville, Ohio, 1,639..C5   78
Ashwaubenon, Wis.,
  2,657..........*A5   88
Asia, cont.,
  1,493,600,000.......F9   16
Asir, reg., Sau. Ar., E6   23
Asmara, Eth., 120,000..E5   23
Asnières [-sur-Seine],
  Fr., 81,768........g10   5
Asotin, co., Wash.,
  12,909...........C8   86
Aspe, Sp., 10,279.....C5   8
Aspen, Colo., 1,101...B4   51
Aspermont, Tex.,
  1,286............C2   84
Aspinwall, Pa., 3,727..A6   81
As Salṭ, Jordan,
  15,478........B3, g5   15
Assam, state, India,
  11,872,772........C9   20
Assen, Neth., 29,500...A7   5
Assens, co., Den.,
  58,005..........*J3   11
Assiniboia, Sask., Can.,
  2,491............H3   39
Assinie, I.C., 1,000...G4   22
Assis, Braz., 30,207...C2   30
Assisi, It., 5,100.....C4   9
Assumption, Ill., 1,439.D4   58
Assumption, par., La.,
  17,991...........E4   63
As Suwaydā', Syr.,
  18,200..........F11   14
Asti, It., 45,000.....B2   9
Aston, Pa., 1,200....*G11   81
Astorga, Sp., 10,101...A2   8
Astoria, Ill., 1,206...C3   58
Astoria, Oreg., 11,239..A3   80
Astrakhan, Sov. Un.,
  313,000...........E7   13
Asturias, reg., Sp.,
  989,344..........A2   8
Asunción, Par., 205,605.E4   29
Aswān, Eg., U.A.R.,
  28,400...........D4   23
Asyūṭ, Eg., U.A.R.,
  106,001..........C4   23
Atacama, prov., Chile,
  114,277..........E1   29
Atami, Jap., 52,163...n18   18
Atascadero, Calif.,
  5,983............E3   50
Atascosa, co., Tex.,
  18,828...........E3   84
Atbara, Sud., 36,298...E4   23
Atbasar, Sov. Un.,
  22,300...........D9   13
Atchison, Kans.,
  12,529........A8, C8   61
Atchison, co., Kans.,
  20,898...........C8   61
Atchison, co., Mo.,
  9,213............A2   69
Atco, N.J., 2,400.....D3   74
Athabasca, Alta., Can.,
  1,487........B4, D1   38
Athena, Oreg., 950....B8   80
Athens, Ala., 9,330...A3   46
Athens, Ont., Can., 935.C9   41

Athens, Ga., 31,355....C3   55
Athens (Athinai), Grc.,
  627,564 (*1,852,709).D4   14
Athens, Ill., 1,035....D4   58
Athens, Mich., 966....F5   66
Athens, N.Y., 1,754...C7   75
Athens, Ohio, 16,470...C5   78
Athens, Pa., 4,515....C8   81
Athens, Tenn., 12,103..D9   83
Athens, Tex., 7,086...C5   84
Athens, W. Va., 1,086..D3   87
Athens, co., Ohio,
  46,998...........C5   78
Atherton, Calif., 7,717.*B5   50
Athinai, see Athens, Grc.
Athis-Mons, Fr.,
  24,004...........h10   5
Athlone, Ire., 9,624...D3   4
Athok, Bur., 4,770....E10   20
Athol, Mass., 11,637...A3   65
Atibaia, Braz., 8,957...m8   30
Atikokan, Ont., Can.,
  6,674............E8
Atkarsk, Sov. Un.,
  39,800..........F15   41
Atkins, Ark., 1,391...B3   12
Atkinson, Ill., 944...B3   49
Atkinson, Nebr., 1,324.B7   58
Atkinson, co., Ga.,
  6,188............E4   71
Atlanta, Ga., 487,455 C3   55
  (*1,011,100).....B5, C2
Atlanta, Ill., 1,568...C4   55
Atlanta, Tex., 4,076...C5   58
Atlantic, Iowa, 6,890..C2   84
Atlantic, co., N.J.,
  160,880..........E3   60
Atlantic Beach, Fla.,
  3,125............B6   74
Atlantic Beach, N.Y.,
  1,500..........*G2   54
Atlantic City, N.J., 59,544   75
  (*129,800).......E4   74
Atlantic Highlands, N.J.,
  4,119............C4   74
Atlántico, dept., Col.,
  514,490..........A2   32
Atlas, Pa., 1,574....*D8   81
Atlixco, Mex., 30,433..n14   34
Atmore, Ala., 8,173...D2   46
Atoka, Okla., 2,877...C5   79
Atoka, co., Okla.,
  10,352...........C5   79
Atotonilco el Alto, Mex.,
  14,190...........m12   34
Atrisco, N. Mex.,
  3,000..........*B5   48
Atsugi, Jap., 20,800...n18   18
Aṭ Ṭafīlah, Jordan,
  8,588............D3   15
Aṭ Ṭā'if, Sau. Ar.,
  25,000...........E3   15
Attala, co., Miss.,
  21,335...........B4   68
Attalla, Ala., 8,257...A3   46
At Tayyibah, Jordan,
  2,000............C3   15
Attica, Ind., 4,341...D3   59
Attica, N.Y., 2,758...C2   75
Attica, Ohio, 965....A5   78
Attica, reg., Grc....*C4   14
Attiki, prov., Grc.,
  2,057,974........*C4   14
Attleboro, Mass.,
  27,118...........C5   65
Åtvidaberg, Swe.,
  7,800............H6   11
Atwater, Calif., 7,318..D3   50
Atwater, Minn., 899...E4   68
Atwood, Ill., 1,258...D5   58
Atwood, Kans., 1,906..C2   61
Atwood Heights, Ill.,
  1,000..........*F3   58
Atzcapotzalco, Mex.,
  49,617.........h9, n14   34
Aubagne, Fr., 12,612..F3   5
Aube, dept., Fr.,
  255,099.........*C6   5
Aubenas, Fr., 5,754...E6   5
Aubervilliers, Fr.,
  70,632...........g10   5
Aubin, Fr., 7,821....E5   5
Auburn, Ala., 16,261..C4   46
Auburn, Calif., 5,586..C3   55
Auburn, Ill., 2,209...D4   58
Auburn, Ind., 6,350...B7   59
Auburn, Kans., 200...D8   61
Auburn, Ky., 1,013...D3   62
Auburn, Maine,
  24,449........D2, D5   64
Auburn, Mass., 14,047.B4   65
Auburn, Mich., 1,497..E6   66
Auburn, Nebr., 3,229.D10   71

Auburn, N.Y., 35,249..C4   75
Auburn, Pa., 936......E9   81
Auburn, Wash.,
  11,933........B3, D2   86
Auburndale, Fla., 5,595.D5   54
Auburn Heights, Mich.,
  2,500............F7   66
Aubusson, Fr., 5,669...E5   5
Auch, Fr., 18,918.....F4   5
Auckland, N.Z., 143,583
  (*448,365)........L15   26
Aude, dept., Fr.,
  269,782.........*F5   5
Audincourt, Fr., 12,433.D7   5
Audrain, co., Mo.,
  26,079...........B6   69
Audubon, Iowa, 2,928..C3   60
Audubon, N.J., 10,440.D2   74
Audubon, co., Iowa,
  10,919...........C3   60
Audubon Park, Ky.,
  1,867..........*A4   62
Audubon Park, N.J.,
  1,713..........*C3   74
Aue, Ger., 31,200....C6   6
Auglaize, co., Ohio,
  36,147...........B3   78
Augsburg, Ger.,
  208,700..........D5   6
Augusta, Ga., 70,626
  (*160,600)........C5   55
Augusta, Ill., 1,568...C3   58
Augusta, It., 27,950...F5   9
Augusta, Kans.,
  6,434........B6, E7   61
Augusta, Ky., 1,458...B6   62
Augusta, Maine, 21,680.D3   64
Augusta, Mich., 972...F5   66
Augusta, Wis., 1,338..D2   88
Augusta, co., Va.,
  37,363...........C3   85
Augustow, Pol., 12,700.B7   7
Aulander, N.C., 1,083..A6   76
Aulnay-sous-Bois, Fr.,
  47,507...........g11   5
Aurangabad, India,
  87,579...........F6   20
Auray, Fr., 8,118.....D2   5
Aurelia, Iowa, 904....B2   60
Aurich, Ger., 13,000..B3   6
Aurillac, Fr., 24,563...E5   5
Aurora, Ont., Can.,
  8,791............D5   42
Aurora, Colo., 48,548..B6   51
Aurora, Ill., 63,715....F1   58
Aurora, Ind., 4,756...F8   59
Aurora, Minn., 2,799...C6   67
Aurora, Mo., 4,683....E4   69
Aurora, Nebr., 2,576..D7   71
Aurora, Ohio, 4,049...A6   78
Aurora, co., S. Dak.,
  4,749............G7   77
Au Sable Forks, N.Y.,
  2,026............B3   75
Aust-Agder, co., Nor.,
  76,900..........*H3   12
Austell, Ga., 1,867...B4   55
Austin, Ind., 3,838...G6   59
Austin, Minn., 27,908..C6   67
Austin, Tex., 186,545
  (*210,000).......D4   84
Austin, co., Tex.,
  13,777...........E4   84
Austin Lake, Mich.,
  3,520..........*F5   66
Austintown, Ohio,
  5,000..........*A7   78
Australia, country,
  Oceania, 10,508,189....   25
Australian Capital
  Territory, Austl.,
  58,828..........*G8   25
Austria, country, Eur.,
  7,073,807........E6   6
Autauga, co., Ala.,
  18,739...........C3   46
Autlán de Navarro, Mex.,
  17,069.......D4, n11   34
Autun, Fr., 15,305....D6   5
Auvergne, former prov.,
  Fr., 838,000......E5   5
Auxerre, Fr., 31,178...D5   5
Auxier, Ky., 800.....C7   62
Ava, Mo., 1,581......E5   69
Avalon, Calif., 1,536..F4   50
Avalon, Pa., 6,859...A5   81
Avanos, Tur., 5,700...C10   14
Avaré, Braz., 20,334..C3   34
Aveiro, Port., 13,423..B1   8
Avella, Pa., 1,310....F1   81
Avellaneda, Arg.,
  329,626........A5, g7   28
Avellino, It., 33,500...D5   9

Avenal, Calif., 3,147...E3   50
Avenel, N.J., 9,000....E4   74
Aversa, It., 40,336....D5   9
Avery, co., N.C.,
  12,009...........A2   76
Avesta, Swe., 10,900..G7   11
Aveyron, dept., Fr.,
  290,442.........*E5   5
Avezzano, It., 25,000..C4   9
Avigliano, It., 4,554..D5   9
Avignon, Fr., 72,717..F6   5
Ávila, Sp., 26,807....B3   8
Ávila, prov., Sp.,
  238,372.........*B3   8
Avilés, Sp., 48,503....A3   8
Avilla, Ind., 919.....B7   59
Avis, Pa., 1,262......D7   81
Avoca, Ala., 400.....A2   46
Avoca, Iowa, 1,540...C2   60
Avoca, N.Y., 1,086...C3   75
Avoca, Pa., 3,562....B9   81
Avola, It., 27,453....F5   9
Avon, Conn., 5,273...B5   52
Avon, Ill., 996......C3   58
Avon, Mass., 4,301...E3   65
Avon, N.Y., 2,772...C3   75
Avon, Ohio, 6,002...A5   78
Avon, Pa., 1,212....*F9   81
Avon by the Sea, N.J.,
  1,707............C4   74
Avondale, Ariz.,
  6,151............D1   48
Avondale, Pa., 1,016..G10   81
Avondale Estates, Ga.,
  1,646............B5   55
Avon Lake, Ohio,
  9,403............A5   78
Avonmore, Pa., 1,351..B3   81
Avon Park, Fla., 6,073..E5   54
Avoyelles, par., La.,
  37,606...........C3   63
Avranches, Fr., 8,854..C3   5
Axim, Ghana, 4,647...H4   22
Axis, Ala., 300......E1   46
Ay, Fr., 6,806.......C5   6
Ayabe, Jap., 21,500...n14   18
Ayacucho, Arg., 9,220..B5   28
Ayacucho, Peru,
  21,531...........D3   31
Ayacucho, dept., Peru,
  469,396..........D3   31
Ayaguz, Sov. Un.,
  52,400...........E11   13
Ayamonte, Sp., 8,908..D2   8
Ayan, Sov. Un.,
  9,300...........D16   13
Ayaviri, Peru, 6,586...D3   31
Ayden, N.C., 3,108...B6   76
Aydin, Tur., 35,700...D6   14
Ayer, Mass., 14,927.A4, C1   65
Ayios Dhimitrios, Grc.,
  21,365..........*C4   14
Aylesbury, Eng.,
  27,891...........E6   4
Aylmer East, Que.,
  Can., 6,286.......D2   42
Aylmer West, Ont.,
  Can., 4,201.......E4   41
Ayora, Sp., 6,634....C5   8
Ayr, Scot., 45,297....C4   4
Ayr, co., Scot.,
  342,855.........*C4   4
Aytos, Bul., 9,972....D8   11
Ayutthaya, Thai.,
  33,187...........C2   19
Ayvalik, Tur., 16,100..C6   14
Azalea Park, Fla.,
  6,500..........*D5   54
Azemmour, Mor.,
  12,449...........B3   22
Azerbaidzhan (S.S.R.),
  rep., Sov. Un.,
  3,973,000.......*E7   16
Azle, Tex., 2,969....B5   84
Azogues, Ec., 6,579...B2   31
Azores Is., reg.,
  Port., 327,500.....C3   21
Azov, Sov. Un.,
  10,000..........H12   13
Azrou, Mor., 14,143...B3   22
Aztec, N. Mex., 4,137..A5   48
Azua, Dom. Rep.,
  12,350...........F8   35
Azuaga, Sp., 17,518...C3   8
Azuay, prov., Ec.,
  277,772..........B2   31
Azul, Arg., 28,609....B5   28
Azusa, Calif., 20,497..F3   50
Aẕ Ẕahrān (Dhahran),
  Sau. Ar., 75,000...D5   15
Az Zaqāzīq, Eg., U.A.R.,
  81,813...........B4   23

B

Baalbek, Leb., 9,623....f6   15
Babaeski, Tur., 11,700..E8   10
Babahoyo, Ec., 9,045..B2   31

Babayevo, Sov. Un.,
  10,000..........B11   12
Babbit, Nev., 2,159...*B2   72

Babbitt, Minn., 2,587..C7   67
Bābol, Iran, 36,194....A8   23
Babyak, Bul., 6,211....E6   10

Babylon, N.Y., 11,062..E3   75
Baca, co., Colo., 6,310..D8   51
Bacău, Rom., 54,138...B8   10

Baccarat, Fr., 6,067....C7   5
Backa Palanka, Yugo.,
  16,487..............C4   10
Bac Kan, Viet.,
  10,000............*G5   17
Backa Topola, Yugo.,
  15,057.............C4   10
Backbay, Va., 500.....E6   85
Bac Lieu, Viet.,
  10,000............*D3   19
Bacliff, Tex., 1,707.....E5   84
Bac Ninh, Viet.,
  25,000..............G6   17
Bacolod, Phil., 52,000..C6   19
Bacon, co., Ga., 8,359..E4   55
Bacsalmas, Hung.,
  7,344...............B4   10
Bács-Kiskun, co., Hung.,
  587,028............*B4   10
Badajoz, Sp., 80,000...C2   8
Badajoz, prov., Sp.,
  834,340............*C2   8
Badalona, Sp., 92,257..B7   8
Bad Axe, Mich., 2,998..E7   66
Bad Doberan, Ger.,
  12,600..............A5   6
Baden, Aus., 22,484...D8   6
Baden, Ont., Can.,
  977................D4   41
Baden, Pa., 6,109..A5, E1   81
Baden, Switz., 13,949..E4   6
Baden, reg., Ger.......D4   6
Baden-Baden, Ger.,
  40,000..............D4   6
Baden-Württemberg, state,
  Ger., 7,759,200.....*D4   6
Bad Freienwalde, Ger.,
  12,200..............B7   6
Badger, Newf., Can.,
  1,036..............D3   44
Bad Hersfeld, Ger.,
  23,000..............C4   6
Badin, N.C., 1,905.....B3   76
Bad Ischl, Aus., 12,703.E6   6
Bad Kissingen, Ger.,
  12,900..............C5   6
Bad Kreuznach, Ger.,
  35,100..............D3   6
Bad Oldesloe, Ger.,
  16,000..............B5   6
Bad Reichenhall, Ger.,
  13,100..............E6   6
Bad Tölz, Ger., 11,700..E5   6
Badulla, Cey., 17,323..G7   20
Baena, Sp., 17,761.....D3   8
Baeza, Sp., 15,176.....D4   8
Baffin, isl., N.W. Ter.,
  Can................C19   36
Bafra, Tur., 20,800...B10   14
Bagé, Braz., 47,930....E2   30
Bagdad, Ariz., 1,462...B2   48
Baghdad, Iraq, 355,958.C3   15
Bagheria, It., 34,201...E4   9
Baghlan, Afg., 24,410..A4   20
Bagley, Minn., 1,385...C3   67
Bagnara [Calabra], It.,
  10,000..............E5   9
Bagnères-de-Bigorre, Fr.,
  8,996...............F4   5
Bagnolet, Fr., 31,576..g10   5
Bagnols [-sur-Cèze], Fr.,
  12,905..............E6   5
Bagot, co., Que., Can.,
  21,390..............D5   42
Bagotville, Que., Can.,
  5,629...............A7   42
Bahama Is., Br. dep.,
  N.A., 131,000......C6   35
Bahawalpur, Pak.,
  84,000..............C5   20
Bahia, see Salvador, Braz.
Bahia, state, Braz.,
  5,990,605...........A4   30
Bahía Blanca, Arg.,
  136,000.............B4   28
Bahía de Caráquez, Ec.,
  7,993...............B1   31
Bahrain, country, Asia,
  109,650.............C8   23
Baia-Mare, Rom.,
  35,920..............B6   10
Baie Comeau, Que.,
  Can., 7,956........A2   42
Baie St. Paul, Que.,
  Can., 4,674........B7   42
Baile Átha Cliath, see
  Dublin, Ire.
Bailén, Sp., 11,245.....C4   8
Băilești, Rom., 15,932..C6   10
Bailey, co., Tex., 9,090.B1   84
Bainbridge, Ga., 12,714.F2   55
Bainbridge, N.Y.,
  1,712...............C5   75
Bainbridge, Ohio, 1,001.C4   78
Baird, Tex., 1,633.....C3   84
Baixo Alentejo, prov.,
  Port., 380,236......*C2   8
Baja, Hung., 30,355....B4   10
Baja California, state,
  Mex., 520,913.......A1   34

Baja California Sur., ter.,
  Mex., 83,433........C2   34
Baker, La., 4,823.....*D4   63
Baker, Mont., 2,365..D12   70
Baker, Oreg., 9,986....C9   80
Baker, co., Fla., 7,363..B4   54
Baker, co., Ga., 4,543..F2   55
Baker, co., Oreg.,
  17,295..............C9   80
Bakersfield, Calif., 56,848
  (*158,000).........E4   50
Bakerton, see Elmora, Pa.
Baku, Sov. Un.,
  671,000.............E7   13
Bala-Cynwyd, Pa.,
  8,000.............*B11   81
Balaguer, Sp., 8,342...B6   8
Balakleya, Sov. Un.,
  5,000..............G11   12
Balanda, Sov. Un.,
  10,000.............F15   12
Balanga, Phil., 5,061...C6   19
Balashov, Sov. Un.,
  67,000.............F14   12
Balasore, India,
  33,931.............D8   20
Balassagyarmat, Hung.,
  12,457.............A4   10
Balboa, C.Z., 3,139...*B2   32
Balcarce, Arg., 15,210..B5   28
Balch Springs, Tex.,
  6,821.............*A6   84
Balcones Heights, Tex.,
  950...............*E3   84
Bald Eagle, Minn.,
  1,200..............E7   67
Bald Knob, Ark.,
  2,096..............B4   49
Baldwin, Fla., 1,272...B5   54
Baldwin, La., 1,548....E4   63
Baldwin, N.Y., 30,204..G2   52
Baldwin, Pa., 24,489..*F1   81
Baldwin, Wis., 1,184...C1   88
Baldwin, co., Ala.,
  49,088..............E2   46
Baldwin, co., Ga.,
  34,064..............C3   9
Baldwin City, Kans.,
  1,877..............D8   5
Baldwin Park, Calif.,
  33,951.............*F3   50
Baldwinsville, N.Y.,
  5,985..............B4   75
Baldwinville, Mass.,
  1,631..............A3   65
Baldwyn, Miss., 2,023..A5   68
Baleares (Balearic Islands),
  prov., Sp., 443,327..*C7   8
Balearic, is., Sp.......C6   8
Baler, Phil., 2,769.....B6   19
Balfour, N.C., 1,106...D3   76
Bali, isl., Indon.......G5   19
Balikesir, Tur., 61,000..C6   14
Balikpapan, Indon.,
  88,534.............F5   19
Balkh, Afg., 12,466....A4   20
Balkhash, Sov. Un.,
  61,000.............E10   13
Balki, Sov. Un.,
  25,000.............H10   12
Ballarat, Austl., 41,028.G7   25
Ballard, co., Ky., 8,291.A2   62
Ballard Vale, Mass.,
  1,000............A5, C2   65
Ballina, Ire., 6,027....C2   4
Ballinasloe, Ire., 5,711..D2   4
Ballinger, Tex., 5,043..D3   84
Ballston Spa, N.Y.,
  4,991..............B7   75
Ballville, Ohio, 1,424..*A4   78
Ballwin, Mo., 5,710....B7   69
Bally, Penn., 1,033....F10   81
Ballymena, N. Ire.,
  14,740.............C3   4
Balm, Fla., 250.......E4   54
Balmazujvaros, Hung.,
  16,312.............B5   10
Balmville, N.Y.,
  1,538.............*D6   75
Balotra, India, 12,110..C5   20
Balș, Rom., 6,956....C7   10
Balta Sov.Un., 47,400.H7   12
Baltic, Conn., 1,366...C8   52
Baltimore, Ohio, 2,116..C5   78
Baltimore, co., Md.,
  492,428.............B4   53
Baltimore (Independent
  City), Md., 939,024
  (*1,636,500).....B4, C2   53
Baluchistan, reg., Pak..C4   20
Bamako, Mali, 68,200..F3   22
Bamberg, Ger., 74,100.D5   6
Bamber, S.C., 3,081....E5   82
Bamberg, co., S.C.,
  16,274.............E5   82
Banaras, India, 471,258
  (*489,864).........C7   20
Banat, prov., Rom.,
  948,596............*C5   10

Banat, reg., Rom.,
  Yugo..............C5   10
Banbridge, N. Ire.,
  6,115..............C3   4
Banbury, Eng., 20,996.D6   4
Banco, see El Banco, Col.
Bancroft, Ont., Can.,
  1,669..............B7   41
Bancroft, Iowa, 1,000..A3   60
Banda, India, 37,744...C7   20
Bandar 'Abbās, Iran,
  14,278.............C2   20
Bande, Sp., 6,275.....A2   8
Bandera, Tex., 950....E3   84
Bandera, co., Tex.,
  3,892..............E3   84
Bandirma,Tur., 28,900.B6   14
Bandjermasin, Indon.,
  212,683............F4   19
Bandon, Oreg., 1,653..D2   80
Bandung, Indon.,
  966,359............G3   19
Banes, Cuba, 20,257...E6   35
Banff, Alta., Can.,
  3,429..............D3   38
Banff, co., Scot.,
  46,400............*B5   4
Bangalore, India,
  905,134............F6   20
Banggai, Indon........F6   19
Bangka, isl., Indon....F3   19
Bangkok (Krung Thep),
  Thai., 1,394,513....C2   19
Bangor, Maine, 38,912.D4   64
Bangor, Mich., 2,109...F4   66
Bangor, N. Ire., 23,865.C4   4
Bangor, Pa., 5,766....E11   81
Bangor, Wales, 13,977.D4   4
Bangor, Wis., 928.....E3   88
Bangs, Tex., 967......D3   84
Bangued, Phil., 5,663..B6   19
Bangui, Cen. Afr. Rep.,
  80,000.............H1   23
Banhã, Eg., U.A.R.,
  42,600.............G8   14
Baní, Dom. Rep.,
  14,472.............F8   35
Bani Suwayf, Eg.,
  U.A.R., 65,600......C4   23
Banja Luka, Yugo.,
  50,463.............C3   10
Banjuwangi, Indon.,
  25,185.............G4   19
Banks, co., Ga., 6,497..B3   55
Bankura, India, 62,833.D8   20
Banner, co., Nebr.,
  1,269..............C2   71
Banner Hill, Tenn.,
  1,100............*C11   83
Bannertown, N.C.,
  1,096.............*A3   76
Banning, Calif., 10,250.F5   55
Bannock, co., Idaho,
  49,342.............G6   57
Bannu, Pak., 20,509...B5   20
Bañolas, Sp., 8,075...A7   8
Banska Bystrica, Czech.,
  22,600.............D5   7
Banska Stiavnica, Czech.,
  9,500..............D5   7
Bansko, Bul., 6,161...E6   10
Bantam, Conn., 833....C4   52
Bar, Sov. Un., 22,100..G6   12
Barabinsk, Sov. Un.,
  38,900............D10   13
Baraboo, Wis., 7,660...E4   88
Baracaldo, Sp., 77,802.A4   8
Baracoa, Cuba, 11,459..E6   35
Baradero, Arg., 10,194..f7   28
Baraga, Mich., 991....B2   66
Baraga, co., Mich.,
  7,151..............B2   66
Barahona, Dom. Rep.,
  20,398.............F8   35
Baramula, India,
  19,854.............B5   20
Baranovichi, Sov. Un.,
  63,000.............E5   12
Baranya, co., Hung.,
  285,316............*B4   10
Barbacena, Braz.,
  41,931............C4, g6   30
Barbados, Br. dep.,
  N.A., 232,085......p17   35
Barbastro, Sp., 10,227..A6   8
Barbate, Sp., 10,720...D3   8
Barber, co., Kans.,
  8,713..............E5   61
Barberton, Ohio,
  33,805.............A6   78
Barberton, S. Afr.,
  11,016.............F6   24
Barbour, co., Ala.,
  24,700.............D4   46
Barbour, co., W. Va.,
  15,474.............B4   87
Barboursville, W. Va.,
  2,331..............C2   87
Barbourville, Ky.,
  3,211..............D6   62

Barbuda, isl.,
  Barbados..........n16   35
Barcarrota, Sp., 7,898..C2   8
Barcellona [Pozzo di
  Gotto], It., 20,500...E5   9
Barcelona, Sp., 1,557,863
  (*2,020,000).......B7   8
Barcelona, Ven.,
  40,773.............A5   32
Barcelona, prov., Sp.,
  2,877,966..........*B7   8
Barcelos, Port., 7,875..B1   8
Bardejov, Czech.,
  6,572..............D6   7
Bardstown, Ky., 4,798..C4   62
Bardwell, Ky., 1,067...A2   62
Bareilly, India, 254,409.C6   20
Baresville, Pa., 1,700..*G8   81
Barguzin, Sov. Un.,
  5,600.............D13   13
Bar Harbor, Maine,
  2,444..............D4   64
Bari, It., 312,023......D6   9
Barinas, state, Ven.,
  139,271............B3   32
Baripada, India,
  20,301.............D8   20
Barirí, Braz., 8,403.C3, m7   30
Barking, Eng., 72,282..k13   4
Barköl (Chensi), China,
  10,000.............C3   17
Barlad, Rom., 32,043..B8   10
Bar-le-Duc, Fr., 18,346.C6   5
Barletta, It., 68,035...D6   9
Barling, Ark., 1,518...B1   49
Barmer, India, 27,600..C5   20
Barnaul, Sov. Un.,
  338,000...........D11   13
Barnes, Oreg., 5,076..*D3   80
Barnes, co., N. Dak.,
  16,719.............C7   77
Barnesboro, Pa., 3,035..E4   81
Barnesville, Ga., 4,919..C2   55
Barnesville, Minn.,
  1,632..............D2   67
Barnesville, Ohio,
  4,425..............C6   78
Barnhill, Ohio, 350....B6   78
Barnsdall, Okla., 1,663.A5   79
Barnstable, co., Mass.,
  70,286.............C7   65
Barnstaple, Eng.,
  15,907.............E4   4
Barnwell, S.C., 4,568..E5   82
Barnwell, co., S.C.,
  17,659.............E5   82
Baroda, India, 295,144.D5   20
Barquisimeto, Ven.,
  196,557............A4   32
Barra, Braz., 7,237...*E5   27
Barraba, Austl., 1,469..E8   26
Barrackville, W. Va.,
  950.............A7, B4   87
Barra do Piraí, Braz.,
  29,398...........C4, h6   30
Barra Mansa, Braz.,
  47,398...........C4, h6   30
Barrancabermeja, Col.,
  25,046.............B3   32
Barranquilla, Col.,
  356,920............A3   32
Barranquitas, P.R.,
  4,684............*m13   35
Barre, Mass., 1,065...B3   65
Barre, Vt., 10,387....C3   73
Barreiras, Braz., 7,175.*E5   27
Barreiro, Port.,
  22,190...........C1, f9   8
Barreiros, Braz.,
  10,402.............D7   27
Barren, co., Ky.,
  28,303.............D4   62
Barretos, Braz., 39,950.C3   30
Barrett, Tex., 1,200..*F5   84
Barrhead, Alta., Can.,
  2,286..............B7   38
Barrie, Ont., Can.,
  21,169.............C5   41
Barrigada, Guam,
  1,729.............*F6   2
Barrington, Ill.,
  5,434...........A5, E2   58
Barrington, N.J.,
  7,943.............*D2   74
Barrington, R.I.,
  9,800.............C11   52
Barrington Hills, Ill.,
  1,726...........A5, E2   58
Barron, Wis., 2,338....C2   88
Barron, co., Wis.,
  34,270.............C2   88
Barrow, Alsk., 1,314...A8   47
Barrow, co., Ga.,
  14,485.............B3   55
Barrow-in-Furness, Eng.,
  64,824.............C5   4
Barruelo de Santullán, Sp.,
  7,770..............A3   8
Barry, Ill., 1,422.....D2   58
Barry, co., Mich.,
  31,738.............F5   66

Barry, co., Mo., 18,921..E4 69
Barrys Bay, Ont., Can.,
  1,366..............B7 41
Barsi, India, 50,389....E6 20
Barstow, Calif., 11,644.E5 50
Barth, Fla., 200......G2 54
Barth, Ger., 12,200....A6 6
Bartholomew, co., Ind.,
  48,198............F6 59
Bartin, Tur., 11,700....B9 14
Bartlesville, Okla.,
  27,893............A6 79
Bartlett, Ill., 1,540....E2 58
Bartlett, Tex., 1,540...D4 84
Barton, Ala., 300.....A2 46
Barton, Ohio, 975....B7 78
Barton, Vt., 1,169....B3 73
Barton, Wis., 1,569...E5 88
Barton, co., Kans.,
  32,368............D5 61
Barton, co., Mo.,
  11,113............D3 69
Bartonville, Ill., 7,253..C4 58
Bartonwoods, Ga.,
  3,000...........*C2 55
Bartow, Fla., 12,849..E5 54
Bartow, co., Ga.,
  28,267............B2 55
Barvas, Scot.........A3 4
Barvenkovo, Sov. Un.,
  10,000............G11 12
Barwick, Ky., 300.....C6 62
Basel, Switz., 206,746..E3 6
Basel-Land, sub canton,
  Switz., 148,282.....*E3 6
Basel-Stadt, sub canton,
  Switz., 225,588.....*E3 6
Basile, La., 1,932......D3 63
Basilicata, pol. dist., It.,
  644,297...........*D5 9
Basin, Wyo., 1,319....A4 89
Basingstoke, Eng.,
  25,940............E6 4
Baskin, Fla., 500.....E1 54
Basking Ridge, N.J.,
  2,438.............B3 74
Basque Provinces, reg.,
  Sp., 1,371,654......A4 8
Basra, Iraq, 164,623...B7 23
Bas-Rhin, dept., Fr ,
  770,150...........*C7 5
Bassac, Laos, 5,000....C3 19
Bassano del Grappa, It.,
  23,800............B3 9
Bassein, Bur., 77,905...E9 20
Basses-Alpes, dept., Fr.,
  91,843............*E7 5
Basses-Pyrénées, dept.,
  Fr., 466,038.......*F3 5
Basse-Terre, Guad.,
  9,124.............o16 35
Basseterre, St. Kitts-
  Nevis-Anguilla,
  15,742............n15 35
Bassett, Calif., 2,000..*F3 50
Bassett, Nebr., 1,023...B6 71
Bassett, Va., 3,148.....E3 85
Bastia, Fr., 50,117.....C2 9
Bastogne, Bel., 5,927..B6 5
Bastrop, La., 15,193...B4 63
Bastrop, co., Tex.,
  16,925............D4 84
Basutoland (Lesotho), Br.
  dep., Afr., 685,000....F5 24
Bata, Equat. Gui.,
  4,000.............H6 22
Bataan, prov., Phil.,
  145,900...........*C6 19
Batala, India, 51,300...B6 20
Batanes, prov., Phil.,
  10,300............*A6 19
Batangas, Phil.,
  15,000............p13 19
Batangas, prov., Phil.,
  682,900...........*C6 19
Bataszek, Hung., 6,235.B4 10
Batatais, Braz., 15,266.C3 30
Batavia, Ill., 7,496.B5, F1 58
Batavia, see Djakarta,
  Indon.
Batavia, N.Y., 18,210..C2 75
Batavia, Ohio, 1,729...C3 78
Bataysk, Sov. Un.,
  70,000............H12 12
Bates, co., Mo., 15,905.C3 69
Batesburg, S.C., 3,806..D4 82
Batesville, Ark., 6,207..B4 49
Batesville, Ind., 3,349..F7 59
Batesville, Miss., 3,284.A4 68
Bath, Eng., 80,856....E5 4
Bath, Maine,
  10,717.........E3, E6 64
Bath, N.Y., 6,166.....C3 75
Bath, Pa., 1,736......E11 81
Bath, S.C., 1,419.....D4 82
Bath, co., Ky., 9,114...B6 62
Bath, co., Va., 5,335...C3 85
Bathurst, Austl.,
  16,939............F8 25
Bathurst, N.B., Can.,
  5,494.............B4 43

Bathurst, Gam., 21,022.F1 22
Batna, Alg., 14,732....A6 22
Baton Rouge, La., 152,419
  (*248,700)......B5, D4 63
Batouri, Cam.........H7 22
Batroun, Leb., 5,000....f5 15
Battambang, Camb.,
  16,000............C2 19
Batticaloa, Cey.,
  17,662............G7 20
Battle Creek, Mich.,
  48,774 (*107,300)....F3 66
Battleford, Sask., Can.,
  1,627.............E1 39
Battonya, Hung.,
  9,216.............B5 10
Batumi, Sov. Un.,
  87,000............E7 13
Batu Pahat, Mala.,
  39,294...........*E2 19
Baturité, Braz., 7,198..D7 27
Bauchi, Nig., 1,344....F6 22
Baudette, Minn., 1,597.B4 67
Baurú, Braz., 85,237...C3 30
Bautzen, Ger., 41,900..C7 6
Bauxite, Ark., 950.C3, E5 49
Bavaria, reg., Ger.....D5 6
Bawcomville, La.,
  1,500...........*B3 63
Baxley, Ga., 4,268....E4 55
Baxter, Minn., 1,037...D4 67
Baxter, co., Ark., 9,943.A3 49
Baxter Estates, N.Y.,
  932..............*D2 75
Baxter Springs, Kans.,
  4,498.............E9 61
Bay, co., Fla., 67,131..G3 54
Bay, co., Mich.,
  107,042...........E6 66
Baya Dzur-Gunen,
  Mong., 5,000.......B5 17
Bayamo, Cuba, 20,178.E5 35
Bayamón, P.R.,
  15,109............m13 35
Bayanovka, Sov. Un...C8 13
Bayard, Nebr., 1,519...C2 71
Bayard, N. Mex., 2,327.C4 48
Baybay, Phil., 9,500...*C6 19
Bayburt, Tur., 12,000.B13 14
Bay City, Mich.,
  53,604............E7 66
Bay City, Oreg., 996...B3 80
Bay City, Tex.,
  11,656.........E5, G4 84
Bay de Verde, Newf.,
  Can., 906.........D5 44
Bayern, state, Ger.,
  9,513,900........*D5 6
Bayeux, Fr., 9,678.....C3 5
Bayfield, Wis., 969....B3 88
Bayfield, co., Wis.,
  11,910............B2 88
Bay Harbor Island, Fla.,
  3,249............*F3 54
Bayindir, Tur., 11,300..C6 11
Baylor, co., Tex., 5,893.C3 84
Bay Minette, Ala.,
  5,197.............E2 46
Bayombong, Phil.,
  6,929............*B6 19
Bayonne, Fr., 36,941...F3 5
Bayonne, N.J.,
  74,215.........B4, E5 74
Bayou Cane, La.,
  3,173............*E5 63
Bayou La Batre, Ala.,
  2,572.............E1 46
Bay Park, N.Y.,
  1,500............*G2 75
Bayport, Minn.,
  3,205.........E6, E8 67
Bayport, N.Y., 3,000...D3 75
Bayreuth, Ger., 61,800.D5 6
Bay Roberts, Newf., Can.,
  1,306.............E5 44
Bay St. Louis, Miss.,
  5,073.........E2, E4 68
Bayshore, Calif.,
  1,500............*D2 50
Bay Shore, N.Y.,
  20,000.........E3, E7 75
Bayshore Gardens, Fla.,
  2,297............*E4 54
Bayside, Va., 6,000....B7 85
Bayside, Wis., 3,181...E6 88
Bay Springs, Miss.,
  1,544.............D4 68
Bayt Lahm (Bethlehem),
  Jordan, 19,155...C3, h5 15
Baytown, Tex.,
  28,159.........E5, F5 84
Bayview, Ala., 1,081...E4 46
Bayview, Calif., 1,800.*B1 50
Bayview, Mass. (part of
  Gloucester).........A6 65
Bay Village, Ohio,
  14,489............B1 78
Bayville, N.Y., 3,962...F2 52
Baza, Sp., 14,880.....D4 8
Baztán, Sp., 1,534....A5 8

Beach (Dunes Park), Ill.,
  1,800............*A6 58
Beach, N. Dak., 1,460..D2 77
Beach City, Ohio,
  1,151.............B6 78
Beach Haven, N.J.,
  1,041.............D4 74
Beachwood, N.J.,
  2,765.............D4 74
Beachwood, Ohio,
  6,089............*A6 78
Beacon, N.Y., 13,922..D7 75
Beacon Falls, Conn.,
  2,886.............D4 52
Beacon Hill, Wash.,
  1,019............*C3 86
Beaconsfield, Que., Can.,
  10,064............D8 42
Beadle, co., S. Dak.,
  21,682............F7 77
Beadling, Pa., 1,500...*F1 81
Bealwood, Ga. (part of
  Columbus).........D2 55
Beamsville, Ont., Can.,
  2,198.............D5 41
Bearden, Ark., 1,268...D3 49
Bearden, Tenn.,
  3,600.........D9, E11 83
Beardstown, Ill., 6,294.C3 58
Bear Lake, co., Idaho,
  7,148.............G7 57
Béarn, former prov., Fr.,
  275,000...........F3 5
Bear River, N.S., Can.,
  830..............E4 43
Bear Town (McComb
  South), Miss., 1,865..D3 68
Beas de Segura, Sp.,
  9,251.............C4 8
Beatrice, Nebr., 12,132.D9 71
Beattyville, Ky., 1,048.C6 62
Beaucaire, Fr., 8,243...F6 5
Beauce, co., Que., Can.,
  62,264............C7 42
Beauceville Est, Que.,
  Can., 1,920........*C7 42
Beauceville Ouest, Que.,
  Can., 1,645........*C7 42
Beaufort, N.C., 2,922...C7 76
Beaufort, S.C., 6,298...G6 82
Beaufort, co., N.C.,
  36,014............B6 76
Beaufort, co., S.C.,
  44,187............G6 82
Beaufort West, S. Afr.,
  16,323............G4 24
Beauharnois, Que., Can.,
  8,704.........D4, D8 42
Beauharnois, co., Que.,
  Can., 49,667.......D3 42
Beaumont, Calif., 4,432.F4 50
Beaumont, Tex., 119,175
  (*266,600).........D5 84
Beaumont Place, Tex.,
  1,500............*E5 84
Beaune, Fr., 15,367....D6 6
Beauport, Que., Can.,
  9,192.............C9 42
Beauport Est, Que.,
  Can., 1,417........*C9 42
Beaupre, Que., Can.,
  2,587.............B7 42
Beauregard, par., La.,
  19,191............D2 63
Beaurepaire, Que., Can.,
  2,400.............D8 42
Beausejour, Man., Can.,
  1,770.............D3 40
Beauvais, Fr., 33,995...C5 5
Beaver, Okla.,
  2,087.........A1, D4 79
Beaver, Pa., 6,160.....E1 81
Beaver, Utah, 1,548...B5 72
Beaver (Glen Hedrick),
  W. Va., 1,230..D3, D7 87
Beaver, co., Okla.,
  6,965.............A1 79
Beaver, co., Pa.,
  206,948...........E1 81
Beaver, co., Utah,
  4,331.............B5 72
Beaver City, Nebr.,
  818..............D6 71
Beaverdale, Pa., 1,000..F4 81
Beaver Dam, Ky.,
  1,648.............C3 62
Beaver Dam, Wis.,
  13,118............E5 88
Beaver Falls, Pa.,
  16,240............E1 81
Beaverhead, co., Mont.,
  7,194.............E3 70
Beaver Meadows, Pa.,
  1,392............E10 81
Beaverton, Ont., Can.,
  1,099.............C5 42
Beaverton, Mich., 926..E6 66
Beaverton, Oreg.,
  5,937.........B2, B3 80
Beawar, India, 53,931..C1 20

Bebedouro, Braz.,
  18,249............C3 30
Bečej, Yugo., 24,853...C5 10
Béchar, Alg., 18,090..B4 22
Bechuanaland
  (Botswana), Br. dep.,
  Afr., 337,000.......E4 24
Beckenham, Eng.,
  77,265............m12 4
Becker, co., Minn.,
  23,959............D3 67
Beckham, co., Okla.,
  17,782............B2 79
Beckley, W. Va.,
  18,642.........D3, D7 87
Bédarieux, Fr., 7,263..F5 5
Bedford, N.S., Can.,
  2,021.............E6 43
Bedford, Que., Can.,
  2,855.............D5 42
Bedford, Eng., 63,317..D6 4
Bedford, Ind., 13,024..G5 59
Bedford, Iowa, 1,807...D3 60
Bedford, Mass.,
  10,969.........B5, C2 65
Bedford, Ohio,
  15,223.........A6, B2 78
Bedford, Pa., 3,696....F4 81
Bedford, Tex., 2,706...*C4 84
Bedford, Va., 5,921....D3 85
Bedford, co., Eng.,
  380,704...........*D6 4
Bedford, co., Pa.,
  42,451............G4 81
Bedford, co., Tenn.,
  23,150............B5 83
Bedford, co., Va.,
  31,028............D3 85
Bedford Heights, Ohio,
  5,275............*B2 78
Bedford Hills, N.Y.,
  3,000.............D3 75
Bédja, see Béja, Tun.
Bedlington, Eng.,
  29,373............C6 4
Bedzin, Pol., 39,000...g10 7
Bee, co., Tex., 23,755..E4 84
Beebe, Ark., 1,697.....B4 49
Beebe, Que., Can.,
  1,363.............D5 42
Beecher, Ill., 1,367....B6 58
Beech Grove, Ind.,
  10,973.........E5, H8 59
Beechwood Village, Ky.,
  1,903............*A4 62
Bee Ridge, Fla.,
  2,043.........E4, F2 54
Beersheba, Isr.,
  43,158.........C2, h5 15
Beeskow, Ger., 7,571..B7 6
Beeville, Tex., 13,811..E4 84
Bègles, Fr., 24,388.....E3 5
Beida, Libya, 12,800...B2 23
Beira, Moz., 25,000...D6 24
Beira, reg., Port.,
  2,039,800..........B2 8
Beira Alta, prov., Port.,
  703,231...........*B2 8
Beira Baixa, prov., Port.,
  361,191...........*C2 8
Beira Litoral, prov., Port.,
  985,135...........*B1 8
Beirut (Beyrouth), Leb.,
  400,000...........g5 15
Béja, Tun., 34,645.....A6 22
Bejaïa (Bougie), Alg.,
  43,934............A5 22
Békés, Hung., 17,661..B5 10
Békés, co., Hung.,
  468,303...........*B5 10
Bekescsaba, Hung.,
  40,965............B5 10
Bela, India, 21,397....C7 20
Bela Crkva, Yugo.,
  10,749............C5 10
Bel Air, Md., 4,300....A5 53
Belalcázar, Sp., 8,793..C3 8
Bela Vista, Braz.,
  8,878.............C1 30
Belaya Tserkov, Sov. Un.,
  76,000............G8 12
Belchertown, Mass.,
  900..............B3 65
Belding, Mich., 4,887..E5 66
Belém, Braz., 359,988..D6 27
Belen, N. Mex., 5,031..B5 48
Belén, Par., 6,647.....D4 29
Belev, Sov. Un.,
  10,000............E11 12
Belfair, Wash., 400....B3 86
Belfast, Maine, 6,140..D3 64
Belfast, N. Ire.,
  416,094...........C4 4
Belfield, N. Dak.,
  1,064.............D3 77
Belford, N.J., 3,500...C4 74
Belfort, Fr., 48,070...D7 5
Belfort, dept., Fr.,
  109,371...........*D7 5
Belfry, Ky., 950......C7 62

Belgaum, India, 127,885............E5 20
Belgium, country, Eur., 9,189,741...........B6 5
Belgorod, Sov. Un., 81,000............F11 12
Belgorod-Dnestrovskiy, Sov. Un., 38,600....H8 12
Belgrade, Mont., 1,057.E5 70
Belgrade (Beograd), Yugo., 587,899......C5 10
Belhaven, N.C., 2,386..B7 76
Belington, W. Va., 1,528............B5 87
Belize, Br. Hond., 32,813.............D7 34
Belknap, co., N.H., 28,912.............D5 73
Bell, Calif., 19,450....F2 50
Bell, co., Ky., 35,336..D6 62
Bell, co., Tex., 94,097..D4 84
Bell Acres, Pa., 1,283.............*E1 81
Bellaire, Ohio, 11,502..C7 78
Bellaire, Tex., 19,872..F5 84
Bellary, India, 85,673..E6 20
Bella Unión, Ur., 2,519.............E1 30
Bella Vista, Arg., 8,352.E2 29
Bella Vista, Arg., 7,922.E4 29
Bella Vista, Par., 5,762.D4 29
Bellbrook, Ohio, 941...C3 78
Belle, Mo., 1,016...C6 69
Belle, W. Va., 2,559...C6 87
Belleair, Fla., 2,456...E1 54
Belle Center, Ohio, 949................B4 78
Bellechasse, co., Que., Can., 26,054...C7 42
Bellefontaine, Ohio, 11,424.............B4 78
Bellefontaine Neighbors, Mo., 13,650.......*A8 69
Bellefonte, Del., 1,536..A7 53
Bellefonte, Pa., 6,088..E6 81
Belle Fourche, S. Dak., 4,087...........F2 77
Bellegarde-sur-Valserine, Fr., 6,588...........D6 5
Belle Glade, Fla., 11,273............F6 54
Belle Isle, Fla., 2,344...D5 54
Bellemead, Md., 1,400.............*C4 53
Belle Meade, Tenn., 3,082........A5, E9 83
Belle Plaine, Iowa, 2,923..............C5 60
Belle Plaine, Kans., 1,579.............E6 61
Belle Plaine, Minn., 1,931.............F5 67
Bellerive, Que., Can., 1,000.............E8 42
Belle River, Ont., Can., 1,814.............*E2 41
Bellerose, N.Y., 1,083............*E3 75
Belleterre, Que., Can., 638.............*E10 41
Belle Vernon, Pa., 1,784.............F2 81
Belleview, Va., 3,500..*B5 85
Belleville, Ont., Can., 30,655.............C7 41
Belleville, Ill., 37,264..E4 58
Belleville, Kans., 2,940.C6 61
Belleville, Mich., 1,921.A7 66
Belleville, N.J., 35,005...........B4, D5 74
Belleville, Pa., 1,539..E6 81
Belleville North, Mich., 1,128.............A7 66
Bellevue, Ill., 1,561..*C4 58
Bellevue, Iowa, 2,181..B7 60
Bellevue, Ky., 9,336...A7 62
Bellevue, Mich., 1,277.F5 66
Bellevue, Nebr., 8,831..........C9, E3 71
Bellevue, Ohio, 8,286...A5 78
Bellevue, Pa., 11,412...........B5, F1 81
Bellevue, Wash., 12,809.............D2 86
Belley, Fr., 4,609......E6 5
Bellflower, Calif., 45,909.............*F2 50
Bell Gardens, Calif., 26,467.............*F2 50
Bellingham, Wash., 34,688.............A3 86
Bellinzona, Switz., 13,435.............E4 6
Bell Island, see Wabana, Newf., Can.
Bellmawr, N.J., 11,853.D2 74
Bellmead, Tex., 5,127.*D4 84
Bellmore, N.Y., 12,784.G2 52
Bello, Col., 28,398...B2 32
Bellows Falls, Vt., 3,831.............E3 73

Bellport, N.Y., 2,461...G5 52
Bells, Tenn., 1,232....B2 83
Belluno, It., 22,500....A4 9
Bell Ville, Arg., 15,796..A4 28
Bellville, Ohio, 1,621...B5 78
Bellville, Tex., 2,218...E4 84
Bellwood, Ill., 20,729..F2 58
Bellwood, Pa., 2,330...E5 81
Belmar, N.J., 5,190...C4 74
Bélmez, Sp., 8,068.....C3 9
Belmond, Iowa, 2,506..B4 60
Belmont, Calif., 15,996.B5 50
Belmont, Fla., 2,000...*E4 54
Belmont, Mass., 28,715.............C2 65
Belmont, Miss., 901...A5 68
Belmont, N.Y., 1,146...C2 75
Belmont, N.C., 5,007..B2 76
Belmont, co., Ohio, 83,864.............C6 78
Belmonte, Braz., 7,897.............*E7 27
Bel-Nor, Mo., 2,388...A8 69
Beloeil Village, Que., Can., 6,283........*D4 42
Belo Horizonte, Braz., 642,912.............E2 34
Beloit, Kans., 3,837...C5 61
Beloit, Wis., 35,199...F4 88
Beloit West, Wis., 2,162.............*F4 88
Belomorsk, Sov. Un., 17,400.............C6 13
Belopolye, Sov. Un.,...F10 13
Beloretsk, Sov. Un., 61,000.............D8 13
Belovo, Sov. Un., 115,000..........*D11 13
Belpre, Ohio, 5,418....C6 78
Bel-Ridge, Mo., 4,878.*A8 69
Belton, Mo., 4,897....C3 69
Belton, S.C., 5,106...B3 82
Belton, Tex., 8,163....D4 84
Beltrami, co., Minn., 23,425.............B3 67
Beltsville, Md., 3,500..B4 53
Beltsy, Sov. Un., 67,000.............H6 13
Belvedere, Calif., 2,148.............*B5 50
Belvedere Marittimo, It., 9,069.............E5 9
Belvedere, Va., 1,100..*B5 85
Belvidere, Del., 1,000..A6 53
Belvidere, Ill., 11,223..A5 58
Belvidere, N.J., 2,636..B2 74
Belzoni, Miss., 4,142..B3 68
Bement, Ill., 1,558.....D5 58
Bemidji, Minn., 9,958..C4 67
Bemis, Tenn., 3,127...B3 83
Benavente, Sp., 11,080.A3 8
Benavides, Tex., 2,459..F3 84
Ben Avon, Pa., 2,553..*E1 81
Benbrook, Tex., 3,254.*C4 84
Bend, Oreg., 11,936...C5 80
Bendale, S.C., 1,544...C6 82
Ben Davis, Ind., 900...H7 59
Bendery, Sov. Un., 38,000.............H7 13
Bendigo, Austl., 30,204.G7 25
Benesov, Czech., 9,000...........D3, o18 7
Benevento, It., 40,000..D5 9
Benewah, co., Idaho, 6,036.............B2 57
Bengal, reg., India, Pak..............D8 20
Bengasi (Banghāzī), Libya, 69,718.............B2 23
Bengkulu, Indon., 16,800.............F2 19
Benguela, Ang., 15,399.C2 24
Benguela, dist., Ang., 487,871.............C3 24
Benham, Ky., 1,874..D7 62
Ben Hill, co., Ga., 13.633...........E3 55
Beni, dept., Bol., 119,770.............B3 29
Benicarló, Sp., 10,627..B6 8
Benicia, Calif., 6,070..B5 50
Benin, Nig., 53,753...G6 22
Benisa, Sp., 6,036......C6 8
Benkelman, Nebr., 1,400.............D4 71
Benld, Ill., 1,848......D4 58
Ben Lomond, Calif., 1,814.............C3 50
Bennett, co., S. Dak., 3,053.............G4 77
Bennettsville, S.C., 6,963.............B8 82
Bennettsville Southwest, S.C., 1,022.............B8 82
Bennington, Vt., 8,023..F1 73
Bennington, co., Vt., 25,088.............E1 73
Bensenville, Ill., 11,057...........B6, E2 58
Bensheim, Ger., 24,100.D4 6
Benson, Ariz., 2,494...D3 48

Benson, Minn., 3,678..E3 67
Benson, N.C., 2,355...B5 76
Benson, co., N. Dak., 9,435...........B6 77
Bent, co., Colo., 7,419..D7 51
Bentleyville, Pa., 3,160.F1 81
Benton, Ark., 10,399...C3 49
Benton, Ill., 7,023.....E5 58
Benton, Ky., 3,074....B3 62
Benton, La., 1,336.....B2 63
Benton, Pa., 981.....D9 81
Benton, Tenn., 638....D9 83
Benton, co., Ark., 36,272.............A1 49
Benton, co., Ind., 11,912.............C3 59
Benton, co., Iowa, 23,422.............B5 60
Benton, co., Minn., 17,287.............E4 67
Benton, co., Miss., 7,723.............A4 68
Benton, co., Mo., 8,737.C4 69
Benton, co., Oreg., 39,165.............C3 80
Benton, co., Tenn., 10,662.............A3 83
Benton, co., Wash., 62,070.............C6 86
Benton City, Wash., 1,210.............C6 86
Benton Harbor, Mich., 19,136.............F4 66
Benton Heights, Mich., 6,112.............*F4 66
Bentonville, Ark., 4,015.............A1 49
Benwood, W. Va., 2,850...........A4, B2 87
Benzie, co., Mich., 7,834.............D4 66
Beograd, see Belgrade, Yugo.
Beppu, Jap., 107,734...J5 18
Berat, Alb., 15,700....*B2 14
Berat, pref., Alb., 176,000..........*B2 14
Berber, Sud., 10,977...E4 23
Berbera, Som., 20,000..F7 23
Berchtesgaden, Ger., 4,800.............E6 6
Berck-sur-Mer, Fr., 12,877.............B4 5
Berdichev, Sov. Un., 56,000.............G7 12
Berea, Ky., 4,302...C5 62
Berea, Ohio, 16,592...A6 78
Beregovo, Sov. Un., 5,000.............G4 12
Beresford, S. Dak., 1,794.............G9 77
Berettyoujfalu, Hung., 11,377.............B5 10
Berezhany, Sov. Un., 5,000.............G5 12
Berezna, Sov. Un., 10,000.............F8 12
Berezniki, Sov. Un., 117,000.............D8 13
Berg, Nor............q27 11
Berga, Sp., 9,822....A6 8
Bergama, Tur., 21,800.*C6 14
Bergamo, It., 114,907..B2 9
Bergen, see Mons, Bel.
Bergen, Ger., 10,500...A6 7
Bergen, N.Y., 964....B3 75
Bergen, Nor., 115,900..G1 11
Bergen, co., N.J., 780,255.............B4 74
Bergenfield, N.J., 27,203...........B5, D5 74
Bergen op Zoom, Neth., 35,500.............B6 5
Bergerac, Fr., 21,236...E4 5
Bergholz, Ohio, 955....B7 78
Bergisch Gladbach, Ger., 41,900.............C3 6
Berhampore, India, 76,931.............D8 20
Berhampur, India, 62,317.............E7 20
Berislav, Sov. Un., 10,000.............H9 12
Berja, Sp., 6,425.....D4 8
Berkeley, Calif., 111,268...........B5, D2 50
Berkeley, Ill., 5,792...*F2 58
Berkeley, Mo., 18,676..A8 69
Berkeley, R.I., 1,000..B11 52
Berkeley, co., S.C., 38,196.............E8 82
Berkeley, co., W. Va., 33,791.............B6 87
Berkeley Heights, N.J., 8,721.............B4 74
Berkeley Springs (Bath), W. Va., 1,138...B6 87
Berkley, Mich., 23,275...........A7, F7 66
Berkovitsa, Bul., 6,870.D6 10
Berks, co., Pa., 275,414.F9 81

Berkshire, Md., 1,200.*C4 53
Berkshire, co., Eng., 503,357.............*E6 4
Berkshire, co., Mass., 142,135.............B1 65
Berlin (P.O.), Conn., 3,500.............C6 52
Berlin, Ger., 3,343,200..B6 6
Berlin, East, Ger., 1,055,300..........*B6 6
Berlin, West, Ger., 2,197,600..........*B6 6
Berlin, Md., 2,046.....D7 53
Berlin, N.H., 17,821...C5 73
Berlin, N.J., 3,578...D3 74
Berlin, N.Y., 800...C7 75
Berlin, Pa., 1,600...G4 81
Berlin, Wis., 4,838...E5 88
Bermeo, Sp., 13,781...A4 8
Bermuda, Br. dep., N.A., 53,326.............D16 2
Bern, Switz., 163,172...E3 6
Bern, canton, Switz., 889,523.............*E3 6
Bernalillo, N. Mex., 2,574...........B5, D6 48
Bernalillo, co., N. Mex., 262,199.............B5 48
Bernardsville, N.J., 5,515.............B3 74
Bernau, Ger., 13,600..B6 6
Bernay, Fr., 7,418.....C4 5
Bernburg, Ger., 44,500.C5 6
Berndorf, Aus., 8,992..E8 6
Berne, Ind., 2,644.....C8 59
Bernice, La., 1,641...B3 63
Bernie, Mo., 1,578...E8 69
Bernville, Pa., 884.....F9 81
Beroun, Czech., 15,600.........D3, o17 7
Berrien, co., Ga., 12,038.............E3 55
Berrien, co., Mich., 149,865.............G4 66
Berrien Springs, Mich., 1,953.............G4 66
Berry, former prov., Fr., 464,000............D4 5
Berry Hill, Tenn., 1,551.............E9 83
Berryville, Ark., 1,999..A2 49
Berryville, Va., 1,645...B5 85
Bershad, Sov. Un., 10,000.............G7 12
Berthier, co., Que., Can., 27,325.............C3 42
Berthierville, Que., Can., 3,708.............C4 42
Berthoud, Colo., 1,014..A5 51
Bertie, co., N.C., 24,350.............A6 76
Bertrand, Mich., 3,500.............*G4 66
Berwick, N.S., Can., 1,282.............D5 43
Berwick, La., 3,880...E4 63
Berwick, Maine, 1,557..E2 64
Berwick, Pa., 13,353...D9 81
Berwick, co., Scot., 22,441.............*C5 4
Berwick-on-Tweed, Eng., 12,166.............C6 4
Berwind, W. Va., 950..D3 87
Berwyn, Ill., 54,224...F2 58
Berwyn, Pa., 5,000...A10 81
Berwyn Heights, Md., 2,376.............*B4 53
Besa, Indon..............E7 19
Besançon, Fr., 95,642..D7 5
Besni, Tur., 11,200...D11 14
Bessèges, Fr., 5,770...E6 5
Bessemer, Ala., 33,054...........B3, E4 46
Bessemer, Mich., 3,304.A5 66
Bessemer, Pa., 1,491..E1 81
Bessemer City, N.C., 4,017.............B2 76
Betanzos, Sp., 7,561...A1 8
Bethalto, Ill., 3,235...E3 58
Bethany, Conn., 2,384.D5 52
Bethany, Ill., 1,118....D5 58
Bethany, Mo., 2,771...A3 69
Bethany, Okla., 12,342.B4 79
Bethany, W. Va., 992..B2 87
Bethayres-Huntingdon Valley, Pa., 2,500..*F11 81
Bethel, Alsk., 1,258...C7 47
Bethel, Conn., 8,200..D3 52
Bethel, Maine, 1,117...D2 64
Bethel, N.C., 1,578...B6 76
Bethel, Ohio, 2,019...D3 78
Bethel, Oreg., 1,500...*C3 80
Bethel (Bethel Park), Pa., 23,650.......*F1 81
Bethesda, Md., 56,527.........C1, C3 53
Bethesda, Ohio, 1,178..B6 78
Bethlehem, Pa., 75,408.............E11 81
Bethlehem, S. Afr., 24,125.............F5 24

Bethlehem, W. Va., 2,308...........B2 87
Bethpage, N.Y., 30,000..............G3 52
Bettendorf, Iowa, 11,534..........C7, D7 60
Betul, India, 19,860...D6 20
Beulah, N. Dak., 1,318.C4 77
Beulaville, N.C., 1,062.C6 76
Beverley, Eng., 16,024.D6 4
Beverly, Alta., Can., 9,041..............C4 38
Beverly, Mass., 36,108........A6, C3 65
Beverly, N.J., 3,400....C3 74
Beverly, Ohio, 1,194...C6 78
Beverly Gardens, Ohio, 2,200............*C3 78
Beverly Hills, Calif., 30,817............F2 50
Beverly Hills, Mich., 8,633............*F7 66
Beverly Park, Wash., 950.............B3 86
Beverwijk, Neth., 36,600............A6 5
Bexar, co., Tex., 687,151...........E3 84
Bexhill-on-Sea, Eng., 28,926............E7 4
Bexley, Ohio, 14,319...C2 78
Beypazari, Tur., 8,900............B8 14
Beyrouth, see Beirut, Leb.
Bezerros, Braz., 7,737.*D7 27
Bezhetsk, Sov. Un., 25,000...........C11 12
Bezhitsa, Sov. Un., 85,000...........E10 12
Béziers, Fr., 73,538...F5 5
Bezons, Fr., 22,061.....g9 5
Bhagalpur, India, 143,850...........C8 20
Bhakkar, Pak., 12,397.B5 20
Bhamo, Bur., 9,817...D10 20
Bharatpur, India, 49,776............C6 20
Bhatpara, India, 147,630...........D8 20
Bhavnagar, India, 171,039...........D5 20
Bhind, India, 28,208...C6 20
Bhopal, India, 185,374.D6 20
Bhor, India, 8,627.....E5 20
Bhuj, India, 40,180....D4 20
Bhutan, country, Asia, 300,000...........C9 20
Biala, Eg., U.A.R., 10,005...........*G8 14
Biala Podlaska, Pol., 15,300............B7 7
Bialogard, Pol., 15,200.A4 7
Bialystok, Pol., 95,000..B7 7
Bianco, It., 5,057.....E6 9
Biarritz, Fr., 25,231...F3 5
Bibai, Jap., 62,500....E10 18
Bibb, co., Ala., 14,357..C2 46
Bibb, co., Ga., 141,249.D3 55
Bibb City, Ga., 1,213..D2 55
Biberach, Ger., 21,500.D4 6
Bic, Que., Can., 1,177..A9 42
Bicknell, Ind., 3,878....G3 59
Bicske, Hung., 8,148....B4 10
Bida, Nig., 19,346....G6 22
Bidar, India, 32,420...E6 20
Biddeford, Maine, 19,255............E2, E4 64
Bideford, Eng., 10,265..E4 4
Biel, Switz., 59,216....E3 6
Bielawa, Pol., 28,000...C4 7
Bielefeld, Ger., 174,600.B4 6
Biella, It., 50,209......B2 9
Bielsko-Biala, Pol., 76,000..........D5, h10 7
Bielsk Podlaski, Pol., 6,203............B7 7
Bienville, par., La., 16,726............B2 63
Biga, Tur., 10,800....*B7 14
Big Bear City, Calif., 800.............E5 50
Big Bear Lake, Calif., 1,562............*E5 50
Big Beaver, Pa., 2,381.*E1 81
Biggar, Sask., Can., 2,702............E1 39
Big Horn, co., Mont., 10,007............E9 70
Big Horn, co., Wyo., 11,898............A4 89
Big Lake, Tex., 2,668..D2 84
Biglerville, Pa., 923...G7 81
Big Rapids, Mich., 8,686............E5 66
Big River, Sask., Can., 896..............D2 39
Big Sandy, Mont., 954.B6 70
Big Spring, Tex., 31,230............C2 84
Big Stone, co., Minn., 8,954............E2 67

Big Stone Gap, Va., 4,688............B2 85
Big Timber, Mont., 1,660............E7 70
Big Wells, Tex., 801...E3 84
Bihać, Yugo., 15,552...C3 10
Bihar, India, 78,581....C8 20
Bihar, state, India, 46,455,610..........D8 20
Bijapur, India, 78,854..E6 20
Bijeljina, Yugo., 15,682.C4 10
Bijou, Calif., 2,000.....C4 50
Bikaner, India, 150,634.C5 20
Bikin, Sov. Un., 10,000.C7 18
Bilaspur, India, 86,706.D7 20
Bilbao, Sp., 297,942....A4 8
Bileća, Yugo., 2,489....D4 10
Bilin, Bur., 5,265.....E10 20
Billerica, Mass., 1,600..........A5, C2 65
Billings, Mont., 52,851.E8 70
Billings, co., N. Dak., 1,513............C2 77
Billings Bench, Mont., 1,500............*E8 70
Billings Heights, Mont., 2,500............*E8 70
Biloela, Austl., 2,048...B8 26
Biloxi, Miss., 44,053.........E2, E5 68
Bilqas Qism Awwal, Eg., U.A.R., 43,200......*G8 14
Biltmore Forest, N.C., 1,004............D3 76
Binalbagan, Phil., 6,979............*C6 19
Bindura, Rh., 25,000...D6 24
Bingen, Ger., 20,200...D3 6
Bingham, Maine, 1,180.C3 64
Bingham, co., Idaho, 28,218............F6 57
Bingham Canyon, Utah, 1,516..........A5, D2 72
Binghamton, N.Y., 75,941 (*212,600)........C4 75
Bintulu, Mala., 3,957...E4 19
Bío-Bío, prov., Chile., 167,286...........B2 28
Birakan, Sov. Un., 5,000.............B5 18
Bi'r ar Rummānah, Eg., U.A.R., 1,000......G9 14
Birch Cliff, Ont., Can., 960..........D5, E7 41
Bird Island, Minn., 1,384............F4 67
Birdsboro, Pa., 3,025.F10 81
Birecik, Tur., 13,100..D11 14
Birkenhead, Eng., 141,683...........D5 4
Birmingham, Ala., 340,887 (*624,000).....B3, E4 46
Birmingham, Eng., 1,105,651..........D6 4
Birmingham, Mich., 25,525........A7, F7 66
Birobidzhan, Sov. Un., 41,000...........E16 12
Bisbee, Ariz., 9,914....D4 48
Biscayne Park, Fla., 2,911............F3 54
Bisceglie, It., 41,451...D6 9
Biscoe, N.C., 1,053....B4 76
Bishop, Calif., 2,875...D4 50
Bishop, Tex., 3,722....F4 84
Bishop's Falls, Newf., Can., 4,099.........D4 44
Bishop's Stortford, Eng., 18,308............E7 4
Bishopville, S.C., 3,586.C7 82
Biskra, Alg., 52,511....B6 22
Bismarck, Mo., 1,237..D7 69
Bismarck, N. Dak., 27,670............D5 77
Bistrita, Rom., 20,292..B7 10
Bitlis, Tur., 16,600...C14 14
Bitola, Yugo., 49,101...E5 10
Bitonto, It., 33,300....D6 9
Bitterfeld, Ger., 31,000.C6 6
Biwabik, Minn., 1,836..C6 67
Bixby, Okla., 1,711....B6 79
Biysk, Sov. Un., 162,000...........D11 12
Bizerte, Tun., 44,721...A6 22
Bizuta, Mong., 10,000..B8 17
Bjelovar, Yugo., 15,637.C3 10
Blackburn, Eng., 106,114...........D5 4
Black Diamond, Alta., Can., 1,043........D3 38
Black Diamond, Wash., 1,026..........B3, D2 86
Black Eagle, Mont., 2,000.............C5 70
Blackfoot, Idaho, 7,378............F6 57
Blackford, co., Ind., 14,792............D7 59
Black Forest, Colo., 1,000.............C6 51

Black Hawk, co., Iowa, 122,482...........B5 60
Black Lake, Que., Can., 4,180............C6 42
Black Mountain, N.C., 1,313............D4 76
Black Oak, Ind., 15,000............*A3 59
Black Point, Calif., 650.............B5 50
Blackpool, Eng., 152,133...........D5 4
Black River, N.Y., 1,237............A5 75
Black River Falls, Wis., 3,195............D3 88
Blacksburg, S.C., 2,174.A4 82
Blacksburg, Va., 7,070.D2 85
Blackshear, Ga., 2,482.E4 55
Blackstone, Mass., 2,000............B4 65
Blackstone, Va., 3,659.D5 85
Blackville, S.C., 1,901..E5 82
Blackwell, Okla., 9,588............A4 79
Blackwood, N.J., 3,000............*D2 74
Bladen, co., N.C., 28,881...........C5 76
Bladensburg, Md., 3,103............C2 53
Blagoevgrad (Gorna Dzhumaya), Bul., 14,066..........D6 10
Blagoveshchensk, Sov. Un., 99,000.......D15 13
Blain, Fr., 2,009.......D3 5
Blaine, Minn., 7,570...E7 67
Blaine, Wash., 1,735...A3 86
Blaine, co., Idaho, 4,598............F4 57
Blaine, co., Mont., 8,091............B7 70
Blaine, co., Nebr., 1,016............C6 71
Blaine, co., Okla., 12,077...........B3 79
Blair, Nebr., 4,931.....C9 71
Blair, Wis., 909.......D2 88
Blair, co., Pa., 137,270.E5 81
Blairgowrie [& Rattray], Scot., 5,168........B5 4
Blairmore, Alta., Can., 1,980............E3 38
Blairsville, Pa., 4,930...F3 81
Blaj, Rom., 8,731.....B7 10
Blakely, Ga., 3,580....E2 55
Blanchard, Okla., 1,377.B4 79
Blanchester, Ohio, 2,944............C4 78
Blanco, co., Tex., 3,657.D3 84
Bland, co., Va., 5,982..D1 85
Blanding, Utah, 1,805..C7 72
Blandinsville, Ill., 853..C3 58
Blankenburg, Ger., 19,500...........C5 6
Blasdell, N.Y., 3,909...C2 75
Blato, Yugo., 5,140....D3 10
Blauvelt, N.Y., 3,000..*C5 75
Blawnox, Pa., 2,085....A6 81
Bleckley, co., Ga., 9,642............D3 55
Bled-Grad, Yugo., 4,120............B2 10
Bledsoe, co., Tenn., 7,811............D8 83
Blekinge, co., Swe., 145,000...........*I6 11
Blenheim, Ont., Can., 2,844............E2 41
Blenheim, N.Z., 11,957...........N14 76
Blida, Alg., 67,913.....A5 22
Blind River, Ont., Can., 3,633............A2 41
Blissfield, Mich., 2,653.G7 66
Bloemfontein, S. Afr., 112,606 (*145,273)...F5 24
Blois, Fr., 33,838......D4 5
Blonie, Pol., 6,416....m13 7
Bloomer, Wis., 2,834...C2 88
Bloomfield, Conn., 5,000............B6 52
Bloomfield, Ga., 4,381............*D3 55
Bloomfield, Ind., 2,224.F4 59
Bloomfield, Iowa, 2,771............D5 60
Bloomfield, Ky., 916...C4 62
Bloomfield, Mo., 1,330.E8 69
Bloomfield, Nebr., 1,349............B8 71
Bloomfield, N.J., 51,867............D4 74
Bloomfield, N. Mex., 1,292............A5 48
Bloomfield Hills, Mich., 2,378............A7 66
Bloomfield Village, Mich., 3,500............*F7 66

Bloomingdale, Ga., 1,000.............D5 55
Bloomingdale, Ill., 1,262............E2 58
Bloomingdale, N.J., 5,293............A4 74
Blooming Grove, Wis., 8,500............*E4 88
Blooming Prairie, Minn., 1,778............G5 67
Bloomington, Calif., 3,500............*F3 50
Bloomington, Ill., 36,271............C5 58
Bloomington, Ind., 31,357............F4 59
Bloomington, Minn., 50,498............F7 67
Bloomington, Tex., 1,756............E4 84
Bloomsburg, Pa., 10,655............E9 81
Blossburg, Pa., 1,956...C7 81
Blossom Hill, Pa., 1,000............*F9 81
Blount, co., Ala., 25,449...........B3 46
Blount, co., Tenn., 57,525...........D10 83
Blountstown, Fla., 2,375............B1 54
Bludenz, Aus., 11,127..E4 6
Blue Ash, Ohio, 8,341..D2 78
Blue Bell, Pa., 1,000..*F11 81
Blue Earth, Minn., 4,200............G4 67
Blue Earth, co., Minn., 44,385...........G4 67
Bluefield, Va., 4,235...B3 85
Bluefield, W. Va., 19,256............D3 87
Bluefields, Nic., 11,900............E8 34
Blue Hills, Conn., 4,000............*B6 52
Blue Island, Ill., 19,618........B6, F3 58
Blue Lake, Calif., 1,234............B2 50
Blue Mound, Ill., 1,038............D4 58
Blue Point, N.Y., 2,300.G4 52
Blue Rapids, Kans., 1,426............C7 61
Blue Ridge, Ga., 1,406.B2 55
Blue Springs, Mo., 2,555............E2 69
Bluff City, Tenn., 948.C11 83
Bluff Park, Ala., 3,000............*B3 46
Bluffton, Ind., 6,238...C7 59
Bluffton, Ohio, 2,591..B4 78
Blumenau, Braz., 46,591............D3 30
Bly, Calif., 1,554.....*F3 50
Blyth, Eng., 35,933....C6 4
Blythe, Calif., 6,023...F6 50
Blytheville, Ark., 25,883............B6 49
Bnei Braq, Isr., 47,080............*B2 15
Boac, Phil., 3,262.....C6 19
Boardman, Ohio, 20,000............*A7 78
Boaz, Ala., 4,654......A3 46
Bobbili, India, 25,592..E7 20
Bobcaygeon, Ont., Can., 1,210............C6 41
Bobigny, Fr., 37,010..g10 5
Bobo-Dioulasso, Upper Volta, 45,000......F4 22
Bobrinets, Sov. Un., 10,000............G9 12
Bobrka, Sov. Un., 10,000............G5 12
Bobruysk, Sov. Un., 104,000...........E7 12
Bobtown, Pa., 1,167...G2 81
Bobures, Ven., 9,397...B3 32
Boca Raton, Fla., 6,961............F6 54
Bochnia, Pol., 11,000..D6 7
Bochum, Ger., 361,400.C3 6
Bodaybo, Sov. Un., 14,700...........D14 13
Boden, Swe., 13,700...E9 11
Bodmin, Eng., 6,209...E4 4
Bodö, Nor., 12,700....D6 11
Boerne, Tex., 2,169...E3 84
Bogalusa, La., 21,423..D6 63
Bogata, Tex., 1,112....C5 84
Boger City, N.C., 2,200............*B2 76
Bogo, Phil., 6,371.....*C6 19
Bogodukhov, Sov., Un., 10,000...........F10 12
Bogor, Indon., 146,907.G3 19
Bogoroditsk, Sov. Un., 10,000...........E12 12
Bogorodsk, Sov. Un., 36,200...........C14 12

Bogotá, Col., 954,120..C3 32
Bogota, N.J., 7,965...D5 74
Bogra, Pak., 25,303...D8 20
Boguslav, Sov. Un., 10,000...........G8 12
Bohain [-en-Vermandois], Fr., 6,726........C5 5
Bohemia, N.Y., 2,000...........*G4 75
Bohemia, reg., Czech., 6,035,500.........D3 7
Bohol, prov., Phil., 602,500..........*D6 19
Boiling Springs, N.C., 1,311............B2 76
Boiling Springs, Pa., 1,182...........F7 81
Boischatel, Que., Can., 1,576...........C6 42
Bois-Colombes, Fr., 29,938..........G10 5
Bois des Filion, Que., Can., 2,499.......D8 42
Boise, Idaho, 34,481...F2 57
Boise, co., Idaho, 1,646...........F3 57
Boise City, Okla., 1,978...........D2 79
Boissevain, Man., Can., 1,303............E1 40
Boissevain, Va., 600..B3 85
Bolbec, Fr., 12,212....C4 5
Bolgrad, Sov. Un., 10,000............I7 12
Boling, Tex., 950.....G4 84
Bolívar, Arg., 14,010..B4 28
Bolivar, Mo., 3,512...D4 69
Bolivar, N.Y., 1,405...C2 75
Bolivar, Ohio, 932....B6 78
Bolivar, Tenn., 3,338..B3 83
Bolivar, co., Miss., 54,464..........B3 68
Bolívar, prov., Ec., 123,205.........B2 31
Bolívar, dept., Col., 737,890..........B2 32
Bolívar, state, Ven., 213,543..........B4 32
Bolivia, country, S.A., 3,311,000........C2 29
Bolkhov, Sov. Un., 10,000...........E11 12
Bollinger, co., Mo., 9,167............D7 69
Bollnäs, Swe., 10,679..G7 11
Bollullos, Sp., 10,947..D2 8
Bologna, It., 444,872..B3 9
Bologoye, Sov. Un., 22,000...........C10 12
Bolshaya Lepetikha, Sov. Un., 5,000........H9 12
Bolshaya Viska, Sov. Un., 10,000.......G8 12
Bolshoy Tokmak, Sov., Un., 10,000.......H10 12
Bolton, Ont., Can., 2,104...........D5 41
Bolton, Eng., 160,887..D5 4
Bolton Landing, N.Y., 900.............B7 75
Bolu, Tur., 13,700....B8 14
Bolvadin, Tur., 16,100..C8 14
Bolzano, It., 88,799...A3 9
Boma, Con. L., 31,500..B2 24
Bombay, India, 4,152,056........E5 20
Bom Conselho, Braz., 6,840............*D7 27
Bom Despacho, Braz., 13,568..........B3 30
Bon Air, Pa., 1,000..*G11 81
Bon Air, Va., 1,500...C7 85
Bonaventure, Que., Can., 804............*B3 42
Bonaventure, co., Que., Can., 42,962......A3 43
Bonavista, Newf., Can., 4,186...........D5 44
Bond, co., Ill., 14,060..E4 58
Bondy, Fr., 38,039...G10 5
Bône, see Annaba, Alg.
Bonham, Tex., 7,357..C4 84
Bon Homme, co., S. Dak., 9,229...........G8 77
Bonifay, Fla., 2,222..G3 54
Bonita, Calif., 2,000..*E2 50
Bonn, Ger., 143,900...C3 6
Bonner, co., Idaho, 15,587..........A2 57
Bonners Ferry, Idaho, 1,921...........A2 57
Bonner Springs, Kans., 3,171..........B8, C9 61
Bonne Terre, Mo., 3,219...........D7 69
Bonneville, co., Idaho, 46,906..........F7 57
Bonnyville, Alta., Can., 1,736...........B5 38
Bonorva, It., 6,669...D2 9

Bonthain, Indon., 6,711............G5 19
Bontoc, Phil., 4,471...*B6 19
Boomer, W. Va., 1,657.........C3, D6 78
Boone, Iowa, 12,468...B4 60
Boone, N.C., 3,686....A2 76
Boone, co., Ark., 16,116...........A2 49
Boone, co., Ill., 20,326..A5 58
Boone, co., Ind., 27,543..........D4 59
Boone, co., Iowa, 28,037..........B4 60
Boone, co., Ky., 21,940.B5 62
Boone, co., Mo., 55,202..........B5 69
Boone, co., Nebr., 9,134............C7 71
Boone, co., W. Va., 28,764..........C3 87
Booneville, Ark., 2,690.B2 49
Booneville, Miss., 3,480............A5 68
Boonsboro, Md., 1,211.A2 53
Boon Terrace, Pa., 1,100...........*F1 81
Boonton, N.J., 7,981...B4 74
Boonville, Ind., 4,801..H3 59
Boonville, Mo., 7,090..C5 69
Boonville, N.Y., 2,403..B5 75
Boothbay Harbor, Maine, 1,850...........E3 64
Boothwyn, Pa., 5,000...........*G11 81
Boppard, Ger., 8,600...C3 6
Boqueron, dept., Par., 28,082..........D3 29
Borås, Swe., 67,700....I5 11
Bordeaux, Fr, 249,688.E3 5
Borden, co., Tex., 1,076...........C2 84
Borden Springs, Ala., 500............B4 46
Bordentown, N.J., 4,974...........C3 74
Bordighera, It., 8,621..C1 9
Borgå, Fin., 11,800...G11 11
Borger, Tex., 20,911..B2 84
Borgomanero, It., 7,900............B2 9
Borgo Val di Taro, It., 11,809..........B2 9
Borislav, Sov. Un., 47,500...........G7 12
Borisoglebsk, Sov. Un., 56,000..........F13 12
Borisov, Sov. Un., 63,000...........D7 12
Borispol, Sov. Un., 25,000..........F8 12
Borja, Sp., 4,381....B5 8
Borkou, reg., Chad...E1 23
Borlänge, Swe., 26,700.G6 11
Bornholm, co., Den., 48,632..........*A3 7
Bornos, Sp., 8,697...D3 8
Boromlya, Sov. Un., 10,000..........F10 12
Borovan, Bul., 5,905...D6 10
Borovichi, Sov. Un., 47,100..........B9 12
Borovskoye, Sov. Un., 5,000...........q21 12
Borsod-Abauj-Zemplen, co., Hung., 583,001..*A5 10
Bort-les-Orgues, Fr., 5,115...........E5 5
Borzna, Sov. Un., 10,000..........F9 12
Bosa, It., 8,169.......D2 9
Bosanska Gradiska, Yugo., 6,373...........C3 10
Bosanska Kostajnica, Yugo., 2,037.......C3 10
Bosanski Novi, Yugo., 7,082...........C3 10
Boscobel, Wis., 2,608...E3 88
Boskovice, Czech., 6,396...........D4 7
Bosnia, reg., Yugo.....C3 10
Bosnia-Hercegovina, rep., Yugo., 3,274,886....*C3 10
Bosque, co., Tex., 10,809..........D4 84
Bossier, La., 32,776...B2 63
Bossier, par., La., 57,622..........B2 63
Boston, Eng., 24,903..D6 4
Boston, Ga., 1,357....F3 55
Boston, Mass., 697,197 (*2,913,500)....B5, D3 65
Boston, Pa., 2,300....*F2 81
Botetourt, co., Va., 16,715..........D3 85
Botevgrad, Bul., 5,925.D6 10
Botoşani, Rom., 29,569..........E8 10
Botswana, see Bechuanaland, Br. dep., Afr.

Bottineau, N. Dak., 2,613...........A5 77
Bottineau, co., N. Dak., 11,315..........B5 77
Botucatú, Braz., 33,878.........C3, m7 30
Botwood, Newf., Can., 2,800...........D4 44
Bouaké, I.C., 45,000...G3 22
Boucherville, Que., Can., 7,403.........D4, D9 42
Bouches-du-Rhône, dept., Fr., 1,248,355.....*F6 5
Bougie, see Bejaïa, Alg.
Boulder, Austl., 5,773..F3 25
Boulder, Colo., 37,718..A5 51
Boulder, Mont., 1,394..D4 70
Boulder, co., Colo., 74,254..........A5 51
Boulder City, Nev., 4,059...........D4 72
Boulder Creek, Calif., 1,306...........C5 50
Boulogne-Billancourt, Fr., 106,641.....C5, g9 5
Boulogne-sur-Mer, Fr., 49,281 (*98,000)....B4 5
Boundary, co., Idaho, 5,809...........A2 57
Bound Brook, N.J., 10,263..........B3 74
Bountiful, Utah, 17,039.........A6, C2 72
Bourbon, Ind., 1,522..B5 59
Bourbon, co., Kans., 16,090..........E9 61
Bourbon, co., Ky., 18,178..........B5 62
Bourbonnais, Ill., 3,336............B6 58
Bourbonnais, former prov., Fr., 318,000......D5 5
Bourg-de-Péage, Fr., 7,804...........E6 5
Bourg [-en-Bresse], Fr., 32,596..........D6 5
Bourges, Fr., 60,632...D5 5
Bourg-la-Reine, Fr., 17,694..........g10 5
Bourgoin, Fr., 9,240...E6 5
Bourlamaque, Que., Can., 3,344...........*E9 41
Bournemouth, Eng., 153,965.........E6 4
Bovey, Minn., 1,086...C5 67
Bovina, Tex., 1,029...B1 84
Bowdon, Ga., 1,548...C1 55
Bowie, Md., 1,072....B4 53
Bowie, Tex., 4,566....C4 84
Bowie, co., Tex., 59,971..........C5 84
Bow Island, Alta., Can., 1,122...........E5 38
Bowling Green, Fla., 1,171...........E5 54
Bowling Green, Ky., 28,338..........D3 62
Bowling Green, Mo., 2,650...........B6 69
Bowling Green, Ohio, 13,574.........A2, A4 78
Bowling Green, S.C., 700............A5 82
Bowman, N. Dak., 1,730...........D2 77
Bowman, S.C., 1,106...E6 82
Bowman, co., N. Dak., 4,154...........D2 77
Bowmanville, Ont., Can., 7,397...........D6 41
Bowness, Alta., Can., 9,184............D3 38
Box Butte, co., Nebr., 11,688..........B2 71
Box Elder, co., Utah, 25,061..........A5 72
Boxtel, Neth., 11,000..B6 5
Boyacá, dept., Col., 824,700.........B3 32
Boyce, La., 1,094.....C3 63
Boyd, co., Ky., 52,163..B7 62
Boyd, co., Nebr., 4,513.B7 71
Boyertown, Pa., 4,067.F10 81
Boyes Hot Springs, Calif., 2,462...........B5 50
Boyle, co., Ky., 21,257..C5 62
Boylston, Ala., 1,300...C3 46
Boyne City, Mich., 2,797...........C5 66
Boynton Beach, Fla., 10,467..........F6 54
Boys Town, Nebr., 997.D3 71
Bozeman, Mont., 13,361..........E7 70
Bozuyuk, Tur., 9,200..C8 14
Bra, It., 13,100......B1 9
Brabant, prov., Bel., 1,992,139.......*B6 5
Bracciano, It., 6,783...g8 9
Bracebridge, Ont., Can., 2,927...........B5 41

Bracken, co., Ky., 7,422...........B5 62
Brackenridge, Pa., 5,697...........A7 81
Brackettville, Tex., 1,662...........E2 84
Brad, Rom., 9,963....B6 10
Bradbury Heights, Md., 1,100...........*C3 53
Braddock, Pa., 12,337..B6 81
Braddock Hills, Pa., 2,414...........*B5 81
Bradenton, Fla., 19,380.........E4, F2 54
Bradenton Beach, Fla., 1,124...........*E4 54
Bradenville, Pa., 1,000.F3 81
Bradford, Ont., Can., 2,342...........C5 41
Bradford, Eng., 295,768.........D6 4
Bradford, Ill., 857...B4 58
Bradford, Ohio, 2,148..B3 78
Bradford, Pa., 15,061..C4 81
Bradford, R.I., 950...D10 52
Bradford, co., Fla., 12,446..........C4 54
Bradford, co., Pa., 54,925..........C8 81
Bradley, Fla., 1,035...E5 54
Bradley, Ill., 8,082....B6 58
Bradley, co., Ark., 14,029..........D3 49
Bradley, co., Tenn., 38,324..........D9 83
Bradley Beach, N.J., 4,204...........C4 74
Bradley Gardens, N.J., 1,800...........*B3 74
Bradner, Ohio, 994...A4 78
Bradshaw, W. Va., 950.D3 87
Brady, Tex., 5,338....D3 84
Braga, Port., 41,000...B1 8
Bragado, Arg., 16,104.........B4, g6 28
Bragança, Braz., 12,848..........*D6 27
Bragança, Port., 8,245...........B2 8
Braganca Paulista, Braz., 27,328.........C3, m8 30
Braidwood, Ill., 1,944..B5 58
Brăila, Rom., 102,500..C8 10
Brainerd, Minn., 12,898.........D4 67
Braintree, Mass., 31,069........B5, D3 65
Brampton, Ont., Can., 18,467.......D9, E6 41
Bramwell, W. Va., 1,195...........D3 87
Branch, co., Mich., 34,903..........G5 66
Branchville, S.C., 1,182.E6 82
Brandenburg, Ger., 86,700..........B6 6
Brandenburg, Ky., 1,542...........C3 62
Brandenburg, reg., Ger.............B6 6
Brandenburg, former state, Ger., 2,527,492.....B6 6
Brandon, Man., Can., 28,166..........E2 40
Brandon, Fla., 1,665...E4 54
Brandon, Miss., 2,139..C4 68
Brandon, S.C., 2,200...B3 82
Brandon, Vt., 1,675...D1 73
Brandys nad Labem, Czech., 13,300.....n18 7
Branford, Conn., 2,371...........D5 52
Branson, Mo., 1,887...E4 69
Brant, co., Ont., Can., 83,839..........D4 41
Brantford, Ont., Can., 55,201..........D4 41
Brantley, Ala., 1,014...D3 46
Brantley, co., Ga., 5,891...........E4 55
Brasília, Braz., 150,000.........B3 30
Braşov, Rom., 123,882.........C7 10
Bratenahl, Ohio, 1,332.B2 78
Bratislava, Czech., 242,100.........D4 7
Bratslav, Sov. Un., 10,000..........G7 12
Brattleboro, Vt., 11,734..........F2 73
Braunau [am Inn], Aus., 14,449..........D6 6
Braunschweig, Ger., 246,200.........B5 6
Brawley, Calif., 13,752.F6 50
Braxton, co., W. Va., 15,152..........C4 87
Bray, Ire., 11,688....D3 4
Braymer, Mo., 874....B4 69

Brazil, Ind., 8,853.....E9 59
Brazil, country, S.A., 70,967,185.......C3 30
Brazoria, Tex., 1,291.........E5, G4 84
Brazoria, co., Tex., 76,204.............E5 84
Brazos, co., Tex., 44,895.............D4 84
Brazzaville, Con. B., 99,000.............A3 24
Brčko, Yugo., 17,834...C4 10
Brea, Calif., 8,487.....F3 50
Breathitt, co., Ky., 15,490.............C6 62
Breaux Bridge, La., 3,303.............D4 63
Brechin, Scot., 7,114..B5 4
Breckenridge, Mich., 1,131.............E6 66
Breckenridge, Minn., 4,335.............D2 67
Breckenridge, Tex., 6,273.............C3 84
Breckenridge Hills, Mo., 6,299............*A8 69
Breckinridge, co., Ky., 14,734.............C3 62
Brecknock, co., Wales, 55,544............*E5 4
Brecksville, Ohio, 5,435.........A6, B2 78
Břeclav, Czech., 11,800.............D4 7
Brecon, Wales, 6,466...E5 4
Breda, Neth., 108,700..B6 5
Breese, Ill., 2,461.....E4 58
Bregenz, Aus., 21,428..E4 6
Bregovo, Bul., 5,271...C6 10
Bremen, Ga., 3,132....C1 55
Bremen, Ger., 564,500..B4 6
Bremen, Ind., 3,062...B5 59
Bremen, Ohio, 1,417...C5 78
Bremen, state, Ger., 706,400............*B4 6
Bremer, co., Iowa, 21,108.............B5 60
Bremerhaven, Ger., 141,800............B4 6
Bremerton, Wash., 28,922.........B3, D1 86
Bremerton East (Enetai), Wash., 2,539........*B3 86
Bremond, Tex., 803....D4 84
Brenham, Tex., 7,740..D4 84
Brent, Ala., 1,879......C2 46
Brent, Fla., 7,000......G2 54
Brentford (Brentford and Chiswick), Eng., 54,832............m11 4
Brenton, W. Va., 500..D3 87
Brentwood, Calif., 2,186.............B6 50
Brentwood, Md., 3,693.C1 53
Brentwood, Mo., 12,250.............A8 69
Brentwood, N.Y., 15,387.............F4 52
Brentwood, Pa., 13,706.............B6 81
Brescia, It., 172,744....B3 9
Breslau, see Wroclaw, Pol.
Bressanone, It., 9,100..A3 9
Bressler, Pa., 1,000....*F8 31
Bressuire, Fr., 6,528...D3 5
Brest, Fr., 136,104.....C1 5
Brest, Sov. Un., 78,000.E4 12
Breton Woods, N.J., 1,292.............C4 74
Bretton Woods, Mich., 1,500............*F6 66
Brevard, N.C., 4,857...D3 76
Brevard, co., Fla., 111,435.............D6 54
Brewer, Maine, 9,009..D4 64
Brewster, N.Y., 1,714.........D3, D7 75
Brewster, Ohio, 2,025..B6 78
Brewster, co., Tex., 6,434.............E1 84
Brewton, Ala., 6,309...D2 46
Brezno, Czech., 9,900..D5 7
Briançon, Fr., 7,570...E7 5
Briarcliff, Pa., 9,000..*G11 81
Briarcliff Manor, N.Y., 5,105.............D7 75
Briceville, Tenn., 1,217.............C9 83
Bridgeport, Mich., 1,326.............E7 66
Bridge City, La., 3,000............*C7 63
Bridge City, Tex., 4,677............*D6 84
Bridgehampton, N.Y., 900.............D4 75
Bridgeport, Ala., 2,906.A4 46
Bridgeport, Ont., Can., 1,672............*D4 41
Bridgeport, Conn., 156,748 (*322,800).........E4 52

Bridgeport, Ill., 2,260..E6 58
Bridgeport, Nebr., 1,645.............C2 71
Bridgeport, Ohio, 3,824.B7 78
Bridgeport, Pa., 5,306.........A10, F11 81
Bridgeport, Tex., 3,218.............C4 84
Bridgeport, Wash., 876.A6 86
Bridgeport, W. Va., 4,199.........B4, B7 87
Bridgeton, Mo., 7,820.........A8, C7 69
Bridgeton, N.J., 20,966.............E2 74
Bridgetown, Barb., 11,289 (*110,000)....p17 35
Bridgetown, N.S., Can., 1,043...........E4 43
Bridgetown, Ohio, 5,000............*D2 78
Bridgeview, Ill., 7,334.*F3 58
Bridgeville, Del., 1,469.C6 53
Bridgeville, Pa., 7,112..B5 81
Bridgewater, N.S., Can., 4,497.............E5 43
Bridgewater, Mass., 4,296.............C6 65
Bridgewater, Va., 1,815.............C4 85
Bridgman, Mich., 1,454.............G4 66
Bridgton, Maine, 1,715.............D2 64
Bridgwater, Eng., 25,582.............E5 4
Bridlington, Eng., 26,007.............C6 4
Brielle, N.J., 2,619.....C4 74
Brigantine, N.J., 4,201.E4 74
Brigham City, Utah, 11,728.........A5, C2 72
Brighton, Ala., 2,884.........B3, E4 46
Brighton, Ont., Can., 2,403.............C7 41
Brighton, Colo., 7,055..B6 51
Brighton, Eng., 162,757 (*400,000)...E6 4
Brighton, Ill., 1,248...D3 58
Brighton, Mich., 2,282..F7 66
Brighton, N.Y., 27,849............*B3 75
Brightwaters, N.Y., 3,193.............E3 75
Brignoles, Fr., 5,347...F7 5
Brilliant, Ohio, 2,174...B7 78
Brillion, Wis., 1,783.........A6, D5 88
Brindisi, It., 70,657...D6 9
Brinkley, Ark., 4,636...C4 49
Brioude, Fr., 6,184.....E5 5
Brisbane, Austl., 593,668.............E9 25
Brisbane, Calif., 5,000............*B5 50
Briscoe, co., Tex., 3,577.............B2 84
Bristol, Conn., 45,499..C5 52
Bristol, Eng., 436,440..E5 4
Bristol, Ind., 991......A6 59
Bristol, N.H., 1,054....D4 73
Bristol, Pa., 12,364....F12 81
Bristol, R.I., 14,570...C11 52
Bristol, Tenn., 17,582.C11 83
Bristol, Vt., 1,421.....C1 73
Bristol, Va., 17,144....B2 85
Bristol, co., Mass., 398,488.............C5 65
Bristol, co., R.I., 37,146.............C11 52
Bristol Terrace No. 2, Pa., 1,300............*F12 81
Bristow, Okla., 4,795...B5 79
Britannia Beach, B.C., Can., 771..........E6 37
British Columbia, prov., Can., 1,629,082........ 37
British Guiana, see Guyana, country, S.A.
British Honduras, dep., N.A., 90,381........D7 34
British North Borneo, see North Borneo, reg., Mala.
Britt, Iowa, 2,042.....A4 60
Brittany, former prov., Fr., 3,072,000.......C2 5
Britton, S. Dak., 1,442.E8 77
Brive [-la-Gaillarde], Fr., 40,175.............E4 5
Brno, Czech., 314,400..D4 7
Broach, India, 73,639..D5 20
Broadalbin, N.Y., 1,438.............B6 75
Broad Brook, Conn., 1,389.............B6 52
Broadmoor, Colo., 2,000.............C6 51

Broadview, Sask., Can., 1,008.............G4 39
Broadview, Ill., 8,588..*F2 58
Broadview, Ind., 1,865............*F4 59
Broadview Heights, Ohio, 6,209.............B2 78
Broadwater, co., Mont., 2,804.............D5 70
Brockport, N.Y., 5,256.B3 75
Brockton, Mass., 72,813.............B5 65
Brockville, Ont., Can., 17,744.............C9 41
Brockway, Pa., 2,563..D4 81
Brocton, N.Y., 1,416...C1 75
Brod, Yugo., 28,729...C4 10
Broderick, Calif., 5,000.A6 50
Brodhead, Wis., 2,444..F4 88
Brodnica, Pol., 12,600..B5 7
Brody, Sov. Un., 10,000.............F5 12
Broken Arrow, Okla., 5,928.............A6 79
Broken Bow, Nebr., 3,482.............C6 71
Broken Bow, Okla., 2,087.............C7 79
Broken Hill, Austl., 31,267.............F7 25
Broken Hill, Zambia, 22,000.............C5 24
Brome, co., Que., Can., 13,691.............D5 42
Bromley, Eng., 68,169............m13 4
Bromptonville, Que., Can., 2,726.............D6 42
Bronson, Mich., 2,267..G5 66
Bronte, Tex., 999......D2 84
Bronx, borough and co., N.Y., 1,424,815 (part of New York City)....D2 75
Bronxville, N.Y., 6,744.............D2 75
Brook, Ind., 845.......C3 59
Brooke, co., W. Va., 28,940.............A4 87
Brookfield, Ill., 20,429..F2 58
Brookfield, Mass., 950..B3 65
Brookfield, Mo., 5,694..B4 69
Brookfield, Wis., 19,812.............E1 88
Brookhaven, Ga., 8,000.............A5 55
Brookhaven, Miss., 9,885.............D3 68
Brookhaven, Pa., 5,280............*G11 81
Brookings, Oreg., 2,637.............E2 80
Brookings, S. Dak., 10,558.............F9 77
Brookings, co., S. Dak., 20,046.............F9 77
Brooklands, Man., Can., 4,369............*E3 40
Brooklands, Mich., 1,800............*F7 66
Brooklawn, N.J., 2,504.D2 74
Brookline, Mass., 54,044.........B5, D2 65
Brookline, Mich., 1,600............*F6 66
Brooklyn, Conn., 900..B9 52
Brooklyn (Lovejoy), Ill., 1,922.............B8 69
Brooklyn, Iowa, 1,415..C5 60
Brooklyn, Mich., 986...F6 66
Brooklyn, Ohio, 10,733.B2 78
Brooklyn, borough (Kings co.), N.Y., 2,627,319 (part of New York City).............E1 75
Brooklyn Center, Minn., 24,356.............E6 67
Brooklyn Park, Md., 1,800............*B4 53
Brooklyn Park, Minn., 10,197............*E6 67
Brookneal, Va., 1,070..D4 85
Brook Park, Ohio, 12,856.............B2 78
Brookport, Ill., 1,154..F5 58
Brooks, Alta., Can., 2,827.............D5 38
Brooks, co., Ga., 15,292.............F3 55
Brooks, co., Tex., 8,609.............F3 84
Brookshire, Tex., 1,339.........E5, F4 84
Brookside, Ala., 999...E4 46
Brookside, Del., 5,000.A6 53
Brookston, Ind., 1,202..C4 59
Brooksville, Fla., 3,301.D4 54
Brookview, Fla., 1,500............*B5 54
Brookville, Ind., 2,596..F7 59
Brookville, Mass., 3,000.............E3 65

Brookville, N.Y., 1,468............*G2 52
Brookville, Ohio, 3,184.C3 78
Brookville, Pa., 4,620..D3 81
Broomall, Pa., 19,772............*B10 81
Broome, co., N.Y., 212,661.............C5 75
Broomfield, Colo., 4,535.............B5 51
Broughton, Pa., 3,500..*B6 81
Broussard, La., 1,600..D4 63
Broward, co., Fla., 333,946.............F6 54
Brown, co., Ill., 6,210..D3 58
Brown, co., Ind., 7,024.F5 59
Brown, co., Kans., 13,229.............C8 61
Brown, co., Minn., 27,676.............F4 67
Brown, co., Nebr., 4,436.............B6 71
Brown, co., Ohio, 25,178.............D4 78
Brown, co., S. Dak., 34,106.............E7 77
Brown, co., Tex., 24,728.............D3 84
Brown, co., Wis., 125,082.............D6 88
Brown City, Mich., 993.............E8 66
Brown Deer, Wis., 11,280.............E2 88
Brownfield, Tex., 10,286.............C1 84
Browning, Mont., 2,011.............B3 70
Brown Lee Park, Mich., 3,307............*F5 66
Brownsburg, Que., Can., 3,617.............D3 42
Brownsburg, Ind., 4,478.............E5 59
Browns Mill, N.J., 792.D3 74
Brownstown, Ind., 2,158.............G8 59
Brownstown, Pa., 1,379............*F4 81
Browns Valley, Minn., 1,033.............E2 67
Brownsville, La., 3,000............*B3 63
Brownsville, Oreg., 875.C4 80
Brownsville, Pa., 6,055.F2 81
Brownsville, Tenn., 5,424.............B2 83
Brownsville, Tex., 48,040 (*141,000).........G4 84
Brownville, Ala., 534...E4 46
Brownville, N.Y., 1,082.............A5 75
Brownville Junction, Maine, 900.........C3 64
Brownwood, Tex., 16,974.............D3 84
Broxton, Ga., 907......E4 55
Brozas, Sp., 5,634.....C2 8
Bruay-en-Artois, Fr., 30,902.............B5 5
Bruce, Miss., 1,698....B4 68
Bruce, co., Ont., Can., 43,036.............C3 41
Bruceton, Tenn., 1,158.A3 83
Bruchsal, Ger., 22,600..D4 6
Bruck, Aus., 16,087....E7 6
Bruck, Aus., 6,791....D8 6
Brugge (Bruges), Bel., 52,220.............B5 5
Brule, co., S. Dak., 6,319.............G6 77
Brumath, Fr., 6,801....C7 5
Brundidge, Ala., 2,523.D4 46
Brunei, Bru., 9,702....E4 19
Brunei, Br. dep., Asia, 40,657.............E4 19
Brunswick, Ga., 21,703.............E5 55
Brunswick, Maine, 12,500.........E3, E5 64
Brunswick, Md., 3,555.B2 53
Brunswick, Mo., 1,493.B4 69
Brunswick, Ohio, 11,725.............A6 78
Brunswick, co., N.C., 20,278.............C5 76
Brunswick, co., Va., 17,779.............E5 85
Brush, Colo., 3,621....A7 51
Brusly, La., 544...B5, D4 63
Brusque, Braz., 16,127.............D3 30
Brussels (Bruxelles), Bel., 170,489 (*1,930,000) B6 5
Bruxelles, see Brussels, Bel.
Bryan, Ohio, 7,361....A3 78
Bryan, Tex., 27,542....D4 84
Bryan, co., Ga., 6,226..D5 55
Bryan, co., Okla., 24,252.............D5 79

Bryansk, Sov. Un.,
231,000............E10 12
Bryant, Fla., 400.....F6 54
Bryn Athyn, Pa.,
1,057.............A12 81
Bryn Mawr, Pa.,
9,000.............A11 81
Bryn Mawr, Wash.,
10,000.............D2 86
Bryson City, N.C.,
1,084.............D2 76
Bryte, Calif., 3,000...*A6 50
Brzeg, Pol., 24,000.....C4 7
Brzeziny, Pol., 6,008...C5 7
Bucaramanga, Col.,
153,790............B3 32
Buchanan, Mich.,
5,341.............G4 66
Buchanan, N.Y.,
2,019.............*D7 75
Buchanan, Va., 1,349..D3 85
Buchanan, co., Iowa,
22,293.............B6 60
Buchanan, co., Mo.,
90,581.............B3 69
Buchanan, co., Va.,
36,724.............B3 85
Buchans, Newf., Can.,
2,413.............D3 44
Bucharest, Rom., 1,177,661
(*1,250,000).........C8 10
Buchloe, Ger., 5,700...D5 6
Buckeye, Ariz.,
2,286.........C2, D1 48
Buckeye Lake, Ohio,
2,129.............C5 78
Buckhannon, W. Va.,
6,389.............C4 87
Buckhaven [& Methil],
Scot., 21,104.......B5 4
Buckhorn, Ariz.,
400.............D2 48
Buckie, Scot., 7,666....B5 4
Buckingham, Que., Can.,
7,421.............D2 42
Buckingham, co., Eng.,
486,183...........*E6 4
Buckingham, co., Va.,
10,877.............D4 85
Buckley, Wash., 3,538..B3 86
Bucknell Manor, Va.,
2,000.............*B5 85
Buckner, Mo., 1,198..*B3 69
Bucks, co., Pa.,
308,567...........F11 81
Bucksport, Maine,
2,327.............D4 64
Bucksport, S.C., 600...D9 82
Bucovina, prov., Rom.,
Sov. Un...........B7 10
Bucovina, reg., Rom.,
Sov. Un...........B7 10
Bucuresti, see Bucharest,
Rom.
Bucyrus, Ohio, 12,276..B5 78
Budapest, Hung.,
1,807,299..........B4 10
Budd Lake, N.J.,
1,520.............B3 74
Bude, Eng., 5,095.....E4 4
Bude, Miss., 1,185.....D3 68
Budrio, It., 16,364.....B3 9
Buechel, Ky.,
8,000.........A4, B4 62
Buena, N.J., 3,243.....D3 74
Buena Park, Calif.,
46,401...........*F3 50
Buenaventura, Col.,
35,087.............C2 32
Buena Vista, Colo.,
1,806.............C4 51
Buena Vista, Ga.,
1,574.............D2 55
Buena Vista (Independent
City), Va., 6,300....D3 85
Buena Vista, co., Iowa,
21,189.............B2 60

Buenos Aires, Arg.,
2,966,816
(*6,975,000).....A5, g7 28
Buenos Aires, prov., Arg.,
6,734,548.......B4, g5 28
Buffalo, Iowa,
1,088.........C7, D7 60
Buffalo, Minn., 2,322..E5 67
Buffalo, Mo., 1,477....D4 69
Buffalo, N.Y., 532,759
(*1,330,000)........C2 75
Buffalo, Okla., 1,618...A2 79
Buffalo, S.C., 1,209...B4 82
Buffalo, Tex., 1,108...D4 84
Buffalo, Wyo., 2,907..A6 89
Buffalo, co., Nebr.,
26,236.............D6 71
Buffalo, co., S. Dak.,
1,547.............F6 77
Buffalo, co., Wis.,
14,202.............D2 88
Buffalo Center, Iowa,
1,140.............A4 60
Buffalo Grove, Ill.,
1,497.............*E2 58
Buford, Ga., 4,168....B2 55
Buga, Col., 32,016....C2 32
Bugojno, Yugo., 5,411..C3 10
Buhl, Idaho, 3,059....G4 57
Buhl, Minn., 1,526....C6 67
Buhuși, Rom., 12,382..B8 10
Bujalance, Sp., 11,475..D3 8
Bujumbura, Burundi,
18,000.............I3 23
Bukama, Con. L......B5 24
Bukavu, Con. L.,
33,500.............I3 23
Bukhara, Sov. Un.,
79,000.............F9 13
Bukidnon, prov., Phil.,
195,600...........*D6 19
Bukoba, Tan., 5,297...I4 23
Bulacan, prov., Phil.,
557,700...........*C6 19
Bulan, Ky., 500......C6 62
Bulan, Phil., 14,279...*C6 19
Bulawayo, Rh.,
160,000............E5 24
Bulgaria, country, Eur.,
7,022,206..........D7 10
Bullas, Sp., 8,936.....C5 8
Bullitt, co., Ky.,
15,726.............C4 62
Bulloch, co., Ga.,
24,263.............D11 55
Bullock, co., Ala.,
13,462.............C4 46
Bulun, Sov. Un., 800..B15 13
Bulun Tokhoi
(Puluntohai), China,
10,000.............B2 17
Bunbury, Austl.,
13,186.............F2 25
Buncombe, co., N.C.,
130,074............D3 76
Bundaberg, Austl.,
22,799.............D9 25
Bunia, Con. L., 5,000..H4 23
Bunker Hill, Ill., 1,524..D4 58
Bunker Hill, Ind.,
1,049.............C5 59
Bunker Hill, Oreg.,
1,655.............*D2 80
Bunker Hill, Tex.,
2,216.............*E5 84
Bunkie, La., 5,188....D3 63
Bunnell, Fla., 1,860...C5 54
Bunny Run, Mich.,
1,058.............*F7 66
Buo Ha, Viet., 10,000.*G5 17
Burao, Som., 10,000...G7 23
Buras, La., 4,000.....E6 63
Buraydah, Sau. Ar.,
20,000.............D3 15
Burbank, Calif.,
5,000.............*B6 50
Burbank, Calif.,
90,155.............F2 50

Burdur, Tur., 25,400...D8 14
Burdwan, India,
108,224............D8 20
Bureau, co., Ill.,
37,594.............B4 58
Bureya, Sov. Un.,
5,000.............B4 18
Burgas, Bul., 43,684...D8 10
Burgas, co., Bul.,
629,593...........*D8 10
Burgaw, N.C., 1,750...C6 76
Burgdorf, Switz., 13,936
(*16,966)..........E3 6
Burgeo, Newf., Can.,
1,138.............E3 44
Burgettstown, Pa.,
2,883.............F1 81
Burgos, Sp., 82,177...A4 8
Burgos, prov., Sp.,
380,791............A4 8
Burgundy, former prov.,
Fr., 1,264,000.......D6 5
Burhanpur, India,
82,090.............D6 20
Burien, Wash.,
10,000...........*D1 86
Burin, Newf., Can.,
1,116.............E4 44
Buriram, Thai.,
12,352...........*C2 19
Burkburnett, Tex.,
7,621.............B3 84
Burke, co., Ga., 20,596.C4 55
Burke, co., N.C.,
52,701.............B2 76
Burke, co., N. Dak.,
5,886.............B3 77
Burke City, Mo., 1,500.A8 69
Burkesville, Ky., 1,688.D4 62
Burks Falls, Ont., Can.,
926.............B5 41
Burleigh, co., N. Dak.,
34,016.............D5 77
Burleson, Tex., 2,345..B5 84
Burleson, co., Tex.,
11,177.............D4 84
Burley, Idaho, 7,508...G5 57
Burlingame, Calif.,
24,036.............B5 50
Burlingame, Kans.,
1,151.............D8 61
Burlington, Ont., Can.,
47,008.............D5 41
Burlington, Colo.,
2,090.............B8 51
Burlington, Iowa,
32,430.............D6 60
Burlington, Kans.,
2,113.............D8 61
Burlington, Mass.,
12,852............C2 65
Burlington, N.J.,
12,687............C3 74
Burlington, N.C.,
33,199............A4 76
Burlington, Vt., 35,531.C1 73
Burlington, Wash.,
2,968.............A3 86
Burlington, Wis.,
5,856.........F1, F5 88
Burlington, co., N.J.,
224,499............D3 74
Burlington Beach, Ont.,
Can., 3,314.......*D5 41
Burma, country, Asia,
19,856,000.........D10 20
Burnet, Tex., 2,214...D3 84
Burnet, co., Tex., 9,265.D3 84
Burnett, co., Wis.,
9,214.............C1 88
Burney, Calif., 1,294...B3 50
Burnham, Ill., 2,478...*F3 58
Burnham, Pa., 2,755...E6 81
Burnie, Austl., 14,201.o15 25
Burnley, Eng., 80,588..D5 4
Burns, Oreg., 3,523....D7 80
Burns Flat, Okla.,
2,280.............B2 79

Burns Lake, B.C., Can.,
1,041.............B5 37
Burnsville, N.C.,
1,388.............C4 76
Burnwell, Ala., 500....E4 46
Burriana, Sp., 15,154...C5 8
Bursa, Tur., 153,600...B7 14
Burt, co., Nebr., 10,192.C9 71
Burton, Calif., 4,635..*D4 50
Burton, Ohio, 1,085...A6 78
Burton-on-Trent, Eng.,
50,766............D6 4
Burundi, country, Afr.,
2,300,000..........I3 23
Būshehr, Iran, 27,317..G8 16
Bushnell, Ill., 3,710...C3 58
Buskerud, co., Nor.,
168,500...........*H4 11
Busko, Pol., 5,975.....C6 7
Bussum, Neth., 39,800.A6 5
Busto Arsizio, It.,
64,367.............B2 9
Buta, Con. L., 11,200..H2 23
Bute, co., Scot.,
15,129...........*C4 4
Butler, Ala., 1,765.....C1 46
Butler, Ga., 1,346.....D2 55
Butler, Ind., 2,176....B8 59
Butler, Mo., 3,791....C3 69
Butler, N.J., 5,414....B4 74
Butler, Ohio, 899.....B5 78
Butler, Pa., 20,975....E2 81
Butler, Wis., 2,274....E1 88
Butler, co., Ala.,
24,560.............D3 46
Butler, co., Iowa,
17,467.............B5 60
Butler, co., Kans.,
38,395.............E7 61
Butler, co., Ky., 9,586..C3 62
Butler, co., Mo., 34,656.E7 69
Butler, co., Nebr.,
10,312.............C8 71
Butler, co., Ohio,
199,076............C3 78
Butler, co., Pa.,
114,639............E2 81
Butner, N.C., 1,000...*A5 76
Butte, Mont., 27,877..D4 70
Butte, co., Calif.,
82,030.............C3 50
Butte, co., Idaho,
3,498.............F5 57
Butte, co., S. Dak.,
8,592.............F2 77
Butterworth, Mala.,
42,504.............D2 19
Butts, co., Ga., 8,976..C3 55
Butuan, Phil., 15,000..D7 19
Buturlinovka, Sov. Un.,
39,800............F13 12
Bützow, Ger., 10,900...B5 6
Buxtehude, Ger.,
15,700............B4 6
Buxton, Guy.,
5,164.............C5 27
Buzău, Rom., 47,595...C8 10
Buzet, Yugo., 444.....C1 10
Buzzards Bay, Mass.,
2,170.............C6 65
Byala Slatina, Bul.,
9,357.............D6 10
Bydgoszcz, Pol.,
231,000............B5 7
Byelorussia (S.S.R.)
(White Russia), rep.,
Sov. Un., 8,226,000..E5 12
Byesville, Ohio, 2,447..C6 78
Bykovo, Sov. Un.,
10,000............G15 12
Byron, Ga., 1,138.....D3 55
Byron, Ill., 1,578.....A4 58
Bystrzyca, Pol., 9,564..C4 7
Bytom, Pol.,
182,000.........C5, G9 7
Bytosh, Sov. Un.,
10,000............E10 12

C

Caacupé, Par., 15,834..E4 29
Caaguazú, dept., Par.,
2,610.............D4 29
Caapucú, Par., 6,608...E4 29
Caazapá, Par., 16,588..E4 29
Caazapá, dept., Par.,
3,003.............E4 29
Cabaceiras, Braz., 581.*D4 27
Cabanatuan, Phil.,
20,000............o13 19
Cabano, Que., Can.,
2,695.............B9 42
Cabarrus, co., N. Car.,
68,137............B13 76
Cabedelo, Braz.,
10,738.........C4, H6 34
Cabell, co., W. Va.,
108,202............C2 87

Cabeza del Buey, Sp.,
11,737.............C3 8
Cabimas, Ven., 93,347..A3 32
Cabinda, Ang., 1,554...B2 24
Cabinda, reg., Ang.,
58,453.............B2 24
Cabin John, Md.,
2,000.........C1, C3 53
Cabo, Braz., 6,029....*D7 27
Cabo Frio, Braz.,
13,117.............C4 30
Cabool, Mo., 1,284....D5 69
Caborca, Mex., 9,285..A2 34
Cabo Rojo, P.R.,
3,086...........*M13 35
Cabot, Ark., 1,321.....C3 49
Cabra, Sp., 15,995.....D3 8
Čačak, Yugo., 27,356..D5 10

Caçapava, Braz.,
7,987.............C3 30
Cacequi, Braz., 8,458..D2 30
Cáceres, Sp., 48,005...C2 8
Cáceres, prov., Sp.,
544,407............C2 8
Cachan, Fr., 23,282..G10 5
Cache, Okla., 1,003....C3 79
Cache, co., Utah,
35,788.............A6 72
Cachi, Arg............E2 29
Cachoeira do Sul, Braz.,
38,661............E2 30
Cachoeira, Braz.,
11,415...........*E7 27
Cachoeiro do Itapemirim,
Braz., 39,470.......C4 30
Caddo, co., Okla.,
28,621.............B3 79

Caddo, par., La.,
223,859............B2 63
Cadillac, Que., Can.,
1,077.............*E9 41
Cadillac, Mich., 10,112.D5 66
Cadiz, Ky., 1,980......D2 62
Cadiz, Ohio, 3,259....B6 78
Cádiz, Sp., 117,871...D2 8
Cádiz, prov., Sp.,
818,847...........*D2 8
Caen, Fr., 91,336
(*120,000)..........C3 5
Caernarvon, Wales,
8,998.............D4 4
Caernarvon, co., Wales,
121,194...........*D4 4
Cagayan, Phil., 23,000.D6 19
Cagayan, prov., Phil.,
445,700...........*B6 19

Cagli, It., 3,235......C4 9
Cagliari, It., 183,784...E2 9
Cagnes-sur-Mer, Fr., 15,392......F7 5
Caguas, P.R., 32,015.M13 35
Cahaba Heights, Ala., 2,000......*B3 46
Cahokia, Ill., 15,829..B8 58
Cahors, Fr., 17,046....E4 5
Caibarién, Cuba, 22,657......D4 35
Caicedonia, Col., 10,681......C2 32
Caicó, Braz., 15,826..*D7 27
Cairnbrook, Pa., 1,100..F4 81
Cairns, Austl., 25,204..C8 25
Cairo (Al Qāhirah), Eg., U.A.R., 2,877,195...B4 23
Cairo, Ga., 7,427.....F2 55
Cairo, Ill., 9,348.....F4 58
Caithness, co., Scot., 27,345......*A5 4
Cajamarca, Peru, 18,324......C2 31
Cajamarca, dept., Peru, 651,068......C2 31
Cajàzeiras, Braz., 15,884......*D7 27
Cakovec, Yugo., 9,647..B3 10
Calabria, pol. dist., It., 2,045,047......*E5 9
Calabria, reg., It E6 9
Calafat, Rom., 8,069..D6 10
Calahorra, Sp., 14,462..A4 8
Calais, Fr., 70,372....B4 5
Calais, Maine, 4,223...C5 64
Calamar, Col., 5,393...A3 32
Calamba, Phil., 7,600..C6 19
Calañas, Sp., 4,059...D2 8
Calapan, Phil., 6,113..C6 19
Călărasi, Rom., 25,555......C8 10
Calarcá, Col., 15,707...C2 32
Calasparra, Sp., 8,155..C5 8
Calatayud, Sp., 15,792.B5 8
Calauag, Phil., 4,260..P14 19
Calaveras, co., Calif., 10,289......C3 50
Calcasieu, par., La., 145,475......D2 63
Calceta, Ec., 3,680.....B1 31
Calcutta, India, 2,927,289 (*6,350,000)......D8 20
Calcutta, Ohio, 2,221..B7 78
Caldas, dept., Col., 1,212,450......B2 32
Caldas da Rainha, Port., 10,039......C1 8
Caldwell, Idaho, 12,230.F2 57
Caldwell, Kans., 1,788..E6 61
Caldwell, N.J., 6,942..B4 74
Caldwell, Ohio, 1,999..C6 78
Caldwell, Tex., 2,204..D4 84
Caldwell, co., Ky., 13,073......C2 62
Caldwell, co., Mo., 8,830......B3 69
Caldwell, co., N.C., 49,552......B2 76
Caldwell, co., Tex., 17,222......E4 84
Caldwell, par., La., 9,004......B3 63
Caledonia, Ont., Can., 2,198......D5 41
Caledonia, Minn., 2,563......G7 67
Caledonia, N.Y., 1,917.C3 75
Caledonia, co., Vt., 22,786......C3 73
Calella, Sp., 7,947....B7 8
Calera, Ala., 1,928...B3 46
Calera, Chile, 13,047..A2 28
Calexico, Calif., 7,992.F6 50
Calgary, Alta., Can., 249,641 (*279,062)..D3 38
Calhoun, Ga., 3,587..B2 55
Calhoun, co., Ala., 95,878......B4 46
Calhoun, co., Ark., 5,991......D3 49
Calhoun, co., Fla., 7,422......B1 54
Calhoun, co., Ga., 7,341......E2 55
Calhoun, co., Ill., 5,933......D3 58
Calhoun, co., Iowa, 15,923......B3 60
Calhoun, co., Mich., 138,858......F5 66
Calhoun, co., Miss., 15,941......B4 68
Calhoun, co., S.C., 12,256......D6 82
Calhoun, co., Tex., 16,592......E4 84
Calhoun, co., W. Va., 7,948......C3 87
Calhoun City, Miss., 1,714......B4 68

Calhoun Falls, S.C., 2,525......C3 82
Cali, Col., 429,170.....C2 32
Calico Rock, Ark., 773.A3 49
Calicut, see Kozhikode, India.
Caliente, Nev., 792...C4 72
California, Mo., 2,788..C5 69
California, Pa., 5,978..F2 81
California, state, U.S., 15,717,204......C2 50
Calipatria, Calif., 2,548......F6 50
Calistoga, Calif., 1,514......A5, C2 50
Callahan, co., Tex., 7,929......C3 84
Callao, Peru, 84,232...D2 31
Callaway, co., Mo., 23,858......C6 69
Calloway, co., Ky., 20,972......B3 62
Calmar, Alta., Can., 700......C4 38
Calmar, Iowa, 954.....A6 60
Caltagirone, It., 36,000.F5 9
Caltanissetta, It., 48,500......F5 9
Caluire [-et-Cuire], Fr., 25,754......E6 5
Calumet, Mich., 1,139..A6 66
Calumet, Pa., 1,241...*F3 81
Calumet, co., Wis., 22,268......D5 88
Calumet City, Ill., 25,000......B6, F3 58
Calumet Park, Ill., 8,448......*F3 58
Calvados, dept., Fr., 480,686......*C3 5
Calvert, Tex., 2,073...D4 84
Calvert, co., Md., 15,826......C4 53
Calvert City, Ky., 1,505......A3 62
Calverton Park, Mo., 1,714......A8 69
Calwa, Calif., 8,000...*D4 50
Calzada de Calatrava, Sp., 9,140......C4 8
Camagüey, Cuba, 110,388......E5 35
Camagüey, prov., Cuba, 618,256......E5 35
Camanche, Iowa, 2,225......C7 60
Camarillo, Calif., 2,359......*E4 50
Camarines Norte, prov., Phil., 188,600.....*C6 19
Camarines Sur, prov., Phil., 826,600......*C6 19
Camas, Wash., 5,666...D3 86
Camas, co., Idaho, 917.F4 57
Cambodia, country, Asia, 3,800,000......C2 19
Camborne [-Redruth], Eng., 36,090......E4 4
Cambrai, Fr., 32,897..B5 5
Cambria, Calif., 700...E3 50
Cambria, co., Pa., 203,283......E4 81
Cambrian Park, Calif., 4,000......*D3 50
Cambridge, Eng., 95,358......D7 4
Cambridge, Ill., 1,665..B3 58
Cambridge, Md., 12,239......C5 53
Cambridge, Mass., 107,716......B5, D3 65
Cambridge, Minn., 2,728......E5 67
Cambridge, Nebr., 1,090......D5 71
Cambridge, N.J., 1,900......*C3 74
Cambridge, N.Y., 1,748......B7 75
Cambridge, Ohio, 14,562......B6 78
Cambridge, co., Eng., 189,913......*D7 4
Cambridge City, Ind., 2,569......E7 59
Cambridge Springs, Pa., 2,031......C1 81
Camden, Ala., 1,121..D2 46
Camden, Ark., 15,823..D3 49
Camden, Del., 1,125..B6 53
Camden, Maine, 3,523.D3 64
Camden, N.J., 117,159.D2 74
Camden, N.Y., 2,694..B5 75
Camden, Ohio, 1,308...C3 78
Camden, S.C., 6,842...C6 82
Camden, Tenn., 2,774..A3 83
Camden, Tex., 1,131..D5 84
Camden, co., Ga., 9,975......F5 55
Camden, co., Mo., 9,116......C5 69

Camden, co., N.J., 392,035......D3 74
Camden, co., N.C., 5,598......A7 76
Camdenton, Mo., 1,405......D5 69
Camerino, It., 4,200...C4 9
Cameron, Mo., 3,674..B3 69
Cameron, Tex., 5,640..D4 84
Cameron, W. Va., 1,652......B4, C2 87
Cameron, Wis., 982...C2 88
Cameron, co., Pa., 7,586......D5 81
Cameron, co., Tex., 151,098......F4 84
Cameron, par., La., 6,909......E2 63
Cameroon, country, Afr., 4,129,000......G7 22
Camiling, Phil., 7,765..o13 19
Camilla, Ga., 4,753....E2 55
Camillus, N.Y., 1,416.*B4 75
Cammack, Ark., 1,355......C3, D5 49
Camocim, Braz., 10,788......D6 27
Camp, co., Tex., 7,849.C5 84
Campagna di Roma, reg., It......h9 9
Campana, Arg., 14,452. g7 28
Campanario, Sp., 9,660.C3 8
Campania, pol. dist., It., 4,760,759......*D5 9
Campania, reg., It.....D5 9
Campbell, Calif., 11,863......C5 50
Campbell, Mo., 1,964..E7 69
Campbell, Ohio, 13,406......A7 78
Campbell, co., Ky., 86,803......B5 62
Campbell, co., S. Dak., 3,531......E5 77
Campbell, co., Tenn., 27,936......C9 83
Campbell, co., Va., 32,958......D3 85
Campbell, co., Wyo., 5,861......A7 89
Campbellford, Ont., Can., 3,478......E7 41
Campbellpur, Pak., 10,135 (*17,689)......B5 20
Campbell River, B.C., Can., 3,737......D5 37
Campbells Bay, Que., Can., 1,024......B8 41
Campbellsport, Wis., 1,472......E5 88
Campbellsville, Ky., 6,966......C4 62
Campbellton, N.B., Can., 9,873......A3 43
Campbelltown, Pa., 1,061......*F9 81
Campbeltown, Scot., 6,525......C4 4
Campeche, Mex., 44,426......D6 34
Campeche, state, Mex., 164,256......D6 34
Camp Hill, Ala., 1,270.C4 46
Camp Hill, Pa., 8,559..F8 81
Campiglia Marittima, It., 2,716......C3 9
Câmpina, Rom., 18,680.C7 10
Campina Grande, Braz., 116,226......D7 27
Campinas, Braz., 179,797......C3, m8 30
Campobasso, It., 26,500......D5 9
Campo Belo, Braz., 15,742......C3 30
Campo de Criptana, Sp., 14,608......C4 8
Campo Grande, Braz., 64,477......C2 30
Campo Maior, Braz., 13,939......*D6 27
Campo Maior, Port., 8,086......C2 8
Campos, Braz., 90,601..C4 30
Camp Point, Ill., 1,092.C2 58
Campti, La., 1,045.....C2 63
Campton Heights, Calif., 1,200......*B1 50
Câmpulung, Rom., 18,880......C7 10
Câmpulung, Moldovenesc, Rom., 13,627......B7 10
Camrose, Alta., Can., 6,939......C4 38
Canaan, Conn., 1,146..A3 52
Canada, Ky., 400......C7 62
Canada, country, N.A., 18,238,247......D10 33
Cañada de Gómez, Arg., 12,354......A4 28
Canadian, Tex., 2,239..B2 84

Canadian, co., Okla., 24,727......B4 79
Canajoharie, N.Y., 2,681......C6 75
Canakkale, Tur., 19,500......B6 29
Canal Fulton, Ohio, 1,555......B6 78
Canal Point, Fla., 900..F6 54
Canal Winchester, Ohio, 1,976......C2, C5 78
Canal Zone, U.S. dep., N.A., 42,122......B2 32
Canandaigua, N.Y., 9,370......C3 75
Cananea, Mex., 19,895.A2 34
Cañar, prov., Ec., 107,701......B2 31
Canary Is., reg., Sp., 944,448......C1 22
Cañas, C.R., 5,929...*E7 34
Canastota, N.Y., 4,896.B5 75
Canavieiras, Braz., 10,264......E7 27
Canberra, Austl., 56,449......G8 25
Canby, Minn., 2,146...F2 67
Canby, Oreg., 2,168......B2, B4 80
Candeleda, Sp., 6,983..B3 8
Candia, see Iraklion, Grc.
Candler, Ga., 4,753....D4 55
Cando, N. Dak., 1,566.B6 77
Candor, N.Y., 956.....C4 75
Canea, see Khania, Grc.
Canelones, Ur., 8,041..E1 30
Canelones, dept., Ur., 182,100......*E1 30
Caney, Kans., 2,682...E8 61
Canfield, Ohio, 3,252..A7 78
Cangas, Sp., 4,008....A1 8
Cangas de Narcea, Sp., 2,528......A2 8
Cangas de Onís, Sp., 9,936......A3 8
Canicatti, It., 31,800...F4 10
Caniles, Sp., 8,040....D4 8
Canisteo, N.Y., 2,731..C3 75
Çankiri, Tur., 20,000...B9 14
Cannelton, Ind., 1,829.I4 59
Cannes, Fr., 58,079....F7 5
Cannington, Ont., Can., 1,024......C5 41
Cannon, co., Tenn., 8,537......B5 83
Cannon Falls, Minn., 2,055......F6 67
Canoinhas, Braz., 9,252.D2 30
Canon City, Colo., 8,973......C5 51
Canonsburg, Pa., 11,877......F1 81
Canora, Sask., Can., 2,117......F4 39
Canosa, It., 34,015....D6 10
Canso, N.S., Can., 1,151......D8 43
Cantal, dept., Fr., 172,977......*E5 5
Canterbury, Eng., 30,376......E7 4
Can Tho, Viet., 27,000......*C3 19
Cantilan, Phil., 4,141.*D7 19
Canton, China, 1,840,000......G7 17
Canton, Ga., 2,411....B2 55
Canton, Ill., 13,588....C3 58
Canton, Mass., 12,771......B5, D2 65
Canton, Miss., 9,707...C3 68
Canton, Mo., 2,562....A6 69
Canton, N.Y., 5,046...B2 75
Canton, N.C., 5,068...D3 76
Canton, Ohio, 113,631 (*281,900)......B6 78
Canton, Okla., 887....A3 79
Canton, Pa., 2,102....C8 81
Canton, S. Dak., 2,511.G9 77
Canton, Tex., 1,114...C5 84
Cantonment, Fla., 2,499......G2 54
Cantwell, Mo., 900...D7 69
Canutillo, Tex., 1,377..E1 84
Canyon, Tex., 5,864..B2 84
Canyon, co., Idaho, 57,662......F2 57
Canyonville, Oreg., 1,089......E3 80
Cao Bang, Viet., 25,000.G6 17
Capac, Mich., 1,235...F8 66
Cap Chat, Que., Can., 2,035......G20 36
Cap de la Madeleine, Que., Can., 26,925......C5 42
Cape Breton, co., N.S., Can., 131,507......D9 43
Cape Canaveral, Fla., 3,500......D6 54
Cape Charles, Va., 2,041......D6 85

Cape Coast, Ghana,
56,730.............G4   22
Cape Elizabeth, Maine,
5,505.........E2, E5   64
Cape Girardeau, Mo.,
24,947.............D8   69
Cape Girardeau, co., Mo.,
42,020.............D8   69
Capels, W. Va., 800...D3   87
Cape May, N.J., 4,477..F3   74
Cape May, co., N.J.,
48,555.............E3   74
Cape May Court House,
N.J., 1,749.........E3   74
Cape of Good Hope, prov.,
S. Afr., 5,355,368....G4   24
Capesterre, Guad.,
3,725.............n16   35
Cape Town, S. Afr.,
508,341 (*807,211)...G3   24
Cape Verde Is., Port. dep.,
Afr., 147,328.......o12   22
Cape Vincent, N.Y.,
770...............A4   75
Cap-Haïtien, Hai.,
24,957.............F7   35
Capiatá, Par., 14,942..E4   29
Capistrano Beach, Calif.,
2,026............*F5   50
Capitan, N. Mex., 552..C6   48
Capitola, Calif., 2,021.*C6   50
Capitol Heights, Md.,
3,138..........C2, C4   53
Capivarí, Braz., 10,961.m8   30
Capiz, prov., Phil.,
314,800...........*C6   19
Capreol, Ont., Can.,
3,003.............E9   41
Cap St. Ignace, Que.,
Can., 1,247........B7   42
Captain Cook, Haw.,
1,687.............D6   56
Capua, It., 13,200.....D5   9
Caquetá, intendencia, Col.,
63,970.............C3   32
Carabobo, state, Ven.,
381,636............A4   32
Caracal, Rom., 19,082..C7   10
Caracas, Ven., 786,710.A4   32
Caraguatay, Par.,
15,315.............E4   29
Carangola, Braz.,
11,896.............C4   30
Caransebes, Rom.,
15,195.............C6   10
Carapeguá, Par.,
23,675.............E4   29
Caraquet, N.B., Can.,
1,214.............B5   43
Caratinga, Braz.,
22,275.............B4   30
Caravaca, Sp., 10,678..C5   8
Caraway, Ark., 821....B5   49
Caràzinho, Braz.,
18,162.............D2   30
Carballino, Sp., 9,639..A1   8
Carballo, Sp., 3,110....A1   8
Carberry, Man., Can.,
1,113.............E2   40
Carbon, co., Mont.,
8,317.............E7   70
Carbon, co., Pa.,
52,889............E10   81
Carbon, co., Utah,
21,135.............B6   72
Carbon, co., Wyo.,
14,937.............D5   89
Carbondale, Ill.,
14,670.............F4   58
Carbondale, Pa.,
13,595............C10   81
Carbonear, Newf., Can.,
4,234.............E5   44
Carbon Hill, Ala.,
1,944.............B2   46
Carbonia, It., 34,400...E2   9
Carcagente, Sp.,
17,937.............C5   8
Carcar, Phil., 5,344...*C6   19
Carcassonne, Fr.,
40,897.............F5   5
Carchi, prov., Ec.,
84,738.............A2   31
Cardale, Pa., 900.....*G2   81
Cárdenas, Cuba,
43,750.............D3   35
Cárdenas, Mex.,
12,344............k14   34
Cardiff, Wales, 256,270.E5   4
Cardiff-by-the-Sea, Calif.,
1,500............*F5   50
Cardigan, co., Wales,
53,564............*D4   4
Cardinal, Ont., Can.,
1,994.............C9   41
Cardington, Ohio,
1,613.............B5   78
Cardston, Alta., Can.,
2,801.............E4   38
Cardwell, Mo., 816....E7   69
Carei, Rom., 16,780....B6   61

Carencro, La., 1,519...D3   63
Carenero, Ven.........A4   32
Caretta, W. Va., 1,092.D3   87
Carey, Ohio, 3,722.....B4   78
Cariati, It., 5,204.....E6   9
Caribou, Maine, 8,305..B5   64
Caribou, co., Idaho,
5,976.............G7   57
Carini, It., 16,723.....E4   9
Carinthia, reg., Aus...E6   6
Caripito, Ven., 19,003..A5   32
Carle Place, N.Y.,
5,100............*G2   52
Carleton, Mich., 1,379..F7   66
Carleton, co., N.B., Can.,
23,507.............C2   43
Carleton, co., Ont., Can.,
352,931............B9   41
Carleton Place, Ont., Can.,
4,796.............B8   41
Carlin, Nev., 1,023.....A3   72
Carlinville, Ill., 5,440..D4   58
Carlisle, Ark., 1,514....C4   49
Carlisle, Eng., 71,112..C5   4
Carlisle, Iowa, 1,317...C4   60
Carlisle, Ky., 1,601....B5   62
Carlisle, Pa., 16,623....F7   81
Carlisle, co., Ky., 5,608.B2   62
Carl Junction, Mo.,
1,220.............D3   69
Carloforte, It., 7,275...E2   9
Carlos Casares, Arg.,
7,558.............B4   28
Carlow, Ire., 7,708.....D3   4
Carlow, co., Ire.,
33,342............*D3   4
Carlsbad, Calif., 9,253..F5   50
Carlsbad, N. Mex.,
25,541.............C6   48
Carlstadt, N.J., 6,042...D5   74
Carlton, Oreg., 959.B1, B3   80
Carlton, co., Minn.,
27,932.............D6   67
Carlyle, Ill., 2,903.....C4   58
Carmagnola, It., 4,800..B1   9
Carman, Man., Can.,
1,930.............E2   40
Carman, N.Y., 1,500..*C6   75
Carmarthen, Wales,
13,249.............E4   4
Carmarthen, co., Wales,
167,736...........*E4   4
Carmaux, Fr., 11,136...E5   5
Carmel, Calif.,
4,580..........C6, D3   50
Carmel, Ind., 1,442....E5   59
Carmel, N.Y., 2,735...D7   75
Carmelo, Ur., 11,800...E1   30
Carmel Valley, Calif.,
1,143............*D3   50
Carmel Woods, Calif.,
1,043............*D3   50
Carmen del Paraná, Par.,
10,699.............E4   29
Carmen de Patagones,
Arg., 5,243........C4   28
Carmi, Ill., 6,152.....E5   58
Carmichael, Calif.,
20,455.............A6   50
Carmona, Sp., 28,216..D3   8
Carnegie, Okla., 1,500..B3   79
Carnegie, Pa.,
11,887..........B5, F1   81
Carneys Point, N.J.,
3,500.............D2   74
Caro, Mich., 3,534.....E7   66
Carol City, Fla.,
21,749.............E3   54
Caroleen, N.C., 1,168..B2   76
Carolina, P.R., 3,075.*m13   35
Carolina Beach, N.C.,
1,192.............C6   76
Caroline, co., Md.,
19,462.............C6   53
Caroline, co., Va.,
12,725.............D5   85
Caroline Is., U.S. trust.,
Pac. O.............F6   2
Carora, Ven., 22,251...A3   32
Carouge, Switz., 12,760.E3   6
Carpentersville, Ill.,
17,424.............E2   58
Carpentras, Fr., 14,169.E6   5
Carpi, It., 21,000.....B3   9
Carpinteria, Calif.,
4,998.............E4   50
Carrabelle, Fla., 1,146..C2   54
Carrara, It., 64,901....B3   9
Carrboro, N.C., 1,997..B4   76
Carrickfergus, N. Ire.,
10,211.............C4   4
Carriers Mills, Ill.,
2,006.............F5   58
Carrington, N. Dak.,
2,438.............C6   77
Carrizo Springs, Tex.,
5,699.............E3   84
Carrizozo, N. Mex.,
1,546.............C6   48
Carroll, Iowa, 7,682....B3   60

Carroll, co., Ark.,
11,284.............A2   49
Carroll, co., Ga., 36,451.C1   55
Carroll, co., Ill., 19,507.A4   58
Carroll, co., Ind.,
16,934.............C4   59
Carroll, co., Iowa,
23,431.............B3   60
Carroll, co., Ky., 7,978.B4   62
Carroll, co., Md.,
52,785.............A3   53
Carroll, co., Miss.,
11,177.............B4   68
Carroll, co., Mo.,
13,847.............B4   69
Carroll, co., N.H.,
15,829.............D5   73
Carroll, co., Ohio,
20,857.............B6   78
Carroll, co., Tenn.,
23,476.............B3   83
Carroll, co., Va., 23,178.E2   85
Carrollton, Ga., 10,973.C1   55
Carrollton, Ill., 2,558..D3   58
Carrollton, Ky., 3,218..B4   62
Carrollton, Md., 3,385..A4   53
Carrollton, Mich.,
6,718.............E7   66
Carrollton, Mo., 4,554..B4   69
Carrollton, Ohio, 2,786.B6   78
Carrollton, Tex., 4,242.B5   84
Carrolltown, Pa., 1,525.E4   81
Carrville, Ala., 1,081...C4   46
Carsamba, Tur.,
14,800............B11   14
Carshalton, Eng.,
61,000............m12   4
Carson, Iowa, 583....C10   71
Carson, co., Tex., 7,781.B2   84
Carson City, Mich.,
1,201.............E5   66
Carson City, Nev.,
5,163.............B2   72
Carsonville, Mo.,
4,500............*A8   69
Carswell, W. Va., 500.*D3   87
Cartagena, Col.,
152,380............A2   32
Cartagena, Sp.,
100,000............D5   8
Cartago, Col., 31,051..C2   32
Cartago, C.R., 18,900..F8   34
Cartago, prov., C.R.,
154,200...........*H12   33
Cartaxo, Port., 5,920...C1   8
Cartaya, Sp., 9,002....D2   8
Carter, co., Ky., 20,817.B6   62
Carter, co., Mo., 3,973.E7   69
Carter, co., Mont.,
2,493.............E12   70
Carter, co., Okla.,
39,044.............C4   79
Carter, co., Tenn.,
41,578............C11   83
Carteret, N.J.,
20,502.........B4, E4   74
Carteret, co., N.C.,
30,940.............C7   76
Carter Lake, Iowa,
2,287.............C2   60
Cartersville, Ga., 8,668.B2   55
Carterville, Ill., 2,643..F4   58
Carterville, Mo., 1,443.D3   69
Carthage, Ill., 3,325...C2   58
Carthage, Ind., 1,043..E6   59
Carthage, Miss., 2,442..C4   68
Carthage, Mo., 11,264..D3   69
Carthage, N.Y., 4,216..B5   75
Carthage, N.C., 1,190..B4   76
Carthage, Tenn., 2,021.C8   83
Carthage, Tex., 5,262..C5   84
Caruaru, Braz., 64,471.D7   27
Carúpano, Ven., 38,210.A5   32
Caruthersville, Mo.,
8,643.............E8   69
Carver, Minn., 467....E5   67
Carver, co., Minn.,
21,358.............F5   67
Carville, La., 950.....B5   63
Cary, Ill., 3,204......A5   58
Cary, N.C., 3,356.....B5   76
Caryville, Tenn., 950...C9   83
Casablanca, Mor.,
965,277............B3   22
Casa Branca, Braz.,
8,980..........C3, k8   30
Casa de Oro, Calif.,
1,500............*E2   50
Casa Grande, Ariz.,
8,311.............C3   48
Casale Monferrato, It.,
33,200.............B2   9
Casalmaggiore, It.,
5,656.............B3   9
Casarano, It., 14,744...D7   9
Casas Adobes, Ariz.,
5,000............*C3   48
Cascade, Idaho, 923...E2   57
Cascade, Iowa, 1,601..B6   60
Cascade, co., Mont.,
73,418.............C5   70

Cascais, Port.,
7,887...........C1, f9   8
Caserta, It., 38,000...D5   9
Casey, Ill., 2,890.....D6   58
Casey, co., Ky.,
14,327.............C5   62
Caseyville, Ill.,
2,455............*E3   58
Cashion, Ariz., 1,000..D1   48
Cashmere, Wash.,
1,891.............B5   86
Casilda, Arg., 11,023...A4   28
Casino, Austl., 8,091..D9   26
Caslav, Czech., 10,100.D3   7
Caspe, Sp., 9,033.....B5   8
Casper, Wyo., 38,930..C6   89
Caspian, Mich., 1,493..B2   66
Cass, co., Ill., 14,539..D3   58
Cass, co., Ind., 40,931..C5   59
Cass, co., Iowa, 17,919.C3   60
Cass, co., Mich.,
36,932.............G4   66
Cass, co., Minn., 16,720.D4   67
Cass, co., Mo., 29,702..C3   69
Cass, co., Nebr.,
17,821.............D9   71
Cass, co., N. Dak.,
66,947.............C8   77
Cass, co., Tex., 23,496.C5   84
Cass City, Mich., 1,945.E7   66
Casselberry, Fla.,
2,463............*D5   54
Casselman, Ont., Can.,
1,277.............B9   41
Casselton, N. Dak.,
1,394.............D8   77
Cassia, co., Idaho,
16,121.............G5   57
Cassino, It., 8,000....D4   9
Cass Lake, Minn.,
1,586.............C4   67
Cassopolis, Mich.,
2,027.............G4   66
Cassville, Mo., 1,451...E4   69
Cassville, Wis., 1,290..F3   88
Castalia, Ohio, 954....A5   78
Castanea, Pa., 1,218...D7   81
Castellón, prov., Sp.,
339,229...........*C5   8
Castellón de la Plana, Sp.,
62,493.............C5   8
Castelnaudary, Fr.,
8,071.............F4   5
Castelo Branco, Port.,
13,056.............C2   8
Castelvetrano, It.,
31,282.............F4   9
Castile, N.Y., 1,146....C2   75
Castilla, Peru, 8,892...C1   31
Castlegar, B.C., Can.,
2,253.............E9   37
Castle Hill, Iowa, 932..B5   60
Castle Hills, Tex.,
2,622............*E3   84
Castlemaine, Austl.,
7,217.............H5   26
Castle Park, Calif.,
1,800............*E2   50
Castle Rock, Colo.,
1,152.............B6   51
Castle Rock, Wash.,
1,424.............C3   86
Castle Shannon, Pa.,
11,836.............B5   81
Castleton-on-Hudson,
N.Y., 1,752........C7   75
Castor, Alta., Can.,
1,025.............C5   38
Castres, Fr., 36,978...F5   5
Castries, St. Lucia,
17,505............o16   35
Castro, Braz., 9,249...C3   30
Castro, Sp., 11,842....D3   8
Castro, co., Tex., 8,923.B1   84
Castro Alves, Braz.,
7,388............*E7   27
Castropol, Sp., 7,368...A2   8
Castro Urdiales, Sp.,
6,222.............A4   8
Castro Valley, Calif.,
37,120............*B5   50
Castrovillari, It.,
12,500.............E6   9
Castroville, Calif.,
2,838..........C6, D3   50
Castroville, Tex., 1,508.E3   84
Castuera, Sp., 10,166..C3   8
Caswell, co., N.C.,
19,912.............A4   76
Catacaos, Peru, 8,526..C1   31
Catacocha, Ec., 2,754..B2   31
Cataguases, Braz.,
21,476..........C4, g6   30
Catahoula, par., La.,
11,421.............C4   63
Cataiñgan, Phil.,
7,462............*C6   19
Catalão, Braz., 11,471..B3   30
Catalca, Tur., 4,800...B7   14
Catamarca, Arg.,
31,067.............E2   29

Catamarca, prov., Arg., 172,407....E2 29
Catanduva, Braz., 37,307....C3 30
Catania, It., 363,928...F5 9
Cataño, P.R., 8,276..*m13 35
Catanzaro, It., 74,037..E6 9
Catarman, Phil., 11,293....C6 19
Catarroja, Sp., 11,680..C5 8
Catasauqua, Pa., 5,062....E11 81
Catawba, co., N.C., 73,191....B2 76
Catawissa, Pa., 1,824..E9 81
Catbalogan, Phil., 10,757....C6 19
Cathedral City, Calif., 1,855....F5 50
Catlettsburg, Ky., 3,874....B7 62
Catlin, Ill., 1,263....C6 58
Catonsville, Md., 37,372....B4, C2 53
Catoosa, co., Ga., 21,101....B1 55
Catron, co., N. Mex., 2,773....C4 48
Catskill, N.Y., 5,825....C7 75
Cattaraugus, N.Y., 1,258....C2 75
Cattaraugus, co., N.Y., 80,187....C2 75
Cattolica, It., 12,969...C4 9
Cauca, dept., Col., 481,980....C2 32
Caudebec, Fr., 9,270...C4 5
Caudéran, Fr., 28,715..E3 5
Caudete, Sp., 7,544....C5 8
Caudry, Fr., 13,207...B5 5
Caughnawaga, Que., Can., 2,200....D4, D9 42
Cauquenes, Chile, 14,849....B2 28
Causapscal, Que., Can., 3,463....*B3 42
Cautín, prov., Chile, 393,041....B2 28
Cavaillon, Fr., 12,067..F6 5
Cavalier, N. Dak., 1,423....B8 77
Cavalier, co., N. Dak., 10,064....B7 77
Cavan, co., Ire., 56,594....*D3 4
Cavarzere, It., 5,600...B4 9
Cave., It., 5,856....h9 9
Cave City, Ky., 1,418..C4 62
Cave Junction, Oreg., 248....E3 80
Cave Spring, Ga., 1,153.B1 55
Cavite, Phil., 54,900..o13 19
Cavite, prov., Phil., 379,900....*C6 19
Cawnpore, see Kanpur, India
Cawood, Ky., 800....D6 62
Caxias, Braz., 19,092..D6 27
Caxias do Sul, Braz., 60,607....D2 30
Caxito, Ang., 8,690..B2 31
Cayambe, Ec., 7,364...A2 31
Cayce, S.C., 8,517....D5 82
Cayenne, Fr. Gu., 10,961....C5 77
Cayey, P.R., 19,738..m13 35
Cayman Islands, Br. dep., N.A., 7,616....F3 35
Cayuga, Ind., 904....E3 59
Cayuga, co., N.Y., 73,942....C4 75
Cayuga Heights, N.Y., 2,788....*C4 75
Cazalla de la Sierra, Sp., 9,284....D3 8
Cazenovia, N.Y., 2,584....C5 75
Cazorla, Sp., 8,699...D4 8
Ceará, state, Braz., 3,337,856....*D7 27
Ceará Mirim, Braz., 8,290....D7 27
Cebu, Phil., 259,200...C6 19
Cebu, prov., Phil., 1,340,400....*C6 19
Cecil, Pa., 900....F1 81
Cecil, co., Md., 48,408.A6 53
Cecina, It., 6,741....C3 9
Cedar, co., Iowa, 17,791....C6 60
Cedar, co., Mo., 9,185..D4 69
Cedar, co., Nebr., 13,368....B8 71
Cedar Bluff, Va., 995..*A3 85
Cedarburg, Wis., 5,191....E1, E6 88
Cedar City, Utah, 7,543....C5 72
Cedar Falls, Iowa, 21,195....B5 60

Cedar Grove. N.J., 14,603....*B4 74
Cedar Grove, W. Va., 1,569....C3, C6 87
Cedar Grove, Wis., 1,175....E6 88
Cedar Hammock, Fla., 3,089....*E4 54
Cedar Heights, Md., 1,900....*C4 53
Cedar Hill, Tex., 1,848.B5 84
Cedar Hills, Fla., 8,000....*B5 54
Cedar Hills, Oreg., 4,000....*B4 80
Cedarhurst, N.Y., 6,954....E2 75
Cedar Key, Fla., 668...C3 54
Cedar Knolls, N.J., 3,300....B4 74
Cedar Lake, Ind., 5,766....B3 59
Cedar Rapids, Iowa, 92,035 (*119,600)....C6 60
Cedar Springs, Mich., 1,768....E5 66
Cedar Terrace, S.C., 1,000....*D5 82
Cedartown, Ga., 9,340..B1 55
Cedar Vale, Kans., 859.E7 61
Cedarville, Calif., 750..B3 50
Cedarville, N.J., 1,095..E2 74
Cedarville, Ohio, 1,702.C4 78
Cedarwood Park, N.J., 1,052....*C4 74
Cefalù, It., 10,700....E5 9
Cegled, Hung, 30,310..B4 10
Ceglie Messapico, It., 16,500....D6 9
Cehegín, Sp., 7,084....C5 8
Celakovice, Czech., 6,041....n18 7
Celanese Village, Ga., 1,500....*B1 55
Celaya, Mex., 58,762.m13 34
Celina, Ohio, 7,659....B3 78
Celina, Tenn., 1,228..C8 83
Celina, Tex., 1,204....C4 84
Celje, Yugo., 16,487..B2 10
Celle, Ger., 58,500....B5 6
Celoron, N.Y., 1,507..C1 75
Cement, Okla., 959....C3 79
Cementon, Pa., 1,800.E10 81
Cenon, Fr., 13,821....E3 5
Center, Colo., 1,600...D4 51
Center, Tex., 4,510....D5 84
Centerburg, Ohio, 963..B5 78
Centereach, N.Y., 8,524....*E3 75
Center Line, Mich., 10,164....A8 66
Center Moriches, N.Y., 2,521....D4 75
Center Point, Ala., 7,500....E5 46
Center Point, Iowa, 1,236....B6 60
Centerport, N.Y., 3,628....*D3 75
Centerville, Ill., 12,769.E3 58
Centerville, Ind., 2,378.E8 59
Centerville, Iowa, 6,629....D5 60
Centerville, Mont., 950.D4 70
Centerville, Ohio, 3,490.C3 78
Centerville, Pa., 5,088..F2 81
Centerville, S. Dak., 887....G9 77
Centerville, Tenn., 1,678....B4 83
Centerville, Tex., 836..D5 84
Centerville, Utah, 2,361....A6, C2 72
Central, N. Mex., 1,075.C4 48
Central, S.C., 1,473....B2 82
Central African Republic, country, Afr., 1,227,000....G2 23
Central America, reg., N.A., 9,699,000....E6 34
Central Avenue Park, Ohio, 900....*A2 78
Central City, Ill., 1,422.E4 58
Central City, Iowa, 1,087....B6 60
Central City, Ky., 3,694....C2 62
Central City, Nebr., 2,406....C8 71
Central City, Pa., 1,604.F4 81
Central Falls, R.I., 19,858....B11 52
Central Heights, Ariz., 2,486....*C3 48
Central Heights, Iowa, 900....A4 60
Centralia, Ill., 13,904..E4 58
Centralia, Mo., 3,200..B5 69
Centralia, Pa., 1,435..*E9 81
Centralia, Wash., 8,586.C3 86

Central Islip, N.Y., 10,000....D3, E7 75
Central Nyack, N.Y., 1,400....*D7 75
Central Park, Ill., 2,676....*C6 58
Central Park, Wash., 1,622....*C2 86
Central Point, Oreg., 2,289....E4 80
Central Provinces, see Madhya Pradesh, state, India
Central Square, N.Y., 935....B4 75
Central Valley, Calif., 2,854....B2 50
Central Valley, N.Y., 950....D2, D6 75
Centre, Ala., 2,392....A4 46
Centre, co., Pa., 78,580.E6 81
Centre Hall, Pa., 1,109.E6 81
Centreville, Ala., 1,981.C2 46
Centreville, Md., 1,863.B5 53
Centreville, Mich., 971....*D5 50
Centreville, Miss., 1,737....D2 68
Century, Fla., 2,046...G2 54
Ceram, isl., Indon.....F7 19
Ceredo, W. Va., 1,387..C2 87
Ceres, Calif., 4,406....D3 50
Ceres Northwest, Calif., 1,126....D3 50
Cerignola, It., 49,287..D5 9
Cernavodă, Rom., 8,802....C9 10
Cerritos, Mex., 9,849..C4 34
Cerro de Pasco, Peru, 22,688....D2 31
Cerro Gordo, Ill., 1,067.D5 58
Cerro Gordo, co., Iowa, 49,894....A4 60
Cerro Largo, dept., Ur., 67,500....*E2 30
Cervantes, Sp., 7,011..A2 9
Cervera del Río Alhama, Sp., 7,101....A2 9
Cesena, It., 38,000....B4 9
Cesenatico, It., 5,935..B4 9
Ceska Lipa, Czech., 14,000....C3 7
Ceska Trebova, Czech., 13,000....D4 7
Ceske Budejovice, Czech., 63,900....D3 7
Cesky Brod, Czech., 5,754....n8 7
Cesky Krumlov, Czech., 8,900....D3 7
Cessnock, Austl., 35,282....F9 25
Cetinje, Yugo., 9,345..D4 10
Cetraro, It., 9,366....E5 9
Ceuta, Sp. dep., Afr., 73,182....A3 22
Ceylon, country, Asia, 8,929,000....G7 20
Chacabuco, Arg., 12,530....A4, g6 28
Chachapoyas, Peru, 6,480....C2 31
Chaco, prov., Arg., 535,443....E3 29
Chad, country, Afr., 2,675,000....F1 23
Chadbourn, N.C., 2,323....C5 76
Chadron, Nebr., 5,079..B3 71
Chadwicks, N.Y., 1,000....*B5 75
Chaffee, Mo., 2,862....D8 69
Chaffee, co., Colo., 8,298....C4 51
Chaffins, Mass., 3,500.*B4 75
Chagrin Falls, Ohio, 3,458....A6 78
Chahar Burjak, Afg., 5,000....B3 20
Chaibasa, India, 22,019....D8 20
Chakradharpur, India, 20,260....D8 20
Chakwal, Pak., 13,319..B5 20
Chalchuapa, Sal., 13,680....*E7 34
Chalfant, Pa., 1,414...*F2 81
Chalk River, Ont., Can., 1,135....A7 41
Chalkville, Ala., 1,000....*E4 46
Chalmette, La., 10,000....C7, E6 63
Châlons-sur-Marne, Fr., 41,705....C6 6
Chalon-sur-Saône, Fr., 43,655....D6 5
Chama, N. Mex., 900...A5 48
Chamalières, Fr., 14,700....E5 5
Chaman, Pak., 7,161...B4 20

Chamberlain, S. Dak., 2,598....G6 77
Chamberlayne Heights, Va., 1,000....*D5 85
Chambers, co., Ala., 37,828....C4 46
Chambers, co., Tex., 10,379....E5 84
Chambersburg, Pa., 17,670....G6 81
Chambéry, Fr., 44,246.E6 5
Chamblee, Ga., 6,635...A5 55
Chambly, co., Que., Can., 146,745....D4 42
Chambly, Que., Can., 3,737....D4 42
Chambly-Canton, Que., Can., 1,885....*D4 42
Chambord, Que., Can., 1,188....A5 42
Champaign, Ill., 49,583....C5 58
Champaign, co., Ill., 132,436....C5 58
Champaign, co., Ohio, 29,714....B4 78
Champigny-sur-Marne, Fr., 57,876....g11 5
Champion, Ohio, 2,500....*A7 78
Champlain, N.Y., 1,549....A3 75
Champlain, co., Que., Can., 111,953....B4 42
Champlin, Minn., 1,271....E6 67
Chanda, India, 51,484.E6 20
Chandigarh, India, 89,321....B6 20
Chandler, Ariz., 9,531....C3, D2 48
Chandler, Que., Can., 3,406....B3 42
Chandler, Ind., 1,784..H3 59
Chandler, Okla., 2,524..B5 79
Chandpur, Pak., 32,048....D9 20
Changchow, China, 296,500....E8 17
Changchun (Hsinking), China, 975,000....C10 17
Change Islands, Newf., Can., 804....D4 44
Changhua, Taiwan, 52,340....*G9 17
Changjin, Kor., 5,000..F3 18
Changsha, China, 703,000....F7 17
Changte, China, 94,800.F7 17
Changting, China, 27,000....F8 17
Changyon, Kor., 18,072....G2 18
Changkiang, China, 166,000....G7 17
Channel, is., Eur......F5 4
Channel Lake, Ill., 1,969....*A6 58
Channel-Port aux Basques, Newf., Can., 4,105...E2 44
Channelview, Tex., 7,500....F5 84
Chantada, Sp., 2,262...A2 8
Chanthaburi, Thai., 10,649....C2 19
Chantilly, Fr., 8,197...C5 6
Chanute, Kans., 10,849.E8 61
Chaoan (Chaochow), China, 101,300....G8 17
Chaochou, China, 5,000....D2 18
Chaoyang, China, 66,000....*G8 17
Chaoyang, China, 16,000....C9 17
Chaparral, Col., 11,705.C2 32
Chapayevsk, Sov. Un., 85,000....*D7 13
Chapel Hill, N.C., 12,573....B4 76
Chapleau, Ont., Can., 3,350....E9 41
Chaplygin, Sov. Un., 10,000....E12 12
Chapman, Ala., 617....D3 46
Chapman, Kans., 1,095....D7 61
Chapmanville, W. Va., 1,241....D2 87
Chappaqua, N.Y., 6,000....D7 75
Chappell, Nebr., 1,280.C3 71
Chapra, India, 75,580..C7 20
Charcas, Mex., 9,058..C4 34
Chardon, Ohio, 3,154..A6 78
Chardzhou, Sov. Un., 72,000....F9 13
Charente, dept., Fr., 327,658....*E4 5
Charente-Maritime, dept., Fr., 470,897....*D3 5

Chareton-le-Pont, Fr., 22,530............g10 6
Charikar, Afg., 21,070..A4 20
Chariton, Iowa, 5,042..C4 60
Chariton, co., Mo., 12,720.............B4 69
Charlack, Mo., 1,493..*A8 69
Charlemagne, Que., Can., 3,068............D4, D9 42
Charleroi, Bel., 26,175.B6 5
Charleroi, Pa., 8,148...F2 81
Charles, co., Md., 32,572.............C3 53
Charlesbourg, Que., Can., 14,308............C9 42
Charles City, Iowa, 9,964.............A5 60
Charles City, co., Va., 5,492.............D5 85
Charles Mix, co., S. Dak., 11,785.............G7 77
Charleston, Ark., 1,036.B1 49
Charleston, Ill., 10,505.D5 58
Charleston, Miss., 2,538.............A3 68
Charleston, Mo., 5,911.E8 69
Charleston, S.C., 65,925 (*203,100).......F3, F8 82
Charleston, W. Va., 85,796 (*213,900)......C3, C6 87
Charleston, co., S.C., 216,382............F8 82
Charleston Heights, S.C., 25,000.............F3 82
Charlestown, Ind., 5,726.............H6 59
Charlestown, N.H., 1,173.............E3 73
Charles Town, W. Va., 3,329.............B7 87
Charleville, Fr., 24,668.C6 5
Charlevoix, Mich., 2,751.............C5 66
Charlevoix, co., Mich., 13,421.............C5 66
Charlevoix East, co., Que., Can., 16,450.......B7 42
Charlevoix West, co., Que., Can., 14,562.......B7 42
Charlieu, Fr., 4,911....D6 5
Charlotte, Mich., 7,657.F6 66
Charlotte, N.C., 201,564 (*272,700).........B3 76
Charlotte, Tex., 1,465..E3 84
Charlotte, co., N.B., Can., 23,285.............D3 43
Charlotte, co., Fla., 12,594.............F4 54
Charlotte, co., Va., 13,368.............D4 85
Charlotte Amalie, Vir. Is., 12,880............m14 35
Charlottesville (Independent City) Va., 29,427............C4 85
Charlottetown, P.E.I., Can., 18,318.......C6 43
Charlton, co., Ga., 5,313.............F4 55
Charmco, W. Va., 700.D4 87
Charny, Que., Can., 4,189..........C6, C9 42
Charter Oak, Calif., 4,000.............*F3 50
Charters Towers, Austl., 7,633.............D8 25
Chartres, Fr., 31,495...C4 5
Chascomús, Arg., 9,105.B5 28
Chase, Kans., 922.....D5 61
Chase, co., Kans., 3,921.............D7 61
Chase, co., Nebr., 4,317.............D4 71
Chase City, Va., 3,207.E4 85
Chaska, Minn., 2,501..F5 67
Chasong, Kor., 5,000..F3 18
Chasov Yar, Sov. Un., 10,000.............q20 12
Chataignier, La., 550..D3 63
Châteaubriant, Fr., 10,852.............D3 5
Châteaudun, Fr., 11,982.............C4 5
Chateaugay, N.Y., 1,097.............A3 75
Château-Gontier, Fr., 7,065.............D3 5
Chateauguay, Que., Can., 7,570.........D4, D8 42
Chateauguay, co., Que., Can., 34,042.........D4 42
Chateauguay Station, Que., Can., 3,265...*D8 42
Châteauroux, Fr., 45,063.............D4 5
Château-Thierry, Fr., 10,006.............C5 5
Châtellerault, Fr., 27,079.............D4 5
Chatfield, Minn., 1,841.G6 67

Chatham, N.B., Can., 7,109.............B4 43
Chatham, Ont., Can., 29,826.............E2 41
Chatham, Ill., 1,069...D4 58
Chatham, Mass., 1,479.C8 65
Chatham, N.J., 9,517..B4 74
Chatham, N.Y., 2,426..C7 75
Chatham, Va., 1,822...E3 85
Chatham, co., Ga., 188,299............E5 55
Chatham, co., N.C., 26,785.............B4 76
Chatom, Ala., 993.....D1 46
Chatsworth, Ga., 1,184.B2 55
Chatsworth, Ill., 1,330.C5 58
Chattahoochee, Fla., 9,699.............B2 54
Chattahoochee, co., Ga., 13,011............D2 55
Chattanooga, Tenn., 130,009 (*286,700).....D8, E10 83
Chattaroy, W. Va., 950.............D2 87
Chattooga, co., Ga., 19,954.............B1 55
Chatwood, Pa., 3,621............*G10 81
Chau Doc, Viet., 5,000.C3 19
Chauk, Bur., 24,466...D9 20
Chaumont, Fr., 21,717.C6 5
Chauncy, Ohio, 996....C5 78
Chauny, Fr., 12,626...C5 5
Chautauqua, co., Kans., 5,956.............E7 61
Chautauqua, co., N.Y., 145,377............C1 75
Chaves, Port., 11,286..B2 8
Chaves, co., N. Mex., 57,649.............C6 48
Chavinda, Mex., 5,418.............m12 34
Chazelles [-sur-Lyon], Fr., 5,076.............E6 5
Cheatham, co., Tenn., 9,428.............A4 83
Cheb, Czech., 20,600...C2 7
Chebanse, Ill., 995.....C6 58
Cheboksary, Sov. Un., 123,000...........C16 12
Cheboygan, Mich., 5,859.............C6 66
Cheboygan, co., Mich., 14,550.............C6 66
Checotah, Okla., 2,614.B6 79
Cheddar, S.C., 500.....B3 82
Cheektowaga, N.Y., 52,362.............C2 75
Cheektowaga-Southwest, N.Y., 12,766........C2 75
Chefoo, China, 116,000.D9 17
Chehalis, Wash., 5,199.C3 86
Cheju, Kor., 34,300....J3 68
Chekhov, Sov. Un., 10,000.............C10 18
Chekiang, prov., China, 25,280,000...........F9 17
Chelan, Wash., 2,402...B6 86
Chelan, co., Wash., 40,744.............B7 86
Chelkar, Sov. Un., 19,300.............E8 13
Chełm [Lubelski], Pol., 27,000.............C7 7
Chelmno, Pol., 14,400..B5 7
Chelmsford, Ont., Can., 2,559.............*E9 41
Chelmsford, Eng., 49,810.............E7 4
Chelmsford, Mass., 3,500.............A5, C2 65
Chelmza, Pol., 12,200..B5 7
Chelsea, Mass., 33,749.........B5, D3 65
Chelsea, Mich., 3,355..F6 66
Chelsea, Okla., 1,541...A6 79
Cheltenham, Eng., 71,968.............E5 4
Cheltenham, Md., 500..C4 53
Cheltenham, Pa., 7,000.............A12 81
Chelyabinsk, Sov. Un., 733,000............D9 13
Chemainus, B.C., Can., 1,518.........B9, E6 37
Chemnitz, see Karl-Marx-Stadt, Ger.
Chemung, co., N.Y., 98,706.............C4 75
Chenango, co., N.Y., 43,243.............C5 75
Chenango Bridge, N.Y., 2,000.............*C5 75
Cheney, Kans., 1,101.............B4, E6 61
Cheney, Wash., 3,173.............B8, D7 86
Cheneyville, La., 1,037.C3 63
Chengchow, China, 766,000............E7 17

Chenghwa, see Sharasume, China
Chengteh (Jehol), China, 92,900.............C8 17
Chengtu, China, 1,107,000...........E5 17
Chenoa, Ill., 1,523.....C5 58
Chepén, Peru, 8,214....C2 31
Chepstow, Wales, 6,041.............E5 4
Cher, dept., Fr., 293,514............*D5 6
Cheraw, S.C., 5,171...B8 82
Cherbourg, Fr., 37,486.C3 6
Cheremkhovo, Sov. Un., 122,000...........D3 13
Cherepovets, Sov. Un., 113,000...........B11 12
Cherkassy, Sov. Un., 95,000.............G9 12
Chernigov, Sov. Un., 101,000...........F8 12
Chernobay, Sov. Un., 25,000.............G9 12
Chernobyl, Sov. Un., 10,000.............F8 12
Chernovtsy, Sov. Un., 147,000...........G5 12
Chernyakhovsk (Insterburg), Sov. Un., 33,000....D3 13
Cherokee, Ala., 1,349..A2 46
Cherokee, Iowa, 7,724.B2 60
Cherokee, Kans., 797..E9 61
Cherokee, Okla., 2,410.A3 79
Cherokee, co., Ala., 16,303.............A4 46
Cherokee, co., Ga., 23,001.............B2 55
Cherokee, co., Iowa, 18,598.............B2 60
Cherokee, co., Kans., 22,279.............E9 61
Cherokee, co., N.C., 16,335.............D2 76
Cherokee, co., Okla., 17,762.............B6 79
Cherokee, co., S.C., 35,205.............A4 82
Cherokee, co., Tex., 33,120.............D5 84
Cherokee Ranch, Pa., 1,200............*F10 81
Cherry, co., Nebr., 8,218.............B4 71
Cherry Grove, Ohio, 2,000.............*C3 78
Cherry Hills Village, Colo., 1,931............*B6 51
Cherryvale, Kans., 2,783.............E8 61
Cherry Valley, Mass., 1,500.............*B4 65
Cherryville, N.C., 3,607.............B2 76
Chesaning, Mich., 2,770.............E6 66
Chesapeake, Ohio, 1,396.............D5 78
Chesapeake, Va., 73,647.........B7, E6 85
Chesapeake, W. Va., 2,699.............C3 87
Chesapeake City, Md., 1,104.............A6 53
Cheshire, Conn., 4,072.D5 52
Cheshire, Mass., 1,078.A1 65
Cheshire, co., Eng., 1,367,860...........D5 4
Cheshire, co., N.H., 43,342.............F3 73
Chesley, Ont., Can., 1,697.............C3 41
Chesnee, S.C., 1,045...A4 82
Chester, Calif., 1,553..*B3 50
Chester, N.S., Can., 990.............E5 43
Chester, Conn., 1,414..D7 52
Chester, Eng., 59,283..D5 4
Chester, Ill., 4,460....F4 58
Chester, Md., 900.....C5 53
Chester, Mass., 950....B2 65
Chester, Mont., 1,158..B6 70
Chester, N.J., 1,074...B3 74
Chester, N.Y., 1,492.........D2, D6 75
Chester, Pa., 63,658.........B10, G11 81
Chester, S.C., 6,906...B5 82
Chester, Vt., 923......E3 73
Chester, Va., 2,000.............C7, D5 85
Chester, W. Va., 3,787.............A2, A4 87
Chester, co., Pa., 210,608............G10 81
Chester, co., S.C., 30,888.............B5 82
Chester, co., Tenn., 9,569.............B3 83

Chesterfield, Eng., 67,833.............D6 4
Chesterfield, Ind., 2,588.............D6 59
Chesterfield, S.C., 1,532.............B7 82
Chesterfield, co., S.C., 33,717.............B7 82
Chesterfield, co., Va., 71,197.............D5 85
Chesterton, Ind., 4,335.A3 59
Chestertown, Md., 3,602.............B5 53
Chesterville, Ont., Can., 1,248.............B9 41
Cheswick, Pa., 2,734...A6 81
Chetek, Wis., 1,729...C2 88
Chetopa, Kans., 1,538..E8 61
Cheverly, Md., 5,223..*C1 53
Cheviot, Ohio, 10,701.........C3, D2 78
Chevy Chase, Md., 2,405.........C1, C3 53
Chevy Chase Heights, Pa., 1,160............*E3 81
Chevy Chase Lake, Md., 2,500.............*C3 53
Chevy Chase Section Four, Md., 2,243.......*C3 53
Chevy Chase View, Md., 1,000.............*C3 53
Chewelah, Wash., 1,525.............A8 86
Chews, N.J., 1,500....*C4 74
Cheyenne, Okla., 930..B2 79
Cheyenne, Wyo., 43,505.............D8 89
Cheyenne, co., Colo., 2,789.............C8 51
Cheyenne, co., Kans., 4,708.............C2 61
Cheyenne, co., Nebr., 14,828.............C2 71
Cheyenne Wells, Colo., 1,020.............C8 51
Chiahsing, China, 78,300.............E9 17
Chiai, Taiwan, 83,400.*G9 17
Chiamussu, see Kiamusze, China.
Chian, China, 52,800...F3 18
Chiang Khong, Thai., 3,320.............A2 19
Chiangling, China, 15,000.............E7 17
Chiang Mai, Thai., 66,019.............B1 19
Chiang Rai, Thai., 13,494.............B1 19
Chiapa de Corzo, Mex., 6,972.............D6 34
Chiapas, state, Mex., 1,215,475...........D6 34
Chiari, It., 9,000......B2 9
Chiavari, It., 24,603...B2 9
Chiba, Jap., 241,615........I10, n19 18
Chiba, pref., Jap., 2,306,010..........*I10 18
Chicago, Ill., 3,550,404 (*6,517,600)....B6, F3 58
Chicago Heights, Ill., 34,331.........B6, F3 58
Chicago Ridge, Ill., 5,748.............*F3 58
Chichester, Eng., 20,118.............E6 4
Chichibu, Jap., 43,700.n18 18
Chickamauga, Ga., 1,824.............B1 55
Chickasaw, Ala., 10,002.............E1 46
Chickasaw, co., Iowa, 15,034.............A5 60
Chickasaw, co., Miss., 16,891.............B5 68
Chickasha, Okla., 14,866.............B4 79
Chiclana, Sp., 21,524..D2 8
Chiclayo, Peru, 38,517.C2 31
Chico, Calif., 14,757...C3 50
Chico, Tex., 654.......C4 84
Chico, Wash., 300.....B3 86
Chicopee, Ga., 900....B3 55
Chicopee, Mass., 61,553.............B2 65
Chicora (Millerstown), Pa., 1,156..........E2 81
Chicot, co., Ark., 18,990.............D4 49
Chicoutimi, Que., Can., 31,657...........A6, B2 42
Chicoutimi, co., Que., Can., 157,196........A6 42
Chico Vecino, Calif., 4,688.............*C3 50
Chiefland, Fla., 1,459..C4 54
Chieri, It., 11,900....B1 9
Chieti, It., 36,000.....C5 9
Chigirin, Sov. Un., 10,000.............G9 12

Chigwell, Eng., 61,001.k13   4
Chihchiang, China, 19,000............F6   17
Chihfeng, China, 40,000............C8   17
Chihuahua, Mex., 149,437............B3   34
Chihuahua, state, Mex., 1,235,891............B3   34
Chikura, Jap., 10,900..o18   18
Chilapa, Mex., 7,105............D5, o14   34
Childersburg, Ala., 4,884............B3   46
Childress, Tex., 6,399..B2   84
Childress, co., Tex., 8,421............B2   84
Chile, country, S.A., 7,339,546............E2   29
Chilecito, Arg., 6,121...E2   29
Chilhowie, Va., 1,169..B3   85
Chillán, Chile, 65,000..B2   28
Chillicothe, Ill., 3,054..C4   58
Chillicothe, Mo., 9,236.B4   69
Chillicothe, Ohio, 24,957............C5   78
Chillicothe, Tex., 1,161.B3   84
Chilliwack, B.C., Can., 8,259............B11, E7   37
Chillum, Md., 10,000..*C3   53
Chiloé, prov., Chile, 98,662............C2   28
Chiloquin, Oreg., 945...E5   80
Chilpancingo [de los Bravos], Mex., 17,942............D5, o14   34
Chilton, Tex., 400.....D4   84
Chilton, Wis., 2,578............B5, D5   88
Chilton, co., Ala., 25,693............C3   46
Chilung (Keelung), Taiwan, 165,200...F9   17
Chimaltenango, Guat., 6,138............*E6   34
Chimayo, N. Mex., 700.B6   48
Chimbay, Sov. Un., 16,100............E8   13
Chimborazo, prov., Ec., 241,258............B2   31
Chimkent, Sov. Un., 171,000............E9   13
China (excl. Taiwan), country, Asia, 646,530,000............E4   17
China Grove, N.C., 1,500............B3   76
Chinandega, Nic., 19,800............E7   34
Chincha Alta, Peru, 15,053............D2   31
Chinchilla, Pa., 1,100............*D10   81
Chinchow, China, 352,200............C9   17
Chincoteague, Va., 2,131............D1   85
Chingford, Eng., 45,777............k13   4
Chingpu, China, 45,000............*E9   17
Chinhae, Kor., 60,000..I4   18
Chinhua, China, 46,200.F8   17
Chining, China, 86,200.D8   17
Chiniot, Pak., 39,070...B5   20
Chinju, Kor., 68,000....I4   18
Chinkiang, China, 207,600............E8   17
Chinnampo (Nampo), Kor., 82,162.......G2   18
Chino, Calif., 10,305...F3   50
Chinook, Mont., 2,326.B7   70
Chinwangtao, China, 186,800............D8   17
Chioggia, It., 47,151..B4   9
Chipley, Fla., 3,159...G3   54
Chipman, N.B., Can., 1,490............C4   43
Chippawa, Ont., Can., 3,256............D5   41
Chippewa, co., Mich., 32,655............B6   66
Chippewa, co., Minn., 16,320............E3   67
Chippewa, co., Wis., 45,096............C2   88
Chippewa Falls, Wis., 11,708............D2   88
Chiquimula, Guat., 8,840............E7   34
Chiquinquirá, Col., 10,143............B3   32
Chiriqui Grande, Pan., 98............B1   32
Chirpan, Bul., 13,231..D7   10
Chisago, co., Minn., 13,419............E6   67
Chisholm, Ala., 1,500..C3   46
Chisholm, Maine, 1,193............D2   64
Chisholm, Minn., 7,144.C6   67

Chisineu-Cris, Rom., 6,124...............B5   10
Chislehurst [& Sidcup] Eng., 86,907......m13   4
Chistyakovo, Sov. Un., 90,000.............q21   12
Chita, Sov. Un., 182,000.............A7   13
Chitai (Kuchêng), China, 25,000.............C2   17
Chitaldroog, India, 33,336.............F6   20
Chitré, Pan., 9,120....B1   32
Chittagong, Pak., 180,000 (*364,205).....D9   20
Chittenango, N.Y., 3,180.............*B5   75
Chittenden, co., Vt., 74,425.............C1   73
Chittoor, India, 47,876.F6   20
Chiusi, It., 8,498......C3   9
Chivasso, It., 8,800...B1   9
Chivilcoy, Arg., 23,386.............A4, g6   28
Chochiwon, Kor., 16,700.............H3   18
Chocó, dept., Col., 139,380.............C2   32
Choctaw, co., Ala., 17,870.............C1   46
Choctaw, co., Miss., 8,423.............B4   68
Choctaw, co., Okla., 15,637.............C6   79
Chodziez, Pol., 7,694...B4   7
Choisy-le-Roi, Fr., 40,950.............g10   6
Chojna, Pol., 1,484....B3   7
Chojnice, Pol., 20,000.B4   7
Chojnow, Pol., 5,467...C3   7
Cholet, Fr., 36,565....D3   5
Choluteca, Hond., 5,275.............E7   34
Chomutov, Czech., 33,200.............C2   7
Chonan, Kor., 36,500..H3   18
Chon Buri, Thai., 33,086.............C2   19
Chone, Ec., 8,030.....B1   31
Chŏngjin, Kor., 184,301.............F4   18
Chongju, Kor., 92,300..H3   18
Chonju, Kor., 152,000..I3   18
Chorrillos, Peru, 6,996.D2   31
Chorwon, Kor., 30,085.G3   18
Chorzow, Pol., 147,000.........C5, g9   7
Chosen, see Korea, Asia.
Chosen, Fla., 1,858....F6   54
Chōshi, Jap., 71,500............I10, n19   18
Choteau, Mont., 1,966.C4   70
Chouchiakou, China, 85,500.............*E7   17
Choum, Maur.......D2   22
Chouteau, co., Mont., 7,348.............C6   70
Chowan, co., N.C., 11,729.............A7   76
Chowchilla, Calif., 4,525.............D3   50
Chrisman, Ill., 1,221..D6   58
Christchurch, N.Z., 151,671 (*220,510)..O14   26
Christian, co., Ill., 37,207.............D4   58
Christian, co., Ky., 56,904.............D2   62
Christian, co., Mo., 12,359.............E4   69
Christiana, Pa., 1,069..G9   81
Christiansburg, Va., 3,653.............D2   85
Christiansted, Vir. Is., 5,137.............*A14   35
Christmas Island, Austl. dep., Oceania, 3,099.F10   2
Christopher, Ill., 2,854.F4   58
Chrudium, Czech., 15,500.............D3   7
Chrzanow, Pol., 21,000.............g10   7
Chüanchow, China, 107,700.............G8   17
Chubut, prov., Arg., 142,195.............C3   28
Chugiak, Alsk., 1,500.......C10, g17   47
Chuguyev, Sov. Un., 10,000.............G11   12
Chuho, China, 5,000...D3   18
Chühsien, China, 32,000.............F8   17
Chula Vista, Calif., 42,034.............E2, F5   50
Chulucanas, Peru, 14,874.............B1   31
Chumikan, Sov. Un., 1,100.............D16   13
Chunchon, Kor., 83,000.............H3   18

Chungju, Kor., 47,600..H3   18
Chungking, China, 1,800,000.............F6   17
Chuquisaca, dept., Bol., 282,980.............D3   29
Chur, Switz., 24,825...E4   6
Churchill, Man., Can., 1,878.............C5   40
Church Hill, Tenn., 769.............C11   83
Churchill, Pa., 3,428..*F2   81
Churchill, co., Nev., 8,452.............B2   72
Churchland, Va., 3,000.B6   85
Church Point, La., 3,606.............D3   63
Churchville, Pa., 1,500.............*F11   81
Churubusco, Ind., 1,284.............B7   59
Chusovoy, Sov. Un., 63,000.............D8   13
Cicero, Ill., 69,130....F3   58
Cicero, Ind., 1,284....D5   59
Ciechanow, Pol., 20,000.............B6   7
Ciego de Avila, Cuba, 35,178.............E4   35
Ciénaga, Col., 24,358..A3   32
Cienfuegos, Cuba, 57,991........ D3   35
Cieszyn, Pol., 23,000..D5   7
Cieza, Sp., 20,000.....C5   8
Cimarron, Kans., 1,115.E3   61
Cimarron, N.M., 997...A6   48
Cimarron, co., Okla., 4,496.............D2   79
Cincinnati, Ohio, 502,550 (*1,203,300).....C3, D2   78
Cinnaminson Township, N.J., 8,302.............*C2   74
Circle, Mont., 1,117..C11   70
Circle Pines, Minn., 2,789.............*E5   67
Circleville, Ohio, 11,059.............C5   78
Cirencester, Eng., 11,836.............E6   4
Ciso, Tex., 4,499......C3   84
Cisneros, Col., 5,489..B2   32
Cisterna di Latina, It., 8,000.............h9   9
Citronelle, Ala., 1,918.D1   46
Citrus, co., Fla., 9,268.D4   54
Citrus Heights, Calif., 9,000.............*C3   50
Cittadella, It., 5,002...B3   9
Città di Castello, It., 11,300.............C4   9
City Park, Ill., 1,133..*D4   58
City Terrace, Calif., 6,000.............*F4   50
City View, S.C., 2,475..B2   82
Ciudad Bolívar, Ven., 56,032.............B5   32
Ciudad Camargo, Mex., 11,940.............B3   34
Ciudad Chetumal, Mex., 12,775.............D7   34
Ciudad de las Casas, Mex., 23,355.............D6   34
Ciudad del Carmen, Mex., 20,901.............D6   34
Ciudad de Valles, Mex., 23,620.......C5, m14   34
Ciudad Dr. Hernández Alvarez, Mex., 8,553.............m13   34
Ciudadela, Sp., 9,804..B7   8
Ciudad García [Salinas], Mex., 14,948.............C4   34
Ciudad Guzmán, Mex., 30,971.......D4, n12   34
Ciudad Hidalgo, Mex., 17,060.............n13   34
Ciudad Juárez, Mex., 261,683.............A3   34
Ciudad Lerdo, Mex., 17,537.............B4   34
Ciudad Madero, Mex., 53,526.............C5   34
Ciudad Mante, Mex., 22,701.............C5   34
Ciudad Melchor Múzquiz, 12,659.............B4   34
Ciudad Obregón, Mex., 68,010.............B3   34
Ciudad Real, Sp., 37,081.............C4   8
Ciudad Real, prov., Sp., 583,948.............*C4   8
Ciudad Rodrigo, Sp., 9,919.............B2   8
Ciudad Serdán, Mex., 9,584.............n15   34
Ciudad Victoria, Mex., 50,727.............C5   34
Cividale del Fruiuli, It., 7,074.............A4   9
Civitanova Marche, It., 12,300.............C4   9

Civitavecchia, It., 38,138.............C3   9
Cizre, Tur., 6,700...D14   14
Clackamas, co., Oreg., 113,038.............B4   80
Clackmannan, co., Scot., 41,391.............*B5   4
Claflin, Kans., 891...D5   61
Claiborne, co., Miss., 10,845.............D3   68
Claiborne, co., Tenn., 19,067.............C10   68
Claiborne, par., La., 19,407.............B2   63
Clairfield, Tenn., 500..C10   83
Clair Haven, Mich., 1,365.............*F8   66
Clairton, Pa., 18,389..F2   81
Callam, co., Wash., 30,022.............B2   86
Clamart, Fr., 47,991...g10   5
Clamecy, Fr., 5,520....D5   5
Clanton, Ala., 5,683...C3   46
Clara Barton, N.J., 3,500.............*B4   74
Clara City, Minn., 1,358.............F3   67
Clare, Mich., 2,442....E6   66
Clare, co., Ire., 73,702.*D2   4
Clare, co., Mich., 11,647.............E6   66
Claremont, Calif., 12,633.............F3   50
Claremont, N.H., 13,563.............E3   73
Claremore, Okla., 6,639.............A6   79
Clarence, Mo., 1,103..B5   69
Clarence, N.Y., 1,456..*C2   75
Clarendon, Ark., 2,293.C4   49
Clarendon, Tex., 2,172.B2   84
Clarendon, co., S.C., 29,490.............D7   82
Clarendon Hills, Ill., 5,885.............F2   58
Clarenville, Newf., Can., 1,195.............D4   44
Claresholm, Alta., Can., 2,143.............D4   38
Claridge, Pa., 1,100...F2   81
Clarinda, Iowa, 5,901.............D2   60
Clarion, Iowa, 3,232...B4   60
Clarion, Pa., 4,958.....D3   81
Clarion, co., Pa., 37,408.............D3   81
Clark, N.J., 12,195....*B4   74
Clark, S. Dak., 1,484..F8   77
Clark, co., Ark., 20,950.C2   49
Clark, co., Idaho, 915..E6   57
Clark, co., Ill., 16,546..D6   58
Clark, co., Ind., 62,795.H6   59
Clark, co., Kans., 3,396.............E4   61
Clark, co., Ky., 21,075.C5   62
Clark, co., Mo., 8,725..A6   69
Clark, co., Nev., 127,016.............C4   72
Clark, co., Ohio, 131,440.............C4   78
Clark, co., S. Dak., 7,134.............F8   77
Clark, co., Wash., 93,809.............D3   86
Clark, co., Wis., 31,527.............D3   88
Clarkdale, Ariz., 1,095..B2   48
Clarke, co., Ala., 25,738.............D2   46
Clarke co., Ga., 45,363.C3   55
Clarke, co., Iowa, 8,222.............D4   60
Clarke, co., Miss., 16,493.............C5   68
Clarke, co., Va., 7,942.B4   85
Clarkes Harbour, N.S., Can., 945.............F4   43
Clarkesville, Ga., 1,352.B3   55
Clarkfield, Minn., 1,100.............F3   67
Clark Mills, N.Y., 1,148.............*B5   75
Clarks, La., 940......B3   63
Clarksburg, W. Va., 28,112.............B4, B6   87
Clarksdale, Miss., 21,105.............A3   68
Clarks Green, Pa., 1,256.............*D10   75
Clarkson, Ont., Can., 1,400.............D5   41
Clarks Summit, Pa., 3,693.............A9   81
Clarkston, Ga., 1,524..B5   55
Clarkston, Wash., 6,209.............C8   86
Clarksville, Ark., 3,919.B2   49
Clarksville, Ga., 1,352..B3   55
Clarksville, Ind., 8,088.H6   59
Clarksville, Iowa, 1,328.B5   60

Clarksville, Tenn., 22,021....A4 83
Clarksville, Tex., 3,851.C5 84
Clarksville, Va., 1,530..E4 85
Clarkton, Mo., 1,049...E8 69
Clatskanie, Oreg., 797..A3 80
Clatsop, co., Oreg., 27,380...............A3 80
Claude, Tex., 895......B2 84
Clausthal-Zellerfeld, Ger., 15,200.............C5 6
Clawson, Mich., 14,795..............A7 66
Claxton, Ga., 2,672...D5 55
Clay, Ky., 1,343........C2 62
Clay, co., Ala., 12,400..B4 46
Clay, co., Ark., 21,258..A5 49
Clay, co., Fla., 19,535..B5 54
Clay, co., Ga., 4,551...E2 55
Clay, co., Ill., 15,815...E5 58
Clay, co., Ind., 24,207..F3 59
Clay, co., Iowa, 18,504.A2 60
Clay, co., Kans., 10,675.C6 61
Clay, co., Ky., 20,748..C6 62
Clay, co., Minn., 39,080.............D2 67
Clay, co., Miss., 18,933.B5 68
Clay, co., Mo., 87,474..B3 69
Clay, co., Nebr., 8,717..D7 71
Clay, co., N.C., 5,526..D2 76
Clay, co., S. Dak., 10,810..............H9 77
Clay, co., Tenn., 7,289.C8 83
Clay, co., Tex., 8,351...C3 84
Clay, co., W. Va., 11,942..............C3 87
Clay Center, Kans., 4,613................C6 61
Clay City, Ill., 1,144...E5 58
Clay City, Ind., 950....F3 59
Claycomo, Mo., 1,423.*B3 69
Claymont, Del., 10,000.A7 53
Claypool, Ariz., 1,800...........C3, D3 48
Claysburg, Pa., 1,439..F5 81
Claysville, Pa., 986....F1 81
Clayton, Ala., 1,313...D4 46
Clayton, Del., 1,028...B6 53
Clayton, Ga., 1,507....B3 55
Clayton, Ill., 774......C3 58
Clayton, La., 882......C4 63
Clayton, Mo., 15,245..........B8, C7 69
Clayton, N.J., 4,711...D2 74
Clayton, N. Mex., 3,314..............A7 48
Clayton, N.Y., 1,996.............A4, B1 75
Clayton, N.C., 3,302...B5 76
Clayton, Okla., 615....C6 79
Clayton, co., Ga., 46,365.............C2 55
Clayton, co., Iowa, 21,962.............B6 60
Clear Creek, co., Colo., 2,793..............B5 51
Clearfield, Pa., 9,270..D5 81
Clearfield, Utah, 8,833...........A5, C2 72
Clearfield, co., Pa., 81,534.............D5 81
Clear Lake, Iowa, 6,158................A4 60
Clear Lake, S. Dak., 1,137................F9 77
Clear Lake Shores, Tex., 700................F5 84
Clearwater, Fla., 34,653...........E1, E4 54
Clearwater, Kans., 1,073...............E6 61
Clearwater, S.C., 1,450.E4 82
Clearwater, co., Idaho, 8,548................C3 57
Clearwater, co., Minn., 8,864................C3 67
Cleburne, Tex., 15,381...........B5, C4 84
Cleburne, co., Ala., 10,911.............B4 46
Cleburne, co., Ark., 9,059................B3 49
Cle Elum, Wash., 1,814.B5 86
Clementon, N.J., 3,766.D3 74
Clemson College, S.C., 3,500.............*B2 82
Clendenin, W. Va., 1,510...........C3, C6 87
Cleona, Pa., 1,988.....F9 81
Clermont, Que., Can., 3,114..............B7 42
Clermont, Fla., 3,313..D5 54
Clermont, Ind., 1,058............E5, H7 59
Clermont, co., Ohio, 80,530.............C3 78
Clermont-Ferrand, Fr., 127,684............E5 5
Clermont-l'Hérault, Fr., 5,538................F5 5

Cleveland, Miss., 10,172.............B3 68
Cleveland, Ohio, 876,050 (*2,090,800).....A6, B2 78
Cleveland, Okla., 2,519.A5 79
Cleveland, Tenn., 16,196.............D9 83
Cleveland, Tex., 5,838.D5 84
Cleveland, co., Ark., 6,944..............D3 49
Cleveland, co., N.C., 66,048.............D2 76
Cleveland, co., Okla., 47,600.............B4 79
Cleveland Heights, Ohio, 61,813.........A6, B2 78
Cleves, Ohio, 1,025...*C3 78
Clewiston, Fla., 3,144..F6 54
Clichy [-la-Garenne], Fr., 56,316.........C5, g10 5
Cliffside, N.C., 1,275...........B2, D4 76
Cliffside Park, N.J., 17,642.........B5, D5 74
Cliffwood, N.J., 3,000.*C4 74
Cliffwood Beach, N.J., 3,000.............*C4 74
Clifton, Ariz., 4,191....C4 48
Clifton, Ill., 1,018.....C6 58
Clifton, N.J., 82,084.........B4, D5 74
Clifton, S.C., 1,249...B4 82
Clifton, Tex., 2,335...D4 84
Clifton Forge, Va., 5,268..............D3 85
Clifton Heights, Pa., 8,005............B11 81
Clifton Springs, N.Y., 1,953.............C3 75
Climax, Colo., 1,609...B4 51
Clinch, co., Ga., 6,545.F4 55
Clinchfield, N.C., 950.*D4 76
Clincho, Va., 975......B2 85
Clint, Tex., 800........F1 84
Clinton, Ark., 744.....B3 49
Clinton, Ont., Can., 3,491..............D3 41
Clinton, Conn., 4,166..D6 52
Clinton, Ill., 7,355.....C5 58
Clinton, Ind., 5,843....E3 59
Clinton, Iowa, 33,589..C7 60
Clinton, Ky., 1,647....B2 62
Clinton, La., 1,568....D4 63
Clinton, Md., 1,578....C4 53
Clinton, Mass., 12,848.B4 65
Clinton, Mich., 1,481..F7 66
Clinton, Miss., 3,438..C3 68
Clinton, Mo., 6,925...C4 69
Clinton, N.J., 1,158...B3 74
Clinton, N.Y., 1,855...B5 75
Clinton, N.C., 7,461...C5 76
Clinton, Ohio, 924....*B6 78
Clinton, Okla., 9,617..B3 79
Clinton, S.C., 7,937...C4 82
Clinton, Tenn., 4,943.........C9, E11 83
Clinton, Utah, 1,025...B3 72
Clinton, Wis., 1,274...F5 88
Clinton, co., Ill., 24,029.E4 58
Clinton, co., Ind., 30,765.............D4 59
Clinton, co., Iowa, 55,060.............C7 60
Clinton, co., Ky., 8,886.D4 62
Clinton, co., Mich., 37,969.............F6 66
Clinton, co., Mo., 11,588.............B3 69
Clinton, co., N.Y., 72,722.............A3 75
Clinton, co., Ohio, 30,004.............C4 78
Clinton, co., Pa., 37,619.............D6 81
Clintonville, Wis., 4,778..............D5 88
Clintwood, Va., 1,400..B2 85
Clio, Ala., 929........D4 46
Clio, Mich., 2,212....E7 66
Clonmel, Ire., 10,640..D3 4
Cloquet, Minn., 9,013..D6 67
Closter, N.J., 7,767.B5, D5 74
Clothier, W. Va., 500..D5 87
Cloud, co., Kans., 14,407.............C6 61
Clover, S.C., 3,500....A5 82
Cloverdale, Calif., 2,848..............C2 50
Cloverdale, B.C., Can., 569................A10 37
Cloverleaf, Tex., 3,000.E5 84
Cloverport, Ky., 1,334..C3 62
Clovis, Calif., 7,704...D4 50
Clovis, N. Mex., 23,713.............B7 48
Cluj, Rom., 154,752...B6 13
Clute, Tex., 4,501.....G5 84
Clyde, Kans., 1,025...C6 61
Clyde, N.Y., 2,693....B4 75
Clyde, Ohio, 4,826.....A5 78
Clyde, Tex., 1,116.....C3 84

Clydebank, Scot., 47,654.............C4 4
Clyde Hill, Wash., 1,871.............*B4 86
Clymer, Pa., 2,251....E3 81
Coachella, Calif., 4,854.F5 50
Coahoma, Tex., 1,239..C2 84
Coahoma, co., Miss., 46,212.............A3 68
Coahuila, state, Mex., 896,509............B4 34
Coal, co., Okla., 5,546.C5 79
Coal City, Ill., 2,852..B5 58
Coaldale, Alta., Can., 2,592..............E4 38
Coaldale, Pa., 3,949...E10 81
Coal Fork, W. Va., 1,000..............C6 87
Coalgate, Okla., 1,689..C5 79
Coalgood, Ky., 800....D6 62
Coal Grove, Ohio, 2,961..............D5 78
Coal Hill, Ark., 704....B2 49
Coalinga, Calif., 5,965.D3 50
Coalport, Pa., 821.....E4 81
Coaltown, Pa., 1,033.*D1 81
Coalville, Utah, 907.............A6, C2 72
Coalwood, W. Va., 1,199..............D3 87
Coamo, P.R., 12,146.m13 35
Coatbridge, Scot., 53,946.............C5 4
Coatepec, Mex., 18,081.............n15 34
Coatepeque, Guat., 6,281.............*E6 34
Coatesville, Pa., 12,971.............G10 81
Coaticook, Que., Can., 6,906..............D6 42
Coats, N.C., 1,049.....B5 76
Coatzacoalcos (Puerto México), Mex., 36,989.............D6 34
Cobalt, Ont., Can., 2,209..............E9 41
Cobán, Guat., 7,911...D6 34
Cobb, co., Ga., 114,174.C2 55
Cobden, Ont., Can., 942................B8 41
Cobden, Ill., 918......F4 58
Cobh, Ire., 5,266.....E2 4
Cobleskill, N.Y., 3,471.C6 75
Cobourg, Ont., Can., 10,646.............D6 41
Coburg, Ger., 44,200..C5 6
Cocentaina, Sp., 8,108.C5 8
Cochabamba, Bol., 80,795.............C2 29
Cochabamba, dept., Bol., 490,475............C2 29
Cochin, India, 35,076..G6 20
Cochin China, reg., Viet., 6,500,000..........D3 19
Cochise, co., Ariz., 55,039.............D4 48
Cochituate, Mass., 4,000..............D1 65
Cochran, Ga., 4,714...D3 55
Cochran, co., Tex., 6,417..............C1 84
Cochrane, Ont., Can., 4,521..............E9 41
Cochrane, co., Ont., Can., 95,666.............D8 41
Cochranton, Pa., 1,139.C1 81
Cocke, co., Tenn., 23,390.............D10 83
Cockeysville, Md., 2,582..............B4 53
Cockrell Hill, Tex., 3,104..............B5 84
Cocoa, Fla., 12,294...D6 54
Cocoa Beach, Fla., 3,475..............D6 54
Cocoa West, Fla., 3,975.............*D6 54
Coconino, co., Ariz., 41,857.............B2 48
Cocos (Keeling) Is., Austl., dep., Oceania, 606...G3 2
Cocula, Mex., 10,148.........C4, m12 34
Codington, co., S. Dak., 20,220.............F8 77
Codogno, It., 10,500...B2 9
Cody, Wyo., 4,838.....A3 89
Coeburn, Va., 2,471...B2 85
Coesfeld, Ger., 20,300.C3 7
Coeur d'Alene, Idaho, 14,291.............B2 57
Coffee, co., Ala., 30,583.............D3 46
Coffee, co., Ga., 21,953.E4 55
Coffee, co., Tenn., 28,603.............B5 83
Coffey, co., Kans., 8,403..............D8 61
Coffeyville, Kans., 17,382.............E8 61

Coff's Harbour, Austl., 7,185..............E9 26
Cognac, Fr., 20,798....E3 5
Cohasset, Mass., 2,748.D4 65
Cohocton, N.Y., 929...C3 75
Cohoes, N.Y., 20,129..C7 75
Coimbatore, India, 286,305............F6 20
Coimbra, Port., 45,500.B1 8
Coín, Sp., 11,828.....D3 8
Cojedes, state, Ven., 72,652.............B4 32
Cojutepeque, Sal., 11,617............*E7 34
Cokato, Minn., 1,356..E4 67
Coke, co., Tex., 3,589..D2 84
Cokeburg, Pa., 989...*F1 81
Colac, Austl., 9,257.....I4 26
Colbert, co., Ala., 46,506.............A2 46
Colborne, Ont., Can., 1,336..............C7 41
Colby, Kans., 4,210...C2 61
Colby, Wis., 1,085....D3 88
Colchagua, prov., Chile, 158,024............A2 28
Colchester, Conn., 2,260..............C7 52
Colchester, Eng., 65,072.............E7 4
Colchester, Ill., 1,495..C3 58
Colchester, co., N.S., Can., 34,307.............D6 43
Cold Lake, Alta., Can., 1,307..............B5 38
Cold Spring, Ky., 1,095.........A7, B5 62
Cold Spring, Minn., 1,760..............E4 67
Cold Spring, N.Y., 2,083.............*D7 75
Cold Spring Harbor, N.Y., 1,705.............F3 52
Coldwater, Kans., 1,164..............E4 61
Coldwater, Mich., 8,880..............G5 66
Coldwater, Miss., 1,264..............A4 68
Coldwater, Ohio, 2,766.B3 78
Cole, co., Mo., 40,761..C5 69
Colebrook, N.H., 1,550.B5 73
Coleman, Alta., Can., 1,713..............E3 38
Coleman, Fla., 921....D4 54
Coleman, Mich., 1,264.E6 66
Coleman, Tex., 6,371..D3 84
Coleman, co., Tex., 12,458.............D3 84
Coleraine, N. Ire., 11,912.............C3 4
Coleraine, Minn., 1,346.C5 67
Coles, co., Ill., 42,860..D5 58
Colfax, Calif., 915....C3 50
Colfax, Iowa, 2,331...C4 60
Colfax, La., 1,934.....C3 63
Colfax, Wash., 2,860..C8 86
Colfax, Wis., 885.....D2 88
Colfax, co., Nebr., 9,595..............C8 71
Colfax, co., N. Mex., 13,806.............A6 48
Colima, Mex., 44,860.........D4, n12 34
Colima, state, Mex., 157,338.........D4, n12 34
College, Alsk., 1,755..C10 47
Collegedale, Tenn., 1,500.............E10 83
College Heights, Ark., 1,000..............D4 49
College Heights, S.C., 1,330..............C7 82
College Park, Fla., 950.C5 54
College Park, Ga., 23,469.........B5, C2 55
College Park, Md., 18,482.............C2 53
College Place, Wash., 4,031..............C7 86
College Station, Tex., 11,396.............D4 84
Collegeview, Colo., 1,800.............*B6 51
Collegeville, Ind., 1,400..............C3 59
Collegeville, Minn., 1,600.............*E4 67
Collegeville, Pa., 2,254.F11 81
Colleton, co., S.C., 27,816.............F6 82
Colleyville, Tex., 1,491.B5 84
Collier, co., Fla., 15,753.............F5 54
Collierville, Tenn., 2,020..............B2 83
Collin, co., Tex., 41,247.............C4 84
Collingdale, Pa., 10,268............B11 81

Collingswood, N.J.,
17,370.............D2 74
Collingsworth, co., Tex.,
6,276..............B2 84
Collingwood, Ont., Can.,
8,385..............C4 41
Collins, Miss., 1,537..D4 68
Collins Park, Del.,
2,500..............*A6 53
Collins View, Oreg.,
1,500..............*B4 80
Collinsville, Ala., 1,199.A4 46
Collinsville, Conn.,
1,682..............B5 52
Collinsville, Ill., 14,217.E4 58
Collinsville, Okla.,
2,526..............A6 79
Collinsville, Va., 3,586.*E3 85
Collister, Idaho, 5,436..F2 57
Colmar, Fr., 47,305....C7 5
Colmar Manor, Md.,
1,772..............C1 53
Colmenar Viejo, Sp.,
8,375..............o17 8
Cologne, see Köln, Ger.
Coloma, Mich., 1,473..F4 66
Colomb-Béchar, see
Béchar, Alg.
Colombes, Fr., 76,918..g10 5
Colombia, country, S.A.,
12,939,140..........C3 32
Colombo, Cey.,
424,816............G6 20
Colón, Arg., 8,335.....A5 28
Colón, Cuba, 15,755...D3 35
Colon, Mich., 1,055...G5 66
Colón, Pan., 59,598....B2 32
Colón, Archipielago de
(Galápagos Islands),
prov., Ec., 1,546.....g5 31
Colonia, N.J., 6,000...*B4 74
Colonia, Ur., 7,500....E1 30
Colonia, dept., Ur.,
95,400..............*E1 30
Colonia Gustavo A.
Madero, Mex.,
60,239..............h9 34
Colonial Beach, Va.,
1,769..............C6 85
Colonial Heights, Va.,
9,587..............C7, D5 85
Colonial Manor, N.J.,
1,300..............*D2 74
Colonial Park, Pa.,
2,500..............*F8 81
Colonia Suiza, Ur.,
4,307..............g8 28
Colonie, N.Y., 6,992..*C7 75
Colorado, co., Tex.,
18,463.............E4 84
Colorado, state, U.S.,
1,753,947........... 51
Colorado City, Tex.,
6,457..............C2 84
Colorado Springs, Colo.,
70,194 (*139,500)....C6 51
Colored Hill, W. Va.,
1,115..............*D3 87
Colquitt, Ga., 1,556....E2 55
Colquitt, co., Ga.,
34,048.............E3 55
Colton, Calif., 18,666..F3 50
Columbia, Ill., 3,174...E3 58
Columbia, Ky., 2,255..C4 62
Columbia, La., 1,021...B3 63
Columbia, Miss., 7,117.D4 68
Columbia, Mo., 36,650.C5 69
Columbia, N.C., 1,099..B7 76
Columbia, Pa., 12,075..F9 81
Columbia, S.C., 97,433
(*213,400)..........D5 82
Columbia, Tenn.,
17,624.............B4 83
Columbia, co., Ark.,
26,400.............D2 49
Columbia, co., Fla.,
20,077.............B4 54
Columbia, co., Ga.,
13,423.............C4 55
Columbia, co., N.Y.,
47,322.............C7 75
Columbia, co., Oreg.,
22,379.............B3 80
Columbia, co., Pa.,
53,489.............D9 81
Columbia, co., Wash.,
4,569..............C7 86
Columbia, co., Wis.,
36,708.............E4 88
Columbia City, Ind.,
4,803..............B7 59
Columbia Falls, Mont.,
2,132..............B2 70
Columbia Heights, Minn.,
17,533.............E7 67
Columbia Heights, Wash.,
2,227..............*C3 86
Columbiana, Ala.,
2,264..............B3 46
Columbiana, Ohio,
4,164..............B7 78

Columbiana, co., Ohio,
107,004............B7 78
Columbia Park, Calif.,
1,977..............*B5 50
Columbia Station, Ohio,
1,000..............*A6 78
Columbus, Ga., 116,779
(*201,500).........D2 55
Columbus, Ind., 20,778.F6 59
Columbus, Kans.,
3,395..............E9 61
Columbus, Miss.,
24,771.............B5 68
Columbus, Mont.,
1,281..............E7 70
Columbus, Nebr.,
12,476.............C8 71
Columbus, Ohio, 471,316
(*715,400).......C2, C5 78
Columbus, Tex., 3,656..E4 84
Columbus, Wis., 3,467..E4 88
Columbus, co., N.C.,
48,973.............C5 76
Columbus Grove, Ohio,
2,104..............B3 78
Columbus Junction, Iowa,
1,016..............C6 60
Columbus Manor, Ill.,
2,500..............*B6 58
Colusa, Calif., 3,518...C2 50
Colusa, co., Calif.,
12,075.............C2 50
Colver, Pa., 1,261......E4 81
Colville, Wash., 3,806..A8 86
Colwyn, Pa., 3,074...*G11 81
Comacchio, It., 10,200..B4 9
Comal, co., Tex.,
19,844.............E3 84
Comalapa, Guat.,
7,404..............E6 34
Comanche, Okla.,
2,082..............C4 79
Comanche, Tex., 3,415.D3 84
Comanche, co., Kans.,
3,271..............E4 61
Comanche, co., Okla.,
90,803.............C3 79
Comanche, co., Tex.,
11,865.............C3 84
Combined Locks, Wis.,
1,421..............A5 88
Combs, Ky., 900.......C6 62
Comerío, P.R., 5,232..m13 35
Comfort, Tex., 950....E3 84
Comilla, Pak., 47,526..D9 20
Comiso, It., 25,904....F5 9
Comitán, Mex., 15,378.D6 34
Commack, N.Y.,
9,613..............*F3 75
Commentry, Fr.,
9,711..............D5 5
Commerce, Calif.,
9,555..............*F2 50
Commerce, Ga., 3,551..B3 55
Commerce, Mich.,
1,200..............*A7 66
Commerce, Okla.,
2,378..............A7 79
Commerce, Tex., 5,789.C5 84
Commerce Town, Colo.,
8,970..............B6 51
Commercy, Fr., 7,043..C6 5
Como, It., 81,983.....B2 9
Comodoro Rivadavia,
Arg., 25,651........D3 28
Comores Is., Fr. dep.,
Afr., 183,133........C8 24
Comox, B.C., Can.,
1,756..............E5 37
Compiègne, Fr.,
24,427.............C5 5
Compton, Calif.,
71,812.............F2 50
Compton, co., Que., Can.,
24,410.............D6 42
Comstock, Mich.,
3,000..............F5 66
Comstock Park, Mich.,
2,500..............*E5 66
Conakry, Guinea,
43,000.............G2 22
Concarneau, Fr.,
11,691.............D2 5
Concepción, Arg.,
12,338.............E2 29
Concepción, Chile,
150,000............B2 28
Concepción, Par.,
32,556.............D4 29
Concepción, dept., Par.,
14,640.............D4 29
Concepción, prov., Chile,
537,711............B2 28
Concepción del Uruguay,
Arg., 31,498........A5 28
Concho, co., Tex.,
3,672..............D3 84
Concord, Calif.,
36,208.............B5 50
Concord, Mass.,
3,188..........B5, C2 6

Concord, Mich., 990...F6 66
Concord, N.H., 28,991..E4 73
Concord, N.C., 17,799..B3 76
Concordia, Arg.,
64,000.............A5 28
Concordia, Kans.,
7,022..............C6 61
Concordia, Mo., 1,471..C4 69
Concordia, par., La.,
20,467.............C4 63
Concord North, N.C.,
2,199..............B3 76
Condon, Oreg., 1,149...B6 80
Conecuh, co., Ala.,
17,762.............D2 46
Conegliano, It., 11,300.B4 9
Conejos, co., Colo.,
8,428..............D4 51
Conemaugh, Pa.,
3,334..............*E8 81
Coney, isl., N.Y.......E1 75
Conflans-Ste. Honorine,
Fr., 21,874.........g9 5
Confluence, Pa., 938...G3 81
Congers, N.Y.,
3,000..............*D7 75
Congo (Brazzaville),
country, Afr., 795,000
...................I7 22
Congo (Léopoldville),
country, Afr.,
13,284,300.........B4 24
Conil, Sp., 9,002......D2 8
Coniston, Ont., Can.,
2,692..............E9 41
Conjeeveram, see
Kancheepuram, India.
Connacht, prov., Ire.,
419,465............*D2 4
Conneaut, Ohio, 10,557.A7 78
Conneautville, Pa.,
1,100..............C1 81
Connecticut, state, U.S.,
2,535,234........... 52
Connell, Wash., 906...C7 86
Connellsville, Pa.,
12,814.............F2 81
Connersville, Ind.,
17,698.............E7 59
Conning Towers, Conn.,
3,457..............*D8 52
Conover, N.C., 2,281..B2 76
Conrad, Mont., 2,665..B5 70
Conroe, Tex., 9,192...D5 84
Conselheiro Lafaiete,
Braz., 29,208.......C4 30
Conshohocken, Pa.,
10,259.........A11, F11 81
Consolación del Sur, Cuba,
5,392..............D2 35
Constanta, Rom.,
99,690.............C9 10
Constantina, Sp.,
11,910.............D3 8
Constantine, Alg.,
148,725............A6 22
Constantine, Mich.,
1,710..............G5 66
Constantinople, see
Istanbul, Tur.
Constitución, Chile,
8,285..............B2 28
Constitution, Ga., 900.*B5 55
Consuegra, Sp., 10,572.C4 8
Continental, Ohio,
1,147..............A3 78
Contra Costa, co., Calif.,
409,030............D2 50
Contrecoeur, Que., Can.,
2,007..............D4 42
Contreras, Mex.,
10,112.............h9 34
Convent, La., 400..B6, D5 63
Converse, Ind., 1,044..C6 59
Converse, S.C., 950...B4 82
Converse, co., Wyo.,
6,366..............B7 89
Convoy, Ohio, 976.....B3 78
Conway, Ark., 12,500..B3 49
Conway, Fla., 1,000..*D5 54
Conway, N.H., 1,143..D5 73
Conway, Pa., 1,926....E1 81
Conway, S.C., 8,563...D9 82
Conway, co., Ark.,
15,430.............B3 49
Conway Springs, Kans.,
1,057..............E6 61
Conyers, Ga., 2,881.B6, C2 55
Conyngham, Pa.,
1,163..............*D9 81
Cooch-Behār, India,
41,922.............C8 20
Cook, co., Ga., 11,822.E3 55
Cook, co., Ill.,
5,129,725..........B6 58
Cook, co., Minn., 3,377.A6 67
Cooke, co., Tex.,
22,560.............C4 84
Cookeville, Tenn.,
7,805..............C8 83

Cookshire, Que., Can.,
1,412..............D6 42
Cooksville, Ont., Can.,
1,750.........D5, E6 41
Cooleemee, N.C.,
1,609..............B3 76
Coolidge, Ariz.,
4,990.........C3, E2 48
Coolidge, Tex., 913....D4 84
Cool Ridge, W. Va.,
400..............D3 87
Cool Valley, Mo.,
1,492..............*C7 69
Coon Rapids, Iowa,
1,560..............C3 60
Coon Rapids, Minn.,
14,931.............E7 67
Cooper, Tex., 2,213....C5 84
Cooper, co., Mo.,
15,448.............C5 69
Coopersburg, Pa.,
1,800..............E11 81
Cooperstown, N.Y.,
2,553..............C6 75
Cooperstown, N. Dak.,
1,424..............C7 77
Coopersville, Mich.,
1,584..............E5 66
Cooper Village, N.J.,
1,500..............*D2 74
Coos, co., N.H., 37,140.B5 73
Coos, co., Oreg.,
54,955.............D2 80
Coosa, co., Ala., 10,726.C3 46
Coos Bay, Oreg., 7,084.D2 80
Cootamundra, Austl.,
5,938..............G7 26
Copenhagen (København),
Den., 721,381.......J5 11
Copiague, N.Y., 14,081.G3 52
Copiah, co., Miss.,
27,051.............D3 68
Copiapó, Chile, 28,000.E1 29
Coplay, Pa., 3,701...*E11 81
Copley, Ohio, 4,000...*A6 78
Copparo, It., 5,800....B3 9
Copperas Cove, Tex.,
4,567..............D4 84
Copperhill, Tenn., 631.D9 83
Coquilhatville, Con. L.,
37,500.............H1 23
Coquille, Oreg., 4,730..D2 80
Coquimbo, Chile,
31,000.............E1 29
Coquimbo, prov., Chile,
306,384............A2 28
Cora, W. Va., 500....*D2 87
Corabia, Rom., 11,502.D7 10
Coral Gables, Fla.,
34,793.........F3, G6 54
Coralville, Iowa, 2,357.C6 60
Coraopolis, Pa.,
9,643.........A5, F1 81
Corato, It., 39,452....D6 9
Corbeil, Fr., 26,804...C5 5
Corbin, Ky., 7,119....D5 62
Corcoran, Calif., 4,976.D4 50
Corcoran, Minn.,
1,237..............*E5 67
Cordele, Ga., 10,609...E3 55
Cordell, Okla., 3,589..B3 79
Cordillera, dept., Par.,
145,232............D4 29
Córdoba, Arg., 580,000.A4 28
Córdoba, Mex., 47,390.n15 34
Córdoba, Sp., 198,148..D3 8
Córdoba, prov., Arg.,
1,759,997..........A4 28
Córdoba, prov., Sp.,
798,437............*D3 8
Cordova, Ala., 3,184...B2 46
Cordova, Alsk.,
1,128.........C10, g19 47
Cordova, N.C., 950....C4 76
Cori, It., 9,681......h9 9
Corigliano Calabro, It.,
16,300.............E6 9
Corinne, W. Va.,
1,273..............D3 87
Corinth, see Korinthos,
Grc.
Corinth, Miss.,
11,453.............A5 68
Corinth, N.Y., 3,193...B7 75
Corinto, Braz., 12,247.B4 30
Cork, Ire., 77,980.....E2 4
Cork, co., Ire.,
330,443............*E2 4
Corleone, It., 14,682..F4 9
Corlu, Tur., 22,000....B6 14
Cormeilles-en-Parisis,
Fr., 11,486.........g9 5
Cornelia, Ga., 2,936...B3 55
Cornelius, N.C., 1,444..B3 76
Cornelius, Oreg.,
1,146..............*B3 80
Cornell, Wis., 1,685....C2 88
Corner Brook, Newf.,
Can., 25,185........D3 44
Corning, Ark., 2,565...A5 49

Corning, Calif., 3,006..C2 50
Corning, Iowa, 2,041...D3 60
Corning, N.Y., 17,085 .C3 75
Corning, Ohio, 1,065...C5 78
Cornwall, Ont., Can.,
  43,639.............B10 41
Cornwall, N.Y., 2,824 .D6 75
Cornwall, Pa., 1,934...F9 81
Cornwall, co., Eng.,
  345,612.............*E4 4
Cornwall [-on-the-Hudson]
  N.Y., 2,785.........D6 75
Cornwells Heights, Pa.,
  10,000............*A12 81
Coro, Ven., 44,757....A4 31
Corona, Calif.,
  13,336..........F3, F5 50
Coronado, Calif.,
  18,039..........E2, F5 50
Coronell, Chile, 28,000 . B2 28
Coronel Dorrego, Arg.,
  7,245..............B4 28
Coronel Oviedo, Par.,
  34,442.............E4 29
Coronel Pringles, Arg.,
  12,844.............B4 28
Coronel Pringles, Arg..C4 28
Coronel Suárez, Arg.,
  11,133.............B4 28
Corpus Christi, Tex.,
  167,690
  (*195,200).........F4 84
Corral de Almaguer, Sp.,
  8,261..............C4 8
Correctionville, Iowa,
  912...............B2 60
Corrèze, dept., Fr.,
  237,926...........*E4 5
Corrientes, Arg.,
  104,000...........E4 29
Corrientes, prov., Arg.,
  543,226...........E4 29
Corrigan, Tex., 986...D5 84
Corry, Pa., 7,744....C2 81
Corse, dept., Fr.,
  275,465...........*C2 9
Corsicana, Tex., 20,344.C4 84
Corson, co., S. Dak.,
  5,798.............E4 77
Cortegana, Sp., 7,179 .D2 8
Corte Madera, Calif.,
  5,962.............*B5 50
Cortez, Colo., 6,764...D1 51
Cortland, N.Y., 19,181.C4 75
Cortland, Ohio, 1,957 .A7 78
Cortland, co., N.Y.,
  41,113.............C4 75
Cortona, It., 4,000.....C3 9
Çorum, Tur., 34,600..B10 14
Corumbá, Braz.,
  36,744.............B1 30
Corunna, Mich., 2,764..F6 66
Corvallis, Oreg.,
  20,669.........C1, C3 80
Corydon, Ind., 2,701..H5 59
Corydon, Iowa, 1,687..D4 60
Coryell, co., Tex.,
  23,961.............D4 84
Cosenza, It., 78,611....E6 9
Coshocton, Ohio,
  13,106.............B6 78
Coshocton, co., Ohio,
  32,224.............B6 78
Cosmopolis, Wash.,
  1,312.............C2 86
Cosne [-sur-Loire], Fr.,
  8,802.............D5 5
Costa Mesa, Calif.,
  37,550.............F2 50
Costa Rica, country, N.A.,
  1,251,300.........E8 34
Costermansville, see
  Bukavu, Con. L.
Costilla, N. Mex., 300..A6 48
Costilla, co., Colo.,
  4,219.............D5 51
Cotabato, Phil., 17,000.D6 19
Cotabato, prov., Phil.,
  1,152,500.........*D6 19
Cotati, Calif., 1,852....B5 50
Côte-d'Or, dept., Fr.,
  387,869...........*D6 5
Côte St. Luc, Que., Can.,
  13,266............*D4 42
Cote St. Michel, Que.,
  Can., 55,978.......*D4 42
Côtes-du-Nord, dept., Fr.,
  501,923...........*C2 5
Cotonou, Dah., 21,140.G5 22
Cotopaxi, prov., Ec.,
  179,965............B2 31
Cottage City, Md.,
  1,099.............*C1 53
Cottage Grove, Oreg.,
  3,895.............D3 80
Cottage Grove, Wis.,
  413...............*E4 88
Cottage Hills, Ill.,
  3,976.............*E3 58
Cottbus, Ger., 67,700..C7 6
Cotter, Ark., 683......A3 49

Cottle, co., Tex., 4,207.B2 84
Cotton, co., Okla.,
  8,031.............C3 79
Cotton Mills, Tex.,
  950...............*C4 84
Cotton Plant, Ark.,
  1,704.............B4 49
Cottonport, La., 1,581.D3 63
Cotton Valley, La.,
  1,145.............B2 63
Cottonwood, Ala., 953 .D4 46
Cottonwood, Ariz.,
  1,879.............B3 48
Cottonwood, Calif.,
  700...............B2 50
Cottonwood, Idaho,
  1,081.............C2 57
Cottonwood, co., Minn.,
  16,166............F3 67
Cottonwood Falls, Kans.,
  971...............D7 61
Cottonwood Heights,
  Utah, 1,500.......*D2 72
Cotulla, Tex., 3,960...E3 84
Coudekerque-Branche,
  Fr., 20,757........B5 5
Coudersport, Pa., 2,889.C5 81
Coulee City, Wash.,
  654...............B6 86
Coulee Dam, Wash.,
  1,344.............B7 86
Coulommiers, Fr.,
  8,561.............C5 5
Coulterville, Ill., 1,022.E4 58
Council Bluffs, Iowa,
  55,641............C2 60
Council Grove, Kans.,
  2,664.............D7 61
Country Club Hills, Ill.,
  4,771.............*B6 58
Country Club Hills, Mo.,
  1,763.............*A8 69
Country Homes, Wash.,
  1,600.............*B8 86
Courbevoie, Fr.,
  59,491............g10 5
Courtdale, Pa., 845...*D9 81
Courtenay, B.C., Can.,
  3,485.............E5 37
Courtland, Calif., 550..B6 50
Courtrai, see Kortrijk, Bel.
Courville, Que., Can.,
  4,670.............*C9 42
Coushatta, La., 1,663..B2 63
Coutances, Fr., 7,806..C3 5
Coutras, Fr., 3,688.....E3 5
Cove City, Tex.,
  1,749.............*D6 84
Covedale, Ohio, 10,000.D2 78
Coventry, Conn., 3,568.B7 52
Coventry, Eng.,
  305,060...........D6 4
Coventry, R.I., 4,500 .C10 52
Covilhã, Port., 20,423..B2 8
Covina, Calif., 20,124 .*F3 50
Covington, Ga., 8,167..C3 55
Covington, Ind., 2,759.D3 59
Covington, Ky.,
  60,376.........A5, A7 62
Covington, La.,
  6,754.........B7, D5 63
Covington, Ohio, 2,473.B3 78
Covington, Tenn.,
  5,298.............B2 83
Covington, Va., 11,062.D3 85
Covington, co., Ala.,
  35,631............D3 46
Covington, co., Miss.,
  13,637............D4 68
Cowan, Tenn., 1,979..B5 83
Cowansville, Que., Can.,
  7,050.............D5 42
Cowansville, Pa., 400..E2 81
Cowes, Eng., 16,974..E6 4
Coweta, Okla., 1,858..B6 79
Coweta, co., Ga.,
  28,893............C2 55
Cowley, co., Kans.,
  37,861............E7 61
Cowlitz, co., Wash.,
  57,801............C3 86
Cowpens, S.C., 2,038..A4 82
Cowra, Austl., 6,289..F7 26
Coxsackie, N.Y., 2,849.C7 75
Coyoacán, Mex.,
  46,031.........h9, n14 34
Cozad, Nebr., 3,184...D6 71
Crab Orchard, W. Va.,
  1,953.............D7 87
Crabtree, Pa., 950.....F3 81
Crabtree Mills, Que.,
  Can., 1,313.......D4 42
Cradock, S. Afr.,
  19,476............G5 24
Crafton, Pa., 8,418....B5 81
Craig, Colo., 3,984....A3 51
Craig, co., Okla.,
  16,303............A6 79
Craig, co., Va., 3,356 ..D2 85
Craig Beach, Ohio,
  1,139............*A7 78

Craighead, co., Ark.,
  47,253............B5 49
Craigsville, Va., 978...C3 85
Crailsheim, Ger.,
  14,400............D5 6
Craiova, Rom., 96,929.C6 10
Cramerton, N.C.,
  3,123.............B2 76
Cranbrook, B.C., Can.,
  5,549.............E10 37
Cranbury, N.J., 1,038..C3 74
Crandon, Wis., 1,679..C5 88
Crane, Mo., 954.......E4 69
Crane, Tex., 3,796....D1 84
Crane, co., Tex., 4,699.D1 84
Cranford, N.J.,
  26,424............B4 74
Cranston, R.I.,
  66,766............B11 52
Crateús, Braz.,
  14,572...........*D6 27
Crato, Braz., 27,649..*D7 27
Craven, co., N.C.,
  58,773............B6 76
Crawford, Nebr., 1,588.B2 71
Crawford, co., Ark.,
  21,318............B1 49
Crawford, co., Ga.,
  5,816.............D3 55
Crawford, co., Ill.,
  20,751............D6 58
Crawford, co., Ind.,
  8,379.............H4 59
Crawford, co., Iowa,
  18,569............B2 60
Crawford, co., Kans.,
  37,032............E9 61
Crawford, co., Mich.,
  4,971.............D6 66
Crawford, co., Mo.,
  12,647............D6 69
Crawford, co., Ohio,
  46,775............B5 78
Crawford, co., Pa.,
  77,956............C1 81
Crawford, co., Wis.,
  16,351............E3 88
Crawfordsville, Ind.,
  14,231............D4 59
Crawfordville Ga., 786.C4 55
Creek, co., Okla.,
  40,495............B5 79
Creighton, Sask., Can,,
  1,729.............*C5 39
Creighton, Nebr., 1,388.B8 71
Creighton, Pa., 2,865 ..A6 81
Creil, Fr., 19,235......C5 5
Crema, It., 30,035.....B2 9
Cremona, It., 73,902..B3 9
Crenshaw, Miss., 1,382.A3 68
Crenshaw, co., Ala.,
  14,909............D3 46
Cresaptown, Md.,
  1,680.............D2 53
Crescent, Okla., 1,264..B4 79
Crescent City, Calif.,
  2,958.............B1 50
Crescent City, Fla.,
  1,629.............C5 54
Crescent City Northwest,
  Calif., 3,086......*B1 50
Crescent Springs, Ky.,
  946...............A7 62
Cresco, Iowa, 3,809...A5 60
Cresskill, N.J., 7,290...D5 74
Cresson, Pa., 2,659...F4 81
Cressona, Pa., 1,854...E9 81
Crest, Fr., 4,494......E6 5
Crest Hill, Ill., 5,887 .*F2 58
Crestline, Calif., 1,290.*E5 50
Crestline, Ohio, 5,521..B5 78
Crestmont, Pa.,
  2,000............*F11 81
Crestmore, Calif.,
  2,000............*E5 50
Creston, B.C., Can.,
  2,460.............E9 37
Creston, Iowa, 7,667...C3 60
Creston, Ohio, 1,522...B6 78
Crestview, Fla., 7,467..G2 54
Crestwood, Ill., 3,918 .*B6 58
Crestwood, Mo.,
  11,106............*B8 69
Crestwood, Va., 2,200.*E6 85
Crete, Ill., 3,463......B6 58
Crete, Nebr., 3,546...D9 71
Crete, isl., Grc.......E5 14
Creuse, dept., Fr.,
  163,515...........*D4 5
Creutzwald, Fr.,
  13,649............C7 5
Creve Coeur, Ill., 6,684.C4 58
Creve Coeur, Mo.,
  5,122.............*C7 69
Crevillente, Sp., 14,047.C5 8
Crewe, Eng., 53,394...D5 4
Crewe, Va., 2,012....D4 85
Cridersville, Ohio,
  1,053.............B3 78
Crieff, Scot., 5,773....B5 4

Crimmitschau, Ger.,
  31,300............C6 6
Crisana-Maramures, prov.,
  Rom., 1,391,672....B6 10
Crisfield, Md., 3,540...E6 53
Crisp, co., Ga., 17,768..E3 55
Crittenden, co., Ark.,
  47,564............B5 49
Crittenden, co., Ky.,
  8,648.............A3 62
Croatia, rep., Yugo.,
  4,148,122.........*C2 10
Croatia, reg., Yugo....C2 10
Crockett, Calif., 4,500..B5 50
Crockett, Tex., 5,356..D5 84
Crockett, co., Tenn.,
  14,594............B2 83
Crockett, co., Tex.,
  4,209.............D2 84
Cromona, Ky., 950....C7 62
Cromwell, Conn., 6,780.C6 52
Crook, co., Oreg., 9,430.C6 80
Crook, co., Wyo., 4,691.A8 89
Crookston, Minn.,
  8,546.............C2 67
Crooksville, Ohio,
  2,958.............C5 78
Crosby, Minn., 2,629..D5 67
Crosby, Miss., 705.....D2 68
Crosby, N. Dak., 1,759.A2 77
Crosby, Tex., 1,200...F5 84
Crosby, co., Tex.,
  10,347............C2 84
Crosbyton, Tex., 2,088.C2 84
Cross, co., Ark., 19,551.B5 49
Cross City, Fla., 1,857.C3 54
Crossett, Ark., 5,370...D4 49
Cross Keys, Ga.,
  1,000............*D3 55
Cross Mill, N.C., 700..D4 76
Cross Plains, Tex.,
  1,168.............C3 84
Cross Plains, Wis.,
  1,066.............E4 88
Crossville, Tenn.,
  4,668.............D8 83
Croswell, Mich., 1,817..E8 66
Crothersville, Ind.,
  1,449.............G6 59
Crotone, It., 43,256....E6 9
Croton-on-Hudson, N.Y.,
  6,812.........D3, D7 75
Crouse, N.C., 901.....B2 76
Crow Agency, Mont.,
  600...............E9 70
Crowell, Tex., 1,703...C3 84
Crowley, La., 15,617...D3 63
Crowley, co., Colo.,
  3,978.............C7 51
Crown Point, Ind.,
  8,443.............B3 59
Crown Point, N.Y.,
  500...............B7 75
Crow Wing, co., Minn.,
  32,134............D4 67
Croydon, Eng.,
  252,387.......E6, m12 4
Croydon, Pa., 9,000...F12 81
Cruces, Cuba, 10,704..D3 35
Crucible, Pa., 1,064....G1 81
Crum Lynne, Pa.,
  3,500............*B10 81
Cruz Alta, Braz.,
  33,190............D2 30
Cruz del Eje, Arg.,
  15,563............A4 28
Cruzeiro, Braz., 27,005.C4 30
Crystal, Minn., 24,283.E6 67
Crystal Beach, Ont., Can.,
  1,886............*D5 41
Crystal Beach, Fla.,
  1,000.............D4 54
Crystal City, Mo.,
  3,678.........B8, C7 69
Crystal City, Tex.,
  9,101.............E3 84
Crystal Falls, Mich.,
  2,203.............B2 66
Crystal Lake, Ill.,
  8,314.........A5, E1 58
Crystal Lakes, Ohio,
  1,569.............C3 78
Crystal River, Fla.,
  1,423.............D4 54
Crystal Springs, Miss.,
  4,496.............D3 68
Csongrad, Hung.,
  16,801............B5 10
Csongrad, co., Hung.,
  335,565...........*B5 10
Csorna, Hung., 9,208..B3 10
Cuautla [Morelos], Mex.,
  11,847............n14 34
Cuba, Ill., 1,380......C3 58
Cuba, Mo., 1,672.....C6 69
Cuba, N.Y., 1,949....C2 75
Cuba, country, N.A.,
  5,829,029.........E4 35
Cuba City, Wis., 1,673.F3 88
Cucamonga, Calif.,
  2,500.............F3 50

Cúcuta, Col., 86,300...B3 32
Cudahy, Calif., 12,000.*F2 50
Cudahy, Wis.,
  17,975............E2, F6 88
Cuddalore, India,
  79,168.............F6 20
Cuddapah, India,
  49,027.............F6 20
Cuddy, Pa., 1,400....*B5 81
Cuéllar, Sp., 7,514....B3 8
Cuenca, Ec., 46,428....B2 31
Cuenca, Sp., 27,007....B4 8
Cuenca, prov., Sp.,
  315,433...........*B4 8
Cuernavaca, Mex.,
  35,824.........D5, n14 34
Cuero, Tex., 7,338.....E4 84
Cuevas, Sp., 9,530.....D5 8
Cuiabá, Braz., 43,112..B1 30
Culberson, co., Tex.,
  2,794.............F2 84
Culbertson, Mont.,
  919..............B12 70
Culiacán, Mex.,
  84,602............C3 34
Cúllar de Baza, Sp.,
  9,502.............D4 8
Cullen, La., 2,194.....B2 63
Cullera, Sp., 14,103....C5 8
Cullman, Ala., 10,883..A3 46
Cullman, co., Ala.,
  45,572............A3 46
Culloden, W. Va., 700..C2 87
Cullowhee, N.C., 1,500.D3 76
Culmore, Va., 1,700...*B5 85
Culpeper, Va., 2,412...C4 85
Culpeper, co., Va.,
  15,088............C5 85
Culver, Ind., 1,558.....B5 59

Culver City, Calif.,
  32,163............F2 50
Cumaná, Ven., 71,563..A5 32
Cumberland, B.C., Can.,
  1,303.............E5 37
Cumberland, Ky.,
  4,271.............D7 62
Cumberland, Md.,
  33,415............D2 53
Cumberland, R.I.,
  7,500............B11 52
Cumberland, Wis.,
  1,860.............C1 88
Cumberland, co., N.S.,
  Can., 37,767........D5 43
Cumberland, co., Eng.,
  294,162...........*C5 4
Cumberland, co., Ill.,
  9,936.............D5 58
Cumberland, co., Ky.,
  7,835.............D4 62
Cumberland, co., Maine,
  182,751...........E2 64
Cumberland, co., N.J.,
  106,850...........E2 74
Cumberland, co., N.C.,
  148,418...........B5 76
Cumberland, co., Pa.,
  124,816...........F7 81
Cumberland, co., Tenn.,
  19,135............D8 83
Cumberland, co., Va.,
  6,360.............D4 85
Cuming, co., Nebr.,
  12,435............C9 71
Cumming, Ga., 1,561..B2 55
Cumra, Tur., 7,100....D9 14
Cundinamarca, dept.,
  Col., 1,840,890......C3 32

Cuneo, It., 34,000.....B1 9
Cupertino, Calif., 3,664.C5 50
Curaçao, isl., Neth.
  Antilles...........A4 32
Curacautín, Chile,
  9,201.............B2 28
Curicó, Chile, 35,000...A2 28
Curicó, prov., Chile,
  107,160...........A2 28
Curitiba, Braz.,
  344,560...........D3 30
Currais Novos, Braz.,
  7,782............*D7 27
Currituck, co., N.C.,
  6,601.............A7 76
Curry, co., N. Mex.,
  32,691............B7 48
Curry, co., Oreg.,
  13,983............E2 80
Curtea-de-Arges, Rom.,
  10,764............C7 10
Curtici, Rom., 8,050...B5 10
Curtis, Nebr., 868.....D5 71
Curtisville, Pa.,
  1,376.........A6, E2 81
Curug, Yugo., 9,457...C5 10
Curuzú Cuatia, Arg.,
  15,440............E4 29
Curvelo, Braz., 21,772..B4 30
Curwensville, Pa.,
  3,231.............E4 81
Cusco, Peru, 53,242...D3 31
Cusco, dept., Peru,
  649,643...........D3 31
Cushing, Okla., 8,619..B5 79
Cusset, Fr., 11,468....D5 5
Custer, S. Dak., 2,105..G2 77
Custer, co., Colo.,
  1,305.............C5 51

Custer, co., Idaho,
  2,996............E4 57
Custer, co., Mont.,
  13,227...........D11 70
Custer, co., Nebr.,
  16,517............C6 71
Custer, co., Okla.,
  21,040............B2 79
Custer, co., S. Dak.,
  4,906............G2 77
Cut Bank, Mont.,
  4,539.............B4 70
Cutchogue, N.Y., 950..D4 75
Cuthbert, Ga., 4,300...E2 55
Cutler, Calif., 2,191..*D4 50
Cutler Ridge, Fla.,
  7,005............*G6 54
Cuttack, India,
  146,308...........D8 20
Cutten, Calif., 1,572..*B1 50
Cuxhaven, Ger., 44,100.B4 6
Cuyahoga, co., Ohio,
  1,647,895.........A6 78
Cuyahoga Falls, Ohio,
  47,922............A6 78
Cyclades, is., Grc......D5 14
Cynthiana, Ky., 5,641..B5 62
Cypress, Calif., 1,753.*F2 50
Cyprus, country, Asia,
  528,618...........B4 23
Cyrenaica, prov., Libya,
  291,328...........B2 23
Cyril, Okla., 1,284....C3 79
Czechoslovakia, country,
  Eur., 13,741,700....D4 7
Czersk, Pol., 7,092....B4 7
Częstochowa, Pol.,
  164,000...........C5 7

D

Dab, Pol., 9,096......B3 7
Dab, Pol., 13,666.....g9 7
Dablice, Czech., 5,378.n18 7
Dabrowa, Pol., 4,520...C6 7
Dabrowa Gornicza, Pol.,
  42,000.........C5, g10 7
Dacca, Pak., 556,712
  (*720,000).........D9 20
Dachau, Ger., 29,100..D5 6
Dade, co., Fla.,
  935,047...........G6 54
Dade, co., Ga., 8,666..B1 55
Dade, co., Mo., 7,577.D4 69
Dade City, Fla., 4,759.D4 54
Dadeville, Ala., 2,940..C4 46
Dadu, Pak., 13,716....C4 20
Daet, Phil., 20,000....*C6 19
Daggett, co., Utah,
  1,164.............A7 72
Dagupan, Phil.,
  17,000............n13 19
Dahlgren, Va., 475....C5 85
Dahlonega, Ga., 2,604..B3 55
Dahomey, country, Afr.,
  2,000,000..........G5 22
Daigleville, La., 5,906.*E5 63
Dailey, W. Va., 800....C5 87
Daimiel, Sp., 19,625...C4 8
Daingerfield, Tex.,
  3,133.............C5 84
Dairen (Talien), China,
  950,000...........D9 17
Dairy Valley, Calif.,
  3,508............*F4 50
Daisetta, Tex., 1,500..D5 84
Daisy, Tenn.,
  1,508.........D8, E10 83
Daisytown, Pa., 1,396.*F2 81
Dakar, Sen., 231,000..F1 22
Dakota, co., Minn.,
  78,303............F5 67
Dakota, co., Nebr.,
  12,168............B9 71
Dakota City, Nebr.,
  928..............B9 71
Dalat, Viet., 5,217.....C3 19
Dale, Ind., 900........H4 59
Dale, Pa., 2,807......*F4 81
Dale, co., Ala., 31,066..D4 46
Daleville, Ind., 1,548..D6 59
Dalhart, Tex., 5,160....A1 84
Dalhousie, N.B., Can.,
  5,856.............A3 43
Dallam, co., Tex.,
  6,302.............A1 84
Dallas, Ga., 2,065.....C2 55
Dallas, N.C., 3,270....B2 76
Dallas, Oreg., 5,072...C3 80
Dallas, Pa., 2,586.B8, D10 81
Dallas, Tex., 679,684
  (*1,022,300)....B5, C4 84
Dallas, co., Ala.,
  56,667............C2 46
Dallas, co., Ark.,
  10,522............D3 49
Dallas, co., Iowa,
  24,123............C3 60

Dallas, co., Mo., 9,314.D3 69
Dallas, co., Tex.,
  951,527...........C4 84
Dallas Center, Iowa,
  1,083.............C4 60
Dallas City, Ill., 1,276..C2 58
Dallastown, Pa., 3,615.G8 81
Dalmatia, reg., Yugo...D3 10
Dalmellington, Scot.,
  4,702.............C4 4
Dalnyaya, Sov. Un.,
  10,000...........D11 18
Dalton, Ga., 17,868...B2 55
Dalton, Mass., 6,436..B1 65
Dalton, Ohio, 1,067...B6 78
Dalton, Pa., 1,229....C10 81
Daltonganj, India,
  25,270............D7 20
Dalton Gardens, Idaho,
  1,083.............B2 57
Daly City, Calif.,
  44,791............B5 50
Damanhūr, Eg., U.A.R.,
  99,000............G8 14
Damão, Ind., 10,000...D5 20
Damascus, Md., 1,500..B3 53
Damascus (Dimashq),
  Syr., 408,744.......C2 15
Damascus, Va., 1,485..B3 85
Damietta (Dumyāt), Eg.,
  U.A.R., 63,100......G8 14
Da Nang, Viet.,
  109,000...........B3 19
Dana Point, Calif.,
  1,186............*F5 50
Danbury, Conn.,
  22,928............D3 52
Dandenong, Austl.,
  24,914............H5 26
Dane, co., Wis.,
  222,095...........E4 88
Dania, Fla., 7,065..E3, F6 54
Daniels, co., Mont.,
  3,755............B11 70
Danielson, Conn.,
  4,642.............B9 52
Dannemora, N.Y.,
  4,835.............A3 75
Dannevirke, N.Z.,
  5,508............N16 26
Dansalan, Phil., 4,882..D6 19
Dansville, N.Y., 5,460..C3 75
Dante, Som.............F8 23
Dante, Va., 1,436.....B2 85
Danubyu, Bur.,
  10,000...........*E10 20
Danvers, Mass.,
  21,926.........A6, C3 65
Danville, Ark., 955....B2 49
Danville, Calif., 3,585..B5 50
Danville, Que., Can.,
  2,562.............D5 42
Danville, Ill., 41,856...C6 58
Danville, Ind., 3,287...E4 59
Danville, Ky., 9,010...C5 62
Danville, Ohio, 926....B5 78
Danville, Pa., 6,889....E8 81
Danville, Va., 46,577...E3 85

Danville East, Pa.,
  1,758............*E8 81
Danzig, see Gdańsk, Pol.
Daphne, Ala., 1,527....E2 46
Darabani, Rom.,
  11,379............A8 10
Darasun, Sov. Un.,
  18,000...........D14 13
Darbhanga, India,
  103,016...........C8 20
Darby, Pa.,
  14,059........B11, G11 81
Dardanelle, Ark.,
  2,098.............B2 49
Dardenne, Tur., 6,900..C11 14
Dare, co., N.C., 5,936..B8 76
Dar es Salaam, Tan.,
  128,742...........B7 24
Darien, Conn., 18,437..E3 52
Darien, Ga., 1,569.....E5 55
Darjeeling, India,
  40,651............C8 20
Darke, co., Ohio,
  45,612............B3 78
Darlington, Eng.,
  84,162............C6 4
Darlington, S.C., 6,710.C8 82
Darlington, Wis.,
  2,349.............F3 88
Darlington, co., S.C.,
  52,928............C8 82
Darlowo, Pol., 5,262...A4 7
Darmstadt, Ger.,
  136,400...........D4 6
Darnah, Libya, 15,891..B2 23
Darrington, Wash.,
  1,272.............A4 86
Darrow, La., 400......B5 63
Dartmouth, N.S., Can.,
  46,966............E6 43
Dartmouth, Eng.,
  5,757.............E5 4
Daruvar, Yugo., 6,280.C3 10
Darwin, Austl., 12,335.B5 25
Dasē, Eth., 40,000.....F5 23
Dassel, Minn., 863....E4 67
Daugavpils, Sov. Un.,
  70,000............D6 12
Dauphin, Man., Can.,
  7,374.............D1 40
Dauphin, co., Pa.,
  220,255...........F8 81
Dauphiné, former prov.,
  Fr., 1,016,000......E6 5
Davao, Phil., 135,000..D7 19
Davao, prov., Phil.,
  903,200...........*D7 19
Davenport, Fla., 1,209.D5 54
Davenport, Iowa, 88,981
  (*260,300)......C7, D7 60
Davenport, Wash.,
  1,494.............B7 86
David, Pan., 14,969...B1 32
David City, Nebr.,
  2,304.............C8 71
Davidson, N.C., 2,573..B3 76
Davidson, co., N.C.,
  79,493............B3 76

Davidson, co., Tenn.,
  399,743...........A5 83
Davie, Fla., 1,500..E3, F6 54
Davie, co., N.C.,
  16,728............B3 76
Daviess, co., Ind.,
  26,636............G3 59
Daviess, co., Ky.,
  70,588............C3 62
Daviess, co., Mo.,
  9,502.............B3 69
Davis, Calif., 8,910.A6, C3 50
Davis, Okla., 2,203....C4 79
Davis, W. Va., 898....B5 87
Davis, co., Iowa,
  9,199.............D4 60
Davis, co., Utah,
  64,760............A5 72
Davison, Mich., 3,761.E7 66
Davison, co., S. Dak.,
  16,681............G7 77
Davisville, R.I., 1,800.C11 52
Davos, Switz., 9,588...E4 6
Davy, W. Va., 1,331...D3 87
Dawes, co., Nebr.,
  9,536.............B2 71
Dawson, Yukon, Can.,
  881..............D6 36
Dawson, Ga., 5,062...E2 55
Dawson, Minn., 1,766..F2 67
Dawson, Tex., 911....D4 84
Dawson, co., Ga.,
  3,590.............B2 55
Dawson, co., Mont.,
  12,314...........C11 70
Dawson, co., Nebr.,
  19,405............D6 71
Dawson, co., Tex.,
  19,185............C1 84
Dawson Creek, B.C.,
  Can., 10,946......*B7 37
Dawson Springs, Ky.,
  3,002............*C2 62
Dax, Fr., 17,051......F3 5
Day, co., S. Dak.,
  10,516............E8 77
Daylight, Tenn., 20....D8 83
Dayrūt, Eg., U.A.R.,
  5,000.............C4 23
Dayton, Ky., 9,050....A7 62
Dayton, Ohio, 262,332
  (*648,600).........C3 78
Dayton, Tenn., 3,500..D8 83
Dayton, Tex.,
  3,367.........D5, F5 84
Dayton, Va., 930......C4 85
Dayton, Wash., 2,913..C8 86
Daytona Beach, Fla.,
  37,395............C6 54
Daytona Beach Shores
  (South Peninsula),
  Fla., 3,741........*C6 54
Dayville, Conn., 900...B9 52
De Aar, S. Afr.,
  14,357............G4 24
Deadwood, S. Dak.,
  3,045.............F2 77

Deaf Smith, co., Tex.,
13,187.............B1 84
Deal, N.J., 1,889......C4 74
Deán Funes, Arg.,
13,840.............A4 28
Deanwood, Ga., 2,758..E4 55
Dearborn, Mich.,
112,007.........A7, F7 66
Dearborn, co., Ind.,
28,674.............F8 59
Dearborn Heights, Ill.,
1,300.............*B6 58
Deauville, Fr., 5,051...C4 5
De Baca, co., N. Mex.,
2,991.............B6 48
Debaltsevo, Sov. Un.,
33,800.............q21 12
Debar, Yugo., 6,341....E5 10
DeBary, Fla., 2,362....D5 54
Debica, Pol., 19,000...C6 7
Debno, Pol., 3,341.....B3 7
Debrecen, Hung.,
129,679.............B5 10
Decatur, Ala., 29,217..A3 46
Decatur, Ga.,
22,026..........B5, C2 55
Decatur, Ill., 78,004
(*111,300)..........D5 58
Decatur, Ind., 8,327...C8 59
Decatur, Mich., 1,827..F5 66
Decatur, Miss., 1,340..C4 68
Decatur, Tex., 3,563...C4 84
Decatur, co., Ga.,
25,203.............F2 55
Decatur, co., Ind.,
20,019.............F6 59
Decatur, co., Iowa,
10,539.............D4 60
Decatur, co., Kan.,
5,778.............C3 61
Decatur, co., Tenn.,
8,324.............B3 83
Decazeville, Fr.,
11,855.............E5 5
Deccan, reg., India....E6 20
Decherd, Tenn., 1,704..B5 83
Decin, Czech., 39,400...C3 7
Decorah, Iowa, 6,435...A6 60
Dededo, Guam, 2,247..*F6 2
Dedham, Mass.,
23,869..........B5, D2 65
Dedinovo, Sov. Un.,
5,000.............n19 12
Deephaven, Minn.,
3,286.............F5 67
Deep River, Conn.,
2,166.............D7 52
Deepwater, N.J., 700..D1 74
Deerfield, Ill.,
11,786.........A6, E2 58
Deerfield Beach, Fla.,
9,573.............F6 54
Deer Lake, Newf., Can.,
3,481.............D3 44
Deer Lodge, Mont.,
4,681.............D4 70
Deer Lodge, co., Mont.,
18,640.............D3 70
Deer Park, N.Y.,
11,725.............F3 75
Deer Park, Ohio, 8,423.D2 78
Deer Park, Tex., 4,865.*E5 84
Deer Park, Wash.,
1,333.............B8 86
Deer River, Minn.,
992.............C5 67
Defense Highway, Md.,
1,000.............*C4 53
Defiance, Ohio, 14,553..A3 78
Defiance, co., Ohio,
31,508.............A3 78
De Forest, Wis., 1,223..E4 88
De Funiak Springs, Fla.,
5,282.............G3 54
Degerfors, Swe., 9,500..E8 11
Deggendorf, Ger.,
17,100.............D6 6
Degraff, Ohio, 996....B4 78
Dehra Dun, India,
126,918 (*156,341)...B6 20
Dej, Rom., 19,281.....B6 10
De Kalb, Ill., 18,486...B5 58
De Kalb, Miss., 880....C5 68
De Kalb, Tex., 2,042...C5 84
De Kalb, co., Ala.,
41,417.............A4 46
De Kalb, co., Ga.,
256,182.............C2 55
De Kalb, co., Ill.,
51,714.............B5 58
De Kalb, co., Ind.,
28,271.............B7 59
De Kalb, co., Mo.,
7,226.............B3 69
De Kalb, co., Tenn.,
10,174.............D8 83
Delafield, Wis., 2,334.*E5 88
Del Aire, Calif., 5,000.*F2 50
Delanco, N.J., 4,011...C3 74
De Land, Fla., 10,775..C5 54
Delano, Calif., 11,913..E4 50

Delano, Minn., 1,612...E5 67
Delavan, Ill., 1,377....C4 58
Delavan, Wis., 4,846...F5 88
Delavan Lake, Wis.,
1,884.............*F5 88
Delaware, Ohio, 13,282.B4 78
Delaware, co., Ind.,
110,938.............D7 59
Delaware, co., Iowa,
18,483.............B6 60
Delaware, co., N.Y.,
43,540.............C6 75
Delaware, co., Ohio,
36,107.............B4 78
Delaware, co., Okla.,
13,198.............A7 79
Delaware, co., Pa.,
553,154.............G11 81
Delaware, state, U.S.,
446,292............. 53
Delaware City, Del.,
1,658.............A6 53
Delbarton, W. Va.,
1,122.............D2 87
Delcambre, La., 1,857..E4 63
Del City, Okla., 12,934.B4 79
Delémont, Switz.,
9,542.............E3 6
De Leon, Tex., 2,022...C3 84
De Léry, Que., Can.,
1,957.............*D4 42
Delft, Neth., 74,500...A6 5
Delfzijl, Neth., 16,600..A7 5
Delhi, Calif., 1,175....*D3 50
Delhi, Ont., Can.,
3,427.............E4 41
Delhi, India, 2,061,758
(*2,658,612).......C6 20
Delhi, La., 2,514.....B4 63
Delhi, N.Y., 2,307.....C6 75
Delhi Hills, Ohio,
5,000.............*D2 78
Delitzsch, Ger., 22,900.C6 6
Dell Rapids, S. Dak.,
1,863.............G9 77
Dellwood, Mo., 4,720..*C7 69
Del Mar, Calif., 3,124..E2 50
Delmar, Del., 934.....D6 53
Delmar, Md., 1,291....D6 53
Delmar, N.Y., 7,000...*C7 75
Del Mar-Heights, Calif.,
1,907.............*E3 50
Delmenhorst, Ger.,
57,300.............B4 6
Delmont, Pa., 1,313...*F6 81
Del Monte Heights,
Calif., 1,174.......*C6 50
Del Monte Park, Calif.,
2,177.............*D3 50
Del Norte, Colo., 1,856.D4 51
Del Norte, co., Calif.,
17,771.............B2 50
Deloraine, Man., Can.,
916.............E1 40
Del Paso Heights, Calif.,
11,495.............*A6 50
Delphi, Ind., 2,517....C4 59
Delphos, Ohio, 6,961...B3 78
Delray Beach, Fla.,
12,230.............F6 54
Del Ray Oaks, Calif.,
1,831.............*D3 50
Del Rio, Tex., 18,612..E2 84
Del Rosa, Calif.,
6,000.............*E5 50
Delta, Colo., 3,832.....C2 51
Delta, Ohio, 2,376.....A4 78
Delta, Utah, 1,576.....B5 72
Delta, co., Colo.,
15,602.............C3 51
Delta, co., Mich.,
34,298.............C4 69
Delta, co., Tex., 5,860..C5 81
Delta Amacuro, ter.,
Ven., 33,979.......B5 32
Demarest, N.J., 4,231..D5 74
Demidov, Sov. Un.,
10,000.............D8 12
Deming, N. Mex.,
6,764.............C5 48
Demirci, Tur., 8,700...C7 14
Demmin, Ger., 16,400..B6 6
Demopolis, Ala., 7,377.C2 46
Demorest, Ga., 1,029...B3 55
Denain, Fr., 29,467....B5 5
Denbigh, Wales, 8,044.D5 4
Denbigh, co., Wales,
173,843.............*D5 4
Denham Springs, La.,
5,991...........A5, D5 63
Den Helder, Neth.,
49,200.............A6 5
Denia, Sp., 7,876.....C6 8
Denison, Iowa, 4,930...B2 60
Denison, Tex., 22,748..C4 84
Denizli, Tur., 49,000...D7 14
Denmark, S.C., 3,221...E5 82
Denmark, Wis.,
1,106...........A6, D6 88
Denmark, country, Eur.,
4,585,256.............I3 11

Dennison, Ohio, 4,158..B6 78
Dennis Port, Mass.,
1,271.............C7 65
Denny Terrace, S.C.,
3,000.............D5 82
Denpasar, Indon.,
16,639.............G5 19
Dent, co., Mo., 10,445..D6 69
Denton, Ga., 255......E4 56
Denton, Md., 1,938....C6 53
Denton, Tex., 26,844...C4 84
Denton, co., Tex.,
47,432.............C4 84
Dentsville, S.C., 1,500..C6 82
Denver, Colo., 493,887
(*858,300).........B6 51
Denver, Pa., 1,875.....F9 81
Denver, co., Colo.,
493,887.............B6 51
Denver City, Tex.,
4,302.............C1 84
Denville, N.J., 10,632..B4 74
De Pere, Wis.,
10,045.........A6, D5 88
Depew, N.Y., 13,580...C2 75
Deposit, N.Y., 2,025...C5 75
Depue, Ill., 1,920.....B4 58
DeQueen, Ark., 2,859..C1 49
DeQuincy, La., 3,928..D2 63
Der'a, Syr., 15,635....F11 14
Dera Ghazi Khan, Pak.,
36,239.............B5 20
Dera Ismail Khan, Pak.,
39,846 (*41,663).....B5 20
Derby, Colo., 10,124..*B6 51
Derby, Conn., 12,132..D4 52
Derby, Eng., 132,325..D6 4
Derby, Kans., 6,458...E6 61
Derby, N.Y., 3,500....C2 75
Derby, co., Eng.,
877,458.............*D6 4
Derecske, Hung., 9,970.B5 10
De Ridder, La., 7,188..D2 63
Derita, N.C., 1,500....B3 76
Dermott, Ark., 3,665..D4 49
Derry, N.H., 4,468....F5 73
Derry, Pa., 3,426.....F3 81
Derventa, Yugo., 9,795.C3 10
Derzhavinskoye,
Sov. Un.............D9 16
Des Arc, Ark., 1,482...C4 49
Desbiens, Que., Can.,
1,970.............A6 42
Deschaillons sur St.
Laurent, Que., Can.,
1,283.............*C5 42
Deschambault, Que.,
Can., 1,056........C6 42
Deschenes, Que.,
Can., 2,090.......*D2 42
Deschutes, co., Oreg.,
23,100.............D5 80
Deseronto, Ont., Can.,
1,797.............C7 41
Desert Hot Springs,
Calif., 1,472.......*F5 50
Desha, co., Ark.,
20,770.............D4 49
Deshler, Nebr., 956....D8 71
Deshler, Ohio, 1,824...A4 78
Desloge, Mo., 2,308...D7 69
De Smet, S. Dak., 1,324.F8 77
Des Moines, Iowa, 208,982
(*261,900).......A7, C4 60
Des Moines, Wash.,
1,987.........B3, D1 86
Des Moines, co., Iowa,
44,605.............D6 60
De Soto, Kans.,
1,271.........B8, D9 61
De Soto, Mo., 5,804....C7 69
De Soto, Tex., 1,969..*C4 84
De Soto, co., Fla.,
11,683.............E5 54
De Soto, co., Miss.,
23,891.............A3 68
De Soto, par., La.,
24,248.............B2 63
Despard, W. Va.,
1,763.............B7 87
Des Peres, Mo., 4,362..B8 69
Des Plaines, Ill.,
41,209.........A6, E2 58
Dessau, Ger., 94,000...C6 6
Detmold, Ger., 31,200..C4 6
Detroit, Mich., 1,670,144
(*4,028,500).....A8, F7 66
Detroit Beach, Mich.,
1,571.............*G7 66
Detroit Lakes, Minn.,
5,633.............D3 67
Detva, Czech., 7,786...D5 7
Deuel, co., Nebr., 3,125.C3 71
Deuel, co., S. Dak.,
6,782.............F9 77
Deurne, Bel., 68,703...B6 5
Deux-Sèvres, dept., Fr.,
321,118.............*D3 5
Deva, Rom., 16,879....C6 10
Devavanya, Hung.,
10,828.............B5 10

Deventer, Neth.,
56,600.............A7 5
Devils Lake, N. Dak.,
6,299.............B7 77
Devine, Tex., 2,522....E3 84
Devon, Alta., Can.,
1,418.............*C4 38
Devon, Pa., 1,500...*G11 81
Devon, co., Eng.,
822,906.............*E5 4
Devon, isl., N.W. Ter.,
Can.............m33 36
Devonport, Austl.,
13,068.............o15 25
Devonport, N.Z.,
10,976.............L15 26
Dewar, Okla., 817.....B6 79
Dewey, Okla., 3,994...A6 79
Dewey, co., Okla.,
6,051.............B2 79
Dewey, co., S. Dak.,
5,257.............E5 77
DeWitt, Ark., 3,019....C4 49
DeWitt, Iowa, 3,224...C7 60
DeWitt, Mich., 1,238..F6 66
DeWitt, N.Y., 3,500..*B4 75
DeWitt, co., Ill.,
17,253.............C5 58
DeWitt, co., Tex.,
20,683.............E4 84
Dewsbury, Eng.,
52,942.............A6 4
Dexter, Maine, 2,720...C3 64
Dexter, Mich., 1,702...F7 66
Dexter, Mo., 5,519....E8 69
Dexter, N.Y., 1,009...A4 75
Dhamār, Yemen,
20,000.............G3 15
Dharamjaygarh, India,
5,000.............D7 20
Dharmapuri, India,
28,031.............F6 20
Dharmsala, India,
10,255.............B6 20
Dharwar, India,
77,163.............E6 20
Dhidhimotikhon, Grc.,
8,111.............E8 10
Dhulia, India, 98,893..D5 20
Diablo, Calif., 2,096..*D2 50
Diablo Heights, C.Z.,
1,647.............k11 39
Diamante, Arg.,
13,600.............A4 28
Diamantina, Braz.,
14,252.............B4 30
Diamond Springs, Va.,
1,500.............*E6 85
Diber, pref., Alb.,
96,000.............*E5 10
D'Iberville, Miss.,
3,005.........E2, E5 68
Diboll, Tex., 2,506.....D5 84
Dickens, co., Tex.,
4,963.............C2 84
Dickenson, co., Va.,
20,211.............B2 85
Dickey, co., N. Dak.,
8,147.............D7 77
Dickinson, N. Dak.,
9,971.............D3 77
Dickinson, Tex.,
4,715.............*G5 84
Dickinson, co., Iowa,
12,574.............A2 60
Dickinson, co., Kans.,
21,572.............D6 61
Dickinson, co., Mich.,
23,917.............B3 66
Dickson, Tenn.,
5,028.............A4 83
Dickson, co., Tenn.,
18,839.............A4 83
Dickson City, Pa.,
7,738.........A9, D10 81
Didsbury, Alta., Can.,
1,254.............D3 38
Diégo-Suarez, Malag.,
30,254.............C9 24
Dien Bien Phu, Viet.,
10,000.............*A2 19
Diepholz, Ger., 10,900.B4 6
Dieppe, N.B., Can.,
4,032.............C5 43
Dieppe, Fr., 29,967....C4 5
Dierks, Ark., 1,276....C1 49
Digboi, India, 18,235..C10 20
Digby, N.S., Can.,
2,308.............E4 43
Digby, co., N.S., Can.,
20,216.............E4 43
Dighton, Kans., 1,526.D3 61
Digne, Fr., 10,299.....E7 5
Digoin, Fr., 8,529.....D5 5
Dijon, Fr., 139,694....D6 5
Dikson, Sov. Un.,
10,000.............B10 16
Dilley, Tex., 2,118....E3 84
Dillingen [an der Donau],
Ger., 11,200.......D5 6
Dillon, Mont., 3,690...E4 70

Dillon, S.C., 6,173.....C9 82
Dillon, co., S.C.,
  30,584.............C9 82
Dillonvale, Ohio, 1,232.B7 78
Dillsburg, Pa., 1,322...F7 81
Dilworth, Minn., 2,102.D2 67
Dimitrovgrad, Bul.,
  45,000............D7 10
Dimitrovo (Pernik), Bul.,
  28,504............D6 10
Dimmit, co., Tex.,
  10,095............E3 84
Dimmitt, Tex., 2,935...B1 84
Dinan, Fr., 12,847.....C3 5
Dinant, Bel., 6,851....B6 5
Dinard, Fr., 9,270.....C2 5
Dindigul, India,
  92,947............F6 20
Dinh Lap, Viet.,
  10,000...........*G6 17
Dinsmore, Fla.,
  2,000.........B5, B6 54
Dinuba, Calif., 6,103..D4 50
Dinwiddie, co., Va.,
  22,183............D5 85
Diourbel, Sen., 20,600..F1 22
Dipolog, Phil., 8,770..*D6 19
Dirēdawā, Eth.,
  30,000............G6 23
Diriamba, Nic., 13,100.E7 34
Dishman, Wash., 5,000.D7 86
Disraeli, Que., Can.,
  3,067.............D6 42
District of Columbia,
  U.S., 763,956........C1 53
District Heights, Md.,
  7,534.............*C4 53
Distrito Federal, fed. dist.,
  Mex., 4,829,402.....D5 34
Distrito Federal, fed. dist.,
  Ven., 1,257,515.....A4 32
Disūq, Eg., U.A.R.,
  36,600............*G8 14
Diu, India 4,856.....D5 20
Divernon, Ill., 997....D4 58
Dives-sur-Mer, Fr.,
  6,258.............C3 5
Divide, co., N. Dak.,
  5,566.............B2 77
Divinópolis, Braz.,
  41,544............C4 30
Divnoye, Sov. Un.,
  17,300............I14 12
Dixfield, Maine, 1,298.D2 64
Dixiana, Ala., 500....B3 46
Dixie, co., Fla., 4,479..C3 54
Dixmoor, Ill., 3,076..*F3 58
Dixon, Calif.,
  2,970.........A6, C3 50
Dixon, Ill., 19,565.....B4 58
Dixon, Mo., 1,473.....D5 69
Dixon, co., Nebr.,
  8,106.............B9 71
Diyarbakir, Tur.,
  80,600............D3 14
Djakarta, Indon.,
  2,922,000.........G3 19
Djakovica, Yugo.,
  20,741............D5 10
Djakovo, Yugo.,
  12,069............C4 10
Djambi, Indon.,
  108,834...........F2 19
Djelfa, Alg., 10,070....B5 22
Djibouti, Fr. Som.,
  31,500............F6 23
Djurdevac, Yugo.,
  6,408.............B3 10
Djursholm, Swe.,
  7,400.............t36 11
Dmitriyevka, Sov. Un.,
  10,000.......H12, r21 12
Dmitriyev-Lgovskiy, Sov.
  Un., 10,000......E10 12
Dmitrov, Sov. Un.,
  10,000...........C11 12
Dmitrovsk-Orlovskiy,
  Sov. Un., 10,000...E10 12
Dneprodzerzhinsk,
  Sov. Un., 203,000...G10 12
Dnepropetrovsk, Sov. Un.,
  707,000...........G10 12
Dno, Sov. Un.,
  10,000............C7 12
Dobbs Ferry, N.Y.,
  9,260.............D1 75
Döbeln, Ger., 28,900...C6 6
Doboj, Yugo., 13,445..C4 10
Dobritch, see Tolbukhin,
  Bul.
Dobrogea, prov., Rom.,
  503,217..........*C9 10
Dobruja, reg., Bul.,
  Rom..............C9 10
Docena, Ala., 1,400....E4 46
Dock Junction, Ga.,
  3,920............*E5 55
Doddridge, co., W. Va.,
  6,970.............B4 87
Dodge, co., Ga.,
  16,483............D3 55

Dodge, co., Minn.,
  13,259............G6 67
Dodge, co., Nebr.,
  32,471............C9 71
Dodge, co., Wis.,
  63,170............E5 88
Dodge Center, Minn.,
  1,441.............F6 67
Dodge City, Kans.,
  13,520............E3 61
Dodgeville, Wis., 2,911.F3 88
Dodoma, Tan., 13,435..B7 24
Doerun, Ga., 1,037....E3 55
Doha, Qatar, 10,000...C8 23
Dolbeau, Que., Can.,
  6,052............G19 36
Dole, Fr., 24,525.....D6 5
Dolgeville, N.Y., 3,058.B6 75
Dolina, Sov. Un.,
  5,000.............D8 7
Dolinsk (Ochiai), Sov.
  Un., 30,000......C11 18
Dolomite, Ala.,
  1,300.........B3, E4 46
Dolores, Arg., 14,438...B5 28
Dolores, Ur., 13,300...E1 30
Dolores, co., Colo.,
  2,196.............D2 51
Dolores Hidalgo, Mex.,
  11,733...........m13 34
Dolton, Ill., 18,746.....F3 58
Dolzhanskaya, Sov. Un.,
  5,000.............q22 12
Domazlice, Czech.,
  8,500.............D2 7
Dominguez, Calif.,
  6,000............*F2 50
Dominican Republic,
  country, N.A.,
  3,013,525.........F8 35
Dominion, N.S., Can.,
  2,999.............C9 43
Domodossola, It.,
  16,728............A2 9
Dom Pedrito, Braz.,
  15,429............E2 30
Dona Ana, co., N. Mex.,
  59,948............C5 48
Donaldsonville, La.,
  6,082.........B5, D4 63
Donalsonville, Ga.,
  2,621.............E2 55
Don Benito, Sp., 25,248.C3 8
Doncaster, Eng.,
  86,402............D6 4
Donegal, co., Ire.,
  113,842..........*C2 4
Doneraile, S.C., 1,043..C8 82
Donetsk, Sov. Un.,
  749,000.......H11, r20 12
Dong Hoi, Viet., 10,000.B3 19
Dongola, Sud., 3,350...E4 23
Doniphan, Mo., 1,421..E7 69
Doniphan, co., Kans.,
  9,574.............C8 61
Donley, co., Tex., 4,449.B2 84
Donna, Tex., 7,522....F3 84
Donnacona, Que., Can.,
  4,812.........C6, C8 42
Donora, Pa., 11,131....F2 81
Donzère, Fr., 1,544....E6 5
Doolittle, Mo., 449....D6 69
Dooly, co., Ga., 11,474.D3 55
Door, co., Wis., 20,685.D6 88
Dora, Ala., 1,776.....B2 46
Doraville, Ga., 4,437...A5 55
Dorchester, N.B., Can.,
  1,779.............D5 43
Dorchester, Eng.,
  12,266............E5 4
Dorchester, co., Que.,
  Can., 34,711......C7 42
Dorchester, co., Md.,
  29,666............D5 53
Dorchester, co., S.C.,
  24,383............E7 82
Dordogne, dept., Fr.,
  375,455..........*E4 5
Dordrecht, Neth., 83,800
  (*130,000).........B6 5
Dores do Indaiá, Braz.,
  10,354............B3 30
Dorgali, It., 7,189.....D2 9
Dorion-Vaudreuil, Que.,
  Can., 4,996.......*D3 42
Dormont, Pa., 13,098..B5 81
Dornbirn, Aus., 28,075.E4 6
Dorohoi, Rom., 14,771.B8 10
Dorris, Calif., 973.....B3 50
Dorset, co., Eng.,
  309,176..........*F5 4
Dortmund, Ger.,
  641,500...........C3 6
Dorton, Ky., 700......C7 62
Dortyol, Tur., 10,200.D11 14
Dorval, Que., Can.,
  18,592............D8 42
Dos Hermanas, Sp.,
  22,700............D3 8
Dos Palos, Calif., 2,373.D3 50
Dothan, Ala., 31,440...D4 46

Douai, Fr., 47,639
  (*135,000)........B5 5
Douala, Cam., 125,000.H6 22
Douarnenez, Fr.,
  19,887............C1 5
Doubs, dept., Fr.,
  384,881..........*D7 5
Dougherty, co., Ga.,
  75,680............E2 55
Douglas, Alsk.,
  1,042.........D13, k22 47
Douglas, Ariz., 11,925.D4 48
Douglas, Ga., 8,736....E4 55
Douglas, I. of Man,
  18,837............C4 4
Douglas, Wyo., 2,822...C7 89
Douglas, co., Colo.,
  4,816.............B6 51
Douglas, co., Ga.,
  16,741............C2 55
Douglas, co., Ill.,
  19,243............D5 58
Douglas, co., Kans.,
  43,720............D8 61
Douglas, co., Minn.,
  21,313............E3 67
Douglas, co., Mo.,
  9,653.............E5 69
Douglas, co., Nebr.,
  343,490...........C9 71
Douglas, co., Nev.,
  3,481.............B2 72
Douglas, co., Oreg.,
  68,458............D3 80
Douglas, co., S. Dak.,
  5,113.............G7 77
Douglas, co., Wash.,
  14,890............B6 86
Douglas, co., Wis.,
  45,008............B2 88
Douglass, Kans., 1,058.E7 61
Douglasville, Ga.,
  4,462.............C2 55
Doullens, Fr., 6,321....B5 5
Douro Litoral, prov.,
  Port., 1,240,149...*B1 8
Dove Creek, Colo.,
  986...............D2 51
Dover, Del., 7,250.....B6 53
Dover, Eng., 35,248...E7 4
Dover, Mass., 1,400...D2 65
Dover, N.H., 19,131...E6 73
Dover, N.J., 13,034....B3 74
Dover, Ohio, 11,300...B6 78
Dover, Pa., 975.......F8 81
Dover, Tenn., 736.....A4 83
Dover-Foxcroft, Maine,
  2,481.............C3 64
Dowagiac, Mich.,
  7,208.............G4 66
Down, co., N. Ire.,
  267,013..........*C4 4
Downers Grove, Ill.,
  21,154............F2 58
Downey, Calif., 82,505.*F2 50
Downington, Pa.,
  5,598...........F10 81
Downs, Kans., 1,206...C5 61
Dows, Iowa, 882.....B4 60
Doylestown, Ohio,
  1,873.............B6 78
Doylestown, Pa.,
  5,917...........F11 81
Doyle, La., 1,061.....B2 63
Doyline, La., 1,061....B2 63
Dracut, Mass., 10,000..A5 65
Draganovo, Bul.,
  5,465.............D7 10
Drăgăsani, Rom., 9,963.C7 10
Dragerton, Utah,
  2,959............*B6 72
Draguignan, Fr.,
  11,814............F7 5
Drain, Oreg., 1,052....D3 80
Drakesboro, Ky., 832..C2 62
Drama, Grc., 32,195...B5 14
Drama, prov., Grc.,
  121,006..........*B5 14
Drammen, Nor.,
  31,300.........H4, p28 11
Drancy, Fr., 65,890...g10 5
Draper, N.C., 3,382....A4 76
Draper, Utah,
  1,000.........A6, D2 72
Dravosburg, Pa., 3,458.B6 81
Drayton, N. Dak., 940.A8 77
Drayton, S.C., 1,128...B4 82
Drayton Plains, Mich.,
  6,000.............F7 66
Drayton Valley, Alta.,
  Can., 3,854.......*C3 38
Drenthe, prov., Neth.,
  314,400..........*A7 5
Dresden, Ont., Can.,
  2,346.............E2 41
Dresden, Ger., 491,700
  (*700,000).........C6 6
Dresden, Ohio, 1,338..B5 78
Dresden, Tenn., 1,510.A3 83
Dresden Village, Mich.,
  5,500............*F7 66
Dreux, Fr., 21,588.....C4 5

Drew, Miss., 2,143.....B3 68
Drew, co., Ark., 15,213.D4 49
Drexel, N.C., 1,146....B2 76
Drexel, Ohio, 2,500....C3 78
Drexel Gardens, Ind.,
  1,000............*E5 59
Drexel Hill, Pa.,
  39,000...........*B11 81
Drift, Ky., 800........C7 62
Drifton, Pa., 900.....D10 81
Driggs, Idaho, 824.....F7 57
Drissa, Sov. Un.,
  10,000............D6 12
Drogheda, Ire., 17,085.D3 4
Drogobych, Sov. Un.,
  42,000............G4 12
Drôme, dept., Fr.,
  304,227..........*E6 5
Druid Hills, Ga.,
  2,000............*C2 55
Druid Hills, N.C.,
  1,207.............D3 76
Drumheller, Alta., Can.,
  2,931.............D4 38
Drummond, co., Que.,
  Can., 58,220......D5 42
Drummondville, Que.,
  Can., 27,909......D5 42
Drummondville Ouest,
  Que., Can., 2,057..*D5 42
Drumright, Okla.,
  4,190.............B5 79
Druzhkovka, Sov. Un.,
  39,800............q20 12
Dryden, Ont., Can.,
  5,728.............E8 41
Dryden, N.Y., 1,263...C4 75
Duarte, Calif., 13,962.*F3 50
Dubach, La., 1,013....B3 63
Dubayy, Tr. Coast,
  40,000............D6 15
Dubbo, Austl., 14,121..F8 25
Dublin, Ga., 13,814....D4 55
Dublin, Ind., 1,021....E7 59
Dublin (Baile Átha Cliath),
  Ire., 537,448
  (*690,000).........D3 4
Dublin, Tex., 2,443....C3 84
Dublin, Va., 1,427.....D2 85
Dublin, co., Ire.,
  718,332...........D3 4
Dublin Gulch, Mont.,
  2,450............*D4 70
Du Bois, Pa., 10,667...D4 81
Dubois, co., Ind.,
  27,463............H4 59
Duboistown, Pa., 1,358.D7 81
Dubossary, Sov. Un.,
  25,000............H7 12
Dubovka, Sov. Un.,
  12,300............G15 12
Dubrovnik, Yugo.,
  22,961............D4 10
Dubsdread, Fla.,
  1,400............*D5 54
Dubuque, Iowa,
  56,606............B7 60
Dubuque, co., Iowa,
  80,048............B7 60
Duchesne, co., Utah,
  7,179.............A6 72
Duchov, Czech., 8,229..C2 7
Ducktown, Tenn., 741.D9 83
Dudinka, Sov. Un.,
  17,000...........C11 13
Dudley, Eng., 61,748..D5 4
Due West, S.C., 1,166..C3 82
Dufferin, co., Ont., Can.,
  16,095............C4 41
Dugger, Ind., 1,062....F3 59
Duisburg, Ger.,
  503,000...........C3 6
Dukes, co., Mass.,
  5,829.............D6 65
Dulawan, Phil.,
  16,376...........*D6 19
Duluth, Ga., 1,483.A5, B2 55
Duluth, Minn., 106,884
  (*165,200).........D6 67
Dumaguete, Phil.,
  13,000............D6 19
Dumas, Ark., 3,540....D4 49
Dumas, Tex., 8,477....B2 84
Dumbarton, co., Scot.,
  184,546..........*B4 4
Dumfries, Scot., 27,275.C5 4
Dumfries, Va., 1,368...C5 85
Dumfries, co., Scot.,
  88,423...........*C5 4
Dumont, N.J.,
  18,882.........B5, D5 74
Dunafoldvar, Hung.,
  11,251............B4 10
Dunapataj, Hung.,
  4,846.............B4 10
Dunaujváros, Hung.,
  31,048............B4 10
Dunayevtsy, Sov. Un.,
  10,000............G6 12
Dunbar, Pa., 1,536....G2 81

Dunbar, W. Va.,
11,006...........C3, C6 87
Duncan, Ariz., 862.....C4 48
Duncan, B.C., Can.,
3,726.............B9, E6 37
Duncan, Okla., 20,009..C4 79
Duncan, S.C., 1,186....B3 82
Duncannon, Pa., 1,800.F7 81
Duncansville, Pa.,
1,396...............F5 81
Duncanville, Tex.,
3,774................B5 84
Dundalk, Ire., 19,790...C3 4
Dundalk, Md.,
82,428...........B4, C3 53
Dundas, Ont., Can.,
12,912...............D5 41
Dundas, co., Ont., Can.,
17,162...............B9 41
Dundee, Fla., 1,554....D5 54
Dundee (West Dundee),
Ill., 2,530.......A5, E2 58
Dundee, Mich., 2,377...G7 66
Dundee, N.Y., 1,468...C4 75
Dundee, Scot., 182,959.B5 4
Dundee, S. Afr.,
10,943..............F6 24
Dundy, co., Nebr.,
3,570...............D4 71
Dunean, S.C., 3,950..*B3 82
Dunedin, Fla.,
8,444...........D4, E1 54
Dunedin, N.Z., 73,245
(*105,003).........P13 26
Dunellen, N.J., 6,840..B4 74
Dunfermline, Scot.,
47,159..............B5 4
Dungarvan, Ire., 5,188.D3 4

Dunkerque, Fr., 27,616
(*120,000).........B5 5
Dunkirk, see Dunkerque,
Fr.
Dunkirk, Ind., 3,117...D7 59
Dunkirk, N.Y., 18,205..C1 75
Dunkirk, Ohio, 1,006...B4 78
Dunklin, co., Mo.,
39,139..............E7 69
Dún Laoghaire, Ire.,
47,792..............D3 4
Dunlap, Ind., 1,935...A6 59
Dunlap, Iowa, 1,254...C2 60
Dunlap, Tenn., 1,026..D8 83
Dunlo, Pa., 950.......F4 81
Dunmore, Pa.,
18,917.........A9, D10 81
Dunn, N.C., 6,350.....B5 76
Dunn, co., N. Dak.,
6,350...............C3 77
Dunn, co., Wis., 26,156.D2 88
Dunnellon, Fla., 1,079..C4 54
Dunn Loring, Va.,
1,500..............*C5 85
Dunnville, Ont., Can.,
5,181...............E5 41
Dunoon, Scot., 9,211..C4 4
Dunseith, N. Dak.,
1,017...............A5 77
Dunsmuir, Calif., 2,873.B2 50
Du Page, co., Ill.,
313,459.............B5 58
Duparquet, Que., Can.,
978..............*E10 41
Duplin, co., N.C.,
40,270..............C6 76
Dupnitsa, see Stanke
Dimitrov, Bul.
Dupo, Ill., 2,937.......E3 58

Dupont, Pa., 3,669....B9 81
Dupontonia, Tenn.,
1,896..............*A5 83
Duquesne, Pa.,
15,019............B6, F2 81
Du Quoin, Ill., 6,558...E4 58
Dūrā, Jordan, 10,000...C3 15
Durand, Mich., 3,312..F6 66
Durand, Wis., 2,039...D2 88
Durango, Colo., 10,530.D3 51
Durango, Mex., 97,520.C4 34
Durango, state, Mex.,
754,220.............C4 34
Durant, Iowa, 1,266...C7 60
Durant, Miss., 2,617...B4 68
Durant, Okla., 10,467..D5 79
Durazno, dept., Ur.,
49,500.............*E1 30
Durazno, Ur., 18,900...E1 30
Durban, S. Afr., 560,010
(*659,934)..........F6 24
Düren, Ger., 49,100....C3 6
Durham, Calif., 700....C3 50
Durham, Ont., Can.,
2,180...............C4 41
Durham, Eng., 20,484..C6 4
Durham, N.H., 4,688...E6 73
Durham, N.C., 78,302
(*106,200)..........B5 76
Durham, co., Ont., Can.,
39,916..............C6 41
Durham, co., Eng.,
1,517,039..........*C6 4
Durham, co., N.C.,
111,995.............A5 76
Durres, Alb., 32,300...*B2 14
Duryea, Pa.,
5,626...........B8, D10 81

Dushanbe, Sov. Un.,
248,000.............F9 13
Duson, La., 1,033.....D3 63
Düsseldorf, Ger.,
702,600.............C3 6
Dutchess, co., N.Y.,
176,008.............D7 75
Duval, co., Fla.,
455,411.............B5 54
Duval, co., Tex., 13,398.F3 84
Duxbury, Mass., 1,069.B6 65
Duzce, Tur., 18,200...B8 14
Dvůr Králové, Czech.,
15,000..............C3 7
Dwight, Ill., 3,086....B5 58
Dyer, Ind., 3,993.....B2 59
Dyer, Tenn., 1,909....A3 83
Dyer, co., Tenn.,
29,537..............A2 83
Dyersburg, Tenn.,
12,499..............A2 83
Dyersville, Iowa, 2,818.B6 60
Dyrlow, see Darlowo, Pol.
Dysart, Iowa, 1,197...B5 60
Dzaudzhikau, see
Ordzhonikidze, Sov. Un.
Dzerzhinsk, Sov. Un.,
176,000............C14 12
Dzerzhinsk, Sov. Un.,
26,200.............q20 12
Dzhambul, Sov. Un.,
131,000............E10 13
Dzhankoy, Sov. Un.,
10,000.............I10 12
Dzialdowo, Pol., 5,139..B6 7
Dzierzlow, see Darlowo,
Pol.
Dzierzoniow, Pol.,
27,000..............C4 7

E

Eads, Colo., 929.......C8 51
Eagan, Tenn., 500....C10 83
Eagle, W. Va., 200.C3, D6 87
Eagle, co., Colo., 4,677.B4 51
Eagle Grove, Iowa,
4,381...............B4 60
Eagle Lake, Fla., 1,364.E5 54
Eagle Lake, Maine, 900.A4 64
Eagle Lake, Tex., 3,565.E4 84
Eagle Pass, Tex.,
12,094..............E2 84
Eagle River, Wis.,
1,367...............C4 88
Eagleton Village, Tenn.,
5,068.............*D10 83
Ealing, Eng., 183,151..k11 4
Earle, Ark., 2,391......B5 49
Earlimart, Calif., 2,897.E4 50
Earlington, Ky., 2,786..C2 62
Earlville, Ill., 1,420....B5 58
Earlville, N.Y., 1,004...C5 75
Early, co., Ga., 13,151..E2 55
Early, Tex., 1,104.....B1 84
Earth, Tex., 1,104.....B1 84
Easley, S.C., 8,283....B2 82
East, div., Ice., 9,794.*n15 11
East Alamosa, Colo.,
800................D5 51
East Alliance, Ohio,
1,275.............*B6 78
East Alton, Ill., 7,630..E3 58
East Angus, Que., Can.,
4,756...............D6 42
East Ashtabula, Ohio,
4,179...............A7 78
East Aurora, N.Y.,
6,791...............C2 75
East Bangor, Pa., 970.E11 81
Eastbank, W. Va.,
1,023...............C6 87
East Barnet, Eng.,
40,599.............k12 4
East Baton Rouge, par.,
La., 230,058........D4 63
East Berlin, Pa., 1,037.G8 81
East Bernstadt, Ky.,
594................C5 62
East Berwick, Pa.,
1,258.............*D9 81
East Bethel, Minn.,
1,408.............*E5 67
Eastborough, Kans.,
1,001...............B5 61
Eastbourne, Eng.,
60,897..............E7 4
East Brady, Pa., 1,282.E2 81
East Brewton, Ala.,
2,511...............D2 46
East Bridgewater, Mass.,
3,000...............B6 65
East Brookfield, Mass.,
1,150.............*B3 65
East Brooklyn, Conn.,
1,213.............*B9 52
East Broughton, Que.,
Can., 1,136.........C6 42
East Brunswick, N.J.,
12,000.............*B4 74

East Butler, Pa.,
1,007...............E2 81
East Canon, Colo.,
1,101...............C5 51
East Canton, Ohio,
1,521.............*B6 78
East Carroll, par., La.,
14,433..............B4 63
East Chelmsford, Mass.,
1,500.............*A5 65
Eastchester, N.Y.,
12,000.............*E7 75
East Chicago, Ind.,
57,669..............A3 59
East Chicago Heights,
Ill., 4,295.........*F3 58
East Cleveland, Ohio,
37,991..............B2 78
East Cleveland, Tenn.,
1,452.............*D9 83
East Conemaugh, Pa.,
3,334...............F4 81
East Coulee, Alta., Can.,
683................D4 38
East Detroit, Mich.,
45,756..............A8 66
East Douglas, Mass.,
1,695...............B4 65
East Dublin, Ga.,
1,677.............*D4 55
East Dubuque, Ill.,
2,082...............A3 58
East Dundee, Ill.,
2,221.............*A5 58
East Ely, Nev.,
1,796...............D7 72
Eastern, reg., Nig.,
12,394,462.........G6 22
Eastern Valley, Ala.,
1,000.............*E4 46
East Falmouth, Mass.,
1,655...............C6 65
East Farmington Heights,
Conn., 1,800......*B6 52
East Faxon, Pa.,
3,641.............*D8 81
East Fayetteville, N.C.,
2,797.............*B5 76
East Feliciana, par.,
La., 20,198.........D4 63
East Flanders, prov.,
Bel., 1,272,005.....*B5 5
East Flat Rock, N.C.,
1,700...............D3 76
East Gaffney, S.C.,
4,779...............A4 82
East Gary, Ind.,
9,309...............A3 59
East Gastonia, N.C.,
3,326.............*B2 76
Eastgate, Wash.,
3,000.............*D2 86
East Glenville, N.Y.,
5,000.............*C7 75
East Grand Forks,
Minn., 6,998.......C2 67
East Greenbush, N.Y.,
1,325.............*C7 75

East Greenville, Pa.,
1,931.............F10 81
East Greenwich, R.I.,
6,100..............C11 52
East Griffin, Ga.,
1,715.............*C2 55
East Ham, Eng.,
105,359............k13 4
East Hampden, Maine,
1,500.............*D4 64
East Hampton, Conn.,
3,000...............C6 52
Easthampton, Mass.,
12,326..............B2 65
East Hampton, N.Y.,
1,772...............D4 75
East Hartford, Conn.,
43,977..............B6 52
East Haven, Conn.,
21,388..............D5 52
East Hazel Crest, Ill.,
1,457.............*F3 58
East Helena, Mont.,
1,490...............D5 70
East Herkimer, N.Y.,
1,068.............*B6 75
East Hills, N.Y.,
7,184.............*E3 75
East Indies, see Indonesia
East Islip, N.Y., 7,000.G4 52
East Jordan, Mich.,
1,919...............C5 66
East Keansburg, N.J.,
3,000.............*C4 74
East Kingsford, Mich.,
1,063.............*C2 66
Eastlake, Ohio, 12,467..A6 78
Eastland, Tex., 3,292...C3 84
Eastland, co., Tex.,
19,526..............C3 84
East Lansdowne, Pa.,
3,224.............*G11 81
East Lansing, Mich.,
30,198..............F6 66
Eastlawn, Mich.,
2,500.............*F7 66
East Liverpool, Ohio,
22,306..............B7 78
East London, S. Afr.,
113,746 (*115,677)...G5 24
East Longmeadow,
Mass., 10,294......B2 65
East Los Angeles,
Calif., 98,000......*E4 50
East Lothian, co., Scot.,
52,653.............*C5 4
East McKeesport, Pa.,
3,470.............*F2 81
Eastman, Ga., 5,118...D3 55
East Marion, N.C.,
2,442.............*D4 76
East Massapequa, N.Y.,
6,000.............*G3 75
East Meadow, N.Y.,
46,036.............*E7 75
East Middleton, N.Y.,
1,752.............*D6 75

East Millcreek, Utah,
6,000...............C2 72
East Millinocket, Maine,
2,392...............C4 64
East Moline, Ill.,
16,732..............B3 58
East Moriches, N.Y.,
1,210...............F5 52
East Naples, Fla.,
1,500...............F5 54
East Newark, N.J.,
1,872...............E5 74
East Newnan, Ga.,
500..............*C2 55
East Northport, N.Y.,
8,381...............F3 52
East Norwich, N.Y.,
2,500.............*F2 52
East Omaha, Nebr.,
684..............*D3 71
Easton, Calif., 2,500..*D4 50
Easton, Maine, 550...B5 64
Easton, Md., 6,337....C5 53
Easton, Pa., 31,955..E11 81
East Orange, N.J.,
77,259..............D4 74
East Palatka, Fla.,
1,133...............C5 54
East Palestine, Ohio,
5,232...............B7 78
East Palo Alto, Calif.,
12,000.............*B5 50
East Patchogue, N.Y.,
5,500...............G5 52
East Paterson, N.J.,
19,344.............*B4 74
East Pea Ridge, W.
Va., 1,500.........*C2 87
East Peoria, Ill.,
12,310..............C4 58
East Pepperell, Mass.,
1,200...............A4 65
East Petersburg, Pa.,
2,053...............F9 81
East Pines, Md.,
1,800.............*C4 53
East Pittsburgh, Pa.,
4,122.............*F2 81
East Point, Ga.,
35,633..........B5, C2 55
Eastport, Newf., Can.,
438................D5 44
Eastport, Maine, 2,537.D6 64
Eastport, N.Y., 950....D6 75
East Prairie, Mo.,
3,449...............E8 69
East Providence, R.I.,
41,955.............B11 52
East Quincy, Calif.,
1,020.............*C3 50
East Quoque, N.Y.,
1,000...............F6 75
East Rainelle, W. Va.,
1,244...............D4 87
East Richmond, Calif.,
4,000.............*B5 50
East Ridge, Tenn.,
19,570.............E10 83

East Rochester, N.Y.,
8,152..............B3 75
East Rochester, Pa.,
1,025.............*E1 81
East Rockaway, N.Y.,
10,721..............G2 52
East Rockingham,
N.C., 3,212.......C4 76
East Rockwood,
Mich., 1,000.......*F7 66
East Rutherford, N.J.,
7,769..............D5 74
East St. Louis, Ill.,
81,712.............E3 58
East Setauket, N.Y.,
1,127..............F4 52
Eastside, Miss., 4,318..E3 68
Eastside, Oreg., 1,380..D2 80
Eastside Galesburg, Ill.,
1,147.............*C3 58
East Somerset, Ky.,
3,645..............C5 62
East Sparta, Ohio, 961.B6 78
East Spencer, N.C.,
2,171..............B3 76
East Spokane, Wash.,
6,000..........B8, D7 86
East Stroudsburg, Pa.,
7,674.............D11 81
East Syracuse, N.Y.,
4,708..............B4 75
East Tawas, Mich.,
2,462..............D7 66
East Thomaston, Ga.,
2,237..............D2 55
East Troy, Wis., 1,455.F5 88
East Tulare, Calif.,
1,342.............*D4 50
East Uniontown, Pa.,
2,424.............*G2 81
East Vandergrift, Pa.,
1,388.............*E2 81
Eastview, Ont., Can.,
24,555.............A9 41
East View, W. Va.,
1,704.............*B4 87
East Walpole, Mass.,
2,000..............D2 65
East Washington, Pa.,
2,483..............F1 81
East Wenatchee Beach,
Wash., 2,327.......B5 86
East Whittier, Calif.,
19,884............*F4 50
East Williston, N.Y.,
2,940..............G2 52
East Wilmington, N.C.,
5,520.............*C6 76
Eastwood, Mich.,
6,000.............*E5 66
East York, Pa., 1,800.*G8 81
Eaton, Colo., 1,267....A6 51
Eaton, Ind., 1,529.....D7 59
Eaton, Ohio, 5,034.....C3 78
Eaton, co., Mich.,
49,684.............F6 66
Eaton Rapids, Mich.,
4,052..............F6 66
Eatonton, Ga., 3,612...C3 55
Eatontown, N.J.,
10,334.............C4 74
Eatonville, Wash., 896.C3 86
Eau Claire, Wis.,
37,987.............D2 88
Eau Claire, co., Wis.,
58,300.............D2 88
Eau Gallie, Fla.,
12,300.............D6 54
Eberswalde, Ger.,
32,100.............B6 6
Ebingen, Ger., 21,100..D4 6
Eboli, It., 20,500.....D5 9
Eburne, B.C., Can.,
1,000..............A9 37
Eccles, W. Va.,
1,145..........D3, D6 87
Eceabat (Maydos), Tur.,
2,800.............*B6 14
Echigawa, Jap., 3,400.n15 18
Echols, co., Ga., 1,876.F4 55
Ecija, Sp., 36,200.....D3 9
Eckernförde, Ger.,
19,500.............A4 6
Eckert, Colo., 1,021...C3 51
Eckhart, Md., 900.....D2 53
Eckman, W. Va.,
1,125..............D3 87
Eclectic, Ala., 926....C3 46
Economy, Pa., 5,925..*E1 81
Ecorse, Mich., 17,328..A7 66
Ector, co., Tex.,
90,995.............D1 84
Ecuador, country, S.A.,
3,796,000................ 31
Edcouch, Tex., 2,814..F4 84
Ed Damer, Sud., 5,458.E4 23
Eddiceton, Miss., 300..D3 68
Ed Dueim, Sud.,
12,319.............F4 23
Eddy, co., N. Mex.,
50,783.............C6 48

Eddy, co., N. Dak.,
4,936..............C7 77
Eddystone, Pa., 3,006.B10 81
Eddyville, Iowa, 1,014.C5 60
Eddyville, Ky., 1,858..A3 62
Ede, Neth., 21,200.....A6 5
Edea, Cam., 11,000....H7 22
Eden, N.Y., 2,366.....C2 75
Eden, Tex., 1,486.....D3 84
Edenborn, Pa., 800....G2 81
Edenburg, Pa., 4,111..F4 81
Edenton, N.C., 4,458..A7 76
Edgar, co., Ill., 22,550.D6 58
Edgartown, Mass.,
1,181..............D6 65
Edgecombe, co., N.C.,
54,226.............B6 76
Edgefield, S.C., 2,876..D4 82
Edgefield, co,, S.C.,
15,735.............D4 82
Edgeley, N. Dak., 992..D7 77
Edgely, Pa., 950.....*F12 81
Edgemere, Md., 2,200.*B5 53
Edgemont, Calif.,
1,628.............*F5 50
Edgemont, Colo.,
1,500.............*B5 51
Edgemont, S. Dak.,
1,772..............G2 77
Edgerton, Minn., 1,019.G2 67
Edgerton, Ohio, 1,566..A3 78
Edgerton, Wis., 4,000..F4 88
Edgewater, Ala., 1,200.E4 46
Edgewater, Colo.,
4,314..............B5 51
Edgewater, Fla., 2,051.D6 54
Edgewater, Md., 3,000.C4 53
Edgewater, N.J., 4,113.D5 74
Edgewater Park, Miss.,
750................E2 68
Edgewater Park, N.J.,
2,866..............C3 74
Edgewood, Ind., 2,119.*D6 59
Edgewood, Ky., 1,100..A7 62
Edgewood, Md., 2,240..B5 53
Edgewood, Pa., 3,399.*E8 81
Edgewood, Pa., 5,124..F2 81
Edgeworth, Pa., 2,030..A5 81
Edhessa, Grc., 15,534..B4 14
Edina, Minn., 28,501..E6 67
Edina, Mo., 1,457.....A5 69
Edinboro, Pa., 1,703..C1 81
Edinburg, Ill., 1,003..D4 58
Edinburg, Ind., 3,664.F6 59
Edinburg, Miss., 200..C4 68
Edinburg, Tex., 18,706.F3 84
Edinburgh, Scot.,
468,378.............C5 4
Edirne, Tur., 31,900..B6 14
Edison, Ga., 1,232....E2 55
Edison, N.J., 11,000..*B4 74
Edisto Island, S.C.,
240............F7, G1 82
Edmond, Okla., 8,577..B4 79
Edmonds, Wash., 8,016.B3 86
Edmonson, co., Ky.,
8,085..............C3 62
Edmonston, Md.,
1,197.............*C1 53
Edmonton, Alta., Can.,
281,027 (*337,568)...C4 38
Edmonton, Eng.,
92,062.............K12 4
Edmore, Mich., 1,234..E5 66
Edmunds, co., S. Dak.,
6,079..............E6 77
Edmundson, Mo.,
1,428.............*C7 69
Edmundston, N.B., Can.,
12,791.............B1 43
Edna, Tex., 5,038.....E4 84
Edremit, Tur., 22,200.*C6 14
Edson, Alta., Can.,
3,198..........C2, D1 38
Edwards, Miss., 1,206..C3 68
Edwards, co., Ill.,
7,940..............E5 58
Edwards, co., Kans.,
5,118..............E4 61
Edwards, co., Tex.,
2,317..............E2 84
Edwardsburg, Mich.,
902................G4 66
Edwardsville, Ill.,
9,996..............E4 58
Edwardsville, Pa.,
5,711..............B8 81
Edwight, W. Va., 70...D6 87
Eel River, N.J., Can.,
1,549..............B7 41
Eganville, Ont., Can.,
1,549..............B7 41
Eger, Hung., 35,375...B5 10
Egg Harbor City, N.J.,
4,416..............D3 74
Egirdir, Tur., 7,100...D8 14
Egypt, Pa., 1,500.....E10 81

Egypt, see United Arab
Republic, country, Afr.
Ehime, pref., Jap.,
1,500,687...........*J6 18
Ehrenfeld, Pa., 566....F4 81
Éibar, Sp., 31,725.....A4 8
Eichstätt, Ger., 10,600.D5 6
Eidsberg, Nor.,
233.............H4, p29 11
Eidsvoll, Nor., 11,104..G4 11
Eilenburg, Ger., 19,400.C6 6
Einbeck, Ger., 18,600..C4 6
Eindhoven, Neth.,
168,900............B6 5
Eisenach, Ger., 48,100..C5 6
Eisenhüttenstadt, Ger.,
24,400.............B7 6
Eisleben, Ger., 34,500..C5 6
Ejea de los Caballeros,
Sp., 8,438.........A5 8
Ekalaka, Mont., 738..E12 70
Eksjö, Swe., 10,100....I6 11
El Arahal, Sp., 17,361..D3 8
El Asnam (Orléansville),
Alg., 40,432........A5 22
Elazig, Tur., 60,400..C12 14
Elba, Ala., 4,321.....D3 46
El Banco, Col., 9,636   B3 32
El Barco, Sp., 7,041...A2 8
Elbasan, Alb., 26,000..B3 14
Elbasan, pref., Alb.,
115,000...........*B3 14
Elbert, W. Va., 950...D3 87
Elbert, co., Colo., 3,708.B6 51
Elbert, co., Ga., 17,835.B4 55
Elberton, Ga., 7,107...B4 55
Elbeuf, Fr., 18,988....C4 5
Elbing, see Elblag, Pol.
Elbistan, Tur., 10,300.C11 14
Elblag, Pol., 77,000...A5 7
El Bonillo, Sp., 5,286..C4 8
Elbow Lake, Minn.,
1,521..............E3 67
Elburn, Ill., 960.......B5 58
El Cajon, Calif.,
37,618.............E2 50
El Campo, Tex., 7,700.E4 84
El Campo North, Tex.,
1,086.............*E4 84
El Campo South,
Tex., 1,884........*E4 84
El Carmen, Col., 9,647.B2 32
El Centro, Calif.,
18,340.............F6 50
El Cerrito, Calif.,
25,437.............B5 50
Elche, Sp., 45,000.....C5 8
Elda, Sp., 28,151......C5 8
Eldon, Iowa, 1,386....D5 60
Eldon, Mo., 3,158.....C5 69
Eldora, Iowa, 3,225...B4 60
El Dorado, Ark.,
25,292.............D3 49
Eldorado, Ill., 3,573..F5 58
El Dorado, Kans.,
12,523.........B6, E7 61
Eldorado, Tex., 1,815..D2 84
El Dorado, co., Calif.,
29,390.............C3 50
El Dorado Springs, Mo.,
2,864..............D3 69
Eldoret, Ken., 8,193..H5 23
Eldred, Pa., 1,107.....C5 81
Eleanor, W. Va., 700...C3 87
Electra, Tex., 4,759...B3 84
Electric City, Wash.,
404...............*B6 86
Electric Mills, Miss.,
100................C5 68
Eleele, Haw., 950.....B2 56
Elevsís, Grc., 15,527..*C4 14
El Fasher, Sud.,
26,161.............F3 23
El Ferrol, Sp., 74,799..A1 8
Elgin, Ill., 49,447...A5, E2 58
Elgin, Iowa, 644......B6 60
Elgin, N. Dak., 944...D4 77
Elgin, Oreg., 1,315.....B9 80
Elgin, Scot., 11,971...B5 4
Elgin, Tex., 3,511.....D4 84
Elgin, co., Ont., Can.,
62,862.............E3 41
El Grullo, Mex.,
9,028.............n11 34
El Hasîheisa, Sud.,
6,600..............F4 23
Elida, Ohio, 1,215.....B3 78
Elim, Pa., 1,000.....*F4 81
Eliot, Maine, 1,730....E2 64
Elisabethville, Con. L.,
183,000............C5 24
Elizabeth, Ga.,
1,620...........A4, C2 55
Elizabeth, La., 1,030...D3 63
Elizabeth, N.J.,
107,698........B4, E4 74
Elizabeth, Pa., 2,597..*F2 81
Elizabeth City, N.C.,
14,062.............A7 76
Elizabeth Lake Estates,
Mich., 2,000.......*F7 66

Elizabethton, Tenn.,
10,896............C11 83
Elizabethtown, Ky.,
9,641..............C4 62
Elizabethtown, N.C.,
1,625..............C5 76
Elizabethtown, Pa.,
6,780..............F8 81
Elizabethville, Pa.,
1,455..............E8 81
Elk, Pol., 16,900......B7 7
Elk, co., Kans., 5,048..E7 61
Elk, co., Pa., 37,328...D4 81
Elkader, Iowa, 1,526..B6 60
Elk City, Okla., 8,196..B2 79
Elk Grove, Calif.,
2,205..........A6, C3 50
Elk Grove Village, Ill.,
4,771.............*A6 58
Elkhart, Ind., 40,274..A6 59
Elkhart, Kans., 1,780..E2 61
Elkhart, co., Ind.,
106,790............A6 59
Elkhorn, W. Va., 900..D3 87
Elkhorn, Wis., 3,586..F5 88
Elkhorn City, Ky.,
1,085..............C7 62
Elkhovo, Bul., 6,749...D8 10
Elkin, N.C., 2,868.....A3 76
Elkins, W. Va., 8,307..C5 87
Elkins Park, Pa.,
12,000............A11 81
Elkland, Pa., 2,189....C7 81
Elk Mountain, N.C.,
300................D3 76
Elko, Nev., 6,298......A4 72
Elko, co., Nev., 12,011.A4 72
Elk Point, S. Dak.,
1,378..............H9 77
Elk Rapids, Mich.,
1,015..............D5 66
Elkridge, Md.,
2,000..........B4, C2 57
Elkridge, W. Va., 400..D6 87
Elk River, Idaho, 382..C2 57
Elk River, Minn., 1,763.E5 67
Elk Run Heights, Iowa,
1,124.............*B5 60
Elkton, Ky., 1,448....D2 62
Elkton, Md., 5,989.....A6 53
Elkton, Mich., 1,014...E7 66
Elkton, Va., 1,506.....C4 85
Elkville, Ill., 743......F4 58
Ellaville, Ga., 905.....D2 55
Ellendale, N. Dak.,
1,800..............E7 77
Ellensburg, Wash.,
8,625..............C5 86
Ellenville, N.Y., 5,003.D6 75
Ellesmere, isl., N.W.,
Ter., Can.........k34 36
Ellettsville, Ind., 1,222.F4 59
Ellicott City, Md.,
2,000..............B4 53
Ellicottville, N.Y.,
1,150..............C2 75
Ellijay, Ga., 1,320.....B2 55
Ellinwood, Kans.,
2,729..............D5 61
Elliott, co., Ky., 6,330..B6 62
Ellis, Kans., 2,218....D4 61
Ellis, co., Kans., 21,270.D4 61
Ellis, co., Okla., 5,457..A2 79
Ellis, co., Tex., 43,395..C4 84
Ellisville, Miss., 4,592..D4 68
Ellisville, Mo., 2,732..B7 69
Elloree, S.C., 1,031...D6 82
Ellport, Pa., 1,458.....E1 81
Ellsworth, Kans.,
2,361..............D5 61
Ellsworth, Maine,
4,444..............D4 64
Ellsworth, Pa., 1,456..F1 81
Ellsworth, Wis., 1,701.D1 88
Ellsworth, co., Kans.,
7,677..............D5 61
Ellwangen, Ger.,
12,500.............D5 6
Ellwood City, Pa.,
12,413.............E1 81
Elma, N.Y., 4,000....*C2 75
Elma, Wash., 1,811...B2 86
Elmali, Tur., 7,800...*D7 14
Elmcrest, Mich.,
1,000.............*E7 66
Elmer, N.J., 1,505....D2 74
Elm Grove, Wis.,
4,994.............*E5 88
Elmhurst, Ill.,
40,329.........B6, F2 58
Elmira, Ont., Can.,
3,337..............D4 41
Elmira, N.Y., 46,517...C4 75
El Mirage, Ariz., 1,723.D1 48
Elmira Heights, N.Y.,
5,157..............C4 75
El Moderno, Calif.,
1,000.............*F5 50
Elmont, N.Y., 42,000.*G2 52
El Monte, Calif.,
13,163.............F3 50

El Monte, Calif.,
4,186.............*B5 50
Elmora, Pa., 1,057.....E4 81
Elmore, Minn., 1,078..G4 67
Elmore, Ohio, 1,302....A4 78
Elmore, co., Ala.,
30,524.............C3 46
Elmore co., Idaho,
16,719.............F3 57
Elmore City, Okla.,
982................C4 79
Elmsford, N.Y., 3,795.D2 75
Elmshorn, Ger., 35,000.B4 6
Elmwood, Ill., 1,882...C4 58
Elmwood Park, Ill.,
23,866.............F2 58
Elmwood Place, Ohio,
3,813..............D2 78
El Obeid, Sud.,
52,372.............F4 23
Eloise, Fla., 3,256.....E5 54
Elon College, N.C.,
1,284..............A4 76
Elora, Ont., Can.,
1,486..............D4 41
El Oro, prov., Ec.,
103,950............B2 31
Eloy, Ariz., 4,899......C3 48
El Paso, Ill., 1,964.....C4 58
El Paso, Tex., 276,687
(*599,000)..........E1 84
El Paso, co., Colo.,
143,742............C6 51
El Paso, co., Tex.,
314,070............E1 84
El Portal, Fla., 2,079..*G6 54
El Porto Beach, Calif.,
1,200..............*F2 50
El Puerto de Santa María,
Sp., 35,505.........D2 8
Elrama, Pa., 800.......F2 81
El Reno, Okla., 11,015..B4 79
El Rio, Calif., 6,966....E4 50
Elroy, Wis., 1,505.....E3 88
Elsa, Tex., 3,847......F3 84
El Salvador, country,
N.A., 2,501,278......E7 34
Elsberry, Mo., 1,491...B6 69
El Segundo, Calif.,
14,219.............F2 50
Elsie, Mich., 933......E6 66
Elsinore, Calif.,
2,432...........F3, F5 50
Elsmere, Del., 7,319...A6 53
Elsmere, Ky., 4,607.A7, B5 62
El Sobrante, Calif.,
15,000.............*B5 50
Elsterwerda, Ger.,
9,749..............C6 6
El Tigre, Ven., 41,550..B5 32
El Tocuyo, Ven.,
14,803.............B4 32
Elton, La., 1,595.......D3 63
Elvas, Port., 10,821....C2 8
El Verano, Calif.,
1,236..............*C2 50
Elverum, Nor., 3,595...G4 11
Elvins, Mo., 1,818.....D7 69
El Vista, Ill., 2,000...*C4 58
Elwood, Ind., 11,793...D6 59
Elwood, Kans., 1,191..C9 61
Elwood, N.Y., 2,000..*F3 75
Elwyn, Pa., 1,500....*G10 81
Ely, Eng., 9,815.......D7 4
Ely, Minn., 5,438......C7 67
Ely, Nev., 4,018.......B4 72
Elyria, Ohio, 43,782...A5 78
Elysburg, Pa., 1,100...E8 81
Emanuel, co., Ga.,
17,815.............D4 55
Embetsu, Jap., 3,000..D10 18
Embreeville Junction,
Tenn., 1,204......*C11 83
Emden, Ger., 45,700...B3 6
Emerson, Man., Can.,
932................E3 40
Emerson, N.J., 6,849..D5 74
Emery, co., Utah, 5,546.B6 72
Emeryville, Calif.,
2,686..............*B5 50
Emilia, reg., It........B3 9
Emilia-Romagna, pol.
dist., It., 3,666,680..B3 9
Eminence, Ky., 1,958..B4 62
Emirdag, Tur., 10,000..C8 14
Emlenton, Pa., 844....D2 81
Emmaus, Pa., 10,262..E11 81
Emmen, Neth., 7,500..A7 5
Emmerich, Ger.,
16,800.............C3 6
Emmet, co., Iowa,
14,871.............A3 60
Emmet, co., Mich.,
15,904.............C6 66
Emmetsburg, Iowa,
3,887..............A3 60
Emmett, Idaho, 3,769..F2 57
Emmitsburg, Md.,
1,369..............A3 53
Emmons, co., N. Dak.,
8,462..............D5 77

Emory University, Ga.,
4,200..............*B5 55
Empire, Calif., 1,635..*D3 50
Empire, La., 450.......E6 63
Empire, Nev., 650......A2 72
Empire, Oreg., 3,781...D2 80
Empoli, It., 28,500.....C3 9
Emporia, Kans.,
18,190.............D7 61
Emporia, Va., 5,535....E5 85
Emporium, Pa., 3,397..C5 81
Emsdetten, Ger.,
25,000.............B3 6
Emsworth, Pa., 3,341..A5 81
Encarnación, Par.,
39,804.............E4 29
Encarnación de Díaz,
Mex., 8,638........m12 34
Encinal, Tex., 800......E3 84
Encinitas, Calif., 2,786.F5 50
Ende, Indon., 7,226....G6 19
Enderby, B.C., Can.,
1,075..............D8 37
Enderlin, N. Dak.,
1,596..............D8 77
Endicott, N.Y., 18,775.C4 75
Endwell, N.Y., 12,000.*C4 75
Enfield, Conn., 3,000..B6 52
Enfield, Eng., 109,524.*E6 4
Enfield, Ill., 791.......E5 58
Enfield, N.H., 1,121...D3 73
Enfield, N.C., 2,978...A6 76
Engaru, Jap., 11,000..D11 18
Engels, Sov. Un.,
102,000............F16 12
Enghien, Fr., 12,504...g10 5
England, Ark.
2,861..........C4, E6 49
England, reg., U.K.,
41,572,585.........D6 4
Englehart, Ont., Can.,
1,786............*G18 36
Englewood, Colo.,
33,398.............B6 51
Englewood, Fla.,
5,000..............*B5 54
Englewood, Fla., 2,877.F4 54
Englewood, Ind.,
1,232..............*G5 59
Englewood, N.J.,
26,057.............D5 74
Englewood, Ohio, 1,515.C3 78
Englewood, Ore.,
1,382..............*D2 80
Englewood, Tenn.,
1,574..............D9 83
Englewood Cliffs, N.J.,
2,913..............*D5 74
Englishtown, N.J.,
1,143..............C4 74
Enguera, Sp., 5,663....C5 8
Enhaut, Pa., 2,000....*F8 81
Enid, Okla., 38,859....A4 79
Enka, N.C., 1,400......D3 76
Enköping, Swe.,
13,200.........H7, t35 11
Enna, It., 28,323......F5 9
En Nahud, Sud., 16,499.F3 23
Ennis, Ire., 5,699......D2 4
Ennis, Tex., 9,347.....C4 84
Enniscorthy, Ire.,
5,754..............D3 4
Enniskillen, N. Ire.,
7,438..............C3 4
Enns, Aus., 8,919......D7 6
Enola, Pa., 4,500......F8 81
Enon, Ohio, 1,227.....C4 78
Enoree, S.C., 950......B4 82
Enosburg Falls, Vt.,
1,321..............B2 73
Enschede, Neth.,
126,100............A7 5
Ensenada, Arg., 24,925.g8 28
Ensenada, P.R.,
3,299............*m13 35
Ensley, Fla., 1,836.....G1 54
Entebbe, Ug., 10,941..H4 23
Enterprise, Ala.,
11,410.............D4 46
Enterprise, Calif.,
4,946..............*B2 50
Enterprise, Kans.,
1,015..............D6 61
Enterprise, Oreg.,
1,932..............B9 80
Entre Minho e Douro, reg.,
Port., 2,067,900.....B1 8
Entre Ríos, prov., Arg.,
803,505.........A5, f7 28
Enugu, Nig., 62,764...G6 22
Enumclaw, Wash.,
3,269..............B4 86
Enzan, Jap., 12,500...n17 18
Épernay, Fr., 21,882...C5 5
Ephraim, Utah, 1,801..B6 72
Ephrata, Pa., 7,688....F9 81
Ephrata, Wash., 6,548.B6 86
Epila, Sp., 5,072......B5 8
Epileptic Village, Ind..E7 59
Épinal, Fr., 30,313.....C7 5

Epinay [-sur-Seine], Fr.,
34,167.............g10 5
Epirus, reg., Grc.....*C3 14
Epping, N.H., 980.....E5 73
Equatorial Guinea, Sp.
dep., Afr., 245,989...H6 22
Erath, La., 2,019......E3 63
Erath, co., Tex., 16,236.C3 84
Erciş, Tur., 9,900.....C14 14
Érd, Hung., 23,177....B4 10
Erdek, Tur., 6,700....*B6 14
Erdenheim, Pa., 3,700.A11 81
Erding, Ger., 11,300...D5 6
Eregli, Tur., 6,360.....B8 14
Eregli, Tur., 32,100...D10 14
Erfurt, Ger., 186,400..C5 6
Erice, It., 18,021......E4 9
Erick, Okla., 1,342....B2 79
Erie, Colo., 875.......A5 51
Erie, Ill., 1,215.......B3 58
Erie, Kans., 1,309.....E8 61
Erie, Pa., 138,440
(*212,000).........B1 81
Erie, co., N.Y.,
1,064,688..........C2 75
Erie, co., Ohio, 68,000..A5 78
Erie, co., Pa., 250,682..C1 81
Erin, Tenn., 1,097.....A4 83
Eritrea, prov., Eth.,
1,100,000..........E5 23
Erlangen, Ger., 69,600.D5 6
Erlanger, Ky.,
7,072...........A5, A7 62
Erlton, N.J., 1,000....*D6 74
Ermenek, Tur., 7,500..D6 14
Ermont, Fr., 19,263...g10 5
Ernest, Pa., 950.......E3 81
Errol Heights, Oreg.,
10,000............*B4 80
Erstein, Fr., 6,165.....C7 5
Erwin, N.C., 3,183....B5 76
Erwin, Tenn., 3,210...C11 83
Erzincan, Tur., 36,500.C12 14
Erzurum, Tur., 91,200.C13 14
Esashi, Jap., 7,700...D11 18
Esashi, Jap., 9,700...F10 18
Esbjerg, Den., 55,171..J3 11
Escada, Braz., 13,761.*D7 27
Escalante, Utah, 702...C6 72
Escalon, Calif., 1,763..*C3 50
Escambia, co., Ala.,
33,511.............D2 46
Escambia, co., Fla.,
173,829............G1 54
Escanaba, Mich.,
15,391.............C3 66
Escatawpa, Miss.,
1,464...........E3, E5 68
Esch-sur-Alzette, Lux.,
27,954.............C7 5
Eschwege, Ger., 24,100.C5 6
Eschweiler, Ger.,
39,600.............C3 6
Escondido, Calif.,
16,377.............F5 50
Escoublac-La-Baule, Fr.,
13,004.............D2 5
Escuinapa, Mex., 9,875.C3 34
Escuintla, Guat.,
9,760.............*E6 34
Eşfahān (Isfahan), Iran,
254,876............B8 23
Eskdale, W. Va.,
800.............C3, D6 87
Eskilstuna, Swe.,
59,900...........H7, t34 11
Eskisehir, Tur.,
153,200............C8 14
Esmeralda, co., Nev.,
619................C3 72
Esmeraldas, Ec.,
14,046.............A2 31
Esmeraldas, prov., Ec.,
87,870.............A2 31
Esmond, R.I., 4,500..B10 52
Esmont, Va., 100......D4 85
Espanola, Ont., Can.,
5,353..............A3 41
Espanola, N. Mex.,
1,976..............B5 48
Esperanza, Arg.,
10,035.............A4 28
Espinal, Col., 9,389....C3 32
Espírito Santo, Braz.,
31,027.............C4 30
Espírito Santo, state,
Braz., 1,188,665.....C4 30
Espy, Pa., 1,375.......D9 81
Esquel, Arg., 5,584....C2 28
Esquimalt, B.C., Can.,
10,500..........B9, E6 37
Essen, Ger., 726,600...C3 6
Essex, Ont., Can.,
3,428..............E2 41
Essex, Conn., 1,470...D7 52
Essex, Md., 35,205....B5 53
Essex, co., Ont., Can.,
258,218............E2 41
Essex, co., Eng.,
2,286,970.........*E7 4

Essex, co., Mass.,
568,831............A5 65
Essex, co., N.J.,
923,545............B7 75
Essex, co., N.Y., 35,300.B4 74
Essex, co., Vt., 6,083...B4 73
Essex, co., Va., 6,690..D6 85
Essex Fells, N.J.,
2,174..............*B4 74
Essex Junction, Vt.,
5,340..............C1 73
Essexville, Mich.,
4,590..............E7 66
Essington, Pa.,
3,300.............*B11 81
Esslingen, Ger., 83,200.D4 6
Estacada, Oreg., 957...B4 80
Estância, Braz.,
16,106............*E7 27
Estancia, N. Mex., 797.B5 48
Este, It., 10,600......B3 9
Estelí, Nic., 8,500.....E7 34
Estepa, Sp., 9,476.....D3 8
Estepona, Sp., 10,935..D3 8
Estes Park, Colo.,
1,175..............A5 51
Estevan, Sask., Can.,
7,728..............H4 39
Esther, Mo., 1,033....*D7 69
Estherville, Iowa, 7,927.A3 60
Estill, S.C., 1,865......F5 82
Estill, co., Ky., 12,466..C6 62
Eston, Sask., Can.,
1,695..............F1 39
Estonia (S.S.R.), rep., Sov.
Un., 1,221,000......B5 12
Estremadura, prov.,
Port., 1,592,858....*C1 8
Estremadura, reg.,
Port., 2,404,300.....C1 8
Estremadura, reg., Sp.,
2,626,400..........C2 8
Estremoz, Port., 7,057..C2 8
Esztergom, Hung.,
23,065.............B4 10
Étampes, Fr., 13,515...C5 5
Étaples, Fr., 8,628....B4 5
Etawah, India, 59,986..C6 20
Ethel, W. Va., 650....D5 87
Ethiopia, country, Afr.,
21,600,000.........G5 23
Etna, Pa., 5,519.......A6 81
Etowah, Tenn., 3,223..D9 83
Etowah, co., Ala.,
96,980.............A3 46
Ettrick, Va., 2,998.C7, D5 85
Etzatlán, Mex., 8,752.m11 34
Eu, Fr., 7,029.........B4 5
Euclid, Ohio,
62,998.........A6, B2 78
Euclid Center, Mich.,
2,343.............*F4 66
Euclid Heights, Ark.,
2,030.............*C2 49
Eudora, Ark., 3,598...D4 49
Eudora, Kans.,
1,526..........B8, D8 61
Eufaula, Ala., 8,357....D4 46
Eufaula, Okla., 2,382..B6 79
Eugene, Oreg., 50,977
(*122,200).........C3 80
Euless, Tex., 2,062...*B5 84
Eunice, La., 11,326....D3 63
Eunice, N. Mex., 3,531.C7 48
Eupen, Bel., 14,445...B7 5
Eupora, Miss., 1,468...B4 68
Eure, dept., Fr.,
361,904...........*C4 5
Eure-et-Loir, dept., Fr.,
277,546...........*C4 5
Eureka, Calif., 28,137..B1 50
Eureka, Ill., 2,538.....C4 58
Eureka, Kans., 4,055..E7 61
Eureka, Mo., 1,134....B7 69
Eureka, Mont., 1,229..B1 70
Eureka, S. Dak., 1,555.E6 77
Eureka, Utah, 771.....B5 72
Eureka, co., Nev., 767..B3 72
Eureka East (Ryans
Slough), Calif., 3,634.B1 50
Eureka Springs, Ark.,
1,437..............A2 48
Europe, cont.,
553,300,000............ 3
Euskirchen, Ger.,
20,300.............C3 6
Eustis, Fla., 6,189.....D5 54
Eutaw, Ala., 2,784....C2 46
Evangeline, par., La.,
31,639.............D3 63
Evans, Colo., 1,453...A6 51
Evans, co., Ga., 6,952..D5 55
Evans City (Evansburg),
Pa., 1,825..........E1 81
Evansdale, Iowa, 5,738.B5 60
Evanston, Ill.,
79,283.........A6, E2 78
Evanston, Wyo., 4,901.D2 89
Evansville, Ind.,
141,543............I2 59
Evansville, Wis., 2,858.F4 88

Evart, Mich., 1,775....E5 66
Evarts, Ky., 1,473....D6 62
Eveleth, Minn., 5,721..C6 67
Even Yehuda, Isr.,
2,549.............*B2 15
Everett, Mass., 43,544..C3 65
Everett, Pa., 2,279.....F5 81
Everett, Wash., 40,304.B3 86
Evergreen, Ala., 3,703..D3 46
Evergreen Park, Ill.,
25,284.............F3 58

Everman, Tex., 1,076.*B5 84
Everson, Pa., 1,304....F2 81
Évora, Port., 25,678...C2 8
Évreux, Fr., 23,647....C4 5
Évros, prov., Grc.,
157,760.............*B5 14
Évvoia, prov., Grc.,
166,097.............*C4 14
Ewa, Haw., 3,257..B3, g9 56

Ewa Beach, Haw.,
2,459.............g9 56
Ewing, Va., 500......B1 85
Ewing Township, N.J.,
26,628.............*C3 24
Excelsior, Minn., 2,020.F5 67
Excelsior Springs,
Mo., 6,473....B3, D2 69
Exeter, Calif., 4,264...D4 50
Exeter, Ont., Can.,
3,047.............D3 41

Exeter, Eng., 80,215...E5 4
Exeter, N.H., 7,243....F6 73
Exeter, Pa.,
4,747.........B8, D10 81
Exira, Iowa, 1,111....C3 60
Exmore, Va., 1,566...D7 85
Exmouth, Eng.,
19,740.............E5 4
Experiment, Ga., 2,497.C2 55
Export, Pa., 1,518....F2 81
Ezine, Tur., 7,500.....C6 14

F

Fabens, Tex., 3,134....F1 84
Fabriano, It., 12,700...C4 9
Facatativá, Col.,
13,479.............C3 32
Factoryville, Pa., 991.C10 81
Fada N'Gourma, Upper
Volta, 5,200........F5 22
Faenza, It., 26,500....B3 9
Faeroe Is., Dan. dep.,
Eur., 34,596........C6 3
Fafe, Port., 5,855......B1 8
Făgăras, Rom., 17,256..C7 10
Fagatogo, Am. Sam.,
1,344.............*G9 2
Fagersta, Swe., 15,500..G6 11
Faifo, Viet., 5,000.....B3 19
Fairbanks, Alsk.,
13,311.............C10 47
Fair Bluff, N.C., 1,030.C4 76
Fairborn, Ohio, 19,453..C3 78
Fairburn, Ga.,
2,470............B4, C2 55
Fairbury, Ill., 2,937....C5 58
Fairbury, Nebr., 5,572.D8 71
Fairchance, Pa., 2,120.G2 81
Fairdale, Kans.,
2,100............B8, C9 61
Fairdale, Ky., 6,000...A4 62
Fairfax, Ala., 3,107...C4 46
Fairfax, Calif., 5,813...C2 50
Fairfax, Del., 1,000....*A6 53
Fairfax, Minn., 1,489..F4 67
Fairfax, Ohio, 2,430...*C3 78
Fairfax, Okla., 2,076..A5 79
Fairfax, S.C., 1,814....F5 82
Fairfax, Va.,
13,585..........B4, C5 85
Fairfax, co., Va.,
262,482...........C5 85
Fairfield, Ala.,
15,816..........B3, E4 46
Fairfield, Calif.,
14,968..........B5, C2 50
Fairfield, Conn., 46,183.E3 52
Fairfield, Ill., 6,362....E5 58
Fairfield, Iowa, 8,054...C6 60
Fairfield, Maine, 3,766.D3 64
Fairfield, Mont., 752...C5 70
Fairfield, N.J., 3,310..*B4 74
Fairfield, Ohio, 9,734...C2 78
Fairfield, Oreg., 2,000.*C3 80
Fairfield, Tex., 1,781..D4 84
Fairfield, co., Conn.,
653,589...........D3 52
Fairfield, co., Ohio,
63,912............C5 78
Fairfield, co., S.C.,
20,713............C5 82
Fairfield Highlands, Ala.,
4,500.............*B3 46
Fair Grove, N.C.,
1,500.............*B3 76
Fairhaven, Mass.,
14,339.............C6 65
Fair Haven, Mich., 225.F8 66
Fair Haven, N.J., 5,678.C4 74
Fair Haven, Vt., 2,378.D1 73
Fairhope, Ala., 4,858...E2 46
Fairhope, Pa., 1,700...*F2 81
Fair Lawn, N.J.,
36,421.............D5 74
Fairlawn, Va., 1,325..*D2 85
Fair Lawn Heights,
Ohio, 2,000........*A6 78
Fairless Hills, Pa.,
8,000.............*F12 81
Fairmont, Ill., 2,000...*F2 58
Fairmont, Minn., 9,745.G4 67
Fairmont, N.C., 2,286..C4 76
Fairmont, Wash.,
1,227.............*B3 86
Fairmont, W. Va.,
27,477..........A7, B4 87
Fairmont City, Ill.,
2,688.............B8 69
Fairmount, Ind., 3,080.D6 59
Fairmount, N.Y.,
3,000.............*B4 75
Fairmount Heights, Md.,
2,308.............C2 53
Fair Oaks, Calif., 9,000.A6 50
Fair Oaks, Calif.,
1,622.............*E3 50
Fair Oaks, Ga., 7,969.*C2 55
Fairoaks, Pa., 1,239....A5 81

Fair Plain, Mich.,
7,998.............*F4 66
Fairpoint, Ohio, 600...B7 78
Fairport, N.Y., 5,507..B3 75
Fairport Harbor, Ohio,
4,267.............A6 78
Fairview, Alta., Can.,
1,506.............A1 38
Fairview, Ga., 2,000..*B1 55
Fairview, Ill., 544....*E3 58
Fairview, Mont.,
1,006.............C12 70
Fairview, N.J., 4,500.*C4 74
Fairview, N.J., 9,399..D5 74
Fairview, N.Y., 8,626.*D7 75
Fairview, Ohio, 14,624.B2 78
Fairview, Okla., 2,213..A3 79
Fairview, Pa., 1,399...B1 81
Fairview, Pa., 2,100..*E8 81
Fairview, Pa., 1,146..*E11 81
Fairview, Tenn., 1,017.B4 83
Fairview, Utah, 655....B6 72
Fairview, Wash.,
2,758.............*C5 86
Fairview Park, Ind.,
1,039.............E3 59
Fairview Shores,
Fla., 900........*D5 54
Fairvilla, Fla., 1,000..*D5 54
Fairway, Kans., 5,398.B9 61
Fairyland, Ga., 1,000.*B1 55
Faizabad, Afg., 25,770.A5 20
Faizabad, India, 76,582
(*82,498)...........C7 20
Fajardo, P.R., 12,409.m14 35
Fălciu, Rom., 5,124....B9 10
Falcón, state, Ven.,
340,450............A3 32
Falconer, N.Y., 3,343..C1 75
Falcon Heights, Minn.,
5,927.............E7 67
Falconwood, N.Y.,
1,000.............*B2 75
Faleshty, Sov. Un.,
5,000.............B8 10
Falfurrias, Tex., 6,515..F3 84
Falkirk, Scot., 38,043..C5 4
Falkland Is., Br. dep.,
S.A., 2,439.........I5 27
Falköping, Swe.,
14,400.............H5 11
Fall Branch, Tenn.,
950.............C11 83
Fallbrook, Calif., 4,814.F5 50
Fallon, Nev., 2,734....B2 72
Fallon, co., Mont.,
3,997.............D12 70
Fall River, Mass., 99,942
(*139,200)..........C5 65
Fall River, co., S. Dak.,
10,688.............G2 77
Fall Rock, Ky., 500....C6 62
Falls, co., Tex., 21,263..D4 84
Falls Church (Independent
City), Va., 10,192...B5 85
Falls City, Nebr.,
5,598.............D10 71
Falls Creek, Pa., 1,344.D4 81
Fallsington, Pa.,
1,000.............*F12 81
Fallsview, W. Va., 525.*C3 87
Falmouth, Eng., 15,427.E4 4
Falmouth, Ky., 2,568..B5 62
Falmouth, Maine,
5,976.............E5 64
Falmouth, Mass., 3,308.C6 65
Falmouth, Va., 1,478..C5 85
Fălticeni, Rom., 13,305.B8 10
Falun, Swe., 18,700...G6 11
Fannin, co., Ga.,
13,620.............B2 55
Fannin, co., Tex.,
23,880.............C4 84
Fano, It., 23,000......C4 9
Fanwood, N.J., 7,963.*B4 74
Farafangana, Malag.,
7,300.............E9 24
Farah, Afg., 15,258....B3 20
Faranah, Guinea, 2,250.F2 22
Fargo, N. Dak., 46,662.D9 77
Faribault, Minn.,
16,926.............F5 67
Faribault, co., Minn.,
23,685.............G5 67
Farley, Iowa, 920......B6 60
Farmer City, Ill., 1,838.C5 58

Farmers Branch, Tex.,
13,441.............*C4 84
Farmersburg, Ind.,
1,027.............F3 59
Farmersville, Calif.,
3,101.............*D4 50
Farmersville, Tex.,
2,021.............C4 84
Farmerville, La., 2,727.B3 63
Farmingdale, N.J., 959.C4 74
Farmingdale, N.Y.,
6,128.............G3 52
Farmington, Conn.,
2,500.............C5 52
Farmington, Ill., 2,831.C3 58
Farmington, Iowa, 902.D6 60
Farmington, Maine,
2,749.............D2 64
Farmington, Mich.,
6,881.............A7 66
Farmington, Minn.,
2,300.............F5 67
Farmington, Mo.,
5,618.............D7 69
Farmington, N.H.,
2,241.............E5 73
Farmington, N. Mex.,
23,786............A4 48
Farmington, Utah,
1,951..........A6, C2 72
Farmingville, N.Y.,
2,134.............*D4 75
Farmland, Ind., 1,102..D7 59
Farmville, N.C., 3,997..B6 76
Farmville, Va., 4,293...D4 85
Farnham, Que., Can.,
6,534.............D5 42
Faro, Port., 17,631....D2 8
Farrell, Pa., 13,793....D1 81
Farrukhabad, India,
87,793 (*94,591).....C6 20
Farwell, Tex., 1,009....B1 84
Fasano, It., 16,100....D6 9
Fastov, Sov. Un.,
10,000.............F7 12
Fatehpur, India, 28,232.C7 20
Fatsa, Tur., 6,800....B11 14
Faulk, co., S. Dak.,
4,397.............E6 77
Faulkner, co., Ark.,
24,303.............B3 49
Faulkton, S. Dak.,
1,051.............E6 77
Fauquier, co., Va.,
24,066.............C5 85
Faust, N.Y., 880...A6, B2 75
Favara, It., 27,909....F4 9
Faxon, Pa., 1,841....*D8 81
Fayette, Ala., 4,227...B2 46
Fayette, Iowa, 1,597...B6 60
Fayette, Miss., 1,626..D2 68
Fayette, Mo., 3,294...B5 69
Fayette, Ohio, 1,090...A3 78
Fayette, co., Ala.,
16,148.............B2 46
Fayette, co., Ga., 8,199.C2 55
Fayette, co., Ill.,
21,946.............D4 58
Fayette, co., Ind.,
24,454.............E7 59
Fayette, co., Iowa,
28,581.............B6 60
Fayette, co., Ky.,
131,906............B5 62
Fayette, co., Ohio,
24,775.............C4 78
Fayette, co., Pa.,
169,340............G2 81
Fayette, co., Tenn.,
24,557.............B2 83
Fayette, co., Tex.,
20,384.............E4 84
Fayette, co., W. Va.,
61,731.............C3 87
Fayette City, Pa.,
1,159.............*F2 81
Fayetteville, Ark.,
22,887............A1 49
Fayetteville, Ga., 1,389.C2 55
Fayetteville, N.Y.,
4,311.............B5 75
Fayetteville, N.C., 47,106
(*132,000).........B5 76
Fayetteville, Tenn.,
6,804.............B5 83

Fayetteville, W. Va.,
1,848.........C3, D7 87
Fayetteville North,
N.C., 3,071.......*B5 76
Feasterville, Pa.,
6,000.............A12 81
Feather Falls, Calif.,
900.............C3 50
Fécamp, Fr., 19,491....C4 5
Fédala, Mor., 35,010...B3 22
Federalsburg, Md.,
2,060.............C6 53
Federal Way, Wash.,
7,000.............*B3 86
Fedscreek, Ky., 500...C7 62
Feeding Hills, Mass.,
5,000.............B2 65
Feilding, N.Z., 8,172..N15 26
Feira de Santana, Braz.,
61,612............*E7 27
Fejer, co., Hung.,
300,119............*B4 10
Felanitx, Sp., 11,759..C7 8
Feldkirch, Aus., 17,343.E4 6
Felton, Calif.,
1,380...........C5, D2 50
Feltre, It., 8,500.......A3 9
Fenelon Falls, Ont.,
Can., 1,359........C6 41
Fengshan, Taiwan,
5,000.............*G9 17
Fennimore, Wis., 1,747.F3 88
Fennville, Mich., 705...F4 66
Fenton, Mich., 6,142...F7 66
Fentress, co., Tenn.,
13,288.............C9 83
Fenyang, China,
30,000.............D7 17
Feodosiya, Sov. Un.,
43,600............I10 12
Ferdinand, Ind., 1,427.H4 59
Ferentino, It., 16,836..D4 9
Fergana, Sov. Un.,
91,000............E10 13
Fergus, Ont., Can.,
3,831.............D4 41
Fergus, co., Mont.,
14,018.............C7 70
Fergus Falls, Minn.,
13,733.............D2 67
Ferguson, Mo., 22,149..C7 69
Fermanagh, co., N. Ire.,
51,613............*C3 4
Ferme Neuve, Que.,
Can., 1,971........C2 42
Fermo, It., 11,400....C4 9
Fernán Núñez, Sp.,
12,225............D3 8
Fernandina Beach, Fla.,
7,276.........B5, B6 54
Fernando Póo, reg.,
Equat. Gui., 62,612.H6 22
Fern Creek, Ky., 1,500.A5 62
Ferndale, Calif., 1,371..B1 50
Ferndale, Md., 2,500...B4 53
Ferndale, Mich., 31,347.A7 66
Ferndale, Pa., 1,900..*D8 81
Ferndale, Pa., 2,717...F4 81
Ferndale, Wash., 1,442.A3 86
Fernie, B.C., Can.,
2,661............E10 37
Fernwood, N.Y., 2,108.B4 75
Ferozepore, India,
47,060 (*97,932).....B5 20
Ferrara, It., 99,000...B3 9
Ferreñafe, Peru, 8,812..C2 31
Ferriday, La., 4,563....C4 63
Ferris, Tex., 1,807..B6, C4 84
Ferry, co., Wash., 3,889.A7 86
Ferrysburg, Mich.,
2,590.............*E4 66
Ferryville, Tun., 29,353.F2 9
Fertile, Minn., 968....C2 67
Fès, Mor., 830,999....B3 22
Fessenden, N. Dak.,
920.............C6 77
Festus, Mo., 7,021....C7 69
Fetesti, Rom., 15,383..C8 10
Fetters Springs, Calif.,
750.............*B5 50
Ffestiniog, Wales, 6,923.D5 4
Fianarantsoa, Malag.,
16,943............E9 24
Fidenza, It., 9,800....B3 9
Fieldale, Va., 1,499....E3 85
Fier, Alb., 11,000.....*B2 14

Fife, Wash., 1,463....*B3 86
Fife, co., Scot.,
  320,541...........*B5 4
Figeac, Fr., 6,933......E4 5
Figueira da Foz, Port.,
  10,486.............B1 8
Figueras, Sp., 17,548..A7 8
Fiji, Br. dep., Oceania,
  345,737...........H8 2
Filbert, W. Va., 950...D3 87
Filer, Idaho, 1,249.....G4 57
Filiatra, Grc., 9,209..*D3 14
Fillmore, Calif., 4,725..E4 50
Fillmore, Utah, 1,602..B5 72
Fillmore, co., Minn.,
  23,768............G6 67
Fillmore, co., Nebr.,
  9,425.............D8 71
Finchley, Eng., 69,311.k12 4
Finderne, N.J., 1,100..*B3 74
Findlay, Ohio, 30,344..A4 78
Finistère, dept., Fr.,
  727,847...........*C2 5
Finland, country, Eur.,
  4,448,500.........E12 11
Finney, co., Kans.,
  16,093............D3 61
Finneytown, Ohio,
  5,000.............*C3 78
Finnmark, co., Nor.,
  72,000............*B13 11
Finspång, Swe., 15,200.u33 11
Finsterwalde, Ger.,
  20,700............C6 6
Fircrest, Wash., 3,565..D1 86
Firebaugh, Calif., 2,627.D3 50
Firenze (Florence), It.,
  436,516...........C3 9
Firenzuola, It., 743....B3 9
Firminy, Fr., 26,065....E6 5
Fisher, Ill., 1,155....C5 58
Fisher co., Tex., 7,865.C2 84
Fishkill, N.Y., 1,033...D7 75
Fiskeville, R.I., 300...C10 52
Fitchburg, Mass.,
  43,021............A4 65
Fitzgerald, Ga., 8,781..E3 55
Fiume, see Rijeka, Yugo.
Five Points, Calif.,
  15,000............D4 50
Five Points, N. Mex.,
  2,500.............*B3 48
Flagler, co., Fla., 4,566.C5 54
Flagler Beach, Fla., 970.C5 54
Flagstaff, Ariz., 18,214.B3 48
Flanders, N.Y., 1,248..F6 75
Flandreau, S. Dak.,
  2,129.............F9 77
Flat Creek, Ala.,
  800..............B2, E4 46
Flathead, co., Mont.,
  32,965............B2 70
Flatonia, Tex., 1,009...E4 84
Flat River, Mo., 4,515.D7 69
Flat Rock, Mich., 4,696.F7 66
Flat Rock, N.C., 1,808.D3 76
Flatwoods, Ky., 3,741..B7 62
Fleetwing Estates, Pa.,
  1,100.............*F12 81
Fleetwood, Pa., 2,647..F10 81
Fleming, co., Ky.,
  10,890............B6 62
Flemingsburg, Ky.,
  2,067.............B6 62
Flemington, N.J., 3,232.B3 74
Flemington, Pa., 1,608.D7 81
Flensburg, Ger., 98,500.A4 6
Flers, Fr., 14,634......C3 5
Fletcher, N.C., 800....D3 76
Flin Flon, Man., Can.,
  11,104............B1 40
Flint, Mich., 196,940
  (*379,900).........E7 66
Flint, co., Wales,
  149,888...........*D5 4
Flintridge, Calif.,
  5,000.............*F2 50
Flomaton, Ala., 1,454..D2 46
Flora, Ill., 5,331......E5 58
Flora, Ind., 1,742.....C4 59
Florala, Ala., 3,011...D3 46
Floral Park, Mont.,
  4,079.............*E4 70
Floral Park, N.Y.,
  17,499............D2 75
Flordell Hills, Mo.,
  1,119.............*A8 69
Florence, Ala., 31,649..A2 46
Florence, Ariz.,
  2,143.............C3, D2 48
Florence, Calif.,
  38,164............*E4 50
Florence, Colo., 2,821..C5 51
Florence, see Firenze, It.
Florence, Kans., 853...D7 61
Florence, Ky.,
  5,837.............A5, A7 62
Florence, N.J., 4,215...C3 74
Florence, Oreg., 1,642..D2 80
Florence, S.C., 24,722..C8 82
Florence, Wis., 700....C5 88

Florence, co., S.C.,
  84,438............C8 82
Florence, co., Wis.,
  3,437.............C5 88
Flores, dept., Ur.,
  22,900............*E1 30
Floresville, Tex.,
  2,126.............B4, E3 84
Florham Park, N.J.,
  7,222.............B4 74
Floriano, Braz., 16,063.D6 27
Florianópolis, Braz.,
  74,323............D3 30
Florida, N.Y., 1,550...D6 75
Florida, Ur., 15,500...E1 30
Florida, dept., Ur.,
  61,200............*E1 30
Florida, state, U.S.,
  4,951,560.........E10 54
Florida City, Fla.,
  4,114.............F3, G6 54
Florin, Pa., 1,518.....F8 81
Flórina, Grc., 11,933..E5 10
Florina, prov., Grc.,
  67,356............*B3 14
Florissant, Mo., 38,166.A8 69
Flossmoor, Ill., 4,624..F3 58
Flour Bluff, Tex.,
  3,500.............F4 84
Flourtown, Pa., 4,000.A11 81
Flower Hill, N.Y.,
  4,594.............*E3 75
Flower Village, Calif.,
  5,000.............*E4 50
Floyd, co., Ga., 69,130.B1 55
Floyd, co., Ind., 51,397.H6 59
Floyd, co., Iowa, 21,102.A5 60
Floyd, co., Ky., 41,642.C7 62
Floyd, co., Tex., 12,369.B2 84
Floyd, co., Va., 10,462.E2 85
Floydada, Tex., 3,769..C2 84
Flushing, Mich., 3,761..E7 66
Flushing, Ohio, 1,189..B6 78
Fluvanna, co., Va.,
  7,227.............D4 85
Foard, co., Tex., 3,125.B3 84
Focsani, Rom., 28,244..C8 10
Foggia, It., 118,608...D5 9
Fogo, Newf., Can.,
  1,184.............D4 44
Fohnsdorf, Aus., 11,517.E7 6
Foix, Fr., 7,164......F4 5
Folcroft, Pa., 7,013..*G11 81
Foley, Ala., 2,889.....E2 46
Foley, Minn., 1,112....E5 67
Foligno, It., 31,500...C4 9
Folkestone, Eng.,
  44,129............E7 4
Folkston, Ga., 1,810...F4 55
Follansbee, W. Va.,
  4,052.............A4, B2 87
Follonica, It., 7,147...C3 9
Folly Beach, S.C.,
  1,137.............F18, G3 82
Folsom, Calif.,
  3,925.............A6, C3 50
Folsom, Pa., 5,000....*B11 81
Fonda, Iowa, 1,026....B3 60
Fonda, N.Y., 1,004....C6 75
Fond du Lac, Wis.,
  32,719............B5, E5 88
Fond du Lac, co., Wis.,
  75,085............E5 88
Fondi, It., 13,700.....D4 9
Fonsagrada, Sp., 950...A2 8
Fontainebleau, Fr.,
  20,583............C5 5
Fontana, Calif., 14,659.F3 50
Fontana, Wis., 1,326...F5 88
Fontenay-le-Comte, Fr.,
  10,109............D3 5
Fontenay [-sous-Bois], Fr.,
  37,484............g10 5
Fonthill, Ont., Can.,
  1,872.............*D5 41
Foochow (Minhow),
  China, 616,000.....F8 17
Forbach, Fr., 21,704...C7 5
Forbes, Austl., 6,826..F8 25
Forchheim, Ger.,
  20,900............D5 6
Ford, co., Ill., 16,606..C5 58
Ford, co., Kans., 20,938.E4 61
Ford City, Calif., 3,926.E4 50
Ford City, Pa., 5,440..E2 81
Fords, N.J., 10,000...*B4 74
Fords Prarie, Wash.,
  1,404.............*C3 86
Fordyce, Ark., 3,890...D3 49
Foreman, Ark., 1,001..D1 49
Forest, Bel., 51,503...B6 5
Forest, Ont., Can.,
  2,188.............D2 41
Forest, Ill., 1,040....*C5 58
Forest, Miss., 3,917...C4 68
Forest, Ohio, 1,314....B4 78
Forest, co., Pa., 4,485.C3 81
Forest, co., Wis., 7,542.C5 88
Forest Acres, S.C.,
  3,842.............C6 82

Forest City, Iowa,
  2,930.............A4 60
Forest City, N.C.,
  6,556.............B2, D4 76
Forest City, Pa., 2,651.C11 81
Forest Grove, Oreg.,
  5,628.............B1, B3 80
Forest Heights, Md.,
  3,524.............*C1 53
Forest Hill, Ont., Can.,
  20,489............E6 41
Forest Hill, Tex.,
  3,221.............*C4 84
Forest Hills, Pa., 8,796.*F2 81
Forest Hills, Tenn.,
  2,101.............*A5 83
Forest Homes, Ill.,
  2,025.............*E3 58
Forest Knolls, Calif.,
  800..............B5 50
Forest Lake, Minn.,
  2,347.............E6 67
Forest Lawn, Alta., Can.,
  12,263............D4 38
Forest Park, Ga.,
  14,201............B5, C2 55
Forest Park, Ill., 14,452.F2 58
Forest View, Ill., 1,042.*F3 58
Forest View, S.C.,
  1,000.............*B3 82
Forestville, Md., 1,500.*C4 53
Forestville, N.Y., 905..C1 75
Forfar, Scot., 10,252...B5 4
Forges-les-Eaux, Fr.,
  2,914.............C4 5
Forge Village, Mass.,
  1,191.............A5, C1 65
Forks, Wash., 1,156....B1 86
Forlì, It., 59,500......B4 9
Formiga, Braz., 18,763.C3 30
Formosa, Arg., 16,506..E4 29
Formosa, see Taiwan,
  country, Asia
Formosa, prov., Arg.,
  178,458............E4 29
Forney, Tex., 1,544.B6, C4 84
Forrest, Ill., 1,220....C5 58
Forrest, co., Miss.,
  52,722............D4 68
Forrest City, Ark.,
  10,544............B5 49
Forreston, Ill., 1,153..A4 58
Forst, Ger., 28,700....C7 6
Forsyth, Ga., 3,697...C3 55
Forsyth, Mont., 1,879.D10 70
Forsyth, co., Ga.,
  12,170............B2 55
Forsyth, co., N.C.,
  189,428............A3 76
Fortaleza, Braz.,
  354,942............D7 27
Fort Atkinson, Wis.,
  7,908.............F5 88
Fort Bend, co., Tex.,
  40,527............E5 84
Fort Benton, Mont.,
  1,887.............C6 70
Fort Bragg, Calif.,
  4,433.............C2 50
Fort Branch, Ind.,
  1,983.............H2 59
Fort Collins, Colo.,
  25,027............A5 51
Fort Collins West, Colo.,
  1,569.............*A5 51
Fort Coulonge, Que.,
  Can., 1,823........B8 41
Fort Covington, N.Y.,
  976..............A1 75
Fort-Dauphin, Malag.,
  7,253.............E9 24
Fort Davis, Tex., 900..F2 84
Fort-de-France, Mart.,
  60,648............o16 35
Fort Deposit, Ala.,
  1,466.............D3 46
Fort Dodge, Iowa,
  28,399............B3 60
Fort Edward, N.Y.,
  3,737.............B7 75
Fort Erie, Ont., Can.,
  9,027.............E6 41
Fort Fairfield, Maine,
  3,082.............B7 64
Fort Frances, Ont., Can.,
  9,481.............E6 41
Fort Gaines, Ga., 1,320.E1 55
Fort Gibson, Okla.,
  1,407.............B6 79
Fort Hancock, Tex.,
  600..............F1 84
Fort Howard, Md., 375.B5 53
Fort Huachuca, Ariz.,
  1,500.............D3 48
Fort Johnson, N.Y.,
  876..............*C6 75
Fort Kent, Maine,
  2,787.............A4 64
Fort Knox, Ky., 2,900..C4 62
Fort-Lamy, Chad,
  23,470............F8 22

Fort Laperrine,
  see Tamanrasset,
  Alg.
Fort Lauderdale, Fla.,
  83,348............E3, F6 54
Fort Leavenworth, Kans.,
  8,000.............B8, C9 61
Fort Lee, N.J., 21,815..D5 74
Fort Lupton, Colo.,
  2,194.............A6 51
Fort McKinley, Ohio,
  1,000.............*C3 78
Fort Macleod, Alta., Can.,
  2,490.............E4 38
Fort Madison, Iowa,
  15,247............D6 60
Fort Meade, Fla.,
  4,014.............E5 54
Fort Mill, S.C., 3,315..A6 82
Fort Morgan, Colo.,
  7,379.............A7 51
Fort Myers, Fla.,
  22,523............F5 54
Fort Myers Beach, Fla.,
  2,463.............F5 54
Fort Oglethorpe, Ga.,
  2,251.............B1 55
Fort Payne, Ala., 7,029.A4 46
Fort Peck, Mont., 950.B10 70
Fort Pierce, Fla., 25,256.E6 54
Fort Pierre, S. Dak.,
  2,649.............F5 77
Fort Plain, N.Y., 2,809.C6 75
Fort Qu'Appelle, Sask.,
  Can., 1,521........G4 39
Fort Recovery, Ohio,
  1,336.............B3 78
Fort Riley, Kans.,
  1,500.............C7 61
Fort St. John, B.C.,
  Can., 3,619........A7 37
Fort Saskatchewan, Alta.,
  Can., 2,960........C4 38
Fort Scott, Kans., 9,410.E9 61
Fort Shawnee, Ohio,
  4,000.............B3 78
Fort Sheridan, Ill.,
  2,600.............E2 58
Fort Smith, Ark.,
  63,309............B1 49
Fort Stockton, Tex.,
  6,373.............D1 84
Fort Sumner, N. Mex.,
  1,809.............B6 48
Fort Thomas, Ky.,
  14,896............A7 62
Fortuna, Calif., 3,523..B1 50
Fortune, Newf., Can.,
  1,194.............E4 44
Fort Valley, Ga., 8,310.D3 55
Fort Victoria, Rh.,
  12,300............E6 24
Fortville, Ind., 2,209..E6 59
Fort Walton Beach, Fla.,
  12,147............G2 54
Fort Washington, Pa.,
  2,500.............A11 81
Fort Wayne, Ind., 161,776
  (*215,400).........B7 59
Fort William, Ont., Can.,
  45,214 (*93,251)...E8 41
Fort Worth, Tex., 356,268
  (*505,100).......B5, C4 84
Fort Wright, Ky.,
  2,184.............A7 62
Fort Yates, N. Dak.,
  900..............D5 77
Forty Fort, Pa.,
  6,431.............*D10 81
Foshan, China, 500...B11 17
Fossano, It., 11,000...B1 9
Fossombrone, It., 4,659.C4 9
Fosston, Minn., 1,704..C3 67
Foster, co., N. Dak.,
  5,361.............C7 77
Foster Brook, Pa.,
  950..............C4 81
Foster Village, Haw.,
  2,500.............g10 56
Fostoria, Ohio, 15,732..A4 78
Fostoria, Tex., 666....D5 84
Fougères, Fr., 24,279..C3 5
Fouliang, China,
  92,000............E8 17
Fouling, China, 32,000.F6 17
Foumban, Cam.,
  18,000............G7 22
Founing, China, 85,000.E8 17
Fountain, Colo., 1,602..C6 51
Fountain, co., Ind.,
  18,706............D3 59
Fountain City, Tenn.,
  10,365.........C10, E11 83
Fountain City, Wis.,
  934..............D2 88
Fountain Green, Utah,
  544..............B6 72
Fountain Hill, Pa.,
  5,428............E11 81
Fountain Inn, S.C.,
  2,385.............B3 82

Fountain Place, La.,
  5,000..............*D4   63
Fountain Valley, Calif.,
  2,068..............*F5   50
Four Corners, Oreg.,
  4,743..............*C4   80
Fourmies, Fr., 14,508...B6   5
Four Oaks, N.C., 1,010.B5   76
Four Points, Ga., 1,500.E2   55
Fouyang, China,
  65,000..............E8   17
Fowler, Calif., 1,892..D4   50
Fowler, Colo. 1,240...C6   51
Fowler, Ind., 2,491....C3   59
Fowlerville, Mich.,
  1,674..............F6   66
Foxboro, Mass., 5,000..B5   65
Fox Chapel, Pa.,
  3,302..............*F2   81
Fox Farm, Wyo.,
  1,371..............*D8   89
Fox Lake, Ill.,
  3,700..........A5, E2   58
Fox Lake, Wis., 1,181..E5   88
Fox Point, Wis.,
  7,315..........E2, E6   88
Fox River Grove, Ill.,
  1,866..............E2   58
Fox River Heights,
  Ill., 700..........*B5   58
Foxworth, Miss., 950...D4   68
Frackville, Pa., 5,654...E9   81
Fraga, Sp., 8,691......B6   8
Framingham, Mass.,
  44,526..........B5, D1   65
Franca, Braz., 47,244..C3   30
Francavilla Fontana, It.,
  27,000..............D6   9
France, country, Eur.,
  46,520,271.............   5
Francesville, Ind.,
  1,002..............C4   59
Franche-Comté, former
  prov., Fr., 757,000...D6   5
Francistown, Bech.,
  10,000..............E5   24
Franconia, Va., 3,000..*C5   85
Franconville, Fr.,
  11,185..............g9   5
Frankenberg, Ger.,
  8,100..............C4   6
Frankenmuth, Mich.,
  1,728..............E7   66
Frankenthal, Ger.,
  33,900..............D4   6
Frankford, Ont., Can.,
  1,642..............C7   41
Frankfort, Ind., 15,302.D4   59
Frankfort, Kans., 1,106.C7   61
Frankfort, Ky., 18,365.B5   62
Frankfort, Mich.,
  1,690..............D4   66
Frankfort, N.Y., 3,872.B5   75
Frankfurt [am Main], Ger.,
  683,100 (*1,385,000).C4   6
Frankfurt [an der Oder],
  Ger., 57,000........B7   6
Franklin, Idaho, 7,222.*F2   57
Franklin, Ind., 9,453...F5   59
Franklin, Ky., 5,319...D3   62
Franklin, La., 8,673...E4   63
Franklin, Mass., 6,391.B5   65
Franklin, Mich., 2,262.*F7   66
Franklin, Nebr., 1,194.D7   71
Franklin, N.H., 6,742.E4   73
Franklin, N.J., 3,624...A3   74
Franklin, N.C., 2,173..D3   76
Franklin, Ohio, 7,917..C3   78
Franklin, Pa., 9,586...D2   81
Franklin, Pa., 1,352...*E4   81
Franklin, Tenn., 6,977.B5   83
Franklin, Tex., 1,065..D4   84
Franklin (Independent
  City), Va., 7,264....E6   85
Franklin, Wis., 10,006.*F1   88
Franklin, co., Ala.,
  21,988..............A2   46
Franklin, co., Ark.,
  10,213..............B2   49
Franklin, co., Fla.,
  6,576..............C2   54
Franklin, co., Ga.,
  13,274..............B3   55
Franklin, co., Idaho,
  8,457..............G7   57
Franklin, co., Ill.,
  39,281..............E7   58
Franklin, co., Ind.,
  17,015..............F7   59
Franklin, co., Iowa,
  15,472..............B4   60
Franklin, co., Kans.,
  19,548..............D8   61
Franklin, co., Ky.,
  29,421..............B5   62

Franklin, co., Maine,
  20,069..............C2   64
Franklin, co., Mass.,
  54,864..............A2   65
Franklin, co., Miss.,
  9,286..............D3   68
Franklin, co., Mo.,
  44,566..............C6   69
Franklin, co., Nebr.,
  5,449..............D7   71
Franklin, co., N.Y.,
  44,742..............A6   75
Franklin, co., N.C.,
  28,755..............A5   76
Franklin, co., Ohio,
  682,962..............B4   78
Franklin, co., Pa.,
  88,172..............G6   81
Franklin, co., Tenn.,
  25,528..............B5   83
Franklin, co., Tex.,
  5,101..............C5   84
Franklin, co., Vt.,
  29,474..............B2   73
Franklin, co., Va.,
  25,925..............E2   85
Franklin, co., Wash.,
  23,342..............C7   86
Franklin, dist., N. W.
  Ter., Can., 3,424...B13   36
Franklin, par., La.,
  26,088..............B4   63
Franklin, Hartsell, Brown
  and Norcot Mills (West
  Concord), N.C.,
  5,510..............B3   76
Franklin Lakes, N.J.,
  3,316..............*B4   74
Franklin Park, Ill.,
  18,322..............E2   58
Franklin Park, Va.,
  1,300..............*C5   85
Franklin Square, N.Y.,
  32,483..............G2   52
Franklinton, La., 3,141.D5   63
Franklinton, N.C.,
  1,513..............A5   76
Franklinville, N.J., 900.D2   74
Franklinville, N.Y.,
  2,124..............C2   75
Frankston, Tex., 953...C5   84
Frankton, Ind., 1,445..D6   59
Franz Josef Land, is.,
  Sov. Un............A9   16
Frascati, It., 11,500.D4, h9   9
Fraser, Mich., 7,027...A8   66
Fraserburgh, Scot.,
  10,462..............B6   4
Frauenfeld, Switz.,
  14,702..............E4   6
Fray Bentos, Ur.,
  12,900..............E1   30
Frazee, Minn., 1,083...D3   67
Fredericia, Den., 29,870.J3   11
Frederick, Md., 21,744.B3   53
Frederick, Okla.,
  5,879..............C2   79
Frederick, co., Md.,
  71,930..............B3   53
Frederick, co., Va.,
  21,941..............B4   85
Fredericksburg, Pa.,
  700..............*C1   81
Fredericksburg, Tex.,
  4,629..............D3   84
Fredericksburg
  (Independent City),
  Va., 13,639........C5   85
Frederiksted, Vir. Is.,
  277..............*A14   35
Fredericktown, Mo.,
  3,848..............D7   69
Fredericktown, Ohio,
  1,531..............B5   78
Fredericktown, Pa.,
  1,270..............F1   81
Fredericton, N.B.,
  Can., 19,683........D3   43
Frederiksborg, co.,
  Den., 162,889......*J5   11
Frederikshavn, Den.,
  22,522..............I4   11
Fredonia, Kans., 3,233.E8   61
Fredonia, N.Y., 8,477..C1   75
Fredrikstad, Nor.,
  14,549..........H4, p28   11
Freeborn, co., Minn.,
  37,891..............G5   67
Freeburg, Ill., 1,908...E4   58
Freedom, Calif., 4,206..C6   50
Freedom, Pa., 2,895....E1   81
Freehold, N.J., 9,140...C4   74
Freeland, Pa., 5,068..D10   81
Freeman, S. Dak.,
  1,140..............G8   77

Freemansburg, Pa.,
  1,652..............E11   81
Freeport, Ill., 26,628...A4   58
Freeport, Maine,
  1,801..........E2, E5   64
Freeport, N.Y., 34,419.G2   52
Freeport, Pa., 2,439...E2   81
Freeport, Tex.,
  11,619..........E5, G5   84
Freer, Tex., 2,724....F3   84
Freestone, co., Tex.,
  12,525..............D4   84
Freetown, N.Y., 1,365.*D4   75
Freetown, S.L., 100,000.G2   22
Fregenal de la Sierra,
  Sp., 10,498........C2   8
Freiberg, Ger., 47,400..C6   6
Freiburg [im Breisgau],
  Ger., 145,000......D3   6
Freising, Ger., 27,600..D5   6
Freistadt, Aus., 5,375.D7   6
Fréjus, Fr., 13,243....F3   5
Fremantle, Austl.,
  24,343..............F2   25
Fremont, Calif.,
  43,790..............*B5   50
Fremont, Ind., 937....A8   59
Fremont, Mich., 3,384..E5   66
Fremont, Nebr.,
  19,698..........C9, D2   71
Fremont, N.C., 1,609..B6   76
Fremont, Ohio, 17,573.A4   78
Fremont, co., Colo.,
  20,196..............C5   51
Fremont, co., Idaho,
  8,679..............E7   57
Fremont, co., Iowa,
  10,282..............D2   60
Fremont, co., Wyo.,
  26,186..............B4   89
French Camp, Calif.,
  1,000..............B6   50
French Guiana, dep.,
  S.A., 28,506.......C5   27
French Lick, Ind.,
  1,954..............G4   59
French Somaliland, dep.,
  Afr., 69,000.......F6   23
Frenchtown, N.J.,
  1,340..............B2   74
Freshwater, Newf.,
  Can., 1,048.......*f9   44
Fresnillo [de Gonzáles
  Echeverría], Mex.,
  36,919..............C4   34
Fresno, Calif., 133,929
  (*228,000)..........D4   50
Fresno, co., Calif.,
  365,945..............D3   50
Freudenstadt, Ger.,
  14,200..............D4   6
Frewsburg, N.Y., 1,623.C1   75
Friant, Calif., 300....D4   50
Friars Point, Miss.,
  1,029..............A3   68
Frias, Arg., 7,941......E2   29
Fribourg, Switz.,
  32,583..............E2   6
Fribourg, canton,
  Switz., 159,194....*E3   6
Fridley, Minn., 15,173..E7   67
Friedberg, Ger., 17,300.C4   6
Friedland, Ger., 8,500..B6   6
Friedrichshafen, Ger.,
  37,100..............E4   6
Friend, Nebr., 1,069...D8   71
Friendship, N.Y., 1,231.C2   75
Friern Barnet, Eng.,
  28,807..............k12   4
Fries, Va., 1,039......E2   85
Friesland, prov., Neth.,
  479,900............*A6   5
Frio, co., Tex., 10,112..E3   84
Friona, Tex., 2,048....B1   84
Frisco, Pa., 900.......*E1   81
Frisco, Tex., 1,184....*C4   84
Frisco City, Ala., 1,177.D2   46
Fritch, Tex., 1,617....B2   84
Fritzlar, Ger., 8,500....C4   6
Friuli-Venezia Giulia, pol.
  dist., It., 1,204,298.*B4   9
Frontenac, Kans.,
  1,713..............E9   61
Frontenac, Mo., 3,089.*B8   69
Frontenac, co., Ont.,
  Can., 87,534.......C8   41
Frontenac, co., Que.,
  Can., 30,600.......D7   42
Frontier, co., Nebr.,
  4,311..............D5   71
Frontignan, Fr., 5,341..F5   5
Front Royal, Va., 7,949.C4   85
Frosinone, It., 25,000..D4   9
Frostburg, Md., 6,722..D2   53
Frostproof, Fla., 2,664..E5   54

Frouard, Fr., 6,916....C7   5
Fruita, Colo., 1,830....B2   51
Fruitdale, Oreg., 2,158.*E3   80
Fruitdale, Tex., 1,418.*C4   84
Fruitland, Ill., 1,000...*B3   58
Fruitland, Md., 1,147..D6   53
Fruitport, Mich., 1,037.E4   66
Fruitridge, Calif.,
  5,480..............*A6   50
Fruitvale, Wash.,
  3,345..............*C5   86
Fruitville, Fla., 2,131..F2   54
Frunze, Sov. Un.,
  252,000............E10   13
Frydek-Mistek, Czech.,
  27,900..............D5   7
Fryeburg, Maine, 975..D2   64
Fthiotis (Phthiotis), prov.,
  Grc., 160,035.......*C4   14
Fuchin, China, 40,000.B11   17
Fuchow, China, 10,000.F8   17
Fuente-Alamo, Sp.,
  9,270..............D5   8
Fuente de Cantos, Sp.,
  8,941..............C2   8
Fuenteovejuna, Sp.,
  5,914..............C3   8
Fukien, prov., China,
  14,650,000..........F8   17
Fukuchiyama, Jap.,
  35,200..........I7, n14   18
Fukue, Jap., 8,700....o16   18
Fukui, Jap., 149,823..H8   18
Fukui, pref., Jap.,
  752,696............*H8   18
Fukuoka, Jap., 647,122.J5   18
Fukuoka, Jap., 9,500..F10   18
Fukuoka, pref., Jap.,
  4,006,679...........*J5   18
Fukushima, Jap.,
  103,000............H10   18
Fukushima, Jap.,
  6,900..........I8, n16   18
Fukushima, pref., Jap.,
  2,051,137..........*H10   18
Fukuyama, Jap.,
  107,000............I6   18
Fulda, Ger., 45,100...C4   6
Fulda, Minn., 1,202....G3   67
Fullerton, Calif., 56,180.F3   50
Fullerton, Ky., 1,082..B7   62
Fullerton, Md.,
  3,000..........B4, C3   53
Fullerton, Nebr., 1,475.C8   71
Fullerton, Pa., 5,500.*E11   81
Fulton, Ill., 3,387....B3   58
Fulton, Ky., 3,265....B2   62
Fulton, Miss., 1,706..A5   68
Fulton, Mo., 11,131...C6   69
Fulton, N.Y., 14,261..B4   75
Fulton, co., Ark., 6,657.A4   49
Fulton, co., Ga.,
  556,326............C2   55
Fulton, co., Ill., 41,954.C3   58
Fulton, co., Ind.,
  16,957..............B5   59
Fulton, co., Ky., 11,256.B2   62
Fulton, co., N.Y.,
  51,304..............B6   75
Fulton, co., Ohio,
  29,301..............A3   78
Fulton, co., Pa., 10,597.G5   81
Fultondale, Ala., 2,820.E4   46
Fulton Heights, Colo.,
  1,000..............*C6   51
Fumay, Fr., 6,185.....C6   5
Funabashi, Jap.,
  135,038............n19   18
Funchal, Mad. Is.,
  43,300............h12   8
Funkstown, Md., 968..A2   53
Fuquay Springs, N.C.,
  3,389..............B5   76
Furano, Jap., 11,500..E11   18
Furman University,
  S.C., 1,500........*B3   82
Furnas, co., Nebr.,
  7,711..............D6   71
Fürstenfeld, Aus., 6,415.E8   6
Fürstenwalde, Ger.,
  31,600..............B7   6
Fürth, Ger., 97,800...D5   6
Furukawa, Jap.,
  6,200..........H8, m16   18
Fuse, Jap., 212,754.I7, o14   18
Fushun, China,
  985,000............C9   17
Fusin, China, 188,600..C9   17
Füssen, Ger., 10,700..E5   6
Fusung, China, 5,000..E3   18
Futamata, Jap.,
  11,442............o16   18
Fuyu, China, 64,969...C2   18
Fuyu, China, 45,000...B9   17
Fuyuan, China, 5,000..B7   18

G

Gaberones, Bech.,
  10,000..............*E5   24

Gabès, Tun., 24,420....B7   22
Gabin, Pol., 3,108......B5   7

Gabon, country, Afr.,
  440,000............I7   22

Gabrovo, Bul., 21,268..D7   10
Gadag, India, 76,614...E6   20

Gadsden, Ala., 58,088..A3   46
Gadsden, co., Fla.,
    41,989.............B2   54
Gadyach, Sov. Un.,
    10,000.............F9   12
Găeşti, Rom., 7,179....C7   10
Gaeta, It., 20,569.....D4   9
Gaffney, S.C., 10,435..A4   82
Gafsa, Tun., 24,345...B6   22
Gage, co., Nebr.,
    26,818.............D9   71
Gages Lake, Ill.,
    3,395..............*A5   58
Gagny, Fr., 29,004....g11   5
Gaillac, Fr., 6,205....F4   5
Gaines, co., Tex.,
    12,267.............C1   84
Gainesboro, Tenn.,
    1,021..............C8   83
Gainesville, Fla.,
    29,701.............C4   54
Gainesville, Ga., 16,523.B3   55
Gainesville, Tex.,
    13,083.............C4   84
Gainesville East, Fla.,
    2,393..............C4   54
Gainesville North, Fla.,
    4,290..............C4   54
Gainesville West, Fla.,
    2,725..............C4   54
Gainsborough, Eng.,
    17,276.............D6   4
Gaithersburg, Md.,
    3,847..............B3   53
Galacz, see Galati, Rom.
Galapágos Is., see Colón.,
    Archipiélago de, prov.,
    Ec.
Galashiels, Scot.,
    12,374.............C5   4
Galati, Rom., 95,646...C8   10
Galatia, Ill., 830......F5   58
Galatina, It., 18,200...D7   9
Galax (Independent City),
    Va., 5,254.........E2   85
Galdar, Sp., 6,165....m14   8
Galena, Ill., 4,410.....A3   58
Galena, Kans., 3,827...E9   61
Galena Park, Tex.,
    10,852.............F5   84
Galesburg, Ill., 37,243..C3   58
Galesburg, Mich.,
    1,410..............F5   66
Galesville, Wis., 1,199..D2   88
Galeton, Pa., 1,646....C6   81
Galeville, N.Y., 1,500.*B4   75
Galicia, reg., Pol., Sov.
    Un...............D6   7
Galicia, reg., Sp.,
    2,602,962..........A1   8
Galion, Ohio, 12,650..B5   78
Gallarate, It., 35,477..B1   9
Gallatin, Mo., 1,658...B4   69
Gallatin, Tenn., 7,901..A5   84
Gallatin, co., Ill., 7,638.F5   58
Gallatin, co., Ky.,
    3,867..............B5   62
Gallatin, co., Mont.,
    26,045.............E5   70
Galle, Cey., 55,825...G7   20
Gallia, co., Ohio,
    26,120.............D5   78
Gallipoli, It., 16,196...D6   9
Gallipoli, see Gelibolu, Tur.
Gallipolis, Ohio, 8,775..D5   78
Gallitzin, Pa., 2,783...F4   81
Gällivare, Swe.,
    25,363.............D9   11
Galloway, W. Va., 300.B4   87
Gallup, N. Mex.,
    14,089.............B4   48
Galt, Calif., 1,868..B6, C3   50
Galt, Ont., Can.,
    27,830.............D4   41
Galva, Ill., 3,060.....B3   58
Galveston, Ind., 1,111..C5   59
Galveston, Tex., 67,175
    (*138,700).....E5, G5   84
Galveston, co., Tex.,
    140,364............E5   84
Galway, Ire., 22,028..D2   4
Galway, co., Ire.,
    149,887............*D2   4
Gamagori, Jap.,
    55,926.............o16   18
Gamarra, Col., 2,576..B3   32
Gambia, country, Afr.,
    292,000............F1   22
Gambier, Ohio, 1,148..B5   78
Ganado, Tex., 1,626...E4   84
Gananoque, Ont., Can.,
    5,096..............C8   41
Gand, see Gent, Bel.
Gander, Newf., Can.,
    5,725..............D4   44
Gandía, Sp., 15,812....C5   8
Gangaw, Bur., 3,800...D9   20
Gangtok, Sikkim, 2,744.C8   20
Gannat, Fr., 5,376.....D5   5
Gantt, S.C., 900......B2   82

Gao, Mali, 6,500......E5   22
Gap, Fr., 20,478......E7   5
Garanhuns, Braz.,
    34,050.............D7   27
Garber, Okla., 905....A4   79
Garberville, Calif., 900.B2   50
Garça, Braz., 18,155...C3   30
Garciasville, Tex., 900.F3   84
Gard, dept., Fr.,
    435,482............*F6   5
Gardelegen, Ger.,
    12,400.............B5   6
Garden, co., Nebr.,
    3,472..............C3   71
Gardena, Calif.,
    35,943.............F2   50
Garden City, Ga.,
    5,451..............D5   55
Garden City, Idaho,
    1,681..............*F2   57
Garden City, Kans.,
    11,811.............E3   61
Garden City, Mich.,
    38,017.............*F7   66
Garden City, N.Y.,
    23,948.............G2   52
Garden City, Pa.,
    2,000..............*G11   81
Garden City Park, N.Y.,
    15,364.............*G2   52
Gardendale, Ala.,
    4,712...........B3, E4   46
Garden Grove, Calif.,
    84,238.............*F3   50
Garden Home, Oreg.,
    2,000..............*B2   80
Garden Lakes, Ga.,
    1,300..............*B1   55
Garden View, Pa.,
    2,418..............*D7   81
Gardez, Afg., 17,540...B4   20
Gardiner, Maine, 6,897.D3   64
Gardner, Ill., 1,041....B5   58
Gardner, Kans., 1,619.D9   61
Gardner, Mass., 19,038.A4   65
Garfield, N.J., 29,253..D5   74
Garfield, co., Colo.,
    12,017.............B2   51
Garfield, co., Mont.,
    1,981..............C9   70
Garfield, co., Nebr.,
    2,699..............C6   71
Garfield, co., Okla.,
    52,975.............A4   79
Garfield, co., Utah,
    3,577..............C6   72
Garfield, co., Wash.,
    2,976..............C8   86
Garfield Heights, Ohio,
    38,455.............B2   78
Gargalianoi, Grc.,
    7,658..............*D3   14
Garibaldi, Oreg., 1,163.B3   80
Garland, Md., 1,200...*B4   53
Garland, Tex., 38,501..B6   84
Garland, Utah, 1,119...A5   72
Garland, co., Ark.,
    46,697.............C2   49
Garmisch-Partenkirchen,
    Ger., 25,000.......E5   6
Garner, Iowa, 1,990...A4   60
Garner, N.C., 3,451...B5   76
Garnett, Kans., 3,034.D8   61
Garoua, Cam., 7,050...G7   22
Garrard, co., Ky.,
    9,747..............C5   62
Garrett, Ind., 4,364...B7   59
Garrett, Ky., 800.....C7   62
Garrett, co., Md.,
    20,420.............D1   53
Garrett Park, Md.,
    965................B3   53
Garrett Park Estates,
    Md., 2,000.........*B3   53
Garrettsville, Ohio,
    1,662..............A6   78
Garrison, N. Dak.,
    1,794..............C4   77
Garrison, Tex., 951....D5   84
Garrovillas, Sp., 5,764.C2   8
Gartok, China, 5,000...B7   20
Garvin, co., Okla.,
    28,290.............C4   79
Garwolin, Pol., 5,315...C6   7
Garwood, N.J., 5,426..B4   74
Gary, Ind., 178,320....A3   59
Gary, W. Va., 1,393...D3   87
Garyville, La.,
    2,389...........B6, D5   63
Garza, co., Tex., 6,611.C2   84
Gas City, Ind., 4,469..D6   59
Gasconade, co., Mo.,
    12,195.............C6   69
Gascony, former prov.,
    Fr., 996,000.......E3   5
Gaspé, Que., Can.,
    2,603..............B3   42
Gaspé East, co., Que.,
    Can., 41,333.......*B3   42
Gaspé West, co., Que.,
    Can., 20,529.......*B3   42

Gassaway, W. Va.,
    1,223..............C4   87
Gaston, N.C., 1,214....A6   76
Gaston, co., N.C.,
    127,074............B2   76
Gastonia, N.C., 37,276.B2   76
Gatchina, Sov. Un.,
    47,900...........H14, s31   11
Gate City, Va., 2,142..B2   85
Gates, N.Y., 10,000...*B3   75
Gates, co., N.C., 9,254.A7   76
Gateshead, Eng.,
    103,232............C6   4
Gates Mills, Ohio,
    1,588..............*A6   78
Gatesville, Tex., 4,626.D4   84
Gatineau, Que., Can.,
    13,022.............D2   42
Gatineau, co., Que., Car.,
    44,308.............C2   42
Gatlinburg, Tenn.,
    1,764..............D10   83
Gatun, C.Z., 692.....*B2   32
Gauhati, India,
    100,707............C9   20
Gauley Bridge, W. Va.,
    950..............C3, D7   87
Gävle, Swe., 55,900...G7   11
Gävleborg, co., Swe.,
    294,300............*G7   11
Gavrilovka, Sov. Un.,
    10,000.............G11   12
Gawler, Austl., 5,639..G2   26
Gaya, India, 151,105..D7   20
Gaylord, Mich., 2,568..C6   66
Gaylord, Minn., 1,631.F4   67
Gaysin, Sov. Un.,
    10,000.............G7   12
Gaza Area, Eg. occ.,
    Asia, 377,000......C2   15
Gaziantep, Tur.,
    125,500............D11   14
Gdańsk (Danzig), Pol.,
    286,000............A5   7
Gdynia, Pol., 148,000..A5   7
Geary, Okla., 1,416....B3   79
Geary, co., Kans.,
    28,779.............D7   61
Geauga, co., Ohio,
    47,573.............A6   78
Gedaref, Sud., 17,537.F5   23
Gediz, Tur., 7,300....C7   14
Geelong, Austl., 18,022
    (*104,000).........G7   25
Geislingen, Ger.,
    25,800.............D4   6
Geistown, Pa., 3,186..F4   81
Gela, It., 54,774......F5   9
Gelderland, prov., Neth.,
    1,287,800..........*A6   5
Gelibolu (Gallipoli), Tur.,
    13,000.............B6   14
Gelsenkirchen, Ger.,
    382,700............C3   6
Gem, co., Idaho, 9,127.E2   57
Gemlik, Tur., 12,700..B7   14
Geneina, Sud., 11,817.F2   23
General Belgrano, Arg.,
    3,789..............B5   28
General Madariaga, Arg.,
    7,073..............B5   28
General Pico, Arg.,
    11,121.............B4   28
General Roca, Arg.,
    7,449..............B3   28
Genesee, co., Mich.,
    374,313............E7   66
Genesee, co., N.Y.,
    53,994.............B2   75
Geneseo, Ill., 5,169...B3   58
Geneseo, N.Y., 3,284..C3   75
Geneva, Ala., 3,840...D4   46
Geneva, Ill., 7,646....F1   58
Geneva, Ind., 1,053...C8   59
Geneva, Nebr., 2,352..D8   71
Geneva, N.Y., 17,286..C4   75
Geneva, Ohio, 5,677...A7   78
Geneva, see Genève, Switz.
Geneva, co., Ala.,
    22,310.............D4   46
Genève (Geneva), Switz.,
    176,183 (*270,000)..E3   6
Genève, canton, Switz.,
    259,234............*E3   6
Genevia, Ark.,
    6,000...........C3, D6   49
Genichesk, Sov. Un.,
    25,000.............H10   12
Genk, Bel., 47,416....B6   5
Gennevilliers, Fr.,
    42,595.............g10   5
Genoa, Ill., 2,330.....A5   58
Genoa, see Genova, It.
Genoa, Nebr., 1,009...C8   71
Genoa, Ohio,
    1,957...........A2, A4   78
Genoa, Ohio, 1,000...*B6   78
Genoa City, Wis.,
    1,005...........F1, F5   84
Genova (Genoa), It.,
    784,194............B2   9

Gent (Gand) (Ghent), Bel.,
    157,811 (*330,000)..B5   5
Genthin, Ger., 15,200..B6   6
Gentilly, Fr., 19,211...g10   5
Gentry, co., Mo.,
    8,793..............A3   69
Genzano di Roma, It.,
    12,727.............h9   9
George, Iowa, 1,200...A2   60
George, S. Afr.,
    14,505.............G4   24
George, co., Miss.,
    11,098.............E5   68
Georgetown, Guy.,
    92,000.............C5   27
Georgetown, Ont., Can.,
    10,298.............D5   41
Georgetown, Conn.,
    1,100..............D3   52
Georgetown, Del.,
    1,765..............C7   53
Georgetown, Ill., 3,544.D6   58
Georgetown, Ky.,
    6,986..............B5   62
Georgetown, Mass.,
    2,005..............A6   65
Georgetown, Ohio,
    2,674..............D4   78
Georgetown, S.C.,
    12,261.............E9   82
Georgetown, Tex.,
    5,218..............D4   84
Georgetown, co., S.C.,
    34,798.............D9   82
George West, Tex.,
    1,878..............E3   84
Georgia (Georgian S.S.R.),
    rep., Sov. Un.,
    4,200,000..........*A3   15
Georgia, state, U.S.,
    3,943,116..........   55
Georgiana, Ala., 2,093..D3   46
Georgia Southern, Ga.,
    1,400..............D5   55
Gera, Ger., 101,400....C6   6
Geraldton, Austl.,
    10,894.............E1   25
Geraldton, Ont., Can.,
    3,375..............*E8   41
Gering, Nebr., 4,585...C2   71
Germantown, Conn.,
    2,893..............*D3   52
Germantown, Ill., 983..E4   58
Germantown, Ohio,
    3,399..............C3   78
Germantown, Tenn.,
    1,104..............B2   83
Germany, East, country,
    Eur., 17,079,300...   6
Germany, West, country,
    Eur., 56,173,300...   6
Germiston, S. Afr.,
    148,102 (*213,200)..F5   24
Gero, Jap., 16,163....n16   18
Gerona, Sp., 32,784...B7   8
Gerona, prov., Sp.,
    351,369............*B7   8
Gers, dept., Fr.,
    182,264............*F4   5
Getafe, Sp., 21,895.B4, p17   8
Gettysburg, Pa., 7,960.G7   81
Gettysburg, S. Dak.,
    1,950..............E6   77
Ghana (Gold Coast), Afr.,
    6,690,730..........G4   22
Gharyān, Libya, 2,796.B7   22
Ghazni, Afg., 27,084..B4   20
Ghazzah (Gaza), Eg.,
    U.A.R., 100,000...C2   15
Ghent, see Gent, Bel.
Gheorgheni, Rom.,
    11,969.............B7   10
Gherla, Rom., 7,617...B6   10
Gibara, Cuba, 8,045...E5   35
Gibbon, Minn., 896...F4   67
Gibbon, Nebr., 1,083..D7   71
Gibbsboro, N.J.,
    2,141..............*D3   74
Gibbstown, N.J., 4,065.D2   74
Gibraleón, Sp., 8,865..D2   8
Gibraltar, Gib., 23,232.D3   8
Gibraltar, Br. dep., Eur.,
    23,232.............*D3   8
Gibraltar, Mich.,
    2,196..............*F7   66
Gibsland, La., 1,150...B2   63
Gibson, co., Ind.,
    29,949.............H2   59
Gibson, co., Tenn.,
    44,699.............A3   83
Gibsonburg, Ohio,
    2,540...........A2, A4   78
Gibson City, Ill., 3,453.C5   58
Gibsonia, Pa., 1,150...A6   81
Gibsons, B.C., Can.,
    1,091..............E6   37
Gibsonton, Fla., 1,673.E2   54
Gibsonville, N.C.,
    1,784..............A4   76
Giddings, Tex., 2,821..D4   84
Gideon, Mo., 1,411...E8   69

Gien, Fr., 8,812......D5   5
Giessen, Ger., 66,300...C4   6
Giffard, Que., Can.,
  10,129..............C9   42
Gifford, Fla., 3,509.....E6   54
Gifu, Jap., 304,492.I8, n15   18
Gifu, pref., Jap.,
  1,638,399............*I8   18
Gig Harbor, Wash.,
  1,094.............B3, D1   86
Gijón, Sp., 124,714....A3   8
Gila, co., Ariz., 25,745..C3   48
Gila Bend, Ariz., 2,132.C2   48
Gilbert, Ariz.,
  1,833.............C3, D2   48
Gilbert, Minn., 2,591...C6   67
Gilbert & Ellice Islands,
  Br. dep., Oceania,
  36,000..............F8   2
Gilberton, Pa., 1,712..*E9   81
Gilbertville, Mass.,
  1,202...............B3   65
Gilchrist, co., Fla.,
  2,868...............C4   54
Giles, co., Tenn.,
  22,410..............B4   83
Giles, co., Va., 17,219..D2   85
Gilford Park, N.J.,
  1,560..............*D4   74
Gillespie, Ill., 3,569....D4   58
Gillespie, co., Tex.,
  10,048..............D3   84
Gillett, Wis., 1,374....D5   88
Gillette, Wyo., 3,580...A7   89
Gilliam, co., Oreg.,
  3,069...............B6   75
Gillingham, Eng.,
  72,611..............E7   4
Gilly, Bel., 23,858.....B6   5
Gilman, Ill., 1,704.....C5   58
Gilmer, Tex., 4,312....C5   84
Gilmer, co., Ga., 8,922.B2   55
Gilmer, co., W. Va.,
  8,050...............C4   87
Gilmore City, Iowa,
  688................B3   60
Gilpin, co., Colo., 685..B5   51
Gilroy, Calif.,
  7,348............C6, D3   50
Gimli, Man., Can.,
  1,841...............D3   40
Ginosa, It., 17,800.....D6   9
Ginzo, Sp., 9,130......A2   8
Gioia del Colle, It.,
  24,000..............D6   9
Gioiosa Ionica, It.,
  5,002...............E6   9
Girard, Ill., 1,734......D4   58
Girard, Kans., 2,350....E9   61
Girard, Ohio, 12,997...A7   78
Girard, Pa., 2,451.....C1   81
Girardot, Col., 35,665..C3   32
Girardville, Pa., 2,958..E9   81
Giresun, Tur., 19,900..B12   14
Giridih, India, 36,881..D8   20
Girishk, Afg., 5,000....B3   20
Gironde, dept., Fr.,
  935,448.............*E3   5
Girvan, Scot., 6,159....C4   4
Gisborne, N.Z., 21,769
  (*25,065).........M17   26
Gisors, Fr., 6,398......C4   5
Giulianova, It., 9,100...C4   9
Giurgiu, Rom., 32,613..D7   10
Givet, Fr., 7,444......B6   5
Givors, Fr., 17,066.....E6   5
Gjinokaster, Alb.,
  13,100..............B3   14
Gjinokaster, pref., Alb.,
  168,000.............*B3   14
Gjövik, Nor., 7,900.....G4   11
Glace Bay, N.S., Can.,
  24,186.............C10   43
Glacier, co., Mont.,
  11,565..............B3   70
Gladbrook, Iowa, 949..B5   60
Glades, co., Fla., 2,950.F5   54
Glade Spring, Va.,
  1,407...............B3   85
Gladewater, Tex.,
  5,742...............C5   84
Gladstone, Austl.,
  7,181...............D9   25
Gladstone, Mich.,
  5,267...............C3   66
Gladstone, Mo.,
  14,502..............E2   69
Gladstone, N.J., 1,804..B3   74
Gladstone, Oreg.,
  3,854............B2, B4   80
Gladwin, Mich., 2,226..E6   66
Gladwin, co., Mich.,
  10,769..............D6   66
Gladwyne, Pa., 2,500.*A11   81
Glamoč, Yugo., 986...C3   10
Glamorgan, co., Wales,
  1,227,828...........*E5   4
Glarus, Switz., 5,852...E4   6
Glarus, canton, Switz.,
  40,148.............*E4   6
Glasco, N.Y., 950......C7   75

Glascock, co., Ga.,
  2,672...............C4   55
Glasford, Ill., 1,012....C4   58
Glasgow, Ky., 10,069...C4   62
Glasgow, Mo., 1,200...B5   69
Glasgow, Mont.,
  6,398.............B10   70
Glasgow, Scot.,
  1,054,913...........C4   4
Glasgow, Va., 1,091...D3   85
Glasgow, W. Va., 914..C6   87
Glassboro, N.J., 10,253.D2   74
Glasscock, co., Tex.,
  1,118...............D2   84
Glassport, Pa., 8,418...F2   81
Glastonbury, Conn.,
  3,400...............C6   52
Glauchau, Ger., 33,700.C6   6
Gleason, Tenn., 900....A3   83
Glenarden, Md., 1,336.*C4   53
Glen Avon Heights,
  Calif., 3,416........*F5   50
Glen Burnie, Md.,
  15,000..............B4   53
Glen Carbon, Ill.,
  1,241...............E4   58
Glencliff, Tenn., 3,000.*A5   83
Glencoe, Ala., 2,592...B4   46
Glencoe, Ont., Can.,
  1,156...............E3   41
Glencoe, Ill.,
  10,472...........A6, E3   58
Glencoe, Minn., 3,216..F4   67
Glen Cove, N.Y.,
  23,817..............D2   75
Glencullen, Oreg.,
  1,000...............B2   80
Glendale, Ariz.,
  15,696..........C2, D1   48
Glendale, Calif.,
  119,442.............F2   50
Glendale, Mo., 7,048..*C7   69
Glendale, Ohio,
  2,823............C3, D2   78
Glendale, S.C., 600....B4   82
Glendale, Tenn., 9,000.*A5   83
Glen Dale, W. Va.,
  1,905...............B4   87
Glendale, Wis., 10,432.*E6   88
Glendive, Mont.,
  7,058.............C12   70
Glendora, Calif., 20,752.F3   50
Glendora, N.J., 5,000.*D2   74
Glen Ellyn, Ill., 15,972.F2   58
Glengarry, co., Ont., Can.,
  19,217.............B10   41
Glen Haven, Ga.,
  2,000..............*C2   55
Glen Head, N.Y.,
  4,900..............*F2   52
Glen Innes, Austl.,
  5,719...............E9   25
Glen Jean, W. Va.,
  900.............D3, D7   87
Glen Lyon, Pa., 4,173..D9   81
Glenmora, La., 1,447..D3   63
Glen Moore, Pa.,
  1,700.............*G10   81
Glenn, co., Calif.,
  17,245..............C2   50
Glenns Ferry, Idaho,
  1,374...............G3   57
Glennville, Ga., 2,791..E5   55
Glen Oak Acres, Ill.,
  1,500..............*A6   58
Glen Olden, Pa., 7,249.B11   81
Glen Raven, N.C.,
  2,418...............A4   76
Glen Rock, N.J.,
  12,896...........B4, D5   74
Glen Rock, Pa., 1,546.G8   81
Glenrock, Wyo., 1,584..C7   89
Glen Rogers, W. Va.,
  950................*D3   87
Glen Rose, Tex., 1,422.C4   84
Glens Falls, N.Y.,
  18,580..............B7   75
Glenshaw, Pa., 24,939.*B6   81
Glenside, Pa., 22,500.*A11   81
Glen Ullin, N. Dak.,
  1,210...............D4   77
Glenview, Ill., 18,132..E2   58
Glenview Countryside, Ill.,
  2,000..............*E2   58
Glenville, W. Va.,
  1,828...............C4   87
Glenwillard, Pa.,
  1,100..............*A5   81
Glenwood, Iowa, 4,783.C2   60
Glenwood, Minn.,
  2,631...............E3   67
Glenwood, Va., 1,857.*E3   85
Glenwood Landing, N.Y.,
  3,400..............*F2   52
Glenwood Park, N.Y.,
  1,317..............*D6   75
Glenwood Springs, Colo.,
  3,637...............B3   51
Glidden, Iowa, 993....B3   60
Glidden, Wis., 700.....B3   88

Gliwice, Pol.,
  135,000.........C5, g9   7
Globe, Ariz., 6,217.C3, D3   48
Globino, Sov. Un.,
  10,000..............G9   12
Gloucester, Eng.,
  69,687..............E5   4
Gloucester, Mass.,
  25,789...........A6, C4   65
Gloucester, co., N.B.,
  Can., 66,343........B4   43
Gloucester, co., Eng.,
  1,000,493...........*E5   4
Gloucester, co., N.J.,
  134,840.............D2   74
Gloucester, co., Va.,
  11,919..............D6   85
Gloucester City, N.J.,
  15,511..............D2   74
Glouster, Ohio, 2,255..C5   78
Gloversville, N.Y.,
  21,741..............B6   75
Gloverville, S.C.,
  1,551...............E4   82
Glubczyce, Pol., 5,020..C4   7
Glubokoye, Sov. Un.,
  25,000..............D6   12
Glucholazy, Pol., 7,658.C4   7
Glukhov, Sov. Un.,
  10,000..............F9   12
Glussk, Sov. Un.,
  10,000..............E7   12
Glyndon, Md., 915.....B4   53
Glynn, co., Ga., 41,954.E5   55
Gmunden, Aus., 12,518.E6   6
Gnadenhutten, Ohio,
  1,257...............B6   78
Gniezno, Pol., 44,000..B4   7
Goa, Damão, and Diu, ter.,
  India, 684, 941..D5, E5   20
Goch, Ger., 15,200....C3   6
Goderich, Ont., Can.,
  6,411...............D3   41
Godfrey, Ill., 1,231....E3   58
Goffstown, N.H., 1,052.E4   73
Gogebic, co., Mich.,
  24,370..............A5   66
Goiana, Braz., 19,026.*D7   27
Goiás, Braz., 7,121....B2   30
Goiás, state, Braz.,
  1,954,862...........B2   30
Gojo, Jap., 18,800....o14   18
Golchikha, Sov. Un.,
  1,300.............B11   13
Golconda, Ill., 864....F5   58
Gold Beach, Oreg.,
  1,765...............E2   80
Gold Coast, see Ghana,
  country, Afr.
Golden, Colo., 7,118...B5   51
Golden Acres, Tex.,
  2,500..............*F5   84
Goldendale, Wash.,
  2,536...............D5   86
Golden Glades, Fla.,
  3,000..............*F3   54
Golden Hill, Minn.,
  2,190..............*F6   67
Golden Meadow, La.,
  3,097...............E5   63
Golden Valley, Minn.,
  14,559..............E6   67
Golden Valley, co., Mont.,
  1,203...............D7   70
Golden Valley, co.,
  N. Dak., 3,100......D2   77
Goldsboro, N.C.,
  28,873..............B6   76
Goldsmith, Tex., 670..D1   84
Goldthwaite, Tex.,
  1,383...............D3   84
Goleta, Calif., 4,000...E4   50
Golf Manor, Ohio,
  4,648..............*D2   78
Goliad, Tex., 1,782....E4   84
Goliad, co., Tex., 5,429.E4   84
Gomel, Sov. Un.,
  184,000.............E8   12
Gómez Palacio, Mex.,
  60,765..............B4   34
Gonaïves, Hai., 13,534.F7   35
Gonda, India, 43,496..C7   20
Gondar, Eth., 25,000..F5   23
Gönen, Tur., 10,800...B6   14
Gonesse, Fr., 8,517...g10   5
Gonzales, Calif., 2,138.D3   50
Gonzales, La.,
  3,252...........B5, D5   63
Gonzales, Tex., 5,829..E4   84
Gonzales, co., Tex.,
  17,845..............E4   84
Goochland, co., Va.,
  9,206...............D5   85
Goodhue, co., Minn.,
  33,035..............F6   67
Gooding, Idaho, 2,750.G4   57
Gooding, co., Idaho,
  9,544...............F4   57
Goodland, Ind., 1,202..C3   59
Goodland, Kans., 4,459.C2   61

Goodlettsville, Tenn.,
  3,163............A5, E9   83
Goodman, Miss., 932...C4   68
Goodsprings, Ala., 900.B2   46
Goodview, Minn.,
  1,348...............F7   67
Good Water, Ala.,
  2,023...............B3   46
Goodyear, Ariz.,
  1,654............C3, D2   48
Goose Bay, Newf., Can.,
  3,040............B1, h9   44
Goosport, La., 16,778.*D2   63
Göppingen, Ger.,
  48,900..............D4   6
Gorakhpur, India,
  180,255 (*132,436)...C7   20
Gordo, Ala., 1,714....B2   46
Gordon, Ga., 1,793...D3   55
Gordon, Nebr., 2,223..B3   71
Gordon, Pa., 888.....*E9   81
Gordon, co., Ga.,
  19,228..............B2   55
Gordonsville, Va.,
  1,109...............C4   85
Gorē, Eth., 10,000....G5   23
Gore, N.Z., 7,270.....Q12   26
Gorgas, Ala., 950.....B2   46
Gorham, Maine,
  2,322...........E2, E4   64
Gorham, N.H., 1,945..C5   73
Gorizia, It., 42,187....B4   9
Gorki (Gorkiy), Sov. Un.,
  1,003,000...........D7   13
Gorlice, Pol., 6,100...D6   7
Görlitz, Ger., 89,000..C7   6
Gorlovka, Sov. Un.,
  307,000........G12, q21   12
Gorman, Tex., 1,142...C3   84
Gorna-Dzhumaya, see
  Blagoevgrad, Bul.
Gorna Oryakhovitsa, Bul.,
  10,303..............D7   10
Gorno-Altaysk, Sov. Un.,
  29,000.............D11   12
Gorodenka, Sov. Un.,
  10,000..............G5   12
Gorodische, Sov. Un.,
  10,000.............q21   12
Gorodnya, Sov. Un.,
  10,000..............F8   12
Gorodok, Sov. Un.,
  10,000..............G4   12
Gorodok, Sov. Un.,
  10,000..............D7   12
Gorontalo, Indon.,
  71,232..............E6   19
Gorzow [Wielkopolski],
  Pol., 56,000.........B3   7
Gosford, Austl., 7,317..F8   26
Goshen, Calif., 1,061..*D4   50
Goshen, Ind., 13,718..A6   59
Goshen, N.Y.,
  3,996...........D2, D6   75
Goshen, co., Wyo.,
  11,941..............C8   89
Goslar, Ger., 41,400...C5   6
Gosper, co., Nebr.,
  2,489...............D6   71
Gospić, Yugo., 6,857...C2   10
Gostivar, Yugo.,
  12,776..............E5   10
Gostyn, Pol., 8,021....C4   7
Gostynin, Pol., 7,357..B5   7
Göteborg, Swe.,
  408,300..............I4   11
Göteborg och Bohus, co.,
  Swe., 633,000.......*I4   11
Gotemba, Jap., 28,700.n17   18
Gotha, Ger., 56,200....C5   6
Gothenburg, Nebr.,
  3,050...............D5   71
Gotland, co., Swe.,
  53,700.............*I8   11
Göttingen, Ger.,
  80,900..............C4   6
Gottwaldov (Zlin), Czech.,
  54,200..............D4   7
Gouda, Neth., 43,400..A6   5
Goulburn, Austl.,
  20,544..............F8   25
Gould, Ark., 1,210....D4   49
Goulding, Fla., 900...*G1   54
Goulds, Fla., 5,121....F3   54
Gournay-en-Bray, Fr.,
  3,195...............C4   5
Gouverneur, N.Y.,
  4,946...............B1   75
Gove, co., Kans.,
  4,107...............D3   61
Governador Valadares,
  Braz., 70,494.......B4   30
Gowanda, N.Y., 3,352..C2   75
Gowrie, Iowa, 1,127...B3   60
Goya, Arg., 20,804....E4   29
Graaff-Reinet, S. Afr.,
  16,703..............G4   24
Gračanica, Yugo.,
  7,668...............C4   10
Grace Park, Pa.,
  2,000.............*B10   81

Graceville, Fla., 2,307..G3   54
Graceville, Minn., 823..E2   67
Gradačac, Yugo., 5,897.C4   10
Gradizhsk, Sov. Un.,
    10,000...............G9   12
Grado, Sp., 3,671......A2   8
Grady, co., Ga., 18,015.F2   55
Grady, co., Okla.,
    29,590..............C4   79
Graehl, Alsk., 1,200..*C10   47
Graettinger, Iowa, 879.A3   60
Grafton, Austl., 15,526.E9   25
Grafton, Ill., 1,084.....E3   58
Grafton, Mass., 2,200..B4   65
Grafton, N. Dak.,
    5,885...............B8   77
Grafton, Ohio, 1,683...A5   78
Grafton, W. Va.,
    5,791..........B4, B7   87
Grafton, Wis.,
    3,748..........E2, E6   88
Grafton, co., N.H.,
    48,857..............D4   73
Graham, N.C., 7,723...A4   76
Graham, Tex., 8,505...C3   84
Graham, co., Ariz.,
    14,045..............C3   48
Graham, co., Kans.,
    5,586...............C4   61
Graham, co., N.C.,
    6,432...............D2   76
Grahamstown, S. Afr.,
    32,611..............G5   24
Grainger, co., Tenn.,
    12,506.............C10   83
Grajewo, Pol., 6,171...B7   7
Grambling, La., 3,144..B3   63
Gramercy, La., 2,094...B6   63
Grammichele, It.,
    14,486..............F5   9
Granada, Nic., 34,400..E7   34
Granada, Sp., 157,178..D4   8
Granada, prov., Sp.,
    769,408............*D4   8
Granbury, Tex., 2,227..C4   84
Granby, Que., Can.,
    31,463..............D5   42
Granby, Mass., 1,700..B2   65
Granby, Mo., 1,808....E3   69
Grand, co., Colo., 3,537.A4   51
Grand, co., Utah, 6,345.B7   72
Grand Bank, Newf., Can.,
    2,430...............E4   44
Grand Blanc, Mich.,
    1,565...............F7   66
Grand Bourg, Guad.,
    13,833.............o16   35
Grand Coteau, La.,
    1,165...............D3   63
Grand Coulee, Wash.,
    1,058...............B6   86
Grande Prairie, Alta.,
    Can., 6,302.........B1   38
Grande Riviere, Que.,
    Can., 1,176........*B3   42
Grand Falls, N.B., Can.,
    3,983...............B2   43
Grand Falls, Newf., Can.,
    6,064...............D4   44
Grandfalls, Tex., 1,012.D1   84
Grandfield, Okla.,
    1,606...............C3   79
Grand Forks, B.C., Can.,
    2,347...............E8   37
Grand Forks, N. Dak.,
    48,677..............C8   77
Grand Forks, co.,
    N. Dak., 48,677....C8   77
Grand Haven, Mich.,
    11,066..............E4   66
Grand Island, Nebr.,
    25,742..............D7   71
Grand Island, N.Y.,
    1,700..............*B2   75
Grand Isle, La., 2,074..E6   63
Grand Isle, co., Vt.,
    2,927...............B1   7²
Grand Junction, Colo.,
    18,694..............B2   51
Grand Junction, Iowa,
    949.................B3   60
Grand Ledge, Mich.,
    5,165...............F6   66
Grand Marais, Minn.,
    1,301...............B7   67
Grand 'Mere, Que., Can.,
    15,806..............C5   42
Grand Prairie, Tex.,
    30,386..............B5   84
Grand Rapids, Mich.,
    177,313 (*367,300)...F5   66
Grand Rapids, Minn.,
    7,265...............C5   67
Grand Saline, Tex.,
    2,006...............C5   84
Grand Terrace, Calif.,
    1,450..............*F5   50
Grand Tower, Ill.,
    847.................F4   58
Grand Traverse, co.,
    Mich., 33,490......D5   66

Grand View, Man., Can.,
    1,057...............D1   40
Grandview, Ill.,
    2,214..............*D4   58
Grandview, Mo.,
    6,027...........C3, E2   69
Grandview, Tex., 961..*C4   84
Grandview, Wash.,
    3,366...............C6   86
Grandview Heights, Ohio,
    8,270...............C2   78
Grandview Heights, Pa.,
    3,800..............*F9   81
Grandville, Mich.,
    7,975...............F5   66
Granger, Tex., 1,339...D4   84
Granger, Utah, 1,300..*A5   72
Granger, Wash., 1,424..C5   86
Grangeville, Idaho,
    3,642...............D2   57
Grangeville, Pa.,
    1,100..............*G8   81
Granite, Okla., 952....C2   79
Granite, co., Mont.,
    3,014...............D3   70
Granite City, Ill.,
    40,073..............E3   58
Granite Falls, Minn.,
    2,728...............F3   67
Granite Falls, N.C.,
    2,644...............B2   76
Graniteville, S.C.
    3,000...............D4   82
Granja de Torrehermosa,
    Sp., 6,314..........C3   8
Granollers, Sp., 20,194.B7   8
Grant, Nebr., 1,166....D4   71
Grant, co., Ark., 8,294.C3   49
Grant, co., Ind., 75,741.C6   59
Grant, co., Kans.,
    5,269...............E2   61
Grant, co., Ky., 9,489..B5   62
Grant, co., Minn.,
    8,840...............E2   67
Grant, co., Nebr., 1,009.C4   71
Grant, co., N. Mex.,
    18,700..............C4   48
Grant, co., N. Dak.,
    6,248...............D4   77
Grant, co., Okla., 8,140.A4   79
Grant, co., Oreg., 7,726.C7   80
Grant, co., S. Dak.,
    9,913...............E9   77
Grant, co., Wash.,
    46,477..............B6   86
Grant, co., W. Va.,
    8,304...............B4   87
Grant, co., Wis.,
    44,419..............F3   88
Grant, par., La.,
    13,330..............C3   63
Grant City, Mo., 1,061.A3   69
Grantham, Eng.,
    25,030..............D6   4
Grants, N. Mex.,
    10,274..............B5   48
Grantsboro, N.C., 150..B7   76
Grantsburg, Wis., 900..C1   88
Grants Pass, Oreg.,
    10,118..............E3   80
Grantsville, Utah,
    2,166...........A5, D1   72
Grantsville, W. Va.,
    866.................C3   87
Grant Town, W. Va.,
    1,105...........A7, B4   87
Grantville, Ga., 1,158..C2   55
Granville, Fr., 9,827...C3   5
Granville, Ill., 1,048...B4   58
Granville, N.Y., 2,715..B7   75
Granville, Ohio, 2,868..B5   78
Granville, W. Va.,
    806................*B5   87
Granville, co., N.C.,
    33,110..............A5   76
Grapeland, Tex., 1,113.D5   84
Grapeville, Pa., 1,600.*F2   81
Grapevine, Ky., 500...C2   62
Grapevine, Tex.,
    2,821..........B5, C4   84
Grasonville, Md., 925..C5   53
Grasse, Fr., 26,258....F7   5
Grassflat, Pa., 850.....D5   81
Grass Lake, Mich.,
    1,037...............F6   66
Grass Valley, Calif.,
    4,876...............C3   50
Gratiot, co., Mich.,
    37,012..............E6   66
Graton, Calif., 1,055..*C2   50
Graubünden, canton,
    Switz., 147,458.....*E4   6
Graulhet, Fr., 7,996....F5   5
Gravata, Braz., 15,550.D7   27
Gravelbourg, Sask., Can.,
    1,499...............H2   39
Gravenhurst, Ont., Can.,
    3,077...............C5   41
Graves, co., Ky.,
    30,021..............B2   62

Gravesend, Eng.,
    51,388..............E7   4
Gravina [in Puglia], It.,
    31,977..............D6   9
Gray, Ga., 1,320.......C3   55
Gray, Ky., 800........D5   62
Gray, co., Kans., 4,380.E3   61
Gray, co., Tex., 31,535.B2   84
Grayling, Mich., 2,015.D6   66
Grays Harbor, co., Wash.,
    54,465..............B2   86
Grayslake, Ill.,
    3,762............A5, E2   58
Grayson, Ky., 1,692....B7   62
Grayson, co., Ky.,
    15,834..............C3   62
Grayson, co., Tex.,
    73,043..............C4   84
Grayson, co., Va.,
    17,390..............E1   85
Graysville, Ala., 2,870.*B3   46
Grayville, Ill., 2,280...E5   58
Graz, Aus., 237,080....E7   6
Great Barrington, Mass.,
    4,000...............B4   65
Great Bend, Kans.,
    16,670..............D5   61
Great Britain and
    Northern Ireland, see
    United Kingdom,
    country, Eur.
Greater Antilles, is.,
    W.I................B3   27
Great Falls, Mont.,
    55,357..............C5   70
Great Falls, S.C.,
    3,030...............B6   82
Great Neck, N.Y.,
    10,171..............D2   75
Great Neck Estates, N.Y.,
    3,262..............*D3   75
Great Yarmouth, Eng
    52,860..............D7   4
Greece, N.Y., 25,000..*B3   75
Greece, country, Eur.,
    8,388,553...........C4   14
Greeley, Colo., 26,314..A6   51
Greeley, co., Kans.,
    2,087...............D2   61
Greeley, co., Nebr.,
    4,595...............C7   71
Green, co., Ky., 11,249.C4   62
Green, co., Wis., 25,851.F4   88
Green Acres, Calif.,
    1,000..............*E4   50
Green Acres, Md.,
    1,000..............*C3   53
Green Acres, N.Y.,
    2,500..............*E2   75
Greenacres, Wash.,
    2,074...............B8   86
Greenacres City, Fla.,
    1,026...............F6   54
Greenback, Tenn., 285.D9   83
Green Bay. Wis., 62,888
    (*105,300)......A6, D6   88
Greenbelt, Md., 7,479..B4   53
Greenbrae, Calif.,
    2,000..............*B5   50
Greenbrier, co., W. Va.,
    34,446..............D4   87
Green Brook, N.J.,
    3,622..............*B4   74
Greencastle, Ind.,
    8,506...............E4   59
Greencastle, Pa., 2,988.G6   81
Green Cove Springs, Fla.,
    4,233...........C5, C6   54
Greendale, Ind., 2,861.F8   59
Greendale, Wis.,
    6,843...........F2, F5   88
Greene, Iowa, 1,427....B5   60
Greene, N.Y., 2,051....C5   75
Greene, co., Ala.,
    13,600..............C1   46
Greene, co., Ark.,
    25,198..............A5   49
Greene, co., Ga.,
    11,193..............C3   55
Greene, co., Ill., 17,460.D3   58
Greene, co., Ind.,
    26,327..............F3   59
Greene, co., Iowa,
    14,379..............B3   60
Greene, co., Miss.,
    8,366...............D5   68
Greene, co., Mo.,
    126,276.............D4   69
Greene, co., N.Y.,
    31,372..............C6   75
Greene, co., N.C.,
    16,741..............B6   76
Greene, co., Ohio,
    94,642..............C4   78
Greene, co., Pa., 39,424.G1   81
Greene, co., Tenn.,
    42,163.............C11   83
Greene, co., Va., 4,715.C4   85
Greeneville, Tenn.,
    11,759.............C11   83

Greenfield, Calif.,
    1,680...............D3   50
Greenfield, Ill., 1,064..D3   58
Greenfield, Ind., 9,049..E6   59
Greenfield, Iowa, 2,243.C3   60
Greenfield, Mass.,
    17,690..............A2   65
Greenfield, Mo., 1,172..D4   69
Greenfield, Ohio, 5,422.C4   78
Greenfield, Tenn.,
    1,779...............A3   83
Greenfield, Wis.,
    17,636.............*F1   88
Greenfield Park, Que.,
    Can., 7,807.........D9   42
Greenfield Village, Utah,
    1,000..............*D2   72
Green Forest, Ark.,
    1,038...............A2   49
Green Haven, Md.,
    1,302..............*B2   53
Greenhills, Ohio, 5,407.D2   78
Green Hills, Tenn.,
    14,000.............*A5   83
Green Island, N.Y.,
    3,533..............*C7   75
Green Lake, Wis., 953..E5   88
Green Lake, co., Wis.,
    15,418..............E4   88
Greenland, Dan. dep.,
    N.A., 24,018.......B16   33
Greenlawn, N.Y., 5,422.F3   52
Greenlee, co., Ariz.,
    11,509..............C4   48
Greenmanorville, Conn.,
    1,200..............*B6   52
Green Meadows, Md.,
    1,500..............*C1   53
Greenock, Pa., 1,500...F2   81
Greenock, Scot., 74,578.C4   4
Greenport, N.Y., 2,608.D4   75
Green Ridge, Pa.,
    3,500.............*G11   81
Green River, Utah,
    1,075...............B6   72
Green River, Wyo.,
    3,497...............D3   89
Greensboro, Ala., 3,081.C2   46
Greensboro, Ga., 2,773.C3   55
Greensboro, Md., 1,160.C6   53
Greensboro, N.C., 119,574
    (*156,800)..........A4   76
Greensburg, Ind., 7,492.F7   59
Greensburg, Kans.,
    1,988...............E4   61
Greensburg, Ky., 2,334.C4   62
Greensburg, Pa.,
    17,383..............F2   81
Green Springs, Ohio,
    1,262...............A4   78
Greensville, co., Va.,
    16,155..............E5   85
Greentown, Ind., 1,266.D6   59
Green Tree, Pa., 5,226.*F1   81
Greenup, Ill., 1,477....D5   58
Greenup, Ky., 1,240...B7   62
Greenup, co., Ky.,
    29,238..............B7   62
Greenvale, N.Y.,
    1,650..............*F2   52
Greenville, Ala., 6,894.D3   46
Greenville, Calif., 1,140.B3   50
Greenville, Fla., 1,318..B3   54
Greenville, Ill., 4,569..E4   58
Greenville, Ky., 3,198..C2   62
Greenville, Maine,
    1,400...............C3   64
Greenville, Mich.,
    7,440...............E5   66
Greenville, Miss.,
    41,502..............B2   68
Greenville, N.H., 1,251.F4   73
Greenville, N.Y.,
    2,800..............*D2   75
Greenville, N.C.,
    22,860..............B6   76
Greenville, Ohio,
    10,585..............B3   78
Greenville, Pa., 8,765..D1   81
Greenville, R.I., 3,000.B10   52
Greenville, S.C., 66,188
    (*164,500)..........B3   82
Greenville, Tex.,
    19,087..............C4   84
Greenville, co., S.C.,
    209,776.............B3   82
Greenwich, Conn.,
    53,793..............E2   52
Greenwich, Eng., 85,585
    (part of London)...m12   4
Greenwich, N.Y., 2,263.B7   75
Greenwich, Ohio, 1,371.A5   78
Greenwood, Ark., 1,558.B1   49
Greenwood, Ind.,
    7,169...........E5, I8   59
Greenwood, Miss.,
    20,436..............B3   68
Greenwood, Pa., 1,500.*F5   81
Greenwood, S.C.,
    16,644..............C3   82

Greenwood, Wis.,
1,041............D3 88
Greenwood, co., Kans.,
11,253............E7 61
Greenwood, co., S.C.,
44,346............C3 82
Greenwood Lake, N.Y.,
1,236............*D6 75
Greer, S.C., 8,967....B3 82
Greer, co., Okla., 8,877.C2 79
Gregg, co., Tex.,
69,436............C5 84
Gregory, S. Dak.,
1,478............G6 77
Gregory, Tex., 1,970..*F4 84
Gregory, co., S. Dak.,
7,399............G6 77
Greifswald, Ger.,
47,000............A6 6
Greinwich Terrace, La.,
2,000............*D2 63
Greiz, Ger., 39,100....C6 6
Grenada, Miss., 7,914..B5 68
Grenada, co., Miss.,
18,409............B4 68
Grenada, Br. dep.,
N.A.............p16 35
Grenfell, Sask., Can.,
1,256............G4 39
Grenloch, N.J., 975....D2 74
Grenoble, Fr., 156,707..E6 5
Grenville, Que., Can.,
1,330............D3 42
Grenville, co., Ont., Can.,
22,864............C9 41
Gresham, Oreg., 3,944..B4 80
Gretna, La., 21,967.C7, E5 63
Gretna, Va., 900......E3 85
Grey, co., Ont., Can.,
62,005............C4 41
Greybull, Wyo., 2,286..A4 89
Greymouth, N.Z.,
8,881............O13 26
Gridley, Calif., 3,343...C3 50
Gridley, Ill., 889......C5 58
Griffin, Ga., 21,735....C2 55
Griffing Park, Tex.,
2,267............*E5 84
Griffith, Austl., 7,700..F8 25
Griffith, Ind., 9,483....A3 59
Grifton, N.C., 1,816...B6 76
Griggs, co., N. Dak.,
5,023............C7 77
Griggsville, Ill., 1,240..D3 58
Grimes, co., Tex.,
12,709............D5 84
Grimma, Ger., 16,100..C6 6
Grimsby, Ont., Can.,
5,148............D5 41
Grimsby, Eng., 96,665.D6 4
Grimshaw, Alta., Can.,
1,095............A2 38
Grindstone, Pa., 1,094.*G2 81
Grinnell, Iowa, 7,367...C5 60
Griswold, Iowa, 1,207..C2 60
Grodno, Sov. Un.,
81,000............E4 12
Grodzisk, Pol., 6,015...B4 7
Grodzisk Mazowiecki,
Pol., 17,800........m13 7
Groesbeck, Ohio,
9,000............*C3 78
Groesbeck, Tex., 2,498.D4 84
Grojec, Pol., 6,841.....C6 7
Grombalia, Tun., 5,043.F3 9
Gronau, Ger., 25,600...B3 6
Groningen, Neth.,
146,300............A7 5
Groningen, prov., Neth.,
477,700............*A7 5
Grosse Ile, Mich.,
6,318............*B7 66
Grossenhain, Ger.,
19,500............C6 6

Grosse Pointe, Mich.,
6,631............A8 66
Grosse Pointe Farms,
Mich., 12,172......A8 66
Grosse Pointe Park,
Mich., 15,457......A8 66
Grosse Pointe Shores,
Mich., 2,301......*F8 66
Grosse Pointe Woods,
Mich., 18,580......F8 66
Grosseto, It., 36,000...C3 9
Grossmont, Calif.,
1,000............*F15 50
Groton, Conn., 10,111..D8 52
Groton, Mass., 1,178...C1 65
Groton, N.Y., 2,123....C4 75
Groton, S. Dak., 1,063.E7 77
Grottaferrata, It., 5,377.h9 9
Grottaglie, It., 23,223..D6 9
Grottoes, Va., 969....C4 85
Grove, Okla., 975.....A7 79
Grove City, Ohio,
8,107............C2, C3 78
Grove City, Pa., 8,368.D1 81
Grove Hill, Ala., 1,834.D2 46
Groveland, Fla., 1,747.D5 54
Groveland, Mass.,
1,600............A5 65
Groveport, Ohio,
2,043............C2, C5 78
Grover City, Calif.,
5,210............*E3 50
Groves, Tex., 17,304...E6 81
Groveton, N.H., 2,004..B4 73
Groveton, Pa., 1,300..*B5 81
Groveton, Tex., 1,148..D5 84
Grovetown, Ga., 1,396.C4 55
Groznyy, Sov. Un.,
270,000............E7 13
Grudziadz, Pol.,
65,000............B5 7
Grulla, Tex., 1,436....F3 84
Grundy, Va., 2,287.....B3 85
Grundy, co., Ill., 22,350.B5 58
Grundy, co., Iowa,
14,132............B5 60
Grundy, co., Mo.,
12,220............A4 69
Grundy, co., Tenn.,
11,512............D8 83
Grundy Center, Iowa,
2,403............B5 60
Gruver, Tex., 1,030....A2 84
Gruz, Yugo., 10,000...D4 10
Gryazi, Sov. Un.,
10,000............E12 12
Guadalajara, Mex.,
580,617........C4, m12 34
Guadalajara, Sp.,
30,123............B4 8
Guadalajara, prov., Sp.,
183,545............*B4 8
Guadalcanal, Sp.,
6,931............C3 8
Guadalupe, Ariz.,
1,200............D2 48
Guadalupe, Calif.,
2,614............E3 80
Guadalupe, co., N. Mex.,
5,610............B6 48
Guadalupe, co., Tex.,
29,017............E4 84
Guadix, Sp., 18,500....D4 8
Guaira, dept., Par.,
100,446............E4 29
Gualeguay, Arg.,
23,517............A5 28
Gualeguaychú, Arg.,
37,109............A5 28
Guam, U.S. dep., Oceania,
67,044............F6 2
Guanabacoa, Cuba,
32,490............D2 35
Guanabara, state, Braz.,
3,307,163..........*C4 30

Guanacaste, prov., C.R.,
146,600............*E8 34
Guanajay, Cuba,
12,908............D2 35
Guanajuato, Mex.,
28,135............C4, m13 34
Guanajuato, state, Mex.,
1,728,358............C4 34
Guanare, Ven., 16,935..B4 32
Guánica, P.R.,
4,100............*m13 35
Guantánamo, Cuba,
64,671............E6 35
Guarabira, Braz.,
15,848............*D7 27
Guaranda, Ec., 7,287...B2 31
Guarapuava, Braz.,
13,546............D2 30
Guaratinguetá, Braz.,
38,293............C3 30
Guarda, Port., 7,704...B2 8
Guareña, Sp., 9,742....C2 8
Guárica, state, Ven.,
244,966............B4 32
Guarujá, Braz.,
6,506............n8 30
Guatemala, Guat.,
284,276............E6 34
Guatemala, country, N.A.,
3,301,559............D6 34
Guaxupè, Braz.,
14,168............C3, k8 30
Guayama, P.R.,
19,183............n13 36
Guayaquil, Ec.,
258,966............B2 31
Guayas, prov., Ec.,
663,516............B1 31
Guaymas, Mex., 34,845.B2 34
Gubakha, Sov. Un.,
53,800............*D8 13
Gubat, Phil., 9,045....*C6 19
Gubbio, It., 8,600.....C4 9
Gudur, India, 25,618...F6 20
Guebwiller, Fr., 10,568.D7 5
Guecho, Sp., 22,951....A4 8
Guelma, Alg., 17,225...A6 22
Guelph, Ont., Can.,
39,838............D4 41
Güemes, Arg., 5,688...D2 29
Guéret, Fr., 11,384....D4 5
Guernsey, co., Ohio,
38,579............B6 78
Guernsey, Br. dep., Eur.,
47,178............F5 4
Guerneville, Calif., 900.A4 50
Guerrero, state, Mex.,
1,189,085............D5 34
Gueydan, La., 2,156...D3 63
Guiana, British, see Guyana,
country, S.A.
Guiana, French, see French
Guiana, dep., S.A.
Guiana, Netherlands, see
Surinam, Neth. dep.,
S.A.
Guidonia, It.,
20,205............D4, h9 9
Guildford, Eng., 53,977.E6 4
Guilford, Conn., 2,420.D6 52
Guilford, Maine, 1,372.C3 64
Guilford, N.C., 1,000..*A4 76
Guilford, co., N.C.,
246,520............A4 76
Guilford College, N.C.,
1,700............A4 76
Guimarães, Port.,
18,294............B1 8
Guin, Ala., 1,462.....B2 46
Guinea, country, Afr.,
3,000,000............F2 22
Guinea, Portuguese, see
Portuguese Guinea,
dep., Afr.
Güines, Cuba, 29,226..D2 35

Guingamp, Fr., 8,912..C2 5
Guipúzcoa, prov., Sp.,
478,337............*A4 8
Güira de Melena, Cuba,
13,715............D2 35
Güiria, Ven., 10,704....A5 32
Guise, Fr., 6,284......C5 5
Gujarat, state, India,
20,633,350............D5 20
Gujranwala, Pak.,
196,154............B5 21
Gulbarga, India,
97,069............E6 21
Gulf, co., Fla., 9,937...C1 54
Gulf Hammock, Fla.,
350............C4 54
Gulfport, Fla.,
9,730............E4, F2 54
Gulfport, Miss., 30,204
(*124,200)......E2, E4 68
Gull Lake, Sask., Can.,
1,038............G1 39
Gulyay-Pole, Sov. Un.,
10,000............H11 12
Gumma, pref., Jap.,
1,578,476............*H9 18
Gummersbach, Ger.,
32,000............C3 6
Gunnedah, Austl.,
6,546............E8 26
Gunnison, Colo., 3,477.C4 51
Gunnison, Utah, 1,059.B6 72
Gunnison, co., Colo.,
5,477............C3 51
Guntersville, Ala.,
6,592............A3 46
Guntur, India, 187,122.E7 20
Gurabo, P.R., 3,957..*m13 35
Gurdon, Ark., 2,166...D2 49
Gurnee, Ill., 1,831....E2 58
Guryev, Sov. Un.,
86,000............E8 13
Gusev (Gumbinnen), Sov.
Un., 25,000........A7 7
Gusinje, Yugo., 2,757..D4 10
Gus-Khrustalnyy, Sov.
Un., 58,000........D13 12
Gustine, Calif., 2,300..D3 50
Güstrow, Ger., 38,000..B6 6
Gütersloh, Ger., 52,300.C4 6
Guthrie, Ky., 1,211...D12 62
Guthrie, Okla., 9,502..B4 79
Guthrie, co., Iowa,
13,607............C3 60
Guthrie Center, Iowa,
2,071............C3 60
Guttenberg, N.J.,
5,118............D5 74
Guyana, country,
S.A., 524,000......C5 27
Guyenne, former prov.,
Fr., 2,061,000......E4 5
Guymon, Okla., 5,768.D3 79
Guysborough, co., N.S.,
Can., 13,274......D8 43
Gvardeysk, Sov. Un.,
5,000............A6 7
Gwadar, Pak.........C3 20
Gwalior, India,
300,587............C6 20
Gwelo, Rh., 35,100....D5 24
Gwinn, Mich., 1,009...B3 66
Gwinnett, co., Ga.,
43,541............C2 55
Gyangtse, China,
10,000............C8 20
Gympie, Austl., 11,094.E9 25
Gyongyos, Hung.,
28,668............B4 10
Gyor, Hung., 70,812...B3 10
Györ-Sopron, co., Hung.,
391,734............*B3 10
Gyula Hung., 19,990...B5 10

H

Haakon, co., S. Dak.,
3,303............F4 77
Haapsalu, Sov. Un.,
10,000............B4 12
Haarlem, Neth., 164,500
(*225,000)..........A6 5
Habana (Havana), prov.,
Cuba, 1,538,803......h11 35
Habersham, Ga., 400..B3 55
Habersham, co., Ga.,
18,116............B3 55
Haboro, Jap., 19,800.D10 18
Hachiman, Jap.,
11,700............n15 18
Hachinohe, Jap.,
131,000............F10 18
Hachioji, Jap.,
158,443........I9, n18 18
Hackensack, N.J.,
30,521............B4, D5 74
Hackettstown, N.J.,
5,276............B3 74

Haddonfield, N.J.,
13,201............D2 74
Haddon Heights, N.J.,
9,260............D2 74
Hadera, Isr.,
25,358............B2, g5 15
Haderslev, co., Den.,
71,615............*J3 11
Haditha, Iraq, 5,434...C3 15
Hadley, Mass., 1,000...B2 65
Haeju, Kor., 82,135....G2 18
Hagaman, N.Y.,
1,292............*C6 75
Hagar Shores (Lake
Michigan Beach),
Mich., 1,092......*F4 66
Hagen, Ger., 195,500...C3 6
Hagerman, N. Mex.,
1,144............C6 48
Hagerstown, Ind.,
1,730............E7 59

Hagerstown, Md.,
36,660............A2 53
Hagersville, Ont.,
Can., 2,075........E4 41
Hagi, Jap., 41,000....I5 18
Hagginwood, Calif.,
11,469............*A6 50
Ha Giang, Viet., 25,000.G6 17
Hague, The ('s
Gravenhage), see The
Hague, Neth.
Haguenau, Fr., 20,457..C7 5
Hahira, Ga., 1,297....F3 55
Hahnville, La.,
1,297............C6, E5 63
Hai Duong, Viet.,
25,000............*A3 19
Haifa, Isr., 182,007
(*250,000)......B3, g5 15
Hā'il, Sau. Ar., 11,500.D3 15
Hailar (Hulun), China,
43,200............B8 17

Hailey, Idaho, 1,185...F4 57
Haileybury, Ont., Can.,
2,638............E9 41
Haileyville, Okla., 922..C6 79
Hailun, China, 47,684..C3 18
Hailung, China, 21,000.E2 18
Hainan, isl., China....B4 19
Hainaut, prov., Bel.,
1,248,854............*B5 5
Haines City, Fla.,
9,135............D5 54
Hainesport, N.J.,
2,000............D3 74
Haiphong, Viet.,
143,000............A3 19
Haiti, country, N.A.,
3,097,220............F7 35
Hajdu-Bihar, co., Hung.,
393,332............*B5 10
Hajdúböszörmény,
Hung., 26,918......B5 10

Hajduhadhaz, Hung., 11,221..............B5 10
Hajduki Wielkie, Pol., 25,000...........g9 7
Hajdunanas, Hung., 14,003.............B5 10
Hajduszoboszlo, Hung., 16,709...........B5 10
Hakalau, Haw., 800...D6 56
Hakodate, Jap., 243,012.............F10 18
Halawa Heights, Haw., 2,000............g10 56
Halberstadt, Ger., 45,500.............C5 6
Halden, Nor., 10,000...H4 11
Haldimand, co., Ont., Can., 28,197.........E5 41
Hale, co., Ala., 19,537..C2 46
Hale, co., Tex., 36,798..B2 84
Hale Center, Tex., 2,196.............B2 84
Haledon, N.J., 6,161...B4 74
Haleiwa, Haw., 2,504............B3, f9 56
Hales Corners, Wis., 5,549.............F1 88
Halesite, N.Y., 2,857..*D3 75
Halethorpe, Md., 22,402............C2 53
Haleyville, Ala., 3,740..A2 46
Half Moon Bay, Calif., 1,957.............B5 50
Halfway, Md., 4,256...A2 53
Haliburton, Ont., Can., 853..............B6 41
Haliburton, co., Ont., Can., 8,928.........B6 41
Halifax, N.S., Can., 92,511 (*183,946)....E6 43
Halifax, Eng., 96,073...D6 4
Halifax, co., N.S., Can., 225,723...........E7 43
Halifax, co., N.C., 58,956.............A6 76
Halifax, co., Va., 33,637.............E4 85
Hall, Aus., 10,016.....E5 6
Hall, co., Ga., 49,739...B3 55
Hall, co., Nebr., 35,757.............D7 71
Hall, co., Tex., 7,322...B2 84
Halland, co., Swe., 171,200...........I15 11
Hallandale, Fla., 10,483..........E3, G6 54
Halle [an der Saale], Ger., 276,200........C5 6
Hallein, Aus., 13,329...E6 6
Hallettsville, Tex., 2,808.............E4 84
Hallock, Minn., 1,527..B2 67
Hallowell, Maine, 3,169.............D3 64
Halls, Tenn., 1,890.....B2 83
Hallstead, Pa., 1,580..C10 81
Halmstad, Swe., 39,700.I5 11
Hälsingborg, Swe., 77,000............I5 11
Halstead, Kans., 1,598.............A5, D6 61
Haltom City, Tex., 23,133.............C4 84
Halton, co., Ont., Can., 106,967.........D5 41
Hamada, Jap., 33,200...I6 18
Hamadān, Iran, 99,909............F7 16
Hamāh, Syr., 97,400..E11 14
Hamamatsu, Jap., 333,009.........I8, o16 18
Hamar, Nor., 13,500...G4 11
Hambantota, Cey., 4,345.............G7 20
Hamblen, co., Tenn., 33,092............C10 83
Hamburg, Ark., 2,904..D4 49
Hamburg, Ger., 1,832,400...........B5 6
Hamburg, state, Ger., 1,832,400.........*B5 6
Hamburg, Iowa, 1,647.D2 60
Hamburg, N.J., 1,532..A3 74
Hamburg, N.Y., 9,145..C2 75
Hamburg, Pa., 3,747..E10 81
Hamden, Conn., 41,056............D6 52
Hamden, Ohio, 1,035...C5 78
Häme, dept., Fin., 519,015...........*G11 11
Hämeenlinna, Fin., 28,300............G11 11
Hamel, Minn., 1,472..*E5 67
Hameln, Ger., 50,400..B4 6
Hamhŭng, Kor., 112,184............G3 18
Hami (Kumul), China, 30,000............C3 17
Hamilton, Ala., 1,934..A2 46
Hamilton, Aust., 9,498.G7 25

Hamilton, Ont., Can., 273,991 (*395,189)...D5 41
Hamilton, Ill., 2,228...C2 58
Hamilton, Mo., 1,701..B3 69
Hamilton, Mont., 2,475.............D2 70
Hamilton, N.Y., 3,348..C5 75
Hamilton, N.Z., 42,212 (*50,505)..........L15 26
Hamilton, Ohio, 72,354 (*103,200)......C2, C3 78
Hamilton, Scot., 41,928.C4 4
Hamilton, Tex., 3,106..D3 84
Hamilton, co., Fla., 7,705.............B3 54
Hamilton, co., Ill., 10,010.............E5 58
Hamilton, co., Ind., 40,132.............D5 59
Hamilton, co., Iowa, 20,032.............B4 60
Hamilton, co., Kans., 3,144.............E2 61
Hamilton, co., Nebr., 8,714.............D7 71
Hamilton, co., N.Y., 4,267.............B6 75
Hamilton, co., Ohio, 864,121.............C3 78
Hamilton, co., Tenn., 237,905.............D8 83
Hamilton, co., Tex., 8,488.............D3 84
Hamilton Acres, Alsk., 960.............*C10 47
Hamilton Park, Pa., 3,500.............*F9 81
Hamilton Square (Hamilton Township), N.J., 65,035.........C3 74
Hamina, Fin., 9,800...G12 11
Hamirpur, India, 10,000............C7 20
Hamlet, N.C., 4,460...C4 76
Hamlin, Tex., 3,791...C2 84
Hamlin, co., S. Dak., 6,303.............F8 77
Hamm [in Westfalen], Ger., 68,800........C3 6
Hammond, Ind., 111,698............A2 59
Hammond, La., 10,563..........A6, D5 63
Hammond East, La., 1,462...........*A6 63
Hammondsport, N.Y., 1,176.............C3 75
Hammonton, N.J., 9,854.............D3 74
Hampden, co., Mass., 429,353............B2 65
Hampden Highlands, Maine, 1,000........D4 64
Hampshire, Ill., 1,309..A5 58
Hampshire (Southampton), co., Eng., 1,336,084..E6 4
Hampshire, co., Mass., 103,229............B2 65
Hampshire, co., W. Va., 11,705............B6 87
Hampstead, Que., Can., 4,551........*D4 42
Hampton, Ark., 1,011..D3 49
Hampton, Ga., 1,253...C2 55
Hampton, Iowa, 4,501..B4 60
Hampton, N.H., 3,281..F6 73
Hampton, N.J., 1,135..B3 74
Hampton, S.C., 2,486..F5 82
Hampton, Tenn., 1,048.............C11 83
Hampton (Independent City), Va., 89,258........B6, D6 85
Hampton, co., S.C., 17,425.............F5 82
Hampton Bays, N.Y., 2,000.............D4 75
Hamtramck, Mich., 34,137.............A8 66
Hana, Haw., 547......C6 56
Hanahan, S.C., 4,000...F2 82
Hanamaulu, Haw., 950.B2 56
Hanapepe, Haw., 1,383.B2 56
Hanau, Ger., 47,200....C4 6
Hanceville, Ala., 1,174..A3 46
Hancock, Md., 2,004...A1 53
Hancock, Mich., 5,022..A2 66
Hancock, Minn., 942...E3 67
Hancock, N.Y., 1,830..D5 75
Hancock, co., Ga., 9,979.............C3 55
Hancock, co., Ill., 24,574.............C2 58
Hancock, co., Ind., 26,665.............E6 59
Hancock, co., Iowa, 14,604.............A4 60
Hancock, co., Ky., 5,330.............C3 62

Hancock, co., Maine, 32,293.............D4 64
Hancock, co., Miss., 14,039.............E4 68
Hancock, co., Ohio, 53,686.............A4 78
Hancock, co., Tenn., 7,757.............C10 83
Hancock, co., W. Va., 39,615.............A4 87
Hand, co., S. Dak., 6,712.............F6 77
Handa, Jap., 71,380...o15 18
Handley, W. Va., 900...C6 87
Handsboro, Miss., 1,577............E2, E4 68
Haney, B.C., Can., 1,538...........A10, E6 37
Hanford, Calif., 10,133.D4 50
Hanford Northwest, Calif., 1,364........D4 50
Hangchow, China, 784,000............E9 17
Hangö, Fin., 8,200....H10 11
Hankinson, N. Dak., 1,285.............D9 77
Hanley Hills, Mo., 3,308...........*A8 69
Hanna, Alta., Can., 2,645.............D5 38
Hanna, Wyo., 625.....D6 89
Hanna City, Ill., 1,056.C4 58
Hannibal, Mo., 20,028..B6 69
Hannover, Ger., 573,100............B4 6
Hanoi, Viet., 237,500..G6 17
Hanover, Ont., Can., 4,401.............C3 41
Hanover, Ill., 1,396....A3 58
Hanover, Ind., 1,170...G7 59
Hanover, N.H., 5,649..D3 75
Hanover, N.J., 4,379..*B4 74
Hanover, Pa., 15,538..G8 81
Hanover, co., Va., 27,550.............D5 85
Hanover, reg., Ger.....B4 6
Hanover Greene, Pa., 1,000...........*D10 81
Hansford, co., Tex., 6,208.............A2 84
Hanson, co., S. Dak., 4,584.............G8 77
Hants, co., N.S., Can., 26,444.............D6 43
Hantsport, N.S., Can., 1,381.............D5 43
Hapeville, Ga., 10,082..........B5, C2 55
Harahan, La., 9,275....C2 63
Haralson, co., Ga., 14,543.............C1 55
Harār, Eth., 25,000....G6 23
Harbin, China, 1,814,000............D3 18
Harbor Beach, Mich., 2,282.............E8 66
Harbor Isle, N.Y., 1,300...........*E3 75
Harbor Springs, Mich., 1,433.............C5 66
Harbour Breton, Newf., Can., 989............E4 44
Harbour Grace, Newf., Can., 2,545..........E5 44
Harbour Main, Newf., Can., 469............E5 44
Hardee, co., Fla., 12,370.............E5 54
Hardeman, co., Tenn., 21,517.............B2 83
Hardeman, co., Tex., 8,275.............B3 84
Hardin, Ill., 1,040....*D3 58
Hardin, Mont., 2,789..E9 70
Hardin, co., Ill., 5,879..F5 58
Hardin, co., Iowa, 22,533.............B4 60
Hardin, co., Ky., 67,789.............C4 62
Hardin, co., Ohio, 29,633.............B4 78
Hardin, co., Tenn., 17,397.............B3 83
Hardin, co., Tex., 24,629.............D5 84
Harding, co., N. Mex., 1,874.............B7 48
Harding, co., S. Dak., 2,371.............E2 77
Hardinsburg, Ky., 1,377.............C3 62
Hardshell, Ky., 350....C6 62
Hardwar, India, 58,513.C6 20
Hardwick, Ga., 3,500...C3 55
Hardwick, Vt., 1,521..B3 73
Hardy, co., W. Va., 9,308.............B6 87
Harfleur, Fr., 10,514...C4 5
Harford, co., Md., 76,722.............A5 53
Hargeisa, Som., 53,000.G6 23

Harihar, India, 22,829..F6 20
Harkers Island, N.C., 1,362.............C7 76
Harlan, Iowa, 4,350....C2 60
Harlan, Ky., 4,177....D6 62
Harlan, co., Ky., 51,107.............D6 62
Harlan, co., Nebr., 5,081.............D6 71
Harlem, Fla., 1,256...*F6 54
Harlem, Ga., 1,423....C4 55
Harlem, Mont., 1,267..B8 70
Harlingen, Neth., 12,000.............A6 5
Harlingen, Tex., 41,207.............F4 84
Harlowton, Mont., 1,734.............D7 70
Harmarville, Pa., 2,000.A6 81
Harmon, co., Okla., 5,852.............C2 79
Harmony, Ind., 700....E3 59
Harmony, Minn., 1,214.............G6 67
Harmony, Pa., 1,412...E1 81
Harnett, co., N.C., 48,236.............B5 76
Harney, co., Oreg., 6,744.............D7 80
Härnösand, Swe., 17,200.............F8 11
Haro, Sp., 8,554.......A4 8
Harper, Kans., 1,899...E5 61
Harper, Lib., 5,000....H3 22
Harper, co., Kans., 9,541.............E5 61
Harper, co., Okla., 5,956.............A2 79
Harper Woods, Mich., 19,995...........*F7 66
Harrah, Okla., 934....B4 79
Harriman, Tenn., 5,931.............D1 83
Harrington, Del., 2,495.............C6 53
Harrington Park, N.J., 3,581.............D5 74
Harris, co., Ga., 11,167.............D2 55
Harris, co., Tex., 1,243,158...........E5 84
Harrisburg, Ark., 1,907.............B5 49
Harrisburg, Ill., 9,171..F5 58
Harrisburg, Oreg., 939.C3 80
Harrisburg, Pa., 79,697 (*257,600)........F8 81
Harris Hill, N.Y., 3,944...........*C2 75
Harrison, Ark., 6,580..A2 49
Harrison, Mich., 1,072.D6 66
Harrison, N.J., 11,743..D5 74
Harrison, N.Y., 19,201.D2 75
Harrison, Ohio, 3,878..C3 76
Harrison, co., Ind., 19,207.............H5 59
Harrison, co., Iowa, 17,600.............C2 60
Harrison, co., Ky., 13,704.............B5 61
Harrison, co., Miss., 119,489.............E4 68
Harrison, co., Mo., 11,603.............A3 69
Harrison, co., Ohio, 17,995.............B6 78
Harrison, co., Tex., 45,594.............C5 84
Harrison, co., W. Va., 77,856.............B4 87
Harrison [Township] (Natrona Heights), Pa., 15,710......A7, E2 81
Harrisonville, Mo., 3,510.............C3 69
Harriston, Ont., Can., 1,631.............D4 41
Harrisville, Pa., 896...D1 81
Harrisville, R.I., 1,024.............B10 52
Harrisville, W. Va., 1,428.............B3 87
Harrodsburg, Ky., 6,061.............C5 62
Harrogate, Eng., 50,332.............D6 4
Harrow, Ont., Can., 1,787.............E2 41
Harrow, Eng., 208,963.*E6 4
Hart, Mich., 1,990....E4 66
Hart, co., Ga., 15,229..B4 55
Hart, co., Ky., 14,119..C4 62
Hartford, Ala., 1,956..D4 46
Hartford, Conn., 162,178 (*763,700)........B6 52
Hartford, Ill., 2,355...E3 58
Hartford, Ky., 1,618...C3 62
Hartford, Mich., 2,305.F4 66

Hartford, Wis., 5,627....E1, E5 88
Hartford, co., Conn., 689,555....B5 52
Hartford City, Ind., 8,053....D7 59
Hartington, Nebr., 1,648....B8 71
Hartland, N.B., Can., 1,025....C2 43
Hartland, Maine, 1,016....D3 64
Hartland, Wis., 2,088....E1, E5 88
Hartlepool, Eng., 17,674....C6 4
Hartley, Iowa, 1,738..A2 60
Hartley, co., Tex., 2,171....B1 84
Hartsdale, N.Y., 9,000....*D2 75
Hartselle, Ala., 5,000..A3 46
Hartshorne, Okla., 1,903....C2 79
Hartsville, S.C., 6,392..C7 82
Hartsville, Tenn., 1,712....A5 83
Hartville, Ohio, 1,353..B6 78
Hartwell, Ga., 4,599..B4 55
Harvard, Ill., 4,248..A5 58
Harvard, Nebr., 1,261..D7 71
Harvey, Ill., 29,071.B6, F3 58
Harvey, La., 10,000....C7, E5 63
Harvey, N. Dak., 2,365....C6 77
Harvey, co., Kans., 25,865....D6 61
Harwich, Eng., 13,569..E7 4
Harwick, Pa., 1,500...*A6 81
Harwood Heights, Ill., 5,688....*B6 58
Hasbrouck Heights, N.J., 13,046....D7 74
Hashimoto, Jap., 16,700....o14 18
Haskell, Okla., 1,887..B6 79
Haskell, Tex., 4,016...C3 84
Haskell, co., Kans., 2,990....E3 61
Haskell, co., Okla., 9,121....B6 79
Haskell, co., Tex., 11,174....C3 84
Haslett, Mich., 1,500..*F6 66
Hassan, India, 32,172..F6 20
Hasselt, Bel., 36,618..B6 5
Hässleholm, Swe., 13,500....I5 11
Hastings, Eng., 66,346.E7 4
Hastings, Fla., 617....C5 54
Hastings, Mich., 6,375..F5 66
Hastings, Minn., 8,965....F6, F7 62
Hastings, Nebr., 21,412....D7 71
Hastings, N.Z., 23,383 (*32,490)....M16 26
Hastings, Pa., 1,751...E4 81
Hastings, co., Ont., Can., 93,377....C7 41
Hastings-on-Hudson, N.Y., 8,979....D1 75
Hatboro, Pa., 7,315...F11 81
Hatch, N. Mex., 888...C5 48
Hatfield, Mass., 1,330..B2 65
Hatfield, Pa., 1,941...F11 81
Hatfield, Rh., 8,500...D6 24
Ha Tien, Viet., 5,000...C2 19
Hatteras, N.C., 700...B8 76
Hattiesburg, Miss., 34,989....D4 68
Hatton, N. Dak., 856..C8 77
Hatton Fields, Calif., 2,362....*D3 50
Hatvan, Hung., 19,952.B4 10
Haubstadt, Ind., 1,029.H2 59
Haugesund, Nor., 27,100....H1 11
Hauppauge, N.Y., 1,500....*D3 75
Haute-Garonne, dept., Fr., 594,633....*F4 5
Haute-Loire, dept., Fr., 211,036....*E5 5
Haute-Marne, dept., Fr., 208,446....*C6 5
Hautes-Alpes, dept., Fr., 85,436....*E7 5
Haute-Saône, dept., Fr., 208,440....*D6 5
Haute-Savoie, dept., Fr., 329,230....*D7 5
Hautes-Pyrénées, dept., Fr., 211,433....*F4 5
Haute-Vienne, dept., Fr., 332,514....*E4 5
Hautmont, Fr., 18,594.B6 5
Haut-Rhin, dept., Fr., 547,920....*C7 5
Hauula, Haw., 950.B4, f10 56

Havana (La Habana), Cuba, 785,455 (*1,217,674)....D2, h11 35
Havana, Fla., 2,090....B2 54
Havana, Ill., 4,363....C3 58
Havelock, Ont., Can., 1,260....C7 41
Havelock, N.C., 2,433..C7 76
Haven, Kans., 982....B4 61
Haverford, Pa., 5,000....*B11 81
Haverhill, Mass., 46,346....A5 65
Haverstraw, N.Y., 5,771....D2, D7 75
Havertown, Pa., 35,000....*B11 81
Havlickuv Brod, Czech., 14,900....D3 7
Havre, see Le Havre, Fr.
Havre, Mont., 10,740..B7 70
Havre Aubert, Que., Can., 494....B8 43
Havre de Grace, Md., 8,510....A5 53
Havza, Tur., 4,539....B10 14
Hawaii, co., Haw., 61,332....D5 56
Hawaii, state, U.S., 632,772.... 56
Hawaiian Gardens, Calif., 15,000....*F4 50
Hawarden, Iowa, 2,544....A1 60
Hawera, N.Z., 7,542..M15 26
Hawesville, Ky., 882...C3 62
Hawi, Haw., 800....C6 56
Hawick, Scot., 16,204..C5 4
Hawkesbury, Ont., Can., 8,661....B10 41
Hawkins, co., Tenn., 30,468....C10 83
Hawkinsville, Ga., 3,967....D3 55
Hawley, Minn., 1,270..D2 67
Hawley, Pa., 1,433...D11 81
Haworth, N.J., 3,215..D5 74
Haw River, N.C., 1,410....A4 76
Hawthorne, Calif., 33,035....F2 50
Hawthorne, Fla., 1,167.C4 54
Hawthorne, Nev., 2,838....B2 72
Hawthorne, N.J., 17,735....B4 74
Hawthorne, N.Y., 4,000....D2 75
Haxtun, Colo., 990....A8 51
Hayange, Fr., 11,009...C7 5
Hayden, Ariz., 1,760....C3, D3 48
Hayden, Idaho, 901..B2 57
Haydenville, Ohio, 800.C5 78
Hayes, co., Nebr., 1,919....D4 71
Hayesville, Oreg., 4,568....*C4 80
Haynau, see Chojnow, Pol.
Haynesville, La., 3,031.B2 63
Hay River, N.W. Ter., Can., 1,338....D10 36
Hays, Kans., 11,947..D4 61
Hays, co., Tex., 19,934....D3 84
Hay Springs, Nebr., 823....B3 71
Haysville, Kans., 5,836....*B5 61
Hayti, Mo., 3,737....E8 69
Hayward, Calif., 72,700....B5 50
Hayward, Wis., 1,540..B2 88
Haywood, co., N.C., 39,711....D3 76
Haywood, co., Tenn., 23,393....B2 83
Hazard, Ky., 5,958....C6 62
Hazardville, Conn., 4,000....B6 52
Hazebrouck, Fr., 17,446....B5 5
Hazel Crest, Ill., 6,205..F3 58
Hazel Dell, Wash., 2,500....*D3 86
Hazel Park, Mich., 25,631....A8 66
Hazelwood, Mo., 6,045....*C7 69
Hazelwood, N.C., 1,925....D3 76
Hazen, Ark., 1,456...C4 49
Hazen, N. Dak., 1,222..C4 77
Hazlet, N.J., 9,000....*C4 74
Hazlehurst, Ga., 3,699....E4 55
Hazlehurst, Miss., 3,400....D3 68
Hazleton, Pa., 32,056....E10 81
Headland, Ala., 2,650..D4 46

Healdsburg, Calif., 4,816....A4, C2 50
Healdton, Okla., 2,898.C4 79
Heard, co., Ga., 5,333..C1 55
Hearne, Tex., 5,072....D4 84
Hearst, Ont., Can., 2,373....E9 41
Heart's Content, Newf., Can., 607....E5 44
Heath, Ohio, 2,426....*B5 78
Heavener, Okla., 1,891.C7 79
Hebbronville, Tex., 3,987....F3 84
Heber, Utah, 2,936....A6, D2 72
Heber Springs, Ark., 2,265....B3 49
Hebertville, Que., Can., 1,604....A6 42
Hebertville Station, Que., Can., 1,257..*A6 42
Hebrides, is., Scot....B3 4
Hebron, Ind., 1,401....B3 59
Hebron, Nebr., 1,920..D8 71
Hebron, N. Dak., 1,340....D3 77
Hebron, Ohio, 1,260...C5 78
Hechingen, Ger., 9,600....D4 6
Hector, Minn., 1,297..F4 67
Hedemora, Swe., 6,000.G6 11
Hedmark, co., Nor., 177,200....*G4 11
Hedwig Village, Tex., 1,182....*E5 84
Heerlen, Neth., 72,400..B6 5
Heflin, Ala., 2,400....B4 46
Hegeler, Ill., 1,640...*C6 58
Hegins, Pa., 800....E9 81
Heide, Ger., 20,000...A4 6
Heidelberg, Ger., 125,300....D4 6
Heidelberg, Miss., 1,049....D5 68
Heidelberg, Pa., 2,118....*F1 81
Heidenheim, Ger., 48,800....D5 6
Heidrick, Ky., 500....D6 62
Heilbronn, Ger., 89,100....D4 6
Heiligenstadt, Ger., 12,500....C5 6
Heilungkiang, prov., China, 14,860,000...B10 17
Hejaz, pol. div., Sau. Ar., 2,000,000....E2 15
Helena, Ark., 11,500...C5 49
Helena, Ga., 1,290....D4 55
Helena, Mont., 20,227..D5 70
Helensburgh, Scot., 9,605....B4 4
Hellam, Pa., 1,234...G8 81
Hellertown, Pa., 6,716....E11 81
Hellín, Sp., 12,900....C5 8
Hellville, Malag., 9,321.C9 23
Helmond, Neth., 43,400....B6 5
Helmstedt, Ger., 29,600....B5 6
Helper, Utah, 2,459..B6 72
Helsingfors, see Helsinki, Fin.
Helsingør, Den., 26,658.I5 11
Helsinki, Fin., 452,800....G11 11
Hemet, Calif., 5,416....F4, F5 50
Hemingford, Nebr., 904....B2 71
Hemingway, S.C., 951.D9 82
Hemlock (Eureka), S.C., 1,423....B5 82
Hemphill, Tex., 913...D6 84
Hemphill, co., Tex., 3,185....B2 84
Hempstead, N.Y., 34,641....D2 6
Hempstead, Tex., 1,505....D4 84
Hempstead, co., Ark., 19,661....D2 49
Hendaye, Fr., 7,204....F3 5
Hendek, Tur., 9,900...B8 14
Henderson, Ky., 16,892.C2 62
Henderson, Nev., 12,525....C4 72
Henderson, N.C., 12,740....A5 76
Henderson, Tenn., 2,691....B3 83
Henderson, Tex., 9,666.C5 84
Henderson, co., Ill., 8,237....C2 62
Henderson, co., Ky., 33,519....C3 58
Henderson, co., N.C., 36,163....D3 76
Henderson, co., Tenn., 16,115....B3 83

Henderson, co., Tex., 21,786....C5 84
Hendersonville, N.C., 5,911....D3 76
Hendersonville, Tenn., 950....A5 83
Hendon, Eng., 151,500....k12 4
Hendricks, co., Ind., 40,896....E4 59
Hendry, co., Fla., 8,119.F5 54
Hengelo, Neth., 62,000.A7 5
Hengyang, China, 235,000....F7 17
Henlawson, W. Va., 1,670....D5 87
Hennebont, Fr., 7,623..D2 5
Hennepin, co., Minn., 842,854....E5 67
Hennessey, Okla., 1,228....A4 79
Henning, Minn., 980...D3 67
Henrico, co., Va., 117,339....D5 85
Henrietta, N.C., 950....B2, D4 76
Henrietta, Tex., 3,062..C3 84
Henry, Ill., 2,278....B4 58
Henry, co., Ala., 75,286.D4 46
Henry, co., Ga., 17,619.C2 55
Henry, co., Ill., 49,317..B3 58
Henry, co., Ind., 48,899.E7 59
Henry, co., Iowa, 18,187....C6 60
Henry, co., Ky., 10,987.B4 62
Henry, co., Mo., 19,226.C4 69
Henry, co., Ohio, 25,392....A3 78
Henry, co., Tenn., 22,275....A3 83
Henry, co., Va., 40,335.E3 85
Henryetta, Okla., 7,987.B6 79
Henzada, Bur., 61,972.E10 20
Heppner, Oreg., 1,661..B7 80
Herat, Afg., 75,642...B3 20
Hérault, dept., Fr., 516,658....*F5 5
Herbert, Sask., Can., 1,008....G2 39
Herblay, Fr., 10,220...g9 5
Hercegovina, reg., Yugo....D4 10
Herculaneum, Mo., 1,767....B8, C7 69
Heredia, C.R., 19,000..E8 34
Heredia, prov., C.R., 77,300....*E8 34
Hereford, Eng., 40,431.D5 4
Hereford, Tex., 7,652...B1 84
Hereford, co., Eng., 130,919....*D5 4
Herencia, Sp., 8,606....C4 8
Herford, Ger., 55,700..B4 6
Herington, Kans., 3,702....D7 61
Herisau, Switz., 14,361.E4 6
Herkimer, N.Y., 9,396.B6 75
Herkimer, co., N.Y., 66,370....B6 75
Hermann, Mo., 2,536..C6 69
Hermansville, Mich., 750....C3 66
Hermantown, Minn., 1,000....D6 67
Herminie, Pa., 1,571...F2 81
Hermiston, Oreg., 4,402....B7 80
Hermosa Beach, Calif., 16,115....F2 50
Hermosillo, Mex., 96,122....B2 34
Hernando, Miss., 1,898.A4 68
Hernando, co., Fla., 11,205....D4 54
Herndon, Va., 1,960....A4, C5 85
Herning, Den., 24,790..I3 11
Herrin, Ill., 9,474....F4 58
Herrington, Wis., 2,405....*E2 88
Hershey, Pa., 6,851....F8 81
Herstal, Bel., 29,606..B6 5
Hertford, Eng., 15,734.E6 4
Hertford, N.C., 2,068..A7 76
Hertford, co., Eng., 832,088....*E6 4
Hertford, co., N.C., 22,718....A6 76
Herzliya, Isr., 26,809....B2, g5 15
Hespeler, Ont., Can., 4,519....D4 41
Hesse, reg., Ger....C4 6
Hessen, state, Ger., 4,814,400....*C4 6
Hesston, Kans., 1,103....A5, D6 61
Hettinger, N. Dak., 1,769....D3 77
Hettinger, co., N. Dak., 6,317....D3 77

Heves, Hung., 9,923...B5 10
Heves, co., Hung., 348,756.......*B5 10
Hewlett, N.Y., 7,500..*G2 52
Hewlett Harbor, N.Y., 1,610............*G2 52
Heyworth, Ill., 1,196...C7 58
Hialeah, Fla., 66,972.........F3, G6 54
Hiawatha, Iowa, 1,336............*C6 60
Hiawatha, Kans., 3,391.C8 61
Hiawatha, Utah, 439...B6 72
Hibbing, Minn., 17,731............C6 67
Hibernia, N.J., 450...B4 74
Hickman, Ky., 1,537...B2 62
Hickman, co., Ky., 6,747............B2 62
Hickman, co., Tenn., 11,862............B4 83
Hickory, N.C., 19,328..B2 76
Hickory, co., Mo., 4,516............D4 69
Hickory East, N.C., 3,274............*B2 76
Hickory Hills, Ill., 2,707............*F3 58
Hicksville, N.Y., 50,405.........D3, E7 75
Hicksville, Ohio, 3,116.A3 78
Hico, Tex., 1,020.....D3 84
Hidalgo, Tex., 1,078..*F3 84
Hidalgo, co., N. Mex., 4,961............D4 48
Hidalgo, co., Tex., 180,904............F3 42
Hidalgo, state, Mex., 983,161........C5, m14 34
Hidalgo del Parral, Mex., 41,461......B3 34
Higginsville, Mo., 403..B4 69
High Bridge, N.J., 2,148............B3 74
Highgrove, Calif., 2,000............*F5 50
Highland, Calif., 7,000..F3 50
Highland, Ill., 4,943...E4 58
Highland, Ind., 16,284..A3 59
Highland, N.Y., 2,931..D7 75
Highland, co., Ohio, 29,716............C4 78
Highland, co., Va., 3,221............C3 85
Highland City, Fla., 1,020............*E5 54
Highland Creek, Ont., Can., 1,300........D5 41
Highland Crest, Kans., 4,000............*B8 61
Highland Falls, N.Y., 4,469............*D7 75
Highland Heights, Ky., 3,491............A7 62
Highland Heights, Ohio, 2,929.........*A6 78
Highland Park, Ill., 25,532........A6, E2 58
Highland Park, Mich., 38,063............A8 66
Highland Park, Pa., 1,534............*E6 81
Highland Park, Tex., 10,411............B5 81
Highland Park, Va., 2,500............*E6 85
Highlands, Fla., 5,000............*F6 54
Highlands, N.J., 3,536..C5 74
Highlands, Tex., 4,336..F5 84
Highlands, co., Fla., 21,338............E5 54
Highland Springs, Va., 5,000.........C7, D5 85
Highmore, S. Dak., 1,078............F6 77
High Point, N.C., 62,063 (*100,600).........B3 77
High Prairie, Alta., Can., 1,756........B2 38
High River, Alta., Can., 2,276........D4 38
Highshoals, N.C., 900..B2 76
High Spire, Pa., 2,999..F8 81
High Springs, Fla., 2,329............C4 54
Highstown, N.J., 4,317.C3 74
Highway City, Calif., 1,381............*D4 50
Highway Village, Tex., 1,927............*F4 84
Highwood, Ill., 4,499.........A6, E2 58
High Wycombe, Eng., 50,301............E6 4
Higüey, Dom. Rep., 10,084............F9 35
Hikone, Jap., 41,400..n15 18
Hildburghausen, Ger., 7,870............C5 6

Hildesheim, Ger., 96,300............B4 6
Hill, co., Mont., 18,653.B6 70
Hill, co., Tex., 23,650..D4 84
Hilla, Iraq, 46,441.....B6 23
Hillburn, N.Y., 1,114..*D6 75
Hill City, Kans., 2,421..C4 61
Hillcrest, N.J., 1,922..*B2 74
Hillcrest, N.Y., 1,500..*C5 75
Hillcrest, N.Y., 1,800..*D1 75
Hillcrest Center, Calif., 15,000............*E4 50
Hillcrest Heights, Md., 15,295............*C3 53
Hiller, Pa., 1,746.....*G5 81
Hillgrove, Calif., 3,500............*F3 50
Hilliard, Fla., 1,075...B5 54
Hilliard, Ohio, 5,633..*C2 78
Hillsboro, Ill., 4,232...D4 58
Hillsboro, Kans., 2,441.D6 61
Hillsboro, N.H., 1,645..E4 73
Hillsboro, N.C., 1,349..A4 76
Hillsboro, N. Dak., 1,278............C8 77
Hillsboro, Ohio, 5,474..C4 78
Hillsboro, Oreg., 8,232.........B1, B3 80
Hillsboro, Tex., 7,402..C4 84
Hillsboro, Wis., 1,366..E3 88
Hillsboro, co., N.H., 178,161............F4 73
Hillsborough, Calif., 7,554............*B5 50
Hillsborough, N.B., Can., 679............D5 43
Hillsborough, co., Fla., 397,788............E4 54
Hillsdale, Mich., 7,629.G6 66
Hillsdale, N.C., 2,788..*A8 69
Hillsdale, N.J., 8,734..C5 74
Hillsdale, co., Mich., 34,742............G6 66
Hillside, Ill., 7,794....*F2 58
Hillside, N.J., 22,304..E4 74
Hillsville, Pa., 950....D1 81
Hillside Manor, N.Y., 8,000............*G2 52
Hillsville, Va., 905....E5 85
Hilltop, N.J., 1,000...*D2 74
Hillwood, Va., 1,400..*B5 85
Hilo, Haw., 25,966.........D6, n16 56
Hilton, N.Y., 1,334....B3 75
Hilversum, Neth., 102,000............A6 5
Himeji, Jap., 328,689...I7 18
Hinche, Hai., 4,511....F7 35
Hinckley, Minn., 851..D6 67
Hindenburg, see Zabrze, Pol.
Hinds, co., Miss., 187,045............C3 68
Hines, Oreg., 1,207....D7 80
Hinesville, Ga., 3,174..E5 55
Hingham, Mass., 10,500.........B6, D3 65
Hinojosa [del Duque], Sp., 14,767........C3 8
Hinsdale, Ill., 12,859..F2 58
Hinsdale, Mass., 990...B1 65
Hinsdale, N.H., 1,235..F3 73
Hinsdale, co., Colo., 208............D3 51
Hinton, Okla., 907.....B3 79
Hinton, W. Va., 5,197............D4 87
Hiram, Ohio, 1,011....A6 78
Hiratsuka, Jap., 108,279......I9, n18 18
Hirosaki, Jap., 80,000............F10 18
Hiroshima, Jap., 431,336............I6 18
Hiroshima, pref., Jap., 2,184,043........*I6 18
Hirson, Fr., 11,715.....C5 5
Hissar, India, 60,222...C4 20
Hitachi, Jap., 161,226.H10 18
Hitchcock, Tex., 5,216.G5 84
Hitchcock, co., Nebr., 4,829............D4 71
Hitchins, Ky., 600.....B7 62
Hitoyoshi, Jap., 27,200............J5 18
Hixon, Tenn., 1,500.........D8, E10 83
Hjørring, Den., 15,038..I3 11
Hjørring, co., Den., 173,233............*I3 11
Hlohovec, Czech., 12,700............D4 7
Hlomsak, Thai., 7,906............*E11 20
Hoa Binh, Viet., 25,000............*A3 19
Hobart, Austl., 54,021 (*116,000)........o15 25
Hobart, Ind., 18,680...A3 59
Hobart, Okla., 5,132...B2 79

Hobbs, N. Mex., 26,275............C7 48
Hoboken, Bel., 30,557..B6 5
Hoboken, N.J., 48,441.D5 74
Hocking, co., Ohio, 20,168............C5 78
Hockley, Tex., 200.....F4 84
Hockley, co., Tex., 22,340............C1 84
Hodge, La., 878........B3 63
Hodgeman, co., Kans., 3,115............D4 61
Hodgenville, Ky., 1,985............C4 61
Hodgkins, Ill., 1,126..*F3 58
Hodmezovasarhely, Hung., 40,047......B5 10
Hodonin, Czech., 18,000............D4 7
Hoeryong, Kor., 24,330............E4 18
Hof, Ger., 57,100......C5 6
Hofei, China, 304,000..E8 17
Hoffman Estates, Ill., 8,296............*E2 58
Hofu, Jap., 96,821......I5 18
Hogansville, Ga., 3,658............C2 55
Hohenwald, Tenn., 2,194............B4 83
Ho-Ho-Kus, N.J., 3,988.A4 74
Hoisington, Kans., 4,248............D5 61
Hoke, co., N.C., 16,356.B4 76
Hokendauqua, Pa., 1,400............*E11 81
Hokes Bluff, Ala., 1,619............B4 46
Hokkaido, isl., Jap....E10 18
Hokkaido, ter., Jap., 5,039,206........*E10 18
Hokoda, Jap., 7,100..m10 18
Holbaek, co., Den., 127,127............*J4 11
Holbrook, Ariz., 3,438..B3 48
Holbrook, Mass., 6,000.........B5, D3 65
Holbrook, N.Y., 3,441............*C3 75
Holden, Mass., 2,000..B4 65
Holden, Mo., 1,951....C4 69
Holden, W. Va., 1,900..D2 87
Holdenville, Okla., 5,712............B5 79
Holdrege, Nebr., 5,226.D6 71
Holgate, Ohio, 1,374..A3 78
Holguín, Cuba, 57,573..E5 35
Hollabrunn, Aus., 5,832............D8 6
Holladay, Utah, 28,000............*C3 72
Holland, Mich., 24,777.F4 66
Holland, Ohio, 924............A1, A4 78
Hollandale, Miss., 2,646............B3 68
Holley, N.Y., 1,788....B2 75
Holliday, Tex., 1,139...C3 84
Hollidaysburg, Pa., 6,475............F5 81
Hollins, Va., 1,000....D3 85
Hollis, Alsk., 292.....n23 47
Hollis, Okla., 3,006....C2 79
Hollister, Calif., 6,071.........C6, D3 50
Holliston, Mass., 2,477.D1 65
Holloway Terrace, Del., 1,500............*A6 53
Holly, Colo., 1,108....C8 51
Holly, Mich., 3,269....F7 66
Holly Hill, Fla., 4,182..C5 54
Holly Hill, S.C., 1,235..E7 82
Holly Oak, Del., 1,000..A7 53
Holly Ridge, N.C., 731.C6 76
Holly Springs, Miss., 5,621............A4 68
Hollywood, Fla., 35,237.........E3, F6 54
Hollywood, La., 1,750............*D2 63
Hollywood, Pa., 2,000............*F12 81
Hollywood Heights, Ill., 1,000............*E3 58
Holmdel Gardens, Kans., 1,436............*D6 61
Holmes, Pa., 3,000...*B11 81
Holmes, co., Fla., 10,844............G3 54
Holmes, co., Miss., 27,096............B3 68
Holmes, co., Ohio, 21,591............B6 78
Holmes Beach, Fla., 1,143............*E4 54
Holmes Run Acres, Va., 1,000..........*B5 85
Holmes Run Park, Va., 1,000..........*B5 85
Holon, Isr., 42,102....B2 15
Holopaw, Fla., 250....D5 54

Holstebro, Den., 18,563............I3 11
Holstein, Iowa, 1,413..B2 60
Holt, Ala., 2,800......B2 46
Holt, Mich., 4,818.....F6 66
Holt, co., Mo., 7,885..A2 69
Holt, co., Nebr., 13,722............B7 71
Holton, Kans., 3,028.........A6, C8 61
Holtville, Calif., 3,080..F6 50
Holyhead, Wales, 10,408............D4 4
Holyoke, Colo., 1,555..A8 51
Holyoke, Mass., 52,689.B2 65
Holzminden, Ger., 22,500............C4 6
Homalin, Bur., 10,000..D9 20
Homburg, see Bad-Homburg, Ger.
Homeacre, Pa., 3,508..*E2 81
Home Corner, Ind., 2,636............*C6 59
Homécourt, Fr., 10,141.C6 5
Homedale, Idaho, 1,381............F2 57
Homedale, Ohio, 670..*C2 78
Home Gardens, Calif., 1,541............*F5 50
Homer, Alsk., 1,247.........D6, h16 47
Homer, Ill., 1,276.....C6 58
Homer, La., 4,665.....B2 63
Homer, Mich., 1,629...F6 66
Homer, N.Y., 3,622....C4 75
Homer City, Pa., 2,471.E3 81
Homerville, Ga., 2,634.E4 55
Homestead, Fla., 9,152.........F3, G6 54
Homestead, Pa., 7,502..B6 81
Homestead Valley, Calif., 1,000............*B5 50
Hometown, Ill., 7,479.*F3 58
Homewood, Ala., 20,289............E4 46
Homewood, Ill., 13,371.........B6, F3 58
Hominy, Okla., 2,866..A5 79
Homs, Syr., 137,200...B5 23
Honan, prov., China, 48,670,000........E7 17
Honda, Col., 16,051....B3 32
Hondo, Tex., 4,992....E3 84
Honduras, country, N.A., 1,883,480..........D7 34
Honea Path, S.C., 3,453............C3 82
Honeoye Falls, N.Y., 2,143............C3 75
Honesdale, Pa., 5,569.C11 81
Honey Brook, Pa., 1,023............F10 81
Honey Grove, Tex., 2,071............C5 84
Honfleur, Fr., 8,970....C4 5
Hon Gay, Viet., 25,000............*A3 19
Hong Kong, Br. dep., Asia, 3,133,131......G7 17
Honokaa, Haw., 1,247..C6 56
Honolulu, Haw., 294,179 (*486,400)......B4, g10 56
Honolulu, co., Haw., 500,409............B3 56
Honto, see Nevelsk, Sov. Un.
Hood, co., Tex., 5,443..C4 84
Hood River, Oreg., 3,657............B5 80
Hood River, co., Oreg., 13,395............B5 80
Hooker, Okla., 1,684...D3 79
Hooker, co., Nebr., 1,130............C4 71
Hooks, Tex., 2,048....*C5 84
Hooksett, N.H., 900...E5 73
Hoolehua, Haw., 973...B4 56
Hooper, Utah, 300..A5, C2 72
Hooper Bay, Alsk., 460.C6 47
Hoopeston, Ill., 6,606..C6 58
Hoorn, Neth., 16,100...A6 5
Hoosick Falls, N.Y., 4,023............C7 75
Hooverson Heights, W. Va., 1,800......*B2 87
Hooversville, Pa., 1,120............F4 81
Hopatcong, N.J., 3,391.B3 74
Hope, Ark., 8,399.....D2 49
Hope, B.C., Can., 2,751.E7 37
Hope, Ind., 1,489......F6 59
Hopedale, La., 720.....E6 63
Hopedale, Mass., 3,987.........B4, E1 65
Hopedale, Ohio, 932...B7 78
Hopeh, prov., China, 42,500,000........D8 17
Hopelawn, N.J., 2,000............*B4 74
Hope Mills, N.C., 1,109............C5 76

Hope Ranch, Calif., 1,000....*E4 50
Hope Valley, R.I., 900....C10 52
Hopewell, N.J., 1,928..C3 74
Hopewell (Independent City), Va., 17,895....C7, D5 85
Hopewell, W. Va., 1,230....*B4 87
Hopkins, Minn., 11,370....E6 67
Hopkins, co., Ky., 38,458....C2 62
Hopkins, co., Tex., 18,594....C5 84
Hopkinsville, Ky., 19,465....D2 62
Hopkinton, Mass., 2,754....B4, D1 65
Hopland, Calif., 600...C2 50
Hoppo, China, 67,000..G6 67
Hopwood, Pa., 1,615..G2 81
Hoquiam, Wash., 10,762....C2 86
Hordaland, co., Nor., 225,300....*G1 11
Horicon, Wis., 2,996..E5 88
Horine, Mo., 590....C7 69
Hornell, N.Y., 13,907..C3 75
Hornersville, Mo., 752..E7 69
Horni Pocernice, Czech., 7,579....n18 7
Hornsea, Eng., 5,949...D6 4
Hornsey, Eng., 97,885....k12 4
Horqueta, Par., 17,389....D4 29
Horry, co., S.C., 68,247....D10 82
Horse Cave, Ky., 1,780....C4 62
Horseheads, N.Y., 7,207....C4 75
Horsens, Den., 37,261..J3 11
Horsham, Austl., 9,241....G7 25
Horsham, Pa., 4,000.*F10 81
Horta, Az. Is., 8,564...k9 22
Horten, Nor., 13,500....H4, p28 11
Horton, Kans., 2,361..C8 61
Hortonville, Wis., 1,366....D5 88
Hoshiarpur, India, 50,739....B6 20
Hospitalet, Sp., 122,803.B7 8
Hot Spring, co., Ark., 21,893....C2 49
Hot Springs, see Truth or Consequences, N. Mex.
Hot Springs, S. Dak., 4,943....G2 77
Hot Springs, co., Wyo., 6,365....B4 89
Hot Springs [National Park], Ark., 29,212....C2, C6 49
Houghton, Mich., 3,393....A2 66
Houghton, N.Y., 1,200.C2 75
Houghton, Wash., 2,426....D2 86
Houghton, co., Mich., 35,654....B2 66
Houghton Lake Heights, Mich, 1,195....D6 66
Houilles, Fr., 26,370....g9 5
Houlton, Maine, 5,976..B5 64
Houma, La., 22,561....C6, E5 63
Houston, Minn., 1,082.G7 67
Houston, Miss., 2,577..B5 68
Houston, Mo., 1,660..D6 69
Houston, Pa., 1,865...F1 81
Houston, Tex., 938,219 (*1,251,700)....E5, F5 84
Houston, co., Ala., 50,718....D4 46
Houston, co., Ga., 39,154....D3 55
Houston, co., Minn., 16,588....G7 67
Houston, co., Tenn., 4,794....A4 83
Houston, co., Tex., 19,376....D6 84
Houtzdale, Pa., 1,239..E5 81
Hove, Eng., 72,843....E6 4
Howard, Kans., 1,017..E7 61
Howard, S. Dak., 1,208....F8 77
Howard, Wis., 3,485..*D5 88
Howard, co., Ark., 10,878....C2 49
Howard, co., Ind., 69,509....C5 59
Howard, co., Iowa, 12,734....A5 60
Howard, co., Md., 36,152....B4 53

Howard, co., Mo., 10,859....B5 69
Howard, co., Nebr., 6,541....C7 71
Howard, co., Tex., 40,139....C2 84
Howard City, Mich., 1,004....E5 66
Howard Lake, Minn., 1,007....E4 67
Howe, Ind., 550....A7 59
Howell, Mich., 4,861...F7 66
Howell, co., Mo., 22,027....E6 69
Howland, Maine, 1,362....C4 64
Howrah, India, 512,598....D8 20
Hoxie, Ark., 1,886....A5 49
Hoxie, Kans., 1,289...C3 61
Hoya, Ger., 4,300....B4 6
Hoyerswerda, Ger., 24,500....C7 6
Hoyt Lakes, Minn., 3,186....*C6 67
Hradec Kralove, Czech., 55,100....C3 7
Hranice, Czech., 10,800....D4 7
Hrinova, Czech., 6,831.D5 7
Hrubieszow, Pol., 11,300....C7 7
Hsian, China, 5,000....E2 18
Hsichang (Sichang), China, 50,000....F5 17
Hsifeng, China, 33,886....C9 17
Hsinchu, Taiwan, 97,600....G9 17
Hsinmin, China, 35,000....C9 17
Hsipaw, Bur., 5,000..*D10 20
Huacho, Peru, 16,039..D2 31
Huaiyin, China, 77,000....E8 17
Hualein, Taiwan, 29,455....G9 17
Huamantla, Mex., 9,811....n15 34
Huancavelica, Peru, 9,594....D2 31
Huancavelica, dept., Peru, 305,619....D2 31
Huancayo, Peru, 33,790....D2 31
Huanjen, China, 5,000..F2 18
Huánuco, Peru, 15,180.C2 31
Huánuco, dept., Peru, 315,025....C2 31
Huaral, Peru, 5,012...D2 31
Huarás, Peru, 14,250..C2 31
Huatabampo, Mex., 10,030....B3 34
Huatien, China, 35,000....C10 17
Huatusco [de Chicuellar], Mex., 8,673....n15 34
Huauchiango, Mex., 12,053....m14 34
Hubbard, Ohio, 7,137..A7 78
Hubbard, Tex., 1,628..D4 84
Hubbard, co., Minn., 9,962....C4 67
Hubbell, Mich., 1,429..A2 66
Huber Heights, Ohio, 5,000....*C3 78
Hubli, India, 171,326..E6 20
Huddersfield, Eng., 130,302....D6 4
Huddy, Ky., 600....C7 62
Hudiksvall, Swe., 12,000....G7 11
Hudson, Que., Can., 1,671....D3 42
Hudson, Iowa, 1,085..B5 60
Hudson, Mass., 9,666....B4, D1 65
Hudson, Mich., 2,546..G6 66
Hudson, N.H., 3,651...F5 73
Hudson, N.Y., 11,075..C7 75
Hudson, N.C., 1,536...B2 76
Hudson, Ohio, 2,438..A6 78
Hudson, Pa., 900....*B8 81
Hudson, Wis., 4,325..D1 88
Hudson, co., N.J., 610,734....B4 74
Hudson Bay, Sask., Can., 1,601....E4 39
Hudson Falls, N.Y., 7,752....B7 75
Hudson Heights, Que., Can., 1,540....D8 42
Hudsonville, Mich., 2,649....F5 66
Hudspeth, co., Tex., 3,343....F1 84
Hue, Viet., 113,000...B3 19
Huedin, Rom., 5,134..B6 10
Huehuetenango, Guat., 6,187....*D6 34
Huelma, Sp., 7,739...D4 8

Huelva, Sp., 74,384....D2 8
Huelva, prov., Sp., 399,934....*D2 8
Huércal-Overa, Sp., 13,016....D5 8
Huerfano, co., Colo., 7,867....D5 51
Huesca, Sp., 24,377....A5 8
Huesca, prov., Sp., 233,543....*A5 8
Huéscar, Sp., 5,499....D4 8
Hueytown, Ala., 5,997.E4 46
Hughes, Ark., 1,960...C5 49
Hughes, co., Okla., 15,144....B5 79
Hughes, co., S. Dak., 12,725....F6 77
Hughes Springs, Tex., 1,813....*C5 84
Hughestown, Pa., 1,615....*D10 81
Hughesville, Pa., 2,218....D8 81
Hughson, Calif., 1,898....*D3 50
Hugo, Colo., 811....B7 51
Hugo, Okla., 6,287....C6 79
Hugoton, Kans., 2,912.E2 61
Huguley, Ala., 2,189..*C4 46
Huhehot (Kweisui) China 314,000....C7 17
Huichon, Kor., 14,619.F3 18
Huila, dept., Col., 330,270....C2 32
Huixtla, Mex., 12,344..D6 34
Hukou, China, 5,000...F8 17
Hulan, China, 60,000..B10 17
Hulen, Ky., 500....D6 62
Hull, Que., Can., 56,929....D2 42
Hull, Eng., 303,268....D6 4
Hull, Iowa, 1,289....A1 60
Hull, Mass., 7,055. B6, D3 65
Hull, co., Que., Can., 84,803....D2 42
Hulmeville, Pa., 968.*F12 81
Hulwân, Eg., U.A.R., 8,000....H8 14
Humacao, P.R., 8,005....m14 35
Humber, dist., Newf., Can., 20,560....D3 44
Humble, Tex., 1,711....E5, F5 84
Humboldt, Sask., Can., 3,245....E3 39
Humboldt, Iowa, 4,031.B3 60
Humboldt, Kans., 2,285....E8 61
Humboldt, Nebr., 1,322....D10 71
Humboldt, Tenn., 8,482....B3 83
Humboldt, co., Calif., 104,892....B2 50
Humboldt, co., Iowa, 13,156....B3 60
Humboldt, co., Nev., 5,708....A2 72
Humenné, Czech., 11,100....D6 7
Humeston, Iowa, 638..D4 60
Hummelstown, Pa., 4,474....*F8 81
Humphreys, co., Miss., 19,093....B3 68
Humphreys, co., Tenn., 11,511....A4 83
Humpolec, Czech., 5,083....D3 7
Hunan, prov., China, 36,220,000....F7 17
Hunchun, China, 25,000....C11 17
Hunedoara, Rom., 36,498....C6 10
Hungary, country, Eur., 9,976,530....B4 10
Hungnam, Kor., 143,600....G3 18
Hunt, co., Tex., 39,399....C4 84
Hunterdon, co., N.J., 54,107....B3 74
Huntersville, N.C., 1,004....B3 76
Huntingburg, Ind., 4,146....H4 59
Huntingdon, Que., Can., 3,134....D3 42
Huntingdon, Pa., 7,234.F5 81
Huntingdon, Tenn., 2,119....A3 83
Huntingdon, co., Que., Can., 14,752....D3 42
Huntingdon, co., Eng., 79,879....*D7 4
Huntingdon, co., Pa., 39,457....F5 81
Huntington, Ind., 16,185....C7 59

Huntington, Mass., 900....B2 65
Huntington, N.J., 1,879....*B2 74
Huntington (P.O.), N.Y., 11,255....D3, E7 75
Huntington, Tex., 1,009....D5 84
Huntington, Utah, 787.B6 72
Huntington, W. Va., 83,627 (*231,100)....C2 87
Huntington, co., Ind., 33,814....C6 59
Huntington Bay, N.Y., 1,267....*G3 52
Huntington Beach, Calif., 11,492....F3 50
Huntington Beach, N.Y., 3,789....*D3 75
Huntington Park, Calif., 29,920....F2 50
Huntington Station, N.Y., 23,438....F3 52
Huntington Woods, Mich., 8,746....A7 66
Huntingtown, Md., 165....C4 53
Huntley, Ill., 1,143...A5 58
Huntsville, Ala., 72,365....A3 46
Huntsville, Ark., 1,050.A2 49
Huntsville, Ont., Can., 3,189....B5 41
Huntsville, Mo., 1,526..B5 69
Huntsville, Tex., 11,999....D5 84
Hupeh, prov., China, 30,790,000....E7 17
Hurley, N. Mex., 1,851....C4 48
Hurley, Wis., 2,763...B3 88
Hurlock, Md., 1,035...C6 53
Huron, Calif., 1,269..*D3 50
Huron, Ohio, 5,197...A5 78
Huron, S. Dak., 14,180....F7 77
Huron, co., Ont., Can., 53,805....D3 41
Huron, co., Mich., 34,006....E7 66
Huron, co., Ohio, 47,326....A5 78
Hurricane, Utah, 1,251.C5 72
Hurricane, W. Va., 1,970....C2 87
Hurst, Ill., 863....F4 58
Hurst, Tex., 10,165...*C4 84
Hurtsboro, Ala., 1,056..C4 46
Huşi, Rom., 18,055...B9 10
Huskerville, Nebr., 1,000....D9 71
Huskvarna, Swe., 13,800....I6 11
Husum, Ger., 23,800...A4 6
Hutchins, Tex., 1,100..B5 84
Hutchinson, Kans., 37,574....A4, D6 61
Hutchinson, Minn., 6,207....F4 67
Hutchinson, co., S. Dak., 11,085....G8 77
Hutchinson, co., Tex., 34,419....B2 84
Huttig, Ark., 936....D3 49
Huy, Bel., 13,447....B6 5
Hvittingfoss, Nor., 576....p28 11
Hwaining, see Anking, China
Hyannis, Mass., 5,139..C7 65
Hyattsville, Md., 15,168....C1, C4 53
Hybla Valley, Va., 1,500....*C5 85
Hyde, co., N.C., 5,765....B7 76
Hyde, co., S. Dak., 2,602....F6 77
Hyde Park, N.Y., 1,979....D7 75
Hyde Park, Pa., 2,500....*F10 81
Hyde Villa, Pa., 1,300....*F10 81
Hyderabad, India, 1,085,722....E6 20
Hyderabad, Pak., 420,000 (*434,537)....C4 20
Hyères, Fr., 18,671...F7 5
Hymera, Ind., 1,015...F3 59
Hyndman, Pa., 1,124..G4 81
Hyogo, pref., Jap., 3,906,487....*I7 18
Hyopchon, Kor., 7,000....I4 18
Hyrum, Utah, 1,728..A6 72
Hyrynsalmi, Fin., 1,300....E13 11
Hythe, Alta., Can., 449.B1 38
Hythe, Eng., 10,026...E7 4

Iaeger, W. Va., 930....D3 87
Iaşi, Rom., 94,075.....B8 10
Iba, Phil., 3,064......*B5 19
Ibadan, Nig., 459,196..G5 22
Ibagué, Col., 65,500....C2 32
Ibaraki, pref., Jap.,
   2,047,024........*H10 18
Ibarra, Ec., 14,221....A2 31
Ibb, Yemen, 25,000....G3 15
Iberia, par., La.,
   51,657.............E4 63
Iberville, Que., Can.,
   7,588.............D4 42
Iberville, co., Que., Can.,
   18,080.............D4 42
Iberville, par., La.,
   29,939.............D4 63
Ibitinga, Braz., 8,881..C3 30
Ibiza, Sp., 11,259.....C6 8
Ica, Peru, 25,273.....D2 31
Ica, dept., Peru,
   158,783...........D2 31
Iceland, country, Eur.,
   180,058..........n23 11
Ichang, China, 81,000..E7 17
Ichikawa, Jap.,
   157,301..........N18 18
Ichinomiya, Jap.,
   182,984..........n15 18
Ichinoseki, Jap.,
   25,700..........G10 18
Ichnya, Sov. Un.,
   10,000............F9 12
Ida, co., Iowa, 10,269..B2 60
Idabel, Okla., 4,967....D7 79
Ida Grove, Iowa,
   2,265.............B2 60
Idaho, co., Idaho,
   13,542............D3 57
Idaho, state, U.S.,
   667,191........... 57
Idaho Falls, Idaho,
   33,161............F6 57
Idaho Springs, Colo.,
   1,480.............B5 51
Idalou, Tex., 1,274.....C2 84
Idamay, W. Va.,
   800...........A7, B4 87
Idanha-a-Nova, Port.,
   4,459.............C2 8
Idrija, Yugo., 6,024....B2 10
Ieper, Bel., 18,121.....B5 5
Ierapetra, Grc., 5,521..E5 14
Iesi, It., 21,900.......C4 9
Ifni, Sp. dep., Afr.,
   52,000............C2 22
Igarapava, Braz.,
   9,083.............C3 30
Igarka, Sov. Un.,
   33,800..........C11 13
Iğdir, Tur., 12,700....C15 14
Ighil Izane, Alg.,
   27,120............A5 22
Iglesias, It., 28,004....E2 9
Igloo, S. Dak., 750....G2 77
Igualada, Sp., 19,866..B6 8
Iguatu, Braz., 16,540..D7 27
Ihsing, China, 93,000..*E8 17
Iida, Jap., 44,300..I8, n16 18
Iisalmi, Fin., 6,000....F12 11
Ijebu Ode, Nig.,
   27,558............G5 22
Ijuí, Braz., 19,671.....D2 30
Ikeda, Jap., 59,688...D14 18
Ikhtiman, Bul., 6,516..D6 11
Ilagan, Phil., 7,436....B6 19
Ilan, Taiwan, 38,910..*G9 17
Ilan (Sanhsing), China,
   40,000..........B10 17
Ile-de-France, former
   prov., Fr., 7,733,000..C5 5
Ile Perrot, Que., Can.,
   3,106.............D8 42
Ilford, Eng., 178,210..k13 4
Ilfracombe, Eng.,
   8,701.............E4 4
Ilgin, Tur., 3,100.....C8 14
Ilhavo, Port., 6,969...B1 8
Ilhéus, Braz., 45,712..E7 27
Ilia, prov., Grc.,
   188,861..........*D3 14
Ilinskaya, Sov. Un.,
   10,000...........I13 12
Ilion, N.Y., 10,199....B5 75
Illapel, Chile, 8,266....A2 28
Ille-et-Vilaine, dept., Fr.,
   614,268..........*C3 5
Illinois, state, U.S.,
   10,081,158......... 58
Illiopolis, Ill., 995....D4 58
Illmenau, Ger., 17,700..C5 6
Illmo, Mo., 1,174....D8 69
Illora, Sp., 13,458....D4 8
Ilocos Norte, prov., Phil.,
   287,000..........*B6 19
Ilocos Sur, prov., Phil.,
   338,600..........*B6 19
Iloilo, Phil., 120,000...C6 19

Iloilo, prov., Phil.,
   966,100...........*C6 19
Ilorin, Nig., 40,994.....G5 22
Ilovaysk, Sov. Un.,
   10,000............r21 12
Imabari, Jap., 81,000...I6 18
Iman, Sov. Un.,
   18,000...........E16 13
Imazu, Jap., 4,300....n15 18
Imbabura, prov., Ec.,
   157,356...........A2 31
Imlay City, Mich.,
   1,968.............E7 66
Immenstadt, Ger.,
   10,000............E5 6
Immokalee, Fla.,
   3,224.............F5 54
Imola, It., 27,300.....B3 9
Imperia, It., 34,995....C2 9
Imperial, Calif., 3,007..F6 50
Imperial, Nebr., 1,423..D4 71
Imperial, Pa., 2,000....B5 81
Imperial, co., Calif.,
   72,105............F6 50
Imperial Beach, Calif.,
   17,773...........*F5 50
Imperoyal, N.S., Can.,
   490..............E6 43
Imphal, India,
   67,717............D9 20
Ina, Jap., 18,300.....n16 18
Inatori, Jap., 9,100....o18 18
Inca, Sp., 13,816......C7 8
Inchon, Kor., 402,000..H3 18
Indaw, Bur., 2,138....D10 20
Independence, Calif.,
   950..............D4 50
Independence, Iowa,
   5,498.............B6 60
Independence, Kans.,
   11,222............E8 61
Independence, La.,
   1,941.............D5 63
Independence, Minn.,
   1,446...........*F5 67
Independence, Mo.,
   62,328.........B3, E2 69
Independence, Ohio,
   6,868.............B2 78
Independence, Oreg.,
   1,930..........C1, C3 80
Independence, Wis.,
   954..............D2 88
Independence, co., Ark.,
   20,048............B4 49
Independence Hill, Ind.,
   1,824...........*B3 59
India, country, Asia,
   439,072,893........D6 20
Indialantic, Fla.,
   1,653...........*D6 54
Indiana, Pa., 13,005...E3 81
Indiana, co., Pa.,
   75,366............E3 81
Indiana, state, U.S.,
   4,662,498.......... 59
Indianapolis, Ind., 476,258
   (*806,900)......E5, H8 59
Indian Head, Sask., Can.,
   1,802.............G4 39
Indian Head, Md., 780.C3 53
Indian Hill, Ohio,
   4,526.............D2 78
Indianola, Iowa, 7,062..C4 60
Indianola, Miss., 6,714.B3 68
Indianola, Pa., 1,000..*E2 81
Indian River, co., Fla.,
   25,309............E6 54
Indian Rocks Beach, Fla.,
   1,940.............E1 54
Indiantown, Fla.,
   1,411.............E6 54
Indio, Calif., 9,745.....F5 50
Indochina, reg., Asia,
   28,000,000.........B3 19
Indonesia, country, Asia,
   95,189,000.........F6 19
Indore, India,
   394,941...........D6 20
Indre, dept., Fr.,
   251,432..........*D4 5
Indre-et-Loire, dept., Fr.,
   395,210..........*D4 5
Industrial, S.C., 1,000..B6 82
Industrial City, Ala.,
   1,000...........*E4 46
Industry, Pa., 2,338...*E2 81
Infantes, Sp., 9,909...C4 8
Infiesto, Sp., 1,650....A3 8
Ingalls Park, Ill.,
   6,890...........*B6 58
Ingersoll, Ont., Can.,
   6,874.............D4 41
Ingham, co., Mich.,
   211,296...........F6 66
Ingleside, Nebr., 400..D7 71
Ingleside, Tex., 3,022...F4 84

Inglewood, Calif.,
   63,390............F2 50
Inglewood, Nebr.,
   805..........C9, D2 71
Inglewood, Tenn.,
   26,527...........*A5 83
Ingolstadt, Ger.,
   53,400............D5 6
Ingomar, Pa., 1,500....A5 81
Ingram, Pa., 4,730....B5 81
Inhambane, Moz.,
   10,000............E7 24
Inharrime, Moz.,
   10,000............E7 24
Inkerman, Pa., 1,000..*B8 81
Inkster, Mich., 39,097..A7 66
Inman, S.C., 1,714.....A3 82
Inman Mills, S.C.,
   1,769...........*A3 82
Inner Mongolia, prov.,
   China, 9,200,000....C8 17
Innisfail, Alta., Can.,
   2,270.............C4 38
Innsbruck, Aus.,
   100,695...........E5 6
Inowroclaw, Pol.,
   47,000............B5 7
Insein, Bur., 27,030...E10 20
Institute, W. Va.,
   2,500.............C3 87
Intercity, Wash.,
   1,475...........*B3 86
Interlaken, N.J.,
   1,168...........*C4 74
International Falls, Minn.,
   6,778.............B5 67
Invercargill, N.Z.,
   29,094 (*35,100)....Q12 26
Inverell, Austl., 8,208..E9 25
Inverness, N.S., Can.,
   2,109.............C8 43
Inverness, Fla., 1,878..D4 54
Inverness, Ill., 1,110..*E2 58
Inverness, Miss., 1,039.B3 68
Inverness, Scot.,
   29,773............B4 4
Inverness, co., N.S., Can.,
   18,718............C8 43
Inverness, co., Scot.,
   83,425...........*B4 4
Inwood, N.Y., 10,362..E2 75
Inyo, co., Calif.,
   11,684............D5 50
Ioannina, Grc.,
   34,997............C3 14
Ioannina, prov., Grc.,
   155,326..........*C3 14
Iola, Kans., 6,885.....E8 61
Ione, Calif., 1,118....C3 50
Ionia, Mich., 6,754....F5 66
Ionia, co., Mich.,
   43,132............F5 66
Iosco, co., Mich.,
   16,505............D7 66
Iota, La., 1,245.......D3 63
Iowa, La., 1,857.......D2 63
Iowa, co., Iowa,
   16,396............C5 60
Iowa, co., Wis.,
   19,631............E3 88
Iowa, state, U.S.,
   2,757,537......... 60
Iowa City, Iowa,
   33,443............C6 60
Iowa Falls, Iowa,
   5,565.............B4 60
Iowa Park, Tex., 3,295.C3 84
Ipameri, Braz., 8,987..B3 30
Ipiales, Col., 11,569...C2 32
Ipin, China, 177,500...F5 17
Ipoh, Mala., 125,770..E2 19
Ipswich, Austl., 48,679.E9 25
Ipswich, Eng., 117,325.D7 4
Ipswich, Mass., 5,400..A6 65
Ipswich, S. Dak., 1,131.E6 77
Iquique, Chile, 50,000..D2 29
Iquitos, Peru, 40,408..B3 31
Iraan, Tex., 1,255.....D2 84
Iraklion, Grc., 63,458..E5 14
Iraklion, prov., Grc.,
   208,374..........*E5 14
Iran (Persia), country,
   Asia, 20,042,000.....F8 16
Irapuato, Mex.,
   83,555..........C4, m13 34
Iraq, country, Asia,
   5,047,635..........C3 15
Irbid, Jordan,
   23,157.........B3, g5 15
Irbil, Iraq, 34,313....D15 14
Iredell, co., N.C.,
   62,526............B3 76
Ireland (Eire), country,
   Eur., 2,818,341.....D3 4
Iri, Kor., 53,400......I3 18
Iringa, Tan., 9,587....B7 24
Irion, co., Tex., 1,183..D2 84

Irkutsk, Sov. Un.,
   380,000..........D13 13
Iron, co., Mich.,
   17,184............B2 66
Iron, co., Mo., 8,041...D3 69
Iron, co., Utah, 10,795..C5 72
Iron, co., Wis., 7,830..B3 88
Irondale, Ala., 3,501...E5 46
Irondale, Ohio, 705....B7 78
Irondequoit, N.Y.,
   55,337............B3 75
Iron Mountain, Mich.,
   9,299.............C2 66
Iron River, Mich.,
   3,754.............B2 66
Iron River, Wis., 900..B2 88
Ironton, Mo., 1,310....D7 69
Ironton, Ohio, 15,745..D5 78
Ironwood, Mich.,
   10,265............A5 66
Iroquois, Ont., Can.,
   1,136.............C9 41
Iroquois, co., Ill.,
   33,562............C6 88
Iroquois Falls, Ont., Can.,
   1,681.............E9 41
Irosin, Phil., 7,394....*C6 19
Irún, Sp., 29,814.....A5 8
Irvine, Ky., 2,955.....C6 62
Irvine, Scot., 16,910...C4 4
Irving, Tex., 45,985...B5 84
Irvington, Ky., 1,190..D3 62
Irvington, N.J., 59,379.E4 74
Irvington, N.Y., 5,494.D1 75
Irvona, Pa., 781.......E4 81
Irwin, Pa., 4,270......F2 81
Irwin, S.C., 1,113.....*B6 82
Irwin, co., Ga., 9,211..E3 55
Irwindale, Calif.,
   1,518...........*E4 50
Isabela, prov., Phil.,
   442,800..........*D6 19
Isabella, P.R.,
   7,302...........*m13 35
Isabella, Pa., 900.....G2 81
Isabella, Tenn., 415...D9 83
Isabella, co., Mich.,
   35,348............E6 66
Isahaya, Jap., 31,900...J5 18
Isanti, co., Minn.,
   13,530............E5 67
Iselin, N.J., 14,000....B4 74
Iselin, Pa., 500.......E3 81
Isère, dept., Fr.,
   729,789..........*E6 5
Isernia, It., 8,600....D5 9
Iseyin, Nig., 49,690...G5 22
Isezaki, Jap.,
   54,500.......H9, m18 18
Ishikawa, pref., Jap.,
   973,418..........*H8 18
Ishim, Sov. Un.,
   39,000............D9 13
Ishimbay, Sov. Un.,
   53,500...........*D8 13
Ishinomaki, Jap.,
   83,947...........G10 18
Ishioka, Jap., 17,800..m19 18
Ishpeming, Mich.,
   8,857.............B3 66
Isigny-sur-Mer, Fr.,
   2,391.............C3 5
Iskenderun (Alexandretta),
   Tur., 63,700......D11 14
Iskilip, Tur.,
   12,300..........B10 14
Isla Cristina, Sp.,
   8,276.............D2 8
Island, co., Wash.,
   19,638............A3 86
Island Heights, N.J.,
   1,150.............D4 74
Island Lake, Ill.,
   1,639...........*E2 58
Island Park, N.Y.,
   3,846...........*E3 75
Island Pont, Vt.,
   1,319.............B4 73
Isle Maligne, Que., Can.,
   2,070.............A6 42
Isle of Ely, co., Eng.,
   89,112...........*D7 4
Isle of Hope, Ga.,
   1,500...........*D6 55
Isle of Man, Br. dep.,
   Eur., 48,151........C4 4
Isle of Palms, S.C.,
   1,186.............F3 82
Isle of Wight, co., Eng.,
   95,479...........*E6 4
Isle of Wight, co., Va.,
   17,164............E6 85
Isle Royale, isl., Mich..A2 66
Isle Verte, Que., Can.,
   1,517.............A8 42
Isleton, Calif.,
   1,039.........B6, C3 50

Islington, Ont., Can.,
2,550................E6   41
Islington, Mass., 4,500.D2   65
Islip, N.Y., 8,000.....G4   75
Islip Terrace, N.Y.,
3,000.............*G4   75
Isola Capo Rizzuto, It.,
9,218..............E6   9
Isparta, Tur., 36,200...D8   14
Israel, country, Asia,
2,170,082...........C2   15
Issaquah, Wash., 1,870.B3   86
Issaquena, co., Miss.,
3,576..............C2   68
Issoire, Fr., 10,444.....E5   5
Issoudun, Fr., 13,900..D4   5
Issy [-les-Moulineaux],
Fr., 51,776........g10   5
Istanbul (Constantinople),
Tur., 1,459,500.....B7   14
Itá, Par., 18,777......E4   29
Itabaiana, Braz.,
11,847............*D7   27
Itabaiana, Braz.,
11,050............*E7   27
Itaberaba, Braz.,
8,555.............*E6   27
Itabira, Braz., 15,539..B4   30
Itabuna, Braz., 54,268..E7   27

Itajaí, Braz., 38,889...D3   30
Itajubá, Braz., 31,262..C3   30
Italy, Tex., 1,183......C4   84
Italy, country, Eur.,
50,623,569...........9
Itami, Jap., 86,455....o14   18
Itaperuna, Braz.,
18,095.............C4   30
Itapetininga, Braz.,
29,468.........C3, m7   30
Itapevá, Braz.,
13,510.............C3   30
Itápolis, Braz., 7,430...k7   30
Itapúa, dept., Par.,
111,424............E4   29
Itaqui, Braz., 13,223...D1   30
Itararè, Braz., 12,812..C3   30
Itasca, Ill., 3,564......E2   58
Itasca, Tex., 1,383....C4   84
Itasca, co., Minn.,
38,006.............C5   67
Itatiba, Braz., 12,336..m8   30
Itaúna, Braz., 22,319..C4   30
Itawamba, co., Miss.,
15,080.............A5   68
Ithaca, Mich., 2,611...E6   66
Ithaca, N.Y., 28,799...C4   75
Ito, Jap., 43,600.....o18   18

Itta Bena, Miss.,
1,914.............B3   68
Itú, Braz.,
23,435.........C3, m8   30
Ituiutaba, Braz.,
29,724.............B3   30
Itung, China, 5,000...C10   17
Itzehoe, Ger., 36,100..B4   6
Iuka, Miss., 2,010....A5   68
Iva, S.C., 1,357.......C2   82
Ivanhoe, Calif.,
1,616.............*D4   50
Ivano-Frankovsk, Sov.
Un., 72,000.........G5   12
Ivanovka, Sov. Un.,
5,000.............q21   12
Ivanovo, Sov. Un.,
352,000...........C13   12
Ivanteyevka, Sov. Un.,
10,000............n17   12
Ivory Coast, country,
Afr., 2,490,000....G3   22
Ivoryton, Conn., 950..D7   52
Ivrea, It., 23,723.....B1   9
Ivry-sur-Seine, Fr.,
53,406............g10   5
Ivywild, Colo., 11,065..C6   51
Iwakuni, Jap.,
100,346...........I6   18

Iwamisawa, Jap.,
37,800............E10   18
Iwamurada, Jap.,
7,600.............m17   18
Iwanai, Jap., 21,100..E10   18
Iwate, pref., Jap.,
1,448,517.........*G10   18
Iwaya, Jap., 13,700..o14   18
Iwo, Nig., 100,006.....G5   22
Ixtacalco, Mex., 10,896.h9   34
Ixtapalapa, Mex.,
17,372.............h9   34
Izamal, Mex., 8,675...C7   34
Izard, co., Ark., 6,766..A4   49
Izhevsk, Sov. Un.,
312,000............D8   13
Izmail, Sov. Un.,
52,000.............I7   12
Izmir (Smyrna), Tur.,
370,900............C6   14
Izmit (Kocaeli), Tur.,
73,700.............B7   14
Izúcar de Matamoros,
Mex., 16,175......n14   34
Izuhara, Jap., 15,300..I4   18
Izumo, Jap., 34,500...I6   18
Izyum, Sov. Un.,
34,000............G11   12

J

Jabalpur, India, 295,375
(*367,014).........D6   20
Jaboatão, Braz.,
33,963............*D7   27
Jaboticabal, Braz.,
20,231.........C3, k7   30
Jaca, Sp., 9,856......A5   8
Jacareí, Braz., 28,131..m9   30
Jacarèzinho, Braz.,
14,813.............C3   30
Jachymov, Czech.,
6,806..............C2   7
Jacinto City, Tex.,
9,547..............F5   84
Jack, co., Tex., 7,418..C3   84
Jacksboro, Tex., 3,816..C3   84
Jackson, Ala., 4,959...D2   46
Jackson, Calif., 1,852..C3   50
Jackson, Ga., 2,545....C3   55
Jackson, Ky., 1,852....C6   62
Jackson, La., 1,824....D4   63
Jackson, Mich., 50,720
(*121,400).........F6   66
Jackson, Minn., 3,370..G4   67
Jackson, Miss., 144,422
(*191,200).........C3   68
Jackson, Mo., 4,875...D8   69
Jackson, Ohio, 6,980..C5   78
Jackson, S.C., 1,746...E4   82
Jackson, Tenn., 34,376.B3   83
Jackson, Wyo., 1,437..B2   89
Jackson, co., Ala.,
36,681.............A3   46
Jackson, co., Ark.,
22,843.............B4   49
Jackson, co., Colo.,
1,758.............A4   51
Jackson, co., Fla.,
36,208.............B1   54
Jackson, co., Ga.,
18,499.............B3   55
Jackson, co., Ill.,
42,151.............F4   58
Jackson, co., Ind.,
30,556.............G5   59
Jackson, co., Iowa,
20,754.............B7   60
Jackson, co., Kans.,
10,309.............C8   61
Jackson, co., Ky.,
10,677.............C5   62
Jackson, co., Mich.,
131,994............F6   66
Jackson, co., Minn.,
15,501.............G3   67
Jackson, co., Miss.,
55,522.............E5   68
Jackson, co., Mo.,
622,732............C3   69
Jackson, co., N.C.,
17,780.............D3   76
Jackson, co., Ohio,
29,372.............C5   78
Jackson, co., Okla.,
29,736.............C2   79
Jackson, co., Oreg.,
73,962.............E4   80
Jackson, co., S. Dak.,
1,985.............G4   77
Jackson, co., Tenn.,
9,233.............C8   83
Jackson, co., Tex.,
14,040.............E4   84
Jackson, co., W. Va.,
18,541.............C3   87
Jackson, co., Wis.,
15,151.............D3   88

Jackson, par., La.,
15,828.............B3   63
Jackson Center, Ohio,
980..............B3   78
Jacksonville, Ala.,
5,678.............B4   46
Jacksonville, Ark.,
14,488.........C3, D6   49
Jacksonville, Fla., 201,030
(*456,700).....B5, B6   54
Jacksonville, Ill.,
21,690.............D3   58
Jacksonville, N.C.,
13,491.............C6   76
Jacksonville, Oreg.,
1,172.............E4   80
Jacksonville, Tex.,
9,590.............D5   84
Jacksonville Beach, Fla.,
12,049.........B5, B6   54
Jacmel, Hai., 8,545...F7   35
Jacobabad, Pak.,
22,835.............C4   20
Jacobina, Braz., 12,373.D2   34
Jacomino, Cuba, 6,121.h12   35
Jacques Cartier, Que.,
Can., 40,807.......*D4   42
Jacques Cartier, co., Que.,
Can., 1,747,696.....D8   42
Jadotville, Con. L.,
74,500.............C5   24
Jaén, Sp., 64,917......D4   8
Jaén, prov., Sp.,
736,391...........*D4   8
Jaffna, Cey., 76,664...G7   20
Jaffrey, N.H., 1,648...F3   73
Jaguarão, Braz.,
12,336.............E2   30
Jaipur, India, 403,444..C6   20
Jaisalmer, India, 8,362.C5   20
Jajce, Yugo., 6,839....C3   10
Jajpur, India, 13,802..D8   20
Jakarta, see Djakarta,
Indon.
Jakobstad, Fin., 7,378.F10   11
Jal, N. Mex., 3,051....C7   48
Jalalabad, Afg., 14,756.B5   20
Jalapa, Guat., 6,610...*F6   34
Jalapa Enríquez, Mex.,
51,166........D5, n15   34
Jalgaon, India, 80,351..D6   20
Jalisco, state, Mex.,
2,402,884.....C4, m12   34
Jalna, India, 67,158....E6   20
Jamaica, country, N.A.,
1,613,148...........F5   35
Jamesburg, N.J., 2,853.C4   74
James City, N.C.,
1,474.............B6   76
James City, co., Va.,
11,539.............D6   85
Jamestown, Calif., 900.D3   50
Jamestown, Ont., Can.,
4,040..............E8   41
Jamestown, Ky., 792..D4   62
Jamestown, N.Y.,
41,818.............C1   75
Jamestown, N.C.,
1,247.............B4   76
Jamestown, N. Dak.,
15,163.............D7   77
Jamestown, Ohio,
1,730.............C4   78
Jamestown, Pa., 897..D1   81
Jamestown, R.I.,
2,267.............D11   52
Jamestown, Tenn.,
1,727.............C9   83

Jamesville, N.Y.,
1,000.............*C4   75
Jammu, India, 102,738.B5   20
Jammu and Kashmir, dis-
puted reg., India, Pak.,
3,560,976..........B6   20
Jamnagar, India,
139,692............D5   20
Jamshedpur, India,
291,791............D8   20
Jämtland, co., Swe.,
137,600...........*F6   11
Janesville, Minn.,
1,426.............F5   67
Janesville, Wis., 35,164.F4   88
Janin, Jordan, 12,663..B3   15
Janoshalma, Hung.,
10,767.............B4   10
Janow Lubelski, Pol.,
3,793.............C7   7
Januária, Braz., 9,741.B4   30
Jaoho (Tuanshantzu),
China, 30,000......B11   17
Japan, country, Asia,
83,408,026.........I6   18
Jaral [del Progreso], Mex.,
7,040............m13   34
Jarales, N. Mex., 200..B5   48
Jarocin, Pol., 19,100...C4   7
Jaroslaw, Pol., 26,000..C7   7
Jasonville, Ind., 2,436..F3   59
Jasper, Ala., 10,799....B2   46
Jasper, Alta., Can.,
2,360.............C1   38
Jasper, Fla., 2,103....B4   54
Jasper, Ga., 1,036.....B2   55
Jasper, Ind., 7,910....H4   59
Jasper, Tenn., 1,450...D8   83
Jasper, Tex., 4,889....D6   84
Jasper, co., Ga., 6,135..C3   55
Jasper, co., Ill., 11,346.D5   58
Jasper, co., Ind., 18,842.B3   59
Jasper, co., Iowa,
35,282.............C4   60
Jasper, co., Miss.,
16,909.............C4   68
Jasper, co., Mo.,
78,863.............D3   69
Jasper, co., S.C.,
12,237.............G5   82
Jasper, co., Tex.,
22,100.............D6   84
Jasper Place, Alta., Can.,
30,530............*C4   38
Jaszapati, Hung., 9,423.B5   10
Jaszbereny, Hung.,
22,284.............B4   10
Játiva, Sp., 19,896.....C5   8
Jau, Braz., 31,229.C3, m7   30
Jauja, Peru, 8,276....D2   31
Jaunpur, India, 61,851.C7   20
Java, isl., Indon.......G3   19
Jawor, Pol., 11,900....C4   7
Jaworzno, Pol., 53,500.g10   7
Jay, Okla., 1,120......A7   79
Jay, co., Ind., 22,572..D7   59
Jeanerette, La., 5,568..E4   63
Jeannette, Pa., 16,565..F2   81
Jedrzejow, Pol., 12,000.C6   7
Jeff, Ky., 500.........C6   62
Jeff Davis, co., Ga.,
8,914.............E4   55
Jeff Davis, co., Tex.,
1,582.............F2   84
Jefferson, Ga., 1,746...B3   55
Jefferson, Iowa, 4,570..B3   60
Jefferson, La., 35,000.*E5   63
Jefferson, Ohio, 2,116..A7   78

Jefferson, Pa., 8,280...*F2   81
Jefferson, Tex., 3,082..C5   84
Jefferson, Wis., 4,548..E5   88
Jefferson, co., Ala.,
634,864............B3   46
Jefferson, co., Ark.,
81,373.............C3   49
Jefferson, co., Colo.,
127,520............B5   51
Jefferson, co., Fla.,
9,543.............B3   54
Jefferson, co., Ga.,
17,468.............C4   55
Jefferson, co., Idaho,
11,672.............F6   57
Jefferson, co., Ill.,
32,315.............E5   58
Jefferson, co., Ind.,
24,061.............G7   59
Jefferson, co., Iowa,
15,818.............C6   60
Jefferson, co., Kans.,
11,252.............C8   61
Jefferson, co., Ky.,
610,947............B4   62
Jefferson, co., Miss.,
10,142.............D2   68
Jefferson, co., Mo.,
66,377.............C7   69
Jefferson, co., Mont.,
4,297.............D4   70
Jefferson, co., Nebr.,
11,620.............D8   71
Jefferson, co., N.Y.,
87,835.............A5   75
Jefferson, co., Ohio,
99,201.............B7   78
Jefferson, co., Okla.,
8,192.............C4   79
Jefferson, co., Oreg.,
7,130.............C5   80
Jefferson, co., Pa.,
46,792.............D3   81
Jefferson, co., Tenn.,
21,493............C10   83
Jefferson, co., Tex.,
245,659............E5   84
Jefferson, co., Wash.,
9,639.............B2   86
Jefferson, co., W. Va.,
18,665.............B7   87
Jefferson, co., Wis.,
50,094.............E5   88
Jefferson, par., La.,
208,769............E5   63
Jefferson City, Mo.,
28,228.............C5   69
Jefferson City, Tenn.,
4,550............C10   83
Jefferson Davis, co., Miss.,
13,540.............D4   68
Jefferson Davis, par., La.,
29,825.............D3   63
Jeffersontown, Ky.,
3,431.........A4, B4   62
Jefferson Village, Va.,
2,000.............*B5   85
Jeffersonville, Ga.,
1,013.............D3   55
Jeffersonville, Ind.,
19,522.............H6   59
Jeffersonville, Ky., 500.C6   62
Jeffersonville, Ohio,
897..............C4   78
Jekabpils, Sov. Un.,
10,000.............C5   12
Jelenia Gora, Pol.,
50,000.............C3   7

Jelgava, Sov. Un.,
 35,000...........C4 12
Jellico, Tenn., 2,210....C9 83
Jemison, Ala., 977.....C3 46
Jena, Ger., 81,400.....C5 6
Jena, La., 2,098......C3 63
Jenison, Mich., 2,000..*F4 66
Jenkinjones, W. Va.,
 300.............*D3 87
Jenkins, Ky., 3,202....C7 62
Jenkins, co., Ga., 9,148.D5 55
Jenkinsville, S.C., 500..C5 82
Jenkintown, Pa.,
 5,017.........F11, A11 81
Jenks, Okla., 1,734.....A6 79
Jenners, Pa., 900.....F3 81
Jennings, La., 11,887..D3 63
Jennings, Mo., 19,965..A8 69
Jennings, co., Ind.,
 17,267...........G6 59
Jennings Lodge, Oreg.,
 1,000...........*B4 80
Jequié, Braz., 40,158..*E6 27
Jerauld, co., S. Dak.,
 4,048...........F7 77
Jérémie, Hai., 11,138..F6 35
Jerez de la Frontera, Sp.,
 97,500...........D2 8
Jerez de los Caballeros,
 Sp., 12,446........C2 8
Jericho, N.Y., 10,795..F2 75
Jericho, Va., 2,300....*E6 85
Jermyn, Pa., 2,568....C10 81
Jerome, Ariz., 243.....B2 48
Jerome, Idaho, 4,761..G4 57
Jerome, Ill., 1,666...*D4 58
Jerome, Pa., 1,241....F4 81
Jerome, co., Idaho,
 11,712...........G4 57
Jersey, Br. dep., Eur.,
 63,300...........F5 4
Jersey, co., Ill., 17,023.D3 58
Jersey City, N.J.,
 276,101.........B4, E5 74
Jersey Shore, Pa.,
 5,613...........D7 81
Jerseyville, Ill., 7,420..D3 58
Jerusalem, Isr., 166,301
 (*240,000).......C3, h5 15
Jerusalem, Jordan,
 46,713..........C3, h5 15
Jeseník, Czech., 5,873..C4 7
Jessamine, co., Ky.,
 13,625...........C5 62
Jesselton, Mala.,
 5,000...........D5 19
Jessup (Winton), Pa.,
 5,456...........A9 81
Jesup, Ga., 7,304.....E5 55
Jesup, Iowa, 1,488....B5 60
Jesús María, Arg.,
 6,284...........A4 28
Jetmore, Kans., 1,028..D4 61
Jever, Ger., 9,400.....B3 6
Jewell, Iowa, 1,113...B4 60
Jewell, co., Kans.,
 7,217...........C5 61
Jewell Ridge, Va., 500..B3 85
Jewett, Ohio, 925.....B6 78
Jewett City, Conn.,
 3,608...........C9 52
Jeypore, India, 25,291.E7 20
Jhalrapatan, India,
 9,128...........D6 20
Jhansi, India, 140,217
 (*169,712).........C4 20

Jhelum, Pak., 47,409
 (*56,617)..........B5 20
Jibhalanta (Uliassutai),
 Mong., 25,000......B4 17
Jicin, Czech., 12,200...C3 7
Jihlava, Czech., 34,700.D3 7
Jimā, Eth., 10,000.....G5 23
Jimbolia, Rom., 11,281.C5 10
Jimena, Sp., 10,123...D3 8
Jiménez, Mex., 14,922..B4 34
Jim Hogg, co., Tex.,
 5,022............F3 84
Jim Thorpe, Pa.,
 5,945............E10 81
Jim Wells, co., Tex.,
 34,548............F3 84
Jindrichuv Hradec,
 Czech., 10,300......D3 7
Jinja, Ug., 29,741....H4 23
Jinotepe, Nic., 16,400..E7 34
Jipijapa, Ec., 7,605....B1 31
Jiquilpan de Juárez, Mex.,
 12,013...........n12 34
Jirgalanta (Kobdo),
 Mong., 5,000.......B3 17
Joanna, S.C.,
 1,831............C4 82
João Pessoa, Braz.,
 135,820............D7 27
Jocobus, Pa., 968....*G8 81
Jódar, Sp., 14,424.....D4 8
Jo Daviess, co., Ill.,
 21,821............A3 58
Jodhpur, India,
 224,760...........C5 20
Joe Batts Arm, Newf.,
 Can., 1,058........D4 44
Joensuu, Fin., 28,300..F13 11
Joeuf, Fr., 12,588.....C6 5
Joggins, N.S., Can.,
 909.............D5 43
Jogjakarta, Indon.,
 308,530............G4 19
Johannesburg, S. Afr.,
 594,290 (*2,075,000)..F5 24
John Day, Oreg., 1,520.C8 80
Johns Island, S.C.,
 500............F2, F7 82
Johnson, Kans., 860...E2 61
Johnson, Vt., 941......B2 73
Johnson, co., Ark.,
 12,421............B2 49
Johnson, co., Ga.,
 8,048.............D4 55
Johnson, co., Ill., 6,928.F5 58
Johnson, co., Ind.,
 43,704............F5 59
Johnson, co., Iowa,
 53,663............C6 60
Johnson, co., Kans.,
 143,792...........D9 61
Johnson, co., Ky.,
 19,748............C7 62
Johnson, co., Mo.,
 28,981............C4 69
Johnson, co., Nebr.,
 6,281............D9 71
Johnson, co., Tenn.,
 10,765............C12 83
Johnson, co., Tex.,
 34,720............C4 84
Johnson, co., Wyo.,
 5,475............A6 89
Johnsonburg, Pa.,
 4,966............D4 81
Johnson City, N.Y.,
 19,118............C5 75

Johnson City, Tenn.,
 31,187............C11 83
Johnson City, Tex.,
 611.............D3 84
Johnson City Southeast,
 Tenn., 2,435......*C11 83
Johnston, Iowa, 1,000..A7 60
Johnston, R.I.,
 17,160............B10 52
Johnston, S.C., 2,119..D4 82
Johnston, co., N.C.,
 62,936............B5 76
Johnston, co., Okla.,
 8,517.............C5 79
Johnston City, Ill.,
 3,891............F5 78
Johnstown, Colo., 976..A6 51
Johnstown, N.Y.,
 10,390............B6 75
Johnstown, Ohio, 2,881.B5 78
Johnstown, Pa., 53,949
 (*125,500).........F4 81
Johore, state, Mala.,
 926,850...........E2 19
Johore Bahru, Mala.,
 74,909............E2 19
Joigny, Fr., 7,144.....D5 5
Joinville, Braz., 44,255.D3 30
Joliet, Ill., 66,780
 (*132,100).....B5, F2 58
Joliette, Que., Can.,
 18,088............C4 42
Joliette, co., Que., Can.,
 44,969............C3 42
Jolo, Phil., 22,000....D6 19
Jonava, Sov. Un.,
 10,000............A8 7
Jones, co., Ga., 8,468..C3 55
Jones, co., Iowa,
 20,693............B6 60
Jones, co., Miss.,
 59,542............D4 68
Jones, co., N.C., 11,005.B6 76
Jones, co., S. Dak.,
 2,066.............G5 77
Jones, co., Tex., 19,299.C3 84
Jonesboro, Ark., 21,418.B5 49
Jonesboro, Ga., 3,014..C2 55
Jonesboro, Ill., 1,636..F4 58
Jonesboro, Ind., 2,260.D6 59
Jonesboro, La., 3,848..B3 63
Jonesboro, Tenn.,
 1,148............C11 83
Jones Mills, Ark.,
 950..........C2, C6 49
Jonesport, Maine, 800..D5 64
Jonesville, La., 2,347...C4 63
Jonesville, Mich., 1,896.G6 66
Jonesville, N.C., 1,895..A3 76
Jonesville, S.C., 1,439..B4 82
Jönköping, Swe.,
 51,000............I6 11
Jönköping, co., Swe.,
 286,300...........*I5 11
Jonquière, Que., Can.,
 28,588 (*54,500).....A6 42
Joplin, Mo., 38,958....D3 69
Jordan, Minn., 1,479..F5 67
Jordan, N.Y., 1,390...B4 75
Jordan, country, Asia,
 1,329,174..........D3 15
Jorhat, India, 24,953...C9 20
Jos, Nig., 31,582
 (*38,527)..........G6 22
José Batlle y Ordóñez,
 Ur., 1,781........E1 30

Josephine, co., Oreg.,
 29,917............E3 80
Jourdanton, Tex.,
 1,504............E3 84
Jovellanos, Cuba,
 10,444............D3 35
Juab, co., Utah, 4,597..B5 72
Juana Díaz, P.R.,
 4,618...........*m13 35
Juan Aldama, Mex.,
 7,672............C4 34
Juanita, Wash., 1,500.*B3 86
Juárez, Arg., 7,602....B5 28
Juàzeiro, Braz., 21,196.D6 27
Juàzeiro do Norte, Braz.,
 53,421...........*D7 27
Juba, Sud., 10,660....H4 23
Juchitán [de Zaragoza],
 Mex., 20,031.......D5 34
Juddah (Jidda), Sau. Ar.,
 160,000...........E2 15
Judenburg, Aus.,
 9,869............E7 6
Judith Basin, co., Mont.,
 3,085.............C6 70
Judson, S.C., 2,000...*B3 82
Judsonia, Ark., 1,470..B4 49
Juiz de Fora, Braz.,
 124,979........C4, g6 30
Jujuy, Arg., 31,091...D2 29
Jujuy, prov., Arg.,
 239,763...........D2 29
Jukao, China, 80,000..*E9 17
Julesburg, Colo., 1,840.A8 51
Juliaca, Peru, 7,002...E3 31
Jullundur, India, 222,569
 (*265,030).........B6 20
Jumet, Bel., 28,713...B6 5
Jumilla, Sp., 16,199...C5 8
Junagadh, India,
 74,298............D5 20
Juncos, P.R., 6,247...m14 35
Junction, Tex., 2,441...D3 84
Junction City, Ark.,
 749.............D3 49
Junction City, Kans.,
 17,700............C7 61
Junction City, Ky.,
 1,047............C5 62
Junction City, Oreg.,
 1,614............C3 80
Jundiaí, Braz.,
 79,536..........C3, m8 30
Juneau, Alsk.,
 6,797.......D13, k22 47
Juneau, Wis., 1,718...E5 88
Juneau, co., Wis.,
 17,490............E3 88
Juniata, co., Pa.,
 15,874............F7 81
Juniata Terrace, Pa.,
 1,130............E6 81
Junín, Arg., 36,149...A4 28
Junín, dept., Peru,
 431,082...........D2 31
Jupiter, Fla., 1,058...F6 54
Jura, dept., Fr.,
 225,682..........*D6 5
Jurbarkas, Sov. Un.,
 5,000............A7 7
Justice, Ill., 2,803....*F3 58
Jüterbog, Ger., 13,500.C6 6
Jutiapa, Guat., 5,162..E7 34
Juwain, Afg., 5,000...B3 20
Jyväskylä, Fin.,
 39,600............F11 11

K

Kaalaea, Haw., 300...g10 56
Kabul, Afg., 206,208..B4 20
Kachuga, Sov. Un.,
 53,500...........D13 13
Kadinhan, Tur., 4,338..C9 14
Kadiri, India, 24,307...F6 20
Kadiyevka, Sov. Un.,
 191,000......G12, q21 12
Kaduna, Nig., 22,511..F6 22
Kaédi, Maur., 8,500...E2 22
Kaeryong, Kor., 6,200..H4 18
Kaesŏng, Kor.,
 139,900...........G3 18
Kāf, Sau. Ar., 10,000..C2 15
Kafr az Zayyāt, Eg.,
 U.A.R., 25,100.....D2 14
Kagawa, pref., Jap.,
 918,867..........*I7 18
Kagizman, Tur., 7,200.B14 14
Kagoshima, Jap.
 296,003...........K5 18
Kagoshima, pref., Jap.,
 1,963,104........*K5 18
Kagul, Sov. Un.,
 20,000...........C9 10
Kahoka, Mo., 2,160...*A6 69
Kahuku, Haw.,
 1,238.........B4, f10 56
Kahului, Haw., 4,223..C5 56

Kaifeng, China,
 299,100...........E7 17
Kailua, Haw.,
 25,622...........g11 56
Kainan, Jap., 42,100...I7 18
Kaiping, China, 40,000.C9 17
Kairouan, Tun.,
 33,968............A7 22
Kaiserslautern, Ger.,
 86,300............D3 6
Kaiyuan, China,
 25,000............E2 18
Kaizuka, Jap., 61,067..o14 18
Kajaani, Fin., 14,700..E12 11
Kajikazawa, Jap.,
 4,500............n17 18
Kakegawa, Jap.,
 27,600............o17 18
Kakinada, India,
 122,865...........E7 20
Kalabagh, Pak., 10,523.B5 20
Kalach, Sov. Un.,
 16,900............F13 12
Kalaheo, Haw., 1,185..B2 56
Kalama, Wash., 1,088..C3 86
Kalamai, Grc., 38,211..D4 14
Kalamazoo, Mich., 82,089
 (*170,000).........F5 66
Kalamazoo, co., Mich.,
 169,712............F5 66

Kalat-i-Ghilzai, Afg.,
 5,000.............B4 20
Kalgan (Changkiakow),
 China, 299,300.....C7 17
Kalgoorlie, Austl., 9,696
 (*21,773).........F3 25
Kalimnos, Grc., 10,211.D6 14
Kalinin, Sov. Un.,
 279,000...........C10 12
Kaliningrad (Königsberg),
 Sov. Un., 226,000...D3 12
Kaliningrad, Sov. Un.,
 74,000............n17 12
Kalinkovichi, Sov. Un.,
 10,000............E7 12
Kalispell, Mont.,
 10,151............B2 70
Kalisz, Pol., 70,000....C5 7
Kalkaska, Mich., 1,321.D5 66
Kalkaska, co., Mich.,
 4,382.............D5 66
Kallithea, Grc.,
 54,720..........*D4 14
Kalmar, Swe., 31,400...I7 11
Kalmar, co., Swe.,
 234,800...........*I7 11
Kalocsa, Hung.,
 13,663............B4 10
Kalona, Iowa, 1,235...C6 60

Kaluga, Sov. Un.,
 145,000...........D11 12
Kalush, Sov. Un.,
 10,000............G5 12
Kamaishi, Jap.,
 87,511............G10 18
Kamakura, Jap.,
 98,617............n18 18
Kamenets-Podolskiy,
 Sov. Un., 25,000....G6 12
Kamen-na-Obi, Sov. Un.,
 37,000............D11 13
Kamensk-Shakhtinskiy,
 Sov. Un., 60,000...G13 12
Kamensk-Uralskiy, Sov.
 Un., 151,000.......D9 13
Kamenz, Ger., 14,900..C7 6
Kameoka, Jap.,
 17,300...........o14 18
Kamiah, Idaho, 1,245..C2 57
Kamioka, Jap.,
 20,100...........m16 18
Kamloops, B.C., Can.,
 10,076............D7 37
Kamouraska, co., Que.,
 Can., 27,138.......B8 42
Kampala, Ug., 46,735..H4 23
Kampen, Neth., 23,322.A6 5
Kampot, Camb., 5,000.C2 19

Kamsack, Sask., Can., 2,968..............F5 39
Kamuela, Haw., 950...C6 56
Kamyshin, Sov. Un., 62,000.............F15 12
Kanab, Utah, 1,645....C5 72
Kanabec, co., Minn., 9,007..............E5 67
Kanagawa, pref., Jap., 3,443,176..........*I9 18
Kanash, Sov. Un., 29,000.............D16 12
Kanawha, co., W. Va., 252,925............C3 87
Kanazawa, Jap., 298,972.............H8 18
Kanchanaburi, Thai., 13,357.............C1 19
Kancheepuram, India, 92,714.............F6 20
Kandahar, Afg., 77,186.B4 20
Kandalaksha, Sov. Un., 37,500.............C6 13
Kandangan, Indon., 9,774..............F5 19
Kandira, Tur., 4,900..B8 14
Kandiyohi, co., Minn., 29,987.............E3 67
Kandy, Cey., 57,013...G7 20
Kane, Pa., 5,380......C4 81
Kane, co., Ill., 208,246.B5 58
Kane, co., Utah, 2,667..C5 72
Kaneohe, Haw., 14,414........B4, g10 56
Kanggye, Kor., 30,013..F3 18
Kangnung, Kor., 37,300.............H4 18
Kangting, China, 30,000.............E5 17
Kanhsien, China, 98,600.............F7 17
Kanjiža, Yugo., 10,709.B5 10
Kankakee, Ill., 27,666..B6 58
Kankakee, co., Ill., 92,063.............B6 58
Kankan, Guinea, 24,600.............F3 22
Kanker, India, 6,437..D7 20
Kannan, China, 5,000..C1 18
Kannapolis, N.C., 34,647............B3 76
Kano, Nig., 93,016...F6 22
Kanoya, Jap., 31,700..K5 18
Kanpur, India, 881,177 (*1,000,000)........C7 20
Kansas, state, U.S., 2,178,611...........61
Kansas City, Kans., 121,901........B9, C9 61
Kansas City, Mo., 475,539 (*1,025,900).....B3, E2 69
Kansk, Sov. Un., 88,000............D12 13
Kansong, Kor., 5,000..G4 18
Kansu, prov., China, 12,800,000.........D5 17
Kanye, Bech., 22,922..E5 24
Kaohsiung, Taiwan, 267,516...........G9 17
Kaolack, Sen., 46,600..F1 22
Kaoyao, China, 49,000.............G7 17
Kapaa, Haw., 3,439...A2 56
Kapanga, Con. L., 5,000..............B4 24
Kapfenberg, Aus., 23,859.............E7 6
Kaplan, La., 5,267.....D3 63
Kaposvar, Hung., 43,458.............B3 10
Kapuskasing, Ont., Can., 6,870..............E9 41
Kapuvár, Hung., 10,902.............B3 10
Karachev, Sov. Un., 10,000............E10 12
Karachi, Pak., 1,600,000..........C4 20
Karaga, Sov. Un., 10,000............D19 13
Karaganda, Sov. Un., 441,000...........E10 13
Karakose, Tur., 19,800...........C14 14
Karaman, Tur., 21,700.D9 14
Karapinar, Tur., 10,800.............D9 14
Kara Shahr (Yenki), China, 10,000......C2 17
Karatsu, Jap., 55,000..J4 18
Karbalā', Iraq, 44,600.............C3 15
Karcag, Hung., 20,803.B5 10
Kardhitsa, Grc., 23,708.............C3 14
Karelia (Karelo-Finnish S.S.R.), former rep., Sov. Un...........*C6 16
Kargil, India, 5,000...B6 20
Kargopol, Sov. Un., 5,000.............A12 12

Kariba, Rh., 6,170....D5 24
Karikal, India, 22,252..F6 20
Karima, Sud., 5,989....E4 23
Karkaralinsk, Sov. Un., 12,200............E10 13
Karl-Marx-Stadt (Chemnitz), Ger., 286,100.............C6 6
Karlovac, Yugo., 38,803.............C2 10
Karlovasi, Grc., 5,024..............*D6 14
Karlovy Vary, Czech., 42,800.............C2 7
Karlshamn, Swe., 11,700.............I6 11
Karlskoga, Swe., 36,100.............H6 11
Karlskrona, Swe., 33,200.............I6 11
Karlsruhe, Ger., 241,900.............D4 6
Karlstad, Swe., 43,600.H5 11
Karnak, Ill., 667.......F5 58
Karnes, co., Tex., 14,995.............E4 84
Karnes City, Tex., 2,693..............E4 84
Kars, Tur., 32,000....B14 14
Karsakpay, Sov. Un., 12,000............E9 13
Karshi, Sov. Un., 19,000.............F9 13
Kartal, Tur., 10,800...*B7 14
Kartaly, Sov. Un., 33,400.............D9 13
Kartuzy, Pol., 5,991...A5 7
Karviná, Czech., 46,800.............D5 7
Karwar, India, 12,134..F5 20
Kasaragod, India, 27,635.............F6 20
Kasba Tadla, Mor., 11,733.............B3 22
Kāshān, Iran, 45,955.............B8 23
Kashgar, China, 91,000.............F10 16
Kashira, Sov. Un., 47,314.............*C3 14
Kashiwazaki, Jap., 39,800.............H9 18
Kashmir, see Jammu and Kashmir, disputed reg., India, Pak.
Kasimov, Sov. Un., 33,500............D13 12
Kassala, Sud., 35,621..E5 23
Kassel, Ger., 207,500...C4 6
Kasson, Minn., 1,732...F6 67
Kastamonu, Tur., 19,500.............B9 14
Kastoria, Grc., 10,162..B3 14
Kasukabe, Jap., 18,500.............n18 18
Kasumi, Jap., 12,100...I7 18
Kasur, Pak., 63,086....B5 20
Katanga, prov., Con. L., 1,664,200..........C5 24
Katerini, Grc., 28,046..B4 14
Kathwood, S.C., 2,000..............*D5 82
Katiola, I.C., 7,900....G3 22
Katmandu, Nep., 106,579 (*300,000).........C8 20
Katni, India, 46,169...D7 20
Katonah, N.Y., 3,000..A5 74
Katoomba (Blue Mountains), Austl., 28,119.............F8 26
Katowice, Pol., 269,000........C5, g10 7
Katrineholm, Swe., 19,000.......H7, u34 11
Katsuyama, Jap., 19,300...........m15 18
Katy, Tex., 1,569.....F4 84
Kauai, co., Haw., 28,176.............B2 56
Kaufbeuren, Ger., 34,700.............E5 6
Kaufman, Tex., 3,087..C4 84
Kaufman, co., Tex., 29,931.............C4 84
Kaukauna, Wis., 10,096.........A5, D5 88
Kaumakani, Haw., 950..............B2 56
Kaunakakai, Haw., 900..............B4 56
Kaunas, Sov. Un., 232,000............D4 12
Kavaje, Alb., 13,700..*B2 14
Kaválla, Grc., 44,517..B5 14
Kaválla, prov., Grc., 140,751............*B5 14
Kavarna, Bul., 5,625...D9 10
Kawagoe, Jap., 70,000.............n18 18
Kawaguchi, Jap., 170,066...........n18 18

Kawasaki, Jap., 632,975........I9, n18 18
Kawkareik, Bur., 10,000.............*B1 19
Kay, co., Okla., 51,042.A4 79
Kayes, Mali, 19,600....F2 22
Kayford, W. Va., 400.............C3, D6 87
Kayseri, Tur., 102,809...........C10 14
Kaysville, Utah, 3,608...........A6, C2 72
Kazachye, Sov. Un., 900.............B16 13
Kazakh S.S.R., rep., Sov. Un., 10,387,000.....*E9 16
Kazan, Sov. Un., 693,000............D7 13
Kazanlŭk, Bul., 19,386.............D7 10
Keansburg, N.J., 6,854.C4 74
Kearney, Nebr., 14,210.D6 71
Kearney, co., Nebr., 6,580..............D7 71
Kearns, Utah, 17,172..*A5 72
Kearny, N.J., 37,472...D5 74
Kearny, co., Kans., 3,108..............D2 61
Kearsarge, Mich., 400..A2 66
Keasbey, N.J., 1,500..*B4 74
Kecskemet, Hung., 45,904.............B4 10
Kedah, state, Mala., 701,964............*D2 19
Kedainiai, Sov. Un., 8,602..............A7 7
Keego Harbor, Mich., 2,761..............A7 66
Keene, N.H., 17,562...F3 73
Keene, Tex., 1,532....B5 84
Keeseville, N.Y., 2,213.B3 75
Keewatin, Ont., Can., 1,197.............E4 40
Keewatin, Minn., 1,651.............C5 67
Keewatin, dist., N.W. Ter., Can., 2,301..D15 36
Kefallinia, prov., Grc., 47,314............*C3 14
Keighley, Eng., 55,852.D6 4
Keiser, Pa., 1,132....*E8 81
Keith, co., Nebr., 7,958..............C4 71
Keithsburg, Ill., 963...B3 58
Keizer, Oreg., 5,288..*C4 80
Kekaha, Haw., 2,082...B2 56
Kelantan, state, Mala., 505,522...........*D2 19
Kellerman, Ala., 500...B2 46
Kellogg, Idaho, 5,061..B2 57
Kelly Lake, Minn., 900..............C5 67
Kelowna, B.C., Can., 13,188.............E8 37
Kelso, Wash., 8,379...C3 86
Keltys, Tex., 1,056...*D5 84
Kelvington, Sask., Can., 885..............E4 39
Kem, Sov. Un., 10,000............E16 11
Kemah, Tex., 950.....F5 84
Kemerovo, Sov. Un., 298,000...........D11 13
Kemi, Fin., 28,800....E11 11
Kemmerer, Wyo., 2,028.............D2 89
Kemp, Tex., 816.......C4 84
Kemper, co., Miss., 12,277.............C5 68
Kempsey, Austl., 8,016.F9 25
Kempten, Ger., 43,100.E5 6
Kemptville, Ont., Can., 1,959.............B9 41
Kenbridge, Va., 1,188..E4 85
Kendal, Eng., 18,595...C5 4
Kendall, Fla., 3,000...F3 54
Kendall, co., Ill., 17,540.............B5 58
Kendall, co., Tex., 5,889..............E3 84
Kendallville, Ind., 6,765..............B7 59
Kendari, Indon........F6 19
Kendrapara, India, 15,830............D8 20
Kenedy, Tex., 4,301...E4 84
Kenedy, co., Tex., 884..F4 84
Kenhorst, Pa., 2,815..*F10 81
Kenilworth, Ill., 2,959..E3 58
Kenilworth, N.J., 8,379.............*B4 74
Kenitra, Mor., 86,775..B3 22
Kenly, N.C., 1,147....B5 76
Kenmare, N. Dak., 2,463.............B3 77
Kenmawr, Pa., 3,000..*F1 81
Kenmore, N.Y., 21,261.C2 75
Kenmore, Wash., 1,000.............*B3 86
Kennebec, co., Maine, 83,881............D3 64

Kennebunk, Maine, 2,804..............E2 64
Kennebunk Port, Maine, 700..............E2 64
Kennedale, Tex., 1,521.B5 84
Kenner, La., 17,037....E5 63
Kennesaw, Ga., 1,507...........A4, B2 55
Kenneth City, Fla., 2,114.............*E4 54
Kennett, Mo., 9,098...E7 69
Kennett Square, Pa., 4,355............G10 81
Kennewick, Wash., 14,244............C6 86
Kennydale, Wash., 3,500.............D2 86
Kenogami, Que., Can., 11,816............A6 42
Kenora, Ont., Can., 10,904............E7 41
Kenora, co., Ont., Can., 51,474............D8 41
Kenosha, Wis., 67,899.........F2, F6 88
Kenosha, co., Wis., 100,615............F5 88
Kenova, W. Va., 4,577.C2 87
Kensington, Calif., 6,161.............*B5 50
Kensington, Conn., 4,500.............C5 52
Kensington, Md., 2,175.B3 53
Kensington, N.Y., 1,166.............*G2 52
Kensington Estates, Md., 1,600.............*B3 53
Kensington Park, Fla., 2,969.............*E4 54
Kensington Park, Ga., 1,000.............*D6 55
Kent, Ala., 500.......C4 46
Kent, Ohio, 17,836....A6 78
Kent, Wash., 9,017.B3, D2 86
Kent, co., N.B., Can., 26,667............C4 43
Kent, co., Ont., Can., 89,247............E2 41
Kent, co., Del., 65,651..B6 53
Kent, co., Eng., 1,701,083.........*E7 4
Kent, co., Md., 15,481..B5 53
Kent, co., Mich., 363,187............E5 66
Kent, co., R.I., 112,619............C10 52
Kent, co., Tex., 1,727...C2 84
Kentfield, Calif., 5,000.............*B5 50
Kentland, Ind., 1,783..C3 59
Kentland, Md., 1,800.*C4 53
Kenton, Ohio, 8,747...B4 78
Kenton, Tenn., 1,095..A2 83
Kenton, co., Ky., 120,700............B5 62
Kentucky, state, U.S., 3,038,156...........62
Kent Village, Md., 2,500.............*C4 53
Kentville, N.S., Can., 4,612.............D5 43
Kentwood, La., 2,607..D5 63
Kenvil, N.J., 2,000....B3 74
Kenvir, Ky., 950......D6 62
Kenwood, Ohio, 2,000.*C3 78
Kenya, country, Afr., 7,287,000..........H5 23
Kenyon, Minn., 1,624..F6 67
Keokuk, Iowa, 16,316..D6 60
Keokuk, co., Iowa, 15,492.............C5 60
Keosauqua, Iowa, 1,023.............D6 60
Keota, Iowa, 1,096....C6 60
Kepno, Pol., 7,810....C5 7
Kerala, state, India, 16,903,715.........F6 20
Kerch, Sov. Un., 104,000............I11 12
Kerens, Tex., 1,123...C4 84
Kerkira, Grc., 26,991..C2 14
Kerkira, prov., Grc., 101,770............*C2 14
Kerkrade, Neth., 49,400.............B7 5
Kerman, Calif., 1,970.*D4 50
Kermān, Iran, 62,157..B2 20
Kermānshāh, Iran, 125,439............B7 23
Kermit, Tex., 10,465...D1 84
Kermit, W. Va., 743...D2 87
Kern, co., Calif., 291,984............E4 50
Kernersville, N.C., 2,942.............A3 76
Kerr, co., Tex., 16,800.D3 84
Kerrobert, Sask., Can., 1,220.............F1 39
Kerrville, Tex., 8,901..D3 84
Kerry, co., Ire., 116,458............*D2 4

Kershaw, S.C., 1,567...B6   82
Kershaw, co., S.C.,
    33,585..............C6   82
Kesan, Tur., 15,100....B6   14
Kesennuma, Jap.,
    37,200.............G10   18
Keszthely, Hung.,
    14,854..............B3   10
Keta, Ghana, 11,380...G5   22
Ketapang, Indon.,
    4,385...............F3   19
Ketchikan, Alsk.,
    6,483....:...D13, n24   47
Ketchum, Idaho, 746...F4   57
Ketona, Ala., 900......E5   46
Ketrzyn Mazowiecki, Pol.,
    13,900..............A6   7
Kettering, Eng.,
    38,631..............D6   4
Kettering, Ohio,
    54,462.............*C3   78
Kettle Falls, Wash.,
    905................A7   86
Kety, Pol., 6,581..D5, h10   7
Kewanee, Ill., 16,324...B4   58
Kewaskum, Wis.,
    1,572...............E5   88
Kewaunee, Wis., 2,772.D6   88
Kewaunee, co., Wis.,
    18,282.............D6   88
Keweenaw, co., Mich.,
    2,417..............A2   66
Keya Paha, co., Nebr.,
    1,672..............B6   71
Key Biscayne, Fla.,
    2,500.............*G6   54
Keyes, Calif., 1,546..*D4   50
Keyport, N.J., 6,440...C4   74
Keyser, W. Va., 6,192..B6   87
Keystone, W. Va.,
    6,457..............D3   87
Key West, Fla.,
    33,956..............H5   54
Kezhma, Sov. Un.,
    3,000.............D13   13
Kezmarok, Czech.,
    7,372..............D6   7
Kfar Ata, Isr., 14,245..B3   15
Kfar Sava, Isr., 18,635.B2   15
Khabarovsk, Sov. Un.,
    349,000............E16   13
Khairpur, Pak., 18,186.C4   20
Khalkidhiki, prov., Grc.,
    79,849.............*B4   14
Khalkis, Grc.,
    24,745.............C4   14
Khambhaliya, India,
    20,064.............D5   20
Khanabad, Afg.,
    18,042.............A4   20
Khanaqin, Iraq,
    10,090.............C4   15
Khandwa, India,
    63,505.............D6   20
Khania, Grc., 38,467...E5   14
Khania, prov., Grc.,
    131,061............*E4   14
Khanpur, Pak., 13,484.C5   20
Khan Yunis, Eg., U.A.R.,
    12,350.........C2, h5   15
Kharagpur, India,
    147,253............D8   20
Kharkov, Sov. Un.,
    976,000...........G11   12
Kharmanli, Bul., 9,240.E7   10
Kharovsk, Sov. Un.,
    5,000.............B13   12
Khartoum, Sud., 93,103
    (*260,000)..........E4   23
Khartoum North, Sud.,
    39,082.............E4   23
Khartsyzsk, Sov. Un.,
    10,000.............q21   12
Khash, Afg., 5,000.....B3   20
Khaskovo, Bul., 27,394.E7   10
Khatanga, Sov. Un.,
    10,000............B13   16
Khenifra, Mor.,
    18,503.............B5   22
Kherson, Sov. Un.,
    174,000............H9   12
Khilok, Sov. Un.,
    18,600............D14   13
Khimki, Sov. Un.,
    43,000.............n17   12
Khios, Grc., 24,053....C6   14
Khios, prov., Grc.,
    62,223.............*C6   14
Khmelnik, Sov. Un.,
    10,000.............G6   12
Khmelnitskiy, Sov. Un.,
    62,000.............G6   12
Kholm, Sov. Un.,
    10,000.............C8   12
Kholmsk (Maoka), Sov.
    Un., 33,000.......E17   16
Khong, Laos, 10,000...C3   19
Khong Sedone, Laos,
    10,000............*B3   19
Khorog, Sov. Un.,
    9,000.............F10   13

Khorol, Sov. Un.,
    10,000.............G9   12
Khotan (Hotien), China,
    50,000.............A6   20
Khotin, Sov. Un.,
    10,000.............G6   12
Khulna, Pak., 127,970..D8   20
Khust, Sov. Un.,
    10,000.............G4   12
Kiamusze (Chiamussu),
    China, 146,000......C5   18
Kiangsi, prov., China,
    18,610,000.........F9   17
Kiangsu, prov., China,
    42,630,000.........E8   17
Kiaohsien, China,
    75,000.............D9   17
Kičevo, Yugo., 10,273..E5   10
Kidder, co., N. Dak.,
    5,386..............C6   77
Kidderminster, Eng.,
    40,822.............D5   4
Kiel, Ger., 273,300....A5   6
Kiel, Wis., 2,524...B5, E5   88
Kielce, Pol., 89,000....C6   7
Kiev (Kiyev), Sov. Un.,
    1,174,000..........F8   12
Kifisia, Grc., 14,193..*C24   14
Kigali, Rwanda, 4,000..I4   23
Kikinda, Yugo., 33,906.C5   10
Kikladhes, prov., Grc.,
    99,959............*D5   14
Kikwit, Con. L.,
    11,000.............B3   24
Kilchu, Kor., 30,026...F4   18
Kildare, co., Ire.,
    64,420............*D3   4
Kilgore, Tex., 10,092...C5   84
Kilis, Tur., 33,300....D11   14
Kiliya, Sov. Un., 10,000.I7   12
Kilkenny, Ire., 1,159...D3   4
Kilkenny, co., Ire.,
    61,668............*D3   4
Kilkis, Grc., 10,963....E6   10
Kilkis, prov., Grc.,
    102,812...........*B4   14
Killarney, Man., Can.,
    1,729..............E2   40
Killarney, Ire., 6,825...D2   4
Killeen, Tex., 23,377...D4   84
Killian, S.C., 800......C6   82
Killona, La., 650......C6   63
Kilmallie, Scot., 5,049.B4   4
Kilmarnock, Scot.,
    47,509.............C4   4
Kilmarnock, Va., 927..D6   85
Kimball, Nebr., 4,384..C2   71
Kimball, S. Dak., 912..G7   77
Kimball, W. Va.,
    1,175.............*D3   87
Kimball, co., Nebr.,
    7,975..............C2   71
Kimberley, B.C., Can.,
    6,013..............E9   37
Kimberley, S. Afr.,
    75,376 (*79,031).....F4   24
Kimberly, Ala., 763....B3   46
Kimberly, Idaho, 1,298.G4   57
Kimberly, W. Va., 900.D6   87
Kimberly, Wis., 5,322..A5   88
Kimble, co., Tex.,
    3,943..............D3   84
Kimchaek (Sŏngjin), Kor.,
    67,778.............F4   18
Kimry, Sov. Un.,
    40,000............C11   12
Kincaid, Ill., 1,544....D4   58
Kincardine, Ont., Can.,
    2,841..............C3   41
Kincardine, co., Scot.,
    25,556............*B5   4
Kinder, La., 2,299....D3   63
Kinderhook, N.Y.,
    1,078..............C7   75
Kindersley, Sask., Can.,
    2,990..............F1   39
Kindia, Guinea, 13,000.F2   22
Kindu [-Port Empain],
    Con. L., 14,200.....I3   23
Kineshma, Sov. Un.,
    90,000............C14   12
King, Ont., Can., 898..E6   41
King, N.C., 950.......A3   76
King, co., Tex., 640....C2   84
King, co., Wash.,
    935,014............B4   86
King and Queen, co.,
    Va., 5,889.........D6   85
King City, Calif., 2,937.D3   50
King City, Mo., 1,009..A3   69
Kingfisher, Okla., 3,249.B4   79
Kingfisher, co., Okla.,
    10,635.............B4   79
King George, co., Va.,
    7,243..............C5   85
Kingman, Ariz., 4,525..B1   48
Kingman, Kans.,
    3,582..........B3, E5   61
Kingman, co., Kans.,
    9,958..............E5   61

King of Prussia, Pa.,
    6,000.............*F11   81
Kings, co., Calif.,
    49,954.............D4   50
Kings, co., N.B., Can.,
    25,908.............D4   43
Kings, co., N.S., Can.,
    41,747.............E5   43
Kings, co., P.E.I., Can.,
    17,893.............C7   43
Kings, co. (Brooklyn
    borough), N.Y.,
    2,627,319 (part of New
    York City).........E1   75
Kingsburg, Calif.,
    3,093..............D4   50
Kingsbury, co., S. Dak.,
    9,227..............F8   77
Kingsford, Mich.,
    5,084..............C2   66
Kingsford Heights, Ind.,
    1,276.............*A4   59
Kings Gardens, Kans.,
    400................A4   61
Kingsland, Ga., 1,536..F5   55
Kingsley, Iowa, 1,044..B2   60
King's Lynn, Eng.,
    27,554.............D7   4
Kings Mills, Ohio,
    700............C2, C3   78
Kings Mountain, N.C.,
    8,008..............B2   76
Kings Park, N.Y.,
    4,949..............D3   75
Kings Point, N.Y.,
    5,410..............F1   52
Kingsport, Tenn.,
    26,314............C11   83
Kingston, Ont., Can.,
    53,526.............C8   41
Kingston, Jam.,
    421,718............F5   35
Kingston, Mass., 2,000.C6   65
Kingston, N.Y.,
    29,260.............D6   75
Kingston, Ohio, 1,066..C5   78
Kingston, Pa.,
    20,261.........B8, D10   81
Kingston, R.I., 2,616..D10   52
Kingston, Tenn., 2,010.D9   83
Kingston, W. Va.,
    400...........D3, D6   87
Kingston-on-Thames,
    Eng., 36,450.......m11   4
Kingstree, S.C., 3,847..D8   82
Kingsville, Ont., Can.,
    3,041..............E2   41
Kingsville, Ohio, 950...A7   78
Kingsville, Tex., 25,297.F4   84
King William, co., Va.,
    7,563..............D5   85
King William's Town,
    S. Afr., 14,646.....G5   24
Kingwood, W. Va.,
    2,530..............B5   87
Kinloch, Mo., 6,501....A8   69
Kinmundy, Ill., 813....E5   58
Kinnaird, B.C., Can.
    2,123.............*E9   37
Kinnelon, N.J., 4,431..B4   74
Kinney, co., Tex.,
    2,452..............E2   84
Kinomoto, Jap.,
    5,600..............n15   18
Kinross, co., Scot.,
    6,704.............*B5   4
Kinsley, Kans., 2,263...E4   61
Kinsman, Ohio, 900....A7   78
Kinston, N.C., 24,819..B6   76
Kinwood, Tex., 2,500..*F5   84
Kiowa, Kans., 1,674....E5   61
Kiowa, co., Colo.,
    2,425..............C8   51
Kiowa, co., Kans.,
    4,626..............E4   61
Kiowa, co., Okla.,
    14,825.............C3   79
Kiparissia, Grc.,
    5,027.............*D3   14
Kipushi, Con. L.,
    15,100.............C5   24
Kirbyville, Tex., 1,680.D6   84
Kirensk, Sov. Un.,
    12,500............D13   13
Kirghiz S.S.R., rep., Sov.
    Un., 2,225,000.....E10   16
Kirin (Chilin), China,
    568,000............E3   18
Kirin, prov., China,
    12,550,000........C10   17
Kirkagac, Tur., 11,300.C6   14
Kirkcaldy, Scot.,
    52,371.............B5   4
Kirkcudbright, co., Scot.,
    28,877............*C4   4
Kirkland, Ill., 928....A5   58
Kirkland, Wash.,
    6,025..........B3, D2   86
Kirkland Lake, Ont.,
    Can., 15,366.......E9   41

Kirklareli, Tur.,
    20,200.............B6   14
Kirksville, Mo., 13,125.A5   69
Kirkuk, Iraq, 120,593..B3   15
Kirkwood, Md., 2,500.*C3   53
Kirkwood, Mo., 29,421.B7   69
Kirn, Ger., 9,600......D3   6
Kirov, Sov. Un.,
    269,000............D7   13
Kirovabad, Sov. Un.,
    116,000............E7   13
Kirovograd, Sov. Un.,
    134,000............G9   12
Kirovsk, Sov. Un.,
    52,800.............C6   13
Kirsanov, Sov. Un.,
    10,000.............E14   12
Kirsehir, Tur., 20,200.C10   14
Kirtland, Ohio, 1,500..*A6   78
Kiruna, Swe., 19,348...D9   11
Kiryu, Jap.,
    123,010.........H9, m18   18
Kisarazu, Jap.,
    29,200.............n18   18
Kiselevsk, Sov. Un.,
    141,000...........*D11   13
Kishangarh, India,
    25,244.............C5   20
Kishinev, Sov. Un.,
    236,000............H7   12
Kishiwada, Jap.,
    120,265............o14   18
Kishorganj, Pak.,
    19,067.............D9   20
Kiskoros, Hung., 9,972.B4   10
Kiskundorozsma, Hung.,
    8,705..............B5   10
Kiskunfelegyhaza, Hung.,
    22,925.............B4   10
Kiskunhalas, Hung.,
    18,314.............B4   10
Kiskunmajsa, Hung.,
    7,611..............B4   10
Kislovodsk, Sov. Un.,
    82,000.............*E7   13
Kissimmee, Fla., 6,845.D5   54
Kistler, W. Va.,
    1,084..........D3, D5   87
Kisujszallas, Hung.,
    11,304.............B5   10
Kisumu, Ken., 10,899...I4   23
Kisvarda, Hung.,
    13,284...........:.A6   10
Kitakyūshū, Jap.,
    1,335,000..........J5   18
Kitale, Ken., 6,338....H4   23
Kitami, Jap., 38,200..E11   18
Kit Carson, co., Colo.,
    6,957..............B8   51
Kitchener, Ont., Can.,
    74,485.............D4   41
Kitega, Burundi,
    5,000..............I4   23
Kitimat, B.C., Can.,
    8,217..............B3   37
Kitsap, co., Wash.,
    84,176.............B3   86
Kittanning, Pa., 6,793..E2   81
Kittery, Maine, 8,051..E2   64
Kittery Point, Maine,
    1,259..............E2   64
Kittias, co., Wash.,
    20,467.............B5   86
Kitts, Ky., 950.......D6   62
Kittson, co., Minn.,
    8,343..............B2   67
Kityang, China,
    54,000.............G8   17
Kitzbühel, Aus.,
    7,744..............E6   6
Kitzingen, Ger., 17,800.D5   6
Kiukiang, China,
    64,600.............F8   17
Kizel, Sov. Un.,
    61,000............*D8   13
Kizyl-Arvat, Sov. Un.,
    26,000.............F8   13
Kladno, Czech.,
    49,600.........C3, n17   7
Klagenfurt, Aus.,
    69,218.............E7   6
Klaipeda (Memel),
    Sov. Un., 100,000...D3   12
Klamath, co., Oreg.,
    47,475.............E5   80
Klamath Falls, Oreg.,
    16,949.............E5   80
Klang, Mala., 75,649...E2   19
Klatovy, Czech.,
    14,000.............D2   7
Kleberg, Tex., 3,572..*B6   84
Kleberg, co., Tex.,
    30,052.............F4   84
Kletnya, Sov. Un.,
    10,000.............E9   12
Kletsk, Sov. Un.,
    10,000.............E6   12
Klickitat, co., Wash.,
    13,455.............D5   86

Klintsy, Sov. Un.,
40,000.............E9   12
Ključ, Yugo., 2,322....C3   10
Klobuck, Pol., 6,533...C5   7
Klodzko, Pol., 20,200..C4   7
Klosterneuburg,Aus.,
22,787.............D8   6
Kluczbork, Pol.,
11,800.............C5   7
Knezha, Bul., 13,133...D7   10
Knightstown, Ind.,
2,496.............E6   59
Knittelfeld, Aus.,
14,259.............E7   6
Knob Noster, Mo.,
2,292.............C4   69
Knollwood, Ohio,
2,500.............*C3   78
Knollwood Park, Mich.,
2,100.............*F6   66
Knott, co., Ky.,
17,362.............C6   62
Knowlton, Que., Can.,
1,396.............D5   42
Knox, Ind., 3,458.....B4   59
Knox, Pa., 1,247.....*D3   81
Knox, co., Ill., 61,280...B3   58
Knox, co., Ind., 41,561.G3   59
Knox, co., Ky., 25,258..D6   62
Knox, co., Maine,
28,575.............D4   64
Knox, co., Mo., 6,558...A5   69
Knox, co., Nebr.,
13,300.............B8   71
Knox, co., Ohio,
38,808.............B5   78
Knox, co., Tenn.,
250,523.............C10   83
Knox, co., Tex., 7,857..C3   84
Knox City, Tex., 1,805.C3   84
Knoxville, Ill., 2,560...C3   58
Knoxville, Iowa, 7,817..C4   60
Knoxville, Tenn., 111,827
(*286,000)....D10, E11   83
Knysna, S. Afr.,
11,085.............G4   24
Kobe, Jap., 1,113,977...o14   18
Kobelyaki, Sov. Un.,
10,000.............G10   12
København, co., Den.,
1,269,336...........*J5   11
Koblenz, Ger., 99,200..C3   6
Kobrin, Sov. Un.,
25,000.............E5   12
Kočani, Yugo., 10,986..E6   10
Kochi, Jap., 196,288....J6   18
Kochi, pref., Jap.,
854,595...........*J6   18
Kodak, Ky., 500.....C6   62
Kodiak, Alsk., 2,628...D9   47
Kodiak, isl., Alsk......D9   47
Koforidua, Ghana,
17,806.............G4   22
Kofu, Jap.,
160,963.........I9, n17   18
Koga, Jap., 42,474...m18   18
Kohala, Haw., 950...C6   56
Kohat, Pak., 30,719....B5   20
Kohler, Wis., 1,524.B6, E6   88
Kokand, Sov. Un.,
113,000.............E10   13
Kokchetav, Sov. Un.,
59,000.............D9   13
Kokkola, Fin., 16,200.F10   11
Kokomo, Ind., 47,197..D5   59
Kokstad, S. Afr.,
7,984.............G5   24
Kolar Gold Fields, India,
146,811.............F6   20
Kolarovo, Bul., 31,169.D8   10
Kolarovo, Czech.,
10,800.............E4   7
Kolhapur, India,
187,442.............E5   20
Kolin, Czech., 23,200..C3   7
Köln (Cologne), Ger.,
809,000.............C3   6
Kolo, Pol., 10,600.....B5   7
Koloa, Haw., 1,426....B2   56
Kolomna, Sov. Un.,
124,000......D12, n18   12
Kolomyya, Sov. Un.,
45,000.............G5   2
Kolonodale, Indon.,
10,000.............F6   19
Kolpino, Sov. Un.,
50,000.............s31   11
Kolwezi, Con. L.,
48,000.............C5   24
Kolyberovo, Sov. Un.,
10,000.............n18   12
Komádi, Hung., 7,362.B5   10
Komandorski Village,
Calif., 1,006........*B6   50
Komarno, Czech.,
24,000.............E5   7
Komarno, Sov. Un.,
5,000.............D7   7
Komárom, Hung.,
9,862.............B4   10

Komárom, co., Hung.,
270,208.............*B4   10
Komatsu, Jap., 54,900.H8   18
Kommunarsk, Sov. Un.,
107,000.......G12, q21   12
Komotini, Grc., 32,906.B5   14
Kompong Cham, Camb.,
25,000.............*C2   19
Kompong Chhnang, Camb.,
25,000.............*C2   19
Kompong Kleang, Camb.,
10,000.............*C2   19
Kompong Speu, Camb.,
5,000.............*C2   19
Kompong Thom, Camb.,
25,000.............C2   19
Komrat, Sov. Un.,
10,000.............H7   12
Komsomolsk [-na-Amure],
Sov. Un., 189,000...D16   13
Konawa, Okla., 1,555...C5   79
Kondoa, Tan., 2,816...A7   24
Kondopoga, Sov. Un.,
5,000.............F16   11
Kong, reg., I.C.......G4   22
Kongju, Kor., 23,400...H3   18
Kongsberg, Nor., 9,700.H3   11
Konin, Pol., 3,500.....B5   7
Konosha, Sov. Un.,
10,000.............A13   12
Konotop, Sov. Un.,
56,000.............F9   12
Konskie, Pol., 7,386....C6   7
Konstantinovka, Sov. Un.,
93,000............q20   12
Konstanz, Ger., 52,700.E4   6
Kontum, Viet., 10,000..C3   19
Konya, Tur.,
122,700.............D9   14
Konyang, Kor., 2,000...I3   18
Koochiching, co., Minn.,
18,190.............B4   67
Kootenai, co., Idaho,
29,556.............B2   57
Kopeysk, Sov. Un.,
168,000...........*D9   13
Köping, Swe.,
17,700.........H6, t33   11
Kopparberg, co., Swe.,
286,600...........*G6   11
Koppel, Pa., 1,389.....E1   81
Kopperston, W. Va.,
950.............*D3   87
Koprivnica, Yugo.,
1,329.............B3   10
Kopychintsy, Sov. Un.,
10,000.............G5   12
Korçë, Alb., 34,400....B3   14
Korçë, pref., Alb.,
175,000...........*B3   14
Korea, North, country,
Asia, 10,029,500.....F4   37
Korea, South, country,
Asia, 24,994,117....H3   37
Korets, Sov. Un.,
10,000.............F6   12
Korhogo, I.C., 14,000..G3   22
Kórinthos (Corinth), Grc.,
15,892.............D4   14
Koriyama, Jap.,
102,636.............H10   18
Korkino, Sov. Un.,
87,000...........*D9   13
Kormend, Hung., 7,581.B3   10
Korneuburg, Aus.,
8,276.............D8   6
Koropi, Grc., 7,128...*D4   14
Korosten, Sov. Un.,
33,800.............F7   12
Korsakov (Otomari),
Sov. Un., 43,800....E17   13
Kortrijk, Bel., 43,606..B5   5
Kos, Grc., 8,844......D6   14
Koscian, Pol., 12,900..B4   7
Koscierzyna, Pol.,
7,820.............A4   7
Kosciusko, Miss.,
6,800.............B4   68
Kosciusko, co., Ind.,
40,373.............B6   59
Koshan, China,
25,000.............B10   17
Košice, Czech., 79,600.D6   7
Kosong, Kor., 14,842..G4   18
Kosove, pref., Alb.,
53,000...........*A3   14
Kosovska Mitrovica,
Yugo., 26,620......D5   10
Kossuth, co., Iowa,
25,314.............A3   60
Kosti, Sudan, 22,688...F4   23
Kostroma, Sov. Un.,
184,000.............C13   12
Kostrzyn, Pol., 23,000.B3   7
Koszalin, Pol., 44,000..A4   7
Koszeg, Hung., 9,818..B3   10
Kotabaru, see
Sukarnapura, W. Irian
Kota Bharu, Mala.,
38,103.............D2   19
Kotah, India, 120,345..C6   20

Kotelnikovskiy, Sov. Un.,
10,000.............H14   12
Köthen, Ger., 37,600...C5   6
Kotka, Fin., 30,300...G12   11
Kotlas, Sov. Un.,
55,000.............C7   13
Kotor, Yugo., 4,833...D4   10
Kotovsk, Sov. Un.,
10,000.............H7   12
Kotung, China, 5,000..B7   18
Kotzebue, Alsk.,
1,290...........*B7   47
Koudougou, Upper Volta,
8,000.............F4   22
Kountze, Tex., 1,768...D5   84
Kouts, Ind., 1,007.....B3   59
Kouvola, Fin., 18,200.G12   11
Kovel, Sov. Un.,
42,600.............F5   12
Kovrov, Sov. Un.,
103,000.............C13   12
Kowa, Jap., 10,300....o15   18
Kowloon, Hong Kong,
726,976.............G7   17
Kowon, Kor., 5,000....G3   18
Kozan, Tur., 15,200..D10   14
Kozani, Grc., 21,537..*B3   14
Kozani, prov., Grc.,
190,835...........*B3   14
Kozhikode, India,
192,521.............F6   20
Kozienice, Pol., 4,099..C6   7
Kozle, Pol., 8,277.....C5   7
Kozloduy, Bul., 7,422..D6   10
Kozuchow, Pol., 8,782..C3   7
Kragujevac, Yugo.,
52,491.............D5   10
Krakow, Pol., 479,000..C5   7
Kraljevo, Yugo.,
20,409.............D5   10
Kralupy [nad Vltavou],
Czech., 11,100......n17   7
Kramatorsk, Sov. Un.,
123,000.......G11, q20   12
Kranj, Yugo., 21,354...B2   10
Kraslice, Czech., 6,294.C2   7
Krasnik Lubelski, Pol.,
9,158.............C7   7
Krasnoarmeysk, Sov. Un.,
54,000.............F15   12
Krasnodar, Sov. Un.,
343,000.............I12   12
Krasnograd, Sov. Un.,
10,000.............G10   12
Krasnoselye, Sov. Un.,
10,000.............G9   12
Krasnoslobodsk, Sov. Un.,
5,000.............D14   12
Krasnovodsk, Sov. Un.,
38,000.............E8   13
Krasnoyarsk, Sov. Un.,
468,000.............D12   13
Krasnystaw, Pol.,
10,300.............C7   7
Krasnyy Liman, Sov. Un.,
10,000............q20   12
Krasnyy Luch, Sov. Un.,
98,000............q21   12
Krasnyy Sulin, Sov. Un.,
66,600.............H13   12
Krasnyy Yar, Sov. Un.,
10,000.............F15   12
Kratie, Camb., 25,000..C3   19
Krebs, Okla., 1,342....C6   79
Krefeld, Ger., 213,100..C3   6
Kremenchug, Sov. Un.,
95,000.............G9   12
Kremenets, Sov. Un.,
10,000.............F5   12
Kremennaya, Sov. Un.,
5,000.............p21   12
Krems, Aus., 21,046...D7   6
Kreole, Miss.,
1,870.........E5, E3   68
Krichev, Sov. Un.,
5,000.............E8   12
Krishnagiri, India,
19,774.............F6   20
Kristiansand, Nor.,
27,900.............H2   11
Kristianstad, Swe.,
26,100.............I6   11
Kristianstad, co., Swe.,
256,600...........*I5   11
Kristiansund, Nor.,
17,200.............F2   11
Krivoy Rog, Sov. Un.,
436,000.............H9   12
Križevci, Yugo., 6,498..B3   10
Krnov, Czech., 21,600..C4   7
Kromeriz, Czech.,
20,600.............D4   7
Kromy, Sov. Un.,
10,000.............E10   12
Kronoberg, co., Swe.,
151,000...........*I6   11
Kronshtadt, Sov. Un.,
59,000.............B7   12
Kroonstad, S. Afr.,
42,438.............F5   24

Kropotkin, Sov. Un.,
57,000.............I13   12
Krosno, Pol., 20,000...D6   7
Krosno Odrzanskie, Pol.,
5,841.............B3   7
Krotoszyn, Pol., 16,300.C4   7
Krotz Springs, La.,
1,057.............D4   63
Krsko, Yugo., 629.....C2   10
Krugersdorp, S. Afr.,
89,947.............F5   24
Krumroy, Ohio,
1,400...........*A6   78
Kruševac, Yugo.,
22,140.............D5   10
Kruševo, Yugo.,
4,099.............E6   10
Krymskaya, Sov. Un.,
10,000.............I11   12
Krynki, Pol., 5,290....B7   7
Ksar el Kebir, Mor.,
34,035.............B3   22
Ksar es Souk, Mor.,
6,554.............B4   22
Kuala Lipis, Mala.,
8,753.............E2   19
Kuala Lumpur, Mala.,
316,230.............E2   19
Kuala Trengganu, Mala.,
29,446.............D2   19
Kuantan, Mala.,
23,034.............E2   19
Kuching, Mala.,
37,949.............E4   19
Kuerhlo (Korla), China,
10,000.............C2   17
Kufstein, Aus., 11,215..E6   6
Kuji, Jap., 14,750.....F10   18
Kuki, Jap., 11,300....m18   18
Kukong, China,
73,000.............G7   17
Kula, Bul., 5,566.....D6   10
Kula, Tur., 9,180.....*C7   14
Kula, Yugo., 13,612...C4   10
Kulebaki, Sov. Un.,
34,000.............D14   12
Kuling, China, 5,000..F8   17
Kulmbach, Ger.,
23,500.............C5   6
Kulpmont, Pa., 4,288..E9   81
Kumagaya, Jap.,
60,100.............m18   18
Kumamoto, Jap.,
373,922.............J5   18
Kumamoto, pref., Jap.,
1,856,192...........*J5   18
Kumanovo, Yugo.,
30,734.............D5   10
Kumasi, Ghana, 220,922
(*78,483)..........G4   22
Kumbakonam, India,
92,581.............F6   20
Kumla, Swe.,
10,000.........H6, t33   11
Kungchuling, China,
25,000.............E2   18
Kunming, China,
880,000.............F5   17
Kunsan, Kor., 90,500...I3   18
Kunszentmarton, Hung.,
8,783.............B5   10
Kuolayarvi, Sov. Un.,
10,000.............D13   11
Kuopio, Fin., 45,000..F12   11
Kuopio, dept., Fin.,
453,881...........*F12   11
Kupang, Indon., 7,171.H6   19
Kupyansk, Sov. Un.,
32,400.............G11   12
Kurashiki, Jap., 90,000..I6   18
Kurdzhali, Bul., 10,480.E7   10
Kure, Jap., 210,032....I6   18
Kuressaare, Sov. Un.,
10,000.............B4   12
Kurgan, Sov. Un.,
164,000.............D9   13
Kuri, India, 10,000....C5   20
Kuril, is., Sov. Un....E17   16
Kurnool, India,
100,815.............E6   20
Kursk, Sov. Un.,
222,000.............F11   12
Kurthwood, La., 70....C2   63
Kurtistown, Haw.,
1,025.............D6   56
Kurume, Jap., 155,041..J5   18
Kurunegala, Cey.,
13,510.............G7   20
Kusatsu, Jap., 17,800..n14   18
Kushchevskaya, Sov. Un.,
10,000.............H12   12
Kushevat, Sov. Un.,
1,000.............C9   13
Kushiro, Jap., 150,624.E12   18
Kushka, Sov. Un.,
7,100.............F9   13
Kustanay, Sov. Un.,
98,000.............D9   13
Kutahya, Tur., 39,900..C7   14
Kutaradja, Indon.,
34,207.............k11   19

Kutna Hora, Czech.,
16,900............D3 7
Kutno, Pol., 20,000....B5 7
Kutztown, Pa.,
3,321............E10 81
Kuwait, Kuw.,
104,551............D4 15
Kuwait, country, Asia,
206,177............D4 15
Kuwana, Jap.,
69,391............I8, n15 18
Kuybyshev, Sov. Un.,
863,000............D8 13
Kuznetsk, Sov. Un.,
62,000............E16 12
Kwangju, Kor., 240,000. I3 18

Kwangsi Chuang, auton.
reg., China,
19,390,000.........G6 17
Kwangtung, prov., China,
37,960,000.........G7 17
Kweichow, prov., China,
16,890,000.........F6 17
Kweilin, China,
145,100............F7 17
Kweisui, see Huhehot,
China.
Kweiyang, China,
504,000............G7 17
Kwidzyn, Pol.,
20,000............B5 7
Kyaiklat, Bur.,
15,781............E10 20

Kyaikto, Bur.,
10,000............*B1 19
Kyakhta, Sov. Un.,
21,700............D13 13
Kyaukse, Bur.,
8,659............D10 20
Kybartai, Sov. Un.,
7,274............A7 7
Kyje, Czech., 5,836....n18 7
Kyle, Tex., 1,023....E4 84
Kylestrome, Scot.....*A4 4
Kyllburg, Ger., 1,250..*C3 6
Kymi, dept., Fin.,
247,913............*G12 11
Kynlyn, Del., 1,600...*A6 53

Kyŏngju, Kor.,
42,100............I4 18
Kyoto, Jap.,
1,284,818......I7, n14 18
Kyoto, pref., Jap.,
1,993,403......*I7 18
Kyritz, Ger., 8,679....B6 6
Kyshtym, Sov. Un.,
31,000............*D9 13
Kyustendil, Bul.,
19,309............D6 10
Kyzyl, Sov. Un.,
38,000............D12 13
Kzyl-Orda, Sov. Un.,
71,000............E9 13

L

Laa, Aus., 4,925......D8 6
La Baie Shawinigan, Que.,
Can., 1,085.........C5 42
La Banda, Arg., 16,953. E3 19
La Barca, Mex.,
16,330........C4, m12 34
Labé, Guinea, 11,800...F2 22
Labelle, Que., Can.,
1,224............C3 42
La Belle, Fla., 1,262...F5 54
Labelle, co., Que., Can.,
29,084............C2 42
Labette, co., Kans.,
26,805............E8 61
Labin, Yugo., 6,152....C2 10
La Boca, C.Z., 48.....*B2 32
Laboulaye, Arg., 9,032. A4 28
Labrador, reg., Newf.,
Can., 10,814........g9 44
Laburnum Manor, Va.,
2,500............*D5 85
La Canada, Calif.,
13,340............*F2 50
La Carlota, Phil.,
7,213............*C6 19
La Carolina, Sp.,
12,138............C4 8
Lac au Saumon, Que.,
Can., 1,548........*B3 42
Laccadive, is., India....F5 20
La Ceiba, Hond.,
24,864............D7 34
Lac Etchemin, Que., Can.,
1,485............C7 42
Lacey, Wash., 6,630...B3 86
Lacey Park, Pa.,
4,000............*F11 81
La Chaux-de-Fonds,
Switz., 38,906......E3 6
Lachine, Que., Can.,
38,630..........D4, D9 42
La Chorrera, Pan.,
8,626............B2 32
Lachute, Que., Can.,
7,560............D3 42
La Ciotat, Fr., 18,827..F6 5
Lackawanna, N.Y.,
29,564............C2 75
Lackawanna, co., Pa.,
234,531............D10 81
Lac la Biche, Alta., Can.,
1,314............B5 38
Laclede, co., Mo.,
18,991............D5 69
Lac Megantic, Que., Can.,
7,015............D7 42
Lacolle, Que., Can.,
1,187............D4 42
Lacombe, Alta., Can.,
3,029............C4 38
Lacombe, La., 650.....D6 63
Lacon, Ill., 2,175......B4 58
Laconia, N.H., 15,288..D5 73
Lacoochee, Fla., 1,523. D4 54
La Coruña, Sp.,
177,502............A1 8
La Coruña, prov., Sp.,
971,641............*A1 8
La Courneuve, Fr.,
25,792............g10 5
Lacq, Fr., 319.........F3 5
Lac qui Parle, co., Minn.,
13,330............F2 67
La Crescent, Minn.,
2,624............G7 67
La Crescenta, Calif.,
12,000............*F2 50
La Cresta Village, Calif.,
10,000............*E4 50
La Crosse, Kans.,
1,767............D4 61
La Crosse, Wis., 47,575. E2 88
La Crosse, co., Wis.,
72,465............E2 88
La Cygne, Kans., 810..D9 61
Lacy-Lakeview, Tex.,
2,272............*D4 84
Ladd, Ill., 1,255......B4 58
Ladera Heights, Calif.,
1,500............*F2 50

Ladner, B.C., Can.,
2,000............A10, E6 37
Ladoga, Ind., 974......E4 59
Ladonia, Tex., 890.....C5 84
La Dorado, Colo.,
14,577............B3 32
Ladue, Mo., 9,466....*C7 69
Ladysmith, B.C., Can.,
2,173............B9, E6 37
Ladysmith, S. Afr.,
22,955............F5 24
Ladysmith, Wis., 3,584. C2 88
La Estrada, Sp., 2,540. A1 8
La Farge, Wis., 833....E3 88
Lafayette, Ala., 2,605..C4 46
Lafayette, Calif.,
7,114............*B5 50
Lafayette, Colo., 2,612. B5 51
La Fayette, Ga., 5,588. B1 55
Lafayette, Ind., 42,330. D4 59
Lafayette, La., 40,400..D3 63
Lafayette, N.J., 350....A3 74
Lafayette, Tenn., 1,590. C7 83
Lafayette, co., Ark.,
11,030............D2 49
Lafayette, co., Fla.,
2,889............C3 54
Lafayette, co., Miss.,
21,355............A4 68
Lafayette, co., Mo.,
25,274............B4 69
Lafayette, co., Wis.,
18,142............F3 88
Lafayette, par., La.,
84,656............D3 63
Lafayette Hill, Pa.,
3,500............*A7 81
Lafayette Southwest, La.,
6,682............D3 63
La Feria, Tex., 3,047...F4 84
La Ferté-Bernard, Fr.,
5,979............C4 5
Lafferty, Ohio, 850.....B6 78
La Flèche, Fr., 9,439...D3 5
La Follette, Tenn.,
6,204............C9 83
Lafourche, par., La.,
55,381............E5 63
La France, S.C., 900...B2 82
Laghouat, Alg., 11,058. B5 22
Lagny, Fr., 11,945.....C5 5
Lagos, Nig., 364,000...G5 22
Lagos, Port., 7,143....D1 8
Lagos de Moreno, Mex.,
23,298............C4, m13 34
La Grand' Combe, Fr.,
14,440............E5 5
La Grande, Oreg.,
9,014............B8 80
La Grange, Ga., 23,632. C1 55
La Grange, Ill.,
16,326............B6, F2 58
Lagrange, Ind., 1,990..A7 59
La Grange, Ky., 2,168. B4 62
La Grange, Mo., 1,347. A6 69
La Grange, N.C., 2,133. B6 76
Lagrange, Ohio, 1,007. A5 78
La Grange, Tex., 3,623. E4 84
Lagrange, co., Ind.,
17,380............A7 59
La Grange Highlands, Ill.,
5,000............*F2 58
La Grange Park, Ill.,
13,793............F3 58
La Guadeloupe, Que.,
Can., 1,728........D7 42
La Guaira, Ven., 20,275
(*55,000)............A4 32
La Guajira, intendencia,
Col., 112,190........A3 32
La Guardia, Sp., 9,311. B1 8
Laguna, Braz., 17,451. D3 61
Laguna, prov., Phil.,
472,200............*C6 19
Laguna Beach, Calif.,
9,288............F5 50
Laguna Shores, Tex.,
1,500............*F4 84
La Habana, see Havana,
Cuba

La Habra, Calif.,
25,136............F3 50
La Habra Heights, Calif.,
1,500............*F3 50
Lahaina, Haw., 3,423..C5 56
La Harpe, Ill., 1,322...C3 58
Lahij, S. Arabia,
10,000............G3 15
Lahore, Pak., 1,225,000. B5 20
Lahr, Ger., 22,600....D3 6
Lahti, Fin., 66,600....G11 11
Laie, Haw., 1,767..B4, f10 56
Laigle, Fr., 5,520......C4 5
Laingsburg, Mich.,
1,057............F6 66
La Jara, Colo., 724....D5 51
La Junta, Colo., 8,026. D7 51
Lajes, Braz., 35,112....D2 30
Lajosmizse, Hung.,
4,735............B4 10
Lake, co., Calif., 13,786. C2 50
Lake, co., Colo., 7,101. B4 51
Lake, co., Fla., 57,383. D5 54
Lake, co., Ill., 293,656. A6 58
Lake, co., Ind., 513,269. B3 59
Lake, co., Mich., 5,338. E5 66
Lake, co., Minn.,
13,702............C7 67
Lake, co., Mont.,
13,104............C2 70
Lake, co., Ohio,
148,700............A6 78
Lake, co., Oreg., 7,158. E6 80
Lake, co., S. Dak.,
11,764............F8 77
Lake, co., Tenn., 9,572. A2 83
Lake Alfred, Fla.,
2,191............D5 54
Lake Andes, S. Dak.,
1,097............G7 77
Lake Arrowhead, Calif.,
500............E5, F3 50
Lake Arthur, La.,
3,541............D3 63
Lake Barcroft, Va.,
1,800............*B5 85
Lake Benton, Minn.,
905............F2 67
Lake Bluff, Ill.,
3,494............A6, E2 58
Lake Burien Heights,
Wash., 2,000........*B3 86
Lake Butler, Fla.,
1,311............B4 54
Lake Charles, La., 63,392
(*127,200)............D2 63
Lake City, Fla., 9,465. B4 54
Lake City, Iowa, 2,114. B3 60
Lake City, Minn.,
3,494............F6 67
Lake City, Pa., 1,722. B1 81
Lake City, S.C., 6,059. D8 82
Lake City, Tenn.,
1,914............C9 83
Lake Cowichan, B.C.,
Can., 2,149........*E5 37
Lake Crystal, Minn.,
1,652............F4 67
Lake Erie Beach, N.Y.,
2,117............*C1 75
Lake Fenton, Mich.,
1,500............*F7 66
Lakefield, Ont., Can.,
2,167............C6 41
Lakefield, Minn.,
1,789............G3 67
Lake Forest, Fla.,
8,000............*B5 54
Lake Forest, Ill.,
10,687............A6, E2 58
Lake Forest, S.C.,
1,500............*B3 82
Lake Forest Park, Wash.,
1,500............*B3 86
Lake Geneva, Wis.,
4,929............F5 88
Lake George, N.Y.,
1,0?6............B7 75
Lake Hamilton, Fla.,
930............*D5 54

Lake Harbor, Fla., 500. F6 54
Lake Helen, Fla., 1,096. D5 54
Lake Hiawatha, N.J.,
4,000............B4 74
Lake Hills, Wash.,
4,500............*D2 86
Lake Holloway, Fla.,
3,172............*D5 54
Lake Hopatcong, N.J.,
1,107............*B3 74
Lakehurst, N.J., 2,780. C4 74
Lake in the Hills, Ill.,
2,046............*A5 58
Lake Jackson, Tex.,
9,651............G5 84
Lakeland, Fla., 41,350. D5 54
Lakeland, Ga., 2,236...E3 55
Lakeland, Miss., 900...C3 68
Lakeland Village, Calif.,
3,593............*F5 50
Lake Linden, Mich.,
1,314............A2 66
Lake Lotawana, Mo.,
1,499............*C3 69
Lake Luzerne, N.Y.,
900............B7 75
Lake Mills, Iowa, 1,758. A4 60
Lakemills, Wis., 2,951. E5 88
Lake Mohawk, N.J.,
4,647............*A3 74
Lakemont, Pa., 1,500..F5 81
Lakemore, Ohio, 2,765. A6 78
Lake Odessa, Mich.,
1,806............F5 66
Lake of the Woods, co.,
Minn., 4,304........B4 67
Lake Orion, Mich.,
2,698............F5 66
Lake Orion Heights,
Mich., 1,918........*F7 66
Lake Oswego, Oreg.,
8,906..........B2, B4 80
Lake Ozark, Mo., 500..C5 69
Lake Park, Fla., 3,589. F6 54
Lake Park, Iowa, 952...A2 60
Lake Placid, Fla., 1,007. E5 54
Lake Placid, N.Y.,
2,998............A7, B3 75
Lakeport, Calif., 2,303. C2 50
Lake Preston, S. Dak.,
955............F8 77
Lake Providence, La.,
5,781............B4 63
Lake Ronkonkoma, N.Y.,
4,841............F4 52
Lake St. John East, co.,
Que., Can., 43,920...A6 42
Lake St. John West, co.,
Que., Can., 61,310...A5 42
Lake Shore, Fla.,
11,000............B6 54
Lakeside, Calif.,
6,000............E2, F5 50
Lakeside, La., 1,233...*C3 63
Lakeside, Ohio, 950....A5 78
Lakeside, Va., 19,000..*C7 85
Lakeside Park, Ky.,
2,214............A7 62
Lake Stevens, Wash.,
1,538............A3 86
Lake Success, N.Y.,
2,954............D2 75
Lake Telemark, N.J.,
1,000............*B3 74
Lakeview, Ga., 1,000..*B1 55
Lake View, Iowa, 1,165. B2 60
Lakeview, Mich., 1,126. E5 66
Lakeview, Mich.,
10,384............*F5 66
Lakeview, N.Y., 9,000. *E7 75
Lake View, N.Y.,
4,000............*C2 75
Lakeview, Ohio, 1,008. B4 78
Lakeview, Oreg., 3,260. E6 80
Lakeview, Tex., 1,200. *B6 84
Lakeview, Tex., 3,849. *E6 84
Lake Villa, Ill., 903....E2 58
Lake Village, Ark.,
2,998............D4 49
Lakeville, Conn., 950..B3 52

Lakeville, Minn., 924..F5 67
Lakeville, Ohio, 4,181..A7 78
Lake Wales, Fla., 8,346.E5 54
Lakewood, Calif.,
  67,126............*F2 50
Lakewood, Colo.,
  36,209.............*B5 51
Lakewood, Fla., 7,000.*B5 83
Lakewood, N.J., 16,020.C4 74
Lakewood, N.Y., 3,933.C1 75
Lakewood, Ohio,
  66,154.........A6, B2 78
Lakewood, Tex., 1,882.*E5 84
Lakewood Center, Wash.,
  20,000............*E1 86
Lake Worth, Fla.,
  20,758.............F6 54
Lake Worth Village, Tex.,
  3,833..............*B5 84
Lake Zurich, Ill., 3,458.E2 58
Lakhimpur, India,
  25,055.............C7 20
Lakin, Kans., 1,432....E2 61
Lakonia, prov., Grc.,
  118,661............*D4 14
Lakota, N. Dak., 1,066.B7 77
La Laguna, Sp.,
  18,000...........m13 8
La Libertad, dept., Peru,
  462,026............C2 31
Lalín, Sp., 1,353......A1 8
La Línea, Sp., 59,456..D3 8
Lalitpur, India,
  20,792.............D6 20
La Loma, Calif.,
  5,700.............*D3 50
La Maddalena, It.,
  11,169.............D2 9
La Malbaie, Que., Can.,
  2,580..............B7 42
Lamar, Colo., 7,369....C8 51
Lamar, Mo., 3,608.....D3 69
Lamar, S.C., 1,121....C7 82
Lamar, co., Ala.,
  14,271.............B1 46
Lamar, co., Ga., 10,240.C2 55
Lamar, co., Miss.,
  13,675.............D4 68
Lamar, co., Tex.,
  34,234.............C5 84
La Marque, Tex.,
  13,969.............G5 84
Lamartine, Que., Can.,
  66.................B7 42
Lamas, Peru, 5,625....C2 31
Lamb, co., Tex., 21,896.B1 84
Lamballe, Fr., 5,069...C2 5
Lambayeque, Peru,
  6,846..............C2 31
Lambayeque, dept., Peru,
  229,958............C2 31
Lambert, Miss., 1,181.A3 68
Lamberton, Minn.,
  1,141..............F3 67
Lambertville, Mich.,
  1,168.............*G7 67
Lambertville, N.J.,
  4,269..............C3 74
Lambton, co., Ont., Can.,
  102,131............E2 41
Lamego, Port., 7,449..B2 8
La Mesa, Calif.,
  30,441.............E2 50
Lamesa, Tex., 12,438..C2 84
Lamia, Grc., 25,509....C4 14
La Mirada, Calif.,
  22,444............*F4 50
Lamoille, co., Vt.,
  11,027.............B2 73
Lamoni, Iowa, 2,173...D4 60
Lamont, Calif., 6,177..E4 50
La Moure, N. Dak.,
  1,068..............D7 77
La Moure, co., N. Dak.,
  8,705..............D7 77
Lampang, Thai.,
  35,460............*B1 19
Lampasas, Tex., 5,061.D3 84
Lampasas, co., Tex.,
  9,418..............D3 84
Lamphun, Thai.,
  9,862.............*B1 19
Lanai, isl., Haw.......C5 56
Lanai City, Haw.,
  2,056..............C5 56
Lanao del Norte, prov.,
  Phil., 280,500.....*D6 19
Lanark, Ill., 1,473.....A4 58
Lanark, Scot., 8,436...C5 4
Lanark, co., Ont., Can.,
  40,313.............B8 41
Lanark, co., Scot.,
  1,626,317.........*C5 4
Lancashire, co., Eng.,
  5,131,646.........*C5 4
Lancaster, Calif.,
  26,012.............E4 50
Lancaster, Eng., 48,887.C5 4
Lancaster, Ky., 3,021..C5 62
Lancaster, N.H., 2,392.C4 73

Lancaster, N.Y.,
  12,254.............C2 75
Lancaster, Ohio,
  29,916.............C5 78
Lancaster, Pa., 61,055
  (*125,100).........F9 81
Lancaster, S.C., 7,999.B6 82
Lancaster, Tex., 7,501.B5 84
Lancaster, Wis., 3,703.F3 88
Lancaster, co., Nebr.,
  155,272............D9 71
Lancaster, co., Pa.,
  278,359............G9 81
Lancaster, co., S.C.,
  39,352.............B6 82
Lancaster, co., Va.,
  9,174..............D6 85
Lancaster Mills, S.C.,
  6,255.............*B6 82
Lancer, Ky., 500.......C7 62
Lanchow, China,
  699,000............D5 17
Lanciano, It., 13,300...C5 9
Lancut, Pol., 9,106....C7 7
Landau [an der Isar],
  Ger., 6,000........D6 6
Landau [in die Pfalz],
  Ger., 28,700.......D4 6
Landeck, Aus., 6,514...E5 6
Lander, Wyo., 4,182...C4 89
Lander, co., Nev.,
  1,566..............A3 72
Landerneau, Fr.,
  11,834.............C1 5
Landes, dept., Fr.,
  260,495...........*F3 5
Landing, N.J., 1,068..*B3 74
Landis, N.C., 1,763....B3 76
Landisville, Pa.,
  1,690............*F11 81
Landivisiau, Fr., 4,121.C1 5
Landover Hills, Md.,
  1,850.............*C1 53
Landrum, S.C., 1,930..A3 82
Landsberg, Ger.,
  13,400.............D5 6
Landshut, Ger., 49,500.D6 6
Landskrona, Swe.,
  28,900.............J5 11
Lane, co., Kans., 3,060.D3 61
Lane, co., Oreg.,
  162,890............D4 80
Lanesboro, Minn.,
  1,063..............G7 67
Lanett, Ala., 7,674....C4 46
Langadhas, Grc.,
  7,590.............*B4 14
Langdale, Ala., 2,528..C4 46
Langdon, N. Dak.,
  2,151..............B7 77
Langeloth, Pa., 1,112..F1 81
Langensalza, Ger.,
  16,200.............C5 6
Langenthal, Switz.,
  10,978.............E3 6
Langesund, Nor.,
  2,200.........H3, p27 11
Langhorne, Pa., 1,924.F12 81
Langlade, co., Wis.,
  19,916.............C4 88
Langley, B.C., Can.,
  2,365.............B10 37
Langley, Ky., 700.....C7 62
Langley, S.C., 1,216...D4 82
Langley Park, Md.,
  11,510............*C3 53
Langnau [in Emmental]
  Switz., 9,201......E3 6
Langon, Fr., 4,197....E3 5
Langreo, Sp., 7,138...A3 8
Langres, Fr., 9,577....D6 6
Lang Son, Viet.,
  25,000...........*G13 16
Languedoc, former prov.,
  Fr., 2,413,000......F5 5
Lanham, Md., 2,500...C4 53
Lanhsi, China, 5,000...C3 18
Lanier, co., Ga., 5,097.E3 55
Lannion, Fr., 6,497....C2 5
Lannon, Wis., 1,084...E1 88
Lansdale, Pa., 12,612.F11 81
Lansdowne, Md.,
  13,134.............B4 53
Lansdowne, Pa.,
  12,601.......B11, G11 81
L'Anse, Mich., 2,397..B2 66
Lansford, Pa., 5,958..E10 81
Lansing, Ont., Can.,
  4,000..............E6 41
Lansing, Ill.,
  19,366.........B6, F3 58
Lansing, Iowa, 1,325...A6 60
Lansing, Kans., 1,264.B8 61
Lansing, Mich., 107,807
  (*209,100).........F6 66
Lansing, Ohio, 1,200..B1 87
Lantana, Fla., 5,021..*F6 54
Laoag, Phil., 26,000...B6 19
Laoighis, co., Ire.,
  45,069...........*D3 4

Lao Kay, Viet.,
  25,000...........*G13 16
Laon, Fr., 25,078......C5 5
Laona, Wis., 950......C5 88
La Oroya, Peru, 17,076.D2 31
Laos, country, Asia,
  1,200,000..........B2 19
Lapa, Braz., 7,167.....D3 30
La Palma, Sp., 8,969..D2 8
La Pampa, prov., Arg.,
  158,489............B3 28
La Paz, Arg., 15,006...A5 28
La Paz, Bol., 321,073..C2 29
La Paz, Mex., 23,324..C2 34
La Paz, dept., Bol.,
  948,446............C2 29
Lapeer, Mich., 6,160...E7 66
Lapeer, co., Mich.,
  41,926.............E7 56
Lapel, Ind., 1,772....D6 59
La Piedad [Cabadas],
  Mex., 24,306.......m12 34
Laplace, La., 3,541....B6 63
Lapland, reg., Eur...C12 11
La Plata, Arg.,
  295,000........A5, g8 28
La Plata, Md., 1,214...C4 53
La Plata, Mo., 1,365...A5 69
La Plata, co., Colo.,
  19,225.............D3 51
La Pola, Sp., 5,430...A3 8
La Porte, Ind., 21,157..A4 59
La Porte, Tex., 4,512..F5 84
La Porte, co., Ind.,
  95,111.............A4 59
La Porte City, Iowa,
  1,953..............B5 60
Lappeenranta, Fin.,
  21,600............G13 11
Lappi, dept., Fin.,
  152,607..........*D11 11
Laprairie, Que., Can.,
  7,228..............D4 42
Laprairie, co., Que., Can.,
  31,157.............D4 42
La Presa, Calif., 1,300.*E2 50
La Providence, Que.,
  Can., 4,251.......*D5 42
La Pryor, Tex., 900....E3 84
La Puebla, Sp., 9,931..C7 8
La Puebla de Montalbán,
  Sp., 7,700.........C3 8
La Puente, Calif.,
  24,723............*F3 50
La Quiaca, Arg., 6,768.D2 29
L'Aquila, It., 36,000...C4 9
Lara, state, Ven.,
  489,140............A3 32
Larache, Mor., 30,763..A3 22
Laramie, Wyo., 17,520.D7 89
Laramie, co., Wyo.,
  60,149.............D8 89
Larchmont, N.Y.,
  6,789..............D2 75
Laredo, Sp., 6,206....A4 8
Laredo, Tex., 60,678
  (*152,500).........F3 84
Largo, Fla., 5,302..E1, E4 54
Lariat, Colo., 900....D4 51
La Ricamarie, Fr.,
  11,902.............E6 5
Larimer, Pa., 1,500..*F3 81
Larimer, co., Colo.,
  53,343.............A5 51
Larimore, N. Dak.,
  1,714..............C8 77
Larino, It., 8,678....D5 9
La Rioja, Arg., 23,809.E2 29
La Rioja, prov., Arg.,
  128,270............E2 29
Lárisa, Grc., 55,391...C4 14
Lárisa, prov., Grc.,
  237,776...........*C4 14
Larkana, Pak., 33,414..C4 20
Larkspur, Calif., 5,710.B5 50
Larksville, Pa., 4,390..B8 81
Larne, N. Ire., 16,341..C4 4
Larned, Kans., 5,001..D4 61
La Rochelle, Fr.,
  66,590.............D3 5
La Roche-sur-Yon, Fr.,
  24,019.............D3 5
La Roda, Sp., 12,190..C4 8
La Romana, Dom. Rep.,
  24,058.............F9 35
Larose, La., 2,796....E5 63
Larue, co., Ky., 10,346.C4 62
Larvik, Nor.,
  10,600.........H4, p28 11
Larwill, Ind., 994.....B6 59
La Salle, Que., Can.,
  30,904...........*D9 42
La Salle, Colo., 1,070..A6 51
La Salle, Ill., 11,897..B4 58
La Salle, co., Ill.,
  110,800............B5 58
La Salle, co., Tex.,
  5,972..............E3 84
La Salle, par., La.,
  13,011.............C3 63

Las Animas, Colo.,
  3,402..............C7 51
Las Animas, co., Colo.,
  19,983.............D6 51
La Sarre, Que., Can.,
  3,944..............E9 41
Las Conchas, Arg.,
  24,809.............g7 28
Las Cruces, N. Mex.,
  29,367.............C5 48
La Serena, Chile,
  40,000.............E1 29
La Seyne [-sur-Mer], Fr.,
  33,570.............F6 5
Las Flores, Arg., 8,955.B5 28
La Sierra, Calif., 7,000.F3 50
Lasithi, prov., Grc.,
  73,880............*E5 14
Las Matas de Farfan,
  Dom. Rep., 3,585...F8 35
La Solana, Sp., 14,948.C4 8
Las Palmas [de Gran
  Canaria], Sp.,
  193,862...........m14 8
Las Palmas, prov., Sp.,
  453,973...........m14 8
La Spezia, It., 121,923.B2 19
Las Piedras, Ur.,
  15,400.............E1 30
Lassen, co., Calif.,
  13,597.............B3 50
L'Assomption, Que.,
  Can., 4,448.......D4 42
L'Assomption, co., Que.,
  Can., 39,440.......D4 42
Las Varillas, Arg.,
  5,950..............A4 28
Las Vegas, N. Mex.,
  6,028.........B6, D7 48
Las Vegas, Nev., 64,405
  (*119,300).........C4 72
Las Villas, prov., Cuba,
  1,030,162..........D4 35
Latacunga, Ec., 10,340.B2 31
Latah, co., Idaho,
  21,170.............C2 57
La Teste-de-Buch, Fr.,
  8,907..............E3 5
Latham, N.Y., 5,000..*C7 75
Lathrop, Mo., 1,006...B3 69
Lathrope, Calif., 1,123.B6 50
Lathrup Village, Mich.,
  3,556.............*A7 66
Latimer, co., Okla.,
  7,738..............C6 79
Latina, It., 24,500...D4, k9 9
Latium, reg., It.......C4 9
Laton, Calif., 1,052...D4 50
Latrobe, Pa., 11,932..F3 81
Latta, S.C., 1,901.....C9 82
Lattimer Mines, Pa.,
  600...............E10 81
Lattingtown, N.Y.,
  1,461............*E7 75
La Tuque, Que., Can.,
  13,023.............B5 42
Latvia (S.S.R.), rep.,
  Sov. Un., 2,142,000.C4 12
Lauderdale, Minn.,
  1,676.............E7 67
Lauderdale, co., Ala.,
  61,622.............A2 46
Lauderdale, co., Miss.,
  67,119.............C5 68
Lauderdale, co., Tenn.,
  21,844.............B2 83
Lauderdale-by-the-Sea,
  Fla., 1,327.......*F6 54
Launceston, Austl.,
  38,118 (*56,721)...o15 25
La Unión, Chile, 9,830.C2 28
La Unión, Sal., 10,687.E7 34
La Unión, Sp., 11,687..D5 8
La Union, prov., Phil.,
  295,200...........*B6 19
Laupheim, Ger., 8,700.D4 6
Laurel, Del., 2,709....C6 53
Laurel, Fla., 1,000....E4 54
Laurel, Md., 8,503.....B4 53
Laurel, Miss., 27,889..D4 68
Laurel, Mont., 4,601...E8 70
Laurel, Nebr., 922....B8 71
Laurel, co., Ky., 24,901.C5 62
Laureldale, Pa., 4,051.F10 81
Laurel Gardens, Pa.,
  1,500.............*B6 81
Laurel Heights, Wash.,
  900...............*B3 86
Laurel Run, Pa., 855..B8 81
Laurel Springs, N.J.,
  2,028.............*D3 74
Laurence Harbor, N.J.,
  3,000..............C4 74
Laurens, Iowa, 1,799..B3 60
Laurens, S.C., 9,598..B3 82
Laurens, co., Ga.,
  32,313.............D4 55
Laurens, co., S.C.,
  47,609.............C4 82
Lauria Inferiore, It.,
  4,530..............D5 9

Laurinburg, N.C., 8,242............C4 76
Laurium, Mich., 3,058..A2 66
Lausanne, Switz., 126,328 (*173,000).........E3 6
Lautaro, Chile, 9,255...B2 28
Lauzon, Que., Can., 11,533............C6, C9 42
Lavaca, co., Tex., 20,174.............E4 84
Lavadores, Sp., 38,462.A1 8
Laval, Fr., 39,283.....C3 5
Laval, co., Que., Can., 124,741.............D4 42
La Vale, Md., 4,031..*D2 53
Lavalleja, dept., Ur., 62,200.............*E1 30
Lavaltrie, Que., Can., 1,034.............D4 42
Lavaur, Fr., 4,137.....F4 5
La Vega, Dom. Rep., 19,884.............F8 35
Lavello, It., 13,745...D5 9
La Verne, Calif., 6,516.F3 50
Laverne, Okla., 1,937..A2 79
Laviana, Sp., 12,455...A3 8
La Victoria, Ven., 23,126.............A4 32
La Villa, Tex., 1,261..*F4 84
La Vista, Ga., 3,000..*C2 55
Lavonia, Ga., 2,088....B3 55
Lavras de Mangabeira, Braz., 23,793........C3 30
Lawndale, Calif., 21,740.............*F2 50
Lawndale, N.C., 723...B2 76
Lawnside, N.J., 2,155.*D2 74
Lawnton, Pa., 3,500..*F8 81
Lawrence, Ind., 10,103.............E5, H8 59
Lawrence, Kans., 32,858.............B7, D8 61
Lawrence, Mass., 70,933 (*196,500).........A5 65
Lawrence, N.Y., 5,907.G2 52
Lawrence, Pa., 1,048...F1 81
Lawrence, co., Ala., 24,501.............A2 46
Lawrence, co., Ark., 17,267.............A4 49
Lawrence, co., Ill., 18,540.............E6 58
Lawrence, co., Ind., 36,564.............G5 59
Lawrence, co., Ky., 12,134.............B7 62
Lawrence, co., Miss., 10,215.............D3 68
Lawrence, co., Mo., 23,260.............D4 69
Lawrence, co., Ohio, 55,438.............D5 78
Lawrence, co., Pa., 112,965............D1 81
Lawrence, co., S. Dak., 17,075.............F2 77
Lawrence, co., Tenn., 28,049.............B4 83
Lawrenceburg, Ind., 5,004.............F8 59
Lawrenceburg, Ky., 2,523.............B5 62
Lawrenceburg, Tenn., 8,042.............B4 83
Lawrence Park, Pa., 4,403.............*B1 81
Lawrenceville, Ga., 3,804...........A6, C3 55
Lawrenceville, Ill., 5,492.............E6 58
Lawrenceville, N.J., 2,000.............C3 74
Lawrenceville, Va., 1,941.............E5 85
Lawton, Mich., 1,402..F5 66
Lawton, Okla., 61,697..C3 79
Layland, W. Va., 400..D7 87
Layton, Utah, 9,027....C2 72
Lazio, pol. dist., It., 3,958,957.........*D4 9
Lea, co., N. Mex., 53,429.............C7 48
Leachville, Ark., 1,507.B5 49
Lead, S. Dak., 6,211...F2 77
Leader, Sask., Can., 1,211.............G1 39
Leadville, Colo., 4,008..B4 51
Leadwood, Mo., 1,343..D7 69
League City, Tex., 2,622.............*E6 84
Leake, co., Miss., 18,660.............C4 68
Leakesville, Miss., 1,014.............D5 68
Leakey, Tex., 587......E3 84
Leaksville, N.C., 6,427.A4 76
Lealman, Fla., 13,000..E2 54
Leamington, Ont., Can., 9,030.............E2 41
Leamington, Eng., 43,236.............D6 4

Leaside, Ont., Can., 18,579.............E6 41
Leatherwood, Ky., 1,283.............C6 62
Leavenworth, Kans., 22,052.............B8, C9 61
Leavenworth, Wash., 1,480.............B5 86
Leavenworth, co., Kans., 48,524.............C8 61
Leavittsburg, Ohio, 3,300.............A7 78
Leawood, Kans., 7,466.D9 61
Lebanon, Ill., 2,853....E4 58
Lebanon, Ind., 9,593...D5 59
Lebanon, Ky., 4,813....C4 62
Lebanon, Mo., 8,220...D5 69
Lebanon, N.H., 9,299..D3 73
Lebanon, Ohio, 5,993..C3 78
Lebanon, Oreg., 5,858.........C4, D4 80
Lebanon, Pa., 30,045...F9 81
Lebanon, Tenn., 10,512.A5 83
Lebanon, Va., 2,085....B3 85
Lebanon, co., Pa., 90,853.............F9 81
Lebanon, country, Asia, 1,303,940.........F10 14
Lebanon Junction, Ky., 1,527.............C4 62
Lebedyan, Sov. Un., 10,000.............E12 12
Le Blanc, Fr., 5,279...D4 5
Le Blanc-Mesnil, Fr., 35,708.............g10 5
Lebork, Pol., 21,000...A4 7
Le Bourget, Fr., 10,077.............g10 5
Le Bouscat, Fr., 21,404.............E3 5
Lebrija, Sp., 12,297...D2 8
Le Cateau, Fr., 9,055..B5 5
Lecce, It., 75,297......D7 9
Lecco, It., 48,230.....B2 9
Le Center, Minn., 1,597.............F7 67
Le Chambon-Feugerolles, Fr., 20,320.........E6 5
Le Chesnay, Fr., 13,249.g9 5
Le Claire, Iowa, 1,546...........C7, D7 60
Lecompte, La., 1,485...C3 63
Le Coteau, Fr., 6,571..D6 5
Le Creusot, Fr., 33,737.D6 5
Leczyca, Pol., 6,755...B7 7
Ledo, India, 5,000....C10 20
Leduc, Alta., Can., 2,356.............C4 38
Lee, Mass., 3,078.....B1 65
Lee, co., Ala., 49,754...C4 46
Lee, co., Ark., 21,001..C5 49
Lee, co., Fla., 54,539..F5 54
Lee, co., Ga., 6,204....E2 55
Lee, co., Ill., 38,749...B4 58
Lee, co., Iowa, 44,207..D6 60
Lee, co., Ky., 7,420....C6 62
Lee, co., Miss., 40,589..A5 68
Lee, co., N.C., 26,561..B4 76
Lee, co., S.C., 21,832..C7 82
Lee, co., Tex., 8,949...D4 84
Lee, co., Va., 25,824...B1 85
Leechburg, Pa., 3,545..E2 81
Leedon Estates, Pa., 1,800.............*B11 81
Leeds, Ala., 6,162...C3, E5 45
Leeds, Eng., 510,597..D6 4
Leeds, co., Ont., Can., 46,889.............C8 41
Leelanau, co., Mich., 9,321.............D5 66
Lee Park, Pa., 3,500.*D10 81
Leer, Ger., 20,500....B3 6
Leesburg, Fla., 11,172..D5 54
Leesburg, Ohio, 932....C4 78
Leesburg, Va., 2,869..B5 85
Lee's Summit, Mo., 8,267...........C3, E2 69
Leesville, La., 4,689...C2 63
Leesville, S.C., 1,619..D4 82
Leetes Island, Conn., 400.............D6 52
Leetonia, Ohio, 2,543..B7 78
Leetsdale, Pa., 2,153..A5 81
Leeuwarden, Neth., 80,928.............A6 5
Leeward Islands, see Antigua, Montserrat, St. Kitts-Nevis-Anguilla, and Virgin Is. (Br.), Br. dep., N.A.
Leflore, co., Miss., 47,142.............B3 68
Le Flore, co., Okla., 29,106.............C7 79
Le François, Mart., 2,189.............o16 35
Leganés, Sp., 8,539....p17 8
Legaspi, Phil., 28,000..C6 19
Leghorn, see Livorno, It.
Legion, Tex., 1,691...*E3 84
Legnano, It., 42,460...B2 9

Legnica, Pol., 64,000...C4 7
Le Havre, Fr., 183,776.C3 5
Lehi, Utah, 4,377..A6, D2 72
Lehigh, co., Pa., 227,536.............E10 81
Lehighton, Pa., 6,318.E10 81
Lehrte, Ger., 21,300...B4 6
Leiah, Pak., 14,914....B5 20
Leicester, Eng., 273,298.............D6 4
Leicester, Mass., 1,750.............B4 65
Leicester, co., Eng., 682,196.............*D6 4
Leiden, Neth., 96,700..A6 5
Leigh Creek, Austl., 1,020.............E2 26
Leighton, Ala., 1,158...A2 46
Leinster, prov., Ire., 1,332,149.........*D3 4
Leipsic, Ohio, 1,802...A4 78
Leipzig, Ger., 585,300..C6 6
Leiria, Port., 7,123....C1 8
Leisure City, Fla., 3,001.............F3 54
Leitchfield, Ky., 2,982..C3 62
Leith, Pa., 1,622......*G2 81
Leitrim, co., Ire., 33,470.............*D3 4
Lejunior, Ky., 900.....D6 62
Le Kef, Tun., 14,743..A6 22
Leksands, Swe., 1,800..G6 11
Leland, Miss., 6,295...B3 68
Leland Grove, Ill., 1,731.............*D4 58
Le Locle, Switz., 13,762.............E3 6
Le Mans, Fr., 132,181..D4 5
Le Mars, Iowa, 6,767..B1 60
Lemay (Luxemburg), Mo., 15,000.............*C7 69
Leme, Braz., 11,785....m8 30
Lemeta, Alsk., 1,227.*C10 47
Lemgo, Ger., 20,400...B4 6
Lemhi, co., Idaho, 5,816.............E4 57
Lemmon, S. Dak., 2,412.............E3 77
Lemon Grove, Calif., 19,348.............E2 50
Lemont, Ill., 3,397.....F2 58
Lemont, Pa., 1,153....E6 81
Lemoore, Calif., 2,561..D4 50
Le Moule, Guad., 5,284.............n16 35
Le Moyne, Que., Can., 8,057.............*D9 42
Lemoyne, Pa., 4,662..*F8 81
Lena, Ill., 1,552.......A4 58
Lena, Sp., 2,252......A3 8
Lenawee, co., Mich., 77,789.............G6 66
Lenexa, Kans., 2,487..D9 61
Leninabad, Sov. Un., 83,000.............E9 13
Leningrad, Sov. Un., 2,997,000 (*3,800,000) H14, s31 11
Leninogorsk, Sov. Un., 68,000.............D11 13
Leninsk, Sov. Un., 5,000.............G15 12
Leninsk-Kuznetskiy, Sov. Un., 138,000........D11 13
Lenkoran, Sov. Un., 30,000.............F7 13
Lennox, Calif., 31,224.*F2 50
Lennox, S. Dak., 1,353.............G9 77
Lennox and Addington co., Ont., Can., 23,717...B7 41
Lennoxville, Que., Can., 3,699.............D6 42
Lenoir, N.C., 10,257..B2 76
Lenoir, co., N.C., 55,276.............B6 76
Lenoir City, Tenn., 4,979.............D9 83
Lenox, Iowa, 2,004.....D4 60
Lenox, Mass., 1,713...B1 65
Lenox, Va., 1,520.....*B7 85
Lenox Avenue, N.Y., 1,500.............*C4 75
Lens, Fr., 42,590......B5 5
Lenwood, Calif., 2,407.*E5 50
Leoben, Aus., 36,257..E7 6
Leominster, Mass., 27,929.............A4 65
Leon, Iowa, 2,004.....D4 60
León, Nic., 52,900....E7 34
León, Sp., 73,483.....A3 8
Leon, co., Fla., 74,225.B2 54
Leon, co., Tex., 9,951..D5 84
León, prov., Sp., 584,594.............*A3 8
León, reg., Sp., 1,291,452.........B3 8
Leonard, Tex., 1,117..C4 84
Leonardo, N.J., 2,000.*C4 74
Leonardtown, Md., 1,281.............D4 53

Leon [de los Aldamas], Mex., 209,469..C4, m13 34
Leonforte, It., 17,927..F5 9
Leonia, N.J., 8,384.B5, D5 74
Leopoldina, Braz., 17,726...........C4, g6 30
Léopoldville, Con. L., 390,000.............A3 24
Leoti, Kans., 1,401....D2 61
Leovo, Sov. Un., 10,000.............H7 12
Lepanto, Ark., 1,585...B5 49
Lepe, Sp., 10,038.....D2 8
Lepel, Sov. Un., 10,000.D7 12
Le Petit-Quevilly, Fr., 21,098.............C4 5
L'Epiphanie, Que., Can., 2,663.............D4 42
Le Puy [-en-Velay], Fr., 25,125.............E5 5
Le Raincy, Fr., 14,908.............g11 5
Lercara Friddi, It., 11,872.............F4 9
Lérida, Sp., 51,200....B6 8
Lérida, prov., Sp., 333,765.............*B6 8
Le Roy, Ill., 2,088.....C5 58
Le Roy, Minn., 971....G6 67
Le Roy, N.Y., 4,662...C3 75
Lerwick, Scot., 5,906..g10 4
Les Cayes, Hai., 11,835.F7 35
Lesh, Alb., 1,609.....B2 14
Leskovac, Yugo., 33,441.............D5 10
Leslie, Mich., 1,807...F6 66
Leslie, co., Ky., 10,941.C6 62
Les Lilas, Fr., 17,721..g10 5
Lesotho, see Basutoland, Br. dep., Afr.
Les Sables-d'Olonne, Fr., 18,401.............D3 5
Lesser Antilles, is., W.I.............B4 27
Lester, Pa., 2,000....*B11 81
Lester, W. Va., 626....D6 87
Lester Prairie, Minn., 966.............F4 67
Le Sueur, Minn., 3,310.F5 67
Le Sueur, co., Minn., 19,906.............F5 67
Lesvos, prov., Grc., 140,251.............*C6 14
Leszno, Pol., 29,000...C4 7
Letcher, co., Ky., 30,102.............C7 62
Le Teil, Fr., 8,236.....E6 5
Lethbridge, Alta., Can., 35,454.............E4 38
Leticia, Col., 1,898...D4 32
Letpadan, Bur., 15,896.............*H12 16
Le Tréport, Fr., 6,136..B4 5
Leucadia, Calif., 5,665.*F5 50
Leuven, Bel., 32,524..B6 5
Levack, Ont., Can., 3,178.............*E9 41
Levadhia, Grc., 12,609.C4 14
Levallois-Perret, Fr., 61,804...........C4, g10 5
Level Green, Pa., 1,500.............*B7 81
Levelland, Tex., 10,153.C1 84
Level Park, Mich., 3,017.............*F5 66
Leven, Scot., 8,872....B5 4
Levice, Czech., 13,800.D5 7
Levin, N.Z., 7,934....N15 26
Levis, Que., Can., 15,112...........C6, C9 42
Levis, co., Que., Can., 51,842.............C6 42
Levittown, N.J., 11,861.............*C3 74
Levittown, N.Y., 65,276.............*G2 52
Levittown, Pa., 58,000.............*F12 81
Levkas, Grc., 6,577....C3 14
Levoca, Czech., 7,584..D6 7
Levy, co., Fla., 10,364..C4 54
Lewes, Del., 3,025....C7 53
Lewes, Eng., 13,637...E7 4
Lewis, co., Idaho, 4,423.............C2 57
Lewis, co., Ky., 13,115.B6 62
Lewis, co., Mo., 10,984.A6 69
Lewis, co., N.Y., 23,249.............B5 75
Lewis, co., Tenn., 6,269.B4 83
Lewis, co. Wash., 41,858.............C3 86
Lewis, co., W. Va., 19,711.............C4 87
Lewis and Clark, co., Mont., 28,006......C4 70
Lewisburg, Ala., 2,500.E4 46
Lewisburg, Ohio, 1,415.C3 78
Lewisburg, Pa., 5,523..E8 81
Lewisburg, Tenn., 6,338.............B5 83

Lewisburg, W. Va., 2,259..........D4 87
Lewisdale, Md., 5,000.*C3 53
Lewis Gardens, Va., 1,380.............*D5 85
Lewisporte, Newf., Can., 2,076.............D4 44
Lewiston, Idaho, 12,691............C2 57
Lewiston, Maine, 40,804......D2, D5 64
Lewiston, N Y., 3,320..B1 75
Lewiston, Utah, 1,336..A6 72
Lewiston Orchards, Idaho, 9,680.............C2 57
Lewistown, Ill., 2,603..C3 58
Lewistown, Mont., 7,408...........C7 70
Lewistown, Pa., 12,640.E6 81
Lewisville, Ark., 1,373.D2 49
Lewisville, Tex., 3,956..........A5, C4 84
Lexington, Ill., 1,244...C5 58
Lexington, Ky., 62,810 (*124,000)........B5 62
Lexington, Mass., 27,691........B5, C2 65
Lexington, Minn., 1,457............*E5 67
Lexington, Miss., 2,839.B3 68
Lexington, Mo., 4,845..B4 69
Lexington, Nebr., 5,572.............D6 71
Lexington, N.C., 16,093............B3 76
Lexington, Ohio, 1,311.B5 78
Lexington, Okla., 1,216.B4 79
Lexington, S.C., 1,127..D5 82
Lexington, Tenn., 3,943............B3 83
Lexington, Va., 7,537..D3 85
Lexington, co., S.C., 60,726............D5 82
Lexington Park, Md., 7,039.............*D5 53
Leyte, prov., Phil., 1,177,400.........*C6 19
Leyton, Eng., 93,857..k12 4
Lézignan [-Corbières], Fr., 6,939.............F5 5
Lezirias, reg., Port...f10 8
Lgov, Sov. Un., 10,000...........F10 12
Lhasa, China, 50,000...F3 17
L'Hay-les-Roses, Fr., 17,968..........g10 5
Liaoning, prov., China, 24,090,000.........C9 17
Liaoyang, China, 135,000...........C9 7
Líbano, Col., 12,019..C3 32
Libby, Mont., 2,828..B1 70
Liberal, Kans., 13,813.E3 61
Liberec, Czech., 55,300.C3 7
Liberia country, Afr., 1,250,000..........G3 22
Liberty, Ind., 1,745...E8 59
Liberty, Ky., 1,578....C5 62
Liberty, Mo., 8,909...E2 69
Liberty, N.Y., 4,704...D6 75
Liberty, N.C., 1,438...B4 76
Liberty, Pa., 3,624...*F2 81
Liberty, S.C., 2,657....B2 82
Liberty, Tex., 6,127...........D5, F5 84
Liberty, co., Fla., 3,138.B2 54
Liberty, co., Ga., 14,487.............E5 55
Liberty, co., Mont., 2,624.............B5 70
Liberty, co., Tex., 31,595.............D5 84
Liberty Acres, Calif., 5,200.............*F2 50
Liberty Corner, N.J., 800..............B3 74
Libertyville, Ill., 8,560............A6, E2 58
Libourne, Fr., 15,170..E3 5
Library, Pa., 3,000....*F1 81
Libreville, Gabon, 19,700...........H6 22
Libya, country, Afr., 1,530,000..........C2 23
Licata, It., 38,655.....F4 9
Lice, Tur., 6,700......C13 14
Licking, Mo., 954.....D6 69
Licking, co., Ohio, 90,242............B5 78
Lida, Sov. Un., 28,000.E5 12
Lidgerwood, N. Dak., 1,081.............D8 77
Lidice, Czech., C3, n17 7
Lidingö, Swe., 30,800........H8, t36 11
Lidköping, Swe., 16,900............H5 11
Liechtenstein, country, Eur., 16,628.........E4 6
Liège, Bel., 153,240 (*550,000).........B6 5

Liège, prov., Bel., 1,003,526..........*B6 5
Lienyün, China, 85,000.E8 17
Lienz, Aus., 11,132....E6 6
Liepāja, Sov. Un., 76,000.............C3 12
Lier, Bel., 28,755.....B6 5
Liestal, Switz., 10,262..E3 6
Lighthouse Point, Fla., 2,453.............*F6 54
Ligonier, Ind., 2,595..B6 59
Ligonier, Pa., 2,276...F3 81
Liguria, pol. dist., It., 1,735,349..........*B2 9
Liguria, reg., It........B2 9
Lihue, Haw., 3,908....B2 56
Likhoslavl, Sov. Un., 5,000.............C10 12
Likino-Dulevo, Sov. Un., 10,000.............n18 12
Lilbourn, Mo., 1,216...E8 69
Lille, Fr., 193,096 (*865,000).........B5 5
Lillehammer, Nor., 6,000.............G4 11
Lillestrøm, Nor., 10,600............H4, p29 11
Lillington, N.C., 1,242.B5 76
Lillooet, B.C., Can., 1,304.............D7 37
Lilly, Pa., 1,642......F4 81
Lilly Grove, W. Va., 1,255.............*D3 87
Lima, N.Y., 1,366.....C3 75
Lima, Ohio, 51,037....B3 78
Lima, Peru, 767,054 (*950,000).........D2 31
Lima, dept., Peru, 1,104,617..........D2 31
Limburg, Ger., 15,600..C4 6
Limburg, prov., Bel., 574,606..........*B6 5
Limburg, prov., Neth., 894,300..........*B6 5
Limeil-Brévannes, Fr., 8,377............h10 5
Limeira, Braz., 45,256..m8 30
Limerick, Ire., 50,786..D2 4
Limerick, co., Ire., 133,339..........*D2 4
Limestone, Maine, 1,772.............B5 64
Limestone, co., Ala., 36,513............A2 46
Limestone, co., Tex., 20,413............D4 84
Limoeiro do Norte, Braz., 5,705............*D7 27
Limoges, Fr., 117,827..E4 5
Limon, Colo., 1,811....B7 51
Limón, C.R., 16,500....F8 34
Limón, prov., C.R., 62,800............*I12 33
Limousin, former prov., Fr., 487,000.........E4 5
Limoux, Fr., 9,603....F5 5
Linares, Chile, 26,000..B2 28
Linares, Mex., 13,318..C5 34
Linares, Sp., 50,200....C4 8
Linares, prov., Chile, 170,278...........B2 28
Lincoln, Arg., 12,695...A4 28
Lincoln, Calif., 3,197...C3 50
Lincoln, Eng., 77,065..D6 4
Lincoln, Ill., 16,890....C4 58
Lincoln (Lincoln Center), Kans., 1,717.......C5 61
Lincoln, Maine, 3,616..C4 64
Lincoln, Mass., 1,700..*C2 65
Lincoln, Nebr., 128,521 (*145,400)......D9, E2 71
Lincoln, N.H., 900....*C4 73
Lincoln, Ohio, 8,004...B5 78
Lincoln, Pa., 1,686...*F2 81
Lincoln, R.I., 7,600...B11 52
Lincoln, co., Ark., 14,447............D4 49
Lincoln, co., Ont., Can., 126,674............D5 41
Lincoln, co., Colo., 5,310.............C7 51
Lincoln, co., Eng., 743,383..........*D6 4
Lincoln, co., Ga., 5,906.C4 55
Lincoln, co., Idaho, 3,686.............G4 57
Lincoln, co., Kansas, 5,556.............C5 61
Lincoln, co., Ky., 16,503............C5 62
Lincoln, co., Maine, 18,497............D3 64
Lincoln, co., Minn., 9,651.............F2 67
Lincoln, co., Miss., 26,759............D3 68
Lincoln, co., Mo., 14,783............B6 69
Lincoln, co., Mont., 12,537............B1 70

Lincoln, co., Nebr., 28,491............D5 71
Lincoln, co., Nev., 2,431.............C4 72
Lincoln, co., N. Mex., 7,744.............C6 48
Lincoln, co., N.C., 28,814............B2 76
Lincoln, co., Okla., 18,783............B5 79
Lincoln, co., Oreg., 24,635............C3 80
Lincoln, co., S. Dak., 12,371............G9 77
Lincoln, co., Tenn., 23,829............B5 83
Lincoln, co., Wash., 10,919............B2 86
Lincoln, co., W. Va., 20,267............C2 87
Lincoln, co., Wis., 22,338............C4 88
Lincoln, co., Wyo., 9,018.............C2 89
Lincoln, par., La., 28,535............B3 63
Lincoln Acres, Calif., 3,500.............*E2 50
Lincoln Heights, Ohio, 7,798.............D2 78
Lincoln Highway, Nebr., 950..............*C5 71
Lincoln Park, Colo., 2,085.............*C5 51
Lincoln Park, Ga., 1,840.............*D2 55
Lincoln Park, Mich., 53,933............A7 66
Lincoln Park, N.J., 6,048.............B4 74
Lincoln Park, N.Y., 1,100.............*D6 75
Lincoln Park, Pa., 1,500.............*G11 81
Lincoln Park, Va., 1,500.............*F10 81
Lincolnton, Ga., 1,450..C4 55
Lincolnton, N.C., 5,699.B2 76
Lincoln Village, Calif., 6,000.............*D3 50
Lincoln Village, Ohio, 2,400.............*C1 78
Lincolnwood, Ill., 11,744............E3 58
Lincroft, N.J., 4,000...C4 74
Linda, Calif., 6,129...*C2 50
Lindale, Ga., 2,600...*B1 55
Lindale, Tex., 1,285...C5 84
Lindau, Ger., 21,700...E4 6
Linden, Ala., 2,516....C2 46
Linden, Mich., 1,146...E7 66
Linden, N.J., 39,931...E4 74
Linden, Tenn., 1,086...B4 83
Linden, Tex., 1,832....C5 84
Lindenhurst, Ill., 1,259.E2 58
Lindenhurst, N.Y., 20,905............G3 52
Lindenwold, N.J., 7,335.............D3 74
Lindesberg, Swe., 6,000.............H6 11
Lindi, Tan., 10,315....B7 24
Lindon, Utah, 1,150..*A6 72
Lindsay, Calif., 5,397..D4 50
Lindsay, Ont., Can., 11,399............C6 41
Lindsay, Okla., 4,258..C4 79
Lindsborg, Kans., 2,609.............D6 61
Linesville, Pa., 1,255...C1 81
Lineville, Ala., 1,612...B4 46
Lingayen, Phil., 8,000..B6 19
Lingen, Ger., 25,200...B3 6
Lingyuan, China, 20,000............C8 17
Linhai, China, 26,000..F9 17
Lini, China, 80,000....D8 17
Liniere, Que., Can., 1,269.............C7 42
Linköping, Swe., 66,000............H6 11
Linn, Mo., 1,050......C6 69
Linn, co., Iowa, 136,899............B6 60
Linn, co., Kans., 8,274.D9 61
Linn, co., Mo., 16,815..B4 69
Linn, co., Oreg., 58,867.C4 80
Linntown, Pa., 1,628..*E8 81
Lino Lakes, Minn., 2,329.............*E5 67
Lins, Braz., 32,204....C3 30
Linthicum Heights, Md., 6,000..........B4, C2 53
Linton, Ind., 5,736....F3 59
Linton, N. Dak., 1,826.D5 77
Linwood, N.J., 3,847...E3 74
Linwood, Pa., 4,460..*G11 81
Linyu, China, 60,000...C8 17
Linz, Aus., 195,978....D7 6
Lipa, Phil., 12,000.C6, p13 19
Lipari, It., 3,731......E5 9

Lipetsk, Sov. Un., 183,000............E12 12
Lipkany, Sov. Un., 10,000.............A8 10
Lipno, Pol., 8,389.....B5 7
Lipova, Rom., 10,064..B5 10
Lippstadt, Ger., 37,500.C4 6
Lipscomb, Ala., 2,811.........B3, E4 46
Lipscomb, co., Tex., 3,406.............A2 84
Liria, Sp., 9,723......C5 8
Lisboa, see Lisbon, Port.
Lisbon, Iowa, 1,227...C6 60
Lisbon, Maine, 1,542..........D2, D5 64
Lisbon, N.H., 1,220...C4 73
Lisbon, N. Dak., 2,093.D8 77
Lisbon, Ohio, 3,579...B7 78
Lisbon (Lisboa), Port., 802,200 (*1,300,000)......C1, f9 8
Lisbon Falls, Maine, 2,640..........D5, E2 64
Lisburn, N. Ire., 17,691............C3 4
Lishu, China, 5,000....E2 18
Lisichansk, Sov. Un., 10,000............q21 12
Lisieux, Fr., 21,156....C4 5
Lisle, Ill., 4,219......F2 58
L'Islet, co., Que., Can., 24,798............B7 42
Lisman, Ala., 909......C1 46
Lismore, Austl., 18,931.E9 25
Listowel, Ont., Can., 4,002.............D4 41
Litchfield, Conn., 1,363.B4 52
Litchfield, Ill., 7,330...D7 58
Litchfield, Mich., 993..F6 68
Litchfield, Minn., 5,078.E4 67
Litchfield, co., Conn., 119,856............B3 52
Litchfield Park, Ariz., 900..............D1 48
Lithgow, Austl., 14,230.F9 25
Lithonia, Ga., 1,667...........B5, C2 55
Lithuania (S.S.R.), rep., Sov. Un., 2,804,000..D4 12
Lititz, Pa., 5,987......F9 81
Litokhoron, Grc., 5,032.............*B4 14
Litomerice, Czech., 16,900............C3 7
Litomysl, Czech., 6,384.............D7 7
Little Canada, Minn., 3,512.............*E5 67
Little Chute, Wis., 5,099..........A5, D5 88
Little Current, Ont., Can., 1,527.............B3 41
Little Falls, Minn., 7,551.............E4 67
Little Falls, N.J., 9,430.B4 74
Little Falls, N.Y., 8,935.............B6 75
Little Ferry, N.J., 6,175.............D5 74
Littlefield, Tex., 7,236..C1 84
Little River, co., Ark., 9,211.............D1 49
Little Rock, Ark., 107,813 (*238,500).....C3, D6 49
Little Silver, N.J., 5,202.............C4 74
Littlestown, Pa., 2,756.G7 81
Littleton, Colo., 13,670.B6 51
Littleton, N.H., 3,355..C4 73
Littleton, N.C., 1,024..A6 76
Littleton Common, Mass., 2,277.............C1 65
Little Valley, N.Y., 1,244.............C2 75
Liuho, China, 5,000....E2 18
Lively, Ont., Can., 2,311.............*E9 41
Live Oak, Calif., 2,276.C3 50
Live Oak, Fla., 6,544..B4 54
Live Oak, co., Tex., 7,846.............E3 84
Livermore, Calif., 16,058............B6 50
Livermore, Ky., 1,506..C2 62
Livermore Falls, Maine, 2,882.............D2 64
Liverpool, N.S., Can., 3,712.............E5 43
Liverpool, Eng., 747,490 (*1,655,000)......D5 4
Liverpool, N.Y., 3,487..B4 75
Livingston, Ala., 1,544.C1 46
Livingston, Calif., 2,188.............D3 50
Livingston, Guat., 2,206.............D7 34
Livingston, Ill., 964...E4 58
Livingston, La., 1,183..........A6, D5 63

Livingston, Mont.,
8,229.............E6 70
Livingston, N.J.,
23,125............*B4 74
Livingston, Tenn.,
2,817.............C8 83
Livingston, Tex., 3,398.D5 84
Livingston, co., Ill.,
40,341............C5 58
Livingston, co., Ky.,
7,029.............A3 62
Livingston, co., Mich.,
38,233............F6 66
Livingston, co., Mo.,
15,771............B4 69
Livingston, co., N.Y.,
44,053............C3 75
Livingston, par., La.,
26,974............D5 63
Livingstone, Zambia,
28,600............D5 24
Livingston Manor, N.Y.,
2,080.............D6 75
Livno, Yugo., 5,170...D3 10
Livny, Sov. Un.,
10,000............E11 12
Livonia, Mich., 66,702.A7 66
Livonia, N.Y., 946.....C3 75
Livorno (Leghorn), It.,
161,077...........C3 9
Livramento, Braz.,
37,666............E1 30
Livry-Gargan, Fr.,
29,679............g11 5
Ljubljana, Yugo.,
133,386...........B2 10
Ljungby, Swe., 9,300...I5 11
Llandudno, Wales,
17,852............D5 4
Llanelly, Wales, 29,994.E4 4
Llanes, Sp., 20,421....A3 8
Llanquihue, prov., Chile,
165,959...........C2 28
Llano, Tex., 2,656.....D3 84
Llano, co., Tex., 5,240.D3 84
Llerena, Sp., 8,217....C2 8
Lloyd, Ky., 600........B7 62
Lloyd Harbor, N.Y.,
2,521.............*G3 52
Lloydminster, Alta. and
Sask., Can., 5,667...D1 39
Lloyd Place, Va.,
2,282.............*E6 85
Lluchmayor, Sp.,
10,664............C7 8
Löbau, Ger., 16,800....C7 6
Lobería, Arg., 7,916....B5 28
Lobito, Ang., 31,630...C2 24
Lobos, Arg., 8,372..B5, g7 28
Locarno, Switz., 10,155.E4 6
Lochdale, B.C., Can.,
900..............A10 37
Lochearn, Md., 2,000.*B4 53
Loches, Fr., 5,902.....D4 5
Loch Raven, Md.,
23,278............*B4 53
Lockeport, N.S., Can.,
1,231.............F4 43
Lockhart, Tex.,
6,084..........A4, E4 84
Lock Haven, Pa.,
11,748............D7 81
Lockland, Ohio, 5,992..A7 62
Lockney, Tex., 2,141...B2 84
Lockport, Ill.,
7,560...........B2, F5 58
Lockport, La.,
2,221...........C6, E5 63
Lockport, N.Y., 26,443.B2 75
Locust Grove, Okla.,
828..............A6 79
Locust Valley, N.Y.,
3,700.............F2 52
Lod (Lydda), Isr.,
19,012.........C2, h5 15
Lodève, Fr., 6,869.....F5 5
Lodeynoye Pole, Sov. Un.,
10,000............A9 12
Lodhran, Pak., 4,890...C5 20
Lodi, Calif., 22,229.B6, C3 50
Lodi, N.J., 23,502.....D5 74
Lodi, Ohio, 2,213.....A5 78
Lodi, Wis., 1,620......E4 88
Łódź, Pol., 708,000....C5 7
Loei, Thai., 7,700....*B2 19
Logan, Iowa, 1,605....C2 60
Logan, Kans., 846.....C4 61
Logan, Ohio, 6,417....C5 78
Logan, Utah, 18,731...A6 72
Logan, W. Va.,
4,185..........D3, D5 87
Logan, co., Ark.,
15,957............B2 49
Logan, co., Colo.,
20,302............A7 51
Logan, co., Ill., 33,656.C4 58
Logan, co., Kans.,
4,036.............D2 61
Logan, co., Ky., 20,896.D3 62
Logan, co., Nebr.,
1,108.............C5 71

Logan, co., N. Dak.,
5,369.............D6 77
Logan, co., Ohio,
34,803............B4 78
Logan, co., Okla.,
18,662............B4 79
Logan, co., W. Va.,
61,570............D3 87
Logansport, Ind.,
21,106............C5 59
Logansport, La., 1,371.C2 63
Loganville, Ga., 926...C3 55
Logroño, Sp., 61,292...A4 8
Logroño, prov., Sp.,
229,852...........*A4 8
Logrosán, Sp., 6,595...C3 8
Lohardaga, India,
13,203............D4 20
Loire, dept., Fr.,
696,348...........*E6 5
Loire-Atlantique, dept.,
Fr., 803,372.......*D3 5
Loiret, dept., Fr.,
389,854...........*D4 5
Loir-et-Cher, dept., Fr.,
250,741...........*D4 5
Loja, Ec., 18,200.....B2 31
Loja, Sp., 12,439.....D3 8
Loja, prov., Ec.,
252,737...........B2 31
Lokhvitsa, Sov. Un.,
10,000............F9 12
Lom, Bul., 15,182.....D6 10
Loma Linda, Calif.,
6,000.............*F3 50
Lomas de Zamora, Arg.,
275,219.........A5, g7 28
Lombard, Ill., 25,296..F2 58
Lombardia, pol. dist., It.,
7,406,152.........*B2 9
Lombardy reg., It.....B2 9
Lomé, Togo, 69,448....G5 22
Lometa, Tex., 817.....D3 84
Lomita, Calif., 14,983.*F2 50
Lomonosov, Sov. Un.,
30,000............s30 11
Lompoc, Calif., 14,415.E3 50
Łomża, Pol., 20,000...B7 7
Lonaconing, Md.,
2,077.............D2 53
London, Ont., Can.,
169,569 (*181,283)...E3 41
London, Eng., 3,195,114
(Greater London,
8,346,137)
(*10,830,000)....E6, k12 4
London, Ky., 4,035....C5 62
London, Ohio, 6,379...C4 78
London, W. Va., 500..*C6 87
London, co., Eng.,
3,195,114.........*E6 4
Londonbridge, Va.,
1,061.............*E6 85
Londonderry, N. Ire.,
53,744............C3 4
Londonderry, co., N. Ire.,
111,565...........*C3 4
Londrina, Braz.,
74,110............C2 30
Lone Oak, Ky., 2,104..A2 62
Lone Pine, Calif.,
1,310.............D4 50
Lone Star, Tex., 1,513.*C5 84
Long, co., Ga., 3,874...E5 50
Long, isl., N.Y.......D3 75
Long Beach, Calif.,
344,168.........F2, F4 50
Long Beach, Ind.,
2,007.............A4 59
Long Beach, Miss.,
4,770...........E2, E4 68
Long Beach, N.Y.,
26,473......E2, E3, E7 75
Longboat Key, Fla.,
1,000.............*E4 54
Long Branch, Ont., Can.,
11,039............E6 41
Long Branch, N.J.,
26,228............C5 74
Longford, co., Ire.,
30,643............*D3 4
Longhurst, N.C., 1,546.A5 76
Long Island, Tenn.,
1,925.............*C11 83
Long Lake, Ill., 3,502.*E2 58
Long Lake, Minn.,
996..............*F5 67
Long Leaf Park, N.C.,
2,238.............*C3 76
Longmeadow, Mass.,
10,565............B2 65
Longmont, Colo.,
11,489............A5 51
Longport, N.J., 1,077.E13 74
Long Prairie, Minn.,
2,414.............E4 67
Longueuil, Que., Can.,
24,131.........D4, D9 42
Long Valley, N.J.,
1,220.............B3 74

Longview, Alta., Can.,
246..............D3 38
Long View, Ky., 500...C4 62
Longview, N.C., 2,997..B2 76
Longview, Tex., 40,050.C5 84
Longview, Wash.,
23,349............C3 86
Longwood, Fla., 1,689.*D5 54
Longwood Park, N.C.,
1,144.............*C4 76
Longwy, Fr., 21,939...C6 5
Long Xuyen, Viet.,
5,000.............*C3 19
Lonoke, Ark., 2,359...D6 49
Lonoke, co., Ark.,
24,551............C4 49
Lons-le-Saunier, Fr.,
15,924............D6 5
Loogootee, Ind., 2,858.G4 59
Lookout, Ky., 900.....C7 62
Lookout Mountain, Tenn.,
1,817.............E10 83
Lopei, China, 5,000....C5 18
Lora, Sp., 11,864.....D3 8
Lorado, W. Va.,
700...........D3, D6 87
Lorain, Ohio, 68,932..A5 78
Lorain, Pa., 1,324....*F4 81
Lorain, co., Ohio,
217,500...........A5 78
Loraine, Tex., 21,000..C2 84
Lorca, Sp............D5 8
Lordsburg, N. Mex.,
3,436.............C4 48
Lorena, Braz., 26,068..C3 30
Lorenzo, Tex., 1,188...C2 84
Loreto, Par., 11,321...D4 29
Loreto, dept., Peru,
350,306...........C3 31
Loretteville, Que., Can.,
6,522...........C6, C8 42
Loretto, Pa., 1,338....E4 81
Loretto, Tenn., 929...B4 83
Lorica, Col., 8,420....B2 32
Lorient, Fr., 60,566...D2 5
L'Orignal, Ont., Can.,
1,189.............B10 41
Loris, S.C., 1,702.....C10 82
Lörrach, Ger., 30,500..E3 6
Lorraine, former prov.,
Fr., 1,956,000.....C6 5
Los Alamitos, Calif.,
4,312.............*F2 50
Los Alamos, N. Mex.,
13,037............B5 48
Los Alamos, co., N. Mex.,
13,037............B5 48
Los Altos, Calif.,
19,696............C5 50
Los Altos Hills, Calif.,
3,412.............C5 50
Los Andes, Chile,
19,162............A2 28
Los Angeles, Calif.,
2,479,015
(*6,565,000).....E4, F2 50
Los Angeles, Chile,
33,000............B2 78
Los Angeles, co., Calif.,
6,038,771.......E4, F2 50
Los Banos, Calif.,
6,090.............D3 50
Los Barrios, Sp., 3,583.D3 8
Los Fresnos, Tex.,
1,289.............F4 84
Los Gatos, Calif.,
9,036...........C5, D3 50
Loshan, China, 5,000...F5 17
Los Mochis, Mex.,
37,682............B3 34
Los Nietos, Calif.,
9,000.............*F2 50
Los Reyes, Mex.,
9,777.........D4, n12 34
Los Ríos, prov., Ec.,
174,335...........B2 31
Los Teques, Ven.,
34,874............A4 32
Lot, dept., Fr.,
149,929...........*E4 5
Lota, Chile, 45,000....B2 78
Lotbiniere, co., Que., Can.,
30,234............C6 42
Lot-et-Garonne, dept., Fr.,
275,028...........*E4 5
Lothair, Ky., 1,082....C6 62
Lott, Tex., 924.......D4 84
Loudon, Tenn., 3,812..D9 83
Loudon, co., Tenn.,
23,757............D9 83
Loudonville, N.Y.,
5,500.............*C4 75
Loudonville, Ohio,
2,611.............B5 78
Loudoun, co., Va.,
24,549............B5 85
Loudun, Fr., 5,587....D4 5
Loughborough, Eng.,
38,621............D6 4
Louisa, Ky., 2,071....B7 62

Louisa, co., Iowa,
10,290............C6 60
Louisa, co., Va., 12,959.D5 85
Louisbourg, N.S., Can.,
1,417.............D10 43
Louisburg, N.C., 2,862.A5 76
Louiseville, Que., Can.,
4,138.............C5 42
Louisiana, Mo., 4,286..B6 69
Louisiana, state, U.S.,
3,257,022............. 63
Louisville, Colo., 2,073.B5 51
Louisville, Ga., 2,413..C4 55
Louisville, Ill., 906....E5 58
Louisville, Ky., 390,639
(*735,800)......A4, B4 62
Louisville, Miss., 5,066.B4 68
Louisville, Nebr.,
1,194.........D9, E3 71
Louisville, Ohio, 5,116..B6 78
Louis Trichardt, S. Afr.,
9,703.............E5 24
Loulé, Port., 6,479....D1 8
Louny, Czech., 12,300..C2 7
Loup, co., Nebr., 1,097.C6 71
Loup City, Nebr.,
1,415.............C7 71
Lourdes, Fr., 16,023...F4 5
Lourenço Marques, Moz.,
99,000............F6 24
Loures, Port., 6,089...f9 8
Louth, Eng., 11,556...D7 4
Louth, co., Ire.,
67,378............*C3 4
Loutrá Aidhipsoú, Grc.,
5,028.............*C4 14
Louvain, see Leuven, Bel.
Louviers, Fr., 13,160...C4 5
Love, co., Okla., 5,862.D4 79
Lovech, Bul., 11,730...D7 10
Lovejoy, Ill., 1,922....*E3 58
Loveland, Colo., 9,734.A5 51
Loveland, Ohio,
5,008...........C3, D2 78
Loveland Park, Ohio,
1,000...........C2, C3 78
Lovell, Wyo., 2,451....A4 89
Lovelock, Nev., 1,948..A2 72
Lovely, Ky., 600......C7 62
Loves Park, Ill., 9,086..A4 58
Loving, N. Mex., 1,646.C6 48
Loving, co., Tex., 226..D1 84
Lovington, Ill., 1,200...D5 58
Lovington, Iowa, 800..A7 60
Lovington, N. Mex.,
9,660.............C7 48
Lowell, Ind., 2,270....B3 59
Lowell, Mass., 92,107
(*147,400)........A5 65
Lowell, Mich., 2,545...F5 66
Lowell, N.C., 2,784...B2 76
Lowell, Wash., 1,086..*B3 86
Lowellville, Ohio, 2,055.A7 78
Lower Burrell, Pa.,
11,952............*E2 81
Lower Hutt, N.Z.,
53,044............*N15 26
Lower Paia, Haw., 950.C5 56
Lowestoft, Eng.,
45,687............D7 4
Lowicz, Pol., 14,400...B5 7
Lowndes, co., Ala.,
15,417............C3 46
Lowndes, co., Ga.,
49,270............F3 55
Lowndes, co., Miss.,
46,639............B5 68
Lowville, N.Y., 3,616..B5 75
Loxton, Austl., 2,321..G3 26
Loyal, Wis., 1,146.....D3 88
Loyalhanna, Pa.,
1,000.............*F3 81
Loyall, Ky., 1,260.....D6 62
Loyalton, Calif., 936...C3 50
Loyalty, is., Pac. O....H8 2
Loyang, China,
171,200...........E7 17
Lozére, dept., Fr.,
81,868............*E5 5
Loznica, Yugo., 10,611.C4 10
Lozovatka, Sov. Un.,
10,000............G9 12
Lualualei, Haw., 2,100..g9 56
Luanda, Ang.,
189,590...........B2 24
Luang Prabang, Laos,
25,000............B2 19
Luanshya, Zambia,
18,000............C5 24
Luarca, Sp., 4,236....A2 8
Luban, Pol., 11,100...C3 7
Lubartow, Pol., 5,542..C7 7
Lübben, Ger., 9,433...C6 6
Lubbock, Tex., 128,691
(*144,300)........C2 84
Lubbock, co., Tex.,
156,271...........C2 84
Lubec, Maine, 1,289...D6 64
Lübeck, Ger., 234,600..B5 6
Lublin, Pol., 181,000...C7 7
Lubliniec, Pol., 12,400.C5 7

Lubny, Sov. Un.,
  10,000............F9 13
Lubrín, Sp., 5,417....D4 8
Lubutu, Con. L., 8,318..I3 23
Lucan, Ont., Can., 986.D3 41
Lucas, co., Iowa,
  10,923............C4 60
Lucas, co., Ohio,
  456,931............A4 78
Lucasville, Ohio,
  1,277..............D5 78
Lucca, It., 88,428......C3 9
Luce, co., Mich., 7,827.B5 66
Lucedale, Miss., 1,977..E5 68
Lucena, Phil.,
  28,000........C6, p13 19
Lucena, Sp., 19,400....D3 8
Lucenec, Czech.,
  16,100..............D5 7
Lucera, It., 24,500.....D5 9
Lucerne, see Luzern,
  Switz.
Lucernemines, Pa.,
  1,524..............E3 81
Luceville, Que., Can.,
  1,419..............A9 42
Luckau, Ger., 6,145....C6 6
Lukenwalde, Ger.,
  28,600..............B6 6
Luckey, Ohio, 946..A2, A4 78
Lucknow, Ont., Can.,
  1,031..............D3 41
Lucknow, India, 595,440
  (*675,000)..........C7 20
Lucknow, Pa., 900....*F8 81
Luçon, Fr., 7,599......D3 5
Lüdenscheid, Ger.,
  58,200..............C3 6
Ludhiana, India,
  244,032............B6 20
Ludington, Mich.,
  9,421..............E4 66
Ludlam, Fla., 20,000..*G6 54
Ludlow, Eng., 6,774...D5 4
Ludlow, Ky., 6,233....A7 62
Ludlow, Mass., 8,000..B3 65
Ludlow, Vt., 1,658....E2 73
Ludowici, Ga., 1,578...E5 55
Ludvika, Swe., 12,300..G6 11
Ludwigsburg, Ger.,
  73,500.............D4 6
Ludwigshafen, Ger.,
  165,800............D4 6
Ludwigslust, Ger.,
  12,000..............B5 6
Lueders, Tex., 654.....C3 84
Lufkin, Tex., 17,641...D5 84
Luga, Sov. Un., 43,000.B7 12
Lugano, Switz., 19,758
  (*33,139)...........E4 6

Lugansk, Sov. Un.,
  300,000......G12, q22 12
Lugo, It., 12,800.....B3 9
Lugo, Sp., 40,900.....A2 8
Lugo, prov., Sp.,
  479,530...........*A2 8
Lugoj, Rom., 30,258...C5 10
Luhsien, China,
  289,000...........F6 17
Luichow, China,
  158,800...........C6 17
Luján, Arg., 19,001....g7 28
Lukovit, Bul., 7,755...D7 10
Lukow, Pol., 8,513.....C7 7
Lukoyanov, Sov. Un.,
  5,000.............D15 12
Luleå, Swe., 31,600..E10 11
Lüleburgaz, Tur.,
  22,300.............B6 14
Luling, La., 2,122.....C7 63
Luling, Tex., 4,412.B4, E4 84
Luluabourg, Con. L.,
  59,500.............B4 24
Lumber City, Ga.,
  1,360.............E4 55
Lumberport, W. Va.,
  1,031...........A6, B4 87
Lumberton, Miss.,
  2,108.............D4 68
Lumberton, N.C.,
  15,305.............C5 76
Lumpkin, Ga., 1,348...D2 55
Lumpkin, co., Ga.,
  7,241.............B2 55
Luna, co., N. Mex.,
  9,839.............C5 48
Luna Pier (Lakewood),
  Mich., 1,815........G7 66
Lund, Swe., 41,000....J5 11
Lunda, dist., Ang.,
  247,449...........A3 24
Lundale, W. Va.,
  500...........D3, D5 87
Lüneburg, Ger., 59,600.B5 6
Lunel, Fr., 7,758......F6 5
Lunenburg, Mass.,
  2,000.............A4 65
Lunenburg, N.S., Can.,
  3,056.............E5 43
Lunenburg, co., N.S.,
  Can., 34,998........E5 43
Lunenburg, co., Va.,
  12,523.............E4 85
Lunéville, Fr., 21,618..C7 5
Lungchi, China, 81,200.G8 17
Lunino, Sov. Un.,
  10,000............E15 12
Lupeni, Rom., 21,188..C6 10
Lupin, see Manchouli,
  China

Luque, Par., 22,469....E4 29
Luray, Va., 3,014......C4 85
Lure, Fr., 6,408.......D7 5
Lurgan, N. Ire., 17,873.C3 4
Lusaka, Zambia,
  30,700.............D5 24
Lusambo, Con. L.,
  9,800..............I2 23
Lusk, Wyo., 1,890....C8 89
Lutcher, La., 3,274.B6, D5 63
Lutherville, Md.,
  12,265.............B4 53
Luton, Eng., 131,505...E6 4
Lutsk, Sov. Un., 63,000.F5 12
Lutugino, Sov. Un.,
  5,000............q22 12
Luverne, Ala., 2,238...D3 46
Luverne, Minn., 4,249..G2 67
Luwuk, Indon.........F6 19
Luxembourg, Lux.,
  71,653.............C7 5
Luxembourg, prov., Bel.,
  216,848...........*C6 5
Luxembourg, country,
  Eur., 314,889.......C7 5
Luxeuil-les-Bains, Fr.,
  8,161.............D7 5
Luxor (Al Uqṣur), Eg.,
  U.A.R., 30,100......C4 23
Luxora, Ark., 1,236....B6 49
Luzern, Switz., 67,433..E4 6
Luzern, canton, Switz.,
  253,446...........*E4 7
Luzerne, Pa., 5,118....B8 81
Luzerne, co., Pa.,
  346,972...........D9 81
Luzon, isl., Phil......B6 19
Lvov, Sov. Un.,
  436,000...........G5 12
Lyallpur, Pak., 425,248.B5 20
Lyaskovets, Bul.,
  5,560.............D7 10
Lycoming, co., Pa.,
  109,367...........D7 81
Lydia Mills, S.C.,
  1,177............*C4 82
Lydick, Ind., 1,217....A5 59
Lyford, Tex., 1,554....F4 84
Lykens, Pa., 2,527....E8 81
Lyman, S.C., 1,261....B3 82
Lyman, co., S. Dak.,
  4,428.............G6 77
Lynbrook, N.Y.,
  19,881.............G2 52
Lynch, Ky., 3,810.....D7 62
Lynchburg, Ohio,
  1,022.............C4 78
Lynchburg, Va.,
  54,790............D3 85

Lynden, Wash., 2,542..A3 86
Lyndhurst, N.J.,
  21,867.............D5 74
Lyndhurst, Ohio,
  16,805.............B2 78
Lyndon, Kans., 953....D8 61
Lyndon, Ky., 5,000....A4 62
Lyndonville, Vt., 1,477.B3 73
Lyndora, Pa., 5,700...E2 81
Lynn, Ind., 1,260.....D8 59
Lynn, Mass.,
  94,478........B6, C3 65
Lynn, co., Tex., 10,914.C2 84
Lynnfield, Mass.,
  8,398.............C3 65
Lynn Garden, Tenn.,
  5,261............*C11 83
Lynn Haven, Fla.,
  3,078.............G3 54
Lynnview, Ky., 1,711.*B4 62
Lynnwood, Pa., 2,230.*F2 81
Lynnwood, Pa.,
  1,200...........*D10 81
Lynnwood, Wash.,
  7,207............*B3 86
Lynwood, Calif.,
  31,614.............F2 50
Lyon, Fr., 528,535.....E6 5
Lyon, co., Iowa,
  14,468............A1 60
Lyon, co., Kans.,
  26,928.............D7 61
Lyon, co., Ky., 5,924..C1 62
Lyon, co., Minn.,
  22,655.............F3 67
Lyon, co., Nev., 6,143..B2 72
Lyon Mountain, N.Y.,
  950...............A3 75
Lyonnais, former prov.,
  Fr., 1,621,000.......E6 5
Lyons, Ga., 3,219.....D4 55
Lyons, Ill., 9,936.....F3 58
Lyons, Kans., 4,592...D5 61
Lyons, Nebr., 972....C9 71
Lyons, N.Y., 4,673...B4 75
Lysa, Czech., 6,500...n18 7
Lysaya Gora, Sov. Un.,
  10,000.............G8 12
Lysekil, Swe., 7,800...H4 11
Lyster Station, Que., Can.,
  912...............C6 42
Lysva, Sov. Un.,
  76,000.............D8 13
Lytle, Tex., 798......E3 84
Lyubar, Sov. Un.,
  10,000.............G6 12
Lyubertsy, Sov. Un.,
  100,000...........n17 12

M

Maastricht, Neth.,
  91,200.............B6 5
Mabank, Tex., 944....C4 84
Mableton, Ga., 7,127...A4 55
Mabscott, W. Va.,
  1,591...........D3, D7 87
Mabton, Wash., 958...C5 86
McAdam, N.B., Can.,
  2,472.............D2 43
McAdenville, N.C.,
  748..............*B2 76
McAdoo, Pa., 3,560...E9 81
Macaé, Braz., 19,830..C4 30
McAfee, Ga., 3,000...*C2 55
McAlester, Okla.,
  17,419.............C6 79
McAllen, Tex., 32,728..F3 84
Macamic, Que., Can.,
  1,388...........*E10 41
Macao, Port. dep., Asia,
  169,299............G7 17
Macapá, Braz., 27,585.C5 27
McArthur, Ohio, 1,529.C5 78
MacArthur, W. Va.,
  1,418............*D3 87
Macau, Braz., 11,876..D7 27
McCall, Idaho, 1,423...E2 57
McCamey, Tex., 3,375.D1 84
McCaysville, Ga.,
  1,871.............B2 55
McChesneytown, Pa.,
  1,140............*F3 81
McClain, co., Okla.,
  12,740.............C4 79
McCleary, Wash.,
  1,115.............B2 86
Macclenny, Fla., 2,671.B4 54
Macclesfield, Eng.,
  37,578.............D5 4
McCloud, Calif., 2,140.B2 50
McClure, Pa., 1,001...E7 81
McColl, S.C., 2,479...B8 82
McComas, W. Va., 950.D3 87
McComb, Miss.,
  12,020.............D3 68
McComb, Ohio, 1,176..A4 78

McCone, co., Mont.,
  3,321............C11 70
McConnellsburg, Pa.,
  1,245.............G6 81
McConnelsville, Ohio,
  2,257.............C6 78
McCook, Nebr., 8,301.D5 71
McCook, co., S. Dak.,
  8,268.............G8 77
McCormick, S.C.,
  1,998.............D3 82
McCormick, co., S.C.,
  8,629.............D3 82
McCracken, co., Ky.,
  57,306............A2 62
McCreary, co., Ky.,
  12,463.............D5 62
McCrory, Ark., 1,053..B4 49
McCulloch, co., Tex.,
  8,815.............D3 84
McCurtain, co., Okla.,
  25,851.............C7 79
McDonald, Ohio, 2,727.A7 78
McDonald, Pa., 3,141..B5 81
MacDonald, W. Va.,
  300............D3, D7 87
McDonald, co., Mo.,
  11,798.............E3 69
McDonough, Ga.,
  2,224.............C2 55
McDonough, co., Ill.,
  28,928.............C3 58
McDowell, co., N.C.,
  26,742.............D4 76
McDowell, co., W. Va.,
  71,359.............D3 87
McDuffie, co., Ga.,
  12,627.............C4 55
Macedonia, reg., Grc.,
  Bul., Yugo.......*B4 14
Macedonia, rep., Yugo.,
  1,404,883.........*D5 10
Maceió, Braz., 153,305.D7 27
Macequece, Moz.,
  5,000.............D6 24
Macerata, It., 24,000...C4 9
McEwen, Tenn., 979...A4 83

McFarland, Calif.,
  3,686.............E4 50
McFarland, Wis., 1,272.E4 88
McGehee, Ark., 4,448..D4 49
McGill, Nev., 2,195...B4 72
McGrann, Pa., 800...*E2 81
McGraw, N.Y., 1,276..C4 75
McGregor, Iowa,
  1,040.............A6 60
McGregor, Tex., 4,642.D4 84
Machado, Braz.,
  8,373..........C3, k9 30
Machala, Ec., 7,491...B2 31
McHenry, Ill.,
  3,336..........A5, E2 58
McHenry, co., Ill.,
  84,210............A5 58
McHenry, co., N. Dak.,
  11,099............B5 77
Machias, Maine, 1,523.D5 64
Măcin, Rom., 6,533...C9 10
McIntosh, co., Ga.,
  6,364.............E5 55
McIntosh, co., N. Dak.,
  6,702.............D6 77
McIntosh, co., Okla.,
  12,371.............B6 79
Mack, Ohio, 3,500....*D2 8
Mackay, Austl., 16,809.D8 5
Mackayville, Que.,
  Can., 9,958.......*D4 42
McKean, co., Pa.,
  54,517............C4 81
McKeesport, Pa.,
  45,489..........B6, F2 81
McKees Rocks, Pa.,
  13,185..........B5, F1 81
McKenzie, Tenn.,
  3,780.............A3 83
McKenzie, co., N. Dak.,
  7,296.............C2 77
Mackenzie, dist., N.W.
  Ter., Can., 10,279..D11 36
Mackinac, co., Mich.,
  10,853............B5 66
Mackinac Island, Mich.,
  942...............C6 66

Mackinaw, Ill., 1,163..C4 58
Mackinaw City, Mich.,
  934..............C6 66
McKinley, Minn., 408..C6 67
McKinley, co., N.
  Mex., 37,209.......B4 48
McKinley Heights,
  Ohio, 1,500.......*A7 78
McKinney, Tex.,
  13,763............C4 84
McKnight, Pa., 15,000.A5 81
McKownville, N.Y.,
  2,000............*C7 75
McLaughlin, S. Dak.,
  983...............E5 77
McLean, Tex., 1,330...B2 84
McLean, Va., 2,000...A5 85
McLean, co., Ill.,
  83,877............C5 58
McLean, co., Ky.,
  9,355.............C2 62
McLean, co., N. Dak.,
  14,030............C4 77
McLeansboro, Ill.,
  2,951.............E5 58
McLennan, Alta.,
  Can., 1,078.......B2 38
McLennan, co., Tex.,
  150,091............D4 84
McLeod, co., Minn.,
  24,401............F4 67
McMasterville, Que.,
  Can., 2,075.......*D4 42
McMechen, W. Va.,
  2,999...........B2, B4 87
McMillan Manor,
  Calif., 1,193......*E4 50
McMinn, co., Tenn.,
  33,662............D9 83
McMinnville, Oreg.,
  7,656..........B1, B3 80
McMinnville, Tenn.,
  9,013.............D8 83
McMullen, co., Tex.,
  1,116.............E3 84
McMurray, Alta.,
  Can., 1,186........A5 38

McNair, Tex., 1,880. .*E5 84
McNairy, co., Tenn.,
18,085..............B3 83
McNary, Ariz., 1,608. .B4 48
Macomb, Ill., 12,135...C3 58
Macomb, co., Mich.,
405,804.............F8 66
Mâcon, Fr., 25,714....D6 5
Macon, Ga., 69,764
(*170,700).........D3 55
Macon, Ill., 1,229....D5 58
Macon, Miss., 2,432..B5 68
Macon, Mo., 4,547.....B5 69
Macon, co., Ala.,
26,717.............C4 46
Macon, co., Ga.,
13,170.............D2 55
Macon, co., Ill.,
118,257............D5 58
Macon, co., Mo.,
16,473.............B5 69
Macon, co., N.C.,
14,935.............D2 76
Macon, co., Tenn.,
12,197.............C7 83
Macoupin, co., Ill.,
43,524.............D4 58
McPherson, Kans.,
9,996..............D6 61
McPherson, co., Kans.,
24,285.............D6 61
McPherson, co., Nebr.,
735................C4 71
McPherson, co., S.
Dak., 5,821........E6 77
McRae, Ga., 2,738....D4 55
McRoberts, Ky., 1,363.C7 62
McSherrystown, Pa.,
2,839..............G7 81
Macungie, Pa., 1,266. .E10 81
McVeigh, Ky., 800....C7 62
Ma'dabā, Jordan,
8,545..............C3 15
Madawaska, Maine,
4,035..............A4 64
Madawaska, co., N.B.,
Can., 38,983.......B1 43
Madeira, Ohio, 6,744...D2 78
Madeira Beach, Fla.,
3,943..............*E4 54
Madeira Is., reg.,
Atl. O., 268,900......B1 22
Madelia, Minn., 2,190..F4 67
Madera, Calif., 14,430.D3 50
Madera, Pa., 900.....E4 81
Madera, co., Calif.,
40,468.............D4 50
Madhya Pradesh, state,
India, 32,372,408....D6 20
Madill, Okla., 3,084...C5 79
Madison, Ala., 1,435...A3 46
Madison, Ala., 900....C3 46
Madison, Conn., 1,416.D6 52
Madison, Fla., 3,239..B3 54
Madison, Ga., 2,680...C3 55
Madison, Ill., 6,861....E3 58
Madison, Ind., 10,488. .G7 59
Madison, Kans., 1,105.D7 61
Madison, Maine, 2,761.D3 64
Madison, Minn., 2,380.E2 67
Madison, Nebr., 1,513..C8 71
Madison, N.J., 15,122..B4 74
Madison, N.C., 1,912..A4 76
Madison, Ohio, 1,347...A6 78
Madison, S. Dak.,
5,420..............G9 77
Madison, Tenn.,
13,583.............A5, E9 83
Madison, W. Va.,
2,215..............C3, D5 87
Madison, Wis., 126,706
(*179,200).........E4 88
Madison, co., Ala.,
117,348............A3 46
Madison, co., Ark.,
9,068..............B2 49
Madison, co., Fla.,
14,154.............B3 54
Madison, co., Ga.,
11,246.............B3 55
Madison, co., Idaho,
9,417..............F7 57
Madison, co., Ill.,
224,689............E4 58
Madison, co., Ind.,
125,819............D6 59
Madison, co., Iowa,
12,295.............C3 60
Madison, co., Ky.,
33,482.............C5 62
Madison, co., Miss.,
32,904.............C4 68
Madison, co., Mo.,
9,366..............D7 69
Madison, co., Mont.,
5,211..............E4 70
Madison, co., Nebr.,
25,145.............C8 71
Madison, co., N.Y.,
54,635.............C5 75

Madison, co., N.C.,
17,217.............C3 76
Madison, co., Ohio,
26,454.............C4 78
Madison, co., Tenn.,
60,655.............B3 83
Madison, co., Tex.,
6,749..............D5 84
Madison, co., Va.,
8,187..............C4 85
Madison, par., La.,
16,444.............B4 63
Madison Heights,
Mich., 33,343.....*F7 66
Madison Heights, Va.,
3,000..............D3 85
Madisonville, Ky.,
13,110.............C2 62
Madisonville, Tenn.,
1,812..............D9 83
Madisonville, Tex.,
2,324..............D5 84
Madoc, Ont., Can.,
1,347..............C7 41
Madras, India,
1,729,141..........F7 20
Madras, Oreg., 1,515...C5 80
Madras, state, India,
33,686,953.........F6 20
Madre de Dios, dept.,
Peru, 26,116.......D3 31
Madrid, Iowa,
2,286.............A7, C4 60
Madrid, Sp.,
2,259,931.....B4, p17 8
Madrid, prov., Sp.,
2,606,254......*B4, p17 8
Madridejos, Phil.,
3,041..............C6 19
Madridejos, Sp., 9,795..C4 8
Madura, India,
361,781............G6 20
Maebashi, Jap.,
135,000.........H9, m18 18
Maeser, Utah, 929.....A7 72
Mafeking, Bech., 8,279.F5 24
Mafra, Braz., 12,981...D3 30
Magadan, Sov. Un.,
65,000.............D18 13
Magallanes, prov.,
Chile, 73,037...E2, h11 28
Magangué, Col.,
17,114.............B3 32
Magdalena, N. Mex.,
1,211..............B5 48
Magdalena, dept., Col.,
450,920............A3 32
Magdalen Islands, co.,
Que., Can., 12,479...B8 43
Magdeburg, Ger.,
262,400............B5 6
Magé, Braz., 10,712...h6 30
Magee, Miss., 2,039...D4 68
Magelang, Indon.,
91,636.............G4 19
Magenta, It., 18,417...B2 9
Maglie, It., 13,028.....D7 9
Magna, Utah,
6,442.............A5, C2 72
Magnitogorsk, Sov.
Un., 328,000.......D8 13
Magnolia, Ark., 10,651.D2 49
Magnolia, Miss., 2,083.D3 68
Magnolia, N.J., 4,199..D2 74
Magnolia, Ohio, 1,596..B6 78
Magoffin, co., Ky.,
11,156.............C6 62
Magog, Que., Can.,
13,139.............D5 42
Magrath, Alta., Can.,
1,338..............E4 38
Magwe, Bur., 13,270...D9 20
Mahanoy City, Pa.,
8,536..............E9 81
Maharashtra, state, India,
39,553,718.........D5 20
Mahaska, co., Iowa,
23,602.............C5 60
Mahbubnagar, India,
35,588.............E6 20
Mahdia, Tun., 10,880..A7 22
Mahe, India, 7,951....F6 20
Mahnomen, Minn.,
1,462..............C3 67
Mahnomen, co., Minn.,
6,341..............C3 67
Mahomet, Ill., 1,367...C5 58
Mahón, Sp., 16,619...C8 4
Mahone Bay, N.S.,
Can., 1,103........E5 43
Mahoning, co., Ohio,
300,480............B7 78
Mahopac, N.Y.,
1,337.............D3, D7 75
Mahtomedi, Minn.,
2,127..............E7 67
Mahwah, N.J., 3,200...A4 74
Maiden, N.C., 2,089...B2 76
Maidstone, Eng.,
59,761.............E7 4

Maiduguri, Nig.,
54,646.............F7 22
Maimana, Afg., 25,698.A3 20
Maine, former prov.,
Fr., 682,000........C3 5
Maine, state, U.S.,
969,265............ 64
Maine-et-Loire, dept.,
Fr., 556,272.......*D3 5
Maintirano, Malag.,
2,594..............D8 24
Mainz, Ger., 134,400...C4 6
Maipú, Arg., 5,469.....B5 28
Maiquetía, Ven.,
73,015.............A4 32
Maisons-Alfort, Fr.,
51,186.............g10 5
Maisons-Laffitte, Fr.,
19,132.............g9 5
Maitland, Austl.,
27,351.............F9 25
Maitland (Lake
Maitland), Fla.,
3,570.............*D5 54
Maizuru, Jap.,
73,200...........I7, n14 18
Majestic, Ky., 503.....C7 62
Major, co., Okla.,
7,808..............A3 79
Majunga, Malag.,
38,042.............D9 24
Makaha, Haw., 2,720...g9 56
Makarov (Shirutoru),
Sov. Un., 5,000.....B11 18
Makarska, Yugo.,
3,637..............D3 10
Makasar, Indon.,
367,882............G5 19
Makawao, Haw., 950..C5 56
Makaweli, Haw., 600..B2 56
Makeyevka, Sov. Un.,
381,000.........G11, q20 12
Makhachkala, Sov. Un.,
129,000............A4 13
Makhalata, Bul., 6,537.D7 10
Makri, India, 5,000....E7 20
Makurazaki, Jap.,
15,600.............K5 18
Makurdi, Nig., 16,713..G6 22
Malacca, Mala., 69,848.E2 19
Malacca, state, Mala.,
291,211............E2 19
Malad City, Idaho,
2,274..............G6 57
Málaga, Col., 6,022....B3 32
Málaga, Sp., 301,048..D3 8
Málaga, prov., Sp.,
775,167...........*D3 8
Malagasy Republic,
country, Afr.,
4,918,000..........E9 24
Malagón, Sp., 9,833....C4 8
Malakal, Sud., 9,680...G4 23
Malakoff, Fr., 33,603..g10 5
Malakoff, Tex., 1,657..C4 84
Malang, Indon.,
332,023............G4 19
Malange, Ang., 12,815..B3 24
Malartic, Que., Can.,
6,998..............E9 41
Malatya, Tur., 84,200.C12 14
Malaya, reg., Mala.,
6,278,758..........E2 19
Malaya Vishera, Sov.
Un., 25,000........B9 12
Malaybalay, Phil.,
2,267..............D7 19
Malaysia, country, Asia,
8,676,635.........E24 19
Malbork, Pol., 25,000..A5 7
Malchin, Ger., 6,825...B6 6
Malden, Mass., 57,676.C3 65
Malden, Mo., 5,007....E8 69
Malden, W. Va., 1,000..C6 87
Maldive Islands, country,
Asia, 82,068.......G5 20
Maldonado, Ur.,
12,100.............E2 30
Maldonado, dept., Ur.,
52,600............*E2 30
Maler-Kotla, India,
32,575.............B6 20
Malheur, co., Oreg.,
22,764.............D6 80
Mali, country, Afr.,
4,100,000..........F3 22
Malibu, Calif., 2,000. .*E4 50
Malinec, Czech., 6,551.D5 7
Malita, Phil., 5,125...*D7 19
Malkara, Tur., 9,300...B6 14
Mallawī, Eg., U.A.R.,
43,200.............C4 23
Malleco, prov., Chile,
174,185............B2 28
Mallow, Ire., 5,545....D2 4
Mallory, W. Va.,
1,133.............*D3 87
Malmédy, Bel., 6,355..B7 5
Malmesbury, S. Afr.,
8,206..............G3 24
Malmö, Swe., 233,400..J5 11

Malmöhus, co., Swe.,
632,200...........*J5 11
Maloarkhangelsk, Sov.
Un., 10,000........E11 12
Malolos, Phil., 3,500..o13 19
Malone, N.Y., 8,737...A2 75
Maloyaroslavets, Sov.
Un., 25,000........D11 12
Malta, Mont., 2,239...B9 70
Malta, Ohio, 983.....C6 78
Malta, country, Eur.,
319,620............A7 22
Malton, Ont., Can.,
2,148.............D5, E6 41
Malvern, Ark.,
9,566.............C3, D6 49
Malvern, Iowa, 1,193...C2 60
Malvern, Ohio, 1,320..B6 78
Malvern, Pa.,
2,268.............A10, F10 81
Malverne, N.Y.,
9,968.............*G2 52
Mamanguape, Braz.,
8,512.............*D7 27
Mamaroneck, N.Y.,
17,673.............D2 75
Mamba, Jap., 1,700. .m17 18
Mamers, Fr., 4,869....C4 5
Mammoth, Ariz., 1,913.C3 48
Mammoth, W. Va.,
800...............C3, C6 87
Mamou, Guinea, 5,100.F2 22
Mamou, La., 2,928....D3 63
Man, W. Va.,
1,486.............D3, D5 87
Man, Isle of, see Isle of
Man, Br. dep., Eur.
Manabí, prov., Ec.,
477,503............B1 31
Manacor, Sp., 19,224...C7 8
Manado, Indon.,
127,614............E6 19
Managua, Nic.,
226,300............E7 34
Manahawkin, N.J.,
400................D4 74
Manakara, Malag.,
6,200..............E9 24
Manama, Bahrain,
39,648.............D5 15
Mananjary, Malag.,
11,269.............E9 24
Manasquan, N.J.,
4,022..............C4 74
Manassas, Va.,
3,555..............B4, C5 85
Manassas Park, Va.,
5,342.............*C5 85
Manatee, co., Fla.,
69,168.............E4 54
Manatí, P.R., 9,682...m13 35
Manaus, Braz., 154,040.C2 36
Manawa, Wis., 1,037. .D5 88
Mancelona, Mich.,
1,141..............D5 66
Mancha, reg., Sp......C4 8
Mancha Real, Sp.,
7,855..............D4 8
Manche, dept., Fr.,
446,878...........*C3 5
Manchester, Conn.,
42,102.............B6 52
Manchester, Eng.,
661,041............D5 4
Manchester, Ga., 4,115.D2 55
Manchester, Iowa,
4,402..............B6 60
Manchester, Ky., 1,868.C6 62
Manchester, Md.,
1,108..............A4 53
Manchester, Mass.,
3,932.............A6, C4 65
Manchester, Mich.,
1,568..............F6 66
Manchester, Mo.,
2,021..............B7 69
Manchester, N.H., 88,282
(*111,900).........F5 73
Manchester, N.Y.,
1,344..............C3 75
Manchester, Ohio,
2,172..............D4 78
Manchester, Pa., 1,454.F8 81
Manchester, Tenn.,
3,930..............B5 83
Manchester Depot, Vt.,
800................E1 73
Manchouli (Lupin),
China, 25,000......B8 17
Manchuria, reg.,
China, 41,700,000...B10 17
Mandalay, Bur.,
190,000............D10 20
Mandan, N. Dak.,
10,525.............D5 77
Mandarin, Fla.,
900..............B5, C6 54
Manderson, Wyo., 167.A5 89
Mandeville, La.,
1,740..............B7, D5 63

Mandsaur, India, 41,876............D6 20
Manduria, It., 22,500..D6 9
Mandvi, India, 29,305..D4 20
Manfalūt, Eg., U.A.R., 23,900............C4 23
Manfredonia, It., 34,000.............D5 9
Mangalore, India, 142,669............F5 20
Mangum, Okla., 3,950..C2 79
Manhasset, N.Y., 8,300..............F2 52
Manhattan, Ill., 1,117.*B6 58
Manhattan, Kans., 22,993............C7 61
Manhattan, borough (New York co.), N.Y., 1,698,281 (part of New York City)........*D6 74
Manhattan Beach, Calif., 34,513.............F2 50
Manheim, Pa., 4,790...F9 81
Manhuaçu, Braz., 10,546............C4 30
Manila, Ark., 1,753....B5 49
Manila, Phil., 1,145,700..........o13 19
Manilla, Iowa, 939.....C2 60
Manisa, Tur., 59,200...C6 14
Manistee, Mich., 8,324.D4 66
Manistee, co., Mich., 19,042.............D4 66
Manistique, Mich., 4,875............C4 66
Manito, Ill., 1,093.....C4 58
Manitoba, prov., Can., 921,686..............40
Manitoulin, co., Ont., Can., 11,176............B2 41
Manitou Beach, Mich., 1,544...........*G6 66
Manitou Springs, Colo., 3,626.........C6 51
Manitowoc, Wis., 32,275.........B6, D6 88
Manitowoc, co., Wis., 75,215............D6 88
Maniwaki, Que., Can., 6,349.............C2 42
Manizales, Col., 147,210.............B2 32
Mankato, Kans., 1,231.C5 61
Mankato, Minn., 23,797..........F5 67
Manlius, N.Y., 1,997...C5 75
Manlléu, Sp., 9,410....A7 8
Manly, Iowa, 1,425....A4 60
Mannar, Cey., 5,190...G6 20
Mannheim, Ger., 313,900 (*1,125,000).........D4 6
Manning, Iowa, 1,676..C2 60
Manning, S.C., 3,917..D7 82
Mannington, W. Va., 2,996.........A7, B4 87
Manono, Con. L., 28,465.............B5 24
Manor, Pa., 1,136....*F2 81
Manorhaven, N.Y., 3,566...........*E3 75
Manosque, Fr., 7,454..F6 5
Manresa, Sp., 52,216..B6 8
Mansfield, Eng., 53,222............D6 4
Mansfield, La., 5,839...B2 63
Mansfield, Mass., 5,500.............B5 65
Mansfield, Mo., 949...D5 69
Mansfield, Ohio, 47,325............B5 78
Mansfield, Pa., 2,678...C7 81
Mansfield, Tex., 1,375..B5 84
Mansfield Southeast, Ohio, 2,961.........*B5 78
Manson, Iowa, 1,789..B3 60
Mansura, La., 1,579...C3 63
Manta, Ec., 19,021...B1 31
Manteca, Calif., 8,242............B6, D3 50
Manteno, Ill., 2,225....B6 58
Mantes [-la-Jolie], Fr., 13,181............C4 5
Manti, Utah, 1,739...B6 72
Manton, Mich., 1,050..D5 66
Mantova, It., 62,411...B3 9
Mantua, N.J., 1,500...D2 74
Mantua, Ohio, 1,194...A6 78
Manville, N.J., 10,995..B3 74
Manville, R.I., 3,600..B11 52
Many, La., 3,164......C2 63
Manzanares, Sp., 17,847............C4 8
Manzanillo, Cuba, 42,252............E5 35
Manzanillo, Mex., 16,591.........D4, N11 34
Maple Bluff, Wis., 1,565............E4 88
Maple Creek, Sask., Can., 2,291..........H1 39

Maple Heights, Ohio, 31,667............B2 78
Maple Lake, Minn., 1,018.............E5 67
Maple Lane, Ind., 2,500.............*A5 59
Maple Mount, Ky., 500...............C2 62
Maple Shade, N.J., 12,947.............D2 74
Mapleton, Iowa, 1,686.B2 60
Mapleton, Maine, 900..B4 64
Mapleton, Minn., 1,107..............G5 67
Mapleton, Utah, 1,516..............D2 72
Maplewood, La., 2,432.D2 63
Maplewood, Minn., 18,519.............E7 67
Maplewood, Mo., 12,552.............B8 69
Maplewood, N.J., 23,977.............B4 74
Maplewood, N.Y., 1,000.............*C7 75
Maplewood Park, Pa., 1,800............*G11 81
Maquoketa, Iowa, 5,909.............B7 60
Maracaibo, Ven., 432,902............A3 32
Maracay, Ven., 134,123............A4 32
Maradi, Niger, 10,100..F6 22
Maragogipe, Braz., 12,575............*E7 27
Marana, Ariz., 500....C3 48
Maranguape, Braz., 8,715.............*D7 27
Maranhão, state, Braz., 2,492,139...........*D6 27
Maraş, Tur., 54,600...D11 14
Marathon, N.Y., 1,079.C4 75
Marathon, Tex., 800.............D1, F2 84
Marathon, Wis., 1,022.D4 88
Marathon, co., Wis., 88,874.............D4 88
Marbella, Sp., 8,982...D3 8
Marble Falls, Tex., 2,161..............D3 84
Marblehead, Mass., 18,521.........B6, C4 65
Marburg [an der Lahn], Ger., 44,900............C4 6
Marceline, Mo., 2,872..B5 69
Marcellus, Mich., 1,073..............G5 66
Marcellus, N.Y., 1,697.C4 75
Marche, pol. dist., It., 1,347,489..........*C4 9
Marche, former prov., Fr., 222,000..........D4 5
Marchena, Sp., 17,030..D3 8
Marches, reg., It......C4 9
Marcos Juárez, Arg., 9,556..............A4 28
Marcus, Iowa, 1,307...B2 60
Marcus Hook, Pa., 3,299..............G11 81
Mardan, Pak., 46,358..B5 20
Mar del Plata, Arg., 203,000............B5 28
Mardin, Tur., 27,400..D3 14
Marechal Deodoro, Braz., 5,269..........*D7 27
Marengo, Ill., 3,568...A5 58
Marengo, Iowa, 2,264..C5 60
Marengo, co., Ala., 27,098.............C2 46
Marfa, Tex., 2,799....F2 84
Margão, India, 17,175..E5 20
Margaret, Ala., 715...B3 46
Margaretville, N.Y., 833..............C6 75
Margate, Eng., 45,708..E7 4
Margate, Fla., 2,646...*F6 54
Margate, N.J., 9,474...E3 74
Margelan, Sov. Un., 73,000.............E10 13
Mariana, is., Pac. O...E6 2
Marianao, Cuba, 219,278.........D2, K11 35
Marianna, Ark., 5,134..C5 49
Marianna, Fla., 7,152..B1 54
Marianna, Pa., 1,088..*F3 81
Marianske Lazne, Czech., 12,600..........D2 7
Maribo, co., Den., 133,870.............*J4 11
Maribor, Yugo., 82,387.B2 10
Maricopa, co., Ariz., 663,510............C2 48
Mariemont, Ohio, 4,120..............D2 78
Marienville, Pa., 800...D3 81
Maries, co., Mo., 7,282.C6 69
Mariestad, Swe., 11,900.............H5 11
Marietta, Ga., 25,565...........A5, C2 55

Marietta, Ohio, 16,847..C6 78
Marietta, Okla., 1,933..D4 79
Marietta, Pa., 2,385...F8 81
Marietta East, Ga., 4,535.............*A5 55
Marieville, Que., Can., 3,809.............D4 42
Marília, Braz., 51,789..C3 30
Marín, Sp., 7,261.....A1 8
Marin, co., Calif., 146,820............C2 50
Marin City, Calif., 2,500.............*B5 50
Marinduque, prov., Phil., 114,900.........*C6 19
Marine City, Mich., 4,404..............F8 66
Marinette, Wis., 13,329.............C6 88
Marinette, co., Wis., 34,660............C5 88
Maringouin, La., 1,168.D4 63
Marinha Grande, Port., 4,698..............C1 8
Marino, It., 9,700.....H9 9
Marion, Ala., 3,807...C2 46
Marion, Ill., 11,274...F5 58
Marion, Ind., 37,854..C6 59
Marion, Iowa, 10,882..B6 60
Marion, Kans., 2,169..D6 61
Marion, Ky., 2,468...A3 62
Marion, Mass., 1,160..C6 65
Marion, Mich., 898...D5 66
Marion, N.C., 3,345..........B2, D4 76
Marion, Ohio, 37,079..B4 78
Marion, S.C., 7,174...C9 82
Marion, Va., 8,385...B3 85
Marion, Wis., 1,200...D5 88
Marion, co., Ala., 21,837............A2 46
Marion, co., Ark., 6,041.............A3 49
Marion, co., Fla., 51,616............C4 54
Marion, co., Ga., 5,477.............D2 55
Marion, co., Ill., 39,349............E5 58
Marion, co., Ind., 697,567..........E5 59
Marion, co., Iowa, 25,886............C4 60
Marion, co., Kans., 15,143...........D6 61
Marion, co., Ky., 16,887............C4 62
Marion, co., Miss., 23,293............D4 68
Marion, co., Mo., 29,522............B6 69
Marion, co., Ohio, 60,221............B4 78
Marion, co., Oreg., 120,888..........C4 80
Marion, co., S.C., 32,014............C9 82
Marion, co., Tenn., 21,036............D8 83
Marion, co., Tex., 8,049.............C5 84
Marion, co., W. Va., 63,717............B4 87
Marionville, Mo., 1,251.............D4 69
Mariposa, co., Calif., 5,064.............D3 50
Marissa, Ill., 1,722.....E4 58
Maris Town, Miss., 500..............C3 68
Mariupol, see Zhdanov, Sov. Un.
Markdale, Ont., Can., 1,090..............C4 41
Marked Tree, Ark., 3,216..............B5 49
Markesan, Wis., 1,060..E5 88
Markham, Ont., Can., 4,294.........C9, D5 41
Markham, Ill., 11,704..F3 58
Markovka, Sov. Un., 5,000.............G12 12
Marks, Miss., 2,572...A3 68
Marksville, La., 4,257..C3 63
Marktredwitz, Ger., 15,500.............C6 6
Marlboro, Mass., 18,819.........B4, D1 65
Marlboro, N.H., 1,097..F3 73
Marlboro, N.Y., 1,733..D6 75
Marlboro, co., S.C., 28,529............B8 82
Marlene Village, Oreg., 1,100.............*B3 80
Marlette, Mich., 1,640.E7 66
Marlin, Tex., 6,918...D4 84
Marlinton, W. Va., 1,586..............C4 87
Marlow, Okla., 4,027...C4 79
Marlow, W. Va., 700..B7 87
Marmande, Fr., 10,199.E4 5

Marmet, W. Va., 2,500...........C3, C6 87
Marmora, Ont., Can., 1,381..............C7 41
Marne, dept., Fr., 442,195............*C6 5
Maroa, Ill., 1,235.....C5 58
Maroantsetra, Malag., 4,412...............D9 24
Maroua, Cam...........F7 22
Marovoay, Malag., 7,217...............D9 24
Marquesas, is., Fr. Polynesia...........G11 2
Marquês de Valença, Braz., 12,935....C4, h6 30
Marquette, Mich., 19,824............B3 66
Marquette Heights, Ill., 2,517.............*C5 58
Marquette, co., Mich., 56,154............B3 66
Marquette, co., Wis., 8,516............E4 88
Marrakech, Mor., 243,134............B3 22
Marrero, La., 19,000...C7 63
Marromeu, Moz., 5,000..............D7 24
Mars, Pa., 1,522.....E1 81
Marsala, It., 39,000...F4 9
Marseille, Fr., 778,071..F6 5
Marseilles, Ill., 4,347..B5 58
Marshall, Ark., 1,095..B3 49
Marshall, Ill., 3,270...D6 58
Marshall, Mich., 6,736.F6 66
Marshall, Minn., 6,681.F3 67
Marshall, Mo., 9,572..B4 69
Marshall, N.C., 926...D3 76
Marshall, Tex., 23,846..C5 84
Marshall, co., Ala., 48,018............A3 46
Marshall, co., Ill., 13,334............B4 58
Marshall, co., Ind., 32,443............B4 59
Marshall, co., Iowa, 37,984............C4 60
Marshall, co., Kans., 15,598...........C7 61
Marshall, co., Ky., 16,736............A3 62
Marshall, co., Minn., 14,262............B2 67
Marshall, co., Miss., 24,503............A4 68
Marshall, co., Okla., 7,263.............C5 79
Marshall, co., S. Dak., 6,663.............E8 77
Marshall, co., Tenn., 16,859............B5 83
Marshall, co., W. Va., 38,041............B4 87
Marshall Northeast, Tex., 1,192...........*C5 84
Marshallton, Del., 1,800..............A6 53
Marshallton, Pa., 2,316.............*E8 81
Marshalltown, Iowa, 22,521............B5 60
Marshallville, Ga., 1,308..............D3 55
Marshfield, Mass., 1,500...........B6, E4 65
Marshfield, Mo., 2,221.D5 69
Marshfield, Wis., 14,153.............D3 88
Mars Hill, Ind., 1,000.............E5, H7 59
Mars Hill, Maine, 1,458..............B5 64
Mars Hill, N.C., 1,574..D3 76
Marshville, N.C., 1,360.C3 76
Mart, Tex., 2,197....D4 84
Martigues, Fr., 9,852..F6 5
Martin, Ky., 992.....C7 62
Martin, S. Dak., 1,184..G4 77
Martin, Tenn., 4,750...A3 83
Martin, co., Fla., 16,932............E6 54
Martin, co., Ind., 10,602............G4 59
Martin, co., Ky., 10,201............C7 62
Martin, co., Minn., 26,986............G4 67
Martin, co., N.C., 27,139............B6 76
Martin, co., Tex., 5,068.............C2 84
Martina [Franca], It., 25,500............D6 9
Martinez, Calif., 9,604...........B5, C2 50
Martinez, Ga., 2,000..*C4 55
Martinique, Fr. dep., N.A., 258,000........o16 35
Martinsburg, Pa., 1,772.............F5 81

Martinsburg, W. Va.,
15,179.............B6 87
Martins Creek, Pa.,
900..............B2 74
Martins Ferry, Ohio,
11,919............B7 78
Martinsville, Ill., 1,351.D6 58
Martinsville, Ind.,
7,525.............F5 59
Martinsville, N.J.,
1,700.............B3 74
Martinsville (Independent
City), Va., 18,798...E3 85
Martos, Sp., 16,900....D4 8
Maruf, Afg., 5,000.....B4 20
Marugame, Jap.,
39,500............I6 18
Marvell, Ark., 1,690...C5 49
Marvin Terrace, Mo.,
1,260............*C7 69
Mary, Sov. Un., 51,000.F9 13
Maryborough, Austl.,
7,235.............G7 25
Maryborough, Austl.,
19,126............E9 25
Maryland, state, U.S.,
3,100,689.............. 53
Maryland Heights, Mo.,
2,000.............A8 69
Maryport, Eng., 12,334.C5 4
Marystown, Newf.,
Can., 1,460......E4 44
Marysville, Calif.,
9,553.............C3 50
Marysville, N.B.,
Can., 3,233........D3 43
Marysville, Kans.,
4,143.............C7 61
Marysville, Mich.,
4,065.............F8 66
Marysville, Ohio, 4,952.B4 78
Marysville, Pa., 2,580..F8 81
Marysville, Wash.,
3,117.............A3 86
Maryvale, Ariz.,
2,000............*C2 48
Maryville, Mo., 7,807..A3 69
Maryville, Tenn.,
10,348........D10, E11 83
Masan, Kor., 159,500...I4 18
Masaya, Nic., 32,100...E7 34
Masbate, Phil., 7,500..C6 19
Masbate, prov., Phil.,
136,700..........*H7 19
Mascara, Alg., 39,830..A5 22
Mascot, Tenn.,
1,000........C10, E12 83
Mascouche, Que.,
Can., 1,152......D4 42
Mascoutah, Ill., 3,625..E4 58
Mashhad (Meshed),
Iran, 241,989......B6 15
Masindi, Ug., 5,000....H4 23
Maskinongé, co., Que.,
Can., 21,274......C4 42
Mason, Mich., 4,522...F6 66
Mason, Ohio,
4,727........C2, C3 78
Mason, Tex., 1,910...D3 84
Mason, W. Va., 1,005..B2 87
Mason, co., Ill., 15,193.C4 58
Mason, co., Ky.,
18,454............B6 62
Mason, co., Mich.,
21,929............D4 66
Mason, co., Tex.,
3,780.............D3 84
Mason, co., Wash.,
16,251............B2 86
Mason, co., W. Va.,
24,459............C3 87
Mason City, Ill., 2,160.C4 58
Mason City, Iowa,
30,642............A4 60
Masontown, Pa., 4,730.G2 81
Masontown, W. Va.,
841..............B5 87
Mass, Mich., 500......A6 66
Massa, It., 56,988.....B3 9
Massac, co., Ill.,
14,341............F5 58
Massachusetts, state,
U.S., 5,148,578........ 65
Massafra, It., 20,005...D6 9
Massa Marittima, It.,
5,700.............C3 9
Massapequa, N.Y.,
30,000............G3 52
Massapequa Park, N.Y.,
19,904...........*G3 75
Massaua, Eth., 25,000..E5 23
Massena, N.Y., 15,478.A2 75
Massey, Ont., Can.,
1,324.............A2 41
Massillon, Ohio, 31,236.B6 78
Masson, Que., Can.,
1,933.............D2 42
Masterton, N.Z.,
15,128...........N15 26
Mastic, N.Y., 1,600...*F5 75

Mastic Beach, N.Y.,
3,035............*F4 52
Mastung, Pak., 2,792...C4 20
Masuda, Jap., 27,400...I5 18
Masulipatnam, India,
101,417...........E7 20
Masuria, reg., Pol.....B6 7
Masury, Ohio, 5,900...A7 78
Matadi, Con. L.,
59,000............B2 24
Matador, Tex., 1,217..B2 84
Matagalpa, Nic.,
15,900............E7 34
Matagorda, co., Tex.,
25,744............E5 84
Matamoras, Pa.,
2,087............D12 81
Matamoros, Mex.,
93,334............B5 34
Matamoros [de la Laguna],
Mex., 13,572.......B4 34
Matane, Que., Can.,
9,190............G20 36
Matane, co., Que., Can.,
35,078...........*G20 36
Matanzas, Cuba,
63,916............D3 35
Matanzas, prov., Cuba,
395,380...........D3 35
Matapedia, co., Que.,
Can., 35,586.....*G20 36
Matara, Cey., 27,735..G7 20
Mataram, Indon.,
10,000............G5 19
Mataró, Sp., 41,128....B7 8
Matawan, N.J., 5,097..C4 74
Matehuala, Mex.,
19,738............C4 34
Matera, It., 38,562....D6 9
Mateszalka, Hung.,
11,249............B6 10
Mateur, Tun., 12,714..F2 9
Matewan, W. Va., 896.D2 87
Mather, Pa., 1,033....G1 81
Mathews, co., Va.,
7,121.............D6 85
Mathis, Tex., 6,075....E4 84
Mathura, India,
116,959...........C6 20
Matoaca, Va., 2,000...C7 85
Matoaka, W. Va., 613..D3 87
Mato Grosso, state,
Braz., 910,262......B1 30
Matozinhos, Port.,
33,400............B1 8
Maṭrah, Mus. & Om.,
3,500.............E6 15
Maṭrūḥ, Eg., U.A.R.,
3,047.............B3 23
Matsue, Jap., 78,000...I6 18
Matsuida, Jap.,
9,300...........m17 18
Matsumoto, Jap.,
108,000.......H9, m16 18
Matsuyama, Jap.,
238,604...........J6 18
Matsuzaka, Jap.,
57,600........I8, o15 18
Matsuzaki, Jap.,
5,708...........o17 18
Mattancheri, India,
83,896............G6 20
Mattapoisett, Mass.,
1,640.............C6 65
Mattawa, Ont., Can.,
3,314.........A6, E9 41
Matteson, Ill., 3,225...F3 58
Mattituck, N.Y., 1,274.D4 75
Mattoon, Ill., 19,088...D5 58
Mattydale, N.Y.,
9,000............*B4 75
Matun, Afg., 5,000....B4 20
Maturín, Ven., 53,445..B5 32
Maubeuge, Fr., 27,214.B5 5
Maubin, Bur., 22,130.*E10 20
Mauch Chunk, see Jim
Thorpe, Pa.
Maud, Okla., 1,137....B5 79
Maud, Tex., 951.....C5 84
Maui, co. (incl. Kalawao),
Haw., 42,855.......B4 56
Mauldin, S.C., 1,462..*B3 82
Maule, prov., Chile,
79,304............B2 28
Maumee, Ohio,
12,063........A2, A4 78
Maunaloa, Haw., 950..B4 56
Mauritania, country, Afr.,
725,000...........E2 22
Maury, co., Tenn.,
41,699............B4 83
Mauston, Wis., 3,531..E3 88
Maverick, co., Tex.,
14,508............E2 84
Maxton, N.C., 1,755...C4 76
Mayagüez, P.R.,
50,147...........m13 35
Maybeury, W. Va.,
900..............D3 87
Maybrook, N.Y., 1,348.D6 75
Mayen, Ger., 17,300...C3 6

Mayenne, Fr., 10,270..C3 5
Mayenne, dept., Fr.,
250,030..........*C3 5
Mayer, Ariz., 300.....B2 48
Mayes, co., Okla.,
20,073............A6 79
Mayfair, S.C., 5,000...*B3 82
Mayfield, Ky., 10,762..B2 62
Mayfield, Ohio, 1,977.*A6 78
Mayfield, Pa., 1,996...C10 81
Mayfield Heights, Ohio,
13,478............A6 78
Mayhew, Okla., 1,223..A4 79
Mayking, Ky., 750....C7 62
Maykop, Sov. Un.,
88,000...........*E7 13
Maymyo, Bur.,
22,287...........D10 20
Maynard, Mass.,
7,695........B5, C1 65
Mayo, Md., 500.......C4 53
Mayo, co., Ire.,
123,330..........*D2 4
Mayodan, N.C., 2,366..A4 76
Mayo Landing, Yuk.,
Can., 342..........D6 36
May Pen, Jam., 14,214.G5 35
Mayport, Fla.,
450.........B5, B6 54
Mays Landing, N.J.,
1,404.............E3 74
Maysville, Ky., 8,484..B6 62
Maysville, Mo., 942...B3 69
Maysville, Okla., 1,530.C4 79
Mayville, Mich., 896...E7 66
Mayville, N.Y., 1,619..C1 75
Mayville, N. Dak.,
2,168.............C8 77
Mayville, Wis., 3,607..E5 88
Maywood, Calif.,
14,588............F2 50
Maywood, Ill., 27,330..F2 58
Maywood, N.J., 11,460.D5 74
Maywood, N.Y.,
1,500............*C7 75
Mazagan, Mor., 40,302.B3 22
Mazamet, Fr., 14,863..F5 5
Mazara del Vallo, It.,
36,827............F4 9
Mazar-i-Sharif, Afg.,
41,960............A4 20
Mazarrón, Sp., 11,569.D5 8
Mazatenango, Guat.,
11,067............E6 34
Mazatlán, Mex.,
74,934............C3 34
Mazomanie, Wis.,
1,069.............E4 88
Mazzarino, It., 17,789..F5 9
Mbaïki, Cen. Afr. Rep.,
1,000.............H1 23
Mbalmayo, Cam.,
6,242.............H7 22
Mbeya, Tan., 6,932....B6 24
Meade, Kans., 2,019...E3 61
Meade, co., Kans.,
5,505.............E3 61
Meade, co., Ky.,
18,938............C3 62
Meade, co., S. Dak.,
12,044............F3 77
Meadowbrook, Ind.,
1,500............*B7 59
Meadowbrook, W. Va.,
500..............A7 87
Meadow Lands, Pa.,
1,967.............F1 81
Meadow Park, Fla.,
3,500.............F6 54
Meadville, Pa., 16,671.C1 81
Meaford, Ont., Can.,
3,834.............C4 41
Meagher, co., Mont.,
2,616.............D6 70
Meath, co., Ire.,
65,122...........*D3 4
Meaux, Fr., 22,251....C5 5
Mebane, N.C., 2,364...A4 76
Mecca, Ind., 500......E3 59
Mecca (Makkah), Sau.
Ar., 200,000........E2 15
Mechanic Falls, Maine,
2,195.............D2 64
Mechanicsburg, Ohio,
1,810.............B4 78
Mechanicsburg, Pa.,
8,123.............F7 81
Mechanicsville, Iowa,
1,010.............C6 60
Mechanicsville, N.Y.,
6,831.............C7 75
Mechelen, Bel., 64,772.B6 5
Mecklenburg, co., N.C.,
272,111...........B3 76
Mecklenburg, co., Va.,
31,428............E4 85
Mecklenburg, reg.,
Ger..............B6 6
Mecklenburg, state, Sov.
Zone, Ger.,
2,139,640.........*B6 6

Mecosta, co., Mich.,
21,051............E5 66
Medan, Indon.,
466,670........E1, m11 19
Médéa, Alg., 7,638.....A5 22
Medellín, Col., 485,250
(*700,000).........B2 32
Medfield, Mass., 2,424.D2 65
Medford, Mass.,
64,971........B5, C3 65
Medford, N.J., 1,480...D3 74
Medford, Okla., 1,223..A4 79
Medford, Oreg., 24,425.E4 80
Medford, Wis., 3,260...C3 88
Medford Lakes, N.J.,
2,876.............D3 74
Medgidia, Rom.,
17,943............C9 10
Media, Pa.,
5,803........B10, G11 81
Mediapolis, Iowa,
1,040.............C6 60
Medias, Rom., 32,503..B7 10
Medical Lake, Wash.,
4,765.........B8, D7 86
Medicine Hat, Alta.,
Can., 24,484......D5 38
Medicine Lodge, Kans.,
3,072.............E5 61
Medina, N.Y., 6,681...B2 75
Medina, Ohio, 8,235...A6 78
Medina, Wash., 2,285.D12 86
Medina, co., Ohio,
63,315............A6 78
Medina, co., Tex.,
18,904............E3 84
Medina del Campo, Sp.,
14,327............B3 8
Medina Sidonia, Sp.,
8,704.............D3 8
Medvezhegorsk, Sov. Un.,
19,200...........F16 11
Medway, Mass.,
1,602.........B5, E1 65
Medzhibozh, Sov. Un.,
10,000............G6 12
Meeker, Colo., 1,655...A3 51
Meeker, co., Minn.,
18,887............E4 67
Meerane, Ger., 24,500..C6 6
Meerut, India, 200,470
(*283,997).........C6 20
Megantic, co., Que.,
Can., 57,400......C6 42
Megara, Grc., 15,450...C4 14
Meggett, S.C., 188.F1, F7 82
Mehun-sur-Yèvre, Fr.,
4,735.............D5 5
Meigs, Ga., 1,236.....E2 55
Meigs, co., Ohio,
22,159............C5 78
Meigs, co., Tenn.,
5,160.............D9 83
Meihsien, China,
85,000............G8 17
Meiktila, Bur., 25,180.D10 20
Meiners Oaks, Calif.,
3,513............*E4 50
Meiningen, Ger.,
23,700............C5 6
Meissen, Ger., 47,900..C6 6
Meknès, Mor., 175,943.B3 22
Melbourne, Austl., 76,834
(*1,667,100).......G7 25
Melbourne, Fla.,
11,982............D6 54
Melbourne Beach, Fla.,
1,004.............D6 54
Melfi, It., 18,208.....D5 9
Melfort, Sask., Can.,
4,039.............E3 39
Melilla, Sp. poss., Afr.,
79,056............A4 22
Melipilla, Chile,
11,525............A2 28
Melita, Man., Can.,
1,038.............E1 40
Melito di Porto Salvo,
It., 8,880..........F5 9
Melitopol, Sov. Un.,
102,000...........H10 12
Mellen, Wis., 1,182....B3 88
Mellette, co., S. Dak.,
2,664.............G5 77
Melnik, Czech.,
13,100...........n18 7
Melo, Ur., 27,100.....E2 30
Melocheville, Que.,
Can., 1,666........D8 42
Melouprey, Camb.,
10,000............C3 19
Melrose, Mass.,
29,619........B5, C3 65
Melrose, Minn., 2,135..E4 67
Melrose, N. Mex., 698..B7 48
Melrose Park, Fla.,
4,000............*F6 54
Melrose Park, Ill.,
22,291............F2 58
Melrose Park, N.Y.,
2,085............*C4 75

Melrose Park, Pa., 6,000.............*G11 81
Melun, Fr., 26,873.....C5 5
Melville, Sask., Can., 5,191.............G4 39
Melville, La., 1,939....D4 63
Melville, isl., N.W. Ter., Can.....A11 36
Melvin, Ky., 750......C7 62
Melvindale, Mich., 13,089.............A8 66
Memel, see Klaipeda, Sov. Un.
Memmingen, Ger., 29,800.............E5 6
Memphis, Fla., 2,647...F2 54
Memphis, Mich., 996...F8 66
Memphis, Mo., 2,106..A5 69
Memphis, Tenn., 497,524 (*628,100).....B1, E8 83
Memphis, Tex., 3,332..B2 84
Mena, Ark., 4,388.....C1 49
Menands, N.Y., 2,314..D3 75
Menard, Tex., 1,914..D3 84
Menard, co., Ill., 9,248.............C4 58
Menard, co., Tex., 2,964.............D3 84
Menasha, Wis., 14,647..........A5, D5 88
Mende, Fr., 8,337.....E5 5
Mendenhall, Miss., 1,946.............D4 68
Mendham, N.J., 2,371..B3 74
Mendocino, co., Calif., 51,059.............C2 50
Mendon, Mass., 900...E1 65
Mendota, Calif., 3,086.D3 50
Mendota, Ill., 6,154...B4 58
Mendota Heights, Minn., 5,028.......*F5 67
Mendoza, Arg., 109,149............A3 28
Mendoza, prov., Arg., 825,535.............A3 28
Menemen, Tur., 15,100..........*C6 14
Menfi, It., 12,492.....F4 9
Mengtzu, China, 9,000.G5 17
Menifee, co., Ky., 4,276.............C6 62
Menlo Park, Calif., 26,957.............B5 50
Menlo Park Terrace, N.J., 2,500.........*B4 74
Menominee, Mich., 11,289.............C3 66
Menominee, co., Mich., 24,685.............C3 66
Menominee, co., Wis., 2,606.............C5 88
Menomonee Falls, Wis., 18,276...........E1, E5 88
Menomonie, Wis., 8,624.............D2 88
Mentana, It., 5,489....g9 9
Menton, Fr., 19,904...F7 5
Mentone, Calif., 2,000.*F3 50
Mentor, Ohio, 4,354....A6 78
Mentor Headlands, Ohio, 1,500.............*A4 78
Mentor-on-the-Lake, Ohio, 3,290.............A6 78
Meppel, Neth., 17,700..A7 5
Meppen, Ger., 14,900..B3 6
Mequon, Wis., 8,543...E2 88
Merano, It., 30,614....A3 9
Merca, Som., 15,000...H6 23
Mercara, India, 14,453.F6 20
Merced, Calif., 20,068..D3 50
Merced, co., Calif., 90,446.............D3 50
Mercedes, Arg., 25,912.A3 28
Mercedes, Arg., 16,932..........A5, g7 28
Mercedes, Arg., 14,813.E4 29
Mercedes, Tex., 10,943.F4 84
Mercedes, Ur., 25,400..E1 30
Mercer, Pa., 2,800.....D1 81
Mercer, co., Ill., 17,149.B3 58
Mercer, co., Ky., 14,596.............C5 62
Mercer, co., Mo., 5,750.A4 69
Mercer, co., N.J., 266,392.............C3 74
Mercer, co., N. Dak., 6,805.............C4 77
Mercer, co., Ohio, 32,559.............B3 78
Mercer, co., Pa., 127,519.............D1 81
Mercer, co., W. Va., 68,206.............D3 87
Mercer Island, Wash., 12,000.........B3, D2 86
Mercersburg, Pa., 1,759.............G6 81
Merchantville, N.J., 4,075.............*D2 74
Meredith, N.H., 950...D4 73
Meredosia, Ill., 1,034..D3 58

Merefa, Sov. Un., 10,000.............G11 12
Mergui, Bur., 33,697..F10 20
Mérida, Mex., 170,513.C7 34
Mérida, Sp., 34,297...C2 8
Mérida, Ven., 40,404..B3 32
Mérida, state, Ven., 270,668.............B3 32
Meridan, Conn., 51,850.............C5 52
Meridian, Idaho, 2,081.F2 57
Meridian, Miss., 49,374.C5 68
Meridian, Pa., 1,649..*E2 81
Meridian, Tex., 993...D4 84
Merino Village, Mass., 3,099.............B4 65
Merioneth, co., Wales, 39,007.............*D5 4
Merion Park, Pa., 1,000.............*F11 81
Merion Station, Pa., 5,500.............*B11 81
Meriwether, co., Ga., 19,756.............C2 55
Merkel, Tex., 2,312...C2 84
Merksem, Bel., 36,098..B6 5
Merlo, Arg., 8,385.....g7 28
Merowe, Sud., 1,620...E4 23
Merriam, Kans., 5,084..B8 61
Merrick, N.Y., 18,789..G2 52
Merrick, co., Nebr., 8,363.............C7 71
Merrifield, Va., 1,000..B5 85
Merrill, Mich., 963....E6 66
Merrill, Wis., 9,451....C4 88
Merrillville, Ind., 3,120.B3 59
Merrillville Lake, Ind., 3,120.............B3 59
Merrimac, Mass., 1,800.A5 65
Merrimac, N.H., 500...F5 73
Merrimack, co., N.H., 67,785.............E4 73
Merrionette Park, Ill., 2,354.............*F3 58
Merritt, B.C., Can., 39,039.............D7 37
Merritt Island, Fla., 3,554.............D6 54
Merryville, La., 1,232..D2 63
Merseburg, Ger., 47,200.............C4 6
Mersin, Tur., 68,600..D10 14
Merthyr Tydfil, Wales, 59,008.............E5 4
Merzifon, Tur., 22,200.............B10 14
Mesa, Ariz., 33,772.C3, D2 48
Mesa, co., Colo., 50,715.C2 51
Mesagne, It., 23,000...D6 9
Meshkovskaya, Sov. Un.............G13 12
Mesilla, N. Mex., 1,264.E3 48
Mesilla Park, N. Mex., 2,400.............E3 48
Mesolongion, Grc., 11,266.............C3 14
Mesquite, Tex., 27,526.B6 84
Messina, It., 254,715..E5 9
Messina, S. Afr., 10,225.............E6 24
Messini, Grc., 7,725...*D3 14
Messinia, prov., Grc., 211,970.............*D4 14
Mestre, It., 73,435....B4 9
Meta, dept., Col., 74,780.............C3 32
Metabetchouan, Que., Can., 1,962.............A6 42
Metairie, La., 65,000..*C7 63
Metamora, Ill., 1,808..C4 58
Metán, Arg., 6,915....E3 29
Metcalfe, co., Ky., 8,367.............D4 62
Methuen, Mass., 28,114.............A5 65
Metković, Yugo., 4,488.D3 10
Metropolis, Ill., 7,339..F5 58
Metter, Ga., 2,362....D4 55
Metuchen, N.J., 14,041.B4 74
Metz, Fr., 102,771 (*150,000).............C7 5
Meudon, Fr., 34,078....g9 5
Meurthe-et-Moselle, dept., Fr., 678,078..*C7 5
Meuse, dept., Fr., 215,985.............*C6 5
Mexia, Tex., 6,121.....D4 84
Mexicali, Mex., 172,554.............A1 34
Mexico, Maine, 5,043..D2 64
Mexico, Mo., 12,889...B6 69
Mexico, N.Y., 1,465...B4 75
Mexico, country, N.A., 34,625,903.............34
México, state, Mex., 1,383,291.............D5, n14 34
Mexico City, Mex., 2,697,994 (*4,800,000).D5, h9, n14 34
Meyersdale, Pa., 2,901.G3 81
Mezen, Sov. Un., 7,300.C7 13

Mézières, Fr., 11,799...C6 5
Mezokovesd, Hung., 18,640.............B5 10
Mezotur, Hung., 16,000.............B5 10
Mglin, Sov. Un., 10,000.E9 12
Miajadas, Sp., 8,632...C3 8
Miami, Ariz., 3,350.C3, D3 48
Miami, Fla., 291,688 (*1,212,000).....F3, G6 54
Miami, Okla., 12,869...A7 79
Miami, W. Va., 500.....C3, D6 87
Miami, co., Ind., 38,000.............C5 59
Miami, co., Kans., 19,884.............D9 61
Miami, co., Ohio, 72,901.............B3 78
Miami Beach, Fla., 63,145.............F3, G6 54
Miamisburg, Ohio, 9,893.............C3 78
Miami Shores, Fla., 8,865.............F3, G6 54
Miami Shores, Ohio, 1,200.............*C3 78
Miami Springs, Fla., 11,229.............F3, G6 54
Mianwali, Pak., 23,341.B5 20
Miaoli, For., 5,000....*G9 17
Miass, Sov. Un., 107,000.............*D9 13
Michalovce, Czech., 16,300.............D6 7
Michigan, state, U.S., 7,823,194.............66
Michigan Center, Mich., 4,611.............F6 66
Michigan City, Ind., 36,653.............A4 59
Michoacán, state, Mex., 1,862,568.....D4, n13 34
Michurinsk, Sov. Un., 84,000.............E13 12
Mickleyville, Ind., 950.H7 59
Middelburg, Neth., 22,600.............B5 5
Middelburg, S. Afr., 6,193.............G5 24
Middleboro, Mass., 6,003.............C6 65
Middleburg, N.Y., 1,317.............C6 75
Middleburg, Pa., 1,366.E7 81
Middleburgh Heights, Ohio, 7,282.............B2 78
Middlebury, Conn., 2,000.............C4 52
Middlebury, Ind., 917..A6 59
Middlebury, Vt., 3,688.C1 73
Middlefield, Ohio, 1,467.............A6 78
Middleport, N.Y., 1,882.............B2 75
Middleport, Ohio, 3,373.............C5 78
Middleport, Pa., 775..*E9 81
Middle River, Md., 10,825.............*B5 53
Middlesboro, Ky., 12,607.............D6 62
Middlesbrough, Eng., 157,308.............C6 4
Middlesex, N.J., 10,520.B4 74
Middlesex, co., Ont., Can., 221,422.............D3 41
Middlesex, co., Conn., 88,865.............D6 52
Middlesex, co., Eng., 2,230,093.............*E6 4
Middlesex, co., Mass., 1,238,742.............A5 65
Middlesex, co., N.J., 433,856.............C4 74
Middlesex, co., Va., 6,319.............D6 85
Middleton, N.S., Can., 1,921.............E4 43
Middleton, Mass., 2,200...........A5, C3 65
Middleton, Wis., 4,410.E4 88
Middletown, Conn., 33,250.............C6 52
Middletown, Del., 2,191.............B6 53
Middletown, Ind., 2,033.............D6 59
Middletown, Ky., 2,764.............A4 62
Middletown, Md., 1,036.............B2 53
Middletown, N.J., 3,500.............C4 74
Middletown, N.Y., 23,475.............D6 75
Middletown, Ohio, 42,115.............C3 78
Middletown, Pa., 11,182.............F8 81

Middletown, R.I., 12,675.............C11 52
Middletown Heights, Pa., 1,000.............*G11 81
Middleville, Mich., 1,196.............F5 66
Midfield, Ala., 3,556..*E4 46
Midland, Ont., Can., 8,656.............C5 41
Midland, Mich., 27,779.E6 66
Midland, Pa., 6,425....E1 81
Midland (uninc.), Pa., 1,317.............*F1 81
Midland, Tex., 62,625..D1 84
Midland, Wash., 3,000.*D3 86
Midland, co., Mich., 51,450.............E6 66
Midland, co., Tex., 67,717.............D1 84
Midland Park, Kans., 3,000.............B5 61
Midland Park, N.J., 7,543.............B4 74
Midlothian, Ill., 8,749..F3 58
Midlothian, Tex., 1,521.............B5, C4 84
Midlothian, co., Scot., 580,332.............*C5 4
Midnapore, India, 59,532.............D8 20
Midstate Mill (Amerotron Mill), N.C., 1,090..*C4 76
Midvale, Utah, 5,802..D2 72
Midway, Ky., 1,044....B5 62
Midway, Oreg., 19,000.............*B4 80
Midway, Pa., 1,012...*F1 81
Midway (uninc.), Pa., 1,568.............G7 81
Midway, isl., Pac. O...E9 2
Midway City, Calif., 2,500.............*F2, F5 50
Midwest City, Okla., 36,058.............B4 79
Mid-Western, reg., Nig., 2,535,839.............G6 22
Midyat, Tur., 9,600...D13 14
Mie, pref., Jap., 1,485,054.............*I8 18
Miechow, Pol., 6,878...C6 7
Miechowice, Pol., 13,831.............g9 7
Miedzyrzec, Pol., 8,696.C7 7
Mielec, Pol., 22,000...C6 7
Mieres, Sp., 17,100....A3 8
Mifflin, co., Pa., 44,348.E6 81
Mifflinburg, Pa., 2,476.E7 81
Mifflintown, Pa., 887..E7 81
Mifflinville, Pa., 1,027.D9 81
Migdal Ashqelon, Isr., 14,400.............C2 15
Migennes, Fr., 6,352...D5 5
Mignon, Ala., 2,271...B3 46
Mikhaylovgrad, Bul., 8,067.............D6 10
Mikhaylovka, Sov. Un., 31,000.............F14 12
Mikhaylovka, Sov. Un., 10,000.............H10 12
Mikindani, Tan., 4,807.C8 24
Mikkeli, Fin., 19,800..G12 11
Mikkeli, dept., Fin., 235,403.............*G12 11
Mikolow, Pol., 16,100..g9 7
Mikulczyce, Pol., 16,336.............g9 7
Mikulov, Czech., 5,220.D4 7
Milaca, Minn., 1,821..E5 67
Milam, co., Tex., 22,263.............D4 84
Milan, Ill., 3,065.....B3 58
Milan, Ind., 1,174.....F7 59
Milan, see Milano. It.
Milan, Mich., 3,616....F7 66
Milan, Mo., 1,670.....A4 69
Milan, N. Mex., 2,658.*B2 48
Milan, Ohio, 1,500....A5 78
Milan, Tenn., 5,208...B3 83
Milano, It., 1,582,534 (*2,600,000).............B2 9
Milas, Tur., 11,700...*D6 14
Milazzo, It., 12,900...E5 9
Milbank, S. Dak., 3,500.............E9 77
Mildred, Pa., 800.....D9 81
Mildura, Austl., 12,279.F7 25
Miles City, Mont., 9,665.............D11 70
Milford, Conn., 41,662.E4 52
Milford, Del., 5,795....C7 53
Milford, Ill., 1,699....C6 58
Milford, Ind., 1,167....B6 59
Milford, Iowa, 1,476...A2 60
Milford, Mass., 15,749.............B4, E1 65
Milford, Mich., 4,323.............A6, F7 66
Milford, Nebr., 1,462..D8 71
Milford, N.H., 3,916...F4 73
Milford, N.J., 1,114...B2 74
Milford, Ohio, 4,131...C3 78

Milford, Pa., 1,198....D12 81
Milford, Utah, 1,471...B5 72
Milford Haven, Wales,
  12,802..............E4   4
Milford Mills, Md.,
  5,000..............*B4 53
Miliana, Alg., 5,983...A5 22
Millard, Nebr., 1,014..*C9 71
Millard, co., Utah,
  7,866..............B5 72
Millau, Fr., 21,229.....E5   5
Millbourne, Pa., 793.*G11 81
Millbrae, Calif., 15,873.B5 50
Millbrook, Ala., 900....C3 46
Millbrook, N.J., 900..*B3 74
Millbrook, N.Y., 1,717.D7 75
Millburn, N.J., 18,799..B4 74
Millbury, Mass., 6,000.B4 65
Mill City, Oreg., 1,289..C4 80
Milledgeville, Ga.,
  11,117..............C3 55
Milledgeville, Ill.,
  1,208..............B4 58
Mille Lacs, co., Minn.,
  14,560..............E5 67
Millen, Ga., 3,633.....D5 55
Miller, S. Dak., 2,081..F7 77
Miller, co., Ark.,
  31,686..............D2 49
Miller, co., Ga., 6,908..E2 55
Miller, co., Mo., 13,800.C5 69
Miller Heights, Pa.,
  1,500.............*E11 81
Millerovo, Sov. Un.,
  32,400.............G13 12
Millersburg, Ky., 913..B5 62
Millersburg, Ohio,
  3,101..............B6 78
Millersburg, Pa., 2,984.E8 81
Millers Falls, Mass.,
  1,199..............A3 65
Millersville, Pa., 3,883.F9 81
Millerton, N.Y., 1,027..D7 75
Millerville, Mass.,
  1,200.............*B4 65
Mill Hall, Pa., 1,891...D7 81
Millington, Mich.,
  1,159..............E7 66
Millington, N.J.,
  1,182.............*B3 74
Millington, Tenn.,
  6,059.............*B1 83
Millinocket, Maine,
  7,453..............C4 64
Millis, Mass., 2,588....D2 65
Millport, Ala., 943....B1 46
Mills, Wyo., 1,477....C6 89
Mills, co., Iowa, 13,050.C2 60
Mills, co., Tex., 4,467..D3 84
Millsboro, Pa., 1,179...G1 81
Millside, Del., 1,000..*A6 53
Millstadt, Ill., 1,830...E3 58
Milltown, N.B., Can.,
  1,892..............D2 43
Milltown, N.J., 5,435..C4 74
Millvale, Pa., 6,624....B6 81
Mill Valley, Calif.,
  10,411..........B5, D2 50
Millville, Mass., 1,567.B4 65
Millville, N.J., 19,096..E2 74
Millville, Pa., 952....D9 81
Millwood, Wash.,
  1,776.............*B8 86
Milmont Park, Pa.,
  2,000.............*B11 81
Milo, Maine, 1,802....C4 64
Milpitas, Calif., 6,572.B6 50
Milroy, Ind., 690.....F7 59
Milroy, Pa., 1,666....E6 81
Milstead, Ga.,
  1,047..........B6, C3 55
Milton, N.S., Can.,
  1,121..............E5 43
Milton, Del., 1,617....C7 53
Milton, Fla., 4,108.....G2 54
Milton, Mass.,
  26,375..........B5, D3 65
Milton, N.J., 400.....A3 74
Milton, N.Y., 800.....D7 75
Milton, Pa., 7,972....D8 81
Milton, Wash., 2,218..*C3 86
Milton, W. Va., 1,714...C2 87
Milton, Wis., 1,671....F5 88
Milton-Freewater, Oreg.,
  4,110..............B8 80
Milton Junction, Wis.,
  1,433..............F5 88
Miltonvale, Kans., 814.C6 61
Milton West, Ont., Can.,
  5,629..............D5 41
Milverton, Ont., Can.,
  1,111..............D4 41
Milwaukee, Wis., 741,324
  (*1,240,700)....E2, E6 88
Milwaukee, co., Wis.,
  1,036,041..........E5 88
Milwaukie, Oreg.,
  9,099..........B2, B4 80
Mimico, Ont., Can.,
  18,212..........D5, D9 41
Mims, Fla., 1,307.....D6 54

Minamata, Jap., 30,400.J5 18
Minas, Ur., 24,400.....E1 30
Minas de Ríotinto, Sp.,
  9,060..............D2   8
Minas Gerais, state,
  Braz., 9,798,880....B4 30
Minatitlan, Mex.,
  34,980.............D6 34
Minato, Jap., 7,100...m19 18
Minbu, Bur., 9,096....D9 20
Minco, Okla., 1,021...B4 79
Mindanao, isl., Phil...D6 19
Minden, Ger., 48,700...B4   6
Minden, La., 12,785...B2 63
Minden, Nebr., 2,383..D7 71
Minden, W. Va.,
  1,114..........D3, D7 87
Minehead, Eng., 7,674.E5   4
Mine Hill, N.J., 3,362.*B4 74
Mineola, N.Y.,
  20,519......D2, D3, E7 75
Mineola, Tex., 3,810...C5 84
Miner, Mo., 548......E8 69
Miner, co., S. Dak.,
  5,398..............G8 77
Mineral, co., Colo., 424.D4 51
Mineral, co., Mont.,
  3,037..............C1 70
Mineral, co., Nev.,
  6,329..............B2 72
Mineral, co., W. Va.,
  22,354.............B6 87
Mineral City, Ohio,
  917...............B6 78
Mineral del Oro, Mex.,
  4,283.............n13 34
Mineral Point, Wis.,
  2,385..............F3 88
Mineral Ridge, Ohio,
  2,000.............*A7 78
Mineral Wells, Tex.,
  11,053.............C3 84
Minersville, Pa., 6,606..E9 81
Minerva, Ohio, 3,833...B6 78
Minerva Park, Ohio,
  1,169.............*C5 78
Minervino Murge, It.,
  18,427.............D6   9
Mineville, N.Y., 1,181..A7 75
Mingo, co., W. Va.,
  39,742.............D2 87
Mingo Junction, Ohio,
  4,987..............B7 78
Mingshui, China,
  5,000..............C2 18
Minho, prov., Port.,
  825,788...........*B1   8
Minhow, see Foochow,
  China
Minidoka, co., Idaho,
  14,394.............G5 57
Minna, Nig., 12,810...G6 22
Minneapolis, Kans.,
  2,024..............C6 61
Minneapolis, Minn.,
  482,872
  (*1,491,000).....E7, F5 67
Minnedosa, Man., Can.,
  2,211..............D2 40
Minnehaha, co., S. Dak.,
  86,575.............G9 77
Minnehaha, Wash.,
  2,000.............*D3 86
Minneota, Minn., 1,297.F3 67
Minnesota, state, U.S.,
  3,413,864.......... 67
Minnetonka, Minn.,
  25,037............*F5 67
Minnetrista, Minn.,
  2,076.............*E5 67
Mino, Jap., 18,700....n15 18
Minoa, N.Y., 1,838...*B4 75
Minocqua, Wis., 700...C4 88
Minokamo, Jap.,
  31,144............n15 18
Minonk, Ill., 2,001....C4 58
Minot, N. Dak., 33,437.B4 77
Minquadale, Del.,
  1,200.............*A6 53
Minsk, Sov. Un.,
  510,000............E6 12
Minsk Mazowiecki, Pol.,
  20,000..........B6, m15   7
Minster, Ohio, 2,193..*B3 78
Minturno, It., 3,125...D4   9
Minûf, Eg., U.A.R.,
  36,900............*G8 14
Minusinsk, Sov. Un.,
  44,600.............D12 13
Miraflores, Peru,
  16,146.............E3 31
Miraj, India, 53,345....E5 20
Mira Loma, Calif.,
  3,982..............F3 50
Miramar, Fla., 5,485...E3 54
Miranda, state, Ven.,
  492,349............A4 32
Miranda de Ebro, Sp.,
  27,881.............A4   8
Mirassol, Braz., 13,674.C3 30
Mirebalais, Hai., 5,200.F7 35

Mirecourt, Fr., 8,572...C7   5
Mirgorod, Sov. Un.,
  10,000.............G9 12
Miri, Mala., 8,810.....E4 19
Mirzapur, India,
  100,097............C7 20
Misakubo, Jap., 5,000.n16 18
Misamis Occidental, prov.,
  Phil., 251,100......*D6 19
Misamis Oriental, prov.,
  Phil., 387,800......*D7 19
Mishan, China, 5,000..D6 18
Mishawaka, Ind.,
  33,361.............A5 59
Mishima, Jap.,
  62,966..........I9, n17 18
Misiones, dept., Par.,
  43,449.............E4 29
Misiones, prov., Arg.,
  331,000............E4 29
Miskolc, Hung.,
  · 143,364...........A5 10
Misrātah, Libya,
  59,902.............B8 22
Missaukee, co., Mich.,
  6,784..............D5 66
Mission, Kans., 4,626.*B9 61
Mission, Tex., 14,081...F3 84
Mission City, B.C.,
  Can., 3,251......A10, E6 37
Mission Hills, Kans.,
  3,621..............B9 61
Missisquoi, co., Que.,
  Can., 29,526........D4 42
Mississippi, co., Ark.,
  70,174.............B5 49
Mississippi, co., Mo.,
  20,695.............E8 69
Mississippi, state, U.S.,
  2,178,141.......... 68
Mississippi City, Miss.,
  4,169..........E2, E4 68
Missoula, Mont.,
  27,090.............D2 70
Missoula, co., Mont.,
  44,663.............D2 70
Missouri, state, U.S.,
  4,319,813.......... 69
Missouri Valley, Iowa,
  3,567..............C2 60
Mistassini, Que., Can.,
  3,461.............*A5 42
Mistelbach [an der Zaya],
  Aus., 5,434.........D8   6
Mistretta, It., 9,979....F5   9
Mitcham, Eng.,
  63,653............m12   4
Mitchell, Ont., Can.,
  2,247..............D3 41
Mitchell, Ind., 3,552...G5 59
Mitchell, Nebr., 1,920..C2 71
Mitchell, S. Dak.,
  12,555.............G7 77
Mitchell, co., Ga.,
  19,652.............E2 55
Mitchell, co., Iowa,
  14,043.............A5 60
Mitchell, co., Kans.,
  8,866..............C5 61
Mitchell, co., N.C.,
  13,906.............C4 76
Mitchell, co., Tex.,
  11,255.............C2 84
Mitchellsburg, Ky.,
  500...............C5 62
Mitchellville, Iowa,
  957...............C4 60
Mitilini (Mytilene),
  Grc., 25,758........C6 14
Mito, Jap.,
  110,000........H10, m19 18
Mitterteich, Ger.,
  6,500..............D6   6
Mittweida, Ger.,
  20,900.............C6   6
Miura (Misaki), Jap.,
  19,334............n18 18
Miyagi, pref., Jap.,
  1,743,195.........*G10 18
Miyako, Jap., 37,400..G10 18
Miyakonojo, Jap.,
  54,600.............K5 18
Miyazaki, Jap.,
  115,000............K5 18
Miyazaki, pref., Jap.,
  1,134,590.........*K5 18
Miyazu, Jap., 21,800..n14 18
Mizil, Rom., 7,460.....C8 10
Mjölby, Swe., 10,700..H6 11
Mlada Boleslav, Czech.,
  25,700..........C3, n18   7
Mlawa, Pol., 14,100...B6   7
Moab, Utah, 4,682.....B7 72
Mobara, Jap., 19,300..n19 18
Moberly, Mo., 13,170..B5 69
Mobile, Ala., 202,779
  (*304,000).........E1 46
Mobile, co., Ala.,
  314,301............E1 46
Mobridge, S. Dak.,
  4,391..............E5 77

Moca, Dom. Rep.,
  13,829.............F8 35
Moçambique, Moz.,
  9,222..............D8 24
Moçâmedes, Ang.,
  7,185..............D2 24
Mocanaqua, Pa., 1,104.D9 81
Mochudi, Bech.,
  11,767.............E5 24
Mocksville, N.C., 2,379.B3 76
Mocoa, Col., 1,698.....C2 32
Mocóca, Braz.,
  14,306.........C3, k8 30
Modena, It., 139,183...B3   9
Modesto, Calif.,
  36,585.............D3 50
Modica, It., 30,000....F5   9
Modlin, Pol.,
  12,000.........B6, k13   7
Mödling, Aus., 17,274..D8   6
Modoc, co., Calif.,
  8,308..............B3 50
Modrany, Czech.,
  10,100............n17   7
Moffat, co., Colo.,
  7,061..............A2 51
Mogadiscio, Som.,
  77,000.............H7 23
Mogador, Mor.,
  26,392.............B3 19
Mogadore, Ohio, 3,851.A6 78
Mogaung, Bur., 2,940.C10 20
Mogí das Cruzes, Braz.,
  63,748.........C3, m8 30
Mogilev, Sov. Un.,
  134,000............E8 12
Mogilev-Podolskiy, Sov.
  Un., 46,300........G6 12
Mogilno, Pol., 5,193...B4   7
Mogí Mirim, Braz.,
  18,345.........C3, m8 30
Mogocha, Sov. Un.,
  18,000.............D14 13
Mogok, Bur., 8,369...D10 20
Moguer, Sp., 7,222....D2   8
Mohacs, Hung., 15,860.C4 10
Mohall, N. Dak., 956...B4 77
Mohave, co., Ariz.,
  7,736..............B1 48
Mohawk, N.Y., 3,533..C5 75
Mohnton, Pa., 2,223..F10 81
Mohon, Fr., 9,043.....C6   5
Moinesti, Rom., 12,934.B8 10
Moissac, Fr., 4,770....E4   5
Mojave, Calif., 1,845..E4 50
Mokena, Ill., 1,332...*B6 58
Mokpo, Kor., 129,700...I3 18
Mol, Yugo., 8,079.....C5 10
Mola [di Bari], It.,
  22,852.............D6   9
Molalla, Oreg., 1,501..B4 80
Mold, Wales, 6,857...*D5   4
Moldavia, reg., Rom...B8 10
Moldavia (S.S.R.), rep.,
  Sov. Un., 3,040,000..H7 12
Moldova, prov., Rom.,
  2,598,258.........*B8 10
Molepolole, Bech.,
  14,805.............E5 24
Molfetta, It., 61,684...D6   9
Molina, Chile, 6,123...B2 28
Molina de Segura, Sp.,
  8,578..............C5   8
Moline, Ill., 42,705....B3 58
Moline Acres, Mo.,
  3,132.............*C7 69
Moliterno, It., 5,657...D5   9
Mollendo, Peru, 14,893.E3 31
Mölndal, Swe., 26,500...I5 11
Molns, Ky., 500......D6 62
Molodechno, Sov. Un.,
  26,000.............D6 12
Molokai, isl., Haw.....B5 56
Molotovsk, Sov. Un.,
  30,000.............E18 11
Molotovskoye, Sov. Un.,
  10,000.............I13 12
Mombasa, Ken.,
  189,800............I5 23
Mombetsu, Jap.,
  28,200.............D11 18
Momence, Ill., 2,949...B6 58
Momostenango, Guat.,
  5,002.............*D6 34
Mompós, Col., 9,192...B3 32
Mona, W. Va., 806....A7 87
Monaca, Pa., 8,394....E1 81
Monaco, country, Eur.,
  22,297.............F7   5
Monagas, state, Ven.,
  246,217............B5 32
Monaghan, S. C., 1,200.B2 82
Monaghan, co., Ire.,
  47,088............*C3   4
Monahans, Tex., 8,567.D1 84
Monarch, S.C., 1,990..B4 82
Monastir, Tun., 12,596.A7 22
Monaville, W. Va.,
  825...............*D5 87
Monchegorsk, Sov. Un.,
  30,000.............D15 11

Mönchengladbach, Ger., 152,200 (*330,000)...C3 6
Moncks Corner, S.C., 2,030...E7 82
Monclova, Mex., 43,333...B4 34
Moncton, N.B., Can., 43,840 (*55,768)...C5 43
Mondoñedo, Sp., 9,153.A2 8
Mondoví, It., 8,800...B1 9
Mondovi, Wis., 2,320..D2 88
Monessen, Pa., 18,424..F2 81
Monett, Mo., 5,359...E4 69
Monette, Ark., 981...B5 49
Monfalcone, It., 26,818...B4 9
Monforte de Lemos, Sp., 13,502...A2 8
Monfort Heights, Ohio, 6,000...*D2 78
Monghyr, India, 89,768...C8 20
Mong Mit, Bur., 5,000...D10 20
Mongolia, country, Asia, 900,000...B5 17
Moniteau, co., Mo., 10,500...C5 69
Monmouth, Ill., 10,372.C3 58
Monmouth, Oreg., 2,229...C1, C3 80
Monmouth, co., N.J., 334,401...C4 74
Monmouth, co., Wales, 424,647...*E5 4
Monmouth Beach, N.J., 1,363...C5 74
Mono, co., Calif., 2,213.D4 50
Monon, Ind., 1,417...C4 59
Monona, Iowa, 1,346...A6 60
Monona, Wis., 8,178...E4 88
Monona, co., Iowa, 13,916...B1 60
Monongah, W. Va., 1,321...A7, B4 87
Monongahela, Pa., 8,388...F2 81
Monongalia, co., W. Va., 55,617...B4 87
Monopli, It., 24,000...D6 9
Monor, Hung., 14,830..B4 10
Monóvar, Sp., 9,933...C5 8
Monreale, It., 18,000..E4 9
Monroe, Conn., 1,000..D3 52
Monroe, Ga., 6,826...C3 55
Monroe, Iowa, 1,366...C4 60
Monroe, La., 52,219...B3 63
Monroe, Mich., 22,968.G7 66
Monroe, N.Y., 3,323...D2, D6 75
Monroe, N.C., 10,882..C3 76
Monroe, Ohio, 1,475..*C3 78
Monroe, Utah, 955...B5 72
Monroe, Va., 800...D3 85
Monroe, Wash., 1,901..B4 86
Monroe, Wis., 8,050...F4 88
Monroe, co., Ala., 22,372...D2 46
Monroe, co., Ark., 17,327...C4 49
Monroe, co., Fla., 47,921...H5 54
Monroe, co., Ga., 10,495...D3 55
Monroe, co., Ill., 15,507...E3 58
Monroe, co., Ind., 59,225...F4 59
Monroe, co., Iowa, 10,463...C5 60
Monroe, co., Ky., 11,799...D4 62
Monroe, co., Mich., 101,120...G7 66
Monroe, co., Miss., 33,953...B5 68
Monroe, co., Mo., 10,688...B5 69
Monroe, co., N.Y., 586,387...B3 75
Monroe, co., Ohio, 15,268...C3 78
Monroe, co., Pa., 39,567...D11 81
Monroe, co., Tenn., 23,316...D9 83
Monroe, co., W. Va., 11,584...D4 87
Monroe, co., Wis., 31,241...E3 88
Monroe City, Mo., 2,337...B6 69
Monroeville, Ala., 3,632...D2 46
Monroeville, Ind., 1,294...C8 59
Monroeville, Ohio, 1,371...A5 78
Monroeville, Pa., 22,446...*B6 81

Monrovia, Calif., 27,079...F3 50
Monrovia, Lib., 41,391.G2 22
Mons, Bel., 29,973...B5 5
Monson, Mass., 2,413..B3 65
Montague, P.E.I., Can., 1,126...C7 43
Montague, Mich., 2,366...E4 66
Montague, co., Tex., 14,893...C4 84
Mont Alto, Pa., 1,039..G6 81
Montalvo, Calif., 2,028...*E4 50
Montana, state, U.S., 674,767...72
Montánchez, Sp., 14,190...C2 8
Montargis, Fr., 15,996.D5 5
Montauban, Fr., 30,242...E4 5
Monta Vista, Calif., 2,000...*B5 50
Montbéliard, Fr., 21,699...D7 5
Mont Belvieu, Tex., 950...E5, F5 84
Montbrison, Fr., 9,051.E6 5
Montcalm, co., Que., Can., 18,766...C3 42
Montcalm, co., Mich., 35,795...E5 66
Montceau-les-Mines, Fr., 29,364...D6 5
Montchanin [-les-Mines], Fr., 6,405...D6 5
Montclair (Monte Vista), Calif., 13,546...*F3 50
Montclair, N.J., 43,129.B4 74
Mont Clare, Pa., 1,124...A10 81
Montcoal, W. Va., 275...D3, D6 87
Mont-de-Marsan, Fr., 21,203...F3 5
Montebello, Calif., 32,097...F2 50
Montebello, Que., Can., 1,486...D3 42
Monte Caseros, Arg., 11,409...A5 28
Montecelio, It., 5,000...g9 9
Montefrío, Sp., 5,137..D3 8
Montego Bay, Jam., 23,471...F5 35
Montélimar, Fr., 15,914...E6 5
Montellano, Sp., 9,334...D3 8
Montello, Wis., 1,021..E4 88
Montemorelos, Mex., 11,525...B5 34
Montemor-o-Novo, Port., 5,047...C1 8
Montenegro, Braz., 14,941...D2 30
Montenegro, rep., Yugo., 471,433...*D4 10
Montepulciano, It., 17,552...C3 9
Montereau [-faut-Yonne], Fr., 8,962...C5 5
Monterey, Calif., 22,618...C6, D3 50
Monterey, Ohio, 1,500...*D2 78
Monterey, Tenn.,2,069.C8 83
Monterey, co., Calif., 198,351...D3 50
Monterey Park, Calif., 37,821...F2 50
Montería, Col., 27,300.B2 32
Monteros, Arg., 7,745..E2 29
Monterotondo, It., 9,340...g9 9
Monterrey, Mex., 596,993...B4 34
Montesano, Wash., 2,486...C2 86
Monte Sant' Angelo, It., 21,601...D5 9
Montes Claros, Braz., 40,545...B4 30
Monte Sereno, Calif., 1,506...*D3 50
Montevallo, Ala., 2,755...B3 46
Montevarchi, It., 9,100...C3 9
Montevideo, Minn., 5,693...F3 67
Montevideo, Ur., 954,700...E1 30
Montevideo, dept., Ur., 954,700...*E1 30
Monte Vista, Colo., 3,385...D4 51
Monte Vista, Wash., 1,500...*B3 86
Montezuma, Ga., 3,744...D2 55

Montezuma, Ind., 1,231...E3 59
Montezuma, Iowa, 1,416...C5 60
Montezuma, co., Colo., 14,024...D2 51
Montgomery, Ala., 134,393 (*155,200)...C3 46
Montgomery, Ill., 2,122...B5 58
Montgomery, Minn., 2,118...F3 67
Montgomery, N.Y., 1,312...D6 75
Montgomery, Ohio, 3,075...*C3 78
Montgomery, Pak., 75,000...B5 20
Montgomery, Pa., 2,150...D8 81
Montgomery, W. Va., 3,000...C3, C6 87
Montgomery, co., Ala., 169,210...C3 46
Montgomery, co., Ark., 5,370...C2 49
Montgomery, co., Ga., 6,284...D4 55
Montgomery, co., Ill., 31,244...D4 58
Montgomery, co., Ind., 32,089...D4 59
Montgomery, co., Iowa, 14,467...C2 60
Montgomery, co., Kans., 45,007...E8 61
Montgomery, co., Ky., 13,461...B6 62
Montgomery, co., Md., 340,928...B3 53
Montgomery, co., Miss., 13,320...B4 68
Montgomery, co., Mo., 11,097...C6 69
Montgomery, co., N.Y., 57,240...C6 75
Montgomery, co., N.C., 18,408...B4 76
Montgomery, co., Ohio, 527,080...C3 78
Montgomery, co., Pa., 516,682...F11 81
Montgomery, co., Tenn., 55,645...A4 83
Montgomery, co., Tex., 26,839...D5 84
Montgomery, co., Va., 32,923...D2 85
Montgomery, co., Wales, 44,228...*D5 4
Montgomery City, Mo., 1,918...C6 69
Monticello, Ark., 4,412.D4 49
Monticello, Fla., 2,490..B3 54
Monticello, Ga., 1,931..C3 55
Monticello, Ill., 3,219..C5 58
Monticello, Ind., 4,035.C4 59
Monticello, Iowa, 3,190.B6 60
Monticello, Ky., 2,940.D5 62
Monticello, Minn., 1,477...E5 67
Monticello, Miss., 1,432...D3 68
Monticello, N.Y., 5,222...D6 75
Monticello, Utah, 1,845...C7 72
Montigny-[lès-Metz], Fr., 22,388...C7 5
Montijo, Port., 13,306...C1, f10 8
Montijo, Sp., 14,961...C2 8
Montilla, Sp., 19,755...D3 8
Montivilliers, Fr., 8,427...C4 5
Mont Joli, Que., Can., 6,178...G20 36
Mont Laurier, Que., Can., 5,859...C2 42
Montluçon, Fr., 55,184...D5 5
Montmagny, Que., Can., 6,850...C7 42
Montmagny, co., Que., Can., 26,450...C7 42
Montmorency, Que., Can., 5,985...C6, C9 42
Montmorency, Fr., 16,369...g10 5
Montmorency, co., Mich., 4,424...C6 66
Montmorency No. 1, co., Que., Can., 20,734..B6 42
Montmorency No. 2, co., Que., Can., 4,974...*C7 42
Montmorillon, Fr., 4,766...D4 5
Montoro, Sp., 14,950..C3 8
Montour, co., Pa., 16,730...D8 81

Montour Falls, N.Y., 1,533...C4 75
Montoursville, Pa., 5,211...D8 81
Montpelier, Idaho, 3,146...G7 57
Montpelier, Ind., 1,954.C7 58
Montpelier, Ohio, 4,131...A3 78
Montpelier, Vt., 8,782..C2 73
Montpelier, Fr., 118,864...F5 5
Montreal, Que., Can., 1,191,062 (*2,109,509)...D4, D9 42
Montreal, Wis., 1,361..B3 88
Montreal East, Que., Can., 5,884...*D4 42
Montreal North, Que., Can., 48,433...D9 42
Montreal South, Que., Can., 5,319...*D4 42
Montreal West, Que., Can., 6,446...*D4 42
Montreuil-sur-Mer, Fr., 3,253...B4 5
Montreux, Switz., 12,222...E3 6
Mont Rolland, Que., Can., 1,457...D3 42
Montrose, Ala., 500...E2 46
Montrose, Calif., 6,000...*F2 50
Montrose, Colo., 5,044.C3 51
Montrose, Mich., 1,466.E7 66
Montrose, Pa., 2,363..C10 81
Montrose, Pa., 1,100..F10 81
Montrose, Scot., 10,702.B5 4
Montrose, co., Colo., 18,286...C2 51
Montrose Hill, Pa., 2,000...*E2 81
Montrouge, Fr., 42,260...g10 5
Mont Royal, Que., Can., 21,182...*D4 42
Montvale, N.J., 3,699...A4, C5 74
Montville, Conn., 1,060...D8 52
Montville, N.J., 4,000..B4 74
Monywa, Bur., 26,172.D10 20
Monza, It., 84,445...B2 9
Moodus, Conn., 1,103..D7 52
Moody, Tex., 1,074...D4 84
Moody, co., S. Dak., 8,810...F9 77
Moonachie, N.J., 3,052...*B4 74
Moon Crest, Pa., 1,500...*E1 81
Moon Run, Pa., 650...B5 81
Moore, Okla., 1,783...B4 79
Moore, co., N.C., 36,733...B4 76
Moore, co., Tenn., 3,454...B5 83
Moore, co., Tex., 14,773...B2 84
Moorefiled, W. Va., 1,434...B6 87
Moorestown, N.J., 12,497...D3 74
Mooresville, Ind., 3,856...E5 59
Mooresville, N.C., 6,918...B3 76
Moorhead, Minn., 22,934...D2 67
Moorhead, Miss., 1,754...B3 68
Moorpark, Calif., 2,902...E4 50
Mooseheart, Ill., 1,100...B5, F1 58
Moose Jaw, Sask., Can., 33,206...C1, G3 39
Moose Lake, Minn., 1,514...D6 67
Moosic, Pa., 4,243...B9 81
Moosomin, Sask., Can., 1,781...G5 39
Moosup, Conn., 2,760..C9 52
Mopti, Mali, 12,700...F4 22
Moquegua, dept., Peru, 41,072...E3 31
Mor, Hung., 11,482...B4 10
Mora, Minn., 2,329...E5 67
Mora, N. Mex., 400...B6 48
Mora, Sp., 10,657...C4 8
Mora, Swe., 6,032...G6 11
Mora, co., N. Mex., 6,028...A6 48
Morada, Calif., 2,156.*D3 50
Moradabad, India, 180,000 (*191,828)..C6 20
Moraine, Ohio, 2,262..*C3 78
Moramanga, Malag., 3,750...D9 24
Morant Bay, Jam., 5,053...G5 35

Moratalla, Sp., 5,879...C5 8
Moravia, reg., Czech., 3,549,700.........D4 7
Moravia, N.Y., 1,575...C4 75
Moray, co., Scot., 49,156............*B5 4
Morbihan, dept., Fr., 530,833............*D2 5
Morden, Man., Can., 2,793.............E2 40
Moree, Austl., 6,795...E8 25
Morehead, Ky., 4,170..B6 62
Morehead City, N.C., 5,583............C7 76
Morehouse, Mo., 1,417.E8 69
Morehouse, par., La., 33,709............B4 63
Moreland Hills, Ohio, 2,188............*A6 78
Morelia, Mex., 100,258.......D4, n13 34
Morelos, state, Mex., 381,346........D5, n14 34
Morenci, Ariz., 2,431...C4 48
Morenci, Mich., 2,053..G6 66
Möre og Romsdal, co., Nor., 213,400......*F2 11
Morez, Fr., 5,777.....D7 5
Morgan, Minn., 975....F4 67
Morgan, Utah, 1,299...A6 72
Morgan, co., Ala., 60,454............A3 46
Morgan, co., Colo., 21,192............A7 51
Morgan, co., Ga., 10,280............C3 55
Morgan, co., Ill., 36,571............D3 58
Morgan, co., Ind., 33,875............F5 59
Morgan, co., Ky., 11,056............C6 62
Morgan, co., Mo., 9,476............C5 69
Morgan, co., Ohio, 12,747............C6 78
Morgan, co., Tenn., 14,304............C9 83
Morgan, co., Utah, 2,837............A6 72
Morgan, co., W. Va., 8,376............B6 87
Morgan City, La., 13,540..........C5, E4 63
Morganfield, Ky., 3,741............C2 62
Morgan Hill, Calif., 3,151..........C6, D3 50
Morganton, N.C., 9,186............B2 76
Morgantown, Ind., 971............F5 59
Morgantown, Ky., 1,318............C3 62
Morgantown, W. Va., 22,487.........A7, B5 87
Morganza, La., 937....D4 63
Mori, Jap., 12,500....E10 18
Morioka, Jap., 157,441..........G10 18
Morlaix, Fr., 18,866...C2 5
Morningside, Md., 1,708............*C4 53
Morningside, Minn., 1,981............*F5 67
Morning Sun, Iowa, 875..............C6 60
Morocco, Ind., 1,341...C3 59
Morocco, country, Afr., 11,626,470.........B4 22
Morogoro, Tan., 14,507............B7 24
Moroleón, Mex., 17,955............m13 34
Morón, Cuba, 18,629...D4 35
Morondava, Malag., 5,300............E8 24
Morón de la Frontera, Sp., 25,800........D3 8
Moroni, Utah, 879.....B6 72
Morozovsk, Sov. Un., 28,000............G13 12
Morrill, co., Nebr., 7,057............C2 71
Morrilton, Ark., 5,997..B3 49
Morris, Ala., 638.....B3 46
Morris, Man., Can., 1,370............E3 40
Morris, Ill., 7,935......B5 58
Morris, Minn., 4,199...E3 67
Morris, Okla., 982.....B6 79
Morris, co., Kans., 7,392............D7 61
Morris, co., N.J., 261,620............B3 74
Morris, co., Tex., 12,576............C5 84
Morrisburg, Ont., Can., 1,820............C9 41
Morrisdale, Pa., 800...E5 81
Morrison, Ill., 4,159....B4 58

Morrison, Tenn., 294..............*C5 83
Morrison, co., Minn., 26,641............D4 67
Morrisonville, Ill., 1,129............D4 58
Morris Plains, N.J., 4,703............B4 74
Morristown, N.J., 17,712............B4 74
Morristown, Tenn., 21,267............C10 83
Morrisville, N.Y., 1,304............C5 75
Morrisville, Pa., 7,790.F12 81
Morrisville, Vt., 2,047..B2 73
Morro Bay, Calif., 3,692............E3 50
Morrow, Ohio, 1,477...C3 78
Morrow, co., Ohio, 19,405............B5 78
Morrow, co., Oreg., 4,871............B7 80
Morshansk, Sov. Un., 48,000............E13 12
Mortara, It., 10,500...B2 9
Morteros, Arg., 5,593...A4 28
Morton, Ill., 5,325.....C4 58
Morton, Minn., 624....F4 67
Morton, Miss., 2,260...C4 68
Morton, Pa., 2,207...*G11 81
Morton, Tex., 2,731...C1 84
Morton, Wash., 1,183..C3 86
Morton, co., Kans., 3,354............E2 61
Morton, co., N. Dak., 20,992............D4 77
Morton Grove, Ill., 20,533............E3 58
Mortons Gap, Ky., 1,308............C2 62
Moruya, Austl., 1,181..G8 26
Moscow, Idaho, 11,183.C2 57
Moscow, Pa., 1,212....B9 81
Moscow (Moskva), Sov. Un., 6,208,000 (*8,075,000)...D11, n17 12
Moselle, dept., Fr., 919,412............*C7 5
Moses Lake, Wash., 11,299............B6 86
Moshi, Tan., 13,726....I5 23
Mosinee, Wis., 2,067...D4 88
Mosjöen, Nor., 4,600...E5 11
Mosonmagyaróvar, Hung., 21,199......B3 10
Moss, Nor., 20,600.........H4, p28 11
Mossel Bay, S. Afr., 12,178............G4 24
Mossoro, Braz., 38,833............*D7 27
Moss Point, Miss., 6,631..........E3, E5 68
Most, Czech., 44,500...C2 7
Mostaganem, Alg., 60,186............A5 22
Mostar, Yugo., 35,242..D3 10
Mosul, Iraq, 179,646...B3 15
Motala, Swe., 27,100...H6 11
Motherwell [& Wishaw], Scot., 72,799........C5 4
Motley, co., Tex., 2,870.B2 84
Motril, Sp., 19,185....D4 8
Mott, N. Dak., 1,463..D3 77
Motul [de Felipe Carrillo Puerto], Mex., 9,965.C7 34
Moulins, Fr., 23,909...D5 5
Moulmein, Bur., 102,777............E10 20
Moulton, Ala., 1,716...A2 46
Moulton, Iowa, 773....D5 60
Moultrie, Ga., 15,764...E3 55
Moultrie, co., Ill., 13,635............D5 58
Mound, Minn., 5,440...F5 67
Mound Bayou, Miss., 1,354............B3 68
Mound City, Ill., 1,669.F4 58
Mound City, Mo., 1,249............A2 69
Moundridge, Kans., 1,214............D6 61
Mounds, Ill., 1,835.....F4 58
Mounds View, Minn., 6,416............*F5 67
Moundsville, W. Va., 15,163..........B2, B4 87
Moundville, Ala., 922..C2 46
Mountain, prov., Phil., 436,200............*B6 19
Mountainair, N. Mex., 1,605............B5 48
Mountain Brook, Ala., 12,680............E5 46
Mountain City, Tenn., 1,379............C12 83
Mountain Grove, Mo., 3,176............D5 69
Mountain Home, Ark., 2,105............A3 49

Mountain Home, Idaho, 10,075............F3 57
Mountain Iron, Minn., 1,808............C6 67
Mountain Lake, Minn., 1,943............G4 67
Mountain Lakes, N.J., 4,037............B4 74
Mountain Pine, Ark., 1,279..........C2, C5 49
Mountainside, N.J., 6,325............B4 74
Mountain View, Ark., 983............B3 49
Mountain View, Calif., 30,889............B5 50
Mountainview, Haw., 747............D6 56
Mountain View, Idaho, 4,898............*F2 57
Mountain View, Mo., 936............D6 69
Mountain View, Okla., 864............B3 79
Mountain View, Wyo., 1,721............*C6 89
Mount Airy, Md., 1,352............B3 53
Mount Airy, N.C., 7,055............A3 76
Mount Angel, Oreg., 1,428............B2, B4 80
Mount Arlington, N.J., 1,246............B3 74
Mount Athos (Ayion Oros), prov. Grc., 2,687............B5 14
Mount Ayr, Iowa, 1,738............D3 60
Mount Berry, Ga., 1,000............B1 55
Mount Carmel, Ill., 8,594............E6 58
Mount Carmel, Pa., 10,760............E9 81
Mount Carroll, Ill., 2,056............A4 58
Mount Clare, W. Va., 900............B4 87
Mount Clemens, Mich., 21,016..........A8, F8 66
Mount Dora, Fla., 3,756............D5 54
Mount Edgecumbe, Alsk., 1,884......*m22 47
Mount Ephraim, N.J., 5,447............*D2 74
Mount Forest, Ont., Can., 2,623............D4 41
Mount Gambier, Austl., 15,388............G7 25
Mount Gay, W. Va., 3,386............*D3 87
Mount Gilead, N.C., 1,229............B4 76
Mount Gilead, Ohio, 2,788............B5 78
Mount Healthy, Ohio, 6,553............D2 78
Mount Holly, N.J., 13,271............D3 74
Mount Holly, N.C., 4,037............B2 76
Mount Holly Springs, Pa., 1,840............F7 81
Mount Hope, N.J., 500.B3 74
Mount Hope, W. Va., 2,000..........D3, D7 87
Mount Horeb, Wis., 1,991............E4 88
Mount Houston, Tex., 2,500............*F5 84
Mount Jewett, Pa., 1,226............C4 81
Mount Joy, Pa., 3,292..F9 81
Mount Kisco, N.Y., 6,805..........D3, D7 75
Mountlake Terrace, Wash., 9,122......*B3 86
Mount Lebanon, Pa., 35,361............F1 81
Mount Morris, Ill., 3,075............A4 58
Mount Morris, Mich., 3,484............E7 66
Mount Morris, N.Y., 3,250............C3 75
Mount Olive, Ala., 1,800..........B3, E4 46
Mount Olive, Ill., 2,295............D4 58
Mount Olive, N.C., 4,673............B5 76
Mount Oliver, Pa., 5,980............B5 81
Mount Orab, Ohio, 1,058............C4 78
Mount Pearl Park-Glendale, Newf., Can., 1,979............*f9 44

Mount Penn, Pa., 3,574............*F10 81
Mount Pleasant, Iowa, 7,339............D6 60
Mount Pleasant, Mich., 14,875............E6 66
Mount Pleasant, N.C., 1,041............B3 76
Mount Pleasant, Pa., 6,107............F2 81
Mount Pleasant, S.C., 5,116............F3, F8 82
Mount Pleasant, Tenn., 2,921............B4 83
Mount Pleasant, Tex., 8,027............C5 84
Mount Pleasant, Utah, 1,572............B6 72
Mount Pocono, Pa., 935............D11 81
Mount Prospect, Ill., 22,945..........A6, E2 58
Mount Pulaski, Ill., 1,689............C4 58
Mountrail, co., N. Dak., 10,077............B3 77
Mount Rainier, Md., 9,855............C1 53
Mount Savage, Md., 1,639............D2 53
Mount Shasta, Calif., 1,272............B2 50
Mount Sterling, Ill., 2,262............D3 58
Mount Sterling, Ky., 5,370............B6 62
Mount Sterling, Ohio, 1,338............C4 78
Mount Union, Pa., 4,091............E6 81
Mount Vernon, Ala., 553............D1 46
Mount Vernon, Ga., 1,166............D4 55
Mount Vernon, Ill., 15,566............E5 58
Mount Vernon, Ind., 5,970............I2 59
Mount Vernon, Iowa, 2,593............C6 60
Mount Vernon, Ky., 1,177............C5 62
Mount Vernon, Mo., 2,381............D4 69
Mount Vernon, N.Y., 4,000............*C2 75
Mount Vernon, N.Y., 76,010............D2 75
Mount Vernon, Ohio, 1,000............*A2 78
Mount Vernon, Ohio, 13,284............B5 78
Mount Vernon, Tex., 1,338............C5 84
Mount Vernon, Wash., 7,921............A3 86
Mountville, Pa., 1,411.*F9 81
Mount Washington, Ky., 1,173..........A4, B4 62
Mount Wolf, Pa., 1,514.F8 81
Mount Zion, Ill., 925..*D5 58
Moura, Port., 9,509....C2 8
Mouscron, Bel., 36,554.B5 5
Mousie, Ky., 500......C7 62
Moville, Iowa, 1,156...B1 60
Moweaqua, Ill., 1,614..D4 58
Mower, co., Minn., 48,498............G6 67
Moyeuvre-Grande, Fr., 15,146............C7 5
Moyobamba, Peru, 8,850............C2 31
Mozambique, Port. dep., Afr., 6,234,000......D7 24
Mozhaysk, Sov. Un., 10,000............D11 12
Mozyr, Sov. Un., 25,000............E7 12
Mtsensk, Sov. Un., 10,000............E11 12
Muang Hot, Thai., 10,000............*B1 19
Muang Nan, Thai., 13,624............*B2 19
Muang Ubon, Thai., 25,442............B2 19
Muchkap, Sov. Un., 10,000............F14 12
Mudanya, Tur., 5,900.*B7 14
Mudgee, Austl., 5,313..F7 26
Muenster, Tex., 1,190..C4 84
Mufulira, Zambia, 18,000............C5 24
Mugía, Sp., 7,061......A1 8
Mugla, Tur., 14,000...D7 14
Mühldorf, Ger., 10,800.D6 6
Muhlenberg, co., Ky., 27,791............C2 62
Muhlenberg Park, Pa., 1,000............*F10 81

Mühlhausen, Ger.,
47,011..............C5   6
Mukachevo, Sov. Un.,
33,000..............G4   12
Mukden (Shenyang),
China, 2,411,000.....C9   17
Mukilteo, Wash., 1,128.B3   86
Mukwonago, Wis.,
1,877..........F1, F5   88
Mula, Sp., 14,312......C5   8
Mulberry, Ark., 934....B1   49
Mulberry, Fla., 2,922..E5   54
Mulberry, Ind., 1,062..D4   59
Mulberry, Kans., 642..E9   61
Mulchén, Chile, 7,324..B2   28
Muldraugh, Ky., 1,743.C4   62
Muldrow, Okla., 1,137..B7   79
Muleng, China, 5,000..D5   18
Muleshoe, Tex., 3,871..B1   84
Mulga Mine, Ala.,
950...........*B2, E4   46
Mulgrave, N.S., Can.,
1,145..............D8   43
Mülheim, Ger.,
185,700............C3   6
Mulhouse, Fr., 108,995.D7   5
Mullan, Idaho, 1,477...B3   57
Mullens, W. Va., 3,544.D3   87
Mullingar, Ire., 5,894..D3   4
Mullins, S.C., 6,229....C9   82
Multan, Pak., 340,000..B5   20
Multnomah, co., Oreg.,
522,813............B4   80
Mulvane, Kans., 2,981.E6   61
München, Ger.,
1,084,500...........D5   6
Muncie, Ind., 68,603
(*100,500)..........D7   59
Muncy, Pa., 2,830......D8   81
Munday, Tex., 1,978...C3   84
Mundelein, Ill.,
10,526..........A5, E2   58
Münden, Ger., 20,200..C4   6
Munford, Tenn., 1,014.B2   83
Munfordville, Ky.,
1,157..............C4   62
Munhall, Pa., 17,312...B6   81

Munich, see München,
Ger.
Munising, Mich., 4,228.B4   66
Munroe Falls, Ohio,
1,828.............*A6   78
Munsan, Kor., 5,000...H3   18
Munsey Park, N.Y.,
2,847.............*E3   75
Munster, Fr., 4,965....C7   5
Munster, Ind., 10,313..A2   59
Munster, prov., Ire.,
849,203...........*D2   4
Münster [in Westfalen],
Ger., 182,700.......C3   6
Muntenia, prov., Rom.,
4,991,289.........*C8   10
Muntenia, reg., Rom...C7   10
Muntok, Indon., 6,929..F3   19
Muong Hou Nua, Laos,
10,000............*D11   20
Muong Sing, Laos,
10,000............D11   20
Murakami, Jap.,
23,200............G9   18
Murcia, Sp., 126,000...D5   8
Murcia, prov., Sp.,
800,463...........*D5   8
Murcia, reg., Sp.,
1,171,439..........C5   8
Murfreesboro, Ark.,
1,096..............C2   49
Murfreesboro, N.C.,
2,643..............A6   76
Murfreesboro, Tenn.,
18,991............B5   83
Muriaé, Braz., 22,571..C4   30
Murmansk, Sov. Un.,
237,000...........C15   11
Murom, Sov. Un.,
81,000............D13   12
Muroran, Jap.,
145,679...........E10   18
Muros, Sp., 2,420......A1   8
Murphy, N.C., 2,235...D2   76
Murphysboro, Ill.,
8,673..............F4   58
Murray, Ky., 9,303....B3   62

Murray, Utah,
16,806.........A6, C2   72
Murray, co., Ga.,
10,447............B2   55
Murray, co., Minn.,
14,743............F3   67
Murray, co., Okla.,
10,622............C4   79
Murrysville, Pa.,
1,200..............B7   81
Murud, India, 9,744...E5   20
Murwillumbah, Austl.,
7,153.............D9   26
Mürzzuschlag, Aus.,
11,586............E7   6
Mus, Tur., 12,000....C13   14
Muscat, Mus. & Om.,
5,000..............D2   20
Muscat and Oman,
country, Asia,
550,000...........F6   15
Muscatine, Iowa,
20,997............C6   60
Muscatine, co., Iowa,
33,840............C6   60
Muscle Shoals, Ala.,
4,084.............A2   46
Muscoda, Wis., 927....E3   88
Muscogee, co., Ga.,
158,623...........D2   55
Muse, Pa., 1,386......F1   81
Mushketovo, Sov. Un.,
10,000............r20   12
Muskego, Wis., 2,000.*E5   88
Muskegon, Mich., 46,485
(*167,400).........E4   66
Muskegon, co., Mich.,
149,943...........E4   66
Muskegon Heights,
Mich., 19,552.......E4   66
Muskingum, co., Ohio,
79,159............B6   78
Muskö, Swe., 5,000...u36   11
Muskogee, Okla.,
38,059............B6   79
Muskogee, co., Okla.,
61,866............B6   79

Muskoka, co., Ont.,
Can., 26,705.......B5   41
Musselburgh, Scot.,
17,273............C5   4
Musselshell, co., Mont.,
4,888.............D8   70
Mustafa Kemalpasa, Tur.,
209,000...........B7   14
Mutankiang, China,
151,400...........D4   18
Muttontown, N.Y.,
1,265.............*E7   75
Muzaffarpur, India,
109,048...........C8   20
Muzambinho, Braz.,
6,731..............k8   30
Mwanza, Tan., 19,877..I4   23
Myaungmya, Bur.,
20,770............*E9   20
Myers, S.C., 1,000.....F3   82
Myerstown, Pa., 3,268..F9   81
Myingyan, Bur.,
36,536............D10   20
Myitkyina, Bur.,
12,833............C10   20
Myjava, Czech., 9,935.D4   7
Mymensingh, Pak.,
45,315............D9   20
Myrtle Beach, S.C.,
7,834.............D10   82
Myrtle Creek, Oreg.,
2,231..............D3   80
Myrtle Grove, Fla.,
3,000..............G2   54
Myrtle Point, Oreg.,
2,886..............D2   80
Mysen, Nor., 2,525....p29   11
Myslenice, Pol., 6,520..D5   7
Mysolwice, Pol.,
40,000............g10   7
Mysore, India, 253,865.F6   20
Mysore, state, India,
23,586,772.........F6   20
Mystic, Conn., 2,536...D9   52
Mystic, Iowa, 761.....D5   60
My Tho, Viet., 5,000...C3   19
Mytishchi, Sov. Un.,
104,000...........n17   12

N

Naalehu, Haw., 950...D6   56
Nabeul, Tun., 14,047...A7   22
Nabnasset, Mass.,
1,381.............*A5   65
Nābulus, Jordan,
42,499..........B3, g5   15
Nachod, Czech., 17,800.C4   7
Nacogdoches, Tex.,
12,674.............D5   84
Nacogdoches, co., Tex.,
28,046............D5   84
Nadlac, Rom., 12,284..B5   10
Nadvornaya, Sov. Un.,
10,000............G5   12
Naesong, Kor., 5,000..H4   18
Naestved, Den., 19,617.J4   11
Naga, Phil., 8,000.....C6   19
Nagano, Jap., 160,522..H9   18
Nagano, pref., Jap.,
1,981,433.........*H9   18
Nagaoka, Jap., 99,000..H9   18
Nagasaki, Jap., 344,153.J4   18
Nagasaki, pref., Jap.,
1,760,421.........*J4   18
Nagercoil, India,
106,207...........G6   20
Nagoya, Jap.,
1,591,935......I8, n15   18
Nagpur, India,
643,659...........D6   20
Nagykanisza, Hung.,
34,222............B3   10
Nagykoros, Hung.,
19,908............B4   10
Naha, Okinawa,
63,630............F10   17
Nahant, Mass., 3,960...C3   65
Nahariya, Isr., 14,537..A3   15
Nahunta, Ga., 952.....E5   55
Nairn, co., Scot.,
8,421.............*B5   4
Nairobi, Ken., 297,000..I5   23
Najin, Kor., 34,338....E5   18
Nakatsu, Jap., 40,900..J5   18
Nakhichevan [na Arakse],
Sov. Un., 27,000.....F7   16
Nakhon Ratchasima,
Thai., 43,698.......C2   19
Nakiri, Jap., 7,000....o15   18
Naklo, Pol., 12,000....B4   7
Nakskov, Den., 16,639..J4   11
Nakuru, Ken., 17,625...I5   23
Nakusp, B.C., Can.,
992...............D9   37
Nalchik, Sov. Un.,
98,000............*E7   13
Namangan, Sov. Un.,
134,000...........E10   12

Nam Dinh, Viet.,
25,000............A3   19
Nampa, Idaho, 18,897..F2   57
Nampula, Moz., 2,561..D7   24
Namur, Bel., 32,511....B6   5
Namur, prov., Bel.,
369,432...........*B6   5
Namwŏn, Kor., 25,900..I3   18
Nanaimo, B.C., Can.,
14,135.........A8, E6   37
Nanakuli, Haw.,
2,745...........B3, g9   56
Nanam, Kor., 21,258...F4   18
Nanao, Jap., 29,700....H8   18
Nance, co., Nebr.,
5,635..............C7   71
Nanchang, China,
508,000...........F8   17
Nancheng, China,
59,000............E6   17
Nanchung, China,
164,700...........E6   17
Nancy, Fr., 128,677....C7   5
Nanhai, China,
122,500...........*G7   17
Nanking, China,
1,419,000.........E8   17
Nanning (Yungning),
China, 264,000......G6   17
Nanping, China,
29,000............F8   17
Nansemond, co., Va.,
31,366............E6   85
Nanterre, Fr., 83,416...g9   5
Nantes, Fr., 240,028...D3   5
Nanticoke, Pa.,
15,601........B7, D10   81
Nanton, Alta., Can.,
1,054..............D4   38
Nantucket, Mass.,
2,804..............D7   65
Nantucket, co., Mass.,
3,559..............D7   65
Nantung, China,
260,400...........*E9   17
Nanty Glo, Pa., 4,608..F4   81
Nanuet, N.Y., 5,000...D1   75
Nanyang, China,
50,000............E7   17
Naoma, W. Va.,
600...........D3, D6   87
Naousa, Grc., 15,492..*B4   14
Napa, Calif.,
22,170.........B5, C2   50
Napa, co., Calif.,
65,890............C2   50
Napanee, Ont., Can.,
4,500..............C8   41
Napanoch, N.Y., 950..D6   75

Naperville, Ill.,
12,933.........B5, F2   58
Napier, N.Z., 24,579
(*32,716).........M16   26
Napierville, Que., Can.,
1,812..............D4   42
Napierville, co., Que.,
Can., 11,216.......D4   42
Naples, Fla., 4,655....F5   54
Naples, see Napoli, It.
Naples, N.Y., 1,237....C3   75
Naples, Tex., 1,692....C5   84
Napo, prov., Ec.......B2   31
Napoleon, N. Dak.,
1,078.............D6   77
Napoleon, Ohio, 6,739.A3   78
Napoleonville, La.,
1,148.........C5, E4   63
Napoli (Naples), It.,
1,182,815.........D5   9
Nappanee, Ind., 3,895..B5   59
Nara, Jap., 134,577...o14   18
Nara, pref., Jap.,
781,058...........*I7   18
Naranja, Fla.,
2,509..........F3, G6   54
Narberth, Pa., 5,109..F11   81
Narbonne, Fr., 33,891..F5   5
Nardó, It., 24,000....D7   9
Nariño, dept., Col.,
571,940...........C2   32
Narita, Jap., 17,900...n19   18
Naro-Fominsk, Sov. Un.,
10,000............D11   12
Narragansett, R.I.,
1,741.............D11   52
Narrows, Va., 2,508...D2   85
Narva, Sov. Un.,
43,600............B7   12
Narvik, Nor., 13,300...C7   11
Naryan-Mar, Sov. Un.,
11,400............C8   13
Nash, Tex., 1,124.....C5   84
Nash, co., N.C., 61,002.A6   76
Nashua, Iowa, 1,737...B5   60
Nashua, Mont., 796...B10   70
Nashua, N.H., 39,096..F5   73
Nashville, Ark., 3,579..D2   49
Nashville, Ga., 4,070...E3   55
Nashville, Ill., 2,606...E4   58
Nashville, Mich., 1,525.F5   66
Nashville, N.C., 1,423..B6   76
Nashville, Tenn., 170,874
(*411,500)......A5, E9   83
Nashwauk, Minn.,
1,712.............C5   67
Našice, Yugo., 4,157...C4   10
Nasik, India, 131,303..E5   20
Nassau, Ba. Is., 6,000..C5   35

Nassau, N.Y., 1,248...C7   75
Nassau, co., Fla.,
17,189............B5   54
Nassau, co., N.Y.,
1,300,171.........E7   75
Nässjö, Swe., 18,400...I6   11
Natal, Braz., 154,276..D7   27
Natal, prov., S. Afr.,
2,979,920.........F6   24
Natalia, Tex., 1,154...E3   84
Natchez, Miss., 23,791.D2   68
Natchitoches, La.,
13,924............C2   63
Natchitoches, par., La.,
35,653............C2   63
Natick, Mass.,
28,831.........B5, D2   65
National City, Calif.,
32,771............E2   50
National Park, N.J.,
3,380.............*D2   74
Natrona, co., Wyo.,
49,623............C6   89
Naturita, Colo., 979...C2   51
Naudville, Que., Can.,
4,475.............*A6   42
Nauen, Ger., 12,300....B6   6
Naugatuck, Conn.,
19,511............D4   52
Naumburg [an der Saale],
Ger., 37,400.......C5   6
Nauvoo, Ill., 1,039.....C2   58
Navajo, co., Ariz.,
37,994............B3   48
Navalmoral de la Mata,
Sp., 9,073.........C3   8
Navarra, prov., Sp.,
402,042...........*A5   8
Navarre, Ohio, 1,698...B6   78
Navarre, reg., Sp.,
402,042...........A5   8
Navarro, co., Tex.,
34,423............C4   84
Navasota, Tex., 4,937..D4   84
Navesink, N.J., 2,000..C4   74
Navojoa, Mex., 30,762.B3   34
Navolato, Mex., 7,119..C3   34
Navplion, Grc., 8,456.*D4   14
Navy Yard City, Wash.,
3,341.............*B3   86
Nayarit, state, Mex.,
391,970.......C4, m11   34
Nayoro, Jap., 23,400..D11   18
Nazaré, Braz., 14,634..*E7   27
Nazaré, Port., 9,241...C1   8
Nazareth, Isr.,
25,066.........B3, g5   15
Nazareth, Ky., 500....C4   62
Nazareth, Pa., 6,209..E11   81

Nazilli, Tur., 36,000...D7 14
Nchanga, Zambia, 21,800..............C5 24
Ndola, Zambia, 84,500.C5 24
Neath, Wales, 30,888...E5 4
Nebraska, state, U.S., 1,411,330............. 71
Nebraska City, Nebr., 7,252..........D10, F3 71
Necochea, Arg., 17,808.B5 28
Nederland, Tex., 12,036..............E6 84
Nedrow, N.Y., 2,000.*C4 75
Needham, Mass., 25,793.............D2 65
Needles, Calif., 4,590...E6 50
Needville, Tex., 861..............E5, F4 84
Ñeembucu, dept., Par., 50,861.............E4 29
Neenah, Wis., 18,057..........A5, D5 88
Neepawa, Man., Can., 3,191.............D2 40
Neffs, Ohio, 950......B7 78
Negapattinam, India, 57,854.............F6 20
Negaunee, Mich., 6,126.B3 66
Negotin, Yugo., 8,639..C6 10
Negreira, Sp., 7,725....A1 8
Negri Sembilan, state, Mala., 364,524.....*E2 19
Negros Occidental, prov., Phil., 1,332,000....*C6 19
Negros Oriental, prov., Phil., 598,800....*D6 19
Neillsville, Wis., 2,728..D3 88
Neiva, Col., 41,100.....C2 32
Nejd, pol. div., Sau. Ar., 5,000,000.........D3 15
Nekoosa, Wis., 2,515...D4 88
Neligh, Nebr., 1,776...B7 71
Nellore, India, 106,776.F6 20
Nelson, B.C., Can., 7,074..............E9 37
Nelson, Nebr., 695...D7 71
Nelson, N.Z., 23,971 (*25,321)..........N14 26
Nelson, co., Ky., 22,168.............C4 62
Nelson, co., N. Dak., 7,034..............C7 77
Nelson, co., Va., 12,752.............D4 85
Nelsonville, Ohio, 4,834.............C5 78
Nemacolin, Pa., 1,404..G2 81
Nemaha, co., Kans., 12,897.............C7 61
Nemaha, co., Nebr., 9,099.............D10 71
Nemuro, Jap., 42,740..E12 18
Neodesha, Kans., 3,594.E8 61
Neoga, Ill., 1,145.....D5 58
Neon, Ky., 776........C7 62
Neopit, Wis., 1,359...D5 88
Neosho, Mo., 7,452....E3 69
Neosho, co., Kans., 19,455.............E8 61
Nepal, country, Asia, 8,700,000.........C7 20
Nephi, Utah, 2,566....B6 72
Neptune, N.J., 16,000..C4 74
Neptune Beach, Fla., 2,868...........B5, B6 54
Neptune City, N.J., 4,013...........*C4 74
Nerchinsk, Sov. Un., 28,700...........D14 13
Nerekhta, Sov. Un., 19,900...........C13 12
Nerja, Sp., 7,224....D4 8
Nerva, Sp., 12,686.....D2 8
Nesconset, N.Y., 1,964.F4 52
Nescopeck, Pa., 1,934..D9 81
Neshoba, co., Miss., 20,927.............C4 68
Nesquehoning, Pa., 2,714.............E10 81
Ness, co., Kans., 5,470.D3 61
Ness City, Kans., 1,653.............D4 61
Nes Ziona, Isr., 10,917...........*C2 15
Netcong, N.J., 2,765...B3 74
Netherlands, country, Eur., 11,556,000.....A6 5
Netherlands Antilles, (Netherlands West Indies), dep., N.A., 187,000...........*A4 32
Netherlands West Indies, see Netherlands Antilles, dep., N.A.
Nettleton, Miss., 1,389.A5 68
Nettuno, It., 14,100...k9 9
Neubrandenburg, Ger., 33,400.............B6 6
Neuburg, Ger., 16,500.D5 6
Neuchâtel, Switz., 33,430 (*45,930).........*E3 6

Neuchâtel, canton, Switz., 147,633...........*E3 6
Neufchâtel-en-Bray, Fr., 5,590..............C4 5
Neuhaldensleben, Ger., 22,000.............B5 6
Neuilly [-sur-Marne], Fr., 15,082.............g11 5
Neuilly-sur-Seine, Fr., 72,773.............g10 5
Neumarkt [in der Oberpfalz], Ger., 15,800.............D5 5
Neumünster, Ger., 75,100.............A4 5
Neunkirchen, Aus., 10,027.............E8 5
Neuquén, Arg., 7,498..B3 28
Neuquén, prov., Arg., 111,008.............B3 28
Neuruppin, Ger., 22,000.............B6 6
Neustadt [an der Aisch], Ger., 8,900.........C5 6
Neustadt [an der Weinstrasse], Ger., 31,600.............D4 6
Neustadt [bei Coburg], Ger., 12,600.........D4 6
Neustadt [im Schwarz-wald], Ger., 6,900....A5 6
Neustadt [in Holstein], Ger., 14,500.........C5 6
Neustrelitz, Ger., 28,000.............B6 6
Neu-Ulm, Ger., 24,300.D5 6
Neuwied, Ger., 26,400..C3 6
Nevada, Iowa, 4,227...B4 60
Nevada, Mo., 8,416....D3 69
Nevada, Ohio, 919....B4 78
Nevada, co., Ark., 10,700.............D2 49
Nevada, co., Calif., 20,911.............C3 50
Nevada, state, U.S., 285,278............. 72
Nevada City, Calif., 2,353.............C3 50
Nevelsk (Honto), Sov. Un., 10,980.............C10 18
Nevers, Fr., 39,085....D5 5
Nevesinje, Yugo., 2,272.............D4 10
Neville Island, Pa., 2,400.............*B5 81
Nevşehir, Tur., 18,800.............C10 14
New Albany, Ind., 37,812.............H6 59
New Albany, Miss., 5,151.............A4 68
New Alexandria, Va., 1,500.............*C5 85
New Amsterdam, Guy., 12,304.............C5 27
Newark, Ark., 728....B4 49
Newark, Calif., 9,884..B5 50
Newark, Del., 11,404..A6 53
Newark, Eng., 24,610..D6 4
Newark, N.J., 405,220...........B4, E4 74
Newark, N.Y., 12,868..B3 75
Newark, Ohio, 41,790..B5 78
Newark Valley, N.Y., 1,234.............C4 75
New Athens, Ill., 1,923.E4 58
Newaygo, Mich., 1,447.E5 66
Newaygo, co., Mich., 24,160.............E5 66
New Baden, Ill., 1,464..E4 58
New Baltimore, Mich., 3,159.............F8 66
New Beaver, Pa., 1,338.............*E1 81
New Bedford, Mass., 102,477 (*146,400)...C6 65
Newberg, Oreg., 4,204............B1, B4 80
New Berlin, N.Y., 1,262.............C5 75
New Berlin, Wis., 15,788.............E1 88
New Berlinville, Pa., 1,151.............*F10 81
New Bern, N.C., 15,717.............B6 76
Newbern, Tenn., 1,695.A2 83
Newberry, Fla., 1,105..C4 54
Newberry, Mich., 2,612.............B5 66
Newberry, S.C., 8,208..C4 82
Newberry, co., S.C., 29,416.............C4 82
New Bethlehem, Pa., 1,599.............D3 81
New Bloomfield (Bloom-field), Pa., 987......F7 81
New Boston, Ohio, 3,984.............D5 78
New Boston, Tex., 2,773.............C5 84

New Braunfels, Tex., 15,631..........A4, E3 84
New Bremen, Ohio, 1,972.............B3 78
New Brighton, Minn., 6,448.............*E5 67
New Brighton, Pa., 8,397.............E1 81
New Britain, Conn., 82,201.............C5 52
New Brockton, Ala., 1,093.............D4 46
New Brunswick, N.J., 40,139.............C4 74
New Brunswick, prov., Can., 597,936.......C3 43
New Brunswick Heights, N.J., 1,000.........*C4 74
New Buffalo, Mich., 2,128.............G4 66
Newburg, Mo., 884....D6 69
Newburgh, Ind., 1,450.I3 59
Newburgh, N.Y., 30,979 (*104,000)........D7 75
Newburgh Heights, Ohio, 3,512.............B2 78
Newbury, Eng., 20,386.E6 4
Newburyport, Mass., 14,004.............A6 65
New Caledonia, Fr. dep., Oceania, 63,000.....H7 2
New Canaan, Conn., 13,466.............E3 52
New Carlisle, Que., Can., 1,333.............A4 43
New Carlisle, Ind., 1,376.............A4 59
New Carlisle, Ohio, 4,107.............C3 78
New Cassel, N.Y., 7,000.............*E3 75
New Castile, reg., Sp., 4,210,817.........C4 8
New Castle, Ala., 950.............B3, E5 46
Newcastle, Austl., 142,580.............F9 25
Newcastle, Calif., 900..C3 50
Newcastle, N.B., Can., 5,236.............B4 43
Newcastle, Ont., Can., 1,272.............D6 41
New Castle, Del., 4,469.............A6 53
New Castle, Ind., 20,349.............E7 59
New Castle, Pa., 44,790.............D1 81
Newcastle, Tex., 617...C3 84
Newcastle, Wyo., 4,345.B8 89
New Castle, co., Del., 307,446.............A6 53
Newcastle Mine, Alta., Can., 900.........D4 38
New Castle Northwest, Pa., 2,007.........*D1 81
Newcastle-on-Tyne, Eng., 269,389.............C6 4
New Chicago, Ind., 2,312.............A3 59
New City, N.Y., 4,000...........D3, D7 75
Newcomerstown, Ohio, 4,273.............B6 78
New Concord, Ohio, 2,127.............C6 78
New Cumberland, Pa., 9,257.............F8 81
New Cumberland, W. Va., 2,076...........A2, A4 87
New Cumnock, Scot., 3,871.............C4 4
New Delhi, India, 261,545.............C6 20
New Eagle, Pa., 2,670 *F2 81
New Egypt, N.J., 1,737.............C3 74
Newell, W. Va., 1,842...........A2, A4 87
New Ellenton, S.C., 2,309.............E4 82
Newellton, La., 1,435..B4 63
New England, N. Dak., 1,095.............D3 77
Newfane, N.Y., 1,423..B2 75
Newfield, N.J., 1,299..D2 74
New Florence, Pa., 958.............F3 81
Newfoundland, prov., Can., 457,852........ 44
New Franklin, Mo., 1,096.............B5 69
New Freedom, Pa., 1,395.............G8 81
New Glarus, Wis., 1,468.............F4 88
New Glasgow, N.S., Can., 9,782.............D7 43
New Guinea, Territory of, Austl. trust., Oceania, 1,409,000.........h12 25

Newgulf, Tex., 1,419..*E5 84
Newhall, Calif., 4,705...........E4, F2 50
New Hamburg, Ont., Can., 2,181.........D4 41
New Hampshire, state, U.S., 606,921........ 73
New Hampton, Iowa, 3,456.............A5 60
New Hanover, co., N.C., 71,742.............C6 76
New Harmony, Ind., 1,121.............H2 59
New Hartford, Conn., 1,034.............B5 52
New Hartford, N.Y., 2,468.............*B5 75
New Haven, Conn., 152,048 (*320,800)...D5 52
New Haven, Ind., 3,396.............B7 59
New Haven, Ky., 1,009.............C4 62
New Haven, Mich., 1,198.............F8 66
New Haven, Mo., 1,223.............C6 69
New Haven, W. Va., 1,314.............C3 87
New Haven, co., Conn., 660,315.............D4 52
New Hebrides Is., Br. and Fr. dep., Oceania, 49,000.............H8 2
New Holland, Ga., 1,000.............B3 55
New Holland, Pa., 3,425.............F9 81
New Holstein, Wis., 2,401...........B6, E5 88
New Hope, Ala., 953...A3 46
New Hope, Minn., 3,552.............*E5 67
New Hope, Pa., 958...F12 81
New Hyde Park, N.Y., 10,808.............G2 52
New Iberia, La., 29,062.............D4 63
Newington, Conn., 17,664.............C6 52
New Jersey, state, U.S., 6,066,782......... 74
New Kensington, Pa., 23,485...........A7, E2 81
New Kent, co., Va., 4,504.............D6 85
Newkirk, Okla., 2,092..A4 79
New Lebanon, Ohio, 1,459.............*C3 78
New Lenox, Ill., 1,750...........B6, F2 58
New Lexington, Ohio, 4,514.............C5 78
New Lisbon, Wis., 1,337.............E3 88
New Liskeard, Ont., Can., 4,896.........*E9 41
New London, Conn., 34,182 (*104,600)...D8 52
New London, Iowa, 1,694.............D6 60
New London, N.H., 1,007.............E4 73
New London, Ohio, 2,392.............A5 78
New London, Wis., 5,288.............D5 88
New London, co., Conn., 185,745.............C8 52
New Madison, Ohio, 910.............C3 78
New Madrid, Mo., 2,867.............E8 69
New Madrid, co., Mo., 31,350.............E8 69
New Malden, Eng., 46,587.............m11 4
Newman, Calif., 2,148.D3 50
Newman, Ill., 1,097...D6 58
Newman Grove, Nebr., 880.............C8 71
Newmanstown, Pa., 1,200.............F9 81
Newmarket, Ont., Can., 8,932.............C5 41
Newmarket, N.H., 2,745.............E6 73
New Market, N.J., 3,500.............*B4 74
New Martinsville, W. Va., 5,607.............B4 87
New Matamoras, Ohio, 925.............C6 78
New Mexico, state, U.S., 951,023............. 48
New Miami, Ohio, 2,360.............C3 78
New Milford, Conn., 3,023.............C3 52
New Milford, N.J., 18,810.............D5 74

New Milford, Pa.,
1,129..............C10 81
Newnan, Ga., 12,169...C2 55
New Norfolk, Austl.,
5,445..............o15 25
New Orleans, La., 627,525
(*885,200).......C7, E5 63
New Oxford, Pa., 1,407.G7 81
New Paltz, N.Y., 3,041.D6 75
New Paris, Ohio, 1,679.C3 78
New Philadelphia, Ohio,
14,241.............B6 78
New Philadelphia, Pa.,
1,702..............E9 81
New Plymouth, Idaho,
940................F2 57
New Plymouth, N.Z.,
29,368 (*32,387)...M15 26
Newport, Ark., 7,007...B4 49
Newport, Del., 1,239...A6 53
Newport, Eng.,
105,285............E5   4
Newport, Eng., 19,482..E6   4
Newport, Ky.,
30,070..........A7, B5 62
Newport, Maine, 1,589.D3 64
Newport, Mich., 650...G7 66
Newport, Minn., 2,349.E7 67
Newport, N.H., 3,222..E3 73
Newport, Oreg., 5,344..C3 80
Newport, Pa., 1,861....F7 81
Newport, R.I., 47,049.D11 52
Newport, Tenn.,
6,448.............D10 83
Newport, Vt., 5,019....B3 73
Newport, Wash., 1,513.A8 86
Newport, co., R.I.,
81,891............C11 52
Newport Beach, Calif.,
26,564.........F3, F4 50
Newport News (Independ-
ent City), Va., 113,662
(*219,200).....B6, E6 85
New Port Richey, Fla.,
3,520..............D4 54
Newportville, Pa.,
700.............*F12 81
New Prague, Minn.,
2,533..............F5 67
New Providence, N.J.,
10,243............*B4 74
New Providence, Tenn.,
4,451..............A4 83
Newquay, Eng.,
11,877.............E4   4
New Richland, Minn.,
1,046..............G5 67
New Richmond, Que.,
Can., 411..........A4 43
New Richmond, Ohio,
2,834..............D3 78
New Richmond, Wis.,
3,316..............C1 88
New Roads, La., 3,965.D4 63
New Rochelle, N.Y.,
76,812.........D2, D3 75
New Rockford, N. Dak.,
2,177..............C6 77
Newry, N. Ire., 12,450.C3   4
New Salem, N. Dak.,
986................D4 77
New Salem, Pa., 860..*G2 81
New Sarpy, La., 1,259..C7 63
New Sharon, Iowa,
1,063..............C5 60
New Shrewsbury, N.J.,
7,313.............*C4 74
New Smyrna Beach, Fla.,
8,781..............C6 54
New South Wales, state,
Austl., 3,917,016.....F8 25
New Straitsville, Ohio,
1,019..............C5 78
New Tazewell, Tenn.,
768...............C10 83
Newton, Ala., 958....D4 46
Newton, Ill., 2,901...E5 58
Newton, Iowa, 15,381..C4 60
Newton, Kans.,
14,877.........A5, D6 61
Newton, Mass.,
92,384.........B5, D2 65
Newton, Miss., 3,178...C4 68
Newton, N.J., 6,563...A3 74
Newton, N.C., 6,658...B2 76
Newton, Tex., 1,233...D6 84
Newton, co., Ark.,
5,963..............B2 49
Newton, co., Ga.,
20,999.............C3 55
Newton, co., Ind.,
11,502.............B3 59
Newton, co., Miss.,
19,517.............C4 68
Newton, co., Mo.,
30,093.............E3 69
Newton, co., Tex.,
10,372.............D6 84
Newton Brook, Ont.,
Can., 1,600........E6 41

Newton Falls, Ohio,
5,038..............A7 78
Newtonville, N.Y.,
1,000.............*C7 75
New Toronto, Ont., Can.,
13,384.........D5, E6 41
Newtown, Conn.,
1,261..............D3 52
New Town, N. Dak.,
1,586..............C3 77
Newtown, Ohio, 1,750..C3 78
Newtown, Pa., 2,400..B8 81
Newtown, Pa., 2,323..F12 81
Newtown [&
Llanllwchaiarn], Wales,
5,512..............D5   4
Newtownards, N. Ire.,
13,090.............C4   4
New Ulm, Minn.,
11,114.............F4 67
Newville, Pa., 1,656...F7 81
New Washington, Ohio,
1,162..............B5 78
New Waterford, N.S.,
Can., 10,592......C9 43
New Westminster, B.C.,
Can., 33,654...A10, E6 37
New Whiteland, Ind.,
3,488.............*E5 59
New Wilmington, Pa.,
2,203..............D1 81
New Windsor (Windsor),
Eng., 27,126......*E6   4
New Windsor, N.Y.,
4,041.............*D6 75
New York, N.Y., 7,781,984
(*15,404,300)
...........D1, D3, E7 75
New York, co.
(Manhattan borough),
N.Y., 1,689,281 (part
of New York City)..D1 75
New York, state, U.S.,
16,782,304............ 75
New York Mills, Minn.,
828................D3 67
New York Mills, N.Y.,
3,788.............*B5 75
New Zealand, country,
Oceania, 2,414,984..N15 26
Nezhin, Sov. Un.,
59,000.............F8 12
Nez Perce, co., Idaho,
27,066.............C2 57
N'Gaoundéré, Cam.,
10,090.............G7 22
Nha Trang, Viet.,
5,000..............C3 19
Niagara, Wis., 2,098...C5 88
Niagara, co., N.Y.,
242,269............B2 75
Niagara Falls, Ont., Can.,
53,365 (*56,621)...D5 41
Niagara Falls, N.Y.,
102,394............B1 75
Niagara-on-the-Lake,
Ont., Can., 2,712...D5 41
Niagara University, N.Y.,
1,500.............*B1 75
Niamey, Niger, 30,000..F5 22
Niantic, Conn., 2,788..D8 52
Nicaragua, country, N.A.,
1,551,500..........E7 34
Nicastro, It., 21,500...E6   9
Nice, Fr., 292,958....F7   5
Niceville, Fla., 4,517...G2 54
Nicholas, co., Ky.,
6,677..............B6 62
Nicholas, co., W. Va.,
25,414.............C4 87
Nicholasville, Ky.,
4,275..............C5 62
Nicholl, Ga., 930.....E4 55
Nichols Hills, Okla.,
4,897..............B4 79
Nicholson, Pa., 942...C10 81
Nickerson, Kans.,
1,091..........A3, D5 61
Nicobar, is., India.....G9 20
Nicolet, Que., Can.,
4,441..............C5 42
Nicolet, co., Que., Can.,
30,827.............C5 42
Nicollet, co., Minn.,
23,196.............F4 67
Nicoma Park, Okla.,
1,263..............B4 79
Nicosia, Cyp., 48,864..A4 23
Nicosia, It., 17,600...F5   9
Nicotera, It., 9,143....E5   9
Nicoya, C.R., 10,461...E7 34
Niedersachsen (Lower
Saxony), state, Ger.,
6,641,400.........*B4   6
Nienburg, Ger., 22,100.B4   6
Nièvre, dept., Fr.,
245,921...........*D5   5
Niğde, Tur., 18,000...D10 14
Niger, country, Afr.,
2,850,000..........F6 22

Nigeria, country, Afr.,
34,228,000.........G6 22
Nigrita, Grc., 8,399...*B4 14
Niigata, Jap., 314,528..H9 18
Niigata, pref., Jap.,
2,442,037.........*H9 18
Niihama, Jap., 125,688..J6 18
Níjar, Sp., 2,052.....D4   8
Nijmegen, Neth.,
131,600............B6   5
Nikitovka, Sov. Un.,
10,000............q21 12
Nikko, Jap., 33,348...H9 18
Nikolayev, Sov. Un.,
242,000............H9 12
Nikolayevskiy, Sov. Un.,
30,000............F15 12
Nikolayevsk [-na-Amure],
Sov. Un., 40,000...D17 13
Nikopol, Sov. Un.,
92,000............H10 12
Niksar, Tur., 10,600..B11 14
Niles, Ill., 25,073....E2 58
Niles, Mich., 13,842...G4 66
Niles, Ohio, 19,545...A7 78
Nimes, Fr., 92,802....F6   5
Nimmonsburg, N.Y.,
1,500.............*C5 75
Ninety Six, S.C., 1,435.C3 82
Ningan, China, 40,000.D4 18
Ninghsien, see Ningpo,
China
Ningpo (Ninghsien),
China, 237,500.....F9 17
Ningsia, see Yinchwan,
China
Ningsia Hui, prov., China,
1,822,000..........D6 17
Ningte, China, 30,000..F8 17
Ninh Binh, Viet.,
25,000.............A3 19
Niobrara, co., Wyo.,
3,750..............B8 89
Niort, Fr., 37,512....D3   5
Niota, Tenn., 679....D9 83
Nipawin, Sask.,.Can.,
3,836..............D3 39
Nipissing, co., Ont., Can.,
70,568............*A5 41
Nipomo, Calif., 550...E3 50
Niquero, Cuba, 5,437..E5 35
Nirasaki, Jap., 11,500..n17 18
Niš, Yugo., 81,073....D5 10
Nisa, Port., 5,617....C2   8
Nisko, Pol., 6,590....C7   7
Niterói, Braz.,
228,826.......C4, h6 30
Nitra, Czech., 34,200..D5   7
Nitro, W. Va., 6,894...C3 87
Nivelles, Bel., 14,345..B6   5
Nivernais, former prov.,
Fr., 236,000.......D5   5
Nixa, Mo., 944.......D4 69
Nixon, N.J., 14,000..*B4 74
Nixon, Tex.,
1,751..........B4, E4 84
Nizhneudinsk, Sov. Un.,
35,900............D12 13
Nizhneye, Sov. Un.,
10,000............q21 12
Nizhniy-Tagil, Sov. Un.,
355,000............D9 13
Nkana, Zambia,
53,500.............C5 24
Nkongsamba, Cam.,
12,000.............H6 22
Noank, Conn., 1,116..D9 52
Nobeoka, Jap.,
100,000............J5 18
Noble, Okla., 995....B4 79
Noble, co., Ind.,
28,162.............B7 59
Noble, co., Ohio,
10,982.............C6 78
Noble, co., Okla.,
10,376.............A4 79
Nobles, co., Minn.,
23,365.............G3 67
Noblesville, Ind., 7,664.D5 59
Nocona, Tex., 3,127...C4 84
Nodaway, co., Mo.,
22,215.............A3 69
Nogales, Ariz., 7,286..D3 48
Nogales, Mex., 37,565..A2 34
Nogales, Mex., 11,179.n15 34
Nogata, Jap., 62,179...J5 18
Nogent-le-Rotrou, Fr.,
9,428..............C4   5
Nogent [-sur-Marne], Fr.,
24,501............g10   5
Noginsk, Sov. Un.,
97,000........D12, n18 12
Nogoya, Arg., 12,051..A5 28
Nógrád, co., Hung.,
236,393...........*A4 10
Nohar, India, 13,728...C5 20
Noheji, Jap., 9,900...F10 18
Noisy-le-Sec, Fr.,
31,187............g10   5
Nokomis, Fla., 2,253...E4 54
Nokomis, Ill., 2,476...D4 58

Nola, It., 16,400......D5   9
Nolan, co., Tex.,
18,963.............C2 84
Nome, Alsk., 2,316....C6 47
Nomme, Sov. Un.,
18,026............*B5 12
Noranda, Que., Can.,
11,477...........*E9 41
Nora Springs, Iowa,
1,275..............A5 60
Norborne, Mo., 965...B4 69
Norco, Calif., 4,964..*F5 50
Norco, La., 4,682..B6, D5 63
Norcross, Ga.,
1,605..........A5, C2 55
Nord, dept., Fr.,
2,293,112.........*B5   5
Nordegg, Alta., Can.,
1,000..........C2, D1 38
Norden, Ger., 16,200..B3   6
Nordenham, Ger.,
26,900.............B4   6
Nordhausen, Ger.,
39,900.............C5   6
Nordhorn, Ger.,
39,400.............B3   6
Nordland, co., Nor.,
225,394...........*D6 11
Nördlingen, Ger.,
14,400.............D5   6
Nordrhein-Westfalen,
state, Ger.,
15,901,700........*C3   6
Nord-Trøndelag, co., Nor.,
112,185...........*E4 11
Nordvik, Sov. Un.,
2,500.............B14 13
Norfolk, Nebr., 13,640..B8 71
Norfolk, N.Y., 1,353...A2 75
Norfolk (Independent
City), Va., 304,869
(*574,900).....B7, E7 85
Norfolk, co., Ont., Can.,
50,475.............E4 41
Norfolk, co., Eng.,
561,980...........*D7   4
Norfolk, co., Mass.,
510,256............B5 65
Norfolk Highlands, Va.,
1,000.............*E6 85
Norilsk, Sov. Un.,
109,000...........C11 13
Norlina, N.C., 927....A5 76
Normal, Ala., 1,500...*A3 46
Normal, Ill., 13,357...C5 58
Norman, Okla., 33,412.B4 79
Norman, co., Minn.,
11,253.............C2 67
Normandin, Que., Can.,
1,838............*G19 36
Normandy, Fla.,
1,900.............*B5 54
Normandy, Mo., 4,452.A8 69
Normandy, former prov.,
Fr., 2,407,000......C4   5
Normandy Park, Wash.,
3,224.............*B4 86
Norrbotten, co., Swe.,
262,600..........*E10 11
Norridge, Ill., 14,087..*E3 58
Norris, Tenn., 1,389...C9 83
Norris Arm, Newf., Can.,
1,226..............D4 44
Norris City, Ill., 1,243..F5 58
Norristown, Pa.,
38,925.........A10, F11 81
Norrköping, Swe.,
91,400.........H7, u34 11
Norrtälje, Swe.,
8,900.........H8, t36 11
Norte de Santander, dept.,
Col., 403,420.......B3 32
North, S.C., 1,047....D5 82
North, div., Ice.,
28,388...........*n23 11
North Abington, Mass.,
4,900..............B6 65
North Adams, Mass.,
19,905.............A1 65
North Agawam, Mass.,
2,000.............*B2 65
North America, cont.,
229,700,000........... 33
North Amherst, Mass.,
1,009..............B2 65
North Amityville, N.Y.,
6,000.............*E7 75
Northampton, Eng.,
105,361............D6   4
Northampton, Mass.,
30,058.............B2 65
Northampton, Pa.,
8,866.............E11 81
Northampton, co., Eng.,
398,132...........*D6   4
Northampton, co., N.C.,
26,811.............A6 76
Northampton, co., Pa.,
201,412...........E11 81
Northampton, co., Va.,
16,966.............D7 85

North Andover, Mass.,
10,908.............A5   65
North Apollo, Pa.,
1,741.............E2   81
North Arlington, N.J.,
17,477.............D5   74
North Asheboro, N.C.,
3,805.............*B4   76
North Atlanta, Ga.,
12,661.............A5   55
North Attleboro, Mass.,
14,777.............C5   65
North Augusta, S.C.,
10,348.............D4   82
North Aurora, Ill.,
2,088.............*B5   58
North Babylon, N.Y.,
12,000.............*E3   75
North Baltimore, Ohio,
3,011.............A4   78
North Battleford, Sask.,
Can., 11,230.......E1   39
North Bay, Ont., Can.,
23,781.........A5, E9   41
North Bay, Fla.,
2,006.............*G6   54
North Belle Vernon, Pa.,
3,148.............*F2   81
North Bellmore, N.Y.,
19,639.............*G2   75
North Bellport, N.Y.,
2,000.............*F5   75
North Belmont, N.C.,
3,000.............B2   76
North Bend, Nebr.,
1,174.............C9   71
North Bend, Oreg.,
7,512.............D2   80
North Bend, Pa., 800..D6   81
North Bend, Wash.,
945.............B4   86
North Bennington, Vt.,
1,437.............F1   73
North Bergen, N.J.,
42,387.............D5   74
North Berwick, Maine,
1,295.............E2   64
North Billerica, Mass.,
3,000.............A5, C2   65
Northboro, Mass.,
2,516.............B4   65
North Brabant, prov.,
Neth., 1,512,800....*B6   5
North Braddock, Pa.,
13,204.............B6   81
North Branch, Mich.,
901.............E7   66
North Branch, Minn.,
949.............E6   67
Northbridge, Mass.,
2,128.............B4   65
Northbrook, Ill.,
11,635.............E2   58
North Brookfield, Mass.,
2,615.............B3   65
North Brunswick, N.J.,
10,099.............*C4   74
North Caldwell, N.J.,
4,163.............B4   74
North Canton, Ga.,
1,996.............B2   55
North Canton, Ohio,
7,727.............B6   78
North Carolina, state,
U.S., 4,556,155.....   76
North Catasauqua, Pa.,
2,805.............*E11   81
North Cedar, Iowa,
1,500.............*B5   60
North Charleroi, Pa.,
2,259.............*F2   81
North Charleston, S.C.,
22,339.............F2, F8   82
North Chelmsford, Mass.,
3,500.............A5   65
North Chicago, Ill.,
20,517.............A6, E2   58
North Chili, N.Y.,
2,000.............*B3   75
North Chillicothe, Ill.,
2,259.............C4   58
North City, Wash.,
2,000.............*B3   86
North College Hill, Ohio,
12,035.............D2   78
North Collins, N.Y.,
1,574.............C2   75
North Conway, N.H.,
1,104.............B4   73
North Corbin, Ky.,
950.............D5   62
Northcrest, Calif.,
1,945.............*B1   50
North Dakota, state,
U.S., 632,446.....   77
North Dartmouth, Mass.,
4,000.............C6   65
North Decatur, Ga.,
10,000.............*C2   55

North Dighton, Mass.,
1,167.............C5   65
North Druid Hills, Ga.,
4,000.............*C2   55
North East, Md.,
1,628.............A6   53
North East, Pa.,
4,217.............B2   81
Northeastern Polder,
prov., Neth., 28,800.*A6   5
Northeast New Guinea,
reg., N. Gui.,
875,000.............k12   25
North Easton, Mass.,
4,000.............B5   65
Northeim, Ger.,
19,300.............C4   6
North English, Iowa,
1,004.............C5   60
Northern, reg., Nig.,
29,758,875.........F6   22
Northern Ireland, reg.,
U.K., 1,425,462.....C3   4
Northern Territory, ter.,
Austl., 27,095.....B5   25
Northfield, Ill., 4,005..*E3   58
Northfield, Mass.,
1,179.............A3   65
Northfield, Minn.,
8,707.............F5   67
Northfield, N.H.,
1,243.............E4   73
Northfield, N.J., 5,849..E3   74
Northfield, Ohio,
1,055.............B2   78
Northfield (P.O.), Ohio,
2,427.............*B2   78
Northfield, Vt., 2,159..C2   73
North Fond du Lac, Wis.,
2,549.............B5, E5   88
Northfork, W. Va.,
798.............*D3   87
North Gamboa, C.Z.,
3,489.............*B2   32
North Glen Ellyn, Ill.,
1,500.............*F2   58
North Grafton, Mass.,
2,600.............B4   65
North Great River, N.Y.,
1,500.............*G4   75
North Greenville, Miss.,
2,516.............*B2   68
North Grosvenor Dale,
Conn., 1,874.......B9   52
North Gulfport, Miss.,
3,323.............*E4   68
North Haledon, N.J.,
6,026.............*B4   74
North Hartsville, S.C.,
1,899.............*C7   76
North Haven, Conn.,
15,935.............D5   52
North Henderson, N.C.,
1,995.............*A5   76
North Highlands, Calif.,
21,271.............*A6   50
North Holland, prov.,
Neth., 2,073,100....*A6   5
North Hornell, N.Y.,
917.............*C3   75
North Hudson, Wis.,
1,019.............*D1   88
North Industry, Ohio,
1,800.............B6   78
North Irwin, Pa.,
1,143.............*F2   81
North Judson, Ind.,
1,942.............B4   59
North Kamloops, B.C.,
Can., 6,456.......D7   37
North Kansas City, Mo.,
5,657.............B3, E2   69
North Kingstown, R.I.,
3,500.............C11   52
North Kingsville, Ohio,
1,854.............A7   78
North La Junta, Colo.,
950.............C7   51
North Lake, Ill.,
12,318.............*F2   58
North Larchmont, N.Y.,
9,000.............*D2   75
North Las Vegas, Nev.,
18,422.............C4   72
North Liberty, Ind.,
1,241.............A5   59
North Lindenhurst, N.Y.,
10,000.............G3   75
North Little Rock, Ark.,
58,032.............C3, D6   49
North Manchester, Ind.,
4,377.............C6   59
North Mankato, Minn.,
5,927.............F4   67
North Massapequa, N.Y.,
12,300.............G3   75
North Merrick, N.Y.,
12,976.............*G2   75
North Miami, Fla.,
28,708.............F3, G6   54

North Miami Beach, Fla.,
21,405.............E3   54
North Muskegon, Mich.,
3,855.............E4   66
North New Hyde Park,
N.Y., 9,930.........*E7   75
North Ogden, Utah,
2,621.............A6, C2   72
North Olmsted, Ohio,
16,290.............B1   78
North Oxford, Mass.,
1,466.............B4   65
North Palm Beach, Fla.,
2,684.............*F6   54
North Park, Ill., 1,500.*A4   58
North Patchogue, N.Y.,
6,000.............*D4   75
North Pekin, Ill.,
2,025.............*C4   58
North Pelham, N.Y.,
5,326.............*D1   75
North Plainfield, N.J.,
16,993.............B4   74
North Platte, Nebr.,
17,184.............C5   71
North Pleasanton, Tex.,
1,018.............*E3   84
Northport, Ala., 5,245..B2   46
Northport, N.Y.,
5,972.............D3   75
North Princeton, N.J.,
4,506.............*C3   74
North Providence, R.I.,
18,220.............B11   52
North Pulaski, Va.,
1,156.............*D2   85
North Quincy, Ill.,
2,256.............*D2   58
North Reading, Mass.,
8,331.............C3   65
North Richland Hills,
Tex., 8,662........*B5   84
Northridge, Ohio,
1,500.............*C3   78
North Riverside, Ill.,
8,401.............*F3   58
North Rockville Center,
N.Y., 1,500........*E3   75
North Royalton, Ohio,
9,290.............B2   78
North Sacramento, Calif.,
12,922.............A6   50
North St. Paul, Minn.,
8,520.............E7   67
North Salt Lake, Utah,
1,655.............*A6   72
North Scituate, Mass.,
3,421.............D4   65
North Seaford, N.Y.,
3,000.............*G3   75
North Shreveport, La.,
7,701.............*B2   63
North Springfield, Va.,
5,000.............*B5   85
North Sydney, N.S., Can.,
8,657.............C9   43
North Syracuse, N.Y.,
7,412.............B4   75
North Tarrytown, N.Y.,
8,818.........D2, D3, D7   75
North Terre Haute, Ind.,
1,100.............E3   59
North Tonawanda, N.Y.,
34,757.............B2   75
North Troy, Vt., 961...B3   73
North Tunica, Miss.,
1,025.............*A3   68
North Turlock, Calif.,
2,535.............*D3   50
Northumberland, Pa.,
4,156.............E8   81
Northumberland, co.,
N.B., Can., 47,223...B3   43
Northumberland, co.,
Ont., Can., 41,892...C7   41
Northumberland, co.,
Eng., 818,988.......*C6   4
Northumberland, co., Pa.,
104,138.............D8   81
Northumberland, co., Va.,
10,185.............D6   85
North Uxbridge, Mass.,
1,882.............B4   65
Northvale, N.J.,
2,892.............A5, C5   74
North Valley Stream,
N.Y., 5,000........*E2   75
North Vancouver, B.C.,
Can., 23,656...A10, E6   37
North Vandergrift, Pa.,
1,827.............*E2   81
North Vernon, Ind.,
4,307.............F6   59
Northville, Mich.,
3,967.............A7   66
Northville, N.Y., 1,156.B6   75
North Virginia Beach, Va.,
2,587.............*E7   85
North Wales, Pa.,
3,673.............F11   81

North Warren, Pa.,
1,458.............C3   81
Northwest Park Apart-
ments, Md., 3,000..*B3   53
North Westport, Mass.,
3,000.............C5   65
Northwest Territories,
ter., Can., 22,998...C4   36
North Whittier Heights,
Calif., 12,200......*E4   50
North Wilbraham, Mass.,
2,000.............B3   65
North Wildwood, N.J.,
3,598.............F3   74
North Wilkesboro, N.C.,
4,197.............A2   76
Northwood, Iowa,
1,768.............A4   60
Northwood, Mich.,
4,000.............*E5   66
Northwood, N.H., 350..E5   73
Northwood, N. Dak.,
1,195.............C8   77
Northwoods, Ga.,
1,000.............*A5   55
Northwoods, Mo.,
4,701.............*C7   69
North York, Pa.,
2,290.............G8   81
Norton, Kans., 3,345...C4   61
Norton, Mass., 1,501...C5   65
Norton (Independent
City), Va., 5,013...B2   85
Norton, co., Kans.,
8,035.............C4   61
Norton Center, Ohio,
2,000.............*A6   78
Nortonville, Ky., 775...C2   62
Norvelt, Pa., 1,211....*F3   81
Norwalk, Calif.,
88,739.............*F2   50
Norwalk, Conn.,
67,775.............E3   52
Norwalk, Iowa,
1,328.............A7, C4   60
Norwalk, Ohio, 12,900..A5   78
Norway, Maine, 2,654..D2   64
Norway, Mich., 3,171...C3   66
Norway, country, Eur.,
3,596,300.........E5   11
Norwayne, Mich.,
6,000.............*A7   66
Norwich, Ont., Can.,
1,703.............E4   41
Norwich, Conn., 38,506.C8   52
Norwich, Eng.,
119,904.............D7   4
Norwich, N.Y., 9,175...C5   75
Norwood, Ont., Can.,
1,060.............C7   41
Norwood, Mass.,
24,898.............B5, D2   65
Norwood, Minn., 945..F5   67
Norwood, N.J., 2,852...C5   74
Norwood, N.Y., 2,200..A2   75
Norwood, N.C., 1,844..B3   76
Norwood, Ohio, 34,580.D2   78
Norwood, Pa., 6,729...B11   81
Norwood, Tenn.,
5,000.............*D10   83
Noshiro, Jap., 36,500..F10   18
Nossa Senhora das Dores,
Braz., 4,740.......*E7   27
Noto, It., 21,000.....F5   9
Notodden, Nor., 7,600..H3   11
Notre Dame, Ind.,
6,500.............*A5   59
Notre Dame du Lac, Que.,
Can., 1,680........B9   42
Nottingham, Eng.,
311,645.............D6   4
Nottingham, co., Eng.,
902,966.............*D6   4
Nottingham, Pa.,
2,500.............*A12   81
Nottoway, co., Va.,
15,141.............D7   85
Nova Cruz, Braz.,
6,780.............*D7   27
Nova Friburgo, Braz.,
49,901.............C4, h6   30
Nova Iguaçu, Braz.,
134,708.............h6   30
Nova Lima, Braz.,
21,135.............C4   30
Nova Lisboa, Ang.,
37,381.............C3   24
Novara, It., 87,704....B2   9
Nova Scotia, prov., Can.,
737,007.............D6   43
Novato, Calif.,
17,881.............B5, C2   50
Nova Varos, Yugo.,
3,186.............D4   10
Novaya Ladoga, Sov. Un.,
25,000.............A9   12
Novaya Zemlya, is., Sov.
Un.............B8   16
Nova Zagora, Bul.,
11,031.............D8   10
Novelda, Sp., 8,887....C5   8

Nové Zámky, Czech., 22,000............E5 7
Novgorod, Sov. Un., 68,000............B8 12
Novgorod-Severskiy, Sov. Un., 10,000........E9 12
Novi, Mich., 6,390.....A7 66
Novigrad, Yugo., 531..C2 10
Novi Ligure, It., 26,972............B2 9
Novi Pazar, Bul., 5,461.D8 10
Novi Pazar, Yugo., 20,712............D5 10
Novi Sad, Yugo., 102,385............C4 10
Novoaydar, Sov. Un., 10,000........G12, q21 12
Novocherkassk, Sov. Un., 96,000............H13 12
Novoekonomicheskoye, Sov. Un., 10,000....q20 12
Novogrudok, Sov. Un., 25,000............E5 12
Novo-Kazalinsk, Sov. Un., 10,000............E9 16
Novokuznetsk, Sov. Un., 405,000............D11 13
Novomoskovsk, Sov. Un., 112,000............D12 12
Novomoskovsk, Sov. Un., 37,500............G10 12
Novorossiysk, Sov. Un., 101,000............I11 12
Novoskakhtinsk, Sov. Un., 108,000........H12 12
Novosibirsk, Sov. Un., 963,000............D11 13

Novosil, Sov. Un., 10,000............E11 12
Novoukrainka, Sov. Un., 10,000............G8 12
Nový Bohumín, Czech., 11,000............D5 7
Novy Bydzov, Czech., 6,120............C3 7
Novy Jicin, Czech., 16,600............D5 7
Novyye Senzhary, Sov. Un., 4,700........G10 12
Novyy Oskol, Sov. Un., 10,000............F11 12
Nowa Sól, Pol., 25,000............C3 7
Nowata, Okla., 4,163...A6 79
Nowata, co., Okla., 10,848............A6 79
Nowra, Austl., 6,221...G8 26
Nowshera, Pak., 23,122.B5 20
Nowy Dwor, Pol., 5,046............k13 7
Nowy Sacz, Pol., 34,000............D6 7
Nowy Targ, Pol., 12,600............D6 7
Noxubee, co., Miss., 16,826............B5 68
Noya, Sp., 4,236......A1 8
Noyon, Fr., 9,317......C5 5
Nsawam, Ghana, 8,731.G4 22
Ñuble, prov., Chile, 284,516............B2 28
Nuckolls, co., Nebr., 8,217............D7 71

Nucla, Colo., 906......C2 51
Nueces, co., Tex., 221,573............F4 84
Nueva Ecija, prov., Phil., 608,700............*C6 19
Nueva Esparta, state, Ven., 89,492......A5 32
Nueva Imperial, Chile, 6,450............B2 28
Nueva Rosita, Mex., 32,294............B4 34
Nueva San Salvador, Sal., 26,911............*E7 34
Nueva Vizcaya, prov., Phil., 138,000......*B6 34
Nueve de Julio, Arg., 13,678............B4 28
Nuevitas, Cuba, 12,390.E5 35
Nuevo Laredo, Mex., 93,787............B5 34
Nuevo León, state, Mex., 1,063,399............B5 34
Nules, Sp., 8,460......C5 8
Numazu, Jap., 142,609..........I9, n17 18
Nu Mine, Pa., 500......E3 81
Nunda, N.Y., 1,224....C3 75
Nungan, China, 35,000............C10 17
Nunkiang, China, 5,000............B10 17
Nuoro, It., 23,033.....D2 9
Nuremberg, Pa., 900...E9 81
Nürnberg, Ger., 454,500............D5 6
Nushki, Pak., 2,142...C4 20

Nutley, N.J., 29,513............B4, D5 74
Nutter Fort, W. Va., 2,440............B4 87
Nutting Lake, Mass., 1,600............C2 65
Nuwara Eliya, Cey., 11,983............G7 20
Nyack, N.Y., 6,062.....D1, D3, D7 75
Nyamandhlovu, Rh., 10,000............D5 24
Nyandoma, Sov. Un., 17,800............A13 12
Nybro, Swe., 8,700.....I6 11
Nye, co., Nev., 4,374..B3 72
Nyiregyhaza, Hung., 39,662............B5 10
Nykøbing Falster, Den., 17,850............A1 7
Nykøbing [Mors], Den., 9,326............I3 11
Nykoping, Swe., 24,300............H7, u34 11
Nyland Acres, Calif., 1,619............*E4 50
Nymburk, Czech., 12,600............C3, n19 7
Nynäshamn, Swe., 9,400............H7, u35 11
Nyngan, Austl., 2,414............F8 25
Nysa, Pol., 23,000............C4 7
Nyssa, Oreg., 2,611...D10 80

O

Oahu, isl., Haw........g9 56
Oak Bluffs, Mass., 1,419............D6 65
Oakbrook Terrace, Ill., 1,121............*F2 58
Oak Creek, Colo., 666.A4 51
Oak Creek, Wis., 9,372............*F6 88
Oakdale, Calif., 4,980.D3 50
Oakdale, La., 6,618....D3 63
Oakdale, N.Y., 1,500.*C5 75
Oakdale, Pa., 1,695....B5 81
Oakes, N. Dak., 1,650.D7 77
Oakfield, N.Y., 2,070...B2 75
Oakford, Ill., 2,000........A12, F12 81
Oak Forest, Ill., 5,850.F3 58
Oak Grove, Ga., 3,500.*C2 55
Oak Grove, La., 1,797..B4 63
Oak Grove, Oreg., 4,000............B2, B4 80
Oakharbor, Ohio, 2,903.A4 78
Oak Harbor, Wash., 3,942............A3 86
Oak Hill, Ohio, 1,748..D5 78
Oak Hill, Tenn., 4,490.*A5 83
Oak Hill, W. Va., 4,711............D3, D7 87
Oakhurst, N.J., 4,374..C4 74
Oakhurst, Okla., 3,000.*A5 79
Oakland, Calif., 367,548............B5, D2 50
Oakland, Ill., 939......D5 58
Oakland, Iowa, 1,340..C2 60
Oakland, Maine, 1,880.D3 64
Oakland, Md., 1,977...D1 53
Oakland, Mo., 1,552..*C7 69
Oakland, Nebr., 1,429.C9 71
Oakland, N.J., 9,446..A4 74
Oakland, Pa., 2,303...*D1 81
Oakland, co., Mich., 690,259............F7 66
Oakland City, Ind., 3,016............H3 59
Oakland Park, Fla., 5,331............E3, F6 54
Oakland Park, Ohio, 10,000............*C5 78
Oaklawn, Ill., 31,476..F3 58
Oaklawn, Kans., 5,000.B5 61
Oakley, Kans., 2,190..C3 61
Oakley Park, Mich., 1,100............*A7 66
Oaklyn, N.J., 4,778....D2 74
Oakman, Ala., 849....B2 46
Oakmont, Pa., 7,504............A6, E2 81
Oak Park, Ill., 61,093..F2 58
Oak Park, Mich., 36,632............A7 66
Oakridge, Oreg., 1,973.D4 80
Oak Ridge, Tenn., 27,169............C9 83
Oak View, Calif., 2,448............*E4 50
Oak View, Md., 1,000.*C3 53
Oakville, Ont., Can., 10,366............D5 41
Oakville, Conn., 6,000.C4 52
Oakville, Mo., 1,300...B8 69

Oakville, Tenn., 6,000............B2, E8 83
Oakwood (Oakwood Village), Ohio, 3,283............*B2 78
Oakwood (Far Hills), Ohio, 10,493........C3 78
Oakwood, Pa., 2,267.*D1 81
Oakwood, Tex., 716...D5 84
Oakwood Villa, Fla., 4,500............*B5 54
Oamaru, N.Z., 12,429.P13 26
Oaxaca, Mex., 72,313..D5 34
Oaxaca, state, Mex., 1,675,926............D5 34
Obama, Jap., 20,400..n14 18
Oban, Scot., 6,859.....B4 4
Oberhausen, Ger., 256,800............C3 6
Oberlin, Kans., 2,337..C3 61
Oberlin, La., 1,794....D3 63
Oberlin, Ohio, 8,198...A5 78
Oberlin, Pa., 2,500....*F8 81
Oberstdorf, Ger., 8,300.E5 6
Obetz, Ohio, 1,984.C2, C5 78
Obihiro, Jap., 83,000..E11 18
Obion, Tenn., 1,097....A2 83
Obion, co., Tenn., 26,957............A2 83
Oblong, Ill., 1,817.....D6 58
Obluchye, Sov. Un., 15,000............E16 13
O'Brien, co., Iowa, 18,840............A2 59
Obuasi, Ghana, 15,876.G4 22
Ocala, Fla., 13,598....C4 54
Ocaña, Col., 15,214...B3 32
Ocaña, Sp., 6,686......C4 8
Ocean, co., N.J., 108,241............D4 74
Oceana, Va., 2,448....B4 85
Oceana, W. Va., 1,303.D3 87
Oceana, co., Mich., 16,547............E4 66
Ocean City, Md., 983..D7 53
Ocean City, N.J., 7,618.E3 74
Ocean Falls, B.C., Can., 3,056............C4 37
Ocean Gate, N.J., 706.D4 74
Ocean Grove, Mass., 1,200............*C5 65
Ocean Grove, N.J., 5,000............C4 74
Oceanlake, Oreg., 1,342.C3 80
Oceano, Calif., 1,317.*E3 50
Oceanport, N.J., 4,937.C4 74
Oceanside, Calif., 24,971............F5 50
Oceanside, N.Y., 30,448............*G2 52
Ocean Springs, Miss., 5,025............E3, E5 68
Oceanway, Fla., 1,271.B6 54
Ochiltree, co., Tex., 9,380............A2 84
Ocilla, Ga., 3,217......E3 55
Ockelbo, Swe., 2,490..G7 11
Ocnele Mari, Rom., 4,420............C7 10
Ocoee, Fla., 2,628.....D5 54

Oconee, co., Ga., 6,304.C3 55
Oconee, co., S.C., 40,204............B1 82
Oconomowoc, Wis., 6,682............E5 88
Oconto, Wis., 4,805...D6 88
Oconto, co., Wis., 25,110............D5 88
Oconto Falls, Wis., 2,331............D5 88
Ocotlán, Mex., 25,435........C4, m12 34
Oda, Ghana, 8,374.....G4 22
Odawara, Jap., 124,813............I9, n18 18
Odda, Nor., 5,197......G2 11
Odebolt, Iowa, 1,331..B2 60
Odell, Ill., 936........B5 58
Odem, Tex., 2,088.....F4 84
Odemis, Tur., 28,500..C6 14
Odendaalsrus, S. Afr., 15,126............F5 24
Odense, Den., 111,145..J4 11
Odense, co., Den., 196,213............*J4 11
Odenton, Md., 1,914...B4 53
Odessa, Mo., 2,034....C4 69
Odessa, Sov. Un., 696,000............H8 12
Odessa, Tex., 80,338...D1 84
Odessa, Wash., 1,231..B7 86
Odin, Ill., 1,242.......E4 58
Odon, Ind., 1,192......G4 59
O'Donnell, Tex., 1,356.C2 84
Odorhei, Rom., 14,162.B7 10
Oella, Md., 860........B4 53
Oelsnitz, Ger., 18,500.C6 6
Oelwein, Iowa, 8,282..B6 60
O'Fallon, Ill., 4,705...E4 58
O'Fallon, Mo., 3,770..A7 69
Offaly, co., Ire., 51,533............*D3 4
Offenbach, Ger., 116,200............C4 6
Offenburg, Ger., 27,600.D3 6
Ogaki, Jap., 102,478............I8, n15 18
Ogallala, Nebr., 4,250..C4 71
Ogbomosho, Nig., 139,535............G5 22
Ogden, Iowa, 1,525...B3 60
Ogden, Kans., 1,780...C7 61
Ogden, Pa., 1,600....*G11 81
Ogden, Utah, 70,197 (*141,400)......A6, C2 72
Ogden Dunes, Ind., 947............*A3 59
Ogdensburg, N.J., 1,212............A3 74
Ogdensburg, N.Y., 16,122............A1 75
Ogemaw, co., Mich., 9,680............D6 66
Ogle, co., Ill., 38,106..A4 58
Ogles, Ill., 1,000.....*E4 58
Oglesby, Ill., 4,215....B4 58
Oglethorp, Ga., 1,169.D2 55
Oglethorpe, co., Ga., 7,926............C3 55
Ogletown, Del., 3,500.*A6 53

Ogulin, Yugo., 3,519...C2 10
Ohara, Jap., 10,500...n19 18
O'Higgins, prov., Chile, 259,135............A2 28
Ohio, co., Ind., 4,165..G7 59
Ohio, co., Ky., 17,725..C3 62
Ohio, co., W. Va., 68,437............A4 87
Ohio, state, U.S., 9,706,397............ 78
Ohioville, Pa., 3,050.*E1 81
Ohrid, Yugo., 16,626..E5 10
Oil City, La., 1,430....B2 63
Oil City, Pa., 17,692..D2 81
Oildale, Calif., 19,000.E4 50
Oilton, Okla., 1,100...A5 79
Oise, dept., Fr., 481,289............*C5 5
Oita, Jap., 124,807....J5 18
Oita, pref., Jap., 1,239,655............*J5 18
Ojai, Calif., 4,495.....E4 50
Ojocaliente, Mex., 6,642............C4 34
Ojus, Fla., 5,000.....E3, G6 54
Oka, Que., Can., 1,243............D3, D8 42
Okaloosa, co., Fla., 61,175............G2 54
Okanogan, Wash., 2,001............A6 86
Okanogan, co., Wash., 25,520............A6 86
Okauchee, Wis., 1,879.*E5 88
Okawville, Ill., 931....E4 58
Okaya, Jap., 52,256............H9, m17 18
Okayama, Jap., 260,773............I6 18
Okayama, pref., Jap., 1,670,454............I6 18
Okazaki, Jap., 137,000.o16 18
Okecie, Pol., 10,000............B6, m13 7
Okeechobee, Fla., 2,947.E6 54
Okeechobee, co., Fla., 6,424............E6 54
Okeene, Okla., 1,164...A3 79
Okemah, Okla., 2,836.B5 79
Okemos, Mich., 1,000.*F6 66
Okfuskee, co., Okla., 11,706............B5 79
Okha, Sov. Un., 35,000............D17 13
Okhotsk, Sov. Un., 2,000............D17 13
Okinawa, isl., Ryukyu Is., 698,590............F10 17
Oklahoma, Pa., 983...*F2 81
Oklahoma, co., Okla., 439,506............B4 79
Oklahoma, state, U.S., 2,328,284............ 79
Oklahoma City, Okla., 324,253 (*448,300)...B4 79
Okmulgee, Okla., 15,951............B6 79
Okmulgee, co., Okla., 36,945............B6 79
Okolona, Ky., 7,000...A4 62

Okolona, Miss., 2,622..B5 68
Oktibbeha, co., Miss.,
  26,175..............B5 68
Olaa (Keaau), Haw.,
  1,334...............D6 56
Olathe, Kans., 10,987..D9 61
Olavarría, Arg., 24,204.B4 28
Olawa, Pol., 6,410......C4 7
Olbia, It., 11,000......D2 9
Olcott, N.Y., 1,215.....B2 75
Old Bethpage, N.Y.,
  3,000..............*G3 75
Old Bridge, N.J., 6,000.C4 74
Old Brookville, N.Y.,
  1,126..............*F2 75
Old Castile, reg., Sp.,
  2,218,884...........B4 8
Oldenburg [in Holstein]
  Ger., 9,350.........A5 6
Oldenburg [in Oldenburg]
  Ger., 125,200.......B4 6
Old Forge, Pa.,
  8,928.........A9, D10 81
Oldham, Eng., 115,426.D5 4
Oldham, co., Ky.,
  13,388.............B4 62
Oldham, co., Tex.,
  1,928..............B1 84
Old Hickory, Tenn.,
  5,000..........A5, E9 83
Old Hometown, Tenn.,
  2,500.............*B1 83
Old Orchard Beach,
  Maine, 4,580....E2, E5 64
Olds, Alta., Can., 2,433.D3 38
Old Saybrook, Conn.,
  1,671.............*D7 52
Old Tappan, N.J.,
  2,330.............*B4 74
Old Town, Maine,
  8,626..............D4 64
Oldtown, N.C., 1,000.*A3 76
Old Westbury, N.Y.,
  2,064.............*E3 75
Olean, N.Y., 21,868....C2 75
Oleiros, Sp., 76........A1 8
Olekminsk, Sov. Un.,
  5,500.............C15 13
Olesno, Pol., 6,058.....C5 7
Olhão, Port., 16,592...D2 8
Olímpia, Braz., 14,629..C3 30
Olimpo, dept., Par.,
  2,705..............D4 29
Olinda, Braz., 100,545.*D7 27
Oliva, Sp., 14,579......C5 8
Oliva de la Frontera, Sp.,
  11,314.............C2 8
Olive (Alexander Park),
  Va., 7,000........*E6 85
Olive Hill, Ky., 1,398..B6 62
Olivehurst, Calif.,
  4,835..............C2 50
Oliveira, Braz., 12,919..C4 30
Olivenza, Sp., 11,469...C2 8
Oliver, B.C., Can.,
  1,774..............E8 37
Oliver, Pa., 1,250......G2 81
Oliver, co., N. Dak.,
  2,610..............C4 77
Oliver Springs, Tenn.,
  1,163..............C9 83
Olivet, Mich., 1,185....F6 66
Olivette, Mo., 8,257..*C7 69
Olivia, Minn., 2,355....F4 67
Olkusz, Pol., 10,500...g11 17
Olla, La., 1,246.......C3 63
Olmos Park, Tex.
  2,457..............B3 84
Olmsted, Ohio, 4,773.*B1 78
Olmsted, co., Minn.,
  65,532.............G6 67
Olmsted Falls, Ohio,
  2,144..............B1 78
Olney, Ill., 8,780......E5 58
Olney, Md., 650........B3 53
Olney, Tex., 3,872.....C3 84
Olomouc, Czech.,
  70,100.............D4 7
Oloron-Ste. Marie, Fr.,
  12,778.............F3 5
Olot, Sp., 17,185......A7 8
Olshany, Sov. Un.,
  10,000............F10 12
Olsztyn, Pol., 68,000..B6 7
Olten, Switz., 20,044..E3 6
Oltenia, prov., Rom.,
  1,717,982.........*C6 10
Oltenia, reg., Rom....C6 10
Oltenita, Rom., 14,111.C8 10
Olton, Tex., 1,917.....B1 84
Olvera, Sp., 8,341.....D3 8
Olympia, Wash.,
  18,273.............B3 86
Olympia Fields, Ill.,
  1,503.............*B6 58
Olyphant, Pa.,
  5,864.........A9, D10 81
Omagh, N. Ire., 8,109..C3 4
Omaha, Nebr., 301,598
  (*434,800).....C9, D3 71
Omak, Wash., 4,068...A6 86

Omar, W. Va.,
  900............D3, D5 87
Omdurman, Sud.,
  113,551...........E4 23
Omega, Ga., 940......E3 55
Omigawa, Jap., 6,800..n19 18
Ominato, Jap., 21,600.F10 18
Ōmiya, Jap.,
  169,996.......I9, n18 18
Omro, Wis., 1,991....D5 88
Omsk, Sov. Un.,
  630,000...........D10 13
Omuta, Jap., 205,776...J5 18
Onalaska, Wis., 3,161..E2 88
Onancock, Va., 1,759..D7 85
Onarga, Ill., 1,397....C5 58
Onawa, Iowa, 3,176...B1 60
Onaway, Mich., 1,338..C6 66
Onda, Sp., 7,304......C5 8
Ondor Haan, Mong.,
  10,000............B7 17
Oneco, Fla.,
  1,530.........E4, F2 54
Onega, Sov. Un.,
  17,000............C6 13
Oneida, N.Y., 11,677..B5 75
Oneida, Ohio, 4,000...C3 78
Oneida, Tenn., 2,480..C9 83
Oneida, co., Idaho,
  3,603.............G6 57
Oneida, co., N.Y.,
  264,401...........B5 75
Oneida, co., Wis.,
  22,112............C4 88
Onega, Sov. Un.,
  17,000...........F18 11
O'Neill, Nebr., 3,181..B7 71
Oneonta, Ala., 4,136..B3 46
Oneonta, N.Y., 13,412.C5 75
Ono, Jap., 20,000....n15 18
Onomichi, Jap., 64,800.I6 18
Onondaga, N.Y.,
  1,500............*C4 75
Onondaga, co., N.Y.,
  423,028...........C4 75
Onset, Mass., 1,714...C6 65
Onslow, co., N.C.,
  82,706............C6 76
Ontario, Calif.,
  46,617........E5, F3 50
Ontario, Ohio, 3,049...B5 78
Ontario, Oreg., 5,101..C10 80
Ontario, co., Ont., Can.,
  135,895...........C5 41
Ontario, co., N.Y.,
  68,070............C3 75
Ontario, prov., Can.,
  6,236,092......... 41
Onteniente, Sp.,
  18,787............C5 8
Ontonagon, Mich.,
  2,358.............A5 66
Ontonagon, co., Mich.,
  10,584............A5 66
Oolitic, Ind., 1,140...G4 59
Oostburg, Wis., 1,065..E6 88
Oostende, Bel., 56,494..B5 5
Ootacamund, India,
  50,140............F6 20
Oot Park, N.Y., 1,500.*B4 75
Opal Cliffs, Calif.,
  3,825............*D2 50
Opa-Locka, Fla., 9,810.F3 54
Opatow, Pol., 5,459...C6 7
Opava, Czech., 42,500.D4 7
Opdal, Nor., 5,156....F3 11
Opelika, Ala., 15,678..C4 46
Opelousas, La., 17,417.D3 63
Opochka, Sov. Un.,
  10,000............C7 12
Opoczno, Pol., 7,433..C6 7
Opole, Pol., 61,000....C5 7
Opole Lubelskie, Pol.,
  5,574.............C6 7
Opp, Ala., 5,535......D3 46
Oppeln, see Opole, Pol.
Oppland, co., Nor.,
  162,519..........*G4 11
Opportunity, Wash.,
  12,465........B8, D8 86
Oquawka, Ill., 1,090...C3 58
Oradea, Rom., 99,007..B5 10
Oradell, N.J., 7,487...D5 74
Oran (Ouahran), Alg.,
  299,008...........A4 22
Oran, Mo., 1,090.....D8 69
Oran, dept., Alg.,
  1,990,729........*B5 22
Orange, Austl., 18,978..F8 25
Orange, Calif., 26,444..F3 50
Orange, Conn., 8,547..D4 52
Orange, Fr., 17,520...E6 5
Orange, Mass., 4,000..A3 65
Orange, N.J., 35,789...B4 74
Orange, Ohio, 2,006..*A6 78
Orange, Tex., 25,605..D6 84
Orange, Va., 2,955....C4 85
Orange, co., Calif.,
  703,925...........F5 50
Orange, co., Fla.,
  263,540...........D5 54

Orange, co., Ind.,
  16,877............G4 59
Orange, co., N.Y.,
  183,734...........D6 75
Orange, co., N.C.,
  42,970............A4 76
Orange, co., Tex.,
  60,357............D6 84
Orange, co., Vt.,
  16,014............D3 73
Orange, co., Va., 12,900.C4 85
Orangeburg, N.Y.,
  1,000.............C5 75
Orangeburg, S.C.,
  13,852............E6 82
Orangeburg, co., S.C.,
  68,559............E6 82
Orange City, Fla.,
  1,598.............D5 54
Orange City, Iowa,
  2,707.............B1 60
Orange Cove, Calif.,
  2,885............*D4 50
Orange Free State, prov.,
  S. Afr., 1,386,547..F5 24
Orange Grove, Tex.,
  1,109.............F4 84
Orange Park, Fla.,
  2,624.........B5, C6 54
Orangevale, Calif.,
  8,000............*C3 50
Orangeville, Ont., Can.,
  4,593.............D4 41
Oranienburg, Ger.,
  21,100............B6 6
Oras, Phil., 5,422.....H8 18
Orăştie, Rom., 10,488..C6 10
Oravița, Rom., 8,175...C5 10
Orchard Avenue, Wash.,
  5,000............*B8 86
Orchard Beach, Md.,
  1,691............*B4 53
Orchard Lake, Mich.,
  1,127............*F7 66
Orchard Park, N.Y.,
  3,278.............C2 75
Orcutt, Calif., 1,414...E3 50
Ord, Nebr., 2,413.....C7 71
Órdenes, Sp., 1,311...A1 8
Ordu, Tur., 20,200....B11 14
Orduña, Sp., 5,950....A4 8
Ordville, Nebr., 950...C2 71
Ordway, Colo., 1,254...C7 51
Ordzhonikidze, see
  Yenakiyevo, Sov. Un.
Ordzhonikidze
  (Dzaudzhikau),
  Sov. Un., 175,000....E7 13
Ordzhonikidzegrad, see
  Bezhitsa, Sov. Un.
Örebro, Swe.,
  76,200........H6, t33 11
Örebro, co., Swe.,
  263,300..........*H6 11
Oregon, Ill., 3,732....G4 58
Oregon, Mo., 887.....B2 69
Oregon, Ohio,
  13,319........A2, A4 78
Oregon, Wis., 1,701...F4 88
Oregon, co., Mo., 9,845.E6 69
Oregon, state, U.S.,
  1,768,687......... 80
Oregon City, Oreg.,
  7,996.........B2, B4 80
Orekhov, Sov. Un.,
  10,000...........H10 12
Orekhovo-Zuyevo, Sov.
  Un., 112,000...D12, n18 12
Orel, Sov. Un.,
  167,000..........E11 12
Oreland, Pa., 6,700..*F11 81
Orenburg, Sov. Un.,
  282,000...........D8 13
Orense, prov., Sp.,
  451,474..........*A2 8
Orestias, Grc., 10,281..B6 14
Orgeyev, Sov. Un.,
  10,000............H7 12
Oriente, prov., Cuba,
  1,797,606.........E6 35
Orihuela, Sp., 14,200..C5 8
Orillia, Ont., Can.,
  15,345............C5 41
Orinda, Calif., 10,280.*B5 50
Orion, Ill., 1,135.....B5 58
Oriskany, N.Y., 1,580..B5 75
Oriskany Falls, N.Y.,
  972...............C5 75
Orissa, state, India,
  17,548,846........E7 20
Oristano, It., 14,300...E2 9
Orizaba, Mex.,
  69,672........D5, n15 34
Orkney, co., Scot.,
  18,743...........*A5 4
Orkney, is., Scot.....*A5 4
Orland, Calif., 2,534...C2 50
Orlando, Fla., 88,135
  (*255,800).........D5 54
Orland Park, Ill., 2,592.F2 58

Orléanais, former prov.,
  Fr., 782,000.......D4 5
Orléans, Fr., 84,233...D4 5
Orleans, Ind., 1,659...G5 59
Orleans, Mass., 900...C8 65
Orleans, Nebr., 608...D6 71
Orleans, Vt., 1,240....B3 73
Orleans, co., N.Y.,
  34,159............B2 75
Orleans, co., Vt.,
  20,143............B3 73
Orleans, par., La.,
  627,525...........E6 63
Orléansville, see El
  Asnam, Alg.
Orlovista, Fla., 4,000..D5 54
Orlovo, Sov. Un.,
  9,000............E17 13
Ormoc, Phil., 8,000..*C6 19
Ormond Beach, Fla.,
  8,658.............C5 54
Ormsby, co., Nev.,
  8,063.............B2 72
Ormstown, Que., Can.,
  1,527.............D3 42
Orne, dept., Fr.,
  280,549..........*C3 5
Örnsköldsvik, Swe.,
  8,400.............F8 11
Orofino, Idaho, 2,471..C2 57
Oro Grande, Calif., 800.E5 50
Orono, Maine, 8,341...D4 64
Orono, Minn., 5,643..*E5 67
Oronogo, Mo., 513....D3 69
Oroquieta, Phil.,
  7,233............*D6 19
Oroshaza, Hung.,
  26,000............B5 10
Oroville, Calif., 6,115..C3 50
Oroville, Wash., 1,437..A6 86
Orpington, Eng.,
  80,271...........m13 4
Orrville, Ohio, 6,511...B6 78
Orsha, Sov. Un.,
  71,000............D8 12
Orsk, Sov. Un.,
  195,000...........D8 13
Orșova, Rom., 6,527...C6 10
Orthez, Fr., 5,125.....F3 5
Ortigueira, Sp., 1,590..A2 8
Orting, Wash., 1,520..B3 86
Ortona a Mare, It.,
  10,700............C5 9
Ortonville, Minn.,
  2,674.............E2 67
Oruro, Bol., 62,975....C2 29
Oruro, dept., Bol.,
  210,260...........C2 29
Orvieto, It., 9,600....C4 9
Orwigsburg, Pa., 2,131.E9 81
Oryakhovo, Bul., 6,972.D6 10
Osage, Iowa, 3,753....A5 60
Osage, co., Kans.,
  12,886............D8 61
Osage, co., Mo., 10,867.C6 69
Osage, co., Okla.,
  32,441............A4 79
Osage Beach, Mo., 741.C5 69
Osage City, Kans.,
  2,213.............D8 61
Osaka, Jap., 3,011,563
  (*8,050,000)....I7, o14 18
Osaka, Jap., 2,700....n16 18
Osaka, pref., Jap.,
  5,504,746........*I7 18
Osakis, Minn., 1,396...E3 67
Osawatomie, Kans.,
  4,622.............D9 61
Osborne, Kans., 2,049..C5 61
Osborne, co., Kans.,
  7,506.............C5 61
Osbornsville, N.J., 900.C4 74
Osburn, Idaho, 1,788..B3 57
Osceola, Ark., 7,055...B6 49
Osceola, Ind., 1,350...A5 59
Osceola, Iowa, 3,350...C4 60
Osceola, Mo., 1,066...C4 69
Osceola, Nebr., 1,013..C8 71
Osceola, Wis., 942....C1 88
Osceola, co., Fla.,
  19,029............D5 54
Osceola, co., Iowa,
  10,064............A2 60
Osceola, co., Mich.,
  13,595............E5 66
Osceola Mills, Pa.,
  1,777.............E5 81
Oschatz, Ger., 15,500..C6 6
Oschersleben, Ger.,
  19,100............B5 6
Oscoda, co., Mich.,
  3,447.............D6 66
Osgood, Ind., 1,434...F7 59
Osh, Sov. Un., 79,000.E10 13
Oshamambe, Jap.,
  10,500...........E10 18
Oshawa, Ont., Can.,
  62,415............D6 41
Oshkosh, Nebr., 1,025..C3 71

Oshkosh, Wis.,
45,110.........B5, D5 88
Oshogbo, Nig., 122,728.G5 22
Osijek, Yugo., 58,600...C4 10
Osinniki, Sov. Un.,
71,000.........*D11 13
Osipenko, Sov. Un.,
70,000.........H11 12
Oskaloosa, Iowa,
11,053.........C5 60
Oskarshamn, Swe.,
12,900.........I7 12
Oslo, Nor., 477,100
(*635,000).....H4, p28 12
Osmaniye, Tur.,
29,300.........D11 14
Osnabrück, Ger.,
138,800.........B4 6
Osorno, Chile, 55,000..C2 28
Osorno, prov., Chile,
143,955.........C2 28
Oss, Neth., 30,700.....B6 5
Osseo, Minn., 2,104...E6 67
Osseo, Wis., 1,144....D2 88
Ossian, Ind., 1,108....C7 59
Ossining, N.Y.,
18,662.........D3, D7 75
Ostashkov, Sov. Un.,
10,000.........C9 12
Östergötland, co., Swe.,
358,000.........*H6 11
Osterode, see Ostrod, Pol.
Östersund, Swe., 24,900.F6 11
Osterville, Mass., 1,094.C7 65
Östfold, co., Nor.,
202,700.........*H4 11
Ostrava, Czech.,
234,700.........D5 7
Ostróda, Pol., 15,200...B5 7
Ostrogozhsk, Sov. Un.,
10,000.........F12 12
Ostroleka, Pol., 11,700.B6 7
Ostrov, Czech., 16,600..C2 7
Ostrov, Sov. Un.,
10,000.........C7 12
Ostrow, Pol., 12,900...B6 7
Ostrowiec, Pol., 38,000.C6 7
Ostrow Wielkopolski, Pol.,
42,000.........C4 7
Ostrzeszow, Pol., 5,403.C4 7
Ostuni, It., 23,500....D6 9
Osuna, Sp., 19,569.....D3 8
Oswego, Ill., 1,510....B5 58
Oswego, Kans., 2,027..E8 61
Oswego, N.Y., 22,155..B4 75
Oswego, co., N.Y.,
86,118.........B4 75

Oswestry, Eng.,
11,193.........D5 4
Oswiecim, Pol.,
31,000.........C5, G10 7
Otaki, Jap., 4,600.....N19 18
Otaru, Jap., 198,511..E10 18
Otavalo, Ec., 8,379....A2 31
Otay, Calif., 1,500....*F5 50
Oteen, N.C., 1,000....D3 76
Otero, co., Colo.,
24,128.........D7 51
Otero, co., N. Mex.,
36,976.........C6 48
Othello, Wash., 2,669..C6 86
Otisville, N.Y., 896...*D6 75
Otoe, co., Nebr.,
16,503.........D9 71
Otsego, Mich., 4,142...F5 66
Otsego, co., Mich.,
7,545.........C6 66
Otsego, co., N.Y.,
51,942.........C5 75
Ōtsu, Jap., 38,402....*o14 18
Ōtsu, Jap., 113,547...o14 18
Ottawa, Ont., Can.,
268,206
(*429,750).....A9, B9 41
Ottawa, Ill., 19,408...B5 58
Ottawa, Kans., 10,673.D8 61
Ottawa, Ohio, 3,245...A3 78
Ottawa, co., Kans.
6,779.........C6 61
Ottawa, co., Mich.
98,719.........F4 66
Ottawa, co., Ohio,
35,323.........A4 78
Ottawa, co., Okla.,
28,301.........A7 79
Ottawa Hills, Ohio,
3,870.........A2, A4 78
Otter Tail, co., Minn.,
48,960.........D3 67
Ottumwa, Iowa,
33,871.........C5 60
Otwock, Pol., 36,000..M14 7
Ouachita, co., Ark.,
31,641.........D3 49
Ouachita, par., La.,
101,663.........B3 63
Ouagadougou, Upper
Volta, 63,000.........F4 22
Ouahigouya, Upper Volta,
10,000.........F4 22
Ouargla, Alg., 6,456...B6 22
Oudtshoorn, S. Afr.,
22,229.........G4 24
Ouezzane, Mor., 26,203.B3 22
Ouidah, Dah., 14,000..G5 22

Oullins, Fr., 24,356....E6 5
Oulu, Fin., 58,300....E11 11
Oulu, dept., Fin.,
338,243.........*E11 11
Ouray, Colo., 785......C3 51
Ouray, co., Colo.,
1,601.........C3 51
Ourinhos, Braz.,
25,717.........C3 30
Ouro Fino, Braz.,
8,044.........C3, M8 30
Ouro Prêto, Braz.,
14,722.........C4 30
Outagamie, co., Wis.,
101,794.........D5 88
Outes, Sp., 869........A1 8
Outlook, Sask., Can.,
1,340.........F2 39
Outreau, Fr., 13,548...B4 5
Outremont, Que., Can.,
30,753.........D4 42
Ovada, It., 9,594.....B2 9
Ovalle, Chile, 26,000...A2 28
Ovar, Port., 7,298....B1 8
Overijssel, prov., Neth.,
783,400.........*A7 5
Overland, Mo., 22,763..C7 69
Overland Park, Kans.,
21,110.........B9 61
Overlea, Md.,
10,795.........B4, C3 53
Overton, Nev., 700....C4 72
Overton, Tex., 1,950...C5 84
Overton, co., Tenn.,
14,661.........C8 83
Ovid, Mich., 1,505....E6 66
Oviedo, Fla., 1,926...D5 54
Oviedo, Sp., 127,058...A3 8
Oviedo, prov., Sp.,
989,344.........*A3 8
Ovruch, Sov. Un.,
10,000.........F7 12
Owasso, Okla., 2,032...A6 79
Owatonna, Minn.,
13,409.........F5 67
Owego, N.Y., 5,417....C4 75
Owen, Wis., 1,098.....D3 88
Owen, co., Ind.,
11,400.........F4 59
Owen, co., Ky., 8,237..B5 62
Owens, N.C., 5,207...*B5 76
Owensboro, Ky.,
42,471.........C3 62
Owensboro East, Ky.,
2,244.........*C3 62
Owensboro West, Ky.,
1,366.........*C3 62
Owen Sound, Ont., Can.,
17,421.........C4 41

Owensville, Ind., 1,121.H2 59
Owensville, Mo., 2,379.C6 69
Owenton, Ky., 1,376...B5 62
Owings Mills, Md.,
3,810.........*B4 53
Owingsville, Ky., 1,040.B6 62
Owosso, Mich., 17,006..E6 66
Owsley, co., Ky., 5,369.C6 62
Owyhee, co., Idaho,
6,375.........G2 57
Oxbow, Mich., 1,700..*F7 66
Oxelösund, Swe.,
10,000.........u35 11
Oxford, Ala., 3,603....B4 46
Oxford, N.S., Can.,
1,471.........D6 43
Oxford, Eng., 106,124..E6 4
Oxford, Ga., 1,047....C3 55
Oxford, Ind., 1,108....C3 59
Oxford, Kans., 989....E6 61
Oxford, Mass., 6,985..B4 65
Oxford, Mich., 2,357...F7 66
Oxford, Miss., 5,283...A4 68
Oxford, Nebr., 1,090..D6 71
Oxford, N.J., 950.....B3 74
Oxford, N.Y., 1,871...C5 75
Oxford, N.C., 6,978...A5 76
Oxford, Ohio, 7,828...C3 78
Oxford, Pa., 3,376....G10 81
Oxford, co., Ont., Can.,
70,499.........D4 41
Oxford, co., Eng.,
309,458.........*E6 4
Oxford, co., Maine,
44,345.........D2 64
Oxnard, Calif., 40,265..E4 50
Oxnard Beach, Calif.,
2,000.........*E4 50
Oyo, Nig., 72,133.....G5 22
Oyonnax, Fr., 14,830..D6 5
Oyrot-Tura, see Gorno-
Altaysk, Sov. Un.
Oyster Bay, N.Y.,
6,500.........D3, E7 75
Oyster Bay Cove, N.Y.,
988.........*E7 75
Ozamiz, Phil., 13,000..D6 19
Ozark, Ala., 9,534....D4 46
Ozark, Ark., 1,965....B2 49
Ozark, Mo., 1,536....D4 69
Ozark, co., Mo., 6,744.E5 69
Ozaukee, co., Wis.,
38,441.........E6 88
Ozd, Hung., 34,155.....A5 10
Ozieri, It., 11,884....D2 9
Ozona, Fla., 700......E1 54
Ozona, Tex., 3,361....D2 84
Ozorkow, Pol., 14,800..C5 7
Ozu, Jap., 17,100.....J6 18

P

Paarl, S. Afr., 41,540..G3 24
Paauilo, Haw., 1,059...C6 56
Pabianice, Pol., 56,000.C5 7
Pabna, Pak., 32,240...D8 20
Pacasmayo, Peru,
6,615.........C2 31
Pace, Fla., 900.......C2 54
Pacheco, Calif., 1,518.*C2 50
Pachuca [de Soto], Mex.,
64,564.........C5, m14 34
Pacific, Mo., 2,795.B7, C7 69
Pacific, Wash., 1,577...D2 86
Pacific, co., Wash.,
14,674.........C2 86
Pacifica, Calif., 20,995.*B5 50
Pacific Grove, Calif.,
12,121.........C6, D3 50
Pacolet, S.C., 1,252....B4 82
Pacolet Mills, S.C.,
1,476.........B4 82
Paczkow, Pol., 6,955...C4 7
Padang, Indon.,
143,615.........F2 19
Paden City, W. Va.,
3,137.........B4 87
Paderborn, Ger.,
54,000.........C4 6
Paducah, Ky., 34,479.A2 62
Paducah, Tex., 2,392..B2 84
Pagadian, Phil., 9,839.*D6 19
Page, Ariz., 2,960.....A4 48
Page, W. Va., 800.C3, D6 87
Page, co., Iowa, 21,023.D2 60
Page, co., Va., 15,572..C4 85
Pagedale, Mo., 5,106..*A8 69
Pageland, S.C., 2,020...B7 82
Page Manor, Ohio,
5,000.........C3 78
Pago Pago, Am. Sam.,
1,251.........*G9 2
Pagosa Springs, Colo.,
1,374.........D3 51
Pahala, Haw., 1,602...D6 56
Pahang, state, Mala.,
315,058.........E2 19
Pahlavi, Iran., 37,511..A7 23
Pahoa, Haw., 1,046....D7 56

Pahokee, Fla., 4,709...F6 54
Paia, Haw., 3,195.....C5 56
Painesville, Ohio,
16,116.........A6 78
Paint, Pa., 1,275.....*F4 81
Painted Post, N.Y.,
2,570.........C3 75
Paintsville, Ky., 4,025..C7 62
Paisley, Scot., 95,753..C4 4
Paita, Peru, 7,177....C1 31
Pajaro, Calif., 1,273..*D3 50
Pakistan, country, Asia,
93,831,982......C4, D9 20
Pak Lay, Laos, 10,000.*B2 19
Pakokku, Bur.,
30,943.........D10 20
Paks, Hung., 10,452...B4 10
Pakse, Laos, 25,000...B3 19
Palacios, Tex., 3,676..E4 84
Palafrugell, Sp., 7,905.B7 8
Palaiseau, Fr., 16,326..h9 5
Palamós, Sp., 7,639...B7 8
Palana, Sov. Un.,
1,000.........D19 13
Palanpur, India,
29,139.........D5 20
Palas de Rey, Sp.,
769.........A2 9
Palatine, Ill.,
15,189.........A5, E2 58
Palatka, Fla., 11,028..C5 54
Palawan, prov., Phil.,
162,900.........C5 19
Palazzolo Acreide, It.,
11,024.........F5 9
Palembang, Indon.,
458,661.........F2 19
Palencia, Sp., 48,216..A3 9
Palencia, prov., Sp.,
231,977.........*A3 8
Palermo, It., 587,985..E4 9
Palestine, Ill., 1,564..D6 58
Palestine, Tex., 13,974.D5 84
Palestine, reg., Asia...C2 15
Palestrina, It., 9,154..h9 9
Palghat, India, 77,620..F6 20
Palisades, Idaho, 75..*F7 57

Palisades Park, N.J.,
11,943.........D5 74
Palma del Rio, Sp.,
11,324.........D3 8
Palma [de Mallorca], Sp.,
159,084.........C7 7
Palmares, Braz.,
17,327.........*D7 27
Palma Soriano, Cuba,
25,241.........E6 35
Palm Bay, Fla., 2,808..D6 54
Palm Beach, Fla., 6,055.F6 54
Palm Beach, co., Fla.,
228,106.........F6 54
Palmdale, Calif.,
11,522.........E4 50
Palm Desert, Calif.,
1,295.........*F5 50
Palmeira dos Indios,
Braz., 15,642.....*D7 27
Palmer, Alsk.,
1,181.........C10, g17 47
Palmer, Mass., 3,888..B3 65
Palmer, Tenn., 1,069..D8 83
Palmer Heights, Pa.,
2,597.........*E11 81
Palmer Park, Md.,
4,000.........*C4 53
Palmerston, Ont., Can.,
1,554.........D4 41
Palmerston North, N.Z.,
41,014 (*43,185)...N15 26
Palmerton, Pa., 5,942.E10 81
Palmetto, Fla.,
5,556.........E4, F2 54
Palmetto, Ga., 1,466...C2 55
Palm Harbor, Fla.,
1,000.........E2 54
Palmi, It., 15,400.....E5 9
Palmira, Col., 54,293..C2 32
Palmira, Cuba, 5,865..D3 35
Palm Springs, Calif.,
13,468.........F5 50
Palm Springs, Fla.,
2,503.........*F6 54
Palmyra, Mo., 2,933..B6 69
Palmyra, N.J., 7,036...C2 74
Palmyra, N.Y., 3,476..B3 75

Palmyra, Pa., 6,999....F8 81
Palmyra, Wis., 1,000...F5 88
Palo Alto, Calif.,
52,287.........B5, D2 50
Palo Alto, Pa., 1,445..*E9 81
Palo Alto, co., Iowa,
14,736.........A3 60
Palombara Sabina, It.,
6,215.........g9 9
Palo Pinto, co., Tex.,
20,516.........C3 84
Palos Heights, Ill.,
3,775.........*F3 58
Palos Hills, Ill., 3,766.*F2 58
Palos Park, Ill., 2,169.*A6 58
Palos Verdes Estates,
Calif., 9,654.....*F2 50
Palouse, Wash., 926...C8 86
Pameskasan, Indon.,
24,912.........G4 19
Pamiers, Fr., 13,297...F4 5
Pamlico, co., N.C.,
9,850.........B7 76
Pampa, Tex., 24,664...B2 84
Pampanga, prov., Phil.,
615,800.........*B6 19
Pampas, reg., Arg....G4 27
Pamplico, S.C., 988...D8 82
Pamplona, Col., 16,396.B3 32
Pamplona, Sp., 97,880..A5 8
Pana, Ill., 6,432......D4 58
Panagyurishte, Bul.,
12,015.........D7 10
Panama, Okla., 937...B7 79
Panamá, Pan., 273,440.B2 32
Panama, country, N.A.,
1,075,541.........B1 32
Panama City, Fla.,
33,275.........G3 54
Panay, isl., Phil......*C6 19
Pancevo, Yugo., 40,740.C5 10
Pandharpur, India,
45,421.........E6 20
Pando, Ur., 6,248....E1 30
Pando, dept., Bol.,
19,804.........B2 29
Panevezys, Sov. Un.,
37,100.........D5 12

Panfilov, Sov. Un.,
27,300.............E10 13
Pangasinan, prov., Phil.,
1,124,800...........*B6 19
Pangkalpinang, Indon.,
58,540..............F3 19
Panguitch, Utah, 1,435.C5 72
Panjim, India, 31,950..E5 20
Panna, India, 16,737...D7 20
Panola, co., Miss.,
28,791..............A3 68
Panola, co., Tex.,
16,870..............C5 84
Panora, Iowa, 1,019....C3 60
Pantelleria, It., 2,294...F3 9
Pantin, Fr., 46,292....g10 5
Pánuco, Mex.,
8,688............C5, k14 34
Paola, It., 9,197......E6 9
Paola, Kans., 4,784....D9 61
Paoli, Ind., 2,754.....G5 59
Paoli, Pa., 5,000......A10 81
Paonia, Colo., 1,083...C3 51
Paoting (Tsingyuan),
China, 265,000.....D8 17
Paotow, China,
400,000............C7 17
Paoying, China,
85,000.............C7 17
Papa, Hung., 25,629...B3 10
Papaikou, Haw., 1,427.D6 56
Papantla, Mex.,
18,579...........C5, m15 34
Papeete, Fr. Polynesia,
12,428.............H11 2
Papenburg, Ger.,
15,000.............B3 6
Papillion, Nebr.,
2,235...........C9, E3 71
Papineau, co., Que., Can.,
32,697.............D2 42
Papineauville, Que., Can.,
1,300..............D2 42
Papua, Austl. dep.,
Oceania, 374,000....k12 25
Pará, state, Braz.,
1,550,935..........*D6 27
Paracatú, Braz., 5,909..B3 30
Paracin, Yugo., 15,627.D5 10
Paradise, Calif., 8,268..C3 50
Paradise, Pa., 750.....F9 81
Paradise Valley, Ariz.,
1,000..............D2 48
Paragould, Ark., 9,947.A5 49
Paraguaçu Paulista, Braz.,
11,391.............C2 30
Paraguarí, Par., 12,405.E4 29
Paraguarí, dept., Par.,
159,161............E4 29
Paraguay, country, S.A.,
1,638,000..........D4 29
Paraíba, state, Braz.,
2,018,023..........*D7 27
Paraíba do Sul, Braz.,
7,675..............h6 30
Paraiso, C.Z., 3,113...*B2 32
Paraisópolis, Braz.,
6,582..............C3 30
Parakhino-Poddubye,
Sov. Un., 20,000....B9 12
Paramaribo, Sur.,
75,233.............C5 27
Paramé, Fr., 8,811....C2 5
Paramount, Calif.,
27,249.............*F2 50
Paramus, N.J., 23,238.*B4 74
Paraná, Arg., 110,000..A4 28
Paraná, state, Braz.,
4,227,763..........C2 30
Paranaguá, Braz.,
27,728.............D3 30
Paray-le-Monial, Fr.,
9,557..............D6 5
Parchim, Ger., 18,900.B5 6
Parchment, Mich.,
1,565..............F5 66
Pardeeville, Wis., 1,331.E4 88
Pardes Hanna, Isr.,
7,073..............B2 15
Pardubice, Czech.,
52,700.............C3 7
Parent, Que., Can.,
1,298.............*B5 42
Parintins, Braz.,
9,068.............*D5 27
Paris, Ark., 3,007....B2 49
Paris, Ont., Can.,
5,820..............D4 41
Paris, Fr., 2,790,091
(*7,750,000)....C5, g10 5
Paris, Idaho, 746.....G7 57
Paris, Ill., 9,823.....D6 58
Paris, Ky., 7,791.....B5 62
Paris, Mo., 1,393.....B5 69
Paris, S.C., 1,000....*B3 82
Paris, Tenn., 9,325....A3 83
Paris, Tex., 20,977...C5 84
Park, co., Colo., 1,822..B5 51
Park, co., Mont.,
13,168.............E6 70

Park, co., Wyo., 16,874.A3 89
Park City, Ill., 1,408..*A6 58
Park City, Kans.,
2,687..............B5 61
Park City, Utah,
1,366...........A6, C2 72
Parkdale, P.E.I., Can.,
1,735.............*C6 43
Parke, co., Ind., 14,804.E3 59
Parker, Ariz., 1,642...B1 48
Parker, Fla., 2,669....G3 54
Parker, Pa., 945......D2 81
Parker, S. Dak., 1,142.G8 77
Parker, co., Tex.,
22,880.............C4 84
Parker City, Ind.,
1,181..............D7 59
Parkersburg, Iowa,
1,468..............B5 60
Parkersburg, W. Va.,
44,797.............B3 87
Parkers Prairie, Minn.,
884................D3 67
Parkes, Austl., 8,223..F7 26
Parkesburg, Pa.,
2,759.............G10 81
Park Falls, Wis., 2,919.C3 88
Park Forest, Ill., 29,993.F3 58
Park Hill, Ont., Can.,
1,169..............D3 41
Park Hills, Ky., 4,076..A7 62
Parkin, Ark., 1,489....B5 49
Parkland, Pa., 1,200..*F11 81
Parkland, Wash.,
15,000.............E1 86
Parklawn, Va., 1,000..*C5 85
Park Place, S.C.,
1,600.............*B3 82
Park Rapids, Minn.,
3,047..............D3 67
Park Ridge, Ill., 35,430.E2 58
Park Ridge, N.J.,
6,389..............C5 74
Park Ridge Manor, Ill.,
1,000.............*E2 58
Park River, N. Dak.,
1,813..............B8 77
Parkrose, Oreg.,
24,000............*B2 80
Parkside, Pa., 2,426..*G11 81
Parkston, S. Dak.,
1,514..............G8 77
Parksville, B.C., Can.,
1,183.............*E5 37
Parkton, N.C., 906....C4 76
Parkview, Ohio, 2,018.*A6 78
Parkview, Pa., 1,000..*E2 81
Parkville, Md., 27,236..C3 53
Parkville, Mo.,
1,229..........B3, E2 69
Parkville, Pa., 1,300...*G8 81
Parkway Village, Ky.,
949...............*B4 62
Parkwood, Md., 1,400.*B3 53
Parlier, Calif., 1,366..*D4 50
Parma, Idaho, 1,295...F2 57
Parma, It., 141,203...B3 9
Parma, Mo., 1,060....E8 96
Parma, Ohio,
82,845..........A6, B2 78
Parma Heights, Ohio,
18,100.............B2 78
Parmer, co., Tex.,
9,583..............B1 84
Parnaiba, Braz.,
39,951.............D6 27
Pärnu, Sov. Un.,
43,000.............B5 12
Parowan, Utah, 1,486..C5 72
Parral, Chile, 10,717..B2 28
Parras de la Fuente, Mex.,
19,499.............B4 34
Parrish, Ala., 1,608...B2 46
Parrish, Fla., 800..E4, F2 54
Parrsboro, N.S., Can.,
1,834..............D5 43
Parry Is., N.W. Ter.,
Can...............m30 36
Parry Sound, co., Ont.,
Can., 29,632.......B4 41
Parry Sound, Ont., Can.,
6,004..........B4, F9 41
Parshall, N. Dak.,
1,216..............C3 77
Parsippany, N.J.,
3,500.............*B4 74
Parsons, Kans., 13,929.E8 61
Parsons, Tenn., 1,859..B3 83
Parsons, W. Va., 1,798.B5 87
Parthenay, Fr., 8,350..D3 5
Partinico, It., 26,119...E4 9
Pasadena, Calif.,
116,407.........E4, F2 50
Pasadena, Md., 2,000..B4 53
Pasadena, Tex., 58,737.F5 84
Pasadena Hills, Mo.,
1,315.............*C7 69
Pasadena Park, Wash.,
2,000.............*B8 86
Pasay (Rizal), Phil.,
132,200........C6, o13 19

Pascagoula, Miss.,
17,155..........E3, E5 68
Pașcani [-Garǎ], Rom.,
15,008.............B8 10
Pasco, Wash., 14,522...C6 86
Pasco, co., Fla., 36,785.D4 54
Pasco, dept., Peru,
130,507............D2 31
Pascoag, R.I., 2,983..B10 42
Pas-de-Calais, dept., Fr.,
1,366,282..........B5 5
Pasewalk, Ger., 12,400.B7 6
Pasig, Phil., 61,900....o13 19
Paso de los Libres, Arg.,
11,665.............E4 29
Paso Robles, Calif.,
6,677..............E3 50
Pasquotank, co., N.C.,
25,630..............A7 76
Pasrur, Pak, 9,403....B5 20
Passaic, N.J.,
53,963..........B4, D5 74
Passaic, co., N.J.,
406,618............A4 74
Passau, Ger., 31,800...D6 6
Pass Christian, Miss.,
3,881..........E2, E4 68
Passo Fundo, Braz.,
47,299.............D2 30
Passos, Braz., 28,555...C3 30
Pastaza, prov., Ec.....B2 31
Pasto, Col., 59,500.....C2 32
Pasuruan, Indon.,
62,872.............G4 19
Patagonia, reg., Arg...H4 27
Pataskala, Ohio, 1,046..B5 78
Patchogue, N.Y., 8,938.D4 75
Paternò, It., 42,935....F5 9
Paterson, N.J.,
143,663.........B4, D5 74
Pathankot, India,
46,330.............B6 20
Pathfork, Ky., 500....D6 62
Patiala, India, 125,234.B6 20
Patna, India, 363,700..C8 20
Patos, Braz., 27,275..*D7 27
Patos de Minas, Braz.,
31,471.............B3 30
Patrai, Grc., 95,364....C3 14
Patrick, co., Va.,
15,282.............E2 85
Patrocínio, Braz.,
13,933.............B3 30
Pattani, Thai., 16,534..D2 19
Patten, Maine, 1,099...C4 64
Patterson, Calif., 2,429.B6 50
Patterson, La., 2,923...E4 63
Patterson Gardens, Mich.,
1,747.............*G7 63
Patton, Pa., 2,880....E4 81
Pátzcuaro, Mex.,
14,281........D4, n13 34
Patzicía, Guat., 5,021.*E6 34
Patzún, Guat., 5,103..*E6 34
Pau, Fr., 59,937......F3 5
Paudalho, Braz.,
6,889.............*D7 27
Pauk, Bur., 5,000....D9 20
Paulding, Ohio, 2,936..A3 78
Paulding, co., Ga.,
13,101............C2 55
Paulding, co., Ohio,
16,792.............A3 78
Paulina (Remy), La.,
1,014.............*D5 63
Paulis, Con. L., 9,700..H3 23
Paullina, Iowa, 1,329..B2 60
Paulsboro, N.J., 8,121.D2 74
Pauls Valley, Okla.,
6,856..............C4 79
Paungde, Bur., 17,286.E10 20
Pavia, It., 74,962.....B2 9
Pavlodar, Sov. Un.,
107,000...........D10 13
Pavlograd, Sov. Un.,
43,000............G10 12
Pavlovo, Sov. Un.,
53,000............D14 12
Pavlovsk, Sov. Un.,
30,000............F13 12
Pavlovskiy Posad, Sov.
Un., 58,000........n18 12
Pawcatuck, Conn.,
6,000..............D9 52
Paw Creek, N.C.,
2,000..............B3 76
Pawhuska, Okla., 5,414.A5 79
Pawling, N.Y., 1,734...D7 75
Pawnee, Ill., 1,517....D4 58
Pawnee, Okla., 2,303...A5 79
Pawnee, co., Kans.,
10,254.............D4 61
Pawnee, co., Nebr.,
5,356..............D9 71
Pawnee, co., Okla.,
10,884.............A5 79
Pawnee City, Nebr.,
1,343..............D9 71
Paw Paw, Mich., 2,970.F5 66
Paw Paw, W. Va., 789.B6 87

Paw Paw Lake, Mich.,
3,518.............*F4 66
Pawtucket, R.I.,
81,001............B11 52
Paxtang, Pa., 1,916...*F8 81
Paxton, Ill., 4,370.....C5 58
Payen, China, 5,000...C3 18
Payette, Idaho, 4,451..E2 57
Payette, co., Idaho,
12,363.............E2 57
Payne, Ohio, 1,287.....A3 78
Payne, co., Okla.,
44,231.............A5 79
Paynesville, Minn.,
1,754..............E4 67
Paysandú, Ur., 44,800..E1 30
Paysandú, dept., Ur.,
78,400............*E1 30
Payson, Utah,
4,237..........A6, D2 72
Pazardzhik, Bul.,
30,430.............D7 10
Pazin, Yugo., 3,004....C1 10
Peabody, Kans.,
1,309..........A6, D6 61
Peabody, Mass.,
32,202.........A6, C3 65
Peace Dale, R.I.,
2,000.............D11 52
Peace River, Alta., Can.,
2,543..............A2 38
Peach, co., Ga.,
13,846.............D3 55
Peach Creek, W. Va.,
700................D5 87
Pearisburg, Va., 2,268..D2 85
Pearl, Miss., 5,081....*C3 68
Pearland, Tex., 1,497..F5 84
Pearl Beach, Mich.,
1,224............*F8 66
Pearl City, Haw.,
8,200........B4, g10 56
Pearl River, La., 964..D6 63
Pearl River, N.Y.,
9,000..............D1 57
Pearl River, co., Miss.,
22,411............E4 68
Pearl Ridge, Tex.,
3,470..............E2 63
Pearsall, Tex., 4,957...E3 84
Pearson, Ga., 1,615....E4 55
Pebane, Moz., 5,000...D7 24
Peč, Yugo., 28,297....D5 10
Peçanha, Braz., 3,602..B4 30
Pecatonica, Ill., 1,659..A4 58
Pechenga, Sov. Un.,
13,200.............C6 13
Peckville (Blakely), Pa.,
6,374..............A9 81
Pecos, N. Mex., 584..*B6 48
Pecos, Tex., 12,728.D1, F2 84
Pecos, co., Tex., 11,957.D1 84
Pecs, Hung., 114,713..B4 10
Pedley, Calif., 1,600...*F3 50
Pedreiras, Braz.,
10,189............*D6 27
Pedricktown, N.J.,
645................D2 74
Pedro Juan Caballero,
Par., 12,521.......D4 29
Pedro Velho, Braz.,
2,041..............D7 27
Peebles, Ohio, 1,601...D4 78
Peebles, Scot., 5,545...C4 4
Peebles, co., Scot.,
14,117............*C5 4
Peekskill, N.Y.,
18,737.........D3, D7 75
Peel, co., Ont., Can.,
111,575............D5 41
Pego, Sp., 8,291......C5 8
Pegu, Bur., 47,378....E10 20
Pehan, China,
18,000............B10 17
Pehuajo, Arg., 13,537..B4 28
Peilintzu, see Suihua,
China
Peine, Ger., 29,800....B5 6
Peiping, see Peking, China
Pekalongan, Indon.,
100,261............G3 19
Pekan, Mala., 2,070....E2 19
Pekin, Ill., 28,146.....C4 58
Peking (Peiping), China,
3,500,000..........D8 17
Pelahatchie, Miss.,
1,066..............C4 68
Pelaihari, Indon., 5,000.F4 19
Pelham, Ga., 4,609....E2 55
Pelham, N.Y., 1,964..*D1 75
Pelham Manor, N.Y.,
6,114..............D1 75
Pelhrimov, Czech.,
7,200..............D3 7
Pelican Rapids, Minn.,
1,693..............D2 67
Pella, Iowa, 5,198.....C5 60
Pella, prov., Grc.,
133,224...........*B4 14
Pell City, Ala., 4,165...B3 46

Peloponnesos, reg., Grc.............D4 14
Pelotas, Braz., 121,280..E2 30
Pelzer North, S.C., 1,400.............*B3 76
Pemberton, N.J., 1,250.............D3 74
Pemberville, Ohio, 1,237.........A2, A4 78
Pembina, co., N. Dak., 12,946.............B8 77
Pembroke, Ont., Can., 16,791........B7, E10 41
Pembroke, Ga., 1,450..D5 55
Pembroke, Mass., 1,300.............B6 65
Pembroke, N.C., 1,372.C4 76
Pembroke, Va., 1,038..D2 85
Pembroke, Wales, 12,737.............E4 4
Pembroke, co., Wales, 93,980............*E4 4
Pembroke Pines, Fla., 1,429.............*F6 54
Pemiscot, co., Mo., 38,095.............E8 69
Penang, Mala., 234,903.............D2 19
Penang, state, Mala., 572,100.............D2 19
Penápolis, Braz., 14,400.............C2 30
Pen Argyl, Pa., 3,693.E11 81
Peñarroya-Pueblonuevo, Sp., 24,152.........C3 8
Penbrook, Pa., 3,671...F8 81
Pender, Nebr., 1,165...B9 71
Pender, co., N.C., 18,508.............C6 76
Pendleton, Ind., 2,472..E6 59
Pendleton, Oreg., 14,434.............B8 80
Pendleton, S.C., 2,358..B2 82
Pendleton, co., Ky., 9,968.............B5 62
Pendleton, co., W. Va., 8,093.............C5 87
Pend Oreille, co., Wash., 6,914.............A8 86
Penedo, Braz., 17,084..E7 27
Penetanguishene, Ont., Can., 5,340.........C5 41
Penfield, N.Y., 3,500..*B3 75
Penfield Junction, Ohio, 2,300............*A5 78
Pengpu, China, 253,000.............E8 17
Peniche, Port., 10,057..C1 8
Peninsula, Ohio, 644...A6 78
Penki, China, 449,000..C9 17
Penn, Pa., 858.........*F3 81
Penndel, Pa., 2,158..*F12 81
Penne, It., 5,054.....C4 9
Pennington, Ala., 400..C1 46
Pennington, N.J., 2,063.............C3 74
Pennington, co., Minn., 12,468.............B2 67
Pennington, co., S. Dak., 58,195.............G3 77
Pennington Gap, Va., 1,799.............B2 85
Pennsauken, N.J., 33,771.............D2 74
Pennsboro, W. Va., 1,660.............B4 87
Pennsburg, Pa., 1,698.F11 81
Penns Grove, N.J., 6,176.............D2 74
Pennside, Pa., 3,000..*F10 81
Pennsville, N.J., 7,000.D2 74
Pennsylvania, state, U.S., 11,319,366......... 81
Penn Valley, Pa., 3,500............*F11 81
Penn Wynne, Pa., 4,500............*C11 81
Penn Yan, N.Y., 5,770.C3 75
Penny Hill, Del., 1,000............*A6 53
Penobscot, co., Maine, 126,346............C4 64
Pensacola, Fla., 56,752 (*165,400).........G2 54
Pentecost, Miss., 100..B3 68
Penticton, B.C., Can., 13,859.............E8 37
Penton, Miss., 100.....A3 68
Pentwater, Mich., 1,030.............E4 66
Penza, Sov. Un., 277,000.............E15 13
Penzance, Eng., 19,433.E4 4
Penzberg, Ger., 10,300.E5 6
Penzhino, Sov. Un., 600.............C19 13
Peoria, Ariz., 2,593.C2, D1 48
Peoria, Ill., 103,162 (*265,000).........C4 58
Peoria, co., Ill., 189,044.............C4 58

Peoria Heights, Ill., 7,064.............C4 58
Peotone, Ill., 1,788.....B6 58
Pepin, co., Wis., 7,332.D2 58
Pepper Pike, Ohio, 3,217.............*B2 78
Pequannock, N.J., 4,600.............B4 74
Perak, state, Mala., 1,221,446..........*E2 19
Percy, Ill., 810.......E4 58
Pereira, Col., 76,262...C2 32
Pereira Barreto, Braz., 7,173.............C2 30
Perekop, Sov. Un., 10,000.............H9 12
Pereslavl-Zalesskiy, Sov. Un., 22,200........C12 12
Pereyaslav-Khmelnitskiy, Sov. Un., 10,000....F8 12
Pergamino, Arg., 32,382.............A4 28
Pergine Valsugana, It., 3,879.............A3 9
Perham, Minn., 2,019..D3 67
Périgueux, Fr., 38,529..E4 5
Perkasie, Pa., 4,650..F11 81
Perkins, co., Nebr., 4,189.............D4 71
Perkins, co., S. Dak., 5,977.............E3 77
Perleberg, Ger., 13,500.B5 6
Perlis, state, Mala., 90,885............*D2 19
Perl-Mack, Colo., 3,000............*B6 51
Perm, Sov. Un., 678,000.............D8 13
Përmet, Alb., 2,302...B3 14
Pernambuco, state, Braz., 4,136,900.........*D7 27
Perpignan, Fr., 83,025..F5 5
Perquimans, co., N.C., 9,178.............A7 76
Perrine, Fla., 6,424.F3, G6 54
Perris, Calif., 2,950.F3, F5 50
Perry, Fla., 7,979.....B3 54
Perry, Ga., 6,032......D3 55
Perry, Iowa, 6,442.....C3 60
Perry, Mich., 1,370....F6 66
Perry, N.Y., 4,629.....C3 75
Perry, Okla., 5,210....A4 79
Perry, co., Ala., 17,358.C2 46
Perry, co., Ark., 4,927..C3 49
Perry, co., Ill., 19,184..E4 58
Perry, co., Ind., 17,232.H4 59
Perry, co., Ky., 34,961..C6 62
Perry, co., Miss., 8,745.D4 68
Perry, co., Mo., 14,642.D8 69
Perry, co., Ohio, 27,864.C5 78
Perry, co., Pa., 26,582..F7 81
Perry, co., Tenn., 5,273.B4 83
Perrygo Place, Wis., 4,475............*F4 88
Perry Hall (Fullerton), Md., 3,800.........B5 53
Perryopolis, Pa., 1,799............*F2 81
Perrysburg, Ohio, 5,519.........A2, A4 78
Perryton, Tex., 7,903..A2 84
Perryville, Mo., 5,117..D8 69
Pershing, co., Nev., 3,999.............A2 72
Persia, see Iran, country, Asia
Persimmon Grove, Ky., 100.............A7 62
Person, co., N.C., 24,361.............A4 76
Perth, Austl., 94,508 (*450,000).........F2 25
Perth, Ont., Can., 5,360.............C8 41
Perth, Scot., 41,199....B5 4
Perth, co., Ont., Can., 57,452.............D3 41
Perth, co., Scot., 127,018............*B5 4
Perth Amboy, N.J., 38,007.........B4, E4 74
Pertuis, Fr., 6,774....F6 5
Peru, Ill., 10,460.....B4 58
Peru, Ind., 14,453.....C5 59
Peru, Nebr., 1,151....D10 71
Peru, country, S.A., 8,132,793.........D3 31
Perugia, It., 71,500...C4 9
Pervomaysk, Sov. Un., 30,000.............G8 12
Pervomaysk, Sov. Un., 10,000.............q21 12
Pervouralsk, Sov. Un., 101,000.............D8 13
Pesaro, It., 45,000.....C4 9
Pescara, It., 87,436....C5 9
Peshtera, Bul., 8,946...D7 10
Peshtigo, Wis., 2,504..C6 88
Peski, Sov. Un., 25,500.............F14 12

Peso da Régua, Port., 5,623.............B2 8
Pesqueira, Braz., 19,778.............D7 27
Pest, co., Hung., 783,108............*B4 10
Petah-Tiqva, Isr., 37,500.............B2 15
Petal, Miss., 4,007.....D4 68
Petaluma, Calif., 14,035.........B5, C2 50
Peterborough, Ont., Can., 47,185.............C6 41
Peterborough, Eng., 62,031.............D6 4
Peterborough (Peterboro), N.H., 1,931.........F4 73
Peterborough, co., Ont., 76,375.............C6 41
Peterhead, Scot., 12,497.............B6 4
Petersburg, Alsk., 1,502.......D13, m23 47
Petersburg, Ill., 2,359..C4 58
Petersburg, Ind., 2,939.H3 59
Petersburg, Mich., 1,018............*G7 66
Petersburg, Tex., 1,400.C2 84
Petersburg (Independent City), Va., 36,750 (*100,300).....C7, D5 85
Petersburg, W. Va., 2,079.............B5 87
Petilia Policastro, It., 8,662.............E6 9
Pétionville, Hai., 9,570.F7 35
Petit-Goâve, Hai., 5,536.............F7 35
Peto, Mex., 6,995......C7 34
Petoskey, Mich., 6,138.C6 66
Petrich, Bul., 13,456...E6 10
Petrikov, Sov. Un., 10,000.............E7 12
Petrinja, Yugo., 7,345..C3 10
Petrodvorets, Sov. Un., 30,000.............s30 11
Petrokrepost, Sov. Un., 30,000.............s32 11
Petroleum, co., Mont., 894.............C8 70
Petrolia, Ont., Can., 3,708.............E2 41
Petrolina, Braz., 14,652............*D6 27
Petropavlovsk, Sov. Un., 140,000.............D9 13
Petropavlovsk [-Kamchatskiy], Sov. Un., 96,000...D18 13
Petrópolis, Braz., 93,849.........C4, h6 30
Petros, Tenn., 850.....C9 83
Petroseni, Rom., 23,052.............C6 10
Petrovgrad, see Zrenjanin, Yugo.
Petrovsk, Sov. Un., 10,000.............E15 12
Petrovskoye, Sov. Un., 29,000.............I14 12
Petrovsk-Zabaykalskiy, Sov. Un., 59,000...D13 13
Petrozavodsk, Sov. Un., 139,000.............A10 12
Pettis, co., Mo., 35,120.C4 69
Pewaukee, Wis., 2,484.........E1, E5 88
Pézenas, Fr., 7,198....F5 5
Pforzheim, Ger., 82,500.............D4 6
Phalodi, India, 15,722..C5 20
Phang Rang, Viet., 5,000.............C3 19
Phan Thiet, Viet., 5,000.............C3 19
Pharr, Tex., 14,106....F3 84
Phelps, Ky., 725.......C7 62
Phelps, N.Y., 1,887....C3 75
Phelps, co., Mo., 25,396.............D6 69
Phelps, co., Nebr., 9,800.............D6 71
Phenix City, Ala., 27,630.............C4 46
Phet Buri, Thai., 14,288.............C1 19
Phetchabun, Thai., 5,733.............B2 19
Phichit, Thai., 9,477..*B2 19
Philadelphia, Miss., 5,017.............C4 68
Philadelphia, Pa., 2,002,512 (*3,969,500)...B11, G11 81
Philadelphia, co., Pa., 2,002,512.........G11 81
Phil Campbell, Ala., 898.............A2 46
Philip, S. Dak., 1,114..C4 77
Philippeville, see Skikda, Alg.

Philippi, W. Va., 2,228.B4 87
Philippines, country, Asia, 27,455,500.........B6 19
Philippolis, S. Afr., 2,078.............G5 24
Philipsburg, Mont., 1,107.............D3 70
Philipsburg, Pa., 3,872.E5 81
Philips, Tex., 3,605...B2 84
Philips, Wis., 1,524...C3 88
Phillips, co., Ark., 43,997.............C5 49
Phillips, co., Colo., 4,440.............A8 51
Phillips, co., Kans., 8,709.............C4 61
Phillips, co., Mont., 6,027.............B8 70
Phillipsburg, Ga., 2,037............*E3 55
Phillipsburg, Kans., 3,233.............C4 61
Phillipsburg, N.J., 18,502.............B2 74
Phillipsville, N.C., 1,311............*D3 76
Philmont, N.Y., 1,750..C7 75
Philo, Ohio, 913.......C6 78
Philomath, Ga., 200...C4 55
Philomath, Oreg., 1,359.............C3 80
Philrich, Tex., 2,067..*B2 84
Phitsanulok, Thai., 32,659.............B2 19
Phnom Penh, Camb. 420,000.............C2 19
Phoenix, Ariz., 439,170 (*619,600)......C2, D2 48
Phoenix, Ill., 4,203....F3 58
Phoenix, N.Y., 2,408...B4 75
Phoenixville, Pa., 13,797.........A10, F10 81
Phong Saly, Laos, 10,000.............G5 17
Phrae, Thai., 15,616..*B2 19
Phuket, Thai., 27,021..D1 19
Piacenza, It., 88,541..B2 10
Pialba, Austl., 3,544...B9 26
Piaseczno, Pol., 13,800.............m14 7
Piatra-Neamt, Rom., 32,648.............B8 10
Piatt, co., Ill., 14,960..D5 58
Piauí, state, Braz., 1,263,368..........*D6 27
Piazza Armerina, It., 24,887.............F5 9
Picadome, Ky., 900....B5 62
Picardy, former prov., Fr., 1,051,000.........C5 5
Picayune, Miss., 7,834..E4 68
Picher, Okla., 2,553...A7 79
Pichincha, prov., Ec., 424,655.............B2 31
Pickaway, co., Ohio, 35,855.............C4 78
Pickens, S.C., 2,198...B2 82
Pickens, co., Ala., 21,882.............B1 46
Pickens, co., Ga., 8,903.............B2 55
Pickens, co., S.C., 46,030.............B2 82
Pickering, Ont., Can., 1,755.............D5 41
Pickett, co., Tenn., 4,431.............C8 83
Pickstown, S. Dak., 600.............H7 77
Pico Rivera, Calif., 49,150............*F2 50
Picton, Ont., Can., 4,862.............D7 41
Pictou, N.S., Can., 4,534.............D7 43
Pictou, co., N.S., Can., 43,908.............D7 43
Piedmont, Ala., 4,794..B4 46
Piedmont, Calif., 11,117.............B5 50
Piedmont, Mo., 1,555..D7 69
Piedmont, S.C., 2,108..B3 82
Piedmont, W. Va., 2,307.............B5 87
Piedmont, reg., It.....B1 9
Piedrabuena, Sp., 6,210.............C3 8
Piedras Negras, Mex., 42,649.............B4 34
Pieksämäki, Fin., 10,600.............F12 11
Piélagos, Sp., 8,040...A4 8
Piemonte, pol. dist., It., 3,914,250.........*B1 9
Pierce, Fla., 800......E5 54
Pierce, Nebr., 1,216...B8 71
Pierce, co., Ga., 9,678..E4 55
Pierce, co., Nebr., 8,722.............B8 71
Pierce, co., N. Dak., 7,394.............B5 77

Pierce, co., Wash., 321,590..........C3 86
Pierce, co., Wis., 22,503...........D1 88
Pierce City, Mo., 1,006............E3 69
Pierceton, Ind., 1,186...B6 59
Piermont, N.Y., 1,906..D7 75
Pierre, S. Dak., 10,088.F5 77
Pierrefitte [-sur-Seine], Fr., 14,770...........g10 5
Pierreville, Que., Can., 1,559............C5 42
Piestany, Czech., 18,700...........D4 7
Pietermaritzburg, S. Afr., 91,178......F6 24
Pietersburg, S. Afr., 28,071...........E5 24
Pigeon, Mich., 1,191...E7 66
Pigeon Cove, Mass., 1,064............A6 65
Piggott, Ark., 2,776...A5 49
Pigüé, Arg., 5,869.....B4 28
Pike, co., Ala., 25,987.D4 46
Pike, co., Ark., 7,864...C2 49
Pike, co., Ga., 7,138...C2 55
Pike, co., Ill., 20,552..D3 58
Pike, co., Ind., 12,797..H3 59
Pike, co., Ky., 68,264..C7 62
Pike, co., Miss., 35,063.D3 68
Pike, co., Mo., 16,706..B6 69
Pike, co., Ohio, 19,380..C4 78
Pike, co., Pa., 9,158..D11 81
Pikesville, Md., 18,737.C2 53
Piketon, Ohio, 1,244...C4 78
Pikeville, Ky., 4,754...C7 62
Pikeville, Tenn., 951..D8 83
Piła, Pol., 27,000.....B4 7
Pilar, Braz., 7,201....*D7 27
Pilar, Par., 10,062....E4 29
Pilgrim Gardens, Pa., 5,000............*B11 81
Pilot Mountain, N.C., 1,310............A3 76
Pilot Point, Tex., 1,254.C4 85
Pilot Rock, Oreg., 1,695............B8 80
Pima, co., Ariz., 265,660...........C2 48
Pimmit Hills, Va., 1,000............*B5 85
Pinal, co., Ariz., 62,673...........C3 48
Pinar del Río, Cuba, 38,885...........D2 35
Pinar del Río, prov., Cuba, 448,442...........D2 35
Pinardville, N.H., 1,500............*E4 73
Pincher Creek, Alta., Can., 2,961.......E4 38
Pinckneyville, Ill., 3,085............E4 58
Pinconning, Mich., 1,329............E7 66
Pindamonhangaba, Braz., 19,144...........C3 30
Pine, co., Minn., 17,004...........D6 67
Pine Beach, N.J., 985.*D4 74
Pine Bluff, Ark., 44,037.C3 49
Pine Bluff, Wyo., 1,121.D8 89
Pine Bluff Southeast, Ark., 2,679.......*C4 49
Pine Bush, N.Y., 1,016.D6 75
Pine Castle, Fla., 6,000.D5 54
Pine City, Minn., 1,972.E6 67
Pineda, Fla., 150.....D6 54
Pinedale, Calif., 3,202.D4 50
Pinedale, Wyo., 965...C3 89
Pine Grove, Pa., 2,267.E9 81
Pine Hill, N.J., 3,939..D3 74
Pine Hills, Fla., 7,000.*D5 54
Pinehurst, Idaho, 1,432............B2 57
Pinehurst, Mass., 1,991.C2 65
Pinehurst, N.C., 1,124..B4 76
Pinehurst, Tex., 1,703.*D6 84
Pinehurst, Wash., 3,000............B3 86
Pine Island, Minn., 1,308............F6 67
Pine Knot, Ky., 750...D5 62
Pinelake, Ind., 1,400..*A4 59
Pineland, Tex., 1,236..D6 84
Pine Lawn, Mo., 5,943............C7 69
Pinellas, co., Fla., 374,665...........E4 54
Pinellas Park, Fla., 10,848..........E1, E4 54
Pine Ridge, S. Dak., 1,256............G3 77
Pinerolo, It., 24,500...B1 9
Pinetops, N.C., 1,372..B6 76
Pineville, Ky., 3,181...D6 62
Pineville, La., 8,636...C3 63
Pineville, N.C., 1,514..B3 76
Pineville, W. Va., 1,137............D3 87

Piney Point, Tex., 1,790............*E5 84
Piney View, W. Va., 800............D3, D7 87
Pinghsiang, China, 22,000...........F7 17
Pingliang, China, 55,000...........D6 17
Pingtung, Taiwan, 81,020...........*G9 17
Pinhal, Braz., 14,260...........C3, m8 30
Pinhsien, China, 6,000.D3 18
Pinkney (South Gastonia), N.C., 3,762........*B2 76
Pinole, Calif., 6,064....B5 50
Pinon, Ariz., 100.....A3 48
Pinoso, Sp., 5,114.....C5 8
Pinos-Puente, Sp., 8,653............D4 8
Pinsk, Sov. Un., 39,000............E6 12
Pinson, Ala., 1,121....E5 46
Pinsonfork, Ky., 800..*C7 62
Pioche, Nev., 900.....C4 72
Piombino, It., 36,102..C3 9
Piotrkow (Trybunalski), Pol., 53,000.......C5 7
Pipestone, Minn., 5,324............G2 67
Pipestone, co., Minn., 13,605...........F2 67
Piqua, Ohio, 19,219....B3 78
Piracicaba, Braz., 80,670...........C3, m8 30
Piraçununga, Braz., 12,546...........C3, k8 30
Piraeus, see Piraievs, Grc.
Piraievs (Piraeus), Grc., 183,877...........D4 14
Pirajú, Braz., 10,658...C3 30
Pirajuí, Braz., 6,465...C3 30
Piran, Yugo., 5,464....B4 9
Pirapora, Braz., 13,772.B4 30
Pirgos, Grc., 20,558...D3 14
Piriápolis, Ur., 4,400...E1 30
Pirmasens, Ger., 53,200...........D3 6
Pirna, Ger., 41,100.....C6 6
Pirot, Yugo., 18,585...D6 10
Piryatin, Sov. Un., 10,000............F9 12
Pisa, It., 90,928.......C3 9
Piscataquis, co., Maine, 17,379...........C3 64
Pisco, Peru, 17,222....D2 31
Pisek, Czech., 19,500..D3 7
Pisinimo, Ariz., 200....C2 48
Pismo Beach, Calif., 1,762............E3 50
Pisticci, It., 13,300....D6 9
Pistoia, It., 75,915.....C3 9
Pitangui, Braz., 7,421..B4 30
Pitcairn, Pa., 5,383....F2 81
Piteå, Swe., 7,400.....E9 11
Pitești, Rom., 38,333...C7 10
Pithiviers, Fr., 7,318...C5 5
Pitkin, co., Colo., 2,381.B4 51
Pitman, N.J., 8,644....D2 74
Pitrufquén, Chile, 5,193............B2 28
Pitt, co., N.C., 69,942..B6 76
Pittsboro, N.C., 1,215..B4 76
Pittsburg, Calif., 19,062...........B5 50
Pittsburg, Kans., 18,678...........E9 61
Pittsburg, Tex., 3,769..C5 84
Pittsburg, co., Okla., 34,360...........C6 79
Pittsburgh, Pa., 604,332 (*1,957,700)...B6, F1 81
Pittsfield, Ill., 4,089...D3 58
Pittsfield, Maine, 3,232.D3 64
Pittsfield, Mass., 57,879...........B1 65
Pittsfield, Mich., 1,500............*F7 66
Pittsfield, N.H., 1,407..E5 73
Pittsford, N.Y., 1,749..B3 75
Pittston, Pa., 12,407..........B8, D10 81
Pittsylvania, co., Va., 58,296...........E3 85
Piuka, Jap., 5,200....D11 18
Piura, Peru, 23,678....C1 31
Piura, dept., Peru, 431,487...........C1 31
Piute, co., Utah, 1,436.B5 72
Pixley, Calif., 1,327....E4 50
Pizzo, It., 9,560.......E6 9
Placentia, Calif., 5,861............*F3 50
Placentia, Newf., Can., 1,610............E5 44
Placer, co., Calif., 56,998...........C3 50
Placerville, Calif., 4,439............C3 50
Placetas, Cuba, 25,226.D4 35
Placida, Fla., 150......F4 54

Plage Laval, Que., Can., 3,818............*D8 42
Plain City, Ohio, 2,146............B4 78
Plain Dealing, La., 1,357............B2 63
Plainfield, Conn., 2,044.C9 52
Plainfield, Ill., 2,183...........B5, F2 58
Plainfield, Ind., 5,460..E5 59
Plainfield, N.J., 45,330.B4 74
Plainfield, Tenn., 2,127............*D10 83
Plainfield Heights, Mich., 1,000............*F5 66
Plainsboro, N.J., 600...C3 74
Plainsville, Pa., 500...*B8 81
Plainview, Minn., 1,833............F6 67
Plainview, Nebr., 1,467.B8 71
Plainview, N.Y., 27,710...........*G3 52
Plainview, Tex., 18,735.B2 84
Plainville, Conn., 13,149...........C5 52
Plainville, Kans., 3,104.C4 61
Plainwell, Mich., 3,125.F5 66
Plaistow, N.H., 1,500..F5 73
Planada, Calif., 1,704.*D3 50
Plandome, N.Y., 1,379............*E3 75
Plandome Heights, N.Y., 1,025............*F2 75
Plano (Doyle Colony), Calif., 1,500.......*D4 50
Plano, Ill., 3,343......B5 58
Plano, Tex., 3,695..A6, C4 84
Plant City, Fla., 15,711...........D4 54
Plantsite, Ariz., 1,552.*D6 48
Plantsville, Conn., 2,793............C5 52
Plaquemine, La., 7,689...........B5, D4 63
Plaquemines, par., La., 22,545...........E6 63
Plaquemine Southwest, La., 1,272.......*D4 63
Plasencia, Sp., 21,297..B2 8
Plato, Col., 8,039......B3 32
Platte, S. Dak., 1,167..G7 77
Platte, co., Mo., 23,350.B3 69
Platte, co., Nebr., 23,992...........C8 71
Platte, co., Wyo., 7,195.C7 89
Platteville, Wis., 6,957..F3 88
Plattsburg, Mo., 1,663.B3 69
Plattsburg, N.Y., 20,172...........A3 75
Plattsmouth, Nebr., 6,244..........C10, E3 71
Plauen, Ger., 78,900...C6 6
Pleasant Dale, Nebr., 190............D8 71
Pleasant Gap, Pa., 1,389............E6 81
Pleasant Grove, Ala., 3,097............E4 46
Pleasant Grove, Utah, 4,772..........A6, D2 72
Pleasant Hill, Calif., 23,844..........*D2 50
Pleasant Hill, Ill., 950..D3 58
Pleasant Hill, La., 907..C2 63
Pleasant Hill, Mo., 2,689............C3 69
Pleasant Hill, Ohio, 1,060............B3 78
Pleasant Hill, Pa., 1,200............*F9 81
Pleasant Hill, Va., 2,636............*E6 85
Pleasant Hills, Pa., 8,573..........*F1, B5 81
Pleasanton, Calif., 4,203............B6 50
Pleasanton, Kans., 1,098............D9 61
Pleasanton, Tex., 3,467.E3 84
Pleasant Ridge, Mich., 3,807............A7 66
Pleasants, co., W. Va., 7,124............B3 87
Pleasant Valley, Mo., 1,109............*B3 69
Pleasant View, Colo., 1,500............*B5 51
Pleasant View, Utah, 927............A5 72
Pleasantville, Iowa, 1,025............C4 60
Pleasantville, N.J., 15,172...........E3 74
Pleasantville, N.Y., 5,877............D3 75
Pleasantville, Pa., 940..C2 81
Pleasure Beach, Conn., 1,264............*E4 52
Pleasure Ridge Park, Ky., 10,612...........A4 62

Pleasureville, Pa., 1,000............*G8 81
Pleiku, Viet., 10,000..*C3 19
Plenita, Rom., 6,735...C6 10
Plentywood, Mont., 2,121............B12 70
Plesetsk, Sov. Un., 18,000...........E6 13
Plessisville, Que., Can., 6,570............C6 42
Pleszew, Pol., 8,760....C4 7
Pleven, Bul., 38,997...D7 10
Pleven, co., Bul., 1,056,436.........*D7 10
Pljevlja, Yugo., 10,240.D4 10
Plock, Pol., 42,000.....B5 7
Ploërmel, Fr., 3,840....D2 5
Ploești, Rom., 114,560..C8 10
Plomarion, Grc., 5,889.*C6 14
Plonsk, Pol., 7,578....B6 7
Plovdiv, Bul., 125,440..D7 10
Plovdiv, co., Bul., 876,993..........*D7 10
Plum, Pa., 10,241....*F2 81
Plumas, co., Calif., 11,620...........B3 50
Plymouth, Conn., 950..C4 52
Plymouth, Eng., 204,279...........E4 4
Plymouth, Ind., 7,558..B5 59
Plymouth, Mass., 11,000...........C6 65
Plymouth, Mich., 8,766...........A7, F7 66
Plymouth, Minn., 9,576............*F5 67
Plymouth, N.H., 2,244.D4 73
Plymouth, N.C., 4,666..B7 76
Plymouth, Ohio, 1,822..B5 78
Plymouth, Pa., 10,401..........B8, D10 81
Plymouth, Wis., 5,128............B6, E6 88
Plymouth, co., Iowa, 23,906...........B1 60
Plymouth, co., Mass., 248,449..........C6 65
Plymouth Meeting, Pa., 4,000............*A11 81
Plymouth Valley, Pa., 1,700............*F11 81
Plymptonville, Pa., 1,220............*D5 81
Plzen, Czech., 137,800.D2 7
Pocahontas, Ark., 3,665............A5 49
Pocahontas, Iowa, 2,011............B3 60
Pocahontas, Va., 1,313.B3 85
Pocahontas, co., Iowa, 14,234...........B3 60
Pocahontas, co., W. Va., 10,136...........C4 87
Pocatello, Idaho, 27,140...........G6 57
Pochep, Sov. Un., 10,000............E9 12
Pocomoke City, Md., 3,329............D6 53
Poços de Caldas, Braz., 32,291.........C3, k8 30
Podgorica, see Titograd, Yugo.
Podolsk, Sov. Un., 139,000........D11, n17 12
Podor, Sen., 3,400.....E2 22
Poe, S.C., 1,000......*B3 82
Poggibonsi, It., 7,236..C3 9
Pohang, Kor., 47,500..H4 18
Poinsett, co., Ark., 30,834...........B5 49
Point Comfort, Tex., 1,453............*E4 84
Pointe-à-Pitre, Guad., 26,160...........n16 35
Pointe au Pic, Que., Can., 1,333............B7 42
Pointe aux Trembles, Que., Can., 21,926........D9 42
Pointe Claire, Que., Can., 22,709..........D4, D8 42
Pointe Coupee, par., La., 21,841..........D4 63
Point Edward, Ont., Can., 2,744...........*D2 41
Pointe-Gatineau, Que., Can., 8,854........*D1 42
Pointe Noire, Con. B., 31,199............I7 22
Point Lookout, Mo., 200............E4 69
Point Marion, Pa., 1,853............F2 81
Point Pleasant, N.J., 10,182...........C4 74
Point Pleasant, W. Va., 5,785............C2 87
Point Pleasant Beach, N.J., 3,873........*C4 74
Poissy, Fr., 28,499.....C4 5

Poitiers, Fr., 62,178....D4 5
Poitou, former prov., Fr.,
1,037,000.............D3 5
Pokaran, India, 5,284..C5 20
Pokotu, China, 5,000...B9 17
Pokrovskoye, Sov. Un.,
10,000...........H12 12
Poland, Ohio, 2,766...*A7 78
Poland, country, Eur.,
29,731,200...........C5 7
Polgar, Hung., 7,697...B5 10
Poli, China, 35,000...B11 17
Polikhnitos, Grc.,
6,071.............*C6 14
Polk, Pa., 3,574......D2 81
Polk, co., Ark., 11,981..C1 49
Polk, co., Fla., 195,139.E5 54
Polk, co., Ga., 28,015...C1 55
Polk, co., Iowa,
266,315............C4 60
Polk, co., Minn.,
36,182.............C2 67
Polk, co., Mo., 13,753..D4 69
Polk, co., Nebr., 7,210..C8 71
Polk, co., N.C., 11,395.D4 76
Polk, co., Oreg., 26,523.C3 80
Polk, co., Tenn.,
12,160.............D9 83
Polk, co., Tex., 13,861..D5 84
Polk, co., Wis., 24,968..C1 88
Pollensa, Sp., 8,984....C7 8
Pollocksville, N.C., 416.B6 76
Polo, Ill., 2,551......B4 58
Polotsk, Sov. Un.,
30,000.............D7 12
Polson, Mont., 2,314...C2 70
Poltava, Sov. Un.,
151,000...........G10 12
Pombal, Braz., 8,120..*D7 27
Pombetsu, Jap., 6,600.E11 18
Pomerania, reg., Pol...B4 7
Pomeroy, Ohio, 3,345..C5 78
Pomeroy, Pa., 1,085..*G10 81
Pomeroy, Wash.,
1,677..............C8 86
Pomoho Camp, Haw.,
350................f9 56
Pomona, Calif., 67,157
(*212,000)......E5, F5 50
Pompano Beach, Fla.,
15,992...........E3, F6 54
Pompton Lakes, N.J.,
9,445..............A4 74
Pompton Plains, N.J.,
5,800..............B4 74
Ponca City, Okla.,
24,411.............A4 79
Ponce, P.R., 114,286..m13 35
Ponchatoula, La.,
4,727...........B6, D5 63
Pondcreek, Okla., 935..A4 79
Pondera, co., Mont.,
7,653..............B4 70
Pondicherry, India,
40,421.............F6 20
Ponferrada, Sp.,
37,053.............A2 8
Ponoka, Alta., Can.,
3,938..............C4 38
Ponta Delgada, Az. Is.,
22,300...........m10 22
Ponta Grossa, Braz.,
77,803.............D2 30
Pont-à-Mousson, Fr.,
12,802.............C7 5
Ponta Porã, Braz.,
9,160..............C1 30
Pontarlier, Fr., 15,382..D7 5
Pontedera, It., 12,400..C3 9
Ponte Nova, Braz.,
22,536.............C4 30
Pontevedra, Sp.,
21,400.............A1 8
Pontevedra, prov., Sp.,
680,229...........*A1 8
Pontiac, Ill., 8,435.....C5 58
Pontiac, Mich.,
82,233..........A7, F7 66
Pontiac, co., Que., Can.,
19,947.............A7 41
Pontianak, Indon.,
146,547............F3 19
Pontivy, Fr., 8,775....C2 5
Pont-l'Abbé, Fr., 5,541.D1 5
Pontoise, Fr., 15,853...C4 5
Pontotoc, Miss., 2,108..A4 68
Pontotoc, co., Miss.,
17,232.............A4 68
Pontotoc, co., Okla.,
28,089.............C5 79
Pontremoli, It., 4,839..B2 9
Pont Rouge, Que., Can.,
2,988.........C6, C8 42
Pont Viau, Que., Can.,
16,077.............D4 42
Poole, Eng., 88,088....E6 4
Pooler, Ga., 1,073.....D5 55
Poona, India, 597,562
(*800,000).........E5 20
Popasnaya, Sov. Un.,
10,000............q21 12

Popayán, Col., 37,400..C2 32
Pope, co., Ark., 21,177.B2 49
Pope, co., Ill., 4,061....F5 58
Pope, co., Minn.,
11,914.............E3 67
Poplar, Calif., 1,478...*D4 50
Poplar, Mont., 1,565..B11 70
Poplar Bluff, Mo.,
15,926.............E7 69
Poplar Heights, Va.,
1,000.............*B5 85
Poplarville, Miss.,
2,136..............E4 68
Popovka, Sov. Un.,
10,000............H11 12
Popovo, Bul., 6,469...D8 10
Poquonock, Conn., 600.B6 52
Poquonock Bridge, Conn.,
3,000..............D8 52
Poquoson, Va., 4,278...B6 85
Porbandar, India,
74,476.............D4 20
Porcuna, Sp., 10,516...D3 8
Pordenone, It., 34,055..B4 9
Poreč, Yugo., 2,992....C1 10
Pori, Fin., 54,000......G9 11
Porlamar, Ven., 20,807.A5 32
Poronaysk, Sov. Un.,
33,000............E17 13
Porrentruy, Switz.,
7,095..............E3 6
Porsgrunn, Nor.,
10,700............p27 11
Port Adelaide, Austl.,
38,923.............F6 25
Portadown, N. Ire.,
18,605.............C3 4
Portage, Ind., 13,659..*A3 59
Portage, Mich., 6,000..*F5 66
Portage, Pa., 3,933....F4 81
Portage, Wis., 7,822....E4 88
Portage, co., Ohio,
91,798.............A6 78
Portage, co., Wis.,
36,964.............D4 88
Portage Lakes, Ohio,
10,000...........*B6 78
Portage la Prairie, Man.,
Can., 12,388....D5, E2 40
Portageville, Mo.,
2,505..............E8 69
Port Alberni, B.C., Can.,
11,560.............E5 37
Portalegre, Port.,
10,510.............C2 8
Portales, N. Mex.,
9,695..............B7 48
Port Alfred, Que., Can.,
9,066..............A7 42
Port Alfred, S. Afr.,
6,171..............G5 24
Port Allegany, Pa.,
2,742..............C5 81
Port Allen, La.,
5,026...........B5, D4 63
Port Angeles, Wash.,
12,653.............A2 86
Port Angeles East, Wash.,
1,283.............*A2 86
Port Antonio, Jam.,
7,827..............F5 35
Port Arthur, Ont., Can.,
45,276.............E8 41
Port Arthur (Lushun),
China, 126,000....D9 17
Port Arthur, Tex.,
66,676.............E6 84
Port-au-Prince, Haiti,
134,117............F7 35
Port Barre, La., 1,876..D4 63
Port Byron, Ill., 1,153..B3 58
Port Byron, N.Y.,
1,201..............B4 75
Port Carbon, Pa.,
2,775.............*E9 81
Port Charlotte, Fla.,
3,197.............*F4 54
Port Chester, N.Y.,
24,960....D2, D3, E7 75
Port Chicago, Calif.,
1,746..............B5 50
Port Clinton, Ohio,
6,870..............A5 78
Port Colborne, Ont., Can.,
14,886.............E5 41
Port Coquitlam, B.C.,
Can., 8,111....A10, E6 37
Port Credit, Ont., Can.,
7,203..........D5, E6 41
Port-de-Bouc, Fr.,
12,510.............F6 5
Port-de-Paix, Hai.,
6,309..............F7 35
Port Deposit, Md., 953.A5 53
Port Dickinson, N.Y.,
2,295..............C5 75
Port Dickson, Mala.,
4,415..............E2 19
Port Dover, Ont., Can.,
3,064..............E4 41

Port Edwards, Wis.,
1,849..............D4 88
Port Elgin, Ont., Can.,
1,632..............C3 41
Port Elizabeth, S. Afr.,
249,211, (*274,180)..G5 24
Porter, Ind., 2,189.....A3 59
Porter, co., Ind.,
60,279.............B3 59
Porterdale, Ga., 2,365..C3 55
Porterville, Calif.,
7,991..............D4 50
Porterville West (Burton),
Calif., 4,635.......*D4 50
Port Étienne, Maur.,
1,200..............D1 22
Port Ewen, N.Y.,
2,622..............D7 75
Port-Francqui, Con. L.,
3,553..............I2 23
Port-Gentil, Gabon,
16,600.............I6 22
Port Gibson, Miss.,
2,861..............D3 68
Port Hammond, B.C.,
Can., 1,267.......A10 37
Port Harcourt, Nig.,
71,634.............H6 22
Port Hawkesbury, N.S.,
Can., 1,346........D8 43
Port Henry, N.Y.,
1,767..............A7 75
Port Hope, Ont., Can.,
8,091..............D6 41
Port Hueneme, Calif.,
11,067.............E4 50
Port Huron, Mich., 36,084
(*124,000).........F8 66
Portimão, Port.,
12,066.............D1 8
Port Isabel, Tex., 3,575.F4 84
Port Jefferson, N.Y.,
2,336..............F4 52
Port Jefferson Station,
N.Y., 1,041.......*D3 75
Port Jervis, N.Y.,
9,268..............D6 75
Portland, Conn., 7,496.C6 52
Portland, Ind., 6,999...D8 59
Portland, Maine, 72,566
(*142,700)......E2, E5 64
Portland, Mich., 3,330..F6 66
Portland, Oreg., 372,676
(*731,200).....B2, B4 80
Portland, Tenn., 2,424.A5 83
Portland, Tex., 2,538...F4 84
Port Lavaca, Tex.,
8,864..............E4 84
Port Leyden, N.Y.,
898................B5 75
Port Monmouth, N.J.,
4,000..............C4 74
Port Moody, B.C., Can.,
4,789..........A10, E6 37
Port Neches, Tex.,
8,696..............E6 84
Portneuf, Que., Can.,
1,380..............C6 42
Portneuf, co., Que., Can.,
50,711.............C5 42
Port Norris, N.J.,
1,789..............E2 74
Pôrto, Port., 303,400
(*750,000).........B1 8
Pôrto Alegre, Braz.,
617,629............E2 30
Porto Alexandre, Ang.,
2,874..............D2 24
Pôrto Amélia, Moz.,
10,000.............C8 24
Pôrto Feliz, Braz.,
11,786.........C3, M8 30
Portoferraio, It.,
6,000..............C3 9
Port-of-Spain, Trin.,
94,100.............A5 32
Portogruaro, It.,
7,100..............B4 9
Portola, Calif., 1,874...C3 50
Portomaggiore, It.,
4,300..............B3 9
Porto-Novo, Dah.,
30,800.............G5 22
Port Orange, Fla.,
1,801..............C6 54
Port Orchard, Wash.,
2,778..........B3, D1 86
Port Orford, Oreg.,
1,171..............E2 80
Portotorres, It.,
9,166..............D2 9
Pôrto União, Braz.,
9,954..............D2 30
Pôrto Velho, Braz.,
19,387.............D2 36
Portoviejo, Ec., 18,082.B1 31
Port Perry, Ont., Can.,
2,262..............C6 41
Port Pirie, Austl.,
14,003.............F6 25

Port Reading, N.J.,
3,000..............E4 74
Port Richey, Fla.,
1,931..............D4 54
Port Said (Būr Saʿïd), Eg.,
U.A.R., 212,963.....G9 14
Port St. Joe, Fla.,
4,217..........C1, H3 54
Port Sewall, Fla., 200..E6 54
Portsmouth, Eng., 215,198
(*415,000).........E6 4
Portsmouth, N.H.,
26,900.............E6 73
Portsmouth, Ohio,
33,637.............D5 78
Portsmouth, R.I.,
3,000.............C12 52
Portsmouth (Independent
City), Va.,
80,039.........B6, E6 85
Port Staley, Ont., Can.,
1,460..............E3 41
Port Sudan, Sud.,
47,562.............E5 23
Port Sulphur, La.,
2,868..............E6 63
Port Townsend, Wash.,
5,074..............A3 86
Portugal, country, Eur.,
8,889,300..........C1 8
Portugalete, Sp.,
22,584.............A4 8
Portuguesa, state, Ven.,
203,707............B4 32
Portuguese Guinea, dep.,
Afr., 559,000.......F1 22
Portuguese Timor, dep.,
Asia, 439,000......G7 19
Portville, N.Y., 1,336..C2 75
Port Vue, Pa., 6,635..*F2 81
Port Washington, N.Y.,
15,657.............D2 75
Port Washington, Wis.,
5,984..............E6 88
Port Wentworth, Ga.,
3,705..............D5 55
Posadas, Arg., 37,588..E4 29
Posadas, Sp., 8,999....D3 8
Posen, Ill., 4,517......F3 58
Posen, see Poznan, Pol.
Posey, co., Ind., 19,214.H2 59
Poseyville, Ind., 997...H2 59
Post, Tex., 4,663......C2 84
Post Falls, Idaho,
1,983..............B2 57
Postojna, Yugo., 4,848.C2 10
Poston, S.C., 250......D9 82
Postville, Iowa, 1,554..A6 60
Potchefstroom, S. Afr.,
41,927.............F5 24
Poteau, Okla., 4,428...B7 79
Poteet, Tex., 2,811....E3 84
Potenza, It., 29,500...D5 9
Potgietersrust, S. Afr.,
11,438.............E5 24
Poth, Tex., 1,119......E3 84
Potomac Park, Md.,
1,016.............*D2 53
Potosí, Bol., 45,758...C2 29
Potosí, Mo., 2,805.....D7 69
Potosí, dept., Bol.,
534,399............C2 29
Pototan, Phil., 4,812..*C6 19
Potsdam, Ger., 114,500.B6 6
Potsdam, N.Y., 7,765..A2 75
Pottawatomie, co., Iowa,
83,102.............C2 60
Pottawatomie, co., Kans.,
11,957.............C7 61
Pottawatomie, co., Okla.,
41,486.............B5 79
Potter, co., Pa., 16,483.C6 81
Potter, co., S. Dak.,
4,926..............E5 77
Potter, co., Tex.,
115,580............B2 84
Potterville, Mich.,
1,028.............*F6 66
Pottstown, Pa.,
26,144............F10 81
Pottsville, Pa., 21,659..E9 81
Pouch Cove, Newf., Can.,
1,324..............E5 44
Poughkeepsie, N.Y.,
38,330 (*124,700)...D7 75
Poulsbo, Wash., 1,505..B3 86
Poultney, Vt., 1,810...D1 73
Pound, Va., 1,135.....B2 85
Pouso Alegre, Braz.,
18,852.........C3, M9 30
Póvoa de Varzim, Port.,
16,913.............B1 8
Powassan, Ont., Can.,
1,064..............A5 41
Powder River, co., Mont.,
2,485.............E11 70
Powell, Mo., 100......E3 69
Powell, Wyo., 4,740...A4 89
Powell, co., Ky., 6,674.C6 62
Powell, co., Mont.,
7,002..............D4 70

Powell River, B.C., Can.,
5,500...............E5 37
Powellton, W. Va.,
1,256...........C3, D6 87
Power, co., Idaho,
4,111...............G6 57
Powers, Oreg., 1,366...E2 80
Powerview, Man., Can.,
902...............*D3 41
Poweshiek, co., Iowa,
19,300..............C5 60
Powhatan, co., Va.,
6,747..............D5 85
Powhatan Point, Ohio,
2,147...............C7 78
Poynette, Wis., 1,090..E4 88
Požarevac, Yugo.,
24,293..............C5 10
Poznan, Pol., 408,000..B4 7
Pozoblanco, Sp.,
16,020..............C3 8
Pozzallo, It., 12,253...F5 9
Pozzuoli, It., 51,308...D5 9
Prachin Buri, Thai.,
13,308..............C2 19
Prachuap Khiri Khan,
Thai., 6,799.......*C1 19
Praco, Ala., 900......E4 46
Prades, Fr., 5,676.....F5 5
Praestø, co., Den.,
123,328............*J5 11
Prague, Czech.,
1,003,300........C3, n17 7
Prague, Okla., 1,545...B5 75
Praha, see Prague, Czech.
Prairie, co., Ark.,
10,515 ....C4 49
Prairie, co., Mont.,
2,318.............D11 70
Prairie City, Iowa,
943...............*C4 60
Prairie du Chien, Wis.,
5,649..............E2 88
Prairie du Sac, Wis.,
1,676..............E4 88
Prairie Grove, Ark.,
1,056..............B1 49
Prairie View, Tex.,
2,326.............*D5 84
Prairie Village, Kans.,
25,356............*B9 61
Pran Buri, Thai.,
5,000..............C1 19
Prato, It., 111,285.....C3 9
Pratt, Kans., 8,156....E5 61
Pratt, W. Va., 602....*C6 87
Pratt, co., Kans.,
12,122..............E5 61
Prattville, Ala., 6,616..C3 46
Prattville, Okla.,
2,530.............*A5 79
Pravdinsk (Friedland),
Sov. Un., 10,000.....A6 7
Pravia, Sp., 1,804.....A2 8
Preble, Wis., 12,245...A6 88
Preble, co., Ohio,
32,498..............C3 78
Premont, Tex., 3,049...F3 84
Prentiss, Miss., 1,321..D4 68
Prentiss, co., Miss.,
17,949..............A5 68
Prenzlau, Ger., 19,700..B6 6
Prerov, Czech.,
30,500..............D4 7
Prescott, Ariz., 12,861..B2 48
Prescott, Ark., 3,533...D2 49
Prescott, Ont., Can.,
5,366..............C9 41
Prescott, Wis., 1,536..D1 88
Prescott, co., Ont., Can.,
27,226.............B10 41
Presidencia Roque Saenz
Peña, Arg., 23,100...E3 29
Presidente Hayes, dept.,
Par., 23,490........D4 29
Presidente Prudente,
Braz., 54,055.......C2 30
Presidio, Tex., 1,062...G2 84
Presidio, co., Tex.,
5,460..............F2 84
Presov, Czech., 35,100.D6 7
Presque Isle, Maine,
12,886.............B4 64
Presque Isle, co., Mich.,
13,117.............C6 66
Preston, Ont., Can.,
11,557.............D4 41
Preston, Eng., 113,208.D5 4
Preston, Idaho, 3,640..G7 57
Preston, Ky., 200.....B6 62
Preston, Minn., 1,491..G6 67
Preston, co., W. Va.,
27,233.............B5 87
Prestonsburg, Ky.,
3,133..............C7 62
Prestonville, Ky., 211..B4 62
Prestwick, Scot.,
12,564............*C4 4
Pretoria, S. Afr.,
303,684 (*422,590)..F5 24
Preveza, Grc., 11,162..C3 14

Préveza, prov., Grc.,
62,523............*C3 14
Prey Veng, Camb.,
5,000............*C3 19
Pribilof, is., Alsk.....D6 47
Pribram, Czech.,
25,700.............D3 7
Price, Que., Can.,
3,049............*G20 36
Price, Tex., 800.....C5 84
Price, Utah., 6,802.....B6 72
Price, co., Wis., 14,370.C3 88
Pricedale, Pa., 1,300..*F2 81
Prichard, Ala., 47,371..E1 46
Priego, Sp., 13,801....D3 8
Priest River, Idaho,
1,749..............A2 57
Prilep, Yugo., 37,486..E5 10
Priluki, Sov. Un.,
40,000..............F9 12
Primera, Tex., 1,066..*F4 84
Primghar, Iowa, 1,131..A2 60
Primorsk, Sov. Un.,
8,000..............A6 7
Primorsko-Akhtarsk,
Sov. Un., 10,000...H12 12
Primos, Pa., 1,000...*B11 81
Primrose, Pa., 950....*E9 81
Prince, co., P.E.I., Can.,
40,894..............C5 43
Prince Albert, Sask., Can.,
24,168.............D3 39
Prince Edward, co., Ont.,
Can., 21,108........C7 41
Prince Edward, co., Va.,
14,121.............D4 85
Prince Edward Island,
prov., Can.,
104,629............C6 43
Prince George, B.C., Can.,
13,877.............C6 37
Prince George, co., Va.,
20,270.............D5 85
Prince Georges, co., Md.,
357,395............C4 53
Prince Rupert, B.C., Can.,
11,987.............B2 37
Princess Anne, Md.,
1,351..............D6 53
Princeton, Ala., 150...A3 46
Princeton, B.C., Can.,
2,163..............E7 37
Princeton, Fla.,
1,719..........F3, G6 54
Princeton, Ill., 6,250...B4 58
Princeton, Ind., 7,906..H2 59
Princeton, Ky., 5,618..C2 62
Princeton, Minn.,
2,353..............E5 67
Princeton, Mo., 1,443..A4 69
Princeton, N.J., 11,890.C3 74
Princeton, N.C., 948...B5 76
Princeton, W. Va.,
8,393..............D3 87
Princeton, Wis., 1,509..E4 88
Princeville, Que., Can.,
3,174..............C6 42
Princeville, Ill., 1,281..C4 58
Princeville, N.C., 797..B6 76
Prince William, co., Va.,
50,164.............C5 85
Prineville, Oreg., 3,263.C6 80
Prineville Southeast,
Oreg., 1,299.......*C6 80
Pringle, Pa., 1,418...*D10 81
Prinsburg, Minn., 462..F3 67
Priozersk, Sov. Un.,
32,800............G14 11
Pristina, Yugo.,
38,891.............D5 10
Pritzwalk, Ger., 9,416..B6 6
Privas, Fr., 8,663.....E6 5
Privolnoye, Sov. Un.,
9,000..............H9 12
Prizren, Yugo., 28,050.D5 10
Prizzi, It., 9,752.....F4 9
Probolinggo, Indon.,
68,378.............G4 19
Proctor, Minn., 2,963..D6 67
Proctor, Vt., 1,978....D1 73
Progreso, Hond.,
6,921.............*D7 34
Progreso, Mex., 13,659.C7 34
Progress, Pa., 1,700..*F8 84
Project City, Calif.,
950...............B2 50
Prokopyevsk, Sov. Un.,
292,000...........D11 13
Prokuplje, Yugo.,
13,690.............D5 10
Proletarskaya, Sov. Un.,
10,000............H13 12
Prome, Bur., 36,997..E10 20
Prophetstown, Ill.,
1,802..............B4 58
Propriá, Braz.,
15,947............*D7 27
Prosotsani, Grc.,
6,276............*B4 14
Prospect, Conn., 4,367.C5 52
Prospect, Ohio, 1,607..B4 78

Prospect, Pa., 903.....E1 81
Prospect Heights, Ill.,
2,500............*E2 58
Prospect Park, N.J.,
5,201..............B4 74
Prospect Park, Pa.,
6,596.............B11 81
Prosser, Wash., 2,763..C6 86
Prostejov, Czech.,
33,500.............D4 7
Provadiya, Bul., 8,730.D8 10
Provence, former prov.,
Fr., 1,750,000......F7 5
Providence, Ky., 3,771.C2 62
Providence, R.I., 207,498
(*804,300).......B11 52
Providence, Tenn.,
3,830............*A5 83
Providence, Utah,
1,189..............A6 72
Providence, co., R.I.,
568,778...........B10 52
Provincetown, Mass.,
3,389..............B7 65
Provins, Fr., 10,310...C5 5
Provo, Utah, 36,047
(*101,000)......A6, D2 72
Prowers, co., Colo.,
13,296.............D8 51
Prozor, Yugo., 5,506...D3 10
Pruden, Ky., 100.....*D6 62
Prudnik, Pol., 15,200..C4 7
Pruszkow, Pol.,
37,000........B6, m13 7
Pruzhany, Sov. Un.,
10,000.............E5 12
Pryor (Pryor Creek),
Okla., 6,476.......A6 79
Przasnysz, Pol., 7,015..B6 7
Przemysl, Pol., 46,000..D7 7
Przeworsk, Pol., 8,569..C7 7
Pskov, Sov. Un.,
93,000.............C7 12
Pszczyna, Pol.,
12,800.........D5, h9 7
Ptolemais, Grc.,
12,747............*B3 14
Ptuj, Yugo., 7,365.....B2 10
Puebla, Mex.,
287,952.......D5, n14 34
Puebla, state, Mex.,
1,957,380.....D5, n14 34
Puebla de Don Fadrique,
Sp., 7,142.........D4 8
Puebla del Caramiñal,
Sp., 8,337.........A1 8
Pueblo, Colo., 91,181
(*111,000).........C6 51
Pueblo, co., Colo.,
118,707............C6 51
Puenteareas, Sp.,
14,634.............A1 8
Puente Ceso, Sp., 9,780.A1 8
Puentedeume, Sp.,
7,755..............A2 8
Puente-Genil, Sp.,
25,000.............D3 8
Puerto Alvaro Obregón,
Mex., 8,320........D6 34
Puerto Armuelles, Pan.,
10,712...........*B1 32
Puerto Barrios, Guat.,
15,155.............D7 34
Puerto Berrío, Col.,
8,947..............B3 32
Puerto Cabello, Ven.,
50,973.............A4 32
Puerto Casado, Par.,
6,708..............D4 29
Puerto Cortés, Hond.,
17,412.............D7 34
Puerto de la Cruz,
Sp., 5,855........m13 8
Puerto La Cruz, Ven.,
54,954.............A5 32
Puertollano, Sp.,
53,136.............C3 8
Puerto Montt, Chile,
41,000.............C2 28
Puerto Padre, Cuba,
6,949..............E5 35
Puerto Pinasco, Par.,
7,576..............D4 29
Puerto Plata, Dom. Rep.,
19,073.............F8 35
Puerto Real, Sp.,
10,033.............D2 8
Puerto Rico, U.S. dep.,
N.A., 2,349,544....m13 35
Puerto Sastre, Par.,
5,058..............D4 29
Puerto Tejada, Col.,
8,535..............C2 32

Pula, Yugo., 36,838....C1 10
Pulaski, Miss., 200....C4 68
Pulaski, N.Y., 2,256...B4 75
Pulaski, Tenn., 6,616..B4 83
Pulaski, Va., 10,469...D2 85
Pulaski, Wis., 1,540...D5 88
Pulaski, co., Ark.,
242,980............C3 49
Pulaski, co., Ga., 8,204.D3 55
Pulaski, co., Ill.,
10,490.............F4 58
Pulaski, co., Ind.,
12,837.............B4 59
Pulaski, co., Ky.,
34,403.............C5 62
Pulaski, co., Mo.,
46,567.............D5 69
Pulaski, co., Va.,
27,258.............D2 85
Pulawy, Pol., 11,900...C6 7
Pul-i-Khumri, Afg.,
12,246.............A4 20
Pullman, Wash.,
12,957.............C8 86
Pultusk, Pol., 8,787...B6 7
Puluntohai, see Bulun
Tokhoi, China
Punjab, state, India,
20,306,812.........B6 20
Puno, Peru, 18,852...E3 31
Puno, dept., Peru,
646,385............E3 31
Punta Alta, Arg.,
19,852.............B4 28
Punta Arenas, Chile,
48,000............h11 28
Punta Gorda, Fla.,
3,157..............F4 54
Puntarenas, C.R.,
19,500............*F8 34
Puntarenas, prov., C.R.,
148,100...........*F8 34
Punxsutawney, Pa.,
8,805..............E4 81
Puquio, Peru, 6,183...D3 31
Purcell, Mo., 265.....D3 69
Purcell, Okla., 3,729...B4 79
Purcellville, Va., 1,419.B5 85
Purépero, Mex.,
10,092............n12 34
Puri, India, 60,815....E8 20
Purnea, India, 40,602..C8 20
Pursat, Camb., 25,000..C2 19
Pursglove, W. Va., 600.B4 87
Purulia, India, 48,134..D8 20
Purvis, Miss., 1,614...D4 68
Pusan, Kor., 1,162,600..I4 18
Pushkin, Sov. Un.,
51,000.............B8 12
Pushkino, Sov. Un.,
10,000.........C11, m17 12
Pushmataha, Ala., 200.C1 46
Pushmataha, co., Okla.,
9,088..............C6 79
Puspokladany, Hung.,
15,735.............B5 10
Pustelnik, Pol., 5,000..k14 7
Putao, Bur., 10,000...C10 20
Puteaux, Fr., 39,640...g9 5
Putivl, Sov. Un.,
10,000.............F9 12
Putnam, Conn., 6,952..B9 52
Putnam, co., Fla.,
32,212.............C5 54
Putnam, co., Ga.,
7,798..............C3 55
Putnam, co., Ill., 4,570.B4 58
Putnam, co., Ind.,
24,927.............E4 59
Putnam, co., Mo.,
6,999..............A4 69
Putnam, co., N.Y.,
31,722.............D7 75
Putnam, co., Ohio,
28,331.............B3 78
Putnam, co., Tenn.,
29,236.............C8 83
Putnam, co., W. Va.,
23,561.............C3 87
Puttalam, Cey., 10,162.G6 20
Putumayo, comisaría,
Col., 35,000........C2 32
Puukolii, Haw., 500...C5 56
Puunene, Haw., 3,054..C5 56
Puyallup, Wash.,
12,063.........B3, E2 86
Puy-de-Dôme, dept., Fr.,
508,928...........*E5 5
Puyo, Ec., 1,092.....B2 31
Pyapon, Bur., 19,174..E10 20
Pyatigorsk, Sov. Un.,
73,000...........*E7 13
Pyinmana, Bur.,
22,066............E10 20
Pyŏngyang, Kor.,
653,100............G2 18
Pyrénées-Orientales, dept.,
Fr., 251,231.......*F5 5
Pyskowice, Pol.,
21,000............g9 7
Pyu, Bur., 10,443....E10 20

Q

Qalqīlyah, Jordan,
8,000..............B2 15
Qana, Leb., 5,000.....A3 15
Qatar, country, Asia,
20,000.............D5 15
Qinā, Eg., U.A.R.,
47,700.............C4 23
Quakenbrück, Ger.,
7,800..............B3 15
Quaker Hill, Conn.,
1,671..............D8 52
Quakertown, Pa.,
6,305.............F11 81
Quanah, Tex., 4,564...B3 84
Quang Ngai, Viet.,
5,000..............B3 19
Quang Tri, Viet.,
13,425.............B3 19
Quantico, Va., 1,015...C5 85
Quapaw, Okla., 850....A7 79
Quaraí, Braz., 10,575...E1 30
Quarryville, Pa.,
1,427..............G9 81
Quartu Sant' Elena, It.,
22,916.............E2   9
Quartz Hill, Calif.,
3,325.............*E4 50
Quay, co., N. Mex.,
12,279.............B7 48

Quebec, Que., Can.,
171,979
(*357,568)......C6, C9 42
Quebec, co., Que., Can.,
331,307............B5 42
Quebec, prov., Can.,
5,259,211......... 42
Quebec-Ouest, Que.,
Can., 8,733.......*C6 42
Quedlinburg, Ger.,
30,700.............C5   6
Queen Annes, co., Md.,
16,569.............B5 53
Queen Charlotte, is., B.C.,
Can................C1 37
Queen City, Tex.,
1,081.............*C6 84
Queen Elizabeth, is.,
N.W. Ter., Can....m31 36
Queens, borough and co.,
N.Y., 1,809,578 (part of
New York City).....D2 75
Queens, co., N.B., Can.,
11,640.............D4 43
Queens, co., N.S., Can.,
13,155.............E4 43
Queens, co., P.E.I., Can.,
45,842.............C6 43
Queensland, state, Austl.,
1,518,828..........D7 25

Queenstown, S. Afr.,
33,182.............G5 24
Quelimane, Moz.,
8,000..............D7 24
Querétaro, Mex.,
67,277.........C4, m13 34
Querétaro, state, Mex.,
353,154........C4, m13 34
Quesada, Sp., 7,609...D4   8
Quesnel, B.C., Can.,
4,673..............C6 37
Questa, N. Mex., 900..A6 48
Quetta, Pak., 75,000...B4 20
Quezaltenango, Guat.,
27,672.............E6 34
Quezaltepeque, Sal.,
8,471.............*E7 34
Quezon, prov., Phil.,
656,900...........*C6 19
Quezon City, Phil.,
397,400............C6 19
Quibdó, Col., 9,700...B2 32
Quidnessett, R.I.,
1,000.............C11 52
Quidnick, R.I., 2,000..C10 52
Quiindy, Par., 2,150....E4 29
Quillota, Chile, 27,000..A2 28
Quilmes, Arg., 310,000..g7 28
Quilon, India, 91,018...G6 20

Quilpué, Chile, 26,000..A2 28
Quimper, Fr., 45,989...C2   5
Quimperlé, Fr., 10,272.D2   5
Quincy, Calif., 1,700...C3 50
Quincy, Fla., 8,874...B2 54
Quincy, Ill., 43,793...D2 58
Quincy, Mass.,
87,409.........B5, D3 65
Quincy, Mich., 1,602..G6 66
Quincy, Wash., 3,269..B6 86
Qui Nhon, Viet.,
10,000.............C3 19
Quinnville, R.I., 400..B11 52
Quintana de la Serena, Sp.,
7,861..............C3   8
Quintanar, Sp., 9,483..C4   8
Quintana Roo, ter., Mex.,
52,312.............D7 34
Quinton, Okla., 898....B6 79
Quiroga, Sp., 8,380....A2   8
Quitman, Ga., 5,071...F3 55
Quitman, Miss., 2,030..C5 68
Quitman, Tex., 1,237...C5 84
Quitman, co., Ga.,
2,432..............E1 55
Quitman, co., Miss.,
21,019.............A3 68
Quito, Ec., 209,932....B2 31
Quixadá, Braz., 8,747.*D7 27

R

Raba, Indon., 6,781....G5 19
Rabat, Mor., 227,445..B3 22
Rabun, Ala., 300......D2 46
Rabun, co., Ga., 7,456..B3 55
Raceland, Ky., 1,115..B7 62
Raceland, La.,
3,666..........E5, C6 63
Rach Gia, Viet.,
24,000............*C2 19
Raciborz, Pol.,
32,000.............C5   7
Racine, Wis., 89,144
(*113,500)......F2, F6 88
Racine, co., Wis.,
141,781............F5 88
Rădăuti, Rom., 15,949.B7 10
Radcliff, Ky., 3,384....C4 62
Radeberg, Ger., 16,300.C6   6
Radford (Independent
City), Va., 9,371....D2 85
Radiant Valley, Md.,
1,500.............*C4 53
Radnor, Pa., 1,000..*A10 81
Radnor, co., Wales,
18,431............*D5   4
Radom, Pol., 130,000..C6   7
Radomir, Bul., 5,778..D6 10
Radomsko, Pol., 27,000.C5   7
Radville, Sask., Can.,
1,067..............H3 39
Radzionkow, Pol.,
24,000.............g9   7
Rae Bareli, India,
29,940.............C7 20
Raeford, N.C., 3,058...C4 76
Rafaela, Arg., 23,665..A4 28
Ragland, Ala., 1,166...B3 46
Ragunda, Swe., 202....F7 11
Ragusa, It., 47,000....F5   9
Rahimyar-Khan, Pak.,
14,919.............C5 20
Rahway, N.J.,
27,699.........B4, E4 74
Raichur, India, 63,329..E6 20
Raigarh, India, 36,933.D7 20
Rainbow City, Ala.,
1,625.............*A3 46
Rainier, Oreg., 1,152...A4 80
Rains, co., Tex., 2,993..C5 84
Rainsville, Ala., 398....A4 46
Rainy River, Ont., Can.,
1,168..............E6 41
Rainy River, co., Ont.,
Can., 26,531.......E7 41
Raipur, India, 139,792.D7 20
Rajahmundry, India,
130,002............E7 20
Rajasthan, state, India,
20,155,602.........C5 20
Rajkot, India, 193,498.D5 20
Rakovnik, Czech.,
12,000.............C2   7
Rakvere, Sov. Un.,
25,000.............B6 12
Raleigh, N.C., 93,931
(*130,200).........B5 76
Raleigh, Tenn.,
6,000..........B2, E8 83
Raleigh, W. Va., 750..D7 87
Raleigh, co., W. Va.,
77,826.............D3 87
Ralls, Tex., 2,229....C2 84
Ralls, co., Mo., 8,078..B6 69
Ralston, Nebr., 2,977..D4 71

Rām Allāh, Jordan,
17,145.............C3 15
Ramat Gan, Isr.,
90,234.............B2 15
Rambervillers, Fr.,
7,042..............C7   5
Ramea, Newf., Can.,
970................E3 44
Ramenskoye, Sov. Un.,
10,000.......D12, n18 12
Ramle, Isr., 22,444....C2 15
Ramleh, Eg., U.A.R.,
52,000............*G8 14
Râmnicu-Sărat, Rom.,
19,095.............C8 10
Râmnicu-Vâlcea, Rom.,
18,984.............C7 10
Ramona, Calif., 2,449..F5 50
Rampur, India,
135,407............C6 20
Rampur-Baolia, Pak.,
39,993.............D8 20
Ramsay, Mich., 1,158..A5 66
Ramseur, N.C., 1,258..B4 76
Ramsey, N.J., 9,527...A4 74
Ramsey, co., Minn.,
422,525............E5 67
Ramsey, co., N. Dak.,
13,443.............B7 77
Ramsgate, Eng.,
36,906.............E7   4
Rancagua, Chile,
50,000.............A2 28
Ranches of Taos, N.
Mex., 1,668........A6 48
Ranchi, India, 122,416.D8 20
Rancho Cordova, Calif.,
7,429.............*C3 50
Rand, W. Va., 3,500...C6 87
Randall, co., Tex.,
33,913.............B2 84
Randallstown, Md.,
2,000..............B4 53
Randers, Den., 42,238..I4 11
Randers, co., Den.,
170,802............I4 11
Randleman, N.C.,
2,232..............B4 76
Randolph, Maine,
1,724..............D3 64
Randolph, Mass.,
18,900.........B5, D3 65
Randolph, Nebr., 1,063.B8 71
Randolph, N.Y., 1,414.C2 75
Randolph, Vt., 2,122...D2 73
Randolph, Wis., 1,507..E4 88
Randolph, co., Ala.,
19,477.............B4 46
Randolph, co., Ark.,
12,520.............A4 49
Randolph, co., Ga.,
11,078.............E2 55
Randolph, co., Ill.,
29,988.............E4 58
Randolph, co., Ind.,
28,434.............D7 59
Randolph, co., Mo.,
22,014.............B5 69
Randolph, co., N.C.,
61,497.............B4 76
Randolph, co., W. Va.,
26,349.............C5 87
Randolph Hills, Md.,
2,000.............*B3 53

Ranger, Tex., 3,313....C3 84
Rangley, Colo., 1,464..A2 51
Rangoon, Bur.,
752,000...........E10 20
Rangpur, Pak., 31,759..C8 20
Raniganj, India,
30,113.............D8 20
Rankin, Pa., 5,164....B6 81
Rankin, Tex., 1,214....D2 84
Rankin, co., Miss.,
34,322.............C4 68
Ranlo, N.C., 2,000....*B2 76
Ranshaw, Pa., 1,078..*E9 81
Ransom, W. Va., 1,974.B7 87
Ransom, co., N. Dak.,
8,078..............D8 77
Rantoul, Ill., 22,116...C5 58
Rapallo, It., 20,606....B2   9
Rapid City, S. Dak.,
42,399.............F2 77
Rapides, par., La.,
111,351............C3 63
Rappahannock, co.,
Va., 5,368.........C4 85
Raritan, N.J., 6,137....B3 74
Raseiniai, Sov. Un.,
6,181..............A7   7
Rasht, Iran, 109,491...A7 23
Rasskazovo, Sov. Un.,
43,500...........E13 12
Rastatt, Ger., 24,100..D4   7
Rat Buri, Thai., 19,092.C1 19
Rathenow, Ger., 28,600.B6   6
Ratibor, see Raciborz, Pol.
Ratnagiri, India,
31,901.............E5 20
Raton, N. Mex., 8,146..A6 48
Rauch, Arg., 5,274....B5 28
Rauma, Fin., 21,700...G9 11
Ravalli, co., Mont.,
12,341.............D2 70
Rava-Russkaya, Sov. Un.,
10,000.............F4 12
Raven, Va., 900......B3 85
Ravena, N.Y., 2,410...C7 75
Ravenna, It., 54,000...B4   9
Ravenna, Ky., 921....C6 62
Ravenna, Nebr., 1,417.C7 71
Ravenna, Ohio, 10,918.A6 78
Ravensburg, Ger.,
31,300.............E4   6
Ravenswood, W. Va.,
3,410..............C3 87
Rawalpindi, Pak., 250,000
(*340,175).........B5 20
Rawa Mazowiecka, Pol.,
6,908..............C6   7
Rawdon, Que., Can.,
2,388..............C4 42
Rawicz, Pol., 11,600...C4   7
Rawlins, Wyo., 8,968..D5 89
Rawlins, co., Kans.,
5,279..............C2 61
Ray, Ariz., 1,468..C3, D3 48
Ray, N. Dak., 1,049...B2 77
Ray, co., Mo., 16,075..B3 70
Raybon, Ga., 400.....E5 55
Raychikha, Sov. Un.,
30,000.............B4 18
Raymond, Alta., Can.,
2,362..............E4 38
Raymond, Miss., 1,381.C3 68
Raymond, Wash.,
3,301..............C2 86

Raymondville, Tex.,
9,385..............F4 84
Rayne, La., 8,634.....D3 63
Raynham Center, Mass.,
500................C5 65
Rayong, Thai, 10,776..*C2 19
Raytown, Ga., 100....C4 55
Raytown, Mo., 17,083..E2 69
Rayville, La., 4,052....B4 63
Razgrad, Bul., 15,023..D8 10
Razlog, Bul., 6,857....E6 10
Reading, Eng., 119,870.E6   4
Reading, Mass.,
19,259.........A5, C3 65
Reading, Mich., 1,128..G6 66
Reading, Ohio,
12,832.........C3, D2 78
Reading, Pa., 98,177
(*192,500).......F10 81
Reagan, co., Tex.,
3,782..............D2 84
Real, co., Tex., 2,079..E3 84
Ream, Camb., 5,000...*C2 19
Ream, W. Va., 800...*D3 87
Reamstown, Pa., 950..F9 81
Recanati, It., 6,288....C4   9
Rechitsa, Sov. Un.,
33,800.............E8 12
Recife, Braz., 788,569..D7 27
Recklinghausen, Ger.,
130,600............C3   6
Reconquista, Arg.,
12,729.............E4 29
Rector, Ark., 1,757....A5 49
Red Bank, N.J., 12,482.C4 74
Red Bank-White Oak,
Tenn., 10,777......*D8 83
Red Bay, Ala., 1,954...A1 46
Red Bluff, Calif., 7,202.B2 50
Red Boiling Springs,
Tenn., 597.........C8 83
Red Bud, Ill., 1,942...E4 58
Redcliff, Alta., Can.,
2,221..............D5 38
Red Cloud, Nebr.,
1,525..............D7 71
Red Deer, Alta.,
Can., 19,612....C4, D1 38
Reddell, La., 500.....D3 63
Redding, Calif., 12,773.B2 50
Redfield, Iowa, 966....C3 60
Redfield, S. Dak., 2,952.F7 77
Redford Heights,
Mich., 71,276.....*F7 66
Red Hill, Pa., 1,086..*F11 81
Red Hook, N.Y., 1,719.D7 75
Redington Beach, Fla.,
1,368.............*E4 54
Redington Shores, Fla.,
917...............*E4 54
Red Jacket, W. Va.,
950................D2 87
Red Key, Ind., 1,746..D7 59
Red Lake, Ont., Can.,
2,051..............D5 40
Red Lake, co., Minn.,
5,830..............C2 67
Red Lake Falls, Minn.,
1,520..............C2 67
Redlands, Calif.,
26,829.........E5, F3 50
Red Lion, Pa., 5,594...G8 81
Red Lodge, Mont.,
2,278..............E7 70

Redmond, Oreg., 3,340.C5 80
Redmond, Wash.,
  1,426..............C2 86
Red Oak, Ga., 800.....B5 55
Red Oak, Iowa, 6,421..D2 60
Redon, Fr., 6,444......D3 5
Redondela, Sp., 3,261..A1 8
Redondo Beach, Calif.,
  46,986.............F2 50
Redore, Minn., 170....C6 67
Red River, co., Tex.,
  15,682.............C5 84
Red River, par., La.,
  9,978..............B2 63
Red Springs, N.C.,
  2,767..............C4 76
Redstone, Ala., 1,000..*A2 46
Redstone, Colo., 160...B3 51
Red Tank, C.Z.,
  1,949.............*B2 32
Redtop, Mo., 128.....D4 69
Redwater, Alta., Can.,
  1,135..............C4 38
Red Willow, co., Nebr.,
  12,940.............D5 71
Red Wing, Minn.,
  10,528.............F6 67
Redwood, co., Minn.,
  21,718.............F3 67
Redwood City, Calif.,
  46,290.........B5, D2 50
Redwood Estates, Calif.,
  930...............*C6 50
Redwood Falls, Minn.,
  4,285..............F3 67
Reed City, Mich.,
  2,184..............E5 66
Reedley, Calif., 5,850..D4 50
Reedsburg, Wis., 4,371.E3 88
Reeds Lake, Mich.,
  10,924.............F5 66
Reedsport, Oreg.,
  2,998..............D3 80
Reedsville, Pa., 950...E6 81
Reese Village, Tex.,
  1,433.............*C2 84
Reeves, co., Tex.,
  17,644.............D1 84
Reform, Ala., 1,241...B1 46
Refugio, Tex., 4,944...E4 84
Refugio, co., Tex.,
  10,975.............E4 84
Regensburg, Ger.,
  125,000............D6 6
Reggio [di] Calabria,
  It., 124,000........E5 9
Reggio nell'Emilia, It.,
  86,000.............B3 9
Reghin, Rom., 18,091..B7 10
Regina, Sask., Can.,
  112,141............G3 39
Region Occidental (Chaco),
  dept., Par., 54,277.*D3 29
Regla, Cuba, 26,755...h12 35
Rehoboth Beach, Del.,
  1,507..............C7 53
Rehovot, Isr., 28,740..C2 15
Reichenbach, Ger.,
  29,600.............C6 6
Reidsville, Ga., 1,229..D4 55
Reidsville, N.C., 14,267.A4 76
Reigate, Eng., 53,710..E6 4
Reims, Fr., 133,914....C6 5
Reinbeck, Iowa, 1,621.B5 60
Reinosa, Sp., 10,044..A3 8
Reisterstown, Md.,
  3,300..............B4 53
Relizane, see Ighil
  Izane, Alg.
Rembertow, Pol.,
  22,000.........B6, k14 7
Remedios, Cuba,
  10,602.............D4 35
Remerton, Ga., 571....F3 55
Remington, Ind., 1,207.C3 59
Remiremont, Fr.,
  9,350..............C7 5
Remscheid, Ger.,
  126,900............C3 6
Remsen, Iowa, 1,338..B2 60
Rendsburg, Ger.,
  35,700.............A4 6
Renfrew, Ont., Can.,
  8,935..............B8 41
Renfrew, co., Ont.,
  Can., 89,635........B7 41
Renfrew, co., Scot.,
  338,815...........*C4 4
Rengo, Chile, 9,115....A2 28
Rennes, Fr., 151,948...C3 5
Reno, Nev., 51,470....B2 72
Reno, co., Kans.,
  59,055.............E5 61
Renovo, Pa., 3,316....D6 81
Rensselaer, Ind., 4,740.C3 59
Rensselaer, N.Y.,
  10,506.............C7 75
Rensselaer, co., N.Y.,
  142,585............C7 75
Renton, Wash.,
  18,453.........B3, D2 86

Renville, Minn., 1,373..F3 67
Renville, co., Minn.,
  23,249.............F4 67
Renville, co., N. Dak.,
  4,698..............B4 77
Republic, Mich., 950..B3 66
Republic, Mo., 1,519..D4 69
Republic, Pa., 1,921...G2 81
Republic, Wash.,
  1,064..............A7 86
Republic, co., Kans.,
  9,768..............C6 61
Requena, Sp., 8,228....C5 8
Reserve, La., 5,297....B6 63
Resistencia, Arg.,
  80,000.............E4 29
Reşiţa, Rom., 41,241...C5 10
Restigouche, co., N.B.,
  Can., 40,973........B2 43
Reszel, Pol., 5,693....A6 7
Retalhuleu, Guat.,
  9,304..............E6 34
Rethimni, prov., Grc.,
  69,943............*E5 14
Rethimnon, Grc.,
  14,999.............E5 14
Reus, Sp., 41,014.....B6 8
Reutlingen, Ger.,
  67,400.............D4 6
Revel, Fr., 4,288......F5 5
Revelo, Ky., 500......D5 62
Revelstoke, B.C., Can.,
  3,624..............D8 37
Revere, Mass., 40,080..C3 65
Revere, Minn., 201....F3 67
Revin, Fr., 11,244.....C6 5
Revloc, Pa., 900......F4 81
Rewa, India, 43,065...D7 20
Rewari, India, 36,994..C6 20
Rexburg, Idaho, 4,767.F7 57
Reykjavík, Ice.,
  73,388.............n22 11
Reynolds, Ga., 1,087..D2 55
Reynolds, co., Mo.,
  5,161..............D6 69
Reynoldsburg, Ohio,
  7,793.........C2, C5 78
Reynolds Corners,
  Ohio, 7,000........A2 78
Reynoldsville, Pa.,
  3,158..............D4 81
Reynosa, Mex.,
  74,113.............B5 34
Rezé, Fr., 28,276......D3 5
Rezekne, Sov. Un.,
  13,139.............C6 12
Rhea, co., Tenn.,
  15,863.............D9 83
Rheden, Neth., 7,800..A7 5
Rheine, Ger., 44,300..B3 6
Rheinland-Pfalz, state,
  Ger., 3,417,100......C3 6
Rhinebeck, N.Y.,
  2,093..............D7 75
Rhineland, reg., Ger...C3 6
Rhinelander, Wis.,
  8,790..............C4 88
Rhode Island, state,
  U.S., 859,488.......... 52
Rhodesia, Br. dep., Afr.,
  3,150,000...........D5 24
Rhodhiss, N.C., 837...B2 76
Rhondda, Wales,
  100,314............E5 4
Rhône, dept., Fr.,
  1,116,664..........*E6 5
Rhyl, Wales, 21,825...D5 4
Rialto, Calif., 18,567..*F3 50
Rianjo, Sp., 9,971....A1 8
Ribadavia, Sp., 7,031..A1 8
Ribadeo, Sp., 9,867...A2 8
Ribadesella, Sp., 8,228.A3 8
Ribatejo, prov., Port.,
  464,874...........*C1 8
Ribe, co., Den.,
  178,501...........*J3 11
Ribeirão Prêto, Braz.,
  116,153.........C3, k8 30
Ribera, It., 18,547....F4 9
Ricany, Czech., 6,376..o18 7
Rice, co., Kans.,
  13,909.............D5 61
Rice, co., Minn.,
  38,988.............F5 67
Rice Lake, Wis., 7,303..C2 88
Riceville, Iowa, 898....A5 60
Rich, Miss., 100......A3 68
Rich, co., Utah, 1,685..A6 72
Richardson, Tex.,
  16,810.............B5 84
Richardson, co., Nebr.,
  13,903.............D10 71
Richelieu, co., Que.,
  Can., 38,565........D4 42
Richfield, Calif., 250...C2 50
Richfield, Minn.,
  42,523.............E7 67
Richfield, Utah, 4,412..B5 72
Richfield Springs, N.Y.,
  1,630..............C6 75
Richford, Vt., 1,663...B2 73

Rich Hill, Mo., 1,699...C3 69
Richibucto, N.B.,
  Can., 1,375.........C5 43
Richland, Ga., 1,472...D2 55
Richland, Mo., 1,662..D5 69
Richland, Pa., 1,276..*F9 81
Richland, Wash.,
  23,548.............C6 86
Richland, co., Ill.,
  16,299.............E5 58
Richland, co., Mont.,
  10,504.............C12 70
Richland, co., N. Dak.,
  18,824.............D9 77
Richland, co., Ohio,
  117,761............B5 78
Richland, co., S.C.,
  200,102............D6 82
Richland, co., Wis.,
  17,684.............E3 88
Richland, par., La.,
  23,824.............B4 63
Richland Center, Wis.,
  4,746..............E3 88
Richland Hills, Tex.,
  7,804.............*B5 84
Richlands, N.C., 1,079 C6 76
Richlands, Va., 4,963..B3 85
Richmond, Calif.,
  71,854.........B5, D2 50
Richmond, Que., Can.,
  4,072..............D5 42
Richmond, Eng.,
  41,002.............m11 4
Richmond, Ind., 44,149.E8 59
Richmond, Ky., 12,168.C5 62
Richmond, Maine,
  1,412.........D3, D6 64
Richmond, Mich.,
  2,667..............F8 66
Richmond, Mo., 4,604..B4 69
Richmond, Tex.,
  3,668.........E5, F4 84
Richmond, Utah, 1,991.A6 72
Richmond, Va., 219,958
  (*409,100)......C7, D5 85
Richmond (Staten Island),
  borough and co., N.Y.,
  221,991 (part of New
  York City).........E1 75
Richmond, co., N.S.,
  Can., 11,374........D9 43
Richmond, co., Que.,
  Can., 42,232........D5 42
Richmond, co., Ga.,
  135,601............C4 55
Richmond, co., N.C.,
  39,202.............B4 76
Richmond, co., Va.,
  6,375..............D6 85
Richmond Beach, Wash.,
  2,000..............B3 86
Richmond Heights, Fla.,
  4,311..............F3 54
Richmond Heights, Mo.,
  15,622.............B8 69
Richmond Highlands,
  Wash., 6,000......*B3 86
Richmond Hill, Ont.,
  Can., 16,446....D5, E6 41
Richmond Hill, N.C.,
  2,943.............*A4 76
Rich Square, N.C.,
  1,134..............A6 76
Richton, Miss., 1,089..D5 68
Richwood, Ohio, 2,137.B4 78
Richwood, W. Va.,
  4,110..............C4 87
Ridder, see Leninogorsk,
  Sov. Un.
Ridge, Va., 20,000....*D5 85
Ridgecrest, Calif.,
  5,099.............*E5 50
Ridgecrest, Wash.,
  3,000.............*B3 87
Ridgedale, Mo., 135....E4 69
Ridgedale, Tenn.,
  1,000.............*D10 83
Ridge Farm, Ill., 894..D6 58
Ridgefield, Conn.,
  2,954..............D3 52
Ridgefield, N.J.,
  10,788.............D5 74
Ridgefield Park, N.J.,
  12,701.........B4, D5 74
Ridgeland, S.C., 1,192..G6 82
Ridgeley, W. Va., 1,229.B6 87
Ridgely, Tenn., 1,464..A2 83
Ridgetown, Ont., Can.,
  2,603..............E3 41
Ridgeville, Ga., 200....E5 55
Ridgeville, Ind., 950...D7 59
Ridgewood, Ill., 5,586.*B5 58
Ridgewood, N.J.,
  25,391.............B4 74
Ridgewood Heights, Ohio,
  1,500.............*C3 78
Ridgway, Ill., 1,055...F5 58
Ridgway, Pa., 6,387...D4 81

Ridley Farms, Pa.,
  1,500.............*G11 81
Ridley Park, Pa.,
  7,387.............B11 81
Ried, Aus., 9,471.....D6 6
Riegelsville, Pa., 953...B2 81
Riesa, Ger., 36,800....C6 6
Rieti, It., 23,500......C4 9
Rifle, Colo., 2,135....B3 51
Riga, Sov. Un., 607,000.C5 12
Rigaud, Que., Can.,
  1,990..............D3 42
Rigby, Idaho, 2,281....F7 57
Riihimäki, Fin.,
  20,200............G11 11
Rijeka, Yugo., 100,339.C2 10
Riley, co., Kans.,
  41,914.............C7 61
Rimbey, Alta., Can.,
  1,266..............C3 38
Rimersburg, Pa., 1,323.D2 81
Rimini, It., 63,000.....B4 9
Rimouski, Que., Can.,
  17,739.............A9 42
Rimouski, co., Que.,
  Can., 65,295........A9 42
Rincon, Ga., 1,057....D5 55
Ringgold, Ga., 1,311..B1 55
Ringgold, La., 953....B2 63
Ringgold, co., Iowa,
  7,910..............D3 60
Ringkøbing, co., Den.,
  198,389...........*I3 11
Ringling, Okla., 1,170..C4 79
Ringsaker, Nor.,
  15,017.............G4 11
Ringsted, Den., 9,694..A1 7
Ringwood, N.J., 4,182..A4 74
Rio Arriba, co., N. Mex.,
  24,193.............A5 48
Riobamba, Ec., 29,611.B2 31
Rio Blanco, co., Colo.,
  5,150..............B2 51
Rio Branco, Braz.,
  17,245.............C4 31
Río Caribe, Ven., 7,188.A5 32
Rio Claro, Braz.,
  48,548.........C3, m8 30
Río Cuarto, Arg.,
  70,000.............A4 28
Rio de Janeiro, Braz.,
  3,307,163.......C4, h6 30
Rio de Janeiro, state,
  Braz., 3,402,728..C4, h6 30
Rio Dell, Calif.,
  3,222.............*B1 50
Río Gallegos, Arg.,
  5,880.........E3, h12 28
Rio Grande, Braz.,
  83,189.............E2 28
Rio Grande, Mex.,
  8,208..............C4 34
Rio Grande, N.J.,
  950................E3 74
Rio Grande, co., Colo.,
  11,160.............D4 51
Rio Grande City, Tex.,
  5,835..............F3 84
Rio Grande do Norte,
  state, Braz.,
  1,157,258.........*D7 27
Rio Grande do Sul, state,
  Braz., 5,448,823...E2 30
Ríohacha, Col., 5,953...A3 32
Rio Hondo, Tex., 1,344.F4 84
Rio Linda, Calif.,
  6,000.............*A6 50
Riom, Fr., 14,418......E5 5
Rio Muni, reg., Equat.
  Gui., 183,377.......H7 22
Rio Negro, Braz.,
  10,225............D3 30
Río Negro, dept., Ur.,
  192,595...........*E1 30
Río Negro, prov., Arg.,
  41,400.............C3 28
Rionero in Vulture, It.,
  14,378.............D5 9
Rio Pardo, Braz.,
  14,412.............D2 30
Río Piedras, P.R., 65,406
  (part of San Juan)..m13 35
Ríosucio (Caldas dept.),
  Col., 7,363.........B2 32
Río Tercero, Arg.,
  10,683.............A4 28
Rio Verde, Braz.,
  11,268.............B2 30
Río Verde (Ríoverde),
  Mex., 14,294.......m13 34
Rio Vista, Calif.,
  2,616.........B6, C3 50
Ripley, Miss., 2,668....A5 68
Ripley, N.Y., 1,247....C1 75
Ripley, Ohio, 2,174...D4 78
Ripley, Tenn., 3,782...B2 83
Ripley, W. Va., 2,756..C3 87
Ripley, co., Ind.,
  20,641.............F7 59
Ripley, co., Mo., 9,096.E7 69
Ripoll, Sp., 9,034.....A7 8

Ripon, Calif., 1,894....B6   50
Ripon, Eng., 10,490....C6   4
Ripon, Wis., 6,163.....E5   88
Rishon le-Zion, Isr.,
  27,998.................C3   15
Rising Star, Tex., 997..C3   84
Rising Sun, Ind., 2,230.G8   59
Rison, Ark., 889.....D3   49
Ritchey, Mo., 128.....E3   69
Ritchie, co., W. Va.,
  10,877................B3   87
Rittman, Ohio, 5,410..B6   78
Ritzville, Wash., 2,173.B7   86
Riva, It., 6,839........B3   9
Rivadavia, Arg., 5,643..A3   28
Rive-de-Gier, Fr.,
  16,565................E6   5
Rivera, Ur., 36,700....E1   30
Rivera, dept., Ur.,
  68,700...............*E1   30
Riverbank, Calif.,
  2,786.................D3   50
Riverdale, Calif., 1,012.D4   50
Riverdale, Ga., 1,045..*C2   55
Riverdale, Ill., 12,008..D4   58
Riverdale, Md.,
  4,389............C2, C4   53
Riverdale, N.J., 2,596..B4   74
Riverdale, N. Dak.,
  1,055.................C4   77
Riverdale, Oreg.,
  1,500................*B4   80
Riverdale, Utah,
  1,848................*A6   72
Riverdale Heights, Md.,
  1,800................*C4   53
River Edge, N.J.,
  13,264................D5   74
River Falls, Wis., 4,857.D1   88
River Forest, Ill.,
  12,695................F2   58
River Grove, Ill., 8,464.E2   58
Riverhead, N.Y., 5,830.D4   75
River Hebert, N.S., Can.,
  1,382.................D5   43
River Hills, Wis., 1,257.E2   88
Riverina, reg., Austl...F7   25
Riverland Terrace, S.C.,
  2,400................*F2   82
River Oaks, Tex.,
  8,444................*C4   84
River Pines, Mass.,
  800.................*C2   65
River Plaza, N.J.,
  4,500................*C4   74
River Rouge, Mich.,
  18,147............A7, F7   66
Rivers, Man., Can.,
  1,574.................D1   40
Riverside, Calif.,
  84,332...........F3, F5   50
Riverside, Ont., Can.,
  18,089................E2   41
Riverside, Colo., 180...B5   51
Riverside, Ill., 9,750....F2   58
Riverside, Mo., 1,315..*B3   69
Riverside, N.J., 8,474..C3   74
Riverside, N.Y., 1,030.*C3   75
Riverside, Pa., 1,580...E8   81
Riverside, S.C., 1,200.*B3   82
Riverside, co., Calif.,
  306,191...............F5   50
Riverton, Ill., 1,591....D4   58
Riverton, N.J., 3,324...C2   74
Riverton, Utah, 1,993..D2   72
Riverton, Wyo., 6,845..B4   89
Riverton Heights, Wash.,
  19,000...............*B3   86
River Vale, N.J.,
  5,616................*A5   74
River View, Ala., 1,171.C4   46
Riverview, Calif.,
  7,000................*E4   50
Riverview, Fla., 4,000..B6   54
Riverview, Fla., 1,000..E2   54
Riverview, Mich.,
  7,237.................A7   66
Riverview, Mo., 3,706.*C7   69
Riverview (Pasco West),
  Wash., 2,894........*C6   86
Rives, Mo., 134......E7   69
Rivesville, W. Va.,
  1,191.............A7, B4   87
Riviera Beach, Fla.,
  13,046................F6   54
Riviera Beach, Md.,
  4,902................*B4   53
Riviere Bleue, Que.,
  Can., 1,540..........B8   42
Riviere des Praries, Que.,
  Can., 10,054........*D9   42
Riviere du Loup, Que.,
  Can., 10,835.........B8   42
Riviere du Loup, co., Que.,
  Can., 40,239.........B9   42
Riviere du Moulin, Que.,
  Can., 4,386..........A6   42
Riyadh (Ar Riyāḍ), Sau.
  Ar., 150,000.........E4   15
Rizal, prov., Phil.,
  1,463,500..........*B6   14

Rize, Tur., 22,300....B13   14
Rjukan, Nor., 5,677....H3   11
Roachdale, Ind., 927...E4   59
Roane, co., Tenn.,
  39,133................D9   83
Roane, co., W. Va.,
  15,720................C3   87
Roan Mountain, Tenn.,
  800.................C11   83
Roanne, Fr., 51,723...D5   5
Roanoke, Ala., 5,288..B4   46
Roanoke, Ill., 1,821....C4   58
Roanoke, Ind., 935....C7   59
Roanoke (Independent
  City), Va., 97,110
  (*160,400)..........D3   85
Roanoke, co., Va.,
  61,693................D2   85
Roanoke Rapids, N.C.,
  13,320................A6   76
Roaring Springs, Pa.,
  2,937.................F5   81
Robbins, Ill., 7,511....F3   58
Robbins, N.C., 1,294...B4   76
Robbinsdale, Minn.,
  16,381...........E5, E6   67
Robersonville, N.C.,
  1,684.................B6   76
Robert Lee, Tex., 990..D2   84
Roberts, co., S. Dak.,
  13,190................E9   77
Roberts, co., Tex.,
  1,075.................B2   84
Robertsdale, Ala.,
  1,474.................E2   46
Robertsdale, Pa., 800...F5   81
Robertson, co., Ky.,
  2,443.................B5   62
Robertson, co., Tenn.,
  27,335................A5   83
Robertson, co., Tex.,
  16,157................D4   84
Robertsonville, Que., Can.,
  1,156.................C6   42
Roberval, Que., Can.,
  7,739.................A5   42
Robeson, co., N.C.,
  89,102................C4   76
Robesonia, Pa., 1,579..*F9   81
Robinson, Ill., 7,226...D6   58
Robinson, Pa., 900.....F3   81
Robinson, Tex., 2,111.*D4   84
Robinsonville, Miss.,
  115...................A3   68
Robinwood, Ala.,
  1,000................*B3   46
Roblin, Man., Can.,
  1,368.................D1   40
Robstown, Tex.,
  10,266................F4   84
Roby, Mo., 100.......D5   69
Roby, Tex., 913.......C2   84
Roccastrada, It.,
  3,109.................C3   9
Rocha, Ur., 18,200.....E2   30
Rocha, dept., Ur.,
  53,400...............*E2   30
Rochdale, Eng., 85,785.D5   4
Rochdale, Mass., 1,058.B4   65
Rochefort, Fr., 28,648..E3   5
Rochelle, Ga., 1,235...E3   55
Rochelle, Ill., 7,008....B4   58
Rochelle Park, N.J.,
  6,119.................D5   74
Rochester, Ind., 4,883.B5   59
Rochester, Mich., 5,431.F7   66
Rochester, Minn.,
  40,663................F6   67
Rochester, N.H.,
  15,927................E6   73
Rochester, N.Y., 318,611
  (*594,500)..........B3   75
Rochester, Pa., 5,952...E1   81
Rock, co., Minn.,
  11,864................G2   67
Rock, co., Nebr., 2,554.B6   71
Rock, co., Wis.,
  113,913...............F4   88
Rockaway, N.J., 5,413.B3   74
Rockaway, Oreg., 771..B3   80
Rockbridge, co., Va.,
  24,039................D3   85
Rockcastle, co., Ky.,
  12,334................C5   62
Rockcliffe Park, Ont.,
  Can., 2,084.........*A9   41
Rock Creek Hills, Md.,
  1,500................*B3   53
Rockdale, Ill.,
  1,272.............B5, F2   58
Rockdale, Md., 1,500.*B4   53
Rockdale, Tex., 4,481..D4   84
Rockdale, co., Ga.,
  10,572................C3   55
Rock Fall, Conn., 550..C6   52
Rock Falls, Ill., 10,261.B4   58
Rockford, Ill., 126,706
  (*191,100)..........A4   58
Rockford, Iowa, 941...A5   60
Rockford, Mich., 2,074.E5   66
Rockford, Ohio, 1,155..B3   78

Rockford, Tenn.,
  900...........D10, E11   83
Rock Hall, Md., 1,073..B5   53
Rockhampton, Austl.,
  44,128................D9   25
Rock Hill, Mo., 6,523..*C7   69
Rock Hill, S.C., 29,404.B5   82
Rockingham, N.C.,
  5,512.................C4   76
Rockingham, co., N.H.,
  99,029................E5   73
Rockingham, co., N.C.,
  69,629................A4   76
Rockingham, co., Va.,
  40,485................C4   85
Rock Island, Que., Can.,
  1,608.................D5   42
Rock Island, Ill.,
  51,863................B3   58
Rock Island, co., Ill.,
  150,991...............B3   58
Rockland, Ont., Can.,
  3,037.................B9   41
Rockland, Maine,
  8,769.................B3   64
Rockland, Mass.,
  13,119............B6, E3   65
Rockland, co., N.Y.,
  136,803...............D6   75
Rockledge, Fla., 3,481..D6   54
Rockledge, Pa., 2,587.A11   81
Rocklin, Calif., 1,495..*C3   50
Rockmart, Ga., 3,938..C1   55
Rockport, Ind., 2,474..I3   59
Rockport, Maine, 900..D3   64
Rockport, Mass., 3,511.A6   65
Rock Port, Mo., 1,310..A2   69
Rockport, Tex., 2,989..E4   84
Rock Rapids, Iowa,
  2,780.................A1   60
Rocksprings, Tex.,
  1,182.................D2   84
Rock Springs, Wyo.,
  10,371................D3   89
Rockton, Ill., 1,833....A4   58
Rock Valley, Iowa,
  1,693.................A1   60
Rockville, Conn., 9,478.B7   52
Rockville, Ind., 2,756..E3   59
Rockville, Md., 26,090.B3   53
Rockville Centre, N.Y.,
  26,355................E3   75
Rockwall, Tex.,
  2,166............B6, C4   84
Rockwall, co., Tex.,
  5,878.................C4   84
Rockwell City, Iowa,
  2,313.................B3   60
Rockwood, Mich.,
  2,026.................F7   66
Rockwood, Pa., 1,101..G3   81
Rockwood, Tenn.,
  5,345.................D9   83
Rocky Ford, Colo.,
  4,929.................C7   51
Rockygrove, Pa., 3,168.D2   81
Rocky Hill, Conn.,
  7,404.................C6   52
Rocky Mount, N.C.,
  32,147................B6   76
Rocky Mount, Va.,
  1,412.................D3   85
Rocky Mountain House,
  Alta., Can., 2,360....C3   38
Rocky Point, N.Y.,
  2,261.................F5   75
Rocky Point, Wash.,
  1,000................*B3   86
Rocky Ripple, Ind.,
  967..................H8   59
Rocky River, Ohio,
  18,097............A6, B2   78
Roddickton, Newf., Can.,
  1,185.............C3, h10   44
Rodeo, Calif., 5,400..*B5   50
Roderfield, W. Va.,
  1,020.................D3   87
Rodessa, La., 700.....B1   63
Rodez, Fr., 20,924....E5   5
Rodgers Forge, Md.,
  7,645................*B4   53
Rodhopi, prov., Grc.,
  109,201...............*B5   14
Ródhos, Grc., 27,393...D7   14
Rodney, Ont., Can.,
  1,041.................E3   41
Rodney Village, Del.,
  1,200.................B6   53
Roebling, N.J., 3,272...C3   74
Roebuck Plaza, Ala.,
  1,000................*B3   46
Roeland Park, Kans.,
  8,949.................B9   61
Roermond, Neth.,
  34,500................B6   5
Roeselare, Bel., 35,645..B5   5
Roessleville, N.Y.,
  19,000...............*C7   75
Rogachev, Sov. Un.,
  25,000................E8   12

Rogaland, co., Nor.,
  239,000..............*H1   11
Rogatica, Yugo., 3,044.D4   10
Roger Mills, co., Okla.,
  5,090.................B2   79
Rogers, Ark., 7,600....A1   49
Rogers, Tex., 936.....D4   84
Rogers, co., Okla.,
  20,614................A6   79
Rogers City, Mich.,
  4,722.................C7   66
Rogers Heights, Md.,
  2,000................*C4   53
Rogersville, Tenn.,
  3,121................C10   83
Rogozno, Pol., 5,536...B4   7
Rohnerville, Calif.,
  1,000................*B1   50
Roi Et, Thai., 12,119...B2   19
Rojas, Arg., 6,608.....A4   28
Rokitno, Sov. Un.,
  9,000.................F6   12
Rokycany, Czech.,
  12,000................D2   7
Roland Terrace, Md.,
  2,000................*B4   53
Rolette, co., N. Dak.,
  10,641................B6   77
Rolfe, Iowa, 819.......B3   60
Rolla, Mo., 11,132.....D6   69
Rolla, N. Dak., 1,398..A6   77
Rolling Fork, Miss.,
  1,619.................C3   68
Rolling Hills, Kans.,
  2,000.................B5   61
Rolling Hills Estates,
  Calif., 3,941.........*F2   50
Rolling Meadows, Ill.,
  10,879...............*E2   58
Rollingwood, Calif.,
  2,200................*B5   50
Roma, Austl., 5,571....E8   25
Roma, see Rome, It.
Roma, Tex., 1,496.....F3   84
Roman, Rom., 27,948..B8   10
Romania, country, Eur.,
  17,489,794.............B7   10
Romans [-sur-Isère], Fr.,
  26,377................E6   5
Romblon, Phil., 5,000.*C6   19
Romblon, prov., Phil.,
  132,000..............*C6   19
Rome, Ga., 32,226.....B1   55
Rome, Ill., 1,347......C4   58
Rome (Roma), It.,
  2,188,160.........D4, h8   9
Rome, N.Y., 51,646....B5   75
Rome, Ohio, 1,500....*C5   78
Romeo, Ill., 3,574.....*B5   58
Romeo, Mich., 3,327...F7   66
Romilly [-sur-Seine], Fr.,
  13,753................C5   5
Romita, Mex., 10,377.m11   34
Romney, W. Va.,
  2,203.................B6   87
Romny, Sov. Un.,
  10,000................F9   12
Romorantin, Fr.,
  11,777................D4   5
Romulus, Mich., 3,500.A7   66
Ronan, Mont., 1,334...C2   70
Ronceverte, W. Va.,
  1,882.................D4   87
Ronciglione, It., 7,079..C4   9
Ronda, Sp., 16,100.....D3   8
Rondônia, ter., Braz.,
  70,783................B3   29
Ronkonkoma, N.Y.,
  5,666.................F4   52
Rönne, Den., 13,195...A3   7
Ronse, Bel., 25,106....B5   5
Roodhouse, Ill., 2,352.D3   58
Rooks, co., Kans.,
  9,734.................C4   61
Roosendaal, Neth.,
  38,800................B6   5
Roosevelt, N.Y.,
  12,883................G2   52
Roosevelt, Utah, 1,812.A6   72
Roosevelt, co., Mont.,
  11,731...............B11   70
Roosevelt, co., N. Mex.,
  16,198................B7   48
Roosevelt Park, Mich.,
  2,578.................E4   66
Roquetas, Sp., 5,514...B6   8
Rorschach, Switz.,
  12,759 (*22,358).....E4   6
Rosario, Arg., 595,000.A4   28
Rosário, Braz., 6,999..*D6   27
Rosário, Mex., 11,608..C3   34
Rosário, Par., 6,058...D4   29
Rosario, Ur., 7,600....E1   30
Rosário do Sul, Braz.,
  15,786................E2   30
Rosario Tala, Arg.,
  10,584................A5   28
Roscoe, N.Y., 900.....D6   75
Roscoe, Pa., 1,315....F2   81
Roscoe, Tex., 1,490....C2   84

Roscommon, co., Ire., 59,217............*D2 4
Roscommon, co., Mich., 7,200..............D6 66
Roseau, Minn., 2,146...B3 67
Roseau, Dominica, 10,422..............o16 35
Roseau, co., Minn., 12,154..............B3 67
Rose Blanche, Newf., Can., 626...........E2 44
Roseboro, N.C., 1,354..C5 76
Rosebud, Tex., 1,644..D4 84
Rosebud, co., Mont., 6,187..............D10 70
Roseburg, Oreg., 11,467.............D3 80
Rosedale, Fla., 4,085..*E4 54
Rosedale, Miss., 2,339..B2 68
Rosedale Station, Alta., Can., 1,200........D4 38
Rose Hill, Kans., 273..E6 61
Rosehill, N.C., 1,292...C5 76
Roseland, Fla., 145...E6 54
Roseland, Ind., 971....A5 59
Roseland, La., 1,254...D5 63
Roseland, N.J., 2,804..*B4 74
Roseland, Ohio, 8,204.*B5 78
Roselle, Ill., 3,581...E2 58
Roselle, N.J., 21,032...E4 74
Roselle Park, N.J., 12,546.............E4 74
Rosemead, Calif., 15,476............*F2 50
Rosemere, Que., Can., 6,158..............D8 42
Rosemont, Ill., 978....*A6 58
Rosemont, Ill., 4,000..*E3 58
Rosemont, Pa., 4,000.*A10 81
Rosemount, Minn., 1,068..............F5 67
Rosenberg, Tex., 9,698.F4 84
Rosendael, Fr., 19,960..B5 5
Rosendale, N.Y., 1,033.............*C7 75
Rosenheim, Ger., 31,600..............E6 6
Roseto, Pa., 1,630...E11 81
Rosetown, Sask., Can., 2,450..............C1, F1 39
Rosetta (Rashid), Eg., U.A.R., 32,800......G8 14
Roseville, Calif., 13,421.C3 50
Roseville, Ill., 1,065....C3 58
Roseville, Mich., 50,195..............A8 66
Roseville, Minn., 23,997..............E7 67
Roseville, Ohio, 1,749..C5 78
Rosewood, Calif., 1,100.............*B1 50
Rosewood Heights, Ill., 4,572.............*E3 58
Rosiclare, Ill., 1,700....F5 58
Rosiorii-de-Vede, Rom., 17,320.............C7 10
Roskilde, co., Den., 82,223.............*J5 11
Roslavl, Sov. Un., 36,000.............E9 12
Roslyn, N.Y., 2,681...*E3 75
Roslyn, Pa., 8,500....*A11 81
Roslyn, Wash., 1,283..B4 86
Roslyn Estates, N.Y., 1,289.............*G2 52
Roslyn Harbor, N.Y., 925...............*E7 75
Roslyn Heights, N.Y., 4,000.............D2 75
Rosny-sous-Bois, Fr., 21,001............g10 5
Ross, Calif., 2,551....*D2 50
Ross, co., Ohio, 61,215..C4 78
Ross and Cromarty, co., Scot., 57,607......*B4 4

Rossano, It., 12,400....E6 9
Rossford, Ohio, 4,406...........A2, A4 78
Rossiter, Pa., 950......E4 81
Rossland, B.C., Can., 4,354..............E9 37
Rossmoor, Calif., 9,000............*F2 50
Rossmoyne, Ohio, 2,000............*D2 78
Rossosh, Sov. Un., 10,000............F12 12
Rossville, Ga., 4,665...B1 55
Rossville, Ill., 1,470....C6 58
Rosthern, Sask., Can., 1,264..............E2 39
Rostock, Ger., 161,800.A6 6
Rostov, Sov. Un., 29,200.............C12 12
Rostov [-na-Donu], Sov. Un., 645,000.......H12 12
Roswell, Ga., 2,983.A5, B2 55
Roswell, N. Mex., 39,593..............C6 48
Rotan, Tex., 2,788.....C2 84
Rotenburg [an der Fulda], Ger., 7,700..........B4 6
Rothenburg [ob der Tauber], Ger., 11,100.............D5 6
Rothesay, Scot., 7,656..C4 4
Rothschild, Wis., 2,550.D4 88
Rothsville, Pa., 900....F9 81
Rotondella, It., 5,643..D6 9
Rotorua, N.Z., 19,360.M16 26
Rotterdam, Neth., 729,800 (*990,000)..........B6 5
Rotterdam, N.Y., 16,871............*C6 75
Rottweil, Ger., 17,900..D4 6
Roubaix, Fr., 112,856..B5 5
Roudnice nad Labem, Czech., 8,683.......n17 7
Rouen, Fr., 120,857....C4 5
Roulette, Pa., 700.....C5 81
Round Lake, Ill., 997..E2 58
Roundlake, Miss., 175..A3 68
Round Lake Beach, Ill., 5,011.............*E2 58
Round Lake Heights, Ill., 900...........*E2 58
Round Lake Park, Ill., 2,565...........*E2 58
Round Pond, Ark., 50..B5 49
Round Rock, Tex., 1,878.............D4 84
Roundup, Mont., 2,842.............D8 70
Rouses Point, N.Y., 2,160.............A3 75
Rouseville, Pa., 923...D2 81
Routt, co., Colo., 5,900.A3 51
Rouville, co., Que., Can., 25,979........D4 42
Rouyn, Que., Can., 18,716.............E9 41
Rouzerville, Pa., 900...G6 81
Rovaniemi, Fin., 21,500.............D11 11
Rovato, It., 6,288.....B2 9
Rovenki, Sov. Un., 10,000.......G12, q22 12
Rovereto, It., 25,638..B3 9
Rovigo, It., 33,000.....B3 9
Rovinj, Yugo., 7,156...C1 10
Rovno, Sov. Un., 68,000.............F6 12
Rovnoye, Sov. Un., 10,000.............F16 12
Rowan, co., Ky., 12,808.............B6 62
Rowan, co., N.C., 82,817.............B3 76
Rowan Mill, N.C., 1,089.............*B3 76

Rowes Run, Pa., 950..*F2 81
Rowland, N.C., 1,408..C4 76
Rowland, Pa., 100...D11 81
Rowlesburg, W. Va., 970..............B5 87
Rowlett, Tex., 1,015..*C4 84
Rowley, Mass., 1,223..A6 65
Roxana, Ill., 2,090....A8 69
Roxas (Capiz), Phil., 18,000.............C6 19
Roxboro, N.C., 5,147..A5 76
Roxburgh, co., Scot., 43,171............*C5 4
Roxton, Tex., 950.....C5 84
Roxton Falls, Que., Can., 972...........*D5 42
Roy, N. Mex., 633.....B6 48
Roy, Utah, 9,239..A5, C2 72
Royal, Fla., 200.......D4 54
Royal Center, Ind., 966..............C4 59
Royal Mills, N.C., 600.A5 76
Royal Oak, Mich., 80,612.........A7, F7 66
Royal Oak Township, Mich., 8,147........*A7 66
Royalton, Ill., 1,225....F4 58
Royalton, Pa., 1,128..*F8 81
Royan, Fr., 16,521....E3 5
Royersford, Pa., 3,969.F10 81
Royse City, Tex., 1,274.C4 84
Royston, Ga., 2,333....B3 55
Roznava, Czech., 10,200.............D6 7
Rtishchevo, Sov. Un., 32,000.............E14 12
Rubezhnoye, Sov. Un., 50,000.............p21 13
Rubidoux (West Riverside), Calif., 8,000..*F3 50
Rudbar, Afg., 5,000....B3 20
Rudolstadt, Ger., 27,700..............C5 6
Rueil-Malmaison, Fr., 54,786.............g9 5
Rufino, Arg., 10,987....A4 28
Rufisque, Sen., 37,500..F1 22
Rugby, N. Dak., 2,972.B6 77
Ruidoso, N. Mex., 1,557.............C6 48
Ruidoso Downs, N. Mex., 407................C6 48
Rule, Tex., 1,347......C3 84
Ruleville, Miss., 1,902..B3 68
Ruma, Yugo., 19,570...C4 10
Rumford, Maine, 7,233.D2 64
Rumoe, Jap., 29,100..E10 18
Rumson, N.J., 6,405...C4 74
Runge, Tex., 1,036....E4 84
Runnels, co., Tex., 15,016.............D3 84
Runnelstown, Miss., 125..............D4 68
Runnemede, N.J., 8,396.............D2 74
Rupert, Idaho, 4,153...G5 57
Rupert, W. Va., 921...D4 87
Rural Hall, N.C., 1,503.A3 76
Ruse, Bul., 53,420....D7 10
Ruse, co., Bul., 527,708...........*D8 10
Rush, co., Ind., 20,393..E6 59
Rush, co., Kans., 6,160.D4 61
Rush City, Minn., 1,108.............E6 67
Rushford, Minn., 1,335.G7 67
Rush Springs, Okla., 1,303.............C4 79
Rushville, Ill., 2,819....C3 58
Rushville, Ind., 7,264..E7 59
Rushville, Nebr., 1,228.B3 71
Rusk, Tex., 4,900......D5 84
Rusk, co., Tex., 36,421.C5 84
Rusk co., Wis., 14,794..C2 88
Ruskin, Fla., 1,894.E4, F2 54

Russas, Braz., 7,102...*D7 27
Russell (Russell City), Calif., 1,100........*B5 50
Russell, Man., Can., 1,263..............D1 40
Russell, Kans., 6,113...D5 61
Russell, Ky., 1,458....B7 62
Russell, co., Ala., 46,351.............C4 46
Russell, co., Ont., Can., 20,892.............B9 41
Russell, co., Kans., 11,348.............D5 61
Russell, co., Ky., 11,076.............D4 62
Russell, co., Va., 26,290.B3 85
Russell Gardens, N.Y., 1,156............*E3 75
Russells Point, Ohio, 1,111.............*B5 78
Russell Springs, Ky., 1,125.............D4 62
Russellville, Ala., 6,628.A2 46
Russellville, Ark., 8,921.............B2 49
Russellville, Ky., 5,861.D3 62
Russelton, Pa., 1,613..*F2 81
Russian Soviet Federated Socialist Republic, rep., Sov. Un., 120,554,000........C8 12
Russiaville, Ind., 1,064.D5 59
Ruston, La., 13,991...B3 63
Rutchenkovo, Sov. Un., 25,000............r20 12
Rute, Sp., 10,077.....D3 8
Ruteng, Indon., 5,000.G6 19
Ruth, Miss., 150......D3 68
Ruth, Nev., 800.......B4 72
Ruthenia, reg., Sov. Un..............D7 7
Rutherford, N.J., 20,473..........B4, D5 74
Rutherford, Tenn., 983.A3 83
Rutherford, co., N.C., 45,091.............B2 76
Rutherford, co., Tenn., 52,368.............B5 83
Rutherford Heights, Pa., 1,700.........*F8 81
Rutherfordton, N.C., 3,392..........B2, D4 76
Rutland, Mass., 1,774..B4 65
Rutland, Vt., 18,325...D2 73
Rutland, co., Eng., 23,956............*D6 4
Rutland, co., Vt., 46,719.............D1 73
Rutledge, Pa., 947...*G11 81
Ruvo [di Puglia], It., 23,746.............D6 9
Ruxton, Md., 2,100....C2 53
Ruzayevka, Sov. Un., 34,500.............D15 12
Ruzomberok, Czech., 18,600.............D5 7
Rwanda, country, Afr., 2,725,000.......I3 23
Ryazan, Sov. Un., 240,000.............D12 12
Rybinsk (Shcherbakov), Sov. Un., 192,000...B12 12
Rybink, Pol., 34,000...........C5, g9 7
Rydal, Pa., 1,500....*F11 81
Ryde, Eng., 19,796....E6 4
Rye, N.Y., 14,225.D2, D3 75
Rylsk, Sov. Un., 10,000.............F10 12
Ryozu, Jap., 12,100...G9 18
Rypin, Pol., 7,350....B5 7
Rzeszow, Pol., 62,000..C6 7
Rzhev, Sov. Un., 54,000.............C10 12

S

Saalfeld, Ger., 26,900..C5 6
Saar, state, Ger., 1,072,600..........D3 6
Saarbrücken, Ger., 130,700 (*350,000).........D3 6
Saarlouis, Ger., 36,800.D3 6
Sabac, Yugo., 30,231...C4 10
Sabadell, Sp., 105,152..B7 8
Sabah (North Borneo), state, Mala., 334,141............D5 19
Sabana Grande, P.R., 3,318..........*m13 35
Sabanalarga, Col., 13,982.............A3 32
Sabang, Indon., 6,855.K11 19
Sabará, Braz., 10,004..B4 30
Sabaudia, It., 6,262....D4 9
Sabetha, Kans., 2,318..C8 61
Sabina, Ohio, 2,313....C4 78
Sabinal, Tex., 1,747...E3 84
Sabinas, Mex., 15,953..B4 34

Sabinas Hidalgo, Mex., 11,558.............B4 34
Sabine, co., Tex., 7,302.............D6 84
Sabine, par., La., 18,564.............C2 73
Sablé [-sur-Sarthe], Fr., 6,885.............D3 5
Sabzawar, Afg., 10,000.B3 20
Sac, co., Iowa, 17,007...B2 60
Sac City, Iowa, 3,354..B1 60
Sachsen, former state, Ger., 5,558,566.....*C6 6
Sachsen-Anhalt, former state, Ger., 4,160,539..........*C5 6
Sackets Harbor, N.Y., 1,279.............B4 75
Sackville, N.B., Can., 3,038.............D5 43
Saco, Maine, 10,515..........E2, E4 64

Sacramento, Calif., 191,667 (*536,000)......A6, C3 50
Sacramento, co., Calif., 502,778............C3 50
Sacre-Coeur Saguenay, Que., Can., 1,108....A8 42
Ṣa'dah, Yemen, 25,000.F3 15
Sá da Bandeira, Ang., 13,867............C2 24
Saddle Brook, N.J., 13,834............*A4 74
Saddle River, N.J., 1,776............*A4 74
Saddle Rock, N.Y., 1,109.............*G2 52
Saegertown, Pa., 1,131.C1 81
Saeki, Jap., 32,000....J5 18
Safad, Isr., 10,586..B3, g5 15
Safety Harbor, Fla., 1,787..........D4, E2 54
Safford, Ariz., 4,648....C4 48
Safi, Mor., 81,072......B3 22

Safranbolu, Tur., 7,400.............B9 14
Saga, Jap., 129,888.....J5 18
Saga, pref., Jap., 942,874............*J5 18
Sagadahoc, co., Maine, 22,793.............E3 64
Sagaing, Bur., 15,439.D10 20
Sagamore, Pa., 800....E3 81
Sagamore Hills, Ohio, 3,848.............B2 78
Sagara, Jap., 12,000....o17 18
Sag Harbor, N.Y., 2,346.............D4 75
Saginaw, Mich., 98,265 (*160,900)..........E7 66
Saginaw, Tex., 1,001...B5 84
Saginaw, co., Mich., 190,752............E6 66
Saguache, Colo., 722...C4 51
Saguache, co., Colo., 4,473.............C4 51

Sagua la Grande, Cuba,
26,187............D3   35
Saguenay, co., Que., Can.,
81,900............A8   42
Sagunto, Sp.,
40,293............C5   8
Saharanpur, India,
185,213............C6   20
Sahuayo [de Díaz], Mex.,
25,673............m12   34
Saidpur, Pak.,
61,369............C8   20
Saigo, Jap., 8,000.....H6   18
Saigon, Viet.,
1,383,000............C3   19
St. Affrique, Fr.,
5,670............F5   5
St. Agapit, Que., Can.,
1,117............C6   42
Ste. Agathe des Monts,
Que., Can., 5,173....C3   42
St. Albans, Newf., Can.,
1,547............E4   44
St. Albans, Vt., 8,806..B1   73
St. Albans, W. Va.,
15,103............C3   87
St. Albert, Alta., Can.,
4,059............C4   38
St. Alexandre, Que., Can.,
872............B8   42
St. Amand-Mont-Rond,
Fr., 10,890............D5   5
St. Ambroise, Que., Can.,
1,576............A6   42
St. Andrews, N.B., Can.,
1,531............D2   43
St. Andrews, Scot.,
9,888............B5   4
St. Andrews, S.C.,
1,500............F2, F8   82
Ste. Angele-de-Laval,
Que., Can., 655....D8   42
St. Ann, Mo., 12,155..*A8   69
Ste. Anne, Que., Can.,
900............D4   42
Ste. Anne, Guad.,
2,384............n16   35
St. Anne, Ill., 1,378....B6   58
Ste. Anne de Beaupré,
Que., Can., 1,878....B7   42
St. Anne de Bellevue,
Que., Can., 4,044..D8   42
St. Anselme, Que., Can.,
1,131............C7   42
St. Ansgar, Iowa, 1,014.A5   60
St. Anthony, Newf., Can.,
1,820............C4   44
St. Anthony, Idaho,
2,700............F7   57
St. Anthony, Minn.,
5,084............*F5   67
St. Antoine des
Laurentides, Que.,
Can., 3,005............*D3   42
St. Augustine, Fla.,
14,734............C5, C7   54
St. Avold, Fr., 15,247..C7   5
St. Basile [de Portneuf],
Que., Can., 1,709....C6   42
St. Basile Station, Que.,
Can., 1,635............*C6   42
St. Bernard, Ohio,
6,778............D2   78
St. Bernard, par., La.,
32,186............E6   63
St. Bernice, Ind., 800..E2   59
St. Bonaventure, N.Y.,
2,000............*C2   75
St. Boniface, Man., Can.,
37,600............E3   40
St. Brieuc, Fr., 43,142..C2   5
St. Bruno, Que., Can.,
1,158............B8   42
St. Casimir, Que., Can.,
1,386............C5   42
St. Catharines, Ont., Can.,
84,472 (*95,577)....D5   41
St. Cesaire, Que., Can.,
2,097............D4   42
St. Chamond, Fr.,
17,107............E6   5
St. Charles, I'l.,
9,269............B5, F1   58
St. Charles, Mich.,
1,959............E6   66
St. Charles, Minn.,
1,882............G6   67
St. Charles, Mo.,
21,189............A7, C7   69
St. Charles, co., Mo.,
52,970............C7   69
St. Charles, par., La.,
21,219............E5   63
St. Charles de Bellechasse,
Que., Can., 981....C7   42
St. Clair, Mich., 4,538..F8   66
St. Clair, Mo., 2,711...C6   69
St. Clair, Pa., 5,159...E9   81
St. Clair, co., Ala.,
25,388............B3   46

St. Clair, co., Ill.,
262,509............E4   58
St. Clair, co., Mich.,
107,201............F8   66
St. Clair, co., Mo.,
8,421............C4   69
St. Claire Shores, Mich.,
76,657............A8   66
St. Clairsville, Ohio,
3,865............B7   78
St. Claude [-sur-Bienne],
Fr., 12,114............D6   5
St. Cloud, Fla., 4,353..D5   54
St. Cloud, Fr., 26,476...g9   5
St. Cloud, Minn.,
33,815............E4   67
St. Croix, Que., Can.,
1,363............C6   42
St. Croix, co., Wis.,
29,164............C1   88
St. Croix Falls, Wis.,
1,249............C1   88
St. Cyrille, Que., Can.,
1,138............D5   42
St. Davids, Pa.,
1,200............*A10   81
St. Denis, Que., Can.,
737............B8   42
St. Denis, Fr.,
94,264............C5, g10   5
St. Dié, Fr., 23,108....C7   5
St. Dizier, Fr., 34,407..C6   5
St. Edward, Nebr., 777.C3   71
St. Elmo, Ill., 1,503...D5   58
Saintes, Fr., 25,717....E3   5
St. Étienne, Fr., 201,242
(*285,000)............E6   5
St. Eustache, Que., Can.,
5,463............D4, D8   42
St. Eustache sur le Lac,
Que., Can., 7,274...D8   42
St. Fabien, Que., Can.,
1,466............A9   42
St. Felicien, Que., Can.,
5,133............A5   42
St. Felix de Valois, Que.,
Can., 1,399............C4   42
St. Ferdinand, Que., Can.,
2,706............C6   42
St. Flour, Fr., 5,846....E5   5
Ste, Foy, Que., Can.,
29,716............C6   42
St. Francis, Kans.,
1,594............C2   61
St. Francis, Wis.,
10,065............E2   88
St. Francis, co., Ark.,
33,303............B5   49
St. Francisville, Ill.,
1,040............E6   58
St. Francisville, La.,
1,661............D4   63
St. Francois, co., Mo.,
36,516............D7   69
St. Fulgence, Que., Can.,
1,094............*A6   42
St. Gabriel [-de-Brandon],
Que., Can., 3,425....C4   42
St. Gallen, see Sankt
Gallen, Switz.
St. Gallen, canton, Switz.
St. Gaudens, Fr.,
7,949............F4   5
Ste. Genevieve, Mo.,
4,443............D7   69
Ste. Genevieve, co., Mo.,
12,116............D7   69
Ste. Geneviéve-de-
Pierrefonds, Que., Can.,
2,397............*D4   42
St. George, N.B., Can.,
1,133............D3   43
St. George, Mo.,
1,323............*C7   69
St. George, S.C.,
1,833............E6   82
St. George, Utah,
5,130............C5   72
St. Georges, Que., Can.,
385............D6   42
St. Georges, Que., Can.,
1,775............C5   42
St. George's, Grenada,
19,582............p16   35
St. Georges Ouest, Que.,
Can., 4,755............*C7   42
St. Germain [de
Grantham], Que.,
Can., 1,015............D5   42
St. Germain-en-Laye, Fr.,
34,621............g9   5
St. Gervais, Que., Can.,
576............C7   42
St. Gilles-du-Gard, Fr.,
4,791............F6   5
St. Girons, Fr., 7,368...F4   5
St. Helena, Calif.,
2,722............A5, C2   50
St. Helena, Br. dep.,
Afr., 5,250............H20   2

St. Helena, par., La.,
9,162............D5   63
St. Helens, Eng.,
108,348............*D5   4
St. Helens, Oreg., 5,022.B4   80
St. Helier, Jersey,
25,364............F5   4
St. Henry, Ohio, 978...B3   78
St. Hilaire Est, Que.,
Can., 2,000............D4   42
St. Hyacinthe, Que.,
Can., 22,354............D5   42
St. Hyacinthe, co., Que.,
Can., 44,993............D4   42
St. Ignace, Mich.,
3,334............C6   66
St. Ignatius, Mont.,
940............C2   70
St. Jacques, Que., Can.,
2,038............D4   42
St. James, Man., Can.,
33,977............*E3   40
St. James, Minn., 4,174.G4   67
St. James, Mo., 2,384...D6   69
St. James, N.Y., 3,524..F4   52
St. James, par., La.,
18,369............D5   63
St. Jean, Que., Can.,
26,988............D4   42
St. Jean, co., Que., Can.,
38,470............D4   42
St. Jean Baptiste, Man.,
Can., 521............E3   40
St. Jean-d'Angély, Fr.,
8,660............E3   5
St. Jean de Dieu, Que.,
Can., 1,177............A9   42
St. Jean-de-Luz, Fr.,
10,241............F3   5
St. Jean de Matha, Que.,
Can., 846............C4   42
St. Jean Eudes, Que.,
Can., 2,873............*A7   42
St. Jerome, Que., Can.,
24,546............D3   42
St. Jo, Tex., 977.....C4   84
Saint John, N.B., Can.,
55,153 (*95,563)....D3   43
St. John, Ind., 1,128...B3   59
St. John, Kans., 1,753..E5   61
St. John, Mo., 7,342...*C7   69
St. John, co., N.B., Can.,
89,251............D4   43
St. John's, Antigua,
21,637............n16   35
St. Johns, Ariz., 1,310.B4   48
St. John's, Newf., Can.,
63,633 (*90,838)...E5   44
St. Johns, Mich., 5,629.E6   66
St. Johns, co., Fla.,
30,034............C5   54
St. Johnsbury, Vt.,
6,809............C3   73
St. Johnsville, N.Y.,
2,196............B6   75
St. John the Baptist, par.,
La., 18,439............D5   63
St. Joseph, Ill., 1,210..C5   58
St. Joseph, La., 1,653..C4   63
St. Joseph, Mich.,
11,755............F4   66
St. Joseph, Minn.,
1,487............E4   67
St. Joseph, Mo.,
79,673............B3   69
St. Joseph, co., Ind.,
238,614............A5   59
St. Joseph, co., Mich.,
42,332............G5   66
St. Joseph de Beauce,
Que., Can., 2,484....C7   42
St. Joseph de St.
Hyacinthe, Que.,
Can., 3,799............*D5   42
St. Joseph de Sorel, Que.,
Can., 3,588............*D4   42
St. Jovite, Que., Can.,
2,692............C3   42
St. Junien, Fr., 8,449..E4   5
St. Kitts-Nevis-Anguilla,
Br. dep., N.A.,
56,644............m15, n15   35
St. Lambert, Que., Can.,
14,531............D9   42
St. Landry, par., La.,
81,493............D3   63
St. Laurent, Que., Can.,
49,805............D9   42
St. Lawrence, Newf.,
Can., 2,095............E4   44
St. Lawrence, Pa.,
929............*F10   81
St. Lawrence, co., N.Y.,
111,239............A6   75
St. Leonard, N.B., Can.,
1,666............B2   43
St. Léonard [-de-Noblat],
Fr., 3,671............E4   5
St. Lô, Fr., 15,388....C3   5
St. Louis, Mich., 3,808.E6   66

St. Louis (Independent
City), Mo., 750,026
(*2,050,800)............C7   69
St. Louis, Sen., 39,100..E1   22
St. Louis, co., Minn.,
231,588............C6   67
St. Louis, co., Mo.,
703,532............C7   69
St. Louis Park, Minn.,
43,310............E6   67
St. Lucie, co., Fla.,
39,294............E6   54
St. Maixent-l'École, Fr.,
7,068............D3   5
St. Malo, Fr., 17,137...C2   5
St. Mandé, Fr., 24,325..g10   5
St. Marc, Hai., 10,485..F7   35
St. Marc [des Carrieres],
Que., Can., 2,622....C5   42
Ste. Marie, Que., Can.,
3,662............C6   42
St. Maries, Idaho,
2,435............B2   57
St. Martin, Que., Can.,
6,440............*D8   42
St. Martin, par., La.,
29,063............D4   63
St. Martinville, La.,
6,468............D4   63
St. Mary, par., La.,
48,833............E4   63
St. Mary-of-the-Woods,
Ind., 700............E3   59
St. Marys, Ont., Can.,
4,482............D3   41
St. Marys, Ga., 3,272..F5   55
St. Marys, Ind., 900...A5   59
St. Marys, Kans., 1,509.C7   61
St. Marys, Ohio, 7,737..B3   78
St. Marys, Pa., 8,065..D4   81
St. Marys, W. Va.,
2,443............B3   87
St. Marys, co., Md.,
38,915............D4   53
St. Matthews, Ky.,
8,738............A4, B4   62
St. Matthews, S.C.,
2,433............D6   82
St. Maur-des-Fossés, Fr.,
70,397............g10   5
St. Maurice, co., Que.,
Can., 109,873............C4   42
St. Michael, Minn., 707.E5   67
St. Michael, Pa., 1,292.*F4   81
St. Michaels, Md.,
1,484............C5   53
St. Nazaire, Fr., 58,286.D2   5
St. Noel, Que., Can.,
1,124............*G20   36
St. Omer, Fr., 19,283..B5   5
Saintonge, former prov.,
Fr., 286,000............E3   5
St. Ouen, Fr., 51,956..g10   5
St. Pacome, Que., Can.,
1,242............B8   42
St. Pamphile, Que., Can.,
1,839............C8   42
St. Paris, Ohio, 1,460..B4   78
St. Pascal, Que., Can.,
2,144............B8   42
St. Paul, Alta., Can.,
2,823............B5   38
St. Paul, Minn.,
313,411............E7, F6   67
St. Paul, Nebr., 1,714..C7   71
St. Paul, Va., 1,156....B2   85
St. Paulin, Que., Can.,
920............C4   42
St. Paul Park, Minn.,
3,267............F6, F7   67
St. Pauls, N.C., 2,249..C5   76
St. Peter, Minn., 8,484..F5   67
St. Peter Port, Guernsey,
16,720............F5   4
St. Petersburg, Fla.,
181,298
(*355,200)............E2, E4   54
St. Petersburg Beach, Fla.,
6,268............F1   54
St. Pie, Que., Can.,
1,434............D5   42
St. Pierre, Mart.,
6,218............o16   35
St. Pierre, St. Pierre and
Miquelon, 4,217......E3   44
St. Pierre and Miquelon,
Fr. dep., N.A., 4,606.E3   44
St. Pol-de-Léon, Fr.,
6,037............C2   5
St. Pourçain [-sur-Sioule],
Fr., 3,182............D5   5
St. Prosper, Que., Can.,
425............C7   42
St. Quentin, N.B., Can.,
2,089............B2   43
St. Quentin, Fr., 61,071.C5   5
St. Raphael, Que., Can.,
1,134............C7   42
St. Raphaël, Fr. 9,470.F7   5

St. Raymond, Que., Can.,
3,931...........C6 42
St. Regis, Ky.,
1,179..............*H6 53
St. Remi, Que., Can.,
2,276...........D4, E9 42
St. Romuald, Que., Can.,
4,000...........C6, C9 42
Ste. Rosalie, Que., Can.,
1,255..............*D5 42
Ste. Rose, Que., Can.,
7,571...........D4, D8 42
Ste. Rose, Guad.,
1,288..............n16 35
St. Rose, La., 1,099....C7 63
Ste. Rose de Lima, Que.,
Can., 2,965...........D2 42
Ste. Rose du Degele, Que.,
Can., 1,943...........B9 42
St. Sauveur [-des-Monts],
Que., Can., 1,702....D3 42
Ste. Savine, Fr., 11,864.C5 5
St. Servan [-sur-Mer], Fr.,
14,963.............C3 5
St. Simeon' Que., Can.,
1,197..............B8 42
St. Simons Island, Ga.,
3,199..............E5 55
St. Stephen, N.B., Can.,
3,380..............D2 43
St. Stephen, S.C., 1,462.E8 82
St. Tammany, par., La.,
38,643.............D5 63
Ste. Thecle, Que., Can.,
2,009..............C5 42
Ste. Therese de Blainville,
Que., Can.,
11,771.........D4, D8 42
St. Thomas, Ont., Can.,
22,469.............E3 41
St. Tite, Que., Can.,
3,250..............C5 42
St. Ulric, Que., Can.,
1,021..............*A2 42
St. Vincent de Paul, Que.,
Can., 11,214.......D9 42
St. Yrieix-la-Perche, Fr.,
4,368..............E4 5
Saitama, pref., Jap.,
2,403,871..........*I9 18
Sakākā, Sau. Ar.,
10,000.............D3 15
Sakania, Con. L.,
12,100.............C5 24
Sakashita, Jap., 3,400..n16 18
Sakata, Jap., 55,600....G9 18
Sakchu, Kor., 13,568...F2 18
Sakhalin, isl., Sov.
Un.............D17 16
Sakon Nakhon, Thai.,
14,940.............B2 19
Sakti, India, 8,125....D7 20
Sala, Swe., 11,000.H7, t34 11
Sala Consilina, It.,
6,897..............D5 9
Saladillo, Arg., 7,586...B5 28
Salamá, Guat., 2,760..*D7 34
Salamanca, Mex.,
32,192.............m13 34
Salamanca, N.Y., 8,480.C2 75
Salamanca, Sp., 90,498.B3 8
Salamanca, prov., Sp.,
405,729...........*B3 8
Salamina, Col., 7,940...B2 32
Salamis, Grc., 11,161..*D4 14
Salas, Sp., 2,522......A2 8
Salcedo, Ec., 2,596....B2 31
Saldanha, S. Afr.,
2,195..............G3 24
Saldus, Sov. Un.,
10,000.............C4 12
Sale, Austl., 7,899......I6 26
Salé, Mor., 75,799....B3 22
Salekhard, Sov. Un.,
16,000............*C9 13
Salem, Ill., 6,165.....E5 58
Salem, India, 249,145..F6 20
Salem, Ind., 4,546....G5 59
Salem, Mass.,
39,211.........A6, C3 65
Salem, Mo., 3,870....D6 69
Salem, N.H., 950.....F5 73
Salem, N.J., 8,941....D2 74
Salem, N.Y., 1,076....B7 75
Salem, Ohio, 13,854...B7 78
Salem, Oreg.,
49,142...........C1, C4 80
Salem, S. Dak., 1,188..G8 77
Salem, Utah, 920.....D2 72
Salem, Va., 16,058....D2 85
Salem, W. Va.,
2,366...........B4, B6 87
Salem, co., N.J., 58,711.D2 74
Salem Depot, N.H.,
2,523..............F5 73
Salem Heights, Oreg.,
10,770............*C4 80
Salemi, It., 13,300....F4 9
Salerno, It., 117,363...D5 9
Salford, Eng., 154,963..D5 4
Salge, Idaho, 100.....A2 57

Salgotarjan, Hung.,
26,682.............A4 11
Salida, Calif., 1,109...*D3 50
Salida, Colo., 4,560....C5 51
Salies-de-Béarn, Fr.,
2,859..............F3 5
Salihli, Tur., 24,100...*C7 14
Salin, Bur., 5,000....*D9 20
Salina, Kans., 43,202..D6 61
Salina, Okla., 972.....A6 81
Salina, Utah, 1,618...B6 72
Salinas, Calif.,
28,957.........C6, D3 50
Salinas, P.R., 3,666...m13 35
Salina Springs, Ariz.,
200...............A4 48
Saline, Mich., 2,334...F7 66
Saline, co., Ark., 28,956.C3 49
Saline, co., Ill., 26,227..F5 58
Saline, co., Kans.,
54,715.............D6 61
Saline, co., Mo., 25,148.B4 69
Saline, co., Nebr.,
12,542.............D8 71
Salineville, Ohio, 1,898.B7 78
Salisbury, Eng., 35,471.E6 4
Salisbury, Md., 16,302.D6 53
Salisbury, Mass., 950..A6 65
Salisbury, Mo., 1,787..B5 69
Salisbury, N.C., 21,297.B3 76
Salisbury, Rh.,
190,000...........D6 24
Salisbury West, N.C.,
1,323.............*B3 76
Sallisaw, Okla., 3,351..B7 79
Salmon, Idaho, 2,944..D5 57
Salmon Arm., B.C., Can.,
1,506..............D8 37
Salmon Falls, N.H.,
1,210..............E6 73
Salo, Fin., 11,000....G10 11
Salon-de-Provence, Fr.,
17,267.............F6 5
Salonta, Rom., 16,276..B5 10
Salsk, Sov. Un.,
18,500............H13 12
Salsomaggiore, It.,
8,600..............B2 9
Salta, Arg., 108,000....D2 29
Salta, prov., Arg.,
412,652............D2 29
Saltillo, Mex., 99,101...B4 34
Salt Lake, co., Utah,
383,035............A5 72
Salt Lake City, Utah,
189,454
(*410,200).......A6, C2 72
Salto, Braz., 12,643....m8 30
Salto, Ur., 46,500.....E1 30
Salto, dept., Ur.,
78,600............*E1 30
Saltpond, Ghana, 6,968.G4 22
Salt River, Ky., 400....C4 62
Saltsburg, Pa., 1,054...F3 81
Salt Springs, Fla., 755..C5 54
Saltville, Va., 2,844....B3 85
Saluda, S.C., 2,089....D4 82
Saluda, co., S.C.,
14,554............C4 82
Saluda Gardens, S.C.,
2,000.............*D5 82
Salur, India, 26,111....E7 20
Saluzzo, It., 11,100....B1 9
Salvador, Braz.,
630,878............E7 27
Salvador, El, see El
Salvador, country, N.A.
Salvatierra, Mex.,
14,417............m13 34
Salyersville, Ky.,
1,173..............C6 62
Salzburg, Aus., 108,114.E6 6
Salzburg, state, Aus.,
347,292............E6 6
Salzgitter, Ger.,
110,200............B5 6
Salzwedel, Ger., 20,700.B5 6
Samar, prov., Phil.,
871,900............C7 19
Samarinda, Indon.,
68,095.............F5 19
Samarkand, Sov. Un.,
209,000............F9 13
Samarra, Iraq, 8,867...C3 15
Sambalpur, India,
38,915.............D7 20
Sambas, Indon., 12,000.E3 19
Sambor, Sov. Un.,
41,200.............G4 12
Samokov, Bul., 12,784.D6 10
Samos, prov., Grc.,
52,022............*D6 14
Samoset, Fla., 4,824...F2 54
Sampson, co., N.C.,
48,013.............C5 76
Samson, Ala., 1,932...D3 46
Samsun, Tur., 87,300..B11 14
Samtown, La., 4,008...*C3 63
San'ā', Yemen,
89,000.............F3 15

San Andreas, Calif.,
1,416.............C3 50
San Andres de Giles, Arg.,
5,392..............g7 28
San Andrés Tuxtla, Mex.,
19,830.............D5 34
San Angelo, Tex.,
58,815.............D2 84
San Anselmo, Calif.,
11,584.............B5 50
San Antonio, Chile,
27,000.............A2 28
San Antonio, Tex., 587,718
(*689,700).....B3, E3 84
San Antonio de Areco,
Arg., 7,436.........g7 28
San Antonio de los Baños,
Cuba, 17,783.......D2 35
San Antonio Heights,
Calif., 1,100......*E5 50
Sanatorium, Tex.,
1,800..............D2 84
San Augustine, Tex.,
2,584..............D5 84
San Augustine, co., Tex.,
7,722..............D5 84
San Bartolomeo in Galdo,
It., 8,767..........D5 9
San Benedetto del Tronto,
It., 22,500.........C4 9
San Benito, Tex.,
16,422.............F4 84
San Benito, co., Calif.,
15,396.............D3 50
San Bernardino,
Calif., 91,922
(*460,000).....E5, F3 50
San Bernardino, co.,
Calif., 503,591.......E5 50
San Bernardo, Chile,
53,000.............A2 28
Sanborn, Iowa, 1,323..A2 60
Sanborn, co., S. Dak.,
4,641..............G7 77
San Bruno, Calif.,
29,063.........B5, D2 50
San Carlos, Arg., 6,362.C2 28
San Carlos, Calif.,
21,370.............B5 50
San Carlos, Chile,
11,094.............B2 28
San Carlos, Phil.,
12,000............o13 19
San Carlos, Ur., 12,400..E2 30
San Carlos [de Bariloche],
Arg., 6,562........C2 28
San Cataldo, It., 22,544.F4 9
San Clemente, Calif.,
8,527..............F5 50
San Clemente, Sp.,
6,948..............C4 8
San Cristóbal, Dom. Rep.,
15,525............*F8 35
San Cristóbal, Ven.,
96,102.............B3 32
San Cristóbal de las
Casas, Mex., 23,355..D6 34
Sancti-Spíritus, Cuba,
37,741.............E4 35
Sanda, Jap., 16,300...o14 18
Sandakan, Mala.,
15,000.............D5 19
Sandefjord, Nor.,
7,000..............p28 11
Sanders, co., Mont.,
6,880..............C1 70
Sanderson, Tex., 2,189.D1 84
Sandersville, Ga.,
5,425..............D4 55
San Diego, Calif., 573,224
(*1,065,000).....E2, F5 50
San Diego, Tex., 4,351..F3 84
San Diego, co., Calif.,
1,033,011..........F5 50
Sandikli, Tur., 9,400...C8 14
Sandila, India, 18,407..C7 20
San Dimas, Calif.,
7,200.............*F3 50
Sandoa, Con. L., 5,000.B4 24
Sandomierz, Pol., 8,357.C6 7
San Donà di Piave, It.,
11,100.............B4 9
Sandoval, Ill., 1,356...E4 58
Sandoval, co., N. Mex.,
14,201.............B5 48
Sandpoint, Idaho,
4,355..............A2 57
Sands Point, N.Y.,
2,161.............*G2 52
Sand Springs, Okla.,
7,754..............A5 79
Sandston, Va., 4,500...C7 85
Sandstone, Minn.,
1,552..............D6 67
Sandusky, Mich.,
2,066..............E8 66
Sandusky, Ohio, 31,989.A5 78
Sandusky South, Ohio,
4,724.............*A5 78
Sandusky, co., Ohio,
56,486.............A4 78

Sandviken, Swe.,
22,000.............G7 11
Sandwich, Ill., 3,842...B5 58
Sandwich, Mass., 1,099.C7 65
Sandy, Oreg., 1,147....B4 80
Sandy, Pa., 2,070.....*D4 81
Sandy, Utah, 3,322...D2 72
Sandy Beach, N.Y.,
1,000.............*B2 75
Sandy Hook, Conn.,
950...............D3 52
Sandy Springs, Ga.,
5,000..............A5 55
San Elizario, Tex.,
1,064..............F1 84
San Estanislao, Par.,
10,948.............D4 29
San Felipe, Chile,
15,476.............A2 28
San Felipe, N. Mex.,
1,034...........B5, D6 48
San Felipe, Ven.,
27,774.............A4 32
San Felíu de Guixols, Sp.,
10,307.............B7 8
San Fernando, Arg.,
84,000.........A5, g7 28
San Fernando, Calif.,
16,093.............F2 50
San Fernando, Chile,
22,500.............A2 28
San Fernando, Phil.,
10,000............o13 19
San Fernando, Phil.,
4,636..........B6, n13 19
San Fernando, Sp.,
52,389.............D2 8
San Fernando, Trin.,
41,800.............A5 32
San Fernando de Apure,
Ven., 21,544.......B4 32
Sanford, Fla., 19,175...D5 54
Sanford, Maine, 10,936.E4 64
Sanford, N.C., 12,253..B4 76
San Francisco, Arg.,
24,354.............A4 28
San Francisco,
Calif., 740,316
(*3,275,000)....B5, D2 50
San Francisco, co., Calif.,
740,316............D2 50
San Francisco del Oro,
Mex., 11,317.......B3 34
San Francisco del Rincón,
Mex., 20,864......m13 34
San Francisco de Macorís,
Dom. Rep., 26,000...F8 35
San Gabriel, Calif.,
22,561.............F2 50
San Gabriel, Ec., 6,382.A2 31
San Gabriel Chilac, Mex.,
6,131...........D5, n15 34
Sangamon, co., Ill.,
146,539............D4 58
Sanger, Calif., 8,533...D4 50
Sanger, Tex., 1,190....C4 84
Sangerhausen, Ger.,
23,800.............C5 6
San Germán, P.R.,
7,790.............m13 35
San Gil, Col., 10,149...B3 32
San Giovanni in Fiore, It.,
17,400.............E6 9
Sangju, Kor., 21,600...H4 18
Sanhsing, see Ilan, China
San Ignacio, Par.,
10,766.............E4 29
Sanilac, co., Mich.,
32,314.............E8 66
San Isidro, Arg.,
196,168............g7 28
San Jacinto, Calif.,
2,553..........F4, F5 50
San Jacinto, co., Tex.,
6,153..............D5 84
San Javier, Chile, 7,006.B2 28
Sanjo, Jap., 48,800....H9 18
San Joaquin, co., Calif.,
249,989............C3 50
San Jose, Ariz., 100....C4 48
San Jose, Calif.,
204,196.........C6, D3 50
San José, C.R.,
115,700............F8 34
San Jose, Fla., 8,000..*B5 54
San Jose, Ill., 1,093...C4 58
San José, Ur., 21,200...E1 30
San José, dept., Ur.,
67,200............*E1 30
San José, prov., C.R.,
430,300...........*F8 34
San José de Feliciano,
Arg., 7,643........A5 28
San Juan, Arg., 106,746
(*105,000)........A3 28
San Juan, Colo., 100...D6 51
San Juan, Dom. Rep.,
20,449.............F8 35
San Juan, P.R., 432,377
(*588,805).........m13 35
San Juan, Tex., 4,371..F3 84

San Juan, co., Colo.,
　849...............D3　51
San Juan, co., N. Mex.,
　53,306............A4　48
San Juan, co., Utah,
　9,040.............C6　72
San Juan, co., Wash.,
　2,872.............A3　86
San Juan, prov., Arg.,
　352,461...........A3　28
San Juan Bautista, Calif.,
　1,046.............C6　50
San Juan Bautista, Par.,
　9,054.............E4　29
San Juan Capistrano,
　Calif., 1,120........F5　50
San Juan de los Lagos,
　Mex., 22,713......m12　34
San Juan de los Morros,
　Ven., 25,821........B4　32
San Juan del Río, Mex.,
　11,179...........m13　34
Sankt Gallen, Switz.,
　76,279............E4　6
Sankt Gallen, canton,
　Switz., 327,600.....*E4　6
Sankt Pölten, Aus.,
　40,112............D7　6
Sankt Veit [an der Glan],
　Aus., 10,950........E7　6
San Leandro, Calif.,
　65,962............B5　50
San Lorenzo, Arg.,
　11,109............A4　28
San Lorenzo, Calif.,
　23,773...........*B5　50
San Lorenzo, P.R.,
　5,551...........*m14　35
San Lorenzo del Escorial,
　Sp., 7,965.....B3, o16　8
Sanlúcar, Sp., 34,000...D2　8
San Luis, Arg., 25,147..A3　28
San Luis, Colo., 800...D5　51
San Luis, Cuba,
　11,110............E6　35
San Luis, prov., Arg.,
　174,251...........A3　28
San Luis de la Paz, Mex.,
　8,268............m13　34
San Luis Obispo, Calif.,
　20,437............E3　50
San Luis Obispo, co.,
　Calif., 81,044.......E3　50
San Luis Potosí, Mex.,
　159,640........C4, k13　34
San Luis Potosí, state,
　Mex., 1,054,206.C4, k13　34
San Manuel, Ariz.,
　4,524............*C3　48
San Marco [in Lamis],
　It., 19,014.........D5　9
San Marcos, Tex.,
　12,713.........A4, E5　84
San Marino, Calif.,
　13,658............F2　50
San Marino, country,
　Eur., 12,950........C4　9
San Martín, Arg.,
　8,748.............A3　28
San Martín (General San
　Martín), Arg.,
　279,213............g7　28
San Martin, Calif.,
　1,162.............C6　50
San Martín, dept., Peru,
　120,913...........C2　31
San Mateo, Calif.,
　69,870............B5　50
San Mateo, Ven., 1,829. B5　32
San Mateo, co., Calif.,
　444,387...........D2　50
San Miguel, Sal.,
　38,330............E7　34
San Miguel, co., Colo.,
　2,944.............D2　51
San Miguel, co., N. Mex.,
　23,468............B6　48
San Miguel de Allende,
　Mex., 14,853.......m13　34
San Nicolás, Arg.,
　25,926............A4　28
Sannicolaul-Mare, Rom.,
　9,956.............B5　10
Sannois, Fr., 16,490...g10　5
Sanok, Pol., 13,800....D7　7
San Pablo, Calif.,
　19,687............B5　50
San Patricio, co., Tex.,
　45,021............F4　84
San Pedro, Arg.,
　12,798..........A5, f7　28
San Pedro, Arg., 6,105..D3　29
San Pedro, Par., 16,691.D4　29
San Pedro, Tex., 7,634.*F4　84
San Pedro, dept., Par.,
　64,534............D4　29
San Pedro de las Colonias,
　Mex., 25,183........B4　34
San Pedro de Lloc, Peru,
　5,286.............C2　31

San Pedro de Macorís,
　Dom. Rep., 22,935...F9　35
San Pedro Sula, Hond.,
　58,126............D7　34
Sanpete, co., Utah,
　11,053............B6　72
San Rafael, Arg.,
　28,847............A3　28
San Rafael, Calif.,
　20,460.........B5, D2　50
San Ramon, Ur., 3,982..g9　28
San Remo, It., 43,500..C1　9
San Roque, Sp., 13,676. D3　8
San Saba, Tex., 2,728..D3　84
San Saba, co., Tex.,
　6,381.............D3　84
San Salvador, Sal.,
　248,100...........E7　34
San Sebastian, P.R.,
　4,019...........*m13　35
San Sebastián, Sp.,
　135,149...........A4　8
San Sepolcro, It.,
　7,242.............C4　9
San Severo, It.,
　48,443............D5　9
Sansom Park Village,
　Tex., 4,175.......*B5　84
Sans Souci, S.C., 7,000.*B3　82
Santa Ana, Calif.,
　100,350........F5, F3　50
Santa Ana, Sal., 73,864. E7　34
Santa Anna, Tex.,
　1,320.............D3　84
Santa Barbara, Calif.,
　58,768............E4　50
Santa Bárbara, Mex.,
　15,892............B3　34
Santa Barbara, co., Calif.,
　168,962...........E3　50
Santa Bárbara [d'Oeste],
　Braz., 13,571......m8　30
Santa Catalina, isl.,
　Calif..............F4　50
Santa Catarina, state,
　Braz., 2,146,909....D2　30
Santa Clara, Calif.,
　58,880........D3, C6　50
Santa Clara, Cuba,
　77,398............D4　35
Santa Clara, Ur.,
　2,499.............E2　30
Santa Clara, co., Calif.,
　642,315...........D3　50
Santa Cruz, Bol.,
　34,837............C3　29
Santa Cruz, Calif.,
　25,596.........D2, C5　50
Santa Cruz, C.R.,
　7,430.............E7　34
Santa Cruz, co., Ariz.,
　10,808............D3　48
Santa Cruz, co., Calif.,
　84,219............D2　50
Santa Cruz, dept., Bol.,
　286,145...........C3　29
Santa Cruz, prov., Arg.,
　52,853............D3　28
Santa Cruz de la Palma,
　Sp., 8,835........m13　8
Santa Cruz de la Zarza,
　Sp., 5,588.........C4　8
Santa Cruz de Tenerife,
　Sp., 133,100......m13　8
Santa Cruz de Tenerife,
　prov., Sp., 490,655.*m13　8
Santa Cruz do Rio Pardo,
　Braz., 13,789.......C3　30
Santa Cruz do Sul, Braz.,
　18,898............D2　30
Santa Elena, Tex., 250. F3　84
Santa Eugenia [de Ribeira],
　Sp., 4,543.........A1　8
Santa Eulalia del Río, Sp.,
　7,564.............C6　8
Santa Fe, Arg., 208,000. A4　28
Santa Fe, N. Mex.,
　33,394.........B6, D6　48
Santafé, Sp., 8,387....D4　8
Santa Fe, co., N. Mex.,
　44,970............B5　48
Santa Fe, prov., Arg.,
　1,865,537..........A4　28
Santa Fe Springs, Calif.,
　16,342...........*F2　50
Santai, China, 24,000.. E6　17
Santa Isabel, Equat.
　Gui., 11,098.......H6　22
Santa Isabel, P.R.,
　4,712...........*A13　35
Santa Lucia, Ur.,
　8,258.............E1　30
Santa Margarita, Calif.,
　600...............E3　50
Santa María, Braz.,
　78,682............D2　30
Santa Maria, Calif.,
　20,027............E3　50
Santa Maria [Capua
　Vetere], It., 30,024..D5　9

Santa Marta, Col.,
　42,700............A3　32
Santa Marta, Sp.,
　5,142.............C2　8
Santa Monica, Calif.,
　83,249............F2　50
Santana, Port.,
　4,953............h12　8
Santander, Sp.,
　118,435...........A4　8
Santander, prov., Sp.,
　432,132..........*A4　8
Santander, dept., Col.,
　804,490...........B3　32
Santañy, Sp., 6,295....C7　8
Santa Paula, Calif.,
　13,279............E4　50
Santarém, Braz.,
　24,924............D5　27
Santarém, Port.,
　13,114............C1　8
Santa Rita, Braz.,
　4,427...........*D7　27
Santa Rita, Guam,
　1,630...........*F6　2
Santa Rita, N. Mex.,
　1,772.............C4　48
Santa Rosa, Arg.,
　3,564.............B4　28
Santa Rosa, Calif.,
　31,027.........A5, C2　50
Santa Rosa, N. Mex.,
　2,220.............B6　48
Santa Rosa, Tex.,
　1,572...........*F4　84
Santa Rosa, co., Fla.,
　29,547............G2　54
Santa Rosa de Copán,
　Hond., 7,972......*E7　34
Santa Rosalía, Mex.,
　5,361.............B2　34
Santa Susana, Calif.,
　2,310...........*E4　50
Santa Venetia, Calif.,
　3,000...........*D2　50
Santa Vitória do Palmar,
　Braz., 8,224........E2　30
Santee, Calif., 2,000...*E2　50
Santiago, Braz., 15,140.D2　30
Santiago, Chile,
　646,000...........A2　28
Santiago, Dom. Rep.,
　83,523............F8　35
Santiago, Pan., 8,746...B1　32
Santiago, Par., 7,834...E4　29
Santiago, Sp., 34,000..A1　8
Santiago, prov., Chile,
　2,429,539..........A2　28
Santiago de Cuba, Cuba,
　163,237...........E6　35
Santiago del Estero, Arg.,
　80,000............E3　29
Santiago del Estero, prov.,
　Arg., 477,156......E3　29
Santiago Ixcuintla, Mex.,
　10,985.........C3, m11　34
Santiago Morona, prov.,
　Ec., 22,329........B2　31
Santisteban del Puerto,
　Sp., 8,678.........C4　8
Santo Amaro, Braz.,
　17,226...........*E7　27
Santo Angelo, Braz.,
　25,415............D2　30
Santo Antônio, Braz.,
　2,978...........*E7　27
Santo Domingo, Dom.
　Rep., 367,053......F9　35
Santo Domingo, N. Mex.,
　900...........B5, D6　48
San Tomas, Calif.,
　1,500...........*D3　50
Santoña, Sp., 9,082....A4　8
Santos, Braz.,
　262,048.........C3, m8　30
Santos Dumont, Braz.,
　20,414.........C4, g6　30
Santo Tomé de
　Guayama, Ven.,
　75,000............B5　32
San Vicente, Sal.,
　15,189............E7　34
San Vicente de Alcántara,
　Sp., 8,212.........C2　8
San Vito al Tagliamento,
　It., 5,065.........B4　9
Sao Bernardo [do Campo],
　Braz., 61,645...C3, m8　30
São Borja, Braz.,
　20,339............D1　30
São Carlos, Braz.,
　50,010.........C3, m8　30
São Cristovão, Braz.,
　7,624...........*E7　27
São Francisco do Sul,
　Braz., 11,593......D3　30
São Gabriel, Braz.,
　22,967............E2　30
São João de Boa Vista,
　Braz., 25,226....C3, K8　30

São João del Rei, Braz.,
　34,654........C4, g5　30
São João Nepomuceno,
　Braz., 9,436.....C4, g6　30
São José do Rio Pardo,
　Braz., 14,186.......k8　30
São José do Rio Prêto,
　Braz., 66,476......C3　30
São José dos Campos,
　Braz., 55,349....C3, m9　30
São Leopoldo, Braz.,
　41,023............D2　30
São Lourenço, Braz.,
　14,680............C3　30
São Luís, Braz.,
　124,606...........D6　27
São Luís Gonzaga, Braz.,
　12,926............D2　30
São Manuel, Braz.,
　10,009.........C3, m7　30
Saône-et-Loire, dept.,
　Fr., 535,772......*D6　5
São Paulo, Braz.,
　3,825,351.......C3, m8　30
São Paulo, state, Braz.,
　12,974,699......C3, m8　30
São Roque, Braz.,
　12,409...........m8　30
São Salvador, see Salvador,
　Braz.
São Sebastião do Paraíso,
　Braz., 14,451......C3　30
São Tomé & Principe,
　Port. dep., Afr.,
　60,159............H6　22
São Vicente, Braz.,
　73,578............C3　30
São Vicente, Port.,
　6,663............h11　8
Sapai, Grc., 5,698....*B5　14
Sapozhok, Sov. Un.,
　10,000...........E13　12
Sappington, Mo.,
　10,000............B8　69
Sapporo, Jap.,
　523,839..........E10　18
Sapri, It., 6,188......D5　9
Sapulpa, Okla., 14,282. B5　79
Sara Buri, Thai.,
　20,245...........*C2　19
Sarah, Miss., 125......A3　68
Sarajevo, Yugo.,
　142,423...........D4　10
Sara Kaeo, Thai.,
　25,000...........*C2　19
Saraland, Ala., 4,595...E1　46
Saranac, Mich., 1,081..F5　66
Saranac Lake, N.Y.,
　6,421.............B3　75
Saranap, Calif., 6,450..*B5　50
Sarandí del Yí, Ur.,
　4,437.............E1　30
Sarandí Grande, Ur.,
　4,539.............E1　30
Saransk, Sov. Un.,
　108,000..........D15　12
Sarapul, Sov. Un.,
　76,000............D8　12
Sarasota, Fla.,
　34,083.........E4, F2　54
Sarasota, co., Fla.,
　76,895............E4　54
Saratoga, Calif., 14,861. C5　50
Saratoga, Tex., 800...*D5　84
Saratoga, Wyo., 1,133.*D6　89
Saratoga, co., N.Y.,
　89,096............B7　75
Saratoga Place, Va.,
　1,478...........*E6　85
Saratoga Springs, N.Y.,
　16,630............B7　75
Saratov, Sov. Un.,
　622,000..........F15　12
Saravane, Laos,
　25,000...........*B3　19
Sarawak, state, Mala.,
　546,385...........E4　19
Saraykoy, Tur., 6,900..D7　14
Sarcelles, Fr., 35,885..g10　5
Sarcoxie, Mo., 1,056...D3　69
Sardegna, pol. dist., It.,
　1,419,362........*E2　9
Sardinia, isl., It.......D2　9
Sardis, Ala., 300......C3　46
Sardis, Miss., 2,098...A4　68
Sargent, co., N. Dak.,
　6,856.............D8　77
Sarikamis, Tur.,
　17,600...........B14　14
Sariwon, Kor., 42,957..G2　18
Sarlat, Fr., 5,251......E4　5
Sarnia, Ont., Can.,
　50,976............E2　41
Sarny, Sov. Un.,
　10,000............F6　12
Saronno, It., 25,190...B2　9
Sarospatak, Hung.,
　9,610.............A5　10
Sarpsborg, Nor.,
　13,300...........p29　11

Sarpy, co., Nebr., 31,281............C9 71
Sarreguemines, Fr., 17,866..............C7 5
Sarria, Sp., 3,935......A2 8
Sartène, Fr., 4,067.....D2 9
Sarthe, dept., Fr., 443,019.........*D4 5
Sartrouville, Fr., 31,267.............g9 5
Sarvar, Hung., 11,021..B3 10
Sarzana, It., 8,600.....B2 9
Sasaram, India, 37,782.D7 20
Sasebo, Jap., 262,484...J4 18
Saskatoon, Sask., Can., 95,526...........E2 39
Saskatchewan, prov., Can., 925,181..........39
Sasovo, Sov. Un., 26,000...........D13 12
Sassari, It., 90,037....D2 9
Saticoy, Calif., 2,283...E4 50
Satka, Sov. Un., 38,900.............*D8 13
Satoraljaujhely, Hung., 16,197.............A5 10
Satsuma, Ala., 1,491...E1 46
Sattahip, Thai., 4,478.*C2 19
Satu-Mare, Rom., 52,099.............B6 10
Sauda, Nor., 3,055....H2 11
Saudi Arabia, country, Asia, 6,036,000......D3 15
Saugatuck, Mich., 927..F4 66
Saugerties, N.Y., 4,286.C7 75
Saugor, India, 85,491...D6 20
Saugus, Mass., 20,666..........B5, C3 65
Sauk, co., Wis., 36,179..E4 88
Sauk Centre, Minn., 3,573.............E4 67
Sauk City, Wis., 2,095..E4 88
Sauk Rapids, Minn., 4,038.............E4 67
Sauk Village, Ill., 5,774...........*B6 58
Sault Ste. Marie, Ont., Can., 43,088........E9 41
Sault Ste. Marie, Mich., 18,722............B6 66
Saumur, Fr., 20,773....D4 5
Saunders, co., Nebr., 17,270............C9 71
Sauquoit, N.Y., 1,715.*B5 75
Sausalito, Calif., 5,331............B5, D2 50
Savage, Md., 1,341....B4 63
Savage, Minn., 1,094..........F5, F6 67
Savanna, Ill., 4,950....A3 58
Savannah, Ga., 149,245 (*189,200)..........D5 55
Savannah, Mo., 2,455..B3 69
Savannah, Tenn., 4,315.B3 83
Savannah Beach, Ga., 1,385.............D6 55
Saveni, Rom., 6,470....B8 10
Saverne, Fr., 9,056.....C7 5
Savigliano, It., 14,800..B1 9
Savoie, dept., Fr., 266,678..........*F3 6
Savona, It., 72,115.....B2 9
Savona, N.Y., 904.....C3 75
Savonlinna, Fin., 14,700...........G13 11
Savoy, former prov., Fr., 546,000...........E7 5
Savran, Sov. Un., 10,000............G8 12
Sawankhalok, Thai., 7,742.............B1 19
Sawbill Landing, Minn., 100...............C7 67
Sawhāj, Eg., U.A.R., 48,300............C4 23
Sawyer, Mich., 1,300...G4 66
Sawyer, co., Wis., 9,475.C2 88
Sawyerwood, Ohio, 1,600.............*A6 78
Saxon, S.C., 3,917.....B4 82
Saxony, reg., Ger......C6 6
Saxton, Pa., 977.......F5 81
Sayabec, Que., Can., 2,314............*G20 36
Sayhūt, S. Arabia,.....F5 15
Sayre, Ala., 1,200.....B3 46
Sayre, Okla., 2,913.....B2 79
Sayre, Pa., 7,917......C3 81
Sayreton, Ala., 1,000............C3, E4 46
Sayreville, N.J., 22,553.C4 74
Sayula, Mex., 11,596...........D4, n12 34
Sayville, N.Y., 6,500...G4 52
Scalp Level, Pa., 1,445..F4 81
Scanlon, Minn., 1,126..D6 67
Scansano, It., 8,560.....C3 9
Scappoose, Oreg., 923..B4 80
Scarborough, Ont., Can., 900...............E7 41

Scarborough, Eng., 42,597.............C6 4
Scarbro, W. Va., 900...D7 87
Scarsdale, N.Y., 17,968.D2 75
Sceaux, Fr., 19,024....g10 5
Schaefferstown, Pa., 800................F9 81
Schaffhausen, Switz., 30,904 (*40,400).....E4 6
Schaffhausen, canton, Switz., 65,981......*E4 6
Schaller, Iowa, 896....B2 60
Schaumberg, Ill., 3,296.E2 58
Schenectady, N.Y., 81,682.............C7 75
Schenectady, co., N.Y., 152,896............C6 75
Schererville, Ind., 2,875.............B3 59
Schertz, Tex., 2,281....B4 84
Schiedam, Neth., 8,600.............B6 5
Schiltigheim, Fr., 25,081.............C7 5
Schiller Park, Ill., 5,867.E2 58
Schio, It., 28,289......B3 9
Schivelbein, see Swidwin, Pol.
Schleicher, co., Tex., 2,791.............D2 84
Schleswig, Ger., 33,800.A4 6
Schleswig-Holstein, reg., Ger...............A4 6
Schleswig-Holstein, state, Ger., 2,316,600......A4 6
Schley, co., Ga., 3,256..D2 55
Schlüchtern, Ger., 5,800.............C4 6
Schmalkalden, Ger., 14,000.............C5 6
Schneidemühl, see Piła, Pol.
Schofield, Wis., 3,038..D4 88
Schoharie, N.Y., 1,168..C6 75
Schoharie, co., N.Y., 22,616............C6 75
Schönebeck, Ger., 44,000.............B5 6
Schongau, Ger., 8,800..E5 6
Schoolcraft, Mich., 1,205.............F5 66
Schoolcraft, co., Mich., 8,953.............B4 66
Schramberg, Ger., 18,100.............D4 6
Schreiber, Ont., Can., 2,230............*E8 41
Schrobenhausen, Ger., 8,700.............D5 6
Schulenburg, Tex., 2,207.............E4 84
Schuyler, Nebr., 3,096..C8 71
Schuyler, co., Ill., 8,746.C3 58
Schuyler, co., Mo., 5,052.............A5 69
Schuyler, co., N.Y., 15,044............C4 75
Schuylerville, N.Y., 1,361.............B7 75
Schuylkill, co., Pa., 173,027............E9 81
Schuylkill Haven, Pa., 6,470.............E9 81
Schwabach, Ger., 23,700.............D5 6
Schwäbisch Gmünd, Ger., 41,100............D4 6
Schwäbisch Hall, Ger., 21,900............D4 6
Schwandorf, Ger., 16,100.............D6 6
Schwaz, Aus., 9,455....E5 6
Schwedt, Ger., 5,961...B7 6
Schweinfurt, Ger., 56,900.............C5 6
Schwenningen, Ger., 31,700.............D4 6
Schwerin, Ger., 92,900.B5 6
Schwyz, Switz., 11,007.E4 6
Schwyz, canton, Switz., 78,048............*E4 6
Sciacca, It., 25,000....F4 9
Scio, Ohio, 1,135......B6 78
Scioto, co., Ohio, 84,216............D4 78
Sciotodale, Ohio, 800..*D5 78
Scituate, Mass., 3,229..........B6, D4 65
Scobey, Mont., 1,726..B11 70
Scotch Plains, N.J., 18,491............B4 74
Scotia, Calif., 1,122....B1 50
Scotia, N.Y., 7,625....C7 75
Scotland, S. Dak., 1,077.............G8 77
Scotland, reg., U.K., 5,178,490..........B4 4
Scotland, co., Mo., 6,484.............A5 69
Scotland, co., N.C., 25,183............C4 76

Scotland Neck, N.C., 2,974.............A6 76
Scotlandville, La., 10,000..........A5, D4 63
Scotstown, Que., Can., 1,038.............D6 42
Scott, La., 902........D3 63
Scott, co., Ark., 7,297..C1 49
Scott, co., Ill., 6,377...D3 58
Scott, co., Ind., 14,643..G6 59
Scott, co., Iowa, 119,067............C7 60
Scott, co., Kans., 5,228.D3 61
Scott, co., Ky., 15,376..B5 62
Scott, co., Minn., 21,909............F5 67
Scott, co., Miss., 21,187.C4 68
Scott, co., Mo., 32,748..D8 69
Scott, co., Tenn., 15,413............C9 83
Scott, co., Va., 25,813..B2 85
Scott City, Kans., 3,555.............D3 61
Scott City, Mo., 1,963.*D8 69
Scottdale, Ga., 4,000..*B5 55
Scottdale, Pa., 6,244...F2 81
Scottsbluff, Nebr., 13,377............C4 71
Scotts Bluff, co., Nebr., 33,809............C2 71
Scottsboro, Ala., 6,449..A3 46
Scottsburg, Ind., 3,810.G6 59
Scottsdale, Ariz., 10,026............C3, D2 48
Scottsville, Ky., 3,324..D3 62
Scottsville, N.Y., 1,863.B3 75
Scottville, Mich., 1,245.E4 66
Scranton, Pa., 111,443 (*215,600).....A9, D10 81
Screven, Ga., 1,010....E4 55
Screven, co., Ga., 14,919............D5 55
Scribner, Nebr., 1,021..C9 71
Scunthorpe, Eng., 67,257............D6 4
Scurry, co., Tex., 20,369............C2 84
Sea Bright, N.J., 1,138.C5 74
Seabrook, Md., 3,000..*C4 53
Seabrook, N.J., 1,798..*E2 74
Seabrook, Tex., 950....F5 84
Sea Cliff, N.Y., 5,669..F2 52
Seadrift, Tex., 1,082...E4 84
Seaford, Del., 4,430....C6 53
Seaford, N.Y., 14,718..G3 52
Seaforth, Ont., Can., 2,255.............D3 41
Sea Girt, N.J., 1,798....C4 74
Seagoville, Tex., 3,745..B6 84
Seagraves, Tex., 2,307..C1 84
Seahurst, Wash., 2,500.D1 86
Sea Isle City, N.J., 1,393.............E3 74
Seal Beach, Calif., 6,994.............*F2 50
Sealy, Tex., 2,328.....E4 84
Searcy, Ark., 8,215.....B4 49
Searcy, co., Ark., 8,124..I3 49
Seaside, Calif., 19,353..C6 50
Seaside, Oreg., 3,877...B3 80
Seaside Heights, N.J., 954...............D4 74
Seaside Park, N.J., 1,054.............D4 74
Seatack, Va., 3,120...*E7 85
Seat Pleasant, Md., 5,365...........C2, C4 53
Seattle, Wash., 557,087 (*938,400).....B3, D1 86
Sebastian, co., Ark., 66,685............B1 49
Sebastopol, Calif., 2,694...........A5, C2 50
Sebeş, Rom., 11,628...C6 10
Sebewaing, Mich., 2,026.............E7 66
Sebinkarahisar, Tur., 8,800.............B12 14
Sebnitz, Ger., 14,800...C7 6
Sebree, Ky., 1,139.....C2 62
Sebring, Fla., 6,939....E5 54
Sebring, Ohio, 4,439...B6 78
Secane, Pa., 2,000....*B11 81
Secaucus, N.J., 12,154..D5 74
Secor Gardens, Ohio, 3,000............*A2 78
Secunderabad, India, 187,471............E6 20
Security, Colo., 10,000..C6 51
Sedalia, Mo., 23,874...E6 20
Sedan, Fr., 20,336.....C6 5
Sedan, Kans., 1,677....E7 61
Sedgefield, N.C., 1,000............*A4 76
Sedgwick, Kans., 1,095............B5, E6 61
Sedgwick, co., Colo., 4,242.............A8 51
Sedgwick, co., Kans., 343,231............E6 61

Sedro Woolley, Wash., 3,705.............A3 86
Seekonk, Mass., 8,399..C5 65
Seelyville, Ind., 1,114..F3 59
Segorbe, Sp., 7,538....C5 8
Ségou, Mali, 17,400....F3 22
Segovia, Sp., 33,360....B3 8
Segovia, prov., Sp., 195,602...........*B3 8
Segré, Fr., 5,203......D3 5
Seguin, Tex., 14,299.........:.B4, E4 84
Sehwan, Pak., 3,827...C4 20
Seiling, Okla., 910.....A3 79
Seinäjoki, Fin., 15,800...........F10 11
Seine, dept., Fr., 5,646,446........*C5, g10 5
Seine-et-Marne, dept., Fr., 524,486...........*C5 5
Seine-et-Oise, dept., Fr., 2,298,931.........*C5 5
Seine-Maritime, dept., Fr., 1,035,844.......*F7 4
Seis de Septiembre, Arg., 110,344............g7 28
Seixal, Port., 4,125.....f9 8
Sekondi-Takoradi, Ghana, 26,757............H4 22
Selah, Wash., 2,824....C5 86
Selangor, state, Mala., 1,012,929..........E2 19
Selanovtsi, Bul., 7,259..D7 10
Selb, Ger., 19,200.....C6 6
Selby, S. Dak., 979....E5 77
Selbyville, Del., 1,080..D7 53
Selden, N.Y., 1,604...*E3 75
Sélestat, Fr., 13,818...C7 5
Selidovka, Sov. Un., 10,000............q20 12
Selinsgrove, Pa., 3,948.E8 81
Selkirk, Man., Can., 8,576.............D3 40
Selkirk, Scot., 5,634...*C5 4
Selkirk, co., Scot., 21,055............H6 59
Sellersburg, Ind., 2,679.H6 59
Sellersville, Pa., 2,497.F11 81
Selma, Ala., 28,385....C2 46
Selma, Calif., 6,934....D4 50
Selma, N.C., 3,102....B5 76
Selmer, Tenn., 1,897...B3 83
Selvas, reg., Braz......D4 27
Semarang, Indon., 487,006............G4 19
Semenovka, Sov. Un., 9,000.............E9 12
Seminole, Ala., 200....E2 46
Seminole, Fla., 1,500..*E4 54
Seminole, Okla., 11,464.B5 79
Seminole, Tex., 5,737...C1 84
Seminole, co., Fla., 54,947............D5 54
Seminole, co., Ga., 6,802.............F2 55
Seminole, co., Okla., 28,066............B5 79
Semipalatinsk, Sov. Un., 177,000............D11 13
Semnān, Iran, 23,078..A8 23
Senador Pompeu, Braz., 8,210.............D7 27
Senath, Mo., 1,369.....E7 69
Senatobia, Miss., 3,259.A4 68
Sendai, Jap., 425,272..G10 18
Sendai (Kagoshima pref.), Jap., 25,600.......K5 18
Seneca, Ill., 1,719.....B5 58
Seneca, Kans., 2,072...C7 61
Seneca, Mo., 1,478....E3 69
Seneca, S.C., 5,227....B2 82
Seneca, co., N.Y., 31,984............C4 75
Seneca, co., Ohio, 59,326............A4 78
Seneca Falls, N.Y., 7,439.............C4 75
Seneca Gardens, Ky., 928..............*H6 62
Senegal, country, Afr., 2,973,000..........F2 22
Senftenberg, Ger., 21,000............C7 6
Senhor do Bonfim, Braz., 13,950............E7 27
Senigallia, It., 16,700...C4 9
Senlis, Fr., 9,371.....C5 5
Senneterre, Que., Can., 3,246.............B2 42
Sens, Fr., 20,015......C5 42
Senta, Yugo., 24,987...C5 10
Sentinel, Okla., 1,154..B2 79
Seoul (Sŏul), Kor., 2,444,900..........H3 18
Sept Iles (Seven Islands), Que., Can., 14,196..B3 42
Sequatchie, co., Tenn., 5,915.............D8 83
Sequim, Wash., 1,164..A2 86
Sequoyah, co., Okla., 18,001............B7 79

Serafimovich, Sov. Un.,
  8,800.............G14 12
Seraing, Bel., 41,239...B6   5
Serbia, reg., Yugo.....D5 10
Serbia, rep., Yugo.,
  7,629,113..........*D5 10
Serdobsk, Sov. Un.,
  10,000.............E15 12
Sered, Czech., 6,208...D4   7
Seremban, Mala.,
  52,091.............E2 19
Sergipe, state, Braz.,
  760,263...........*E7 27
Seria, Bru., 17,595....E4 19
Seringapatam, India,
  11,423.............F6 20
Serón, Sp., 7,091.....D4   8
Serov, Sov. Un.,
  102,000...........*D9 13
Serowe, Bech., 15,935..E5 24
Serpa, Port., 7,273....D2   8
Serpukhov, Sov. Un.,
  111,000............D11 12
Sérrai, Grc., 40,063...B4 14
Sérrai, prov., Grc.,
  248,041...........*B4 14
Serra Talhada, Braz.,
  5,353............*D7 27
Serrinha, Braz.,
  10,284...........*E7 27
Sesser, Ill., 1,764.....E4 58
Sesto [Fiorentino], It.,
  22,453.............C3   9
Sestroretsk, Sov. Un.,
  34,000 (part of
  Leningrad).......A8 12
Sestri Levante, It.,
  9,100..............B2   9
Setana, Jap., 4,100....E9 18
Setauket, N.Y., 1,207..F4 52
Sète, Fr., 36,301......F5   5
Sete Lagoas, Braz.,
  36,302.............B4 30
Seth, W. Va., 800..C3, D6 87
Seth Ward, Tex.,
  1,328............*B2 84
Sétif, Alg., 53,057....A6 22
Seto, Jap., 82,101..I8, n16 18
Settat, Mor., 29,617...B3 22
Setúbal, Port., 44,600..C1   8
Sevastopol., Sov. Un.,
  163,000............I9 12
Seven Harbors, Mich.,
  2,748..............F7 66
Seven Hills, Ohio,
  5,708............*A6 78
Severna Park, Md.,
  3,100..............B4 53
Sevier, co., Ark.,
  10,156.............D1 49
Sevier, co., Tenn.,
  24,251.............D10 83
Sevier, co., Utah,
  10,565.............B6 72
Sevierville, Tenn.,
  2,890.............D10 83
Sevilla, Col., 17,210...C2 32
Sevilla, Sp., 442,300...D3   8
Sevilla, prov., Sp.,
  1,234,435.........*D3   8
Seville, Ohio, 1,190...A6 78
Sevlievo, Bul., 9,856...D7 10
Sevran, Fr., 17,969...g11   5
Sèvres, Fr., 20,129.....g9   5
Sewanee, Tenn., 1,464.B6 83
Seward, Alsk.,
  1,891.........C10, g17 47
Seward, Nebr., 4,208...D8 71
Seward, co., Kans.,
  15,930.............E3 61
Seward, co., Nebr.,
  13,581.............D8 71
Sewaren, N.J., 1,500...E4 74
Sewell, Ky., 265......C6 62
Sewell, N.J., 900......D2 74
Sewickley, Pa.,
  6,157...........A5, E1 81
Sewickley Heights, Pa.,
  931..............*E1 81
Seychelles, Br. dep., Afr.,
  34,632............G24   2
Seymchan, Sov. Un...C18 12
Seymour, Conn.,
  10,100.............D4 52
Seymour, Ind., 11,629..G6 59
Seymour, Iowa, 1,117..D4 60
Seymour, La., 1,788...B5 63
Seymour, Mo., 1,046...D5 69
Seymour, Tex., 3,789...C3 84
Seymour, Wis.,
  2,045...........A5, D5 88
Sezimbra, Port., 6,957..C1   8
Sezze, It., 7,544......D4   9
Sfantul-Gheorghe, Rom.,
  17,638.............C7 10
Sfax, Tun., 65,645.....B7 22
's Gravenhage, see The
  Hague, Neth.
Shackelford, co., Tex.,
  3,990..............C3 84
Shadyside, Ohio, 5,028.C7 78

Shaft (William Penn), Pa.,
  850..............*E9 81
Shafter, Calif., 4,576...E4 50
Shafter, Tex., 975......F2 84
Shahjahanpur, India,
  110,432 (*117,702)...C6 20
Shārūd, Iran, 23,132...B6 15
Shaker Heights, Ohio,
  36,460..........A6, B2 78
Shakhty, Sov. Un.,
  201,000...........H13 12
Shaki, Nig., 22,983....G5 22
Shakopee, Minn., 5,201.F5 67
Shallowater, Tex.,
  1,001..............C2 84
Shamokin, Pa., 13,674..E8 81
Shamokin Dam, Pa.,
  1,093..............E8 81
Shamrock, Fla., 600....C3 54
Shamrock, Tex., 3,113..B2 84
Shanee, Colo., 100....B5 51
Shangchiu, China,
  134,400............E8 17
Shanghai, China,
  6,900,000..........E9 17
Shannon, Ga., 1,629...B1 55
Shannon, co., Mo.,
  7,087..............D6 69
Shannon, co., S. Dak.,
  6,000..............G3 77
Shannontown, S.C.,
  7,064............*D7 82
Shansi, prov., China,
  15,960,000.........D7 17
Shantung, prov., China,
  54,030,000.........D8 17
Shaohsing, China,
  130,600............E9 17
Shaoyang, China,
  117,700............F7 17
Sharasume (Chenghwa),
  China, 25,000......B2 17
Shari, Jap., 8,100....E12 18
Sharkey, co., Miss.,
  10,738.............C3 68
Sharon, Mass.,
  10,070..........B5, E2 65
Sharon, Pa., 25,267...D1 81
Sharon, Tenn., 966....A3 83
Sharon, Wis., 1,167...F5 88
Sharon Hill, Pa.,
  7,123.............G11 81
Sharon Springs, Kans.,
  966..............D2 61
Sharonville, Ohio,
  6,457..............D2 78
Sharp, co., Ark., 6,319..A4 49
Sharpsburg, Pa., 6,096..A5 81
Sharpsville, Pa., 6,067..D1 81
Shasi, China, 85,800...E7 17
Shasta, co., Calif.,
  59,468.............B3 50
Shatsk, Sov. Un.,
  10,000............D13 12
Shattuck, Okla., 1,625..A2 79
Shaunavon, Sask., Can.,
  2,154..............H1 39
Shavertown, Pa.,
  2,000............*B8 81
Shaw, Miss., 2,062....B3 68
Shawano, Wis., 6,103..D5 88
Shawano, co., Wis.,
  34,351.............D5 88
Shawinigan Est, Que.,
  Can., 2,451.......*C5 42
Shawinigan, Que., Can.,
  28,597 (*58,698).....C5 42
Shawmut, Ala., 1,898..C4 46
Shawnee, Kans., 9,072..B8 61
Shawnee, Ohio, 1,000...C5 78
Shawnee, Okla., 24,326.B5 79
Shawnee, co., Kans.,
  141,286............D8 61
Shawneetown, Ill.,
  1,399..............F5 58
Shawsheen Village, Mass.,
  3,000..............A5 65
Shawville, Que., Can.,
  1,534..............B8 41
Shchelkovo, Sov. Un.,
  65,000.............n18 12
Shchetovo, Sov. Un.,
  10,000.............q22 12
Shchigry, Sov. Un.,
  10,000.............F11 12
Shchors, Sov. Un.,
  10,000.............F8 12
Sheboygan, Wis.,
  45,747..........B6, E6 88
Sheboygan, co., Wis.,
  86,484.............E6 88
Sheboygan Falls, Wis.,
  4,061...........B6, E6 88
Shediac, N.B., Can.,
  2,159..............C5 43
Sheerness, Eng., 14,123.E7   4
Sheet Harbour, N.S., Can.,
  883..............E7 43
Sheffield, Ala., 13,491..A2 46
Sheffield, Eng., 493,954
  (*725,000).........D6   4

Sheffield, Ill., 1,078....B4 58
Sheffield, Iowa, 1,156...B4 60
Sheffield, Ohio, 1,664...A5 78
Sheffield, Pa., 1,971....C3 81
Sheffield Lake, Ohio,
  6,884............*A5 78
Shefford, co., Que., Can.,
  54,963.............D5 42
Shelbiana, Ky., 500....C7 62
Shelbina, Mo., 2,067...B5 69
Shelburn, Ind., 1,299...F3 59
Shelburne, Ont., Can.,
  1,239..............C4 41
Shelburne, N.S., Can.,
  2,408..............F4 43
Shelburne, co., N.S., Can.,
  15,208.............F4 43
Shelburne Falls, Mass.,
  2,097..............A2 65
Shelby, Mich., 1,603...E4 66
Shelby, Miss., 2,384...B3 68
Shelby, Mont., 4,017...B5 70
Shelby, N.C., 17,698...B2 76
Shelby, Ohio, 9,106...B5 78
Shelby, co., Ala.,
  32,132.............B3 46
Shelby, co., Ill.,
  23,404.............D5 58
Shelby, co., Ind.,
  34,093.............E6 59
Shelby, co., Iowa,
  15,825.............C2 60
Shelby, co., Ky.,
  18,493.............B4 62
Shelby, co., Mo.,
  9,063..............B5 69
Shelby, co., Ohio,
  33,586.............B3 78
Shelby, co., Tenn.,
  627,019............B2 83
Shelby, co., Tex.,
  20,479.............D5 84
Shelby City, Ky., 500...C5 62
Shelby Village, Mich.,
  1,900............*F7 66
Shelbyville, Ill., 4,821..D5 58
Shelbyville, Ind.,
  14,317.............E6 59
Shelbyville, Ky., 4,525.B4 62
Shelbyville, Tenn.,
  10,466.............B5 83
Sheldon, Ill., 1,137....C6 58
Sheldon, Iowa, 4,251...A2 60
Shell Beach, Calif.,
  1,820............*E3 50
Shell Brook, Sask., Can.,
  1,042..............D2 39
Shell Camp, Tex.,
  500..............*C5 84
Shelley, Idaho, 2,612...F6 57
Shell Lake, Wis., 1,016.C2 88
Shellman, Ga., 1,050...E2 55
Shellman Bluff, Ga.,
  150...............E5 55
Shell Rock, Iowa,
  1,112..............B5 60
Shelton, Conn., 18,190.D4 52
Shelton, Nebr., 904....D7 71
Shelton, Wash., 5,651..B2 86
Shenandoah, Iowa,
  6,567..............D2 60
Shenandoah, Pa.,
  11,073.............E9 81
Shenandoah, Va., 1,839.C4 85
Shenandoah, co., Va.,
  21,825.............C4 85
Shenandoah Heights, Pa.,
  1,721............*E9 81
Shendi, Sud., 11,031...E4 23
Shenorock, N.Y.,
  1,402............*D7 75
Shensi, prov., China,
  18,130,000.........E6 17
Shenyang, see Mukden,
  China
Shepetovka, Sov. Un.,
  10,000.............F6 12
Shepherd, Mich., 1,293.E6 66
Shepherdstown, W. Va.,
  1,328..............B7 87
Shepherdsville, Ky.,
  1,525..............D4 62
Shepparton, Austl.,
  13,579.............H5 26
Sheppton, Pa., 800....E9 81
Sherbrooke, Que., Can.,
  66,554.............D6 42
Sherbrooke, co., Que.,
  Can., 80,490.......D5 42
Sherburn, Minn., 1,227.G4 67
Sherburne, N.Y., 1,647.C5 75
Sherburne, co., Minn.,
  12,861.............E5 67
Shereshevo, Sov. Un.,
  10,000.............B8   7
Sheridan, Ark., 1,938...C3 49
Sheridan, Colo., 3,559..B6 51
Sheridan, Ind., 2,165...D5 59
Sheridan, Oreg., 1,763..B3 80
Sheridan, Wyo., 11,651.A6 89

Sheridan, co., Kans.,
  4,267.............C3 61
Sheridan, co., Mont.,
  6,458.............B12 70
Sheridan, co., Nebr.,
  9,049.............B3 71
Sheridan, co., N. Dak.,
  4,350.............C5 77
Sheridan, co., Wyo.,
  18,989.............A5 89
Sheridan Beach, Wash.,
  1,500............*B3 86
Sherman, Ohio, 1,000..*B6 78
Sherman, Tex., 24,988..C4 84
Sherman, co., Kans.,
  6,682..............C2 61
Sherman, co., Nebr.,
  5,382..............C6 71
Sherman, co., Oreg.,
  2,446..............B6 80
Sherman, co., Tex.,
  2,605..............A2 84
Sherridon, Man., Can.,
  88................B1 40
Sherrill, N.Y., 2,922...B5 75
's Hertogenbosch, Neth.,
  76,700.............B6   5
Sherwood, Ark., 1,222..D5 49
Sherwood, Tenn., 650..B6 83
Sheshebee, Minn., 100..D5 67
Shetland, co., Scot.,
  17,809...........*g10   4
Shetland, is., Scot....g10   4
Shiawassee, co., Mich.,
  53,446.............F6 66
Shibām, S. Arabia,
  8,000..............F4 15
Shibarghan, Afg.,
  22,464.............A4 20
Shibetsu, Jap., 12,750.D11 18
Shibīn al Kawm, Eg.,
  U.A.R., 47,100......G8 14
Shickshinny, Pa., 1,843.D9 81
Shields, Ky., 900....*D6 62
Shiga, pref., Jap.,
  842,695...........*I8 18
Shigatse (Zhikatse),
  China, 10,000......C8 20
Shihchiachuang, China,
  126,000..........*D7 17
Shikarpur, Pak., 45,376.C4 20
Shikoku, isl., Jap.....J6 18
Shilka, Sov. Un.,
  23,000............D14 13
Shillington, Pa., 5,639.F10 81
Shillong, India, 72,438..C9 20
Shiloh, Ohio, 9,500....C3 78
Shimabara, Jap., 28,200.J5 18
Shimada, Jap., 36,500..o17 18
Shimane, pref., Jap.,
  888,886..........*I16 18
Shimanovsk, Sov. Un.,
  17,000............D15 13
Shimizu, Jap.,
  142,983..........I9, n17 18
Shimoda, Jap., 16,200..o17 18
Shimodate, Jap.,
  23,000.............m18 18
Shimoga, India, 63,764.F6 20
Shimonoseki, Jap.,
  246,941............I5 18
Shimotsuma, Jap.,
  9,700............*m18 18
Shiner, Tex., 1,945.....E4 84
Shinglehouse, Pa.,
  1,298..............C5 81
Shingu, Jap., 39,114...J7 18
Shinjo, Jap., 22,100..G10 18
Shinkolobwe, Con. L.,
  10,900.............C5 24
Shinnston, W. Va.,
  2,724...........A7, B4 87
Shinshiro, Jap., 14,100.o16 18
Shiogama, Jap.,
  55,325............G10 18
Shiojiri, Jap., 13,500..m16 18
Shippegan, N.B., Can.,
  1,631..............B5 43
Shippensburg, Pa.,
  6,138..............F6 81
Shīrāz, Iran, 170,659...G8 16
Shirbīn, Eg., U.A.R.,
  13,293.............G8 14
Shiremanstown, Pa.,
  1,212............*F8 81
Shirley, Ind., 1,038....E6 59
Shirley, Mass., 1,762...A4 65
Shirley, Mont., 3......D11 70
Shirley, N.Y., 1,800...*D4 75
Shirutoru, see Makarov,
  Sov. Un.
Shishido, Jap., 11,018.m19 18
Shively, Ky.,
  15,155..........A4, B4 62
Shizuoka, Jap.,
  323,819..........I9, o17 18
Shizuoka, pref., Jap.,
  2,756,271.........*I9 18
Shkodër, Alb., 40,900..A2 14
Shkodër, pref., Alb.,
  150,000..........*A2 14

Shoals, Ind., 1,022.....G4   59
Shoemakersville, Pa.,
1,464...............E10   81
Sholapur, India, 337,583
(*277,087)...........E6   20
Shore Acres, Calif.,
3,093...............*B5   50
Shore Acres, Mass.,
980................*B6   65
Shoreview, Minn.,
7,157...............*F5   67
Shorewood, Minn.,
3,197...............*F5   67
Shorewood, Wis.,
15,990.............E2, E6   88
Shorewood Hills, Wis.,
2,320...............*E4   88
Short Beach, Conn.,
950.................D5   52
Shortsville, N.Y., 1,382.C3   75
Shoshone, Idaho, 1,416.G4   57
Shoshone, co., Idaho,
20,876..............B3   57
Show Low, Ariz., 1,625.B3   48
Shpola, Sov. Un.,
10,000..............G8   12
Shreve, Ohio, 1,617....B5   78
Shreveport, La., 164,372
(*245,200)..........B2   63
Shrewsbury, Eng.,
49,726.............D5   4
Shrewsbury, Mass.,
16,622.............B4   65
Shrewsbury, Mo.,
4,730...............*C7   69
Shrewsbury, N.J.,
3,222...............C4   74
Shrewsbury, Pa., 943..G8   81
Shropshire, co., Eng.,
297,313............*D5   4
Shrub Oak, N.Y.,
1,874...............*D7   75
Shuangcheng, China,
81,000.............D3   18
Shuangshan, China,
5,000...............E1   18
Shuangyang, China,
5,000...............E2   18
Shulan, China, 5,000...D3   18
Shullsburg, Wis., 1,324.F3   88
Shumen, co., Bul.,
1,408,188..........*D8   10
Shumerlya, Sov. Un.,
26,800............D16   12
Shuya, Sov. Un.,
67,000............C13   12
Shuzenji, Jap., 7,800..o17   18
Shwangliao
(Chengchiatun),
China, 120,100......C9   18
Shwebo, Bur., 17,842.D10   20
Shwegyin, Bur.,
10,000.............*B1   19
Sialkot, Pak., 135,000..B5   20
Siam, see Thialand,
country, Asia
Sian (Hsian), China,
1,310,000..........E6   17
Siangtan, China,
183,600............F7   17
Siauliai, Sov. Un.,
65,000.............D4   12
Sibenik, Yugo., 26,253.D2   10
Sibert, Ky., 700......C6   62
Sibi, Pak., 11,842......C4   20
Sibiu, Rom., 90,478....C7   10
Sibley, Iowa, 2,852....A2   60
Sibley, co., Minn.,
16,228.............F4   67
Sibolga, Indon., 37,171.E1   19
Sibsagar, India, 15,106.C9   20
Sibu, Mala., 9,983....E4   19
Sicard, La., 2,000.....*B3   63
Sicilia, pol. dist., It.,
4,721,001.........*F4   9
Sicily, isl., It........F4   9
Sicuaní, Peru, 7,036...D3   31
Siderno Marina, It.,
6,915..............E6   9
Sidhirokastron, Grc.,
9,022..............*B4   14
Sidi-bel-Abbès, Alg.,
80,632.............A4   22
Sidi Ifni, Ifni, 7,991...C2   22
Sidmouth, Eng.,
11,139.............E5   4
Sidney, B.C., Can.,
1,558............B9, E6   37
Sidney, Iowa, 1,057...D2   60
Sidney, Mont., 4,564..C12   70
Sidney, Nebr., 8,004...C3   71
Sidney, N.Y., 5,157...C5   75
Sidney, Ohio, 14,663..B3   78
Siedlce, Pol., 32,000...B7   7
Siegburg, Ger., 34,000..C3   6
Siegen, Ger., 49,400....C4   6
Siemianowice Slaskie,
Pol., 62,000.......g10   7
Siem Reap, Camb.,
10,000.............C2   19
Siena, It., 47,000......C3   9

Sieradz, Pol., 11,700...C5   7
Siero, Sp., 30,931.....A3   8
Sierpc, Pol., 10,200...B5   7
Sierra, co., Calif.,
2,247..............C3   50
Sierra, co., N. Mex.,
6,409..............C5   48
Sierra Blanca, Tex.,
800................F1   84
Sierra Leone, country,
Afr., 2,400,000......G2   22
Sierra Madre, Calif.,
9,732..............F2   50
Sierraville, Calif., 150..C3   50
Sierra Vista, Ariz.,
3,121..............*D3   48
Sifton, Man., Can.,
245................D1   40
Sighet, Rom., 22,361..B6   10
Sighisoara, Rom.,
20,363.............B7   10
Sigli, Indon., 3,327...*G10   20
Signal Hill, Calif.,
4,627..............*F2   50
Signal Hill, Ill., 1,200..*E3   58
Signal Mountain, Tenn.,
3,413..........D8, E10   83
Sigourney, Iowa, 2,387.C5   60
Siguiri, Guinea, 11,400.F3   22
Siirt, Tur., 22,900....D13   14
Sikar, India, 50,636....C6   20
Sikasso, Mali, 13,600..F3   22
Sikeston, Mo., 13,765..E8   69
Sikionía, Grc., 5,113...*C4   14
Sikkim, country, Asia,
162,189............C8   20
Silao, Mex., 24,138...m13   34
Silchar, India, 41,062..D9   20
Siler City, N.C., 4,455..B4   76
Silesia, reg., Pol......C4   7
Silifke, Tur., 9,200....D9   14
Siliguri, India, 65,471..C8   20
Silistra, Bul., 16,180...C8   10
Sillery, Que., Can.,
14,109.............C9   42
Siloam Springs, Ark.,
3,953..............A1   49
Silsbee, Tex., 6,277...D5   84
Siluria, Ala., 736......B2   46
Silva, Mo., 100.......D7   69
Silva Jardim, Braz.,
1,774..............h6   30
Silver Bay, Minn.,
3,723..............C7   67
Silver Bow, co., Mont.,
46,454.............E4   70
Silver Bow Park, Mont.,
4,798.............*D4   70
Silver City, C.Z.,
3,688.............*B2   32
Silver City, N. Mex.,
6,972..............C4   48
Silver Creek, N.Y.,
3,310..............C1   75
Silver Grove, Ky.,
1,207..............A7   62
Silver Lake, Mass.,
4,654..............C2   65
Silver Lake, Ohio,
2,655.............*A6   78
Silver Lake, Wis.,
1,077...........F1, F5   88
Silver Spring, Md.,
66,348..........C1, C3   53
Silverton, Colo., 822...D3   51
Silverton, Ohio, 6,682..D2   78
Silverton, Oreg.,
3,081...........B4, C2   80
Silverton, Tex., 1,098..B2   84
Silvis, Ill., 3,953......B3   58
Silvis Heights, Ill.,
1,500.............*B3   58
Silwān, Jordan, 5,000.*C3   15
Simav, Tur., 6,300....C7   14
Simcoe, Ont., Can.,
8,754..............E4   41
Simcoe, co., Ont., Can.,
141,271............C5   41
Simferopol, Sov. Un.,
196,000...........I10   12
Simi, Calif., 2,107....*E4   50
Simla, India, 42,597...B6   20
Simleul-Silvaniei, Rom.,
8,560..............B6   10
Simmesport, La., 2,125.D4   63
Simpson, N.C., 302....B6   76
Simpson, Pa., 1,800...C11   81
Simpson, co., Ky.,
11,548.............D3   62
Simpson, co., Miss.,
20,454.............D4   68
Simpsonville, S.C.,
2,282..............B3   82
Simsbury, Conn., 2,745.B5   52
Sinaia, Rom., 9,006....C7   10
Sinajana, Guam, 2,861.*F6   2
Sinaloa, state, Mex.,
791,679............C3   34
Sinanju, Kor., 16,493..G2   18
Sincé, Col., 7,112.....B2   32
Sincelejo, Col., 21,625.B2   32

Sind, reg., Pak.......C4   20
Sinelnikovo, Sov. Un.,
10,000............G10   12
Sines, Port., 4,893.....D1   8
Singa, Sud., 9,436....F4   23
Singapore, Singapore,
925,241............E2   19
Singapore, country, Asia,
1,476,694..........E2   19
Singaradja, Indon.,
12,345.............G5   19
Singkawang, Indon.,
7,127..............E3   19
Sinhung, Kor., 7,583...F3   18
Sining, China, 300,000.D5   17
Siniscola, It., 6,559....D2   9
Sinj, Yugo., 4,133.....D3   10
Sinkiang Uighur, prov.,
China, 5,640,000....C2   17
Sinking Spring, Pa.,
2,244.............*F9   81
Sinnuris, Eg., U.A.R.,
23,537.............H8   14
Sinop, Tur., 9,900....A10   14
Sint-Niklaas, Bel.,
47,811.............B6   5
Sinton, Tex., 6,008....E4   84
Sintra, Port., 7,150....f9   8
Sinuiju, Kor., 118,414..F2   18
Sion, Switz., 16,051...E3   6
Sioux, co., Iowa,
26,375.............A1   60
Sioux, co., Nebr., 2,575.B2   71
Sioux, co., N. Dak.,
3,662..............D5   77
Sioux Center, Iowa,
2,275..............A1   60
Sioux City, Iowa, 89,159
(*101,500).........B1   60
Sioux Falls, S. Dak.,
65,466.............G9   77
Sioux Lookout, Ont.,
Can., 2,453.........E8   41
Sioux Rapids, Iowa,
962................B2   60
Sipes (Midway), Fla.,
1,500.............*D5   54
Sipsey, Ala., 900.....B2   46
Siracusa, It., 89,407...F5   9
Sirājganj, Pak., 37,858.D8   20
Siret, Rom., 5,664....B8   10
Siros, Grc., 16,953....D5   14
Sirpur, India, 4,466....E6   20
Sirsa, India, 33,363...C6   20
Sisak, Yugo., 19,238...C3   10
Siskiyou, co., Calif.,
32,885.............B2   50
Sisseton, S. Dak., 3,218.E9   77
Sistersville, W. Va.,
2,331..............B4   87
Sitapur, India, 53,884..C7   20
Sitka, Alsk., 3,237....D12   47
Sivas, Tur., 93,800....C11   14
Siverek, Tur., 26,100..D21   14
Sivrihisar, Tur., 7,200..C8   14
Skagit, co., Wash.,
51,350.............A4   86
Skamania, co., Wash.,
5,207..............D4   86
Skanderborg, co., Den.,
136,495............I3   11
Skaneateles, N.Y.,
2,921..............C4   75
Skara, Swe., 9,100....H5   11
Skaraborg, co., Swe.,
249,900...........*H5   11
Skegness, Eng., 12,843.D7   4
Skelleftea, Swe., 22,700.E9   11
Skien, Nor., 15,500
(*47,861).......H3, p27   11
Skierniewice, Pol.,
22,000.............C6   7
Skikda (Philippeville),
Alg., 70,406........A6   22
Skokie, Ill., 65,281....E3   58
Skole, Sov. Un., 5,000..D7   7
Skopin, Sov. Un.,
10,000............E13   12
Skopje, Yugo., 161,983.D5   10
Skövde, Swe., 23,900..H5   11
Skovorodino, Sov. Un.,
26,000............D15   13
Skowhegan, Maine,
6,667..............D3   64
Skradin, Yugo., 928....D2   10
Skvira, Sov. Un.,
10,000.............G7   12
Skyland, N.C., 1,500...D3   76
Slagelse, Den., 20,562..A1   7
Slănic-Prahova, Rom.,
6,842..............C7   10
Slany, Czech., 12,000..n17   7
Slater, Mo., 2,767....B4   69
Slatersville, R.I.,
1,000.............B10   52
Slatina, Rom., 13,381..C7   10
Slatington, Pa., 4,316.E10   81
Slaton, Tex., 6,568....C2   84
Slavgorod, Sov. Un.,
44,000............D10   13
Slavonia, reg., Yugo...C3   10

Slavonska Pozega, Yugo.,
13,112.............C3   10
Slavyanoserbsk, Sov.
Un., 5,000.........q21   12
Slavyansk, Sov. Un.,
86,000.........G11, q20   12
Slavyanskaya, Sov. Un.,
83,000............I12   12
Slayton, Minn., 2,487..G3   67
Sleepy Eye, Minn.,
3,492..............F4   67
Sleepy Hollow, Calif.,
1,200.............*B5   50
Sleepy Hollow, Va.,
1,200.............*C5   85
Slickville, Pa., 950....F2   81
Slidell, La., 6,356..B8, D6   63
Sligo, Ire., 13,145....C2   4
Sligo, Pa., 814.......D3   81
Sligo, co., Ire., 53,561.*C2   4
Slinger, Wis., 1,141...E5   88
Slingerlands, N.Y.,
1,500.............*C7   75
Slippery Rock, Pa.,
2,563..............D1   81
Sliven, Bul., 35,553...D8   10
Sloan, N.Y., 5,803....C2   75
Sloatsburg, N.Y., 2,565.A4   74
Slobozia, Rom., 9,632..C8   10
Slocomb, Ala., 1,368..D4   46
Slonim, Sov. Un.,
10,000.............E5   12
Slope, co., N. Dak.,
1,893..............D2   77
Slough, Eng., 80,503...E6   4
Slovakia, reg., Czech.,
4,175,000..........D5   7
Slovan, Pa., 1,018.....F1   81
Slovenia, reg., Yugo...C2   10
Slovenia, rep., Yugo.,
1,584,368.........*C2   10
Slupca, Pol., 5,133....B4   7
Slupsk, Pol., 53,000...A4   7
Slutsk, Sov. Un., 5,000.s31   11
Slyudyanka, Sov. Un.,
17,500............D13   13
Smackover, Ark., 2,434.D3   49
Smederevo, Yugo.,
27,104.............C5   10
Smela, Sov. Un.,
45,000.............G8   12
Smelterville, Idaho,
1,127..............B2   57
Smethport, Pa., 1,725..C5   81
Smethwick, Eng.,
68,372.............D6   4
Smidovich, Sov. Un.,
5,000..............B6   18
Smith, co., Kans.,
7,776..............C5   61
Smith, co., Miss.,
14,303.............C4   68
Smith, co., Tenn.,
12,059.............C8   83
Smith, co., Tex., 86,350.C5   84
Smith Center, Kans.,
2,379..............C5   61
Smithers, B.C., Can.,
2,487..............B4   37
Smithers, W. Va.,
1,696...........C3, C6   87
Smithfield, N.C., 6,117.B5   76
Smithfield, Ohio, 1,312.B7   78
Smithfield, Pa., 939...G2   81
Smithfield, Pa., 2,547..*E5   81
Smithfield, Utah, 2,512.A6   72
Smithfield, Va.,
917.............B6, E6   85
Smithmill, Pa., 600....E5   81
Smith Falls, Ont.,
Can., 9,603.........C8   41
Smithtown, N.Y.,
4,000..............F4   52
Smithville, Mo., 1,254..B3   69
Smithville, Ohio, 1,024.B6   78
Smithville, Tenn.,
2,348..............D8   83
Smithville, Tex., 2,933.D4   84
Smock, Pa., 1,012....*G2   81
Smolensk, Sov. Un.,
159,000............D8   12
Smooth Rock Falls,
Ont., Can., 1,131...*D8   41
Smyre, N.C., 1,197...*B2   76
Smyrna, Del., 3,241...B6   53
Smyrna, Ga.,
10,157..........A5, C2   55
Smyrna, Tenn., 3,612..B5   83
Smyrna, see Izmir, Tur.
Smyth, co., Va., 31,066.B3   85
Sneads, Fla., 1,399....B1   54
Sneek, Neth., 21,100..A6   5
Snezhnoye, Sov. Un.,
10,000............q21   12
Snohomish, Wash.,
3,894..............B3   86
Snohomish, co., Wash.,
172,199............A4   86
Snoqualmie, Wash.,
1,216..............B4   86
Snow Flake, Ariz., 982..B3   48

Snow Hill, Md., 2,311..D7 53
Snow Hill, N.C., 1,043..B6 76
Snyatyn, Sov. Un., 10,000............A7 10
Snyder, Okla., 1,663...C3 79
Snyder, Tex., 13,850...C2 84
Snyder, co., Pa., 25,922.E7 81
Soap Lake, Wash., 1,591..............B6 86
Sobinka, Sov. Un., 10,000.............D13 12
Sobota Rimavska, Czech., 10,700......D6 7
Sobral, Braz., 32,281..*D6 27
Sochaczew, Pol., 13,300.B6 7
Sochi, Sov. Un., 101,000............*E6 13
Social Circle, Ga., 1,780..............C3 55
Society, is., Fr. Polynesia..........H10 2
Socorro, Col., 11,842...B3 32
Socorro, N. Mex., 5,271..............B5 48
Socorro, co., N. Mex., 10,168...........C5 48
Socotra, isl., S. Arabia.G5 15
Soc Trang, Viet., 16,890............D3 19
Socuéllamos, Sp., 14,828.............C4 8
Soda Springs, Idaho, 2,424.............G7 57
Soddy, Tenn., 2,206......D8, E10 83
Söderhamn, Swe., 13,000.............G7 11
Södermanland, co., Swe., 230,400.......H7 11
Södertälje, Swe., 35,300.........t35 11
Sodus, N.Y., 1,645.....B3 75
Soest, Ger., 33,300.....C4 6
Sofia (Sofiya), Bul., 366,925 (*434,888)..D6 10
Sofiya, see Sofia, Bul.
Sofiya, co., Bul., 1,457,742..........*D6 10
Sofiyevka, Sov. Un., 10,000.............G9 12
Sogamoso, Col., 13,574.B3 32
Sogn og Fjordane, co., Nor., 99,900.......*G1 11
Soissons, Fr., 23,150...C5 5
Sokal, Sov. Un., 10,000.F5 12
Soke, Tur., 23,400.....D6 14
Soke of Peterborough, co., Eng., 74,442.....*D6 4
Sokol, Sov. Un., 36,000..............B13 12
Sokolow, Pol., 7,515....B7 7
Sokoto, Nig., 47,643...F6 22
Sokoto, reg., Nig......F6 22
Solana Beach, Calif., 3,000...........*F5 50
Solano, Phil., 9,497...*B6 19
Solano, co., Calif., 134,597...........C2 50
Soledad, Calif., 2,837..D3 50
Soledad, Col., 20,158..A3 32
Solikamsk, Sov. Un., 84,000..........:D8 13
Soliman, Tun., 6,980..F3 9
Solingen, Ger., 162,800.C3 6
Sollefteå, Swe., 9,900..F7 11
Sóller, Sp., 6,817......C7 8
Solna, Swe., 53,300....H7 11
Solomon, Kans., 1,008..D6 61
Solomon Is., Br. dep., Oceania, 102,000...G7 2
Solon, Ohio, 6,333.....A6 78
Solonika, see Thessaloniki, Grc.
Solothurn, Switz., 18,394 (*30,405).....E3 6
Solothurn, canton, Switz., 200,816.....E3 6
Solovyevsk, Sov. Un., 10,000.............D15 13
Soltau, Ger., 14,400....B4 6
Solun, China..........B9 17
Solvang, Calif., 1,325..*E3 50
Solvay, N.Y., 8,732....B4 75
Soma, Tur., 13,100....*C6 14
Somaliland, French, see French Somaliland, dep., Afr.
Somali Republic, country, Afr., 1,980,000....H6 23
Sombor, Yugo., 37,802.C4 10
Sombrerete, Mex., 9,260..............C4 34
Somerdale, N.J., 4,839.D2 74
Somers, Conn., 950....B7 52
Somerset, Ky., 7,112...C5 62
Somerset, Md., 1,444..*C3 53
Somerset, Mass., 12,196............C5 65
Somerset, Ohio, 1,361..C5 78
Somerset, Pa., 6,347...F3 81

Somerset, co., Eng., 598,556.............E5 4
Somerset, co., Maine, 39,749..............C2 64
Somerset, co., Md., 19,623.............D6 53
Somerset, co., N.J., 143,913............B3 74
Somerset, co., Pa., 77,450.............G3 81
Somerset East, S. Afr., 9,779.............G5 24
Somers Point, N.J., 4,504.............E3 74
Somersworth, N.H., 8,529.............E6 73
Somerton, Ariz., 1,613.C1 48
Somervell, co., Tex., 2,577.............C4 84
Somerville, Mass., 94,697.......B5, D3 65
Somerville, N.J., 12,458...........B3 74
Somerville, Tenn., 1,820..............B2 83
Somerville, Tex., 1,177.D4 84
Somme, dept., Fr., 488,225............C5 5
Somogy, co., Hung., 371,783.........*B3 10
Sonchon, Kor., 22,725..G2 18
Sønderborg, Den., 20,653.............A4 6
Sønderborg, co., Den., 49,604..........*A4 6
Sondershausen, Ger., 19,000.............C5 6
Sondrio, It., 18,944...A2 9
Sŏngjin, see Kimchaek, Kor.
Songkhla, Thai., 31,001.............D2 19
Son La, Viet., 10,000...G5 17
Sonneberg, Ger., 28,900.............C5 6
Sonobe, Jap., 7,300....n14 18
Sonoma, Calif., 3,023.......B5, C2 50
Sonoma, co., Calif., 147,375...........C2 50
Sonora, Ariz., 1,244...........C3, D3 48
Sonora, Calif., 2,725...D3 50
Sonora, Tex., 2,619...D2 84
Sonora, state, Mex., 771,663............B2 34
Sonpur Raj, India, 7,108..............D7 20
Sonsón, Col., 10,913...B2 32
Sonsonate, Sal., 23,137.E7 34
Son Tay, Viet., 16,640..G6 17
Soochow (Suchou), China, 663,000.....E9 17
Soperton, Ga., 2,317...D4 55
Sophia, W. Va., 1,284..D3 87
Sopot, Pol., 44,000....A5 7
Sopron, Hung., 41,246..B3 10
Sora, It., 9,000.......D4 9
Sorbas, Sp., 5,961....D4 8
Sorel, Que., Can., 17,147 (*27,500)....C4 42
Soresina, It., 9,100...B2 9
Soria, Sp., 19,301....B4 8
Soria, prov., Sp., 147,052.........*B4 8
Soriano, dept., Ur., 70,500..........*E1 30
Sorø, co., Den.,128,176.*J4 11
Sorocaba, Braz., 109,258.........C3, m8 30
Soroki, Sov. Un., 15,000.............G7 12
Soroti, Ug., 6,645....H4 23
Sorrento, It., 7,900...D5 9
Sorrento, La., 1,151..........B6, D5 63
Sorsogon, Phil., 14,000.C6 19
Sorsogon, prov., Phil., 348,700.........*C6 19
Sortavala, Sov. Un., 16,400..........G14 11
Sör-Tröndelag, co., Nor., 211,700.........*F4 11
Sosnovka, Sov. Un., 10,000.............E13 12
Sosnowiec, Pol., 132,000.......C5, g10 7
Sotteville-lès-Rouen, Fr., 25,625.............C4 5
Soudan, Minn., 810....C6 67
Souderton, Pa., 5,381.F11 81
Souflion, Grc., 7,435...*B6 14
Soufriere, St. Lucia, 3,550.............p16 35
Souk-el-Arba, Tun., 6,469..............F2 9
Sŏul, see Seoul, Kor.
Soulanges, co., Que., Can. 10,075........D3 42
Sound Beach, N.Y., 1,625.............*D4 75

Soure, Braz., 6,666....*D6 27
Souris, Man., Can., 1,759..............E1 40
Souris East, P.E.I., Can., 1,537..............C7 43
Sourlake, Tex., 1,602..D5 84
Sousse, Tun., 48,185...A7 22
South, div., Ice., 13,416..........*n21 11
South Acton, Mass., 1,700..............C1 65
South Africa, country, Afr., 15,995,312.....F5 24
South Amboy, N.J., 8,422.........C4, E4 24
South America, cont., 118,100,000........... 27
South Amherst, Ohio, 1,657..............A5 78
Southampton, Ont., Can., 1,640........C3 42
Southampton, Eng., 204,707...........E6 4
Southampton, N.Y., 4,582..............D4 75
Southampton, Pa., 4,500..........*F11 81
Southampton, co., Va., 27,195..........E5 85
South Apopka, Fla., 2,484.........*D5 54
South Arabia, Br. prot., Asia, 758,000.....G4 15
South Australia, state, Austl., 969,340.....F6 25
South Barre, Mass., 900.............B3 65
South Bay, Fla., 1,631..F6 54
South Bellingham, Mass., 2,300............B5 65
South Belmar, N.J., 1,537..............C4 74
South Belmont, N.C., 2,286.........*B2 76
South Beloit, Ill., 3,781............A4 58
South Bend, Ind., 132,445 (*265,100).......A5 59
South Bend, Wash., 1,671............C2 86
South Bennettsville, S.C., 1,025.........*B8 82
South Berwick, Maine, 1,773............E2 64
South Boise, Idaho, 1,452.........*F2 57
Southboro, Mass., 1,114.........B4, D1 65
South Boston, Va., 5,974............E4 85
South Bound Brook, N.J., 3,626........B3 74
Southbridge, Mass., 16,523..........B3 65
South Bridgeview, Ill., 1,000.........*B6 58
South Broadway, Wash., 3,661.........*C5 86
South Burlington, Vt., 6,903.........*C1 73
South Carolina, state, U.S., 2,382,594....... 82
South Charleston, Ohio, 1,505............C4 78
South Charleston, W. Va., 19,180..........C6 87
South Chelmsford, Mass., 950............C1 55
South Chicago Heights, Ill., 4,043........F3 58
South Cleveland, Tenn., 1,512.........*D9 83
South Clinton, Tenn., 1,356.........*C9 83
South Coatesville, Pa., 2,032........*G10 81
South Connellsville, Pa., 2,434.........G2 81
South Corning, N.Y., 1,448.........*C3 75
South Dakota, state, U.S., 680,514......... 77
South Dartmouth, Mass., 6,000.......C6 65
South Daytona, Fla., 1,954............C5 54
South Decatur, Ga., 15,000.........*C2 55
South Deerfield, Mass., 1,253............B2 65
South Duxbury, Mass., 900.............B6 65
South Elgin, Ill., 2,624.E2 58
South El Monte, Calif., 4,850.........*E5 50
Southend-on-Sea, Eng., 164,976..........E7 4
Southern Pines, N.C., 5,198............B4 76
Southern Shops, S.C., 1,435.........*B4 82

Southern View, Ill., 1,485...........*D4 58
South Euclid, Ohio, 27,569..........B2 78
South Fallsburg, N.Y., 1,290............D6 75
South Farmingdale, N.Y., 16,318.......*E7 75
South Fayetteville, N.C., 3,411.......*B5 76
Southfield, Mich., 31,501.........*F7 66
South Floral Park, N.Y., 1,090........*E3 75
South Fork, Pa., 2,053..F4 81
South Fort Mitchell, Ky., 4,086..........A7 62
South Fulton, Tenn., 2,512.............A3 83
South Gate, Calif., 53,831............F2 50
Southgate, Ky., 2,070..A7 62
Southgate, Mich., 29,404.........*F7 66
South Glastonbury, Conn., 1,000......C6 52
South Glens Falls, N.Y., 4,129........*B7 75
South Grafton (Fisherville), Mass., 3,000..*B4 65
South Greensburg, Pa., 3,058.......*F2 81
South Greenwood, S.C., 2,520...........C3 82
South Hackensack, N.J., 1,841.......*D5 74
South Hadley, Mass., 5,000...........B2 65
South Hadley Falls, Mass., 3,100........B3 65
South Hamilton, Mass., 2,000........A6, C3 65
South Harriman, Tenn., 2,884...........D9 83
South Haven, Mich., 6,149...........F4 66
South Hempstead, N.Y., 3,000........*D2 75
South Henderson, N.C., 2,017........*A5 76
South Hill, Va., 2,569..E4 85
South Holland, Ill., 12,603.........*F3 58
South Holland, prov., Neth., 2,726,200....*A6 5
South Hooksett, N.H., 1,700............D4 73
South Houston, Tex., 7,523............F5 84
South Huntington, N.Y., 7,250........*D3 75
South Hutchinson, Kans., 1,672........A4 61
Southington, Conn., 14,000...........C5 52
South International Falls, Minn., 2,479.....B5 77
South Jacksonville, Ill., 2,340...........D3 58
South Jordan, Utah, 1,354..........*A6 72
South Kent, Mich., 15,000.............**F5 66
South Laguna, Calif., 2,000.........*F5 50
South Lake, Tex., 1,023..........*C4 84
South Lancaster, Mass., 1,891...........B4 65
Southland, Mich., 2,000.........*F6 66
Southlawn, Ill., 2,300.*D4 58
South Lebanon, Ohio, 2,720...........C3 78
South Lyon, Mich., 1,753..........A6, F7 66
South Macon, Ga., 9,000...........*D3 55
South Medford, Oreg., 2,306.........*E4 80
South Miami, Fla., 9,846.........F3, G6 54
South Milwaukee, Wis., 20,307....F2, F6 88
South Modesto, Calif., 9,000.........*D3 50
South Monroe, Mich., 2,919.........*G7 66
Southmont, Pa., 2,857.*F4 81
South Mt. Vernon, Ohio, 1,420........*B5 78
South New Castle, Pa., 955.........*D1 81
South Nyack, N.Y., 3,113...........C6 74
South Ogden, Utah, 7,405........A6, C2 72
Southold, N.Y., 950...D4 75
South Orange, N.J., 16,175.............B4 74

South Oroville, Calif.,
3,704...............*C3 50
South Paris, Maine,
2,063.............D2 64
South Park, Ill., 2,063.*B5 58
South Pasadena, Calif.,
19,706............F2 50
South Pekin, Ill., 1,007.C4 58
South Pittsburg, Tenn.,
4,130.............D8 83
South Plainfield, N.J.,
17,879............B4 74
South Point, Ohio,
1,663.............*D5 78
Southport, Austl.,
33,716............F9 25
Southport, Eng.,
81,976............D5 4
Southport, N.Y.,
6,698.............*C4 75
Southport, N.C., 2,034.D5 76
South Portland, Maine,
22,788..........E2, E5 64
South Pottstown, Pa.,
1,850.............*F10 81
South Range, Mich.,
760..............A2 66
South Renovo, Pa.,
777..............D6 81
South River, Ont.,
Can., 1,044........B5 42
South River, N.J.,
13,397............C4 74
South Rockwood,
Mich., 1,337.......*F7 66
South Roxana, Ill.,
2,010.............*E3 58
South Russell, Ohio,
1,276.............*A6 78
South St. Paul, Minn.,
22,032..........E7, F5 67
South Sacramento,
Calif., 10,960......*C3 50
South Salisbury, N.C.,
3,065.............*B3 76
South Salt Lake, Utah,
9,520.............C2 72
South San Francisco,
Calif., 39,418.......B5 50
South San Gabriel,
Calif., 26,213......*F2 50
South San Leandro,
Calif., 17,150......*B5 50
South Shields, Eng.,
109,533...........C6 4
South Shore, Mo., 200..A7 69
Southside Estates, Fla.,
4,000.............*B5 83
South Side Place, Tex.,
1,282.............F5 84
South Sioux City, Nebr.,
7,200.............B9 71
South Stickney, Ill.,
23,000............*B6 58
South Streator, Ill.,
1,923.............*B5 58
South Swansea, Mass.,
1,100.............C5 65
South Taft, Calif.,
1,910.............*E4 50
South Temple, Pa.,
1,500.............*F10 81
South Toms River,
N.J., 1,603........*D4 74
South Torrington, Wyo.,
950..............C8 89
South Trail, Fla.,
5,471.............*E4 54
South Tucson, Ariz.,
7,004.............C3 48
South Uniontown, Pa.,
3,603.............*G2 81
South Waverly, Pa.,
1,382.............C8 81
South West, div., Ice.,
77,976............*n22 11
South West Africa,
S. Afr. mandate, Afr.,
512,496...........E3 24
South Westbury, N.Y.,
11,977............*D3 75
Southwest Dillon, S.C.,
1,048.............*C9 82
South West Fargo,
N. Dak., 3,328......D9 77
Southwest Greensburg,
Pa., 3,264.........*F2 81
Southwest Harbor,
Maine, 900.........D4 64
South Whitley, Ind.,
1,325.............B6 59
Southwick, Mass.,
1,242.............B2 65
South Williamson, Ky.,
1,097.............C7 62
South Williamsport,
Pa., 6,972.........D7 81
South Windermere, S.C.,
1,500.............*F8 82
South Windham,
Maine, 1,142....E2, E4 64

South Windsor, Conn.,
900..............B6 52
South Wisconsin Rapids,
Wis., 1,464........*D4 88
Southwood Acres, Conn.,
3,000.............*B6 52
South Yarmouth, Mass.,
2,029.............C7 65
South Zanesville, Ohio,
1,557.............C5 78
Sovetsk (Tilsit), Sov.
Un., 85,900........A6 7
Sovetskaya Gavan, Sov.
Un., 49,000........E7 13
Soviet Union (U.S.S.R.),
country, Eur., Asia,
208,826,000........ 13
Spa, Bel., 9,055.....B6 5
Spain, country, Eur.,
30,430,698......... 8
Spalding, Eng., 14,821.D6 4
Spalding, co., Ga.,
35,404............C2 55
Spanaway, Wash.,
2,500.............B3 86
Spaniard's Bay, Newf.,
Can., 1,289........E5 44
Spangler, Pa., 2,658...E4 81
Spanish Fork, Utah,
6,472...........A6, D2 72
Spanish Sahara, dep.,
Afr., 19,000........D2 22
Spanish Town, Jam.,
14,439............G5 35
Sparkill, N.Y., 1,100...C5 75
Sparkman, Ark., 787...D3 49
Sparks, Ga., 1,158.....E3 55
Sparks, Nev., 16,618...B2 72
Sparlingville, Mich.,
1,877.............*F8 66
Sparrows Point, Md.,
3,300.............B5 53
Sparta, Ga., 1,921.....C4 55
Sparta, Ill., 3,452.....E4 58
Sparta, Mich., 2,749...E5 66
Sparta, N.C., 1,047....A2 76
Sparta, Tenn., 4,510...D8 83
Sparta, Wis., 6,080....E3 88
Spartanburg, S.C.,
44,352............B4 82
Spartanburg, co., S.C.,
156,830...........B5 82
Spárti (Sparta), Grc.,
10,412............D4 14
Spassk-Dalniy, Sov. Un.,
29,400............E16 13
Spearfish, S. Dak.,
3,682.............F2 77
Spearman, Tex., 3,555..A2 84
Speed, Ind., 950......H6 59
Speedway, Ind.,
9,624...........E5, H7 59
Speers, Pa., 1,479.....*F2 81
Speight, Ky., 500.....C7 62
Spenard, Alsk., 9,074.*g17 47
Spencer, Ind., 2,557...F4 59
Spencer, Iowa, 8,864...A2 60
Spencer, Mass., 5,593..B4 65
Spencer, N.C., 2,904...B4 76
Spencer, Okla., 1,189.*B4 79
Spencer, W. Va., 2,660..C3 87
Spencer, Wis., 897....D3 88
Spencer, co., Ind.,
16,074............H4 59
Spencer, co., Ky., 5,680.B4 62
Spencerport, N.Y.,
2,461.............B3 75
Spencerville, Ohio,
2,061.............B3 78
Speyer, Ger., 38,500...D4 6
Spinazzola, It., 10,850.D6 9
Spindale, N.C., 4,082...B2 76
Spink, co., S. Dak.,
11 706............F7 77
Spirit Lake, Idaho, 693.B2 57
Spirit Lake, Iowa,
2,685.............A2 60
Spiro, Okla., 1,450....B7 79
Spišská Nová Ves, Czech.,
16,900............D6 7
Spittal, Aus., 10,045...E6 6
Spotswood, N.J., 5,788.C4 74
Spotsylvania, co., Va.,
13,819............C5 85
Sprague, W. Va., 3,073.D7 87
Spray, N.C., 4,565.....A4 76
Spreckles, Calif., 800..C6 50
Sprecklesville, Haw.,
950..............C5 56
Spremberg, Ger.,
22,900............C7 6

Spring, Tex., 950......F5 84
Springboro, Ohio, 917..C3 78
Spring City, Pa., 3,162.F10 81
Spring City, Tenn.,
1,800.............D9 83
Springdale, Ark.,
11,895............A1 49
Springdale, Newf.,
Can., 1,638........D3 44
Springdale, Ohio,
3,550.............*D2 78
Springdale, Pa.,
5,602...........A7, E2 81
Springdale, S.C.,
1,002.............*D5 82
Springer, N. Mex.,
1,564.............A6 43
Springfield, Colo.,
1,791.............D8 51
Springfield, Fla., 4,628.G3 54
Springfield, Ill., 83,271
(*122,700).........D4 58
Springfield, Ky., 2,382.C4 62
Springfield, Mass., 174,463
(*429,400).........B2 65
Springfield, Minn.,
2,701.............F4 67
Springfield, Mo., 95,865
(*108,700).........D4 69
Springfield, Nebr.,
506............C9, E3 71
Springfield, N.J.,
14,467............*B4 74
Springfield, Ohio, 82,723
(*112,100).........C4 78
Springfield, Oreg.,
19,616............C4 80
Springfield, Pa.,
26,733............*B11 81
Springfield, S. Dak.,
1,194.............H8 77
Springfield, Tenn.,
9,221.............A5 83
Springfield, Vt., 6,600..E3 73
Springfield, W. Va., 10,783.B5 85
Springfield Place, Mich.,
5,136.............*F5 66
Spring Glen, Fla.,
5,000.............*B5 54
Spring Green, Wis.,
1,146.............E3 88
Spring Grove, Minn.,
1,342.............G7 67
Spring Grove, Pa.,
1,675.............G8 81
Springhill, N.S., Can.,
5,836.............D6 43
Spring Hill, Kans.,
909..............D9 61
Springhill, La., 6,437...A2 63
Spring Hill, Pa., 1,127.*F4 81
Spring Hope, N.C.,
1,336.............B4 76
Spring Lake, Mich.,
2,063.............E4 66
Spring Lake, N.J.,
2,922.............C4 74
Spring Lake Heights,
N.J., 3,309........C4 74
Spring Lake Park,
Minn., 3,260.......*E5 67
Springlee, Ky., 987...*H6 62
Spring Mills, S.C.,
1,069.............*B6 82
Springmont, Pa.,
1,000.............*F10 81
Springvale, Maine,
2,379.............E2 64
Spring Valley, Calif.,
7,000.............*E2 50
Spring Valley, Ill.,
5,371.............B4 58
Spring Valley, Minn.,
2,628.............G6 67
Spring Valley, N.Y.,
6,538.............D1 75
Spring Valley, Tex.,
3,004.............*E5 84
Spring Valley, Wis.,
977..............D1 88
Springville, N.Y., 3,852.C2 75
Springville, Utah,
7,913...........A6, D2 72
Spruce Pine, N.C.,
2,504.............C4 76
Spur, Tex., 2,170.....C2 84
Squamish, B.C., Can.,
1,557.............E6 37
Squaw Lake, Minn.,
129..............C4 67
Srbobran, Yugo.,
14,392............C4 10
Sredne-Kolymsk, Sov.
Un., 3,000.........C18 13
Sremska Mitrovica,
Yugo., 20,790......C4 10
Sretensk, Sov. Un.,
24,600............D14 13
Srinagar, India,
285,257...........B6 20
Stade, Ger., 30,500....B4 6

Stafford, Eng., 47,814..D5 4
Stafford, Kans., 1,862..E5 61
Stafford, Tex., 1,485..*F5 84
Stafford, co., Eng.,
1,733,887..........*D5 4
Stafford, co., Kans.,
7,451.............D5 61
Stafford, co., Va.,
16,876............C5 85
Stafford Springs, Conn.,
3,322.............B7 52
Staffordsville, Ky., 700.C7 62
Stains, Fr., 27,503.....g10 5
Stambaugh, Mich.,
1,876.............B2 66
Stamford, Conn.,
92,713............E2 52
Stamford, N.Y., 1,166..C6 75
Stamford, Tex., 5,259..C3 84
Stamps, Ark., 2,591...D2 49
Stanaford, W. Va.,
950...........D3, D7 87
Stanberry, Mo., 1,409..A3 69
Standale, Mich., 1,000.*F5 66
Standerton, S. Afr.,
16,868............F5 24
Standish, Mich., 1,214..E7 66
Stanford, Calif., 9,000.*D2 50
Stanford, Ky., 2,019...C5 62
Stanhope, N.J., 1,814..B3 74
Stanislaus, co., Calif.,
157,294...........D3 50
Stanke Dimitrov, Bul.,
19,239............D6 10
Stanley, N.C., 1,980...B2 76
Stanley, N. Dak., 1,795.B3 77
Stanley, Va., 1,039....C4 85
Stanley, Wis., 2,014...D3 88
Stanley, co., S. Dak.,
4,085.............F5 77
Stanleytown, Va., 500..E3 85
Stanleyville, Con. L.,
80,000............H3 23
Stanleyville, N.C.,
1,138.............*A3 76
Stanly, co., N.C.,
40,873............B3 76
Stanstead, co., Que.,
Can., 36,095.......D5 42
Stanton, Calif., 11,163.F3 50
Stanton, Del., 2,000...*A6 53
Stanton, Mich., 1,139..E5 66
Stanton, Nebr., 1,317..C8 71
Stanton, Tex., 2,228...C2 84
Stanton, co., Kans.,
2,108.............E2 61
Stanton, co., Nebr.,
5,783.............C8 71
Stantonsburg, N.C.,
897..............B6 76
Staples, Minn., 2,706..D4 67
Starachowice, Pol.,
36,000............C6 7
Staraya Russa, Sov. Un.,
35,400............C8 12
Stara Zagora, Bul.,
37,057............D7 10
Stara-Zagora, co., Bul.,
821,764...........*D7 10
Starbuck, Minn., 1,099.E3 67
Star City, Ark., 1,573..D4 49
Star City, W. Va.,
1,236.............B5 87
Stargard, Pol., 31,000..B3 7
Stargo, Ariz., 1,075....C4 48
Starjunction, Pa.,
1,142.............*G2 81
Stark, co., Ill., 8,152..B4 58
Stark, co., N. Dak.,
18,451............D3 77
Stark, co., Ohio,
340,345...........B6 78
Starke, Fla., 4,806....C4 54
Starke, co., Ind., 17,911.B4 59
Starkville, Miss., 9,041.B5 68
Starobelsk, Sov. Un.,
10,000............G12 12
Starodub, Sov. Un.,
10,000............E9 12
Starogard, Pol., 26,000.B5 7
Starr, co., Tex., 17,137.F3 84
Staryy Oskol, Sov.
Un., 10,000........F11 12
Stassfurt, Ger., 26,300..C5 6
State Center, Iowa,
1,142.............B4 60
State College, Miss.,
5,000.............B5 68
State College, Pa.,
22,409............E6 81
Staten Island, see
Richmond, borough and
co., N.Y.
Statesboro, Ga., 8,356.D5 55
Statesville, N.C.,
19,844............B3 76
Staunton, Ill., 4,228...D4 58
Staunton, Va., 22,232..C3 85
Stavanger, Nor., 52,800
(*101,000).........H1 11

Stavropol, Sov. Un., 151,000............I13 12
Stawell, Austl., 5,504......H4 26
Stayner, Ont., Can., 1,671............C4 41
Stayton, Oreg., 2,108............C2, C4 80
Steamboat Springs, Colo., 1,843.........A4 51
Stearns, Ky., 950......D5 62
Stearns, co., Minn., 80,345............E4 67
Steblev, Sov. Un., 10,000.............G8 12
Steele, Mo., 2,301.....E8 69
Steele, co., Minn., 25,029............F5 67
Steele, co., N. Dak., 4,719............C8 77
Steeleville, Ill., 1,569...E4 58
Steelton, Pa., 11,266...F8 81
Steelville, Mo., 1,127..D6 69
Steep Rock Lake, Ont., Can., 80............E8 41
Stefanesti, Rom., 7,770.B8 10
Steger, Ill., 6,432......B6 58
Steiermark, state, Aus., 1,137,865............*E7 6
Steilacoom, Wash., 1,569..............E1 86
Stein, Aus., 5,157......D7 6
Steinbach, Man., Can., 3,739.............E3 40
Stellarton, N.S., Can., 5,327..............D7 43
Stendal, Ger., 37,000...B5 6
Stephens, Ark., 1,275..D2 49
Stephens, co., Ga., 18,391.............B3 55
Stephens, co., Okla., 37,990............C4 79
Stephens, co., Tex., 8,885..............C3 84
Stephenson, co., Ill., 46,207............A4 58
Stephenville, Newf., Can., 6,043............D2 44
Stephenville, Tex., 7,359..............C3 84
Stephenville Crossing, Newf., Can., 2,209..D2 44
Stepnoy, Sov. Un., 30,000.............H15 12
Sterling, Colo., 10,751..A7 51
Sterling, Ill., 15,688...B4 58
Sterling, Kans., 2,303..D5 61
Sterling, co., Tex., 1,177..............D2 84
Sterlington, La., 1,200..B3 63
Sterlitamak, Sov. Un., 125,000............D8 13
Sternberk, Czech., 11,200............D4 7
Stettin, see Szczecin, Pol.
Stettler, Alta., Can., 3,638............C4 38
Steuben, co., Ind., 17,184............A7 59
Steuben, co., N.Y., 97,691............C3 75
Steubenville, Ohio, 32,495 (*121,300).........B7 78
Stevens, co., Kans., 4,400............E3 61
Stevens, co., Minn., 11,262............E3 67
Stevens, co., Wash., 17,884............A8 86
Stevenson, Ala., 1,456..A4 46
Stevenson, Wash., 927.D4 86
Stevens Point, Wis., 17,837............D4 88
Steveston, B.C., Can., 2,207............A9 37
Stewart, co., Ga., 7,371.D2 55
Stewart, co., Tenn., 7,851............A4 83
Stewart Manor, N.Y., 2,422............*E3 75
Stewartstown, Pa., 1,164............G8 81
Stewartville, Minn., 1,670............G6 67
Stewiacke, N.S., Can., 1,042............D6 43
Steyr, Aus., 38,306....D7 6
Stickney, Ill., 6,239...*F3 58
Stigler, Okla., 1,923....B6 79
Stillwater, Minn., 8,310............E6, E8 67
Stillwater, N.Y., 1,398..C7 75
Stillwater, Okla., 23,965............A4 79
Stillwater, co., Mont., 5,526............E7 70
Stilwell, Okla., 1,916..B7 79
Stinnett, Tex., 2,695..B2 84
Štip, Yugo., 18,650..E6 10
Stirling, Ont., Can., 1,315............C7 41

Stirling, N.J., 1,382....B4 74
Stirling, Scot., 27,553..B4 4
Stirling, co., Scot., 194,858............*B4 4
Stockbridge, Ga., 1,201.C2 55
Stockbridge, Mass., 900..............B1 65
Stockbridge, Mich., 1,097.............F6 66
Stockdale, Tex., 1,111............B4, E4 84
Stockerau, Aus., 11,853.D8 6
Stockholm, Swe., 807,100 (*1,130,000)....H8, t36 11
Stockholm, co., Swe., 487,100............*H8 11
Stockport, Eng., 142,469............D5 4
Stockton, Ala., 950....E2 46
Stockton, Calif., 86,321 (*160,000)......B6, D3 50
Stockton, Ill., 1,800...A3 58
Stockton, Kans., 2,073.C4 61
Stockton-on-Tees, Eng., 81,198............C6 4
Stoddard, co., Mo., 29,490............E8 69
Stoke-on-Trent, Eng., 265,506............D5 4
Stokes, co., N.C., 22,314............A3 76
Stokke, Nor., 5,000...p28 11
Stolberg, Ger., 37,500.C3 6
Stone, Ky., 728............C7 62
Stone, co., Ark., 6,294.B3 49
Stone, co., Miss., 7,013.E4 68
Stone, co., Mo., 8,176..E4 69
Stoneboro, Pa., 1,267..D1 81
Stoneham, Mass., 17,821............C3 65
Stoneleigh, Md., 8,000.*B4 53
Stone Mountain, Ga., 1,976............B5, C2 55
Stone Park, Ill., 3,038.*F2 58
Stones River Homes, Tenn., 1,800.......*B5 83
Stoneville, N.C., 951...A4 76
Stonewall, Man., Can., 1,420.............D3 40
Stonewall, Miss., 1,126.C5 68
Stonewall, co., Tex., 3,017............C2 84
Stonewood, W. Va., 2,202............*B4 87
Stoney Creek, Ont., Can., 6,043............*D5 41
Stonington, Conn., 1,622............D9 52
Stonington, Ill., 1,076.D4 58
Stony Brook, N.Y., 3,548............F4 75
Stony Creek Mills, Pa., 1,500............*F10 81
Stony Plain, Alta., Can., 1,311............C3 38
Stony Point, N.Y., 3,330............A5 74
Stony Point, N.C., 1,015............B2 76
Storey, co., Nev., 568..B2 72
Storm Lake, Iowa, 7,728............B2 60
Stormont, co., Ont., Can., 57,867........B10 41
Stornoway, Scot., 5,221.A3 4
Storozhinets, Sov. Un., 10,000............G5 12
Storrs, Conn., 6,054....B7 52
Story, co., Iowa, 49,327............B4 60
Story City, Iowa, 1,773.B4 60
Story Prairie, Ohio, 1,720............*A4 78
Stottville, N.Y., 1,040..C7 75
Stouffville, Ont., Can., 3,188............D5, E7 41
Stoughton, Mass., 16,328............B5, E3 65
Stoughton, Wis., 5,555..F4 88
Stovall, Miss., 125.....A3 68
Stow, Ohio, 12,194....A6 78
Stowe, Pa., 3,501.....F10 81
Stowe Township, Pa., 11,730............*B5 81
Strabane, N. Ire., 7,786............C3 4
Strabane, Pa., 1,940...F1 81
Strafford, Mo., 300....D4 69
Strafford, Pa., 2,500.*A10 81
Strafford, co., N.H., 59,799............E5 73
Strakonice, Czech., 14,100............D2 7
Straldzha, Bul., 5,348..D8 10
Stralsund, Ger., 66,100.A6 6
Strängnäs, Swe., 8,300.t35 11
Stranraer, Scot., 9,249..C4 4
Strasbourg, Fr., 228,971 (*320,000)............C7 5
Strasburg, N. Dak., 612............D5 77

Strasburg, Ohio, 1,687..B6 78
Strasburg, Pa., 1,416...G9 81
Strasburg, Va., 2,428...C4 85
Stratford, Ont., Can., 20,467............D4 41
Stratford, Conn., 45,012............E4 52
Stratford, N.J., 4,308..D2 74
Stratford, Okla., 1,058..C5 79
Stratford, Tex., 1,380..A1 84
Stratford, Wis., 1,106..D3 88
Stratford Hills, Va., 2,500............*D5 85
Stratford-on-Avon, Eng., 16,847............D6 4
Strathmore, Calif., 1,095............D4 50
Strathroy, Ont., Can., 5,150............E3 41
Straubing, Ger., 36,300.D6 6
Strawberry Point, Calif., 1,500............*B5 50
Strawberry Point, Iowa, 1,303............B6 60
Strawn, Tex., 817.....C3 84
Straznice, Czech., 4,989............D4 7
Streamwood, Ill., 6,751............*A5 58
Streator, Ill., 16,868...B5 58
Streetsboro, Ohio, 1,000............*A6 78
Streetsville, Ont., Can., 5,056............*D5 41
Strehaia, Rom., 8,545..C6 10
Stringtown, Ky., 300...B5 62
Stromsburg, Nebr., 1,244............C8 71
Strongsville, Ohio, 8,504............A6, B2 78
Stroud, Okla., 2,456...B5 79
Stroudsburg, Pa., 6,070............E11 81
Stroudsburg West, Pa., 1,569............*E11 81
Struer, Den., 8,335....I3 11
Strumica, Yugo., 15,978............E6 10
Struthers, Ohio, 15,631.A7 78
Stryker, Ohio, 1,205....A3 78
Stryy, Sov. Un., 47,000.G4 12
Strzegom, Pol., 7,137...C4 7
Strzelce, Pol., 10,300...C5 7
Strzelin, Pol., 7,334...C4 7
Strzelno, Pol., 5,264...B5 7
Strzemieszyce, Pol....g10 7
Stuart, Fla., 4,791....E6 54
Stuart, Iowa, 1,486....C3 60
Stuart, Va., 974....E2 85
Stung Treng, Camb., 10,000............C3 19
Sturbridge, Mass., 400..B3 65
Sturgeon, Pa., 1,000...*F1 81
Sturgeon Bay, Wis., 7,353............D6 88
Sturgeon Falls, Ont., Can., 6,288............A5 41
Sturgis, Ky., 2,209....C2 62
Sturgis, Mich., 8,915...G5 66
Sturgis, S. Dak., 4,639.F2 77
Sturtevant, Wis., 1,488............F2, F6 88
Stutsman, co., N. Dak., 25,137............C7 77
Stuttgart, Ark., 9,661..C4 49
Stuttgart, Ger., 637,500 (*1,350,000)........D4 6
Styria, reg., Aus....E7 6
Suakin, Sud., 4,228....E5 23
Suao, Taiwan, 5,000...G9 17
Sublette, Kans., 1,077..E3 61
Sublette, co., Wyo., 3,778............C2 89
Subotica, Yugo., 74,832............B4 11
Succasunna, N.J., 2,500............B3 74
Suceava, Rom., 20,949.B8 10
Sucha, Pol., 5,866....D5 7
Suchan, Sov. Un., 47,200............E16 13
Suchitoto, Sal., 4,380..*E7 34
Süchow, China, 676,000............E8 17
Sucre, Bol., 40,128.....C2 32
Sucre, state, Ven., 401,992............A5 32
Sucy-en-Brie, Fr., 13,258............g11 5
Sudan, Tex., 1,235.....B1 84
Sudan, country, Afr., 11,390,000............F3 23
Sudbury, Ont., Can., 80,120 (*110,694)......A4, E9 41
Sudbury, Mass., 1,800.D1 65
Sudbury, co., Ont., Can., 165,862............A3 41
Sudzha, Sov. Un., 10,000............F10 12
Sueca, Sp., 20,612....C5 8

Suez, Eg., U.A.R., 162,826............H9 14
Suffern, N.Y., 5,094..........D1, D2, D6 75
Suffield, Conn., 1,069...B6 52
Suffolk (Independent City), Va., 12,609..........B6, E6 85
Suffolk, co., Eng., 472,665............*D7 4
Suffolk, co., Mass., 791,329............B5 65
Suffolk, co., N.Y., 666,784............D3 70
Sugar Creek, Mo., 2,663............E2 69
Sugar Creek, Ohio, 982............*B6 78
Sugar Grove, Va., 800............B3, E1 85
Sugar Hill, Ga., 1,175..B2 55
Sugar Land, Tex., 2,802............E5, F4 84
Sugar Notch, Pa., 1,524............B8 81
Şuḥār, Mus. & Om., 5,000............E6 15
Suhl, Ger., 25,500.....C5 6
Suihua (Peilintzu), China, 40,000............B10 17
Suileng, China, 5,000...C3 18
Suipin, China, 5,000....C5 18
Suitland, Md., 10,300..C2 53
Sukabumi, Indon., 78,806............G3 19
Sukarnapura (Hollandia), W. Irian, 16,300....F10 19
Sukkur, Pak., 103,216..C4 20
Sulaimaniya (As Sulaymānīyah), Iraq, 35,352............B4 15
Sullana, Peru, 26,330...B1 31
Sulligent, Ala., 1,346..B1 46
Sullivan, Ill., 3,946...D5 58
Sullivan, Ind., 4,979...F3 59
Sullivan, Mo., 4,098...C6 69
Sullivan, co., Ind., 21,721............F3 59
Sullivan, co., Mo., 8,783............A4 69
Sullivan, co., N.H., 28,067............E3 73
Sullivan, co., N.Y., 45,272............D6 75
Sullivan, co., Pa., 6,251.D8 81
Sullivan, co., Tenn., 114,139............C11 83
Sullivans Island, S.C., 1,358............F3 82
Sully, co., S. Dak., 2,607............F5 77
Sulmona, It., 18,400...C4 9
Sulphur, La., 11,429...D2 63
Sulphur, Okla., 4,737...C5 79
Sulphur South, La., 1,351............*D2 63
Sulphur Springs, Tex., 9,160............C5 84
Sulu Archipelago, Phil.D6 19
Sulu, prov., Phil., 327,100............*D6 19
Sumach, Wash., 1,345.*C5 86
Sumatra, isl., Indon....F2 19
Sumenep, Indon., 17,824............G4 19
Sumiton, Ala., 1,287...B2 46
Summerdale, Pa., 1,200............*F8 81
Summerland, B.C., Can., 2,500............E8 37
Summers, co., W. Va., 15,640............D4 87
Summerside, P.E.I., Can., 8,611............C6 43
Summersville, W. Va., 2,008............C4, C7 87
Summerton, S.C., 1,504............D7 82
Summerville, Ga., 4,706............B1 55
Summerville, Pa., 895..D3 81
Summerville, S.C., 3,633............E2, E7 82
Summit, Ill., 10,374...F2 58
Summit, Miss., 1,663..D3 68
Summit, N.J., 23,677..B4 74
Summit, co., Colo., 2,073............B4 51
Summit, co., Ohio, 513,569............A6 78
Summit, co., Utah, 5,673............A6 73
Summit Hill, Pa., 4,386............E10 81
Summitville, Ind., 1,048............D6 59
Sumner, Ill., 1,035...E6 58
Sumner, Iowa, 2,170...B5 60
Sumner, Wash., 3,156..B3 86
Sumner, co., Kans., 25,316............E6 61

Sumner, co., Tenn., 36,217.............A5 83
Sumoto, Jap., 34,000...I7 18
Sumperk, Czech., 19,400.............D4 7
Sumter, S.C., 23,062...D7 82
Sumter, co., Ala., 20,041.............C1 46
Sumter, co., Fla., 11,869.............D4 54
Sumter, co., Ga., 24,652.............D2 55
Sumter, co., S.C., 74,941.............D7 82
Sumy, Sov. Un., 108,000...........F10 12
Sun, La., 224.............D6 63
Sunagawa, Jap., 24,200.............E10 18
Sunbury, Ohio, 1,360...B5 78
Sunbury, Pa., 13,687...E8 81
Sunbury, co., N.B., Can., 22,796.............D3 43
Sunchon, Kor., 20,682..G2 18
Sunchon, Kor., 44,400..I3 18
Sun City, Ariz., 2,000...*C2 48
Suncook, N.H., 3,807..E5 73
Sun Crest, Calif., 1,166.............*F5 50
Sundance, Wyo., 908...A8 89
Sundbyberg, Swe., 27,100.............t35 11
Sunderland, Eng., 189,629.............C6 4
Sundown, Tex., 1,186..C1 84
Sundre, Alta., Can., 853.............D3 38
Sundsvall, Swe., 29,800.............F7 11
Sunflower, co., Miss., 45,750.............B3 68
Sungchiang, China, 70,000.............E7 17
Sungurlu, Tur., 10,500.............B10 14
Suniland, Fla., 1,500..*G6 54
Sunny Acres, Ky., 844..A7 62
Sunnyland, Fla., 4,761.*E4 54
Sunnyland, Ill., 1,000..C4 58
Sunnymead, Calif., 3,404.............*F5 50
Sunnyside, Utah, 1,740.B6 72
Sunnyside, Wash., 6,208.............C5 86
Sunnyvale, Calif., 52,898.............B5 50
Sunol, Calif., 750.............B6 50
Sun Prairie, Wis., 4,008.E4 88
Sunray, Tex., 1,967...B2 84
Sunrise Heights, Mich., 1,569.............*F5 66
Sunset, La., 1,307...D3 63
Sunset, Utah, 4,235..*A5 72
Sunset Beach, Calif., 1,300.............*F2 50
Sunset Hills, Mo., 3,525.............*B8 69
Sunset Park, Kans., 1,000.............*B5 61
Sunshine, Calif., 9,000.*F4 50
Sunwui, China, 85,000..G7 17
Superior, Ariz., 4,875.............C3, D3 48
Superior, Mont., 1,242..C2 70
Superior, Nebr., 2,935..D7 71
Superior, W. Va., 900.*D3 87
Superior, Wis., 33,563..B1 88
Superior, Wyo., 241...D4 89
Suquamish, Wash., 950.............B3 86
Şūr, Mus. & Om......E6 15
Surabaja, Indon., 989,734...........G4 19

Surakarta, Indon., 363,167...........G4 19
Surany, Czech., 5,381..D5 7
Surat, India, 288,026..D5 20
Surbiton, Eng., 62,940.............m11 4
Suresnes, Fr., 39,100...g9 5
Surfside, Fla., 3,157...F3 54
Surgoinsville, Tenn., 1,132.............C11 83
Surgut, Sov. Un., 3,500.............C10 13
Suri, India, 22,841.....D8 20
Surigao, Phil., 12,870..D7 19
Surigao, prov., Phil., 360,100.............*D7 19
Surinam, Neth. dep., S.A., 237,000.......C5 27
Surrey, co., Eng., 1,733,036.............*E6 4
Surry, N.H., 200.....E3 73
Surry, co., N.C., 48,205.............A3 76
Surry, co., Va., 6,220.............D6 85
Susa, It., 5,891.............B1 9
Susana Knolls, Calif., 900.............*E4 50
Susanville, Calif., 5,598.B3 50
Susice, Czech., 6,793...D2 7
Susquehanna, Pa., 2,591.............C10 81
Susquehanna, co., Pa., 33,137.............C10 81
Sussex, N.B., Can., 3,457.............D4 43
Sussex, N.J., 1,656...A3 74
Sussex, Wis., 1,087...E1 88
Sussex, co., Del., 73,195.............C6 53
Sussex, co., Eng., 1,075,893.............*E7 4
Sussex, co., N.J., 49,255.............A3 74
Sussex, co., Va., 12,411.E5 85
Susurluk, Tur., 6,752...C7 14
Suterville, Pa., 964....*F2 81
Sutherland, co., Scot., 13,442.............*B4 4
Sutherlin, Oreg., 2,452.D3 80
Sutter, Calif., 1,219...*C3 50
Sutter, co., Calif., 33,380.............C3 50
Sutter Creek, Calif., 1,161.............C3 50
Sutton, Que., Can., 1,755.............D5 42
Sutton, Eng., 78,969..m12 4
Sutton, Nebr., 1,252...D8 71
Sutton, W. Va., 967...C4 87
Sutton, co., Tex., 3,738.............D2 84
Sutton-in-Ashfield, Eng., 40,438......D6 4
Sutton West, Ont., Can., 1,470.............C5 41
Suva, Fiji Is., 37,371..H8 2
Suwa, Jap., 31,400....m17 18
Suwalki, Pol., 20,000..A7 7
Suwannee, Fla., 200...C3 54
Suwannee, co., Fla., 14,961.............B3 54
Suzuka, Jap., 44,800..o15 18
Svalbard (Spitsbergen), Nor. dep., Eur., 1,200 (no permanent pop.).............A22 2
Svedala, Swe., 3,114..A2 7
Svendborg, co., Den., 150,365.............*J4 11
Sverdlovsk, Sov. Un., 832,000.............D9 13
Sverdrup, is., N.W. Ter., Can.............m30 36

Svetlaya, Sov. Un., 10,000.............C9 18
Svilajnac, Yugo., 5,905.C5 10
Svilengrad, Bul., 9,918.E8 10
Svirstroy, Sov. Un., 10,000.............A9 12
Svishtov, Bul., 12,949..D7 10
Svitavy, Czech., 13,900.D4 7
Svobodnyy, Sov. Un., 58,000.............D15 13
Swain, co., N.C., 8,387.D2 76
Swainsboro, Ga., 5,943.D4 55
Swampscott, Mass., 13,294.............B6, C3 65
Swan Lake, Idaho, 150.G6 57
Swan Lake, Miss., 300..B3 68
Swannanoa, N.C., 2,189.............D4 76
Swan River, Man., Can., 3,163.........C1 40
Swansboro, N.C., 1,104.C6 76
Swansea, Ont., Can., 9,628.............E6 41
Swansea, Ill., 3,018...B9 69
Swansea, Mass., 1,000..C5 65
Swansea, Wales, 166,740.............E5 4
Swanton, Ohio, 2,306...A4 78
Swanton, Vt., 2,390...B1 73
Swarthmore, Pa., 5,753.............B10 81
Swartz Creek, Mich., 3,006.............F7 66
Swastika, Ont., Can., 643.............*E9 41
Swatow, China, 280,400.............G8 17
Swaziland, Br. dep., Afr., 267,000.............F6 24
Swedeborg, Mo., 175...D5 69
Swedeland, Pa., 950...A11 81
Sweden, country, Eur., 7,542,600.............F7 11
Swedesboro, N.J., 2,449.............D2 74
Sweeny, Tex., 3,087...G4 84
Sweet, Idaho, 100....F2 57
Sweet Grass, co., Mont., 3,290.............E7 70
Sweet Home, Oreg., 3,353.............C4 80
Sweetsers, Ind., 896...C6 59
Sweet Springs, Mo., 1,452.............C4 69
Sweetwater, Tenn., 4,145.............D8 83
Sweetwater, Tex., 13,914.............C2 84
Sweetwater, co., Wyo., 17,920.............D3 89
Swepsonville, N.C., 800.............A4 76
Swidnica, Pol., 39,000..C4 7
Swidwin, Pol., 6,098...B3 7
Swiebodzice, Pol., 6,078.............C4 7
Swiebodzin, Pol., 11,200.............B3 7
Swiecie, Pol., 8,358...B5 7
Swietochlowice, Pol., 57,000.............g9 7
Swift, co., Minn., 14,936.............E3 67
Swift Current, Sask., Can., 12,186.......G2 39
Swindon, Eng., 91,736..E6 4
Swinemünde, see Swinoujscie, Pol.
Swinoujscie, Pol., 10,600.............A3 7
Swisher, co., Tex., 10,607.............B2 84

Swissvale, Pa., 15,089..B6 81
Switzer, W. Va., 1,131.D5 87
Switzerland, co., Ind., 7,092.............G7 59
Switzerland, country, Eur., 5,429,061.....E4 6
Swoyersville, Pa., 6,751.............B8, D10 81
Sycamore, Ill., 6,961...B5 58
Sycamore, Ohio, 998...B4 78
Sycamore Hills, Mo., 942.............*C7 69
Sydney, Austl., 172,192 (*2,235,000).............F9 25
Sydney, N.S., Can., 33,617.............C9 43
Sydney Mines, N.S., Can., 9,122.............C9 43
Sykesville, Md., 1,196..B4 53
Sykesville, Pa., 1,479..D4 81
Syktyvkar, Sov. Un., 73,000.............C8 13
Sylacauga, Ala., 12,857.............B3 46
Sylhet, Pak., 33,124..D9 20
Sylva, N.C., 1,564....D3 76
Sylvan, Oreg., 600....B2 80
Sylvan Hills, Ark., 2,000.............*C3 49
Sylvania, Ala., 400....A4 46
Sylvania, Ga., 3,469...D5 55
Sylvania, Ky., 1,200...A3 62
Sylvania, Ohio, 5,187.............A1, A4 78
Sylvan Lake, Alta., Can., 1,381.............C3 38
Sylvan Lake, Mich., 2,004.............F7 66
Sylvan Shores, Fla., 1,214.............*D5 54
Sylvester, Ga., 3,610...E3 55
Syosset, N.Y., 14,000..F2 52
Syracuse, Ind., 1,595..B6 59
Syracuse, Kans., 1,888..E2 61
Syracuse, Nebr., 1,261.............D9, F3 71
Syracuse, N.Y., 216,038 (*442,300).............B4 75
Syracuse, Utah, 1,061..C2 72
Syria, country, Asia, 4,565,000.............F6 16
Syriam, Bur., 15,070..*B1 19
Syzran, Sov. Un., 157,000.............D7 13
Szabadszallas, Hung., 4,878.............B4 10
Szabolcs-Szatmár, co., Hung., 587,257.....*B5 10
Szamotuly, Pol., 10,800.B4 7
Szarvas, Hung., 12,277.B5 10
Szczebrzeszyn, Pol., 5,122.............C7 7
Szczecin (Stettin),Pol., 269,000.............B3 7
Szczecinek, Pol., 23,000.............B4 7
Szechwan, prov., China, 72,160,000.............E5 17
Szeged, Hung., 99,061..B5 10
Szekesfehervar, Hung., 55,943.............B4 10
Szekszard, Hung., 16,409.............B4 10
Szentendre, Hung., 10,307.............B4 10
Szentes, Hung., 24,807.B5 10
Szeping, China, 125,900.............C9 17
Szolnok, Hung., 45,553.B5 10
Szolnok, co., Hung., 462,516.............*B5 10
Szombathely, Hung., 54,465.............B3 10

T

Tabaco, Phil., 8,308...*C6 19
Tabasco, state, Mex., 471,808.............D6 34
Taber, Alta., Can., 3,951.............E4 38
Taboada, Sp., 8,162....A2 8
Tabor, Czech., 19,600..D3 7
Tabor, Iowa, 909.....D2 60
Tabor, N.J., 1,000....*B4 74
Tabora, Tan., 15,361..B6 24
Tabor City, N.C., 2,338.............C5 76
Tabrīz, Iran, 290,195..B4 15
Tabūk, Sau. Ar., 10,000.............D2 15
Tachikawa, Jap., 67,949.............n18 18
Táchira, state, Ven., 399,163.............B3 32
Tacloban, Phil., 37,000.C6 19
Tacna, Peru, 13,514...E3 31
Tacna, dept., Peru, 42,874.............E3 31

Tacoma, Wash., 147,979 (*298,000)......B3, D1 86
Tacuarembó, Ur., 21,200.............E1 30
Tacuarembó, dept., Ur., 71,100.............*E1 30
Tadoussac, Que., Can., 1,083.............A8 42
Tadzhik, rep., Sov. Un., 2,104,000......F9 16
Taegu, Kor., 678,300...I4 18
Taejon, Kor., 229,400..H3 18
Tafalla, Sp., 7,320....A5 8
Tafí Viejo, Arg., 15,374.E2 29
Taft, Calif., 3,822.....E4 50
Taft, Fla., 1,214......D5 54
Taft, Tex., 3,463.....F4 84
Taft Heights, Calif., 2,661.............*E4 50
Taft Southwest, Tex., 1,927.............*F4 84

Taganrog, Sov. Un., 214,000...........H12 12
Taguchi, Jap., 4,400...n16 18
Tahlequah, Okla., 5,840.............B7 79
Tahoka, Tex., 3,012...C2 84
Tahoua, Niger, 12,400..F6 22
Taian, China, 80,000..*D8 17
T'aichung, Taiwan, 188,000.............G9 17
Taihsien, China, 131,000.............*E8 17
Taikang, China, 5,000..C2 18
Tailai, China, 5,000....C1 18
T'ainan, Taiwan, 239,300.............G9 17
Taipei, Taiwan, 813,800.............G9 17
Taiping, Mala., 48,206.E2 19
Taira, Jap., 71,115...H10 18
T'aitung, Taiwan, 8,886.............G9 17

Taiwan (Formosa), country, (Nationalist China), Asia, 8,265,000.............G9 17
Taiyüan (Yangkü), China, 1,020,000.............D7 17
Ta'izz, Yemen, 5,000..G3 15
Tajimi, Jap., 53,793.............I8, n16 18
Tajūrā', Libya, 2,670..B7 22
Tak, Thai., 12,918....*B1 19
Takada, Jap., 46,200..H9 18
Takamatsu, Jap., 228,172.............I7 18
Takaoka, Jap., 135,190.H8 18
Takasaki, Jap., 125,000.............H9, m18 18
Takata, Jap., 23,025...H9 18
Takatsuki, Jap., 79,043.............o14 18
Takayama, Jap., 34,800...H8, m16 18
Takefu, Jap., 37,100...n15 18

Takeo, Camb., 5,000..*C2 19
Takingeun, Indon., 1,411.........*m11 19
Takoma Park, Md., 16,799............C1 53
Takut, Bur., 5,000...*D10 20
Talā, Eg., U.A.R., 18,570............*G8 14
Tala, Mex., 12,541...m12 34
Tala, Ur., 1,957......E1 30
Talagante, Chile, 7,966............A2 28
Talai, China, 24,921...D2 18
Talara, Peru, 12,985...B1 31
Talavera de la Reina, Sp., 31,900............B2 8
Talbert, Ky., 150.....C6 62
Talbot, co., Ga., 7,127..D2 55
Talbot, co., Md., 21,578............C5 53
Talbotton, Ga., 1,163..D2 55
Talca, Chile, 70,000....B2 28
Talca, prov., Chile, 205,448............B2 28
Talcahuano, Chile, 82,000............B2 28
Talcher, India, 8,147...D8 20
Talco, Tex., 1,024.....C5 84
Tali, China, 15,000...E6 17
Taliaferro, co., Ga., 3,370............C4 55
Talien, see Dairen, China
Talihina, Okla., 1,048..C6 79
Talisayan, Phil., 10,646............*D6 19
Talladega, Ala., 17,742.B3 46
Talladega, co., Ala., 65,495............B3 46
Tallahassee, Fla., 48,174............B2 54
Tallahatchie, co., Miss., 24,081............B3 68
Tallapoosa, Ga., 2,744..C1 55
Tallapoosa, co., Ala., 35,007............C4 46
Tallassee, Ala., 4,934...C4 46
Talleyville, Del., 1,000.............*A6 53
Tallinn, Sov. Un., 298,000............B5 12
Tallmadge, Ohio, 10,246............A6 78
Tallulah, La., 9,413....B4 63
Talnoye, Sov. Un., 10,000............G8 12
Talsi, Sov. Un., 10,000..C4 12
Taltal, Chile, 4,901....E1 29
Tama, Iowa, 2,925.....C5 60
Tama, co., Iowa, 21,413............B5 60
Tamale, Ghana, 16,164.G4 22
Taman, Sov. Un., 10,000............I11 12
Tamano, Jap., 65,292...I6 18
Tamanrasset, Alg., 10,089............D6 22
Tamaqua, Pa., 10,173.E10 81
Tamatave, Malag., 36,133............D9 24
Tamaulipas, state, Mex., 1,009,800...........C5 34
Tamazula de Gordiano, Mex., 10,784......n12 34
Tambov, Sov. Un., 170,000 (*190,000)..E13 12
Tampa, Fla., 274,970 (*356,200)......E2, E4 54
Tampere, Fin., 126,600............G10 11
Tampico, Mex., 122,197......C5, k15 34
Tams, W. Va., 500....D3 87
Tamworth, Austl., 18,984............F9 25
Tanabe, Jap., 48,673....J7 18
Tananarive, Malag., 248,000............D6 24
Tanchon, Kor., 32,761..F4 18
Tandag, Phil., 6,735..*D7 19
Tandil, Arg., 32,309....B5 28
Tandjungpandan, Indon., 15,708............F3 19
Taney, co., Mo., 10,238.E4 69
Taneytown, Md., 1,519.A3 53
Tanga, Tan., 38,053....B7 24
Tanger (Tangier), Mor., 141,714............A3 22
Tangermünde, Ger., 13,800............B5 6
Tangier, Va., 876......D7 85
Tangipahoa, par., La., 59,434............D5 63
Tangshan, China, 800,000...........*D8 17
Tangyüan, China, 5,000............C4 18
Tanjay, Phil., 12,503..*D6 19
Tanjore, India, 111,099.F6 20
Tank, Pak., 6,899.....B5 20
Tanque Verde, Ariz., 1,053.............*C4 48

Tanshui, For., 10,000..*F9 17
Tantā, Eg., U.A.R., 151,700............G8 14
Tanzania, country, Afr., 10,127,000..........B6 24
Taonan, China, 65,000.B9 17
Taormina, It., 6,521....F5 9
Taos, N. Mex., 2,163...A6 48
Taos, co., N. Mex., 15,934............A6 48
Taourirt, Mor., 7,343..B4 22
Tapachula, Mex., 41,701............E6 34
Tappahannock, Va., 1,086............D6 85
Tappan, N.Y., 2,100...D1 75
Taquara, Braz., 11,282.D2 30
Taquaritinga, Braz., 11,624............k7 30
Tara, Mo., 2,000.....*C7 69
Tara, Sov. Un., 20,400............D10 13
Tarabulus (Tripoli), Leb., 110,000............E10 14
Tarakan, Indon., 11,589............E5 19
Tarancón, Sp., 7,714...B4 8
Taranto, It., 194,609...D6 9
Tarapacá, prov., Chile, 122,665............D1 29
Tarapoto, Peru, 9,249..C2 31
Tarare, Fr., 12,131.....E6 5
Tarascon [-sur-Ariège], Fr., 6,485............F6 5
Tarazona, Sp., 12,059..B5 8
Tarbes, Fr., 46,600....F4 5
Tarboro, N.C., 8,411...B6 76
Taree, Austl., 10,050...E9 26
Tarentum, Pa., 8,232............A7, E2 81
Tarfaya, Mor., 18,361..C2 22
Târgoviște, Rom., 24,360............C7 10
Tâgul-Jiu, Rom., 19,618............C6 10
Târgul-Neamt, Rom., 10,373............B8 10
Târgul-Ocna, Rom., 11,227............B8 10
Târgul-Săcuesc, Rom., 7,500............B8 10
Targu-Mures, Rom., 65,194............B7 10
Tarifa, Sp., 7,737.....D3 8
Tarija, Bol., 16,869....D3 29
Tarija, dept., Bol., 126,752............D3 29
Tarkio, Mo., 2,160....A2 69
Tarkwa, Ghana, 7,840 (*25,232)..........G4 22
Tarlac, Phil., 30,000..........B6, o13 19
Tarlac, prov., Phil., 427,300............*B6 19
Tarma, Peru, 7,876....D2 31
Tarn, dept., Fr., 319,560............*F5 5
Târnăveni, Rom., 14,883............B7 10
Tarn-et-Garonne, dept., Fr., 175,847..........*E4 5
Tarnobrzeg, Pol., 4,140.C6 7
Tarnow, Pol., 71,000...C6 7
Tarnowskie Gory, Pol., 28,000............C5, g9 7
Taroudant, Mor., 17,141............B3 22
Tarpon Springs, Fla., 6,768............D4 54
Tarquinia, It., 9,776...C3 9
Tarragona, Sp., 43,519.B6 8
Tarragona, prov., Sp., 362,679............*B6 8
Tarrant, Ala., 7,810............C3, E4 46
Tarrant, co., Tex., 538,495............C4 84
Tarrasa, Sp., 92,234...B7 8
Tárrega, Sp., 6,059....B6 8
Tarrytown, N.Y., 11,109........D1, D3 75
Tarshiha, Isr., 639....A3 15
Tarsney, Mo., 400.....E3 69
Tarsus, Tur., 51,300..D10 14
Tartu, Sov. Un., 76,000............B6 12
Taschereau, Que., Can., 950............B2 42
Tashkent, Sov. Un., 971,000............E9 13
Tashkurghan, Afg., 20,000............A4 20
Tasmania, state, Austl., 350,340............o15 25
Tatamagouche, N.S., Can., 581.........D6 43
Tatarbunary, Sov. Un., 10,000............C9 10
Tate, Ga., 900........B2 55
Tate, co., Miss., 18,138.A4 68
Tateville, Ky., 725....D5 62

Tateyamahojo, Jap., 37,291.........I9, o18 18
Tatta, Pak., 9,716.....D4 20
Tattnall, co., Ga., 15,837............D4 5
Tatuí, Braz., 22,550............C3, m8 30
Tatum, N. Mex., 1,168.C7 48
Tatung, China, 228,500.C7 17
Taubaté, Braz., 64,863.C3 30
Taung, S. Afr., 1,496...F4 24
Taungdwingyi, Bur., 16,233............D10 20
Taunggyi, Bur., 8,652.D10 20
Taunton, Eng., 35,178..E5 4
Taunton, Mass., 41,132.C5 65
Taurage, Sov. Un., 10,465............D4 12
Tauranga, N.Z., 13,468............L16 26
Taurianova, It., 14,300.E6 9
Tauste, Sp., 6,634....B5 8
Tavares, Fla., 2,724...D5 54
Tavas, Tur., 7,110...*D7 14
Tavda, Sov. Un., 40,800............D9 13
Tavira, Port., 7,496...D2 8
Tavistock, Ont., Can., 1,232............D4 41
Tavoy, Bur., 40,312...F10 20
Tavsanli, Tur., 11,500.*C7 14
Tawas City, Mich., 1,810............D7 66
Taylor, Mich., 49,658.*F7 66
Taylor, Pa., 6,148.A9, D10 81
Taylor, Tex., 9,434....A4 84
Taylor, co., Fla., 13,168............B3 54
Taylor, co., Ga., 8,311..D2 55
Taylor, co., Iowa, 10,288............D3 60
Taylor, co., Ky., 16,285............C4 62
Taylor, co., Tex., 101,078............C3 84
Taylor, co., W. Va., 15,010............B4 87
Taylor, co., Wis., 17,843............C3 88
Taylor Mill, Ky., 710..A7 62
Taylors, S.C., 1,071...B3 82
Taylorsport, Ky., 200..A7 62
Taylorsville, Ky., 937..B4 62
Taylorsville, Miss., 1,132............D4 68
Taylorsville, N.C., 1,470............B2 76
Taylorville, Ill., 8,801..D4 58
Tayshet, Sov. Un., 28,900............D12 13
Taza, Mor., 31,667....B4 22
Tazewell, Va., 3,000...B3 85
Tazewell, Tenn., 1,264............C10 83
Tazewell, co., Ill., 99,789............C4 58
Tazewell, co., Va., 44,791............B3 85
Tbilisi, Sov. Un., 724,000............E7 13
Tczew, Pol., 34,000....A5 7
Tchula, Miss., 882....B3 68
Teague, Tex., 2,728....D4 84
Teaneck, N.J., 42,085.D5 74
Tecuala, Mex., 10,747..C3 34
Tecuci, Rom., 23,400..C8 10
Tecumseh, Ont., Can., 4,476............F2 41
Tecumseh, Mich., 7,045............F7 66
Tecumseh, Nebr., 1,887............D9 71
Tecumseh, Okla., 2,630.B5 79
Tegucigalpa, Hond., 133,887............E7 34
Teguise, Sp. 5,547....m15 8
Tehachapi, Calif., 3,161............E4 50
Tehama, co., Calif., 25,305............B2 50
Tehrān, Iran, 1,513,164 (*1,590,000)......B5 15
Tehuacán, Mex., 31,724..........D5, n15 34
Tehuantepec, Mex., 13,440............D5 34
Tekamah, Nebr., 1,788.C9 71
Tekax de Alvaro Obregon, Mex., 7,797..........C7 34
Tekirdag, Tur., 23,900.B6 14
Tekoa, Wash., 911.....B8 86
Tela, Hond., 11,662..*D7 34
Tel Aviv-Jaffa, Isr., 386,612 (*640,000)......B2, g5 15
Telde, Sp. 14,100.....m14 8
Telemark, co., Nor., 149,900............*H3 11
Telfair, co., Ga., 11,715.E4 55
Telford, Pa., 2,763...F11 81
Tell City, Ind., 6,609...I4 59

Teller, co., Colo., 2,495.C5 51
Telluride, Colo., 677...D3 51
Telok Anson, Mala., 37,042............E2 19
Teloloapan, Mex., 7,297...........D5, n14 34
Telukbetung, Indon., 132,312............G3 19
Temiscouata, co., Que., Can., 29,079.......B9 42
Tempe, Ariz., 24,897...........C3, D2 48
Temperance, Mich., 2,215............G7 66
Tempio Pausania, It., 8,300............D2 9
Temple, Okla., 1,282...C3 79
Temple, Pa., 1,633...F10 81
Temple, Tex., 30,419..D4 84
Temple City, Calif., 26,500............*F2 50
Temple Hill, Ky., 100..D4 62
Temple Terrace, Fla., 3,812............E2 54
Templeton, Mass., 900.A3 65
Templin, Ger., 11,600.B6 6
Temryuk, Sov. Un., 10,000............I11 12
Temuco, Chile, 68,000.B2 28
Tenafly, N.J., 14,264........B5, D5 74
Tenaha, Tex., 1,097...D5 84
Tenancingo [de Degollado], Mex., 14,769...D5, n14 34
Tenango del Valle, Mex., 7,536............n14 34
Tenasserim, Bur., 1,194............F10 20
Tengchung, China, 82,951............F4 17
Tenino, Wash., 836....C3 86
Tennessee, state, U.S., 3,567,089............ 83
Tennille, Ga., 1,837...D4 55
Tensas, par., La., 11,796............B4 63
Teocaltiche, Mex., 11,066............C4, m12 34
Teófilo Otoni, Braz., 41,013............B4 30
Tepatitán [de Morelos], Mex., 19,609...C4, m12 34
Tepic, Mex., 53,955...........C4, m11 34
Teplice, Czech., 42,900.C2 7
Teramo, It., 25,000....C4 9
Teresina, Braz., 100,006............D6 27
Teresópolis, Braz., 29,540...........C4, h6 30
Termez, Sov. Un., 24,000............F9 13
Termini Imerese, It., 23,690............F4 9
Termoli, It., 9,686.....C5 9
Ternate, Indon., 21,200.E7 19
Terneuzen, Neth., 12,100............B5 5
Terney, Sov. Un., 10,000............D8 18
Terni, It., 95,072.....C4 9
Ternopol, Sov. Un., 56,000............G5 12
Terra Alta, W. Va., 1,504............B5 87
Terrace, B.C., Can., 4,682............B3 37
Terrace Park, Ohio, 2,023............A7 62
Terracina, It., 17,300..D4 9
Terra Linda, Calif., 3,000.............*D2 50
Terrebonne, Que., Can., 6,207........D4, D9 42
Terrebonne, co., Que., Can., 102,275.......D3 42
Terrebonne, par., La., 60,771............E5 63
Terre Haute, Ind., 72,500............F3 59
Terre Hill, Pa., 1,129...F9 81
Terrell, Tex., 13,803...C4 84
Terrell, co., Ga., 12,742.E2 55
Terrell, co., Tex., 2,600.D1 84
Terrell Hills, Tex., 5,572............B4 84
Terry, Mont., 1,140...D11 70
Terry, co., Tex., 16,286............C1 84
Terrytown, La., 5,000.*C7 63
Terry Town, Nebr., 164............C2 71
Terryville, Conn., 5,231............C4 52
Teruel, Sp., 19,726....B5 8
Teruel, prov., Sp., 215,183............*B5 8
Tešanj, Yugo, 3,150...C3 10
Teterow, Ger., 11,100.B6 6
Teton, co., Idaho, 2,639............F7 57

Teton, co., Mont.,
7,295................C4 70
Teton, co., Wyo., 3,062.B2 89
Tétouan, Mor.,
101,352...............A3 22
Tetovo, Yugo., 25,203.D5 10
Tetu, China, 22,024....B3 18
Teutopolis, Ill., 1,140..D5 58
Tewksbury, Mass.,
1,800...........A5, C2 65
Texarkana, Ark.,
19,788...............D1 49
Texarkana, Tex.,
30,218...............C5 84
Texas, Md., 120......B4 53
Texas, co., Mo., 17,758.D5 69
Texas, co., Okla.,
14,162...............D3 79
Texas, state, U.S.,
9,579,677............. 84
Texas City, Tex.,
32,065.........E5, G5 84
Texhoma, Okla., 911...D2 79
Teziutlán, Mex.,
17,384.........D5, n15 34
Thailand (Siam), country,
Asia, 25,520,638.....B2 19
Thames, N.Z., 5,315..L15 26
Thamesville, Ont., Can.,
1,054................E3 41
Thanh Hoa, Viet.,
25,000...............B3 19
Thann, Fr., 7,736.....D7 5
Thaon [-les-Vosges], Fr.,
8,166................C7 5
Tharptown, Pa., 1,085.*E8 81
Tharrawaddy, Bur.,
8,977...............E10 20
Thatcher, Ariz., 1,581..C4 48
Thatcher, Idaho, 100...G7 57
Thaton, Bur., 38,047..E10 20
Thayer, Mo., 1,713....E6 69
Thayer, co., Nebr.,
9,118................D8 71
Thayetmyo, Bur.,
11,164.............*E10 20
The Dalles, Oreg.,
10,493...............B5 80
The Hague ('s
Gravenhage), Neth.,
605,900..............A6 5
The Pas, Man., Can.,
4,671................C1 40
The Plains, Ohio, 1,148.C5 78
Theresa, N.Y., 956.A5, B1 75
Thermalito, Calif.,
1,200...............*C3 50
Thermopolis, Wyo.,
3,955................B4 89
Thesprotía, prov., Grc.,
52,125..............*C3 14
Thessalon, Ont., Can.,
1,725................E9 41
Thessaloniki (Salonika),
Grc., 250,920........B4 14
Thessaloniki, prov.,
Grc., 544,394.......*B4 14
Thessaly, reg., Grc.....C4 14
Thetford Mines, Que.,
Can., 21,618.........C6 42
The Village, Okla.,
12,118.............*B4 79
Thibodaux, La.,
13,403..........C6, E5 63
Thief River Falls, Minn.,
7,151................B2 67
Thiensville, Wis.,
2,507...........E2, E6 88
Thiers, Fr., 12,418.....E5 5
Thiès, Sen., 42,500....F1 22
Thimbu, Bhu.........C8 20
Thionville, Fr., 31,811..C7 5
Thisted, co., Den.,
86,703.............*I3 11
Thívai (Thebes), Grc.,
15,779..............*C4 14
Thomas, Okla., 1,211..B3 79
Thomas, W. Va., 830...B5 87
Thomas, co., Ga.,
34,319...............F3 55
Thomas, co., Kans.,
7,358................C2 61
Thomas, co., Nebr.,
1,078................C5 71
Thomaston, Ala., 857..C2 46
Thomaston, Conn.,
3,579................C4 52
Thomaston, Ga., 9,336.D2 55
Thomaston, Maine,
2,780................D3 64
Thomaston, N.Y.,
2,767..............*E3 75
Thomasville, Ala.,
3,182................D2 46
Thomasville, Ga.,
18,246...............F3 55
Thomasville, N.C.,
15,190...............F3 76
Thompson, Conn., 500.B9 52
Thompson Falls, Mont.,
1,274................C1 70

Thompsonville, Conn.,
19,000...............A6 52
Thomson, Ga., 4,522...C4 55
Thorburn, N.S., Can.,
1,000................D7 43
Thornaby-on-Tees, Eng.,
22,786...............C6 4
Thornbury, Ont., Can.,
1,097................C4 41
Thorndale, Tex., 995...D4 84
Thornton, Colo.,
11,353.............*B6 51
Thornton, Idaho, 200..F7 57
Thornton, Ill., 2,895..*F3 58
Thornton, Miss., 250...B3 68
Thorntown, Ind., 1,486.D4 59
Thornwood, N.Y.,
3,000..............*D7 75
Thorofare, N.J., 1,100..D2 74
Thorold, Ont., Can.,
8,663................D5 41
Thorp, Wis., 1,496....D3 88
Thorpe, W. Va., 1,102..D3 87
Thorsby, Ala., 968....C3 46
Thouars, Fr., 11,257...D3 5
Thousand Oaks, Calif.,
2,934..............*E4 50
Three Forks, Mont.,
1,161................E5 70
Three Hills, Alta.,
Can., 1,491..........D4 38
Three Oaks, Mich.,
1,763................G4 66
Three Rivers, Mass.,
3,082................B3 65
Three Rivers, Mich.,
7,092................G5 66
Three Rivers, Miss.,
150..................E5 68
Three Rivers, Tex.,
1,932................E3 84
Throckmorton, Tex.,
1,299................C3 84
Throckmorton, co.,
Tex., 2,767..........C3 84
Throop, Pa., 4,732.....A9 81
Thule, Grnld., 123....B14 33
Thun, Switz., 29,034...E3 6
Thunder Bay, co., Ont.,
Can., 138,518........E8 41
Thunderbolt, Ga.,
1,925................D5 55
Thurgau, canton,
Switz., 166,420.....*E4 6
Thüringen, former state,
Ger., 2,927,497.....*C5 6
Thuringia, reg., Ger....C5 6
Thurles, Ire., 6,421....D3 4
Thurmont, Md., 1,998..A3 53
Thurso, Que., Can.,
3,310................D2 42
Thurso, Scot., 8,038...A5 4
Thurston, co., Nebr.,
7,237................B9 71
Thurston, co., Wash.,
55,049...............C3 86
Thysville, Con. L.,
11,600...............B2 24
Tiberias, Isr.,
19,782...........B3, g5 15
Tibet, prov., China,
1,270,000............B8 20
Tiburon, Calif., 1,500..*B5 50
Tice, Fla., 4,377.......F5 54
Ticino, canton, Switz.,
195,566............*E4 6
Tickfaw, La., 317......D5 63
Ticonderoga, N.Y.,
3,568................B7 75
Ticul, Mex., 10,809....C7 34
Tidioute, Pa., 860.....C3 81
Tiehling, China, 45,000.C9 17
Tienen, Bel., 22,736...B6 5
Tienshui, China,
63,000...............E6 17
Tientsin, China,
2,850,000............D8 17
Tie Plant, Miss.,
1,491................B4 68
Tierra Blanca, Mex.,
16,474..........D5, n15 34
Tierra del Fuego, ter.,
Arg., 7,064.........h12 28
Tietê, Braz., 8,729.C3, m8 30
Tiff City, Mo., 100.....E3 69
Tiffin, Ohio, 21,478....A4 78
Tiflis, see Tbilisi, Sov. Un.
Tift, co., Ga., 23,487...E3 55
Tifton, Ga., 9,903.....E3 55
Tiftona, Tenn.,
3,520..............*D8 83
Tigard, Oreg., 5,000...B2 80
Tigil, Sov. Un., 1,200..D18 13
Tignish, P.E.I., Can.,
994..................C6 43
Tijuana, Mex., 151,939.A1 34
Tikhvin, Sov. Un.,
34,300...............B9 12
Tiksi, Sov. Un., 1,000.B15 13
Tilburg, Neth., 115,772.B6 5

Tilbury, Ont., Can.,
3,030................E2 41
Tilden, Ill., 808.......E4 58
Tilden, Nebr., 917.....B8 71
Tilghman, Md., 800....C5 53
Tiline, Ky., 150.......A3 62
Tillamook, Oreg., 4,244.B3 80
Tillamook, co., Oreg.,
18,955...............B3 80
Tillicum, Wash., 1,500.*E1 86
Tillman, co., Okla.,
14,654...............C3 79
Tillsonburg, Ont., Can.,
6,600................E4 41
Tilton, Ill., 2,598.....C6 58
Tilton, N.H., 1,129....E4 73
Tiltonsville, Ohio,
2,454................B7 78
Timaru, N.Z., 24,821
(*26,424)...........P13 26
Timbaúba, Braz.,
21,019.............*D7 27
Timber Lake, Va.,
2,700..............*D3 85
Times Beach, Mo.,
986................*C7 69
Timiskaming, co., Ont.,
Can., 50,971.........E9 41
Timiskaming, co., Que.,
Can., 60,288........A6 41
Timiskaming Station,
Que., Can., 2,517....E9 41
Timisoara, Rom.,
142,257..............C5 10
Timmins, Ont., Can.,
29,270...............E9 41
Timmonsville, S.C.,
2,178................C8 82
Timor, Portuguese, see
Portuguese Timor, dep.,
Asia
Timpson, Tex., 1,120..D5 84
Timuning, Guam,
5,380..............*F6 2
Tineo, Sp., 21,338.....A2 8
Tinley Park, Ill., 6,392.F2 58
Tinsley, Miss., 250....C3 68
Tioga, N. Dak., 2,087..B2 77
Tioga, co., N.Y.,
37,802...............C4 75
Tioga, co., Pa., 36,614..C7 81
Tippah, co., Miss.,
15,093...............A5 68
Tipp City, Ohio, 4,267..C3 78
Tippecanoe, co., Ind.,
89,122...............D4 59
Tipperary, Ire., 4,684..D2 4
Tipperary, co., Ire.,
123,822............*D3 4
Tipton, Calif., 900.....D4 50
Tipton, Ind., 5,604....D5 59
Tipton, Iowa, 2,862....C6 60
Tipton, Mo., 1,639....C5 69
Tipton, Okla., 1,117...C2 79
Tipton, co., Ind.,
15,856...............D5 59
Tipton, co., Tenn.,
28,564...............B2 83
Tiptonville, Tenn.,
2,068................A2 83
Tiranë (Tirana), Alb.,
119,000..............B2 14
Tiranë, pref., Alb.,
57,000.............*B2 14
Tirano, It., 7,517......A3 9
Tiraspol, Sov. Un.,
62,000...............H7 12
Tire, Tur., 26,500.....C6 14
Tirnavos, Grc., 10,805.*C4 14
Tirol, reg., Aus........E5 6
Tirol, state, Aus.,
462,899..............E5 6
Tiruchirappalli, India,
249,862..............F6 20
Tirunelveli, India,
87,988...............G6 20
Tisdale, Sask., Can.,
2,402................E3 39
Tishomingo, Okla.,
2,381................C5 79
Tishomingo, co., Miss.,
13,889...............A5 68
Tiskilwa, Ill., 951......B4 58
Tiszafured, Hung.,
10,318...............B5 10
Tiszakecske, Hung.,
6,626................B5 10
Titograd, Yugo.,
29,043...............D4 10
Titovo Užice, Yugo.,
20,069...............D4 10
Titov Veles, Yugo.,
26,618...............E5 10
Titus, co., Tex., 16,785.C5 84
Titusville, Fla., 6,410..D6 54
Titusville, N.J., 1,000..C3 74
Titusville, Pa., 8,356...C2 81
Tiverton, Eng., 12,296.E5 4
Tiverton, R.I., 3,000..C12 52
Tivoli, It., 34,067..D4, h9 9
Tivoli, Tex., 800.......E4 84

Tixtla, Mex., 8,542....o14 34
Tizapán, Mex., 5,620...h9 34
Tizimín, Mex., 14,100..C7 34
Tizi-Ouzou, Alg.,
5,772................A5 22
Tiznit, Mor., 7,694....C3 22
Tjilatjap, Indon.,
28,309...............G3 19
Tjirebon, Indon.,
153,405..............G3 19
Tlalpan, Mex., 18,141..h9 34
Tlaxcala, state, Mex.,
347,334..............D5 34
Tlaxiaco, Mex., 8,228..D5 34
Tlemcen, Alg., 73,445..B4 22
Toast, N.C., 2,023.....A3 76
Toba, Jap., 21,900....o15 18
Tobarra, Sp., 8,243....C5 8
Tobolsk, Sov. Un.,
46,700...............D9 13
Tobyhanna, Pa., 900..D11 81
Tochigi, Jap.,
47,700...........H9, m8 18
Tochigi, pref., Jap.,
1,513,624...........*H9 18
Toccoa, Ga., 7,303....B3 55
Toccoa Falls, Ga., 300..B3 55
Tocopilla, Chile,
21,000...............D1 29
Todd, co., Ky., 11,364..D2 62
Todd, co., Minn.,
23,119...............D4 67
Todd, co., S. Dak.,
4,661................G5 77
Togo, country, Afr.,
1,440,000............G5 22
Tokat, Tur., 32,700...B11 14
Tokenon, Kor., 15,711..G2 18
Tokushima, Jap.,
182,782..............I7 18
Tokushima, pref., Jap.,
847,274............*I7 18
Tokuyama, Jap., 77,246.I6 18
Tōkyō, Jap., 8,310,027
(*14,085,000)....I9, n18 18
Tōkyō, pref., Jap.,
9,983,802..........*I9 18
Tolbukhin (Dobrich),
Bul., 31,049........D8 10
Toledo, Ill., 998......D5 58
Toledo, Iowa, 2,417...C5 60
Toledo, Ohio, 318,003
(*514,200).....A2, A4 78
Toledo, Oreg., 3,053...C3 80
Toledo, Sp., 40,651....C3 8
Toledo, prov., Sp.,
521,637............*C3 8
Toler, Ky., 700........C7 62
Tolima, dept., Col.,
788,030..............C2 32
Tolland, co., Conn.,
68,737...............B7 52
Tolleson, Ariz., 3,886..D1 48
Tolmin, Yugo., 1,638..B1 10
Tolna, Hung., 8,748...B4 10
Tolna, co., Hung.,
267,415............*B4 10
Tolono, Ill., 1,539....D5 58
Tolosa, Sp., 16,281....A4 8
Toluca, Ill., 1,352....B4 58
Toluca, Mex.,
76,871.........D5, n14 34
Tomah, Wis., 5,321...E3 88
Tomahawk, Wis., 3,348.C4 88
Tomakomai, Jap.,
62,384..............E10 18
Tomakovka, Sov. Un.,
10,000..............H10 12
Tomar, Port., 8,034....C1 8
Tomari, Sov. Un.,
16,100..............E17 13
Tomaszow Lubelski,
Pol., 7,338..........C7 7
Tomaszow Mazowiecki,
Pol., 49,000.........C6 7
Tomball, Tex., 1,713..E5 84
Tombouctou (Timbuktu),
Mali, 7,500.........E4 22
Tombstone, Ariz.,
1,283................D4 48
Tomé, Chile, 27,000...B2 28
Tomelloso, Sp., 27,815..C4 8
Tom Green, co., Tex.,
64,630...............D2 84
Tomiño, Sp., 10,281...B1 8
Tomkins Cove, N.Y.,
800............D2, D7 75
Tommot, Sov. Un.,
4,800..............D15 13
Tompkins, co., N.Y.,
66,164...............C4 75
Tompkinsville, Ky.,
2,091................D4 62
Tomsk, Sov. Un.,
269,000.............D11 13
Toms River, N.J.,
6,062................D4 74
Tonalá, Mex., 12,204..D6 34
Tonasket, Wash., 958..A6 86
Tonawanda, N.Y.,
21,561...............B2 75

Tondano, Indon.,
15,007..............E6 19
Tønder, Den., 7,192....A4 6
Tønder, co., Den.,
42,842.............*J3 11
Tonga, Br. dep., Oceania,
47,000.............H9 2
Tonganoxie, Kans.,
1,354.........B8, C8 61
Tonka Bay, Minn.,
1,204.............*F5 67
Tonkawa, Okla., 3,415.A4 79
Tonkin, reg., Viet.,
11,000,000.........A3 19
Tonk Raj (Tonk),
India, 42,833........C6 20
Tonopah, Nev., 1,679..B3 72
Tönsberg, Nor.,
12,400.........H4, p28 11
Tooele, Utah,
9,133...........A5, D2 72
Tooele, co., Utah,
17,868............A5 72
Toole, co., Mont.,
7,904.............B5 70
Toombs, co., Ga.,
16,837............D4 55
Toowoomba, Austl.,
50,134............E9 25
Topanga, Calif., 3,500.*F4 50
Topeka, Kans., 119,484
(*135,800)......B6, C8 61
Topol'čany, Czech.,
10,400............D5 7
Topolovgrad, Bul.,
6,591.............D8 10
Toppenish, Wash.,
5,667.............C5 86
Topsfield, Mass., 2,000.A6 65
Topsham, Maine,
2,240.........E3, E5 64
Topton, Pa., 1,684....F10 81
Torbay, Newf., Can.,
1,445.............E5 44
Torhout, Bel., 13,435..B5 5
Toride, Jap., 13,300...n19 18
Torino (Turin), It.,
1,025,822..........B1 9
Toro, Sp., 10,218......B3 8
Torokszentmiklós, Hung.,
17,952............B5 10
Toronto, Ont., Can.,
672,407
(*1,824,481).....D5, E6 41
Toronto, Ohio, 7,780...B7 78
Toropets, Sov. Un.,
25,000............C8 12
Torquay, Eng., 53,915..E5 4
Torrance, Calif.,
100,991............F2 50
Torrance, co., N. Mex.,
6,497.............B5 48
Torre Annunziata, It.,
58,400............D5 9
Torre del Greco, It.,
77,576............D5 9
Torredonjimeno, Sp.,
14,204............D4 8
Torrelavega, Sp.,
14,800............A3 8
Torremaggiore, It.,
17,318............D5 9
Torrente, Sp., 24,042...C5 8
Torreón, Mex., 179,955.B4 34
Torre Pacheco, Sp.,
9,541.............D5 8
Torres Novas, Port.,
7,291.............C1 8
Torrevieja, Sp., 9,274..D5 8
Torrington, Conn.,
30,045............B4 52
Torrington, Wyo.,
4,188.............C8 89
Torrox, Sp., 7,384.....D4 8
Tortilla Flat, Ariz.,
100...............C3 48
Tortona, It., 20,400....B2 9
Tortosa, Sp., 14,500...B6 8
Torun, Pol., 105,000...B5 7
Torzhok, Sov. Un.,
32,000............C10 12
Toscana, pol. dist., It.,
3,286,160.........*C3 9
Tosno, Sov. Un.,
10,000............C10 12
Tosya, Tur.,
13,700............B10 14
Totana, Sp., 9,949....D5 8
Totkomlos, Hung.,
8,122.............B5 10
Totonicapán, Guat.,
6,405.............D6 34
Totowa, N.J., 10,897...B4 74
Tottenham, Eng.,
113,126...........k12 4
Tottori, Jap., 73,000....I7 18
Tottori, pref., Jap.,
599,135...........*I7 18
Totz, Ky., 700........D6 62
Tougaloo, Miss., 1,000 .C3 68
Toul, Fr., 14,155......C6 5

Toulon, Fr., 161,786...F6 5
Toulon, Ill., 1,213.....B4 58
Toulouse, Fr., 323,724..F4 5
Toungoo, Bur., 31,589.E10 20
Touraine, former prov.,
Fr., 392,000........D4 5
Tourcoing, Fr., 89,258..B5 5
Tourlaville, Fr., 11,569.C3 5
Tours, Fr., 92,944.....D4 5
Towaco, N.J., 2,500....B4 74
Towanda, Kans.,
1,031.........B6, E7 61
Towanda, Pa., 4,293...C9 81
Tower City, Pa., 1,968.E8 81
Town and Country,
Mo., 1,440........*C7 69
Town and Country Village,
Calif., 35,000......*C3 50
Towner, N. Dak., 948..B5 77
Towner, co., N. Dak.,
5,624.............B6 77
Townley, Ala., 649.....B2 46
Town of Pines, Ind.,
939...............*A4 59
Town of Tonawanda,
N.Y., 83,771.......*B2 75
Towns, co., Ga., 4,538..B3 55
Townsend, Mass.,
1,101.............A4 65
Townsend, Mont.,
1,528.............D5 70
Townsville, Austl.,
51,143............C8 25
Towson, Md.,
17,000........B4, C2 53
Toyama, Jap., 207,226.H8 18
Toyama, pref., Jap.,
1,032,614.........*H8 18
Toyohashi, Jap.,
215,513.......I8, o16 18
Tozeur, Tun., 11,820...B6 22
Trabzon, Tur.,
52,700............B12 14
Tracadie, N.B., Can.,
1,651.............B5 43
Tracy, Calif.,
11,289........B6, D3 50
Tracy, Que., Can.,
6,542............*C4 42
Tracy, Minn., 2,862...F3 67
Tracy City, Tenn.,
1,577.............D8 83
Traer, Iowa, 1,623.....B5 60
Trafford, Pa., 4,330...B7 81
Traiguén, Chile, 8,806..B2 28
Trail, B.C., Can.,
11,580............E9 37
Trail Creek, Ind., 1,552.A4 59
Trailer Estates, Fla.,
1,562............*E4 54
Traill, co., N. Dak.,
10,583............C8 77
Trainer, Pa., 2,358...*G11 81
Tralee, Ire., 10,723...D2 4
Tranås, Swe., 15,400...H6 11
Trani, It., 38,129......D6 9
Transcona, Man., Can.,
8,312.............E3 40
Transilvania, prov.,
Rom., 3,420,859....*B6 10
Transvaal, prov., S. Afr.,
6,273,477..........E5 24
Transylvania, co., N.C.,
16,372............D3 76
Transylvania, reg.,
Rom...............B6 10
Trapani, It., 77,139....E4 9
Trappe, Pa., 1,264...*F11 81
Traralgon, Austl.,
12,300.............I6 26
Trás-os-Montes, reg.,
Port., 558,700......B2 8
Trás-os-Montes e Alto
Douro, prov., Port.,
639,846...........*B2 8
Traunstein, Ger.,
14,400............E6 6
Travelers Rest, S.C.,
1,973.............B3 82
Traverse, co., Minn.,
7,503.............E2 67
Traverse City, Mich.,
18,432............D5 66
Travis, co., Tex.,
212,136...........D4 84
Travnik, Yugo., 9,984..C3 10
Treasure, co., Mont.,
1,345.............D9 70
Treasure Island, Fla.,
3,506............*E4 54
Trebic, Czech., 19,200..D3 7
Trebinje, Yugo., 4,072.D4 10
Trebisov, Czech.,
9,300.............D6 7
Trego, co., Kans.,
5,473.............D4 61
Treinta y Tres, Ur.,
18,600............E2 30
Treinta y Tres, dept., Ur.,
41,400...........*E2 30
Trélazé, Fr., 9,400.....D3 5

Trelew, Arg., 5,880....C3 28
Trelleborg, Swe.,
19,200............J5 11
Tremont, Ill., 1,558....C4 58
Tremont, Pa., 1,893....E9 81
Tremonton, Utah,
2,115.............A5 72
Trempealeau, co., Wis.,
23,377............D2 88
Trencin, Czech., 22,300.D5 7
Trengganu, state, Mala.,
278,269...........*D2 19
Trenque Lanquén, Arg.,
10,887............B4 28
Trentino-Alto Adige, pol.
dist., It., 785,967...*A3 9
Trento, It., 75,154.....A3 9
Trenton, Ont., Can.,
13,183............C7 41
Trenton, N.S., Can.,
3,140.............D7 43
Trenton, Fla., 941.....C4 54
Trenton, Ga., 1,301....B1 55
Trenton, Ill., 1,866....E4 58
Trenton, Mich.,
18,439.........B7, F7 66
Trenton, Mo., 6,262...A4 69
Trenton, Nebr., 914...D4 71
Trenton, N.J., 114,167
(*279,800).........C3 74
Trenton, Ohio, 3,064..C3 78
Trenton, Tenn., 4,225.B3 83
Trentwood, Wash.,
1,387............*B8 86
Tres Arroyos, Arg.,
29,996............B4 28
Tresckow, Pa., 1,145.E10 81
Trés Croações, Braz.,
17,498............C3 30
Três Lagoas, Braz.,
14,520............C2 30
Treutlen, co., Ga.,
5,874.............D4 55
Treviglio, It., 23,413..B2 9
Treviso, It., 75,017....B4 9
Trevorton, Pa., 2,597..E8 81
Trevose, Pa., 6,000...*A12 81
Trevose Heights, Pa.,
1,500............*F12 81
Treynor, Iowa, 368....C2 60
Trezevant, Tenn.,
944...............A3 83
Triangle, Va., 2,948....C5 85
Tribbet, Miss., 200....B3 68
Tribune, Kans., 1,036..D2 61
Trichinopoly, see
Tiruchirapalli, India
Trichur, India, 73,038..F6 20
Trier, Ger., 87,100....D3 6
Trieste, It., 272,723...B4 9
Trigg, co., Ky., 8,870.D2 62
Trigueros, Sp., 6,454..D2 8
Trikkala (Tricca), Grc.,
27,876............C3 14
Trikkala, prov., Grc.,
142,781..........*C3 14
Tri Lakes, Ind.,
1,089............*B7 59
Trilby, Ohio, 5,000....A2 78
Trimble, co., Ky.,
5,102.............B4 62
Trimont, Minn., 942...G4 67
Trincomalee, Cey.,
26,356............G7 20
Tring Jonction, Que.,
Can., 1,214........C6 42
Trinidad, Bol., 8,695..B3 29
Trinidad, Colo., 10,691.D6 51
Trinidad, Cuba, 16,756.E4 35
Trinidad, Tex., 786....C4 84
Trinidad, Ur., 13,600..E1 30
Trinidad and Tobago,
country, N.A.,
825,700...........A5 32
Trinité, Mart., 7,732...o16 35
Trinity, Tex., 1,787....D5 84
Trinity, co., Calif.,
9,706.............B2 50
Trinity, co., Tex.,
7,539.............D5 84
Trino, It., 8,100......B2 9
Trion, Ga., 2,227......B1 55
Tripoli, Iowa, 1,179...B5 60
Tripoli, see Tarabulus,
Leb.
Tripoli (Țarābulus),
Libya, 170,000......B7 22
Trípolis (Tripolitza),
Grc., 18,500.......D4 14
Tripp, S. Dak., 837....G8 77
Tripp, co., S. Dak.,
8,761.............G6 77
Tristate Village, Ill.,
1,000............*B6 58
Triumph, La., 900.....E6 63
Trivandrum, India,
239,815...........G6 20
Trnava, Czech., 31,700.D4 7
Trois Pistoles, Que.,
Can., 4,349........A8 42

Trois Rivières, Que.,
Can., 53,477.......C5 42
Troitsk, Sov. Un.,
79,000............D9 13
Trollhättan, Swe.,
32,700............H5 11
Troms, co., Nor.,
127,500..........*C8 11
Tromsö, Nor., 12,400..C8 11
Trona, Calif., 1,138....E5 50
Trondheim, Nor., 58,600
(*109,000).........F4 11
Tropea, It., 6,702......E5 9
Trotwood, Ohio, 4,992..C3 78
Troup, Tex., 1,667....C5 84
Troup, co., Ga., 47,189.C1 55
Trousdale, co., Tenn.,
4,914.............A5 83
Trouville, Fr., 6,662...C3 5
Trowbridge, Eng.,
15,833............E5 4
Troy, Ala., 10,234....D4 46
Troy, Ill., 1,778......E4 58
Troy, Kans., 1,051....C8 61
Troy, Mich., 19,382...*F7 66
Troy, Mo., 1,779......C7 69
Troy, N.Y., 67,492....C7 75
Troy, N.C., 2,346.....B4 76
Troy, Ohio, 13,685....B3 78
Troy, Pa., 1,478......C8 81
Troyes, Fr., 67,406....C6 5
Trubchevsk, Sov. Un.,
10,000............E9 12
Trucial Coast, country,
Asia, 80,000.......E5 15
Trucksville, Pa., 2,300.*B8 81
Trujillo, Peru, 45,899..C2 31
Trujillo, Sp., 13,326...C3 8
Trujillo, Ven., 19,358..B3 32
Trujillo, state, Ven.,
326,634...........B3 32
Truman, Minn., 1,256..G4 67
Trumann, Ark., 4,511..B5 49
Trumansburg, N.Y.,
1,768.............C4 75
Trumbull, Conn.,
20,379............E4 52
Trumbull, co., Ohio,
208,526...........A7 78
Truro, N.S., Can.,
12,421............D6 43
Truro, Eng., 13,328...E4 4
Trussville, Ala.,
2,510.........B3, E5 46
Truth or Consequences,
N. Mex., 4,269.....C5 48
Trutnov, Czech.,
23,000............C3 7
Tryon, N.C., 2,223....D4 76
Trysil, Nor., 8,059.....G5 11
Tsangwu, see Wuchow,
China
Tselinograd, Sov. Un.,
114,000...........D10 13
Tsinan (Chinan), China,
862,000...........D8 17
Tsinghai, prov., China,
2,050,000.........D5 17
Tsingtao (Chingtao),
China, 1,121,000...D9 17
Tsingyuan, see Paoting,
China
Tsitsihar, China,
668,000...........C1 18
Tskhinvali, Sov. Un.,
24,000............A14 14
Tsu, Jap., 110,900.I8, o15 18
Tsuchiura, Jap.,
47,500........H10, m19 18
Tsuni, China, 97,500...F6 17
Tsuruoka, Jap., 56,300.G9 18
Tsuruga, Jap.,
36,000.........I8, n15 18
Tsushima, Jap.,
43,198............n15 18
Tsuyama, Jap., 44,800..I7 18
Tuareg, reg., Alg.....D5 22
Tubarão, Braz., 29,615.D3 30
Tübingen, Ger., 49,600.D4 6
Tuchola, Pol., 5,750...B4 7
Tuckahoe, N.Y., 6,423.D1 75
Tucker, Ga., 5,000....A5 55
Tucker, co., W. Va.,
7,750.............B5 87
Tuckerman, Ark.,
1,539.............B4 49
Tuckerton, N.J., 1,536.D4 74
Tucson, Ariz., 212,892
(*243,000).........C3 48
Tucumán, Arg.,
280,000...........E2 29
Tucumán, prov., Arg.,
780,348...........E2 29
Tucumcari, N. Mex.,
8,143.............B7 48
Tudela, Sp., 16,456....A5 8
Tuguergarao, Phil.,
19,000............B6 19
Tuktoyaktuk, N.W. Ter.,
Can., 409..........C7 36
Tukwila, Wash., 1,804.*B4 86

Tula, Sov. Un., 333,000.........D11 12
Tulancingo, Mex., 26,663........C5, m14 34
Tulare, Calif., 13,824..D4 50
Tulare, co., Calif., 168,403.........D4 50
Tularosa, N. Mex., 3,200.........C5 48
Tulcán, Ec., 10,658....A2 31
Tulcea, Rom., 24,639...C9 10
Tuléar, Malag., 18,648.E8 24
Tulelake, Calif., 950...A3 50
Tulia, Tex., 4,410.....B2 84
Tūl Karm, Jordan, 21,872........B3 15
Tullahoma, Tenn., 12,242........B5 83
Tullamore, Ire., 2,243.D3 4
Tulle, Fr., 19,084......E4 5
Tullytown, Pa., 2,452..........*F12 81
Tulsa, Okla., 261,685 (*360,900).........A6 79
Tulsa, co., Okla., 346,038.........B6 79
Tuluá, Col., 28,715....C2 32
Tulufan, see Turfan, China
Tulun, Sov. Un., 34,000..........D13 13
Tumaco, Col., 12,692...C2 32
Tumbarumba, Austl., 1,511.........G7 26
Tumbes, Peru, 7,416...B1 31
Tumbes, dept., Peru, 30,035.........B1 31
Tumen, China, 28,000.C10 17
Tumkur, India, 47,277..F6 20
Tumwater, Wash., 3,885.........B3 86
Tunbridge Wells, Eng., 39,855..........E7 4
Tunghwa, China, 129,100..........F2 18
Tungliao (Payintala), China, 40,000......C9 17
Tunguragua (Tungurahua), prov., Ec., 204,726........B2 31
Tunhua, China, 24,088..........C10 17
Tunica, Miss., 1,445...A3 68

Tunica, co., Miss., 16,826..........A3 68
Tunis, Tun., 410,000...A7 22
Tunisia, country, Afr., 3,880,000........B6 22
Tunja, Col., 45,680....B3 32
Tunkhannock, Pa., 2,297..........C10 81
Tuntatuliak, Alsk., 145.C7 47
Tuolumne, Calif., 1,403.........D3 50
Tuolumne, co., Calif., 14,404.........C4 50
Tupelo, Miss., 17,221..A5 68
Tupper Lake, N.Y., 5,200..........A6, B2 75
Tura, Sov. Un., 2,000.C13 13
Turbaco, Col., 10,208..A2 32
Turciansky Svaty Martin, Czech., 22,400......D5 7
Turda, Rom., 33,610...B6 10
Turek, Pol., 7,179.....B6 7
Turfan (Tulufan), China, 25,000......C2 17
Turgay, Sov. Un., 5,800..........E9 13
Turgovishte, Bul., 10,505.........D8 10
Turgutlu, Tur., 31,700.C6 14
Turka, Sov. Un., 10,000.........G4 12
Turkestan, Sov. Un., 28,300.........*E9 13
Turkeve, Hung., 10,339.........B5 10
Turkey, Tex., 813.....B2 84
Turkey, country, Asia, 27,809,000........C9 14
Turkmen, S.S.R., rep., Sov. Un., 1,626,000..*F8 16
Turks and Caicos Is., Br. dep., N.A., 5,716..........E8 35
Turku, Fin., 124,200..G10 11
Turku-Pori, dept., Fin., 607,073.........*G10 11
Turley, Okla., 4,000....A6 79
Turlock, Calif., 9,116..D3 50
Turner, Kans., 1,000...B8 61
Turner, co., Ga., 8,439..E3 55
Turner, co., S. Dak., 11,159.........G8 77
Turners Falls, Mass., 4,917..........A2 65

Turner Valley, Alta., Can., 702.........D3 38
Turnhout, Bel., 36,444.B6 5
Turnov, Czech., 11,500.C3 7
Turnovo, Bul., 16,182..D7 10
Turnu-Măgurele, Rom., 18,055.........D7 10
Turnu-Severin, Rom., 32,486.........C6 10
Turtkul, Sov. Un., 23,700.........E9 13
Turtle Creek, Pa., 10,607.........B6 81
Turukhansk, Sov. Un., 5,000..........C11 13
Tuscaloosa, Ala., 63,370.........B2 46
Tuscaloosa, co., Ala., 109,047.........B2 46
Tuscany, reg., It.....C3 9
Tuscarawas, co., Ohio, 76,789.........B6 78
Tuscola, Ill., 3,875...D5 58
Tuscola, co., Mich., 43,305.........E7 66
Tusculum College, Tenn., 1,433.........*C5 83
Tuscumbia, Ala., 8,994.A2 46
Tuskegee, Ala., 7,240..C4 46
Tuskegee Institute, Ala., 5,380..........C4 46
Tustin, Calif., 2,006...F3 50
Tuticorin, India, 124,230.........G6 20
Tutrakan, Bul., 7,203..C8 10
Tuttlingen, Ger., 24,900.........E4 6
Tutwiler, Miss., 912...A3 68
Tuxedo, Man., Can., 1,627.........*E3 40
Tuxedo, Md., 1,000...*C4 53
Tuxedo Park, N.Y., 723.........D2, D6 75
Tuxpan, Mex., 14,863.......C3, m11 34
Tuxpan, Mex., 23,222.......C5, m15 34
Tuxpan, Mex., 10,871.n12 34
Tuxtla Gutiérrez, Mex., 41,532.........D6 34
Tuzla, Yugo., 37,673...C4 10
Tweed, Ont., Can., 1,791.........C7 41

Twentynine Palms, Calif., 1,000.......E5 50
Twickenham, Eng., 100,822..........m11 4
Twig, Minn., 175......D6 67
Twiggs, co., Ga., 7,935.D3 55
Twillingate, Newf., Can., 947.........D4 44
Twin City, Ga., 1,095..D4 55
Twin Falls, Idaho, 20,126.........G4 57
Twin Falls, co., Idaho, 41,842.........G4 57
Twin Lakes, Calif., 1,849..........*D2 50
Twin Lakes, Ohio, 1,000..............*A6 78
Twin Lakes, Wis., 1,497.........F5 88
Twin Oaks, Pa., 1,500..........*G11 81
Twin Orchards, N.Y., 2,000..........*C4 75
Twin Rocks, Pa., 950...F4 81
Twinsburg, Ohio, 4,098.A6 78
Two Harbors, Minn., 4,695.........C7 67
Two Mountains, co., Que., Can., 32,837...D3 42
Two Rivers, Wis., 12,393.........B7, D6 88
Tyler, Minn., 1,138....F2 67
Tyler, Tex., 51,230....C5 84
Tyler, co., Tex., 10,666.D5 84
Tyler, co., W. Va., 10,026.........B4 87
Tyler Heights, W. Va., 3,000..........*C3 87
Tyler Park, Va., 1,000.*C5 85
Tylertown, Miss., 1,532.........D3 68
Tyndall, S. Dak., 1,262.H8 77
Tynemouth, Eng., 70,112.........C6 4
Tyre (Sur), Leb., 10,432.......A3, g5 15
Tyrone, Pa., 7,792.....E5 81
Tyrone, co., N. Ire., 133,930.........*C3 4
Tyrell, co., N.C., 4,520.B7 76
Tyumen, Sov. Un., 168,000.........D9 13
Tzekung, China, 291,300.........F5 17

U

Ubá, Braz., 21,768..C4, g6 30
Ube, Jap., 166,632......J5 18
Ubeda, Sp., 28,956.....C4 8
Uberaba, Braz., 72,053.B3 30
Uberlândia, Braz., 70,719.........B3 30
Uccle, Bel., 71,725.....B6 5
Udaipur, India, 111,139.........D5 20
Uddevalla, Swe., 34,700.........H4 11
Udine, It., 86,188......A4 9
Udon Thani, Thai., 30,407.........B2 19
Ueda, Jap., 44,900........H9, m17 18
Uelen, Sov. Un., 800..C22 13
Uelkal, Sov. Un., 800.C21 13
Uelzen, Ger., 25,000...B5 6
Ueno, Jap., 34,200....o15 18
Ufa, Sov. Un., 588,000.D8 13
Uganda, country, Afr., 6,538,031........H4 23
Uglegorsk (Esutoru), Sov. Un., 20,000....B11 18
Uglich, Sov. Un., 25,600...........C12 12
Uherské Hradiště, Czech., 12,800.........D4 7
Uhrichsville, Ohio, 6,201............B6 78
Uinta, co., Wyo., 7,484............D2 89
Uintah, co., Utah, 11,852............B7 72
Uitenhage, S. Afr., 48,755............G5 24
Ujiyamada, Jap., 99,026.........I8, o15 18
Ujjain, India, 144,161.D6 20
Ukhta, Sov. Un., 15,000.........C8 13
Ukiah, Calif., 9,900....C2 50
Ukraine (S.S.R.), rep., Sov. Un., 43,091,000...*E6 16
Ulan Bator (Urga), Mong., 70,000......B6 17
Ulan-Ude, Sov. Un., 188,000.........D13 13
Ulla, Sov. Un., 10,000.D7 12
Ulm, Ger., 92,700.....D4 6
Ulman, Mo., 100......C5 69

Ulsan, Kor., 18,100.....I4 18
Ulster, co., N.Y., 118,804.........D6 75
Ulster, prov., Ire., 217,524..........*C3 4
Ulverston, Eng., 10,515.C5 4
Ulyanovsk, Sov. Un., 226,000.........D7 13
Ulysses, Kans., 3,157...E2 61
Uman, Sov. Un., 63,000.........G8 12
Umatilla, Fla., 1,717...D5 54
Umatilla, co., Oreg., 44,352.........B8 80
Umbria, pol. dist., It., 794,745.........*C4 9
Umbria, reg., It.......C4 9
Umeå, Swe., 23,200....F9 11
Umm Ruwāba, Sud., 7,805.........F4 23
Umtali, Rh., 36,200.........D6 24
Umvuma, Rh., 10,000.........D6 24
Una, S.C., 1,500......*B4 82
Unadilla, Ga., 1,304...D3 55
Unadilla, N.Y., 1,586..C5 75
'Unayzah, Sau. Ar., 50,000.........D3 15
Uncasville, Conn., 1,381.........D8 52
Underwood, N. Dak., 819.........C4 77
Unecha, Sov. Un., 10,000.........E9 12
Unggi, Kor., 20,882....E5 18
Unicoi, co., Tenn., 15,082.........C11 83
Union, Miss., 1,726....C4 68
Union, Mo., 3,937.....C6 69
Union, N.J., 51,499....B4 74
Union, Ohio, 1,072....*C3 78
Union, Oreg., 1,490....B9 80
Union, S.C., 10,191....B4 82
Union, co., Ark., 49,518.........D3 49
Union, co., Fla., 6,043..B4 54
Union, co., Ga., 6,510..B2 55
Union, co., Ill., 17,645.F4 58
Union, co., Ind., 6,457..E8 59
Union, co., Iowa, 13,712.........C3 60

Union, co., Ky., 14,537.C2 62
Union, co., Miss., 18,904.........A4 68
Union, co., N.J., 504,255.........B4 74
Union, co., N. Mex., 6,068.........A7 48
Union, co., N.C., 44,670.........B3 76
Union, co., Ohio, 22,853.........B4 78
Union, co., Oreg., 18,180.........B8 80
Union, co., Pa., 25,646.E7 81
Union, co., S.C., 30,015.B4 82
Union, co., S. Dak., 10,197.........H9 77
Union, co., Tenn., 8,498.........C10 83
Union, par., La., 17,624.........B3 63
Union Beach, N.J., 5,862.........C4 74
Union City, Calif., 6,618.........B5 50
Union City, Ga., 2,118.C2 55
Union City, Ind., 4,047.........D8 59
Union City, Mich., 1,669.........F5 66
Union City, N.J., 52,180.........D5 74
Union City, Ohio, 1,657.........*B3 78
Union City, Pa., 3,819..C2 81
Union City, Tenn., 8,837.........A2 83
Uniondale, N.Y., 20,041.........*G2 52
Unión de Reyes, Cuba, 5,503.........D3 35
Union Gap, Wash., 2,100.........C5 86
Union Grove, Wis., 1,970.........F1, F5 88
Union Lake, Mich., 2,000.........*F7 66
Union Park, Fla., 1,000..........*D5 54
Union Point, Ga., 1,615.........C3 55

Union Springs, Ala., 3,704.........C4 46
Union Springs, N.Y., 1,066.........C4 75
Uniontown, Ala., 1,993.C2 46
Uniontown, Ky., 1,255.C2 62
Uniontown, Ohio, 1,668.........B6 78
Uniontown, Pa., 17,942.G2 81
Union Village, R.I., 1,500.........B10 52
Unionville, Conn., 2,246.........B5 52
Unionville, Ga., 1,000.*D3 55
Unionville, Ga., 1,607.*E3 55
Unionville, Mo., 1,896..A4 69
United, Pa., 2,044.....F3 81
United Arab Republic (Egypt), country, Afr., 26,059,000.........C3 23
United Kingdom of Great Britain and Northern Ireland, country, Eur., 52,673,221 4
United Provinces, see Uttar Pradesh, state, India
United States, country, N.A., 179,325,100 45
United States Air Force Academy, Colo., 5,000..........C6 51
Unity, Sask., Can., 1,902.........E1 39
University, Miss., 3,597.........A4 68
University City, Mo., 51,249.........A8, C7 69
University Gardens, Md., 1,000..........*C4 53
University Heights, Ohio, 16,641.........B2 78
University Hills, Md., 1,700..........*C4 53
University Park, Md., 3,098.........*C4 53
University Park (State College), N. Mex., 2,400..........*C5 48
University Park, Tex., 23,202.........B5 84

University View, Ohio,
1,000.............*C2 78
Unterwalden, canton,
Switz., 45,323......*E4 6
Unye, Tur., 11,400....B11 14
Upington, S. Afr.,
20,366...........F4 24
Upland, Calif.,
15,918.........E5, F3 50
Upland, Ind., 1,999....D7 59
Upland, Pa., 4,343...*G10 59
Upper Arlington, Ohio,
28,486.........C2, C4 81
Upper Brookville, N.Y.,
1,045.............*D3 78
Upper Darby, Pa.,
44,000........B11, G11 75
Upper Nyack, N.Y.,
1,833..............*D7 81
Upper Saddle River, N.J.,
3,570...............A4 75
Upper Sandusky, Ohio,
4,941...............B4 74
Upper Silesia, reg., Pol..g9 78
Upper Volta, country,
Afr., 3,567,000......F4 7
Uppsala, Swe.,
79,300......H7, t35 22
Uppsala, co., Swe.,
170,000...........*H7 11
Upshur, co., Tex.,
19,793............C5 84
Upshur, co., W. Va.,
18,292............C4 87

Upson, co., Ga., 23,800.D2 55
Upton, Mass.,
1,000........B4, D1 65
Upton, Wyo., 1,224....A8 89
Upton, co., Tex., 6,239.D2 84
Urakawa, Jap., 12,300.E11 18
Uralsk, Sov. Un.,
111,000...........D8 13
Urania, La., 1,063.....C3 63
Uranium City, Sask.,
Can., 1,665........E12 36
Uravan, Colo., 1,005...C2 51
Urawa, Jap.,
168,757.........I9, n18 18
Urbana, Ill., 27,294....C5 58
Urbana, Ohio, 10,461..B4 78
Urbancrest, Ohio,
1,029..............C2 78
Urbandale, Iowa,
5,821.........A7, C4 60
Urbino, It., 6,500......C4 9
Urfa, Tur., 59,900....D12 14
Uri, canton, Switz.,
32,021.............E4 6
Urla, Tur., 10,800....*C6 14
Uruapan [del Progreso],
Mex., 45,580...D4, n13 34
Uruguaiana, Braz.,
48,358.............D1 30
Uruguay, country, S.A.,
2,163,000..........E1 30
Urumchi (Tihwa), China,
275,000............C2 17
Urusha, Sov. Un.,
10,000............D15 13

Uryupinsk, Sov. Un.,
29,900............F14 12
Usak, Tur., 22,000.....C7 14
Üsküdar, Tur., 60,722..B7 14
Usman, Sov. Un.,
50,000............E12 12
Usolye-Sibirskoye,
Sov. Un., 56,000...D13 13
Ussuriysk, Sov. Un.,
111,000...........E16 13
Usti nad Labem, Czech.,
63,800.............C3 7
Ust-Kamenogorsk, Sov.
Un., 173,000......E11 13
Ust-Kut, Sov. Un.,
21,900............D13 13
Ust-Maya, Sov. Un.,
2,300.............C16 13
Ust-Srednikan, Sov. Un.,
800...............C18 13
Ust-Tsilma, Sov. Un.,
7,900..............C8 13
Ust-Usa, Sov. Un.,
2,500..............C8 13
Ustyuzhna, Sov. Un.,
10,000............B11 12
Usumbura, see
Bujumbura, Burundi
Utah, co., Utah,
106,991............A6 72
Utah, state, U.S.,
890,627............ 72
Utica, Ill., 1,014.......B4 58
Utica, Mich., 1,454.A8, F7 66

Utica, N.Y., 100,410
(*160,400).........B5 75
Utica, Ohio, 1,854.....B5 78
Utica. S.C., 1,294....*B1 82
Utica Heights, Mich.,
2,700.............*F8 66
Utiel, Sp., 10,076......C5 8
Utrecht, Neth., 256,300
(*395,000).........A6 5
Utrecht, prov., Neth.,
686,600...........*A6 5
Utrera, Sp., 35,200....D3 8
Utsunomiya, Jap.,
193,000............H9 18
Uttaradit, Thai.,
9,372.............*B2 19
Uttar Pradesh, state,
India, 73,746,401....C6 20
Utuado, P.R., 9,870..m13 35
Uusimaa, dept., Fin.,
668,211...........G11 11
Uvalde, Tex., 10,293...E3 84
Uvalde, co., Tex.,
16,814.............E3 84
Uvaly, Czech., 4.706..n18 7
Uwajima, Jap., 49,500..J6 18
Uxbridge, Ont., Can.,
2,316..............C5 41
Uxbridge, Mass., 3,377.B4 65
Uzbek, rep., Sov. Un.,
8,665,000.........*E9 16
Uzhgorod, Sov. Un.,
52,000............G4 12
Uzunkopru, Tur.,
18,300.............B6 13

V

Vaasa, Fin., 42,700....F9 11
Vaasa, dept., Fin.,
603,964...........*F9 11
Vac, Hung., 24,738....B4 10
Vacaville, Calif.,
10,898.........B5, C3 50
Vacherie, La., 950.....B6 63
Vadnais Heights, Minn.,
2,459.............*F5 67
Vail Homes, N.J.,
1,204.............*C4 74
Valais, canton, Switz.,
177,783............E3 6
Valatie, N.Y., 1,237....C7 75
Val-Brillant, Que.,
Can., 879.........*G20 36
Val David, Que., Can.,
1,118..............C3 42
Valdepeñas, Sp., 25,706.C4 8
Valdese, N.C., 2,941...B2 76
Valdivia, Chile, 50,000.B2 28
Valdivia, prov., Chile,
255,109............B2 28
Val d'Or, Que., Can.,
10,983.............E9 41
Valdosta, Ga., 30,652..F3 55
Vale, Oreg., 1,491.....D9 80
Valença, Braz., 17,137..E7 27
Valence [-sur-Rhone], Fr.,
52,532.............E6 5
Valencia, Sp., 13,159...C2 8
Valencia, Sp., 505,066..C5 8
Valencia, Ven., 161,413.A4 32
Valencia, co., N. Mex.,
39,085.............B4 48
Valencia, prov., Sp.,
1,429,708.........*C2 8
Valenciennes, Fr., 45,379
(*165,000).........B5 5
Valentine, Nebr., 2,875.B5 71
Valera, Ven., 44,566...B3 32
Valhalla, N.Y.,
3,000.........D3, D7 75
Valjevo, Yugo., 22,070.C4 10
Valka, Sov. Un., 25,000.C6 12
Valki, Sov. Un.,
10,000............G10 12
Valladolid, Sp.,
151,807............B3 8
Valladolid, prov., Sp.,
363,106...........*B3 8
Valle d'Aosta, pol. dist.,
It., 100,959........*B1 9
Valle de la Pascua,
Ven., 24,051.......B4 32
Valle del Cauca, dept.,
Col., 1,396,630.....C2 32
Valle de Santiago, Mex.,
20,372...........m13 34
Vallee Jonction, Que.,
Can., 1,405........C7 42
Vallejo, Calif.,
60,877........B5, C2 50
Valletta, Malta,
18,300 (*208,000)....A7 22
Valley, Nebr.,
1,452.........C9, D2 71
Valley, co., Idaho,
3,663.............E3 57
Valley, co., Mont.,
17,080............B10 70

Valley, co., Nebr.,
6,590.............C6 71
Valley Brook, Okla.,
1,378.............*B4 79
Valley Center, Kans.,
2,570.........B5, E6 61
Valley City, N. Dak.,
7,809.............D7 77
Valley Cottage, N.Y.,
2,200.............D1 75
Valleydale, Calif.,
1,000.............*F3 50
Valley Falls, Kans.,
1,193.........B7, C8 61
Valleyfield, Que., Can.,
27,297.........D3, E8 42
Valley Mills, Tex.,
1,061..............D4 84
Valley Park, Miss., 100.C3 68
Valley Park, Mo.,
3,452..............B7 69
Valley Station, Ky.,
10,553.............A4 62
Valley Stream, N.Y.,
38,629.............E2 75
Valley View, Ill.,
1,741.............*A5 58
Valley View, Ohio,
1,221..............A6 78
Valley View, Pa., 1,540.E8 81
Valmiera, Sov. Un.,
10,000............C5 12
Valparaíso, Chile, 255,000
(*440,000).........A2 28
Valparaiso, Fla., 5,975.G2 54
Valparaiso, Ind.,
15,227.............B3 59
Valparaíso, prov., Chile,
613,405............A2 28
Val Verde, co., Tex.,
24,461.............E2 84
Valverde del Camino,
Sp., 10,843.........D2 8
Van, Tex., 1,103.......C5 84
Van, Tur., 22,000.....C14 14
Van Alstyne, Tex.,
1,608..............C4 84
Van Buren, Ark., 6,787.B1 49
Van Buren, Ind., 929...C6 59
Van Buren, Maine,
3,589..............A5 64
Van Buren, co., Ark.,
7,228..............B3 49
Van Buren, co., Iowa,
9,778..............D6 60
Van Buren, co., Mich.,
48,395.............F4 66
Van Buren, co., Tenn.,
3,671..............D8 83
Vance, co., N.C.,
32,002.............A5 76
Vanceburg, Ky., 1,881..B6 62
Vancouver, B.C., Can.,
384,522
(*790,165).....A10, E6 37
Vancouver, Wash.,
32,464.............D3 86
Vancouver, dist., B.C.,
Can................D5 37
Vancouver, isl., B.C.,
Can................E5 37

Vandalia, Ill., 5,537....E4 58
Vandalia, Mo., 3,055...B6 69
Vandalia, Ohio.......*C3 78
Vanderbilt, Pa., 826....F2 81
Vanderburgh, co., Ind.,
165,794............H2 59
Vandercook, Mich.,
4,000.............*F6 66
Vandergrift, Pa., 8,742.E2 81
Vanderhoof, B.C., Can.,
1,460..............C5 37
Vandling, Pa., 578....C11 81
Vänersborg, Swe.,
18,500.............H5 11
Van Horn, Tex., 1,953..F2 84
Vankleek Hill, Ont.,
Can., 1,735.......B10 41
Van Lear, Ky., 921....C7 62
Vannes, Fr., 30,411...D2 5
Vanves, Fr., 25,585.....g9 5
Van Wert, Ohio, 11,333.B3 78
Van Wert, co., Ohio,
28,840.............B3 78
Van Winkle, Miss.,
2,000..............C3 68
Van Yen, Viet.,
10,000............*G5 17
Van Zandt, co., Tex.,
19,091.............C5 84
Var, dept., Fr.,
469,557...........*F7 5
Varaždin, Yugo.,
26,239.............B3 10
Varazze, It., 9,200.....B2 9
Varberg, Swe., 14,500...I5 11
Varel, Ger., 12,400.....B4 6
Varennes, Que., Can.,
2,240.............*D4 42
Varese, It., 69,963.....B2 9
Varginha, Braz., 24,944.C3 30
Varkaus, Fin., 15,400.F12 11
Värmland, co., Swe.,
290,200...........*H5 11
Varna (Stalin), Bul.,
119,769............D8 10
Värnamo, Swe., 13,200..I6 11
Varnsdorf, Czech.,
13,400.............C3 7
Varnville, S.C., 1,461...F5 82
Vas, co., Hung.,
283,096...........*B3 10
Vasilkov, Sov. Un.,
10,000.............F8 12
Vaslui, Rom., 14,850...B8 10
Vassar, Mich., 2,680...E7 66
Västerås, Swe.,
79,200........H7, t34 11
Västerbotten, co., Swe.,
238,600...........*F9 11
Västernörrland, co.,
Swe., 283,300......*F8 11
Västervik, Swe.,
18,200.............I7 11
Västmanland, co., Swe.,
235,200...........*H7 11
Vasto, It., 12,600......C5 9
Vatican City, country,
Eur., 890......D4, h8 19
Vaucluse, dept., Fr.,
303,536...........*F6 5
Vaud, canton, Switz.,
429,512...........*E3 6

Vaudreuil, co., Que.,
Can., 28,681........D3 42
Vaughn, N. Mex.,
1,170..............B6 48
Vaupés, comisaría, Col.,
9,750..............C3 32
Växjö, Swe., 24,000.....I6 11
Veachland, Ky., 700....B4 62
Veazie, Maine, 1,354..*D4 64
Vecses, Hung., 15,537..B4 10
Veedersburg, Ind.,
1,762..............D3 59
Vegas Heights, Nev.,
1,200.............*G6 72
Vegreville, Alta., Can.,
2,908..............C4 38
Vejer, Sp., 10,691.....D2 8
Vejle, Den., 31,362.....J3 11
Vejle, co., Den.,
207,881...........*J3 11
Velda Village Hills,
Mo., 1,365........*A8 69
Vélez-Málaga, Sp.,
13,000.............D3 8
Vélez-Rubio, Sp.,
4,484..............D5 8
Velikiy Ustyug, Sov.
Un., 41,300........C7 13
Velikiye Luki, Sov. Un.,
65,000.............C8 12
Velikiy Ustyug, Sov.
Un., 41,300........*C7 16
Velizh, Sov. Un.,
10,000.............D8 12
Velletri, It., 16,200.D4, h9 9
Vellore, India, 113,742..F6 20
Velma, Okla., 700......C4 79
Velsk, Sov. Un., 14,300.C7 13
Velva, N. Dak., 1,330..B5 77
Venado Tuerto, Arg.,
15,947.............A4 28
Venango, co., Pa.,
65,295.............D2 81
Vendée, dept., Fr.,
408,928...........*D3 5
Venetian Village, Ill.,
2,084.............*E2 58
Veneto, pol. dist., It.,
3,846,562.........*B4 9
Veneto, reg., It........A3 9
Venezia (Venice), It.,
347,347............B4 9
Venezuela, country, S.A.,
7,583,999..........B4 32
Venice, Ill., 5,380.....E3 58
Venice, Fla., 3,444.....E4 54
Vénissieux, Fr., 29,040.E6 5
Venlo, Neth., 55,200...B7 5
Ventimiglia, It., 12,200.C1 9
Ventnor City, N.J.,
8,688..............E4 74
Ventspils, Sov. Un.,
26,200.............C3 12
Ventura, Calif., 29,114.E4 50
Ventura, co., Calif.,
199,138............E4 50
Ventura North
(Chrisman), Calif.,
3,923.............*E4 50
Veracruz, Mex.,
144,232.......D5, n15 34

Veracruz, state, Mex., 2,749,235......D5, n15 34
Veradale, Wash., 2,000.............*B8 86
Veraval, India, 46,637..D5 20
Vercelli, It., 50,907....B2 9
Vercheres, Que., Can., 1,768..............D4 42
Verchères, co., Que., Can., 25,697.......D9 42
Verden, Ger., 17,500...B4 6
Verdun, Que., Can., 78,317............D9 42
Verdun, Fr., 21,982....C6 5
Verdunville, W. Va., 2,260............*D2 87
Vereeniging, S. Afr., 78,835 (*201,000)....F5 24
Verga, N.J., 1,000.....*D2 74
Vergennes, Vt., 1,921...C1 73
Verkhneye, Sov. Un., 10,000.........G12, q21 12
Verkhoyansk, Sov. Un., 1,200.............C16 13
Vermilion, Alta., Can., 2,449.............C5 38
Vermilion, Ohio, 5,220..A5 78
Vermilion, co., Ill., 96,176.............C6 58
Vermilion, par., La., 38,855.............E3 63
Vermilion Heights, Ill., 1,568.............*C6 58
Vermilion-on-the-Lake, Ohio, 1,273.......*A5 78
Vermillion, S. Dak., 5,337.............H9 77
Vermillion, co., Ind., 17,683.............E3 59
Vermont, Ill., 903.....C3 58
Vermont, state, U.S., 389,881............. 73
Vernal, Utah, 3,655....A7 72
Vernon, Ala., 1,492....B1 46
Vernon, B.C., Can., 10,250.........D8, E3 37
Vernon, Fr., 17,247....C4 5
Vernon, N.Y., 913.....*B5 75
Vernon, Tex., 12,141...B3 84
Vernon, co., Mo., 20,540............D3 69
Vernon, co., Wis., 25,663............E3 88
Vernon, par., La., 18,301.............C2 63
Vernonia, Oreg., 1,089..B3 80
Vernon Valley, N.Y., 5,998............*D3 75
Vero Beach, Fla., 8,849.............E6 54
Veroia, Grc., 25,765....B4 14
Verona, It., 221,221....B3 9
Verona, N.J., 13,782...B4 74
Verona, Pa., 4,032....A6 81
Verona, Wis., 1,471...F4 88
Verona Park, Mich., 1,884............*F5 66
Verplanck, N.Y., 1,800............*D7 75
Versailles, Fr., 86,759............C4, g9 5
Versailles, Ind., 1,158..F7 59
Versailles, Ky., 4,060...B5 62
Versailles, Mo., 2,047...C5 69
Versailles, Ohio, 2,159..B3 78
Versailles, Pa., 2,297..*F2 81
Verviers, Bel., 35,453..B6 5
Veseloye, Sov. Un., 25,000............H10 12
Vesoul, Fr., 13,678.....D7 5
Vest-Agder, co., Nor., 109,000............*H2 11
Vestal, N.Y., 7,000....*C4 75
Vestavia Hills, Ala., 4,029............*B3 46
Vestfold, co., Nor., 174,200............*H4 11
Vestry, Miss., 150....E5 68
Veszprem, Hung., 25,495............B3 10
Veszprem, co., Hung., 393,331............*B3 10
Veszto, Hung., 9,645...B5 10
Vevay, Ind., 1,503....G7 59
Vevey, Switz., 16,269..E3 6
Vezirkopru, Tur., 8,100.............B10 14
Viadana, It., 5,587....B3 9
Vian, Okla., 930.......B4 79
Viana do Castelo, Port., 14,023.............B1 8
Viborg, co., Den., 160,018............*I3 11
Vibo Valentia, It., 12,800.............E6 9
Vicco, Ky., 900.......C6 62

Vicenza, It., 98,019....B3 9
Vich, Sp., 12,414......B7 8
Vichada, comisaría, Col., 13,860.............C3 32
Vichy, Fr., 30,614....D5 5
Vicksburg, Mich., 2,224.............F5 66
Vicksburg, Miss., 29,143.............C3 68
Victor, N.Y., 1,180....C3 75
Victoria, Arg., 17,711..A4 28
Victoria, B.C., Can., 54,941 (*154,152).....B9, E6 37
Victoria, Newf., Can., 1,506.............E5 44
Victoria, Chile, 10,671..B2 28
Victoria, Hong Kong, 674,962............G7 17
Victoria, Kans., 1,170..D4 61
Victoria, Tex., 33,047..E4 84
Victoria, Va., 1,737....E4 85
Victoria, co., N.B., Can., 19,712.............B2 43
Victoria, co., N.S., Can., 8,226.............C9 43
Victoria, co., Ont., Can., 29,750........C6 43
Victoria, co., Tex., 46,475.............E4 84
Victoria, state, Austl., 2,930,113............G7 25
Victoria de las Tunas, Cuba, 12,754......E5 35
Victoria Harbour, Ont., Can., 1,066........C5 41
Victoria Park, Calif., 2,400............*F2 50
Victoriaville, Que., Can., 18,720.......C6 42
Victor Mills, S.C., 2,018............*B3 82
Victorville, Calif., 5,000.............E5 50
Victory Gardens, N.J., 1,085............*B4 74
Victory Heights, N.Y., 1,030............*C4 75
Vidal, Calif., 100.....E6 50
Vidalia, Ga., 7,569....D4 55
Vidalia, La., 4,313....C4 63
Vidin, Bul., 18,580....D6 10
Vidor, Tex., 4,938....D6 84
Vienna (Wien), Aus., 1,627,566 (*1,990,000)......D8 6
Vienna, Ga., 2,099.....D3 55
Vienna, Ill., 1,094.....F5 58
Vienna, Va., 11,440.B4, C5 85
Vienna, W. Va., 9,381..B3 87
Vienne, Fr., 26,977....E6 5
Vienne, dept., Fr., 331,619............*D4 5
Vientiane, Laos, 100,000.............B2 19
Vierzon, Fr., 31,549...D5 5
Vieste, It., 12,679....D6 9
Vietnam, reg., Asia....B3 19
Vietnam, North, country, Asia, 14,500,000.....B3 19
Vietnam, South, country, Asia, 11,000,000.....C3 19
View Park, Calif., 2,500............*E4 50
Vigan, Phil., 7,424.....B6 19
Vigevano, It., 57,069...B2 9
Vigo, Sp., 144,914.....A1 8
Vigo, co., Ind., 108,458.F3 59
Vijayavada, India, 230,397............E7 20
Vila Nova de Gaia, Port., 45,700........B1 8
Vilas, co., Wis., 9,332..B4 88
Vila Teixeira da Silva, Ang., 4,897........C3 24
Vileyka, Sov. Un., 10,000.............D6 12
Viljandi, Sov. Un., 12,941............B5 12
Vilkovo, Sov. Un., 20,000.............I7 12
Villacarrillo, Sp., 13,090.............C4 8
Villach, Aus., 32,971..E6 6
Villa Dolores, Arg., 13,835.............A3 28
Villafranca, It., 15,712..B3 9
Villafranca de los Barros, Sp., 16,671........C2 8
Villafranca del Panadés, Sp., 11,985.......B6 8
Villafranca di Verona, It., 6,015..........B3 9
Villagarcía de Arosa, Sp., 4,986..........A1 8
Village Richelieu, Que., Can., 1,612......*D4 42
Villa Grove, Ill., 2,308.D5 58
Villaguay, Arg., 17,607.A5 28
Villahermosa, Mex., 51,611.............D6 34

Villa Heights, Md., 1,000.............*C4 53
Villalba, Sp., 3,180.....A2 8
Villa Maria, Arg., 30,362.............A4 28
Villanova, Pa., 4,000.*A10 81
Villanueva de Córdoba, Sp., 15,719.........C3 8
Villanueva del Arzobispo, Sp., 9,712.........C4 8
Villanueva de la Serena, Sp., 20,812.........C3 8
Villanueva y Geltrú, Sp., 25,669.........B6 8
Villa Obregón, Mex., 25,908............h9 34
Villa Park, Ill., 23,294..F2 58
Villa Rica, Ga., 3,450..C1 55
Villarreal, Sp., 19,700..C5 8
Villarrica, Par., 14,680.E4 29
Villarrobledo, Sp., 21,356.............C4 8
Villas, N.J., 2,085.....E3 74
Villavicencia, Col., 17,126.............C3 32
Villaviciosa, Sp., 2,322.............A3 8
Villefranche-sur-Saône, Fr., 24,516.........E6 5
Villejuif, Fr., 46,116...g10 5
Villemomble, Fr., 24,540............g10 5
Villena, Sp., 15,687....C5 8
Villeneuve-le-Roi, Fr., 22,300............h10 5
Villeneuve-St. Georges, Fr., 28,231........h10 5
Villeneuve-sur-Lot, Fr., 15,296.........E4 5
Ville Platte, La., 7,512.D3 63
Ville St. Georges, Que., Can., 4,082........C7 42
Ville St. Pierre, Que., Can., 6,795.......*D4 42
Villeta, Par., 14,729...E4 29
Villeurbanne, Fr., 105,416............E6 5
Villingen, Ger., 31,900.D4 6
Villisca, Iowa, 1,690...D3 60
Vilnius, Sov. Un., 255,000............D5 12
Vilvoorde, Bel., 31,441.B6 5
Vilyuysk, Sov. Un., 3,600.............C15 13
Vimianzo, Sp., 654.....A1 8
Viña del Mar, Chile, 118,000............A2 28
Vinalhaven, Maine, 950.............D4 64
Vincennes, Fr., 50,436.g10 5
Vincennes, Ind., 18,046.G2 59
Vincent, Ala., 1,402....B3 46
Vincent, Ohio, 2,100...*A6 78
Vine Grove, Ky., 2,435.C4 62
Vine Hill (Martinez East), Calif., 3,958........*C7 50
Vineland, N.J., 37,685..E2 74
Vineyard Haven, Mass., 2,169.............D6 65
Vinh Yen, Viet., 3,820..G6 17
Vinita, Okla., 6,027....A6 79
Vinita Park, Mo., 2,204............*C7 69
Vinkovci, Yugo., 23,113.............C4 10
Vinnitsa, Sov. Un., 131,000............G7 12
Vinton, Iowa, 4,781....B5 60
Vinton, La., 2,987.....D2 63
Vinton, Va., 3,432.....D2 85
Vinton, co., Ohio, 10,274............C5 78
Vintondale, Pa., 938...F4 81
Virden, Man., Can., 2,708.............E1 40
Virden, Ill., 3,309.....D4 58
Virginia, Ill., 1,669....D3 58
Virginia, Minn., 14,034............C6 67
Virginia, state, U.S., 3,966,949............ 85
Virginia Beach (Independent City), Va., 8,091....B7, E7 85
Virginia City, Nev., 500.............B2 72
Virginia Gardens, Fla., 2,159............*G6 54
Virgin Islands of the U.S., dep., N.A., 26,665..m14 35
Viroflay, Fr., 16,004....g9 6
Viroqua, Wis., 3,926...E3 88
Virovitica, Yugo., 14,027............C3 10
Visakhapatnam, India, 108,042............E7 20
Visalia, Calif., 15,791..D4 50
Visalia North (Crowley), Calif., 3,950.......D4 50

Visby, Swe., 15,600.....I8 11
Viseu, Port., 13,190....B2 8
Vista, Calif., 14,795....F5 50
Vista Park, Calif., 3,500............*E4 50
Vitanovak, Yugo., 1,127.............D5 10
Vitebsk, Sov. Un., 162,000............D8 12
Viterbo, It., 29,000....C4 9
Vitim, Sov. Un., 2,300.D14 13
Vitória, Braz., ...*D7 27
Vitória, Braz., 82,748...C4 30
Vitoria, Sp., 73,701....A4 8
Vitória da Conquista, Braz., 46,778........A4 30
Vitry [-sur-Seine], Fr., 65,734............g10 5
Vittoria, It., 45,035....F5 9
Vittorio Veneto, It., 21,500............B4 9
Vivero, Sp., 3,628......A2 8
Vivian, La., 2,624.....B2 63
Vizcaya, prov., Sp., 754,383............*A4 8
Vizianagram, India, 76,808............E7 20
Vizzini, It., 10,806....F5 9
Vlaardingen, Neth., 68,900............B6 5
Vladimir, Sov. Un., 167,000............C13 12
Vladimiro-Aleksandrovskoye, Sov. Un., 10,000.....E6 18
Vladimir-Volynskiy, Sov. Un., 10,000.....F5 12
Vladivostok, Sov. Un., 317,000............E5 18
Vlasotince, Yugo., 5,924.............D6 10
Vlissingen, Neth., 29,400............B5 5
Vlonë, Alb., 32,700....B2 14
Vlonë, pref., Alb., 58,000............*B2 14
Vodnany, Czech., 4,576............*D3 7
Voeune Sai, Camb., 10,000.............F7 22
Voghera, It., 35,747...B2 9
Voiron, Fr., 11,150....E6 5
Volgograd, Sov. Un., 632,000............G14 12
Volkhov, Sov. Un., 16,500............B9 12
Volkovysk, Sov. Un., 10,000.............E5 12
Vologda, Sov. Un., 148,000............B12 12
Volokolamsk, Sov. Un., 10,000.............C10 12
Volos, Grc., 49,221....C4 11
Volsk, Sov. Un., 66,000............*D7 13
Volta Redonda, Braz., 83,973.........C4, h5 30
Volterra, It., 9,300.....C3 9
Volusia, co., Fla., 125,319............C5 54
Voorheesville, N.Y., 1,228............*C7 75
Vorarlberg, state, Aus., 226,323...........*E4 6
Vordingborg, Den., 11,780............A1 7
Vorkuta, Sov. Un., 59,000.............C9 13
Voronezh, Sov. Un., 496,000............F12 12
Vosges, dept., Fr., 380,676............*C7 5
Votkinsk, Sov. Un., 65,000............*D8 13
Voznesensk, Sov. Un., 10,000.............H8 13
Vranje, Yugo., 16,457..D5 10
Vratsa, Bul., 19,448....D6 10
Vratsa, co., Bul., 771,486............D6 10
Vršac, Yugo., 31,551...C5 10
Vsetin, Czech., 18,200..D5 7
Vukovar, Yugo., 25,826............C4 11
Vulcan, Alta., Can., 1,310.............D4 38
Vulcan, Mo., 100.....D7 69
Vyazma, Sov. Un., 26,700............D10 12
Vyazniki, Sov. Un., 42,300............C14 12
Vyborg, Sov. Un., 56,000.............A7 12
Vyksa, Sov. Un., 28,600............D14 12
Vyshniy Volochek, Sov. Un., 70,000.........C10 12
Vysoké Tatry, Czech., 9,000.............D6 7
Vytegra, Sov. Un., 11,800............A11 12

W

Wabana (Bell Island),
Newf., Can., 8,026...E5   44
Wabash, Ind., 12,621..C6   59
Wabash, co., Ill.,
14,047..............E6   58
Wabash, co., Ind.,
32,605..............C6   59
Wabasha, Minn., 2,500.F6   67
Wabasha, co., Minn.,
17,007..............F6   67
Wabasso, Fla., 500.....E6   54
Wabaunsee, co., Kans.,
6,648..............D7   61
Wacissa, Fla., 300.....B3   54
Waco, Tex., 97,808
(*129,000)..........D4   84
Waconia, Minn., 2,048.F5   67
Waddington, N.Y., 921.A2   75
Wadena, Sask., Can.,
1,311..............F4   39
Wadena, Minn., 4,381..D3   67
Wadena, co., Minn.,
12,199..............D4   67
Wadesboro, N.C.,
3,744..............C3   76
Wadi Halfa, Sud.,
11,006..............D4   23
Wadley, Ga., 1,898....D4   55
Wad Medani, Sud.,
47,677..............F4   23
Wadsworth, Ohio,
10,635..............A6   78
Waelder, Tex., 1,270..E4   84
Wagga Wagga, Austl.,
22,087..............G8   25
Wagner, S. Dak., 1,586.G7   77
Wagoner, Okla., 4,469..B6   79
Wagoner, co., Okla.,
15,673..............B6   79
Wagon Mound, N. Mex.,
760..............B6   48
Wagrowiec, Pol.,
10,800..............B4   7
Wahiawa, Haw.,
15,512..........B3, f9   56
Wahkiakum, co., Wash.,
3,426..............C2   86
Wahneta, Fla., 1,796..*E5   54
Wahoo, Nebr.,
3,610..........C9, D2   71
Wahpeton, N. Dak.,
5,876..............D9   77
Waialua, Haw.,
2,689..........B3, f9   56
Waianae, Haw.,
4,120..........B3, g9   56
Waikabubak, Indon.,
10,000..............G5   19
Wailua (Wailua House-
lots), Haw., 1,129...A2   56
Wailuku, Haw., 6,969..C5   56
Waimanalo, Haw.,
3,011..........B4, g11   56
Waimea, Haw., 1,312..B2   56
Waimea, Haw., 400.....f9   56
Wainwright, Alta., Can.,
3,351..............C5   38
Waipahu, Haw.,
7,650..........B3, g9   56
Waipio Acres, Haw.,
1,158..............g9   56
Waite Park, Minn.,
2,016..............E4   67
Waitsburg, Wash.,
1,010..............C7   86
Wajima, Jap., 18,000..H8   18
Wakamatsu, Jap.,
70,200..............H9   18
Wakarusa, Ind., 1,145..A5   59
Wakaw, Sask., Can.,
974..............E3   39
Wakayama, Jap.,
285,155........I7, o14   18
Wakayama, pref., Jap.,
1,002,191..........*I7   18
Wake, co., N.C.,
169,082..............B5   76
WaKeeney, Kans.,
2,808..............C4   61
Wakefield, Mass.,
24,295..........A5, C3   65
Wakefield, Mich.,
3,231..............A5   66
Wakefield, Nebr., 1,068.B9   71
Wakefield, R.I., 3,570.D11   52
Wakefield, Va., 1,015..E6   85
Wake Forest, N.C.,
2,664..............B5   76
Wakulla, co., Fla.,
5,257..............B2   54
Walbridge, Ohio, 2,142.A2   78
Walbrzych, Pol.,
117,000..............C4   7
Walden, N.Y., 4,851..D6   75
Waldo, Ark., 1,722...D2   49
Waldo, co., Maine,
22,632..............D3   64
Waldorf, Md., 1,048...C4   53

Waldron, Ark., 1,758...C1   49
Waldwick, N.J., 10,495.A4   74
Wales, reg., U.K.,
2,640,632..........D5   4
Walhalla, N. Dak.,
1,432..............A8   77
Walhalla, S.C., 3,431..B1   82
Walker, La., 912.....A6   63
Walker, Minn., 1,180..C4   67
Walker, co., Ala.,
54,211..............B2   46
Walker, co., Ga.,
45,264..............B1   55
Walker, co., Tex.,
21,475..............D5   84
Walkersville, Md.,
1,020..............B3   53
Walkerton, Ont., Can.,
3,851..............C3   41
Walkerton, Ind., 2,044.B5   59
Walkertown, N.C.,
1,240..............A3   76
Walkerville, Mont.,
1,453..............D4   70
Wall, Pa., 1,493......*F2   81
Wallace, Idaho, 2,412..B3   57
Wallace, N.C., 2,285...C5   76
Wallace, co., Kans.,
2,069..............D2   61
Wallaceburg, Ont., Can.,
7,881..............E2   41
Wallasey, Eng.,
103,213..............D5   4
Walla Walla, Wash.,
24,536..............C7   86
Walla Walla, co., Wash.,
42,195..............C7   86
Walled Lake, Mich.,
3,550..............A7   66
Waller, Tex., 900......D5   84
Waller, co., Tex.,
12,071..............E4   84
Wallingford, Conn.,
29,920..............D5   52
Wallingford, Vt., 900..E2   73
Wallington, Eng.,
32,500..............m12   4
Wallington, N.J., 9,261.D5   74
Wallis, Tex., 950.....E4   84
Wallkill, N.Y., 1,215..D6   75
Wallowa, Oreg., 989...B9   80
Wallowa, co., Oreg.,
7,102..............B9   80
Wallsend, Eng., 49,785.C6   4
Walnut, Calif., 934...*F3   50
Walnut, Ill., 1,192....B4   58
Walnut Cove, N.C.,
1,288..............A3   76
Walnut Creek, Calif.,
9,903..............B5   50
Walnut Heights, Calif.,
5,080..............*B5   50
Walnut Park, Calif.,
7,500..............*F2   50
Walnutport, Pa.,
1,609..............E10   81
Walnut Ridge, Ark.,
3,547..............A5   49
Walpole, Mass.,
7,000..........B5, E2   65
Walsall, Eng., 117,896..D6   4
Walsenburg, Colo.,
5,071..............D6   51
Walsh, co., N. Dak.,
17,997..............B8   77
Walterboro, S.C.,
5,417..............F6   82
Walters, Okla., 2,825...C3   79
Walthall, co., Miss.,
13,512..............D6   68
Waltham, Mass.,
55,413..........B5, D2   65
Walthamstow, Eng.,
108,788..............k12   4
Walthill, Nebr., 844....B9   71
Walton, Ind., 1,079....C5   59
Walton, Ky., 1,530.A7, B5   62
Walton, N.Y., 3,855...C5   75
Walton, co., Fla.,
15,576..............G3   54
Walton, co., Ga.,
20,481..............C3   55
Walton Hills, Ohio,
1,776..............*A6   78
Walvis Bay, S. Afr.,
12,235..............E2   24
Walworth, Wis., 1,494..F5   88
Walworth, co., S. Dak.,
8,097..............E5   77
Walworth, co., Wis.,
52,368..............F5   88
Wamac, Ill., 1,394.....E4   58
Wamego, Kans., 2,363..C7   61
Wampum, Pa., 1,085..E1   81
Wanamassa, N.J.,
3,928..............C4   74
Wanaque, N.J., 7,126..A4   74

Wanganui, N.Z., 33,316
(*35,694)..........M15   26
Wangaratta, Austl.,
13,783..............H6   26
Wangching, China....C10   17
Wanhsien, China,
90,000..............E6   17
Wankie, Rh.,
18,200..............D5   24
Wantagh, N.Y., 34,172.G2   52
Wapakoneta, Ohio,
6,756..............B3   78
Wapato, Wash., 3,137..C5   86
Wapello, Iowa, 1,745..C6   60
Wapello, co., Iowa,
46,126..............C5   60
Wappingers Falls, N.Y.,
4,447..............D7   75
War, W. Va., 3,006...D3   87
Warangal, India,
156,106..............E6   20
Ward, W. Va., 1,109...C6   87
Ward, co., N. Dak.,
47,072..............B4   77
Ward, co., Tex., 14,917.D1   84
Warden, Wash., 949...C6   86
Ward Ridge, Fla.,
1,886..............*C1   54
Wardville, La., 1,086..*C3   63
Ware, Mass., 6,650...B3   65
Ware, co., Ga., 34,219.E4   55
Wareham, Mass., 1,739.C6   65
Warehouse Point, Conn.,
1,936..............B6   52
Waren, Ger., 19,700...B6   6
Ware Shoals, S.C.,
2,671..............C3   82
Warfield, B.C., Can.,
2,212..............*E9   37
Warner Robins, Ga.,
18,633..............D3   55
Warr Acres, Okla.,
7,135..............B4   79
Warren, Ark., 6,752...D3   49
Warren, Ill., 1,470....A4   58
Warren, Ind., 1,241....C7   59
Warren, Mass., 1,616..B3   65
Warren, Mich., 89,246..F7   66
Warren, Minn., 2,007..B2   67
Warren, Ohio, 59,648..A7   78
Warren, Pa., 14,505...C3   81
Warren, R.I., 8,750...C11   52
Warren, co., Ga., 7,360.C4   55
Warren, co., Ill., 21,587.C3   58
Warren, co., Ind.,
8,545..............D3   59
Warren, co., Iowa,
20,829..............C4   60
Warren, co., Ky.,
45,491..............C3   62
Warren, co., Miss.,
42,206..............C3   68
Warren, co., Mo., 8,750.C6   69
Warren, co., N.J.,
63,220..............B3   74
Warren, co., N.Y.,
44,002..............B7   75
Warren, co., N.C.,
19,652..............A5   76
Warren, co., Ohio,
65,711..............C3   78
Warren, co., Pa.,
45,582..............C3   81
Warren, co., Tenn.,
23,102..............D8   83
Warren, co., Va.,
14,655..............C4   85
Warrensburg, Mo.,
9,689..............C4   69
Warrensburg, N.Y.,
2,240..............B7   75
Warrensville, Ohio,
10,609..............B2   78
Warrensville Heights,
Ohio, 10,609......*A6   78
Warrenton, Ga., 1,770..C4   55
Warrenton, Mo., 1,869.C6   69
Warrenton, N.C.,
1,124..............A5   76
Warrenton, Oreg.,
1,717..............A3   80
Warrenton, Va., 3,522..C5   85
Warrenville, Ill., 3,134..F2   58
Warrenville, S.C.,
1,128..............D4   82
Warrick, co., Ind.,
23,577..............H3   59
Warrington, Eng.,
75,533..............D5   4
Warrington, Fla.,
16,752..............G2   54
Warrior, Ala., 2,448...B3   46
Warrnambool, Austl.,
15,702..............G7   25
Warroad, Minn., 1,309.B3   67
Warsaw, Ill., 1,938....C2   58
Warsaw, Ind., 7,234...B6   59
Warsaw, Mo., 1,054...C4   69

Warsaw, N.Y., 3,653...C2   75
Warsaw, N.C., 2,221...B5   76
Warsaw (Warszawa), Pol.,
1,136,000......B6, m14   7
Warson Woods, Mo.,
1,746..............*C7   69
Warwick, Que., Can.,
2,487..............D6   42
Warwick, Eng., 16,032.D6   4
Warwick, N.Y.,
3,218..........D2, D6   75
Warwick, R.I., 68,504.C10   52
Warwick, co., Eng.,
2,023,289..........*D6   4
Wasatch, co., Utah,
5,308..............A6   72
Wasco, Calif., 6,841....E4   50
Wasco, co., Oreg.,
20,205..............B5   80
Waseca, Minn., 5,898..F5   67
Waseca, co., Minn.,
16,041..............F5   67
Washabaugh, co., S. Dak.,
1,042..............G4   77
Washakie, co., Wyo.,
8,883..............B5   89
Washburn, Ill., 1,064..C4   58
Washburn, Maine,
1,055..............B4   64
Washburn, Wis., 1,896.B3   88
Washburn, co., Wis.,
10,301..............C2   88
Washington, D.C., 763,956
(*2,053,600).....C1, C3   53
Washington, Ga., 4,440.C4   55
Washington, Ill., 5,919.C4   58
Washington, Ind.,
10,846..............G3   59
Washington, Iowa,
6,037..............C6   60
Washington, Kans.,
1,506..............C6   61
Washington, La., 1,291.D3   63
Washington, Mo.,
7,961..............C6   69
Washington, N.J.,
5,723..............B3   74
Washington, N.C.,
9,939..............B7   76
Washington, Pa.,
23,545..............F1   81
Washington, co., Ala.,
15,372..............D1   46
Washington, co., Ark.,
55,797..............A1   49
Washington, co., Colo.,
6,625..............B7   51
Washington, co., Fla.,
11,249..............G3   54
Washington, co., Ga.,
18,903..............C4   55
Washington, co., Idaho,
8,378..............E2   57
Washington, co., Ill.,
13,569..............E4   58
Washington, co., Ind.,
17,819..............G5   59
Washington, co., Iowa,
19,406..............C6   60
Washington, co., Kans.,
10,739..............C7   61
Washington, co., Ky.,
11,168..............C4   62
Washington, co., Maine,
32,908..............D5   64
Washington, co., Md.,
91,219..............A2   53
Washington, co., Minn.,
52,432..............E6   67
Washington, co., Miss.,
78,638..............B3   68
Washington, co., Mo.,
14,346..............D7   69
Washington, co., Nebr.,
12,103..............C9   71
Washington, co., N.Y.,
48,476..............B7   75
Washington, co., N.C.,
13,488..............B7   76
Washington, co., Ohio,
51,489..............C6   78
Washington, co., Okla.,
42,347..............A6   79
Washington, co., Oreg.,
92,237..............B3   80
Washington, co., Pa.,
217,271..............F1   81
Washington, co., R.I.,
59,054..............D10   52
Washington, co., Tenn.,
64,832..............C11   83
Washington, co., Tex.,
19,145..............D4   84
Washington, co., Utah
10,271..............C5   72
Washington, co., Vt.,
42,860..............C2   73

Washington, co., Va., 38,076.............B3 85
Washington, co., Wis., 46,119.............E5 88
Washington, par., La., 44,015.............D5 63
Washington, state, U.S., 2,853,214............ 86
Washington Court House, Ohio, 12,388........C4 78
Washington Heights, N.Y., 1,231.......*D6 75
Washington North, Pa., 2,077.............*F1 81
Washington Park, Ill., 6,601.............E3 58
Washington Terrace, Utah, 6,441.......*A5 72
Washingtonville, N.Y., 1,178.............*D6 75
Washington West, Pa., 3,951.............*F1 81
Washita, co., Okla., 18,121.............B2 79
Washoe, co., Nev., 84,743.............A2 72
Washougal, Wash., 2,672.............D3 86
Washtenaw, co., Mich., 172,440.............F7 66
Waskom, Tex., 1,336...C5 84
Watauga, co., N.C., 17,529.............A2 76
Watchung, N.J., 3,312.............*B4 74
Waterbury, Conn., 107,130 (*190,300).........C4 52
Waterbury, Vt., 2,984..C2 73
Waterford, Calif., 1,780.............*D3 50
Waterford, Ont., Can., 2,221.............E4 41
Waterford, Conn., 5,000.............D8 52
Waterford, Ire., 28,216.............D3 4
Waterford, N.Y., 2,915.C7 75
Waterford, Pa., 1,390..C1 81
Waterford, Wis., 1,500.............F1, F5 88
Waterford, co., Ire., 71,439.............*D3 4
Waterloo, Ont., Can., 21,366.............D4 41
Waterloo, Que., Can., 4,543.............D5 42
Waterloo, Ill., 3,739...E3 58
Waterloo, Ind., 1,432..B7 59
Waterloo, Iowa, 71,755 (*114,300).........B5 60
Waterloo, N.Y., 5,098..C4 75
Waterloo, Wis., 1,947..E5 88
Waterloo, co., Ont., Can., 176,754.............D4 41
Waterman, Ill., 916....B5 58
Water Proof, La., 1,412.............C4 63
Watertown, Conn., 5,500.............C4 52
Watertown, Fla., 2,109.B4 54
Watertown, Mass., 39,092.............D2 65
Watertown, Minn., 1,046.............*F5 67
Watertown, N.Y., 33,306.............B5 75
Watertown, S. Dak., 14,077.............F8 77
Watertown, Tenn., 919.A5 83
Watertown, Wis., 13,943.............E5 88
Water Valley, Miss., 3,206.............A4 68
Waterville, Que., Can., 1,330.............D6 42
Waterville, Maine, 18,695.............D3 64
Waterville, Minn., 1,623.............F5 67
Waterville, N.Y., 1,901.C5 75
Waterville, Ohio, 1,856.............A1, A4 78
Waterville, Wash., 1,013.............B5 86
Watervliet, Mich., 1,818.............F4 66
Watervliet, N.Y., 13,917.............C7 75
Watford, Ont., Can., 1,293.............E3 41
Watford City, N. Dak., 1,865.............C2 77
Watkins Glen, N.Y., 2,813.............C4 75
Watonga, Okla., 3,252..B3 79
Watonwan, co., Minn., 14,460.............F4 67
Watrous, Sask., Can., 1,461.............F3 39
Watseka, Ill., 5,219....C6 58

Watsontown, Pa., 2,431.............D8 81
Watsonville, Calif., 13,293.........C6, D3 50
Wattrelos, Fr., 41,319..B5 5
Wattsville, S.C., 1,438..B4 82
Wauchula, Fla., 3,411..E5 54
Wauconda, Ill., 3,227...E2 58
Waukegan, Ill., 55,719.........A6, E2 58
Waukesha, Wis., 30,004.............E1, F5 88
Waukesha, co., Wis., 158,249.............E5 88
Waukon, Iowa, 3,639..A6 60
Waunakee, Wis., 1,611.E4 88
Waupaca, Wis., 3,984..D4 88
Waupaca, co., Wis., 35,340.............D5 88
Waupun, Wis., 7,935...E5 88
Waurika, Okla., 1,933..C4 79
Wausau, Wis., 31,943..D4 88
Wauseon, Ohio, 4,311..A3 78
Waushara, co., Wis., 13,497.............D4 88
Wautoma, Wis., 1,466..D4 88
Wauwatosa, Wis., 56,923.............E1 88
Waverly, Ill., 1,375....D4 58
Waverly, Iowa, 6,357..B5 59
Waverly, N.Y., 5,950..C4 75
Waverly, Ohio, 3,830..C5 78
Waverly, Tenn., 2,891..A4 83
Waverly, Va., 1,601...D5 85
Waxahachie, Tex., 12,749.........B5, C4 84
Waycross, Ga., 20,944.E4 55
Wayland, Ky., 1,340...C7 62
Wayland, Mass., 2,000.D2 65
Wayland, Mich., 2,019.F5 66
Wayland, N.Y., 2,003..C3 75
Waymart, Pa., 1,106..C11 81
Wayne, Mich., 16,034..A7 66
Wayne, Nebr., 4,217...B8 71
Wayne, N.J., 29,353..*A4 74
Wayne, Pa., 10,000.............A10, F11 81
Wayne, W. Va., 1,274..C2 87
Wayne, co., Ga., 17,921.E5 55
Wayne, co., Ill., 19,008.E5 58
Wayne, co., Ind., 74,039.............E7 59
Wayne, co., Iowa, 9,800.............D4 60
Wayne, co., Ky., 14,700.............D5 62
Wayne, co., Mich., 2,666,297.........F7 66
Wayne, co., Miss., 16,258.............D5 68
Wayne, co., Mo., 8,638.D7 69
Wayne, co., Nebr., 9,959.............B8 71
Wayne, co., N.Y., 67,989.............B3 75
Wayne, co., N.C., 82,059.............B5 76
Wayne, co., Ohio, 75,497.............B6 78
Wayne, co., Pa., 28,237.............C11 81
Wayne, co., Tenn., 11,908.............B4 83
Wayne, co., Utah, 1,728.............B6 72
Wayne, co., W. Va., 38,977.............C2 87
Waynesboro, Ga., 5,359.............C4 55
Waynesboro, Miss., 3,892.............D5 68
Waynesboro, Pa., 10,427.............G6 81
Waynesboro, Tenn., 1,343.............B4 83
Waynesboro (Independent City), Va., 15,694...C4 85
Waynesburg, Ohio, 1,442.............B6 78
Waynesburg, Pa., 5,188.............G1 81
Waynesville, Mo., 2,377.............D5 69
Waynesville, N.C., 6,159.............D3 76
Waynesville, Ohio, 1,298.............C3 78
Waynoka, Okla., 1,794.A3 79
Wayzata, Minn., 3,219.............*F5 67
Weakley, co., Tenn., 24,227.............A3 83
Weatherford, Okla., 4,499.............B3 69
Weatherford, Tex., 9,759.............C4 84
Weatherly, Pa., 2,591.E10 81
Weaver, Ala., 1,401....B4 46
Weaverville, Calif., 1,736.............B2 50

Weaverville, N.C., 1,041.............D3 76
Webb, co., Tex., 64,791.F3 84
Webb City, Mo., 6,740.D3 69
Weber, co., Utah, 110,744.............A6 72
Weber City, Va., 1,274.............*B2 85
Webster, Mass., 13,680.B4 65
Webster, N.Y., 3,060..B3 75
Webster, S. Dak., 2,409.............E8 77
Webster, co., Ga., 3,247.............D2 55
Webster, co., Iowa, 47,810.............B3 60
Webster, co., Ky., 14,244.............C2 62
Webster, co., Miss., 10,580.............B4 68
Webster, co., Mo., 13,753.............D5 69
Webster, co., Nebr., 6,224.............D7 71
Webster, co., W. Va., 13,719.............C4 87
Webster, par., La., 39,701.............B2 63
Webster City, Iowa, 8,520.............B4 60
Webster Groves, Mo., 28,990.............B8 69
Webster Springs (Addison), W. Va., 1,132.......C4 87
Wedgeport, N.S., Can., 665.............F3 43
Wedowee, Ala., 917...B4 46
Weed, Calif., 3,223.....B2 50
Weed Heights, Nev., 1,092.............*B2 72
Weedon, Que., Can., 1,426.............D6 42
Weedsport, N.Y., 1,731.............B4 75
Weehawken, N.J., 13,504.............D5 74
Weeks, La., 1,138......E4 63
Weeping Water, Nebr., 1,048.............D9, E3 71
Weert, Neth., 12,900..B6 5
Weiden, Ger., 41,700..D6 6
Weifang, China, 148,900.............D8 17
Weihai, China, 45,000.D9 17
Weilheim, Ger., 12,400.E5 6
Weimar, Ger., 63,700..C5 6
Weimar, Tex., 2,006...E4 84
Weinan, China, 75,000.E6 17
Weinheim, Ger., 27,900.............D4 6
Weippe, Idaho, 600....C3 57
Weirton, W. Va., 28,201.............A2, A4 87
Weiser, Idaho, 4,208...E2 57
Weissenburg [in Bayern], Ger., 13,900.......D5 6
Weissenfels, Ger., 45,900.............C5 6
Wejherowo, Pol., 25,000.............A5 7
Welborn, Kans., 6,500..B8 61
Welch, W. Va., 5,313..D3 87
Welcome, S.C., 1,500..*B3 82
Weld, co., Colo., 72,344.A6 51
Weldon, N.C., 2,165...A6 76
Weleetka, Okla., 1,231.B5 79
Welland, Ont., Can., 36,079.............E5 41
Welland, co., Ont., Can., 164,741.............D5 41
Wellesley, Mass., 26,071.........B5, D2 65
Wellford, S.C., 1,040..B3 82
Wellington, Austl., 5,597.............F7 26
Wellington, Ont., Can., 1,064.............*C7 41
Wellington, Kans., 8,809.............E6 61
Wellington, N.Z., 123,969 (*249,532)........N15 26
Wellington, Ohio, 3,599.A5 78
Wellington, Tex., 3,137.B2 84
Wellington, Utah, 1,066.............B6 72
Wellington, co., Ont., Can., 84,702.........D4 41
Wellman, Iowa, 1,085..C6 60
Wells, B.C., Can., 740..C7 37
Wells, Minn., 2,897...G5 67
Wells, Nev., 1,071....A4 72
Wells, co., Ind., 21,220.C7 59
Wells, co., N. Dak., 9,237.............C6 77
Wellsboro, Pa., 4,369..C7 81
Wellsburg, W. Va., 5,514.........A4, B2 87
Wellston, Mo., 7,979...A8 69
Wellston, Ohio, 5,728..C5 78
Wellsville, Kans., 984..D8 61
Wellsville, Mo., 1,532..B6 69

Wellsville, N.Y., 5,967.C3 75
Wellsville, Ohio, 7,117..B7 78
Wellsville, Utah, 1,106.A6 72
Wels, Aus., 41,060.....D7 6
Welsh, La., 3,332......D3 63
Wembley, Eng., 124,843.............k11 4
Wenatchee, Wash., 16,726.............B5 86
Wenchow (Yungkia), China, 201,600......F9 17
Wendell, Idaho, 1,232..G4 57
Wendell, N.C., 1,620...B5 76
Wendham, Mass., 2,798.............A6, C3 65
Wenona, Ill., 1,005...*B4 58
Wenonah, N.J., 2,100..D2 74
Wentworth, co., Ont., Can., 358,837.........D4 41
Wentzville, Mo., 2,742.C7 69
Werdau, Ger., 24,500..C6 6
Wernersville, Pa., 1,462.............*F9 81
Wernigerode, Ger., 33,100.............C5 6
Wesconnett, Fla., 5,000.............B6 54
Wesel, Ger., 32,000....C3 6
Weslaco, Tex., 15,649..F3 84
Weslaco North, Tex., 1,049.............*F3 84
Wesleyville, Newf., Can., 1,285.............D5 44
Wesleyville, Pa., 3,534.B2 81
Wessington Springs, S. Dak., 1,488.......F7 77
Wesson, Miss., 1,157...D3 68
West, Tex., 2,352......D4 84
West Alexandria, Ohio, 1,524.............C3 78
West Allis, Wis., 68,157.............E2 88
West Amityville, N.Y., 4,000.............*E7 75
West Ausdale, Ohio, 1,354.............*B5 78
West Babylon, N.Y., 16,000.............*E3 75
West Baden Springs, Ind., 879.............G4 59
West Barrington, R.I., 4,000.............B11 52
West Baton Rouge, par., La., 14,796.........D4 63
West Belmar, N.J., 2,511.............*C4 74
West Bend, Iowa, 910..B3 60
West Bend, Wis., 9,969.E5 88
West Bengal, state, India, 34,926,279.........*D8 20
West Berlin, N.J., 3,363.............*D3 74
West Billings, Mont., 3,500.............*E8 70
West Blocton, Ala., 1,156.............B2 46
Westboro, Ont., Can., 3,450.............A9 41
Westborough, Mass., 4,011.........B4, D1 65
West Bountiful, Utah, 945.............*A6 72
West Boylston, Mass., 2,000.............B4 65
West Branch, Iowa, 1,053.............C6 60
West Branch, Mich., 2,025.............D6 66
West Bridgewater, Mass., 2,000.............B5 65
West Bridgewater, Pa., 1,292.............*E1 81
West Bromwich, Eng., 95,909.............D6 4
Westbrook, Maine, 13,820.........E2, E5 64
Westbrook, Minn., 1,012.............F3 67
West Brookfield, Mass., 1,250.............B3 65
Westbrook Park, Pa., 5,000.............*B11 81
West Brownsville, Pa., 1,907.............*F2 81
West Brunswick, N.J., 2,000.............*C4 74
West Burlington, Iowa, 2,560.............D6 60
Westbury, N.Y., 14,757.............E3 75
Westby, Wis., 1,544....E3 88
West Caldwell, N.J., 8,314.............*B4 74
West Cape May, N.J., 1,030.............F3 74
West Carroll, par., La., 14,177.............B4 63
West Carrollton, Ohio, 4,749.............C3 78
West Carthage, N.Y., 2,167.............B5 75

Westchester, Ill., 18,092.............*F3 58
West Chester, Pa., 15,705............G10 81
Westchester, co., N.Y., 808,891.............D7 75
West Chicago, Ill., 6,854................F2 58
West City, Ill., 814....E5 58
West Clarkston, Wash., 2,851...............*C8 86
West Collingswood, N.J., 2,000..............*D2 74
West Collingswood Heights, N.J., 1,100...............*D2 74
West Columbia, S.C., 6,410.................D5 82
West Columbia, Tex., 2,947............E5, G4 84
West Concord, Mass., 1,556.................B5 65
West Concord, N.C., 5,510................*B3 76
West Conshohocken, Pa., 2,254..............A11 81
West Corners, N.Y., 2,000................*C4 75
West Covina, Calif., 50,645..............*F3 50
Westdale, Ill., 1,000...*F2 58
West Decatur, Pa., 750....................E5 81
West Derry, Pa., 1,000................*F3 81
West Des Moines, Iowa, 11,949.........A7, C4 60
West Easton, Pa., 1,228...............*E11 81
West Elizabeth, Pa., 921.................*F2 81
West Ellicott, N.Y., 1,500................*C1 75
West Elmira, N.Y., 5,763................*C4 75
West End, Ark., 2,208................*C3 49
West End, Fla., 3,124.*C4 54
West End, N.Y., 1,436................*C5 75
West End Anniston, Ala., 5,485...............*B4 46
West Endicott, N.Y., 2,500................*C4 75
Westerly, R.I., 9,698..D9 52
Western, reg., Nig., 10,265,846...........G5 22
Western Australia, state, Austl., 736,629......D3 25
Western Hills, Colo., 1,500...............*B6 51
Western Peninsula, div., Ice., 11,394.......*m21 11
Westernport, Md., 3,559.................D2 53
Western Samoa, country, Oceania, 83,096............G9 2
Western Springs, Ill., 10,838..............F2 58
Westerville, Ohio, 7,011.................B5 78
West Fairview, Pa., 1,718.................F8 81
West Farmington, Maine, 500.................D2 64
West Feliciana, par., La., 12,395..............D4 63
Westfield, Ala., 2,000..E4 46
Westfield, Ind., 1,217..D5 59
Westfield, Mass., 26,302..............B2 65
Westfield, N.J., 31,447...............B4 74
Westfield, N.Y., 3,878..C1 75
Westfield, Pa., 1,333...C6 81
Westfield, Wis., 919....E4 88
West Flanders, prov., Bel., 1,068,976..........*B5 5
West Frankfort, Ill., 9,027................F5 58
Westgate, Fla., 2,500..F6 54
West Glens Falls, N.Y., 2,725................*B7 75
West Grove, Pa., 1,607...............G10 81
West Ham, Eng., 157,186............k13 4
Westhampton Beach, N.Y., 1,460.........D4 75
West Hartford, Conn., 62,382..............B6 52
West Hartlepool, Eng., 77,073................C6 4
West Hartsville, S.C., 2,427................*C7 82
West Haven, Conn., 43,002..............D5 52
West Haverstraw, N.Y., 5,020................*D7 75

West Hazleton, Pa., 6,278................E9 81
West Helena, Ark., 8,385................C5 49
West Hempstead, N.Y., 15,800...............G2 52
West Hill, Ont., Can., 1,800............D5, E7 41
West Hillsboro, N.C., 1,065...............*A4 76
West Hollywood, Calif., 28,870.............*F6 50
West Hollywood, Fla., 52,000...............E3 54
West Homestead, Pa., 4,155...............*F2 81
West Irian, Indon. dep., Asia, 700,000........F9 19
West Islip, N.Y., 22,300..............*G4 75
West Jefferson, N.C., 1,000...............A2 76
West Jefferson, Ohio, 2,774............C1, C4 78
West Jordan, Utah, 3,009............A5, D2 72
West Junction, Tenn., 4,000............B1, E8 83
West Kankakee, Ill., 3,197................B6 58
West Kingston, R.I., 900................D10 52
West Kittanning, Pa., 1,101...............*E3 81
West La Crosse, Wis., 1,440...............*E2 88
West Lafayette, Ind., 12,680..............D4 59
West Lafayette, Ohio, 1,476................B6 78
Westlake, La., 3,311...D2 63
Westlake, Ohio, 12,906.B1 78
Westlands, Mass., 2,100................*A5 65
West Lanham Hills, Md., 1,000................*C4 53
West Lawn, Pa., 2,059.F10 81
West Lebanon, Pa., 1,054...............*F9 81
West Leechburg, Pa., 1,323...............*E2 81
West Leisenring, Pa., 800.................G2 81
West Liberty, Iowa, 2,042................C6 60
West Liberty, Ky., 1,165................C6 62
West Liberty, Ohio, 1,522................B4 78
West Liberty, W. Va., 1,500................B2 87
West Linn, Oreg., 3,933............B2, B4 80
Westlock, Alta., Can., 1,838................B4 38
West Logan, W. Va., 855................*D3 87
West Long Branch, N.J., 5,337................C4 74
West Lorne, Ont., Can., 1,070................E3 41
West Lothian, co., Scot., 92,764..............*C5 4
West Manayunk, Pa., 1,900...............*B11 81
West Marion, N.C., 1,600...............*D4 76
West Mayfield, Pa., 2,201...............*E1 81
Westmeath, co., Ire., 52,861...............*D3 4
West Medway, Mass., 1,818............B5, E1 65
West Melbourne, Fla., 2,266...............*D6 54
West Memphis, Ark., 19,374..............B5 49
West Miami, Fla., 5,296............F3, G6 54
West Middlesex, Pa., 1,301................D1 81
West Mifflin, Pa., 27,289..............F2 81
West Milton, Ohio, 2,972................C3 78
West Milwaukee, Wis., 5,043................E2 88
Westminster, Calif., 25,750..............*F5 50
Westminster, Colo., 13,850..............A6 51
Westminster, Md., 6,123................A4 53
Westminster, Mass., 1,047................A4 65
Westminster, S.C., 2,413................B1 82
West Monroe, La., 15,215..............B3 63
Westmont, Ill., 5,997...F2 58

Westmont, N.J., 14,000..............D2 74
Westmont, Pa., 6,573..F4 81
Westmoreland, co., Pa., 352,629............F2 81
Westmoreland, co., Va., 11,042.............C6 85
Westmoreland City, Pa., 1,300...............*F2 81
Westmorland, Calif., 1,404................F6 50
Westmorland, co., N.B., Can., 93,679........C5 43
Westmorland, co., Eng., 67,222..............*C5 4
Westmount, Que., Can., 25,012.............*D9 42
West Mystic, Conn., 3,268................D9 52
West Newton, Pa., 3,982................F2 81
West New York, N.J., 35,547..............D5 74
West Nyack, N.Y., 3,000................*D7 75
Weston, Ont., Can., 9,715................E6 41
Weston, Conn., 3,000..E3 52
Weston, Mass., 4,000..D2 65
Weston, Mo., 1,057............B3, D1 69
Weston, Ohio, 1,075...A4 78
Weston, W. Va., 8,754.B4 87
Weston, co., Wyo., 7,929................B8 89
Weston-super-Mare, Eng., 43,923..............E5 4
West Orange, N.J., 39,895..............B4 74
West Orange, Tex., 4,848...............*D6 84
Westover, W. Va., 4,749............A7, B5 87
West Palm Beach, Fla., 56,208 (*157,200)....F6 54
West Paterson, N.J., 7,602...............*B4 74
West Pensacola, Fla., 25,000..............G2 54
West Pittston, Pa., 6,998................B8 81
West Plains, Mo., 5,836................E6 69
West Point, Ga., 4,610.D1 55
West Point, Ky., 2,005.C4 62
West Point, Miss., 8,550................B5 68
West Point, Nebr., 2,921................C9 71
West Point, N.Y., 4,000............D2, D7 75
West Point, Va., 1,678.D6 85
Westport, Conn., 20,955..............E3 52
West Portland, Oreg., 2,000...............*B4 80
West Portland Park, Oreg., 2,500...............*B4 80
West Portsmouth, Ohio, 3,100................D4 78
West Pueblo, Colo., 1,700...............*C6 51
West Reading, Pa., 4,938...............F10 81
West Roanoke Rapids, N.C., 2,000.........*A6 76
West Rockingham, N.C., 1,128...............*C4 76
West Rutland, Vt., 2,302................D1 73
West Sacramento, Calif., 10,000.............*A6 50
West St. Paul, Minn., 13,101..............E7 67
West Salem, Ill., 956...E5 58
West Salem, Ohio, 1,017................B5 78
West Salem, Wis., 1,707................E2 88
West Sayville, N.Y., 3,000................G4 52
West Seneca, N.Y., 33,644..............*C2 75
West Slope, Oreg., 9,000................B2 80
West Springfield, Mass., 24,924.............B2 65
West Sterling, Ill., 1,430...............*B4 58
West Summerland, B.C., Can., 2,500........E8 37
West Terre Haute, Ind., 3,006................F3 59
West Union, Iowa, 2,551................B6 60
West Union, Ohio, 1,762................D4 78
West Union, W. Va., 1,186............B4, B6 87

West Unity, Ohio, 1,192...............A3 78
West University Place, Tex., 14,628........F4 84
West Van Lear, Ky., 900.................C7 62
Westview, B.C., Can., 4,000................E5 37
West View, Ohio, 1,303.B1 78
West View, Pa., 8,079..A5 81
West View Park, Tenn., 1,000..............C11 83
Westville, N.S., Can., 4,159................D7 43
Westville, Ill., 3,497...C6 58
Westville, N.J., 4,951..D2 74
Westville Grove, N.J., 2,500...............*D2 74
West Virginia, state, U.S., 1,860,421............ 87
West Warren, Mass., 1,124................B3 65
West Warwick, R.I., 21,414..............C10 52
Westwego, La., 9,815............C7, E5 63
West Wenatchee, Wash., 2,518...............*B5 86
West Winfield, N.Y., 960.................C5 75
West Winter Haven, Fla., 5,050.............*D5 54
Westwood, Calif., 1,209................B3 50
Westwood, Kans., 2,040................B9 61
Westwood, Ky., 6,000..B7 62
Westwood, Mass., 5,800............B5, D2 65
Westwood, Mich., 6,500...............*F5 66
Westwood, N.J., 9,046............B4, D5 74
Westwood Lakes, Fla., 22,517..............F3 54
Westworth Village, Tex., 3,321..............*C4 84
West Wyalong, Austl., 2,399................F6 26
West Wyoming, Pa., 3,166................B8 81
West Wyomissing, Pa., 2,500...............*F9 81
West Yarmouth, Mass., 1,365................C7 65
West York, Pa., 5,526..G8 81
West Yuma, Ariz., 2,781...............*C1 48
Wetaskiwin, Alta., Can., 5,300................C4 38
Wethersfield, Conn., 20,561..............C6 52
Wetumka, Okla., 1,798.B5 79
Wetumpka, Ala., 3,672.C3 46
Wetzel, co., W. Va., 19,347..............B4 87
Wetzlar, Ger., 37,300..C4 6
Wewahitchka, Fla., 1,436................B1 54
Wewoka, Okla., 5,954..B5 79
Wexford, Ire., 11,328..D3 4
Wexford, co., Ire., 83,308..............*D3 4
Wexford, co., Mich., 18,466..............D5 66
Weyauwega, Wis., 1,239................D5 88
Weyburn, Sask., Can., 9,101................H4 39
Weymouth, N.S., Can., 671.................E4 43
Weymouth, Eng., 40,962..............E5 4
Weymouth, Mass., 48,177.........B6, D3 65
Whangarei, N.Z., 17,880.............K15 26
Wharton, N.J., 5,006...B3 74
Wharton, Tex., 5,734..E4 84
Wharton, W. Va., 1,055................D6 87
Wharton, co., Tex., 38,152..............E4 84
Wharton West, Tex., 1,609...............*E4 84
What Cheer, Iowa, 956.C5 60
Whatcom, co., Wash., 70,317.............A4 86
Wheatland, Wyo., 2,350................C8 89
Wheatland, co., Mont., 3,026................D7 70
Wheatley, Ont., Can., 1,362................E2 41
Wheaton, Ill., 24,312...........B5, F2 58
Wheaton, Md., 54,635.*B3 53
Wheaton, Minn., 2,102.E2 67
Wheat Ridge, Colo., 21,619..............*B5 51
Wheeler, Tex., 1,174...B2 84

Wheeler, co., Ga.,
5,342...............D4 55
Wheeler, co., Nebr.,
1,297...............C7 71
Wheeler, co., Oreg.,
2,722...............C6 80
Wheeler, co., Tex.,
7,947...............B2 84
Wheelersburg, Ohio,
2,682...............D5 78
Wheeling, Ill., 9,627..*A6 58
Wheeling, W. Va., 53,400
(*126,600)......A4, B2 87
Wheelwright, Ky.,
1,518...............C7 62
Whippany, N.J., 6,000.B4 74
Whitaker, Pa., 2,130..*F2 81
Whitakers, N.C., 1,004.A6 76
Whitby, Ont., Can.,
14,685..............D6 41
Whitby, Eng., 11,662..C6 4
White, co., Ark., 32,745.B4 49
White, co., Ga., 6,935..B3 55
White, co., Ill., 19,373..E5 58
White, co., Ind., 19,709.C4 59
White, co., Tenn.,
15,577..............D8 83
White Bear Lake, Minn.,
12,849..........E5, E7 67
White Castle, La.,
2,253..........B5, D4 63
White City, Fla., 600..C1 54
White Cloud, Mich.,
1,001...............E5 66
White Deer, Tex.,
1,057...............B2 84
Whitefield, N.H., 1,244.C4 73
Whitefish, Mont.,
2,965...............B2 70
Whitefish Bay, Wis.,
18,390..............E2 88
White Hall, Ill., 3,012..D3 58
Whitehall, Mich., 2,590.E4 66
Whitehall, Mont., 898.*D4 70
Whitehall, N.Y., 4,016.B7 75
Whitehall, Ohio, 20,818.C5 78
Whitehall, Pa.,
16,075........B5, *F1 81
Whitehall, Wis., 1,446..D2 88
Whitehaven, Eng.,
27,541..............C5 4
White Haven, Pa.,
1,778..............D10 81
Whitehaven, Tenn.,
13,894..............E8 83
Whitehorse, Yukon, Can.,
5,031...............D6 36
Whitehouse, Ohio,
1,135..........A1, A4 78
White Lake, Mich.,
800................*F7 66
Whiteland, Ind., 1,368.E5 59
White Oak, N.C., 150..C5 76
White Oak, Ohio,
5,000...............D2 78
White Oak, Pa.,
9,047.........B6, *F2 81
White Oak, Tex.,
1,250...............*C5 84
White Pigeon, Mich.,
1,399...............G5 81
White Pine, Tenn.,
1,035..............C10 83
White Pine, co., Nev.,
9,808...............B4 72
White Plains, N.Y.,
50,485.........D3, D7 75
White River Junction, Vt.,
2,546...............D3 73
White Rock, B.C., Can.,
6,463.........B10, E6 37
White Salmon, Wash.,
1,590...............D4 86
Whitesboro, N.Y.,
4,784...............*B5 75
Whitesboro, Tex.,
2,485...............C4 84
Whitesburg, Ky.,
1,774...............C7 62
Whites Creek, Tenn.,
100................E9 83
White Settlement, Tex.,
11,513.............*B5 84
Whiteside, co., Ill.,
59,887..............B3 58
White Stone, Va., 395..D6 85
White Sulphur Springs,
Mont., 1,519.......D6 70
White Sulphur Springs,
W. Va., 2,676.......D4 87
Whitesville, W. Va.,
774................D6 87
Whiteville, N.C., 4,683.C5 76
Whitewater, Wis.,
6,380...............F5 88
Whitewright, Tex.,
1,315...............C4 84
Whitfield, co., Ga.,
42,109..............B2 55
Whiting, Ind., 8,137..A3 59
Whiting, Wis., 1,193...D4 88

Whitinsville, Mass.,
5,102...............B4 65
Whitley, co., Ind.,
20,954..............B6 59
Whitley, co., Ky.,
25,815..............D5 62
Whitley City, Ky.,
1,034...............D5 62
Whitman, Mass.,
10,485..............B6 65
Whitman, co., Wash.,
31,263..............B8 86
Whitmire, S.C., 2,663..B4 82
Whitmore City, Haw.,
1,820................f9 56
Whitnel, N.C., 1,232..A2 76
Whitney, Idaho,
13,603..............F2 57
Whitney, S.C., 2,502..B4 82
Whitney, Tex., 1,050..D4 84
Whitney Point, N.Y.,
1,049...............C5 75
Whittier, Calif.,
33,663.........F2, F4 50
Whittier Downs, Calif.,
7,000...............*F4 50
Whitwell, Tenn., 1,857.D8 83
Wiarton, Ont., Can.,
2,138...............C3 41
Wibaux, co., Mont.,
1,698..............D12 70
Wichita, Kans., 254,698
(*346,200)......B5, E6 61
Wichita, Oreg., 6,000..*B4 80
Wichita, co., Kans.,
2,765...............D2 61
Wichita, co., Tex.,
123,528.............B3 84
Wichita Falls, Tex.,
101,724 (*116,900)...C3 84
Wickenburg, Ariz.,
2,445...............C2 48
Wickett, Tex., 900.....D1 84
Wickliffe, Ky., 917.....A2 62
Wickliffe, Ohio,
15,760.........A6, B2 78
Wickliffe, Ohio, 6,000.*A7 78
Wicklow, co., Ire.,
58,473.............*D3 4
Wicomico, co., Md.,
49,050..............D6 53
Wiconisco, Pa., 1,402...E8 81
Wielun, Pol., 10,500...C5 7
Wiener Neustadt, Aus.,
33,845..............E8 6
Wiesbaden, Ger.,
253,300.............C4 6
Wiggins, Miss., 1,591..E4 68
Wigtown, co., Scot.,
29,107.............*C4 4
Wilbarger, co., Tex.,
17,748..............B3 84
Wilber, Nebr., 1,358...D9 71
Wilberforce, Ohio,
1,800...............C4 78
Wilbur, Wash., 1,138..B7 86
Wilburton, Okla., 1,772.C6 79
Wilcox, co., Ala.,
18,739..............D2 46
Wilcox, co., Ga., 7,905..E3 55
Wilden, Pa., 1,787...*E11 81
Wilder, Vt., 1,322.....D3 73
Wildwood, Fla., 2,170..D4 54
Wildwood, N.J., 4,690..F3 74
Wildwood, Pa., 2,500..*E2 81
Wildwood Crest, N.J.,
3,011...............F3 74
Wilhelm-Pieck-Stadt
Guben, Ger., 22,500..C7 6
Wilhelmshaven, Ger.,
100,200.............B4 6
Wikes, co., Ga., 10,961.C4 55
Wikes, co., N.C.,
45,269..............A2 76
Wilkes-Barre, Pa., 63,551
(*250,700)......B8, D10 81
Wilkesboro, N.C.,
1,568...............A2 76
Wilkie, Sask., Can.,
1,612...............E1 39
Wilkin, co., Minn.,
10,650..............D2 67
Wilkinsburg, Pa.,
30,066.........B6, F2 81
Wilkinson, co., Ga.,
9,250...............D3 55
Wilkinson, co., Miss.,
13,235..............D2 68
Will, co., Ill., 191,617..B6 58
Willacoochee, Ga.,
1,061...............E3 55
Willacy, co., Tex.,
20,084..............F4 84
Willamina, Oreg., 960..C3 80
Willard, Ohio, 5,457...A5 78
Willcox, Ariz., 2,441..C4 48
Willemstad, Neth.
Antilles, 44,062.....A4 32
Willesden, Eng.,
170,835.......E6, k11 4
Williams, Ariz., 3,559..B2 48

Williams, Calif., 1,370..C2 50
Williams, co., N. Dak.,
22,051..............B2 77
Williams, co., Ohio,
29,968..............A3 78
Williams Bay, Wis.,
1,347...............F5 88
Williamsburg, Iowa,
1,342...............C5 60
Williamsburg, Ky.,
3,478...............D5 62
Williamsburg, Ohio,
1,956...............C3 78
Williamsburg, Pa.,
1,792...............F5 81
Williamsburg
(Independent
City), Va., 6,832....D6 85
Williamsburg, co., S.C.,
40,932..............D8 82
Williams Lake, B.C., Can.,
2,120..........C6, E3 37
Williamson, N.Y.,
1,690...............B3 75
Williamson, W. Va.,
6,746...............D2 87
Williamson, co., Ill.,
46,117..............F5 58
Williamson, co., Tenn.,
25,267..............A5 83
Williamson, co., Tex.,
35,044..............D4 84
Williamsport, Ind.,
1,353...............D3 59
Williamsport, Md.,
1,853...............A2 53
Williamsport, Pa.,
41,967..............D7 81
Williamston, Mich.,
2,214...............F6 66
Williamston, N.C.,
6,924...............B6 76
Williamston, S.C.,
3,721...............B3 82
Williamstown, Ky.,
1,611...............B5 62
Williamstown, Mass.,
5,428...............A1 65
Williamstown, N.J.,
2,722...............D3 74
Williamstown, Pa.,
2,097...............E8 81
Williamstown, W. Va.,
2,632...............B3 87
Williamsville, N.Y.,
6,316...............C2 75
Willimantic, Conn.,
13,881..............C8 52
Willis Beach, Nebr.,
~100...............B9 71
Williston, Fla., 1,582..C4 54
Williston, N. Dak.,
11,866..............B2 77
Williston, S.C.,
2,722..............*E5 82
Williston Park, N.Y.,
8,255...............G2 52
Willits, Calif., 3,410...C2 50
Willmar, Minn., 10,417.E3 67
Willoughby, Ohio,
15,058..............A6 79
Willow Brook, Calif.,
22,000.............*F2 50
Willowdale, Ont., Can.,
9,000..........D5, E6 41
Willow Grove, Pa.,
10,000........A11, F11 81
Willowick, Ohio,
18,749..............B2 78
Willow Run, Mich.,
4,100..............*F7 66
Willows, Calif., 4,139..C2 50
Willow Springs, Ill.,
2,348...............F2 58
Willow Springs, Mo.,
1,913...............E6 69
Wills Point, Tex.,
2,281..............*C5 84
Wilmer, Tex., 1,785....B6 84
Wilmerding, Pa., 4,349.B6 81
Wilmette, Ill.,
28,268.........A6, E3 58
Wilmington, Del., 95,827
(*318,700)..........A6 53
Wilmington, Ill., 4,210.B5 58
Wilmington, Mass.,
2,250.........A5, C2 65
Wilmington, N.C.,
44,013..............C6 76
Wilmington, Ohio,
8,915...............C4 78
Wilmington Manor, Del.,
2,200..............*A6 53
Wilmore, Ky., 2,773...C5 62
Wilson, Ark., 1,191....B5 49
Wilson, Conn., 2,500..B6 52
Wilson, Kans., 905....D5 61
Wilson, N.C., 28,753..B6 76
Wilson, N.Y., 1,320...B2 75
Wilson, Okla., 1,647...C4 79
Wilson, Pa., 8,465....E11 81

Wilson, co., Kans.,
13,077..............E8 61
Wilson, co., N.C.,
57,716..............B6 76
Wilson, co., Tenn.,
27,668..............A5 83
Wilson, co., Tex.,
13,267..............E3 84
Wilton, Conn., 3,500...E3 52
Wilton, Maine, 1,761..D2 64
Wilton, N.H., 1,425....F4 73
Wilton Junction (Wilton),
Iowa, 1,750........C6 60
Wilton Manor, Fla.,
8,257..............*F6 54
Wiltshire, co., Eng.,
442,753.............*E6 4
Wimbledon, Eng.,
56,994.............m12 4
Winamac, Ind., 2,375..B4 59
Winchendon, Mass.,
3,839...............A3 65
Winchester, Ont., Can.,
1,429...............B9 41
Winchester, Eng.,
28,643..............E6 4
Winchester, Ill., 1,657..D3 58
Winchester, Ind., 5,742.D8 59
Winchester, Ky.,
10,187..............C5 62
Winchester, Mass.,
19,376..............C2 65
Winchester, Mo.,
1,299..............*B7 69
Winchester, Nev., 600..C4 72
Winchester, Tenn.,
4,760...............B5 83
Winchester (Independent
City), Va., 15,110....B4 85
Windber, Pa., 6,994...F4 81
Winder, Ga., 5,555....C3 55
Windfall, Ind., 1,135...D6 59
Windgap, Pa., 1,930..E11 81
Windham, Ohio, 3,777.A6 78
Windham, co., Conn.,
68,572..............B8 52
Windham, co., Vt.,
29,776..............F2 74
Windhoek, S.W. Afr.,
36,051..............E3 24
Wind Lake, Wis.,
1,305...............F5 88
Windom, Minn., 3,691.G3 67
Windsor, Newf., Can.,
5,505...............D4 44
Windsor, N.S., Can.,
3,823...............E5 43
Windsor, Ont., Can.,
114,367 (*193,365)...E1 41
Windsor, Que., Can.,
6,589...............D5 42
Windsor, Colo., 1,509.*A6 51
Windsor, Conn., 12,000.B6 52
Windsor, Ill., 1,021....D5 58
Windsor, Mo., 2,714...C4 69
Windsor, N.C., 1,813..B7 76
Windsor, Pa., 1,029...G8 81
Windsor, Vt., 3,256....E3 73
Windsor, co., Vt.,
42,483..............D2 73
Windsor Heights, Iowa,
4,715...............A7 60
Windsor Hills, Calif.,
3,500..............*F2 50
Windsor Locks, Conn.,
11,411..............B6 52
Windward, is., N.A....o16 35
Windy Hill, S.C.,
2,201..............*C8 82
Windy Hills, Ky.,
1,371..............*H6 62
Winfield, Ala., 2,907...B2 46
Winfield, Ill., 1,575...*B5 58
Winfield, Kans., 11,117.E7 61
Winfield, N.J., 2,458..*E4 74
Wingate, N.C., 1,304...C3 76
Wingham, Ont., Can.,
2,922...............D3 41
Wink, Tex., 1,863....D1 84
Winkelman, Ariz.,
1,123...............C3 48
Winkler, Man., Can.,
2,529...............E3 40
Winkler, co., Tex.,
13,652..............D1 84
Winn, par., La., 16,034.C3 63
Winneba, Ghana,
15,171..............G4 22
Winnebago, Ill., 1,059.A4 58
Winnebago, Minn.,
2,088...............G4 67
Winnebago, co., Ill.,
209,765.............A4 58
Winnebago, co., Iowa,
13,099..............A4 60
Winnebago, co., Wis.,
107,928.............D5 88
Winneconne, Wis.,
1,273...............D5 88
Winnemucca, Nev.,
3,453...............A3 72

Winner, S. Dak., 3,705.G6   77
Winneshiek, co., Iowa,
  21,651...............A6   60
Winnetka, Ill.,
  13,368.........A6, E3   58
Winnfield, La., 7,022...C3   63
Winnie, Tex., 1,114...*E5   84
Winnipeg, Man., Can.,
  265,429 (*475,989)...E3   40
Winnipegosis, Man., Can.,
  980...............D2   40
Winnsboro, La., 4,437.B4   63
Winnsboro, S.C., 3,479.C5   82
Winnsboro, Tex., 2,675.C5   84
Winnsboro Mills, S.C.,
  2,411..............*B5   82
Winona, Minn., 24,895.F7   67
Winona, Miss., 4,282..B4   68
Winona, co., Minn.,
  40,937.............F7   72
Winona Lake, Ind.,
  1,928..............B6   59
Winooski, Vt., 7,420...C1   73
Winschoten, Neth.,
  16,600.............A7   5
Winslow, Ariz., 8,862..B3   48
Winslow, Ind., 1,089...H3   59
Winslow, Maine, 3,640.D3   64
Winslow, Wash., 919..D1   86
Winsted, Conn., 1,836..B4   52
Winsted, Minn., 1,163..F4   67
Winston, Fla., 3,323..D4   54
Winston, Oreg., 2,395.*D3   80
Winston, co., Ala.,
  14,858.............A2   46
Winston, co., Miss.,
  19,246.............B4   68
Winston-Salem, N.C.,
  111,135 (*185,700)...A3   76
Winter Garden, Fla.,
  5,513.............D5   54
Winter Haven, Fla.,
  16,277.............D5   54
Winter Park, Fla.,
  17,162.............D5   54
Winters, Calif.,
  1,700.........A5, C3   50
Winters, Tex., 3,266...D3   84
Winterset, Iowa, 3,639.C3   60
Wintersville, Ohio,
  3,597..............B7   78
Winterthur, Switz.,
  80,352.............E4   6
Winterton, Newf., Can.,
  808...............E5   44
Winterville, N.C.,
  1,418..............B6   76
Winthrop, Maine,
  2,260.............D3   64
Winthrop, Mass.,
  20,303.........B6, D3   65
Winthrop, Minn., 1,381.F4   67
Winthrop Harbor, Ill.,
  3,848.............A6   58
Wirt, co., W. Va.,
  4,391..............B3   87
Wisbech, Eng., 17,512..D7   4
Wiscasset, Maine, 950..D3   64
Wisconsin, state, U.S.,
  3,951,777..........   88
Wisconsin Dells, Wis.,
  2,105.............E4   88
Wisconsin Rapids, Wis.,
  15,042.............D4   88
Wise, Va., 2,614......B2   85
Wise, co., Tex., 17,012.C4   84
Wise, co., Va., 43,579..B2   85
Wishek, N. Dak.,
  1,290.............D6   77
Wismar, Ger., 55,400..B5   6
Wisner, La., 1,254....C4   63
Wisner, Nebr.,.1,192...C9   71
Withamsville, Ohio,
  2,811.............A7   78
Witt, Ill., 1,101......D4   58
Wittenberg, Ger.,
  45,700.............C6   6
Wittenberge, Ger.,
  31,600.............B5   6
Wixom, Mich., 1,531...A7   66
Wloclawek, Pol.,
  63,000.............B5   7
Woburn, Mass.,
  31,214........B5, C2   65
Wolcott, Conn., 1,500..C5   52
Wolcott, N.Y., 1,641..B4   75

Wolfe, co., Que., Can.,
  18,335...........D6   42
Wolfe, co., Ky., 6,534..C6   62
Wolfeboro, N.H.,
  1,557.............D5   73
Wolfe City, Tex.,
  1,317.............C4   84
Wolfenbüttel, Ger.,
  38,100.............B5   6
Wolf Lake, Mich.,
  2,525.............E4   66
Wolf Point, Mont.,
  3,585.............B11   70
Wolfsburg, Ger.,
  64,600.............B5   6
Wolfville, N.S., Can.,
  2,413.............D5   43
Wollongong, Austl.,
  131,764............F9   25
Wolseley, Sask., Can.,
  1,031.............G4   39
Wolverhampton, Eng.,
  150,385............D5   4
Wolverine Lake, Mich.,
  2,404.............*F7   66
Wolverton, Eng.,
  13,116.............D6   4
Womelsdorf, Pa., 1,471.F9   81
Wonder Lake, Ill.,
  3,543.............A5   58
Wŏnsan, Kor.,
  112,952............G3   18
Wood, co., Ohio,
  72,596.............A4   78
Wood, co., Tex.,
  17,653.............C5   84
Wood, co., W. Va.,
  78,331.............B3   87
Wood, co., Wis., 59,105.D3   88
Woodbine, Iowa, 1,304.C2   60
Woodbine, N.J., 2,823.E3   74
Woodbine, Tenn.,
  11,500..........A5, E9   83
Woodbourne, N.Y.,
  900..............D6   75
Woodbridge, Ont., Can.,
  2,315.........D5, E6   41
Woodbridge, Conn.,
  5,182.............D4   52
Woodbridge, N.J.,
  17,000.........B4, E4   74
Woodbridge, Va.,
  1,100.............C5   85
Woodburn, Oreg.,
  3,120.........B2, B4   80
Woodbury, Conn.,
  1,000.............C4   52
Woodbury, Ga., 1,230..D2   55
Woodbury, N.J.,
  12,453.............D2   74
Woodbury, N.Y.,
  1,500.............*E7   75
Woodbury, Tenn.,
  1,562.............B5   83
Woodbury, co., Iowa,
  107,849............B1   60
Woodbury Heights, N.J.,
  1,723.............*D2   74
Woodcliff Lake, N.J.,
  2,742.............C5   74
Woodcroft, Ind.,
  2,000.............*E5   59
Wood Dale, Ill., 4,424.*B5   58
Woodford, Eng.,
  61,250............k13   4
Woodford, co., Ill.,
  24,579.............C4   58
Woodford, co., Ky.,
  11,913.............B5   62
Wood Green, Eng.,
  47,897............k12   4
Woodlake, Calif.,
  2,623.............D4   50
Woodland, Calif.,
  13,524.........A6, C3   50
Woodland, Maine,
  1,393.............C5   64
Woodland, Pa., 900...E5   81
Woodland, Wash.,
  1,336.............D3   86
Woodland Beach, Mich.,
  1,944.............*G7   66
Woodlawn, Ky., 1,688..A2   62
Woodlawn, Md.,
  6,000.............*B4   53

Woodlawn, Md.,
  3,000.............*C4   53
Woodlawn, Ohio, 3,007.D2   78
Woodlawn Beach, N.Y.,
  1,800.............C2   75
Woodlawn Orchards,
  Mich., 2,000......*F6   66
Woodlawn Park, Ky.,
  1,137.............*H6   62
Woodley Hills, Va.,
  2,000.............*A5   85
Woodlyn, Pa., 6,000.*B10   81
Wood-Lynne, N.J.,
  3,128.............D2   74
Woodmere, N.Y.,
  14,011.............G2   52
Wood-Ridge, N.J.,
  7,964.............D5   74
Woodridge, N.Y.,
  1,034.............D6   75
Wood River, Ill.,
  11,694.............E3   58
Woodruff, S.C., 3,679..B3   82
Woodruff, co., Ark.,
  13,954.............B4   49
Woodruff Place, Ind.,
  1,501.............H8   59
Woods, co., Okla.,
  11,932.............A3   79
Woodsboro, Tex., 2,081.E4   84
Woods Cross, Utah,
  1,098.............C2   72
Woodsfield, Ohio,
  2,956.............C6   79
Woodside, Calif.,
  3,592.............*D2   50
Woodson, co., Kans.,
  5,423.............E8   61
Woodson Terrace, Mo.,
  6,048.............*C7   69
Woodstock, N.B., Can.,
  4,305.............C2   43
Woodstock, Ont., Can.,
  20,486.............D4   41
Woodstock, Ill., 8,897..A5   58
Woodstock, Vt., 1,415..D2   73
Woodstock, Va., 2,083..C4   85
Woodstown, N.J.,
  2,942.............D2   74
Woodsville, N.H.,
  1,596.............C3   73
Woodville, Calif.,
  1,045.............*D4   50
Woodville, Miss., 1,856.D2   68
Woodville, Ohio,
  1,700.........A2, A4   78
Woodville, Tex., 1,920.D5   84
Woodward, Ala.,
  1,000.........B3, E4   46
Woodward, Iowa, 967..C4   60
Woodward, Okla.,
  7,747.............A2   79
Woodward, co., Okla.,
  13,902.............A2   79
Woodway, Tex.,
  1,244.............*D4   84
Woolwich, Eng., 146,397
  (part of London)...m13   4
Woonsocket, R.I.,
  47,080............A10   52
Woonsocket, S. Dak.,
  1,035.............F7   77
Wooster, Ohio, 17,046..B6   78
Worcester, Eng.,
  65,865.............D5   4
Worcester, Mass., 186,587
  (*316,200).........B4   65
Worcester, N.Y., 799..C6   75
Worcester, S. Afr.,
  32,274.............G3   24
Worcester, co., Eng.,
  568,642............*D5   4
Worcester, co., Md.,
  23,733.............D7   53
Worcester, co., Mass.,
  583,228............A3   65
Worden, Ill., 1,060....E4   58
Workington, Eng.,
  29,507.............C5   4
Worland, Wyo., 5,806..A5   89
World, 2,620,000,000.....   2
Wormleysburg, Pa.,
  1,794.............*F8   81
Worms, Ger., 62,400...D4   6
Worth, Ill., 9,097.....*F3   58

Worth, co., Ga., 16,682.E3   55
Worth, co., Iowa,
  10,259.............A4   60
Worth, co., Mo., 3,936.A3   69
Wortham, Tex., 1,087..D4   84
Worthing, Eng., 80,143.E6   4
Worthington, Ind.,
  1,635.............F4   59
Worthington, Ky.,
  1,235.............B7   62
Worthington, Minn.,
  9,015.............G3   67
Worthington, Ohio,
  9,239.........B4, C2   78
Wrangell, Alsk.,
  1,315........D13, m23   47
Wray, Colo., 2,082....A8   51
Wrens, Ga., 1,628....C4   55
Wrentham, Mass.,
  1,790.............B5   65
Wrexham, Wales,
  35,427.............D5   4
Wright, co., Iowa,
  19,447.............B4   60
Wright, co., Minn.,
  29,935.............E4   67
Wright, co., Mo.,
  14,183.............D5   69
Wright City, Okla.,
  1,161.............C6   79
Wrightstown, N.J.,
  4,846.............C3   74
Wrightsville, Ga.,
  2,056.............D4   55
Wrightsville, Pa.,
  2,345.............F8   81
Wrightview, Ohio,
  2,500.............*C3   78
Wroclaw (Breslau), Pol.,
  429,000............C4   7
Wuchow (Tsangwu),
  China, 110,800......G7   17
Wuhan, China,
  2,146,000..........E7   17
Wuhu, China, 242,100..E8   17
Wuppertal, Ger.,
  420,700............C3   6
Württemberg, reg.,
  Ger...............D4   6
Würzburg, Ger.,
  116,900............D4   6
Wurzen, Ger., 23,500..C6   6
Wusih, China, 613,000.E9   17
Wusu, China, 10,000...C1   17
Wyandanch, N.Y.,
  5,000.............*E7   75
Wyandot, co., Ohio,
  21,648.............B4   78
Wyandotte, Mich.,
  43,519.........A7, F7   66
Wyandotte, co., Kans.,
  185,495............C9   61
Wyckoff, N.J.,
  11,205............*A4   74
Wylie, Tex., 1,804...*C4   88
Wymore, Nebr., 1,975..D9   71
Wyncote, Pa., 6,000.*A11   81
Wyndmoor, Pa.,
  5,800.............*A11   81
Wynne, Ark., 4,922...B5   49
Wynne Wood, Okla.,
  2,509.............C4   79
Wynnewood, Pa.,
  7,200.............*B11   81
Wynyard, Sask., Can.,
  1,686.........C1, F3   39
Wyoming, Del., 1,172..B6   53
Wyoming, Ill., 1,559...B4   58
Wyoming, Mich.,
  45,829.............*F5   66
Wyoming, Minn., 435..E6   67
Wyoming, Ohio, 7,736.D2   78
Wyoming, Pa., 4,127..B8   81
Wyoming, co., N.Y.,
  34,793.............C2   75
Wyoming, co., Pa.,
  16,813.............D9   81
Wyoming, co., W. Va.,
  34,836.............D3   87
Wyoming, state, U.S.,
  330,066............   89
Wyomissing, Pa.,
  5,044.............F10   84
Wythe, co., Va.,
  21,975.............E1   85
Wytheville, Va., 5,634..E1   85

X

Xanthi, Grc., 26,377...B5   14
Xauen, Mor., 13,712...A3   22

Xavier, Kans., 600.....B8   61

Xenia, Ohio, 20,445....C4   78

Xochimilco, Mex.,
  20,687..........h9, n14   34

Y

Yadkin, co., N.C.,
  22,804.............A3   76
Yadkinville, N.C.,
  1,644.............A3   76

Yaizu, Jap., 50,600....o17   18
Yakima, Wash., 43,284.C5   86
Yakima, co., Wash.,
  145,112............C5   86

Yakutsk, Sov. Un.,
  77,000............C15   13
Yalobusha, co., Miss.,
  12,502.............A4   68

Yalta, Sov. Un.,
  47,100............I10   12
Yalu, China, 10,000....B9   17
Yalvac, Tur., 10,400...C8   14

Yamachiche, Que.,
Can., 1,186........C5 42
Yamagata, Jap.,
125,000..........G10 18
Yamagata, pref., Jap.,
1,320,664........*G10 18
Yamaguchi, Jap.,
54,400............I5 18
Yamaguchi, pref., Jap.,
1,602,207.........*I5 18
Yamanashi, pref., Jap.,
782,062..........*I9 18
Yamaska, co., Que.,
Can., 16,058.......C5 42
Yambol, Bul., 30,311..D8 10
Yamethin, Bur.,
12,030...........D10 20
Yamhill, co., Oreg.,
32,478............B3 80
Yanam, India, 7,032...E7 20
Yanbu', Sau. Ar.,
10,000............E2 15
Yancey, co., N.C.,
14,008............C4 76
Yanceyville, N.C.,
1,113.............A4 76
Yangchow, China,
180,200...........E8 17
Yankton, S. Dak.,
9,279.............H8 77
Yankton, co., S. Dak.,
17,551............G8 77
Yaoundé, Cam., 61,750.H7 22
Yaracuy, state, Ven.,
175,291...........A4 32
Yardley, Pa., 2,271...F12 81
Yarīm, Yemen, 20,000..G3 15
Yarkand, China,
80,000...........F10 16
Yarmouth, N.S., Can.,
8,636.............F3 43
Yarmouth, Maine,
2,913........E2, E5 64
Yarmouth, co., N.S.,
Can., 23,386......F4 43
Yaroslavl, Sov. Un.,
433,000..........C12 12
Yartsevo, Sov. Un.,
25,800............D9 12
Yarumal, Col., 10,349..B2 32
Yasinovataya, Sov. Un.,
10,000...........q20 12
Yates, co., N.Y.,
18,614............C3 75
Yates Center, Kans.,
2,080.............E8 61
Yatsushiro, Jap.,67,000.J5 18
Yauco, P.R., 8,996...m13 35

Yaxapai, co., Ariz.,
28,912............B2 48
Yavorov, Sov. Un.,
10,000............G4 12
Yawatahama, Jap.,
35,200............J6 18
Yazd (Yezd), Iran,
63,502............B8 23
Yazoo, co., Miss.,
31,653............C3 68
Yazoo City, Miss.,
11,236............C3 68
Yeadon, Pa., 11,610...B11 81
Yeagertown, Pa., 1,349.E6 81
Yecla, Sp., 18,400....C5 8
Yefremov, Sov. Un.,
42,900...........E12 12
Yegoryevsk, Sov. Un.,
61,000.......D12, n19 12
Yelan, Sov. Un.,
10,000...........F14 12
Yelets, Sov. Un.,
83,000...........E12 12
Yell, co., Ark., 11,940..B2 49
Yellowknife, N.W. Ter.,
Can., 3,141.......D11 36
Yellow Medicine, co.,
Minn., 15,523.....F2 67
Yellow Springs, Ohio,
4,167.............C4 78
Yellowstone, co., Mont.,
79,015............D8 70
Yellowstone National
Park (part), co.,
Wyo., 420.........A2 89
Yemen, country, Asia,
5,000,000.........F3 15
Yenakiyevo
(Ordzhonikidze),
Sov. Un., 93,000....q20 12
Yenangyaung, Bur.,
11,098............G4 17
Yencheng, China,
105,000..........*E9 17
Yenchi (Chutzuchieh),
China, 70,000.....C10 17
Yeniseysk, Sov. Un.,
18,300...........D12 13
Yeovil, Eng., 24,552...E5 4
Yerevan, Sov. Un.,
558,000...........E7 13
Yessey, Sov. Un.,
10,000...........C13 13
Yevpatoriya, Sov. Un.,
60,000............I9 12
Yeysk, Sov. Un.,
60,000...........H12 12
Yiannitsa, Grc.,
19,693...........*B4 14

Yinchwan (Ningsia),
China, 84,000......D6 17
Yingkow, China,
131,400...........C9 17
Yoakum, Tex., 5,761...E4 84
Yoakum, co., Tex.,
8,032.............C1 84
Yoichi, Jap., 18,600...E10 18
Yokkaichi, Jap.,
195,974......I8, o15 18
Yokohama, Jap.,
1,375,710......I9, n18 18
Yokosuka, Jap.,
287,309......I9, n18 18
Yokote, Jap., 24,700..G10 18
Yolo, co., Calif.,
65,727............C2 50
Yolyn, W. Va., 800....D5 87
Yonago, Jap., 62,900...I6 18
Yonezawa, Jap.,
60,300...........H10 18
Yonghung, Kor.,
18,445............G3 18
Yonkers, N.Y.,
190,634....D1, D3, E7 75
Yonne, dept., Fr.,
269,826..........*D5 5
Yorba, Calif., 1,198...*F5 50
York, Ala., 2,932.....C1 46
York, Eng., 104,468...D6 4
York, Maine, 950.....E1 64
York, Nebr., 6,173....D8 71
York, Pa., 54,504
(*146,600).......G8 81
York, S.C., 4,758.....B5 82
York, co., N.B., Can.,
52,672............C3 41
York, co., Ont., Can.,
1,733,108.........D5 43
York, co., Eng.,
4,621,698.........*D6 4
York, co., Maine,
99,402............E2 64
York, co., Nebr.,
13,724............D8 71
York, co., Pa., 238,336.G8 81
York, co., S.C., 78,760..A5 82
York, co., Va., 21,583..D6 85
Yorkton, Sask., Can.,
9,995........C1, F4 39
Yorktown, Ind., 1,137..D6 59
Yorktown, N.Y.,
3,576............*D7 75
Yorktown, Tex., 2,527..E4 84
Yorktown Heights, N.Y.,
2,478.............A5 74
Yorktown Manor, R.I.,
1,300............C11 52
Yorkville, Ill., 1,568...B5 58

Yorkville, N.Y., 3,749..B5 75
Yorkville, Ohio, 1,801..B7 78
Yoshiwara, Jap.,
80,944...........n17 18
Young, co., Tex.,
17,254............C3 84
Youngstown, N.Y.,
1,848.............B2 75
Youngstown, Ohio,
166,689 (*467,600)...A7 78
Youngsville, La., 946..D3 63
Youngsville, Pa., 2,211.C3 81
Youngtown, Ariz.,
1,559.............D1 48
Youngwood, Pa., 2,813.F2 81
Yozgat, Tur., 18,300..C10 14
Ypacaraí, Par., 8,118..E4 29
Ypsilanti, Mich.,
20,957........A6, F7 81
Yreka, Calif., 4,759..*B2 50
Ystad, Swe., 13,700....J5 11
Yuanling, China,
28,000............F7 17
Yuba, co., Calif.,
33,859............C3 50
Yuba City, Calif.,
11,507............C3 50
Yuba City South, Calif.,
3,200.............C3 50
Yubari, Jap., 107,972..E10 18
Yucatán, state, Mex.,
612,047...........C7 34
Yugoslavia, country,
Eur., 18,512,805.....C3 10
Yukon, Fla., 2,000.B5, B6 54
Yukon, Okla., 3,076...B4 79
Yukon, ter., Can.,
14,628............D6 36
Yuma, Ariz., 23,974...C1 48
Yuma, Colo., 1,919....A8 51
Yuma, co., Ariz.,
46,235............C1 48
Yuma, co., Colo., 8,912.A8 51
Yunnan, prov., China,
19,100,000........G5 17
Yurécuaro, Mex.,
12,088...........m12 34
Yuryevets, Sov. Un.,
10,000...........C14 12
Yuryev-Polskiy, Sov.
Un., 10,000.......C12 12
Yuty, Par., 16,262.....E4 29
Yuzha, Sov. Un.,
25,000...........C13 12
Yuzhno-Sakhalinsk
(Toyohara), Sov. Un.,
85,000...........E17 13
Yverdon, Switz.,
16,338............E3 6

Z

Zabkowice, Pol., 10,127.C4 7
Zabrze, Pol.,
189,000........C5, g9 7
Zacapu, Mex., 22,241..n13 34
Zacatecas, Mex.,
31,851............C4 34
Zacatecas, state, Mex.,
798,232......C4, m12 34
Zachary, La., 3,268....D4 63
Zadar, Yugo., 25,132...C2 10
Zagorsk, Sov. Un.,
77,000...........C12 12
Zagreb, Yugo., 427,319.C2 10
Zāhedān, Iran, 5,000...G9 16
Zahle, Leb., 30,387.....g5 15
Zaječar, Yugo., 18,545.D6 10
Zakinthos, Grc.,
9,506.............D3 14
Zakinthos, prov., Grc.,
35,509...........*D3 14
Zakopane, Pol., 25,000.D6 7
Zala, co., Hung.,
274,161..........*B3 10
Zalaegerszeg, Hung.,
23,738............B3 10
Zalau, Rom., 13,378...B6 10
Zambales, prov., Phil.,
213,600..........*B5 19
Zambia (Northern
Rhodesia), country,
Afr., 2,480,000.....C5 24
Zamboanga, Phil.,
25,000............D6 19
Zamboanga del Norte,
prov., Phil.,
280,400..........*D6 19
Zamboanga del Sur, prov.,
Phil., 744,500.....*D6 19
Zamora, Mex.,
31,991........C4, m12 34
Zamora, Sp., 42,060....B3 8

Zamora, prov., Sp.,
301,129..........*B3 8
Zamosc, Pol., 28,000...C7 7
Zanesville, Ohio,
39,077............C6 78
Zanjān, Iran, 47,159...A7 23
Zanzibar, Tan., 45,284.B7 24
Zapata, Tex., 2,031....F3 84
Zapata, co., Tex., 4,393.F3 84
Zaporozhye, Sov. Un.,
475,000..........H10 12
Zaragoza, Sp., 326,316..B5 8
Zaragoza, prov., Sp.,
656,772..........*B5 8
Zárate, Arg., 35,197.A5, g7 28
Zaraysk, Sov. Un.,
10,000...........D12 12
Zaria, Nig., 32,559.....F6 22
Zashiversk, Sov. Un.,
800..............C17 13
Zatec, Czech., 14,800...C2 7
Zavala, co., Tex.,
12,696............E3 84
Zavitaya, Sov. Un.,
14,500...........D15 13
Zawiercie, Pol.,
33,000........C5, g10 7
Zaysan, Sov. Un.,
15,600...........E11 13
Zdolbunov, Sov. Un.,
10,000............F6 12
Zduńska Wola, Pol.,
25,000............C5 7
Zebulon, N.C., 1,534...B5 76
Zeeland, Mich., 3,702..F4 66
Zeeland, prov., Neth.,
283,900...........B5 5
Zehdenick, Ger., 12,800.B6 6
Zeigler, Ill., 2,133.....F4 58
Zeist, Neth., 52,400....A6 5
Zeitz, Ger., 45,400.....C6 6

Zelienople, Pa., 3,284..E1 81
Zella-Mehlis, Ger.,
16,400............C5 6
Zemetchino, Sov. Un.,
10,000...........E14 12
Zenica, Yugo., 32,552..C3 10
Zephyrhills, Fla., 2,887.D4 54
Zerbst, Ger., 17,900...C6 6
Zeya, Sov. Un.,
15,100...........D15 13
Zgierz, Pol., 37,000....C5 7
Zhdanov (Mariupol), Sov.
Un., 310,000......H11 12
Zhitomir, Sov. Un.,
114,000...........F7 12
Zhizdra, Sov. Un.,
10,000...........E10 12
Zhmerinka, Sov. Un.,
25,000............G7 12
Ziebach, co., S. Dak.,
2,495.............F4 77
Zielona Gora, Pol.,
51,000............C3 7
Ziguinchor, Sen.,
22,400............F1 22
Zile, Tur., 21,400.....B10 14
Zilina, Czech., 32,500..D5 7
Zilwaukee, Mich.,
1,800.............E7 66
Zima, Sov. Un.,
33,200...........D13 13
Zimnicea, Rom.,
12,445............D7 10
Zinder, Niger, 13,300...F6 22
Zion, Ill., 11,941...A6, D2 58
Zionsville, Ind.,
1,822........E5, G7 59
Zipaquirá, Col., 12,708.B3 32
Zitácuaro, Mex.,
23,410...........n13 34

Zittau, Ger., 43,200....C7 6
Zlatoust, Sov. Un.,
166,000...........D8 13
Zlynka, Sov. Un.,
10,000............E8 12
Znamenka, Sov. Un.,
37,300............G9 12
Znojmo, Czech., 24,000.D4 7
Zolochev, Sov. Un.,
28,600............G5 12
Zolotonosha, Sov. Un.,
10,000............G9 12
Zonguldak, Tur.,
54,000............B8 14
Zrenjanin (Petrovgrad),
Yugo., 48,954.....C5 10
Zug, Switz., 19,792....E4 6
Zug, canton, Switz.,
52,489...........*E4 6
Zulia, state, Ven.,
919,863...........B3 32
Zumbrota, Minn.,
1,830.............F6 67
Zuni, N. Mex., 3,585...B4 48
Zürich, Switz., 440,170
(*665,000)........*E4 6
Zürich, canton, Switz.,
952,304..........*E4 6
Zutphen, Neth., 25,200.A7 5
Zuwārah, Libya, 2,380.B7 22
Zvenigorodka, Sov. Un.,
10,000............G8 12
Zvolen, Czech., 19,600.D5 7
Zweibrücken, Ger.,
32,900............D3 6
Zwickau, Ger., 128,700.C6 6
Zwolle, La., 1,326.....C2 63
Zwolle, Neth., 56,300..A7 5
Zyrardow, Pol.,
30,000........B6, m12 7

WORLD POLITICAL INFORMATION TABLE

This table lists all countries and dependencies in the world, U.S. States, Canadian provinces, and other important regions and political subdivisions. Besides specifying the form of government for all political areas, the table classifies them into six groups according to their political status. Units labeled **A** are independent sovereign nations. (Several of these are designated as members of the British Commonwealth of Nations.) Units labeled **B** are independent as regards internal affairs, but for purposes of foreign affairs they are under the protection of another country. Areas under military government are also labeled **B**. Units labeled **C** are colonies, overseas territories, dependencies, etc., of other countries. Together the **A**, **B**, and **C** areas comprise practically the entire inhabited area of the world. The areas labeled **D** are physically separate units, such as groups of islands, which are *not* separate countries, but form part of a nation or dependency. Units labeled **E** are States, provinces, Soviet Republics, or similar major administrative subdivisions of important countries. Units in the table with no letter designation are regions or other areas that do not constitute separate political units by themselves.

Region or Political Division	Area in sq. miles	Estimated Population 1/1/1965	Pop. per sq. mi.	Form of Government and Ruling Power	Capital; Largest City (unless same)	Predominant Languages
Aden	80	250,000	3,125	Colony (U.K.) C	Aden	Arabic, English
Afghanistan†	251,000	15,200,000	61	Monarchy .... A	Kabul	Pushtu (Afghan), Persian
Africa	11,685,000	290,200,000	25		........; Cairo	....
Alabama	51,609	3,462,000	67	State (U.S.) .... E	Montgomery; Birmingham	
Alaska	586,400	247,000	0.4	State (U.S.) .... E	Juneau; Anchorage	English, Indian, Eskimo
Albania†	11,099	1,846,000	166	People's Republic .... A	Tiranë	Albanian
Alberta	255,285	1,449,000	5.7	Province (Canada) .... E	Edmonton	English
Algeria†	919,595	10,700,000	12	Republic .... A	Algiers (Alger)	Arabic, French
American Samoa	76	21,000	276	Unincorporated Territory (U.S.) C	Pago Pago	Polynesian, English
Andaman & Nicobar Is.	3,215	74,000	23	Territory (India) .... D	Port Blair	Andaman, Nicobar Malay
Andorra	175	12,000	69	Principality .... A	Andorra	Catalan
Angola	481,351	5,125,000	11	Overseas Province (Portugal) C	Luanda	Bantu languages
Antarctica	5,100,000	....	...		....	....
Antigua (incl. Barbuda)	171	59,000	345	Colony (U.K.) C	St. John's	English
Arabian Peninsula	933,211	14,636,000	16		........; Mecca	Arabic
Argentina†	1,072,070	22,200,000	21	Federal Republic .... A	Buenos Aires	Spanish
Arizona	113,909	1,635,000	14	State (U.S.) .... E	Phoenix	....
Arkansas	53,104	1,889,000	36	State (U.S.) .... E	Little Rock	....
Armenia (S.S.R.)	11,500	2,100,000	183	Soviet Socialist Republic (Sov. Un.) .... E	Yerevan	Armenian
Aruba	69	63,000	913	Division of Netherlands Antilles (Neth.) .... D	Oranjestad	Dutch, Spanish, English, Papiamento
Ascension I.	34	400	12	Dependency of St. Helena (U.K.) .... D	Georgetown	English
Asia	17,085,000	1,877,000,000	110		........; Tōkyō	....
Australia†	2,971,081	11,335,000	3.8	Monarchy (Federal) (Br. Commonwealth of Nations) .... A	Canberra; Sydney	English
Australian Capital Territory	939	86,000	92	Federal Territory (Australia) .... E	Canberra	English
Austria†	32,374	7,235,000	223	Federal Republic .... A	Vienna (Wien)	German
Azerbaidzhan (S.S.R.)	33,450	4,440,000	133	Soviet Socialist Republic (Sov. Un.) .... E	Baku	Turkic languages, Russian, Armenian
Azores Is.	894	332,000	371	Part of Portugal (3 Districts) .... D	........; Ponta Delgada	Portuguese
Baden-Wurttemberg	13,803	8,245,000	597	State (Germany, West) .... E	Stuttgart	German
Bahama Is.	4,375	136,000	31	Colony (U.K.) C	Nassau	English
Bahrain	231	166,000	719	Sheikdom (U.K. protection) .... B	Manama	Arabic
Balearic Is.	1,936	453,000	234	Part of Spain (Baleares Province) .... D	Palma de Mallorca	Catalan
Baltic Republics	67,200	6,350,000	94	Soviet Union .... E	........; Riga	Lithuanian, Latvian, Estonian, Russian
Barbados	166	242,000	1,458	Colony (U.K.) C	Bridgetown	English
Basutoland	11,716	740,000	63	Territory (Protectorate) (U.K.) C	Maseru	Kaffir, other Bantu languages
Bavaria (Bayern)	27,239	9,970,000	366	State (Germany, West) .... E	München (Munich)	German
Bechuanaland	275,000	555,000	2.0	Protectorate (U.K.) C	Gaberones; Kanye	Bechuana, other Bantu languages
Belgium†	11,778	9,400,000	798	Monarchy .... A	Brussels (Bruxelles)	Flemish, French
Benelux	25,726	21,932,000	853		Brussels (Bruxelles)	Dutch, Flemish, French, Luxembourgeois
Berlin, West	186	2,200,000	11,828	State (Germany, West) .... E	Berlin (West)	German
Bermuda	21	60,000	2,857	Colony (U.K.) C	Hamilton	English
Bhutan	19,300	750,000	39	Monarchy (Indian protection) .... B	Thimbu and Paro	Tibetan dialects
Bismarck Archipelago	20,415	193,000	9.5	Part of Australian Trust Ter. of New Guinea (3 Districts) .... D	........; Rabaul	Malay-Polynesian and Papuan languages
Bolivia†	424,163	3,675,000	8.7	Republic .... A	Sucre and La Paz; La Paz	Spanish, Quechua, Aymará, Guaraní
Bonin Islands	40	200	5.0	U.S. Military Administration .... B		English
Borneo, Indonesian (Kalimantan)	208,286	4,470,000	21	Part of Indonesia (4 Provinces) .... D	........; Bandjermasin	Bahasa Indonesia (Indonesian)
Brazil†	3,286,478	80,250,000	24	Federal Republic .... A	Brasília; Rio de Janeiro	Portuguese
Bremen	156	732,000	4,692	State (Germany, West) .... E	Bremen	German
British Columbia	366,255	1,770,000	4.8	Province (Canada) .... E	Victoria; Vancouver	English
British Commonwealth of Nations	10,890,845	796,403,000	73		London	....
British Guiana, see Guyana	....	....				
British Honduras	8,866	105,000	12	Colony (U.K.) C	Belize	English, Spanish, Indian languages
Brunei	2,226	105,000	47	Protectorate (U.K.) C	Brunei	Malay-Polynesian languages
Bulgaria†	42,829	8,175,000	191	People's Republic .... A	Sofia (Sofiya)	Bulgarian
Burma†	261,789	24,500,000	94	Federal Republic .... A	Rangoon	Burmese, English
Burundi (Urundi)†	10,747	2,775,000	258	Monarchy .... A	Bujumbura	Bantu and Hamitic languages
Byelorussia (S.S.R.)†	80,150	8,500,000	106	Soviet Socialist Republic (Sov. Un.) .... E	Minsk	Byelorussian, Polish
California	158,693	18,338,000	116	State (U.S.) .... E	Sacramento; Los Angeles	....
Cambodia†	66,606	6,100,000	92	Monarchy .... A	Phnom Penh	Cambodian (Khmer), French
Cameroon†	183,569	4,750,000	26	Federal Republic .... A	Yaoundé; Douala	Native languages, French
Canada†	3,851,809	19,445,000	5.0	Monarchy (Federal) (Br. Commonwealth of Nations) .... A	Ottawa; Montreal	English, French
Canal Zone	558	50,000	90	Under U.S. Jurisdiction C	Balboa Heights; Rainbow City	Spanish, English
Canary Is.	2,808	1,005,000	358	Part of Spain (2 Provinces) .... D	........; Las Palmas	Spanish
Canton & Enderbury	27	300	11	U.K.-U.S. Administration C	Canton Island	Malay-Polynesian languages, English
Cape of Good Hope	277,543	5,830,000	21	Province (South Africa) .... E	Cape Town	English, Afrikaans, Bantu languages
Cape Verde Is.	1,538	229,000	149	Overseas Province (Portugal) C	Praia; Mindelo	Portuguese
Caroline Is.	457	62,000	136	Part of U.S. Pacific Is. Trust Ter. (4 Districts) .... D		Malay-Polynesian languages
Cayman Is.	100	9,000	90	Colony (U.K.) C	Georgetown	English
Celebes (Sulawesi)	72,987	7,700,000	105	Part of Indonesia (2 Provinces) .... D	........; Makassar	Malay-Polynesian languages
Central African Republic†	238,200	1,350,000	5.7	Republic .... A	Bangui	Bantu languages, French
Central America	200,412	13,800,000	69		........; Guatemala	Spanish, Indian languages
Central Asia, Soviet	478,150	16,800,000	35	Soviet Union .... E	........; Tashkent	Uzbek, Russian, Kirghiz, Turkoman, Tadzhik
Ceylon†	25,332	11,000,000	434	Commonwealth (Br. Commonwealth of Nations) .... A	Colombo	Sinhalese, Tamil, English
Chad†	495,800	2,900,000	5.8	Republic .... A	Fort Lamy	Hamitic languages, Arabic, French
Channel Is. (Guernsey, Jersey, etc.)	75	112,000	1,493		........; St. Helier	English, French
Chile†	286,397	8,450,000	30	Republic .... A	Santiago	Spanish

†*Member of the United Nations (1965).*

Region or Political Division	Area in sq. miles	Estimated Population 1/1/1965	Pop. per sq. mi.	Form of Government and Ruling Power	Capital; Largest City (unless same)	Predominant Languages
China (excl. Taiwan)	3,691,500	700,000,000	190	People's Republic A	Peking (Peiching); Shanghai	Chinese, Mongolian, Turkish, Tungus
China (Nationalist), see Taiwan						
Christmas I. (Indian Ocean)	55	3,500	64	External Territory (Australia) C		Chinese, Malay, English
Christmas I. (Pacific Ocean)	222	400	1.8	Part of Gilbert & Ellice Is. (U.K.); also claimed by U.S.		Malay-Polynesian languages, English
Cocos (Keeling) Is.	5	700	140	External Territory (Australia) C		Malay, English
Colombia†	439,513	15,600,000	35	Republic A	Bogotá	Spanish
Colorado	104,247	2,003,000	19	State (U.S.) E	Denver	
Commonwealth of Nations, see Br. Commonwealth of Nations						
Comoro Is.	838	192,000	229	Overseas Territory (France) C	Dzaoudzi; Moroni	Malagasy, French
Congo (Rep. of Congo; Capital: Brazzaville)†	132,000	1,050,000	8.0	Republic A	Brazzaville	Bantu languages, French
Congo, The (Rep. of The Congo; Capital: Leopoldville)†	905,565	15,500,000	17	Republic A	Léopoldville	Bantu languages, French
Connecticut	5,009	2,752,000	549	State (U.S.) E	Hartford	
Cook Is.	93	19,000	204	Island Territory (New Zealand) C	Avarua	Malay-Polynesian languages
Corsica	3,368	280,000	83	Part of France (Corse Department) D	Ajaccio; Bastia	French, Italian
Costa Rica†	19,600	1,425,000	73	Republic A	San José	Spanish
Crete	3,219	480,000	149	Part of Greece (4 Prefectures) D	........; Iráklion	Greek
Cuba†	44,217	7,100,000	161	Republic A	Havana (La Habana)	Spanish
Curaçao	173	133,000	769	Division of Netherlands Antilles (Neth.) D	Willemstad	Dutch, Spanish, English, Papiamento
Cyprus†	3,572	590,000	165	Republic (Br. Commonwealth of Nations) A	Nicosia	Greek, Turkish, English
Czechoslovakia†	49,370	14,100,000	286	People's Republic A	Prague (Praha)	Czech, Slovak
Dahomey†	44,696	2,300,000	51	Republic A	Porto Novo; Cotonou	Native languages, French
Delaware	2,057	494,000	240	State (U.S.) E	Dover; Wilmington	
Denmark†	16,619	4,740,000	285	Monarchy A	Copenhagen (København)	Danish
Denmark and Possessions	857,159	4,817,000	5.6		Copenhagen (København)	Danish, Faeroese, Greenlandic
District of Columbia	69	810,000	11,739	District (U.S.) E	Washington	
Dominica	305	65,000	213	Colony (U.K.) C	Roseau	English, French
Dominican Republic†	18,704	3,500,000	187	Republic A	Santo Domingo	Spanish
Ecuador†	104,506	4,950,000	47	Republic A	Quito; Guayaquil	Spanish, Quechua
Egypt, see United Arab Republic						
El Salvador†	8,260	2,875,000	348	Republic A	San Salvador	Spanish
England (excl. Monmouthshire)	50,327	45,150,000	897	United Kingdom	........; London	English
England & Wales	58,344	47,825,000	820	Administrative division of United Kingdom E	London	English, Welsh
Equatorial Guinea	10,830	266,000	25	African Province (Spain) C	Bata and Santa Isabel; Santa Isabel	Bantu languages, Spanish
Estonia (S.S.R.)	17,400	1,250,000	72	Soviet Socialist Republic (Sov. Un.) E	Tallinn	Estonian, Russian
Ethiopia†	457,267	21,500,000	47	Monarchy A	Addis Ababa	Amharic and other Semitic languages, English, various Hamitic languages
Eurasia	20,910,000	2,478,900,000	119		........; Tōkyō	
Europe	3,825,000	601,900,000	157		........; London	
Faeroe Is.	540	37,000	69	Self-Governing Territory (Denmark) C	Thórshavn	Danish, Faeroese
Falkland Is. (excl. Deps)	4,618	2,200	0.5	Colony (U.K.) C	Port Stanley	English
Fernando Poo	785	71,000	90	Part of Equatorial Guinea D	........; Santa Isabel	Bantu languages, Spanish
Fiji	7,040	455,000	65	Colony (U.K.) C	Suva	Malaya-Polynesian languages, English, Hindi
Finland†	130,119	4,600,000	35	Republic A	Helsinki	Finnish, Swedish
Florida	58,560	5,913,000	101	State (U.S.) E	Tallahassee; Miami	
France†	212,822	48,800,000	229	Republic A	Paris	French
France and Possessions	276,238	50,366,000	182		Paris	
Franklin	549,253	6,300	0.01	District of Northwest Territories, Canada E	........; Cambridge Bay	English, Eskimo, Indian
French Guiana	35,100	36,000	1.0	Overseas Department (France) C	Cayenne	French
French Polynesia	1,550	89,000	57	Overseas Territory (France) C	Papeete	Malay-Polynesian languages, French
French Somaliland	8,500	80,000	9.4	Overseas Territory (France) C	Djibouti	Somali, French
French Southern & Antarctic Ter. (excl. Adélie Coast)	2,917	150	0.05	Overseas Territory (France) C		French
French West Indies	1,112	620,000	558		........; Fort-de-France	French
Gabon†	103,100	465,000	4.5	Republic A	Libreville	Bantu languages, French
Galápagos Is.	3,028	2,500	0.8	Province (Ecuador) D	Puerto Baquerizo	Spanish
Gambia†	4,008	320,000	80	Self-Governing Member (Br. Comm. of Nations) A	Bathurst	Mandingo, Fula, English
Georgia (S.S.R.)	26,900	4,460,000	166	Soviet Socialist Republic (Sov. Un.) E	Tbilisi	Georgic, Armenian, Russian
Georgia	58,876	4,312,000	73	State (U.S.) E	Atlanta	
Germany (Entire)	137,743	75,800,000	550		........; Berlin	German
Germany, East	41,815	17,250,000	413	People's Republic A	Berlin (East)	German
Germany, West (incl. West Berlin)	95,928	58,550,000	610	Federal Republic A	Bonn; Berlin (West)	German
Ghana†	91,843	7,600,000	83	Republic (Br. Commonwealth of Nations) A	Accra	Twi, Fanti, Ewe-Fon, English
Gibraltar	2	25,000	12,500	Colony (U.K.) C	Gibraltar	Spanish, English
Gilbert & Ellice Is.	369	51,000	138	Colony (U.K.) C	Tarawa	Malay-Polynesian languages
Great Britain & Northern Ireland, see United Kingdom						
Greece†	50,547	8,500,000	168	Monarchy A	Athens (Athínai)	Greek
Greenland	840,000	40,000	0.05	Overseas Territory (Denmark) C	Godthaab	Greenlandic, Danish, Eskimo
Grenada	133	93,000	699	Colony (U.K.) C	St. George's	English
Guadeloupe (incl. Dependencies)	687	308,000	448	Overseas Department (France) C	Basse-Terre; Pointe-à-Pitre	French
Guam	212	70,000	330	Unincorporated Territory (U.S.) C	Agana	English, Chamorro
Guatemala†	42,042	4,375,000	104	Republic A	Guatemala	Spanish, Indian languages
Guernsey (incl. Dependencies)	30	49,000	1,633	Bailiwick (U.K.) C	St. Peter Port	English, French
Guinea†	94,925	3,500,000	37	Republic A	Conakry	Native languages, French
Guyana	83,000	631,000	7.6	Self-Governing Member (Br. Comm. of Nations) A	Georgetown	English
Haiti†	10,714	4,600,000	429	Republic A	Port-au-Prince	Creole, French
Hamburg	288	1,860,000	6,458	State (Germany, West) E	Hamburg	German
Hawaii	6,424	710,000	111	State (U.S.) E	Honolulu	English, Japanese, Hawaiian
Hesse (Hessen)	8,150	5,082,000	624	State (German, West) E	Wiesbaden; Frankfurt am Main	German
Hispaniola	29,530	8,100,000	274		........; Santo Domingo	French, Spanish
Holland, see Netherlands						
Honduras†	43,277	2,125,000	49	Republic A	Tegucigalpa	Spanish
Hong Kong	398	3,750,000	9,422	Colony (U.K.) C	Victoria	Chinese, English
Hungary†	35,919	10,135,000	282	People's Republic A	Budapest	Hungarian
Iceland†	39,800	190,000	4.8	Republic A	Reykjavík	Icelandic
Idaho	83,557	702,000	8.4	State (U.S.) E	Boise (Boise City)	
Ifni	580	51,000	88	African Province (Spain) C	Sidi Ifni	Spanish, Arabic
Illinois	56,400	10,584,000	188	State (U.S.) E	Springfield; Chicago	
India (incl. part of Kashmir)†	1,227,275	479,000,000	390	Republic (Br. Commonwealth of Nations) A	New Delhi; Calcutta	Hindi and other Indo-Aryan languages, Dravidian languages, English
Indiana	36,291	4,914,000	135	State (U.S.) E	Indianapolis	
Indonesia (excl. West Irian)†	574,670	103,350,000	180	Republic A	Djakarta	Bahasa Indonesia (Indonesian), Chinese, English
Iowa	56,290	2,783,000	49	State (U.S.) E	Des Moines	
Iran (Persia)†	636,300	23,100,000	36	Monarchy A	Tehrān	Persian, Turkish dialects, Kurdish
Iraq†	173,260	7,050,000	41	Republic A	Baghdad	Arabic, Kurdish

†*Member of the United Nations (1965).*

Region or Political Division	Area in sq. miles	Estimated Population 1/1/1965	Pop. per sq. mi.	Form of Government and Ruling Power	Capital; Largest City (unless same)	Predominant Languages
Ireland†	27,135	2,855,000	105	Republic.........................A	Dublin	English, Irish
Isle of Man	227	48,000	211	Possession (U.K.)...............C	Douglas	English
Israel†	7,993	2,520,000	315	Republic.........................A	Jerusalem; Tel Aviv-Yafo	Hebrew, Arabic
Italy†	116,303	50,900,000	438	Republic.........................A	Rome (Roma)	Italian
Ivory Coast†	124,504	3,775,000	30	Republic.........................A	Abidjan	French, native languages
Jamaica†	4,411	1,750,000	397	Self-Governing Member (Br. Commonwealth of Nations)...............A	Kingston	English
Japan†	142,726	97,400,000	682	Monarchy........................A	Tōkyō	Japanese
Java (Djawa) (incl. Madura)	51,040	67,000,000	1,313	Part of Indonesia (5 Provinces)...D	.........; Djakarta	Bahasa Indonesia (Indonesian), Chinese, English
Jersey	45	63,000	1,400	Bailiwick (U.K.)................C	St. Helier	English, French
Jordan†	37,301	1,900,000	51	Monarchy........................A	Amman	Arabic
Kansas	82,264	2,251,000	27	State (U.S.).....................E	Topeka; Wichita	
Kashmir, Jammu &	86,024	4,700,000	55	In dispute (India & Pakistan).....	Srinagar	Kashmiri, Punjabi
Kazakh S.S.R.	1,050,000	11,800,000	11	Soviet Socialist Republic (Sov. Un.)..E	Alma-Ata	Turkic languages, Russian
Keewatin	228,160	2,400	0.01	District of Northwest Territories, Canada..E	.........; Chesterfield Inlet	English, Eskimo, Indian
Kentucky	40,395	3,138,000	77	State (U.S.).....................E	Frankfort; Louisville	
Kenya	224,960	9,200,000	41	Republic (Br. Comm. of Nations)....A	Nairobi	Swahili and other Bantu languages, English
Kerguelen	2,700	150	0.06	Part of French Southern & Antarctic Ter. (Fr.)...D		French
Kirghiz S.S.R.	76,650	2,490,000	32	Soviet Socialist Republic (Sov. Un.)..E	Frunze	Turkic languages, Persian
Korea (Entire)	84,540	39,500,000	467		.........; Seoul (Sŏul)	Korean
Korea, North	46,540	11,500,000	247	People's Republic...............A	Pyongyang	Korean
Korea South	38,000	28,000,000	737	Republic.........................A	Seoul (Sŏul)	Korean
Kuwait†	6,000	405,000	68	Sheikdom.......................A	Kuwait	Arabic
Labrador	112,826	16,000	0.1	Part of Newfoundland Province, Canada..D	.........; Goose Bay	English, Eskimo
Laos†	91,400	2,000,000	22	Monarchy........................A	Vientiane	Lao, French
Latin America	7,923,124	237,100,000	30		.........; Buenos Aires	
Latvia (S.S.R.)	24,600	2,200,000	89	Soviet Socialist Republic (Sov. Un.)..E	Riga	Latvian, Russian
Lebanon†	4,000	2,265,000	566	Republic.........................A	Beirut	Arabic, French, English
Liberia†	43,000	1,050,000	24	Republic.........................A	Monrovia	Native languages, English
Libya†	679,362	1,580,000	2.3	Monarchy........................A	Tripoli and Bengasi; Tripoli	Arabic
Liechtenstein	61	18,000	295	Principality.....................A	Vaduz	German
Lithuania (S.S.R.)	25,150	2,900,000	115	Soviet Socialist Republic (Sov. Un.)..E	Vilnius	Lithuanian, Polish, Russian
Louisiana	48,523	3,480,000	72	State (U.S.).....................E	Baton Rouge; New Orleans	
Lower Saxony (Niedersachsen)	18,294	6,855,000	375	State (Germany, West)...........E	Hannover (Hanover)	German
Luxembourg†	998	332,000	333	Grand Duchy....................A	Luxembourg	Luxembourgeois, French
Macao	6	175,000	29,167	Overseas Province (Portugal).....C	Macao	Chinese, Portuguese
Mackenzie	527,490	16,300	0.03	District of Northwest Territories, Canada..E	.........; Yellowknife	English, Eskimo, Indian
Madeira Is.	308	270,000	877	Part of Portugal (Funchal District)..D	Funchal	Portuguese
Maine	33,215	989,000	30	State (U.S.).....................E	Augusta; Portland	
Malagasy Republic (Madagascar)†	227,800	6,200,000	27	Republic.........................A	Tananarive	French, Malagasy
Malawi (Nyasaland)†	45,747	3,900,000	85	Self-Governing Member (Br. Comm. of Nations)......A	Zomba; Blantyre-Limbe	Bantu languages
Malaya	50,700	7,950,000	157	Part of Malaysia	Kuala Lumpur	Malay, Chinese, English
Malaysia†	128,431	9,310,000	72	Self-Governing Member (Br. Comm. of Nations).......A	Kuala Lumpur	Malay, Chinese, English
Maldive Is.	115	95,000	826	Sultanate.......................A	Male	Arabic
Mali†	464,874	4,550,000	9.8	Republic.........................A	Bamako	Native languages, French, Arabic
Malta†	122	325,000	2,664	Self-Governing Member (Br. Comm. of Nations).......A	Valletta	English, Maltese
Manitoba	251,000	963,000	3.8	Province (Canada)...............E	Winnipeg	English
Mariana Is. (excl. Guam)	154	11,000	71	District of U.S. Pacific Is. Trust Ter...D	Saipan	Malay-Polynesian languages
Maritime Provinces (excl. Newfoundland)	51,963	1,489,000	29	Canada...........................	.........; Halifax	English
Marshall Is.	61	17,000	279	District of U.S. Pacific Is. Trust Ter...D	Majuro	Malay-Polynesian languages
Martinique	425	312,000	734	Overseas Department (France).....C	Fort-de-France	French
Maryland	10,577	3,480,000	329	State (U.S.).....................E	Annapolis; Baltimore	
Massachusetts	8,257	5,387,000	652	State (U.S.).....................E	Boston	
Mauritania†	419,230	1,000,000	2.4	Republic.........................A	Nouakchott	Arabic, French
Mauritius (incl. Dependencies)	808	752,000	931	Colony (U.K.)...................C	Port Louis	Indo-Aryan languages, French, Creole
Mexico†	761,602	40,250,000	53	Federal Republic................A	Mexico City	Spanish
Michigan	58,216	8,269,000	142	State (U.S.).....................E	Lansing; Detroit	
Middle America	1,053,124	76,300,000	72		.........; Mexico City	
Midway Is.	2	2,500	1,250	Possession (U.S.)...............C		English
Minnesota	84,068	3,613,000	43	State (U.S.).....................E	St. Paul; Minneapolis	
Mississippi	47,716	2,320,000	49	State (U.S.).....................E	Jackson	
Missouri	69,686	4,446,000	64	State (U.S.).....................E	Jefferson City; St. Louis	
Moldavia (S.S.R.)	13,000	3,250,000	250	Soviet Socialist Republic (Sov. Un.)..E	Kishinev	Moldavian, Russian, Ukrainian
Monaco	0.8	22,000	27,500	Principality.....................A	Monaco	French, Italian
Mongolia†	592,700	1,079,000	1.8	People's Republic...............A	Ulan Bator	Mongolian
Montana	147,138	717,000	4.9	State (U.S.).....................E	Helena; Great Falls	
Montserrat	32	13,000	406	Colony (U.K.)...................C	Plymouth	English
Morocco†	171,305	13,150,000	77	Monarchy........................A	Rabat; Casablanca	Arabic, Berber, French
Mozambique	297,846	6,900,000	23	Overseas Province (Portugal).....C	Lourenço Marques	Bantu Languages, Portuguese
Muscat & Oman	82,000	580,000	7.1	Sultanate.......................A	Muscat; Matrah	Arabic
Natal	35,284	3,270,000	93	Province (South Africa).........E	Pietermaritzburg; Durban	English, Afrikaans, Bantu languages
Nauru	8	5,000	625	Trust Territory (Austl.-U.K.-N.Z.)....C		Malay-Polynesian languages, Chinese, English
Nebraska	77,227	1,507,000	20	State (U.S.).....................E	Lincoln; Omaha	
Nepal†	54,362	9,900,000	182	Monarchy........................A	Katmandu	Nepali, Tibeto-Burman languages
Netherlands†	12,950	12,200,000	942	Monarchy........................A	The Hague ('s Gravenhage) and Amsterdam; Amsterdam	Dutch
Netherlands and Possessions	68,464	12,793,000	187		The Hague and Amsterdam; Amsterdam	
Netherlands Antilles	371	208,000	561	Self-Governing Territory (Netherlands)...C	Willemstad	Dutch, Spanish, English, Papiamento
Netherlands Guiana, see Surinam	....	....	....		....	
Netherlands New Guinea, see West Irian	....	....	....		....	
Nevada	110,540	426,000	3.9	State (U.S.).....................E	Carson City; Las Vegas	
New Brunswick	28,354	620,000	22	Province (Canada)...............E	Fredericton; Saint John	English, French
New Caledonia (incl. Deps.)	6,531	85,000	13	Overseas Territory (France)......C	Nouméa	Malay-Polynesian languages, French
New England	66,608	11,060,000	166	United States....................	.........; Boston	English
Newfoundland	156,185	495,000	3.2	Province (Canada)...............E	St. John's	English
Newfoundland (excl. Labrador)	43,359	479,000	11		.........; St. John's	English
New Guinea, North-East	69,695	1,320,000	19	Part of Australian Trust Ter. of New Guinea (3 Districts).................D	.........; Lae	Papuan and Negrito languages
New Guinea, Ter. of	94,430	1,575,000	17	Trust Territory (Austl.; administered from Papua).....C	Port Moresby, Papua; Rabaul	Papuan and Negrito languages, English
New Hampshire	9,304	639,000	69	State (U.S.).....................E	Concord; Manchester	
New Hebrides	5,700	65,000	11	Condominium (France-U.K.).......C	Vila	Malay-Polynesian languages, French
New Jersey	7,836	6,587,000	841	State (U.S.).....................E	Trenton; Newark	
New Mexico	121,666	1,048,000	8.6	State (U.S.).....................E	Santa Fe; Albuquerque	

†Member of the United Nations (1965).

Region or Political Division	Area in sq. miles	Estimated Population 1/1/1965	Pop. per sq. mi.	Form of Government and Ruling Power	Capital; Largest City (unless same)	Predominant Languages
New South Wales	309,433	4,160,000	13	State (Australia) .... E	Sydney	English
New York	49,576	17,834,000	360	State (U.S.) .... E	Albany; New York	
New Zealand†	103,736	2,625,000	25	Monarchy (Br. Commonwealth of Nations) .... A	Wellington; Auckland	English
Nicaragua†	48,600	1,620,000	33	Republic .... A	Managua	Spanish
Niedersachsen, see Lower Saxony						
Niger†	458,995	3,275,000	7.1	Republic .... A	Niamey	Hausa, Arabic, French
Nigeria†	356,669	43,200,000	121	Republic (Br. Commonwealth of Nations) .... A	Lagos	Hausa, Ibo, Yoruba, English
Niue	100	5,000	50	Island Territory (New Zealand) C	Alofi	Malay-Polynesian languages, English
Norfolk Island	13	1,000	77	External Territory (Australia) C	Kingston	English
North America	9,420,000	289,700,000	31		....; New York	
North Borneo, see Sabah						
North Carolina	52,712	4,877,000	93	State (U.S.) .... E	Raleigh; Charlotte	
North Dakota	70,665	642,000	9.1	State (U.S.) .... E	Bismarck; Fargo	
Northern Ireland	5,459	1,460,000	267	Administrative division of United Kingdom .... E	Belfast	English
Northern Rhodesia, see Zambia						
Northern Territory	523,620	51,000	0.1	Territory (Australia) .... E	Darwin	English, Aboriginal languages
North Polar Regions						
North Rhine-Westphalia (Nordrhein-Westfalen)	13,119	16,540,000	1,261	State (Germany, West) .... E	Düsseldorf; Köln	German
Northwest Territories	1,304,903	25,000	0.02	Territory (Canada) .... E	Ottawa, Ontario; Yellowknife	English, Eskimo, Indian
Norway†	125,181	3,710,000	30	Monarchy .... A	Oslo	Norwegian (Riksmål and Landsmål)
Nova Scotia	21,425	761,000	36	Province (Canada) .... E	Halifax	English
Nyasaland, see Malawi						
Oceania (incl. Australia)	3,295,000	17,400,000	5.3		....; Sydney	
Ohio	41,222	10,372,000	252	State (U.S.) .... E	Columbus; Cleveland	
Oklahoma	69,919	2,512,000	36	State (U.S.) .... E	Oklahoma City	
Ontario	412,582	6,670,000	16	Province (Canada) .... E	Toronto	English
Orange Free State	49,649	1,580,000	32	Province (South Africa) .... E	Bloemfontein	English, Afrikaans, Bantu languages
Oregon	96,981	1,896,000	20	State (U.S.) .... E	Salem; Portland	
Orkney Is.	376	18,400	49	Part of Scotland, U.K. (Orkney County) .... D	Kirkwall	English
Pacific Islands Trust Territory	672	90,000	134	Trust Territory (U.S.)	Saipan	Malay-Polynesian languages, English
Pakistan (incl. part of Kashmir)†	399,373	102,700,000	257	Federal Republic (Br. Comm. of Nations) .... A	Rawalpindi and Dacca; Karachi	Urdu, Bengali, English
Pakistan, East	55,134	54,600,000	990	Province (Pakistan) .... D	Dacca	Bengali, English
Pakistan, West (incl. Karachi and part of Kashmir)	344,239	48,100,000	140	Pakistan	....; Karachi	Urdu, English
Palestine (Gaza Area)	78	400,000	5,128	Military Government (U.A.R.) .... B	Gaza	Arabic
Panama†	29,209	1,225,000	42	Republic .... A	Panamá	Spanish
Papua (excl. New Guinea, Ter. of)	90,600	560,000	6.2	External Territory (Australia) C	Port Moresby	Papuan and Negrito languages, English
Paraguay†	157,048	1,920,000	12	Republic .... A	Asuncion	Spanish, Guaraní
Pennsylvania	45,333	11,511,000	254	State (U.S.) .... E	Harrisburg; Philadelphia	
Persia, see Iran						
Peru†	496,224	11,500,000	23	Republic .... A	Lima	Spanish, Quechua
Philippines†	115,831	31,800,000	275	Republic .... A	Quezon City; Manila	Tagalog and other Malay-Polynesian languages, English
Pitcairn (excl. Dependencies)	2	100	50	Colony (U.K.) C	Adamstown	English
Poland†	120,359	31,350,000	260	People's Republic .... A	Warsaw (Warszawa)	Polish
Portugal†	35,340	9,140,000	259	Republic .... A	Lisbon (Lisboa)	Portuguese
Portugal and Possessions	837,733	22,697,000	27		Lisbon (Lisboa)	
Portuguese Guinea	13,948	525,000	38	Overseas Province (Portugal) C	Bissau	Native languages, Portuguese
Portuguese India (former) (Goa, Damão & Diu; Dadra & Nagar Haveli)						
Portuguese Timor	7,332	548,000	75	Overseas Province (Portugal) C	Dili	Malay, Papuan languages, Portuguese
Prairie Provinces	757,985	3,359,000	4.4	Canada	....; Winnipeg	English
Prince Edward Island	2,184	108,000	49	Province (Canada) .... E	Charlottetown	English
Puerto Rico	3,435	2,600,000	757	Commonwealth (U.S.) C	San Juan	Spanish, English
Qatar	8,500	65,000	7.6	Sheikdom (U.K. protection) .... B	Doha	Arabic
Quebec	594,860	5,620,000	9.4	Province (Canada) .... E	Quebec; Montreal	French, English
Queensland	667,000	1,606,000	2.4	State (Australia) .... E	Brisbane	English
Reunion	969	385,000	397	Overseas Department (France) C	St. Denis	French
Rhineland-Palatinate (Rheinland-Pfalz)	7,657	3,545,000	463	State (Germany, West) .... E	Mainz; Ludwigshafen am Rhein	German
Rhode Island	1,214	897,000	739	State (U.S.) .... E	Providence	
Rhodesia	150,333	4,200,000	28	Self-Governing Colony (U.K.) C	Salisbury	Bantu langues, English
Rhodesia & Nyasaland, Federation of, see Malawi, Rhodesia, and Zambia						
Rio Muni, see Equatorial Guinea						
Rodrigues	42	19,000	452	Dependency of Mauritius (U.K.) .... D	Port Mathurin	English, French
Romania†	91,698	19,025,000	207	People's Republic .... A	Bucharest (Bucureşti)	Romanian, Hungarian
Ruanda-Urundi, see Rwanda and Burundi						
Russian Soviet Federated Socialist Republic	6,592,850	126,300,000	19	Soviet Federated Socialist Republic (Sov. Un.) .... E	Moscow (Moskva)	Russian, Finno-Ugric languages, various Turkic, Iranian, and Mongol languages
Russian S.F.S.R. in Europe	1,527,400	92,900,000	61	Soviet Union	....; Moscow	Russian, Finno-Ugric languages
Rwanda†	10,169	2,800,000	275	Republic .... A	Kigali	Bantu and Hamitic languages
Ryukyu Is. (Southern)	848	940,000	1,108	U.S. Military Administration .... B	Naha	Japanese
Saar (Saarland)	991	1,116,000	1,126	State (Germany, West) .... E	Saarbrücken	German
Sabah (North Borneo)	29,388	515,000	18	Administrative division of Malaysia .... E	Jesselton; Sandakan	Malay, Chinese
St. Helena (incl. Dependencies)	160	4,600	29	Colony (U.K.) C	Jamestown	English
St. Kitts-Nevis-Anguilla	153	64,000	418	Colony (U.K.) C	Basseterre	English
St. Lucia	238	94,000	395	Colony (U.K.) C	Castries	English
St. Pierre & Miquelon	93	5,000	54	Overseas Territory (France) C	St. Pierre	French
St. Vincent	150	85,000	567	Colony (U.K.) C	Kingstown	English
Samoa (Entire)	1,206	145,000	120		....; Apia	Malay-Polynesian languages, English
San Marino	23	17,000	739	Republic .... A	San Marino	Italian
Sao Tome & Principe	372	55,000	148	Overseas Province (Portugal) C	São Tomé	Bantu languages, Portuguese
Sarawak	48,250	845,000	18	Administrative division of Malaysia .... E	....; Kuching	Malay, Chinese, English
Sardinia	9,301	1,440,000	155	Part of Italy (3 Provinces) .... D	....; Caglairi	Italian
Saskatchewan	251,700	947,000	3.8	Province (Canada) .... E	Regina	English
Saudi Arabia†	617,800	7,000,000	11	Monarchy .... A	Riyadh; Mecca	Arabic
Scandinavia (incl. Finland and Iceland)	510,026	20,952,000	41		....; Copenhagen (København)	Swedish, Danish, Norwegian, Finnish, Icelandic
Schleswig-Holstein	6,045	2,405,000	398	State (Germany, West) .... E	Kiel	German
Scotland	30,411	5,215,000	171	Administrative division of United Kingdom .... E	Edinburgh; Glasgow	English
Senegal†	76,124	3,480,000	46	Republic .... A	Dakar	Wolof, Poular, French
Seychelles	156	47,000	301	Colony (U.K.) C	Victoria	French, Creole, English

† *Member of the United Nations (1965).*

Region or Political Division	Area in sq. miles	Estimated Population 1/1/1965	Pop. per sq. mi.	Form of Government and Ruling Power	Capital; Largest City (unless same)	Predominant Languages
Shetland Is.	550	17,500	32	Part of Scotland, U.K. (Zetland County)......D	Lerwick	English
Siam, see Thailand	....	....	....		....	....
Sicily	9,926	4,810,000	485	Part of Italy (Sicilia Autonomous Region)......D	Palermo	Italian
Sierra Leone†	27,925	2,250,000	81	Monarchy (Br. Commonwealth of Nations)......A	Freetown	Temne, Mende, English
Sikkim	2,744	170,000	62	Monarchy (Indian protection)......B	Gangtok	Tibeto-Burman languages
Singapore	224	1,840,000	8,214	Self-Governing Member (Br. Comm. of Nations)......A	Singapore	Chinese, Malay, English
Solomon Is. (Austl. Trust)	4,320	62,000	14	Part of Australian Trust Ter. of New Guinea (Bougainville District)......D	Sohano; Kieta	Malay-Polynesian languages
Solomon Is., British	11,500	133,000	12	Protectorate (U.K.)......C	Honiara	Malay-Polynesian languages
Somali Republic†	246,202	2,350,000	9.5	Republic......A	Mogadiscio	Somali
South Africa†	472,359	17,700,000	37	Federal Republic......A	Pretoria and Cape Town; Johannesburg	English, Afrikaans, Bantu languages
South America	6,870,000	160,800,000	23	....	........; Buenos Aires	....
South Arabia	111,000	1,050,000	9.5	Protectorate (U.K.)......C	Aden; Al Mukallā	Arabic
South Australia	380,070	1,042,000	2.7	State (Australia)......E	Adelaide	English
South Carolina	31,055	2,524,000	81	State (U.S.)......E	Columbia	....
South Dakota	77,047	711,000	9.2	State (U.S.)......E	Pierre; Sioux Falls	....
Southern Rhodesia, see Rhodesia	....	....	....	....	....	....
South Georgia	1,450	500	0.3	Dependency of Falkland Is. (U.K.)......D	Grytviken	English, Norwegian
South Polar Regions	....	....	....		....	....
South West Africa	317,725	555,000	1.7	Mandate (South Africa)......C	Windhoek	Bantu languages, Hottentot, Bushman, Afrikaans, English
Soviet Union (Union of Soviet Socialist Republics)†	8,599,300	229,500,000	27	Federal Soviet Republic......A	Moscow (Moskva)	Russian and other Slavic languages, various Finno-Ugric, Turkic, and Mongol languages, Caucasian languages, Persian
Soviet Union in Europe	1,919,750	156,500,000	82	Soviet Union......	........; Moscow (Moskva)	Russian, Ruthenian, various Finno-Ugric and Caucasian languages
Spain†	194,884	31,500,000	162	Monarchy (Regency)......A	Madrid	Spanish, Catalan, Galician, Basque
Spain and Possessions	309,079	32,020,000	104	....	Madrid	....
Spanish Possessions in North Africa	82	158,000	1,927	Five Possessions (no central government) (Spain)......C	........; Melilla	Spanish, Arabic, Berber
Spanish Sahara	102,703	45,000	0.4	African Province (Spain)......C	Aiún	Arabic, Spanish
Spitsbergen, see Svalbard	....	....	....	....	....	....
Sudan†	967,500	13,350,000	14	Republic......A	Khartoum	Arabic, native languages, English
Sumatra (Sumatera)	182,860	17,150,000	94	Part of Indonesia (6 Provinces)......D	........; Medan	Bahasa Indonesia, English, Chinese
Surinam (Neth. Guiana)	55,143	385,000	7.0	Self-Governing Territory (Netherlands)......C	Paramaribo	Dutch, Indo-Aryan languages
Svalbard (Spitsbergen)	24,101	No perm. pop.	....	Dependency (Norway)......C	Longyearbyen	Norwegian, Russian
Swaziland	6,705	295,000	44	Territory (Protectorate)(U.K.)......C	Mbabane	Swazi and other Bantu languages, English
Sweden†	173,666	7,675,000	44	Monarchy......A	Stockholm	Swedish
Switzerland	15,941	6,075,000	381	Federal Republic......A	Bern (Berne); Zürich	German, French, Italian
Syria†	71,498	5,100,000	71	Republic......A	Damascus (Esh Sham)	Arabic
Tadzhik S.S.R.	55,250	2,410,000	44	Soviet Socialist Republic (Sov. Un.)......E	Dushanbe	Tadzhik, Turkic languages, Russian
Taiwan (Formosa) (Nationalist China)†	13,884	12,250,000	882	Republic......A	Taipei	Chinese
Tanganyika, see Tanzania	....	....	....	....	....	....
Tanzania (Tanganyika & Zanzibar)†	362,820	10,425,000	29	Republic (Br. Comm. of Nations)......A	Dar es Salaam	Swahili and other Bantu languages, English Arabic
Tasmania	26,215	371,000	14	State (Australia)......E	Hobart	English
Tennessee	42,244	3,737,000	88	State (U.S.)......E	Nashville; Memphis	....
Texas	267,339	10,669,000	40	State (U.S.)......E	Austin; Houston	....
Thailand (Siam)†	198,500	30,100,000	152	Monarchy......A	Bangkok (Krung Thep)	Thai, Chinese
Tibet	471,660	1,300,000	2.8	Autonomous Region (China)......E	Lhasa	Tibetan
Togo†	21,850	1,620,000	74	Republic......A	Lomé	Native languages, French
Tokelau (Union) Is.	4	2,000	500	Island Territory (New Zealand)......C	........; Fakaofo	Malay-Polynesian languages
Tonga	270	72,000	267	Protected Monarchy (U.K.)......C	Nukualofa	Malay-Polynesian languages, English
Transcaucasia	71,850	11,000,000	153	Soviet Union......	........; Baku	....
Transvaal	110,450	7,020,000	64	Province (South Africa)......E	Pretoria; Johannesburg	English, Afrikaans, Bantu languages
Trinidad & Tobago†	1,980	960,000	485	Self-Governing Member (Br. Comm. of Nations)......A	Port-of-Spain	English, Spanish
Tristan da Cunha	40	300	7.5	Dependency of St. Helena (UK.)......D	Edinburgh	English
Trucial Coast	32,300	120,000	3.7	Seven Sheikdoms (no central government) (U.K. protection)......B	........; Dubayy	Arabic
Tunisia†	48,332	4,600,000	95	Republic......A	Tunis	Arabic, French
Turkey†	301,381	31,300,000	104	Republic......A	Ankara; Istanbul	Turkish
Turkey in Europe	9,121	2,600,000	285	Turkey......	........; Istanbul	Turkish
Turkmen S.S.R.	188,450	1,850,000	9.8	Soviet Socialist Republic (Sov. Un.)......E	Ashkhabad	Turkic languages, Russian
Turks & Caicos Is.	166	6,000	36	Colony (U.K.)......C	Grand Turk	English
Uganda†	92,525	7,450,000	81	Self-Governing Member (Br. Commonwealth of Nations)......A	Kampala	Bantu languages
Ukraine (S.S.R.)†	232,050	45,500,000	196	Soviet Socialist Republic (Sov. Un.)......E	Kiev	Ukrainian, Russian
Union of Soviet Socialist Republics, see Soviet Union	....	....	....	....	....	....
United Arab Republic (Egypt)†	386,000	29,000,000	75	Republic......A	Cairo (Al Qāhirah)	Arabic
United Kingdom of Great Britain & Northern Ireland†	94,214	54,500,000	578	Monarchy (Br. Commonwealth of Nations)......A	London	English, Welsh, Gaelic
United Kingdom & Possessions	782,011	68,883,000	88	....	London	....
United States†	*3,675,633	193,850,000‡	53	Federal Republic......A	Washington; New York	English
United States and Possessions	3,680,757	196,723,000	53	....	Washington; New York	English, Spanish
Upper Volta†	105,869	4,775,000	45	Republic......A	Ouagadougou	Voltaic and Mande languages, French
Uruguay†	72,172	2,600,000	36	Republic......A	Montevideo	Spanish
Utah	84,916	1,008,000	12	State (U.S.)......E	Salt Lake City	....
Uzbek S.S.R.	171,900	10,050,000	58	Soviet Socialist Republic (Sov. Un.)......E	Tashkent	Turkic languages, Sart, Russian
Vatican City (Holy See)	0.2	1,000	5,000	Ecclesiastical State......A	Vatican City	Italian, Latin
Venezuela†	352,143	8,600,000	24	Federal Republic......A	Caracas	Spanish
Vermont	9,609	396,000	41	State (U.S.)......E	Montpelier; Burlington	....
Victoria	87,884	3,155,000	36	State (Australia)......E	Melbourne	English
Vietnam (Entire)	127,574	33,400,000	262	....	........; Saigon	Annamese, Chinese
Vietnam, North	61,294	17,500,000	286	People's Republic......A	Hanoi	Annamese, Chinese
Vietnam, South	66,280	15,900,000	240	Republic......A	Saigon	Annamese, Chinese
Virgin Is., British	59	8,000	136	Colony (U.K.)......C	Road Town	English
Virgin Is. of the U.S.	133	38,000	286	Unincorporated Territory (U.S.)......C	Charlotte Amalie	English
Virginia	40,815	4,400,000	108	State (U.S.)......E	Richmond; Norfolk	....
Wake I.	3	1,200	400	Possession (U.S.)......C	....	English
Wales (incl. Monmouthshire)	8,017	2,675,000	334	United Kingdom......	Cardiff	English, Welsh
Wallis & Futuna	106	9,000	85	Overseas Territory (France)......C	Mata-Utu	Malay-Polynesian languages
Washington	68,192	3,051,000	45	State (U.S.)......E	Olympia; Seattle	....
Western Australia	975,920	814,000	0.8	State (Australia)......E	Perth	English
Western Samoa	1,133	124,000	111	Self-Governing Member (Br. Commonwealth of Nations)......A	Apia	Malay-Polynesian languages, English
West Indies	91,110	22,250,000	244	....	........; Havana	....
West Irian	160,600	775,000	4.8	Under Indonesian Administration......C	Sukarnapura (Hollandia)	Various Papuan languages
West Virginia	24,181	1,797,000	74	State (U.S.)......E	Charleston; Huntington	....
White Russia, see Byelorussia	....	....	....	....	....	....
Wisconsin	56,154	4,166,000	74	State (U.S.)......E	Madison; Milwaukee	....
World	57,280,000	3,237,000,000	57	....	........; New York	....
Wyoming	97,914	355,000	3.6	State (U.S.)......E	Cheyenne	....
Yemen†	75,300	5,000,000	66	Republic......A	Şan'ā'	Arabic
Yugoslavia†	98,766	19,400,000	196	Socialist Federal Republic......A	Belgrade (Beograd)	Serbo-Croatian-Slovenian, Macedonian
Yukon	207,076	17,000	0.08	Territory (Canada)......E	Whitehorse	English, Eskimo, Indian
Zambia (Northern Rhodesia)†	290,537	3,650,000	13	Republic......A	Lusaka; Kitwe	Bantu languages, English
Zanzibar	1,020	335,000	328	Part of Tanzania......D	........; Zanzibar	Arabic, English

†Member of the United Nations (1965).
**Total area of the United States includes 3,548,974 square miles of land; 66,237 square miles of inland water; and 60,422 square miles of Great Lakes area, not included in any State.*
‡Total 1965 estimated population of the United States includes 193,200,000 residents of the 50 States and D.C., and 650,000 armed forces overseas, not included in any State.

WORLD FACTS AND COMPARISONS

MOVEMENTS OF THE EARTH

The earth makes one complete revolution around the sun every 365 days, 5 hours, 48 minutes, and 46 seconds.

The earth makes one complete rotation on its axis in 23 hours and 56 minutes.

The earth revolves in its orbit around the sun at a speed of 66,700 miles per hour.

The earth rotates on its axis at an equatorial speed of more than 1,000 miles per hour.

MEASUREMENTS OF THE EARTH

Estimated age of the earth, at least 3 billion years.
Equatorial diameter of the earth, 7,926.68 miles.
Polar diameter of the earth, 7,899.99 miles.
Mean diameter of the earth, 7,918.78 miles.
Equatorial circumference of the earth, 24,902.45 miles.
Polar circumference of the earth, 24,818.60 miles.
Difference between equatorial and polar circumference of the earth, 83.85 miles.

Weight of the earth, 6,600,000,000,000,000,000,000 tons, or 6,600 billion billion tons.

Total area of the earth, 196,940,400 square miles.

Total land area of the earth (including inland water and Antarctica), 57,280,000 square miles.

THE EARTH'S INHABITANTS

Total population of the earth is estimated to be 3,237,000,000 (January 1, 1965).

Estimated population density of the earth, 57 per square mile.

THE EARTH'S SURFACE

Highest point on the earth's surface, Mount Everest, China (Tibet)–Nepal, 29,028 feet.

Lowest point on the earth's land surface, shores of the Dead Sea, Israel-Jordan, 1,286 feet below sea level.

Greatest ocean depth, the Marianas Trench, south of Guam, Pacific Ocean, 36,198 feet.

EXTREMES OF TEMPERATURE AND RAINFALL OF THE EARTH

Highest temperature ever recorded, 136.4°F. at Azizia, Libya, Africa, on September 13, 1922.

Lowest temperature ever recorded, −126.9°F. at Vostok, Antarctica, on August 24, 1960.

Highest mean annual temperature, 88°F. at Lugh Ferrandi, Somali Republic.

Lowest mean annual temperature, −67°F at Vostok, Antarctica.

At Baguio, Luzon, in the Philippines, 46 inches of rainfall was reported in a 24-hour period, July 14–15, 1911. This is believed to be the world's record for a 24-hour rainfall.

An authenticated rainfall of 366 inches in 1 month—July, 1861—was reported at Cherrapunji, India. More than 131 inches fell in a period of 7 consecutive days in June, 1931. Average annual rainfall at Cherrapunji is 450 inches.

THE CONTINENTS

CONTINENT	Area (sq. mi.)	Population Estimated Jan. 1, 1965	Population per sq. mi.	Mean Elevation (feet)	Highest Elevation (Feet)	Lowest Elevation (Feet)	Highest Recorded Temperature	Lowest Recorded Temperature
North America	9,420,000	289,700,000	31	2,000	Mt. McKinley, United States (Alaska), 20,320	Death Valley, California, 282 below sea level	Death Valley, California, 134°F.	Snag, Yukon, Canada, −81°F.
South America	6,870,000	160,800,000	23	1,800	Mt. Aconcagua, Argentina, 22,834	Salinas Grandes, Península Valdés, Argentina, 131 below sea level	Rivadavia, Argentina, 120°F.	Sarmiento, Argentina, −27.4°F.
Europe	3,825,000	601,900,000	157	980	Mt. Elbrus, Soviet Union, 18,481	Caspian Sea, Soviet Union–Iran, 92 below sea level	Sevilla (Seville), Spain, 122°F.	Ust-Shchugor, Soviet Union, −67°F.
Asia	17,085,000	1,877,000,000	110	3,000	Mt. Everest, China (Tibet)-Nepal, 29,028	Dead Sea, Israel-Jordan, 1,286 below sea level	Tirat Zvi, Israel, 129.2°F.	Oymyakon, Soviet Union, −89.9°F.
Africa	11,685,000	290,200,000	25	1,900	Mt. Kilimanjaro, Tanzania, 19,340	Qattara Depression, U.A.R. (Egypt), 436 below sea level	Azizia, Libya, 136.4°F.	Ifrane, Morocco, −11.2°F.
Oceania, incl. Australia	3,295,000	17,400,000	5	.....	Mt. Wilhelm, New Guinea, Ter. of, 15,400	Lake Eyre, South Australia, 39 below sea level	Cloncurry, Queensland, Australia, 127.5°F.	Charlotte Pass, New South Wales, Australia, −8°F.
Australia	2,971,081	11,335,000	4	1,000	Mt. Kosciusko, New South Wales, 7,316	Lake Eyre, South Australia, 39 below sea level	Cloncurry, Queensland, 127.5°F.	Charlotte Pass, New South Wales, −8°F.
Antarctica	5,100,000	Uninhabited	...	6,000	Vinson Massif, 16,864	Sea level	Esperanza (Antarctic Peninsula), 58.3°F.	Vostok, −126.9°F.
World	57,280,000	3,237,000,000	57	.....	Mt. Everest, China (Tibet)-Nepal, 29,028	Dead Sea, Israel-Jordan, 1,286 below sea level	Azizia, Libya, 136.4°F.	Vostok, −126.9°F.

APPROXIMATE POPULATION OF THE WORLD, 1650–1965*

AREA	1650	1750	1800	1850	1900	1914	1920	1939	1950	1965
North America	5,000,000	5,000,000	13,000,000	39,000,000	106,000,000	141,000,000	147,000,000	186,000,000	219,000,000	289,700,000
South America	8,000,000	7,000,000	12,000,000	20,000,000	38,000,000	55,000,000	61,000,000	90,000,000	111,000,000	160,800,000
Europe	100,000,000	140,000,000	190,000,000	265,000,000	400,000,000	470,000,000	453,000,000	526,000,000	530,000,000	601,900,000
Asia	335,000,000	476,000,000	593,000,000	754,000,000	932,000,000	1,006,000,000	1,000,000,000	1,247,000,000	1,418,000,000	1,877,000,000
Africa	100,000,000	95,000,000	90,000,000	95,000,000	118,000,000	130,000,000	140,000,000	170,000,000	199,000,000	290,200,000
Oceania, incl. Australia	} 2,000,000	2,000,000	2,000,000	2,000,000	6,000,000	8,000,000	9,000,000	11,000,000	13,000,000	17,400,000
Australia					4,000,000	5,000,000	6,000,000	7,000,000	8,000,000	11,335,000
World	550,000,000	725,000,000	900,000,000	1,175,000,000	1,600,000,000	1,810,000,000	1,810,000,000	2,230,000,000	2,490,000,000	3,237,000,000

Figures prior to 1965 are rounded to the nearest million. Figures in italics represent very rough estimates.

LARGEST COUNTRIES OF THE WORLD IN POPULATION

	Population 1/1/1965
1 China (excl. Taiwan)	700,000,000
2 India (incl. part of Kashmir)	479,000,000
3 Soviet Union	229,500,000
4 United States	193,850,000
5 Indonesia	103,350,000
6 Pakistan (incl. part of Kashmir)	102,700,000
7 Japan	97,400,000
8 Brazil	80,250,000
9 Germany, West (incl. West Berlin)	58,550,000
10 United Kingdom of Great Britain & Northern Ireland	54,500,000
11 Italy	50,900,000
12 France	48,800,000
13 Nigeria	43,200,000
14 Mexico	40,250,000
15 Philippines	31,800,000
16 Spain	31,500,000
17 Poland	31,350,000
18 Turkey	31,300,000
19 Thailand	30,100,000
20 United Arab Republic (Egypt)	29,000,000
21 Korea, South	28,000,000
22 Burma	24,500,000
23 Iran	23,100,000
24 Argentina	22,200,000
25 Ethiopia	21,500,000

LARGEST COUNTRIES OF THE WORLD IN AREA

	Area (sq. mi.)
1 Soviet Union	8,599,300
2 Canada	3,851,809
3 China (excl. Taiwan)	3,691,500
4 United States	3,675,633
5 Brazil	3,286,478
6 Australia	2,971,081
7 India (incl. part of Kashmir)	1,227,275
8 Argentina	1,072,070
9 Sudan	967,500
10 Algeria	919,595
11 Congo, The (Léopoldville)	905,565
12 Greenland (Den.)	840,000
13 Mexico	761,602
14 Libya	679,362
15 Iran	636,300
16 Saudi Arabia	617,800
17 Mongolia	592,700
18 Indonesia	574,670
19 Peru	496,224
20 Chad	495,800
21 Angola (Port.)	481,351
22 South Africa	472,359
23 Mali	464,874
24 Niger	458,995
25 Ethiopia	457,267

PRINCIPAL MOUNTAINS OF THE WORLD

NORTH AMERICA

Mountain	Height (feet)
McKinley, △Alaska (△United States; △North America)	20,320
Logan, △Canada (△St. Elias Mts.)	19,850
Citlaltépetl (Orizaba), △Mexico	18,696
St. Elias, Alaska–Canada	18,008
Popocatepetl, Mexico	17,887
Foraker, Alaska	17,395
Ixtacihuatl, Mexico	17,343
Lucania, Yukon, Canada	17,147
Whitney, △California	14,495
Elbert, △Colorado (△Rocky Mts.)	14,431
Massive, Colorado	14,418
Harvard, Colorado	14,414
Rainier, △Washington (△Cascade Range)	14,410
Williamson, California	14,384
Blanca Pk., Colorado (△Sangre de Cristo Range)	14,317
Uncompahgre Pk., Colorado (△San Juan Mts.)	14,301
Grays Pk., Colorado (△Front Range)	14,274
Evans, Colorado	14,264
Longs Pk., Colorado	14,256
Colima, Nevado de, Mexico	14,235
Shasta, California	14,162
Pikes Peak, Colorado	14,110
Wrangell, Alaska	14,005
Tajumulco, △Guatemala (△Central America)	13,846
Mauna Kea, △Hawaii (△Hawaii I.)	13,796
Gannett Pk., △Wyoming	13,785
Grand Teton, Wyoming	13,766
Mauna Loa, Hawaii	13,680
Kings Pk., △Utah	13,498
Waddington, Canada (△Coast Mts.)	13,260
Cloud Pk., Wyoming (△Big Horn Mts.)	13,175
Wheeler Pk., △New Mexico	13,160
Boundary Pk., △Nevada	13,145
Robson, Canada (△Canadian Rockies)	12,972
Granite Pk., △Montana	12,799
Humphreys Pk., △Arizona	12,670
Borah Pk., △Idaho	12,662
Chirripó Grande, △Costa Rica	12,533
Adams, Washington	12,307
Gunnbjörn, △Greenland	12,139
San Gorgonio, California (△Southern California)	11,485
Chiriquí, △Panama	11,411
Hood, △Oregon	11,245
Lassen Pk., California	10,466
Duarte, Pico, △Dominican Rep. (△West Indies)	10,417
Haleakala, Hawaii (△Maui)	10,025
Paricutín, Mexico	9,100
Selle, Massif de la, △Haiti	8,793
Guadalupe Pk., △Texas	8,751
Olympus, Washington (△Olympic Mts.)	7,954
Santa Ana, △El Salvador	7,812
Blue Mountain Pk., △Jamaica	7,520
Harney Pk., △South Dakota (△Black Hills)	7,242
Mitchell, △North Carolina (△Appalachian Mts.)	6,684
Clingmans Dome, North Carolina–△Tennessee (△Great Smoky Mts.)	6,642
Turquino, Pico de, △Cuba	6,496
Washington, △New Hampshire (△White Mts.)	6,288
Rogers, △Virginia	5,720
Marcy, △New York (△Adirondack Mts.)	5,344
Katahdin, △Maine	5,268
Kawaikini, Hawaii (△Kauai)	5,170
Spruce Knob, △West Virginia	4,860
Pelée, △Martinique	4,800
Mansfield, △Vermont (△Green Mts.)	4,393
Punta, Cerro de, △Puerto Rico	4,389
Black Mtn., △Kentucky	4,145
Kilauea, Hawaii (Hawaii I.)	4,090
Kaala Pk., Hawaii (△Oahu)	4,025

SOUTH AMERICA

Mountain	Height (feet)
Aconcagua, △Argentina (△Andes Mts.; △South America)	22,834
Ojos del Salado, Nudos, Argentina–△Chile	22,590
Pissis, Argentina	22,546
Tupungato, Argentina–Chile	22,310
Huascarán, △Peru	22,205
Llullaillaco, Argentina–Chile	22,146
Mercedario, Argentina	21,885
Yerupaja, Peru	21,758
Incahuasi, Argentina–Chile	21,719
Illampu, △Bolivia	21,490
Ancohuma, Bolivia	21,489
Sajama, Nevado, Bolivia	21,391
Illimani, Bolivia	21,151
Chimborazo, △Ecuador	20,577
Cotopaxi, Ecuador	19,344
Misti, El, Peru	19,144
Cristóbal Colón, △Colombia	18,947
Huila, Colombia (△Cordillera Central)	18,865
Bolívar (La Columna), △Venezuela	16,411
Fitz Roy, Argentina	11,600
Bandeira, Pico da, △Brazil	9,462

EUROPE

Mountain	Height (feet)
Elbrus, Soviet Union (△Caucasus Mts., △Europe)	18,481
Shkhara, Soviet Union	17,059
Dykh-Tau, Soviet Union	17,054
Kazbek, Soviet Union	16,554
Blanc, Mont, △France (△Alps)	15,781
Rosa, Monte (Dufourspitze) △Switzerland	15,200
Rosa, Monte (Grenzgipfel) △Italy–Switzerland	15,194
Weisshorn, Switzerland	14,803
Matterhorn, Switzerland	14,685
Finsteraarhorn, Switzerland	14,026
Jungfrau, Switzerland	13,668
Grossglockner, △Austria	12,461
Teide, Pico de, △Spain (△Canary Is.)	12,162
Mulhacén, △Spain (continental)	11,424
Aneto, Pico de, Spain (△Pyrenees)	11,168
Etna, Italy (△Sicily)	11,122
Perdido (Perdu), Spain	11,007
Clapier, France-Italy (△Maritime Alps)	10,817
Zugspitze, △Germany	9,721
Coma Pedrosa, Andorra	9,665
Musala, △Bulgaria	9,592
Corno, Italy (△Apennines)	9,560
Olympus, △Greece	9,550
Triglav, △Yugoslavia	9,393
Korab, △Albania	9,068
Cinto, France (△Corsica)	8,891
Gerlachovka, △Czechoslovakia (△Carpathian Mts.)	8,737
Negoi, △Romania	8,346
Rysy Pk., Czechoslovakia	8,212
Galdhöpiggen, △Norway (△Scandinavia)	8,097
Parnassós, Greece	8,061
Idhi (Ida), Greece (△Crete)	8,058
Pico, △Portugal (△Azores Is.)	7,713
Kebnekaise, △Sweden	6,962
Hvannadalshnúkur, △Iceland	6,952
Malhão, △Portugal (continental)	6,532
Narodnaya, Soviet Union (△Ural Mts.)	6,184
Marmora, Punta La, Italy (△Sardinia)	6,017
Hekla, Iceland	4,747
Nevis, Ben, △United Kingdom (△Scotland)	4,406
Haltia, △Finland	4,344
Vesuvius, Italy	3,842
Snowdon, △Wales	3,560
Carrantuohill, △Ireland	3,414
Kekes, △Hungary	3,330
Scafell Pike, △England	3,210
Stromboli, Italy	3,038

ASIA

Mountain	Height (feet)
Everest, △China (△Tibet)–△Nepal (△Himalaya Mts.; △Asia; △World)	29,028
Godwin Austen (K²), △Pakistan (△Kashmir) (△Karakoram Range)	28,250
Kanchenjunga, Nepal–△Sikkim	28,168
Makalu, China (Tibet)–Nepal	27,790
Dhaulagiri, Nepal	26,810
Nanga Parbat, Pakistan (Kashmir)	26,660
Annapurna, Nepal	26,504
Gasherbrum, Pakistan (Kashmir)	26,470
Gosainthan, China (Tibet)	26,291
Nanda Devi, △India	25,645
Rakaposhi, Pakistan (Kashmir)	25,551
Kamet, India	25,447
Namcha Barwa, China (Tibet)	25,445
Gurla Mandhata, China (Tibet)	25,355
Ulugh Muztagh, China (△Kunlun Mts.)	25,340
Tirich Mir, Pakistan (△Hindu Kush)	25,230
Minya Konka, China	24,900
Kangri, △Bhutan	24,740
Communism Pk., △Soviet Union (△Pamir-Alay Mts.)	24,590
Pobeda Pk., China–Soviet Union (△Tien Shan)	24,409
Muztagh Ata, China	24,388
Api, Nepal	23,398
Lenin Pk., Soviet Union	23,382
Tengri Khan, Soviet Union	22,940
Kailas, China (Tibet)	22,028
Hkakabo Razi, △Burma	19,296
Demavend, △Iran	18,934
Ararat, △Turkey	16,946
Carstensz, △West Irian (△New Guinea)	16,503
Klyuchevskaya, Soviet Union (△Kamchatka)	15,912
Wilhelmina, West Irian	15,518
Tabun Bogdo (Khuitun), △Mongolia (△Altai Mts.)	15,266
Belukha, Soviet Union	15,157
Turgun Uula, Mongolia	14,052
Kinabalu, △Malaysia (△Borneo)	13,455
Hsinkao, △Taiwan (Formosa)	13,113
Erciyas, Turkey	12,848
Munku-Sardyk, Mongolia–Soviet Union (△Sayan Mts.)	12,821
Kerintji, △Indonesia (△Sumatra)	12,484
Fuji, △Japan (△Honshu)	12,388
Hadūr Shu'ayb, △Yemen (△Arabian Peninsula)	12,336
Rindjani, Indonesia (△Lombok)	12,225
Mahameru, Indonesia (△Java)	12,060
Qalate Qarrāde, △Iraq	12,000
Razih, Jabal, △Saudi Arabia	11,999
Rantemario, Indonesia (△Celebes)	11,286
Qurnet es Sa'uda, △Lebanon	10,131
Shām, Jabal ash, △Muscat and Oman	9,902
Apo, △Philippines (△Mindanao)	9,690
Pulog, Philippines (△Luzon)	9,612
Phu Bia, △Laos	9,242
Hermon, Lebanon–△Syria	9,232
Changpai, △Korea	9,003
Anai Mudi, △India (peninsular)	8,841
Angka, Doi, △Thailand	8,452
Pidurutalagala, △Ceylon	8,281
Mayon, Philippines (Luzon)	8,071
Asahi, Japan (△Hokkaido)	7,513
Tahan, Gunong, Malaysia (△Malaya)	7,186
Troodos, △Cyprus	6,403
Kuju-San, Japan (△Kyushu)	5,866
Atzmon, △Israel	3,962
Krakatoa (Rakata), Indonesia	2,667
Carmel, Israel	1,791

AFRICA

Mountain	Height (feet)
Kilimanjaro (Kibo), △Tanzania (△Africa)	19,340
Kenya, △Kenya	17,040
Margherita, Mt., △Congo L.–△Uganda	16,795
Ras Dashan, △Ethiopia	15,158
Meru, Tanzania	14,980
Elgon, Kenya–Uganda	14,178
Toubkal, Djebal, △Morocco (△Atlas Mts.)	13,661
Cameroon, △Cameroon	13,354
Thabantshonyana, △Basutoland (△Southern Africa)	11,425
Emi Koussi, △Chad (△Tibesti Mts.)	11,204
Injasuti, South Africa	11,182
Neiges, Piton des, △Reunion	10,069
Tahat, △Algeria (△Ahaggar Mts.)	9,852
Maromokotro, △Malagasy Republic	9,462
Santa Isabel, △Equatorial Guinea (△Fernando Poo)	9,350
Cano, △Cape Verde Is.	9,760
Katrīnah, Jabal, △United Arab Republic (Egypt)	8,652
São Tomé, Pico de, △Sao Tome	6,640

OCEANIA

Mountain	Height (feet)
Wilhelm, △New Guinea, Ter. of	15,400
Bangeta, New Guinea, Ter. of	13,434
Giluwe, △Papua	13,660
Victoria, Papua (△Owen Stanley Range)	13,363
Cook, △New Zealand (△South Island)	12,349
Balbi, △Solomon Is. (△Bougainville)	10,170
Ruapehu, New Zealand (△North Island)	9,175
Egmont, New Zealand	8,260
Orohena, △Fr. Polynesia (△Tahiti)	7,618
The Father, New Guinea, Ter. of (△Bismarck Archipelago)	7,546
Kosciusko, △Australia (△New South Wales)	7,316
Mauga Silisili, △Western Samoa	6,095
Hombolt, △New Caledonia	5,380
Panié, New Caledonia	5,348
Ossa, Australia (△Tasmania)	5,305
Bartle Frere, Australia (△Queensland)	5,287
Woodroffe, Australia (△South Australia)	4,970
Victoria, △Fiji (△Viti Levu)	4,341
Bruce, Australia (△Western Australia)	4,024

ANTARCTICA

Mountain	Height (feet)
Vinson Massif (△Antarctica)	16,864
Kirkpatrick	14,600
Markham	14,275
Andrew Jackson	13,747
Sidley	13,717
Wade	13,398

△ Highest mountain in state, country, range, or region named.

GREAT OCEANS AND SEAS OF THE WORLD

OCEANS AND SEAS	Area (sq. mi.)	Average Depth (feet)	Greatest Depth (feet)	OCEANS AND SEAS	Area (sq. mi.)	Average Depth (feet)	Greatest Depth (feet)	OCEANS AND SEAS	Area (sq. mi.)	Average Depth (feet)	Greatest Depth (feet)
Pacific Ocean	63,855,000	14,050	36,198	Bering Sea	876,000	4,710	16,800	Hudson Bay	476,000	420	850
Atlantic Ocean	31,744,000	12,690	27,498	Caribbean Sea	750,000	7,310	24,580	Japan, Sea of	389,000	4,490	12,280
Indian Ocean	28,371,000	13,000	26,400	Gulf of Mexico	596,000	4,960	14,360	North Sea	222,000	310	2,170
Arctic Ocean	5,427,000	5,010	17,880	Okhotsk, Sea of	590,000	2,760	11,400	Black Sea	178,000	3,610	7,360
Mediterranean Sea	967,000	4,780	15,900	East China Sea	482,000	620	9,840	Red Sea	169,000	1,610	7,370
South China Sea	895,000	5,420	18,090	Yellow Sea	480,000	150	300	Baltic Sea	163,000	180	1,440

PRINCIPAL LAKES OF THE WORLD

LAKES	Area (sq. mi.)	LAKES	Area (sq. mi.)	LAKES	Area (sq. mi.)
Caspian, Soviet Union–Iran (salt)	152,084	Ontario, United States–Canada	7,540	Torrens, Australia (salt)	△2,200
Superior, United States–Canada	31,820	Ladoga, Soviet Union	7,092	Albert, Uganda–Congo L.	2,162
Victoria, Kenya–Uganda–Tanzania	26,828	Balkhash, Soviet Union	6,678	Vänern, Sweden	2,156
Aral, Soviet Union (salt)	26,518	Chad, Chad–Nigeria–Cameroon	△6,300	Winnipegosis, Canada	2,103
Huron, United States–Canada	23,010	Onega, Soviet Union	3,821	Bangweulu, Zambia	△1,900
Michigan, United States	22,400	Eyre, Australia (salt)	△3,700	Nipigon, Canada	1,870
Great Bear, Canada	12,275	Titicaca, Peru–Bolivia	3,500	Manitoba, Canada	1,817
Baykal, Soviet Union	12,159	Athabasca, Canada	3,120	Great Salt, United States (salt)	1,700
Great Slave, Canada	10,980	Nicaragua, Nicaragua	2,972	Koko Nor, China	1,650
Tanganyika, Congo L.–Tanzania–Burundi–Zambia	10,965	Rudolf, Kenya–Ethiopia (salt)	2,473	Dubawnt, Canada	1,600
Nyasa, Malawi–Tanzania–Mozambique	10,900	Reindeer, Canada	2,467	Gairdner, Australia (salt)	△1,500
Erie, United States–Canada	9,940	Issyk-Kul, Soviet Union	2,393	Lake of the Woods, United States–Canada	1,485
Winnipeg, Canada	9,465	Urmia, Iran (salt)	△2,229	Van, Turkey (salt)	1,470

△ Due to seasonal fluctuations in water level, areas of these lakes vary considerably.

PRINCIPAL RIVERS OF THE WORLD

	Length (miles)		Length (miles)		Length (miles)
Nile, Africa	4,132	Amu Darya, Asia	1,628	Si, Asia	930
Amazon, South America	3,900	Kolyma, Asia	1,615	Oka, Europe	920
Mississippi–Missouri–Red Rock, North America	3,860	Murray, Australia	1,600	Canadian, North America	906
Ob-Irtysh, Asia	3,461	Ganges, Asia	1,550	Dnestr, Europe	876
Yangtze, Asia	3,430	Pilcomayo, South America	1,550	Brazos, North America	870
Hwang Ho, Asia	2,903	Angara, Asia	1,549	Salado, South America	870
Congo, Africa	2,900	Ural, Asia	1,522	Fraser, North America	850
Amur, Asia	2,802	Vilyuy, Asia	1,513	Parnaíba, South America	850
Irtysh, Asia	2,747	Arkansas, North America	1,450	Colorado, North America (Texas)	840
Lena, Asia	2,653	Colorado, North America (U.S.–Mexico)	1,450	Rhine, Europe	820
Mackenzie, North America	2,635	Irrawaddy, Asia	1,425	Narbada, Asia	800
Mekong, Asia	2,600	Dnepr, Europe	1,420	Athabasca, North America	765
Niger, Africa	2,590	Aldan, Asia	1,392	Donets, Europe	735
Yenisey, Asia	2,566	Negro, South America	1,305	Pecos, North America	735
Missouri, North America	2,466	Paraguay, South America	1,290	Green, North America	730
Paraná, South America	2,450	Kama, Europe	1,261	Elbe, Europe	720
Mississippi, North America	2,348	Juruá, South America	1,250	James, North America	710
Plata-Paraguay, South America	2,300	Xingú, South America	1,230	Ottawa, North America	696
Volga, Europe	2,293	Don, Europe	1,224	White, North America	690
Madeira, South America	2,060	Ucayali, South America	1,220	Cumberland, North America	687
Indus, Asia	1,980	Columbia, North America	1,214	Gambia, Africa	680
Purús, South America	1,900	Saskatchewan, North America	1,205	Yellowstone, North America	671
St. Lawrence, North America	1,900	Peace, North America	1,195	Tennessee, North America	652
Rio Grande, North America	1,885	Orange, Africa	1,155	Gila, North America	630
Brahmaputra, Asia	1,800	Tigris, Asia	1,150	Vistula, Europe	630
Orinoco, South America	1,800	Sungari, Asia	1,140	Loire, Europe	625
São Francisco, South America	1,800	Pechora, Europe	1,118	Tagus, Europe	625
Yukon, North America	1,800	Tobol, Asia	1,093	North Platte, North America	618
Danube, Europe	1,770	Snake, North America	1,038	Albany, North America	610
Darling, Australia	1,750	Uruguay, South America	1,025	Tisza, Europe	607
Salween, Asia	1,730	Red, North America	1,018	Back, North America	605
Euphrates, Asia	1,675	Churchill, North America	1,000	Ouachita, North America	605
Syr Darya, Asia	1,653	Marañón, South America	1,000	Cimarron, North America	600
Zambezi, Africa	1,650	Ohio, North America	981	Sava, Europe	585
Tocantins, South America	1,640	Magdalena, South America	950	Nemunas (Niemen), Europe	582
Araguaia, South America	1,630	Roosevelt (River of Doubt), South America	950	Branco, South America	580
		Godavari, Asia	930	Oder, Europe	565

PRINCIPAL ISLANDS OF THE WORLD

	Area (sq. mi.)		Area (sq. mi.)		Area (sq. mi.)
Greenland, Arctic Region	840,000	Hispaniola, West Indies	29,530	Ceram, Indonesia	6,046
New Guinea, Oceania	316,856	Sakhalin, Soviet Union	29,344	New Caledonia, Oceania	5,671
Borneo, Indonesia	286,967	Tasmania, Australia	26,215	Flores, Indonesia	5,513
Madagascar, Indian Ocean	227,800	Ceylon, Indian Ocean	25,332	Samar, Philippines	5,124
Baffin, Canadian Arctic	183,810	Banks, Canadian Arctic	23,230	Negros, Philippines	4,903
Sumatra, Indonesia	182,859	Devon, Canadian Arctic	20,861	Palawan, Philippines	4,500
Honshū, Japan	88,930	Tierra del Fuego, Argentina-Chile	18,600	Panay, Philippines	4,448
Great Britain, North Atlantic Ocean	88,756	Kyūshū, Japan	16,215	Jamaica, West Indies	4,411
Ellesmere, Canadian Arctic	82,119	Melville, Canadian Arctic	16,141	Hawaii, Oceania	4,030
Victoria, Canadian Arctic	81,930	Southampton, Hudson Bay, Canada	15,700	Cape Breton, Canada	3,970
Celebes, Indonesia	72,986	West Spitsbergen, Arctic Region	15,260	Bougainville, Oceania	3,880
South Island, New Zealand	58,093	New Britain, Oceania	14,592	Mindoro, Philippines	3,794
Java, Indonesia	50,745	Formosa, China Sea	13,884	Cyprus, Mediterranean Sea	3,572
North Island, New Zealand	44,281	Hainan, South China Sea	13,127	Kodiak, Gulf of Alaska	3,569
Cuba, West Indies	44,217	Timor, Timor Sea	13,094	Puerto Rico, West Indies	3,435
Newfoundland, North Atlantic Ocean	43,359	Prince of Wales, Canadian Arctic	12,830	Corsica, Mediterranean Sea	3,367
Luzon, Philippines	40,814	Vancouver, Canada	12,408	Crete, Mediterranean Sea	3,238
Iceland, North Atlantic Ocean	39,800	Sicily, Mediterranean Sea	9,926	New Ireland, Oceania	3,205
Mindanao, Philippines	36,906	Somerset, Canadian Arctic	9,370	Leyte, Philippines	3,090
Ireland, North Atlantic Ocean	32,596	Sardinia, Mediterranean Sea	9,301	Wrangel, Soviet Arctic	2,819
Novaya Zemlya, Soviet Arctic	31,390	Shikoku, Japan	7,245	Guadalcanal, Oceania	2,500
Hokkaidō, Japan	29,950	North East Land, Svalbard Group	6,350	Long Island, United States	1,620

LARGEST METROPOLITAN AREAS AND CITIES
OF THE WORLD, 1964

This table lists every metropolitan area in the world with 1,000,000 or more population. For ease of comparison, each metropolitan area has been defined by Rand McNally & Company according to consistent rules. A metropolitan area includes a central city, neighboring communities linked to it by continuous built-up areas, and more distant communities if the bulk of their population is supported by commuters to the central city. All populations are estimates for January 1, 1964. The "city proper" figures refer to the area locally considered to be the city, provided it is under a single municipal government. Some metropolitan areas, such as Tōkyō–Yokohama, have more than one central city; in such cases the "city proper" figure is for the first-named city only.

Rank 1964		Estimated Population, 1/1/1964 Metropolitan Area	City Proper
1	New York, New York	16,325,000	8,085,000
2	Tōkyō–Yokohama, Japan	15,400,000	8,850,000
3	London, England	11,025,000	3,175,000
4	Ōsaka–Kōbe, Japan	8,700,000	3,250,000
5	Moscow (Moskva), Soviet Union	8,450,000	6,475,000
6	Paris, France	8,000,000	2,800,000
7	Buenos Aires, Argentina	7,700,000	2,950,000
8	Shanghai, China	7,600,000	10,400,000▲
9	Los Angeles, California	7,475,000	2,660,000
10	Chicago, Illinois	7,090,000	3,575,000
11	Calcutta, India	6,700,000	3,000,000
12	Mexico City, Mexico	6,100,000	3,050,000
13	São Paulo, Brazil	5,450,000	4,425,000
14	Rio de Janeiro, Brazil	5,250,000	3,600,000
15	Essen–Dortmund–Duisburg, Germany (West)	5,200,000	729,000
16	Bombay, India	4,700,000	4,500,000
17	Cairo (Al Qāhirah), United Arab Republic	4,600,000	3,800,000
18	Peking (Peiping), China	4,200,000	7,000,000▲
19	Detroit–Windsor, Michigan–Canada	4,170,000	1,610,000
20	Philadelphia, Pennsylvania	4,150,000	2,040,000
21	Berlin, Germany	4,025,000	2,180,000
22	Leningrad, Soviet Union	4,000,000	3,100,000
23	San Francisco–Oakland–San Jose, California	3,730,000	750,000
24	Boston, Massachusetts	3,480,000	665,000
25	Tientsin (Tienching), China	3,400,000	3,800,000▲
26	Victoria, Hong Kong	3,275,000	725,000
27	Seoul, Korea (South)	3,200,000	3,125,000
28	Djakarta, Indonesia	3,150,000	3,150,000
29	Manila, Philippines	2,900,000	1,190,000
30	Delhi–New Delhi, India	2,900,000	2,575,000
31	Manchester, England	2,850,000	652,000
32	Milano (Milan), Italy	2,775,000	1,675,000
33	Mukden (Shenyang), China	2,650,000	2,650,000
34	Birmingham, England	2,640,000	1,115,000
35	Wuhan, China	2,600,000	2,600,000
36	Madrid, Spain	2,575,000	2,450,000
37	Rome (Roma), Italy	2,500,000	2,340,000
38	Santiago, Chile	2,400,000	640,000
39	Sydney, Australia	2,340,000	168,000
40	Lima, Peru	2,300,000	1,975,000
41	Hamburg, Germany (West)	2,300,000	1,855,000
42	Washington, D.C.	2,265,000	785,000
43	Budapest, Hungary	2,265,000	1,920,000
44	Cleveland, Ohio	2,260,000	865,000
45	Montreal, Canada	2,250,000	1,225,000
46	Johannesburg–Germiston, South Africa	2,200,000	575,000
47	Barcelona, Spain	2,175,000	1,650,000
48	St. Louis, Missouri	2,155,000	720,000
49	Nagoya, Japan	2,150,000	1,750,000
50	Madras, India	2,150,000	1,825,000
51	Bangkok (Krung Thep), Thailand	2,100,000	1,500,000
52	Karachi, Pakistan	2,100,000	1,550,000
53	Melbourne, Australia	2,055,000	75,000
54	Chungking (Chungching), China	2,050,000	2,400,000▲
55	Canton (Kuangchou), China	2,050,000	2,050,000
56	Vienna (Wien), Austria	2,025,000	1,660,000
57	Tehrān, Iran	2,000,000	1,900,000
58	Athens (Athínai), Greece	1,975,000	650,000
59	Brussels (Bruxelles), Belgium	1,975,000	169,000
60	Pittsburgh, Pennsylvania	1,975,000	575,000
61	Toronto, Canada	1,960,000	665,000
62	Katowice–Zabrze–Bytom, Poland	1,960,000	285,000
63	Harbin (Haerhpin), China	1,950,000	1,950,000
64	Istanbul, Turkey	1,950,000	1,625,000
65	Glasgow, Scotland	1,885,000	1,030,000
66	Singapore, Singapore	1,825,000	1,100,000
67	Napoli (Naples), Italy	1,765,000	1,225,000
68	Caracas, Venezuela	1,750,000	890,000
69	Amsterdam, Netherlands	1,730,000	866,000
70	Alexandria (Al Iskandarīyah), United Arab Republic	1,700,000	1,650,000

Rank 1964		Estimated Population, 1/1/1964 Metropolitan Area	City Proper
71	Saigon, Vietnam (South)	1,700,000	1,350,000
72	Donetsk–Makeyevka, Soviet Union	1,700,000	785,000
73	Baltimore, Maryland	1,700,000	930,000
74	Liverpool, England	1,685,000	738,000
75	Nanking (Nanching), China	1,650,000	1,650,000
76	Sian (Hsian), China	1,600,000	1,600,000
77	Warsaw (Warszawa), Poland	1,575,000	1,210,000
78	Köln (Cologne), Germany (West)	1,550,000	835,000
79	Kyōto, Japan	1,550,000	1,330,000
80	Havana (La Habana), Cuba	1,550,000	875,000
81	Minneapolis–St. Paul, Minnesota	1,540,000	470,000
82	Miami–Fort Lauderdale, Florida	1,500,000	335,000
83	München (Munich), Germany (West)	1,500,000	1,175,000
84	Lahore, Pakistan	1,450,000	1,350,000
85	Frankfurt am Main, Germany (West)	1,450,000	695,000
86	Taipei, Taiwan	1,425,000	1,025,000
87	Gorki (Gorkiy), Soviet Union	1,425,000	1,060,000
88	Kitakyūshū–Shimonoseki, Japan	1,425,000	1,065,000
89	Houston, Texas	1,420,000	1,045,000
90	Stuttgart, Germany (West)	1,415,000	642,000
91	Bucharest (Bucureşti), Romania	1,400,000	1,265,000
92	Kiev (Kiyev), Soviet Union	1,390,000	1,280,000
93	Copenhagen (København), Denmark	1,380,000	705,000
94	Ahmadabad, India	1,375,000	1,250,000
95	Lisbon (Lisboa), Portugal	1,375,000	825,000
96	Buffalo–Niagara Falls, New York–Canada	1,370,000	515,000
97	Leeds–Bradford, England	1,360,000	514,000
98	Bogotá, Colombia	1,350,000	1,150,000
99	Torino (Turin), Italy	1,350,000	1,110,000
100	Chengtu, China	1,350,000	1,350,000
101	Hyderabad, India	1,350,000	950,000
102	Montevideo, Uruguay	1,335,000	1,180,000
103	Bangalore, India	1,325,000	950,000
104	Cincinnati, Ohio	1,315,000	495,000
105	Milwaukee, Wisconsin	1,315,000	760,000
106	Pusan, Korea (South)	1,300,000	1,300,000
107	Dairen (Talien), China	1,300,000	1,250,000
108	Tsingtao (Chingtao), China	1,300,000	1,300,000
109	Recife (Pernambuco), Brazil	1,250,000	900,000
110	Taiyüan (Yangkü), China	1,250,000	1,250,000
111	Kharkov, Soviet Union	1,250,000	1,020,000
112	Baku, Soviet Union	1,235,000	710,000
113	Tashkent, Soviet Union	1,205,000	1,055,000
114	San Diego–Tijuana, California–Mexico	1,200,000	640,000
115	Fushun, China	1,200,000	1,200,000
116	Dallas, Texas	1,180,000	750,000
117	Stockholm, Sweden	1,180,000	800,000
118	Casablanca, Morocco	1,175,000	1,100,000
119	Mannheim–Ludwigshafen–Heidelberg, Germany (West)	1,170 000	323,000
120	Newcastle-on-Tyne, England	1,155,000	262,000
121	Changchun (Hsinking), China	1,150,000	1,150,000
122	Surabaja, Indonesia	1,125,000	1,050,000
123	Atlanta, Georgia	1,115,000	515,000
124	Kansas City, Missouri	1,110,000	525,000
125	Prague (Praha), Czechoslovakia	1,110,000	1,011,000
126	Dnepropetrovsk, Soviet Union	1,090,000	755,000
127	Kanpur (Cawnpore), India	1,075,000	950,000
128	Kuybyshev, Soviet Union	1,075,000	920,000
129	Bandung, Indonesia	1,075,000	1,025,000
130	Novosibirsk, Soviet Union	1,065,000	1,000,000
131	Kunming, China	1,050,000	1,050,000
132	Düsseldorf, Germany (West)	1,050,000	704,000
133	Sverdlovsk, Soviet Union	1,040,000	885,000
134	Seattle, Washington	1,035,000	565,000
135	Tsinan (Chinan), China	1,025,000	1,025,000
136	Denver, Colorado	1,020,000	520,000
137	Antwerpen (Antwerp), Belgium	1,015,000	248,000
138	Rotterdam, Netherlands	1,010,000	732,000
139	Lyon, France	1,000,000	545,000

▲ *Municipal boundaries of Shanghai, Peking, Tientsin, and Chungking now include extensive rural zones, which have been excluded in estimating their metropolitan populations.*

PRINCIPAL WORLD CITIES AND POPULATIONS

This table includes all cities with 500,000 or more population, as well as many smaller cities of importance. The populations for all United States cities are estimates for January 1, 1965. The populations for foreign cities listed in the table of World Metropolitan Areas on the preceding page are estimates for January 1, 1964. For other cities, the populations are recent census figures or official estimates. Metropolitan populations are given for as many cities as possible, and identified by a star symbol (*). Some metropolitan areas, such as Minneapolis-St. Paul, include more than one large city. In such cases, the entry for the first named city carries the entire metropolitan population, and other cities in the metropolitan area carry a reference to the first-named city with a star symbol.

Aachen, Germany (West) (*450,000)	174,700
Abidjan, Ivory Coast	180,000
Accra, Ghana	337,800
Addis Ababa, Ethiopia	448,512
Adelaide, Australia (*660,000)	21,300
Aden, Aden (*138,441)	99,285
Agra, India (*508,680)	462,020
Ahmadabad, India (*1,375,000)	1,250,000
Akron, Ohio (*615,000)	298,000
Albany, New York (*605,000)	127,000
Aleppo (Halab), Syria	425,467
Alexandria (Al Iskandarīyah), U.A.R. (*1,700,000)	1,650,000
Algiers (Alger), Algeria (*995,000)	883,879
Allahabad, India (*430,730)	411,955
Alma-Ata, Soviet Union	580,000
'Ammān, Jordan (*246,475)	224,974
Amritsar, India (*398,047)	376,295
Amsterdam, Netherlands (*1,730,000)	866,000
Ankara (Angora), Turkey	650,067
Anshan, China	805,000
Antwerpen (Antwerp), Belgium (*1,015,000)	248,000
Apia, Western Samoa	21,699
Asunción, Paraguay	305,200
Athens (Athínai), Greece (*1,975,000)	650,000
Atlanta, Georgia (*1,230,000)	535,000
Auckland, New Zealand (*499,700)	147,900
Baghdad, Iraq (*650,000)	355,958
Baku, Soviet Union (*1,235,000)	710,000
Baltimore, Maryland (*1,730,000)	925,000
Bamako, Mali	135,000
Banaras (Benares), India (*489,864)	471,258
Bandung, Indonesia (*1,075,000)	1,025,000
Bangalore, India (*1,325,000)	950,000
Bangkok (Krung Thep), Thailand (*2,100,000)	1,500,000
Bangui, Central African Republic	79,600
Barcelona, Spain (*2,175,000)	1,650,000
Barranquilla, Colombia	431,000
Basel (Bâle), Switzerland (*505,000)	211,500
Beirut (Beyrouth), Lebanon	400,000
Belém (Pará), Brazil (*405,000)	359,988
Belfast, Northern Ireland (*580,000)	412,500
Belgrade (Beograd), Yugoslavia	585,234
Belo Horizonte, Brazil (*775,000)	642,912
Bengasi (Banghāzī), Libya	136,600
Berlin, East, Germany (*Berlin)	1,061,200
Berlin, West, Germany (*4,025,000)	2,180,000
Bern (Berne), Switzerland (*225,000)	167,400
Bilbao, Spain (*565,000)	297,942
Birmingham, Alabama (*655,000)	345,000
Birmingham, England (*2,640,000)	1,115,000
Bogotá, Colombia (*1,350,000)	1,150,000
Bologna, Italy	475,700
Bombay, India (*4,700,000)	4,500,000
Bonn, Germany (West) (*285,000)	143,000
Bordeaux, France (*480,000)	249,688
Boston, Massachusetts (*3,540,000)	670,000
Bradford, England (*Leeds)	297,000
Brasília, Brazil	150,000
Brazzaville, Congo	133,700
Bremen, Germany (West)	581,000
Brighton, England (*405,000)	162,900
Brisbane, Australia (*649,500)	619,000
Bristol, England (*605,000)	433,900
Brussels (Bruxelles), Belgium (*1,975,000)	169,000
Bucharest (Bucureşti), Romania (*1,400,000)	1,265,000
Budapest, Hungary (*2,265,000)	1,920,000
Buenos Aires, Argentina (*7,700,000)	2,950,000
Buffalo, New York (*1,370,000)	505,000
Cairo (Al Qāhirah), U.A.R. (*4,600,000)	3,800,000
Calcutta, India (*6,700,000)	3,000,000
Cali, Colombia	591,000
Canberra, Australia	77,644
Canton (Kuangchou), China (*2,050,000)	2,050,000
Cape Town, South Africa (*807,211)	508,341
Caracas, Venezuela (*1,750,000)	890,000
Cardiff, Wales (*605,000)	260,600
Casablanca, Morocco (*1,175,000)	1,100,000
Changchun (Hsinking), China (*1,150,000)	1,150,000
Changsha, China	703,000
Chelyabinsk, Soviet Union (*950,000)	767,000
Chengchow, China	766,000
Chengtu, China (*1,350,000)	1,350,000
Chicago, Illinois (*7,225,000)	3,520,000
Chittagong, Pakistan (364,205)	180,000
Chungking (Chungching), China (2,400,000▲)	*2,050,000
Cincinnati, Ohio (*1,310,000)	495,000
Cleveland, Ohio (*2,250,000)	855,000
Colombo, Ceylon (*800,000)	510,947
Columbus, Ohio (*825,000)	540,000
Conakry, Guinea (*109,500)	43,000
Copenhagen (København), Denmark (*1,380,000)	705,000
Córdoba, Argentina	580,000
Coventry, England (*580,000)	313,900
Dacca, Pakistan (*750,000)	362,006
Dairen (Talien), China (*1,300,000)	1,250,000
Dakar, Senegal (*435,000)	374,700
Dallas, Texas (*1,280,000)	790,000
Damascus (Dimashq), Syria	529,963
Dar es Salaam, Tanzania	128,742
Dayton, Ohio (*720,000)	260,000
Delhi, India (*2,900,000)	2,575,000
Denver, Colorado (*1,035,000)	520,000
Detroit, Michigan (*4,370,000)	1,600,000
Djakarta (Batavia), Indonesia (*3,150,000)	3,150,000
Dnepropetrovsk, Soviet Union (*1,090,000)	755,000
Donetsk (Stalino), Soviet Union (*1,700,000)	785,000
Dortmund, Germany (West) (*Essen)	652,000
Dresden, Germany (East) (*625,000)	494,600
Dublin (Baile Átha Cliath), Ireland (*690,000)	537,448
Duisburg, Germany (West) (*Essen)	497,500
Durban, South Africa (*659,934)	560,010
Düsseldorf, Germany (West) (*1,050,000)	704,000
Edinburgh, Scotland (*615,000)	476,200
Edmonton, Canada (*337,568)	281,027
Elisabethville, The Congo	183,700
El Paso, Texas (*650,000)	309,000
Essen, Germany (West) (*5,200,000)	729,000
Firenze (Florence), Italy (*560,000)	455,000
Foochow, China	616,000
Fortaleza, Brazil (*525,000)	354,942
Fort-Lamy, Chad	91,700
Fort Worth, Texas (*540,000)	360,000
Frankfurt [am Main], Germany, (West) (*1,450,000)	695,000
Freetown, Sierra Leone	128,000
Fukuoka, Japan (*790,000)	647,122
Fushun, China (*1,200,000)	1,200,000
Gdańsk (Danzig), Poland (*550,000)	301,700
Genève (Geneva), Switzerland (*305,000)	174,700
Genova (Genoa), Italy (*865,000)	825,500
Gent (Ghent), Belgium (*330,000)	157,811
Georgetown, Guyana (*148,402)	79,965
Glasgow, Scotland (*1,885,000)	1,030,000
Gorkiy (Gorki), Soviet Union (*1,425,000)	1,060,000
Göteborg, Sweden (*515,000)	410,700
Guadalajara, Mexico (*830,000)	736,800
Guatemala, Guatemala	417,200
Guayaquil, Ecuador	510,800
Halle [an der Saale], Germany (East) (*425,000)	278,000
Hamburg, Germany (West) (*2,300,000)	1,855,000
Hamilton, Canada (*395,189)	273,991
Hangchow, China	784,000
Hannover (Hanover), Germany (West) (*740,000)	567,400
Hanoi, Vietnam (North) (*643,576)	414,620
Harbin (Haerhpin), China (*1,950,000)	1,950,000
Hartford, Connecticut (*885,000)	158,000
Havana (La Habana), Cuba (*1,550,000)	875,000
Helsinki, Finland (*635,000)	476,400
Hiroshima, Japan (*560,000)	431,336
Honolulu, Hawaii (*560,000)	315,000
Houston, Texas (*1,490,000)	1,100,000
Howrah, India (*Calcutta)	512,598
Huhehot (Kweisui), China	314,000
Hull (Kingston-upon-Hull), England (*360,000)	301,000
Hyderabad, India (*1,350,000)	950,000
Hyderabad, Pakistan (*460,000)	416,441
Ibadan, Nigeria	459,196
Inchŏn, Korea (South)	430,100
Indianapolis, Indiana (*900,000)	530,000
Indore, India	394,941
Irkutsk, Soviet Union	390,000
İstanbul, Turkey (*1,950,000)	1,625,000
Ivanovo, Soviet Union	368,000
İzmir (Smyrna), Turkey (*500,000)	360,829
Jabalpur (Jubbulpore), India (*367,014)	295,375
Jacksonville, Florida (*525,000)	198,000
Jaipur, India	403,444
Jamshedpur, India (*328,044)	291,791
Jerusalem, Israel (*260,000)	175,500
Jerusalem, Jordan (*Jerusalem)	60,488
Johannesburg, South Africa (*2,200,000)	575,000
Juddah, Saudi Arabia	147,900
Kabul, Afghanistan	236,000
Kalgan, China	299,300
Kampala, Uganda (*123,332)	46,735
Kanpur (Cawnpore), India (*1,075,000)	950,000
Kansas City, Missouri (*1,140,000)	530,000
Karachi, Pakistan (*2,100,000)	1,550,000
Karaganda, Soviet Union	462,000
Karl-Marx-Stadt (Chemnitz), Germany (East) (*400,000)	287,400
Katmandu, Nepal	122,500
Katowice, Poland (*1,960,000)	285,000
Kaunas, Soviet Union	247,000
Kawasaki, Japan (*Tōkyō)	632,975
Kazan, Soviet Union	725,000
Khabarovsk, Soviet Union	377,000
Kharkov, Soviet Union (*1,250,000)	1,020,000
Khartoum, Sudan (*370,000)	132,000
Kiev (Kiyev), Soviet Union (*1,390,000)	1,280,000
Kigali, Rwanda	4,000
Kingston, Jamaica	421,718
Kirin, China	568,000
Kitakyūshū, Japan (*1,425,000)	1,065,000
Kōbe, Japan (*Ōsaka)	1,113,977
Köln (Cologne), Germany (West) (*1,550,000)	835,000
Kowloon, Hong Kong (*Victoria)	726,976
Kraków (Cracow), Poland	495,600
Krasnoyarsk, Soviet Union	483,000
Krivoy Rog, Soviet Union	448,000
Kuala Lumpur, Malaysia (*400,000)	316,230
Kunming, China (*1,050,000)	1,050,000
Kuwait, Kuwait (*151,247)	96,860
Kuybyshev, Soviet Union (*1,075,000)	920,000
Kweiyang, China	504,000
Kyōto, Japan (*1,550,000)	1,330,000
Lagos, Nigeria	665,246
Lahore, Pakistan (*1,450,000)	1,350,000
Lanchow, China	699,000
La Paz, Bolivia	450,000
La Plata, Argentina (*410,000)	295,000
Leeds, England (*1,360,000)	514,000
Le Havre, France (*223,000)	183,776
Leicester, England (*430,000)	270,400
Leipzig, Germany (East) (*735,000)	587,200
Leningrad, Soviet Union (*4,000,000)	3,100,000
Léopoldville, The Congo	402,500
Libreville, Gabon	31,027
Liège, Belgium (*550,000)	153,240
Lille, France (*865,000)	193,096
Lima, Peru (*2,300,000)	1,975,000
Lisbon (Lisboa), Portugal (*1,375,000)	825,000
Liverpool, England (*1,685,000)	738,000
Łódź, Poland (*875,000)	726,800
Lomé, Togo	80,000
London, England (*11,025,000)	3,175,000
Los Angeles, California (*7,635,000)	2,695,000
Louisville, Kentucky (*795,000)	392,000
Lourenço Marques, Mozambique (*183,800)	78,500
Loyang, China	171,200
Luanda, Angola	225,000
Lucknow, India (*675,000)	595,440
Lusaka, Zambia	114,400
Luxembourg, Luxembourg	73,900
Lvov, Soviet Union	469,000
Lyon (Lyons), France (*1,000,000)	545,000
Macao, Macao (*169,299)	153,630
Madras, India (*2,150,000)	1,825,000
Madrid, Spain (*2,575,000)	2,450,000
Madura, India (*500,000)	424,810
Magdeburg, Germany (East) (*370,000)	265,500
Managua, Nicaragua	234,800
Manchester, England (*2,850,000)	652,000
Manila, Philippines (*2,900,000)	1,190,000
Mannheim, Germany (West) (*1,170,000)	323,000
Maracaibo, Venezuela	432,902
Marseille (Marseilles), France (*870,000)	778,071
Mecca (Makkah), Saudi Arabia	158,900
Medan, Indonesia	466,370
Medellín, Colombia (*750,000)	614,000
Melbourne, Australia (*2,055,000)	75,000
Memphis, Tennessee (*700,000)	525,000
Mexico City, Mexico (*6,100,000)	3,050,000
Miami, Florida (*1,500,000)	325,000
Middlesbrough, England (*545,000)	158,100
Milano (Milan), Italy (*2,775,000)	1,675,000
Milwaukee, Wisconsin (*1,330,000)	765,000
Minneapolis, Minnesota (*1,590,000)	465,000
Minsk, Soviet Union	644,000
Mogadiscio, Somali Rep	90,600
Monrovia, Liberia	81,000
Monterrey, Mexico (*695,000)	596,939
Montevideo, Uruguay (*1,335,000)	1,180,000
Montreal, Canada (*2,250,000)	1,225,000
Moscow (Moskva), Soviet Union (*8,450,000)	6,475,000
Mukden (Shenyang), China (*2,650,000)	2,650,000
München (Munich), Germany (West) (*1,500,000)	1,175,000
Nagasaki, Japan	344,153
Nagoya, Japan (*2,150,000)	1,750,000
Nagpur, India (*700,000)	643,659
Nairobi, Kenya	266,795
Nanchang, China	508,000
Nanking (Nanching), China (*1,650,000)	1,650,000
Napoli (Naples), Italy (*1,765,000)	1,225,000
Nashville, Tennessee (*450,000)	261,000
Newark, New Jersey (*New York)	395,000
Newcastle-on-Tyne, England (*1,155,000)	262,000
New Delhi, India (*Delhi)	261,545
New Orleans, Louisiana (*985,000)	655,000
New York, New York (*16,550,000)	8,080,000
Niamey, Niger	30,030
Nice, France	292,958
Norfolk, Virginia (*655,500)	322,000
Nottingham, England (*630,000)	315,100
Novokuznetsk (Stalinsk), Soviet Union	410,000
Novosibirsk, Soviet Union (*1,065,000)	1,000,000
Nürnberg (Nuremberg), Germany (West) (*675,000)	466,200
Oakland, California (*San Francisco)	378,000
Odessa, Soviet Union	709,000
Oklahoma City, Oklahoma (*585,000)	380,000
Omaha, Nebraska (*495,000)	340,000
Omsk, Soviet Union	674,000
Ōsaka, Japan (*8,700,000)	3,250,000
Oslo, Norway (*635,000)	477,100
Ottawa, Canada (*429,750)	268,206
Ouagadougou, Upper Volta	59,126
Palembang, Indonesia	458,661
Palermo, Italy	614,000
Panamá, Panama (*330,000)	306,000
Paotow, China	400,000
Paris, France (*8,000,000)	2,800,000
Patna, India (*450,000)	363,700
Peking (Peiping), China (7,000,000▲)	*4,200,000
Penang (George Town), Malaysia (*325,000)	234,903
Perm, Soviet Union	722,000
Perth, Australia (*485,000)	95,000
Philadelphia, Pennsylvania (*4,200,000)	2,030,000
Phnom Penh, Cambodia	403,500
Phoenix, Arizona (*810,000)	520,000
Pittsburgh, Pennsylvania (*1,955,000)	560,000
Poona, India (*800,000)	597,562
Port-au-Prince, Haiti	240,000
Portland, Oregon (*795,000)	380,000
Pôrto (Oporto), Portugal (*750,000)	303,424
Pôrto Alegre, Brazil (*850,000)	617,629
Port-of-Spain, Trinidad & Tobago (*170,000)	93,954
Porto Novo, Dahomey	65,000
Port Said (Būr Sa'īd), U.A.R.	245,318
Portsmouth, England (*445,000)	224,900
Poznań, Poland	422,700
Prague (Praha), Czechoslovakia (*1,110,000)	1,011,000
Pretoria, South Africa (*422,590)	303,684
Providence, Rhode Island (*850,000)	195,000
Pusan, Korea (South) (*1,300,000)	1,300,000
Pyŏngyang, Korea (North)	653,100
Quebec, Canada (*357,568)	171,979
Quezon City, Philippines (*Manila)	397,990
Quito, Ecuador	355,200
Rabat, Morocco (*310,000)	227,445
Rangoon, Burma	821,800
Rawalpindi, Pakistan (*340,175)	197,370
Recife (Pernambuco), Brazil (*1,250,000)	900,000
Reykjavík, Iceland (*92,000)	75,000
Richmond, Virginia (*455,000)	223,000
Rīga, Soviet Union	632,000
Rio de Janeiro, Brazil (*5,250,000)	3,600,000
Riyadh (Ar Riyād), Saudi Arabia	169,185
Rochester, New York (*645,000)	305,000
Rome (Roma), Italy (*2,500,000)	2,340,000
Rosario, Argentina	595,000
Rostov [-na-Donu], Soviet Union (*780,000)	689,000
Rotterdam, Netherlands (*1,010,000)	732,000
Sacramento, California (*655,000)	265,000
Saigon, Vietnam (South) (*1,700,000)	1,350,000
St. Louis, Missouri (*2,195,000)	710,000
St. Paul, Minnesota (*Minneapolis)	308,000
St. Petersburg, Florida (*415,000)	200,000
Salisbury, Rhodesia (*315,300)	220,000
Salt Lake City, Utah (*488,000)	195,000
Salvador, Brazil	630,878
Şan'ā', Yemen	89,000
San Antonio, Texas (*790,000)	645,000
San Bernardino, California (*575,000)	102,000
San Diego, California (*1,210,000)	636,000
San Francisco, California (*3,805,000)	745,000
San Jose, California (*San Francisco)	308,000
San José, Costa Rica (*320,000)	101,162
San Juan, Puerto Rico (*660,000)	432,377
San Salvador, Salvador (*360,000)	255,744
Santiago, Chile (*2,400,000)	640,000
Santo Domingo, Dominican Republic	367,053
Santos, Brazil (*400,000)	262,048
São Paulo, Brazil (*5,450,000)	4,425,000
Sapporo, Japan (*615,000)	523,839
Saratov, Soviet Union (*770,000)	644,000
Seattle, Washington (*1,045,000)	565,000
Semarang, Indonesia	487,006
Sendai, Japan (*515,000)	425,272
Seoul, Korea (South) (*3,200,000)	3,125,000
Sevilla (Seville), Spain	442,300
Shanghai, China (10,400,000▲)	*7,600,000
Sheffield, England (*735,000)	495,300
Shihchiachuang, China	598,000
Shizuoka, Japan (*485,000)	323,819
Sian (Hsian), China (*1,600,000)	1,600,000
Singapore, Singapore (*1,825,000)	1,100,000
Sofia (Sofiya), Bulgaria (*769,700)	695,400
Soochow (Suchou), China	663,000
Southampton, England (*355,000)	207,200
Springfield, Massachusetts (*495,000)	174,000
Srinagar, India (*295,084)	285,257
Stockholm, Sweden (*1,180,000)	800,000
Stoke-on-Trent, England (*440,000)	266,100
Strasbourg, France (*320,000)	228,971
Stuttgart, Germany (West) (*1,415,000)	642,000
Suchow, China	676,000
Sucre, Bolivia	55,000
Suez, U.A.R.	203,610
Surabaja, Indonesia (*1,125,000)	1,050,000
Sverdlovsk, Soviet Union (*1,040,000)	885,000
Sydney, Australia (*2,340,000)	168,000
Syracuse, New York (*485,000)	216,000
Szczecin (Stettin), Poland	286,300
Taegu, Korea (South)	716,600
Taipei, Taiwan (*1,425,000)	1,025,000
Taiyüan (Yangkü), China (*1,250,000)	1,250,000
Tallinn, Soviet Union	311,000
Tampa, Florida (*395,000)	305,000
Tananarive, Malagasy Republic	254,271
Tangier, Morocco	141,714
Tangshan, China	800,000
Tashkent, Soviet Union (*1,205,000)	1,055,000
Tbilisi, Soviet Union (*860,000)	768,000
Tegucigalpa, Honduras	133,887
Tehrān, Iran (*2,000,000)	1,900,000
Tel Aviv [-Yafo], Israel (*715,000)	392,900
The Hague ('s Gravenhage), Netherlands (*830,000)	602,400
Thessaloniki (Salonika), Greece (*373,635)	250,920
Tientsin (Tienching), China (3,800,000▲)	*3,400,000
Tiranë, Albania	140,300
Tōkyō, Japan (*15,400,000)	8,850,000
Toledo, Ohio (*540,000)	354,000
Torino (Turin), Italy (*1,350,000)	1,110,000
Toronto, Canada (*1,960,000)	665,000
Tripoli (Tarābulus), Libya	212,600
Tsinan (Chinan), China (*1,025,000)	1,025,000
Tsingtao (Chingtao), China (*1,300,000)	1,300,000
Tsitsihar, China	668,000
Tula, Soviet Union	351,000
Tunis, Tunisia	410,000
Ufa, Soviet Union	630,000
Ulan Bator, Mongolia	195,300
Usumbura, Burundi	50,000
Utrecht, Netherlands (*410,000)	264,200
Valencia, Spain (*660,000)	505,066
Valletta, Malta (*208,000)	18,300
Valparaíso, Chile (*440,000)	252,900
Vancouver, Canada (*790,165)	384,522
Venezia (Venice), Italy	355,700
Victoria, Hong Kong (*3,275,000)	725,000
Vienna (Wien), Austria (*2,025,000)	1,660,000
Vientiane, Laos	162,300
Vilnius, Soviet Union	271,000
Vladivostok, Soviet Union	338,000
Volgograd (Stalingrad), Soviet Union (*775,000)	665,000
Voronezh, Soviet Union	535,000
Warsaw (Warszawa), Poland (*1,575,000)	1,210,000
Washington, D.C. (*2,485,000)	810,000
Wellington, New Zealand (*267,400)	125,900
Wiesbaden, Germany (West) (*520,000)	258,200
Winnipeg, Canada (*475,989)	265,429
Wrocław (Breslau), Poland	451,600
Wuhan, China (*2,600,000)	2,600,000
Wuppertal, Germany (West) (*900,000)	421,800
Wusih, China	613,000
Yaoundé, Cameroon	92,600
Yaroslavl, Soviet Union	454,000
Yerevan, Soviet Union	578,000
Yokohama, Japan (*Tōkyō)	1,375,710
Youngstown, Ohio (*490,000)	162,000
Zagreb, Yugoslavia	430,802
Zaporozhye, Soviet Union	507,000
Zürich, Switzerland (*715,000)	440,000

** Population of metropolitan area, including suburbs. See headnote.*

▲ Population of entire municipality or district, including rural area. Starred population in these entries refers to urban portion of municipality only.

HISTORICAL GAZETTEER

A

A B C Countries. Term applied to three South American countries: Argentina, Brazil, and Chile.

Abraham, Plains of. Battlefield near the city of Quebec where the English under Wolfe defeated the French under Montcalm, 1759.

Abydos. Ancient town on the Hellespont, site of the Bridge of Xerxes. Also an ancient Egyptian town on the Nile below Thebes.

Abyssinia. Former name of Ethiopia.

Acadia. Old French colonial territory bounded by the Atlantic, the river and gulf of St. Lawrence, and a line running north from Penobscot Bay.

Achaia. Separate regions of ancient Greece in southern Thessaly and northern Peloponnesus. Later, a Roman province embracing all but the northern part of modern Greece.

Acropolis. Hill in Athens, Greece, where some of the finest monuments of antiquity now stand.

Actium. Off this promontory at the entrance to the Gulf of Amvrakia in northwestern Greece, Octavius won a naval battle against Antony and Cleopatra, 31 B.C.

Aegospotami. Off the mouth of this river in ancient Thrace, the Spartans crushed the Athenian fleet in 405 B.C., in the final battle of the Peloponnesian War.

Aelia Capitolina. Jerusalem in late Roman times.

Aeolian Islands. Ancient name of the Lipari Islands, off the coast of Sicily.

Aetolia. District of ancient Greece along the north shore of the Gulf of Corinth.

Africa. Roman province corresponding with modern Tunisia. Name was later applied to entire continent.

Agassiz, Lake. Prehistoric lake temporarily created by the withdrawal of glaciers. Covered an area which includes parts of present-day Manitoba, Saskatchewan, Ontario, Minnesota, and North Dakota.

Agincourt. Village near Boulogne, France, where outnumbered English forces under Henry V defeated the French, 1415.

Agrigentum. Prosperous commercial center on the southern coast of Sicily in the fifth century, B.C. The modern Agrigento.

Ai. Old city of the Canaanites near Bethel. It was destroyed by Joshua.

Aix-la-Chapelle. Northern capital and residence of Charlemagne, and coronation site of later German emperors. Now Aachen, Germany.

Akkad. Very ancient land of the Akkadians in north Babylonia at the closest approach of the Tigris and Euphrates. The capital was Agade.

Albania. Ancient country west of the Caspian Sea in the territory roughly corresponding to Soviet Azerbaidzhan. Also the small Adriatic republic.

Albion. Ancient name of Britain.

Alsace-Lorraine. Region in northeastern France seized by Germany in 1871, and returned to France following World War I. The capital was at Strasbourg.

America. Inclusive name of the continents and adjacent islands of North and South America. It is also commonly used when referring to the United States.

Amphipolis. City of ancient Macedonia near the mouth of the Struma River, site of a Spartan victory over Athens in 422 B.C.

Anáhuac. Old Indian term, now applied to the high plateau containing Mexico City.

Anatolia. See Asia Minor.

Anau. Ruins of an ancient city in the desert near Ashkhabad, Soviet Union.

Ancyra. Important city of Phrygia, Asia Minor, and later capital of Galatia. The modern Ankara or Angora, the capital of Turkey.

Andalusia. Region comprising the eight provinces of southern Spain in basin of Guadalquivir River.

Angkor. Extensive ruins of magnificent old city in northern Cambodia.

Antarctic Ocean. Obsolete name for southern part of the Pacific, Atlantic, and Indian Oceans bordering the continent of Antarctica.

Antilles. Collective name for the islands of the West Indies which enclose the Caribbean Sea. They consist of the Greater Antilles (Cuba, Jamaica, Hispaniola, and Puerto Rico) to the north and the Lesser Antilles (which include a number of islands and groups) to the east.

Antioch. Capital of ancient Syria and one of the greatest commercial centers of the time, Antioch later became a stronghold of Christianity. The Roman Antiochia, it is now Antakya, Turkey. It was also a city of Pisidia, Asia Minor, prominent in the journeys of Paul.

Antipodes. Name occasionally applied to New Zealand and Australia, because of their location on the globe diametrically opposite the British Isles.

Apulia. Division of southeastern Italy, containing the important cities of Bari, Taranto, and Foggia.

Aquitania. Originally a region in Transalpine Gaul between the Pyrenees and the Garonne, later extending northward to the Loire.

Arabia. Large Asiatic peninsula extending south of Iraq and Jordan between the Red Sea, the Persian Gulf, and the Arabian Sea on the south.

Arab League. A group of Arab states organized in 1945, with headquarters in Cairo. Original members were Egypt, Iraq, Syria, Lebanon, Transjordan (Jordan), Saudi Arabia, and Yemen. The purpose of the League is to coordinate the foreign policy of the member states for the mutual benefit of all Arab countries.

Aragon. Medieval kingdom in northeastern Spain, whose conquests included the Balearic Islands, Sardinia, and Sicily. Its union with Castile in 1479 created the Spanish kingdom.

Aram. Biblical name of Syria. Also called Aramea.

Ararat. Hebrew name of an ancient kingdom in eastern Armenia. Noah's Ark reputedly came to rest on one of its mountains. The Assyrian Urartu.

Araucania. Old name for the land of the Araucanian Indians in southern Chile, between Concepción and Puerto Montt.

Araxes. Ancient name of the Aras River on the border of Armenia and Media.

Arbela. The modern town of Arbil, Iraq, east of Mozul, where Alexander the Great defeated a huge Persian army, 331 B.C.

Argolis. Region of ancient Greece on the east coast of the Peloponnesus. Its principal cities were Argos and Mycenae.

Ariel. Poetic name of Jerusalem.

Armageddon. Greek name of "The Hill of Megid-do," near an Israelite battlefield. In present usage, the name refers to a final battle between the powers of good and evil.

Armenia. Region of western Asia now roughly comprising northeastern Turkey, Soviet Armenia, and adjacent parts of Soviet and Iranian territory.

Arnon. Biblical name of the Wady Mojib, which flows from Jordan into the Dead Sea.

Ascalon. Also called Ashkelon, an ancient Philistine city on the Mediterranean north of Gaza, Palestine. The present village of Askalan is on its site.

Asculum. Capital of ancient Picenum and site of the original "Pyrrhic victory." Here, in 279 B.C., Pyrrhus of Epirus defeated the Romans, suffering very heavy losses. Asculum is modern Ascoli Piceno, Italy.

Ashdod. Ancient city of the Philistines, later called Azotus. Now it is a village in Israel.

Asia. Roman province comprising western part of Asia Minor. Name was later given to entire continent.

Asia Minor. Name of the peninsula in western Asia bounded by the Black, Aegean, and Mediterranean Seas. The area is nearly identical with Anatolia and contains a large part of Asiatic Turkey.

Asshur. First capital and original name of Assyria. Also Assur and Asur.

Assyria. Very ancient empire which developed on the right bank of the upper Tigris. The empire eventually extended from Elam in the east to Egypt and eastern Asia Minor in the west. Its power ended with the fall of the capital, Nineveh, 612 B.C.

Asturias. Located in northwestern Spain in the early Middle Ages, Asturias was the first Christian kingdom to be established on the Iberian peninsula.

Athos, Mount. Mountain southeast of Salonika (Thessaloniki), Greece, where a community of monks has maintained almost complete autonomy since the early Middle Ages.

Atlantis. Legendary island of great size in the Atlantic Ocean west of the Pillars of Hercules. After reaching an advanced state of civilization, it was supposedly destroyed by a subterranean cataclysm.

Attica. Ancient Greek state southeast of Boeotia. Its capital and chief city was Athens.

Augusta Treverorum. Capital of ancient Belgica; the modern Trier, Germany.

Austerlitz. Town near Brno, Czechoslovakia, where Napoleon defeated armies of Russia and Austria, 1805.

Australasia. That part of the southwest Pacific containing Australia, New Zealand, and the islands of Melanesia. Term is often used to include all Oceania.

Austria-Hungary. Dual monarchy which ruled an empire extending from Bohemia to Transylvania and from Galicia to the Adriatic between 1867 and 1918. Its capital was Vienna.

Axis. Term used to denote first the early understanding between Rome and Berlin and later the military alliance that developed in World War II between Germany, Italy, and their allies.

B

Baalbek. Also Baalbec and the Greek Heliopolis, an ancient city of Syria near headwaters of Litani River, now in Lebanon.

Babel. Biblical name of the city, probably Babylon, where the notorious tower of Babel was located.

Babylon. Capital city of ancient Babylonia on both sides of the lower Euphrates.

Babylonia. Very ancient and powerful kingdom— also called Shinar and Chaldea—in the lower valley of the Tigris and Euphrates. Its capital was Babylon. The Chaldean Empire eventually extended westward to the Mediterranean.

Bactria. Ancient country of central Asia between the Oxus River and the Hindu Kush Mountains. Its capital Bactra is the modern Balkh, Afghanistan.

Baden. Old grand duchy and state of Germany along the right bank of the upper Rhine. Karlsruhe was its capital.

Bad Lands. Name applied to barren, badly eroded areas in the western United States. The best known region is located in western South Dakota.

Balaklava. Town in the Crimea, southeast of Sevastopol. Near here the courageous "Charge of the Light Brigade" took place, 1854. Also Balaclava.

Balkan Peninsula. That part of southeastern Europe south of the Sava and Danube Rivers.

Balkan States. Countries located partly or entirely within the Balkan Peninsula: Yugoslavia, Albania, Greece, Romania, Bulgaria, and European Turkey.

Baltic States. Term used for the former republics of Estonia, Latvia, and Lithuania, bordering Baltic Sea. They were absorbed into Soviet Union in 1940.

Banat, The. Region in Central Europe bounded by the Transylvanian Alps and the Danube, Tisza, and Muresul rivers.

Banda Oriental. Old Spanish name for the "eastern shore" of Plata River, now the country of Uruguay.

Bannockburn. Village south of Stirling, Scotland, where Bruce defeated the English under Edward II, 1314, and assured the independence of Scotland.

Bantam. Seaport, formerly of great commercial importance, west of Djakarta, Java.

Barbary States. Old collective term for the countries of Africa along the "Barbary Coast" of the Mediterranean, between Egypt and the Atlantic Ocean.

Basque Provinces. Region along the Bay of Biscay extending from the areas around Bilbao and Vitoria, Spain, across the Pyrenees into southwestern France.

Batavia. Latin name for island home of Batavi on lower Rhine, later applied to all the Netherlands.

Behistun. Place near Kermanshah, Iran, where a famous rock carries ancient Assyrian inscriptions on its precipitous face.

Belgica. Northerly region of Transalpine Gaul between the Rhine and Seine. It eventually extended southward to the Rhône-Saône confluence and eastward to include most of Switzerland.

Benelux. Collective term for Belgium, the Netherlands, and Luxembourg.

Beneventum. The modern Benevento, Italy; in antiquity, the battleground for the decisive Roman victory over Pyrrhus of Epirus, 275 B.C.

Bengal. Former province in eastern British India between the Himalayas and the mouths of the Ganges. In 1947, most of the province, except the western part containing Calcutta, was absorbed into the new state of Pakistan.

Berea. Ancient Macedonian town near Mount Olympus, where Paul found willing converts to Christianity. It is now Verria, Greece.

Bessarabia. Region in southeastern Europe between the Prut and the Dnestr rivers. After its cession by Romania, in 1940, it became a part of the Soviet Union.

Bethabara. Site of the baptism of Jesus by John the Baptist. It may have been located at a ford of the Jordan 13 miles south of the Sea of Galilee.

Bethany. Famous village that once stood at the foot of the Mount of Olives, east of Jerusalem. The ascension of Christ took place near by.

Bethel. Shrine city of ancient Israel north of Jerusalem. The modern Beitin.

Beth-horon. Site of the great victory of Joshua over the Canaanites. The battle took place between the present villages of Beit Ur el Foka and Beit Ur el Tahta, midway between Jerusalem and Lydda.

Bethsaida. Ancient town at the north end of the Sea of Galilee where Jesus fed the five thousand.

Bimini. Island or region of West Indian legend where the Fountain of Youth was supposed to be located. The name has been given to an island group in the western Bahamas.

Black Country, The. Mining and manufacturing area in the vicinity of Birmingham, England.

Blarney. Village near Cork, Ireland, where the castle containing the famous Blarney Stone is located.

Boeotia. Ancient district in central Greece northwest of Attica. The chief city and capital was Thebes.

Bohemia. Medieval duchy and kingdom of varying frontiers and later a crownland of Austria-Hungary. After World War I, Bohemia became the western section of the new republic of Czechoslovakia. Its capital is Prague.

Bonneville, Lake. Extinct lake that covered northwestern Utah during the glacial period.

Borodino. Village 70 miles west of Moscow where Napoleon defeated the Russians, 1812.

Bosnia. Mountainous region south of the Sava River in Yugoslavia. It was formerly a medieval kingdom and part of the Austro-Hungarian Empire.

Bosporus. Name of an ancient Greek kingdom encircling the Sea of Azov, Soviet Union. This name was derived from the Cimmerian Bosporus, now called Kerch, or Yenikale Strait. Also name of famous strait at Istanbul, ancient Thracian Bosporus.

Bourbon. Medieval duchy in central France, the early home of the famous royal house. Also the county and province of Bourbonnais. Capital was Moulins.

Brabant. Old duchy containing the cities of Antwerp, Brussels, and Louvain. The territory is now divided between Belgium and the Netherlands.

Brandenburg. Former Prussia, now divided between Germany and Poland. Its capital was Potsdam.

Brandywine. Creek near Philadelphia where British defeated Americans commanded by Washington, 1777.

Britannia. Roman name for island of Great Britain, specifically, the southern part. Now used poetically.

British America. Name usually restricted to Canada.

British East Africa. Old descriptive name for the British territories of Kenya, Uganda, and Zanzibar. Also applied to Tanganyika.

British India. That part of the subcontinent of India before August, 1947, under the direct control of Great Britain. The relatively independent princely states were not considered in this category.

British West Africa. Name occasionally used collectively for the former British colonies in western Africa—Nigeria, Gold Coast, now Ghana, Sierra Leone, Gambia, Togo, and Cameroon.

Brundisium. Ancient Roman port on Adriatic and terminus of famed Appian Way. Now Brindisi, Italy.

Bukovina. Region on the eastern slope of the Carpathians, formerly a part of Austria-Hungary, now divided between the Soviet Ukraine in the north and Romania in the south. Also Bukowina.

Bull Run. Small river east of Manassas, in northern Virginia. Two battles were fought in this vicinity (1861 and 1862) between the armies of the Union and the Confederacy.

Bunker Hill. Famous hill in Charlestown, Mass. The battle of that name was actually fought on nearby Breed's Hill in 1775.

Burgenland. Fertile region along the Austro-Hungarian border. Its chief city is Sopron, Hungary.

Burgundy. Early medieval kingdom in southeastern France largely east of the Rhône and Saône and west of the Alps, including the western half of present-day Switzerland. Later, a duchy in the Seine, Loire, and Saône river basins of northeastern France.

Byblos. Important port in ancient Phoenicia north of Beirut, Lebanon. Called Gebal in Old Testament.

Bytown. Early name of Ottawa, Canada.

Byzantine Empire. Name for the Eastern Roman Empire, established in 330 A.D. Included in the Empire were the territories of modern U.A.R., Israel, Jordan, Syria, Turkey, Greece, and Bulgaria.

Byzantium. Ancient Greek city on the Hellespont. Constantinople was built on its site in 330 A.D. and became the capital of the Byzantine Empire.

C

Caesarea Philippi. Ancient town of northern Palestine at the foot of Mt. Hermon, near the modern Banias, Syria.

Calabria. Roman name for the "heel" of Italy, now applied to the "toe."

Caledonia. Roman name for that part of Scotland lying north of the Firths of Clyde and Forth. The name is now used poetically to include all Scotland.

Calvary. Latin word for "skull," an unidentified place outside Jerusalem where Christ was crucified. Also Golgotha.

Campagna di Roma. Extensive reclaimed lowlands around Rome, Italy, comprising roughly the territory of ancient Latium.

Campania. Division of Italy containing the cities of Naples and Salerno. Roman cities of importance were Capua and Nola.

Camulodunum. Early Roman city in Britannia; now Colchester, England.

Cana. Town where Jesus performed his first miracle. Probably the modern Kefr Kenna, Israel.

Canaan. The biblical land of Canaan lay west of the Jordan and the Dead Sea, and extended from Mount Lebanon to the southern deserts of Palestine.

Cannae. North of this ancient town in Apulia, a Roman army was almost completely destroyed by Hannibal, 216 B.C.

Capernaum. Biblical town on the west shore of the Sea of Galilee. It was often visited by Christ.

Cappadocia. Ancient country in eastern Asia Minor extending originally from Cilicia to the Euxine. Under the Romans, the region comprised the provinces of Cappadocia to the south and Pontus to the north.

Carchemish. Old capital of the Hittites on the Euphrates, at its closest approach to the Mediterranean. It was the site of a decisive Babylonian victory over Egypt, 605 B.C.

Caria. Ancient country south of the Meander River in southwest Asia Minor. The principal cities were Halicarnassus and Miletus.

Caribbees. General name for the Lesser Antilles.

Carinthia. Mountainous province in southern Austria, a former crownland of Austria-Hungary. The capital is Klagenfurt.

Carmel, Mount. Mountain ridge south of the Bay of Acre, prominent in the Old Testament.

Carniola. Medieval duchy, later a crownland of Austria-Hungary, located in what is now the northwestern part of Yugoslavia. Laibach, now called Ljubljana, was the principal city.

Carthage. Ancient Phoenician city in northern Africa near Tunis. In 146 B.C., it was destroyed by its great commercial rival, Rome.

Castile. Medieval kingdom in northern and central Spain which united with Aragon in 1479 to form the Spanish monarchy. Old Castile was in the northern part of kingdom and New Castile was in southern part.

Catalonia. Originally an independent state in the northeast corner of the Iberian Peninsula, Catalonia united with Aragon in the twelfth century. Barcelona is chief city of region. Spanish name is Cataluña.

Cathay. Old name for China, used by Marco Polo.

Caucasia. General name for that part of the Soviet Union between the Black and Caspian seas and traversed by the Caucasus Mountains.

Celestial Empire. Once a popular name of China.

Central America. Name applied to that portion of North America south of Mexico and often including Panama. Specifically, the area between the isthmuses of Tehuantepec and Panama.

Central Powers. Collective term formerly used for Germany and Austria-Hungary due to their location in central Europe. In World War I the definition was expanded to include Bulgaria and Turkey, the allies of Germany.

Chaco. Low-lying, swampy region in South America between Paraguay River and the Andes, in Argentina, Paraguay, and Bolivia. Also called Gran Chaco.

Chaeronea. Ancient town in western Boeotia, the site of the victory of Philip over the forces of Thebes and Athens, 338 B.C., which introduced the era of Macedonian supremacy.

Chalcedon. Ancient Greek town on the Bosporus opposite Byzantium.

Chalcidice. Three-armed peninsula of ancient Macedonia containing the cities of Olynthus and Potidaea. It was colonized and named by Euboeans from Chalcis—the modern Khalkis, Greece.

Chaldea. Ancient name for the lowlands at the head of the Persian Gulf, but commonly applied to all of Babylonia. The second and final empire of Babylonia was called the Chaldean Empire.

Champagne. Old province of northeastern France whose capital was at Troyes.

Chancellorsville. Village near Spotsylvania, Virginia, the scene of a victory gained over the Union army by the outnumbered Confederates, 1863.

Chapultepec. Rocky hill southwest of Mexico City, the site of Aztec fortifications and the summer residence of the viceroys and presidents of Mexico.

Charcas. Old Spanish colonial province, a part successively of the viceroyalties of Peru and La Plata. It corresponded roughly to modern Bolivia and extended westward to the Pacific.

Chichén Itzá. Principal city of the Mayas. Its ruins lie in the jungles of eastern Yucatán.

Chinnereth. Sea of Galilee in the Old Testament.

Chosen. Native name of Korea.

Christiania. Former name of Oslo, Norway.

Cibola. Old name given to a region of New Mexico containing seven cities, supposedly rich and powerful. Coronado identified them in 1540 as commonplace Zuni Indian villages.

Cimmeria. Ancient country of the Cimmerians, probably located along northern shores of Black Sea.

Cinnamon, Land of. Old name of the Napo River region in Peru, first explored in the 16th century.

Cinque Ports. In medieval England, a group of coastal towns in Kent and Sussex carrying special royal privileges and responsibilities. Included were the cities of Hastings and Dover.

Cipango, or Cipangu. Name given by Marco Polo to an island group east of Asia, probably Japan.

Circassia. Region in the southern Soviet Union, bordering on Kuban River, Black Sea, and Caucasus Mountains.

Cisalpine Republic. Short-lived state in the valley of the Po between Piedmont and Venetia. In 1802, it was reconstituted as the Italian Republic.

Cisleithania. Old name for the Austrian portion of Austria-Hungary to the west and north of Transleithania. Besides Austria, it included what is now western Czechoslovakia, Galicia, northern Bukovina, and Slovenia. Name is derived from Leitha River, which formed part of the boundary south of Vienna.

Colchis. Ancient country on the eastern shores of the Euxine south of the Caucasus, now part of Soviet Georgia. The legendary land of the Golden Fleece.

Colonia Agrippina. Roman colony on the Rhine; the modern Köln (Cologne), Germany.

Colossae. Early Christian stronghold of Phrygia, Asia Minor, whose people were recipients of Paul's Epistle to the Colossians. Also Colosse.

Columbia. Poetic name of the New World or, more specifically, the United States, in honor of Christopher Columbus.

Constantinople. Old name of Istanbul, Turkey, the ancient Byzantium.

Copais. Ancient lake northwest of Thebes, Boeotia. Recent drainage of the lake and its surrounding marshes has altered the map of central Greece.

Courland. Old Baltic duchy with the capital at Mitau. Most of its territory is now contained in the southern part of Soviet Latvia. Also called Kurland.

Crécy. Small town near Abbeville, France, where an English army badly defeated the French, 1346.

Crimea. Large peninsula of the Soviet Union on the northern coast of the Black Sea. Its chief cities are Simferopol, Sevastopol, and Yalta.

Croatia. Important state on the northwestern coast of the Adriatic in early Middle Ages. More recently it became, with Slavonia, a crownland of Austro-Hungarian Empire. Capital is Zagreb, in Yugoslavia.

Cumae. Ancient city, reputedly the earliest Greek settlement in Italy, 10 miles west of Naples.

Cunaxa. Ancient town of north Babylonia, the site of the Persian victory which precipitated the retreat of the Ten Thousand to Trepezus, 401 B.C.

Cush. Biblical name applied to ancient Ethiopia and also to a land in Mesopotamia. Also called Kush.

Cynoscephalae. Heights in southeastern Thessaly, Greece, the site of a Roman victory over the Macedonians, 197 B.C.

Cyzicus. Ancient name for a city and peninsula on the south coast of the Propontis in Asia Minor. In 410 B.C., near here, the Athenian navy won a victory over Sparta.

D

Dacia. Ancient territory of Rome which lay north of the Danube in an area now occupied in large part by Romania.

Dalmatia. Former crownland of Austria-Hungary along the Adriatic, now part of Yugoslavia.

Dalriada. Kingdom of Scots on southwest coast of Scotland in early Middle Ages. They united with the Picts in ninth century, and combined territories eventually formed the greater part of Scotland.

Dan. Biblical town, originally Laish, in the extreme north of Israel. It is noted for the saying, "from Dan to Beersheba."

Danelaw. That part of northeastern England, from the Tyne to the Thames, under Danish law and control in the early Middle Ages. Also called Danelagh.

Darién. Old name of eastern Panama. The name "Isthmus of Darién," formerly applied to the Isthmus of Panama, now pertains particularly to the isthmus between the gulfs of Darién and San Miguel.

Dark Continent. Name popularly applied to Africa.

Dartmoor. Desolate moorland in south Devonshire, England. Site of the famous prison of the same name.

Dauphiné. A medieval province between the Rhône and the Alps, with its capital at Grenoble. From it was derived the French royal title, "Dauphin."

Deccan. In its broadest sense, the peninsula of India south of the Narbada River. In particular, that part of the peninsula north of the Kistna River.

Decelea. Village in northern Attica used as a Spartan base and giving its name to the final stage of the Peloponnesian War between Sparta and Athens.

Delos. Sacred island of the ancient Greeks, in the Cyclades southwest of Mykonos Island.

Delphi. Ancient city of Phocis, Greece, the site of the Delphic oracle. It is now the village of Kastri.

Deseret. Early Mormon name of Utah.

Dixie. Popular term for the southern states of the United States. It may have stemmed from the ten dollar bills or "Dixies" issued in Louisiana before the Civil War. These bills bore the French word "dix," meaning "ten."

Dobruja. Region bounded on the west and north by the Danube, on the east by the Black Sea, and extending south into Bulgaria. Its chief port and town is Constanta, Romania.

Dodecanese. In Greek, literally "twelve islands." Actually there are about fourteen main islands, with numerous smaller ones belonging to this group. The largest of the islands is Rhodes.

Dogger Bank. Shallow sand bank covering a wide area in central North Sea; valuable fishing ground.

Doris. Small mountainous territory in the central part of ancient Greece; also, a maritime region of Caria colonized by Dorians.

Down Under. A British term for the lands south of the equator; specifically, in the Antipodes.

Drogio. Unidentified island to the south of Estotiland on late medieval maps. Modern Cape Breton Island most nearly answers the description.

Dur Sharrukin. Ancient Assyrian city north of Nineveh. For a short time it was a royal residence.

E

East Anglia. Early medieval kingdom comprising present English counties of Norfolk and Suffolk.

Eastern Archipelago. Name for Malaysia or the Malay Archipelago.

Eastern Empire. Name of the Eastern Roman or Byzantine Empire.

East Indies. Old collective name for southeast Asia including India, Indochina, and Malaysia.

Ebal, Mount. In Old Testament, mountain of the curse, overlooking Shechem (now Nābulus, Jordan).

Eburacum. Old Roman town and military base on site of modern York, England. Also Eboracum.

Ecbatana. Capital of ancient Media; it is now the city of Hamadan, Iran.

Eden. In the Bible, first home of man. Some scholars place it in the valley of the Tigris and Euphrates.

Edessa. Capital of an ancient kingdom in Mesopotamia. The modern Urfa, Turkey.

Edom. In the Old Testament, a mountainous district south of Moab and the Dead Sea. The Roman Idumaea extended westward to include the Negev.

Eire. Official name of Ireland.

Ekron. Important city of the ancient Philistines. The modern Akir, Israel.

Elam. Very ancient kingdom east of the Tigris and north of Persian Gulf, later absorbed into Persian Empire as province of Susiana. Capital city was Susa.

El Dorado. Legendary land of opulence sought by early Spanish explorers in northern South America. The name of the country was taken from its fabled king, El Dorado (the gilded one), who ruled in the golden city of Manoa.

Emerald Isle. Popular name of Ireland.

Emilia. Division of northern Italy between the Po River and the Apennines. Its chief city is Bologna.

Ephesus. Metropolis of ancient Ionia, Asia Minor, important as a center of commerce and Christianity through much of the Roman period. Its ruins are located south of Izmir, Turkey.

Ephraim, Mount. In the Old Testament, the land of the tribe of Ephraim in central Palestine. It contained the village of Ephraim (the Old Testament Ophrah) northeast of Bethel, in Jordan.

Epirus. Ancient country along Ionian Sea in northwestern Greece and southern Albania. Capital was Ambracia, modern Arta.

Eridu. Very ancient city of Sumeria. Originally built on the Euphrates near the Persian Gulf, it has now been placed over one hundred miles inland by the growth of the delta.

Erin. Popular name of Ireland.

Esdraelon. Great plain of northern Israel, famous as a battlefield and surrounded by Mounts Carmel, Gilboa, and Tabor.

Estotiland. Unidentified island on late medieval maps, in the general location of Newfoundland.

Ethiopia. Ancient kingdom of the upper Nile extending south from Nubia. It was known in the Bible as the land of Cush, with successive capitals at Napata and Meroe. Also used in antiquity for all of known Africa, name is now restricted to Empire of Ethiopia.

Etruria. Land of ancient Etruscans, extending from outskirts of Rome northward to include Tuscany.

Eurasia. Continental land mass of Europe and Asia.

Euxine, The. Name for the Black Sea, known in Roman times as Pontus Euxinus.

Eylau. Town southeast of Königsberg, East Prussia (now Kaliningrad, Soviet Union), where the Russians and Prussians met Napoleon in a bloody, inconclusive battle, 1807.

F

Faesulae. Ancient Roman city in northern Etruria; the modern Fiesole, near Florence.

Far East. Collective name for all Asiatic countries east of Iran and Afghanistan, including eastern Siberia, Japan, and the islands of Malaysia.

Farther India. Old name for peninsula of Indochina.

Fertile Crescent. Name for the fertile lands of antiquity, which extended in a great crescent around the Syrian desert from Israel and Jordan through the valley of the Tigris and the Euphrates.

Finger Lakes. Beautiful group of long, narrow lakes in the western part of New York state.

Flanders. Medieval country along the North Sea from the Straits of Dover to the mouth of the Schelde River, containing the cities of Ypres, Ghent, and Bruges. It is now divided between Belgium and France.

Flodden. Field southwest of Berwick, England, where the Scots under James IV were defeated by the English, 1513.

Fontenoy. Village near Tournai, Belgium, the site of the French victory over the English and their allies in the War of the Austrian Succession (1745).

Fortunate Isles. Legendary islands in the western seas, also called the Isles of the Blest and the Happy Isles. When the Canary and Madeira Islands were discovered the name was attached to them.

Francia. Early medieval land of the Franks embracing the kingdoms of Neustria and Austrasia. The name was applied later to a region of varying boundaries in the basins of the Seine and Loire. Also the Italian and Spanish names for France.

Franklin. Short-lived state government organized in eastern Tennessee in 1784. Capital was Jonesboro.

French North Africa. Collective name sometimes used when referring to former possessions of France in North Africa—Algeria, French Morocco, and Tunisia.

French Shore. The western coastal regions of Newfoundland where the French for many years exercised exclusive fishing rights.

Friedland. Former German town southeast of Kaliningrad, Soviet Union, where Napoleon won a great victory over the Russians, 1807. A temporary peace with Russia and Prussia was the consequence.

Friesland. Medieval state which included, at its greatest extent, most of the Netherlands north of the Schelde and Meuse. Now a province of northern Netherlands with its capital at Leeuwarden.

G

Gadara. Ancient city southeast of the Sea of Galilee, which gave its name to the region along the eastern shore. The name has been perpetuated by the biblical account of the Gadarene swine.

Gades. Westernmost colony of the Phoenicians, also called Gadeira. On site is modern city of Cadiz, Spain.

Galatia. Region and later Roman province in central Asia Minor settled by, and named after, the Gauls. Chief city was Ancyra, now Ankara, Turkey.

Galicia. Former Austro-Hungarian crownland to the north of the western Carpathians. Its chief cities were Lvov, now in the Soviet Ukraine, and Krakow, now in Poland. Also a coastal region of northwestern Spain.

Galilee. In the Roman period, the northern part of Palestine containing the towns of Nazareth, Capernaum, and Ptolemais. It was located west of the Jordan between Phoenicia and Samaria.

Gascony. Old duchy and province of southwestern France bordering the Bay of Biscay. Auch was the chief city of the region, which later became a part of the province of Guyenne and Gascogne with its capital at Bordeaux.

Gath. Ancient capital of the Philistines, birthplace of giant Goliath. The modern Tell es Safi, Israel.

Gaul. Ancient name for the land of the Gauls, the Roman Gallia. The greater part, located west of the Rhine and Alps and north of the Pyrenees, was called Transalpine Gaul. That part in the Po Basin of northern Italy was called Cisalpine Gaul.

Gedrosia. Country of ancient Persia along the northern coast of the Arabian Sea. Now part of Pakistan and Iran.

Gehenna. New Testament name for Tophet.

Gennesaret, Lake of. The Sea of Galilee.

Germania. Roman name for the region east of the Rhine, north of the Danube, and west of the Vistula.

German Ocean. Former name of the North Sea.

Germantown. Site of a British victory over the Americans under Washington, 1777. Now a part of residential Philadelphia.

Giant's Causeway. Peninsula northeast of Coleraine, Northern Ireland. Its unusual columns of basalt have given rise to the legend that it was constructed by giants as a causeway to Scotland.

Gilead. Mountainous biblical region east of the Jordan River, now the northwestern part of modern Jordan, between the Parmak and the Mojib rivers.

Gilgal. Camp city of the Israelites near Jericho. It was their base during the conquest of Canaan.

Golgotha. Hebrew word for "skull," and the site of the crucifixion of Christ. Also Calvary.

Goshen. Region of ancient Egypt colonized by the early Israelites. It was located between the Nile delta and the present Suez Canal.

Grand Banks. Extensive submarine plateau east of Newfoundland, noted as a fishing ground.

Great Basin. Extensive region of the western United States between Wasatch Mountains and the Sierra Nevadas. It contains no drainage outlet to the sea except at the northern and southern extremities.

Great Britain. The name of the island containing England, Scotland, and Wales.

Great Lakes. Collective name for Lakes Superior, Michigan, Huron, Erie, and Ontario.

Great Plains. A vast elevated region of North America between the Rockies and the central prairies, and extending from the Mackenzie River south to the Rio Grande. Included in the area are western parts of the Dakotas, Nebraska, Kansas, Oklahoma, and Texas, and the eastern sections of Montana, Wyoming, Colorado, and New Mexico.

Guano Islands. Islands off the Peruvian coast famed for their guano deposits. The most important are the Lobos and Chincha Islands.

Guinea. All lands on west coast of Africa between Sénégal River and the southern boundary of Angola.

H

Halicarnassus. Important seaport of ancient Caria whose site is now occupied by Budrum, Turkey.

Hamelin. German city, commonly Hameln, noted for the legend of the Pied Piper. It is located on the Weser southwest of Hanover.

Haran. Ancient city of Mesopotamia, southeast of Urfa, Turkey. It later became the Roman Carrhae, site of a Parthian victory over the Romans, 53 B.C.

Hatay. District around Iskenderon (Alexandretta), Turkey. It was formerly the Syrian mandated Sanjak of Alexandretta and the short-lived republic of Hatay.

Heartland. The vast center of the Eurasian continent, protected on almost every side by great mountains and seas. The largest portion is the Soviet Union.

Heliopolis. Important city of ancient Egypt whose ruins lie a few miles north of Cairo. The biblical On.

Hellas. Ancient Greece, land of the Hellenes.

Hellespont, The. Ancient name of the Dardanelles.

Helluland. Early Norse name for a desolate land southwest of Greenland, possibly Labrador.

Helvetia. That part of Gaul comprising the western part of Switzerland. The word is used poetically with reference to the entire country.

Heraclea. Name of numerous Greek cities of antiquity, the most important of which was located on the Gulf of Taranto, Italy. In the vicinity, Pyrrhus of Epirus defeated the Romans, 280 B.C., in the first known battle between Greeks and Romans.

Hercegovina. Old duchy in the mountains south of Sarajevo, Bosnia, now absorbed into the republic of Yugoslavia. Also Herzegovina.

Herculaneum. Roman city at the foot of Mt. Vesuvius. Destroyed with Pompeii, 79 A.D.

Hermopolis. City of ancient Egypt midway between Memphis and Thebes. Also called Hermopolis Magna.

Heshbon. Biblical capital of the Amorites near Mt. Nebo, now Hesban in Jordan.

Hesperia. Name given by the Greeks to lesser-known lands in the extreme western Mediterranean.

Hesse. Former grand duchy and state in western Germany with capital at Darmstadt. German Hessen.

Hibernia. Ancient name of Ireland.

Hiddekel. Biblical name of the Tigris River.

Hieromax. Old name of the Wady Varmuk, which flows into the Jordan south of the Sea of Galilee.

Hierosolyma. Greek name of Jerusalem.

Himera. Important seaport founded by the ancient Greeks near the Sicilian city of Termini. It was destroyed by Carthage about 408 B.C.

Hindustan. Old name for predominantly Hindu India north of the Vindhya Mountains, including the upper Ganges Basin and much of the Punjab. In a looser sense, the entire subcontinent.

Hispania. Roman name of the Iberian Peninsula.

Hispaniola. Name of the second largest island in the West Indies, a corruption of the Spanish Española. The island contains Haiti and the Dominican Republic.

Holland. Name of a district along the west coast of the Netherlands; now often applied to entire country.

Holy Alliance. Loose agreement signed in 1815 under which the signatories, Russia, Prussia, and Austria, proposed to conduct their affairs in a Christian manner. The alliance, to which all European states except Great Britain, Turkey, and the Papal States adhered, became reactionary and had lost all its significance by 1848.

Holy Land. Familiar term for Palestine, now a region divided between Israel and Jordan.

Holy Roman Empire. Medieval confederation of Germanic peoples of central Europe ruled by emperors claiming succession to the emperors of Rome. Although the empire lost northern Italy at an early date, it retained close connection with the papacy until the Reformation. The last monarch abdicated in 1806 after a long period of imperial decline.

Hondo. Island of Honshu, Japan.

Hump, The. Nickname given the eastern end of the lofty Himalayas, which lay astride the route of the India-China air transport service in World War II.

Hyrcania. Ancient region on the southeastern shores of the Caspian Sea; now part of northern Iran.

I

Iberia. That part of ancient Europe south of the Pyrenees, now called the Iberian Peninsula. Also an ancient name of Georgia, Soviet Union.

Île-de-France. Old French province whose capital was Paris.

Ilium. Roman name of ancient Troy, Asia Minor.

Illyria. Very ancient region along the Adriatic corresponding to western Yugoslavia. The name Illyricum was later applied by the Romans to western Yugoslavia, northern Albania, Hungary, and eastern Austria. The former Austro-Hungarian kingdom of Illyria included Carinthia, Carniola, and Kustenland.

Indies. Name assigned by early geographers to the newly discovered islands and coasts of America, which they believed to be the Indies of Asia. The islands later became known as the West Indies. The Netherlands East Indies, on the other hand, assumed the official title of Indonesia in 1948.

Indochina. That part of southeast Asia between India and China (i.e., Burma, Thailand, Laos, Cambodia, Vietnam, and Malaya), formerly called Farther India.

Ingermanland. Old name of the region of the Soviet Union south of the Neva and the Gulf of Finland, the ancient Ingria.

Inland Empire. Name of the great white-pine lumber region in the interior basin of the Columbia River. It encompasses northern Idaho, western Montana, and eastern Washington and Oregon.

Ionia. Maritime region of western Asia Minor colonized by the Ionian Greeks. Its chief cities were Ephesus, Miletus, and Smyrna.

Ipsus. Famous Phrygian town where successors of Alexander the Great fought over division of his empire, 301 B.C. It was north of Pisidian Antioch.

Isabela. Name of the first known European settlement in New World. Located on north coast of Hispaniola in 1493 by Columbus, it was soon abandoned.

Israel. Northern kingdom of the Jews. Its territory included Samaria, Galilee, Bashan, and Gilead, and was bounded on the south by Judah. The capital was successively at Shechem, Tirzah, and Samaria. Also, the name of the modern Jewish republic.

Issus. Famous town in ancient Cilicia where Alexander the Great defeated the Persians in battle, 333 B.C. It was located on Turkish Gulf of Iskenderun.

Ithaca. The modern island of Ithake, Greece, the legendary home of Ulysses.

Ivry. Village of Ivry-la-Bataille, south of Rouen, France. Here, in 1590, Henry IV led the Huguenots to victory over forces of the Catholic League.

J

Jamestown. First permanent English settlement in the United States, established on a peninsula on the left bank of the James in 1607. The site is now on Jamestown Island, near Williamsburg, Virginia.

Jaxartes. Ancient name of the Syr Darya River.

Jebus. Early name of Jerusalem—also called Salem, Ariel, Hierosolyma, and Aelia Capitolina.

Jericho. Walled city of biblical fame which once stood in the valley of the Jordan northwest of the Dead Sea. A small village remains.

Judah. Southern kingdom of the Jews, to the south of Israel between the Dead Sea and the Mediterranean. Its chief cities were Hebron, Beersheba, and the capital, Jerusalem.

Judea. Also Judaea, the Roman division of Palestine south of Samaria and west of the Dead Sea. At its greatest extent, the province included Idumaea, Samaria, Galilee, and Peraea.

Jutland. The Danish Jylland, the continental peninsula of Denmark.

K

Kadesh. Southernmost capital of the ancient Hittites near the source of the Orontes.

Kadesh-Barnea. Desert headquarters of Moses and his wandering Israelites near the present border of the U.A.R. and Israel.

Karafuto. Japanese name of the southern half of Sakhalin Island, transferred to Soviet Union in 1945.

Karakorum. Medieval capital of Genghis Khan whose ruins lie along the Orkhon River west of Urga, Mongolia.

Karelia. Old name of district between Lake Ladoga and Gulf of Finland, now part of the Soviet Union.

Kaskaskia. Early French settlement in Illinois on the right bank of the Kaskaskia River near its confluence with the Mississippi.

Kedesh. The present village of Kades, town of Old Testament prominence in northern Palestine near the Waters of Merom.

Kingsmill Islands. The Gilbert Islands.

Kiptchak. Medieval khanate or kingdom ruled by the descendants of the Mongol leader, Genghis Khan. Also called the Kingdom of the Golden Horde, it extended from central Asia to the Black Sea. Its capital was at Sarai on the lower Volga.

Kishon. Famous biblical river, watering plain of Esdraelon in northern Israel.

Kittim. Biblical name of the island of Cyprus, probably derived from its Phoenician port of Citium. The name Chittim also referred to Cyprus, as well as to islands and shores of the eastern Mediterranean.

Klondike. Name of a stream which flows westward into the Yukon River at Dawson, Yukon. Since the gold rush of 1897, name has been applied to entire area of gold fields extending westward into Alaska.

Kurdistan. Land of the Kurds, comprising part of Turkey, Iraq, Iran, and Soviet Armenia.

Kustenland. Old province of Austria-Hungary containing Trieste and the Istrian Peninsula.

L

Laconia. In antiquity, the southeastern division of the Peloponnesus, with its capital at Sparta. Also called Lacedaemon.

Ladrone Islands. Old Spanish name of the Mariana or Marianne Islands. Also called the Ladrones.

Lake District. Picturesque, lake-studded mountain region in England north of Morecambe Bay.

Landes, The. Extensive marshy plain in France along the Bay of Biscay south of the Gironde.

Land of the Midnight Sun. Norway.

Languedoc. Medieval government and province of southern France bordering the Rhône, Mediterranean, and eastern Pyrenees. Its capital was at Toulouse.

Lanka. Ancient name of Ceylon.

Laodicea. Capital of ancient Phrygia and site of one of Paul's seven Asiatic churches. Its ruins now lie near Denizli, Turkey.

Lapland. Country of the Lapps in arctic Europe. This region extends westward from the Kola Peninsula in the Soviet Union through northern Finland, Sweden, and Norway.

Latin America. Collective term for all countries and islands south of the United States where people of Spanish, Portuguese, and French ancestry predominate. It includes Mexico, Central and South America, and most of the West Indies.

Latium. Ancient land of the Latins along the Tyrrhenian Sea. Rome lay in the extreme north.

Laurentian Lakes. Lakes of the glacial period that occupied largely the same area as the present Great Lakes. Huge Lake Algonquin (now divided into lakes Superior, Michigan, and Huron) emptied into Lake Iroquois (now Lake Ontario), which in turn emptied into the Atlantic through the Mohawk and Hudson valleys.

Leeward Islands. General name of the northern group of islands in the Lesser Antilles, extending southeastward from Puerto Rico to include Guadeloupe.

León. Kingdom in northwestern Spain in the early Middle Ages. It absorbed the kingdom of Asturias.

Lepanto. Greek strait between the gulfs of Patras and Corinth, the site of an Italo-Spanish naval victory over Turkey, 1571.

Leuctra. Ancient Greek village near Thebes, Boeotia, where the Thebans destroyed the military power of Sparta, 371 B.C.

Levant, The. Collective name for the lands on the eastern shores of the Mediterranean, including the U.A.R. and Asia Minor. The name was derived from the Latin "levare" (to raise), meaning "the rising

sun" or "the east." It was therefore originally applied to all the Mediterranean lands east of Italy.

Lidice. Small village west of Prague, Czechoslovakia, whose inhabitants were put to death by the Germans in World War II.

Lilybaeum. Fortress city on the western tip of ancient Sicily. The modern Marsala.

Little America. Admiral Byrd's base in Antarctica at 78° 40′ S. and 164° 03′ W.

Little Russia. Name given to an old division of Russia, now in the northern part of the Soviet Ukraine. The region contains the cities of Kharkov, Kiev, Poltava, and Chernigov.

Livonia. Medieval country on the Baltic Sea with its capital at Riga. Its territory is now divided between the Soviet republics of Latvia and Estonia.

Llano Estacado. Vast arid plateau in western Texas and eastern New Mexico, called in English "The Staked Plains."

Lombardy. Early medieval kingdom of the Lombards extending originally from the Alps to southern Italy. It was reduced later to the Po Valley region of northern Italy.

Loochoo Islands. The Ryukyu Islands.

Lorraine. Former kingdom, duchy, and province of varying boundaries in the Meuse and Moselle river basins between France and Germany. The chief city is Metz, France.

Lotharingia. Latin name of the kingdom of Lothaire which extended in the early Middle Ages from the Alps along the left bank of the Rhine to its mouth. It dwindled in size and became duchy of Lorraine.

Louisbourg. Famous French fortress south of Sydney, Nova Scotia, destroyed by the British in 1758. The small port of Louisburg survives near its site.

Louisiana Territory. Name given to the vast frontier region which the United States purchased from France in 1803. It extended roughly from the Mississippi to the Rockies and from Texas to Canada.

Low Countries. Term originally applied to the medieval Netherlands, which then included the present Netherlands, Belgium, and Luxembourg. The term still applies to all three countries.

Lugdunensis. Roman province in central Gaul lying largely between the Seine and Loire rivers and extending westward to the ocean. Its capital city of Lugdunum, the modern Lyon, France, lay in its southeastern extremity.

Lutetia. Roman name of Paris. Also called Lutetia Parisiorum.

Lydia. Powerful kingdom of antiquity extending from the Aegean to the Halys River in Asia Minor. It was conquered by Persia in 546 B.C. and reduced to a small Aegean coastal province. The chief cities were Sardes and Smyrna (now Izmir, Turkey).

M

Macedonia. Also called Macedon. An ancient kingdom, empire, and Roman province of varying boundaries in northern Greece around the head of the Gulf of Salonika. Under Alexander the Great the empire extended from Greece eastward to Egypt and India. The northern part of modern Macedonia is contained within Yugoslavia and Bulgaria.

Maeander. Old name of Menderes River, which flows into the Aegean south of Izmir, Turkey. Its winding course has given rise to the modern word "meander."

Maelström. Also Malström. A strait south of Moskenäsö island in the Lofoten Islands, noted for its dangerous current and whirlpool.

Magna Graecia. Latin name of the southern part of ancient Italy colonized by the Greeks. It extended from the Bay of Naples to the eastern shore of the Gulf of Taranto.

Magnesia. Coast district of ancient Thessaly. It has given its name to magnetic ore which may have been first discovered there.

Maine. Old French province south of Normandy.

Maipo. Chilean river which reaches the Pacific south of Santiago. San Martín's victory over the Spanish here, at the town of Maipú in 1818, assured the independence of Chile.

Malacca. Old name occasionally applied to the Malay Peninsula.

Malaysia. General name for all the islands in the East Indies except New Guinea and including the Philippines. Also called the Malay Archipelago.

Mancha, La. Former province of central Spain southeast of Madrid. Famous in fiction as the home of Don Quixote.

Manche, La. French name of the English Channel.

Manchukuo. State created in Manchuria and part of North China through Japanese intervention in 1932. Its existence ended with the fall of Japan in 1945.

Mantinea. Ancient Arcadian city in the Peloponnesus west of Argos, Greece. It was the site of several ancient battles. Also Mantineia.

Marathon. Famous coastal village and plain of ancient Greece northeast of Athens. Here, in 490 B.C., the Athenian army defeated the Persian invaders.

Mareotis, Lake. Ancient name of the Birket-el-Mariut, a large lake southeast of Alexandria, Egypt.

Maritime Provinces. Historic term for the Canadian provinces of New Brunswick, Nova Scotia, and Prince Edward Island.

Markland. Early Norse name of a region southwest of Greenland, probably Newfoundland.

Mason and Dixon Line. Popular name for the dividing line between North and South prior to the Civil War. Originally, it was the boundary between Maryland and Pennsylvania as surveyed by two English astronomers, 1763-1767.

Massilia. Roman name of Marseilles, France.

Mauretania. Ancient name of northwestern Africa, embracing modern Morocco and part of Algeria. Distinguished from Mauritania, the former French protectorate north of Senegal.

Mayapán. Old capital of the Mayas. Its ruins are located south of Merida, Yucatan.

Mazaca. Capital of ancient Cappadocia. The Roman Caesarea and the modern Kayseri, Turkey.

Mecklenburg. Medieval duchy and later a province of Germany along the Baltic, west of Pomerania. Its chief cities are Schwerin and Rostock.

Media. Ancient country of northwestern Iran with its capital at Ecbatana. Once a powerful empire itself it became in the sixth century, B.C., a part of the empire of Persia.

Megaris. District of ancient Greece on the eastern end of the Isthmus of Corinth. The capital was Megara.

Megiddo. Ancient city on the plain of Esdraelon which gave its name to Armageddon, "the mountain of Megiddo."

Melanesia. Collective name for certain islands in the Southwest Pacific whose inhabitants have similar racial characteristics. They comprise the entire chain of islands from New Guinea to the Fijis, including the Admiralties, the Bismarck Archipelago, the Solomons, New Caledonia, and the New Hebrides.

Melita. Ancient name of Malta.

Memphis. Very ancient capital of Egypt on the left bank of the Nile below Cairo.

Mercia. Early medieval kingdom of central England.

Meroe. Capital of the ancient kingdom of Ethiopia on the Nile below Khartoum.

Merom, Waters of. Biblical name of the small lake in the Jordan valley between Mt. Hermon and the Sea of Galilee. Its modern name is Hula.

Mesopotamia. Old name for the land between the Tigris and Euphrates, the biblical Aram Naharaim. Also a Roman province. It is now a part of Iraq.

Messenia. Ancient country in the southwestern Peloponnesus, Greece. Its chief city was Messene. Now a province of Greece.

Michmash. Site of early Israelite victory over Philistines, now Mukhmas, Jordan, northeast of Jerusalem.

Micronesia. Name applied to an extensive chain of islands in the western Pacific whose races are related. The chief Micronesian groups are the Marianas and Palaus (volcanic), and the Carolines, Marshalls, and Gilberts (coral).

Middle East. Originally, a collective name for the lands between the Near and Far East, including Iraq, Iran, Afghanistan, and the countries of the Arabian peninsula. The name has recently been applied also to the countries of the eastern Mediterranean, from the U.A.R. to Turkey, and east to Iran and is replacing "Near East" in official U.S. State Department usage.

Middle West. Collective name for the lowland states of the north-central United States. West of the Mississippi River it includes Missouri and Kansas and all the states to the north; east of the Mississippi it includes all the states north of the Ohio River.

Miletus. Important seaport of ancient Ionia, Asia Minor, south of Ephesus.

Mizpeh. Mountain meeting-place of the ancient Israelites, northwest of Jerusalem. Also Mizpah.

Mizraim. Hebrew name of Egypt.

Moab. Ancient kingdom between Gilead and Edom on the eastern shores of the Dead Sea. Now it is a part of Jordan.

Moldau. The Vltava River which flows through Prague, Czechoslovakia.

Moldavia. Former principality along the right bank of the Prut River, with its capital at Iasi. In 1861 it united with Walachia to create the kingdom of Romania. Also, the name given to the new Soviet republic in previously Romanian Bessarabia.

Mongolia. Vast land of the Mongols in central Asia between China and the Soviet Union. Outer Mongolia is now the Soviet-dominated People's Republic of Mongolia with its capital at Urga. Inner Mongolia comprises an extensive plateau area in north and northeast China. In the Middle Ages the Mongols ruled an empire which reached to western Russia.

Montenegro. Former principality and kingdom in the mountains northwest of Albania. Now part of Yugoslavia.

Mont-Saint-Michel. Famous island and village west of Avranches, France, containing an historic monastery. It is connected to the mainland by a causeway.

Moon, Mountains of the. Mountain range believed by ancient geographers to lie across central Africa, and to give rise to the headwaters of the Nile.

Moravia. Former Austro-Hungarian crownland in the Morava River valley; now the central province of Czechoslovakia. The capital is Brno.

Morgarten. Mountain slope near Lucerne, Switzerland, where an Austrian army was routed, 1315, and the independence of Switzerland assured.

Moriah, Mount. Hill on the east side of Jerusalem, the site of the Temple of Solomon.

Mount of Olives. This mountain, east of Jerusalem, is frequently mentioned in scripture. It is 2,665 ft. high. Also called Mount Olivet.

Muscovy. Old name of Russia derived from Moscow, the capital of a strong medieval grand duchy.

Mutina. Early Roman colony, the modern Italian city of Modena. It was the site of the last resistance of the Cisalpine Gauls to the growing power of Rome, 193 B.C.

Mycale. Promontory east of island of Samos where Greeks destroyed a Persian naval force, 479 B.C.

Mycenae. Very ancient Greek city whose ruins have been of great archaeological interest. It was located in Argolis northeast of Argos.

N

Narbonensis. Roman province extending along the Mediterranean coast of Gaul from the Alps to the Pyrenees. Its important cities were Massilia, Tolosa, and the capital, Narbo Martius (now Narbonne).

Naseby. Village near Northampton in central England; site of the decisive victory of the Parliamentarians under Cromwell over Charles I, 1645.

Naucratis. Ancient Greek trading center on the Nile delta south of Alexandria.

Navarre. Early medieval kingdom in the western Pyrenees. Its capital was at Pamplona, Spain. Most of the kingdom later united with Aragon, while the remainder, on the northern slopes of the Pyrenees, was absorbed by France.

Navigators' Islands. Old name of Samoan Islands.

Neanderthal. Valley between Düsseldorf and Wuppertal, Germany, where the skull of the famed prehistoric man was found.

Near East. Name formerly associated with the Ottoman Empire, and more recently applied to those countries making up the "Middle East."

Nebo (Pisgah), Mount. Mountain of Gilead near the north end of the Dead Sea, with an altitude of 2,631 ft. Now Jebel Neba in Jordan.

Negev. Vast desert region of southern Israel.

New Albion. Name given by Drake to part of the Pacific Coast north of San Francisco Bay.

New Amsterdam. Old name of New York City under the Dutch regime.

New Carthage. Important colony of the Carthaginians; now the city of Cartagena, Spain.

New England. Collective name since the early colonial days for the northeastern part of the United States. It includes the states of Maine, New Hampshire, Vermont, Massachusetts, Connecticut, and Rhode Island.

New France. Old name applied to the French colonies in North America, specifically, those in eastern Canada which were yielded to the British after the capture of Quebec City in 1763.

New Georgia. Old name of Vancouver Island, Canada, and adjacent mainland territory.

New Granada. Old Spanish viceroyalty in that part of Latin America now occupied by the republics of Colombia and Panama.

New Holland. Old name of Australia.

New Netherland. Originally an English land grant to the Duke of York, for lands between the Connecticut and Delaware Rivers. After the English defeat by the Dutch, it became a Dutch colony, roughly comprising much of New Jersey, New York, and Delaware.

New Spain. Early Spanish colony and viceroyalty of varying boundaries, now the republic of Mexico.

New Sweden. Old Swedish colony along the lower Delaware River.

New World. Name first applied in the 15th century to the newly discovered Western Hemisphere.

Nineveh. Capital of the Assyrian Empire and one of the most splendid cities of antiquity. Its ruins lie across the Tigris from Mosul, Iraq. Also called Ninus.

Nippon. Name of the old Japanese Empire, now reduced to the main and adjacent islands of Japan. Name sometimes restricted to Honshu, largest island.

Nod. Unknown land east of Eden to which Cain fled for refuge.

Normandy. Old French duchy and province along the English Channel containing the cities of Rouen (the capital), Le Havre, Caen, and Cherbourg.

Northeast Passage. Maritime passage from the Atlantic to the Pacific Ocean along north coast of Europe and Asia. It is navigable only in summer months.

North Polar Sea. The Arctic Ocean.

North River. Name of Hudson River near mouth.

Northumbria. Powerful kingdom of the early Middle Ages, located in northeastern England between the Humber and the Firth of Forth. Also called the kingdom of Northumberland, it was created by the union of the kingdoms of Bernicia and Deira.

Northwest Passage. A navigable passage from the Atlantic to the Pacific and the Orient, sought for centuries along the northern coast of North America. The Arctic passage finally found proved to be impassable most of the year.

Northwest Territory. Old name of the region west of Pennsylvania bounded by the Mississippi and Ohio rivers and the Great Lakes. It was ceded by England to the United States at close of Revolution, 1783.

North Woods. Popular name for the forest regions of northern Michigan, Wisconsin, and Minnesota.

Norumbega. In early maps of North America, a mysterious city and region on the Atlantic coast. Its existence has never been proven, though speculation has placed it in Massachusetts and Maine.

Notium. Ancient port west of Ephesus in Asia Minor, noted for the Spartan naval victory over Athens in 407 B.C.

Nubia. Name applied since the dawn of history to a region of the upper Nile now lying in the northern Sudan. It was part of the ancient kingdom of Ethiopia.

Numantia. Ancient town near Soria, Spain, famed for resistance to Roman conquest, 143-133 B.C.

Numidia. Ancient kingdom and later Roman province of northern Africa, in the northeastern part of modern Algeria.

O

Oberammergau. Famous resort in the Bavarian Alps, Germany, noted for its decennial "Passion Play."

Occident. The lands toward the setting sun, a general name for Western Europe and the New World in contradistinction to "Orient."

Oceania. Term used for the Pacific island divisions of Melanesia, Micronesia, and Polynesia. Occasionally it includes the islands of Australasia and Malaysia as well. Also called Oceanica.

Oceanus. According to the ancients, a swift and boundless stream flowing around all the known seas and continents.

Old World. Name applied to Eastern Hemisphere, particularly Europe, since discovery of America.

Olivet. Mount of Olives, east of Jerusalem, in Jordan.

Olympia. Valley of ancient Elis, Greece, site of the Olympic games. It was located along the Alfios River in the western Peloponnesus.

Olynthus. City of ancient Chalcidice, the subject of the famed Olynthiac orations of Demosthenes. It was destroyed in 347 B.C.

On. Biblical name of ancient Heliopolis, Egypt.

Ophir. In the Old Testament, a country which supplied Solomon with gold, silver, and other luxuries. It may have been located in India, southern Arabia, or eastern Africa.

Orange. Medieval principality of France, eventually absorbed by the house of Nassau. It has given its name to the royal house of the Netherlands. The capital, Orange, is located north of Avignon.

Orange River Free State. Former independent republic in South Africa with its capital at Bloemfontein. It was defeated by the British in the Boer War (1899-1902) and later became a province of South Africa.

Orient. The lands toward the rising sun; a western term for the countries of Asia and the Far East.

Ormuz. Famous medieval trade emporium on an island at the mouth of the Persian Gulf. Also called Ormus and Hormuz.

Orontes. Chief river of western Syria, the Arabic Nahr el Asi.

Ottoman Empire. Old Turkish Empire which, at its height in the 16th century, embraced parts of three continents: Asia, Europe, and Africa. Turkish power in Europe advanced to the gates of Vienna and nearly encircled the Black Sea. Turkey also ruled Syria and Mesopotamia in Asia and the entire African coast from Egypt to Algeria.

Oxus. Ancient name of the Amu Darya River in central Asia, which flows into the Aral Sea.

P

Paestum. Ancient city of Magna Graecia whose ruins lie on the southern shore of Italy's Gulf of Salerno. An earlier name was Posidonia.

Palatine Hill. One of the "seven hills" of Rome reputedly selected by Romulus as original site of city.

Palmyra. Desert metropolis of ancient Syria which flourished particularly in Roman times. It was the Tadmor of the Bible, and is now a small Syrian village.

Pampas, The. A vast fertile plain of central Argentina extending from the Atlantic and the Paraná in the east to the Andes and from the Gran Chaco in the north to Patagonia.

Panhandle. Name applied to any strip of territory projecting from the main body of a state or territory, for example, northern Texas, Idaho, and West Virginia; western Oklahoma; southeastern Alaska.

Papal States. Formerly an independent country of central Italy ruled by the Papal See. Stretching from coast to coast, it included the cities of Rome, Bologna, and Ancona. The papacy also possessed Venaissin, an enclave at Avignon, France.

Papua. Former name sometimes applied to the entire island of New Guinea, but now restricted to the Australian-owned territory in the southeast.

Paran. Desert wilderness north of Mt. Sinai where the Israelites wandered before reaching Canaan.

Parima. Legendary lake which early explorers vainly sought in northern South America. The name has since been given to a mountain range at the source of the Orinoco.

Parthia. Ancient country southeast of the Caspian Sea containing the city of Hecatompylos. The Parthian Empire extended from the Indus to the Euphrates before its downfall in 226 A.D.

Pas-de-Calais. French name for the Strait of Dover.

Patagonia. That part of South America south of the Argentine Río Negro between Andes and Atlantic.

Patmos. Small Greek island in the Sporades where John the Divine is believed to have experienced the visions of the Apocalypse.

Pella. Capital of ancient Macedonia, west of Salonika (Thessaloniki), Greece.

Peloponnesus. Ancient name of the large peninsula in southern Greece. The modern Morea.

Peraea. In the New Testament, a region east of the Jordan corresponding closely to Gilead.

Pergamum. Also Pergamon and Pergamus, the name of an ancient Greek kingdom and its capital in Mysia, Asia Minor. The city is identified with the biblical Pergamos, site of one of Paul's seven Asiatic churches. The modern Bergama, Turkey.

Persepolis. Capital of the Persian Empire. Its famous ruins are located northeast of Shiraz, Iran.

Persia. Old name of Iran. The original Persia or Persis was a mountainous country on the northeastern shores of the Persian Gulf. It later grew into an empire extending from the Aegean to the Indus.

Petra. The biblical Sela, midway between the Dead Sea and the Gulf of Aqaba; capital of ancient Edom and, later, of Roman province of Arabia Petraea.

Petrograd. The name of Leningrad between 1914 and 1924. Prior to 1914 city was called St. Petersburg.

Pharos. Peninsula near Alexandria, U.A.R. In ancient times it was an island and the site of a great lighthouse that was considered one of the seven wonders of the world.

Pharsalus. City in southern Thessaly near which Caesar defeated Pompey, 48 B.C. The modern Farsala, Greece.

Philadelphia. Ancient Lydian city where Paul established one of his seven Asiatic churches. It is now the town of Alasehir, Turkey. Also an old name of Amman, the capital of Jordan.

Philippi. City of ancient Greece, inland from the present port of Kavalla. Near here, in 42 B.C., Augustus and Antony defeated the Roman Republicans led by Brutus and Cassius. Here also Paul founded the first Christian church in Europe.

Philistia. Ancient country of the Philistines in southwest Palestine. Its chief cities were Gaza, Ashkelon, Ashdod, Ekron, and Gath. The name Palestine was derived from "Philistine."

Phoenicia. The first nation to engage in large-scale Mediterranean commerce and colonization. Its chief cities were Sidon and Tyre, the present ports of Saida and Tyre (Sur), Lebanon.

Phrygia. In the time of Persian power a large country in west-central Asia Minor. Its important cities were Celaenae and, later, Apamea.

Picardy. Old province of northern France with its capital at Amiens.

Pichincha. Lofty volcano west of Quito, Ecuador, in Pichincha province. It is the site of one of the world's highest battlefields. Here, in 1822, Sucre defeated the Spanish and insured the independence of Ecuador.

Piedmont. Originally, a division of northern Italy in the upper basin of the Po, a part of the old duchy of Savoy and kingdom of Sardinia. Now, a name applied to any foothill region, for example, the plateau between the Appalachians and the Atlantic Coastal Plain, extending from Virginia to Alabama.

Pillars of Hercules. Ancient name of the two promontories forming the Strait of Gibraltar.

Pisgah, Mount. The spur of Mount Nebo from which Moses beheld the Promised Land.

Plassey. Indian village north of Calcutta where Clive defeated Bengal army, 1757, assuring British control of lower Ganges basin and, eventually, of all India.

Plataea. Town south of ancient Thebes, Greece, where the Greeks, principally Spartans, decisively defeated an invading Persian army, 479 B.C.

Polish Corridor. Narrow corridor of former German territory assigned to Poland in 1919 to give that country access to the Baltic Sea. As a result of its World War II acquisitions from Germany east and west of corridor, Poland has extensive Baltic frontage.

Polynesia. Collective name of a myriad of islands in the Central and South Pacific inhabited by closely related races. Important in this category are the Hawaiian, Marquesas, Tuamotu, Society, Samoa, Tonga, Ellice, and Phoenix Islands.

Pomerania. Formerly, a Prussian province along the coast of the Baltic Sea. Most of the old province including Stettin, its capital, is now Polish territory. The German Pommern.

Pompeii. Famous Roman city southeast of Naples. Destroyed by the eruption of Mt. Vesuvius in 79 A.D.

Pontine Marshes. Also called Pomptine Marshes. Extensive areas of reclaimed marshland along the southern coast of the Campagna di Roma, Italy.

Pontus. Old kingdom of northeastern Asia Minor, later a Roman province. It took its name from the Euxine, or Pontus Euxinus, on whose shores it lay.

Porto Bello. Famous port for gold shipment in Spanish colonial days. It is now a small Panamanian village (Portobelo) on the Caribbean east of Colón. Also Puerto Bello.

Port Royal. Old French name of Annapolis Royal, Nova Scotia, founded in 1604.

Prairie Provinces. Collective name for the Canadian provinces of Manitoba, Saskatchewan, and Alberta.

Prussia. Medieval duchy on the Baltic around the lower Vistula and Niemen. Under the later kingdom of Prussia it was divided into provinces; East Prussia (capital, Königsberg) and West Prussia (capital, Danzig). The kingdom, around which greater Germany was constructed, extended westward to Rhenish Prussia (capital, Coblenz).

Pteria. Old capital of the Hittites, believed to be the site of a Persian victory over Lydia. Its ruins are near the village of Boghaz-Keui, Turkey.

Punjab. Former province in the lowlands of northwestern British India. In 1947 much of the Punjab including the capital at Lahore became part of the new state of Pakistan.

Puteoli. A leading seaport of ancient Italy; the modern Pozzuoli, west of Naples.

Pydna. Town in ancient Macedonia where the Romans won a final decisive victory over the Macedonians, 168 B.C.

R

Rabbah. Biblical capital of the Ammonites. Later Philadelphia, it is now Amman, capital of Jordan.

Ragae. First capital of ancient Media, on site of modern Tehrān, Iran. Also called Rhagae and Rages.

Ramah. Ancient home of Samuel, north of Jerusalem.

Ramoth-Gilead. Place of biblical importance east of the Jordan River, possibly near Es Salt in Jordan. May be identical with Ramoth-Mizpah.

Ratisbon. A Bavarian city on the Danube northeast of Munich; now called Regensburg. The story of its capture by Napoleon in 1809 is told in Browning's poem "Ratisbon."

Reval. Also Revel, the former name of Tallinn, capital of Soviet Estonia.

Rhaetia. Alpine province of Rome which has given its name to the Rhaetian Alps between Austria and Switzerland. Also called Raetia.

Rhineland. Also called Rhenish Prussia or Rhine Province, in the basin of the German lower Rhine. Important cities are Köln (Cologne) and Düsseldorf.

Rimland. That part of the World Island adjacent to the Heartland but close enough to the temperate seas and oceans to be influenced by sea power. Included are Western Europe, the Middle East, the Far East, and Africa.

Riviera. Popular name for a narrow strip of territory between the mountains and the Mediterranean extending from Hyères, France to La Spezia, Italy. It includes the cities of Nice and Genova (Genoa) and many smaller resorts.

Roman Empire. The greatest empire of ancient times, administered from the city of Rome. The lands under Roman control included entire Mediterranean littoral and extended from Britain to Mesopotamia.

Roncesvalles. Modern French, Roncevaux, a Spanish village near a pass in the Pyrenees northeast of Pamplona; scene of the death of Roland in 778.

Rubicon. Small stream north of Rimini marking the boundary between Cisalpine Gaul and ancient Italy. Caesar crossed the stream in 49 B.C., precipitating a Roman civil war.

Ruhr. Name applied to industrial district in Ruhr River valley of western Germany. Chief city is Essen.

Rumelia. Also Roumelia. Name, loosely used, for the European territory of the Ottoman Empire along the northern shore of the Aegean. It corresponded roughly with ancient Thrace and Macedonia. Eastern Rumelia was annexed by Bulgaria in 1885.

Runnymede. Also Runnimede. A meadow on the right bank of the Thames west of London, where King John signed the Magna Carta, 1215.

Rupert's Land. Also Rupert Land, an early name for the vast area in the basin of Hudson Bay, later known as the Hudson's Bay Territory.

Russia. Popular name of the Union of Soviet Socialist Republics (Soviet Union), formerly the Russian Empire. The name is now applied more properly to two Soviet republics, the Russian Socialist Federated Soviet Republic and White Russia. Soviet Russia is also a popular name of the Soviet Union.

Ruthenia. Land of the Ruthenians in the central Carpathian Mountains. Parts of Ruthenia have at various times been under the control of Poland, Austria-Hungary, Czechoslovakia, and Russia. At the close of World War II, Czechoslovakia ceded that part of Ruthenia south of the Carpathians to the Soviet Union.

Ryswick. Village near the Hague, the Netherlands, where the French signed a treaty with England, the Netherlands, and Spain, 1697; now Rijswijk.

S

Saguntum. Ancient city noted for its valiant resistance to Hannibal, 219 B.C. Later called Murviedro, it is now the town of Sagunto, Spain.

Saikio. Name occasionally given to Kyoto, the old "western capital" of Japan, to distinguish it from Tokio or Tokyo, the present "eastern capital."

Saint Brendan's Island. According to medieval legend, one of several islands in the Atlantic visited by Irish monks and their leader, Saint Brendan.

Saint Petersburg. Name of the former capital of Russia. The name was changed to Petrograd in 1914 and Leningrad in 1924. In 1918, the capital was transferred to Moskva (Moscow).

Salamis. Chief seaport of ancient Cyprus, now a heap of ruins north of Famagusta. Also, an island near Peiraieus (Piraeus), Greece, noted for Athenian naval victory over Persia off its shores, 480 B.C.

Salem. Original name of Jerusalem, still used poetically. Also Shalem.

Salt Sea. One of the biblical names for the Dead Sea, the others being the Sea of the Plain and the East Sea. Known to Romans as Lacus Asphaltites.

Samaria. Name for the capital of the ancient kingdom of Israel, later applied to the entire region between Galilee and Judea. The city of Samaria became the Roman Sebaste and the present village of Sebustieh, northwest of Nābulus, Jordan.

Sandwich Islands. Old name of Hawaiian Islands.

San Juan Hill. Celebrated elevation southeast of Santiago de Cuba, taken by storm by the Americans, 1898, in an engagement in the Spanish-American War. The famous Rough Riders were prominent in the assault.

San Stefano. Small port west of Constantinople, now Istanbul. The treaty signed there, 1878, ended Russo-Turkish War.

Sarai. Capital of the medieval khanate of Kiptchak. Soviet city of Leninsk, east of Volgograd, formerly Stalingrad, now on site.

Sardes. Also Sardis, capital of the early kingdom of Lydia and seat of one of the seven Asiatic churches of Paul. It was located east of what is now Izmir, Turkey.

Sardinia. Old kingdom created in 1720 out of Savoy, Piedmont, Genoa, and the island of Sardinia. The kings of Sardinia passed the royal succession from the dukes of Savoy to the later kings of Italy.

Sargasso Sea. An extensive ocean area northeast of the West Indies, laden with drifting weeds, chiefly Sargassum or gulf weed. Since it is the center of a great elliptical gyration of ocean currents in the North Atlantic, the region is relatively calm.

Satsuma. Formerly a province on Kyushu Island, Japan; famed for its fine porcelain.

Savoy. Old county and duchy in the French and Italian Alps. At its height, the duchy controlled the Piedmont and an outlet to the sea at Nice, France. In 1860, the Nice district and that part of Savoy on the western slopes of the Alps were ceded to France. The early counts of Savoy founded the reigning house of the kingdom of Italy.

Saxony. Early medieval duchy extending from the North Sea almost to Leipzig in the southeast and the Rhine in the southwest. It later became an electorate and a kingdom north of the Erzgebirge (Ore Mountains), with Dresden and Leipzig as the chief cities.

Scandinavia. Sweden, Norway, and Denmark.

Scapa Flow. Large protected bay in southern Orkney Islands. Main anchorage of the British Home (Grand) Fleet. Chief British naval base in World War I and World War II.

Schleswig-Holstein. Old duchy and province north of the Elbe between the North and Baltic Seas, for whose possession Germany and Denmark have contended for centuries. Northern Schleswig (the Danish Slesvig) is now in Danish territory.

Scotia. Early medieval name of Ireland, the original home of the Scots. It was later applied poetically to Scotland, the land to which many Scots emigrated.

Scylla. Prominent rock on the Italian side of the Strait of Messina. It was the legendary home of the sea monster, Scylla, across the strait from the whirlpool, Charybdis.

Sea of the Plain. Biblical name of the Dead Sea, also called in scripture the Salt Sea and the East Sea. The Roman name was Lacus Asphaltites.

Sedgemoor. Moor near Bridgwater, England, where the Royalists of James II defeated the Duke of Monmouth in 1685.

Seleucia. Capital of the Seleucid Empire on the Tigris south of Baghdad. This empire extended from the Mediterranean to the Indus before being absorbed by Rome. Also, a Syrian city, the port for ancient Antioch.

Senlac. Hill near Hastings, England, where the invading Normans, led by William the Conqueror, won their great victory over the Saxons, 1066.

Sepharvaim. Biblical name of Sippar, a city north of Babylon.

Serbia. Formerly an independent kingdom, now a part of eastern Yugoslavia. Also called Servia. The capital was Belgrade.

Sharon. Coastal plain in Israel between Jaffa and Mt. Carmel.

Sheba. Biblical name of Saba or Sabaea, a wealthy kingdom in southwestern Arabia.

Shechem. Also Sichem, the earliest capital of the kingdom of Israel. The Sychar of the New Testament and the Roman Flavia Neapolis, it is now the city of Nābulus, Jordan.

Shiloh. Early religious center of Israelites between Nābulus and Jerusalem. Also a great battlefield near Pittsburg Landing, Tennessee, in the Civil War.

Shinar. Biblical name of Babylonia or its southern part; also called Chaldea or Sumer.

Shire. In England, a land division or county.

Shushan. Biblical name of Susa.

Siberia. Vast expanse of Soviet territory in Asia extending from the Urals to the Pacific. It is bounded on the south by the Soviet republics of central Asia, and by Sinkiang, Mongolia, and Manchuria, and on the north by the Arctic Ocean.

Sick Man of Europe. Term given to the Ottoman or Turkish Empire in the years prior to World War I, when its control over southeastern Europe and its Arabic and North African empire was beginning to weaken.

Sicyon. Important city of ancient Greece northwest of Corinth. The area surrounding the city was called Sicyonia.

Sidon. Principal port of ancient Phoenicia, also called Zidon. Saida, Lebanon, now occupies its site.

Silesia. Industrial region, largely in the valley of the upper Oder. Formerly a province of Prussia and Germany, it now forms the southwestern part of Poland. The chief city is Wroclaw, formerly Breslau, Germany. Austrian Silesia, in the Moravska Ostrava region, was divided between Czechoslovakia and Poland following World War I. German Schlesin.

Sinai, Mount. Famous biblical mountain where Moses received the Ten Commandments. Many identify it with Ras es Sufsafeh or Jebel Musa, near Jebel Katherina on the U.A.R.'s Sinai Peninsula.

Slavonia. Region between Drava and Sava rivers in north-central Yugoslavia, formerly part of Austro-Hungarian crownland of Croatia and Slavonia.

Slot, The. Name given in World War II to the sound which bisects the Solomon Island chain to the northeast and southwest.

Slovakia. Mountainous province of eastern Czechoslovakia. Capital is Bratislava, the German Pressburg.

Slovenia. Region in northwestern Yugoslavia. The chief city is Ljubljana, formerly called Laibach.

Smyrna. Former Greek name of Izmir, Turkey. One of Paul's seven churches of Asia was located here.

Sofala. Seaport of Mozambique, southwest of Beira, taken from the Arabs by Portugal in 1505.

Southern Ocean. Name formerly applied to the ocean waters between 40° South Latitude and the Antarctic Circle.

South Sea. Old name of the Pacific Ocean. It is now applied to the South Pacific, commonly in the plural form, "South Seas."

Spanish America. Those portions of the New World settled by the Spaniards in the early Colonial period.

Spanish Main. Old name of the mainland of Spanish America; particularly the Caribbean coast of South and Central America, the Spanish Tierra Firme. Popularly, the name has become associated with the entire Caribbean area during the colorful pirate period.

Stonehenge. This mysterious roofless monument stands on Salisbury Plain, near Wiltshire, England. It is formed by huge standing stones, apparently the ruins of a prehistoric sacred enclosure. It is believed to have been erected by men of the Bronze Age.

Straits Settlements. Former crown colony of Great Britain on the Malay Peninsula. The principal settlements were at Singapore (the capital), Penang Island, and Malacca.

Straits, The. Name used collectively in referring to the strategic waterway between the Black and the Aegean Seas. It includes the Bosporus, the Sea of Marmara, and the Dardanelles.

Strathclyde. Old Celtic kingdom of northwestern England south of the Clyde, including the districts of Cumbria and Galloway.

Stresa. Resort town on the southwestern shore of Lake Maggiore in northern Italy. It was the site of an important international conference in 1935.

Styria. Crownland of Austria–Hungary located north of the Drava River, largely within the southeastern boundaries of modern Austria.

Sudan. An extensive region south of the Sahara stretching from the horn of Africa on the Atlantic to the southern shores of the Red Sea. Includes most of the independent nation of the same name.

Sudetenland. Strip of territory in northwestern Czechoslovakia across the Erzgebirge (Ore Mountains) from Germany. It contained a majority of Sudeten Germans prior to World War II.

Sumer. That part of ancient Babylonia south of Akkad at the head of the Persian Gulf. Also called Sumeria, Shumer, and the Land of Shinar.

Susa. Capital of ancient Elam or Susiana and royal residence of kings of Persia. Called Shushan in Bible.

Swanee. Musical adaptation by Stephen Foster of the name of the Suwannee River in Georgia and northern Florida.

Sybaris. Wealthy and luxury-loving city of ancient Magna Graecia. Its ruins are now located in northern Calabria near the Gulf of Taranto.

Sychar. The New Testament name of Shechem; now Nābulus, Jordan.

Syrtis. Ancient name applied to two North African gulfs. Syrtis Major, southwest of Bengazi, is now called the Gulf of Sidra. Syrtis Minor, in Tunisia, is now called the Gulf of Gabes.

T

Tabor, Mount. A mountain east of Nazareth, Palestine, prominent in the Old Testament. Its altitude is 1,880 ft.

Tadmor. Biblical name of Palmyra, Syria.

Tanagra. Ancient town in eastern Boeotia, Greece, the site of a Spartan victory over Athens, 457 B.C. Famed also for its terra-cotta figurines.

Tannenberg. Small village south of Ostróda, Poland, formerly within the boundaries of East Prussia. Here, in 1914, a German army surrounded and partially destroyed a large Russian force.

Taprobane. Ancient name of Ceylon. Also, in the domain of the legendary Prester John somewhere in Asia or Africa, a remarkable island containing deposits of pure gold.

Tarraconensis. Largest of the three Roman provinces in Spain, located east of Baetica and north and east of Lusitania. The capital was Tarraco, the modern city of Tarragona.

Tarshish. Biblical name for a region remote from Palestine. It probably refers to the area around Tartessus, a Phoenician city near the mouth of the Guadalquivir in southern Spain.

Tarsus. Town of southeastern Asia Minor, southwest of what is now Adana, Turkey. It is chiefly famous as the birthplace of the Apostle Paul.

Tatary. Old name (commonly, but less correctly, Tartary) of the vast center of the Eurasian continent inhabited by the Tatars. In the Middle Ages, they extended their control from Mongolia westward to the Dnepr River in European Tatary and eastward to the Pacific. An autonomous Tatar republic now exists with its capital at Kazan, Soviet Union.

Tenochtitlán. Capital of the old Aztec Empire, captured by the Spanish in 1521. Modern Mexico City has been built on the same site.

Thapsus. Town southeast of Sousse, Tunisia, where Caesar defeated the followers of Pompey, 46 B.C.

Thebes. Very ancient capital of Egypt on the right bank of the Nile near the present town of Luxor. Also, the chief city of Boeotia, Greece.

Therma. Ancient name for the modern Thessaloniki, or Salonika, Greece.

Thermopylae. Famous pass between the sea marshes and the mountains southeast of Lamia, Greece. It is the site of the heroic stand made by several hundred Spartans against the invading Persians, 480 B.C.

Thessaly. Division of ancient Greece bordering the Aegean Sea and completely surrounded by mountains, including the famous Olympus. The chief city of the region today is Larisa.

Thrace. Region of antiquity bounded by the Danube and the Black and Aegean seas. The subsequent Roman province, Thracia, included only territory south of the Balkan Mountains, what is now southern Bulgaria, European Turkey, and northeastern Greece.

Thule. Ancient name of the most northerly part of the known world, probably Iceland, or Norway, or one of the Shetland Islands. The expression "Ultima Thule" refers to any distant human objective, geographical or otherwise.

Thyatira. City of ancient Lydia, the site of one of Paul's seven churches of Asia. Its ruins lie near Akhisar, Turkey.

Tierra del Fuego. Desolate archipelago at the southern tip of South America, separated from the continent proper by the Strait of Magellan.

Timbuktu. Remote town on the upper Niger in the interior of Mali. The French form is Tombouctou.

Tiphsah. Biblical name of ancient Thapsacus, Syria.

Tippecanoe. River in northwestern Indiana noted for Harrison's victory over the Indians, near its confluence with the Wabash, 1811.

Tipperary. County and city in south-central Ireland, prominent in a popular song of World War I.

Tiryns. Very old city southeast of Argos, Greece. Its ruins are of great archaeological significance.

Tirzah. Early capital of the kingdom of Israel, east of modern Sebustieh in Jordan.

Tolosa. Roman name of Toulouse, France.

Tophet. That part of the Valley of Hinnom south of Jerusalem where the idolatrous Jews of antiquity worshiped their god of fire. Also called Gehenna.

Touraine. Medieval duchy and province of France with its capital at Tours.

Trafalgar. Cape in southern Spain between Cadiz and Gibraltar. Off this promontory, the British fleet under Lord Nelson defeated the combined navies of France and Spain, 1805.

Transcaucasia. That part of the Soviet Union south of the Caucasus Mountains, comprising the republics of Georgia, Azerbaidzhan, and Armenia.

Transleithania. Old name for the Hungarian portion of Austria-Hungary, to the east and south of Cisleithania. It included all of modern Hungary and parts of Yugoslavia, Czechoslovakia, and Romania.

Transylvania. Region in northwestern Romania separated from the rest of the country by the Carpathians and the Transylvanian Alps. A former part of Austria-Hungary, the area has long been a source of conflict between Hungary and Romania. The capital is Cluj.

Trapezus. Ancient name of Trabzon, Turkey.

Trebizond. Medieval empire of the Byzantines along the southeastern coast of the Black Sea. The capital was Trebizond, which is now the city of Trabzon, Turkey.

Tremont. Also Trimontaine, original name of Boston, derived from the three summits of Beacon Hill.

Trinacria. Ancient name of Sicily, so called because of the island's three large promontories to the northeast, southeast, and west.

Troas. Also called the Troad, a region of ancient Asia Minor bordering the Aegean and the Hellespont. Located here was the famous city of Troy or Ilium and the ancient seaport Troas or Alexandria Troas.

Troy. Ancient city of Troas, Asia Minor, destroyed by the Greeks in the Trojan War. The Greek Ilion and the Roman Ilium.

Turkestan. Extensive region in central Asia bounded by the Caspian to the west, Iran and Afghanistan to the south, the Tien Shan Mtns. to the east, and Siberia to the north. It is divided among constituent republics of the Soviet Union.

Tuscany. Medieval duchy in western Italy containing the old cities of Florence and Pisa.

Two Sicilies. United medieval kingdom of Sicily and southern Italy.

Tyrol. Mountainous region which formed, with Vorarlberg, the westernmost crownland in Austria-Hungary. After World War I, the southern part became the Italian Trentino. The capital of the Tyrol, also called Tirol, was Innsbrück, Austria.

U

Ukraine. Formerly, a general name for the lands in the basin of the Dnepr (Dnieper) River of southwestern Russia. In its broadest sense, the name included all of Russia westward to Polish Galicia, and is now applied to a Soviet republic in that area. It has often been called "Little Russia."

Ulster. Northern division of Ireland largely contained within the boundaries of Northern Ireland, a unit of the United Kingdom. The other divisions, Connaught, Leinster, and Munster, are in Eire (Republic of Ireland).

Umbria. Ancient land of the Umbrians in central Italy, probably extending at one time from the Adriatic to the Tyrrhenian Sea. Modern Umbria lies landlocked in the basin of the upper Tiber. Its capital is Perugia.

United Kingdom. Collective name now applied to Great Britain and Northern Ireland. Before 1931, all of Ireland was included.

Ur (Ur of the Chaldees). Capital of a very ancient kingdom in Chaldea. Its ruins, called Mugheir by the Arabs, are located near the left bank of the lower Euphrates.

Urartu. Assyrian name of Ararat.

Utica. After the fall of Carthage, 146 B.C., the capital of the Roman province of Africa. Utica was located northwest of Carthage.

Uxmal. Ruined Maya city in southern Yucatan.

Uz. In the Old Testament, the home of Job, somewhere in northern Arabia.

V

Van Diemen's Land. Former name of Tasmania.

Veii. Ancient Etruscan city which fell to the Romans in 396 B.C. after a ten-year siege. Generally thought to be site of modern Isola Farnese, Italy.

Veld (Veldt). Open plateau country in South Africa. The name is taken from the Dutch word for "field," or "grassland."

Venaissin. Old county and papal possession whose chief city was Avignon. It was ceded to France in 1791.

Venetia. Province of ancient Italy north of the Adriatic and the lower Po. Modern Venetia is divided into three parts: Venetia proper or Veneto (capital, Venice); Venezia Tridentina (capital, Trento); and Venezia Giulia (capital, Trieste), now ceded in part to Yugoslavia.

Vindelicia. Ancient region of north Rhaetia between the Danube and the Alps. Its chief city was Augusta Vindelicorum, now Augsburg, Germany.

Vinland. Name given by Norsemen to an unidentified region, possibly New England, on northeastern coast of North America. In English, Wineland.

W

Wagram. Village northeast of Vienna. It was the site, in 1809, of a Napoleonic victory over Austria.

Wahlstatt. Village in Silesia where the Germans fought the Mongols and checked their westward advance through Europe, 1241.

Walachia. Also Wallachia. That part of southern Romania between the Danube and the Transylvanian Alps. It united with Moldavia in 1861 to form the kingdom of Romania. Chief city is Bucharest.

Waterloo. Belgian village south of Brussels where Napoleon suffered his final defeat, 1815.

Western Reserve. Early name of a vast tract of land on Lake Erie which was claimed by the state of Connecticut. Incorporated in Northwest Territory in 1800, it is now the northeastern corner of Ohio.

Westphalia. Province of northwestern Germany, formerly duchy and kingdom. Capital is Münster.

White Russia. General name of the land of the White Russians in the western Soviet Union and adjacent parts of Poland and Lithuania. The name applies specifically to the Byelorussian (White Russian) Soviet Republic, whose capital is located at Minsk.

Wilderness, The. In the Civil War, a battlefield south of the Rapidan River, Virginia.

Windward Islands. General name of the southern group of islands in the Lesser Antilles, extending from Dominica to Grenada.

World Island. Term used when referring to the combined land mass of Eurasia and Africa.

Wurtemberg. Old kingdom of southern Germany comprising much of medieval Swabia and almost completely encircled by Baden and Bavaria. German name was Württemberg. Capital was Stuttgart.

X

Xanthus. Famous city of western Lycia, destroyed by the Persians in 545 B.C. and the Romans in 43 B.C. Only ruins remain.

Y

Yedo. Also Yeddo, an old name of Tokyo, Japan.

Yellow River. In Chinese, the Hwang Ho, second of the great rivers of China. Rising in Tibet, it flows through Mongolia and China to the Gulf of Pohai, a distance of 2,903 miles. Its periodic floods have earned it the name of "China's sorrow."

Yezo. Former name of island of Hokkaido, Japan.

Z

Zealand. Largest island in Denmark, the Danish Sjaelland. Also, low-lying province of islands in southwestern Netherlands, commonly called Zeeland.

Zela. Ancient town on the site of Zile, Turkey. After defeating the king of Pontus there in 47 B.C., Caesar sent his famous message, "Veni, vidi, vici."

Zidon. Biblical name of Sidon, Phoenicia; the modern Saida, Lebanon.

Zion, Mount. The highest hill in Jerusalem, where the ancient City of David stood. The name "Zion" was later applied to Jerusalem itself and to the Zionist movement. Also called Sion.

Zoar. In early biblical history, the sole Canaanite city on the plain near the Dead Sea which was spared destruction. It stood near Sodom.

Zuider Zee. Inlet of the North Sea which projects into the Netherlands for a distance of 80 miles. The seaward end is enclosed by a dike. It was once a lake but in the 13th century was joined to the sea by a great flood. Since 1920, site of major land reclamation project. Also IJsselmeer.

Zululand. Former native kingdom north of Durban, Natal. Now part of South Africa.

PRINCIPAL DISCOVERIES AND EXPLORATIONS

Ancient and Medieval (to the Discovery of America)

DATE	EXPLORER	COUNTRY REPRESENTED	DESCRIPTION
600 B.C.	Phoenician Sailors	Egypt	Reported by Herodotus to have sailed around Africa from east to west in three years, under orders of King Necho.
500–450 B.C.	Himilco	Carthage	Said to have explored the west coast of Europe, possibly reaching Britain.
500 B.C.	Hanno	Carthage	Explored west coast of Africa to Sierra Leone or about 5° N.
450 B.C.	Herodotus	Greece	Visited Black Sea, eastern Mediterranean, and Egypt, and described the world of his time.
334–323 B.C.	Alexander the Great	Macedonia	Explored and conquered all of southwestern Asia from Egypt to the Jaxartes and Indus rivers.
320 B.C.	Pytheas	Marseilles	Visited Britain and northwestern Europe and, possibly, either Iceland or Norway, which he called Thule.
59–44 B.C.	Julius Caesar	Rome	Added information about Gaul, Britain, and Germany to current geographical knowledge.
20 B.C.	Strabo	Rome	Traveled widely throughout Mediterranean lands; compiled most complete geography of ancient times.
570 A.D.	St. Brendan	Ireland	Alleged to have sailed the western seas for seven years in search of tropical islands; may have reached Madeira or West Indies.
690 A.D.	Bishop Arculf	France	Visited Jerusalem and other holy places; described Egypt.
721–31 A.D.	Willibard	England	Visited and described the Holy Land, Constantinople, and Rome.
890 A.D.	Othere	Norway	Sailed around North Cape, along the Lapland coast, and discovered the White Sea.
925–950 A.D.	Al Masudi	Baghdad	Traveled in India, Ceylon, China, Russia, Persia, and Egypt.
982 A.D.	Eric the Red	Norway	Discovered and colonized southern Greenland.
1000 A.D.	Leif Ericson	Norway	Discovered Labrador, Newfoundland, and nearby coasts.
1003–06 A.D.	Thorfinn Karlsefni	Iceland	Explored and attempted to colonize northeast coast of North America.
1099–1154 A.D.	Idrisi	Spain and Sicily	Traveled in north Africa and Asia Minor; compiled a description and map of the world.
1106 A.D.	Daniel of Kiev	Russia	Visited Jaffa, Jerusalem, the Jordan, and Damascus on pilgrimage to the Holy Land.
1160–73 A.D.	Benjamin of Tudela	Spain	Traveled through Egypt, Assyria, Persia, and central Asia, visiting Jewish centers.
1245–47 A.D.	John de Plano Carpini	Italy	Traveled through Poland, Russia, and central Asia to Karakoram, in Mongolia, as legate of the pope.
1253–55 A.D.	William of Rubruck	France	Visited Karakoram, in Mongolia, by way of southern Russia and Turkestan.
1270 A.D.	Lancelot Malocello	Italy	Rediscovered the Fortunate or Canary Islands.
1271–95 A.D.	Marco Polo	Italy	Journeyed to China by way of central Asia; returned by sea by way of Sumatra, Ceylon, India, and Persia; reported existence of Japan and Madagascar.
1281–91 A.D.	Vivaldi Brothers	Italy	Attempted voyage to India by sea along west coast of Africa, but never returned.
1323–28 A.D.	Friar Odoric	Italy	Traveled to China by way of India and Malaya; returned through central Asia.
1325–54 A.D.	Ibn Battuta	Spain	Visited every Islamic country from Spain to India; traveled widely in Far East, Arabia, and western Africa.
1346 A.D.	Jayme Ferrer	Catalonia	Credited by 14th-century maps with having rounded Cape Bojador on west coast of Africa.
1427–31 A.D.	Diogo de Seville	Portugal	Discovered some of the Azores Islands.
1433–35 A.D.	Gil Eannes	Portugal	Rounded Cape Bojador in exploration of west coast of Africa.
1435–36 A.D.	Affonso Baldaya	Portugal	Landed on coast of Africa in vicinity of Rio de Oro.

America (1492–1850) continued

DATE	EXPLORER	COUNTRY REPRESENTED	DESCRIPTION
1577–80	Francis Drake	England	Explored west coast of North America to 46° or 48° N. and named it New Albion; circumnavigated the earth.
1583	Humphrey Gilbert	England	Made first effort to establish an English colony in North America; ship lost returning to England.
1585–87	John Davis	England	Made several voyages in search of Northwest Passage; discovered Davis Strait and Baffin Bay.
1602–03	Sebastian Vizcaino and Martin Aguilar	Spain	Sailed along coast of California to about 42° or 43° N.; discovered Monterey Bay but missed that of San Francisco; Aguilar reported large river near 43° N.
1603–15	Samuel de Champlain	France	Explored and mapped St. Lawrence R., New England coast, Ottawa R., Lake Huron, Lake Ontario; discovered Lake Champlain (1609).
1607–14	John Smith	England	Explored and mapped vicinity of Jamestown, Virginia (1608) and coast of New England (1614).
1609–11	Henry Hudson	Holland and England	Explored Hudson R. to Albany for Holland (1609); discovered and explored Hudson Bay for England (1610–1611).
1612–13	Thomas Button	England	Explored Hudson Bay in search of strait to the Western Ocean.
1615–16	William Baffin	England	Made two voyages in search of Northwest Passage; explored Baffin Bay to 78° N.
1631–32	Luke Foxe and William James	England	Explored northern and southern extensions of Hudson Bay without finding passage westwards.
1634	Jean Nicollet	France	Crossed Lake Huron to Mackinac Strait and Green Bay; reported "Western Sea" three days distant.
1658–59	Pierre Radisson and Sieur des Groseillers	France	Explored upper Mississippi R. and western shores of Lake Superior.
1669–70	John Lederer	England	Crossed the Blue Ridge and explored the Shenandoah Valley.
1669–87	Robert Cavalier, Sieur de la Salle	France	Explored Lake Ontario and upper Ohio R. (1669) and the Great Lakes to head of Lake Michigan (1679); descended Illinois and Mississippi rivers to Gulf of Mexico (1681–82); killed in Texas after failing to locate Mississippi R. by sea (1684–87).
1673	Jacques Marquette and Louis Joliet	France	Descended Mississippi R. from the Wisconsin R. to the Arkansas and returned to the Great Lakes via the Illinois-Chicago portage.
1680	Louis Hennepin	France	Explored upper Mississippi R. from the Illinois R. to the Minnesota.
1688	Louis de la Hontan	France	Explored upper Mississippi region; spread reports of fictitious "Long River" leading to Western Sea.
1699	Pierre le Moyne, Sieur d' Iberville	France	Entered mouth of Mississippi from Gulf of Mexico and explored delta.
1701–02	Eusebio Francisco Kino	Spain	Explored the Gila and lower Colorado rivers; proved that California was not an island.
1718–19	Bernard de la Harpe	France	Explored the Red and Arkansas rivers.
1721	Pierre Francois Xavier de Charlevoix	France	Visited French settlements in North America from Quebec to New Orleans.
1728–41	Vitus Bering	Russia	Confirmed existence of strait between Asia and America (1728); discovered northwest coast and named Mt. St. Elias (1741).
1730–43	Sieur de La Vérendrye and sons	France	Explored territory northwest of Lake Superior; discovered Lake Winnipeg; sons may have seen Rocky Mountains.
1742	Christopher Middleton	England	Discovered Repulse Bay in search of passage to Western Sea.
1749	Celoron de Bienville	France	Buried plates along the Ohio R., claiming formal possession for France.
1750	Thomas Walker	England	Discovered Cumberland Gap route into Kentucky.
1750	Christopher Gist	England	Explored Ohio R. and Kentucky areas.

Date	Explorer	Country	Achievement
1441–46 A.D.	Nuno Tristam	Portugal	Reached the Sénégal R. along west coast of Africa.
1445 A.D.	Dinis Diaz	Portugal	Rounded Cape Verde on west coast of Africa.
1455–57 A.D.	Alvise da Cadamosto	Portugal	Explored the Sénégal and Gambia rivers; discovered Cape Verde Islands.
1472 A.D.	Fernando Póo	Portugal	Discovered island bearing his name in Gulf of Guinea.
1482–86 A.D.	Diogo Cao	Portugal	Discovered mouth of Congo R. (1482), reached Cape Negro at 16° S. (1486).
1487 A.D.	Pedro de Covilhã	Portugal	Traveled to India via Egypt and Arabia; visited east coast of Africa, south to Zambezi R.
1487–88 A.D.	Bartolomeu Dias	Portugal	Discovered Cape of Good Hope; explored coast east to Mossel Bay.

America (1492–1850)

Date	Explorer	Country	Achievement
1492–1502	Christopher Columbus	Spain	Discovered the West Indies (1492); in three later voyages explored coasts of northern South America and Central America.
1497–98	John and Sebastian Cabot	England	Discovered shores of Nova Scotia and Newfoundland, and visited southern Greenland.
1499–1500	Amerigo Vespucci, Juan de la Cosa and Alonso de Ojeda	Spain	Discovered and explored northeastern coast of South America.
1499–1500	Vincente Yañez Pinzón	Spain	Discovered mouth of Amazon R.
1500	Pedro Álvares Cabral	Portugal	Discovered or visited coast of Brazil on voyage to India.
1500–01	Gaspar Corte Real	Portugal	Made two voyages to northeastern North America, but never returned.
1501–02	Amerigo Vespucci	Portugal	Explored coast of Brazil to 30° S. or farther.
1513	Juan Ponce de León	Spain	Discovered and explored coasts of Florida.
1513	Vasco Núñez de Balboa	Spain	Crossed Isthmus of Panama and discovered the South Sea (Pacific Ocean).
1515	Juan Diaz de Solis	Spain	Explored mouth of Río de la Plata.
1517	Francisco Fernández de Córdoba	Spain	Discovered Yucatán and evidence of Mayan culture.
1518	Juan de Grijalva	Spain	Explored east coast of Mexico north of Yucatán.
1519	Alvárez Pineda	Spain	Explored Gulf of Mexico and may have discovered mouth of Mississippi R.
1519–22	Ferdinand Magellan	Spain	Discovered Strait of Magellan (1520) during first circumnavigation of the earth.
1519–27	Hernando Cortes	Spain	Explored and conquered Mexico.
1523–41	Francisco Pizarro	Spain	Explored northwestern South America and conquered Peru.
1524	Giovanni da Verrazano	France	Discovered New York Bay and explored coast northward.
1524–25	Estéban Gomez	Spain	Sailed along east coast of North America from Nova Scotia to Florida.
1527–37	Cabeza de Vaca	Spain	Wandered for nine years along and near coast of Gulf of Mexico from Florida to Mexico.
1534–41	Jacques Cartier	France	Explored Gulf of St. Lawrence (1534) and river as far as sites of Quebec and Montreal (1536).
1535–36	Diego de Almagro	Spain	Explored and conquered Chile.
1536–38	Gonzalo Jiménez de Quesada	Spain	Explored and conquered New Granada, and founded Bogotá.
1539	Francisco de Ulloa	Spain	Explored Gulf of California to its head.
1539–43	Hernando de Soto	Spain	Explored southeastern United States from Florida to Tennessee; discovered Mississippi R. (1541).
1540	Hernando de Alarcón	Spain	Sailed up Gulf of California and entered Colorado R.
1540–42	Francisco Vasquez de Coronado	Spain	Led expedition into southwestern United States; explored Great Plains northward to Kansas; Grand Canyon of Colorado R. discovered by one of his party.
1541	Francisco de Orellana	Spain	Crossed the Andes and descended Amazon R. to its mouth.
1542–43	Bartolomé Ferrelo and Juan Rodriguez Cabrillo	Spain	Discovered San Diego Bay and explored California coast to about 42° N. or Cape Mendocino.
1562–65	René de Laudonnière and Jean de Ribaut	France	Failed in effort to establish a permanent colony on coast of South Carolina.
1766–68	Jonathan Carver	England	Explored the upper Mississippi region and reported existence of the Oregon or River of the West.
1769–75	Daniel Boone	England	Explored eastern Kentucky (1769–71) and blazed the famous Wilderness Road (1775).
1769	José Ortega	Spain	Discovered San Francisco Bay during overland expedition into upper California.
1770–72	Samuel Hearne	England	Traced the Coppermine R. to the Northern Ocean and discovered Great Slave Lake.
1774–75	Juan Pérez and Bruno Heceta	Spain	Sent to explore northwest coast, reaching 55° N.; Heceta observed entrance to Columbia R.; Pérez discovered Nootka Sound.
1778–79	James Cook	England	Rediscovered Hawaiian Islands; explored and charted northwest coast from 45° N. to Arctic Ocean.
1788–92	Robert Gray	United States	Explored northwest coast; discovered Grays Harbor; entered and named the Columbia R. (1792).
1789–93	Alexander Mackenzie	England	Traced Mackenzie R. to its mouth (1789); crossed Rocky Mountains via Peace R. and reached Pacific Ocean.
1792–94	George Vancouver	England	Explored and mapped Puget Sound; charted inside passage and inlets along northwest coast.
1804–06	Meriwether Lewis and William Clark	United States	Ascended Missouri R. to its source, crossed Rocky Mountains and descended Columbia R. to Pacific Ocean.
1805–07	Zebulon M. Pike	United States	Explored and mapped upper Mississippi R. (1805); and southwestern section of Louisiana Territory (1806–07).
1807–08	Manuel Lisa and John Colter	United States	Explored Northern Rockies (Yellowstone-Big Horn region) as trappers and fur traders.
1811–12	Wilson Price Hunt (Astorians)	United States	Discovered overland route to Pacific via the Snake and Columbia rivers.
1819–20	Stephen H. Long	United States	Explored the high plains between Platte and Arkansas rivers; called the Great Plains the "Great American Desert."
1821	William Becknell	United States	Opened trade route between Missouri R. and Santa Fe.
1823–29	Jedediah Smith	United States	Located famous South Pass across Rocky Mts.; crossed desert between Colorado R. and California.
1824–28	Peter Skene Ogden	England	Explored upper Snake R. and northern Great Basin; discovered Humboldt R. and Great Salt Lake.
1829–30	Ewing Young and party	United States	Opened up Spanish Trail between Santa Fe and Los Angeles.
1832–33	Nathaniel J. Wyeth	United States	Led first expedition along Oregon Trail to Columbia R.
1833	Joseph E. Walker	United States	Crossed Great Basin between Great Salt Lake and California.
1841	Charles Wilkes	United States	Visited Oregon country and California during official Pacific exploring expedition by sea.
1842–45	John C. Frémont	United States	First official government explorer to re-trace explorations of fur trappers in the Far West.

Africa

Date	Explorer	Country	Achievement
1520–27	Francisco Alvarez	Portugal	Visited Ethiopia and described it in detail.
1541	Christopher da Gama	Portugal	Led expedition into Ethiopia.
1578–89	Duarte López	Portugal	Visited the Kingdom of Congo; his reports a chief source of information until 19th century.
1604–22	Pedro Páez	Portugal	First European to visit Ethiopian sources of the Nile R.
1616	Gaspar Boccaro	Portugal	Explored interior from upper Zambezi R. to west coast.
1618–19	George Thompson	England	Explored the Gambia R.
1625–35	Jerome Lobo	Portugal	Lived in Ethiopia as a missionary.
1698–1700	C. J. Poncet	France	Traveled as a physician into Ethiopia to treat the Emperor.
1768–73	James Bruce	England	Explored Ethiopia, especially source of the Blue Nile R.
1777–79	William Patterson	England	Made several trips into the Kaffir country as a naturalist.
1795–1805	Mungo Park	England	Explored the Gambia R. and was first modern European to reach the Niger R.
1797–98	John Barrow	England	Journeyed from Cape of Good Hope to upper Orange R.

PRINCIPAL DISCOVERIES AND EXPLORATIONS (Continued)

DATE	EXPLORER	COUNTRY REPRESENTED	DESCRIPTION
Africa continued			
1797–1800	Frederick Hornemann	England	Traveled from Egypt to Marzūq and the Niger R., disguised as an Arab.
1798–99	Francisco de Lacerda	Portugal	Explored southeastern interior north of Zambezi R.
1801	John Trutter and William Somerville	England	Explored Bechuanaland, north of Orange R.
1802–06	Pedro Baptista and A. Jose	Portugal	Made first recorded crossing of continent eastward from Angola.
1812–14	Johann L. Burckhardt	Switzerland	Traveled up the Nile R. and across to the Red Sea.
1822–25	Dixon Denham and Hugh Clapperton	England	Crossed desert from Tripoli to Lake Chad and westward to the Niger R.
1825–26	Alexander G. Laing	England	Reached Timbuktu from Tripoli, but was murdered on return trip.
1827–28	René Caillé	France	Traveled from Guinea Coast to Fez and Tangier by way of Timbuktu.
1830–34	Richard Lander	England	Explored the lower Niger R. and located its mouth.
1849–73	David Livingstone	England	Discovered Zambezi R. (1851), Victoria Falls (1855), and Lake Nyasa (1859); explored upper Congo tributaries; found by Stanley on Lake Tanganyika in 1871.
1856–59	Richard Burton	England	Discovered Lake Tanganyika and explored surrounding area.
1858–63	John Speke	England	Discovered Victoria Nyanza as source of the Nile R.
1861–69	Samuel Baker	England	Explored upper Nile R.; discovered Lake Albert.
1863–71	Georg A. Schweinfurth	Germany	Explored extensively in the Sudan and equatorial Africa.
1871–90	Henry Stanley	United States	Continued Livingstone's explorations in the lakes region; descended Congo R. to Atlantic Ocean (1877); discovered Stanley Pool and Lake Edward.
1877–86	Serpa Pinto	Portugal	Crossed the continent from Angola to Mozambique.
1879–90	Joseph Thomson	England	Explored new areas in Tanganyika, Kenya, and Uganda.
1888	Samuel Teleki	Hungary	Discovered lakes Rudolph and Stephanie.
Asia			
1497–99	Vasco da Gama	Portugal	Discovered sea route to India by way of South Africa and Indian Ocean.
1502–07	Ludovici di Varthema	Portugal	Traveled as convert to Islam in Arabia, Persia, India, and East Indies.
1511	Mathias Albuquerque	Portugal	Conquered Malacca, East Indian spice center.
1520–58	Thomé Pires	Portugal	Sent to Peking as commercial envoy.
1537–58	Fernão Mendes Pinto	Portugal	Described travels in India, China, and Japan.
1549–51	Francis Xavier	Portugal	Introduced Christianity into Japan.
1561–63	Anthony Jenkinson	England	Visited Persia by overland route from Russia.
1578–1610	Matteo Ricci	Portugal	Established first Christian missions in China.
1603–05	Benedict de Goez	Portugal	Made first overland trip to China after Marco Polo.
1632–68	Jean B. Tavernier	France	Traveled as commercial trader in Persia, India, and East Indies.
1656	Pieter van Goyer and Jacob von Keyser	Holland	Visited Peking by overland route from Canton.
1665–77	John Chardin	France	Described extensive travels in Persia and India.
1683–93	Engelbert Kaempfer	Holland	As physician with Dutch embassy, visited and described Thailand (Siam) and Japan.
1715–47	John Bell	Russia	Traveled as physician with Russian embassies to Persia and through Siberia to China.
1716–21	Ipolito Desideri	Italy	Reached Tibetan city of Lhasa from Kashmir.
1761–64	Carsten Niebuhr	Denmark	Explored Yemen, reaching cities of San'ā and Mocha (Al Mukāh); also visited Oman, Syria, and Palestine.
1795–97	W. R. Broughton	England	Explored coasts of Hokkaido and Korea.

DATE	EXPLORER	COUNTRY REPRESENTED	DESCRIPTION
Arctic Regions continued			
1871–74	Julius Payer and Carl Weyprecht	Austria	Discovered Franz Josef Land Archipelago.
1876	Albert H. Markham	England	Reached 83° 20' on northwest coast of Greenland.
1878–79	Nils A. E. Nordenskjöld	Sweden	Completed the Northeast Passage in two seasons in ship Vega.
1879–81	George W. DeLong	United States	Explored Arctic Ocean northwest of Bering Strait; ship Jeannette and most of party lost.
1881–83	Adolphus W. Greely	United States	Explored northern Greenland and Ellesmere Island; party established new record of 83° 24' N.
1888–96	Fridtjof Nansen	Norway	Made first crossing of Greenland (1888); reached record of 86° 14' during drift of ship Fram (1895).
1897	Salomon A. Andrée	Sweden	Attempted balloon flight to North Pole from Spitsbergen (Svalbard); remains of party found in 1930 on White Island.
1898–1902	Otto Sverdrup	Norway	Explored northern Ellesmere Island and discovered Axel Heiberg Island.
1899–1900	Umberto Cagni	Italy	Reached new record at 86° 34' N. by sledge from Franz Josef Land; member of Abruzzi expedition.
1900–09	Robert E. Peary	United States	Made repeated efforts to reach North Pole, succeeding (April 6, 1909) by sledge from Grant Land.
1903–6	Roald Amundsen	Norway	Completed first trip through Northwest Passage from east to west.
1907–9	Frederick A. Cook	United States	Claimed to have reached North Pole on April 20, 1908.
1925–26	Lincoln Ellsworth	United States	Made flight with Amundsen from Spitsbergen (Svalbard) to 87° 43' N. and return; co-leader of dirigible flight over North Pole (1926).
1926	Richard Byrd and Floyd Bennett	United States	Made successful flight from Spitsbergen (Svalbard) to North Pole and return.
1926–28	Umberto Nobile	Italy	Made numerous dirigible flights across arctic region; rescued after Italia crashed on ice in 1928.
1937–38	Otto Schmidt	Russia	Spent nine months with scientific expedition near North Pole.
Antarctic Regions			
1738–39	J.B.C. Bouvet de Lozier	France	Discovered Bouvet Island south of Africa in latitude 54° S.
1768–75	James Cook	England	Established non-existence of southern continent in habitable latitudes; reached record of 71° 10' S.
1771–73	Yves Joseph de Kerguélen-Trémarec	France	Discovered and explored Kerguélen Island in latitude 49° 50' S., longitude 69° 30' E.
1819	William Smith	England	Discovered South Shetland Islands.
1819–21	Fabian von Bellingshausen	Russia	Circumnavigated Antarctica; discovered Alexander I Land.
1821	Nathaniel Palmer	United States	Discovered Palmer Peninsula on sealing expedition.
1823	James Weddell	England	Discovered Weddell Sea; reached 74° 15' S.
1837–40	Jules Dumont d'Urville	France	Discovered Adélie Land south of Tasmania.
1839–40	Charles Wilkes	United States	Sighted Antarctic coast between 108° and 148° E.
1840–43	James Ross	England	Charted coast in neighborhood of Ross Sea; reached record of 78° 9' S.
1902–04	Robert F. Scott	England	Explored coast of Edward VII Land; reached 82° 17' S.
1903–05	Jean B. Charcot	France	Explored Palmer Peninsula; discovered Loubet Coast.
1908–09	Ernest Shackleton	England	Explored head of Ross Sea; reached 88° 23' S.
1910–12	Roald Amundsen	Norway	Discovered Queen Maud Range; reached South Pole Dec. 16, 1911.
1910–12	Robert Scott	England	Reached South Pole January 18, 1912; entire party perished during return.
1911–13 1929–31	Douglas Mawson	England and Australia	Explored coast from King George V Land to Enderby Land in two expeditions.
1914–17	Ernest Shackleton	England	Discovered Caird coast; ship lost in Weddell Sea, but party rescued after many hardships.

Date	Explorer	Country	Description
1928–30	Hubert Wilkins	England	Made first Antarctic explorations by air.
1928–47	Richard Byrd	United States	Established base at Little America and made first flight over South Pole (1929); second expedition remained through winter of 1934; third expedition (1939–40) made extensive aerial explorations; fourth expedition concentrated on scientific work.
1935–36	Lincoln Ellsworth	United States	Explored by air between Palmer Peninsula and Little America.
1947–48	Finn Ronne	United States	Explored Palmer Peninsula and Weddell Sea by land and air.
1955–58	Vivian Fuchs and Edmund Hillary	United Kingdom and New Zealand	Commonwealth Trans-Antarctic Expedition crossed the Continent through the South Pole from Weddell Sea to McMurdo Sound.
1957–58	I. G. Y. (International Geophysical Year)	Arg.; Austl.; Bel.; Chile; Fr.; Jap.; N.Z.; Nor.; S. Afr.;Sov. Un.; U.K.; U.S.	Established research stations; field expeditions led to new discoveries of physical features, as well as new information on ice conditions; extensive oceanographic surveys and mapping conducted.
1959–61	Australian National Antarctic Expedition	Australia	Gathered data on weather, cosmic rays, geomagnetism, seismology; field explorations and mapping; extensive aerial surveys.

Pacific Ocean and Australia

Date	Explorer	Country	Description
1520–21	Ferdinand Magellan	Spain	Crossed the Pacific from South America to the Philippines during first circumnavigation of the earth.
1542	Lopez de Villalobos	Spain	Sailed from Mexico to the Philippines; discovered Caroline and Palau Islands.
1565	Andrés de Urdaneta	Spain	Discovered northern sailing route from Philippines to Mexico in latitude of the Forties.
1567–95	Alvaro de Mendana	Spain	Discovered Solomon, Marshall, and Ellice Islands (1567); also Marquesas and Santa Cruz (1595).
1578	Francis Drake	England	Crossed the Pacific from California to the East Indies on first English circumnavigation.
1606	Pedro de Quiros	Spain	Discovered Tahiti and New Hebrides Islands.
1606	Luis de Torres	Spain	Sailed through Torres Strait between Australia and New Guinea.
1616	Dirk Hartog	Holland	Explored section of west coast of Australia.
1616	William Van Schouten and Jacob Lemaire	Holland	Rounded Cape Horn and crossed Pacific; discovered Bismarck Archipelago.
1642–44	Abel Tasman	Holland	Discovered Tasmania and part of New Zealand; explored the north coast of Australia.
1699	William Dampier	England	Explored west and northwest coasts of Australia.
1721	Jacob Roggeveen	Holland	Discovered Easter Island and Samoa.
1767–69	Louis de Bougainville	France	Explored South Pacific islands, including Tahiti, Samoa, and the New Hebrides.
1768–79	James Cook	England	Made three voyages into the Pacific; explored coasts of New Zealand and eastern Australia (1769–70); proved non-existence of continental land north of Antarctic Circle (1772–75); discovered Hawaiian Islands and explored northwest coast of North America (1776–79).
1785–88	Jean de La Pérouse	France	Explored North Pacific Ocean, especially coasts of Siberia and Japan; lost at sea.
1798	George Bass	England	Discovered strait separating Tasmania from Australia.
1802–03	Matthew Flinders	England	Explored south coast of Australia and sailed completely around the continent.
1816–22	John Oxley	England	Explored the interior of New South Wales, Australia.
1828–45	Charles Sturt	England	Discovered the Darling R.; descended Murray R. to its mouth; reached center of continent (1845).
1833–35	Charles Darwin	England	Explored South Pacific islands as a naturalist.
1839–41	Edward Eyre	England	Crossed southern Australia from Spencer Gulf to King George Sound.
1844–48	Ludwig Leichhardt	Germany	Explored interior of northern Queensland and Arnhem Land.
1858–62	John Stuart	England	Explored interior of South Australia and made unsuccessful attempt to cross the continent (1860); succeeded (1862).
1860–61	Robert Burke and W. J. Wills	England	Succeeded in crossing Australia from Melbourne to Gulf of Carpentaria.
1873	Peter E. Warburton	England	Crossed western Australia from Alice Springs to the coast, using camels.
1874	John Forrest	England	Crossed desert region of Australia from Perth to Adelaide.
1875–76	Ernest Giles	England	Made trip across desert from Port Augusta to Perth and return.

Date	Explorer	Country	Description
1839–46	Evariste Regis Huc	France	Traveled through interior of China, Mongolia and Tibet.
1851–54	Matthew C. Perry	United States	Opened Japan to foreign trade.
1862–67	Peter Kropotkin	Russia	Made geographical surveys of North Manchuria.
1867–88	Nikolai Przhevalsky	Russia	Led expeditions into Central Asia, Mongolia, and Tibet; rediscovered Lop Nor.
1868–72	Ferdinand Richthofen	Germany	Explored and described most of Chinese Empire.
1869–70	Joseph Halévy	France	Explored interior of southwestern Arabia.
1873	Jean Dupuis	France	Explored Tonkin route into China.
1885–1908	Sven Hedin	Sweden	Traveled extensively in Persia, Turkestan, China, and Tibet.
1886–1904	Francis Younghusband	England	Explored and surveyed in Kashmir, Central Asia, and Tibet.
1889–92	William W. Rockhill	United States	Explored eastern Tibet.
1899–1914	Gertrude Bell	England	Traveled widely in Palestine, Mesopotamia, and inner Arabia.
1899–1926	Aurel Stein	England	Made archaeological explorations in India, Persia, and central Asia.
1901–06	Ellsworth Huntington	United States	Explored upper Euphrates R. and Chinese Turkestan.
1914–29	Roy Chapman Andrews	United States	Explored western China and Mongolia as a naturalist, discovering many animal fossils.
1917–32	St. John Philby	England	Crossed Arabia from sea to sea; explored oases of Nejd.

Arctic Regions

Date	Explorer	Country	Description
1553–54	Hugh Willoughby and Richard Chancellor	England	Attempted exploration of Northeast Passage; Willoughby lost, but Chancellor reached Archangel and opened trade with Russia.
1576–78	Martin Frobisher	England	Made three voyages in search of Northwest Passage; discovered Frobisher Bay.
1580	Arthur Pet and Charles Jackman	England	Reached the Kara Sea, exploring Northeast Passage.
1585–87	John Davis	England	Reached latitude 73° N. in Baffin Bay, exploring Northwest Passage.
1594–97	Willem Barents	Holland	Discovered Spitsbergen (Svalbard) and reached Novaya Zemlya along Northeast Passage.
1607–11	Henry Hudson	England and Holland	Made several voyages in search of both Northeast and Northwest Passages to India; reached 73° N. on east Greenland coast.
1615–16	William Baffin and Robert Bylot	England	Explored Baffin Bay; reached 78° N.
1648	Simon Dezhnev	Russia	Explored northeastern Siberian coast from the Kolyma to Anadyr rivers.
1728	Vitus Bering	Russia	Discovered Bering Strait and the St. Lawrence and Diomede Islands.
1737–42	Dimitri Laptev	Russia	Explored north Siberian coast from Lena R. to Cape Baranov.
1742	T. Chelyuskin	Russia	Discovered northernmost point of Asia by land.
1773	C. J. Phipps	England	Reached 80° 48' north of Spitsbergen (Svalbard).
1818–27	William E. Parry	England	Explored Canadian arctic and Spitsbergen (Svalbard) areas; reached 82° 45' (1827).
1820–22	William Scoresby	England	Discovered Scoresby Sound in eastern Greenland; published standard description of Arctic regions.
1825–28	Frederick W. Beechey	England	Explored arctic coast of North America from Bering Strait to Point Barrow.
1829–49	John and James Ross	England	Discovered Boothia Peninsula and Gulf; James located North Magnetic Pole (1831); both participated in search for Franklin (1848–49).
1845–48	John Franklin	England	Lost two ships and 129 men in attempt to sail through Northwest Passage; reached King William Island.
1850–54	Richard Collinson and Robert McClure	England	Reached Melville Sound from Bering Strait and proved existence of northwest waterway passage.
1853–55	Elisha K. Kane	United States	Explored Smith Sound and Kane Basin; reached 80° 10' N.
1857–58	Francis L. McClintock	England	Discovered McClintock Channel and relics of Franklin expedition on King William Island.
1860–71	Charles F. Hall	United States	On third expedition, explored northern shores of Ellesmere Island and Greenland, reaching 82° 26' N.

WORLD AIR DISTANCE TABLE

	Apia	Azores Islands	Berlin	Bombay	Buenos Aires	Calcutta	Cape Town	Cape Verde Islands	Chicago	Darwin	Denver	Gibraltar	Hong Kong	Honolulu	Istanbul	Juneau	London	Los Angeles	Manila	Melbourne	Mexico City	Moscow
Apia, Western Samoa		9644	9743	8154	6931	7183	9064	10246	6557	3843	5653	10676	5591	2604	10175	5415	9789	4828	4993	3113	5449	9116
Azores Islands	9644		2185	5967	5417	6549	5854	1499	3093	10209	3991	1249	7572	7180	2975	4526	1527	4794	8250	12101	4385	3165
Berlin, Germany	9743	2185		3910	7376	4376	5977	3194	4402	8036	5077	1453	5500	7305	1078	4560	574	5782	6128	9919	6037	996
Bombay, India	8154	5967	3910		9273	1041	5134	6297	8054	4503	8383	4814	2673	8020	2991	6866	4462	8701	3148	6097	9722	3131
Buenos Aires, Argentina	6931	5417	7376	9273		10242	4270	4208	5596	9127	5928	5963	11463	7558	7568	7759	6918	6118	11042	7234	4633	8375
Calcutta, India	7183	6549	4376	1041	10242		6026	7148	7981	3744	8050	5521	1534	7037	3646	6326	4954	8148	2189	5547	9495	3447
Cape Town, South Africa	9064	5854	5977	5134	4270	6026		4509	8449	6947	9327	5076	7372	11532	5219	10330	6005	9969	7525	6412	8511	6294
Cape Verde Islands	10246	1499	3194	6297	4208	7148	4509		4066	10664	4975	1762	8539	8311	3507	5911	2731	5772	9221	10856	4857	3982
Chicago, U.S.A.	6557	3093	4402	8054	5596	7981	8449	4066		9346	920	4258	7790	4244	5476	2305	3950	1745	8128	9668	1673	4984
Darwin, Australia	3843	10209	8036	4503	9127	3744	6947	10664	9346		8557	9265	2642	5355	7390	7105	8598	7835	1979	1964	9081	7046
Denver, U.S.A.	5653	3991	5077	8383	5928	8050	9327	4975	920	8557		5122	7465	3338	6154	1831	4688	831	7661	8759	1434	5485
Gibraltar, Gibraltar	10676	1249	1453	4814	5963	5521	5076	1762	4258	9265	5122		6828	8075	1874	5273	1094	5936	7483	10798	5629	2413
Hong Kong, Asia	5591	7572	5500	2673	11463	1534	7372	8539	7790	2642	7465	6828		5537	4980	5634	5981	7240	693	4607	8776	4439
Honolulu, Hawaii, U.S.A.	2604	7180	7305	8020	7558	7037	11532	8311	4244	5355	3338	8075	5537		8104	2815	7226	2557	5296	5513	3781	7033
Istanbul (Constantinople), Turkey	10175	2975	1078	2991	7568	3646	5219	3507	5476	7390	6154	1874	4980	8104		5498	1551	6843	5659	9088	7102	1088
Juneau, Alaska, U.S.A.	5415	4526	4560	6866	7759	6326	10330	5911	2305	7105	1831	5273	5634	2815	5498		4418	1842	5869	8035	3219	4534
London, United Kingdom	9789	1527	574	4462	6918	4954	6005	2731	3950	8598	4688	1094	5981	7226	1551	4418		5439	6667	10501	5541	1549
Los Angeles, U.S.A.	4828	4794	5782	8701	6118	8148	9969	5772	1745	7835	831	5936	7240	2557	6843	1842	5439		7269	7931	1542	6068
Manila, Philippines	4993	8250	6128	3148	11042	2189	7525	9221	8128	1979	7661	7483	693	5296	5659	5869	6667	7269		3941	8829	5130
Melbourne, Australia	3113	12101	9919	6097	7234	5547	6412	10856	9668	1964	8759	10798	4607	5513	9088	8035	10501	7931	3941		8422	8963
Mexico City, Mexico	5449	4385	6037	9722	4633	9495	8511	4857	1673	9081	1434	5629	8776	3781	7102	3219	5541	1542	8829	8422		6688
Moscow, Soviet Union	9116	3165	996	3131	8375	3447	6294	3982	4984	7046	5485	2413	4439	7033	1088	4534	1549	6068	5130	8963	6688	
New Orleans, U.S.A.	6085	3524	5116	8865	4916	8803	8316	4194	833	9545	1082	4757	8480	4207	6171	2905	4627	1673	8724	9275	934	5756
New York, U.S.A.	7242	2422	3961	7794	5297	7921	7801	3355	713	9959	1631	3627	8051	4959	5009	2854	3459	2451	8493	10355	2085	4662
Nome, Alaska, U.S.A.	5438	4954	4342	5901	8848	5271	10107	6438	3314	6235	2925	5398	4547	3004	5101	1094	4381	2876	4817	7558	4309	4036
Oslo, Norway	9247	2234	515	4130	7613	4459	6494	3444	4040	8022	4653	1791	5337	6784	1518	4045	714	5325	6016	9926	5706	1016
Panamá, Panama	6514	3778	5849	9742	3381	10114	7014	3734	2325	10352	2636	4926	10084	5245	6750	4460	5278	3001	10283	9022	1495	6711
Paris, France	9990	1659	542	4359	6877	4889	5841	2666	4133	8575	4885	964	5956	7434	1401	4628	213	5601	6673	10396	5706	1541
Peking (Peiping), China	5903	6565	4567	2964	11974	2024	8045	7763	6592	3728	6348	6009	1226	5067	4379	4522	5054	6250	1770	5667	7733	3597
Port Said, U.A.R.	10485	3391	1747	2659	7362	3506	4590	3672	6103	7159	6819	2179	4975	8738	693	6215	2154	7528	5619	8658	7671	1710
Quebec, Canada	7406	2240	3583	7371	5680	7481	7857	3355	878	9724	1752	3383	7650	5000	4644	2660	3101	2579	8124	10497	2454	4242
Reykjavik, Iceland	8678	1777	1479	5191	7099	5409	7111	3248	2954	8631	3596	2047	6031	6084	2558	3268	1171	4306	6651	10544	4622	2056
Rio de Janeiro, Brazil	8120	4428	6144	8257	1218	9376	3769	3040	5296	9960	5871	4775	10995	8190	6395	7598	5772	6296	11254	8186	4770	7179
Rome, Italy	10475	2125	734	3843	6929	4496	5249	2772	4808	8190	5561	1034	5768	8022	854	5247	887	6326	6457	9934	6353	1474
San Francisco, U.S.A.	4786	4872	5657	8392	6474	7809	10241	5921	1858	7637	949	5936	6894	2392	6700	1525	5355	347	6963	7854	1885	5868
Seattle, U.S.A.	5222	4501	5041	7741	6913	7224	10199	5714	1737	7619	1021	5462	6471	2678	6063	899	4782	959	6641	8186	2337	5199
Shanghai, China	5399	7229	5215	3133	12197	2112	8059	8443	7053	3142	6698	6646	772	4934	4959	4869	5710	6477	1152	5005	8039	4235
Singapore, Singapore	5850	8326	6166	2429	9864	1791	6016	8700	9365	2075	9063	7231	1652	6710	5373	7235	6744	8767	1479	3761	10307	5238
Tokyo, Japan	4656	7247	5538	4188	11400	3186	9071	8589	6303	3367	5795	6988	1796	3850	5556	4011	5938	5470	1863	5089	7035	4650
Valparaiso, Chile	6267	5678	7795	10037	761	10993	4998	4649	5268	8961	5452	6408	11607	6793	8172	7271	7263	5527	10930	6998	4053	8792
Washington, D.C., U.S.A.	7066	2667	4167	7988	5216	8088	7894	3486	591	9923	1494	3822	8148	4829	5216	2834	3665	2300	8560	10173	1878	4883
Wellington, New Zealand	2062	11269	11265	7677	6260	7042	7019	10363	8349	3310	7516	12060	5853	4708	10663	7475	11682	6714	5162	1595	6899	10279
Vienna, Austria	10010	2291	328	3718	7368	4259	5671	3147	4694	7974	5383	1386	5429	7626	783	4895	772	6108	6120	9792	6306	1044
Winnipeg, Canada	6283	3389	4286	7644	6297	7424	9054	4556	714	8684	798	4435	7096	3806	5361	1597	3918	1525	7414	9319	2097	4687
Zanzibar, Tanzania	9892	5323	4309	2855	6421	3859	2346	4635	8358	6409	9221	4103	5414	10869	3312	8795	4604	10021	5763	6802	9484	4270

WORLD STEAMSHIP DISTANCE TABLE

	Bombay	Buenos Aires	Cape Town	Colombo	Gibraltar	Halifax	Hamburg	Honolulu	Istanbul	Le Havre	Lisbon	Liverpool	Manila	Melbourne	New Orleans	New York	Panama Roads	Port Said	Rio de Janeiro	San Francisco	Shanghai	Singapore	Valparaiso	Wellington	Yokohama
Bombay, India		9601	5469	1042	5639	8760	7552	9631	4412	7024	6036	7156	4361	6365	10927	9413	14921	3511	8998	11247	5328	2824	11356	7961	6155
Buenos Aires, Argentina	9601		4345	9415	6074	6600	7622	8744	8488	7074	6148	7178	12128	8477	7233	6761	6311	8259	1325	10062	13087	10782	3181	6956	13921
Cape Town, South Africa	5469	4345		5070	5982	7386	7388	11948	7058	6861	5912	7001	7821	6998	9382	7814	7417	6148	3769	11154	8787	6511	6977	7531	9614
Colombo, Ceylon	1042	9415	5070		6227	9278	8090	8594	4920	7563	6577	7717	3399	5380	11489	9941	13919	4010	8839	10289	4370	1825	11073	7058	5151
Gibraltar, Gibraltar	5639	6074	5982	6227		3051	1863	10433	2099	1336	350	1490	9641	11257	5271	3714	5038	2217	4816	8775	10553	8008	9006	12847	11353
Halifax, Canada	8760	6600	7386	9278	3051		3480	8152	5147	3082	2792	2891	12591	11876	2517	686	2718	5257	5332	6456	12707	11047	5731	10196	11592
Hamburg, Germany	7552	7622	7388	8090	1863	3480		11283	3939	573	1543	1083	16678	13066	4166	5888	4058	6354	9625	12349	9838	8900	13758	14734	
Honolulu, Hawaii, U.S.A.	9631	8744	11948	8594	10433	8152	11283		12510	10757	10363	10682	5571	5691	7046	7718	5395	12604	9875	2408	4986	6772	6816	4736	3908
Istanbul, Turkey	4412	8488	7058	4920	2099	5147	3939	12510		3421	2430	3543	8245	9928	7384	5315	3640	3521	5820	9095	11822	9312	8347	12801	12649
Le Havre, France	7024	7074	6861	7563	1336	3082	573	10757	3421		1017	578	10856	12540	5315	3640	3521								
Lisbon, Portugal	6036	6148	5912	6577	350	2792	1543	10363	2430	1017		1148	9867	11551	5377	3403	4968	2532	4858	8737	10833	8323	7975	12459	11660
Liverpool, United Kingdom	7156	7178	7001	7717	1490	2891	1083	10682	3543	578	1148		11111	12764	5266	3539	5287	3652	5932	9024	12201	9490	8299	12778	13399
Manila, Philippines	4361	12128	7821	3399	9641	12591	16678	5571	8245	10856	9867	11111		5214	12414	13086	10764	7335	11524	7164	1338	1578	11967	5647	2023

SHOWING GREAT CIRCLE DISTANCES BETWEEN PRINCIPAL CITIES OF THE WORLD IN STATUTE MILES

New Orleans	New York	Nome	Oslo	Panamá	Paris	Peking (Peiping)	Port Said	Quebec	Reykjavik	Rio de Janeiro	Rome	San Francisco	Seattle	Shanghai	Singapore	Tokyo	Valparaiso	Washington, D.C.	Wellington	Vienna	Winnipeg	Zanzibar	
6085	7242	5438	9247	6514	9990	5903	10485	7406	8678	8120	10475	4786	5222	5399	5850	4656	6267	7066	2062	10010	6283	9892	Apia
3524	2422	4954	2234	3778	1659	6565	3391	2240	1777	4428	2125	4872	4501	7229	8326	7247	5678	2667	11269	2291	3389	5323	Azores Islands
5116	3961	4342	515	5849	542	4567	1747	3583	1479	6114	734	5657	5041	5215	6166	5538	7795	4167	11265	328	4286	4309	Berlin
8865	7794	5901	4130	9742	4359	2964	2659	7371	5191	8257	3843	8392	7741	3133	2429	4188	10037	7988	7677	3718	7644	2855	Bombay
4916	5297	8848	7613	3381	6877	11974	7362	5680	7099	1218	6929	6474	6913	12197	9864	11400	761	5216	6260	7368	6297	6421	Buenos Aires
8803	7921	5271	4459	10114	4889	2024	3506	7481	5409	9376	4496	7809	7224	2112	1791	3186	10993	8088	7042	4259	7424	3859	Calcutta
8316	7801	10107	6494	7014	5841	8045	4590	7857	7111	3769	5249	10241	10199	8059	6016	9071	4998	7894	7019	5671	9054	2346	Cape Town
4194	3355	6438	3444	3734	2666	7763	3672	3355	3248	3040	2772	5921	5714	8443	8700	8589	4649	3486	10363	3147	4556	4635	Cape Verde Islands
833	713	3314	4040	2325	4133	6592	6103	878	2954	5296	4808	1858	1737	7053	9365	6303	5268	591	8349	4694	714	8358	Chicago
9545	9959	6235	8022	10352	8575	3728	7159	9724	8631	9960	8190	7637	7619	3142	2075	3367	8961	9923	3310	7974	8684	6409	Darwin
1082	1631	2925	4653	2636	4885	6348	6819	1752	3596	5871	5561	949	1021	6698	9063	5795	5452	1494	7516	5383	798	9221	Denver
4757	3627	5398	1791	4926	964	6009	2179	3383	2047	4775	1034	5936	5462	6646	7231	6988	6408	3822	12060	1386	4435	4103	Gibraltar
8480	8051	4547	5337	10084	5956	1226	4975	7650	6031	10995	5768	6894	6471	772	1652	1796	11607	8148	5853	5429	7096	5414	Hong Kong
4207	4959	3004	6784	5245	7434	5067	8738	5000	6084	8190	8022	2392	2678	4934	6710	3850	6793	4829	4708	7626	3806	10869	Honolulu
6171	5009	5101	1518	6750	1401	4379	693	4644	2558	6395	854	6700	6063	4959	5373	5556	8172	5216	10663	783	5361	3312	Istanbul
2905	2854	1094	4045	4460	4628	4522	6215	2660	3268	7598	5247	1525	899	4869	7235	4011	7271	2834	7475	4895	1597	8795	Juneau
4627	3459	4381	714	5278	213	5054	2154	3101	1171	5772	887	5355	4782	5710	6744	5938	7263	3665	11682	772	3918	4604	London
1673	2451	2876	5325	3001	5601	6250	7528	2579	4306	6296	6326	347	959	6477	8767	5470	5527	2300	6714	6108	1525	10021	Los Angeles
8724	8493	4817	6016	10283	6673	1770	5619	8124	6651	11254	6457	6963	6641	1152	1479	1863	10930	8560	5162	6120	7414	5763	Manila
9275	10355	7558	9926	9022	10396	5667	8658	10497	10544	8186	9934	7854	8186	5005	3761	5089	6998	10173	1595	9792	9319	6802	Melbourne
934	2085	4309	5706	1495	5706	7733	7671	2454	4622	4770	6353	1885	2337	8039	10307	7035	4053	1878	6899	6306	2097	9484	Mexico City
5756	4662	4036	1016	6711	1541	3597	1710	4242	2056	7179	1474	5868	5199	4235	5238	4650	8792	4883	10279	1044	4687	4270	Moscow
	1171	3937	4795	1603	4788	7314	6756	1534	3711	4796	5439	1926	2101	7720	10082	6858	4514	966	7794	5385	1418	8754	New Orleans
1171		3769	3672	2231	3622	6823	5590	439	2576	4820	4273	2571	2408	7357	9630	6735	5094	205	8946	4224	1281	7698	New York
3937	3769		3836	5541	4574	3428	5745	3489	3366	8586	5082	2547	1976	3784	6148	2983	8360	3792	7383	4657	2599	8209	Nome
4795	3672	3836		5691	832	4360	2211	3263	1083	6482	1243	5181	4591	5020	6246	5221	7914	3870	10974	850	3854	4803	Oslo
1603	2231	5541	5691		5382	8906	7146	2659	4706	3294	5903	3322	3651	9324	11687	8423	2943	2080	7433	6026	2998	8245	Panamá
4788	3622	4574	832	5382		5101	1975	3235	1380	5703	682	5441	4993	5752	6671	6033	7251	3828	11791	644	4118	4396	Paris
7314	6823	3428	4360	8906	5101		4584	6423	4903	10768	5047	5902	5396	662	2774	1307	11774	6922	6698	4639	5907	5803	Peking (Peiping)
6756	5590	5745	2211	7146	1975	4584		5250	3227	6244	1317	7394	6759	5132	5088	5842	8088	5796	10249	1429	6032	2729	Port Said
1534	439	3489	3263	2659	3235	6423	5250		2189	5125	3943	2642	2353	6981	9097	6417	5504	610	9228	3858	1199	7443	Quebec
3711	2576	3366	1083	4706	1380	4903	3227	2189		6118	2044	4199	3614	5559	7160	5472	7225	2800	10724	1805	2804	5757	Reykjavik
4796	4820	8586	6482	3294	5703	10768	6244	5125	6118		5684	6619	6891	11340	9774	11535	1855	4797	7349	6136	6010	5589	Rio de Janeiro
5439	4273	5082	1243	5903	682	5047	1317	3943	2044	5684		6240	5659	5677	6232	6124	7420	4435	11524	463	4803	3712	Rome
1926	2571	2547	5181	3322	5441	5902	7394	2642	4199	6619	6240		678	6132	8479	5131	5876	2442	6739	5988	1504	9958	San Francisco
2101	2408	1976	4591	3651	4993	5396	6759	2353	3614	6891	5659	678		5703	8057	4777	6230	2329	7242	5376	1150	9359	Seattle
7720	7357	3784	5020	9324	5752	662	5132	6981	5559	11340	5677	6132	5703		2377	1094	11650	7442	6054	5270	6350	5971	Shanghai
10082	9630	6148	6246	11687	6671	2774	5088	9097	7160	9774	6232	8479	8057	2377		3304	10226	9834	5292	6036	8685	4480	Singapore
6858	6735	2983	5221	8423	6033	1307	5842	6417	5472	11535	6124	5131	4777	1094	3304		10635	6769	5760	5679	5575	7040	Tokyo
4514	5094	8360	7914	2943	7251	11774	8088	5504	7225	1855	7420	5876	6230	11650	10226	10635		4977	5785	7783	5931	7184	Valparaiso
966	205	3792	3870	2080	3828	6922	5796	610	2800	4797	4435	2442	2329	7442	9834	6769	4977		8745	4429	1243	7884	Washington, D.C.
7794	8946	7383	10974	7433	11791	6698	10249	9228	10724	7349	11524	6739	7242	6054	5292	5760	5785	8745		11278	8230	8122	Wellington
5385	4224	4657	850	6026	644	4639	1429	3858	1805	6136	463	5988	5376	5270	6036	5679	7783	4429	11278		4604	3983	Vienna
1418	1281	2599	3854	2998	4118	5907	6032	1199	2804	6010	4803	1504	1150	6350	8685	5575	5931	1243	8230	4604		8416	Winnipeg
8754	7698	8209	4803	8245	4396	5803	2729	7443	5757	5589	3712	9958	9359	5971	4480	7040	7184	7884	8122	3983	8416		Zanzibar

SHOWING STEAMSHIP DISTANCES BETWEEN PRINCIPAL PORTS OF THE WORLD IN STATUTE MILES

	Bombay	Buenos Aires	Cape Town	Colombo	Gibraltar	Halifax	Hamburg	Honolulu	Istanbul	Le Havre	Lisbon	Liverpool	Manila	Melbourne	New Orleans	New York	Panama Roads	Port Said	Rio de Janeiro	San Francisco	Shanghai	Singapore	Valparaiso	Wellington	Yokohama
Melbourne, Australia	6365	8477	6998	5380	11257	11876	13066	5691	9928	12540	11551	12764	5214		10780	11452	9130	9040	9416	8011	6012	4396	7222	1737	5606
New Orleans, U.S.A.	10927	7233	9382	11489	5271	2517	5935	7046	7384	5315	5377	5266	12414	10780		1970	1650	7498	5965	5287	11495	13207	4663	9133	10489
New York, U.S.A.	9413	6761	7814	9941	3714	686	4166	7718	5788	3640	3403	3539	13086	11452	1970		2323	5895	5493	6059	11693	12176	5335	9814	11169
Panama Roads, Canal Zone	14921	6311	7417	13919	5038	2718	5888	5395	7115	5363	4968	5287	10764	9130	1650	2323		7217	5058	3737	9853	12097	3013	7491	8846
Port Said, U.A.R.	3511	8259	6148	4010	2217	5257	4058	12604	910	3521	2532	3652	7335	9040	7498	5895	7217		7006	10986	8301	5791	10225	10630	9128
Rio de Janeiro, Brazil	8998	1325	3769	8839	4816	5332	6354	9875	6897	5820	4858	5932	11524	9416	5965	5493	5058	7006		8794	12490	10179	4191	7915	13317
San Francisco, U.S.A.	11247	10062	11154	10289	8775	6456	9625	2408	10884	9095	8737	9024	7164	8011	5287	6059	3737	10986	8794		6339	8467	5919	6800	5223
Shanghai, China	5328	13087	8787	4370	10553	12707	12349	4986	9210	11822	10833	12201	1338	6012	11495	11693	9853	8301	12490	6339		2545	11806	6184	1199
Singapore, Singapore	2824	10782	6511	1825	8008	11047	9838	6772	6700	9312	8323	9490	1578	4396	13207	12176	12097	5791	10179	8467	2545		12534	5992	3345
Valparaíso, Chile	11356	3181	6977	11073	9006	5731	8900	6816	11020	8347	7975	8299	11967	7222	4663	5335	3013	10225	4191	5919	11806	12534		5799	10740
Wellington, New Zealand	7961	6956	7531	7058	12847	10196	13758	4736	11540	12801	12459	12778	5647	1737	9133	9814	7491	10630	7915	6800	6184	5992	5799		5736
Yokohama, Japan	6155	13921	9614	5151	11353	11592	14734	3908	10037	12649	11660	13399	2023	5606	10489	11169	8846	9128	13317	5223	1199	3345	10740	5736	

GEOGRAPHICAL FACTS ABOUT THE UNITED STATES

ELEVATION

The highest elevation in the United States is Mount McKinley, Alaska, 20,320 feet.

The lowest elevation in the United States is in Death Valley, California, 282 feet below sea level.

The average elevation of the United States is 2,500 feet.

EXTREMITIES

Direction	Location	Latitude	Longitude
North	Point Barrow, Alaska	71°23′N.	156°29′W.
South	South Cape, Hawaii	18°56′N.	155°41′W.
East	West Quoddy Head, Maine	44°49′N.	66°57′W.
West	Cape Wrangell, Alaska	52°55′N.	172°27′E.

The two places in the United States separated by the greatest distance are Kure Island, Hawaii, and Mangrove Point, Florida. These points are 5,848 miles apart.

LENGTH OF BOUNDARIES

The total length of the Canadian boundary of the United States is 5,525 miles.

The total length of the Mexican boundary of the United States is 2,013 miles.

The total length of the Atlantic coastline of the United States is 2,069 miles.

The total length of the Pacific and Arctic coastline of the United States is 8,683 miles.

The total length of the Gulf of Mexico coastline of the United States is 1,631 miles.

The total length of all coastlines and land boundaries of the United States is 19,921 miles.

The total length of the tidal shoreline and land boundaries of the United States is 96,171 miles.

GEOGRAPHIC CENTERS

The geographic center of the United States (including Alaska and Hawaii) is in Butte County, South Dakota at 44°58′N., 103°46′W.

The geographic center of North America is in North Dakota, a few miles west of Devils Lake, at 48°10′N., 100°10′W.

EXTREMES OF TEMPERATURE

The highest temperature ever recorded in the United States was 134°F., at Greenland Ranch, Death Valley, California, on July 10, 1913.

The lowest temperature ever recorded in the United States was —76°F., at Tanana, Alaska, in January, 1886.

PRECIPITATION

The average annual precipitation for the United States is approximately 29 inches.

Hawaii is the wettest state, with an average annual rainfall of 82.48 inches. Nevada, with an average annual rainfall of 8.81 inches, is the driest state.

The greatest local average annual rainfall in the United States is at Mt. Waialeale, Kauai, Hawaii, 460 inches.

Greatest 24-hour rainfall in the United States, 23.22 inches at New Smyrna, Florida, October 10–11, 1924.

Extreme minimum rainfall records in the United States include a total fall of only 3.93 inches at Bagdad, California, for a period of 5 years, 1909–13, and an annual average of 1.78 inches at Death Valley, California.

Heavy snowfall records include 60 inches at Giant Forest, California, in 1 day; 42 inches at Angola, New York, in 2 days; 87 inches at Giant Forest, California, in 3 days; and 108 inches at Tahoe, California, in 4 days.

Greatest seasonal snowfall, 1,000.3 inches, more than 83 feet, at Paradise Ranger Station, Washington, during the winter of 1955–56.

HISTORICAL FACTS ABOUT THE UNITED STATES

TERRITORIAL ACQUISITIONS

Accession	Date	Area (sq. mi.)	Cost in Dollars
Original territory of the Thirteen States	1790	888,811	....
Purchase of Louisiana Territory, from France	1803	827,192	$11,250,000.00
By treaty with Spain: Florida	1819	58,560	$ 5,000,000.00
Other areas	1819	13,443	
Annexation of Texas	1845	390,144	....
Oregon Territory, by treaty with Great Britain	1846	285,580	....
Mexican Cession	1848	529,017	$15,000,000.00
Gadsden Purchase, from Mexico	1853	29,640	$10,000,000.00
Purchase of Alaska, from Russia	1867	586,400	7,200,000.00
Annexation of Hawaiian Islands	1898	6,424	....
Puerto Rico, by treaty with Spain	1899	3,435	....
Guam, by treaty with Spain	1899	212	....
American Samoa, by treaty with Great Britain and Germany	1900	76	....
Panama Canal Zone, by treaty with Panama	1904	553	*$10,000,000.00
Virgin Islands, by purchase from Denmark	1917	133	$25,000,000.00
Total		3,619,620	$83,450,000.00

Note: The Philippines, ceded by Spain in 1898 for $20,000,000.00, were a territorial possession of the United States from 1898 to 1946. On July 4, 1946 they became the independent republic of the Philippines.

$25,000,000.00 was also paid to the republic of Colombia, out of whose territory the republic of Panama was created. In addition, an annual payment of $430,000.00 is made to the republic of Panama.

WESTWARD MOVEMENT OF CENTER OF POPULATION

Year	U.S. Population Total at Census	Approximate Location
1790	3,929,214	23 miles east of Baltimore, Md.
1800	5,308,483	18 miles west of Baltimore, Md.
1810	7,239,881	40 miles northwest of Washington, D.C.
1820	9,638,453	16 miles east of Moorefield, W. Va.
1830	12,866,020	19 miles southwest of Moorefield, W. Va.
1840	17,069,453	16 miles south of Clarksburg, W. Va.
1850	23,191,876	23 miles southeast of Parkersburg, W. Va.
1860	31,443,321	20 miles southeast of Chillicothe, Ohio
1870	39,818,449	48 miles northeast of Cincinnati, Ohio
1880	50,155,783	8 miles southwest of Cincinnati, Ohio
1890	62,947,714	20 miles east of Columbus, Ind.
1900	75,994,575	6 miles southeast of Columbus, Ind.
1910	91,972,266	Bloomington, Ind.
1920	105,710,620	8 miles southeast of Spencer, Ind.
1930	122,775,046	3 miles northeast of Linton, Ind.
1940	131,669,275	2 miles southeast of Carlisle, Ind.
1950	150,697,361	8 miles northwest of Olney, Ill.
1960	179,323,175	6 miles northwest of Centralia, Ill.

STATE AREAS AND POPULATIONS

STATE	Land Area (square miles) in 1960	Water Area (square miles) in 1960	Total Area (square miles) in 1960	Rank in Area	Population in 1960	Population Per Square Mile in 1960	Rank in Population in 1960	Population in 1950	Rank in Population in 1950	Population 1940
Alabama	51,060	549	51,609	29	3,266,740	63	19	3,061,743	17	2,832,961
Alaska	571,065	15,335	586,400	1	226,167	0.4	50	128,643	50	72,524‡
Arizona	113,575	334	113,909	6	1,302,161	11	35	749,587	37	499,261
Arkansas	52,499	605	53,104	27	1,786,272	34	31	1,909,511	30	1,949,387
California	156,573	2,120	158,693	3	15,717,204	99	2	10,586,223	2	6,907,387
Colorado	103,884	363	104,247	8	1,753,947	17	33	1,325,089	34	1,123,296
Connecticut	4,899	110	5,009	48	2,535,234	506	25	2,007,280	28	1,709,242
Delaware	1,978	79	2,057	49	446,292	217	46	318,085	47	266,505
District of Columbia†	61	8	69	..	763,956	11,072	..	802,178	..	663,091
Florida	54,252	4,308	58,560	22	4,951,560	85	10	2,771,305	20	1,897,414
Georgia	58,274	602	58,876	21	3,943,116	67	16	3,444,578	13	3,123,723
Hawaii	6,415	9	6,424	47	632,772	99	43	499,794	45	423,330
Idaho	82,708	849	83,557	13	667,191	8.0	42	588,637	43	524,873
Illinois	55,930	470	56,400	24	10,081,158	179	4	8,712,176	4	7,897,241
Indiana	36,185	106	36,291	38	4,662,498	128	11	3,934,224	12	3,427,796
Iowa	56,032	258	56,290	25	2,757,537	49	24	2,621,073	22	2,538,268
Kansas	82,048	216	82,264	14	2,178,611	26	28	1,905,299	31	1,801,028
Kentucky	39,863	532	40,395	37	3,038,156	75	22	2,944,806	19	2,845,627
Louisiana	45,106	3,417	48,523	31	3,257,022	67	20	2,683,516	21	2,363,880
Maine	31,012	2,203	33,215	39	969,265	29	36	913,774	35	847,226
Maryland	9,874	703	10,577	42	3,100,689	293	21	2,343,001	23	1,821,244
Massachusetts	7,867	390	8,257	45	5,148,578	624	9	4,690,514	9	4,316,721
Michigan	57,019	1,197	58,216	23	7,823,194	134	7	6,371,766	7	5,256,106
Minnesota	80,009	4,059	84,068	12	3,413,864	41	18	2,982,483	18	2,792,300
Mississippi	47,223	493	47,716	32	2,178,141	46	29	2,178,914	26	2,183,796
Missouri	69,138	548	69,686	19	4,319,813	62	13	3,954,653	11	3,784,664
Montana	145,736	1,402	147,138	4	674,767	4.6	41	591,024	42	559,456
Nebraska	76,612	615	77,227	15	1,411,330	18	34	1,325,510	33	1,315,834
Nevada	109,788	752	110,540	7	285,278	2.6	49	160,083	49	110,247
New Hampshire	9,014	290	9,304	44	606,921	65	45	533,242	44	491,524
New Jersey	7,521	315	7,836	46	6,066,782	774	8	4,835,329	8	4,160,165
New Mexico	121,510	156	121,666	5	951,023	7.8	37	681,187	39	531,818
New York	47,939	1,637	49,576	30	16,782,304	339	1	14,830,192	1	13,479,142
North Carolina	49,067	3,645	52,712	28	4,556,155	86	12	4,061,929	10	3,571,623
North Dakota	69,457	1,208	70,665	17	632,446	8.9	44	619,636	41	641,935
Ohio	40,972	250	41,222	35	9,706,397	235	5	7,946,627	5	6,907,612
Oklahoma	68,887	1,032	69,919	18	2,328,284	33	27	2,233,351	25	2,336,434
Oregon	96,248	733	96,981	10	1,768,687	18	32	1,521,341	32	1,089,684
Pennsylvania	45,007	326	45,333	33	11,319,366	250	3	10,498,012	3	9,900,180
Rhode Island	1,058	156	1,214	50	859,488	708	39	791,896	36	713,346
South Carolina	30,272	783	31,055	40	2,382,594	77	26	2,117,027	27	1,899,804
South Dakota	76,378	669	77,047	16	680,514	8.8	40	652,740	40	642,961
Tennessee	41,762	482	42,244	34	3,567,089	84	17	3,291,718	16	2,915,841
Texas	262,840	4,499	267,339	2	9,579,677	36	6	7,711,194	6	6,414,824
Utah	82,339	2,577	84,916	11	890,627	10	38	688,862	38	550,310
Vermont	9,276	333	9,609	43	389,881	41	47	377,747	46	359,231
Virginia	39,838	977	40,815	36	3,966,949	97	14	3,318,680	15	2,677,773
Washington	66,709	1,483	68,192	20	2,853,214	42	23	2,378,963	24	1,736,191
West Virginia	24,079	102	24,181	41	1,860,421	77	30	2,005,552	29	1,901,974
Wisconsin	54,705	1,449	56,154	26	3,951,777	70	15	3,434,575	14	3,137,587
Wyoming	97,411	503	97,914	9	330,066	3.4	48	290,529	48	250,742
United States	3,548,974	66,237	3,675,633*	..	179,323,175	49	..	151,325,798	..	132,165,129

† District. * Includes the United States parts of the Great Lakes (60,422 square miles). These are not included in state figures. ‡ Census taken in 1939.

Arizona's Grand Canyon—Mighty Gorge of the Colorado

PLACES OF INTEREST IN THE UNITED STATES

For the state capital, largest city, highest point, and other general information about each state, see the U.S. State General Information Table on page 233. Also see the U.S. National Park System Table and Map, pages 228-229 , for additional information about the national parks, monuments, historical parks, and other units under the National Park Service.

ALABAMA

Birmingham. Largest city in Alabama and steel center of the South. On top of Red Mountain, overlooking the city, stands the 55-foot statue of Vulcan on a pedestal 124 feet high. Cast in a Birmingham foundry, from pig iron mined in the area, the statue is second in size only to the Statue of Liberty. Other points of interest are Woodrow Wilson Park, in the city, and Vestavia, on nearby Shades Mountain. Built as a circular residence and patterned after the Roman Temple of Vesta, Vestavia now houses a museum and is surrounded by gardens.

Mobile. Important southern seaport and Alabama's first permanent white settlement, the city is famed for its historic old-colonial homes, a five-day Mardi Gras, and a thirty-five mile Azalea Trail. On this Trail, southwest of the city, are beautiful Bellingrath Gardens, containing many kinds of flowers and shrubs. On Dauphin Island, Alabama's annual Deep Sea Fishing Rodeo is held.

Montgomery. Capital of Alabama and first capital of the southern Confederacy. The Capitol and its grounds, situated on Goat Hill, contain many historic relics and monuments. The first White House of the Confederacy, the Montgomery home of Jefferson Davis, has many war relics, as well as some of Davis' personal belongings.

Mound State Monument. Thirty-four prehistoric Indian mounds. The largest is 58½ feet high and covers one and a quarter acres. A museum near the center of the park contains burial exhibits, tools, pottery, beads, and other relics excavated on the site. The monument is near Moundville.

Muscle Shoals. Site of Wilson Dam and two nitrate plants, construction of which was begun in 1916 as a defense measure and which later was expanded into the vast Tennessee Valley Authority project. Wilson Dam, 137 feet high and nearly a mile long, has two navigation locks that lift boats 89 feet in less than an hour. Fifteen miles up the Tennessee is Wheeler Dam.

ALASKA

Aleutian Islands. A 1,000-mile chain of twenty volcanic, treeless islands stretching out from the Alaska Peninsula. Scattered along the archipelago are small native villages peopled by Aleuts.

Anchorage. Largest city in the state and gateway to a fabulous hunting area for bear, mountain sheep and goats, caribou, and moose. Ski areas are nearby. Short trips from the city lead to Portage Glacier and to Matanuska Valley where giant vegetables and fruits are produced.

Barrow. Located on Point Barrow, the northernmost point in the United States. From here the Distant Early Warning (DEW) Line sweeps across the Arctic to the Atlantic Ocean. Here Eskimos hunt polar bear on the ice and harpoon whale.

Fairbanks. Situated on a loop of the Chena River, Alaska's second largest city lies in the heart of a great gold mining region where giant dredges have replaced the early miner's pan. The University of Alaska is at the nearby town of College. Sightseeing trips on the Tanana River can be taken in a "paddlewheeler," and there are air trips to Chena Hot Springs for hunting and fishing.

Glaciers. The best known glaciers are the Columbia, at the head of Columbia Bay, near Valdez; the Mendenhall, the most photographed glacier, available from Juneau; Portage, available from Anchorage; and Glacier Bay National Monument at the uppermost portion of the Panhandle.

Juneau. The State capital nestles on a narrow ledge of land at the foot of the steep slope of Mt. Juneau. A lumbering and fishing center, its early glory is preserved in the Alaska-Juneau Gold Mine.

Ketchikan. Salmon fishing center, noted for its picturesque harbor. Interesting collection of totem poles at Saxman Indian Village.

Mt. McKinley National Park. Twin peaks of Mt. McKinley overlook more than 3,000 square miles, in which ice-capped domes rise above sphagnum growth, and glaciers wait to be explored.

National Monuments. Glacier Bay, west of Juneau; Katmai, on the Alaska Peninsula; Sitka. See U.S. NATIONAL PARK SYSTEM, pages 228-29.

Nome. Metropolis of Seward Peninsula, where gold, silver, and other valuable minerals are mined.

More than 350 varieties of wildflowers bloom in season. Also see King Island ivory carvers.

Pribilof Islands. Breeding grounds for government protected fur seals which arrive each May.

Seward. Lumbering center on terminus of Alaska Railroad; gateway to the interior.

Sitka. Settled in 1799, it became the Russian capital of Alaska in 1802. Points of interest include Alaska Pioneer's Home, St. Michael's Cathedral, the Old Russian Blockhouse, and Sitka National Monument with its eighteen totem poles.

Skagway. Port of entry to Canada at the terminus of the Yukon Railway. White Pass and Chilkoot Pass are points of interest.

Wrangell. Early Russian fur trading post, now lumber and fishing center. Headquarters for the lovely Stikine River trip through a cut in the Coast Range Mountains. Also see the Tlingit Indian Community House and the remarkable totem poles.

ARIZONA

Apache Trail. Now a graveled road, this famous trail winds through rugged mountain scenery.

Bisbee. Center of a rich copper district. Located on the steep upper slopes of Mule Pass Gulch, Bisbee is built in tiers, and many of the houses are reached by steep flights of wooden and stone steps. Sacramento Pit, 435 feet deep and covering 35 acres, is at Bisbee.

Flagstaff. Home of the Lowell Observatory and Arizona State College. Situated near Humphreys Peak, highest point in the state. The city is popular with summer tourists because of its cool climate.

Grand Canyon National Park. One of nature's most magnificent spectacles, 5,000 feet deep Grand Canyon of the Colorado is lined with rocky towers and pinnacles and is filled with constantly changing colors. Many observation points along the North and South Rims afford excellent views of the Canyon from above, and mule trails lead to the bottom of the gorge. Grand Canyon is from four to eighteen miles wide and is more than two hundred miles long.

Hoover (Boulder) Dam and Lake Mead Recreation Area. See NEVADA

Alaska Vis. Ass'n.   *Hole-in-the-Wall Glacier, Near Juneau*

Union Pacific R.R.   *Los Angeles' Fabulous Freeway System*

Redwood Empire Ass'n.   *Historic Golden Gate Bridge, San Francisco*

Indian Reservations. Located in the northeastern part of the state and completely surrounded by NAVAJO reservations, the HOPI reservation is one of the most interesting of the numerous Indian reservations. Most of its eleven villages are built on the tops of mesas. Oraibi has existed since 1400.

The HAVASUPAI reservation is on the bottom of Cataract Canyon in Grand Canyon National Park, and the HUALPAI is south of Grand Canyon. FORT MOJAVE and COLORADO RIVER reservations, near the California border, are the homes of the Mojave and Southern Paiute Indians. Other reservations are the MARICOPA, south of Phoenix, the PAPAGO, west of Tucson, and the Apache reserves—SAN CARLOS and FORT APACHE—near the New Mexico border.

Meteor Crater. This crater, 600 feet deep and a mile wide, was formed centuries ago by a meteor believed to have displaced between five and six million tons of earth; west of Winslow.

Monument Valley. Colorful valley in the northeastern corner of the state. Its red sandstone pillars and spires resemble huge temple ruins.

National Monuments. There are 16 national monuments in Arizona. CANYON DE CHELLY is in the Navajo Reservation and contains more than 300 cliff-dwelling ruins in an area of nearly 84,000 acres.

PETRIFIED FOREST MONUMENT includes six forests of petrified wood, much of it in the form of huge logs. The Administration Building contains many fine specimens of the wood, as well as Indian relics and fern fossils. For other National Monuments, see the U.S. NATIONAL PARK SYSTEM, pages 228-229.

Painted Desert. Three hundred miles of sand, shale, and sandstone formations splashed with brilliant shades of red, amethyst, yellow, and purple that change to other hues in the shifting light. Part of it is in the Petrified Forest National Monument.

Phoenix. Capital of Arizona and, because of its semi-tropical climate, a popular winter tourist resort. The city is built on the site of a prehistoric community; not far from the business district is La Ciudad (the city), an excavation of an ancient pueblo. The Heard Museum contains relics from La Ciudad, relics of other Indians, including a collection of blankets. The Arizona Museum is also in Phoenix, as is the South Mountain Park.

San Xavier del Bac. Founded in 1700 by a Jesuit missionary and completed in 1797 by the Franciscans, this mission, one of the best preserved in the Southwest, is still in use. It is near Tucson.

Southwestern Arboretum. Located near Superior, this 120-acre tract of land contains 10,000 varieties of plants, brought from all over the world. Founded by the late William Boyce Thompson.

Tombstone. Roaring mining camp of the 1880's, noted for its gambling houses and gun fights. In Boothill Graveyard are buried many desperadoes and others who died violent deaths. Some of the old buildings still in existence are the Bird Cage Theater, Crystal Palace Saloon, Oriental Bar, Russ House, and office of the *Epitaph*, Tombstone newspaper.

Tucson. Resort and site of the University of Arizona. In the southern city, modern metropolitan sections rub elbows with the remnants of the old Spanish town. Businessmen and cowboys, students and Indians, mingle on the streets and in the stores.

ARKANSAS

Arkansas Post State Park. Scene of one of the first white settlements in the Mississippi River Valley, made by the French in 1686; also the first capital of Arkansas Territory. The park contains Confederate fortifications and other historical ruins.

Bauxite. Site of numerous bauxite mines and several aluminum refineries. The mines are worked largely by a stripping process.

Devil's Den State Park. A heavily wooded area of more than 4,000 acres in the Boston Mountains, southern section of the Ozarks. Sandstone formations with deep cracks and crevices are a feature.

Diamond Cave. Large, brilliantly colored cave near Jasper, in the Ozark Mountains.

Eureka Springs. A health resort in the Ozarks, northeast of Fayetteville. On steep mountain slopes, town contains many springs and limestone caves.

Fort Smith. Second largest town in Arkansas. The old fort, erected to protect the settlers against the Indians, is still standing.

Hot Springs. Famous tourist resort and site of Hot Springs National Park. Containing 989 acres the Park includes the mountains around the city.

Little Rock. State capital and largest city. A fascinating blend of ante-bellum homes and modern metropolitan buildings. The restored Territorial Capitol was the scene of the last territorial legislature in 1835. The War Memorial Building, one of the most beautiful buildings in Arkansas, was the state Capitol for three-quarters of a century. The present Capitol faces Capitol Avenue and contains, in addition to the legislative chambers and other state offices, the State History Museum. In MacArthur Park, birthplace of General Douglas MacArthur, is the Old Arsenal, last building of the old army post. It now contains the Arkansas Museum of Natural History and Antiquities.

Mammoth Spring. One of the largest springs in the world and the source of Spring River; located in Fulton County, near the Missouri Line.

Murfreesboro. Scene of the only diamond mine in the United States.

Ozark Mountains. Highlands extending from southern Missouri into northern Arkansas and Oklahoma, famous for rugged scenery.

Petit Jean State Park. Situated on Petit Jean Mountain, a wooded plateau on the edge of the Arkansas Valley, near Morrilton. Attractions include Bear Cave and Cedar Falls.

CALIFORNIA

Catalina Island. Famous resort island where fishing and boating are prime attractions.

Coloma. The site of Sutter's Sawmill, where discovery of gold in 1848 precipitated the California gold rush. Placerville, a few miles south, was a typical "rip-roaring" camp and a station for Pony Express, Overland Mail, and freight. Gold is still mined in the area; dredging is in operation at Chico, to the north.

Death Valley National Monument. Almost 3,000 square miles of desert—salt flats, volcanic craters, hills and valleys and jagged peaks weirdly eroded. Its normal colorings of mauve to red and white to nearly black take on sunset shades as the sunlight changes, with deep shadows of purple and blue. Near Badwater, in the sink of the Armargosa River, is the lowest spot in North America, 282 feet below sea level.

Donner Pass. Six miles above Donner Lake and the spot where the hapless Donner party camped through the winter of 1846.

Hollywood. Part of Los Angeles and world motion picture capital.

Kings Canyon National Park. Established in 1940 and incorporating the old General Grant National Park, as well as Redwood Mountain and Redwood Canyon. Much of this park is a roadless wilderness of mountains, canyons, and sequoia forests. In the southern section a paved automobile road traverses Kings Canyon, whose peaks and crags include Sentinel Dome, North Dome, and Lookout Peak. Famous General Grant Grove Section, containing the General Grant Tree, is at the southwest corner.

Lake Tahoe. This colorful mountain lake is shared by Nevada through most of its length.

Lassen Volcanic National Park. Lassen Peak, a dormant volcano, centers the western half of this region of boiling mudpots, steaming sinks, and weird volcanic formations.

Los Angeles. Spreading for miles inland and along the ocean, this great city is the center of far-flung

orange groves and other agriculture and of an important oil-producing area. It is rich in manufactures, with a fine harbor, and its superb beaches are an unexcelled resort attraction. In the Olvera Street district, the point of the city's origin, Mexican pottery and other wares are made and sold in quaint old shops. Fine residential sections, handsome gardens and parks, flowers in exotic masses of color—for these Los Angeles is famous. Here are the Bernheimer Oriental Gardens and a fine botanic garden at the southern branch of the University of California. (Los Angeles is also home-city for the University of Southern California.) Numerous museums include the Southwest, showing early art, handicraft, and history of the American Indians; the Los Angeles County Museum of History, Science, and Art, containing fossils from La Brea Tar Pits, also here; and Lyons Pony Express Museum, with a fine collection of western relics. The Olympic Stadium and the race track at Santa Anita Park are sports attractions; Great Western Livestock Show is held in December. See HOLLYWOOD, PASADENA, and CATALINA ISLAND.

Missions. In the earliest days of the white man in California, the Spanish missions were the outposts of civilization. A day's journey apart, they made a chain that still reaches from San Diego to Sonoma. Soundly and beautifully built, they contain today many examples of the work of skilled artisans. SAN LUIS REY DE FRANCIA MISSION has changed little since 1798; at SAN JUAN CAPISTRANO beautiful grounds are background for swallows whose regularity of migration is legend; at MISSION SANTA BARBARA, the altar fire has never died, since it was first set. The Mission Festival is held in September, at SAN GABRIEL ARCHANGEL.

Monterey and Carmel. South of Monterey Bay, the two towns are at the base of Monterey Peninsula, whose jutting, rocky coast is a series of superb crags, reefs, and white surf. Here are the famous Monterey cypress trees, and the pines. Monterey was the early key-city of the state and its first capital.

Mount Shasta. Famed for its beauty the peak is a favorite of mountain climbers. The region south of it contains Castle Crags State Park, and, farther south, Shasta Lake, with gigantic Shasta Dam.

National Monuments. See DEATH VALLEY NATIONAL MONUMENT, and U. S. NATIONAL PARK SYSTEM, pages 228-229.

Palomar Observatory. Northwest of San Diego. Home of the world's largest reflector telescope.

Pasadena. Home of the famed Rose Bowl. Here each January 1 the Tournament of Roses takes place. Nearby is the Mount Wilson Observatory; and the Huntington Library, Art Gallery, and Gardens are in San Marino to the south.

Redwoods. All along the northern half of California's coast, the redwood forests are spectacular. From Mill Creek Redwoods State Park in the north to the Big Basin Redwoods State Park south of San Francisco, the coastal area is a series of state parks and groves.

Sacramento. California's capital, on the Sacramento River. Sutter's Fort is a faithful restoration of the ranch and fort where Captain John A. Sutter first settled in 1839, and where scores of starving, exhausted pioneers were given succor. The Crocker Art Gallery, partly housed in the Old Crocker Home, is one of the finest in the country.

San Diego. At the southwestern tip of California. San Diego has a huge training station and military base for the United States Marine Corps and a United States Naval Training Center. The ocean drive from Long Beach ends here. Numerous missions are near the highway. Cabrillo National Monument, the Old Spanish Lighthouse, is a half-acre monument. Tijuana is over the line in Old Mexico.

San Francisco. "City of the world, of the hills, and of the sea." The Golden Gate Bridge links it with the mainland to the north; the Bay Bridge connects it with Oakland, across San Francisco Bay; by a narrow neck of land its peninsula joins the mainland. Twin Peaks Scenic Drive offers a superb view of the city, bay, waterfront, and suburban cities across the bay. A scenic highway skirts the ocean along the peninsula's length. Sea-going ships in the harbor, Fisherman's Wharf, the Latin Quarter, and Chinatown's temples and bazaars lend an air of adventure. Beauty spots are the Civic Center and the all-year parks. Other features of interest are the San Francisco Symphony Orchestra, the Opera, the M. H. DeYoung Memorial Museum (art), the Wells Fargo Historical Collection, and the Steinhart Aquarium. Across the bay are Oakland and Berkeley, site of the University of California; Stanford University is at nearby Palo Alto.

San Jose. Key-city of California's prune and apricot industry and world's largest canning center. Lick Observatory is on nearby Mount Hamilton.

Sequoia National Park. Home of the Big Trees. Grove after grove of these gigantic sequoias are the park's greatest attraction. (See also KINGS CANYON and YOSEMITE NATIONAL PARK.) Chief among them is the Giant Forest, where the sequoias are intermingled with white firs, ponderosa pines, sugar pines, and incense cedars. The park rises sharply to the crest of the High Sierras at its eastern border. Here is Mt. Whitney, at 14,495 feet the highest peak in conterminous United States.

Sonoma and Napa Counties. The vineyard of California, one of the greatest grape and wine areas in the world. Luther Burbank conducted his famous experiments here, and his experimental gardens still may be seen at Santa Rosa and Sebastopol. Calistoga, at the northern end of Napa Valley, is a region of mineral springs and geysers.

Yosemite National Park. Yosemite, in California's High Sierras, is a scenic park of mountains, canyons, lakes, streams, waterfalls and mountain parks. Its sights include Yosemite Valley, walled by towering granite cliffs and monoliths such as El Capitan and Half Dome, accented by waterfalls—Yosemite, Bridalveil, Nevada, Vernal; the Mariposa grove of giant sequoia trees (there are two others in the park); and the mule deer and black bear.

COLORADO

Aspen. West of Continental Divide on Roaring Fork River, this early mining camp is now a popular ski center and winter resort, and a summer cultural center. Beautiful Snowmass Mountain, streams, and lakes are in the vicinity.

Black Canyon of the Gunnison National Monument. State road leads to rim of canyon where rock walls drop 2200 feet to Gunnison river. An old trail takes skilled climbers down to the river.

Boulder. Home of University of Colorado and site of Colorado's first schoolhouse. Boulder Canyon, Roosevelt National Forest, and Rocky Mountain National Park are nearby.

Central City. First town on Gregory Gulch, scene of the first great gold rush to the Rockies and called "the richest square mile on earth." Now the town is partly "ghost."

Colorado National Monument. Near Grand Junction, 17,693 acres of canyons and desert hills are filled with red and yellow sandstone monoliths and columns of fantastic size and shape. There are good views from Serpent's Trail, Rimrock Drive, and Cold Shivers Point. Dinosaur beds are numerous.

Colorado Springs. Famed health and pleasure resort. Here are Pikes peak, Garden of the Gods, containing many fantastic formations of red and yellow sandstone, Manitou Springs, Cave of the Winds, Cheyenne Canyon, Seven Falls, Will Rogers Shrine of the Sun on Cheyenne Mountain.

Cripple Creek. In the mining era, one of the richest gold fields in the world.

Denver. The state capital's beautiful Civic Center and Capitol Hill are marked by fine architecture, murals, and statuary. The city park has a color-lighted electric fountain in the center of its lake. Rare western history collections are in the Public Library and the State Museum. Denver is the home

Cliff Palace, Mesa Verde National Park

Spectacular Royal Gorge, Colorado   D.&R.G.W. R.R.

Longs Peak, from Bear Lake, Colorado   D.L. Hopwood

Gr. Nat. Cap. Comm.
Capitol of the United States, Washington, D.C.

Miami, Florida, City of Sunshine
Miami N.B.

of the first Juvenile Court, the Emily Griffith Opportunity School and the University of Denver. A U.S. Mint is here, and the Denver Union Stockyards. The National Western Livestock and Rodeo Show is an annual attraction in January. The Mountain Parks System includes Red Rocks, with its outdoor theater, Echo Lake, Mount Evans, and Lookout Mountain, with Buffalo Bill's grave.

Dinosaur National Monument. Nearly 205,000 acres of dinosaur beds in Colorado and Utah.

Estes Park. Gateway to Rocky Mountain National Park and headquarters for many vacationers.

Glenwood Springs. Hot mineral springs resort at mouth of Glenwood Canyon of the Colorado River.

Grand Mesa. Flat-topped, high-altitude mountain (10,500 feet) in Grand Mesa National Forest—a land of lakes, fishing, camping, and winter sports. Land's End is a vantage point on the Mesa's rim that offers a panoramic view of hundreds of miles.

Leadville. This highest city in the United States (10,200 feet) has around it the storied gold and silver mines of early-day Colorado. It was the home of the fabulous H. A. W. Tabor and the locale of his mines; it is still the heart of a rich mining region. Nearby Mt. Elbert is the highest peak in Colorado.

Mesa Verde National Park. A great plateau carved by deep canyons, in whose walls are hundreds of prehistoric Indian cliff dwellings. Cliff Palace alone contains more than 200 rooms and a score of kivas. The region is reached by the spectacular Million Dollar Highway, through the most rugged mountains and canyons of the Rockies.

National Monuments. See Black Canyon of the Gunnison; Colorado National Monument; Dinosaur National Monument; and U. S. National Park System, pages 228-229.

Ouray. Mountain mining town, famous in goldmining history as the home of Thomas F. Walsh and his Camp Bird Mine, which is still in operation, as are others in the region. Footpaths and horseback trails to mountain viewpoints, towering peaks and mountain cataracts, Box Canyon with its falls and cavern, are attractive to tourists. This is the northern terminal of the Million Dollar Highway to the southwestern tip of the state.

Pagosa Springs. Mineral springs and health resort. It is just west of the Continental Divide, crossed by spectacular Wolf Creek Pass.

Pueblo. Colorado's second largest city, notable for its huge steel and smeltering plants. The Mineral Palace has a fine collection of ore samples.

Rocky Mountain National Park. Astride the Continental Divide, here is a land of snow-capped mountain ranges, sparkling lakes, pine and fir and quaking aspen, elk, deer, and bighorn sheep, and much other wildlife. Trail Ridge Road, a wide and beautiful highway, crosses the park and drops down

the west side of the Divide to Grand Lake. Among many other sights, the Mummy Range, the Never Summer Range, Iceberg Lake, and Specimen Mountain are seen from the Trail Ridge Road.

Royal Gorge. Deep and colorful canyon of the Arkansas River, near Canon City. An 880-foot suspension bridge swings across the top of the Gorge, 1,053 feet above the river.

San Luis Valley. Largest mountain park in Colorado, near the head of the Rio Grande, and a fertile and important agricultural area. The state's earliest-settled region, it still retains the atmosphere of the first Spanish and Mexican settlements. Among many scenic attractions, it contains the Great Sand Dunes National Monument.

Uravan. Site of one of the most extensive uranium deposits in the world; in Montrose county.

CONNECTICUT

Bridgeport. Industrial city, famous as the home of the circusman, P. T. Barnum. Among the points of interest are the Tom Thumb House, P. T. Barnum Museum, and Seaside Park, which contains Barnum's statue.

East Haddam. At the cemetery, above the Connecticut River, stands the schoolhouse where Nathan Hale taught. Uniquely furnished Gillette Castle, once the country estate of William Gillette, the famous actor, has become a state park.

Guilford. More than 150 old houses still remain in this well-preserved village, settled in 1639 by Reverend Henry Whitfield. His stone home is now a historical museum.

Hartford. State capital and famous insurance center. The Capitol, on a swelling crest of land, overlooks the other State buildings to the south and Bushnell Park to the north. Several blocks to the northeast stands the Old State House, designed by the colonial architect, Bulfinch in 1796. Between Main and Prospect Streets are grouped the Wadsworth Atheneum, Morgan Memorial, Colt Memorial, and Avery Memorial.

Marine Historical Museum. At Mystic, former clipper shipbuilding center. The museum houses an outstanding collection of clipper models.

Newgate Prison. In the countryside near East Granby. The dungeons and leg chains serve as grim reminders of punishments used in Colonial days.

New Haven. Graceful elms edge the streets of the home of Yale University. Noteworthy structures connected with the University are Connecticut Hall (built in 1752), Payne Whitney Gymnasium, Harkness Memorial Tower, Sterling Memorial Library, Gallery of Fine Arts, Sprague Memorial Hall, and the Yale Bowl.

New London. Former whaling town. Among its educational institutions are the U. S. Coast Guard

Academy and Connecticut College. Across the river, north of Groton, lies the U. S. Navy Submarine Base.

DELAWARE

Dover. State capital since 1777. The Georgian-Colonial-style State House, first completed in 1792, has undergone several remodelings and additions. Christ Church dates from 1734.

Lewes. Here the first white men of the Delaware River Region settled in 1630. Early Colonial antiques are exhibited in Zwaanendael House, an adapted model of Town Hall at Hoorn, Holland. Cannons used in War of 1812 stand in Memorial Park. Lewes Beach stretches along Delaware Bay.

Newark. University of Delaware campus cuts through the town. Of special interest are Old College, Elliott Hall, and Mitchell Hall.

New Castle. Colonial appearance is preserved by stately 17th-century homes and buildings. Market and Courthouse Squares comprise The Green, plotted by Peter Stuyvesant. The Old Court House was the State Capitol until 1777. Its central portion was completed in 1704, and its east wing was begun before 1698. Immanuel Church dates from 1710. Town Common, a common land grant of the Dutch era, lies west of the city; this farming tract still yields revenue to the city.

Rehoboth Beach. White sand beaches, fronting Atlantic Ocean, draw vacationers throughout the state and give town the title "Delaware's Summer Capital." Annually, art exhibits line the boardwalk near Virginia Avenue.

Wilmington. Largest city in the state and heavily industrialized. A stone monument, at The Rocks, marks the site of Fort Christina, the original Swedish settlement of 1638. Old Swedes (Holy Trinity) Church, built in 1698, presents a gray-stone facade with a hooded gable roof. The approach from Church Street leads through the cemetery where the earliest legible stone marker bears the date 1719. The Historical Society of Delaware, housed in Old Town Hall (1798), includes in its collection a portion of the eastern terminal stone of the Mason and Dixon Line.

DISTRICT OF COLUMBIA

Washington. Considered by many the most beautiful capital in the world. Washington was planned by George Washington, Thomas Jefferson, and the French engineer, Major Pierre Charles L'Enfant.

Among the Government buildings are the Capitol; White House; Library of Congress, largest in the world; the State Treasury, and other department buildings; the Pentagon, home of the Department of Defense; and the United States Supreme Court Building. The Smithsonian Institution administers ten bureaus, including the United States National Museum, the National Zoological Park, the Bureau of American Ethnology, the Freer Gallery of Art, and the National Gallery of Art, home of the Andrew Mellon Collection and others.

The Grecian charm of the Lincoln Memorial, the clean, straight shaft of the 555-foot Washington Monument, and the classic dignity of the Thomas Jefferson Memorial are beauty spots in the capital, which is at its loveliest when the cherry trees blossom in the spring. The Lincoln Museum (Ford's Theatre), containing a great collection of Lincolniana, and the House Where Lincoln Died have been made National Memorials. At Arlington National Cemetery, on the Virginia side of the Potomac, a sentry always stands guard at the Tomb of the Unknown Soldier. The Custis-Lee Mansion, on a hillside in the cemetery, is now a National Memorial.

FLORIDA

Cape Canaveral. Home of the astronauts. From here on May 5, 1961, Commander Alan Shepard became our first man in space.

Daytona Beach. World-famous speedway beach 23 miles long, whose hard-packed white sands are used by motorists, sand sailboaters, and bathers.

Everglades National Park. Including part of the Florida Keys, the Ten Thousand Islands, and Big

Cypress Swamp, the 2,000 square miles of tropical and sub-tropical wilderness, marsh, and semi-aquatic grasslands comprise America's third largest national park. Here are alligator and otter, raccoon, bobcat, and cougar; snowy egret and white and wood ibis; and tropical trees and other plants found nowhere else in the United States.

Jacksonville. Third largest city in Florida and most important commercially on the south Atlantic seaboard. Near the mouth of the St. Johns River, it is a great ship port and yacht harbor. The Oriental Gardens offer an orange grove and lush plantings of Florida flowers.

Key West. At the tip of Florida's long chain of keys, Key West is a tropical city with Latin atmosphere; its most modern note is the superb Overseas Highway that reaches it by traversing the whole chain of keys. Turtle, sponge, and deep-sea fishing are of interest, as are also the quaint old houses built by ships' carpenters. A United States Naval Station has been based there since 1823. Fort Jefferson National Monument is reached by boat or plane.

Lake Okeechobee. Florida's largest fresh-water lake, claiming the country's best black bass fishing.

Miami and Miami Beach. Cosmopolitan Miami, largest city in Florida, is important as a financial, transportation, and recreation center. Sights include the Hialeah Park with its race track, its avenues of royal palms, and its flamingos; the city docks where the fishing fleets unload, and the steamship piers; the International Airport; and the Seminole Indian Village. At nearby Coral Gables is the University of Miami. MacArthur and other causeways cross Biscayne Bay to Miami Beach, fashionable resort.

Ocala. Hub of Florida's thriving Brahman cattle industry, center of an important citrus fruit area, and resort town in the north-central lake district, which is studded with lakes and springs, parks and recreational areas. At Silver Springs, the largest of the state's many springs, the flow of water is estimated at from 500,000,000 to 800,000,000 gallons a day; glass-bottomed boats, a jungle tour, and a fine bathing beach are attractions.

Orlando. Citrus center of lake area. Lake Eola Park and Orlando Zoo are natural homes for Florida's native flowers, trees, and animals.

Palm Beach and West Palm Beach. Luxury resorts popular among the socially elect.

Pensacola. Old and historically interesting city, with a definitely Spanish air. Plaza Ferdinand VII is on the site of the city's first fort; many old forts are around the harbor and elsewhere. Old Christ Church was built in 1835. Modern points of interest are the huge Naval Air Station nearby, the picturesque red snapper fleet, and the fine beaches across the bay on Santa Rosa Island.

St. Augustine. Oldest city in the United States. Founded in 1565. The Plaza de la Constitucion was the parade grounds of the first settlement; other landmarks include America's oldest house and oldest schoolhouse; the Spanish Treasury; Zero Milestone where the Spanish trail to California began; the old city gates; Castillo de San Marcos, the oldest masonry fort in the nation, now a National Monument. The Fountain of Youth Gardens have a central fountain where Ponce de Léon supposedly drank the waters of eternal life.

St. Petersburg. The west coast's important resort, lying on a climatically favorable and sunny peninsula between Tampa Bay and the Gulf of Mexico; numerous causeways and bridges.

Suwannee River. Beautiful river made romantic by the song, "Old Folks at Home." At White Springs is the Stephen Foster Memorial; dioramas in the museum tell his songs' stories.

Tallahassee. The state's capital, of which the grounds are a beautifully wooded park. There are many points of interest, among them Walker Memorial Library, containing Indian relics and pieces of armor dating from De Soto.

Tampa. South Florida's most important commercial city. An early Spanish trading post, it was

Hawaii Vis. Bur.   *Hawaii's Capitol—Iolani Palace*

Hawaii Vis. Bur.   *Iao Needle—Maui*

later a base for José Gaspar and other west coast pirates. Among important exports, its handmade cigars are famous.

GEORGIA

Andersonville Prison Park. Site of famous Confederate Military Prison. Providence Spring, said to have bubbled forth in answer to prayers of prisoners, is still to be seen.

Athens. Home of the University of Georgia, chartered in 1785 and oldest state university. Overlooking Oconee River, Athens retains much of the atmosphere of the old South.

Atlanta. Capital of the state and one of the great railroad and banking centers of the United States. Here is the "Wren's Nest," home of Joel Chandler Harris. In Grant Park stands Fort Walker, historic breastworks of the Battle of Atlanta.

Chickamauga and Chattanooga National Military Park. Battlefields where Confederate and Union armies met in one of the great campaigns of the war.

Fort Benning. Largest infantry school in the United States, located nine miles from Columbus.

Macon. Industrial city in the State's great agricultural belt. A stately city, it is rich in historic tradition. Nearby, at Ocmulgee National Monument, 683 acres of prehistoric mounds disclose homes and relics of six successive Indian cultures.

Okefenokee Swamp. More than 600 square miles of swampland wilderness in southern Georgia and northern Florida. A wonderland of flowers, canopied by forests of gum, pine, bay, and cypress, it is inhabited by deer, bear, panthers, alligators, birds, and great varieties of fish.

Savannah. "Birthplace of Georgia," founded in 1733. Famous resort and great export city, Savannah's traditions are earliest in America.

Stone Mountain. Near Atlanta; immense granite dome, rises 800 feet above the surroundings.

HAWAII

Island of Oahu

Honolulu. This romantic south-seas tourist center, home of fabled Waikiki Beach and its sentinel Diamond Head, an extinct volcano, is the capital of the newest state. Iolani Palace, the present capitol, served as the royal palace from the 1880's; its Throne Room is kept as it was during the reign of King Kalakaua. The world-famous Bishop Museum houses Polynesian and royal Hawaiian objects; other museums include Queen Emma Museum and the Royal Mausoleum. Foster Park Botanical Gardens with its orchid displays and Kapiolani Park with both an aquarium of Pacific marine life and a zoo with a tropical bird aviary are well worth a visit. Also see the National Memorial Cemetery of the Pacific and the University of Hawaii.

Kahana Beach. Here breadfruit, bamboo, and mango trees mark the site of a once populous old-Hawaiian settlement.

Kaneohe. Fantastic coral formations may be viewed from glass-bottomed boats.

Koko Head Park. Named for the volcanic mountain which dominates the head of land that juts into the sea. A feature of the area is lovely Hanauma Bay, created by volcanic action 10,000 years ago. At the Blow Hole the mighty sea forces its way through a tiny hole in the lava ledge to form miniature geysers rising high in the air.

Laie. A quiet Samoan village where visitors are charmed by the splendid white Mormon Temple, often called the Taj Mahal of Hawaii.

Nuuanu Pali. Seven miles from Honolulu, at the head of the Nuuanu Valley, lies this scenic mountain pass which separates the windward and leeward sides of the island. Here in 1795, during the wars to unite the islands, Kamehameha the Great forced defeated Oahuan warriors over the precipice to death on the rocks below.

Pearl Harbor. United States Naval base. In the harbor lie the sunken remains of the battleships *Arizona* and *Utah*, which entomb the heroes who went down with their ships on December 7, 1941. A monument was erected over the sunken battleship *Arizona* and was dedicated on Memorial Day in 1962.

Sacred Falls. Off the highway near Hauula a crystal stream leaps from the sheer cliffs to a beautiful pool below.

Island of Hawaii

Hawaii Volcanoes National Park. The Kilauea-Mauna Loa section of the park features volcanoes, lava flows, and luxuriant tropical forest with giant fern trees. Mauna Loa, largest single mountain mass in the world, rises 13,680 feet above sea level. A trip to the rim of Kilauea is rewarded with a view of lava activity in the firepit. Kilauea last erupted in 1961 and enlarged the Puna Lava Flow, an area of raw cinder cones and steaming lava.

Hilo. Famous as "Orchid Capital," its daily export of blooms numbers in the thousands. The lovely Japanese gardens and a banyan-tree grove in Liluokalani Park delight visitors, as do the ever changing colors in Rainbow Falls, where the Wailuku River cascades over a volcanic ledge. Another spectacular waterfall, Akaka Falls, lies north of the city. The Lyman Memorial Museum features a collection of ancient Hawaiian relics.

Honaunau. The City of Refuge National Historical Park was established in July 1961. It has 180 acres and contains temple foundations dating from the twelfth century.

Kailua-Kona. Site of the old Hulihee Palace, a reminder that the Islands' monarchy sprang from this island. Here also is the First Christian Church, established by missionaries in 1806.

Kalapana Black Sand Beach. A tremendous coco palm grove surrounds a jet-black beach, where the volcanic sands are washed by creamy surf.

Kohala. Birthplace of Kamehameha I, marked by the original of the statue of the king which stands in the Palace Square in Honolulu. Nearby is the scenic Pululu Valley once the site of ancient Hawaiian temples.

Mauna Kea. Its snow-capped majesty marks the highest point in the Islands; 13,796 feet.

Puna Warm Springs. Near Kapoho. Lush tropical vegetation, including green ferns, surround waters warmed by volcanic heat.

Island of Maui

Haleakala National Park. The Park features the enormous Haleakala Crater; its floor measures twenty-five square miles, and the rim extends twenty-one miles around. Along the walls, and in the crater itself, bloom the rare silversword plant. Rain clouds, borne by the trade winds, find their way into this crater to form world-famous cloud effects.

Iao Valley. A dense green gorge west of Wauluku, best known for the Iao Needle. This freak formation, a solid mass of volcanic stone, rises 1,200 feet.

Lahaina. Romantic and easy-going, this town was a favorite spot of ancient Hawaiians. Here Kamehameha II established the royal capital. Nineteenth-century whalers, also delighted with the locale, spent their winters here.

Maui Ditch. On the winding highway between Wailuku and Hana, through dense forests of bamboo and ape plant, here and there are glimpses of the water gates and tunnels of this famous ditch, important in the battles between the warriors of Maui and Hawaii.

Island of Kauai

Hanalei Valley. This majestic valley can be viewed from a look-out on the highway which skirts the northern coast of the island.

Waimea Canyon. Volcanic rock, sculptured and plunging to great depths, reflects varied colors as mist and sunshine alternately sweep the great expanse which stretches miles into the interior of the island from the south shore highway.

Wet and Dry Caves of Haena. Situated at the base of a volcanic cliff, these large caverns were the gathering place of Hawaiian chiefs. The dry cave is large enough to drive in an automobile.

IDAHO

American Falls. Dam and reservoir on the Snake River, adjacent to Fort Hall Indian Reservation.

Boise. Idaho's capital and largest city is the center of a rich agricultural and mining region.

Of interest are the Municipal Art Gallery, the Capitol, the Veterans' Hospital, and the Julia Davis Park. East of Boise is Arrowrock Dam; northwest is Black Canyon Dam.

Coeur d'Alene. Lumber, agricultural, and tourist city in noted Coeur d'Alene mining area. In this region are Coeur d'Alene and Pend Oreille lakes.

Craters of the Moon National Monument. Volcanic area of craters, cinder cones, lava flows, and stalactite caves; resembles craters on the moon.

Hell's Canyon of the Snake River. Spectacular canyon along the Snake at Oregon boundary. From four to nine miles wide and almost 8,000 feet deep at some points; its walls are red, purple, yellow.

Idaho Falls. Center of rich farming region. Idaho Falls of the Snake and the Lavas are nearby.

Primitive Area. In central Idaho, 1,500,000 acres in Boise, Challis, and Sawtooth National Forests; access is by pack-train only. Rugged mountains, gigantic precipices, and sheer canyons.

Sun Valley. World-famous winter sports resort, popular also with summer tourists. To the northwest is the Lost River Range that includes Mt. Borah, Idaho's highest mountain (12,652 feet).

Twin Falls. Center of great irrigated agricultural region. Nearby are the Blue Lakes, the Twin Falls-Jerome Bridge, Twin and Shoshone Falls, and the Thousand Springs.

ILLINOIS

Brookfield Zoo. Chicago Zoological Park, in Brookfield, near Chicago. Most of the lairs are of the natural habitat type, without bars. The zoo contains everything, from insects to elephants.

Cahokia Mounds State Park. Site of Monks Mound, largest Indian mound in United States. A museum exhibits many Indian relics taken from the Cahokia Mounds. The park is near East St. Louis.

Champaign-Urbana. These two cities are the home of the University of Illinois.

Charleston. Scene of fourth Lincoln-Douglas debate and site of the grave of Dennis Hanks. Near town is the Lincoln Log Cabin State Park, containing reconstructed cabin of Lincoln's father, built on the original foundation.

Chicago. Vibrant and noisy, the great metropolis of the Midwest sprawls over a 200-square-mile area at the lower western end of Lake Michigan. It is the greatest railway center in the world and the heart of an arterial system of steel rails, concrete roads, waterways, and airways, radiating in all directions. It is called the Convention City. Outstanding points of interest include the Art Institute,

Chicago Natural History Museum, parks and boulevards, Navy Pier, University of Chicago, Planetarium, Aquarium, Soldier Field, Museum of Science and Industry, Board of Trade, Prudential Building, McCormick Place, Stock Yards, airports, and Chicago Zoological Park in Brookfield, where most of the lairs are of the natural habitat type.

Dickson Mounds State Park. Here 230 Indian remains have been exhumed and left lying in their original postures; located near Havana.

Galena. Scene of famous "lead rush" in first half of the 19th century. Built on terraces cut by the Galena River, Galena's houses are placed like chalets in an Alpine village. The first home of Ulysses S. Grant and the one presented to him after the Civil War are still standing.

Great Lakes Naval Training Center. Only major naval unit in Middle West and one of three naval training centers in the United States.

Lincoln's New Salem State Park. Authentic reproduction of the village, near Springfield, where Lincoln spent six of his early Illinois years.

Peoria. Third largest city of state, on the northwest bank of the Illinois River. Located in the Corn Belt, Peoria distilleries draw a considerable portion of the corn crop of the area.

Rock Island Arsenal. Located on an island in the Mississippi River. Here are stored a portion of the nation's war supplies; War Museum.

Springfield. Capital of Illinois. The Capitol and the Lincoln Home are attractions. The Lincoln Tomb in Oak Ridge Cemetery contains the bodies of Abraham Lincoln, his wife, and three of his children.

Starved Rock State Park. On Starved Rock, rising 140 feet above the Illinois River, La Salle built Fort St. Louis in 1683. Legend has it that a band of Indians starved to death on the rock.

INDIANA

Bedford and Bloomington. In limestone region from which comes stone for world's finest buildings. Visiting parties are taken through quarries.

Brown County State Park. In the heart of Indiana's rolling hills and dense woods, Brown County's scenic beauty is world famous. Nearby Nashville has a world-famous art colony.

Gary. In Gary and nearby cities are northern Indiana's steel and associated industries; most of the large plants have tours for visitors.

Greenfield. Birthplace of James Whitcomb Riley. Riley Memorial Park contains the original "Old Swimmin' Hole," and the old Riley Homestead is an authentic and notable Riley museum.

Indiana Dunes State Park. East of Gary. Three miles of beach and sand dunes on Lake Michigan; wooded inland.

Indianapolis. State capital, Indiana's largest city, and center of a highly developed agricultural area. The city is large and spacious; four great diagonals reach its center, Monument Circle, holding the impressive Soldiers and Sailors Monument. West of the Circle are the Capitol and Indiana University Medical Center for Children, where murals and stained-glass windows illustrate the Riley poems. East of the Circle is the Riley Home. (See also Greenfield.) North are the World War Memorial, Scottish Rite Cathedral with its carillon and gigantic pipe organ, and the Benjamin Harrison Home. At the famous Indianapolis Motor Speedway, Memorial Day races are an annual event.

International Friendship Gardens. A hundred acres of beautifully landscaped gardens of all nations; colorful outdoor theaters. Near Michigan City.

Nancy Hanks Lincoln Memorial. In Lincoln State Park, near Gentryville, are the grave of Nancy Hanks Lincoln and site of the Lincoln cabin, the fireplace reconstructed from the original stones. At nearby Rockport is the Lincoln Pioneer Village.

Ky. Dept. of Cons.

Cumberland Falls, Ky. — Scene of the "Moonbow"

Ewing Galloway

New Orleans' Imposing Jackson Square

New Harmony. Wabash village founded in 1815 by the Rappites, a religious communal sect. Many of the original stone buildings still remain: Old Rappite Fort, the Community Houses, the Rapp-Maclure Home, the Workingmen's Institute.

South Bend. Home of University of Notre Dame and automobile manufacturing city.

Spring Mill State Park. A pioneer village has been restored around an old stone grist mill, powered by water-wheel. Meal is ground for visitors.

Turkey Run State Park. On picturesque Sugar Creek, famed for its lovely gorges cut deep in sandstone. There is much virgin forest.

Vincennes. Mellow old city on the Wabash River, in the midst of rich orchards and farmlands. First settlement in Indiana, a key city of the old Northwest Territory, and Indiana Territory's capital, Vincennes is rich in history. One of its many fine monuments is the George Rogers Clark Memorial.

Wyandotte Cave. Spectacular caverns, with 20 miles of passages on five levels; near Wyandotte.

IOWA

Amana Colonies. Seven former communal villages, the first settled in 1855.

Davenport. See nation's largest roller gate dam which operates even when the Mississippi is frozen. Wild Cat Den with old dam and grist mill nearby.

Des Moines. State capital; atop Capitol Hill, the gold-domed Capitol dominates other State buildings clustered on the slopes.

Dubuque. In lead and zinc region, one of the oldest towns in Iowa. Trappist Monastery nearby.

Effigy Mounds National Monument. Near McGregor. Great Indian mounds, some 300 feet long, trace shapes of eagles, bears, and wolves. Nearby are McGregor State Park and Painted Rocks.

Fort Dodge. Vast gypsum fields surround town. In Dolliver Memorial Park, sandstone bluffs edge the Des Moines River.

Iowa City. The University of Iowa campus includes the Old Capitol, of Territorial days.

Maquoketa Caves State Monument. Natural bridge, balanced rock, and many limestone caves.

Okoboji Region. Fine resort area including East and West Okoboji and Spirit lakes.

Sioux City. Grand View Park offers a natural amphitheater with outdoor pavilion. At War Eagle Park is the grave of the famous Sioux chief.

KANSAS

Abilene. Famous frontier cow town. Site of the Eisenhower family home and the new Dwight D. Eisenhower Museum.

Council Grove. Historic town on the site of an old Santa Fe Trail campground.

Dodge City. On the Arkansas River, the town was famous as a watering place and shipping point for Texas longhorns. "Boot Hill Cemetery" contains early-day memorials.

Emporia. Birthplace and home of the late William Allen White, noted Kansas journalist. His residence is a show place of the city.

Fort Riley. Military reservation and cavalry post established in 1853 to protect travelers on the Santa Fe Trail from the Indians. The Old Territorial Capitol is nearby.

Fort Scott. On the site of an old army post, of which Carroll Plaza was the parade ground.

Hanover. Near town stands the only original unaltered Pony Express station in the country.

Kaufmann & Fabry

Chicago, Giant of the Midwest

John Brown Memorial State Park. This park commemorates the Battle of Osawatomie and includes a museum built around John Brown's cabin, moved from its original site.

Kansas City. Important meat-packing and railroad center. Nearby is Wyandotte County Park and Lake, largest in the state, and also the Old Shawnee Mission.

Lawrence. Scene of the Quantrell raid in 1863; now home of the University of Kansas and Haskell Institute, government Indian school.

Leavenworth. First settlement in Kansas Territory. Nearby Fort Leavenworth, military reservation and officers' training school, was established in 1827. A Federal penitentiary is also at Leavenworth.

Topeka. Capital of Kansas and third largest city. In the Capitol are the "John Brown" murals, by John Steuart Curry. Some of the historical buildings are Constitution Hall, Underground Railroad Station, and the Old Settlers' Memorial Cabin in Gage Park.

Wichita. Largest city in Kansas and important airplane manufacturing and oil refinery center. Points of interest are the Art Museum and the airplane wind tunnel at the University of Wichita campus.

KENTUCKY

Abraham Lincoln Birthplace National Historic Site. At Hodgenville, the birthplace of Abraham Lincoln. Some of the original Lincoln farm is contained within the park. A granite memorial room encloses the birthplace cabin.

Audubon State Park. Near Henderson, once the home of John James Audubon. The museum has superb collection of his bird prints and other Audubonia.

Berea College. Oldest and largest of Kentucky's mountain schools, at Berea; weaving produced by the school is famous throughout America.

Cumberland Falls State Park. Woodland park on the Cumberland River, where a semi-circular cataract makes a "moonbow" under the moon's light.

Cumberland Gap National Historical Park. Daniel Boone blazed a trail into Kentucky through this pass in the Cumberland Mountains. The park is in three states—Kentucky, Tennessee, and Virginia.

Frankfort. Capital of Kentucky. The Capitol and the Governor's Mansion are characteristic of the stately south. The old Capitol now houses the Kentucky Historical Society. Daniel and Rebecca Boone are buried at Frankfort.

Harrodsburg. First white settlement in Kentucky. In Pioneer Memorial State Park is a replica of old Fort Harrod, complete with stockade and blockhouse. The Lincoln Marriage Temple contains the cabin that was the first home of Lincoln's parents.

Kentucky Lake. Man-made lake, formed by Kentucky Dam across the Tennessee River.

Lexington. Home of the University of Kentucky and "Heart of the Bluegrass." Here some of the world's finest race horses have been raised.

Louisville. Kentucky's largest and most important commercial and industrial city; also the famous home of the Kentucky Derby. Points of interest include the Public Library and the Filson Club, with collections of Kentucky history; Iroquois Park; the grave of George Rogers Clark.

Mammoth Cave National Park. In 150 miles of charted passages there are three underground rivers, eight waterfalls, and two lakes, as well as stalactite, stalagmite, and drapery formations.

My Old Kentucky Home State Shrine. The stately old mansion where Stephen Foster was a guest when he wrote the beloved song.

LOUISIANA

Avery Island. Of special interest are the McIlhenny Jungle Gardens and the bird refuges.

Baton Rouge. Winding drives, scenic lakes and bayous, and ante-bellum homes typify the state capital. The present Capitol was built in 1932. The Old Capitol overlooks the river.

Grand Isle. Semitropical island in Gulf of Mexico. Once headquarters for the pirate, Lafitte.

New Iberia and St. Martinville. Both on Bayou Teche and settled by French colonists in 18th century. In cemetery at St. Martinville Church the Evangeline Monument marks grave of Emmeline Labiche, supposedly Longfellow's "Evangeline."

New Orleans. Founded in 1718, the "Crescent City" was nearly 100 years old when it became part of the United States. The flavor of its glamorous past has been preserved in the Vieux Carre, or French Quarter. A tour through the Quarter leads along narrow streets, lined with two- and three-story French and Spanish buildings, many with balconies of exquisite iron-lace grill. Views through doorways and porte-cocheres reveal lovely patios and oleander, camellia, and wistaria gardens. Surrounding Jackson Square are St. Louis Cathedral, the Pontalba buildings, the Presbytere, and the Cabildo, home of the Spanish governors. At the French Market foodstuffs are vended in the open. The Mardi Gras, preceding Lent, is one of the most famous annual events.

MAINE

Augusta. State capital on the Kennebec River, which bisects the town. The State House, started in 1829, retains only the graceful portico of Bulfinch's design; the 1911 enlargement demolished the major portion. The James G. Blaine House serves as the Executive Mansion. Fort Western has been restored to its appearance in 1754.

Warren—Md. Dept. Econ. Develop.
Old Senate Chamber, State House, Annapolis

Massie—Mo. Res. Div.
Interesting Old Mill in Shannon County, Mo.

Bar Harbor. Fashionable resort on Mt. Desert Island, gateway to Acadia National Park. The park, a 41,634-acre tract, preserves a section of the magnificent wilderness that was once part of the French grant to Sieur de Monts.

Baxter State Park. More than 160,000 acres of spectacular wilderness. Within area is Mt. Katahdin, highest point in Maine (5,268 feet).

Brunswick. Seat of Bowdoin College. Longfellow stayed at Emmons House while teaching at the college. Harriet Beecher Stowe wrote her famous book "Uncle Tom's Cabin" at the house bearing her name.

Moosehead Lake. Largest lake in state. It is popular with trout and salmon fishermen.

Portland. State's largest city and principal port since colonial days. A monument in Longfellow Square honors Portland's noted citizen. The Wadsworth-Longfellow House, the writer's boyhood home, is open. The Museum of the Maine Historical Society and the Portland Museum of Art, including Sweat Mansion, are among the cultural institutions in the city. Near South Portland, the Portland Head Light, built in 1791, marks the entrance to the Portland Harbor.

MARYLAND

Annapolis. State capital, famous as the seat of the U. S. Naval Academy and St. John's College. In the Old Senate Chamber of the State House, Washington surrendered his commission and (1784) the peace treaty with Great Britain was ratified.

Baltimore. Maryland's largest city, and an important port and industrial center. Products of its diversified industries leave the city through its great harbor on the Patapsco River. Of the many monuments marking the parks and squares, Washington Monument is best known. Among educational and cultural institutions are Johns Hopkins University, the Walters Art Gallery, Maryland Historical Society, and Enoch Pratt Free Library. Outside the city, on a point-reaching into the harbor, lies Fort McHenry National Monument, site of the terrible bombardment during the War of 1812, which inspired Francis Scott Key to write "The Star-Spangled Banner."

Frederick. Barbara Fritchie House, reconstructed, contains relics supposedly used by the heroine of Whittier's poem. The home of Roger Brooke Taney, Chief Justice who handed down the Dred Scott decision, preserves his personal effects and those of his brother-in-law, Francis Scott Key.

Hagerstown. In a city park the house of the founder, Jonathan Hager, is maintained. It dates from 1739. Nearby is the Antietam National Battlefield Site.

Ocean City. Important seashore and fishing resort, with marlin ranking highest.

MASSACHUSETTS

Adams National Historic Site. Home of four generations of the John Adams and John Quincy Adams family; near Quincy.

Amherst. Home of Emily Dickinson, Noah Webster, and Robert Frost, and seat of two famous institutions of learning, Amherst College, founded in 1821, and the University of Massachusetts.

Boston. "Hub of the Universe," state capital, leading seaport, industrial and cultural center. Greater Boston, at the mouths of the Mystic and Charles Rivers, includes East Boston, Charlestown, South Boston, Roxbury, Dorchester, Brighton, Hyde Park, and other sections. In the crooked streets and narrow alleys of old Boston it is almost impossible to proceed in any direction without passing a spot of historic significance. The first free public school in America was established at Boston in 1635, followed next year by the founding of Harvard University at Cambridge. In Boston Navy Yard is the reconstructed U.S. frigate *Constitution*, revered by the nation as "Old Ironsides." A tablet marks the spot of the Boston Tea Party. Other points of interest are the Paul Revere House, Old North Church, Battle of Bunker Hill Monument, Boston Athenaeum, Faneuil Hall, King's Chapel, Massachusetts Historical Society Museum, Old South Meeting House, Old State House, The Common and Trinity Church.

Cambridge. Home of Harvard University, Massachusetts Institute of Technology, and Radcliffe College. Among the points of interest are the Botanic Garden, Fogg Museum, the noted glass flower collection at University Museum, and the homes of Longfellow and Lowell.

Concord. Noted for its historic and literary associations, it shares with Lexington the honor of being the "Birthplace of the American Revolution." It was the home of Emerson, Hawthorne, Louisa M. Alcott, Thoreau, and Channing. Hawthorne lived at Old Manse and Wayside, both standing; at Orchard House Miss Alcott wrote *Little Women*.

Gloucester. On the peninsula of Cape Ann, this great fishing port has been dominated by the seafaring tradition for more than 300 years.

Lexington. "Birthplace of American Liberty." It was here that the Minute Men faced the British redcoats and fired "the shot heard 'round the world." In the Common stands a bronze statue of a Minute Man, commemorating the event.

Martha's Vineyard. A large triangular island between Buzzard's Bay and Nantucket Sound, a few miles from the mainland. Its variety of scenery and lively villages have made it a popular summer resort.

Nantucket. Last seaward outpost of New England. With its crooked cobbled streets, quaint comfortable homes, yacht club, artists' colony, beaches, it still retains an atmosphere of the great whaling days. Places of interest are its Whaling Museum; Friends

Meetinghouse; Old Mill, dating from 1746; and Oldest House, built in 1686.

Plymouth. Here is enshrined "the cornerstone of the nation," Plymouth Rock, on which the Pilgrims landed in 1620. There are many fine 17th-century houses and other reminders of the Pilgrim era.

Salem. Witches, clipper ships, privateers, exotic wares from the Indies and China, wharves and docks laden with incoming and outgoing merchandise— all these are conjured up by Salem, historic treasure chest of New England. Nathaniel Hawthorne was born in an old gambrel-roofed house built in 1692; the House of Seven Gables, said to be the setting for his novel of that name, is one of the celebrated structures of Salem. Another is the Witch House.

Woods Hole. Cape Cod port; site of Oceanographic Institute and Marine Biological Laboratory.

MICHIGAN

Ann Arbor. Campus of the University of Michigan extends over half the town. The famous Nichol Arboretum features lilacs and peonies.

Benton Harbor and St. Joseph. Central points in the state's southern fruit belt. Benton Harbor holds an annual Blossom Festival; fruit is marketed wholesale at the Municipal Fruit Market.

Dearborn. Home of Henry Ford. Greenfield Village, model of early American town, exhibits historic buildings moved to this site—Henry Ford's Birthplace; Logan County Courthouse, where Lincoln practiced law; Edison Buildings, including Menlo Park Laboratory; and Luther Burbank's office.

Detroit. "Motor Capital of the World." The Rivera Murals at the Institute of Arts depicts its industrial greatness. In the channel of the Detroit River lies the great amusement park, Belle Isle. In the Detroit Zoological Park, at Royal Oak, animals roam in open areas resembling their natural habitat. Grosse Point, residential section, fronts on Lake St. Clair.

Holland. Dutch settled here in 1847. Now famous for the Annual Tulip Festival, the Netherlands Museum, and the Wooden Shoe Factory.

Isle Royale National Park. This island wilderness lies in Lake Superior fifty miles off the Upper Peninsula. Moose, coyote, mink, beaver, and snowshoe rabbit find a haven here. Wildflowers grow in profusion among the hardwoods and conifers.

Lansing. State capital and important automobile manufacturing center.

Mackinac Island. Boats ferry from Mackinaw City, where automobiles are left behind. Horse-drawn buggies and bicycles provide transportation to Ft. Mackinac, Astor Fur Post, and Arch Rock. Father Marquette is buried at St. Ignace, across the Straits of Mackinac.

Sault Ste. Marie. Michigan's first permanent white settlement. Through the famous "Soo" locks and St. Marys Ship Canal passes America's greatest marine commercial tonnage.

Traverse City. Deep-sea fishing resort in the heart of cherry land. Each May the Blessing of the Cherry Blossoms is held and there is an annual Cherry Festival in mid-July.

MINNESOTA

Alexandria. Resort town in western part of state. The much discussed Kensington Runestone is on exhibit here. Runic inscription on stone tells of visit to this area by Norsemen in year 1362.

Bemidji. Named for Chief Bemidji, leader of a band of Chippewa, whose settlement was located at the present site of the city on the southern end of Lake Bemidji. The legendary stories of Paul Bunyan add to the romantic folklore of Bemidji.

Duluth. Third of Minnesota's cities in size. From the western tip of Lake Superior, the city is 800 feet above the lake level. The Duluth-Superior port is fifth only to New York City in annual tonnage.

Grand Marais. Gateway to the Arrowhead country and the Superior-Quetico canoe country.

Hibbing-Virginia. Two important mining towns in the great Mesabi Iron Range. The largest open pit iron mine in the world is at Hibbing.

Indian Reservations. The WHITE EARTH INDIAN RESERVATION is the largest; authentic Indian customs and language are maintained at the RED LAKE RESERVATION. Chippewas are predominant.

Lake of the Woods. On the Canadian border, this region is a paradise for fishers and hunters.

Minneapolis. Largest city in the state, and one of the largest flour-producing cities in the world. It has a wonderful system of boulevards, lakes, and parks, including the Falls of the Minnehaha, immortalized by Longfellow's "Hiawatha." Minneapolis is the home of the University of Minnesota and the well known Minneapolis Symphony Orchestra.

Pipestone National Monument. Famed quarries of red stone, used by the Plains Indians for material for their ceremonial pipes.

Rochester. Home of famed Mayo Clinic. Health seekers descend on Rochester from every state in the Union and from nearly every country in the world. Transient guests double the official population; because of this unique turnover of inhabitants, the town has an amazing number of apartment buildings, rooming houses, and restaurants.

St. Paul. Capitol and second largest city. The industrial, social, and educational life of the entire state revolves around the hub of St. Paul and its Twin City, Minneapolis, just across the Mississippi River.

Superior National Forest. The nation's largest wilderness park. Only by water, foot, or seaplane can the camper or fisherman traverse much of this area. Hunting is prohibited within the greater portion of its boundaries.

MISSISSIPPI

Biloxi. First permanent settlement in the lower Mississippi River Valley. At nearby Ocean Springs, now a resort, d'Iberville founded Ft. Maurepas in 1699. The Old Lighthouse, built in 1848, still blinks its warning to sailors. Beauvoir, Jefferson Davis' last home, is near the city.

Gulfport. Coastal resort. Fort Massachusetts, used as a Federal prison during the Civil War, is on Ship Island, nearby.

Jackson. State capital. At the Old Capitol the Mississippi Ordinance of Secession was passed and Jefferson Davis made his last public appearance. The State Hall of Fame and the Department of Archives and History are housed in the modern War Memorial Building. Mississippi governors since 1842 have resided at the charming old Governor's Mansion. Manship Home was the Confederate headquarters during the siege of the city.

Natchez. Famous for two annual garden pilgrimages, the town is a virtual museum of ante-bellum mansions. The old Natchez Trail, which terminated at Nashville, Tennessee, started at Natchez.

Pascagoula. Modern shipbuilding center on Pascagoula Bay. Old Spanish Fort, constructed of oyster shells and moss, was built in 1718. Horn Island Light, built on stilts over the water, affords an excellent point for study of marine life. It is eight miles from town.

Vicksburg. Site of the famous Civil-War siege which lasted forty-seven days. The battleground of this campaign is well marked in the Vicksburg National Military Park.

Washington. Second Territorial capital and first capital of the state. Under "Burr Oaks," on the campus of Jefferson Military College, Aaron Burr stood his preliminary trial for treason.

MISSOURI

Arrow Rock State Park. On the Missouri River in the central part of the state. Here is the historic

Old Tavern, built in 1834, and the Arrow Rock Academy, furnished with ante-bellum objects.

Hannibal. Important industrial city, and home of Mark Twain. Huck Finn and Tom Sawyer roamed the banks of the Mississippi River in this section. The Mark Twain Museum and Home contains much Mark Twain and Hannibal memorabilia.

Independence. Historic frontier town on the Missouri River, eastern terminal of Santa Fe and Oregon Trails; the Overland Stage started here. Permanent settlers came in 1825; the Jackson County Courthouse, still standing, was erected two years later. Independence is the home of former President Harry S. Truman and here is Truman Museum and Library.

Jefferson City. State capital. In the Capitol, of Carthage marble, are the murals of Thomas Hart Benton—a crowded design of Frankie and Johnny, Huck Finn and Nigger Jim, the James Boys, a political rally, and other subjects.

Kansas City. Second largest city, railroad center, and market place. Kansas City grew out of two frontier towns—Kansas, on the Missouri River, and Westport, four miles south, on the Santa Fe Trail. Incorporated as a city in 1853, it is noted for its packing plants and as one of the nation's largest horse and mule markets. Among the points of interest are William Rockhill Nelson Gallery of Art and Atkins Museum of Fine Arts; the $2,000,000 Liberty Memorial; Union Station, designed by Jarvis Hunt of Chicago; Swope Park, with its Zoological Gardens; and the Kansas City Museum.

Lake of the Ozarks. Large artificial lake, formed by impounding the waters of the Osage River behind Bagnell Dam. The lake is about 130 miles long and has an irregular shoreline of 1,300 miles.

Ste. Genevieve. First permanent settlement in state; noted for 18th-century French buildings.

St. Joseph. Important as a manufacturing, grain, and meat-packing center. Situated on the bluffs above the Missouri River, it was once the focal point of the trade lanes westward. This was the eastern end of the Pony Express route, and the Pony Express stables are still standing.

St. Louis. Largest city in Missouri, situated on the Mississippi River just below its junction with the Missouri. Founded by French fur traders, St. Louis is still an important market for raw furs, as well as a center for grain and the production of stoves, machinery, and other manufactures. Points of interest are the Old Courthouse, historically associated with the Dred Scott case; Wainwright Building, one of the first skyscrapers, completed in 1891; seven bridges across the Mississippi, Missouri Botanical (Shaw's) Garden, containing more than 12,000 species of trees and plants; Forest Park, site of the Louisiana Purchase Exposition in 1904; St. Louis Municipal Opera, an open-air theater seating 10,000; Jefferson Memorial, containing pioneer and

Indian relics, trophies and gifts to Charles A. Lindbergh after his 1927 trans-Atlantic flight; St. Louis Zoological Garden; and the Jefferson Expansion National Memorial, commemorating westward expansion.

MONTANA

Anaconda. Smelting point for the ores of copper and zinc that are mined at Butte; the Anaconda smelter has the world's biggest smokestack.

Bear Tooth Mountains. Spectacular high plateau, (12,799 feet altitude), carved by deep canyons and jutting precipices, in southern Montana and northern Wyoming. A scenic highway travels through the area from Red Lodge to Cooke City, at the northeastern entrance to Yellowstone National Park. One of the many peaks is Granite, highest point in Montana (12,850 feet). Nearby is Grasshopper Glacier, where grasshopper hordes are frozen in the ice.

Butte. Second largest city and center of the state's great copper-producing region. Numerous old homes and other structures compete in interest with the nearby mines.

Custer Battlefield National Monument. Within today's Crow Indian Reservation, General George A. Custer, with a command of about 262 men, made his ill-fated stand against overwhelmingly large numbers of Sioux and Cheyenne Indians. Marble slabs mark the spots where the men fell, and the cemetery also holds the graves of many soldiers and civilians removed from other forts of the Northwest.

Flathead Lake. Largest body of fresh water west of the Great Lakes, surrounded by magnificent mountain scenery. To the south is the Flathead Indian Reservation and the National Bison Range.

Fort Peck Dam. The huge earth-fill dam across the Missouri forms a 175-mile-long lake.

Glacier National Park. Almost 1,600 square miles, high at Montana's Canadian border, this park is a glacier-carved Rocky Mountain wonderland. The park has sixty small glaciers, in the process of disappearing, and nearly 200 glacier-formed lakes. Alpine flowers and other vegetation are of interest, as well as animal life, including the white mountain goat, elk, moose, bighorn sheep, deer, bear, and many others. Park is part of Waterton-Glacier International Peace Park.

Helena. Capital of Montana. Its streets still follow the line of gulches, as they did when this mining town was first laid out. Helena's oldest building still stands; the State Historical Library has a collection of Custer and Indian relics; a feature of the State Capitol is the paintings depicting the state's history.

Lewis and Clark Cavern State Park. Largest limestone cavern in the Pacific Northwest.

Virginia City. This colorful early gold mining camp has been restored to the 1865 period.

Minneapolis—Nation's Flour-Milling Center

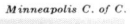

Minneapolis C. of C.

Busy Soo Locks, at Sault Ste. Marie, Michigan

Mich. Tour. Council

Glacier Nat. Park

Grinnell Glacier, in Glacier National Park

Union Pacific R.R.

Immense Hoover Dam at Night

Yellowstone and Powder Rivers. Heading in Wyoming, but traveling most of its length through Montana and draining the whole southeastern corner of the state, the Yellowstone and its tributaries are closely associated with the state's present agricultural economy and with its eventful Indian and cow-country history. On the Yellowstone are Miles City and Billings, rip-roaring cow towns in the day of cattle empires and still holding the flavor now that the range has taken on the character of irrigated ranches. Here, emptying into the Yellowstone near Miles, is the famous Powder River; from this country still comes some of Montana's best beef.

NEBRASKA

Arbor Lodge State Park. At Nebraska City, home of J. Sterling Morton, sponsor of Arbor Day and a distinguished Secretary of Agriculture. The 52-room mansion has fine pioneer and art collections; the arboretum is a mass of color from spring to fall.

Boys Town. A thousand-acre city, 11 miles from Omaha, founded by Father Flanagan for homeless boys, and managed largely by the boys themselves.

Homestead National Monument of America. Site of first land claimed under the Homestead Act of 1862. Includes Daniel Freeman's pioneer cabin.

Kearney. Near Fort Kearney State Park, site of historic Fort Kearney on the Oregon Trail. Farther west is Gothenburg, where a fur-trading post and Pony Express cabin are preserved; lower 96 Ranch, another Pony Express station, is near Gothenburg.

Kingsley Dam. This earthen dam forms the 23-mile-long Lake McConaughy, which affords excellent boating and fishing; near Ogallala.

Lincoln. Capital of the state and home of the University of Nebraska. From far across Nebraska's prairie, the towering 400-foot shaft of the modern Capitol can be seen.

Omaha. Railroad center of Nebraska and the state's largest city. From here the first transcontinental railway was built across the prairies. Points of interest include the Union Passenger Terminal, the Union Stockyards and meat-packing plants. The Joslyn Memorial, tribute to the founder of the Nebraska Western Newspaper Union, houses an art gallery and a concert hall.

Oregon Trail. Crosses the whole state of Nebraska. All along the course of the wide, shallow Platte River, choked with sand, are markers and monuments showing the path of the white-topped wagons, the Pony Express, and the Overland Stage. Later, the first transcontinental railroad was built along this path. Famous Chimney Rock may be seen along this trail.

Pioneer Village. In Minden a two-block area of twelve museum buildings houses pioneer items.

Scotts Bluff National Monument. Scotts Bluff, a great butte of sandstone and clay in the western part, was an important landmark of the Oregon Trail. Mitchell Pass, a defile through the Bluff, was made passable for wagons in 1852 and used thereafter; the Pony Express and the first transcontinental telegraph went through it. Today's Oregon Trail Museum at its foot contains relics, paintings, and dioramas of the Trail; an automobile road leads to the summit for a view of distant Trail landmarks.

Valentine. Near the junction of the Minnechaduza and Niobrara rivers. Here are dozens of small lakes offering boating, fishing, and camping.

NEVADA

Carson City. Smallest state capital; grown from a Pony Express station and mining-boom town named for Kit Carson. Besides the Capitol, points of interest include the Supreme Court and Library Building, the office of the Carson City *Daily Appeal*, where a newspaper has been published since 1865, the old firehouse, the old mint, the Abe Curry House, and other old homes. The Carson Indian Agency, School, and Museum are nearby.

Hoover (Boulder) Dam. Gigantic dam across the Colorado's Black Canyon, vital to water supply of the whole Colorado River Valley; reservoir is enormous Lake Mead, where water backs up for more than a hundred miles and spreads into tributary canyons. Lake Mead National Recreational Area, surrounding almost entire lake, makes it a vast play center.

Las Vegas. Glamorous winter-summer resort featuring gambling and spectacular shows.

Lehman Caves National Monument. Near Baker; delicate, beautiful stalactites and stalagmites.

Reno. Notorious for gambling and easy divorces, Reno is still a mining town and increasingly an all-year sports center. On the Truckee River in the Sierras, with Lake Tahoe to the south and Pyramid Lake to the north, it has great scenic attraction. The University of Nevada is at Reno.

Ruth. Site of large open-cut copper pits.

Tonopah. Famous old mining town and supply center for Nevada's south-central mining country.

Virginia City. Site of the Comstock Lode, colossal gold and silver lode that made endless millions. Largely "ghost" today, the town preserves many famous old buildings—the Crystal Bar, Piper's Opera House, International Hotel, *Territorial Enterprise* office, where Mark Twain reported and edited.

NEW HAMPSHIRE

Berlin. Northern manufacturing city, split by rushing waters of Androscoggin River, which form Berlin Falls; important ski center.

Concord. State capital. Points of interest include granite quarries, the State House, Historical Society and Museum, Kent House, State Library.

Dixville Notch. Sheer rock prominences rise on each side of a two-mile section of highway.

Franconia Notch. Deep cut between the Kinsman and Franconia ranges. Here is the 40-foot granite profile of the Old Man of the Mountain, made famous by Hawthorne's *The Great Stone Face*. In the vicinity are Indian Head, Echo Lake, Cannon Mountain Aerial Tramway, and the Flume, a deep rift with high granite walls.

Hanover. Seat of Dartmouth College, founded as an Indian school in 1769.

Lake Winnipesaukee. The state's largest lake and well-known New England resort area.

Manchester. Largest city and great industrial center. Located on Merrimack River at Amoskeag Falls, Manchester's industrial growth dates from the development of the Amoskeag Mills in 1810. Points of interest include the Manchester Historic Association Building, Home of General John Stark, Stark Park, St. Anselm's College, the Currier Art Gallery, Weston Observatory, and Massabesic Lake.

Mount Washington. Highest point in New Hampshire; a bald, rocky peak of the Presidential Range, 6,288 feet above sea level. The three-mile cog railway and a motor road lead to the summit.

Portsmouth. Port city for New Hampshire since before the Revolutionary War. Today it is a shipping and service center for the United States Navy Yard situated in the harbor. John Paul Jones' *Ranger* was built here; so was the 74-gun ship *Washington* (1815), as well as the *Kearsage* of Civil War fame. There are many notable structures in the vicinity, including Old State House, Pitt Tavern, Fort Constitution, Fort Stark, the John Paul Jones House, and the Jackson House.

NEW JERSEY

Atlantic City. Warmed by the Gulf Stream and protected by the New Jersey pine belt, this pleasure resort on the Atlantic Ocean is visited by some 16,000,000 persons annually. It is famous for its boardwalk and five great piers. The Miss America Pageant is held here every year.

Burlington. Settled by Quakers about 1677 and one time capital of the Province of West New Jersey, Burlington is most noted for its historic associations. Among its interesting old buildings are the James Fenimore Cooper House, Thomas Revel House, Friends Meeting-House, and General Grant House.

Delaware Water Gap. On the Pennsylvania border, where the Delaware River cuts through the rocky ridge of the Kittatinny Mountains, the Gap affords a pass for railroads and highways. It is surrounded by a picturesque resort section.

Edison Laboratory National Monument. At West Orange; the prototype for industrial laboratories of today. Established in 1887.

Elizabeth. Settled in 1664, Elizabeth is a residential suburb of the New York and New Jersey metropolitan area, and an important industrial center. Of interest are the Statue of the Minute Man, Boudinot House, Galloping Hill Monument, Nathaniel Bonnell House, Belcher Mansion, and others.

Highlands. Fishing village and summer resort on the Atlantic Ocean. Nearby is the Navesink Lighthouse, which flashes its beam 22 miles at sea. North of Highlands, on Sandy Hook, is the Sandy Hook Lighthouse, 85 feet high and built in 1763.

Jersey City. Situated on the Hudson River, at the western end of the Holland Tunnel, Jersey City is a shipping, manufacturing, and industrial center. Settled about 1630, the city has many reminders of its Dutch forebears, such as the Old Bergen Church and the Statue of Peter Stuyvesant.

Lakehurst. Famous for many years for the U. S. Naval Air Station for lighter-than-air ships.

Morristown National Historical Park. Headquarters for Washington and his men during the winters of 1777 and 1779-80.

Newark. Largest city in the state, active shipping port, and one of the leading manufacturing centers of the country. Newark's airport is one of the busiest in the world. Among the interesting relics of Newark's past are Military Park, used in colonial days as a drill ground; Trinity Episcopal Church built in 1743; John Plume Home, probably erected in 1710; Newark Academy, founded in 1774 and used as barracks by Revolutionary troops.

Paterson. Known as the "Silk City," because the manufacture of silk is one of its leading industries, Paterson is situated on the Passaic River, which supplies power for many manufacturing plants. Paterson Museum contains an excellent mineral exhibit and the first submarine built by John Holland in 1878.

Princeton. Seat of Princeton University, situated on a 1,300-acre campus. Most famous of the many fine buildings is Nassau Hall, built in 1756. The Chapel is the largest university chapel in America.

Trenton. Situated at the headwaters of the Delaware. Important historically, Trenton was the scene of one of the most decisive battles of the Revolution. See the Trenton Battle Monument. The State House is composed of a part of the original structure of 1792; the Annex houses the state museum.

Washington Crossing State Park. Here Washington made his famous crossing of the Delaware. McKonkey Ferry House, restored to its appearance in colonial days, is maintained as a museum.

NEW MEXICO

Acoma Pueblo. On Acoma Rock 60 miles west of the Rio Grande, this fortress-like Indian village is thought to be the oldest community in the United States. Enchanted Mesa is seen from the pueblo.

Albuquerque. Largest city and important financial and transportation center. Old Town section has much of the picturesque Spanish period; the new town is a modern business and residence section. Buildings of the University of New Mexico are in Spanish-Pueblo architecture, as are many fine residences. Of interest are Old Town Plaza, with the Church of San Felipe de Neri (built in 1706); the Sandia Mountain Rim Drive; and Isleta Indian Pueblo.

Bandelier National Monument. In the beautiful Frijoles Canyon where a northern wall is lined with cliff houses and cave rooms. On the floor of the canyon is the Tyuonyi Pueblo, with its ceremonial kivas, excavated 1908–10.

Carlsbad Caverns National Park. Vast limestone caverns, world-famous for size and beauty, are central feature of 49,448-acre park. Many miles have been explored, on three levels; but the actual size of the caverns is still unknown. In the vast chambers open to the public, huge stalactites and stalagmites and massive draperies form King's Palace, Queen's Chamber, Big Room, Giant Dome, Rock of Ages, and many others. In summer several million bats fly from the caverns every evening.

Chaco Canyon National Monument. Prehistoric Indian ruins, the Pueblo Bonito dates back more than 1,000 years and is believed to have housed in four stories 1,200 people.

Fort Sumner. Ruins of Old Fort Sumner where Kit Carson held 7,000 Navajos prisoner for four years. Billy the Kid is buried nearby.

Fort Union National Monument. Ruins of an important outpost, and guardian, of the Santa Fe Trail; near Watrous.

Gallup. Coal mining center, once an Overland Stage station; today it attracts nation-wide interest with Intertribal Ceremonial each August, when Navajos, Apaches, and Pueblo Indians gather for tribal dances. The Navajo Reservation and the Zuñi Pueblo Reservation are nearby.

Lincoln. Theater of the famous Lincoln County War of the late 1870's. Lincoln County Courthouse State Monument, branch of the Museum of New Mexico, displays local art and traveling exhibits, and houses much historical and archaeological material.

National Monuments. See BANDELIER, CHACO CANYON, FORT UNION and WHITE SANDS and U.S. NATIONAL PARK SYSTEM, pages 228-29.

Pecos. Ranch town and outfitting point for hunting and fishing on Pecos River. Nearby are ruins of Pecos Pueblo (about 1350) and Apache Canyon where Geronimo, great Apache chief, met defeat.

Santa Fe. Capital of New Mexico and a capital city for 300 years under the flags of Spain, Mexico, the Confederacy, and the United States. Oldest city in the West, it was the terminus of the Santa Fe Trail and was trade and supply center for the whole southwest for many years. Points of interest are the Plaza; the adobe Palace of the Governors, dating from the city's earliest years and housing some of the West's finest historical and archaeological collections; ancient San Miguel Church; Cathedral of St. Francis; art and historical museums; Seton Village.

Taos. Famed artists' and writers' colony. There are three settlements: Taos (Don Fernando de Taos), Spanish town, with the home and grave of Kit Carson; Taos Pueblo, with the ruins of the Mission of San Geronimo de Taos, founded in 1600; and Ranchos de Taos, an old Indian farming center, whose massive adobe church, built in 1772, is one of the most impressive in the southwest. Taos Canyon is nearby.

White Sands National Monument. Desert of glistening white gypsum near Alamogordo. In this vicinity the atom bomb was first tested.

NEW YORK

Adirondack Forest Preserve. Covering almost two-thirds of the state north of the Mohawk River, between Lakes Champlain and Ontario, this park consists of several million acres of private and public land, comprising lakes, mountains, and valley regions. Included is Adirondack Forest Preserve, more than 2,000,000 acres of primitive forest land. Famous Ausable Chasm, three miles from Lake Champlain, is in the preserve; also Lake Placid and Saranac Lake.

Albany. State capital, industrial city, and freight center. Founded in 1614 by the Dutch, it is the second oldest permanent white settlement in the thirteen colonies. Points of interest include the Capitol, costing $25,000,000, and Schuyler Mansion.

Buffalo. On the eastern end of Lake Erie, Buffalo is one of the nation's great ports and grain distributing centers. Among the points of interest are the International Peace Bridge, McKinley Monument, and Albright Art Gallery.

Catskills. Scenic wooded mountain area west of the Hudson. Kingston, the first state capital, and Rip Van Winkle country are nearby.

Finger Lakes Region. In central part of state, it includes the lakes Cayuga, Keuka, Seneca, and Watkins Glen State Park.

Lake George. This beautiful body of water lies between majestic mountains in Adirondack Forest Preserve. At its southern end are the ruins of Fort William Henry; at the northern tip is Fort Ticonderoga, captured from the British in 1775 by Ethan Allen.

Long Island. Extends from the mouth of the Hudson River 125 miles along the Connecticut coast, from which it is separated by Long Island Sound. Considered today as one of America's most important playgrounds, with great country estates, beaches, and resorts, Long Island is rich in historic tradition. The Battle of Long Island was fought here; Captain Kidd is said to have buried his gold on nearby Gardiner's Island; the Whaling Museum and Whaler's Church at Sag Harbor are interesting reminders of whaling days. At the extreme tip is Montauk Point Light.

New York City. Greatest metropolis in the world today, New York City embraces five boroughs—Manhattan, business and financial district; Queens, Brooklyn, and the Bronx, industrial and residential areas; and Richmond (Staten Island), reached by bridge. Flags of all nations may be seen on vessels in the harbor; people of all nationalities are a part of its heterogeneous population. Major among its attractions are Wall Street and the New York Stock Exchange; Central Park and other parks, boulevards, highways, and tunnels; Bronx Zoo; Aquarium; Greenwich Village; the Bowery; Chinatown, Harlem; famous cathedrals and churches; Broadway and Times Square; Metropolitan Opera; Empire State, United Nations Building, and other buildings and skyscrapers; City Hall; great museums and art galleries; General Grant's National Memorial; Statue of Liberty National Monument; Radio City; Columbia University; Brooklyn Navy Yard; Governor's Island; Coney Island.

Niagara Falls. Acclaimed one of the seven natural wonders of the world.

Poughkeepsie. Home of Vassar College, founded in 1861 as one of the first institutions in the world to offer women the same educational advantages that universities offered men. Near the city is Hyde Park, estate of the late Franklin D. Roosevelt.

Syracuse. Home of Syracuse University. Once known as "Salt City," because of its production of salt, Syracuse is rich in historic, geologic, and scenic features; Onondaga Indian Reservation nearby.

Thousand Islands. Vacation area of beautiful islands, on the St. Lawrence River.

West Point. Overlooking the Hudson River, West Point is the home of the U. S. Military Academy, established in 1802.

NORTH CAROLINA

Asheville. Mountain resort city and North Carolina's gateway to the Great Smoky Mountains

Niagara Falls, Spectacular Source of Power

Bell Aircraft Corp.

World-famous Brooklyn Bridge, New York

"NYSPIX"

Mount Hood, Oregon's Highest Mountain

Pittsburgh C. of C.

Pittsburgh's "Golden Triangle"

National Park. The magnificent Biltmore House displays a fortune in art objects. A drive over Elk Mountain Scenic Highway affords an excellent view of the plateau on which the city is located.

Cape Hatteras National Seashore Recreational Area. A 28,500-acre area preserving the flora and fauna, with beach recreational areas. Site of the old lighthouse (built in 1793), is part of the area. Wright Brothers National Memorial is also here.

Fayetteville. Market Hall, once a slave market, then the town hall, now houses the public library. Fort Bragg, a large military reservation is nearby.

Fontana Dam. The highest dam in the TVA system has formed the 30-mile-long Fontana Lake, which is a paradise for fishermen. Fontana Village is the center for this resort area.

Fort Raleigh National Historic Site. Scene, on Roanoke Island, of Sir Walter Raleigh's "lost colony." A facsimile of the setting has been made.

Great Smoky Mountains National Park. Overlaps the Tennessee-North Carolina border. This spur of the Appalachian Range contains many peaks 6,000 feet high. Virgin forest and frontier mountain communities lie in the park. See TENNESSEE.

Raleigh. State capital. The Capitol, a noteworthy example of Greek Revival architecture, is surrounded by statuary of state and national heroes. In the Hall of History, the state historical museum, all phases of North Carolina's history, from the Roanoke Colony to modern transportation, are represented.

Winston-Salem. In 1766 a Moravian group settled Salem. The Moravian Brothers' House, dating from 1769, the Home Moravian Church, and the Moravian Graveyard are reminders of the religious settlers and their influence. In 1913 Winston and Salem were united. At nearby Bethabara (Oldtown), the church and graveyard are all that remain of the original communal settlement of 1753.

NORTH DAKOTA

Badlands. A strange and fantastic region along the Little Missouri River, where the land is carved into a jumble of weirdly colored buttes, domes, ridges, pyramids, and other shapes. The Theodore Roosevelt Memorial National Park encloses the heart of the Badlands area.

Bismarck. State capital; located in the south-central part of the state, on the Missouri River. The 19-story Capitol, replacing the former building which burned in 1930, is an outstanding example of modern architecture. There are interesting Indian and pioneer relics in the Historical Society Museum. The log cabin from Theodore Roosevelt's Elkhorn Ranch stands nearby.

Crow Flies High Butte. From this vantage point the French explorer Verendrye first looked across the Missouri River.

Fargo. Largest city in North Dakota, and the chief shipping and distributing center. Because of the location there of the North Dakota State University, it is also state agricultural headquarters.

Fort Abraham Lincoln State Park. Lying on the west bluffs of the Missouri River, near Mandan, this park encloses the site of an old Mandan Indian village, now partially restored, and two frontier forts, also restored to show their original appearance.

Garrison Dam. Huge earth-fill dam at Riverdale forms 200-mile-long Garrison Lake.

International Peace Garden. A formal garden, one mile square, on the international border between North Dakota and Manitoba.

OHIO

Akron. The rubber capital of the world. Points of interest include the rubber plants, Goodyear Air Dock, Baptist Temple, and the parks.

Cincinnati. Metropolis of southern Ohio, the city is a cultural center supported by diversified industry.

Cleveland. Largest city, Lake Erie port, iron and steel center. Severance Hall is the home of the symphony, and the white marble Museum of Art houses a collection of Byzantine and European art. The Cultural Gardens are divided into sections in which each nationality presents a representative display.

Columbus. State capital, situated at the confluence of the Scioto and Olentangy rivers. The Doric-style Capitol and the beautiful Civic Center are the show places of the city.

Dayton. Industrial city and home of Wright-Patterson Air Force Base.

Fort Ancient. Prehistoric earthworks enclosing an area of 100 acres; in Warren County.

Marietta. Peaceful trading center of a large farm area. The Campus Martius Museum is built around Rufus Putnam's Block House, where early pioneers took refuge during Indian attacks.

Mound City Group National Monument. Near Chillicothe. Twenty-three prehistoric burial mounds.

Put-In-Bay. Here Commodore Perry defeated the British in the Battle of Lake Erie (1813). The Perry's Victory and International Peace Memorial National Monument commemorates this event and the subsequent peace between Canada and the United States.

Schoenbrunn Village State Memorial. At New Philadelphia. Schoolhouse, church, and cabins of early Moravian village (1772) have been restored.

Serpent Mound State Memorial. In Adams County. Mound extends for a quarter of a mile in the shape of a snake holding an egg in its mouth.

Toledo. Diversified industry supports this city, originally Anthony Wayne's Fort Industry.

OKLAHOMA

Arbuckle Mountains. Located in the south-central part of the state, these aged mountains, worn down to a height of only 700 feet above the surrounding plains, contain a great variety of geological formations of limestone, sandstone, shale, and granite.

Claremore. Rogers County seat, named for Clem Rogers, father of Oklahoma's well-known citizen, Will Rogers. The state erected the Will Rogers Memorial in Claremore on land donated by his widow.

Lake Texoma and Murray. Denison Dam on the Red River, impounds waters to form Lake Texoma, which nudges the southeastern tip of Lake Murray. Both lakes offer water sports.

Muskogee. Once capital of the Five Civilized Tribes —Cherokee, Choctaw, Chickasaw, Creek and Seminole. The Bacone University for Indians is located here, and Fort Gibson National Cemetery is nearby.

Oklahoma City. State capital and largest city. Settled in the afternoon of April 22, 1889, the date of the "Historic Run." Some of country's largest oil companies have their headquarters here, and there are many oil derricks in the city.

Platt National Park. Well-known for its sulphur, iron, bromide, and fresh water springs. Wild flowers, birds, and small game animals are also abundant.

Sequoyah Shrine. Log cabin of the famous Cherokee Indian statesman and educator. Sequoyah invented the Cherokee syllabry after being intrigued by the white man's language. The Shrine is located near Hulbert and Wagoner.

Tulsa. The state's largest oil refining center. There is a large population of Indians and white people.

Wichita Mountains Wildlife Refuge. Mountainous area lying entirely within Comanche County. Bison, elk, Texas longhorns, wild turkeys and other birds are found in this wildlife sanctuary.

OREGON

Bonneville Dam. This huge dam spans the Columbia River about 42 miles northeast of Portland, supplying electric power over a wide area, and making the Columbia River navigable for seagoing vessels as far as The Dalles. Fish ladders allow the salmon to ascend the Columbia past the dam to their spawning grounds.

Crater Lake National Park. One of the scenic wonders of America, the waters of the lake, 1,996 feet deep, are crystal clear and intensely blue. Hemmed in by steep mountain walls and towering forests, the lake lies 6,000 feet above sea level, in a sunken volcanic crater.

Mount Hood. Oregon's highest mountain, rising 11,245 feet in the Cascade Range east of Portland. Its impressive snow-capped pyramidal peak can be seen from a great distance. Comparatively easy to ascend, by tramway and chairlift, it is a popular recreational area, offering magnificent views from its summit.

Oregon Caves National Monument. A series of caverns in Elijah Mountain in the Siskiyou Range, known as "the Marble Halls of Oregon." The mountain is a labyrinth of corridors and caverns of weird beauty, filled with strange and intricate marble formations. The region around the caves has been set aside as a game refuge.

Portland. The largest city of Oregon and one of the leading lumber-shipping ports in the world; also known as "the City of Roses." The annual Rose Festival is held in June. Points of interest include the Portland Art Museum; the Civic Auditorium, which houses the Oregon Historical Society Collection; the Rough Rider Statue of Theodore Roosevelt; the statue of Sacajawea, the "Bird Woman," in Washington Park; the sunken rose gardens in Peninsula Park; and the Forestry Building.

Snake River Canyon. See IDAHO.

PENNSYLVANIA

Bethlehem. Steel city and music center; home of the Bach Festival, and of the Moravian College (1742). The log Gemein Haus (1741), is the oldest structure in the city.

Chester. Second oldest city in state, settled by the Swedes in 1644. The Caleb Pusey House, in nearby Upland, is the oldest English-built house in the state (1683). Other old-time houses are the Washington House, where General Washington stayed after the Battle of Brandywine, and the Friends Meeting-house, erected in 1736.

Delaware Water Gap. A scenic three-mile gorge in the Kittatinny Mountains near Stroudsburg. Northwest are the beautiful Pocono Mountains.

Erie. State's only port on the Great Lakes. Of historic interest are the Wayne Memorial, a reproduction of the blockhouse where "Mad Anthony" Wayne died in 1796; the Old Custom House; and Perry's flagship, the *Niagara.*

Fort Necessity National Battlefield. Reconstructed stockade, scene of opening of French and Indian Wars.

Gettysburg. Scene of the Battle of Gettysburg and site of the Soldiers' National Monument, where Lincoln delivered his immortal Gettysburg Address.

Harrisburg. State capital, on the Susquehanna River. There are six buildings in the Capitol group, including the Capitol, flanked by the George Gray Barnard sculptured group.

Lancaster County. Pennsylvania Dutch country.

Philadelphia. Fourth largest American city, important port, and great industrial center. Here starts the great Pennsylvania Turnpike, a fast four-lane highway that goes to the Ohio border, via Pittsburgh. Founded in 1682 and first capital of the United States, Philadelphia is second to no other city in historic associations. Among its many points of interest are Independence Hall, where the Liberty Bell is exhibited; Carpenters' Hall, where the first Continental Congress assembled in 1774; Benjamin Franklin's grave in the burial ground of Christ Church; Betsy Ross House; William Penn's House; the United States Mint; Bartram's Gardens; Philadelphia Zoological Gardens; Philadelphia Navy Yard; University of Pennsylvania; Philadelphia Museum of Art, and others.

Pittsburgh. Second largest city in the state and one of the greatest steel centers in the world. Pittsburgh is on the Ohio River, at the junction of the Monongahela and Allegheny rivers. The city began as the French Fort Duquesne (1754), which later became the English Fort Pitt. Points of interest are Carnegie Institute and Library; Carnegie Institute of Technology; University of Pittsburgh's Cathedral of Learning, 42-story skyscraper; Schenley Park; Liberty Tunnels, which pierce the bluff of Mount Washington; Fort Pitt Blockhouse; Stephen Collins Foster Memorial Building, Mellon Institute, and many others.

Valley Forge State Park. Here Washington camped in the winter 1777–78. Remains of entrenchments are to be seen and commemorative buildings.

RHODE ISLAND

Block Island. Pear-shaped and studded with low hills and ponds, it lies in the mouth of Long Island Sound. The Great Salt Pond which covers more than 100 acres almost bisects the island.

Charlestown. The Indian Burial Ground and Fort Neck Lot are nearby.

Narragansett. Fine beach; the old casino, the Towers, at the pier is a landmark.

Newport. Famed as an elite summer capital, the city's historic associations are often overlooked. Washington Square is the center of the old city. Nearby are Old Colony House, once the statehouse, and Friends Meeting House. Touro Synagogue, now a National Historic Site, dates from 1763. The U. S. Naval Base and Goat Island, the Navy's Torpedo Station, are in Newport. The Breakers, Vanderbilt's palatial residence, is open to the public.

Pawtucket. Home of Samuel Slater, the man who built, from memory, the first spinning frame in America, thereby founding the textile industry. The Old Slater Mill, now a memorial, contains some of the original machinery and early relics.

Providence. State capital. Built on three hills, the city was founded by Roger Williams, "Father of Rhode Island," in 1636. Old State House was seat of the General Assembly until 1901. The new Capitol, made of white marble, boasts of a dome which rivals that of St. Peter's in Rome. Rolling woodlands, notable rose gardens, and many lagoons extend throughout Roger Williams Park. Noteworthy collections are found in the Providence Athenaeum and in the libraries at Brown University.

SOUTH CAROLINA

Beaufort. Historic port town on the Intracoastal Waterway. Mellowed residences, surrounded by live oaks, front on narrow, crooked streets. Points of interest are the Oldest House, Tabby Manse, the Beaufort National Cemetery, and Fort Frederick. Parris Island, U. S. Marine base, is nearby.

Charleston. Important city and deep-sea port on the Intracoastal Waterway, six and one-half miles from the ocean. The beautiful harbor with its historic forts spreads before the palmetto-fringed waterfront—"the Battery." In the harbor is Fort Sumter, where the first shots of the Civil War were fired. Charleston gardens and those of nearby plantations have won world acclaim for more than a century. North of the city are the tropical Cypress Gardens, whose moss-laden trees grow in a freshwater lake.

Columbia. State capital. The walls of the gray-granite State House bear scars of Sherman's bombardment. The World War Memorial Building, at the University of South Carolina, houses a historic collection and a shrine to the state's soldiers.

Georgetown. Paper pulp and lumbering center. At the nearby Brookgreen Gardens an outdoor museum of statuary is set among boxwoods, oaks, and flowers. Azaleas and camellias bloom among live oaks at Belle Isle Gardens, also nearby. Myrtle Beach is a little farther up the coast.

Kings Mountain National Military Park. Third largest battlefield park in the United States. In 1780 a Whig force defeated a larger British force entrenched on the summit of the mountain, thus breaking British resistance in the South.

SOUTH DAKOTA

Angostura Dam. This dam impounds the waters of the Cheyenne River, one of the tributaries of the Missouri; near Hot Springs in the southern Black Hills. A reservoir and recreation area are nearby.

Badlands National Monument. Fantastically eroded sedimentary rock formations in many unusual pastel shades. Story book castles and temples seem very real in pink and lavender hues. A weird beauty characterizes this strange land just east of the Black Hills. Numerous fossils and rocks are found among the prickly cactus and wild flowers.

Belle Fourche. Trading center for cattle and sheep empire extending into Montana and Wyoming.

Black Hills. National forest region on the west embracing the highest mountains between the Rockies and the Appalachians. Rising dark against the surrounding colorless plains, the "black" is in reality the brown and green of lofty pines. Popular as a vacation land.

Custer State Park. Features some of the most spectacular scenery in the Black Hills—Needles highway, Sylvan Lake, and Harney Peak (7,242 feet), highest point east of the Rockies. The park covers 128,000 acres and includes a wildlife sanctuary.

Deadwood. Historic mining town and setting for Wild Bill Hickok, Calamity Jane, and other frontier characters. Deadwood Gulch was the center of gold rush of 1876. Adams Memorial Museum houses an excellent collection of pioneer mining devices. In No. 10 Saloon, Wild Bill Hickok was shot in the back holding a poker hand of aces and eights.

Lead. Mile-high city built around the fabulous Homestake Mine, largest gold mine in the Western Hemisphere. Underground shafts go down a mile.

Mt. Rushmore National Memorial. Faces of Washington, Jefferson, Lincoln, and Theodore Roosevelt, carved in granite by Gutzon Borglum, are proportioned to men 465 feet tall. Each head is 60 feet from chin to forehead, twice the height of the Great Sphinx of Egypt. A 500 word history of the United States in letters three feet high is also shown. Three tunnels through adjoining mountains are lined up to focus on Mt. Rushmore.

Pierre. Second smallest capital city in the United States. Nearby Ft. Pierre, built in 1817, is the oldest continuous settlement in the state.

Rapid City. Gateway to the Black Hills, it was the supply point for mining camps during the gold rush of 1876. Stratosphere Bowl was the takeoff point for the 72,395-foot balloon flight by General Orvil Anderson and Albert Stevens on Nov. 11, 1935. South Dakota School of Mines and Technology features fossil and mineral exhibits. Dinosaur Park has five prehistoric monsters, molded of cement.

Sioux Falls. Largest city, located on the Big Sioux River. An important processing center for farm products, it is also a cultural and medical center for a large area. Extensive use is made of locally quarried pink quartzite.

Wind Cave National Park. Located in the southern Black Hills, it is a limestone cavern featuring unusual boxwork formations; several miles of lighted routes. The temperature is always 47°F. There is a buffalo herd in the park area.

Great White Throne, Zion National Park   Union Pacific R.R.   *Mount Vernon—American Shrine*   Va. Dept. of C.&D.

Grand Coulee Dam, Washington

TENNESSEE

Andrew Johnson National Monument. Former president's home and tailor shop; at Greeneville.

Chattanooga. Manufacturing city on the Tennessee River near the Georgia border. Trips from Chattanooga lead to Lookout Mountain (which also may be reached by the Incline Railway) and to Chickamauga and Chattanooga National Military Park. Atop the mountain are the unusual rock formations of Rock City, and Point Park, vantage point for a breath-taking view of Moccasin Bend.

Great Smoky Mountains National Park. Smoky haze hovering about the multi-green mountain tops gives this scenic wonderland its name. The highway from Gatlinburg, headquarters for the Park, passes Mt. Le Conte, Mountaineer Museum, Chimney Tops, and Newfound Gap. At the Gap, trails for mountain climbers wind to the top of Clingman's Dome, highest point in Tennessee. See NORTH CAROLINA.

Knoxville. Industrial center and farm market, especially for tobacco. About 20 miles north is Norris Dam. Oak Ridge, a few miles northwest, features the American Museum of Atomic Energy.

Memphis. Largest city, inland port, and cotton market. The Cotton Exchange is the hub of the city's economy. The annual Cotton Carnival, in May, draws thousands of visitors.

Meriwether Lewis Monument. Honors co-leader of famous western expedition and marks his place of death at Grinder's Inn and his grave.

Nashville. Capital and second largest city. The grounds of the Capitol exhibit statues of Tennessee's prominent people. A replica of Fort Nashborough (1780) is built on its original site; "the Parthenon," a reproduction of the Athenian structure, stands in Centennial Park. Near the city, Andrew Jackson's home, "The Hermitage," remains much as it was when he lived there.

National Military Parks. See U. S. NATIONAL PARK SYSTEM, page 228-229.

TEXAS

Amarillo. Commercial center of the Panhandle section, Amarillo has developed from a barren prairie to a thriving metropolis. Helium gas is produced in large quantities here. Southeast of Amarillo is the spectacular Palo Duro Canyon.

Austin. State capital, commercial city, and home of the University of Texas. Planned by the founders of the Republic of Texas, Austin was the national capital until Texas became a state in the United States. Points of interest are the Capitol and grounds, Governor's Mansion, former French Legation, O. Henry Museum, and others.

Big Bend National Park. Vast frontier area located in a picturesque section of Mexican-border wilderness, in the big bend of the Rio Grande. Spectacular mountains, desert, and canyon areas contain a variety of unusual geological formations.

Dallas. Industrial and commercial city, cotton market and oil center. The city is modern in every way, with beautiful parks and highways, theaters and museums. Points of interest are the John Neely Bryan Cabin, reconstructed on the site where the founder of the city built his home in 1843; Dallas Cotton Exchange; Southern Methodist University; Museum of Fine Arts, and others.

El Paso. Opposite Juarez, Mexico, on the Rio Grande, El Paso dates from the time of the Spanish conquistadores. Today it is a thriving commercial center and important port of entry. Noteworthy are Texas Western College; Fort Bliss, once the largest cavalry post in the United States; and International Bridge.

Galveston. One of the largest cotton ports in the world, year-round resort, and commercial city. Galveston lies on the eastern extremity of Galveston Island, which parallels the Texas mainland. Interesting are the sea wall, built to prevent a disaster similar to the Galveston Flood of 1900; the landlocked harbor; the coast-defense forts.

Houston. Largest city and important port, especially for the export of cotton and oil. Although 50 miles inland, Houston is connected with the Gulf Coast by the Houston Ship Channel. Points of interest are the Hermann Park Zoo, Rice University, and museums. The San Jacinto Battlefield and State Park, where the *Texas* is berthed, is nearby.

Kingsville. Home of Texas College of Arts and Industries; headquarters of million-acre King Ranch.

San Antonio. Historic old city and busy industrial community. Among its many interesting places are the Alamo, where 187 Americans made their last stand; San Fernando Cathedral; Spanish Governor's Palace; Mexican quarter; Franciscan Missions; La Villita; Randolph and Kelly fields.

UTAH

Bingham Canyon. Largest open cut copper mine in world; highway leads to observation points from which operations can be seen in the many-tiered pit. Town is a single street, three miles long.

Bryce Canyon National Park. Vast amphitheater filled with pink and white sandstone eroded into myriads of spires, shafts, minarets, and like formations; sharply defined stratification heightens the color. The highway winds along the west rim with frequent short side roads to viewpoints at the very edge, from which are seen such groups as Fairyland, Queen's Gardens, Fairy Castle, Wall of Windows.

Natural Bridges National Monument. Three massive natural bridges have been cut through red sandstone by the eroding action of the river; Sipapu, largest and most beautifully proportioned, is 220 feet above the canyon floor. Similar natural bridges and arches are found throughout southern Utah. For other National Monuments, see U. S. NATIONAL PARKS SYSTEM, pages 228-229.

Salt Lake City. Capital of the state, home of the University of Utah, and one of the most beautiful cities in America. Wide and shaded streets, green lawns of beautiful homes, spacious grounds of the Capitol, are in sharp contrast to the encroaching desert. The Capitol itself holds a masterful exhibit of the resources and the means by which this green empire has been wrested from an arid wasteland. Famous all over the world are the beautiful Mormon Temple and the Tabernacle with its great dome put together with wooden pegs; in its auditorium a 10,000-pipe, hand-built organ is played every noon in public concert. Nearby is Great Salt Lake, where a swimmer can't sink because the water is so salty. The Great Salt Lake Desert holds the Bonneville Salt Flats that supply much of the world's salt.

Zion National Park. In all the world there is no more awe-inspiring sight than the great shafts and temples and sheer walls that rise from the bottom of Zion Canyon, where the road winds. Vermilion toward the base, they blend to rose, to pink, and finally to white, adding the glow of red and white fire to majestic line and towering height. Some of the formations are the Temple of Sinawava, Angel's Landing, the Great White Throne, the Great Arch.

VERMONT

Barre. Granite center. Cutting and polishing of granite can be watched at the Granite Sheds, which stretch along the floor of the valley.

Bennington. Textile mills and furniture plants in new section. Old First Church, Walloomsac Inn, the Ethan Allen House and the Tichenor Mansion in old section. On a nearby hill is the 300-foot Bennington Battle Monument.

Burlington. Largest city, lake port, and home of the University of Vermont. Historic points are Battery Park, site of big guns in the War of 1812; Green Mountain Cemetery, where Ethan Allen and other soldiers are buried; Ethan Allen Park.

Grand Isle. Several islands and a peninsula, all in Lake Champlain, comprise this resort isle.

Green Mountains. This magnificent chain of rounded, verdant peaks bisects the state and extends from the Massachusetts line to the Canadian border. The highest point in the range, Mt. Mansfield, is also the highest point in the state. Scenic points near here are Smuggler's Notch, Bingham Falls.

Montpelier. From every approach to the city the golden dome of the State Capitol can be viewed. Museum of Natural History contains the Daye Press.

Mount Equinox. Highest mountain overlooking the Vermont valley; has skyline drive to summit.

Rutland. Industrial center surrounded by great marble fields. Methods of cutting and finishing marble and exhibits are shown at nearby Proctor.

VIRGINIA

Appomattox Court House National Historical Park. Commemorates Lee's surrender to Grant on April 9, 1865. For National Military Parks, Battlefield Parks, etc., see U. S. NATIONAL PARK SYSTEM, page 228-229

Arlington National Cemetery. Burial ground of the nation's heroic dead. The Tomb of the Unknown Soldier is here, as is the Custis-Lee Mansion.

Colonial National Historical Park. Park includes Jamestown, first permanent English settlement, which has reconstructed Glasshouse and Jamestown Festival Park; Yorktown, where Cornwallis surrendered; and a parkway between these two places and Williamsburg.

Fredericksburg. Washington's mother's home and Kenmore, his sister's home, are here, as is James Monroe's law office, and the home of John Paul Jones. East of the city, reached by State Route 3, is Stratford Hall, birthplace of Robert E. Lee, and built by his family 1725-30.

Monticello. Home of Thomas Jefferson, third president of the United States. His tomb is here.

Mount Vernon. Famous country place of George Washington, standing since 1743 and filled with Washington treasures.

Natural Bridge. Higher than Niagara, it spans the Cedar Creek; near Lexington.

Norfolk and Portsmouth. Location of Naval Station and Navy Yard, respectively. In vicinity are Newport News, site of immense shipbuilding plant, Hampton Roads, and Virginia Beach, popular resort.

Richmond. State capital since 1779 and Confederate capital from 1861 to 1865. The Capitol, designed by Thomas Jefferson, has Houdon's marble figure of Washington. Other points of interest are the Edgar Allan Poe Shrine, St. John's Church,

Chief Justice John Marshall's Home, Confederate Museum, Hall of Delegates.

Shenandoah National Park. Embraces a portion of the Blue Ridge Mountains. Scenic Skyline Drive traverses the Park. Luray Caverns are nearby.

Williamsburg. Home of the College of William and Mary and subject of extensive restoration to the 18th-century days when Williamsburg was the colonial capital of Virginia.

WASHINGTON

Grand Coulee. A 50-mile dry gorge cut 800 feet deep during glacial times by an ice-diverted Columbia River. At mid point is Dry Falls, once the greatest waterfall known to have existed in North America. Grand Coulee Dam, 550 feet high and 4,173 feet long, furnishes electric power to all parts of the state. Surplus power pumps water 300 feet higher into Grand Coulee, where retaining dams create a huge reservoir. From here it spreads south and east into the Columbia Basin, to irrigate, ultimately, a million acres.

Mt. Rainier National Park. Rising from near sea level to over 14,410 feet, Mt. Rainier, dormant if not extinct volcano, is the dominant natural feature of the state. Park has permanent snow fields and glaciers, high meadows and crystal clear lakes, great variety of trees and flowers. Paradise Valley on south side has hotel and camping; Yakima Park on north, cabin camp and picnic grounds. Summit climb of two days starts from Paradise Inn.

Olympia. New capitol buildings on impressive site overlooking Budd Inlet emphasize character of city as state capital. Suburb of Tumwater, first American settlement on Puget Sound (1845). Gateway to famed Olympic Peninsula recreation area.

Olympic National Park. Occupies the heart of rugged Olympic Peninsula between Pacific Ocean and Puget Sound; preserves primeval forests of giant trees and native animal life, zones ranging from temperate rain forests to mountain glaciers.

Puget Sound Islands. These include beautiful Vashon and Bainbridge, island suburbs of Tacoma and Seattle; Whidbey, the second largest in the United States and connected to the mainland by a bridge across tide-ripped Deception Pass; the San Juan group of nearly 200 habitable islands and hundreds of barren rocks; and scores of others. Protected waters and sheltered coves are a paradise for yachtsman, fisherman, picnicker, and camper.

Seattle. Metropolis of Washington and the Pacific Northwest. Salt water harbor of Elliott Bay rimmed by port facilities for largest ocean going vessels; fresh water harbor via government locks a haven for fishing and pleasure boats. Scenic boulevards link waterfronts with hilltops and provide views of distant mountains. University of Washington, farmers' Public Market, Frozen Fish Museum, Volunteer Park Conservatory, Smith Cove docks, and Lake Washington Bridge are of interest. Industries are varied—lumbering, airplane manufacturing, aluminum fabrication, shipbuilding, and others. Snoqualmie Falls are to the east.

Spokane. Metropolis of the so-called "Inland Empire"—portions of four states between Cascade and Rocky Mountains. Flour mills, lumber mills, and light metal industries are based upon agricultural, timber, and power resources. Spokane Falls in heart of city supplied water-power for original settlement (1871). Nearby lakes and Mt. Spokane provide summer and winter recreation.

Tacoma. Important lumber manufacturing center. Large smelter handles copper ores from all parts of the world. In Point Defiance Park is full size replica of Hudson's Bay Co. Fort Nisqually, first white settlement in the area. Nearby Fort Lewis is one of largest permanent army posts.

Vancouver. River fort and industrial center; dates from Hudson's Bay Co. post of 1825 (Fort Vancouver National Historic Site) when fur-trading and trapping brigades fanned out in all directions. Aluminum industry, based on low-cost power from Bonneville Dam, and wood-processing plants now are major activities.

Walla Walla. Old Fort Walla Walla of fur-trading days was at Wallula; Waiilatpu Mission of Marcus Whitman is now in Whitman National Monument.

WEST VIRGINIA

Berkeley Springs. Historic spa, willed to the state by Lord Fairfax. The Washington Elm, Lovers' Leap, and the Castle are of interest.

Charleston. State capital and state's largest city, near coal, natural gas, and oil fields. The gold-leaf dome of the State Capitol rises 300 feet above the ground. "Stonewall" Jackson Monument and Pioneer Monument are on the Capitol grounds.

Charles Town. In the Eastern Panhandle. The town is named for Charles Washington, brother of George; his home "Harewood" is preserved. John Brown stood trial at the Jefferson County Courthouse and was hanged at Site of John Brown Gallows.

Grave Creek Mound. At Moundsville. It is the largest conical Indian mound in the country.

Harpers Ferry. John Brown Monument marks site of the engine house where the abolitionist made his last stand; "John Brown's Fort," part replica and part reconstruction of the engine house, is on the campus of Storer College. Harpers Ferry National Monument includes Federal hillsides surrendered to Jackson, thus permitting his quick juncture with Lee at Antietam.

Huntington. Picturesquely situated on the Ohio, the state's second largest city is an industrial center primarily known for its huge nickel plant.

Monongahela National Forest. A vacation land along the eastern boundary. Points of interest include Spruce Knob, highest point in the state; Blackwater Falls, which drop 63 feet and rush through a 1,000-foot gorge; "Pictured Rocks" at Petersburg Gap, and nearby Smoke Hole Caverns; the eroded, castle-like white sandstone mountain, Seneca Rock, near Mouth of Seneca; and the Sinks, near Osceola, where the Gandy River goes underground.

Wheeling. Industrial center, leading city of the Northern Panhandle. Oglebay Park contains Mansion Museum, Nature Museum, Greenhouse and Conservatory, and recreational facilities.

White Sulphur Springs. A popular spa since the 1800's. The President's Cottage has housed several Chief Executives since the time of Andrew Jackson, and the Robert E. Lee Cottage remains unchanged.

WISCONSIN

Ashland. Center of hunting area; nearby is beautiful Copper Falls State Park. A side trip leads to Bayfield and from here the offshore Apostle Islands in Lake Superior can be visited.

Big Manitou Falls. Highest waterfall in the state. In Pattison State Park, south of Superior, Black River cascades 165 feet down a narrow, rocky gorge.

Devil's Lake State Park. Unusual rock formations and geological curiosities. Of glacial origin, Devil's Lake is hemmed in by towering cliffs 400 to 500 feet high; near West Baraboo.

Green Bay. State's oldest settlement and gateway to Door Peninsula, famed for cherry blossoms.

Lake Geneva. Fashionable summer resort; many fine estates. Sailboat races are popular on lake. World-famous Yerkes observatory, of the University of Chicago, is at Williams Bay.

Lake Winnebago. Largest lake in state and extensive summer-winter vacation area.

Madison. Capital of Wisconsin and site of the University of Wisconsin; on narrow isthmus between Lake Monona and Lake Mendota, with three other lakes close by. The Capitol, second in height only to the National capitol in Washington, has the only granite dome in the United States.

Milwaukee. Largest city in Wisconsin and important center for the manufacture of heavy machinery. It is also noted for its many large breweries, some of which conduct tours for visitors. Has a Lake Michigan harbor and many fine parks. Among the points of interest are the botanical gardens of Mitchell Park; Court of Honor, with its war memorials; Milwaukee Public Library and Museum.

Prairie du Chien. The second oldest settlement in the state, this picturesque little city has numerous reminders of the old fur-trading days.

Rib Mountain. Near Wausau; 1,941 feet above sea level, highest point in Wisconsin; popular winter sports area, with majestic scenic views from summit.

Superior. Sister city to Duluth. *See* MINN.

Wisconsin Dells. Spectacular rock formations formed by the Wisconsin River as it dashes through eight miles of rocky gorges. Tribal ceremonies by the Winnebago Indians are a summer feature.

WYOMING

Casper. Trading center for rich oil fields (Teapot Dome is to the north) and lively cattle country; on Oregon Trail and rich in frontier history.

Cheyenne. Wyoming's capital; founded as a construction terminus for the building of the first transcontinental railroad, today an important transportation and trade center. Drawing much of its wealth from the cattle industry, it is world-famous for its Cheyenne Frontier Days celebration (July). Points of interest include the Capitol, Ft. Warren, Frontier Park, the State Historical Museum.

Cody. Near entrance of Yellowstone National Park and Shoshone Canyon and Dam; founded by Buffalo Bill Cody; it contains statue and museum of his effects.

Devils Tower National Monument. The first National Monument; of columnar basalt, it rises 865 feet high; northwest of Sundance.

Fort Bridger. Historic trading post established by the famous frontiersman, Jim Bridger.

Fort Laramie National Historic Site. Trade, military, and supply outpost for many years before and during wagon travel on the Oregon Trail; called "Cradle of American civilization in the west." Some original buildings are still standing.

Fort Washakie. Agency for Shoshone Indian Reservation; Sacajawea and Chief Washakie buried here.

Grand Teton National Park. Vistas of shining gray-blue peaks, snow-frosted, reflected in sky-blue lakes amid close ranks of spruce and fir—these are the Tetons. No less typical is the little log Church of the Transfiguration, its altar window framing Grand Teton Peak. Jackson and Jenny are two of several beautiful lakes; adjacent is the famous Jackson Hole country.

Hot Springs State Park. Hot mineral springs. Big Horn Spring is world's largest, flowing 18,000,000 gallons (135°) a day. At Thermopolis.

Independence Rock. On the Sweetwater; famed landmark of Oregon Trail. Called "Register of the Desert" by Father De Smet (1840), it bears 5,000 names scratched by explorers, traders, and emigrants.

Sheridan. Gateway to the Big Horn Mountains; outfitting point for dude and cattle ranches. To the south are sites of Ft. Phil Kearney and Wagon Box Fight, famous turning-point of the Red Cloud War.

Yellowstone National Park. Probably the most famous of all the national parks, the Yellowstone is a fabulous combination of mountains and canyons, lakes and waterfalls, spouting geysers and wildlife that includes moose, buffalo, grizzly bear, and trumpeter swan. Old Faithful Geyser, errupting regularly every hour, is hallmark to the Park. Others that play at more or less regular intervals are Jewel, Daisy, Rocket, and Grotto; the spectacular Grand Geyser performs about every 16 to 20 hours. Many pools, like sparkling blue Morning Glory, terraces like Mammoth Hot Springs, and boiling mud pots are of interest. Yellowstone Canyon and Falls are among the world's most beautiful; from Fishing Bridge almost anyone can catch a trout.

NATIONAL PARKS AND MONUMENTS MAP
OF THE
UNITED STATES

COPYRIGHT BY RAND McNALLY & COMPANY
MADE IN U.S.A.

U.S. NATIONAL PARK SYSTEM Showing Parks, Monuments, and Other National Units

Name	Year Established	Location	Gross Acreage	Description
PARKS				
Acadia	1929	Maine	41,634	Wilderness area on Mount Desert Island, Schoodic Point, and Isle au Haut
Big Bend	1944	Texas	708,221	Spectacular mountains and deserts in bend of Rio Grande
Bryce Canyon	1928	Utah	36,010	Wonderland of colorful rocks and pinnacles
Canyonlands	1964	Utah	257,640	Mesas, canyons, and pinnacles resulting from centuries of erosion
Carlsbad Caverns	1930	N.Mex.	46,786	Immense limestone caverns with brilliantly colored formations
Crater Lake	1902	Oreg.	160,290	High cliffs encircle deep-blue lake in extinct volcano crater
Everglades	1947	Fla.	1,400,533	Subtropical area; mangrove swamps; rare birds and plants
Glacier	1910	Mont.	1,013,129	Part of Waterton-Glacier International Peace Park
Grand Canyon	1919	Ariz.	673,575	Tremendous gorge; ever-changing colors; fantastic rock shapes
Grand Teton	1929	Wyo.	310,350	Majestic, snow-capped peaks, lakes, and evergreen forests
Great Smoky Mountains	1934	N.C.-Tenn.	512,674	Highest eastern mountains; primeval hardwood forests
Haleakala	1961	Hawaii	26,403	One of world's largest dormant volcanoes
Hawaii Volcanoes	1961	Hawaii	220,345	Active volcanoes; tropical forests; tree ferns
Hot Springs	1921	Ark.	1,032	Forty-seven historically famous mineral hot springs
Isle Royale	1940	Mich.	539,347	Forested island in Lake Superior; large moose herd
Kings Canyon	1940	Calif.	454,713	Imposing peaks and canyons; giant sequoias
Lassen Volcanic	1916	Calif.	106,934	Recently active volcano; many lakes and volcanic exhibits
Mammoth Cave	1941	Ky.	51,354	Beautiful limestone caverns, underground rivers, and lakes
Mesa Verde	1906	Colo.	52,074	Well-preserved prehistoric cliff dwellings and pueblo houses
Mount McKinley	1917	Alaska	1,939,493	Highest mountain in N.A.; glaciers; interesting wildlife
Mount Rainier	1899	Wash.	241,983	Glaciers radiating from snow-capped peak; dense forests
Olympic	1938	Wash.	896,599	Mountain wilderness; luxuriant forests of huge evergreens
Petrified Forest	1962	Ariz.	94,189	Spectacular display of petrified wood; part of Painted Desert
Platt	1906	Okla.	912	Cold mineral springs, some of which contain bromides
Rocky Mountain	1915	Colo.	262,324	Magnificent mountain scenery; interesting wildlife
Sequoia	1890	Calif.	386,863	Immense groves of sequoias; Mt. Whitney and other peaks
Shenandoah	1935	Va.	212,304	Blue Ridge Mountains; Skyline Drive
Theodore Roosevelt National Memorial	1947	N.Dak.	70,435	Section of badlands and part of Roosevelt's Elkhorn Ranch
Virgin Islands	1956	Virgin Is.	15,150	A tropical area having historic and prehistoric interest
Wind Cave	1903	S.Dak.	28,059	"Boxwork" limestone caverns in Black Hills; buffalo herd
Yellowstone	1872	Wyo-Mont.-Idaho	2,221,773	World's greatest geyser area; bubbling hot springs and colorful pools; beautiful Yellowstone Falls; wildlife sanctuary
Yosemite	1890	Calif.	760,951	Spectacular gorges, domes, and waterfalls; giant sequoias
Zion	1919	Utah	147,035	Colorful canyon, displaying picturesque rock formations
MONUMENTS				
Arches	1929	Utah	34,010	Giant arches, bridges, windows, spires eroded from sandstone
Aztec Ruins	1923	N.Mex.	27	Ruins of 12th-century prehistoric Indian town
Badlands	1939	S.Dak.	111,530	Deeply eroded hills containing prehistoric animal fossils
Bandelier	1916	N.Mex.	29,661	Prehistoric Indian ruins of the later Pueblo period
Black Canyon of the Gunnison	1933	Colo.	13,683	Remarkably deep, narrow gorge of great geologic interest
Booker T. Washington	1957	Virginia	200	Memorial to the famous educator and reformer
Buck Island Reef	1961	Virgin Is.	850	One of the finest marine gardens in the Caribbean Sea
Cabrillo	1913	Calif.	81	Memorial to Juan Cabrillo, discoverer of San Diego Bay, 1542
Canyon de Chelly	1931	Ariz.	83,840	Prehistoric Indian ruins built in caves; modern Navajo homes
Capitol Reef	1937	Utah	39,173	Twenty-mile-long buttressed cliff of colored sandstone
Capulin Mountain	1916	N.Mex.	775	Large cinder cone of a recently extinct volcano
Casa Grande Ruins	1918	Ariz.	473	Adobe tower built by the Indians 600 years ago
Castillo de San Marcos	1942	Fla.	22	Oldest masonry fort in Continental U.S.—built by Spanish
Castle Clinton	1950	N.Y.	1	Through its door, 1855-90, 7,500,000 people entered America
Cedar Breaks	1933	Utah	6,155	Brilliantly colored amphitheater 2000 feet deep; eroded cliffs
Chaco Canyon	1907	N.Mex.	21,509	Most extensive Indian ruins in the U.S.; shows Pueblo culture
Channel Islands	1938	Calif.	18,167	Sea lion rookery; other interesting wildlife, fossil beds
Chesapeake and Ohio Canal	1961	Md.-W.Va.	4,475	One of the least altered of the older American canals
Chiricahua	1924	Ariz.	10,646	Strange rock shapes depict billion years of geologic history
Colorado	1911	Colo.	17,362	Deep canyons with weirdly eroded red-sandstone walls
Craters of the Moon	1924	Idaho	53,545	Craters, lava flows, caves and other volcanic Phenomena
Custer Battlefield	1946	Mont.	765	Site of battle in which Custer and all his men were killed
Death Valley	1933	Calif.-Nev.	1,907,760	Colorful desert area; lowest point in Western Hemisphere
Devils Postpile	1911	Calif.	798	Sixty-foot basaltic cliff, composed of blue-gray columns
Devils Tower	1906	Wyo.	1,347	Fluted tower of volcanic rock, 865 feet high
Dinosaur	1915	Utah-Colo.	206,234	Well-preserved fossils of many dinosaurs; spectacular canyons
Effigy Mounds	1949	Iowa	1,468	Indian mounds shaped like birds and other animals
El Morro	1906	N.Mex.	1,279	Monolith inscribed by early Spaniards and Americans
Fort Frederica	1945	Ga.	250	Built by Oglethorpe, 1736, as defense against the Spaniards
Fort Jefferson	1935	Fla	47,125	Huge masonry fortification; notable bird refuge; marine life
Fort McHenry National Monument and Historic Shrine	1939	Md.	43	Its defense, 1814, inspired writing of "Star Spangled Banner"
Fort Matanzas	1924	Fla.	258	Historical Spanish fort built, 1737, to protect St. Augustine
Fort Pulaski	1924	Ga.	5,517	Southern fortress important in the Civil War
Fort Sumter	1948	S.C.	2.4	Scene of first battle of the Civil War
Fort Union	1956	N.Mex.	721	Site of an old fort erecteed to protect the Santa Fe Trail
Geo. Washington Birthplace	1930	Va.	394	Memorial house and gardens on site of Washington's birthplace
Geo. Washington Carver	1951	Mo.	210	Site of birthplace and childhood home of famous scientist
Gila Cliff Dwellings	1907	N.Mex.	533	Remains of dwellings built in face of an overhanging cliff
Glacier Bay	1925	Alaska	2,274,595	Area of receding glaciers and post-glacial forests
Grand Canyon	1932	Ariz.	198,280	Portion of the Grand Canyon, including Toroweap Point
Grand Portage	1960	Minn.	770	Portage on principal route of Indians, explorers, missionaries and fur traders into the Northwest
Gran Quivira	1909	N.Mex.	611	Ruins of 17th-century Spanish mission and Indian pueblo
Great Sand Dunes	1932	Colo.	36,740	Very large and high shifting sand dunes
Homestead	1939	Nebr.	163	First claim under the Homestead Act of 1862
Hovenweep	1923	Utah-Colo.	505	Several groups of cliff dwellings, pueblos, and towers
Jewel Cave	1908	S.Dak.	1,275	Series of limestone rooms incrusted with calcite crystals
Joshua Tree	1936	Calif.	557,992	Desert area containing a fine stand of the rare Joshua tree
Katmai	1918	Alaska	2,697,590	Crater of Katmai Volcano; Valley of Ten Thousand Smokes
Lava Beds	1925	Calif.	46,239	Volcanic formations; scene of Modoc Indian War, 1873
Lehman Caves	1922	Nev.	640	Limestone caverns containing stalactites and other formations
Montezuma Castle	1906	Ariz.	842	Unusually well-preserved, 5-story, 20-room cliff dwelling
Mound City Group	1923	Ohio	68	Prehistoric Indian mounds
Muir Woods	1908	Calif.	503	Virgin forest of Coast redwoods and other interesting plants
Natural Bridges	1908	Utah	7,600	Three bridges carved from sandstone walls by running water
Navajo	1909	Ariz.	360	Three large and elaborate cliff dwellings
Ocmulgee	1936	Ga.	683	Mounds and other remains constructed by Southern mound-builders
Oregon Caves	1909	Oreg.	480	Caverns containing unique limestone formations
Organ Pipe Cactus	1937	Ariz.	330,874	Desert area containing rare cactus species
MONUMENTS (Continued)				
Perry's Victory and International Peace Memorial	1936	Ohio	21	Monument to Perry's naval victory and amity with Canada
Pinnacles	1908	Calif.	14,498	Rock spires 500-1200 feet high; caves of volcanic origin
Pipe Spring	1923	Ariz.	40	Historic fort and other Mormon structures
Pipestone	1937	Minn.	283	Quarry from which Indians obtained materials for peace pipes
Rainbow Bridge	1910	Utah	160	Greatest known natural bridge—a rainbow in stone
Russell Cave	1961	Ala.	310	Believed to have been continuously inhabited by stoneage men from 7000 B.C. to 1650 A.D.
Saguaro	1933	Ariz.	78,644	Forest of giant saguaro cactus and other rare desert plants
Scotts Bluff	1919	Nebr.	3,084	High bluff on Oregon Trail—landmark for early wagon trains
Sitka	1910	Alaska	54	Scene of last stand of Kik-Siti Indians against Russians
Statue of Liberty	1924	N.Y.	10	Famous statue on Liberty Island—gift of the French people
Sunset Crater	1930	Ariz.	3,040	Volcanic cone with highly colored rim; ice caves; lava flows
Timpanogos Cave	1922	Utah	250	Brilliantly colored caves on the slope of Mt. Timpanogos
Tonto	1907	Ariz.	1,120	Two 14th-century Pueblo Indian cliff dwellings
Tumacacori	1908	Ariz.	10	Site of historic Spanish mission dating from 1691
Tuzigoot	1939	Ariz.	43	Excavated ruins of large pueblo dating from 1000-1400
Walnut Canyon	1915	Ariz.	1,879	Cliff dwellings built in shallow caves along canyon walls
White Sands	1933	N.Mex.	146,535	Sand dunes 10 to 60 feet high, composed of snow-white gypsum
Wupatki	1924	Ariz.	35,545	Red-sandstone pueblo believed built by ancestors of Hopis
HISTORICAL PARKS, SITES, AND MEMORIALS				
Abraham Lincoln Birthplace	1959	Ky.	117	Log cabin thought to have been Lincoln's birthplace
Adams	1952	Mass.	5	Home of John Adams and John Quincy Adams, U.S. Presidents
Andrew Johnson	1963	Tenn.	17	President Johnson's tailor shop, home, and grave
Appomattox Court House Park	1954	Va.	972	Scene of Robert E. Lee's surrender to Grant in Civil War
Bent's Old Fort	1963	Colo.	178	One of the most significant fur-trading posts of the West
Chalmette Park	1939	La.	136	Part of site of the Battle of New Orleans, War of 1812
City of Refuge Park	1961	Hawaii	182	An area preserving the history of the Polynesian people and early Hawaiian culture
Colonial Park	1936	Va.	9,430	Jamestown Isl., Cape Henry Mem., Yorktown, Williamsburg Parkway
Coronado Mem.	1952	Ariz.	2,834	Place where Coronado entered U.S. (1540-42) to explore southwest
Cumberland Gap Park	1955	Ky.-Tenn.-Va.	20,190	Gap through which passed the main artery of the great trans-Allegheny migration
Custis-Lee Mansion Mem.	1955	Va.	3	Home of the Confederate General Robert E. Lee
De Soto Mem.	1949	Fla.	30	Commemorates landing of De Soto in Florida, 1539
Edison	1962	N.J.	18	Glenmont, home of Thomas Alva Edison from 1886 until his death, 1931; also includes his laboratory, stock room and library
Federal Hall Mem.	1955	N.Y.	.45	Subtreasury building; site of first seat of U.S. Government
Fort Caroline Mem.	1953	Fla.	120	Overlooks site of French colony of 1564
Fort Clatsop Mem.	1958	Ore.	125	Commemorates Lewis & Clark's winter camp
Fort Davis	1963	Texas	460	Ruins of Army post used from 1854 to 1891
Fort Laramie	1960	Wyo.	564	Military post on Oregon Trail, famous in covered-wagon days
Fort Raleigh	1941	N.C.	144	Scene of Sir Walter Raleigh's "Lost Colony" settlement
Fort Smith	1964	Ark.	14	One of the first U.S. military posts in the Louisiana Territory
Fort Vancouver	1961	Wash.	90	Site of stockaded fur trading post from 1824 to 1846
General Grant Mem.	1959	N.Y.	1	Memorial to the commander of the Union armies
Hampton	1948	Md.	45	Eighteenth-century Georgian mansion
Harpers Ferry Park	1963	W. Va.-Md.	1,500	Scene of John Brown's famous raid in 1859
Home of Franklin D. Roosevelt	1945	N.Y.	94	Birthplace and home of President F. D. Roosevelt
Hopewell Village	1938	Pa.	848	Ruins of an 18th- and early 19th-century iron-making village
House Where Lincoln Died Mem.	1896	D.C.	.05	Petersen House, where Lincoln was taken after he was shot
Independence Park	1956	Pa.	22	Structures in Philadelphia associated with the founding of the U.S.
Jefferson National Expansion Mem.	1935	Mo.	85	Riverfront area in St. Louis commemorating westward expansion
Lincoln Boyhood Mem	1963	Ind.	200	Site of Lincoln's residence from ages 7 to 21
Lincoln Mem.	1911	D.C.	.61	White-marble structure enclosing seated figure of Lincoln
Lincoln Museum Mem.	1866	D.C.	.18	Site of Ford's Theatre, where Abraham Lincoln was shot
Minute Man Park	1959	Mass.	750	Site of Revolutionary War skirmish
Morristown Park	1933	N.J.	958	Washington's Headquarters, 1779-80, and other historical sites
Mount Rushmore Mem.	1925	S.Dak.	1,278	Features of four great Presidents carved on face of mountain
Sagamore Hill	1963	N.Y.	75	Victorian-style home of Theodore Roosevelt on Long Island
Salem Maritime	1938	Mass.	11	Several buildings important in New England maritime history
San Juan	1949	P.R.	40	16th Century fortifications guarding San Juan Harbor
Saratoga Park	1948	N.Y.	5,500	Scene of the defeat of Burgoyne, British general, in 1777
Theodore Roosevelt Birthplace	1963	N.Y.	.11	New York City birthplace of President Roosevelt
Thomas Jefferson Mem.	1934	D.C.	1	Structure in classic style introduced in America by Jefferson
Vanderbilt Mansion	1940	N.Y.	212	Palatial residence of the "Gay Nineties"
Washington Monument Mem.	1848	D.C.	.37	An obelisk 555 feet high—memorial to George Washington
Whitman Mission	1963	Wash.	98	Site of mission where Indians massacred Whitman family
Wright Brothers Mem.	1953	N.C.	425	Commemorates Wright brothers' airplane flight at Kitty Hawk
RECREATION AREAS				
Cape Cod National Seashore	1961	Mass.	44,600	An immense area of historical interest, geological significance, and beaches and dunes for recreation
Cape Hatteras Seashore	1953	N.C.	28,500	Extensive beaches with surf fishing and waterfowl refuge
Coulee Dam	1946	Wash.	98,500	Dam forms Franklin D. Roosevelt Lake extending to Canada
Glen Canyon	1958	Ariz.-Utah	1,239,985	Third highest dam in world—forms Lake Powell
Lake Mead	1947	Ariz.-Nev.	1,936,978	Formed by Hoover Dam across the gorge of the Colorado River
Padre Island Seashore	1962	Texas	137,241	80 miles of subtropical offshore bar; excellent fishing
Point Reyes Seashore	1962	Calif.	53,000	Peninsular area containing beaches, meadows and timberland
Shadow Mountain	1952	Colo.	18,240	Included is Shadow Mountain Lake and Granby Reservoir

MILITARY PARKS, BATTLEFIELDS, AND CEMETERIES

Name	Location	Name	Location	Name	Location
Antietam (Battlefield and Cemetery)	Md.	Fredricksburg and Spotsylvania Co. Battlefields Mem.	Va.	Moores Creek (Military Park)	N.C.
Battleground (Cemetery)	D.C.	Fredricksburg (Cemetery)	Va.	Pea Ridge (Military Park)	Ark.
Big Hole (Battlefield)	Mont.	Gettysburg (Military Park and Cemetery)	Pa.	Petersburg (Battlefield)	Va.
Brices Cross Roads (Battlefield)	Miss.	Guilford Courthouse (Military Park)	N.C.	Poplar Grove (Cemetery)	Va.
Chickamauga and Chattanooga (Military Park)	Ga.-Tenn.	Horseshoe Bend (Military Park)	Ala.	Richmond (Battlefield Park)	Va.
Cowpens (Battlefield)	S.C.	Kennesaw Mountain (Battlefield Park)	Ga.	Shiloh (Military Park and Cemetery)	Tenn.
Fort Donelson (Military Park and Cemetery)	Tenn.	Kings Mountain (Military Park)	S.C.	Stones River (Battlefield and Cemetery)	Tenn.
Fort Necessity (Battlefield)	Pa.	Manassas (Battlefield Park)	Va.	Tupelo (Battlefield)	Miss.
				Vicksburg (Park and Cemetery)	Miss.
				Yorktown (Cemetery)	Va.

U.S. STATE CLIMATIC AND ECONOMIC TABLE

State	Topography	Climate Information				Principal Mineral Products	Principal Agricultural Products	Principal Forest and Fishery Products	Principal Manufactures
		Weather Station	Annual Rainfall	January Mean Temp.	July Mean Temp.				
ALABAMA	Mountainous in north and northeast; southward the land gradually slopes to sea level.	Birmingham Mobile	53.52 in., 67.57 in.,	45.2°F., 52.7°F.,	79.6°F. 80.7°F.	Coal, cement, iron ore, stone, lime, sand & gravel, clays, natural gas.	Poultry and eggs, cotton, cattle, dairy products, hogs, peanuts, corn, cottonseed, soybeans, potatoes.	Shortleaf and loblolly pine, longleaf and slash pine, oak, gum, naval stores; shrimp, red snapper.	Steel rolling, textiles, paper products, rubber & plastics, iron & steel products, lumber & wood products.
ALASKA	Very high elevations in E. Broad, rolling, central plateaus, wide river valleys; NE.–W., mountain range sloping gradually to Arctic.	Anchorage Fairbanks	14.27 in., 11.92 in.,	13.0°F., −9.8°F.,	57.3°F. 60.9°F.	Coal, gold, sand & gravel, petroleum, mercury, stone, natural gas, copper, silver, clay.	Dairy products, field crops, poultry & poultry products, vegetables, cattle, sheep, hogs, horses.	Western hemlock, spruce lodgepole pine; salmon, halibut, herring, crabs.	Canned and frozen salmon & other fish products, lumber & wood products, newspapers.
ARIZONA	South—high plains with scattered mountains; north—plateaus, rough mountains, Grand Canyon of Colorado River.	Flagstaff Tucson	18.47 in., 10.66 in.,	25.3°F., 49.7°F.,	65.2°F. 86.2°F.	Copper, sand & gravel, zinc, uranium, molybdenum, stone, gold, silver, lime, lead.	Cotton, cattle, lettuce, dairy products, cottonseed, hay, cantaloups, barley, poultry & eggs.	Ponderosa pine, Douglas fir, true firs, spruce.	Printing & publishing, concrete products, dairy products, lumber & wood products, machinery.
ARKANSAS	Boston Mountains and Ouachita Mountains in northwest, separated by Arkansas River Valley; rest of state slopes southeast to Mississippi River.	Little Rock El Dorado	47.38 in., 51.58 in.,	41.8°F., 47.1°F.,	81.9°F. 82.9°F.	Petroleum, bauxite, stone, sand & gravel, natural gas, natural gas liquids, coal, barite, clays, gypsum, gem stones.	Cotton, poultry & eggs, soybeans, cattle, rice, dairy products, cottonseed, hogs, turkeys, wheat, peaches.	Shortleaf and loblolly pine, oak, gum, hickory, cypress, walnut, cottonwood; buffalofish, catfish.	Lumber & wood products, paper products, chemicals, shoes, primary metals, electrical machinery, clothing, furniture.
CALIFORNIA	Coast Ranges along western edge, bisected by Central Valley; Sierra Nevada inland; low areas in southeast at Death Valley and Imperial Valley.	Los Angeles San Francisco San Diego Sacramento Eureka	14.54 in., 17.43 in., 10.86 in., 16.32 in., 36.15 in.,	55.0°F., 47.9°F., 54.9°F., 45.2°F., 47.2°F.,	72.5°F. 60.4°F. 69.3°F. 75.3°F. 56.4°F.	Petroleum, natural gas, cement, sand & gravel, natural gas liquids, stone.	Cattle, dairy products, cotton, poultry & eggs, grapes, oranges, tomatoes, hay, lettuce, potatoes, turkeys,	Douglas fir, true firs, Ponderosa pine, redwood, sugar pine, lodgepole pine; tuna, sardines, crabs, salmon.	Metal products, electrical machinery, aircraft, machinery, chemicals, printing & publishing, canned & frozen foods.
COLORADO	Great Plains in east rise abruptly westward to high ranges of Rocky Mountains; Colorado Plateau in west central part.	Denver Sterling Pueblo Grand Junction	13.43 in., 14.00 in., 11.87 in., 9.06 in.,	31.4°F., 24.8°F., 29.4°F., 24.0°F.,	73.7°F. 74.2°F. 74.9°F. 78.2°F.	Petroleum, molybdenum, uranium ore, coal, sand & gravel, natural gas, natural gas liquids, zinc.	Cattle, wheat, sugar beets, dairy products, sheep, potatoes, dry edible beans, hay, poultry & eggs, hogs.	Spruce, lodgepole pine, Ponderosa pine, true firs, cottonwood, aspen, Douglas fir.	Machinery, metal products, meat products, dairy products, beverages, newspapers.
CONNECTICUT	Wide central Connecticut Valley; coastal plain rises inland to hills in east, low mountains in west.	Hartford New Haven	40.48 in., 44.99 in.,	27.0°F., 29.1°F.,	73.8°F. 71.2°F.	Stone, sand & gravel, lime, clays, peat, beryllium concentrate, gem stones.	Poultry & eggs, dairy products, tobacco, cattle, potatoes, apples, tomatoes, sweet corn, turkeys.	Oysters, clams, flounders, lobsters, scup or porgy, scallops, shad, cod, swordfish, butterfish, sea bass.	Electrical machinery, rubber & plastics, chemicals, precision instruments, copper rolling, hardware.
DELAWARE	Low plain, swampy along coast; low rolling hills in north.	Dover	46.40 in.,	36.8°F.,	77.2°F.	Sand & gravel, clays, stone.	Poultry & eggs, corn, soybeans, dairy products, potatoes, cattle, lima beans, hogs.	Menhaden, oysters, clams, crabs, sea trout or gray weakfish, flounders, white perch, shad.	Periodicals, chemicals, clothing, metal products, primary metals, rubber & plastics, animal feeds.
FLORIDA	Generally low and flat; many swamps, most extensive in south (The Everglades); many lakes in central part.	Jacksonville Pensacola Tampa Miami	52.08 in., 61.60 in., 49.94 in., 47.20 in.,	55.9°F., 54.0°F., 61.5°F., 68.5°F.,	82.1°F. 81.0°F. 81.7°F. 81.6°F.	Phosphate rock, stone, cement, titanium concentrate, clays, sand & gravel, lime.	Oranges, dairy products, cattle, tomatoes, poultry & eggs, grapefruit, tobacco, potatoes, snap beans.	Naval stores, longleaf and slash pine, cypress, gum; shrimp, mullet, red snapper, catfish and bullheads.	Paper products, canned & frozen food, metal products, concrete & plaster, agricultural chemicals.
GEORGIA	Ridges of the southern Appalachian Mountains in northwest, separated from wide coastal plain by Piedmont.	Atlanta Macon Savannah	49.16 in., 46.31 in., 45.75 in.,	44.6°F., 49.5°F., 51.6°F.,	79.5°F. 82.4°F. 81.2°F.	Clays, stone, cement, sand & gravel, iron ore, mica sheets, talc & soapstone, peat, coal.	Poultry & eggs, cotton, tobacco, hogs, peanuts, cattle, dairy products, corn, pecans, peaches.	Longleaf and slash pine, shortleaf and loblolly pine, gum, oak, cypress, poplars; shrimp, crabs, shad.	Textiles, transportation equipment, paper, clothing, lumber & wood, machinery.
HAWAII	Rugged with young volcanoes, lava slopes, small plains areas.	Honolulu	21.70 in.,	72.2°F.,	78.8°F.	Stone, sand & gravel, pumice, cement.	Pineapples, sugar, poultry & eggs, cattle, coffee, vegetables, hogs.	Sandalwood, ohia, lehua, kukui, koa; tuna, snapper, marlin, big-eye scad.	Sugar products, canned & frozen food, printing, clothing, bakery products.
IDAHO	High Snake River plains in south and west; Bitterroot and other rugged mountain ranges to north, east, and south.	Boise Idaho Falls Lewiston	11.48 in., 7.69 in., 13.12 in.,	27.3°F., 15.7°F., 30.8°F.,	74.8°F. 69.2°F. 75.2°F.	Silver, phosphate rock, lead, zinc, sand & gravel, copper, stone, mercury.	Cattle, potatoes, wheat, dairy products, sugar beets, dry edible beans, sheep, hay, poultry & eggs.	Douglas fir, Ponderosa pine, true firs, sugar and white pines, spruce, lodgepole pines, hemlock.	Lumber & wood products, chemicals, dairy products, frozen fruits & vegetables, printing, machinery.
ILLINOIS	Broad, plain, undulating and ridged in north, hilly in extreme south.	Chicago Rockford Springfield	33.28 in., 36.36 in., 36.65 in.,	27.4°F., 24.0°F., 27.4°F.,	75.2°F. 75.3°F. 76.3°F.	Petroleum, coal, stone, sand & gravel, cement, natural gas, natural gas liquids.	Cattle, hogs, corn, soybeans, dairy products, wheat, poultry & eggs, oats, sheep, hay, turkeys, sweet corn, tomatoes.	Oak, hickory, maple; catfish, buffalofish, carp, chubs.	Electrical machinery, metal products, printing & publishing, primary metals, chemicals, heavy machinery, precision instruments.
INDIANA	Undulating glaciated plains with many lakes in north; sand dunes along Lake Michigan; rocky hill lands in south.	Indianapolis South Bend Evansville	39.69 in., 35.59 in., 41.37 in.,	28.8°F., 24.6°F., 34.7°F.,	76.0°F. 73.4°F. 78.2°F.	Coal, cement, stone, petroleum, sand & gravel, clays.	Hogs, cattle, corn, soybeans, dairy products, poultry & eggs, wheat, turkeys, tomatoes, oats.	Oak, soft maple, hickory, walnut, sugar maple, poplar, gum; buffalofish, carp, catfish.	Steel products, electrical machinery, automobiles & parts, chemicals, machinery, metal products.
IOWA	Land slopes gradually eastward to Mississippi River; undulating to rolling surface.	Des Moines Sioux City Davenport	30.74 in., 24.90 in., 34.27 in.,	22.1°F., 19.1°F., 24.3°F.,	76.2°F. 76.3°F. 77.3°F.	Cement, stone, sand & gravel, gypsum, coal, clays.	Cattle, hogs, corn, dairy products, poultry & eggs, soybeans, turkeys, sheep, oats, hay, wheat.	Oak; catfish, buffalofish, sheepshead.	Meat products, farm machinery, electrical machinery, grain mill products, printing & publishing.
KANSAS	Rolling, valley-cut plain in east; high, gently undulating plain in west. Elevations increase gradually westward.	Topeka Wichita Dodge City	33.28 in., 30.70 in., 20.58 in.,	29.9°F., 32.0°F., 30.3°F.,	80.6°F. 80.9°F. 79.9°F.	Petroleum, natural gas, cement, stone, salt, natural gas liquids, sand & gravel, coal, clays, zinc.	Cattle, wheat, sorghum, dairy products, hogs, poultry & eggs, corn, soybeans, hay, sheep, barley, turkeys.		Aircraft, chemicals, meat products, petroleum refining, machinery, grain mill products.
KENTUCKY	Southeast—Appalachian ridges and valleys; south central—highland rim; north central—Bluegrass plain.	Frankfort Bowling Green	43.55 in., 48.67 in.,	36.6°F., 38.7°F.,	77.7°F. 79.4°F.	Coal, petroleum, stone, natural gas, sand & gravel, fluorspar.	Tobacco, cattle, dairy products, hogs, poultry & eggs, corn, soybeans, wheat, sheep, hay.	Oak, hickory, beech, poplar, shortleaf and loblolly pine, maple, ash, walnut; catfish, buffalofish.	Tobacco, electrical machinery, chemicals, distilled liquor, machinery, metal products.
LOUISIANA	Broad Mississippi Valley on eastern border, with delta at southeast; west undulating to rolling; coastlands marshy.	New Orleans Shreveport	63.54 in., 45.10 in.,	55.9°F., 47.8°F.,	83.1°F. 85.5°F.	Petroleum, natural gas, natural gas liquids, sulfur, salt, sand & gravel, stone.	Cotton, cattle, rice, dairy products, sugarcane, poultry & eggs, soybeans, sweet potatoes.	Shortleaf and loblolly pine, oak, gum, tupelo, hickory, walnut, naval stores; shrimp, menhaden, oysters.	Chemicals, petroleum products, paper, primary metals, lumber & wood products, sugar.
MAINE	Rugged, dissected by numerous stream valleys; coast fringed with promontories and rocky islands.	Portland Farmington	41.78 in., 44.47 in.,	20.7°F., 18.3°F.,	67.8°F. 69.3°F.	Sand & gravel, stone, cement, clay, gem stones.	Poultry & eggs, potatoes, dairy products, cattle, apples, blueberries, hay, oats, hogs, lettuce.	Spruce and balsam fir, red and white pine, birch; shellfish, lobsters, perch, herring, clams, haddock.	Paper, leather, textiles, lumber & wood products, transportation equipment, canned & frozen food.
MARYLAND	Parallel mountain ridges in west; rolling hill lands in central part; coastland lowlands in East, penetrated by Chesapeake Bay.	Baltimore Frederick	42.59 in., 40.23 in.,	34.2°F., 32.7°F.,	76.3°F. 76.7°F.	Stone, sand & gravel, coal, natural gas, clays, gem stones.	Poultry & eggs, dairy products, cattle, tobacco, corn, soybeans, hogs, wheat, tomatoes, apples.	Oak, poplar, gum, pine; shellfish, oysters, crabs, clams, bass, shad, fluke.	Primary metals, chemicals, clothing, communication equipment, machinery, ships, beverages.
MASSACHUSETTS	West—hilly to mountainous, split by Connecticut Valley; Berkshire Hills in far west; rolling lowlands on the coast, with Cape Cod extension.	Boston Springfield New Bedford	38.76 in., 44.87 in., 41.43 in.,	29.1°F., 28.8°F., 31.8°F.,	72.2°F. 74.2°F. 72.0°F.	Sand & gravel, stone, lime, clay, gem stones.	Dairy products, poultry & eggs, tobacco, cattle, apples, hogs, potatoes, sweet corn, turkeys, hay, tomatoes, carrots, lettuce.	Pine, oak; shellfish, haddock, perch, yellowtail, cod, whiting, lobsters, pollock, clams, blackback, fluke, sole, alewives.	Electrical machinery, machinery, leather products, textiles, printing, paper, clothing, rubber & plastics, transportation equipment.
MICHIGAN	Northern peninsula—hilly, with mountain ranges in west; southern peninsula—rolling, glaciated surface with many moraines.	Detroit Grand Rapids Sault Ste. Marie	31.03 in., 31.50 in., 30.19 in.,	26.2°F., 23.5°F., 13.8°F.,	73.1°F. 71.5°F. 63.9°F.	Iron ore, cement, petroleum, sand & gravel, gypsum, salt, stone, clays, natural gas, peat, copper.	Dairy products, cattle, wheat, poultry & eggs, corn, dry edible beans, hogs, apples, cherries.	Maple, hemlock, pine, fir; chubs, herring, trout, pike, perch, whitefish, smelt.	Automobiles & parts, food products, chemicals, metal working machinery, steel products, paper.
MINNESOTA	Glaciated surface dotted with lakes and swamps; Mesabi and other ranges in northeast.	Minneapolis Duluth Bemidji	24.71 in., 29.72 in., 21.95 in.,	14.6°F., 8.3°F., 4.9°F.,	74.1°F. 66.4°F. 68.5°F.	Iron ore, granite, dolomite, sandstone, sand & gravel, clay, manganiferous ore.	Cattle, dairy products, hogs, poultry & eggs, corn, soybeans, turkeys, wheat, oats, barley.	Cottonwood and aspen, oak, red and white pine, jack pine, spruce and balsam fir; herring, pike.	Machinery, meat products, printing, paper, chemicals, electrical machinery.
MISSISSIPPI	Rolling to hilly, sloping gently to south and west; Yazoo-Mississippi Delta in west.	Jackson Greenville Biloxi	50.86 in., 51.69 in., 57.59 in.,	48.3°F., 47.0°F., 54.2°F.,	82.1°F. 82.4°F. 81.8°F.	Petroleum, natural gas, sand & gravel, clays, natural gas liquids, stone.	Cotton, poultry & eggs, cattle, dairy products, soybeans, cottonseed, hogs, corn, rice, pecans.	Shortleaf and loblolly pine, oak, gum, longleaf and slash pine, hickory, naval stores; shellfish, shrimp.	Forest products, paper, clothing, transportation equipment, lumber & wood products, chemicals.
MISSOURI	Highly dissected Ozark Plateau in south; Missouri River traverses northern hill lands from west to east.	St. Louis Kansas City Springfield	37.86 in., 35.31 in., 41.51 in.,	33.3°F., 30.0°F., 32.7°F.,	80.6°F. 80.9°F. 77.5°F.	Cement, stone, lead, lime, sand & gravel, iron ore, barite, zinc, copper, natural gas, silver.	Cattle, hogs, dairy products, soybeans, corn, poultry & eggs, cotton, wheat, turkeys, sheep.	Oak, hickory, shortleaf and loblolly pine, walnut, cottonwood, aspen, maple; buffalofish, catfish, carp.	Automobiles, chemicals, printing, leather, machinery, electrical machinery, clothing.
MONTANA	Rockies cover western third; remainder consists of plateaus and undulating plains.	Butte Great Falls Billings	12.67 in., 14.03 in., 13.10 in.,	14.2°F., 22.7°F., 22.9°F.,	62.4°F. 69.6°F. 73.3°F.	Petroleum, copper, sand & gravel, chromium ore & concentrate, silver, zinc, natural gas, manganese ore.	Cattle, wheat, barley, dairy products, sheep, sugar beets, wool, hay, hogs, poultry & eggs.	Douglas fir, Ponderosa pine, lodgepole pine, spruce, sugar and western white pine.	Lumber & wood products, petroleum, printing & publishing, dairy products, sugar, beverages.

GIVING THE VARIOUS PRINCIPAL PRODUCTS AND MANUFACTURES FOR EACH U.S. STATE

State	Topography	Climate Information				Principal Mineral Products	Principal Agricultural Products	Principal Forest and Fishery Products	Principal Manufactures
		Weather Station	Annual Rainfall	January Mean Temp.	July Mean Temp.				
NEBRASKA	Platte River flows eastward through undulating sand-and-loess-covered plains; foothills of the Rockies in far west.	Omaha Grand Island Scottsbluff	25.90 in., 22.70 in., 15.00 in.,	23.0°F., 23.0°F., 23.5°F.,	78.5°F. 78.5°F. 74.6°F.	Petroleum, sand & gravel, stone, natural gas liquids, natural gas, clays.	Cattle, corn, wheat, hogs, dairy products, poultry & eggs, sorghum grain, sheep, sugar beets, hay, soybeans.		Packed meat, grain mill products, printing & publishing, metal products, dairy products, machinery.
NEVADA	Broken series of roughly parallel ranges and basins with a north to south orientation. High Sierra Nevada on west.	Carson City Las Vegas Elko	11.50 in., 4.35 in., 9.13 in.,	31.7°F., 44.2°F., 21.9°F.,	69.6°F. 90.5°F. 70.2°F.	Copper, sand & gravel, iron ore, manganese ore, gypsum, gold.	Cattle, dairy products, hay, sheep, wool, cotton, wheat, onions, potatoes, hogs, barley, cottonseed.	Ponderosa pine, true firs.	Concrete & plaster products, newspapers, lumber & wood products, dairy products.
NEW HAMPSHIRE	North central—rugged, culminating in White Mountains; high ridges separate Connecticut and Merrimac river valleys; low coastal plain in southeast.	Concord Berlin	37.23 in., 39.13 in.,	20.1°F., 16.0°F.,	69.0°F. 66.6°F.	Sand & gravel, mica, stone, clays, gem stones, feldspar.	Dairy products, poultry & eggs, apples, cattle, hay, potatoes, turkeys, hogs, maple, snap beans.	Red and white pine, birch, maple, spruce and balsam fir, hemlock; shellfish, lobster, smelt.	Leather footwear, textiles, machinery, paper, electrical machinery, lumber & wood products, printing & publishing, food products.
NEW JERSEY	Southern half—low coastal plain, stream-indented coastline with protecting sand bars; northern half—parallel ridges and valleys.	Trenton Atlantic City	40.06 in., 41.77 in.,	32.6°F., 35.8°F.,	75.3°F. 73.6°F.	Stone, sand & gravel, clays, lime, iron ore, uranium, peat.	Poultry & eggs, dairy products, tomatoes, cattle, asparagus, peaches, potatoes, blueberries, apples, corn, hogs.	Oak, beech, maple, gum, poplar; shellfish, menhaden, clams, flounders, oysters, scup or porgy, bass, shad, perch.	Chemicals, electrical machinery, transportation equipment, machinery, metal products, clothing, primary metals.
NEW MEXICO	Rolling plains & plateaus; scattered mountain ranges running north to south; Rio Grande & Pecos valleys drain southward.	Albuquerque Roswell	8.68 in., 12.07 in.,	33.7°F., 39.6°F.,	79.0°F. 79.0°F.	Petroleum, natural gas, potassium salts, uranium ore, natural gas liquids, copper, sand & gravel.	Cattle, cotton, dairy products, wheat, hay, sorghum grain, sheep, poultry & eggs, cottonseed.	Ponderosa pine, Douglas fir, spruce, true firs, cottonwood, aspen.	Food products, lumber & wood products, petroleum & coal products, newspapers.
NEW YORK	Rolling plateau; Adirondacks in northeast, Catskills in southeast, separated by Mohawk Valley; Hudson-Champlain lowland along eastern border.	New York Buffalo Albany	42.03 in., 32.29 in., 35.81 in.,	32.9°F., 25.5°F., 25.2°F.,	74.6°F. 70.6°F. 73.1°F.	Stone, sand & gravel, iron ore, salt, zinc, abrasive garnet, petroleum, gypsum, clays, natural gas.	Dairy products, poultry & eggs, cattle, potatoes, apples, grapes, wheat, snap beans, dry edible beans, hay, onions, tomatoes.	Maples, beech, white and red pine, hemlock, firs; shellfish, clams, oysters, lobster, whiting, bass.	Clothing, printing & publishing, electrical machinery, machinery, chemicals, transportation equipment, precision instruments.
NORTH CAROLINA	Coastal plain in eastern third; Piedmont Uplands in central; Blue Ridge and Smoky Mountains along western border.	Asheville Raleigh Winston-Salem	37.22 in., 45.05 in., 43.15 in.,	39.4°F., 41.4°F., 39.3°F.,	73.8°F. 78.5°F. 77.5°F.	Stone, sand & gravel, feldspar, mica, clays, asbestos, talc & pyrophyllite, silver.	Tobacco, poultry & eggs, dairy products, hogs, corn, cotton, cattle, peanuts, soybeans, wheat, turkeys.	Shortleaf and loblolly pine, oak, gum, cypress, poplar, hickory, hemlock; menhaden, shellfish, crabs.	Textiles, cigarettes, furniture, chemicals, electrical machinery, clothing, paper products.
NORTH DAKOTA	Red River Valley on eastern border; central section, glaciated plains; west, Missouri Plateau cut by Missouri River system.	Bismarck Grand Forks Williston	15.40 in., 20.05 in., 14.66 in.,	9.2°F., 4.4°F., 10.0°F.,	72.1°F. 70.7°F. 70.9°F.	Petroleum, sand & gravel, coal, natural gas, clays, stone, natural gas liquids.	Wheat, cattle, barley, flaxseed, dairy products, hogs, potatoes, poultry & eggs, oats, sheep, sugar beets.	Bullheads, carp, catfish, suckers, buffalofish, perch, burbot, shovelnose.	Dairy products, newspapers, meat products, concrete products.
OHIO	Nearly level plains in north; rolling glacial plains in west; dissected Allegheny Plateau in southeast.	Cleveland Columbus Cincinnati	32.08 in., 34.36 in., 39.34 in.,	28.5°F., 31.1°F., 34.6°F.,	73.7°F. 75.8°F. 78.1°F.	Coal, cement, stone, sand & gravel, lime, salt, petroleum, clays, natural gas.	Dairy products, hogs, cattle, corn, poultry & eggs, wheat, soybeans, tomatoes, oats, turkeys, sheep, tobacco, apples.	Oak, hickory, maple, beech; pike, perch, catfish, bass, carp, sheepshead, whitefish, suckers, bullheads.	Iron & steel products, transportation equipment, machinery, electrical machinery, metal products, rubber products, chemicals.
OKLAHOMA	Ouachita Mountains in southeast; rolling prairies and high plains rising westward.	Oklahoma City Tulsa Lawton	30.22 in., 37.68 in., 29.68 in.,	37.1°F., 37.4°F., 41.1°F.,	82.1°F. 82.1°F. 83.9°F.	Petroleum, natural gas, natural gas liquids, stone, coal, sand & gravel, helium.	Cattle, wheat, cotton, dairy products, poultry & eggs, hogs, peanuts, pecans, hay, sorghum grain.	Shortleaf and loblolly pine, oak, hickory.	Petroleum refining, aircraft, metal products, oilfield machinery, meat products, glass.
OREGON	Broad Cascade Range separates wide Willamette Valley and Coast Range from lava plateaus and basins in southeast, and from mountains in northeast.	Portland Klamath Falls	39.91 in., 13.94 in.,	39.5°F., 29.2°F.,	68.5°F. 68.7°F.	Stone, sand & gravel, nickel, cement, clays, mercury, gold, pumice, gem stones, copper.	Cattle, wheat, dairy products, poultry & eggs, potatoes, barley, hay, beans, pears, strawberries, sheep, hogs, turkeys.	Douglas fir, Ponderosa pine, true firs, hemlock, sugar and western white pine; salmon, tuna, shellfish, crabs, flounders.	Lumber & wood products, canned & frozen fruits & vegetables, paper, iron & steel products, dairy products, machinery.
PENNSYLVANIA	Rolling piedmont in southeast; folded ranges of Appalachians from northeast to southwest; Allegheny Plateau in north and west.	Pittsburgh Philadelphia Scranton	36.23 in., 41.13 in., 40.49 in.,	33.0°F., 33.2°F., 26.9°F.,	75.4°F. 76.3°F. 72.2°F.	Coal, cement, stone, natural gas, petroleum, sand & gravel, clays, lime, zinc.	Dairy products, poultry & eggs, cattle, corn, hogs, wheat, potatoes, tobacco, apples, turkeys, hay, peaches, tomatoes.	Oak, maple, hemlock, white and red pine.	Iron & steel products, heavy machinery, metal products, electrical machinery, chemicals, clothing, glass.
RHODE ISLAND	Glaciated highland in west; Narragansett Bay penetrates rolling eastern lowlands; Block Island lies 10 miles off shore.	Providence	39.63 in.,	28.7°F.,	71.0°F.	Stone, sand & gravel.	Dairy products, poultry & eggs, potatoes, cattle, apples, hogs, tomatoes, sweet corn, turkeys, hay.	Shellfish, clams, scup or porgy, yellowtail, butterfish, fluke, lobster, blackback, menhaden.	Textiles, jewelry, machinery, printing & publishing, metal products, silverware.
SOUTH CAROLINA	Coastal plain occupies three-fifths of state; in remainder, Piedmont Upland rises to Blue Ridge Mountains on northwest border.	Charleston Columbia Greenville	45.99 in., 46.15 in., 47.65 in.,	51.4°F., 47.0°F., 43.0°F.,	81.5°F. 81.4°F. 78.4°F.	Stone, clay, sand & gravel, mica.	Tobacco, cotton, poultry & eggs, dairy products, soybeans, peaches, corn, cottonseed, wheat, oats.	Shortleaf and loblolly pine, gum, oak, cypress, poplar, maple; shellfish, shrimp, oysters, crabs, menhaden.	Textiles, chemicals, clothing, paper, lumber & wood products.
SOUTH DAKOTA	Black Hills and Badlands in southwest; Missouri River Valley separates glaciated plains in east from high, dissected plains of west.	Sioux Falls Aberdeen Rapid City	25.24 in., 19.63 in., 17.10 in.,	14.2°F., 11.0°F., 21.1°F.,	74.8°F. 73.9°F. 72.3°F.	Gold, sand & gravel, stone, cement, uranium ore, feldspar, clays, mica, silver.	Cattle, hogs, wheat, poultry & eggs, dairy products, corn, sheep, oats, flaxseed, wool, barley.	Ponderosa pine, cottonwood and aspen; carp, bullheads, buffalofish, suckers.	Meat products, dairy products, newspapers, wood products.
TENNESSEE	Regions from east to west; Smoky Mountains; parallel valleys; eroded Cumberland Plateau; Nashville Basin; sloping plains to Mississippi River Valley.	Memphis Nashville Chattanooga	46.81 in., 45.03 in., 53.60 in.,	41.9°F., 39.9°F., 41.6°F.,	81.3°F. 80.0°F. 78.3°F.	Stone, cement, zinc, coal, phosphate rock, copper, sand & gravel, clays.	Cotton, cattle, dairy products, tobacco, hogs, poultry & eggs, soybeans, corn, cottonseed, wheat, apples, strawberries, hay.	Oak, hickory, poplar, shortleaf and loblolly pine, gum; catfish, buffalofish, carp, paddlefish.	Chemicals, metal products, plastics, textiles, clothing, paper, printing & publishing, wood products, footwear.
TEXAS	Gulf coastal plain in east; broad, rolling, central plains; high, rolling plateaus in west; mountains extreme southwest.	Houston Dallas Amarillo El Paso San Antonio	45.37 in., 34.42 in., 21.12 in., 7.83 in., 27.93 in.,	53.8°F., 45.7°F., 35.3°F., 43.4°F., 50.6°F.,	83.8°F. 85.5°F. 77.8°F. 81.3°F. 84.2°F.	Petroleum, natural gas, natural gas liquids, cement, sulfur, stone, sand & gravel.	Cotton, cattle, sorghum grain, wheat, cottonseed, rice, hogs, sheep, mohair, wool, peanuts, turkeys.	Shortleaf and loblolly pine, oak, gum, longleaf and slash pine; shellfish, shrimp, menhaden, snapper, trout.	Chemicals, petroleum refining, aircraft & parts, metal products, construction equipment, oilfield machines.
UTAH	High Colorado Plateau in east; basins and ranges in west; Great Salt Lake Plain in northwest; high mountains in northeast.	Salt Lake City Logan Richfield	14.74 in., 17.03 in., 8.19 in.,	26.5°F., 23.6°F., 28.0°F.,	76.6°F. 73.5°F. 71.8°F.	Copper, petroleum, coal, uranium ore, iron ore, gold, asphalt, lead, natural gas.	Cattle, dairy products, poultry & eggs, turkeys, sheep, sugar beets, wheat, hay, wool, potatoes, hogs.	Spruce, lodgepole pine, Ponderosa pine, Douglas fir, true fir, cottonwood and aspen.	Primary metals, petroleum refining, construction machinery, metal products, concrete & plaster products.
VERMONT	The Green Mountains are the main feature; Champlain lowlands in northwest; Connecticut River forms eastern border.	Burlington Rutland	32.22 in., 38.67 in.,	17.9°F., 21.5°F.,	70.4°F. 69.5°F.	Stone, sand & gravel, asbestos, clays, lime, talc, gem stones.	Dairy products, cattle, poultry & eggs, apples, hay, maple, potatoes, hogs, turkeys.	Birch and maple, spruce and balsam, fir, beech, hemlock, white and red pine, oak, walnut.	Machinery & machine tools, paper products, cut stone & stone products, lumber & wood products.
VIRGINIA	Coastal plain merges with Piedmont Upland; Great Valley lies between Blue Ridge and other Appalachian ranges in west.	Richmond Norfolk Roanoke	42.89 in., 43.26 in., 41.58 in.,	38.3°F., 41.5°F., 37.9°F.,	77.5°F. 77.5°F. 75.9°F.	Coal, stone, sand & gravel, lime, zinc, clays, cement, gypsum, gem stones, iron ore.	Dairy products, tobacco, poultry & eggs, cattle, peanuts, hogs, apples, soybeans, turkeys, corn.	Oak, shortleaf and loblolly pine, poplar, gum, hickory, maple and beech, ash, walnut; shellfish, oysters.	Fibers, plastics & rubber, cigarettes, textiles, paper, furniture, chemicals, lumber & wood products.
WASHINGTON	Coast Ranges and Cascade Range, separated by Puget Sound lowland, parallel the west coast; rolling plateau in southeast; Rockies in northeast.	Seattle Spokane Walla Walla	31.92 in., 14.92 in., 15.07 in.,	40.7°F., 24.9°F., 32.0°F.,	65.6°F. 69.6°F. 76.2°F.	Sand & gravel, stone, zinc, uranium ore, lead, coal, barite, pumice, diatomite, clay, peat, gypsum.	Wheat, dairy products, cattle, apples, poultry & eggs, barley, potatoes, hay, hops, sugar beets, green peas, dry field peas.	Douglas fir, western hemlock, true firs, Ponderosa pine, spruce, red alder; salmon, halibut, shellfish, crabs, oysters.	Aircraft, lumber & wood products, pulp & paper, primary metals, chemicals, canned & frozen foods, printing & publishing.
WEST VIRGINIA	Greater portion in Allegheny Plateau; Appalachian ranges and valleys in extreme east.	Charleston Clarksburg	45.00 in., 41.82 in.,	36.4°F., 33.0°F.,	75.4°F. 73.6°F.	Coal, natural gas, natural gas liquids, stone, sand & gravel, salt, clays.	Poultry & eggs, dairy products, cattle, apples, turkeys, sheep, hogs, corn, tobacco.	Oak, maple, birch, beech, yellow poplar, hickory, ash, basswood, walnut, gum, hemlock.	Chemicals, steel rolling & finishing, metal products, electrical machinery, glassware, machinery.
WISCONSIN	Southwest, rough and dissected; remainder, rolling to level glaciated plateau with many lakes and moraines.	Milwaukee Madison Green Bay	27.57 in., 30.71 in., 26.51 in.,	21.9°F., 19.3°F., 16.1°F.,	71.3°F. 73.1°F. 69.9°F.	Sand & gravel, stone, zinc, cement, lime, iron ore, clays.	Dairy products, cattle, hogs, poultry & eggs, corn, potatoes, turkeys, hay, green peas, tobacco, oats, sweet corn, soybeans.	Oak, birch, maple, red and white pine, hemlock, ash, basswood, walnut, cottonwood, aspen; chubs, perch, herring, trout.	Heavy machinery, paper, electrical machinery, automobiles & parts, metal products, dairy products, malt liquors, leather.
WYOMING	Numerous large, high, basins surrounded by high ranges of the Rockies; high plains in northeast quarter.	Cheyenne Sheridan Saratoga Moran	16.25 in., 16.75 in., 9.53 in., 21.21 in.,	25.5°F., 20.1°F., 20.4°F., 10.3°F.,	69.7°F. 70.6°F. 65.8°F. 57.6°F.	Petroleum, uranium ore, natural gas, clays, natural gas liquids, coal, sand & gravel, stone.	Cattle, sheep, wool, wheat, sugar beets, dairy products, dry edible beans, hay, poultry & eggs, hogs.	Lodgepole pine, spruce, Ponderosa pine, Douglas fir.	Petroleum & coal products, food products, stone, clay & glass products, lumber & wood products.

U. S. POPULATION BY STATE OR COLONY

1650 to 1960

STATES	1650	1700	1750	1770	1790	1800	1820	1840	1860	1880	1900	1910	1920	1930	1940	1950	1960
Alabama							127,901	590,756	964,201	1,262,505	1,828,697	2,138,093	2,348,174	2,646,248	2,832,961	3,061,743	3,266,740
Alaska										33,426	63,592	64,356	55,036	59,278	72,524	128,643	226,167
Arizona										40,440	122,931	204,354	334,162	435,573	499,261	749,587	1,302,161
Arkansas							14,273	97,574	435,450	802,525	1,311,564	1,574,449	1,752,204	1,854,482	1,949,387	1,909,511	1,786,272
California									379,994	864,694	1,485,053	2,377,549	3,426,861	5,677,251	6,907,387	10,586,223	15,717,204
Colorado									34,277	194,327	539,700	799,024	939,629	1,035,791	1,123,296	1,325,089	1,753,947
Connecticut	4,139	25,970	111,280	183,881	237,946	251,002	275,248	309,978	460,147	622,700	908,420	1,114,756	1,380,631	1,606,903	1,709,242	2,007,280	2,535,234
Delaware	185	2,470	28,704	35,496	59,096	64,273	72,749	78,085	112,216	146,608	184,735	202,322	223,003	238,380	266,505	318,085	446,292
District of Columbia						8,144	23,336	33,745	75,080	177,624	278,718	331,069	437,571	486,869	663,091	802,178	763,956
Florida								54,477	140,424	269,493	528,542	752,619	968,470	1,468,211	1,897,414	2,771,305	4,951,560
Georgia			5,200	23,375	82,548	162,686	340,989	691,392	1,057,286	1,542,180	2,216,331	2,609,121	2,895,832	2,908,506	3,123,723	3,444,578	3,943,116
Hawaii										32,610	154,001	191,874	255,881	368,300	422,770	499,794	632,772
Idaho											161,772	325,594	431,866	445,032	524,873	588,637	667,191
Illinois						5,641	55,211	476,183	1,711,951	3,077,871	4,821,550	5,638,591	6,485,280	7,630,654	7,897,241	8,712,176	10,081,158
Indiana						5,641	147,178	685,866	1,350,428	1,978,301	2,516,462	2,700,876	2,930,390	3,238,503	3,427,796	3,934,224	4,662,498
Iowa								43,112	674,913	1,624,615	2,231,853	2,224,771	2,404,021	2,470,939	2,538,268	2,621,073	2,757,537
Kansas									107,206	996,096	1,470,495	1,690,949	1,769,257	1,880,999	1,801,028	1,905,299	2,178,611
Kentucky				15,700	73,677	220,955	564,317	779,828	1,155,684	1,648,690	2,147,174	2,289,905	2,416,630	2,614,589	2,845,627	2,944,806	3,038,156
Louisiana							153,407	352,411	708,002	939,946	1,381,625	1,656,388	1,798,509	2,101,593	2,363,880	2,683,516	3,257,022
Maine[3]				31,257	96,540	151,719	298,335	501,793	628,279	648,936	694,466	742,371	768,014	797,423	847,226	913,774	969,265
Maryland	4,504	29,604	141,073	202,599	319,728	341,548	407,350	470,019	687,049	934,943	1,188,044	1,295,346	1,449,661	1,631,526	1,821,244	2,343,001	3,100,689
Massachusetts[3]	16,603	55,941	188,000	235,308	378,787	422,845	523,287	737,699	1,231,066	1,783,085	2,805,346	3,366,416	3,852,356	4,249,614	4,316,721	4,690,514	5,148,578
Michigan							8,896	212,267	749,113	1,636,937	2,420,982	2,810,173	3,668,412	4,842,325	5,256,106	6,371,766	7,823,194
Minnesota									172,023	780,773	1,751,394	2,075,708	2,387,125	2,563,953	2,792,300	2,982,483	3,413,864
Mississippi						8,850	75,448	375,651	791,305	1,131,597	1,551,270	1,797,114	1,790,618	2,009,821	2,183,796	2,178,914	2,178,141
Missouri							66,586	383,702	1,182,012	2,168,380	3,106,665	3,293,335	3,404,055	3,629,367	3,784,664	3,954,653	4,319,813
Montana										39,159	243,329	376,053	548,889	537,606	559,456	591,024	674,767
Nebraska									28,841	452,402	1,066,300	1,192,214	1,296,372	1,377,963	1,315,834	1,325,510	1,411,330
Nevada									6,857	62,266	42,335	81,875	77,407	91,058	110,247	160,083	285,278
New Hampshire	1,305	4,958	27,505	62,396	141,885	183,858	244,161	284,574	326,073	346,991	411,588	430,572	443,083	465,293	491,524	533,242	606,921
New Jersey		14,010	71,393	117,431	184,139	211,149	277,575	373,306	672,035	1,131,116	1,883,669	2,537,167	3,155,900	4,041,334	4,160,165	4,835,329	6,066,782
New Mexico									93,516	119,565	195,310	327,301	360,350	423,317	531,818	681,187	951,023
New York	4,116	19,107	76,696	162,920	340,120	589,051	1,372,812	2,428,921	3,880,735	5,082,871	7,268,894	9,113,614	10,385,227	12,588,066	13,479,142	14,830,192	16,782,304
North Carolina[4]		10,720	72,984	197,200	393,751	478,103	638,829	753,419	992,622	1,399,750	1,893,810	2,206,287	2,559,123	3,170,276	3,571,623	4,061,929	4,556,155
North Dakota[4]										36,909	319,146	577,056	646,872	680,845	641,935	619,636	632,446
Ohio						45,365	581,434	1,519,467	2,339,511	3,198,062	4,157,545	4,767,121	5,759,394	6,646,697	6,907,612	7,946,627	9,706,397
Oklahoma[5]											790,391	1,657,155	2,028,283	2,396,040	2,336,434	2,233,351	2,328,284
Oregon									52,465	174,768	413,536	672,765	783,389	953,786	1,089,684	1,521,341	1,768,687
Pennsylvania		17,950	119,666	240,057	434,373	602,365	1,049,458	1,724,033	2,906,215	4,282,891	6,302,115	7,665,111	8,720,017	9,631,350	9,900,180	10,498,012	11,319,366
Rhode Island	785	5,894	33,226	58,196	68,825	69,122	83,059	108,830	174,620	276,531	428,556	542,610	604,397	687,497	713,346	791,896	859,488
South Carolina		5,704	64,000	124,244	249,073	345,591	502,741	594,398	703,708	995,577	1,340,316	1,515,400	1,683,724	1,738,765	1,899,804	2,117,027	2,382,594
South Dakota[4]									4,837	98,268	401,570	583,888	636,547	692,849	642,961	652,740	680,514
Tennessee				1,000	35,691	105,602	422,823	829,210	1,109,801	1,542,359	2,020,616	2,184,789	2,337,885	2,616,556	2,915,841	3,291,718	3,567,089
Texas									604,215	1,591,749	3,048,710	3,896,542	4,663,228	5,824,715	6,414,824	7,711,194	9,579,677
Utah									40,273	143,963	276,749	373,351	449,396	507,847	550,310	688,862	890,627
Vermont				10,000	85,425	154,465	235,981	291,948	315,098	332,286	343,641	355,956	352,428	359,611	359,231	377,747	389,881
Virginia[6]	18,731	58,560	231,033	447,016	691,737	807,557	938,261	1,025,227	1,219,630	1,512,565	1,854,184	2,061,612	2,309,187	2,421,851	2,677,773	3,318,680	3,966,949
Washington									11,594	75,116	518,103	1,141,990	1,356,621	1,563,396	1,736,191	2,378,963	2,853,214
West Virginia[6]					55,873	78,592	136,808	224,537	376,688	618,457	958,800	1,221,119	1,463,701	1,729,205	1,901,974	2,005,552	1,860,421
Wisconsin								30,945	775,881	1,315,497	2,069,042	2,333,860	2,632,067	2,939,006	3,137,587	3,434,575	3,951,777
Wyoming										20,789	92,531	145,965	194,402	225,565	250,742	290,529	330,066
Total[1]	50,368	250,888	1,170,760	2,148,076	3,929,214	5,308,483	9,638,453	17,069,453[3]	31,443,321	50,189,209	76,212,168	92,228,496	106,021,537	123,202,624	132,164,569	151,325,798	179,323,175

[1] All figures exclude uncivilized Indians. Figures for 1650 through 1770 include only the British colonies that later became the United States. No areas are included prior to their annexation to the United States. However, many of the figures refer to territories prior to their admission as States. U.S. total includes Alaska from 1880 through 1960 and Hawaii from 1900 through 1960.

[2] U.S. total for 1840 includes 6,100 persons on public ships in service of the United States, not credited to any State.

[3] Maine figures for 1770 through 1800 are for that area of Massachusetts which became the State of Maine in 1820. Massachusetts figures exclude Maine from 1770 through 1800, but include it from 1650 through 1750. Massachusetts figure for 1650 also includes Plymouth, a separate colony until 1691.

[4] South Dakota figure for 1860 represents entire Dakota Territory. North and South Dakota figures for 1880 are for the parts of Dakota Territory which later constituted the respective States.

[5] Oklahoma figure for 1900 includes population of Indian Territory (392,060).

[6] West Virginia figures for 1790 through 1860 are for that area of Virginia which became West Virginia in 1863. These figures are excluded from the figures for Virginia from 1790 through 1860.

U.S. STATE GENERAL INFORMATION TABLE

STATE	CAPITAL	LARGEST CITY	ENTERED UNION AS STATE — Date of Entry	Rank of Entry	Greatest N-S Measurement (miles)	Greatest E-W Measurement (miles)	HIGHEST POINT — Location	Altitude (feet)	STATE FLOWER	STATE BIRD	STATE NICKNAME
Alabama	Montgomery	Birmingham	Dec. 14, 1819	22	330	200	Cheaha Mountain	2,407	Camellia	Yellowhammer	Yellowhammer
Alaska	Juneau	Anchorage	Jan. 3, 1959	49	1,332	2,250	Mt. McKinley	20,320	Forget-me-not	Willow Ptarmigan	Last Frontier
Arizona	Phoenix	Phoenix	Feb. 14, 1912	48	390	335	Humphreys Peak	12,670	Saguaro Cactus	Cactus Wren	Grand Canyon
Arkansas	Little Rock	Little Rock	June 15, 1836	25	240	275	Magazine Mtn.	2,823	Apple Blossom	Mockingbird	Land of Opportunity
California	Sacramento	Los Angeles	Sept. 9, 1850	31	800	375	Mt. Whitney	14,495	Golden Poppy	California Valley Quail	Golden
Colorado	Denver	Denver	Aug. 1, 1876	38	270	380	Mt. Elbert	14,431	Rocky Mountain Columbine	Lark Bunting	Centennial
Connecticut*	Hartford	Hartford	Jan. 9, 1788	5	75	90	S. slope of Mt. Frisell	2,380	Mountain Laurel	Robin	Constitution
Delaware*	Dover	Wilmington	Dec. 7, 1787	1	95	35	Ebright Road, New Castle Co.	442	Peach Blossom	Blue Hen Chicken	Diamond
District of Columbia†	Washington	Washington	March 3, 1791	..	15	15	Tenleytown	410	American Beauty Rose	....	....
Florida	Tallahassee	Miami	March 3, 1845	27	460	400	N. boundary, Walton Co.	345	Orange Blossom	Mockingbird	Sunshine
Georgia*	Atlanta	Atlanta	Jan. 2, 1788	4	315	250	Brasstown Bald (mtn.)	4,784	Cherokee Rose	Brown Thrasher	Peach State
Hawaii	Honolulu	Honolulu	Aug. 21, 1959	50	...	1,600	Mauna Kea	13,796	Red Hibiscus	Nene (Hawaiian Goose)	The Aloha
Idaho	Boise	Boise	July 3, 1890	43	480	305	Borah Peak	12,662	Syringa	Mountain Bluebird	Gem
Illinois	Springfield	Chicago	Dec. 3, 1818	21	380	205	Charles Mound	1,241	Native Violet	Cardinal	Prairie
Indiana	Indianapolis	Indianapolis	Dec. 11, 1816	19	265	160	Near Spartanburg	1,253	Peony	Cardinal	Hoosier
Iowa	Des Moines	Des Moines	Dec. 28, 1846	29	205	310	Ocheyedan Mound	1,675	Wild Rose	Eastern Goldfinch	Hawkeye
Kansas	Topeka	Wichita	Jan. 29, 1861	34	205	410	Mt. Sunflower	4,026	Sunflower	Western Meadowlark	Sunflower
Kentucky	Frankfort	Louisville	June 1, 1792	15	175	350	Black Mountain	4,145	Goldenrod	Kentucky Cardinal	Bluegrass
Louisiana	Baton Rouge	New Orleans	April 30, 1812	18	275	300	Driskill Mountain	535	Magnolia	Eastern Brown Pelican**	Pelican
Maine	Augusta	Portland	March 15, 1820	23	310	210	Mt. Katahdin	5,268	White Pine Cone and Tassel	Chickadee	Pine Tree
Maryland*	Annapolis	Baltimore	April 28, 1788	7	120	200	Backbone Mountain	3,360	Black-eyed Susan	Baltimore Oriole	Old Line
Massachusetts*	Boston	Boston	Feb. 6, 1788	6	110	190	Mt. Greylock	3,491	Mayflower	Chickadee	Bay
Michigan	Lansing	Detroit	Jan. 26, 1837	26	400	310	N.E. Baraga Co.	1,980	Apple Blossom	Robin	Wolverine
Minnesota	St. Paul	Minneapolis	May 11, 1858	32	400	350	Eagle Mtn.	2,301	Showy Lady's-slipper	Loon	Gopher
Mississippi	Jackson	Jackson	Dec. 10, 1817	20	340	180	Woodall Mountain	806	Magnolia	Mockingbird	Magnolia
Missouri	Jefferson City	St. Louis	Aug. 10, 1821	24	280	300	Taum Sauk Mountain	1,772	Hawthorne	Bluebird	Show Me
Montana	Helena	Great Falls	Nov. 8, 1889	41	315	570	Granite Peak	12,799	Bitterroot	Western Meadowlark	Treasure
Nebraska	Lincoln	Omaha	March 1, 1867	37	210	415	S.W. corner Kimball Co.	5,424	Goldenrod	Western Meadowlark	Cornhusker
Nevada	Carson City	Las Vegas	Oct. 31, 1864	36	485	315	Boundary Peak	13,145	Sagebrush	Mountain Bluebird**	Silver
New Hampshire*	Concord	Manchester	June 21, 1788	9	185	90	Mt. Washington	6,288	Purple Lilac	Purple Finch	Granite
New Jersey*	Trenton	Newark	Dec. 18, 1787	3	166	70	High Point	1,803	Purple Violet	Eastern Goldfinch	Garden
New Mexico	Santa Fe	Albuquerque	Jan. 6, 1912	47	390	350	Wheeler Peak	13,160	Yucca	Road Runner	Land of Enchantment
New York*	Albany	New York	July 26, 1788	11	310	330	Mt. Marcy	5,344	Rose	Bluebird	Empire
North Carolina*	Raleigh	Charlotte	Nov. 21, 1789	12	200	520	Mt. Mitchell	6,684	Dogwood	Cardinal	Tar Heel
North Dakota	Bismarck	Fargo	Nov. 2, 1889	39	210	360	White Butte	3,530	Wild Prairie Rose	Western Meadowlark	Flickertail
Ohio	Columbus	Cleveland	March 1, 1803	17	230	205	Campbell Hill	1,550	Scarlet Carnation	Cardinal	Buckeye
Oklahoma	Oklahoma City	Oklahoma City	Nov. 16, 1907	46	210	460	Black Mesa	4,978	Mistletoe	Scissor-tailed Flycatcher	Sooner
Oregon	Salem	Portland	Feb. 14, 1859	33	290	375	Mt. Hood	11,245	Oregon Grape	Western Meadowlark	Beaver
Pennsylvania*	Harrisburg	Philadelphia	Dec. 12, 1787	2	180	310	Mt. Davis	3,213	Mountain Laurel	Ruffed Grouse	Keystone
Rhode Island*	Providence	Providence	May 29, 1790	13	50	35	Jerimoth Hill	812	Violet**	Rhode Island Red	Little Rhody
South Carolina*	Columbia	Columbia	May 23, 1788	8	215	285	Sassafras Mountain	3,560	Yellow Jessamine	Carolina Wren	Palmetto
South Dakota	Pierre	Sioux Falls	Nov. 2, 1889	40	240	360	Harney Peak	7,242	American Pasque Flower	Ringnecked Pheasant	Coyote
Tennessee	Nashville	Memphis	June 1, 1796	16	120	430	Clingmans Dome	6,642	Iris	Mockingbird	Volunteer
Texas	Austin	Houston	Dec. 29, 1845	28	710	760	Guadalupe Peak	8,751	Bluebonnet	Mockingbird	Lone Star
Utah	Salt Lake City	Salt Lake City	Jan. 4, 1896	45	345	275	Kings Peak	13,498	Sego Lily	Sea Gull	Beehive
Vermont	Montpelier	Burlington	March 4, 1791	14	155	90	Mt. Mansfield	4,393	Red Clover	Hermit Thrush	Green Mountain
Virginia*	Richmond	Norfolk	June 25, 1788	10	205	425	Mt. Rogers	5,720	American Dogwood	Cardinal	Old Dominion
Washington	Olympia	Seattle	Nov. 11, 1889	42	230	340	Mt. Rainier	14,410	Western Rhododendron	Willow Goldfinch	Evergreen
West Virginia	Charleston	Charleston	June 20, 1863	35	200	225	Spruce Knob	4,860	Big Rhododendron	Cardinal	Mountain
Wisconsin	Madison	Milwaukee	May 29, 1848	30	300	290	Timms Hill	1,952	Wood Violet	Robin	Badger
Wyoming	Cheyenne	Cheyenne	July 10, 1890	44	275	365	Gannett Peak	13,785	Indian Paint Brush	Meadowlark	Equality
United States	Washington, D.C.	New York	...	..	...	...	Mt. McKinley, Alaska	20,320	....	Bald Eagle	....

*One of the Thirteen Original States.   **Unofficial.   †District.

WORLD POPULATION

The most important thing in the world is its people. Many live crowded together; others live miles apart. Belgium has more than 700 people for every square mile of its land, and Brazil has fewer than 25. In Belgium, the people are dispersed evenly over the land. Brazil has more than 250 people for each square mile of land around its big cities, but in its vast interior there are thousands of square miles with scarcely any people at all.

The population of the earth is now somewhat over three billion; exactly how much it is impossible to say. No one knows exactly how many people there were in the world 500 years ago, but it was certainly only a small fraction of the numbers that inhabit the earth today. Then, as now, Europe contained a large population. Since the great age of exploration and discovery which began in the fifteenth century, the population of Europe has increased many fold, even though migrating Europeans have helped to populate the rest of the world.

The spread of Europeans around the world, without diminishing the numbers in the homeland, suggests the two means by which population can grow. One is natural increase, the excess of births over deaths. The other is migration. Natural increase in Europe has been enough to produce an evergrowing population at home, even while thousands of emigrants were moving out to new lands.

The most crowded large areas of the world are in India and China. They have grown almost entirely by natural increase, and comparatively few of their people have moved out to new lands. Neither have many people moved in since the last great invasions several centuries ago. Both China and India are overcrowded. They have too many people for their resources unless they can find a way to bring about great improvement in their method of production. India has no room to expand. China has great stretches of almost unoccupied land in the west, but it is nearly useless.

People have migrated all over the earth in search of land worth settling. It is thought that many thousands of years ago the first human beings lived in one region of the earth. There is reason to believe that man's homeland may have been Africa, although some evidence seems to indicate that it was Asia. From somewhere on this earth then, people moved out into all habitable lands long before they had learned to leave written records.

Wherever people went in the first few thousands of years of their migrations, they were looking for a place where they could find food. When they found such a place some of them would stay. In the beginning they were looking for good hunting grounds and for beaches where fish and shellfish were abundant. When, a long time later, some had learned to farm, they looked for land they could cultivate.

Wherever people have migrated in the world, they have been looking for something of value. Where abundant resources have been found, many people have settled. Although food will always be a prime factor in man's continuing existence, its immediate availability is no longer the only reason large numbers of people gather in certain places to live.

Cities have grown where people could trade with each other. Industries have grown where transportation made it possible to bring together raw materials and to distribute manufactured goods, and people have gone to live in places where they could find work.

In the modern world, urban centers have become larger and larger, until in some places the growing circles of heavy population have met and merged into great urban belts. In one way or another, iron and coal, oil, and the availability of sources of power are as powerful determinants of population concentration as food once was. There are now about 135 metropolitan areas of one million or more people. A century ago there were only four or five. Sixty years ago, well within the memory of many people, there were only about two dozen.

As the world continues its rapid population growth during the next few decades, the number of large cities is almost certain to grow even more rapidly.

The flea market in Madrid, Spain, one of the world's one hundred-odd cities with a population over a million. Although crowded cities seem to be a symbol of our crowded world, only 10 per cent of the world's people live in cities as large as Madrid or larger.

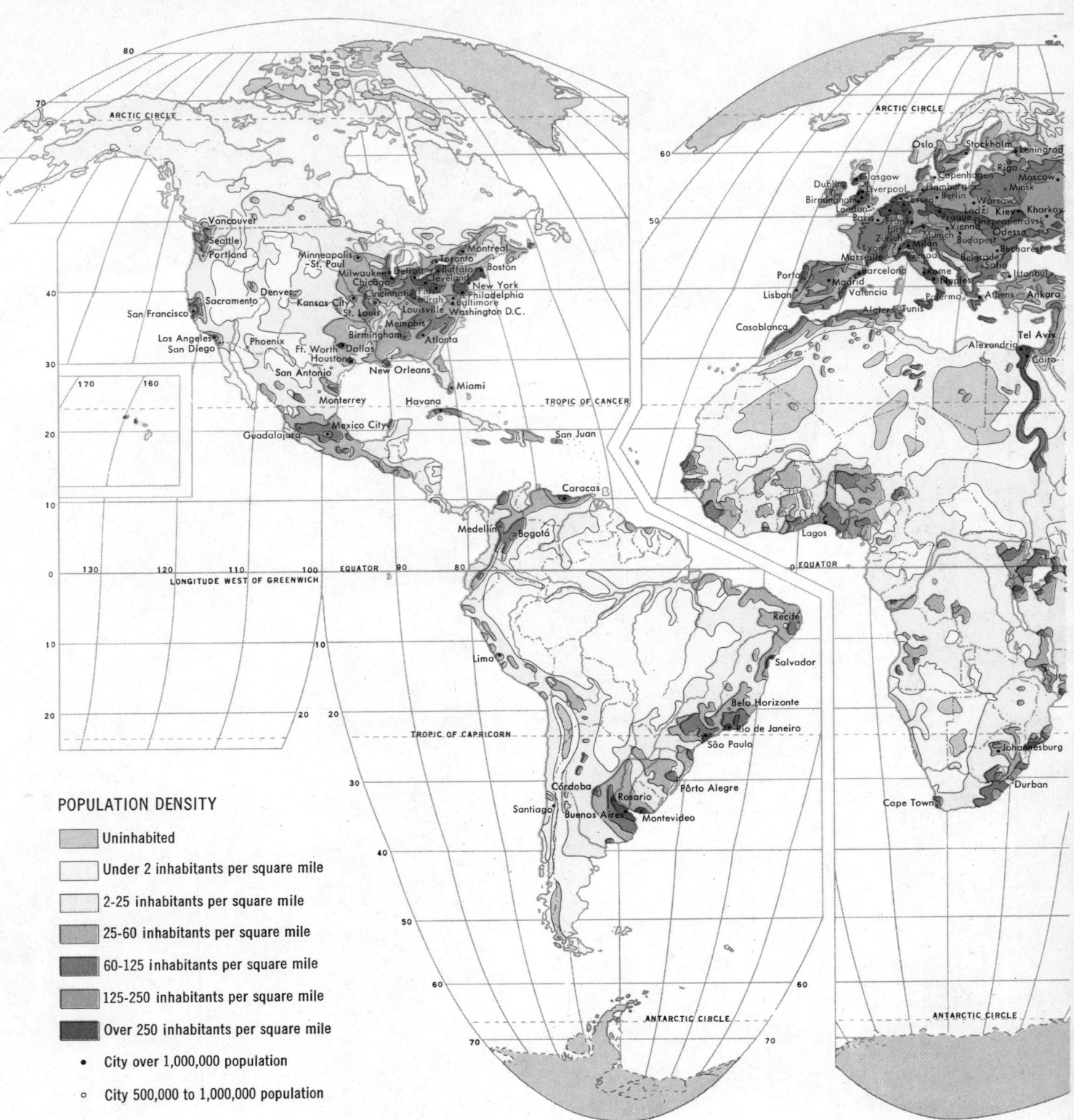

POPULATION DENSITY

- Uninhabited
- Under 2 inhabitants per square mile
- 2-25 inhabitants per square mile
- 25-60 inhabitants per square mile
- 60-125 inhabitants per square mile
- 125-250 inhabitants per square mile
- Over 250 inhabitants per square mile
- • City over 1,000,000 population
- ○ City 500,000 to 1,000,000 population

POPULATION
OF THE WORLD

The colors on the map show the pattern of population on the earth. Despite the fact that the world seems so crowded, the areas of dense population are considerably smaller than those that are unpopulated or very sparsely populated. Some of the reasons that people live where they do and not elsewhere can be found on the world vegetation, climate, and landform maps. Human life depends on the things that support it, and until comparatively recent times these were largely the gifts of nature. As man gains increasing control over his environment the pattern on a population map may be greatly altered.

Sometimes there are very obvious reasons for details of the population pattern. In northeast Africa, what seems to be a red snake with a purple head follows the irrigated Nile Valley. The scanty population on either side of the Nile occupies the Sahara region. The scattered spots of red and orange are oases in the desert.

The wide, dark band across northern India represents the close-packed cities and farm villages of the Ganges Valley. Gray regions at the far north and far south indicate lands where no one lives because they are perpetually buried under ice and snow. Other patches of gray clearly mean the most forbidding depths of the world's great deserts, where there is not even scattered grass for grazing or dry shrubs that camels and goats might eat. The city symbols and names on the map explain some of the small spots of red and purple. In contrast to Asia and Africa, where density seems directly related to fertility of the soil, in North America all the areas of heaviest population are urban—cities or clusters of cities, where industry and commerce have caused people to congregate. Western Europe shows relatively even distribution of heavy population over both rural and urban areas.

In so small a space,

   so many . . . .

The skyscrapers of New York City are one solution to the problem of finding living and working space for millions of people on a small area of land. In general, they indicate a standard of living for most of New York's people that is as high as any other in the world.

Frankfurt, Germany, is in one of the most densely populated regions of western Europe. A flourishing industrial economy creates such problems as rush-hour traffic, but it also creates a prosperous middle class, as can be seen from this well-fed, well-dressed crowd.

Kowloon, on the mainland of the colony of Hong Kong. People living on boats on the rivers and in the harbors is one example of overcrowding along the coast of eastern Asia. Where every scrap of earth is used, there are people who literally cannot find a place on the land for themselves and their families. Here dense population means poverty and a low standard of living.

The Bedouins of Arabia must move constantly from place to place over the bare and empty desert to find what little grass there is to feed their sheep, goats, and camels. Somewhere beyond the horizon the young men of the tribe are watching the herds. When the sparse grass is gone, or when the people hear that rain has fallen elsewhere, they will pack up their tents and travel on.

In so vast a space,

                so few . . . .

Although the Andes Valley in Peru (right) seems populous, with its cultivated fields and numerous houses, it is surrounded by rugged mountains where no human being could make a home, so the region as a whole has a small population. Ushuaia, Argentina (below), is the southernmost town in the world, far from all areas of heavy population on the dry, cold, windswept island of Tierra del Fuego. The region around it suffers the same harsh climate. These towns, in their different but equally difficult environments, show two of the reasons why South America has great expanses of sparsely populated land.

Since man first learned to float down a river on a log, water has carried him and his goods from one place to another. In the highly industrialized modern world, many great metropolitan areas, such as Tokyo, served by its own port and that of Yokohama (shown here), receive most of the food for their millions of people and raw materials for their industries by way of the sea. By sea they send their manufactured goods to all parts of the world. Goods are still carried more cheaply by water than any other way.

WORLD TRANSPORTATION

Transportation maps reflect population density almost as well as a population map does. Railways and highways connect cities and penetrate all areas where there is any significant degree of economic development. The principal continental and international airline routes link the principal metropolitan centers of the world. Heavily laden ocean vessels travel frequented sea routes from busy industrial regions. Furthermore, nowhere in the world is there a cluster, no matter how small, of civilized people without some form of transportation providing them with contact, no matter how infrequent, with the rest of the civilized world.

The modern world could not exist without transportation. Modern transportation routes are man-made, created for the convenience of man. Nearly everywhere in the world people, industries, and transportation routes go together.

Both people and goods travel by land, water, and air. The more complex, the more highly industrialized, and the more densely populated a region is, the more it needs good transportation. Transportation of one kind or another has carried people to every corner of the world. Where large settlements have grown, more transportation has been provided. Where transportation is good, more industries have been started and more people have come.

The development of transportation facilities since the industrial revolution has been incomparably greater and more rapid than any change in either method of travel or extension of routes of travel that preceded it. A few hundred years ago, a community with 20,000 people was considered a large city. Most people produced their own food and probably the materials for their own clothing. The small cities were supplied by the surrounding countryside. Only a few types of goods were carried any distance—salt, dried or salted fish, metal articles, and such luxuries as spices, furs, jewels, and knickknacks. Traffic by water was slow, and ships and river boats too small to carry any but light cargoes. On land, goods were carried by long trains of pack animals over roads that were often mere ruts.

As population increased, and people gathered in cities, the need for trade increased. A vast area of farms would be required to feed a city of a million people. Food and raw materials for manufacturing must be brought into densely populated industrial regions, such as western Europe and Japan. Even in the United States, the great cities along the Atlantic Coast depend upon other parts of the country for food supplies. As industrial regions grow, the industries themselves make more and more use of transportation. Raw materials and fuels are brought from greater distances, and the products go to markets that may become worldwide.

Western Europe is the most highly industrialized region in the world. European farmers produce huge crops, but still they cannot feed all the people of their own countries. Nor can the natural resources of Europe supply all the needs of its industries. It depends on imports from less densely populated lands.

In China, alone, the relationship between transportation patterns and dense population seems to break down. It is a huge area teeming with a multitude of people, but it is poorly supplied with transportation routes. Unlike Europe or North America, most of the people of China live on tiny farms, and each family eats what can be grown on their own acre or two of land. If the crops fail in one area, there is likely to be famine, and people may die by the thousands because it is so difficult to bring them food from elsewhere.

Nearly everywhere else in the world, however, dense population and a dense transportation network go together. In India a tight pattern of roads and railways falls across the Ganges Valley, the most heavily populated part of the country. In Mexico, railways and highways meet near Mexico City. In South America, railways fan out from the ports through the regions that have the most people. In the places where the hoot of a train whistle or the roar of a motor are never heard, there are probably few people to listen for them. Transportation routes go where there are people and industry; and where there is transportation, there people and industry will be found.

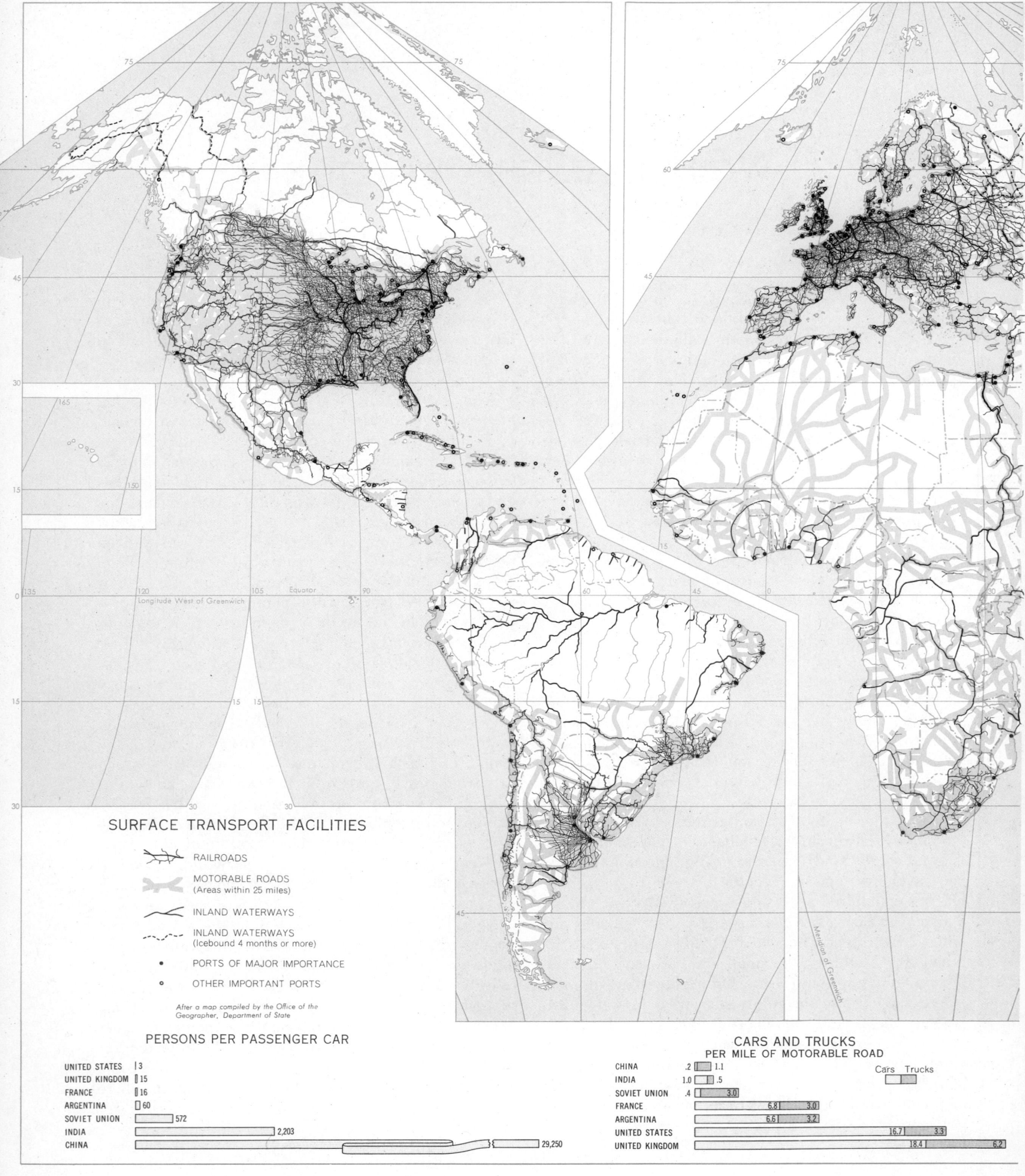

SURFACE TRANSPORT FACILITIES

RAILROADS

MOTORABLE ROADS
(Areas within 25 miles)

INLAND WATERWAYS

INLAND WATERWAYS
(Icebound 4 months or more)

● PORTS OF MAJOR IMPORTANCE

○ OTHER IMPORTANT PORTS

*After a map compiled by the Office of the
Geographer, Department of State*

PERSONS PER PASSENGER CAR

UNITED STATES	3
UNITED KINGDOM	15
FRANCE	16
ARGENTINA	60
SOVIET UNION	572
INDIA	2,203
CHINA	29,250

CARS AND TRUCKS
PER MILE OF MOTORABLE ROAD

Cars   Trucks

	Cars	Trucks
CHINA	.2	1.1
INDIA	1.0	.5
SOVIET UNION	.4	3.0
FRANCE	6.8	3.0
ARGENTINA	6.5	3.2
UNITED STATES	16.7	3.3
UNITED KINGDOM	18.4	6.2

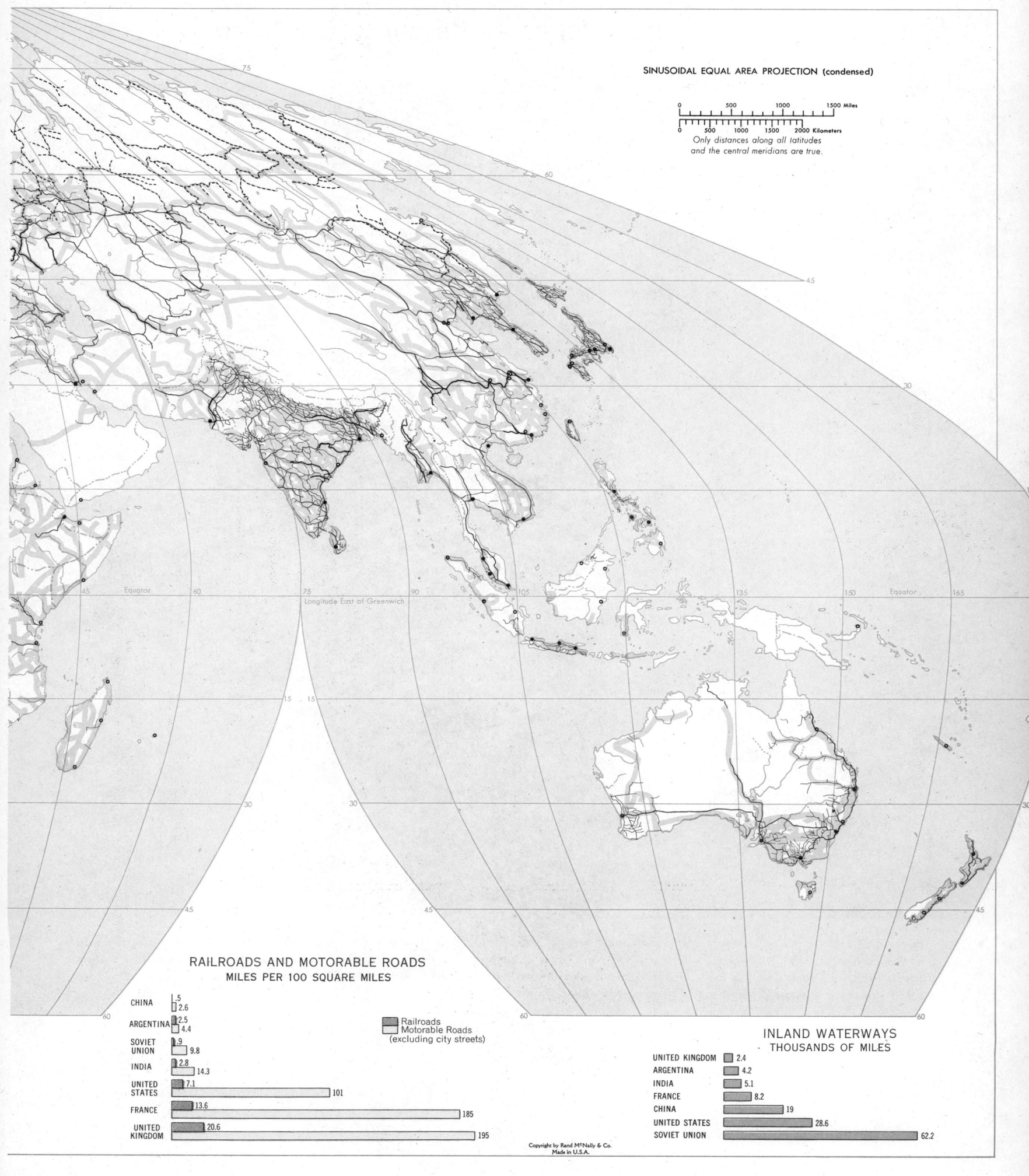

SINUSOIDAL EQUAL AREA PROJECTION (condensed)

0   500   1000   1500 Miles

0   500   1000   1500   2000 Kilometers

Only distances along all latitudes
and the central meridians are true.

Longitude East of Greenwich

RAILROADS AND MOTORABLE ROADS
MILES PER 100 SQUARE MILES

CHINA	.5 / 2.6
ARGENTINA	2.5 / 4.4
SOVIET UNION	.9 / 9.8
INDIA	2.8 / 14.3
UNITED STATES	7.1 / 101
FRANCE	13.6 / 185
UNITED KINGDOM	20.6 / 195

■ Railroads
□ Motorable Roads
(excluding city streets)

INLAND WATERWAYS
THOUSANDS OF MILES

UNITED KINGDOM	2.4
ARGENTINA	4.2
INDIA	5.1
FRANCE	8.2
CHINA	19
UNITED STATES	28.6
SOVIET UNION	62.2

Man journeys endlessly . . . . down rivers,

Boats on small waterways are probably the oldest means of transportation. These Vietnamese, making their way home at the end of the day, are poling themselves along a small canal in a homemade boat of a kind that has been used on quiet, shallow waters for hundreds of centuries. The boat moves hardly faster than a man can walk, but it carries more with much less effort, and where the distances are short or the time long, speed is unimportant.

An extensive system of canals and locks have made the Great Lakes, their connecting rivers, and the mighty St. Lawrence into the St. Lawrence Seaway (right). Through it ocean-going vessels can now travel almost to the heart of the United States Middle West. Iron, coal, wheat, and paper are among the many bulky cargoes that are moved across the lakes.

Wherever there is lumbering and a river, logs are floated away from the forests where they are cut. Sometimes they are tumbled into the water and carried by the current down to a sawmill or paper mill. Sometimes, as in the Fraser River in British Columbia, they are fastened together into a raft and pulled by tugboat. Old as this method is, it is still the easiest and safest.

across cities, countries, continents . . . .

This fantastic tangle of concrete ribbons is a highway interchange in San Francisco, similar to hundreds that are carrying streams of automobiles over, across, and under each other in or near almost every large city in the United States. The tremendous number of cars on modern highways, and the speed at which they travel, have created problems in the control of traffic that could not have existed in the age of the horse and buggy. The larger the city, the greater its traffic problem is.

The Trans-Siberian Railway crosses the Soviet Union from Moscow to Vladivostok on the Pacific. The line of its passage can be clearly seen on a population map—a narrow streak of settlement through vast and almost empty lands.

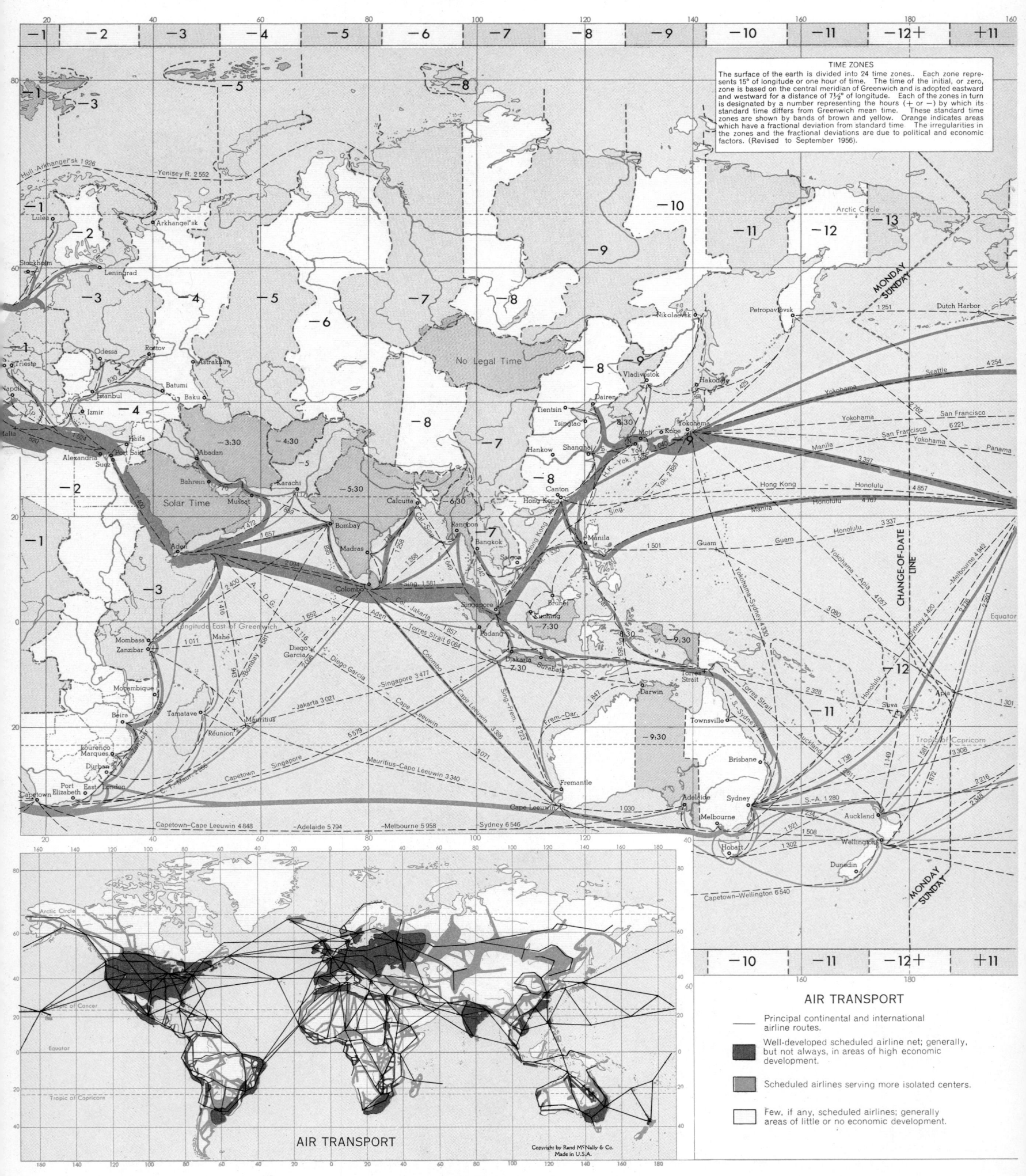

TIME ZONES

The surface of the earth is divided into 24 time zones.. Each zone represents 15° of longitude or one hour of time. The time of the initial, or zero, zone is based on the central meridian of Greenwich and is adopted eastward and westward for a distance of 7½° of longitude. Each of the zones in turn is designated by a number representing the hours (+ or —) by which its standard time differs from Greenwich mean time. These standard time zones are shown by bands of brown and yellow. Orange indicates areas which have a fractional deviation from standard time. The irregularities in the zones and the fractional deviations are due to political and economic factors. (Revised to September 1956.)

AIR TRANSPORT

— Principal continental and international airline routes.

Well-developed scheduled airline net; generally, but not always, in areas of high economic development.

Scheduled airlines serving more isolated centers.

Few, if any, scheduled airlines; generally areas of little or no economic development.

AIR TRANSPORT

Copyright by Rand M⁽ᶜ⁾Nally & Co.
Made in U.S.A.

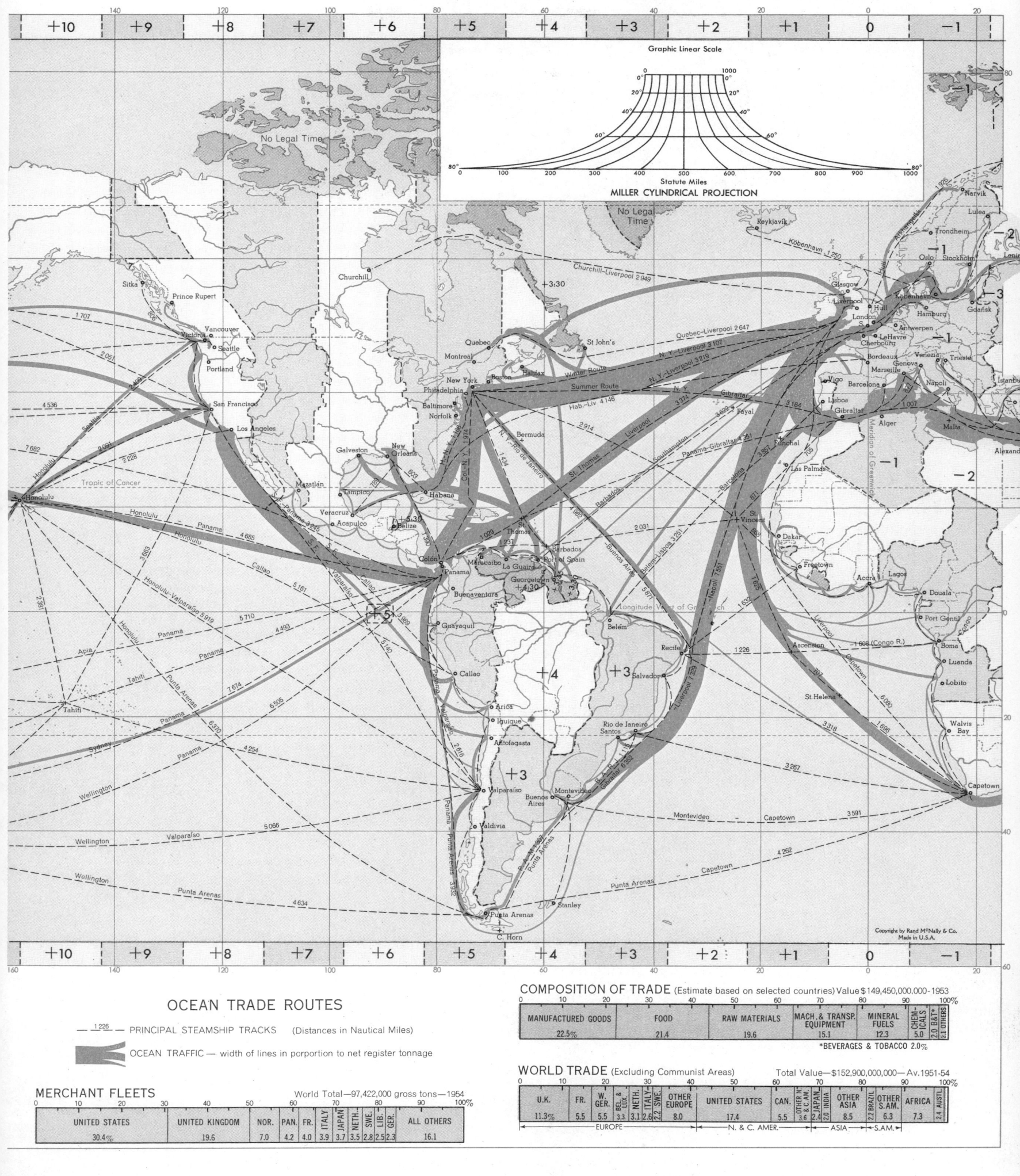

OCEAN TRADE ROUTES

— 1226 — PRINCIPAL STEAMSHIP TRACKS (Distances in Nautical Miles)

OCEAN TRAFFIC — width of lines in proportion to net register tonnage

MERCHANT FLEETS

World Total—97,422,000 gross tons—1954

UNITED STATES	UNITED KINGDOM	NOR.	PAN.	FR.	ITALY	JAPAN	NETH.	SWE.	LIB.	GER.	ALL OTHERS
30.4%	19.6	7.0	4.2	4.0	3.9	3.7	3.5	2.8	2.5	2.3	16.1

COMPOSITION OF TRADE (Estimate based on selected countries) Value $149,450,000,000-1953

MANUFACTURED GOODS	FOOD	RAW MATERIALS	MACH. & TRANSP. EQUIPMENT	MINERAL FUELS	CHEM-ICALS	2.0 B&T* 2.1 OTHERS
22.5%	21.4	19.6	15.1	12.3	5.0	

*BEVERAGES & TOBACCO 2.0%

WORLD TRADE (Excluding Communist Areas)

Total Value—$152,900,000,000—Av.1951-54

U.K.	FR.	W. GER.	BEL. & LUX.	NETH.	ITALY	SWE.	OTHER EUROPE	UNITED STATES	CAN.	OTHER N. & C.AM.	JAPAN	INDIA	OTHER ASIA	BRAZIL	OTHER S.AM.	AFRICA	AUSTL.
11.3%	5.5	5.5	3.3	3.1	2.6	2.2	8.0	17.4	5.5	3.6	2.4	2.0	8.5	2.2	6.3	7.3	2.4

EUROPE — N. & C. AMER. — ASIA — S.AM.

*over oceans,
through the air,
beyond all barriers.*

Great northern ports were once shut in by ice for several months of the year. Now the sea lanes are kept open during the winter by ice-breakers like this Russian atomic-powered vessel, crushing its way through the Berents Sea to Arkhangelsk in the Soviet Union.

The world's largest ships, like the *Queen Elizabeth* shown leaving New York Harbor, sail between the world's largest ports.

Only airports as large or larger than the one at Amsterdam, Netherlands, can accommodate today's giant jets.

DIVIETO TRANSITO
DALLE 8 ALLE 21

DIVIETO PERMANENTE
DI TRANSITO

ANÈNTE
ITO

360

IVIETO PERMANENTE
STA

DIVIETO TRANSITO
DALLE 10 ALLE 21

RICO
DI CARICO
DALLE 8 ALLE 21

BVLGARI

LANGUAGES OF THE WORLD

Language, that set of sounds and symbols by which ideas and feelings are expressed, is a distinctive characteristic of human beings. No people, no matter how primitive, have ever been found who had no language. Man's body is equipped with special mechanisms that make speech possible: an area in the front of the human brain that controls his ability to form and to understand words; muscles in the tongue and throat that he uses to produce the complicated sounds that are spoken language. Not only do all normal human beings have the physical equipment for speech, they are also born with a natural and instinctive desire to talk.

Although speech is instinctive, language is not. Each child must learn a language before he can talk. He learns the one that he hears spoken around him. This language reflects his life and the society in which he lives. It has words for the objects he sees and uses, words for the ceremonies and customs of his people, for the tasks he performs, the games he plays, the food he eats, and words that describe how those foods are prepared. The language he speaks influences the way he thinks. He arranges ideas in his mind as he arranges words in his sentences, and it is almost impossible for him to grasp an abstract thought if his language has no words to express it.

Language is one of the things that binds groups of men together. It is also one of the things that keeps them apart. In the Biblical story of the Tower of Babel, the Lord stopped the descendants of Noah from building their great tower and powerful city by "confounding their speech." When they could no longer understand one another they could no longer work together, and they scattered in all directions over the earth.

Thousands of different languages exist today, and they are so varied that they show no sign of ever having been one common tongue. Most of them, however, belong to one or another of several large language families, and these related languages developed, over the centuries, from the same parent language. English belongs to a family called Indo-European. Languages in this group are spoken from western Europe to India and have been carried to distant parts of the earth. Each Indo-European language has hundreds of words that can be traced to the same origin. The English word *father*, for example, is *fader* in German, *padre* in Spanish, *pater* in Latin, and *pitar* in Sanskrit, an ancient language once spoken in India. Related words in different languages are called "cognate" words, meaning literally "words born together."

Latin, the language of the ancient Romans, is an Indo-European tongue, and although its principal use today is as the official language of the Roman Catholic Church, a family of living languages has descended from it. The Romance languages, French, Italian, Spanish, Portuguese, Romanian, and Romansh, are all spoken in countries that were once part of the Roman Empire.

English belongs to the Germanic group of Indo-European tongues, which includes the Scandinavian languages and Dutch, as well as the various dialects of German. Although English is not a Romance language it has, as an Indo-European tongue, a good many words that are cognates of Latin words, and more important, it has borrowed a great many Latin words. Latin was once the language of government, education, and religion in England; much of it passed from official use into the language spoken by the people.

In time all languages change. They change with changing customs, with the need for new words or because old words are no longer needed, or when any new influence has been exerted on culture. Human languages are the echo of human history.

Some languages are written in words, some in pictures that express ideas. Traffic signs in Rome use both words and pictures, so that he who walks or drives, whether he knows Italian or not, may read and understand. The same kind of sign is used in many places in Europe.

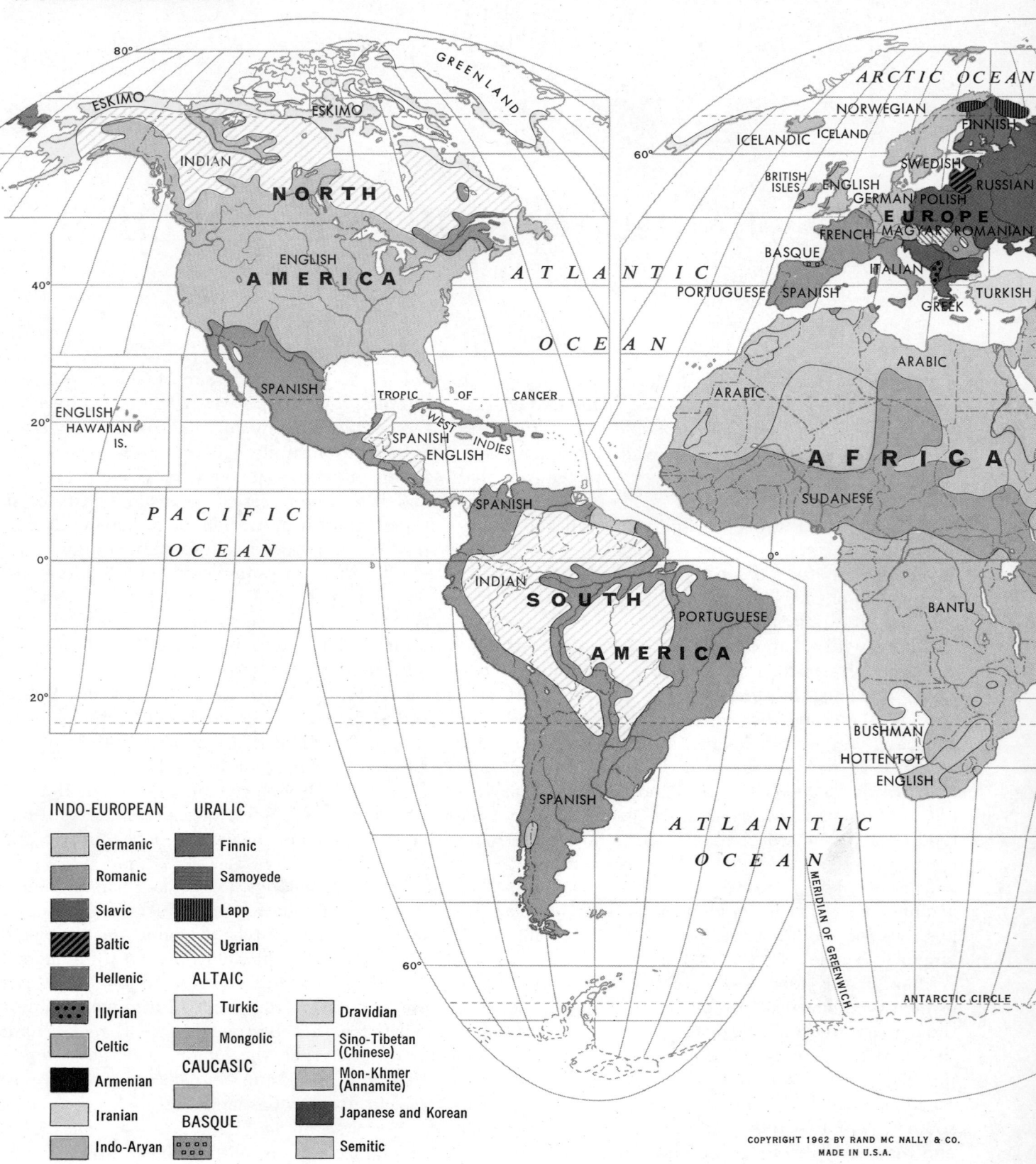

LANGUAGES OF THE WORLD

Thousands of languages are spoken in the world, and no map can show them all. In many areas where more than one language is in use, an attempt to indicate the mixture would only be confusing. The color on the map shows the language spoken by a majority of the people. Indian languages in the Americas, for example, are shown for large areas in South America, but omitted in continental United States, and Bantu is not shown in the Sudanese area of Africa.

INDO-EUROPEAN
- Germanic
- Romanic
- Slavic
- Baltic
- Hellenic
- Illyrian
- Celtic
- Armenian
- Iranian
- Indo-Aryan

URALIC
- Finnic
- Samoyede
- Lapp
- Ugrian

ALTAIC
- Turkic
- Mongolic

CAUCASIC

BASQUE

- Dravidian
- Sino-Tibetan (Chinese)
- Mon-Khmer (Annamite)
- Japanese and Korean
- Semitic

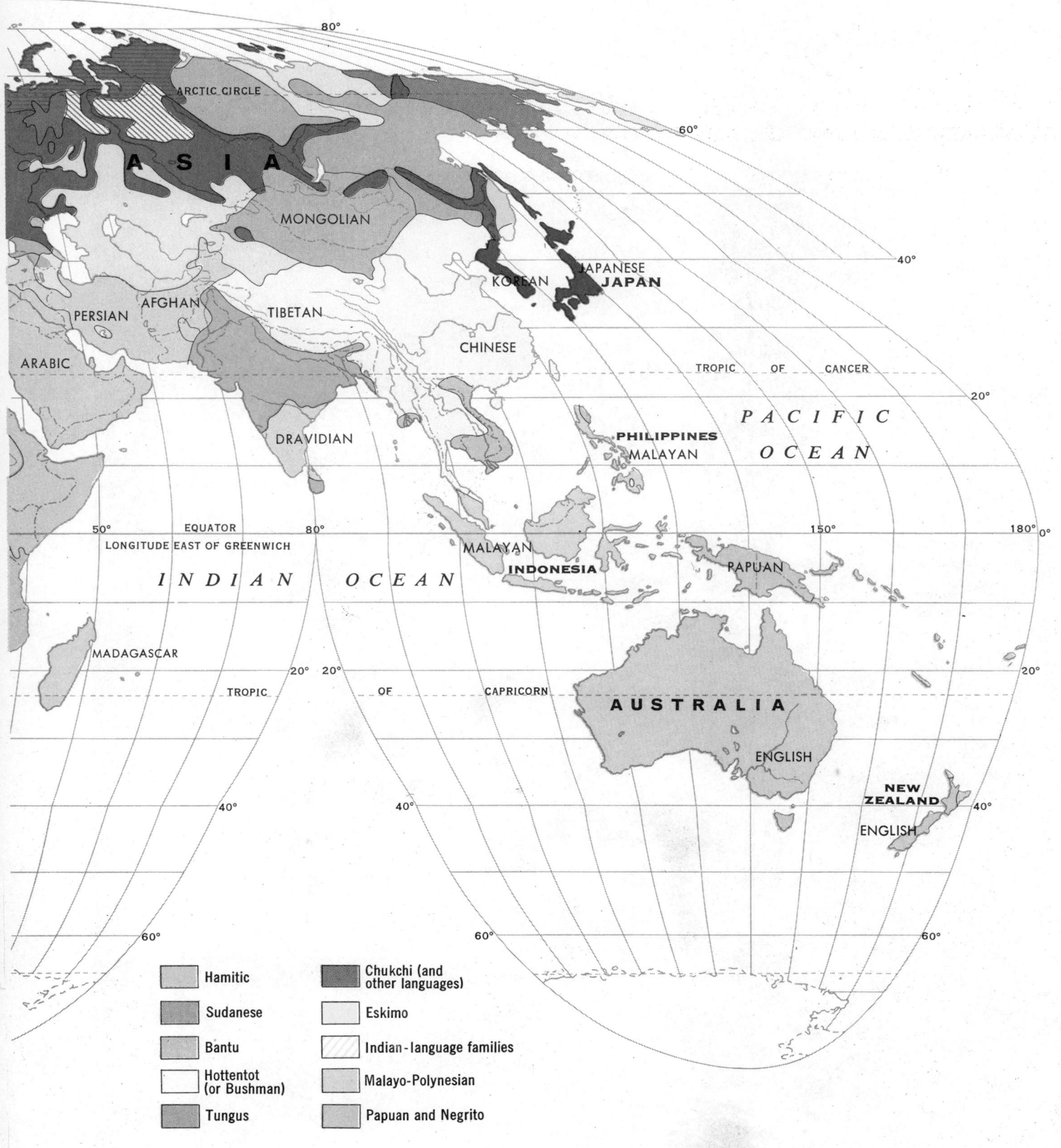

Hamitic	Chukchi (and other languages)
Sudanese	Eskimo
Bantu	Indian-language families
Hottentot (or Bushman)	Malayo-Polynesian
Tungus	Papuan and Negrito

Of all the language families, Indo-European is by far the most important. Indo-European tongues are spoken by almost two-thirds of the human race. Next in importance are the Chinese dialects and related languages, called Sino-Tibetan, spoken by almost a fourth of the world's people. In contrast to these two tremendous families some languages are spoken by only a few people. Basque, for example, which is not related to any other language, is spoken only in one small area along the Spanish-French border. It is one of the great language mysteries, and it has always interested language scholars.

Patterns of conquest and migration can be traced on a language map. Latin, from which the Romantic tongues came, was carried to all parts of the Roman Empire. The wide spread of Arabic reflects the sweep of the Moslems across Africa. The English took their language to North America, and the Spanish and Portuguese took theirs to Central and South America.

Recorded language is the enemy of ignorance....
                          and of the forgetfulness of time.

Egyptian hieroglyphics are symbols that stand for the sound of words. They probably began as picture writing, with drawings standing for the objects they represented. Gradually the drawings came to mean any word that had the same sound as the original object. If this system were used in English, a drawing of the eye, for example, would come in time to mean "I" as well.

The words are Spanish (left), but the same alphabet is used to write English, German, Latin, and a number of other languages. The characters in an alphabet represent sounds. Alphabets are the most highly-developed and convenient form of writing. All the many words in a language can be expressed by combinations of a few interchangeable letters.

In written Chinese (below) the characters stand for ideas or meanings of words and have nothing to do with the sound. Learning to read and write means memorizing thousands of symbols. The Japanese use the same characters although their language is entirely different.

RACES OF THE WORLD

In the largest sense, all human beings belong to the same race: Mankind. We are the speakers of languages, the makers of tools, the shapers and builders, the thinkers of abstract thoughts, the seekers after God. These common qualities transcend all differences and set man apart from all other animals.

Physically, also, all men share certain characteristics. The bodies of men are covered with thin, smooth skin; they have hair, not fur or feathers; human cells are different from the cells of other animals, as is human blood. Large groups of human beings are also distinguished from other large groups by physical characteristics that are determined before birth, by inheritance. On the basis of these traits, mankind has been classified as having three great divisions, the Caucasoid, the Mongoloid, and the Negroid.

The general characteristics that are used to describe these three great divisions are: shape of head; type (straight, wavy, or curly) of hair; color and texture of hair; color of eyes, and presence or absence of a fold in the corners of the eyelids; size and shape of foot; size and shape of hand; skin color; shape of nose; relative proportions of upper and lower leg and upper and lower arm, and many others. No single characteristic is a reliable indication of race, and each characteristic shows great variation within the racial group.

Furthermore, the three principal groups have innumerable subgroups within them, which often differ widely from each other, and some peoples have characteristics of at least two of the three main divisions.

The Caucasoid group includes most Europeans, from the blond northerners to the dark southerners, the peoples of India, the Ainu of northern Japan, and possibly the Polynesians of the western Pacific and some of the aborigines of Australia. The Mongoloid group includes most of the peoples of eastern and central Asia, the Indians of the Americas, and the Eskimos. The Negroid group includes the Negroes of Africa, some of the peoples of the Pacific Islands, and the pygmy peoples of Africa and Malaysia.

There are fascinating groups of people about whom the evidence is not at all clear. For example, the African Bushmen have some characteristics that seem to be Negroid, but there are also many differences between them and other African Negroes. Some scientists think that they may be a remnant of an older race that has disappeared except in a few places. The Melanesians, who live on some of the islands of the southwest Pacific, are classed as Negroid by some scientists and as a separate race by others.

As research yields more knowledge about the world, especially the prehistoric world, the migrations of many racial groups can be traced. Measurement of skeletal remains show that racial groups have wandered over the earth. Some have disappeared from areas where they once lived and been replaced by others. Some have increased in numbers and occupied larger and larger areas. In the course of human history, all groups of people have encountered other groups unlike themselves and have changed them and been changed by them.

The term "race" is often erroneously used with reference to things that have nothing to do with racial characteristics. There is no such thing as racial culture, for example. The customs, language, religion, literature, and art of a people are not inherited characteristics of a racial group. Race has nothing to do with nationality, which is a political division of mankind that was invented by man. People of any race may be a member of any nation, and most nations have had citizens who were members of each of the great races, all of whom help to people Our World.

The population of Hawaii is a happy blend of peoples—European, Asian, and Polynesian—and most racial types and most racial subtypes are represented in it. When Hawaii was discovered by Europeans, it was inhabited by Polynesians.

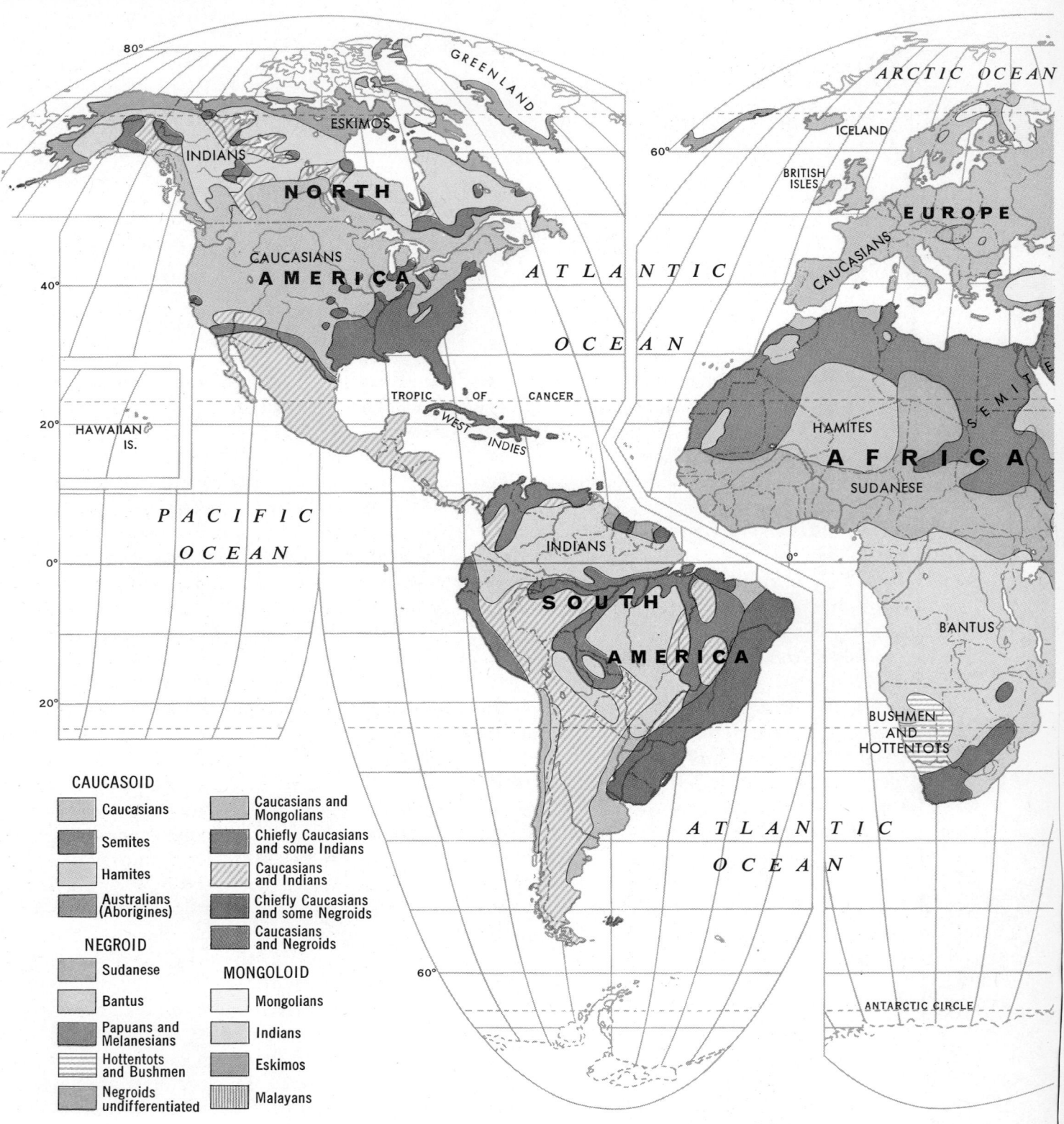

CAUCASOID

Caucasians

Semites

Hamites

Australians (Aborigines)

NEGROID

Sudanese

Bantus

Papuans and Melanesians

Hottentots and Bushmen

Negroids undifferentiated

Caucasians and Mongolians

Chiefly Caucasians and some Indians

Caucasians and Indians

Chiefly Caucasians and some Negroids

Caucasians and Negroids

MONGOLOID

Mongolians

Indians

Eskimos

Malayans

RACES OF THE WORLD

No exact diagram of the distribution of the major races of the world is possible since, during the course of history, so many subdivisions have developed that it is almost impossible to distinguish the root stock in many cases. The map shows what scientists consider the predominant racial types in each area.

Some conclusions concerning man's travels across the world can be drawn from the map. The Caucasoids are the only race to spread in large numbers into every inhabited continent. They occupy nearly all of Europe, southwestern Asia, and North Africa. In northern Asia,

ARCTIC CIRCLE
NORTHERN MONGOLIANS

A S I A

AINUS

JAPAN

SOUTHERN
MONGOLIANS

TROPIC   OF   CANCER

PACIFIC

PHILIPPINES

OCEAN

HAMITES

MALAYANS

INDONESIA

PAPUANS

EQUATOR
LONGITUDE EAST OF GREENWICH

INDIAN   OCEAN

MADAGASCAR

TROPIC   OF   CAPRICORN

AUSTRALIA

NEW
ZEALAND

MAORIS

Russians have settled all across Siberia. Caucasians from Europe are a great majority in North America and a somewhat smaller percentage of the total population in South America. They occupy all but the great desert of Australia.

The Semitic branch of the Caucasoids are believed to have originated in Arabia, the Hamites probably in Africa.

Mongoloids also have wandered a long way over the earth. They occupy a large part of Asia, including all the most densely populated areas except India. Members of the Malayan subrace people Indonesia and the Philippines and are a majority on Madagascar. The most remarkable Mongoloid migration was into the Americas, probably across the Bering Strait; they gradually occupied the land to the southern tip of South America. The Eskimos are part of a relatively late wave of migration from Europe.

Negroes, the people of Africa south of the Sahara, seldom left Africa of their own volition. During the sixteenth, seventeenth, and eighteenth centuries, thousands of them were taken to the Americas as slaves.

*The differences are great,
the likeness greater....*

*These peoples are one race:
CAUCASOID*

In spite of the many differences in appearance, and of the widely separated parts of the world in which they live, all of the people shown in the pictures on these two pages are members of the same large racial group, the Caucasoid. Almost all Europeans are Caucasoid, though Norwegians seem very different from Spaniards or from Greeks. Left, above, are typical eastern European Caucasians, called Slavs. In general, they have wide faces, and rounder heads and darker hair and eyes than western European peoples. The Norwegian girl (right), has coloring typical of certain peoples of northern Europe.

The Australian native to the left is also a Caucasoid. The predominant features that lead scientists to classify him as such are heavy beard and wavy hair, and measurements of the skull and other bones.

Arabs are Semites, one of the almost infinite number of subdivisions of the Caucasoid family. In body measurements and appearance, Semitic peoples are closer to the European types than other non-European Caucasoid groups.

The Ainu man and wife below belong to a small group of people who now live only on Hokkaido, in northern Japan, but probably they once occupied a much larger area in northern Asia. The Ainu have wavy hair and heavy beards, characteristic of Caucasoids.

The face of man has infinite variety. . . .

NEGROID

Most of the people of Uganda, like the two women above, are Bantus, and are called Baganda. The name Bantu refers to speakers of a large group of related languages, and the people themselves differ considerably from tribe to tribe, but there are enough similarities for them to be considered one group.

The people of Ghana (left) are Sudanese, sometimes called the "true Negroes." The traits that distinguish the Negroids can be seen clearly in them; tightly curled hair, and the shape of the nose, mouth, and jaw are distinctive features. The ancestors of most North American Negroes came from the Sudanese area.

There is some mystery about the tribal origin of the Hottentots (below). They share some traits with the Bushmen. Both groups have hair so tightly curled that it forms separate tufts, usually called peppercorns. Bushmen, however, are very short and Hottentots are considerably taller. Those in the picture are boys. Hottentots are probably a mixture of Bushmen and taller tribes.

NATURAL VEGETATION

Except for ice-covered polar lands and mountain tops and the driest cores of the deserts, plants cover the land. Plants grow luxuriously on deep-soiled plains and in valleys; they climb high mountains until they are stopped by perpetual snow near the summits. They flourish in the shallow margins of lakes and in the water of swamps and marshes. Plants grow where the salt ocean water washes their roots at every tide. They crowd to the foot of glaciers, cling to rocks, and grow out of cracks in city sidewalks.

Without plants, there could be no life of any kind on earth. Only plants can take chemicals from air and water, expose them to sunlight, and turn them into food. All animals, including man, must live by eating food that plants have made. The lion that dines on a zebra or the robin that pulls an earthworm from the ground or the man who enjoys a well-browned steak is merely getting his plant food one step removed. Even the gull snatching a fish from the water is dependent on plant food, for there are plants in the ocean. Fish eat them or eat other sea creatures that have eaten them. Every food chain goes back to plants.

Plants must have water to carry chemicals from the soil up to their leaves and flowers and to carry food down for storage in stems and roots. They must be able to obtain the necessary chemicals from soil or water, and they must have warmth and sunshine in order to manufacture food.

Since plants vary in their requirements, the vegetation of the earth varies from region to region. The wild plants of a region—the natural vegetation—are an excellent clue to climate. Settlers in newly-opened lands have used the plants as an indication of what crops are likely to be successful.

There are four main types of natural land vegetation in the world: forest, grassland, desert, and tundra. Each of these has many subdivisions. The basic division in forest types is between needle-leaved and broad-leaved trees. Well-known examples of needle-leaved trees are pine, spruce, fir, hemlock, cedar, and juniper. Not all have truly needle-shaped leaves, but all are closely related. Popularly, they are often called evergreens because most of them keep their leaves the year round, but there are exceptions. In North America the larch or tamarack and the bald cypress shed their leaves in the fall. Needle-leaved trees are the softwoods of the lumber industry, though by no means all of them have wood that is actually soft.

Broad-leaved trees are the lumberman's hardwoods, though the softest known woods, such as balsa, belong to this group. There is great variety in broad-leaved trees—cottonwoods and aspens with wide leaves, narrow-leaved willows, trees with the saw-edged leaves like the elm and birch, and the deeply indented leaves of the oak and maple.

Where winters are cold, most of the broad-leaved trees are deciduous; that is, they lose their leaves in the fall. (There are exceptions, such as the holly.) Where there is warmth all year, the broad-leaved forest is evergreen. Most trees do shed their leaves briefly at some time during the year, but the forest as a whole remains green.

Next to the forests in area are the grasslands. They vary from the thick sod and tall blades of the prairie grasses to the short, scattered tufts of the near desert. On the whole, they occupy lands with a little less moisture than trees require. Grass of some variety will grow almost everywhere. Grass grows on the floor of forests wherever a little light trickles through the trees. It grows in marshes, it invades the tundra, and grows far above the tree line on mountains. Where winters are long and cold or summers are hot and dry, the green blades turn brown and die, but the roots are still alive, ready to cover the earth with a new blanket of green when the season changes. Where a forest is cut or burned, where a lake is drained, where a river builds new land at its mouth, there the grass soon takes over.

To man, forest and grassland are much the most important vegetation regions. Nearly all the densely populated parts of the earth are in areas where trees or grass were the natural vegetation.

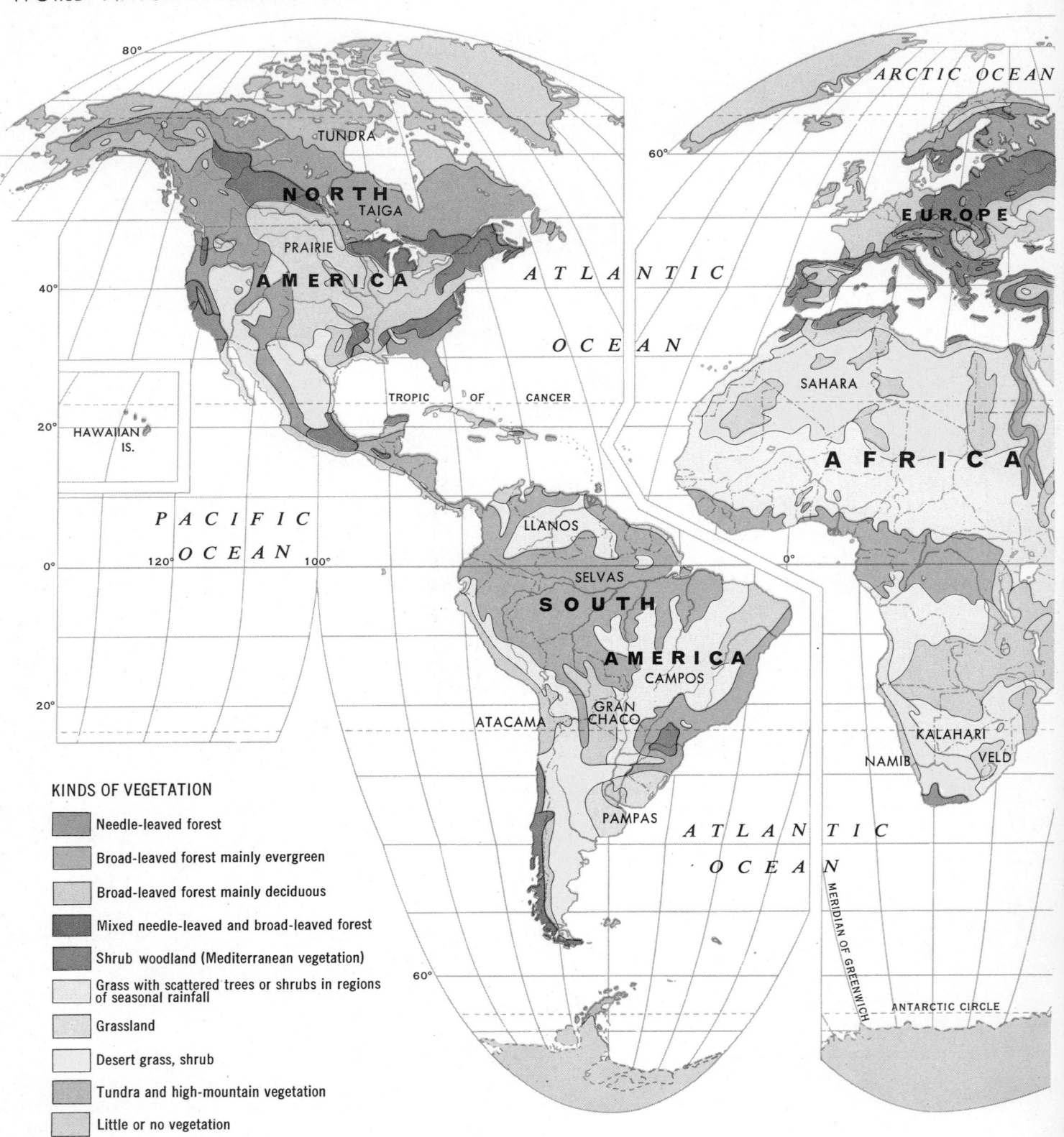

KINDS OF VEGETATION

- Needle-leaved forest
- Broad-leaved forest mainly evergreen
- Broad-leaved forest mainly deciduous
- Mixed needle-leaved and broad-leaved forest
- Shrub woodland (Mediterranean vegetation)
- Grass with scattered trees or shrubs in regions of seasonal rainfall
- Grassland
- Desert grass, shrub
- Tundra and high-mountain vegetation
- Little or no vegetation

NATURAL VEGETATION OF THE WORLD

The pattern on a vegetation map is very similar to the pattern on a world climate map. The most important single factor in the determination of type and extent of vegetation is climate, although soil and altitude also are significant. As vegetation depends on climate, so does population depend on vegetation. Some of the best general-farming land in the world is in broad-leaved forest regions, in North America, western Europe, and eastern Asia, for example, where most forests were cut long ago.

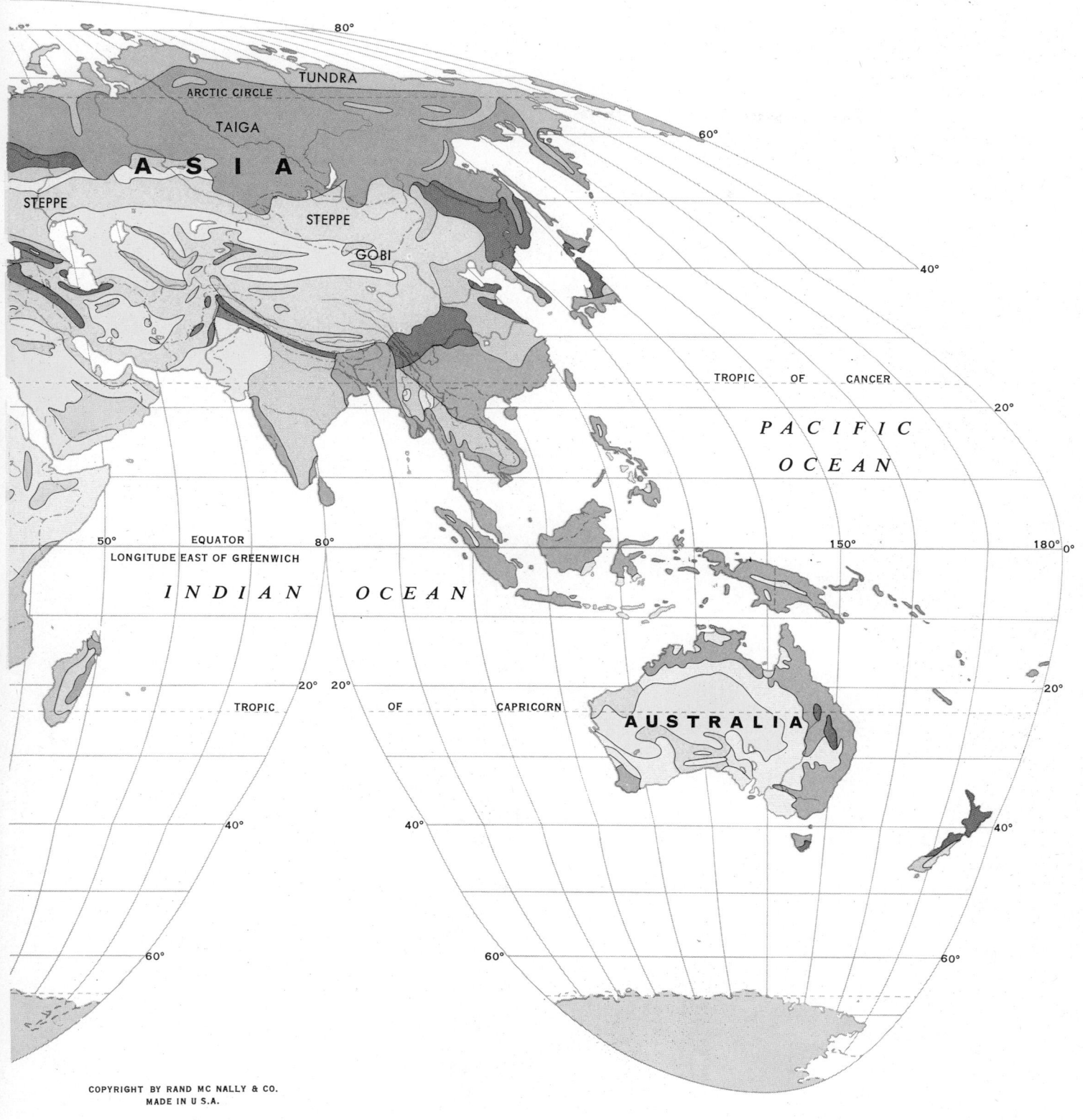

80°

TUNDRA
ARCTIC CIRCLE
60°

TAIGA

A S I A

STEPPE

STEPPE

GOBI

40°

TROPIC   OF   CANCER
20°

P A C I F I C

O C E A N

50°   EQUATOR   80°   150°   180° 0°
LONGITUDE EAST OF GREENWICH

I N D I A N   O C E A N

20° 20°   20°

TROPIC   OF   CAPRICORN

AUSTRALIA

40°   40°   40°

60°   60°   60°

COPYRIGHT BY RAND MC NALLY & CO.
MADE IN U.S.A.

Grasslands have become the world's producers of bread and meat. All the cereal grains, wheat, rye, barley, oats, millet, rice, and corn (maize), belong to the large botanical family of grasses. These grains are grown in the moister grasslands, and the drier lands retain their indigenous grasses and are used as grazing lands, mainly for cattle and sheep.

Two vegetation classes, "shrub woodland" and "grass with scattered trees," belong to the regions with great seasonal differences in rainfall. They make excellent farmland where they can be irrigated.

Most of the tropical broad-leaved forests have never been cleared. It is too difficult, and when the trees have been cut, the soil loses its fertility.

Needle-leaved trees, in general, will tolerate more severe conditions than broad-leaved. They grow where winters are long and cold, where the soil is acid or sandy and infertile, or in the thin soil of mountain slopes.

Trunk, limb, green leaf....great trees adorn the earth.

Slender, pointed, needle-leafed firs form a dense forest on a mountain slope in the Canadian Rockies near Lake Louise. Above treeline the mountainside is bare rock, too high and cold for any but such primitive plants as lichen and mosses. A grassy mountain meadow lies hidden under the snow. In late spring and summer, a profusion of wildflowers will bloom there.

The glorious flames of autumn burn in the Berkshires of Massachusetts. The foliage of the broad-leaved trees turns from the cool green of summer to fiery orange, red, and gold in the crisp, cold air of fall. As the brilliant colors die, the leaves will drop. This color change occurs in North America, western Europe, small regions in Asia, and a few places in southern South America.

Tropical rain forests, found in the humid low latitudes, are green above, dark and shadowy below. Trees grow so close together that their tops form a solid canopy, and young trees can grow only where an old tree falls and lets in the light. Like this one in Puerto Rico, all tropical forests are made up of broad-leaved trees, and they are always green.

No shield against the wind,
No shelter from the sun
  ....these are the treeless lands.

The desert of Saudi Arabia, the desolate "empty quarter." This is one of the regions of "little or no vegetation." It is a nightmare expanse of blowing sand. The dunes in the background show how the sand has blown away from the windward side and into a slope downwind. At the left a moving dune has killed and half buried a shrub that had managed to find a foothold.

In the high mountains of Wyoming, left, plants like those of the far-northern tundra grow. The ground is covered in a scanty fashion, but the plants are dwarfed and meager. Even the woody bushes that grow here and there are only a few inches high.

CLIMATES OF THE WORLD

A generation or two ago, geography textbooks had a very simple scheme for describing world climates. Along the equator, between the Tropic of Cancer and the Tropic of Capricorn, was the torrid zone, which was always hot. Between the Tropic of Cancer and the Arctic Circle, and between the Tropic of Capricorn and the Antarctic Circle, were the temperate zones, which were neither hot nor very cold. Around both poles were the frigid zones, which were always cold.

The pattern was simple and easy to learn, but it had very little relation to the real earth. The "torrid zone" has regions of perpetual snow on its highlands. The "temperate zone" has extreme temperatures ranging from 50 degrees below zero to more than 130 degrees above. Within the "frigid zone" there may be summer days when the temperature rises above 90 degrees. Evidently a useful classification of climates cannot be quite so simple.

The climate of a region is controlled by a combination of many factors. So many combinations are possible that no two regions of the earth have exactly the same climate. In order to classify climates, they must be grouped and small variations must be disregarded.

Distance from the equator, or latitude, is one factor in climate. It is related, not only to temperature, but also to rainfall, wind direction, hours of daylight, number of storms, and the kind and degree of seasonal differences.

Another factor is elevation, height above sea level. High mountains can make a tropical area as icy as Greenland and bring tundra vegetation to equatorial Africa. The temperature drops, on the average, about 3.3 degrees for every thousand feet of elevation. Highlands can bring rain in a desert or dryness to a lowland on their leeward side, as on the east coast of southern South America.

A region in the center of a continent will have a more severe climate, with hotter summers and colder winters, than a region at the same latitude near the ocean. West coasts, in general, have milder climates than east coasts in the same latitudes. Toward the poles from about 40° of latitude north or south, most west coasts have much more rain than east coasts; but from about 20° to 30° north and south, most west-coast regions are very dry. These variations are caused by the difference in prevailing winds. Ocean currents also have an effect on the climate of coastal regions. Warm currents bring heat and rain to the land. Cold currents chill the air.

Another element in climate is the tilt of the earth's axis in relation to the sun. Because of it, the noonday sun shines directly overhead north of the equator during half the year and south of it during the other half. Because of this shift, the seasons change.

The world wind belts shift north and south with the changing position of the sun's vertical rays, and this change helps give the earth its delightful Mediterranean regions. When the sun is south of the equator, the belt of westerly winds shifts far enough south to blow across the Mediterranean Sea. These are moist winds from the Atlantic, and they bring rain. When the direct rays of the sun fall north of the equator, desert conditions shift north, too, and the Mediterranean lands have no rain. In the same latitude in southern California, there is the same effect. At the same distance south of the equator, there are regions of Mediterranean climate in South America, Africa, and Australia.

Temperature around the year, rainfall, seasonal contrasts, the changeability of the weather from day to day—all these make up the climate of any given place. World patterns of climate are closely related to patterns of vegetation, to population density, and to all human activities.

The warmth and humidity of these terraced rice fields in the Philippines are almost visible. The region is classified as "humid low latitude." Low latitude places the area near the equator, and high temperature and moist air make the climate humid.

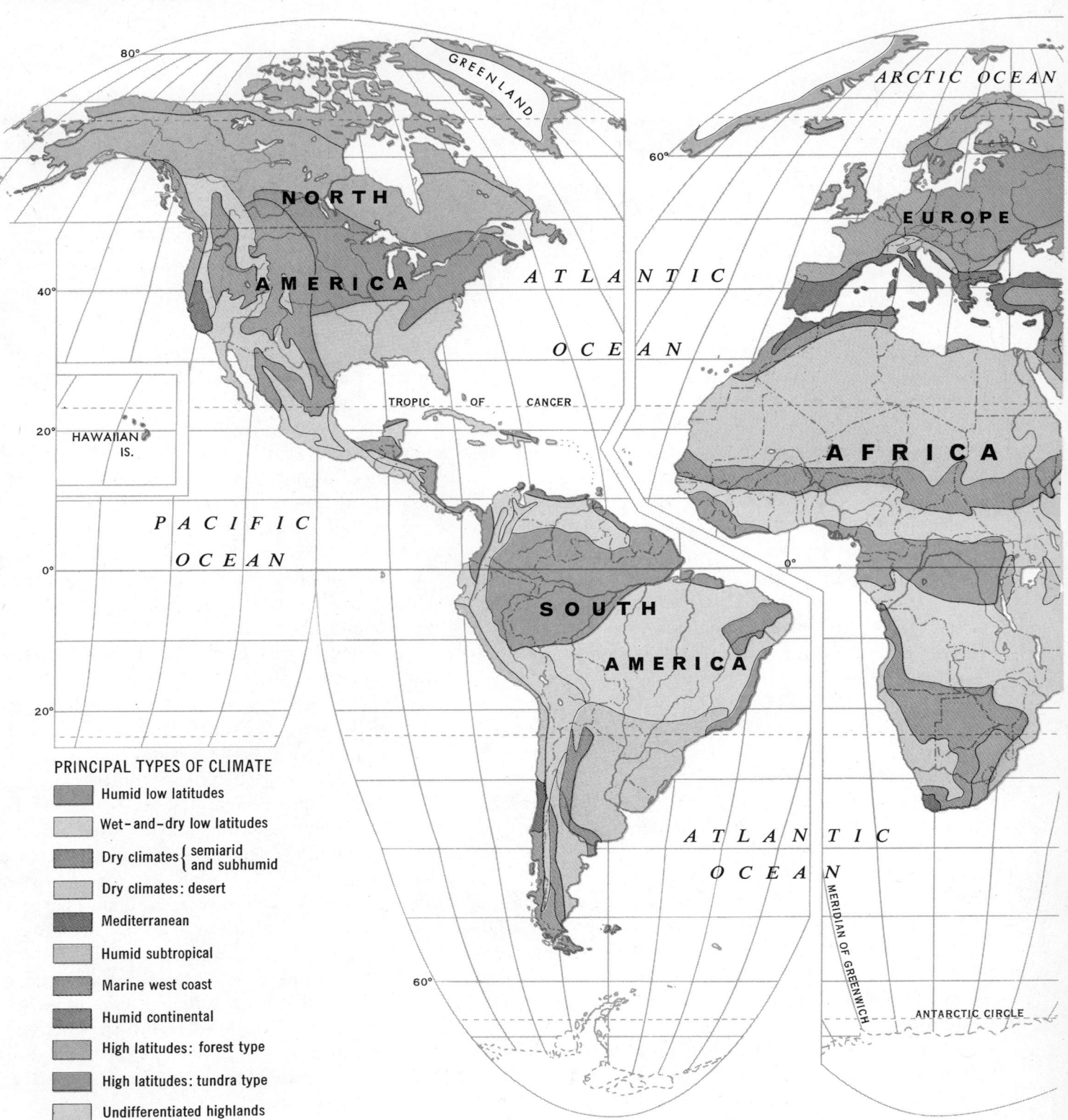

PRINCIPAL TYPES OF CLIMATE

- Humid low latitudes
- Wet-and-dry low latitudes
- Dry climates { semiarid and subhumid
- Dry climates: desert
- Mediterranean
- Humid subtropical
- Marine west coast
- Humid continental
- High latitudes: forest type
- High latitudes: tundra type
- Undifferentiated highlands

CLIMATES OF THE WORLD

Lowlands near the equator are the humid low-latitude regions of the world, warm and wet the year round. The wet-and-dry low latitudes are also near the equator, but they have a distinct dry season during the year. These regions of seasonal rainfall are characteristically grassland with scattered trees or shrubs. Crops must be able to complete their growth during the rainy season unless irrigation is possible. They are also seasonally good pasture lands.

Semiarid and subhumid climates vary from not quite enough moisture for farming to lands that are popularly

*Rain falls or does not
....green land or barren
decrees abundance or want.*

Winters are long and cold, summers hot and often dry, but this field in North Dakota is part of the great North American wheat belt, which produces food for millions of people. There are also many cattle ranches in this area, which is near the western edge of the humid continental region.

"England's green and lovely land" is, in a sense, a gift of the sea. This beautiful farming country with its many trees, along the southwestern coast of England, is typical of regions with a marine west-coast climate. Winds from the Atlantic Ocean keep the temperatures mild and bring rain and many cloudy days.

Mountains are the most conspicuous landforms on the face of the earth. The top of Mount McKinley is the highest point in North America, almost four miles above sea level. The mountain can be seen from many miles away, and the view from its summit is said to encompass 3,000 square miles of Alaska, with lower mountains, valleys, rolling hills, and tundra-covered plains.

LANDFORMS

Since they first had languages for speaking, people have been naming landforms. They have given individual names to specific features, and they have also created general names for whole classes of features, such as "mountains." The numerousness of these names indicates the importance that people have always attached to the various forms that make up the surface of the earth.

Mount McKinley is not the highest mountain in the world. Mount Aconcagua in South America is almost a half mile higher, and Mount Everest in the Himalayas is more than a mile and a half higher. The summit of Mount Everest is the highest point on earth, but jet airliners on regularly scheduled flights climb nearly a mile higher. Anyone who has flown across a coastline (sea level) at 30,000 feet or more has looked down from a height greater than the elevation of the highest mountain on earth. Within those narrow limits, plus the depth of a few small land areas that are slightly below sea level, lie all the earth's landforms. The range of inhabited land is still less. Very few people live at an elevation of as much as 12,000 feet. At much lower levels, most people are made uncomfortable by the thinness of the air and a lack of oxygen.

A great variety of landforms and landform names are associated with mountains. There are mountain peaks, summits, ridges, and ranges. A line following the highest elevations of a range is its crest. Mountain ranges are part of highland regions. At the edge of a mountain range, there are usually foothills. Included in highlands are plateaus, high plains, mountain valleys, and many other features.

Lowlands may be plains, valleys, or basins. Plains may be flat, rolling, or hilly. Special types are coastal plains, high plains, and flood plains of rivers.

Another very large group of landforms is associated with coastlines and the relationships between land and water. Land reaches into the water in peninsulas, capes, points, and headlands. Where the land curves inward instead of projecting into the water, there are bays, inlets, fiords, estuaries, gulfs, sounds, and seas. Straits separate two bodies of land, and isthmuses unite them.

Rivers have sources, channels, and mouths. They cut valleys which may, in special cases, be called ravines, canyons, gulches, and gorges. If a river dries up during part of the year, its valley is an arroyo, or sometimes a draw, in the United States and a wadi in North Africa.

These are only a few of the many landform names commonly used in English. Other languages have their own terms. English has borrowed some of these terms. For instance, fiord is the Norwegian term for a special kind of narrow inlet bordered by mountains. Sierra Nevada Mountains is incorrect usage because "sierra" is Spanish for mountain range.

Another class of names refers to man-made landforms. There are embankments, dikes, levees, mounds, dams, cuts, canals, ditches, polders, and causeways. Other names refer to the use people make of a feature. A valley through mountains is not a pass unless it is used as a transportation route. A bay is not a harbor unless it becomes a shelter for ships.

Geographic terms are hard to define because they have not been applied scientifically. Features were usually named by early explorers and settlers, not by geographers. East and west of India are two extensions of the Indian Ocean of about the same size and general shape. There is no good geographic reason why one should be the Arabian Sea and the other the Bay of Bengal. Hudson Bay is three times as large as the Baltic Sea, and much larger than the Persian Gulf.

There are no definitions that will make sharp distinctions between gulfs, seas, and bays; straits and channels; capes and points. A plateau is almost impossible to define satisfactorily, though many plateaus are named on the map. Features may be called mountains in one place, while very similar features in another place are called hills.

People have invented so many names for landforms because the surface features of the earth are of great importance to human living.

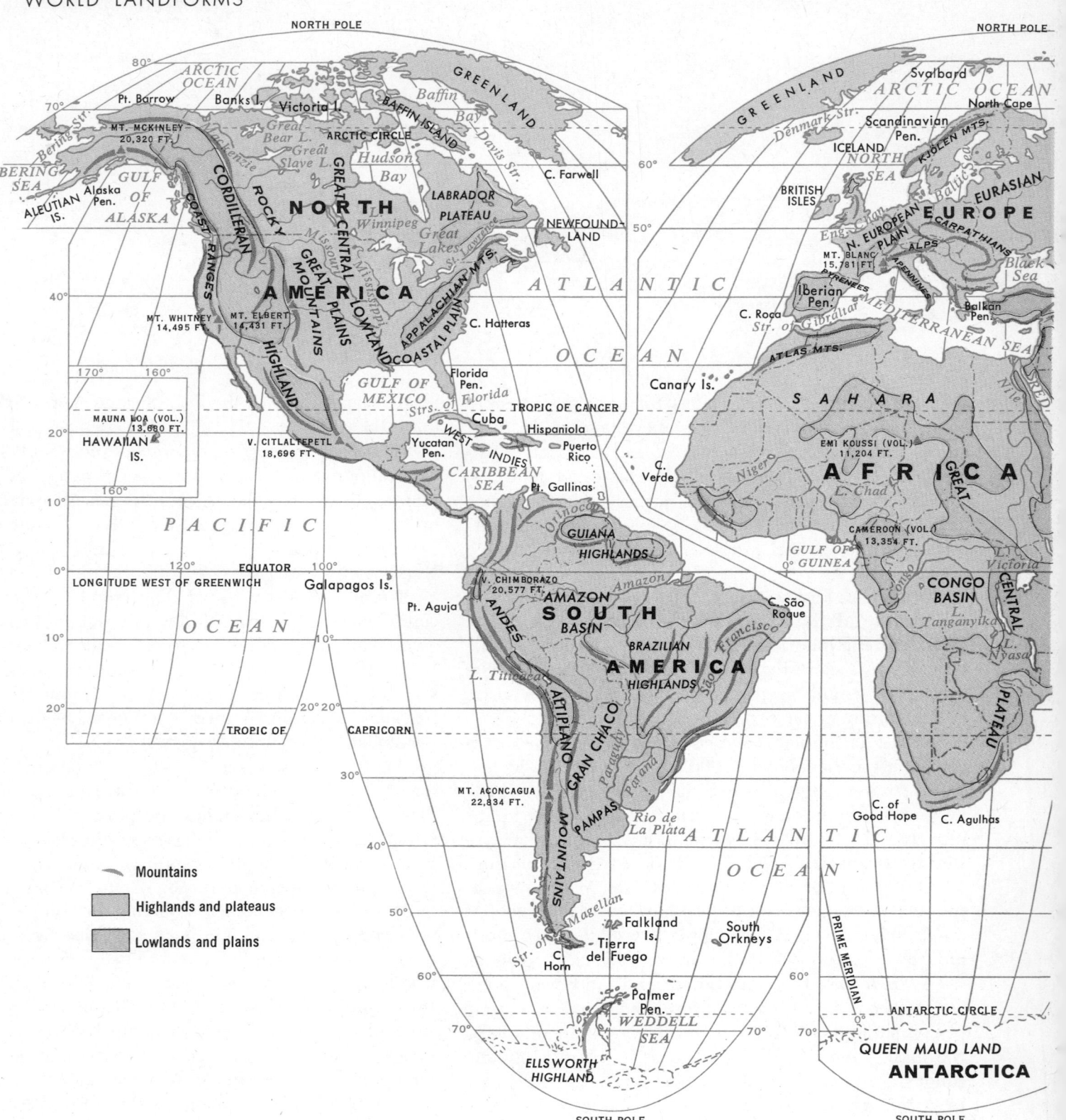

Mountains

Highlands and plateaus

Lowlands and plains

LANDFORMS
OF THE WORLD

The map on these pages is a generalized representation of the landforms of the earth. The major mountain ranges, indicated by wide gray lines, appear as parts of great mountain systems, such as the Rockies. Even these systems are not the end of the story of mountain relationships. The western highlands of the Americas sweep on range after range from northwestern North America to the southern tip of South America, but even that is not the end. They appear again in the spine of the Palmer Peninsula of Antarctica.

Novaya Zemlya
C. Chelyuskin
Taymyr Pen.
ARCTIC CIRCLE
VERKHOYANSK MTS.
CHERSKIV MTS.
80°
70°
60°
Lena
Yenisey
Ob
LOWLAND
URAL MTS.
A S I A
SAYAN MTS.
YABLONOVY MTS.
ALTAI MTS.
Irtysh
L. Baikal
Amur
Kamchatka Pen.
SEA OF OKHOTSK
50°
Volga
Caspian Sea
L. Balkash
Syr Darya
Aral Sea
Amu Darya
TIEN SHAN
PAMIR
TARIM BASIN
PLAT. OF MONGOLIA
KUNLUN MTS.
Sakhalin
Hokkaido
40°
CAUCASUS
GREAT
MT. DEMAVEND 18,934 FT.
CENTRAL
HINDU KUSH
PLATEAU
PLATEAU OF TIBET
NORTH CHINA PLAIN
Hwang
Yellow Sea
Korea Pen.
Japan Sea
Honshu
MT. FUJI (VOL.) 12,388 FT.
PLAT. OF IRAN
HIMALAYA MTS.
Kyushu
Euphrates
Persian G.
Ganges
MT. EVEREST 29,028 FT.
Yangtze
Formosa (Taiwan)
EAST CHINA SEA
PACIFIC
30°
TROPIC OF CANCER
PLATEAU AND PENINSULA OF ARABIA
INDO-GANGETIC PLAIN
THE DECCAN
BAY OF BENGAL
Brahmaputra
Hainan
Luzon
Mariana Islands
20°
SEA
G. of Aden
C. Guardafui
ARABIAN SEA
CEYLON
C. Comorin
SOUTH CHINA SEA
PHILIPPINES
OCEAN
Marshall Islands
10°
Maldive Is.
Strait of Malacca
Malay Pen.
Mindanao
Caroline Islands
MT. KILIMANJARO 19,590 FT.
60°
EQUATOR
LONGITUDE EAST OF GREENWICH
80°
Sumatra
BORNEO
120°
Celebes
MALAYA ARCHIPELAGO
MT. CARSTENSZ 16,503 FT.
New Guinea
Solomon Is.
EQUATOR
180°
0°
INDIAN
OCEAN
SUNDA ISLANDS
Java
Mekong
140°
160°
10°
Mozambique Channel
MADAGASCAR
10°
Torres Str.
New Hebrides
Fiji Is.
20°
TROPIC OF
CAPRICORN
20°
CAPRICORN
North West Cape
THE
WESTERN
AUSTRALIA
PLATEAU
GREAT
PLAINS
GREAT DIVIDING RANGE
GREAT BARRIER REEF
TROPIC OF CAPRICORN
30°
30°
C. Leeuwin
MT. KOSCIUSKO 7,328 FT.
NEW ZEALAND
North I.
40°
40°
Tasmania
South East Cape
Bass Str.
South I.
MT. COOK 12,349 FT.
50°
50°
60°
60°
ANTARCTIC CIRCLE
70°
WILKES LAND
MT. EREBUS 13,200 FT.
ROSS SEA

SOUTH POLE

The Old World has an even more spectacular system of mountains. Starting with the Pyrenees and the Atlas ranges, the mountains curve through the Apennines and Alps to the Carpathians and continue through central Asia. Then the pattern splits up into several branches. One runs through China and southeastern Asia to the islands and continues along the coast of Australia.

Another branch makes a circuit through northeastern Asia, curving back to the south through ranges in Kamchatka, Korea, Japan, the Philippines, and Borneo. At the far northeast of Asia, other ranges link up with those of North America.

Most of the great plateaus of the world are associated with mountains. In western North America, the plateaus lie between two systems of mountains. However, some plateaus have bordering mountains and some do not.

This generalized map does not show details of surface features. Maps on pages 1 to 89 should be used with it. Those maps indicate elevations and surface features by various symbols, as shown on page 90.

The highlands....
thrown up by fire,
rock built on rock....

The most terrifying and dramatic of all nature's great spectacles is the eruption of a volcano. Craters, like that shown at left of a volcano in Peru, are usually formed when the top of the mountain collapses after an explosion. Active volcanoes rise from the great mountain chains that encircle the Pacific.

Peninsulas, capes, isthmuses, bays, and straits—all features associated with shorelines—show in miniature along mountain-bordered Lake Scutari on the boundary between Yugoslavia and Albania. In the far distance a tiny island rises from the water. This part of the lake follows the curve of a narrow valley. The land includes many features characteristic of mountain landscapes.